THE WARS OF AMERICA

BOOKS BY ROBERT LECKIE

HISTORY

None Died in Vain: The Saga of the American Civil War
Delivered from Evil: The Saga of World War II
The Wars of America: A New and Updated Edition
American and Catholic: The Catholic Church in the U.S.
Challenge for the Pacific: The Struggle for Guadalcanal
With Fire and Sword (edited with Quentin Reynolds)
Strong Men Armed: U.S. Marines Against Japan
Conflict: The History of the Korean War
The March to Glory: 1st Marine Division's Breakout from Chosin

AUTOBIOGRAPHY

Helmet for My Pillow   *Lord, What a Family!*

BELLES LETTRES

These Are My Heroes: A Study of the Saints
Warfare: A Study of War
A Soldier-Priest Talks to Youth

FICTION

Ordained   *Forged in Blood*
Marines!   *Blood of the Seventeen Fires*
The Bloodborn   *The General*

FOR YOUNGER READERS

The Battle for Iwo Jima   *The World Turned*
The Story of Football   *Upside-Down*
The Story of World War Two   *1812: The War Nobody Won*
The Story of World War One   *The Big Game*
The War in Korea   *Keeper Play!*
Great American Battles   *Stormy Voyage*

THE WARS

A NEW AND UPDATED EDITION

OF AMERICA

Robert Leckie

CASTLE BOOKS

☆

To Charles Watters
Compassionate Priest and Brave Chaplain
Who Was Killed by Friendly Fire in Vietnam
While Hastening to the Side of a Wounded Soldier.
Simple and Direct, He Was, as Jesus Said of Nathaniel:
"An Israelite, Indeed, in Whom There Is No Guile."

This edition published by Castle Books, 1998
a division of Book Sales, Inc
114 Northfield Avenue
Edison, NJ 08837

by arrangement with and permission of
HarperCollins Publishers, Inc.
10 East 53rd Street
New York, NY 10022

ISBN 0-7858-0914-7
Printed in the United States of America

LIBRARY OF CONGRESS CATALOGING-IN-PUBLICATION DATA

Leckie, Robert.
    The wars of America / Robert Leckie. — 2nd rev. and updated ed.
        p.   cm.
    Includes bibliographical references and index.

    1. United States—History, Military. I. Title.
E181.L45   1992
973—dc20   91-50435

Contents

☆

Maps

☆

x   Maps

Preface

☆

Twenty years ago while discussing war with a Pakistani friend I was astonished to hear him, a Moslem, declare that Islam had never been aggressive. The sons of Mohammed, he insisted, had fought only in self-defense. A few minutes later I found myself maintaining that America had never been imperialist. "Not really," I said. "After all, we gave the Philippines their independence." Now it was my friend's turn to be scornful. "*You* gave *them* their *independence?*" he mocked. Blushing, I realized that my own chauvinism had been no lovelier than his: if I could look upon the Crescent as a bloody scimitar, he could regard the Cross as a sword carried upside down.

The point here is not so much to echo Robert Burns's plea for the gift "to see ourselves as others see us," but rather to accept Voltaire's remark that the study of one's nation's history makes one a better and more loyal citizen. Knowing his national history, a man is less likely to deny the undeniable and more inclined to take the good with the bad and put all into true perspective. This, then, is the purpose of this book: to put the wars of America into perspective.

It is an attempt to show not only how our wars were fought but also why they occurred, as well as to illustrate what this country has gained or lost by appeals to arms. Equally, it is an attempt to portray the men who made and fought in these wars. When military history becomes a dreary compendium of maps and maneuvers, of calibers and compass bearings, as it so often does, the reason usually is that the writer has left out the human heart. War changes, its materials and its methods change, but the hearts of men do not. That is why Marshal Saxe could say, "The human heart is the starting point in all matters pertaining to war," and that is why this book attempts to come down heavily on the human side. I agree with the Englishman who said he liked geography less than biography "because that's about maps, but the other is about chaps." And if, in following this sublime lead, this book sends a few scales flying from the hides of those antediluvian myths—America, the peace-loving nation; man, the peace-loving animal—then I will consider myself to have performed a small service in the interest of international sanity. Obviously, during an age in which an exchange of pushed buttons might very well end mankind's career upon this planet, it would be helpful to understand men as fighting creatures and our own nation as perhaps the fightingest society since the advent of modern warfare. Yet, though America can become martial, she has never been militarist. The distinction is a great one, and it is hoped that a knowledge of American military history may help us to maintain it. To this end, once again, this book was written.

Space limitations in a book of this scope have precluded the listing of a bibliography. A comprehensive one was simply out of the question, while a selected bibliography could well have run to another forty or fifty printed pages. In its place, I have included a list of recommended books and would refer the reader to Colonel Vincent J. Esposito's excellent and longer list in *The West Point Atlas of American Wars,* two volumes, New York: Praeger, 1959. Much of the research for this book was based upon that list.

It should go without saying that, apart from World War II, Korea and Vietnam, in which I had a personal interest, this work depends upon published sources. Nor do I pretend to have read everything published about every American war. When it is considered that one may collect more than 25,000 volumes and articles on the Civil War alone, it may be seen that the problem was not one of finding material but of choosing from it. Therefore, to have gone over ground already spaded by abler men before me would have been not only impossibly time-consuming but also pretentious.

Space limitations have also compelled me to confine reference notes to direct quotations. To footnote every statistic or observation would have been to number every third or fourth sentence. In the interest of smoother reading, all spelling and punctuation has been modernized, except where a certain echo from the past seemed appropriate. All dates are for the Time Zone in which the event occurred, and, to avoid an impression of that precision so rare in warfare, figures for casualties, the size of armies or the number of their arms, as well as the distances they have marched or sailed to battle, are usually rounded off to the nearest zero.

Finally, let me acknowledge my great debt to my editors: to the late Cass Canfield and to Norbert Slepyan for their kindly assistance on the original edition of this work published in 1968; to Corona Machemer for the same reasons on the revised and updated edition of 1981; and to M. S. ("Buz") Wyeth and Daniel Bial for their suggestions, patience and tact on this new, updated revision of 1992—to Mrs. Clarice Browne, librarian at Roxbury (New Jersey) High School, who kindly lent me copies of news magazines I was unable to obtain—and, of course, to my dear wife, who actually runs this lash-up as top kick and mess sergeant, for typing the manuscript while wearing her third hat of company clerk.

ROBERT LECKIE

Polliwog Pond
Byram Township, N.J.
September 23, 1991

PART I

The Colonial Wars

1

☆

In the spring of 1609 Samuel de Champlain prepared to make war upon the Iroquois. Only the previous autumn, soon after Champlain had planted the settlement of Quebec atop a high cliff commanding the broad St. Lawrence, a young Ottawa chief had come to him to propose such an expedition.

The Indian told the Father of New France that the Iroquois were the most ferocious savages in the American wilderness. Known as the Five Nations—Mohawk, Oneida, Onondaga, Cayuga and Seneca —they were the dread of surrounding tribes: killing, torturing, eating or enslaving them, while imposing upon some the humiliating epithet of "women" or exacting from others a ruinous tribute. Should Champlain join with this Ottawa and his kinsmen, as well as with the Hurons and Algonquins, who were also the Frenchman's friends, he might make himself the ally and the leader of all the tribes of Canada. His cannon and arquebuses—his "thunderhorns" as the Indians called them—would surely humble the haughty Iroquois.

Champlain consented, for here was the opportunity to seize power among the savages, and thus carry out French policy in the New World. Unlike those English who had settled at Jamestown in 1607 or the other English who were to come to Plymouth 13 years later, the French did not hold aloof from the Indians but rather mingled with them. They were not in the New World for gold like the Spaniards or land like the English, but rather for furs, for glory and for God. In one way or another, either by gaining the confidence of the Indians or by cowing them, they sought to bind the red men together under French leadership so that Canada's valuable trade in furs might be secured and expanded, and so that the Crown and the Cross might be pushed deeper, ever deeper, into the westward wilderness.

For these reasons, Samuel Champlain joined the war party. He lifted the war hatchet and watched the war dance. Then he dined at the war feast and the following morning—June 28, 1609—he led the war party south to the Iroquois country.

A few days later Champlain came upon a frothing white torrent that marked the rapids of the lower Richelieu. His light sloop could not pass, and he sent the sloop and eight of his 11 Frenchmen back to Quebec while the Indians bore their boats around the rapids. Then Champlain and two other Frenchmen entered war canoes. They paddled upriver and glided into that lovely long lake that was to bear Champlain's name. To either side rose towering forest walls growing darker in the July heat.

Champlain and his Indians paddled on. They intended to move south along Lake Champlain into narrower, lovelier Lake George, and then strike overland to the Hudson River, which they would descend to fall upon some Mohawk village. St. Lawrence River–Richelieu River–Lake Champlain–Lake George–Hudson River, in that order or the reverse, this was the watery warpath of the Iroquois and their enemies, just as it became for 150 years the invasion route of the warring French and English.

But Champlain and his savages did not traverse its length. On July 29 they lay encamped at the foot of Lake Champlain on a promontory which was probably the site of Fort Ticonderoga. A few hours after dark they made out a flotilla of Iroquois war canoes approaching from the south. Both Indian bands exchanged war cries, and then the Iroquois landed on the same shore to erect a barricade of logs in preparation for the morning's fight.

On that morning, Champlain and his fellow Frenchmen vested themselves in steel armor and seized their short, stubby matchlocks in their hands. Each of the three Frenchmen then entered a different canoe and lay hidden on its bottom. The canoes were paddled toward the Iroquois camp. They were beached in sight of the enemy barricade. After Champlain's savages went ashore, their steel-clad allies stealthily slipped from the canoes and followed behind.

Soon the Iroquois began filing out of their makeshift fort. There were about 200 of them. They also were "armored." Some carried shields of wood or hardened hide, or wore vests made of twigs bound by fiber. The Iroquois advanced steadily toward their foemen from the north. Shaken, the allies parted ranks and Champlain strode forward.

"I looked at them," Champlain wrote,

and they looked at me. When I saw them getting ready to shoot their arrows at us, I levelled my arquebuse, which I had loaded with four balls, and aimed straight at one of the three chiefs. The shot brought down two, and wounded another. On this, our Indians set up such a yelling that one could not have heard a thunder-clap, and all the while the arrows flew thick on both sides. The Iroquois were greatly astonished and frightened to see two of their men killed so quickly, in spite of their arrow-proof armor. As I was reloading, one of my companions fired a shot from the woods, which so increased their astonishment that, seeing their chiefs dead, they abandoned the field and fled into the depth of the forest.[1]*

Exultant, the allies closed on the Iroquois camp. They took the scalps of the fallen—both living and dead—and took prisoners on whom they commenced those foul tortures which turned the stomach of their mighty ally.

But Champlain's horror at the spectacle of Indians drinking the blood or eating the hearts of their victims would have been magnified up to the limit of even his considerable endurance had he suspected that his victory in this first pitched battle between French and Indian on American soil would produce in the hearts of the vanquished Iroquois a horrible ache for revenge.

The Father of New France had bequeathed to his heirs a legacy of terror.

In 1641 the Iroquois were ready. An entire new generation had brooded over the insult dealt to the brethren of the Long House. Only fear of the French thunderhorns had restrained them. But now Dutch traders at Fort Orange—renamed Albany after England acquired New York and New Jersey—had supplied them with fire-arms.

With these in their hands they boasted that they would wipe the Hurons, the Algonquins and the French off the face of the earth. They vowed that they would carry the "white girls"—the nuns of the colony—back to their villages. Regarding themselves as peerless warriors destined to conquer all mankind, they went on the warpath: in the west the Senecas and the others attacked the Hurons, while in the east the Mohawks struck at the French and their allies.

There were between 700 and 800 Mohawk braves, 300 of whom

* Notes begin on page 1199.

carried arquebuses, and they came very close to exterminating the 300 French colonists at Quebec, Three Rivers and Montreal.

In parties of ten to a hundred men, they paddled down the river that gave them their name, entered the Hudson at Albany, and stole north along the traditional invasion route. Reaching the St. Lawrence, they lay in ambush for canoes coming downriver with cargoes of fur or outgoing boats bringing supplies to the missions and trading stations in the Great Lakes region.

No one was safe from them. To hunt or fish alone was to risk the war whoop, the sudden shot—and the scalping knife in the brain. Small parties of French soldiers or bushrangers who rushed to the scenes of ambuscades rarely found more than a mangled corpse or heads stuck up on poles, and sometimes, scrawled on trees stripped of their bark, the crude picture writing of the Iroquois vaunting their latest massacre and promising destruction to all who opposed them.

Against the Indian allies of the French they aimed a particular ferocity. They drove the Algonquins from their hunting grounds deep into the wilderness, pursuing them there to destroy their camps and boil and eat the enemy slain in the sight of the survivors. "In a word," wrote the missionary Father Vimont, "they ate men with as much appetite and more pleasure than hunters eat a boar or stag."[2]

But those who were merely killed and eaten were comparatively fortunate, for the Iroquois had brought the practice of torture to an indescribable degree of perfection. In justice to them, it must be stated that none of the Indians regarded cruelty as being wicked. Indeed, its very opposite—pity—was a weakness in their eyes. Compassion in a warrior seemed nothing less than cowardice. To eat the heart of a fallen foe or to drink his blood was to partake of the dead man's courage. To torture a prisoner was not only pleasant; it gave an enemy the opportunity to show by his stoicism that he was a brave man. At times a victim's fortitude so excited the admiration of the Iroquois that they conferred upon him the highest honor, adoption into one of the five tribes.

Nevertheless, they were savages, and if some well-manicured moderns may be able to rationalize their cruelty as being nothing but the ungentle customs of primitive peoples, those who suffered under it had a different explanation.

"They are not men, they are wolves!" a Frenchwoman sobbed, after describing how her baby was burned before her eyes.[3]

Human wolves that they were, they would have devoured New France had they possessed the slightest understanding of the art of warfare or of that discipline which is the chief mark of a military organization. The Iroquois, however, could only make forays or raids. A battle was won or lost in an instant's rush. Stealth and surprise comprised their tactics. A siege was to them an incomprehensible bore, to maneuver in the open a madness. Even so, skulking in the forests by day, charging with a yell out of the dark by night, the Iroquois struck terror into the hearts of the French and came close to achieving the extermination of their enemies.

Gradually, however, the warpath wore them out. Their victories exhausted them, their villages fell silent, and by the year 1660 the Iroquois could count only 2,200 warriors, of whom more than half were adopted prisoners from the Hurons, Eries, neutrals and various Algonquin tribes.

Nevertheless, the Iroquois remained a threat to Canadian security down to the last chapter in the history of New France. Goaded back onto the warpath by the British, they repeatedly hurled themselves against the French and their Indian allies; and it was not until 1763, when the Peace of Paris made Canada a British colony, that they could forget those humiliating shots fired on the shores of Lake Champlain.

That the tolerant French rather than the haughty English should have been the first to incur the wrath of the red men is one of the ironies of American history. True enough, French policy toward the Indians was not one of unmixed altruism: if souls were to be won for the Cross, there were also furs to be gained for the Crown. Yet on balance the French treatment of the Indian tribes seems to have been more humane.

French agents lived in Indian villages and learned their languages. The Indians were befriended and flattered. Whenever they visited a French fort they were saluted with cannon and rolling drums. They were given medals and French uniforms and flags. Their customs—even the most savage ones, especially when they could be turned against the English—were rarely mocked or ridiculed.

It was otherwise with the English. First and foremost, the English colonists sought land. They had come to stay. This, of course, joined to the corollary necessity of learning to govern themselves, was to prove their strength; just as the paternalistic character of the French colony was to be its undoing. But in the beginning this passion for land was the disturbing quality which the Indians marked in the English. Not only the Indians, for Roger Williams, the famous fighter for religious tolerance, once observed: "I fear that . . . God Land will be as great a God with us English as God Gold was with the Spaniard."[4]

English officials were often overbearing in their dealings with proud Indian chiefs. More often than not, the English emissaries among the Indians were the fur traders who were universally hated and despised as "rum-carriers." Some Indians who had beheld the swift, curt justice of French military law were filled with contempt for slower English civil courts, confusing the Englishman's elaborate machinery for safeguarding civil rights with a weak uncertainty. Finally, although there were Protestant ministers such as John Eliot who were as zealous for souls as their Papist rivals to the north, Puritanical colonial legislatures passed blue laws applying to all Indians, converted or no. Thus, in Massachusetts, Indians as well as whites were liable to the death penalty for blasphemy, interpreted to be the denial of God or deprecation of the Christian religion; while in Plymouth no Indian was allowed to fish, hunt or carry burdens during the white man's Sabbath. Such intolerance only served to aggravate the Indian's growing anger at the greatest provocation of all: the shrinking boundaries of his ancestral home.

True enough, the colonists were scrupulously careful to obtain titles to Indian lands; nevertheless it was difficult for the red man to realize that in bartering away hunting preserves for guns or horses or casks of rum he was actually giving up all rights to hunt or fish there or to grow corn on unused parts of it. It might be that the genial Massasoit, friend of the Pilgrims and chief ceder of Wampanoag land, did not complain; but his far fiercer son, King Philip, came to see that the inexorably expanding whites would not be satisfied until they had all the land.

King Philip received his bizarre name after his father had asked the General Court in Plymouth to give English names to his two oldest sons, Wamsutta and Metacom. The English, recalling the kings of ancient Macedon, named the former Alexander and the latter Philip. On the death of Massasoit, in 1661, it was Alexander who succeeded to the chieftainship.

The new sachem quickly showed that he did not share his father's easy trust of the English. Although he did not attack them, he tried to rule his people independently of them. Summoned to appear in Plymouth to give evidence of his loyalty, Alexander refused to go. But colonial soldiers made him go, and he was subjected to a haughty and humiliating interrogation, during which time he contracted a fever that killed him.

King Philip succeeded him, fired by a burning resolve to avenge his brother's death and a determination to wean his people away from the corrupting influences of the white men. Although Philip was only 24, the fame of his ability as an orator and ruler was already great. More warlike and decisive than his brother, he saw with a painful clarity that there was no possibility of compromise for his people: they would either be overwhelmed by the colonists or they would turn and drive the whites into the sea. He realized early that his own outnumbered forces were fragmented, cut up by the sharp knife of tribal jealousies. By the time of the outbreak of King Philip's War in 1675 there were about 40,000 whites in New England, all of whom would certainly close ranks in the face of Indian menace, against 20,000 red men who would rather worry some old bone of tribal contention than rally to a common danger.

Nevertheless, King Philip prepared his war. For 13 years he patiently sought to bind the Indians into a unified whole. By the end of that period, however, it did not appear that he could rely upon more than half of them. Nor did it seem that he could produce any valid reason for taking up arms.

Then, in January, 1675, John Sassamon, a Christianized Indian who had been educated at Harvard College and had served as Philip's trusted aide, came to Plymouth to reveal to Governor Josiah Winslow all the details of Philip's "conspiracy" against the colonists. A few days later Sassamon was found murdered in a pond. The enraged authorities immediately blamed King Philip. They arrested three Wampanoags, and put them on trial. Philip protested that the whites had no right to try red men for crimes committed against other Indians. But the trial went forward, the three men were found guilty, and on June 8 they were hanged.

Twelve days later a group of young Wampanoags came into the settlement at Swansea and shot some cattle. A young colonist retaliated by wounding an Indian—and then, painted and feathered for war, Philip's braves came swarming out of Mount Hope. They surrounded Swansea and shot down settler after settler, until, by the night of June 21, 11 English had received their death wounds.

New England was shocked. From Boston and Connecticut, parties of hastily formed militia came hurrying to Plymouth's rescue. Philip quickly evacuated Mount Hope. His position on the peninsula in Narragansett Bay was untenable. He moved west to the mainland of Rhode Island, while the colonists occupied Mount Hope. From there, Benjamin Church, a colonist knowledgeable in Indian affairs, led a party eastward in pursuit. But they blundered into country infested with rattlesnakes, to the disgust of Church, who thought his men were more afraid of the rattlers "than the black Serpents they were in quest of." Suddenly the "Serpents" appeared and drove the colonists back to Mount Hope.

King Philip now had his war. It had been forced upon him unawares and there was nothing to do but to unleash the ferocity which might rally all the wavering tribes to him while paralyzing the English will to fight. Moving rapidly he struck against settlements in Rehoboth, Taunton and Dartmouth, forcing the residents of Middleborough to flee their village and spreading the dread of his name right into nearby Plymouth. Soon, as he expected, news of his triumphant sorties brought hordes of other tribesmen to his side. Gradually, the fire and ruin, the blood and agony of the tomahawk and the flaming arrow were spread up and down the Connecticut River Valley. It was warfare as barbarous and as pitiless as the horror which the Iroquois spread along the St. Lawrence. Massacre followed massacre, and midnight raids succeeded daylight ambush. With such terror Philip hoped to paralyze the English. But Philip had underestimated his foes. He was the first of the enemies of this country to mistake the peaceful man for the pacifist, and to confuse unreadiness for war with unwillingness to fight. So also were these colonists the first Americans to expose the guardians of their frontiers to a hopeless and bloody fight against overwhelming odds. Even so, the dripping hatchet plunging into the brains of defenseless women and children was also to cut away the last restraints of the English. All their own disciplined ferocity was now let loose upon the Indians. Scalps were taken, bounties were offered for Indian heads, and captive red men were sold into slavery in the Mediterranean and the West Indies.

Six months after Philip had begun his war, the crucial battle was fought on the west side of Narragansett Bay, where the United Colonies of Massachusetts, Connecticut and Plymouth had raised a force of a thousand men. A few miles to the southwest of them 3,000 Indians commanded by the Narragansett sachem Canonchet were entrenched in a fortified village built on an island in a marsh known as the Great Swamp.

On December 19, a cold, snowy day, the colonists marched toward the fort. They crossed the frozen marsh and came upon a walled village protected by masses of felled trees and piles of brush heaped in front of a stockade. There was one gap in the walls, directly opposite the colonists, and they charged it.

Fighting for their lives, the Indians drove the English back with a volley of musket fire. But the colonists rallied and charged again. They fought their way inside the village, and a fierce hand-to-hand fight raged among the wigwams. Then the English set fire to the lodges and the battle swirled on amid flames and smoke, until, as the dusk of a bitterly cold night began to descend, the Indians broke and fled. Now the flames were beyond control, engulfing the Indian dead and wounded, so that, in the words of Cotton Mather, 600 men, women and children were "terribly barbikew'd."

Such a defeat might have discouraged a less ardent spirit than Philip. But he fought on, assisted by the able Canonchet, with whom he had made rendezvous in central Massachusetts. Throughout the winter Philip counseled his allies: burn every house, destroy every village, kill every white man. Before the thaws of spring set in, the war parties set out along the frozen streams and terror was renewed. Town after town was put to the torch. Canonchet struck steadily south until he had reappeared near the scene of his Great Swamp defeat, and King Philip devastated Rhode Island and swept east into Plymouth itself, burning 16 houses.

Of 90 white settlements in New England, 52 had been attacked and 12 had been destroyed. The flower of its manhood was perishing in the battle. However, at the very peak of success, with his goal of utter annihilation almost within his grasp, Philip's own weaknesses became rapidly and ruinously apparent. He had no solid base of operations, no inpregnable position to which he might return to regroup and replan. He had no stores. His war parties lived off the land. Now it was spring and the Indians, denied old hunting and fishing lands, needed to search out new ones if they were to prevent their women and children from starving. And so, one by one, the war parties slipped away, to be defeated piecemeal by the rallying colonists or to be brought over to the English cause.

In April Canonchet was trapped and captured. He was sentenced to be shot. "I shall die before my heart is soft, or I have said anything unworthy of myself," the proud chieftain said before his death.[5] His loss depressed King Philip. It discouraged Philip's followers still more. One by one, the war bands deserted their chief. One of them went straight to the enemy. A chief dispatched by Awashonks, squaw sachem of the Sakonnets, came to Benjamin Church and said: "Sir, if you will please to accept of me and my men, and will head us, we will fight for you, and will help you to Philip's head before the corn be ripe."[6]

Church accepted. Plymouth authorized him to lead a party of colonists and the treacherous Sakonnets against Philip. On July 20, 1676, Church surprised Philip in a swamp, killing or capturing 173 Wampanoags. Philip escaped, but his uncle and adviser was among the slain; his wife and son were among those captives sold into slavery. Now the manhunt began in earnest. Philip flitted from haunt to hideout, never tarrying for fear some new piece of treachery would betray him. His followers were now few. After one of them advised Philip to make peace with the English, he ordered the man killed—setting in motion the final betrayal. The executed man's brother, an Indian named Alderman, deserted to Church and promised to lead him to King Philip.

The Indian leader, like a wild beast coming home to die, had returned to his ancestral stronghold at Mount Hope. In the dead of the night of August 11, 1676, Church led 18 English and 22 Indians across the bay to the peninsula. They surrounded Philip's camp. To the rear of the camp, Church stationed an ambush. Then, at dawn, he attacked.

Driven from their quarters by volleys of musket balls, the startled Wampanoags reacted as Church had envisioned; they turned and fled. Most of them ran straight into the ambush. One of them came sprinting toward a man named Caleb Cook and the traitor, Alderman. Cook's gun misfired, but Alderman's double-barreled weapon roared twice. The fleeing Indian toppled to the ground. Alderman ran forward and rolled the body over. It was King Philip, and there was a hole in his heart and another one two inches above it.

Thus ended King Philip's War. It had been the opening round of a racial conflict which was to rage intermittently for two centuries until it came to its climax on the Western plains. And if the colonists of New France had learned about war by fighting Indians, so had the settlers of New England.

Soon they would be fighting each other.

2

☆

In American folklore the myth of "the most peace-loving nation in the world" still persists. But the fact is that American history is not only concurrent with the annals of American arms, but is as firmly woven into it as a strand of hemp in a rope. Probably it could not have been otherwise, for the birth of both the English and French colonies in the New World was simultaneous with the birth of modern warfare.

Even before the New World was colonized, the Spanish had revolutionized war by introducing an improved matchlock musket and fielding units of professional foot soldiers called infantry. (The name derived from the custom of adopting Spanish princes, or *infantes,* as the honorary colonels of various formations.) With their new though clumsy six-foot muskets, the Spanish foot soldiers were invincible, and their advent opened the age of modern infantry tactics. Deployment and maneuver on the open plain supplanted siege warfare.

However, the true beginning of modern warfare was probably the Thirty Years' War (1618-48), and its true parent was the great Swedish captain, Gustavus Adolphus. It was this warrior king who placed the modern emphasis on infantry firepower. He saw that the real arbiter of battle was the foot soldier holding the hand gun; he shortened and lightened his muskets and increased the number of musketeers while decreasing the number of pikemen. Gustavus Adolphus also introduced modern military discipline into his army and organized the service of supply. He was the first to make widespread use of artillery in the field, using bombardments to cover the shock charges of his cavalry. After Gustavus Adolphus, the heavy, ponderous formations of the Spanish infantry were obsolete, and European kings everywhere adopted the Swedish soldier's light and mobile battalions.

None of these changes had any effect on far-off America. Throughout the Thirty Years' War only one small ripple of Anglo-French conflict backwashed over American shores.

In 1629, while Protestant England came to the side of the French Huguenots resisting Catholic France, an expedition was mounted against Quebec. Samuel Champlain still commanded the struggling settlement then, although he had only 16 starving men inside his rickety fort when Lewis Kirke sailed up the St. Lawrence and summoned him to surrender. Forced to capitulate, Champlain was taken to England as a prisoner. Three years later an Anglo-French treaty brought him his freedom.

Once again the colonists of both crowns were left alone, and they left each other alone. All their fighting was against the Indians, and although their discipline and weapons were always superior, their tactics were scarcely more refined than the bush warfare of the red men. Arms as an art, still less as a profession, was not known in America, and it was not until 1672 that a professional soldier on the new European model arrived in the New World. He was Louis de Buade, the Count Frontenac, a fiery and tumultuous war dog. When Frontenac sailed up the St. Lawrence and entered the widening basin of Quebec, he saw the young city crowning the cliff above him. "I never saw anything more superb than the position of this town," he wrote. "It could not be better situated as the future capital of a great empire."[7]

Ten years later Frontenac was sailing back to France. By his own lights, and by the standards of those days, he had served his King faithfully and well. He had planted Fort Frontenac on the shores of Lake Ontario, thus guarding the routes of the fur trade; but he had also quarreled with the Bishop over the sale of brandy to the

Indians (from which illicit traffic he probably profited), and with the Intendant over the exercise of power. In fine, Frontenac had made too many enemies, and it is safe to say that, as he left, only those friendly Indians who called him the greatest of the *"Onontios,"* or governors of Canada, were sorry to see him go.

In 1689, a crusty and audacious 70 years of age, he was back— and with his arrival came the first blows of New France against New England during the War of the Grand Alliance.

The colonists called this conflict King William's War, and the name is significant. Although Americans generally are fond of pretending that the religious intolerance which erupted in the Thirty Years' War failed to infect the forefathers of America, the fact is that those doctrinal disputes which sundered Christendom were from the very beginning a powerful influence upon American history. Those Pilgrims who fled England to escape the persecution of the Anglican Church set up a harsher and more intolerant persecution of their own once they had planted the New Jerusalem on the uncontaminated shores of Cape Cod. They abhorred the Catholics of New France as idolators and were in turn despised as heretics.

The War of the Grand Alliance was "King William's" to the colonists because William of Orange was a Protestant prince sworn to guarantee Protestantism in England. James II, whom he had supplanted during the "Glorious Revolution" of 1688, was a Catholic who had already attempted to restore that faith in England. Now, in 1689, as Frontenac returned to New France, the Catholic James supported by the Catholic Louis of France was trying to regain the English throne.

Frontenac's first mission was the capture of New York, with explicit instructions to expel all settlers except any Catholics found willing to take an oath of allegiance to the French King. He was foiled by foul weather, which delayed his arrival until September —far too close to winter for military operations. Nevertheless, the religious motive was already present on both sides; and in all the Colonial Wars, as also partially in the Revolutionary War, the religious thrust was never very far away from its emotional twin of racial pride.

Actually, the New York operation was far too grandiose for the forces at Frontenac's command. He arrived at Quebec to find only 700 or 800 soldiers there and the colony itself in terror. Iroquois

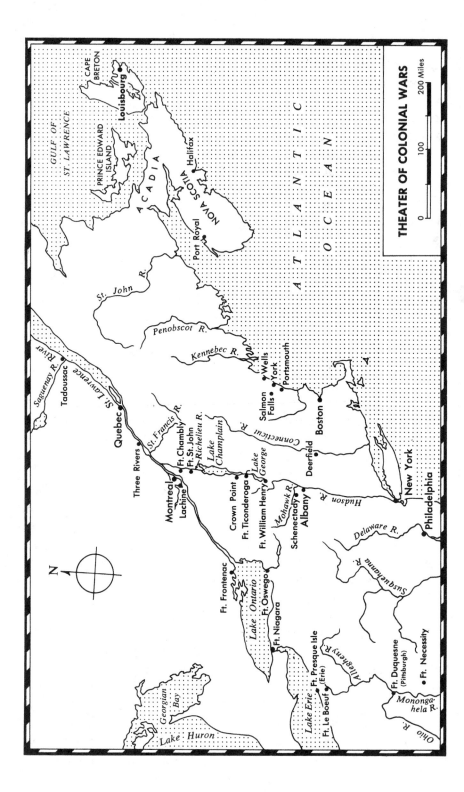

THEATER OF COLONIAL WARS

0   100   200 Miles

had come howling and murdering along the borders again. Frontenac himself inspected the bloody ashes of the massacred settlement at Lachine. He had also, to his disgust, arrived too late to prevent his frightened troops from destroying Fort Frontenac; and Canada's Indian allies, terrified by the English-oriented Iroquois, were on the point of deserting to the enemy.

Frontenac decided that he could only retain his allies, and give a check to Iroquois arrogance, by attacking the English to the south. He formed three war parties: one at Montreal, one at Three Rivers and one at Quebec. In that order they were to strike at Albany, the border villages of New Hampshire and those of what is now Maine. The Albany foray, the largest, was to depart first.

It consisted of 210 men, of whom 96 were Indians. The remainder were Frenchmen, and most of these were *coureurs de bois,* that is, "runners of the woods," or bushrangers, a hardy breed of Canadian to whom the forest was home. Like their Engish counterparts, the American rangers, they were romantic figures of a vanished era. Equally at ease in bucksin or in homespun, dreaming beside the campfire or drunk inside the gambling hall, they could stalk wild beasts as skillfully as any savage—and they could also take a neat scalp.

The Montreal party left in mid-January, 1690, in the dead of winter. They moved on snowshoes, clad in hoods or blanket-coats, with hatchets, knives, tobacco and bullet pouches dangling at their belts, pipes slung about their necks in leather cases, arquebuses in their mittened hands and packs on their backs. Supplies were dragged over the snow on Indian sledges.

Turning left at the Richelieu, they shuffled up that ribbon of ice and debouched on Lake Champlain.

It was a bitter march, and the French gradually came to realize that to attempt Albany would be folly. They would attack its outpost, Schenectady, instead. Reaching the Hudson, the march became even more miserable. A partial thaw had set in and Frontenac's wretched warriors were forced to stumble through slimes of mud and slush, up to their knees in icy swamp water. The weather changed again, to a whistling snowstorm.

But if the weather was against the French and Indians, the complacency of the Dutch burghers in Schenectady was in their favor. The Dutch laughed aside all warnings from Albany, and carried their derision to the length of leaving the settlement gates open with two snowmen as mock sentinels.

The raiders slipped past the snowman at the northern gate. Schenectady slept on. The raiders peeled off, left and right, until, between the palisades and the rows of silent houses stood ranks of French and Indians. And then the night silence was split with the screeching of the war whoops, the doors of the houses were burst open, the tomahawks came plunging down—and the butchery began.

"No pen can write, and no tongue express, the cruelties that were committed," wrote Peter Schuyler. "The women bigg with Childe rip'd up, and the Children alive throwne into the flames, and their heads dashed against the Doors and windows."[8]

In all, 60 persons were killed—of whom 22 were women and children—and between 80 and 90 were taken prisoners. By noon the village of Schenectady was a pile of smoking ashes. Even the Mohawks were shocked when they came upon it a few days later. And Albany was terrified, as were New Hampshire and Maine, when springtime brought the news that raiding parties of French and Indians had destroyed the settlements of Salmon Falls and Casco Bay in like barbarous blood baths.

To Count Frontenac in Quebec the reports were cause for jubilation. "You cannot believe, Monseigneur," he wrote to the Minister in Paris, just after Schenectady, "the joy that this slight success has caused, and how much it contributes to raise the people from their dejection and terror."[9]

The raids may have lifted Canadian hearts, but they had not cast down English ones. Frontenac had not only failed in his second objective; he had created exactly the reverse reaction. Far from being cowed, New York and New England were in a fighting mood. Like King Philip before him, the Count Frontenac had mistaken the temper of his enemy.

The English colonists planned to retaliate with a land-and-sea assault upon Canada. Colonial militia—400 from New York, 350 from Connecticut, Plymouth and Massachusetts—were to rendezvous at Albany with nearly all of the Iroquois, and then advance on Montreal by way of Lake Champlain. Massachusetts alone was mounting the water-borne attack. It was at first intended to fall on Quebec. But the Bay Colony could not afford such an expensive expedition.

Her treasury was empty. French privateers operating out of Port Royal in Acadia (modern Nova Scotia) had been scourging her commerce. Why not, then, take Port Royal? It would put an end to that shark's sanctuary and would give New England command of the entrance to the St. Lawrence. It was agreed, and seven ships carrying about 500 militia were placed under Sir William Phips.

Phips is one of the most remarkable figures in colonial history. Born one of 26 children by the same woman, he was reared in poverty at a rude settlement on the banks of the Kennebec, tending sheep until the age of 18. Then he took up carpentry. Next he came to Boston to marry a widow, better born, better-off and better along in years than himself. In Boston he learned to read and write and to aspire to the command of a king's ship and possession of "a fair brick house in the Green Lane of North Boston."

Phips achieved far more than both dreams combined. Like countless Americans to follow him, he went hunting for sunken treasure. After one fruitless expedition during which Phips, a tall and powerful man, quelled two mutinies, he persuaded the British Admiralty to subsidize a second quest. This time Phips found the wreck of a Spanish galleon in the West Indies and took from it treasure valued at £300,000, and he came home a rich man and a knight.

On May 11, 1690, Phips put his militia ashore at Port Royal and summoned the French Governor, Meneval, to surrender. Meneval had only about 70 soldiers holding a ramshackle fort, and he pulled down his flag with alacrity.

Meanwhile, the overland attack on Montreal was floundering badly. Fitz-John Winthrop, the commander, had met nothing but trial and setback. Only a few reluctant Iroquois had joined his forces. Disputes between the men of the colonies, and quarrels within the New York militia, disrupted discipline. Smallpox reduced Winthrop's strength and scared off the three western tribes of the Iroquois. Finally, there were not enough canoes to ascend Champlain. Winthrop decided to return to Albany after sending Captain John Schuyler forward to make a successful but minor raid at Laprairie.

Frontenac had been at Laprairie. He had rushed there from Montreal—where he had delighted his Indians by seizing a tomahawk and joining them in a whooping war dance—but then, convinced that the English would not attack in force, he had returned to Montreal and then to Quebec.

He arrived in time to gird his beloved "capital city of a great empire" for the all-out assault launched upon it by Sir William Phips.

The triumphant Phips returned from Port Royal to find Boston throbbing with preparation for a much bigger venture: the capture of Quebec.

England had been asked to supply arms, while Massachusetts got ready the ships and men. Even though the Bay Colony's funds were short, it was believed that the plunder of Canada's capital city would more than offset outlays for the expedition. Accordingly, 36 ships of all sizes were assembled and a call for volunteers was issued. After enlistments failed to produce the desired number of men, the colony calmly impressed the rest.

In all, the expeditionary force numbered 2,200 sailors and soldiers, if raw farmers and fishermen may be so designated. At their head was Sir William, a bluff, coarse adventurer-turned-merchant whose military experience consisted of a victory by summons. Beneath him was John Walley—"Major" Walley, now—one of the colony's most respectable citizens, and therefore, by the standards of a merchant republic, eminently qualified to command men in battle.

But vain considerations for the arts of war would have seemed a contradiction to the race chosen by the God of Battles. These citizen-soldiers of New Jerusalem—all these Jonathans and Sauls and Calebs, these Abrahams and Israels and Jedidiahs—could they possibly fail in the holy war against the idolators of the north? Was the New Jerusalem not to be the instrument of God's vengeful wrath upon the New Canaan? Certainly it was, and to suggest that the Almighty's own purpose might be thwarted was to utter a blasphemy. Just to be sure, however, the populace was exhorted to do penance, a day of fasting was ordained, and the Lord was imprecated to look with favor upon the instruments of His will.

Meanwhile, the reply from England had come and the answer was no. King William was too busy with James II in Ireland at that moment. Nevertheless, the expedition sailed. Phips had already waited too long to begin operations, and he left Nantasket on August 9, 1690.

Contrary winds delayed Phips for three more weeks, and it was well into October before he arrived. During that time, Frontenac had fortified Quebec. Entering the basin with the city on the cliff before him, Phips also contemplated a bristling fort. Still, he had taken one French fortress simply by raising his voice—and he summoned Frontenac to surrender. The count's reply to the young subaltern who brought the summons was: "No, I will answer your general only by the mouths of my cannon, that he may learn that a man like me is not to be summoned after this fashion. Let him do his best, and I will do mine."[10]

Sir William called a council of war. It was decided to land at Beauport, a town just below Quebec. The St. Charles River emptied into the St. Lawrence between Quebec and Beauport. Major Walley would take his men up the St. Charles to a ford, cross and strike at the rear of Quebec. The smaller ships would sail up as far as the ford to give fire support. Once the English soldiers had begun attacking Quebec's rear, Phips and the heavier ships would bombard the city from the basin. Neither Phips nor Walley seems to have known that Frontenac had constructed a line of fortifications behind the city. Nor did they pay much attention to French prisoners who told them of a place a mile or two above Quebec where a little-known path led upward to the heights. Seven decades later a red-haired British general named Wolfe would scrutinize similar information a bit closer.

Daylight was fading as the council of war reached its conclusions. At nightfall the colonists heard the peal of fifes and the roll of drums from atop the cliff. The English asked a prisoner named Granville what it meant.

"*Ma foi, Messieurs,*" he answered, smiling, "you have lost the game. It is the governor of Montreal with the people from the country above. There is nothing for you now but to pack and go home."[11]

It was true. Quebec had been reinforced just in time. About 800 men—regular soldiers and unruly *coureurs de bois*—had come downriver to enter the city shouting and singing, to swell the garrison to 3,000 armed men, and to make Sir William's slim chances of success even narrower.

Nevertheless the assault went forward. Walley took some 1,300 militia ashore at Beauport. They were met by a delaying force of 300 sharpshooters. Slowly, taking casualties, Walley's men drove the Canadians back. They gained the St. Charles and made camp for the night. In the morning they would rendezvous with the fire-ships and move upriver.

Unfortunately, the impatient Sir William had gone into action. With neither Walley nor the smaller ships as yet on the St. Charles, he had opened fire on Quebec. Actually, it was Frontenac who had opened fire on him. From the Château St. Louis perched on the brink of the cliff, the count had watched the biggest English ships leave their moorings and sail into position under the town, and he fired the first shot in a furious cannonading that reverberated in one long re-echoing crash around the basin of Quebec. The English ships spat flames and shot, and the cliff belched back with fire and ball. Next day, the duel was resumed. But now the British Crown's failure to provide adequate ammunition, yoked to the colony's faith in God rather than in gunnery practice, began to tell.

The French were superior in shot and in skill. Their 18- and 24-pounders battered the biggest English ships. One cut off Phip's flag-staff and the Cross of St. George fluttered into the river, to be rescued as a prize by Canadian boatmen. Infuriated, the colonists turned their guns on a banner of the Holy Family floating from the spire of the cathedral. They missed it, and the jubilant French—whose priests and nuns had not neglected to imprecate the Virgin for direct hits—promptly proclaimed a miracle. However, as Parkman dryly observed, "The miracle would have been greater if they had hit it."

Riddled and listing, Sir William's ships retired from the combat. He had attacked prematurely, he had exhausted the slender supplies of ammunition needed for the moment when Walley pressed his attack from the rear—and he had, in effect, lost the entire battle. Walley, to his credit, tried to persevere in an impossible situation. Though his small fireships never appeared, probably because their masters also owned them and were loath to risk them under Fron-tenac's cannon, he still attempted to press on to the ford. But he never crossed the St. Charles. Frontenac, with battalions of regulars, militia and Indians, crossed it instead to oppose Walley's frozen troops. A series of inconclusive actions was fought, and four days after they had landed at Beauport the English withdrew to their boats.

The capture of Port Royal and the unsuccessful attempt against Quebec were the only military expeditions of note in King William's War. Once they were over, the fighting degenerated into an exchange of bloody border raids, until, in 1698, England and France ended the War of the Grand Alliance with the Peace of Ryswick.

In that same year Count Frontenac's heart ceased to beat. That very summer he had marched once more against the dreaded Iroquois, but in November he took to his bed in his chamber in the Château St. Louis. He died there, in his 78th year, and New France went into deep mourning.

Perhaps it was understood that something more than a governor of Canada had breathed his last. An era was also perishing. Cartier, La Salle, Champlain, Jogues, Joliet, Marquette, all those bright and shining names which ennoble the history of France in the New World, all these had come before the fiery count from the Pyrenees, and now Frontenac was also dead.

Soldiers and explorers and martyrs were to be replaced by grafting officials, vain and petty governors and worldly priests. It was almost as though the death of Frontenac had been concurrent with the death of the dreams of Louis XIV. All the glory and dominion that the Sun King sought had been his throughout most of the seventeenth century. Now the eighteenth was at hand, and with it disaster for Louis and for France.

3

☆

From a purely military standpoint, it would seem that the advantage during the next three Colonial Wars lay with the French.

Feudal in structure and directed by the strong hand of a centralized government, New France was almost as military as Sparta. Its settlers or *habitants,* as the ordinary French people of Canada are called to this day, were not loosely scattered through the forests as were their southern neighbors of New England. Rather, they were strung out in settlements on either side of the St. Lawrence. A cannon shot from Montreal or Quebec sent them running for the forts. An order from the governor mustered them as militia.

Moreover, the French spent the five-year truce conferred upon

America by the Peace of Ryswick in preparing for the second round of battle. New France's seaward flank had been secured by the restoration of Port Royal to the French Crown. Now, with the power of the Iroquois broken by Frontenac, the way was clear to pen the English colonies between the Alleghenies and the sea. A fort had been built at Michilimackinac at the point where the waters of Lake Michigan enter Lake Huron, and another was erected at Detroit to command the confluence of Lake Huron and Lake Erie. Eventually there was a chain of forts stretching westward from Montreal to the Mississippi; then, with the planting of a new French colony at the mouth of the Father of Waters, French lines of communication reached from the Gulf of the St. Lawrence to the Gulf of Mexico.

Such formidable activity did not seem to trouble the English colonists. More commercial than military, fragmented as a whole and perhaps even looser in its democratic parts, the English society on the Atlantic was quite naturally re-engaged in growth and gain. It was, at the beginning of the eighteenth century, a community of some quarter-million souls. That was perhaps five times larger than the colony on the St. Lawrence, thanks not so much to greater immigration as to a birth rate that was already the astonishment of Europe.

In the South, tobacco made the Chesapeake aristocrats prosper; in the middle colonies it was land and trade; and in the North trade alone. In the Southern and middle colonies—all, except for New York, distant from Canada—there was little fear of French incursions, and little disposition to succor either New York or New England should trouble recommence. True enough, the South and the middle had Indian troubles, but nothing to compare with the howling hell that could burst on the Northern borders upon a fresh outbreak of hostilities between England and France.

And that was to occur after Louis of France had cast his covetous eyes on the crown of Spain.

In simplified terms, the War of the Spanish Succession began because King Louis claimed the Spanish throne for his grandson, Philip of Anjou. In justice to the French King, however, he was all but forced to make that claim. Had Spain gone to the rival house of Austria, the old French fear of encirclement would have been realized. But when Louis followed up his justifiable claim by a series of unwarranted aggressions, and then excluded English merchants from the Spanish colonial trade, the war began. It was a commercial war to the death. Because King William had died of injuries suffered in a fall from his horse, and his sister-in-law, Anne, now reigned in England, the Americans called it Queen Anne's War.

Queen Anne's War brought a return of the scalping horror to the borders between New England and Canada. Then, in 1704, a band of French and Indians sacked the sleeping village of Deerfield in western Massachusetts. With this, New England became enraged. Major Benjamin Church, the old Indian fighter of King Philip's War, was so infuriated that he mounted his horse in Tiverton, Rhode Island, and rode all the way to Boston. He arrived with both himself and his horse in a froth and the poor beast staggering. Church had by then grown so stout that he could not pursue Indians into the woods unless accompanied by a sergeant detailed to hoist him over fallen trees. Nevertheless, he was the only veteran soldier in the colony, and Governor Dudley at once agreed to let him lead an expedition of retaliation.

As usual, Massachusetts was not quite ready for war, and Church was unable to do more than to invade Acadia to destroy Saint-Castin's fort and burn a few houses at Grand Pré. An attempt at Port Royal in 1707 ended in failure after a brief exchange of shots that can best be described as a token fight. Still, the border outrages continued, until at last the exasperated English colonists decided that the only way to end them was to conquer Canada itself.

Captain Samuel Vetch of Boston, the prime mover in this scheme, was sent to England to solicit the help of the mother country. By the time he arrived, Vetch had expanded the plan to include the capture of Newfoundland and the expulsion of the Spanish from Florida. Then he wrote: "Her Majesty shall be sole empress of the vast North American continent."[12]

Queen Anne, however, could be quite content with Canada alone, and Vetch returned to Boston in 1709 empowered to execute a campaign which was to end with himself installed as governor of the conquered province. Montreal was to be attacked by land and Quebec by water. New York with 800 men, New Jersey with 200, Pennsylvania with 150 and Connecticut with 350 were to furnish a total of 1,500 men to be mustered at Albany by the middle of May. This force, under Colonel Francis Nicholson, was to strike at Montreal by way of the Champlain route, while a British squadron bearing five regiments of regular troops—around 3,000 men—and 1,200 militia from Massachusetts, New Hampshire and Rhode Island sailed up the St. Lawrence to invest Quebec.

New York and Connecticut promptly furnished their troops. But New Jersey, far removed from the fires of border warfare, gave no men at all; and Pennsylvania, ruled by pacifist Quakers, supplied only £3,000 with the quaint proviso that the money should not be used to kill people.

Nevertheless Colonel Nicholson was able to move up the Hudson with a force of 1,500 men. He built a stockade fort where Fort Edward now stands and cut a rough road to Wood Creek, which led to Lake Champlain. Then, while canoes were made and flatboats were brought upriver and dragged to Wood Creek, and after an inconclusive brush with a French force which seemed to return to Montreal as suddenly as it had appeared in New York, Nicholson sat down to await word of the arrival of the British fleet in Boston.

The New England soldiery encamped near Boston Harbor also awaited the British squadron. Each morning they arose and searched the horizon for the welcome sight of sails. Days became weeks and weeks months, and as the New Englanders fidgeted and Captain Vetch wrote imploring letters to England, a malignant dysentery broke out in Nicholson's camp far to the west. Men dropped by the scores. The able-bodied were busy tending the sick one day and burying the corpses the next.

At last, as autumn turned that dark green wilderness into a glowing riot of rubies and topazes, the disgusted Nicholson was forced to accept the fact that land operations against Canada were now no longer feasible, and he withdrew to Albany—his men cursing Vetch and swearing that he should be hanged. On October 11 the unfortunate Vetch received a letter from England advising him that the troops promised him had been diverted to Portugal instead.

Though deeply disappointed, the dogged New Englanders did not give up all hope of reprisal; once again they lowered their sights from Quebec to Port Royal. England was again persuaded to provide ships, and in 1710 Massachusetts again rounded up its semidrilled throng of farmers, mechanics, plowboys, clerks and apprentices. The soldiers of 1709 were asked to enlist again, this time lured by the promise that they might keep the muskets supplied them. Once again, when volunteers fell below quotas, the colony calmly drafted the reluctant. Seamen were impressed by the forefathers of that nation which would fight a war to protect its seamen from British press gangs, and the parents of those sturdy provincials who would make mock of the dainties and delicacies in the elaborate war train of Gentleman Johnny Burgoyne did not hesitate to vote 20 sheep, 5 pigs, 100 fowl and 1 pipe of wine for the table of General Nicholson. A dinner was held at the Green Dragon Tavern in honor of Nicholson, Vetch and Sir Charles Hobby, the British squadron commander, and on the following morning, September 18, the expedition numbering about 40 ships, large and small, sailed for Acadia.

Six days later the fleet threaded the narrow entrance to Port Royal. One ship was driven on rocks and sank with the loss of 26 men, but the others anchored safely in sight of the fort. Without interference from the French garrison under Subercase, the new Governor of Acadia, Nicholson began putting his troops ashore. By the following day, September 25, the English had landed four battalions comprised of 400 British marines and about 1,500 militia— no slight achievement in an era when transports were always at the mercy of the wind and the tides.

Moving against the fort, two battalions under Vetch attacked from the north, two under Nicholson from the south. The French harried them with cannon and small arms, but the English continued to move forward until they had occupied ground within artillery range of the fort. Then their own artillery was brought up and emplaced. On October 1, after a desultory—and probably perfunctory—exchange of shots, Subercase asked for terms. Once more the golden Bourbon lilies came fluttering down Port Royal's flagstaff; the French soldiers— about 250 men—came marching out with drums rolling, colors flying and arms reversed; the English troops went marching in, the Union Jack went up the pole, the Queen's health was drunk—and in the morning the distressed French ladies of the fort were treated to a breakfast by the English officers.

For the third time irate New Englanders had responded to Canada's border attacks by seizing the capital of Acadia. This time, however, the city which Nicholson renamed Annapolis Royal in honor of Queen Anne remained British. Eventually, the entire province of Acadia fell to the British Crown.

However, one more expedition—the mightiest of all in Queen Anne's War—was mounted against Quebec.

The third attempt upon the capital of Canada was organized by the mother country, and it sprang from political motives. The new Tory ministry in England was eager to discredit the Duke of Marlborough, whose stunning victories over the French and Spanish had made him the darling of the Whigs. The Tories reasoned that if France could be evicted from America, it could be shown that this triumph would be of greater value to England than all Marlborough's victories, which were already being belittled as of more benefit to Holland and Austria than to Britain. So the new Tory ministry looked across the sea to America. A force of 12,000 men was to be raised to assault Quebec. The sea command was given to an armchair admiral named Sir Hovenden Walker and the ground forces were to be led by Mrs. Masham's brother Jack. Mrs. Masham was the new royal favorite, and her brother, Jack Hill, a man of immense social grace and no military ability, had been promoted to general.

Perhaps the most competent high commander in the entire expedition was the colonial General Nicholson, who was again to move against Montreal by way of Lake Champlain.

Walker and Hill sailed into Boston in June, 1711. They had 9 ships of war, 2 bomb ketches and about 60 transports and supply ships, carrying 7 British infantry regiments, 600 marines and artillery. After picking up 1,500 colonial militia, they steered for the St. Lawrence.

Although it was only August by the time they had reached it, Admiral Walker was already full of misgivings about the Canadian winter. He could think of nothing but ships stove in by freezing ice and men perishing of cold and hunger. "I must confess the melancholy contemplation of this," he wrote later, "for how dismal must it have been to have beheld the seas and the earth locked up by adamantine frosts, and swoln with high mountains of snow, in a barren and uncultivated region; great numbers of brave men famishing with hunger, and drawing lots who should die first to feed the rest."[13]

However, calamities of a different order afflicted Walker's fleet. Because of his own poor seamanship eight transports and two other ships were driven ashore and wrecked during a fog. Perhaps 900 persons perished, and a witness has written: "It was lamentable to hear the shrieks of the sinking, drowning, departing souls."[14] Shaken,

Walker called a council of war. Both he and Jack Hill were eager for an excuse to withdraw. They learned from the ship captains' report that they could not sail up the St. Lawrence without experienced pilots. Walker was aware that Sir William Phips had done that very thing 30 years ago; nevertheless, in the face of opposite—and indignant—counsel by such colonials as Samuel Vetch, he sailed back the way he had come.

At the foot of Wood Creek, prepared to enter Lake Champlain, General Nicholson heard the disgraceful news. "Roguery!" he cried, tearing off his wig and hurling it to the ground. "Treachery!" he screamed, stamping on the wig.[15] Recovering his composure, he ordered his forts burned and marched his force of 2,300 men back to Albany again.

Walker's ordeal was not quite ended. As the British fleet sailed up the Thames, a sailor attempting to steal gunpowder accidentally blew up the flagship, *Edgar*. Five hundred more men were lost in this tragic conclusion to the most ambitious of all projects to conquer Canada. The commanders sent out to eclipse the glory of the great Marlborough had accepted defeat without unsheathing their swords.

4

☆

The debacle on the St. Lawrence made the Tories eager to end hostilities, and in 1713 the Treaty of Utrecht brought the War of the Spanish Succession to a close.

England, Holland and Austria had fought to prevent the union of France and Spain under a Bourbon king, but the war ended with a grandson of Louis of France firmly seated on the Spanish throne. Nevertheless, both France and Spain were exhausted. France was forced to cede Acadia, Hudson's Bay and Newfoundland to England, while Spain handed over Gibraltar at the mouth of the Mediterranean and the sentinel island of Minorca inside it. Both France and

Spain granted England important trade concessions, while Spain, by leasing to England the slave trade to Latin America, indicated to what woeful depths her once proud fleets had sunk.

The British lion had not only obtained its customary share, it had grown stronger at sea at the expense of its ally—but foremost maritime rival—the Dutch Republic. Holland had supplied only three-eighths of the naval forces, against Britain's five-eighths, but she contributed 102,000 soldiers against Britain's 40,000. By accident or design, the Dutch exhausted themselves in an unfamiliar land war while Britain became supreme upon the sea. She was the queen of the waves, not only in her invincible navy but also in her merchant fleet. As Mahan writes: ". . . she was *the* sea power, without any second. This power also she held alone, unshared by friend and unchecked by foe."[16]

Posted now in the Mediterranean, America and the West Indies, Britain began to build that far-flung empire which dazzled the world for two and a half centuries; and she achieved this because she was conscious of the unique value of sea power, as her rivals in the House of Bourbon were not. Her conscious policy was the destruction of the French and Spanish navies and the strengthening of her own. Ports and harbors and strategic islands, not kingdoms, were the objects of her desire; and she sought them as outlets for trade and as bases for her fleets. She could cross no enemy's land frontier, but she could strike at them all from the sea. Without borders of her own, the sea gave her the world for her neighbor.

It was the new Kingdom of Prussia which convulsed Europe again. Once a mere duchy on the Polish border, Prussia was proclaimed a sovereign state in 1701 by the Margrave of Brandenburg, who thereafter became known as King Frederick I of Prussia. After his death, his son, Frederick William, succeeded to the throne.

Frederick William infected Prussia with its demonic spirit of militarism. He was obsessed with his army, with his tall grenadiers whom he had kidnaped from every corner of the world, and with whom he mated tall women similarly enslaved. But Frederick William did not live to lead his splendid army into battle. Instead, it was his son, Frederick II, who lifted the sword the father had forged.

Frederick swung at Austria, because that empire had been left helpless with the death of Emperor Charles VI in 1740. Charles's dominions were bequeathed to his daughter, Maria Theresa, and his will had been guaranteed in advance by the chief powers of Europe. But not a sovereign kept his word. Led by young Frederick of Prussia, who almost at once marched into Maria's province of Silesia and seized it, a pack of bejeweled jackals flocked forward to despoil the beautiful young queen's realm. After Frederick came Spain, Bavaria and then France. England, ever anxious to preserve the balance of power, as well as the Hanoverian holdings of King George II, rushed to Austria's side. Holland followed. Maria Theresa fought back, and the War of the Austrian Succession—the conflict which the colonists called King George's War—had begun.

The first blow struck for King George in America came from the new colony which had been named Georgia in his honor.

In the summer of 1740, James Oglethorpe, Georgia's founder, decided to evict the Spanish from the first European settlement in North America: St. Augustine. Then Florida would fall to the Union Jack and the Atlantic seaboard would be English from the Bay of Fundy to the Gulf of Mexico. But the Spaniards foiled him. They reinforced St. Augustine from Havana, and Oglethorpe's motley of 2,000 English and Indians sailed back to Georgia sunburned and hungry.

Three years later, the commander at St. Augustine, Don Manuel de Monteano, attempted a reverse expedition. He hoped to expel the English from the weak colony which stood as a buffer between New Spain and the rich and populous Carolinas. Even Virginia—and thus the entire South—would be annexed to Spain.

Monteano's force was much larger than Oglethorpe's had been. About 50 ships carrying about 6,000 men and artillery sailed up to St. Simon's Island off the Georgia coast. Here Oglethorpe had entrenched himself with a few thousand American Rangers and wild Highlanders from Scotland, and here he proved himself a more capable commander on defense than on offense. Though outnumbered, he took ship and struck boldly at the Spanish vessels; after which he returned to land, forced Monteano into attacking him piecemeal, destroyed the pieces, and finally frightened the Spaniards off with a bogus letter which, planted on Monteano by an "escaped" Spanish soldier bribed for the occasion, warned of the approach of a huge English fleet.

The first and only land clash of any consequence between England and Spain in North America had ended in stalemate. There was no more colonial fighting under the Southern sun. Thereafter, the Colonial Wars were fought within the familiar gloom of primeval forests or the mistbound coasts of the North.

Louis XIV had hated to give up Acadia. He had even offered to bar French fishermen from those Newfoundland coasts which they had patrolled for centuries if the English would allow him to keep those lands now called Nova Scotia. But all that he could obtain by way of compromise was the restoration of Cape Breton Island just a few miles east of Acadia. Even in this, the English ministers at Utrecht were not wise; in relinquishing Cape Breton Island they at once destroyed the military value of Acadia.

King Louis saw that the island wilderness was the true guardian of the St. Lawrence, and before he died he caused a port to be fortified to that end, and against the day when war would be resumed and France might attack New England and attempt to recover Acadia.

The new port grew into a fishing village of 4,000 persons. It became a harbor so well defended and a privateering refuge so secure that it was called the "Dunkirk of America." And it was named Louisbourg in the king's honor.

The power of Louisbourg was demonstrated when the French captured Canso and attempted but failed to take Annapolis Royal. Obviously, Acadia was at the mercy of the new French base on Cape Breton Island. Because of this, and because the French had renewed their border warfare, the colonists of Massachusetts decided to capture Louisbourg.

Governor William Shirley invited other colonies as far south as Pennsylvania to join the expedition. As usual, all but the New Englanders declined, and even Rhode Island did not provide troops in time for battle. Of the force finally assembled, 3,300 came from Massachusetts, 516 from Connecticut and 454 from New Hampshire, of which 150 were paid by Massachusetts. Some of these men— particularly the hardy borderers from Maine—had fought in the recent war against the Norridgewock Indians; but few, if any, had the sort of experience required for siege warfare against the ramparts and casemented batteries of a fortified town.

"Fortified towns are hard nuts to crack," Benjamin Franklin had written to his brother in Boston, "and your teeth are not accustomed to it. But some seem to think that forts are as easy taken as snuff."[17]

In Boston such good advice was regarded as typical of pacifist Philadelphia. Tough nut or no, Louisbourg and its Papists had already been consigned to the jaws of the Lord. What Cotton Mather once called "the wheel of prayer" was whirring night and day. The very man whom Governor Shirley had appointed to lead the expedition was known to be a pious man of God. William Pepperrell, a highly successful merchant as well as a man of extreme good sense—though no military experience, as he would himself declare—counted many clergymen among his friends. With him at the very moment Shirley appointed him a lieutenant general was none other than George Whitefield, that squint-eyed breather of fire whose archangelic voice had summoned New England to its Great Awakening. At the moment, that revivalist frenzy seemed to be subsiding, and another of Pepperrell's clerical friends was already complaining: "The heavenly shower [is] over; from fighting the devil they must turn to fighting the French."

Pepperrell himself would have preferred to continue with the devil, for he was aware that his forces included not an officer of experience, not even an engineer. Nevertheless he was persuaded to accept. Whitefield, meanwhile, was persuaded to supply a motto. He offered, *"Nil desperandum Christo duce,"* or "Despair not when Christ leads." Old Parson Moody, he of the iron lungs and marathon sermons, also joined the crusade against the antichrist. He brought along an ax to hew down his abominable altars.

Such was the crusading character of the expedition, and it was this ardor of intolerance which brought Parson Moody and General Pepperrell and 90 ships and 4,200 raw recruits to Louisbourg on the morning of April 28, 1745.

To enter Louisbourg basin would have been suicide. Even the warships of the British squadron which had joined the colonists would not attempt it. Instead, they blockaded the port.

To the east or the right of the town itself was a small entrance barely a half-mile wide. Commanding this was the "Island Battery" mounted on a rocky island to the west or left of the entrance. Directly ahead of the entrance on the basin's north shore was the "Grand

Battery." Ships attempting to force the harbor would be raked port and forward. So General Pepperrell sagely decided to put his troops ashore at Flat Point, three miles west of the town.

The Chevalier Duchambon, Governor of Louisbourg, sent 120 men to repulse them. Although Duchambon had 560 regulars and 1,400 militia, he probably did not send a larger force because he could not rely on rough and untried conscripts or soldiers ready to mutiny over pay and rations. So a Captain Morpain led his handful of defenders to Flat Point. They dug in, awaiting the English rowing toward them. Suddenly the English veered away, as though they dared not risk the surf boiling over Flat Point's rocky coast. Captain Morpain relaxed. He began to flatter himself on a bloodless repulse. But then, to his dismay, he saw that more English boats had been lowered away and that the reinforced body was rowing madly for Fresh-Water Cove another two miles to the west.

Morpain and his French soldiers went flying up the coast. But they were too late. The invaders were already ashore. Turning, they fell upon the French, killed six and captured six, and routed the rest against only two of their own men wounded. More and more boats came bobbing through the surf and soon General Pepperrell had a firm beachhead.

Louisbourg had been flanked.

On May 2 Captain William Vaughan, a bold though sometimes rash man, led 400 troops through the hills to the northwest of the town. His men saluted Louisbourg with three rousing cheers, and the inhabitants, surprised by the ragged and disorderly appearance of this crowd of colonists, were also startled by their vigor. Then Vaughan marched to the hills to the rear of the Grand Battery and put a supply of naval stores to the torch. Thick oily coils of smoke swirled skyward, to the dismay of the occupants of Louisbourg— and to the unseemly fright of the troops holding the Grand Battery.

Imagining that Vaughan had come to attack them, they hastily spiked their guns, threw gunpowder into the well and withdrew to the town in boats—leaving 30 of the King's good cannon to fall into the hands of Vaughan, who quickly occupied the battery in their absence. Soon a squad of soldier-mechanics had drilled out the cannons' spiked touchholes, and, in the words of an *habitant* of Louisbourg: "The enemy saluted us with our own cannon, and made a terrific fire, smashing everything within range."[18]

The ragged rabble which the civilian Pepperrell commanded was amazingly constant and cheerful. They built an encampment near Fresh-Water Cove, making tepees by stretching old sails over poles, or building sod huts with spruce boughs for roofs. They unloaded boats by wading up to the waist through ice-cold surf, and at night they threw themselves down, dripping wet, on soggy ground discharging the mists and chills of the thaw.

Next, in tatters and sometimes barefoot, they began dragging Pepperrell's cannon eastward toward Louisbourg. The first attempt to move a gun through the intervening marsh resulted in the loss of the piece, which vanished in the slime. Sledges of timber 16 by 5 feet were then made; cannon were placed on top of them, and teams of 200 men harnessed in breast straps and rope traces, sloshing through knee-deep mud and mush, began hauling them over the marsh. But this could only be done under cover of night or thick fog. Toiling "under almost incredible hardships," as Pepperrell was to write in admiration, they got the guns in place.

Battery after battery was planted under the strangely languorous nose of the Chevalier Duchambon. Louisbourg was hammered from the west, northwest, north and northeast. In all, the bellowing of five new batteries had been added to the cannonade issuing from the captured Grand Battery. Still, Duchambon sent forth no sallies to destroy the guns that were destroying him. Perhaps he still feared mutiny, although mutiny would seem less dangerous than the torrent of balls that was shredding Louisbourg's walls and forcing a terrified citizenry to take refuge within stifling casements.

It may also have been that Duchambon was aware that the New England army was in dire straits. Their food supply was low, ammunition was running out, Louisbourg's cannon and the accurate small-arms fire of the French soldiers had whittled their ranks, and diarrhea and fever had ravaged the remainder. In all, Pepperrell had only 2,100 men fit for duty. The disadvantages which always work against the besiegers in siege warfare were beginning to work in Duchambon's favor. And if the French ship *Vigilant* arrived with promised reinforcements, he might still be saved.

Vigilant, carrying 64 guns and 560 men and munitions and stores for the relief of Louisbourg, was commanded by the Marquis de la Maisonfort. On May 19 *Vigilant* came upon a small English cruiser. The little Englishman attacked. *Vigilant* replied with broadsides. The cruiser fled, still firing; *Vigilant* pursued, and found that she had been led straight into the massed guns of a British squadron. Maisonfort and his men fought gallantly, but after 80 men had been lost, the French commander was forced to strike his colors.

British sea power had saved Pepperrell's army and doomed the French. "We were victims devoted to appease the wrath of Heaven," wrote the *habitant,* "which turned our own arms into weapons for our enemies."[19]

Nevertheless, Duchambon did not know that he was doomed until after the English had also incurred the Heavenly wrath.

The impetuous Captain Vaughan was certain that the Island Battery was the key to Louisbourg. Capture it, and British troops could enter the harbor while Pepperrell's men stormed the town from the land. Vaughan proposed this before news of *Vigilant's* fall reached Pepperrell.

After midnight of May 23, about 300 men clambered into boats beached off the Grand Battery. It was a dark night and they hoped to gain the Island Battery undetected. They used paddles to make no noise. A rising wind also covered their approach. The leading boats reached the island's breakers, drove boldly through them, and scrambled ashore—still unseen.

And then they gave three cheers!

Island Battery "blazed with cannon, swivels, and small-arms." A withering fire plunged into these foolish commandos, and into the following boats piled up on the shore. The English fought back bravely. They even succeeded in placing a dozen scaling ladders against the walls of the fort, but with daybreak it was hopeless to fight on. Those who did not escape surrendered, to the number of 119. In all, English losses were 189, or more than half of the attacking force.

The only pitched battle had ended in an English defeat, although Louisbourg was already undone. The town's fate was sealed when Pepperrell wisely decided to mount another battery on Lighthouse Point across the harbor entrance from Island Battery. The Lighthouse guns gradually reduced the island to impotence. All was in readiness for a final land-sea assault jointly commanded by General Pepperrell and Commodore Peter Warren, commander of the British squadron. It was to commence June 15. On that day, Captain Joseph Sherburn at the advanced battery, wrote in his diary: "By 12 o'clock we had got all our platforms laid, embrazures mended, guns in order, shot in place, cartridges ready, dined, gunners quartered, matches lighted to return their favours, when we heard their drums beat a parley; and soon appeared a flag of truce, which I received midway between our battery and their walls."[20]

Duchambon was asking for terms. Two days later Louisbourg was occupied by the English. "Never was a town more mauled with cannon and shells," Pepperrell wrote to Governor Shirley, "neither have I read in History of any troops behaving with greater courage."[21]

He was right. The disorderly rabble had taken a fortified city with the bold precision of troops trained in siege warfare. Pepperrell's New Englanders had won the only outstanding engagement of King George's War. True, there would be skirmishes to follow, and a French fleet more powerful than the English one which Admiral Walker and Jack Hill had led to disaster and disgrace in the last war was to encounter ordeals even more dreadful and to achieve as little in its attempt to retake Louisbourg and succor Canada.

Even if it had done so, its success would have been superfluous. Much to the indignant disgust of *"les Bastonnais,"* the Peace of Aix-la-Chapelle which ended the War of the Austrian Succession in 1748 returned Louisbourg to the French Crown.

5

☆

Aix-la-Chapelle solved next to nothing,

It gave Europe a breathing spell during which the contending powers realigned themselves, and it bestowed upon the American colonies of England and France a fitful peace soon to degenerate into undeclared war.

Both colonies knew that they could not remain at peace. Between their rival claims and conflicting ambitions there could be no compromise.

France claimed the continent from the Alleghenies to the Rockies, from Florida and Mexico to the North Pole. She possessed the two great waterways—the St. Lawrence and the Mississippi—and two bases of operations in Canada in the north and Louisiana in the south. Moreover, by the middle of the century she had occupied all the points controlling the waterways between Montreal and New Orleans and had even entered New York to plant a stone fort at Crown Point on Lake Champlain. The English colonies had thus been penned between the barrier of the Allegheny Mountains and the Atlantic Ocean. France desired to keep them there while she explored and exploited the vast American interior.

The English, however, not only rejected the French claim, but also aspired to enter the interior—not to exploit but to settle. Should they break out of the Allegheny enclave, they would cut New France in two. To prevent this, the French began to seal off the passes to the west.

They built a fort at Presque Isle on Lake Erie, at the point where the city of Erie, Pennsylvania, now stands; and then cut a road about ten miles long to French Creek, placing at the road's end another outpost called Fort Le Boeuf. They could now cross Lake Erie from Canada to Presque Isle, march overland to Fort Le Boeuf and follow French Creek to the Allegheny River, descending that swift stream to the Ohio River. This was done in 1753. Just before winter, the French evicted an English trader from his house at Venango, the place where French Creek enters the Allegheny.

Venango was France's farthest outpost. It was a clearing in the wilderness, caught between the steady roar of merging waters and the eternal silence of the forests. One day in December the three French officers who occupied the house there thought that they heard the thud of horses' hoofs approaching. A tall young Englishman came riding out of the woods.

He was only 21, but he was already a commanding figure. Tall at six feet three inches, strongly built, his angular cheeks pitted by the scars of the smallpox which had threatened his life a few years before, his humorless eyes full of his unbending determination,

Major George Washington of the Virginia Militia had come to Venango on a mission for Governor Robert Dinwiddie.

Washington had been in Williamsburg at the end of October, 1753, just after Governor Dinwiddie had received the King's approval for his plan to evict the French from the Ohio country. His Majesty promised military equipment, and in the meantime Dinwiddie was to warn the French that they were encroaching upon English lands and to call upon them to retire. Although the icy hand of winter would soon hold the Ohio in its grip, Dinwiddie, an aggressive man, wished to notify the French before they could build any more strong points. Who better than Washington to carry the message?

On Dinwiddie's orders, Washington assembled his party: horses, baggage, four orderlies and hostlers and a veteran of the Dutch army named Jacob van Braam who said he could speak French. On November 15, 1753, they set out for the Ohio country. It was a difficult journey, over strange terrain and beneath the cold rains of the dying autumn. But on December 4 Washington and his companions rode out of the dripping woods at Venango.

The French officers there greeted Washington with flawless courtesy. They also tried to lure his Indians to their side. Failing in this, they suavely refused the young Virginian's message and sent him up French Creek to Fort Le Boeuf to their superior officer, Legardeur de St. Pierre. At Le Boeuf, Washington presented Dinwiddie's demand that the French leave the Ohio country. It was politely refused by St. Pierre. "He told me," Washington wrote later, "that the country belonged to [the French]; that no Englishman had a right to trade upon those waters; and that he had orders to make every person prisoner who attempted it on the Ohio, or the waters of it."[22]

On December 16, bearing St. Pierre's reply, Washington and his party started downriver for Venango. They hurried, plying their paddles furiously, for the creek had begun to freeze. Leaving Venango, Washington discovered that his horses which had been quartered there were too feeble to carry riders. They dismounted and began to walk. Snow was falling regularly. The temperatures fell. Some of the men were so frostbitten they had to be left in a temporary shack. Washington pressed on grimly, eager to get the French answer to Dinwiddie as soon as possible. If he delayed, he might be snowed in until spring, when the French would be already on the move. Eventually, the young major struck out on foot with his guide.

"I took my necessary papers, pulled off my clothes, and tied myself up in a match coat. Then with gun in hand and pack at my back, I set out with Mr. Gist, fitted in the same manner."[23]

They were shot at—and missed—by a false Indian guide. Attempting to cross the Allegheny by a log raft, Washington was thrown into the icy water—only saving himself by throwing one long arm across the raft. But both men could not pole through the current to either shore, and they waded ashore on a little island, spending the night sheeted in ice. In the morning, to their inexpressible joy, they beheld the treacherous river locked in a silent white vise of ice. They crossed, and on January 16, 1754—exactly one month after his departure from Fort Le Boeuf—George Washington placed the French refusal in Governor Dinwiddie's hand.

At the age of 21 the Father of America had already entered his nation's history.

With hindsight, it seems incredible that New France should have even thought of victory in the contest for North America. By 1754 the continent held barely 80,000 Frenchmen, of whom only 55,000 were in Canada. In contrast, the English colonies numbered 1,250,-000 souls. They were richer, they lived in a less exhausting climate, and some of them possessed infant industries capable of producing some of the necessities of war. However, where New France was military and feudal, they were peaceful and democratic. A Canadian governor, usually a veteran military commander, had only to issue his order to send canoes and bateaux swarming down the rivers to the Ohio country. A colonial governor had no such power over people extremely sensitive of their liberties and their right to self-rule. Abhorring war and waste, loving peace and gain, they could rarely be made to see that in the America of that day war was only slightly less avoidable than the continent's twin scourges of smallpox and malaria.

Moreover, there were 13 governors whereas Canada—the actual instrument of French policy—had only one. Canada was unified in race and religion, as the 13 colonies were not. Anticipating the pluralist character of the American nation, the colonies were a welter of races and creeds and a mosaic of differing interests and forms of government. New England was, of course, almost wholly English and Puritan and representative. But other colonies, though predominantly Anglo-Saxon, included many more races. Pennsylvania was a conglomerate of English, Germans, Irish, Dutch, Scotch-Irish (or Ulster Scots) and Swedes. They were Anglicans, Quakers, Lutherans, Catholics, Presbyterians and Moravians, to say nothing of lesser-known sects already beginning to splinter and resplinter under the double impetus of border life and the American ideal of private judgment. Delaware, New York, New Jersey and Maryland had racial and religious variety to a lesser degree, and there were large settlements of Ulster Scots on the western borders of North Carolina and Virginia.

Virginia herself differed almost as much from New England society as did Canada. She was Anglican, and her tobacco-growing aristocracy openly adopted the airs of those cavaliers of King Charles I whom the Roundhead ancestors of the Puritans had detested. Virginia society was nearly as finely structured as Canadian feudalism, a pyramid based on the Negro slaves in the field and rising upward through indentured servants and other poor whites—all unlettered—proceeding next to the despised though literate merchants and mechanics, and then to the farmers and smaller planters, most of whom struggled and schemed to rise to the apex of the structure where the great landowners resided and ruled with almost regal elegance.

Finally, only New York and New England, under the guns and hatchets of the French and Indians, could be made to see that England's war with France was also their own. Even Virginia, mother of so many American captains, kept "out of it" until the French began to invade those western lands which Virginia considered her own. Even so, Governor Dinwiddie's attempts to raise forces to evict those French illustrates how even an aroused aristocracy was reluctant to take the rough road to war.

The Burgesses gave Dinwiddie a most frugal grant of money, and then, jealous of their prerogatives, placed that in the hands of a committee of their own. Of the other colonies to whom Dinwiddie appealed for help, only North Carolina—also claiming western lands—replied with men and money of her own.

The final proof of French capacity to move and English reluctance to take preventive action came when Dinwiddie attempted to fortify that point which today is called Pittsburgh and which then was a fork of land where the confluence of the Allegheny and Monongahela gives birth to the great Ohio River.

"The land in the forks," young George Washington had written, "I think extremely well situated for a fort, as it has the absolute command of both rivers. The land at the point is twenty or twenty-five feet above the common surface of the water; and a considerable bottom of flat, well-timbered land all around it, very convenient for building."[24]

Dinwiddie resolved to fortify the Ohio forks and in February of 1754 he sent a band of backwoodsmen to seize them and build a fort there. In the meanwhile, he argued with the Burgesses over funds, began rounding up independent companies of British regulars, and got half of the Virginia militia regiment of 300 men moving toward the Ohio under young Washington, now a lieutenant colonel. Before the Governor could get the other half moving, the French came bobbing down the Allegheny, took the English fort by summons, demolished it and replaced it with a larger one of their own.

Fort Duquesne now held the West for France.

Lieutenant Colonel Washington was just across the Alleghenies—perhaps 110 miles southeast of Duquesne—when he heard of the disaster. Immediately, he began pushing northwest to establish a forward base for the arrival of reinforcements and artillery. On May 28, 1754, halfway to Duquesne, he surprised an advance party of French.

Jumonville de Villiers, the French leader, was slain in the first volley. After Washington's Indians had brained and scalped the wounded, there were 10 French dead, 1 wounded and 21 captured, against Washington's losses of one wounded. It had been the youthful commander's first fight, and he was elated at the near-perfect result. In fact, his biggest difficulty came in keeping his fierce ally, Half King, from killing and scalping his prisoners. Half King swore that he would be avenged on the French for killing, boiling and eating his father.

But Washington dissuaded him, after which the young Virginian withdrew ten miles to a place called Great Meadows. Here he threw up a ramshackle stockade aptly named Fort Necessity. Meanwhile, all Canada and later France seethed with rage over the "murder" of Villiers by "the cruel Vvasington [sic]." The dead man's brother, the Sieur Coulon de Villiers, came marching hotly from Montreal to avenge "l'assassin." On July 3 his 900 men clashed with Washington's 400 at Fort Necessity.

The French quickly drove the English into rain-filled trenches, and then they carefully shot down every horse, cow or dog within the fort. In a half-hour the English realized that their transport and meat were gone. By nightfall it was obvious that the English were beaten, and the disconsolate young Washington, certain that a glorious career had ended before it had barely begun, sent his old comrade Jacob van Braam out into the night to ask for terms.

The French were generous. They could not have known that van Braam had mistaken the French word for assassination for the word death and they were pleased that Washington was willing to acknowledge his crime of murdering Jumonville. Unaware of a concession he would certainly never have made, Washington capitulated. Next day the English were accorded the honors of war.

Drums beating, colors flying, arms sloped, they marched out of the slime of Fort Necessity while the Indians went rushing in to plunder all that had been left behind. Though the English attempted to show a proud face, they were weary and hungry, many of them carried wounded men on their backs, and they had barely enough powder and ball to drive off the hostile Indians who harried them along the 60 miles back to Wills Creek. A heart-breaking march had begun, and the youth who led it never forgot the day that it started.

It was the fourth of July.

6

☆

The skirmish with Jumonville de Villiers and the fight at Fort Necessity were the tiny sparks which set battlefields blazing in the Old World, in India and in North America.

As yet, neither England nor France had found it convenient to make a formal declaration of war; and the Seven Years' War was still 19 months away. Nevertheless, both France and England seemed content to allow their colonists in the New World to continue to strike at each other in what was nothing less than a head start on the fourth and final round in the Anglo-French war for empire.

Again, the early advantage seemed to lie with the French. Coulon de Villiers' victory over Washington had brought almost all of the wavering western Indians to their side. Flanked by the Spanish of Florida and the French of Louisiana in the South, by the French in the West and the North, with the sea at their backs, divided and disorganized, the 13 colonies at last resolved to act.

A congress was convened at Albany and the famous Indian agent, William Johnson, was sent to the Iroquois to persuade the Five Nations to remain loyal to the English. At the Albany congress, however, neither the colonies nor the Crown could sink their mutual distrust, and the famous plan for union proposed by Benjamin Franklin was rejected by the Crown because it gave too much power to the colonies and by the colonies because it gave too much power to the Crown. Neither side was willing to relinquish governmental functions to the central council proposed by Franklin.

So the colonies continued to flounder along their separate ways, and as they did the French mother country prepared their destruction. Eighteen ships carrying six battalions of regulars—3,000 men in all —sailed from France for America. With them went their commander, the German veteran Baron Dieskau, who had served under the great Marshal Saxe, as well as Canada's new governor, Pierre François Rigaud, Marquis de Vaudreuil, son of an early governor of the colony.

England, however, learned of the French preparations. At once, plans were made to send two regiments of regulars to America, and Admiral Edward Boscawen was ordered to intercept the French force sailing for Canada.

Boscawen stationed his squadron off the mouth of the St. Lawrence. But a fog which had scattered the French fleet also enabled all but two of the ships to elude Boscawen and arrive safely at Quebec and Louisbourg. The other two—*Alcide* and *Lis*—were attacked and overpowered by the British, and two French battalions were taken prisoner. With this action of June 8, 1755, the two mother countries at last crossed swords.

Major General Edward Braddock commanded the British and colonial forces in America. Short, stout and choleric, Braddock was as brave as he was bullheaded, and he had not been in America very long before he had condemned most colonials as a crowd of ignorant sloths, reserving a special contempt for colonial troops.

Braddock was schooled in the tactics of European warfare which had been developed since the turn of the century. After the flintlock had replaced the firelock, and with the development of the socket bayonet, infantry tactics had been simplified. Four kinds of infantry —pikemen, musketeers, fusiliers and grenadiers—were now reduced to one general type of foot soldier armed with bayoneted flintlock. He was drilled incessantly and subjected to a barbarously brutal discipline, which made him, in effect, a battlefield automaton.* He fought in the open against other automatons also taught to wheel and to dress ranks amid the very smoke and stress of battle, to load and advance, fire and reload—and to drive home the assault with the bayonet under the smoke of the final volley.

A musket's killing range was only a few hundred paces, and firing was not very accurate; in fact, the British fire drill of the period did not include the order "Aim." The object was not so much to riddle the enemy as to frighten him and pin him down for the shock action of the cavalry. Such tactics, adjusted to terrain and weapons as tactics always are, were almost the opposite of American bush fighting in which the forests imposed a premium upon dispersion, cover and accuracy. To say that Braddock could not or would not see this difference is only to say, after all, that he was an ordinarily competent commander not gifted with the insights of genius. New wars are always being fought with the fixations of the old, and Edward Braddock was no exception to that dreary axiom as he reached Wills Creek on the tenth of May to take command of his army.

Braddock had a fourfold plan for eviction of the French. He would personally lead the operation against Duquesne, while another force destroyed Fort Niagara on Lake Ontario, a third reduced the French bastion at Crown Point on Lake Champlain and a fourth sailed to Acadia to rid that province of the French forever. All these points were to be attacked at once, neither Braddock nor the colonial governor seeming to question the feasibility of coordinating multiple operations in a wilderness passable only along its waterways or by painfully cleared roads, and in an age when all forms of transport were still at the mercy of the weather.

For his own expedition against Duquesne, Braddock had some-

---

* In 1712 a British guardsman was sentenced to 12,600 lashes and nearly died after he received the first 1,800.

thing over 2,000 men divided among 1,400 British regulars in bright red coats, perhaps 450 Virginia militia—those contemptible "blues" of whom Braddock said "their slothful and languid disposition renders them very unfit for military service"—about 300 axmen assembled to cut the road, and an unknown number of Indians. Of these, Braddock would lead an advance force of 1,500 men while Colonel Thomas Dunbar followed with the remainder. At the end of May, working parties began cutting the road.

The French had decided not to await the English. Scouting reports had made it clear that the approaching enemy possessed enough artillery to batter down even the stout log walls of Fort Duquesne. Accordingly, the Sieur de Contrecoeur ordered Captain Daniel Beaujeu to ambush Braddock's force.

Beaujeu was aware that the terrain would probably force the British to cross and recross the Monongahela. About seven miles from Fort Duquesne lay the second or lower ford which would allow the enemy to return inside the triangle again. It was a place made for ambush, and on July 8 Beaujeu led about 900 men—650 Indians, 100 French, 150 Canadians—southeast toward it.

Unfortunately for Beaujeu, half of his Indians strayed away from him during the day's march, and he was unable to prepare his ambuscade. On July 9, under the covering guns of an advance party led by Lieutenant Colonel Thomas Gage, Braddock's army successfully recrossed the Monongahela. Only seven miles of easy going now separated the English from Fort Duquesne. The men were in high spirits. Some officers predicted that before they reached the French fort the enemy would blow it up.

George Washington was also jubilant. Though racked with pain and weakened by an illness which had kept him an invalid with Colonel Dunbar's rear echelon, he had risen from his pallet on a jolting pack wagon, fastened a pillow to his horse's saddle to ease the agony of riding, mounted and overtaken Braddock so that he, George Washington of Mount Vernon, the first Englishman to lay eyes on the site of Fort Duquesne, might also have the honor of witnessing its fall.

Gradually, the marching column straightened out. From point to point it measured 2,000 yards. There were guides in front and flankers to either side. All seemed secure as Harry Gordon, the army's engineer, rode forward looking for the guides. Suddenly they came running back to tell him that they had seen the enemy. Then Gordon saw a white man in Indian dress come sprinting through the woods. It was Beaujeu. Behind him were about 300 French and Indians, also approaching on the run. Beaujeu caught sight of the scarlet coats behind Gordon. He stopped. He waved his arms to right and left, and Gordon stiffened in the saddle to hear the blood-curdling Indian war whoop. Then Beaujeu's men parted and vanished in the woods on either side of the English, and began raking both flanks.

Gage's troops wheeled into line almost immediately. Shouting "God save the King!" they discharged volley after volley. They killed Beaujeu and sent his Canadians flying away in fright. Captain Dumas, now in command, rallied the Indians, who had stood their ground. They hid behind trees or fallen trunks, they crouched in gullies or ravines, and thus invisible they poured a heavy fire into the close-packed red coats of the British soldiery.

Soon the British fell silent. In their ears was a frightful cacophony. The endless yelling of the Indians, the screams of their own stricken, the rolling musket fire of the battle, all were picked up and sent reverberating through the encircling gloom of the forest. Rare was the British regular who saw his enemies, and rarer still was the survivor who ever forgot that whooping and screeching.

Only the despised Virginians seemed capable of fighting back. A party of them led by Captain Thomas Waggener dashed for a huge fallen tree. They threw themselves down behind it and began picking off red men flitting from cover to cover or darting to the road to scalp a dead or wounded soldier. But the British regulars mistook their only friends for foemen and they opened fire on the Virginia rear, killing many colonials and forcing the rest to withdraw.

Now from a hill to the English right came a plunging fire. Demoralized and then terrified, the redcoats fired volley after volley into thin air. They riddled the trees and chipped the rocks. Some of them tried to take cover like the colonials, but their officers would not allow them. They yanked them erect or away from trees and strode among them with bared swords, crying angrily: "Stand and fight!" Back came the pitiful plea: "We would fight if we could see anybody to fight with."[25] And so, rather than disperse, they stood fast; they huddled together, shrinking from the bullets that swept among them, presenting to their tormentors larger and ever larger targets of red.

Suddenly the rumor spread that the French and Indians were attacking the baggage train in the rear. Gage's men turned and ran. They thundered over St. Clair's working party, abandoned their cannon to the enemy, and came tumbling eastward into the ranks of the British main body even as General Braddock led these soldiers forward.

Now both British regiments were mixed and confusion reigned unchecked. The towering fury of Braddock riding among them failed to rally this disorganized mass. How could it have? Braddock beat his men with the flat of his sword rather than allow them to adopt the "cowardly" cover which is the only way to fight in a forest. He refused George Washington's request to allow him to take the provincials against the hill on the right in Indian style. Instead, he ordered Lieutenant Colonel Ralph Burton to storm the height with dressed ranks. Burton obeyed. He rallied a hundred regulars, who followed him until he fell wounded, after which they melted away.

Gage was also wounded, as were Horatio Gates and Braddock's two aides, Robert Orme and William Morris. The carnage among the officers was frightful. Mounted, resplendent in laced regimentals, the English leaders were choice targets. Sir Peter Halkett was shot dead. So was young William Shirley, son of the Massachusetts Governor. Of 86 officers, 63 were killed or wounded.

Washington himself had four shots through his clothes, and two mounts were shot from under him. Braddock lost four horses, mounted a fifth—and took a musket ball that passed through his right arm and pierced his lung. He fell gasping into the bushes beside the road.

It was then that the retreat which Braddock had ordered became a frenzied rout. The English simply turned and fled for the river in their rear. Some of them were scalped by pursuing Indians even as they plunged into the ford. Washington saw that it was useless to attempt to rally them on the right bank of the Monongahela. Instead, he came to Braddock's side, placed the wounded general in a cart, and conveyed him across the river.

Behind him, howling hideously, the Indians took possession of the field.

It had not been possible to rally the fleeing army on the left bank of the Monongahela, either. Throughout the horrible blackness of the night of July 9, the routed remnants of Braddock's army stumbled steadily southeastward. All along the road back were the sounds of lost horses blundering blindly through the bush, of soldiers cursing as they stumbled over the dying bodies of men who could crawl no longer, or of other wounded crying piteously to be carried away from the dreaded scalping knives of the red men.

Nor was it possible to make a stand when Dunbar's camp was reached, 50 miles back. Here the wagons were burned, cannon and cohorns burst and their shells buried, barrels of gunpowder stove in, and food scattered through the forests. Here, too, the wounded bulldog Braddock came to the end of the trail.

He had remained silent throughout the day and night of the tenth, looking up only to say, "Who would have thought it?"[26] Another day passed in giving orders, and then, after another prolonged silence, Braddock added, "We shall better know how to deal with them another time."[27] Next day, cursing his redcoats while praising his officers and "the blues" of Virginia, Edward Braddock died.

Washington buried him with the honors of war. The corpse was lowered into a short, deep trench. It was covered without a marker. To efface the grave from the sight of marauding Indians, the defeated army passed over it on the retreat to Wills Creek.

7

☆

While Braddock was marching to his defeat, the colonies were launching the remaining three operations in his fourfold plan to evict the French. Of these, the expedition to Nova Scotia was the most successful.

Although the Acadians, who were the sole inhabitants of Nova Scotia, had taken an oath of allegiance to the British King, the French from Canada had begun to encroach upon these now English lands. They had built a fort at Beauséjour on the isthmus linking Nova Scotia with present-day New Brunswick.

This fort was captured on the lucky chance of an English shell having pierced a French bombproof at the moment when its occupants—the officers of Beauséjour—were sitting down to breakfast. Six of them were killed, and the English, having only just begun their bombardment, were astonished to see a white flag waving above Beauséjour's ramparts.

With Beauséjour fallen, the English proceeded with the roundup and expulsion of the Acadians from their more than a century-old home. Militia visited settlement after settlement to tear these sturdy though illiterate peasants away from the harvest and march them to deportation points. About 6,500 Acadians were deported or driven into the wilderness. Their settlements were destroyed, their possessions were seized, and they themselves were herded aboard ships and distributed among the English colonies where, alien in race, language and religion, they passed a miserable existence. Others entered Canada, only to be cruelly exploited by their fellow Frenchmen. Another group reached Louisiana, where their descendants dwell to this day; and still more, having endured an odyssey of indescribable travail, finally made their way back to their homeland.

Thus the cruel mass deportation which, although defensible on military grounds, remains the one crime staining the otherwise admirable record of British colonialism in America. It is true that the Acadians were always a Trojan horse inside Nova Scotia. In faith and race truer to the French Crown than to the British, and maintained in that attitude by their priestly leaders, they were ever ready to rise for France. To prevent this, they were deported. This is the reason, though never the justification, for the uprooting of an entire people; nor does it explain why the Acadians were stripped of most of their possessions before being scattered like barren seeds on unfriendly soil.

In the meantime, while this virtual writ of attainder was executed against an entire province, the French began a counterattack from Canada.

The Marquis de Vaudreuil, the new governor of Canada, had intended to send Baron Dieskau and the newly arrived French regulars against the English outpost of Oswego on Lake Ontario. However, papers of General Braddock found on the Monongahela battlefield gave away the English design against Crown Point and

Dieskau went to Lake Champlain instead. Finding that General William Johnson was farther south in Fort William Henry at the foot of Lake George, Dieskau attacked him there.

He led 700 French and 600 Indians against 2,200 men holding a fixed position, and the result was all but foreordained. The English, skillfully led by General Phineas Lyman, who took command after Johnson was wounded, repulsed charge after charge. Baron Dieskau was himself wounded. He sat helpless behind a tree while his forces fled before the English sallying fiercely from the fort. He turned to see an enemy soldier aiming his musket at him. He signed to the man not to shoot. But the soldier did, sending a bullet across Dieskau's hips, leaping on him and commanding him in French to surrender.

"You rascal!" Dieskau roared. "Why did you fire? You see a man lying in his blood on the ground, and you shoot him!"

"How did I know that you had not got a pistol?" the indignant soldier replied. "I had rather kill the devil than have the devil kill me."[28]

More soldiers fell on the defeated general, stripping him of his clothes. Then they took him to General Johnson, who treated him kindly. Johnson's Mohawk allies, who had lost their great sachem Hendricks to Dieskau's soldiers, would have done otherwise. They burst into Johnson's tent in a fury and demanded his prisoner. Johnson refused, and they filed out, glancing fiercely at Dieskau.

"What did they want?" Dieskau asked.

"What did they want!" Johnson repeated forcefully. "To burn you, by God, to eat you, and smoke you in their pipes. . . . But never fear. You shall be safe with me, or else they shall kill us both."[29]

Johnson was truer to his word than he was to his purpose of expelling the French from New York. He still could have sent General Lyman to Lake Champlain to follow up the advantage gained at Lake George. But he did not, probably because he was already jealous of Lyman. Contenting himself with strengthening his fort, while the French quickly reinforced Ticonderoga, he allowed the opportunity to slip away. A cold and raw November arrived, and with it came mutiny and desertions among the men. At a council of war presided over by Lyman, to whom Johnson was now willing to transfer responsibility, it was voted to withdraw.

William Johnson's outraged army jeered him all the way home, but the reluctant general was still able to make himself a hero abroad. He had already flattered King George by renaming Lac St. Sacrement after him, and now he proceeded to name his stockade there Fort William Henry in honor of one of the king's grandsons, and to change Fort Lyman to Fort Edward to compliment another. Then he wrote a long account of the fight at Lake George in which he exaggerated both its value and his own part in it, while neglecting to mention Lyman's name. Mightier with pen than with sword, William Johnson was made a baronet and Parliament gave him a gift of 5,000 pounds. And Crown Point remained French.

Fort Niagara also remained French.

Governor Shirley of Massachusetts led about 1,500 men to Oswego on Lake Ontario, and there, staring across the lake toward Fort Frontenac, he came to the unhappy conclusion that the French outpost made it impossible for him to move to his west or left to attack Fort Niagara. If he did, the French in Frontenac would merely cross the lake to take Oswego and occupy his rear. So he left part of his force in Oswego to strengthen the garrison and returned to Albany.

Of General Braddock's fourfold plan to destroy the French in America, only the minor operation against the Acadians had succeeded.

8

☆

Although France and England had already declared war, the general European conflict known as the Seven Years' War did not begin until 1756.

It was started by Frederick of Prussia, and England, forsaking her old ally in Austria, and still anxious to protect her sovereign's lands in Hanover, again sided with Prussia. France once more made common cause with Maria Theresa of Austria, while Czarina Catherine of Russia also came to Maria's side. Catherine had been insulted by Frederick, who called her "the Apostolic Hag," and she brought Sweden with her against her detractor.

Frederick's taunts also annoyed Maria Theresa, and they had enraged Madame de Pompadour. Pompadour ruled France. From being the mistress of the libertine Louis XV, she had become his procuress—and therefore his master. Frederick had called Pompadour "Mademoiselle Fish," in a biting reference to the favorite's mother, reputed to have been a fishwife. Thus three angry women were allied against the captain of his age, and he was to chastise them more severely with his sword than with his tongue.

Unfortunately for Canada, Pompadour's pique led her to neglect America. She sent 100,000 troops to help Maria, but could spare only 1,200 for the New World. However, Canada did get a splendid new military chief: Louis Joseph, Marquis de Montcalm-Gozen de Saint-Véran. Scholarly and courteous, Montcalm was also a veteran soldier who had been in many battles and been frequently wounded. He sailed for Canada in April, 1756.

Opposing him was a new British commander: the Earl of Loudoun. Akin to Braddock in his contempt for the colonials, Loudoun was also of the same irascible temper. He was not, however, as energetic. He arrived in America in July, 1756, sat still while Montcalm destroyed Oswego, and did not move until the spring of 1757.

Then he sailed against Louisbourg, found it defended by a mighty French fleet, and sailed back to New York in disgust. Meanwhile, his unsuccessful expedition had left Fort William Henry exposed to the French in Ticonderoga. On August 1 Montcalm left that fort with about 7,500 men. He sailed down Lake George. For the last time the French and their Indian allies took the watery road to the English. In swarms of canoes and hundreds of bateaux, with oar, sail and paddle, while Canadians in buckskin and French regulars in white coats mingled with naked savages radiant as rainbows, the twin perfections of civility and barbarism glided down King George's beautiful lake to fall upon his fort at the foot.

Fort William Henry fought back valiantly, but it never received the reinforcements it needed. Using European siege tactics, Montcalm worked his artillery ever closer to the English position, at last compelling its surrender after his guns were within point-blank range.

And then his Indians went screeching out of control, rushing inside the helpless fort to slaughter the sick and wounded in their beds. A French missionary named Roubaud witnessed the butchery and wrote: "I saw one of these barbarians come out of the casemates with a human head in his hand, from which the blood ran in streams, and which he paraded as if he had got the finest prize in the world."[30]

Nor could Montcalm curb the frenzied Indians as the English began to depart for home. They fell whooping on the rear of the New Hampshire regiment and dragged off 80 men. Montcalm rushed among them, crying, "Kill me, but spare the English!"[31] The massacre continued. In all, 50 prisoners were killed, and perhaps 200 more carried captive to Canada. There, many of them were ransomed by the French, who also bought back the clothes which the Indians had torn from the backs of their terrified captives.

Nevertheless, the massacre was a bloody breach of honor. Montcalm's only excuse for not using his own troops to restrain the Indians was that to do so would have lost the red men as allies. This he would not do, and the Indians and their grisly trophies were still with him when he burned Fort William Henry and withdrew to Montreal.

English defeat in the New World had been joined by English reversal in the Old. In 1757 the inept Duke of Cumberland, son of the King, was defeated in Hanover by the French, and Britain's great ally, King Frederick of Prussia, was unable to prevent a Russian army from invading his kingdom. Yet Frederick rallied in the year's last two months to crush the French at Rossbach and rout the Austrians at Leuthen. The tide was turning, and in London an event occurred which prompted Frederick to say: "England has long been in labor, and at last she has brought forth a man."[32]

The man was William Pitt, Pitt the Elder, the Great Commoner, the father—if ever there has been one—of the British Empire. First and foremost, William Pitt sought the destruction of France. It was his policy to fight her and to crush her wherever she was found: in Europe, in India, in Africa, on the seas and especially in America. Pitt saw at once that the three keys to the New World were Fort Duquesne, Ticonderoga and Louisbourg-Quebec, and he opened his campaign to conquer a continent with another assault upon the French base at Louisbourg.

On the morning of June 1, 1758, Louisbourg's southeastern horizon was fringed with the sails of the English. A fleet of 22 ships of the line, 15 frigates and 120 transports under Admiral Boscawen had arrived with Major General Jeffrey Amherst and 12,000 soldiers, of whom only 500 were colonials.

Inside Louisbourg were about 3,200 French regulars, besides a body of armed inhabitants and some Indians. Five ships of the line and seven frigates lay inside the harbor. However, the fortifications were not completed and ramparts made with bad mortar had already begun to fall down. Breaches in the wall were stuffed with fascines. But the Chevalier de Drucour, Governor of Louisbourg, was an able soldier who was determined to fight.

Colonel James Wolfe was perhaps even more eager for battle. His reckless battlefield gallantry had already amazed his colleagues and impressed William Pitt, and now he was to lead the assault on Fresh-Water Cove. This was the crescent-shaped beach which William Pepperrell's colonials had seized to begin their successful siege of 13 years ago, and Amherst was going to try to duplicate that maneuver —with the added diversion of a double feint at Flat Point and White Point closer to the town.

About a thousand white-coated Frenchmen held the beaches from White Point to Fresh-Water Cove. Wolfe had perhaps more than that. After a few days of high surf and fog, the English went over the side into their landing boats and pulled for the little quarter-mile beach lying between two piles of rocks.

The French opened up. Volleys of grape and musketry raked the English. Wolfe raised his hand to withdraw, but three boats of light infantry either missed his signal or ignored it. They rowed on, driving through the surf and landing among the leftward rocks. They leaped ashore. Wolfe saw them and ordered his other boats to follow. Another party of ten men hurdled the rocks and ran up the beach. French fire cut down half of them. Now other boats battled through the breakers. Some were hurled upon the rocks and stove in, others were broached or overturned, emptying their occupants into the surf. Infantrymen and grenadiers, weighted with cartridges, went down. Some arose without their muskets, others never got up. But the assault was going forward against a nearby French battery, and Colonel James Wolfe, his long lank red locks tied neatly behind his head, only a cane in hand, was leaping among the rocks, urging his men forward and calling upon others to come into line.

Now another division of British came ashore to Wolfe's right, and the French, fearing to be cut off from Louisbourg, broke and ran for the woods.

Once again Louisbourg had been flanked, and now the reduction of the fort was begun in steps almost identical to those of Pepperrell's campaign.

Amherst made his camp between Fresh-Water Cove and Flat Point, brought his guns and supplies ashore, and prepared to work his trenches and batteries forward within range of the fort. The French again abandoned the Grand Battery on the north shore of the harbor (although this time they left it useless), and Colonel Wolfe took 1,200 men around to Lighthouse Point just opposite the Island Battery. Once more British cannon pounded the island's guns into silence, while Amherst's siege works snaked closer and closer to Louisbourg. The English guns roared night and day. Louisbourg's rotten walls crumbled and fell apart.

On July 26 the last of the French guns before the town were silenced and the walls so breached as to admit an assault. At that point, Drucour asked for terms. Amherst and Boscawen were stern. Their master in London desired an end to the French in the New World. There would be no honors of war so that men allowed to depart with their arms sloped might one day return with muskets leveled. No, the garrison must surrender as prisoners of war.

Drucour refused. He would fight on, and he sent his reply by messenger. The courier had hardly departed before Intendant Prevost came to Drucour, beseeching him to spare the town and its inhabitants further ruin and misery. He warned of the dangers of exposing the people and their possessions to an assault by storm. Drucour submitted. He sent another messenger to recall the first one, and notified the English that he accepted their terms.

For the last time in history the golden Bourbon lilies fluttered down the flagstaff at Louisbourg. In England there was great rejoicing at the news of the victory. Cannon were fired and the captured flags of Louisbourg were hung in St. Paul's. Throughout New England bells were rung and bonfires lighted from Boston to Newport.

Most ominous for New France, the tall, thin, nervous redhead who had been foremost in the battle sailed home to England on fire for the final thrust up to Quebec.

Pitt had recalled Loudoun and allowed the American command to devolve upon the next in line, Major General James Abercrombie.

Pitt thought of Abercrombie only less disdainfully than he had thought of Loudoun, but even the Great Commoner could not ignore certain influences at court. Moreover, Pitt was hopeful that the real commander of the expedition against Ticonderoga would be Abercrombie's junior, Brigadier Lord Augustus Howe.

Howe was the younger brother of two other Howes—Richard and William—who appeared ten years later in American history, one as an admiral and the other as a general of British arms. Like his brother William, who had been with Amherst at Louisbourg, Augustus was an excellent soldier. Moreover, he was one British commander who respected the colonials. He had served with the Rangers led by Captain Robert Rogers, and he insisted that the 6,350 regulars, as well as 9,000 colonials, whom Abercrombie was to lead against Ticonderoga, learn to live and fight as the Rangers did.

On July 5 the Ticonderoga force embarked from the ruins of Fort William Henry upon the shining surface of Lake George. Rogers and his Rangers led the way in whaleboats, Colonel Gage—the veteran of the Monongahela who remained in American history for yet another war—was behind with the light infantry, and then Lord Howe with the main body.

The following day the army began landing on the western shore of the lake. It was intended to march around the rapids of Lake George's outlet as they ran northeast and then turned west to Ticonderoga. In this way, the English could attack the French fort from the rear.

Lord Howe and Major Israel Putnam went forward to reconnoiter. They encountered a party of about 350 French which Montcalm had sent down to harass the English. A sharp fight began, and Lord Augustus Howe fell dead, shot through the chest. With one shot the French had saved themselves.

"In Lord Howe the soul of General Abercrombie's army seemed to expire," Major Thomas Mante wrote. "From the unhappy moment the General was deprived of his advice, neither order nor discipline was observed, and a strange kind of infatuation usurped the place of resolution."[33]

Worse, from wavering and hesitating, Abercrombie moved to the conviction that he must do something—anything—and he attacked Montcalm exactly where that astute Frenchman expected him.

Montcalm had deduced that Ticonderoga was not to be attacked from the front, and he had ordered a huge breastwork constructed on a ridge behind the fort. Even officers had stripped to the waist to join the throng of axmen bringing thousands of trees crashing down. When completed, the breastwork stood eight to nine feet high. Firing platforms were provided behind it, and the entire line was zigzagged so that the front could be swept with flanking fire. On the sloping ground in front of the breastwork the French also built an abatis. An entire forest was felled with the trunks pointing inward to the breastwork and the sharpened boughs of the treetops outward toward the approaching English.

Such a formidable position should not have been assaulted. Instead, Abercrombie might have waited for his cannon to be brought up from Lake George to batter the breastwork down; or he might have occupied Mount Defiance overlooking the redoubt and directed a plunging fire into it. Best of all, he could have left a holding force in front of Montcalm while marching through the woods to occupy the road to Crown Point in his rear. Turning the French line in this way, he could have starved Montcalm into submission, for the French had only a week's provisions. But Abercrombie, outnumbering Montcalm 15,000 to 4,000, superior in equipment and supply, holding the initiative and operating at the end of a shorter and unmenaced supply line, chose to storm a fixed position!

The result was disaster. The English fought bravely, and so did the French. "God save the King!" roared the red-coated English, and the French in white cried out *"Vive le Roi!"* and *"Vive notre Général!"* Seven times Abercrombie pressed the assault and each time his men were repulsed in blood and agony. At last, he ordered a retreat. Two thousand dead, wounded and missing had been sacrificed to his foolish conviction that men in the open with muskets could overwhelm men behind breastworks with muskets and cannon.

The second phase of Pitt's threefold campaign for 1758 had failed because "Mrs. Nanny Cromby," as the embittered English soldiery called their general, had not cut his enemy's supply line. Against Fort Duquesne in the third phase, the English succeeded because they did cut it.

This maneuver was undertaken on the initiative of Lieutenant Colonel John Bradstreet. Sailing up the Mohawk River at the head of 3,000 men, he reached Oswego, crossed Lake Ontario and captured and destroyed Fort Frontenac. By this action he severed the

French supply line to the west and left Fort Duquesne at the mercy of the advancing English. Thus it was that the prediction made under Braddock was at last fulfilled: as the English, with George Washington again among them, approached Duquesne in November of 1758, they heard a great roar followed by explosion after explosion. Rushing forward they found that the French had blown up their fort and fled up the Allegheny.

Now it was the turn of the English to fortify the forks. As the year ended they began to build the bastion called Fort Pitt on the site of the modern city of Pittsburgh. With this, they won the West and cut New France in two. Canada was now flanked on the west by Fort Pitt and on the east by Louisbourg, and her capital city of Quebec lay open to attack.

9

☆

When the Duke of Newcastle complained to King George II that James Wolfe, the 32-year-old soldier whom William Pitt had chosen to capture Quebec, was not only too young to command such an important expedition but was also slightly demented, the old King looked up and growled: "Mad is he? Then I hope he will bite some of my other generals."[34]

In fairness to the protesting duke, James Wolfe certainly did not look or act like a "normal" British officer. Tall, thin and very awkward, pallid in complexion and constantly picking at his cuffs and buttons with long, tapering fingers, he seemed more of a sissy than a soldier. He did not even wear the customary military wig, but allowed his bright red hair to grow loose and long, pinning it together at the back of his head like any jackanapes. Yet James Wolfe's pale and bulging blue eyes were hard, and they usually blazed with a zealous fire.

He was a soldier born and bred. He was one of two sons of an

Anglo-Irish colonel of marines, and he had got himself attached to his father's regiment at the age of 13. Only the ill-health which afflicted him throughout his life prevented him from entering battle at that age. Yet at 15 he was an ensign; at 16 he was his battalion's adjutant fighting at Dettingen; and at 18 he was aide-de-camp to the brutal General "Hangman" Hawley during the Jacobite rising of 1745. Wolfe rather liked Hawley, cruel as he might be to the defeated Highlanders. Like St. Paul he was "approving everything that was being done against them." There was much of Saul of Tarsus in James Wolfe. He too was intense, ugly and zealous, thirsting to fight for the King just as Paul hungered to serve the Lord. It was this very single-mindedness that had impressed William Pitt. That was why he had given him command of the chief operation in another three-pronged campaign with which Pitt intended to complete the destruction of the French in America during the year 1759.

Amherst was to take Ticonderoga and move on Montreal by way of Lake Champlain, General Prideaux was to take Fort Niagara on Lake Ontario and open the way to Lake Erie and the West, and Wolfe was to crack the hard nut at Quebec.

Certainly this would be the most difficult of all three operations. Wolfe, however, was supremely confident, so much so that he prevailed upon the caste-conscious British Army to allow him to select two of the three brigadiers who were to accompany him.

One was Robert Monckton, who had commanded the Acadian operations in 1755, and the other a capable officer named James Murray. Monckton was only six months older than Wolfe and Murray only two years older. Thus there were three general officers 34 or under, to whom was added a fourth only a few years older: the Hon. George Townshend. Townshend had not served in the army as continuously as the others, but he did have a reputation for coolness under fire. Once, as he watched an attack, an exploding shell blew off the head of a German officer standing near him, splattering Townshend with gore. "I never knew before," Townshend murmured, calmly mopping his chest with a handkerchief, "that Scheiger had so many brains."[35] Clever and quarrelsome, Townshend was also an artist of talent whose savagely funny caricatures had lost him friends and led him to the field of honor. He did not, of course, get along with Wolfe, who disliked him from the first; but the youthful commander put on a face of politeness while arranging for his departure in February of 1759.

The night before Wolfe sailed, he dined with Pitt and Lord Temple, Pitt's brother-in-law. Toward the end of the meal he suddenly jumped erect, drew his sword and rapped on the table for attention. He then began striding around the room flourishing his sword while boasting of his military prowess and threatening his enemy with doom; after which he turned and walked from the room without a word.

"Good God!" Pitt exclaimed. "That I should have entrusted the fate of the country and of the administration to such hands!"[36]

The Great Commoner might have felt better for his country had he known that his guest, a teetotaler, had been drinking a little wine.

Admiral Charles Saunders commanded the fleet which was to transport Wolfe's army to Quebec. In all, he was to have some 170 sail manned by some 18,000 seamen. Part of his force, under Rear Admiral Philip Durell, had been sent ahead to blockade the St. Lawrence so that the French could not reinforce Quebec.

But Admiral Durell did not enter the river, choosing to stay clear of its treacherous ice, and the French did get men and supplies into the fortress city on the cliff. With them was the Sieur de Bougainville, whom Montcalm had sent to Paris. Bougainville stepped onto the strand of the Lower Town bearing a copy of an intercepted letter from General Jeffrey Amherst.

It revealed the English plan.

Montcalm had planned to resist Amherst at Lake Champlain and Fort Niagara. Now, seeing the major thrust directed at Quebec, he prepared to meet Wolfe there.

First, under Vaudreuil's orders, all French ships were sent upriver to be out of harm's way, and to release about 1,000 sailors for duty in Quebec. Vaudreuil, and Montcalm as well, was confident that Quebec's guns could prevent the English from getting above the city to cut the supply line westward to Montreal. Confident also that the fortress on the cliff was impregnable, Vaudreuil entrusted its defense to the Chevalier de Ramesay with about 2,000 men, and allowed Montcalm to move the main body east along the St. Lawrence.

Montcalm built a line about seven miles long. His left rested on the gorge and falls of the Montmorenci and his right on the St. Charles. The mouth of the St. Charles was guarded by a boom of logs chained together and two sunken ships mounting cannon. A mile up the St. Charles was a bridge of boats which linked Montcalm's right with Quebec. In the center of this bristling line of men and redoubts was the little town of Beauport, and there Montcalm made his headquarters.

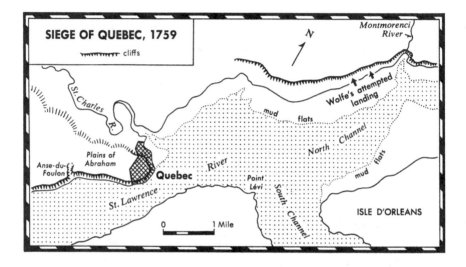

Thus Quebec's only weak point, its landward flank on the left, had been protected against encirclement. The city with its 106 guns was inaccessible from its sheer front and from its impassable heights on its right. Even if the British landed on the unoccupied south bank of the St. Lawrence, they could not possibly force the stream.

All that Montcalm needed to do was to hold his position until October, when the advent of the harsh Canadian winter would force the English to retire. He had 14,000 men, besides his Indians, and Amherst's letter indicated that Wolfe would have only 12,000.

Wolfe had only 8,500 men, of whom many were those Americans whom he despised as "the dirtiest, most contemptible, cowardly dogs that you can conceive."[37] He accepted them, nevertheless, and after he arrived at Louisbourg he divided his army into three brigades under Murray, Monckton and Townshend. While at Louisbourg, Wolfe received a letter from his mother informing him that his father had died. At once, he put on the sleeve of his red coat the black armband of mourning, which he wore constantly, and which was to become as familiar to his men as the little ornamental cane he wore slung at his hip like a toy sword.

On June 5, 1759, a foggy, windless day, the English fleet began working slowly and with flapping sails out of the harbor at Louisbourg.

When the British fleet came up the St. Lawrence about 60 miles below Quebec, it was flying the French flag.

Canadians to the fleet's right cheered and hugged themselves for joy. They had been dreading the appearance of the enemy armada, and now, it appeared, relief from France had come instead and they were saved. Jubilant river pilots quickly launched their canoes and put out to the ships. They clambered aboard, but instead of a smile and the promise of a fee, they met a pistol and a pledge of sudden death if they did not work the vessels through the treacherous Traverse ahead.

Aboard the leading transport *Goodwill,* one enraged pilot vowed that Canada would be the graveyard of the British Army and the walls of Quebec would be hung with English scalps. Captain Killick, the ancient master of the *Goodwill,* angrily pushed the Canadian aside and went forward to the forecastle to guide the ship through himself. The pilot shouted that the ship would be wrecked, for no French ship had ever attempted the Traverse without a pilot.

"Ay, ay, my dear," old Killick shouted back, fiercely shaking his speaking trumpet, "but, damn me, I'll convince you that an Englishman shall go where a Frenchman dare not show his nose."[38]

Behind *Goodwill,* the captain of the following ship was alarmed to learn that *Goodwill* had no pilot.

"Who's your master?" he yelled, and Killick replied, "It's old Killick! And that's enough."[39]

Leaning over the bow, the old man chatted gaily with the sailors in the sounding boats, giving his orders easily while pointing out the different shades of blue and gray indicating the depth of the water, warning of submerged ridges marked by telltale ripples or the sudden disturbance of smoothly flowing waters. Eventually *Goodwill* emerged from the zigzag Traverse into easier water. Killick put down his trumpet and handed the ship over to his mate. "Well, damn me," he snorted. "Damn me if there are not a thousand places in the Thames more hazardous than this. I am ashamed that Englishmen should make such a rout about it."[40]

Gradually, all the following transports were safely through. The fleet was moving now through the South Channel. To the right lay the lower tip of the Island of Orléans, an island about 20 miles long and five miles wide in the center of the broad St. Lawrence. Off the island's upper tip was the basin of Quebec and four miles across the water was the city itself.

Here, on the 26th of June, the fleet anchored. That night, 40 American Rangers under Lieutenant Meech landed on the Island of Orléans and drove off a party of armed inhabitants. In the morning Wolfe's army began coming ashore to build a base camp. A few days later, General Wolfe went forward to a high point on the island's tip to examine his objective, and it was then that he saw the true magnitude of the mission on which Pitt had sent him.

High, high above him, beautiful and white in the sunlight, was the city. He could see the stone houses, the churches, the palaces, the convents, the hospitals, the forest of spires and steeples and crosses glinting beneath the white flag whipping in the breeze. Everywhere he saw thick square walls and gun batteries, even along the strand of the Lower Town straggling out of sight to his left beyond Cape Diamond. To his right as he swung his glass slowly like a swiveling gun, Wolfe perceived the entrenchments of Montcalm. He saw the sealed mouth of the St. Charles and the thundering falls of the Montmorenci guarding the French left flank. He saw the little town of Beauport and the mud flats before it beneath the grape and muskets of Montcalm's redoubts. From left to right he saw steep brown cliffs scarred with the raw red earth of fresh entrenchments, the stone houses with windows reduced to firing slits by piles of logs, and behind them the tops of the Indian wigwams and the white tents of the regulars. If Wolfe could have seen beyond Cape Diamond to his left, he would have been appalled by natural obstacles more formidable than Montcalm's fortifications. Here for seven or eight miles west to Cape Rouge rose steep after inaccessible steep, ranges of cliffs atop which a few men might hold off an army, all ending at another river and waterfall like the Montmorenci.

James Wolfe held his telescope delicately. A soldier near him noticed the marks of scurvy on the back of his long thin hands. No one spoke except his engineer. Wolfe listened mutely, silencing him with a gesture and gazing eagerly at what appeared a likely landing place or a flaw in his enemy's line; but then, shaking his head petulantly, he moved on. At last, he snapped his telescope shut and strode back to camp.

Wolfe had seen that he could not land upriver or between the St. Charles and the Montmorenci as the colonists under Sir William Phips had done six decades before. In fact, there did not seem to be any place to land. As he was to notify William Pitt, he had gazed upon "the strongest country in the world."

That night a black thunderstorm drenched his troops. After it had passed, sentries on Orléans Point thought that they heard movement on the river. They saw flashes of light and the glow of torches and heard the sound of excited voices—and then the world seemed to explode.

Sheets of fire shot up from the river, roar after roar shook the camp, while the air was filled with flying pieces of burning wood and whizzing bits of metal. The sentries turned and ran. As they did, the flames and the roar pursued them like dragons from hell, belching out columns of suffocating smoke and drenching the air with the sulphurous reek of their breath.

The French had launched their fireships downriver against the English fleet anchored off the island. Flames ran up masts and sails like fiery snakes and then vessels soaked in pitch and tar and stuffed with bombs, grenades, old iron, fireworks, rusty cannon swivels and muskets loaded to the muzzle burst apart like floating volcanoes. But the French sailors had applied their torches too soon. Before the fireships could drift down on the English vessels and ignite them, British sailors had jumped into their boats, rowed bravely within range of the blazing hulks, secured them with grappling irons, and towed them ashore where they were allowed to burn themselves out.

The fireship fizzle depressed the Marquis de Vaudreuil, who was watching glumly from the steeple of the little church at Beauport. He had spent two million francs on this military bauble, and had hoped, with characteristic naïveté, that it would drive off the British with one stroke.

Unfortunately for the defense of Canada, the Marquis de Vaudreuil fancied himself a conqueror. Jealous of Montcalm's military prowess, he sometimes pretended that Montcalm's victories were won by Vaudreuil. Such vanity disgusted Montcalm, who already despised the Governor for failing to check the corruption of the greedy officials around him. With the Governor and the general thus divided, delay and indecision were bound to ensue, and this was at once apparent when Wolfe moved to bring Quebec under bombardment.

On June 29 Wolfe seized a tip of land called Point Lévi across the South Channel from the Island of Orléans. Between this point and Quebec the St. Lawrence narrowed to a width of less than a mile. On June 30 Monckton's brigade came ashore in force and began to emplace Wolfe's guns. By the time the French moved to evict the English from Point Lévi, it was too late. They were there in force, and soon their guns were pounding the cliff city's walls.

Next, Wolfe moved to draw Montcalm out of his secure fortifications. Leaving a light guard around the camp on the Island of Orléans, he landed Townshend's and Murray's brigades on the east bank of the Montmorenci, just across from Montcalm's left flank. Wolfe now had thrice divided and dispersed his army into a light guard at Orléans, Monckton at Point Lévi and himself with Townshend and Murray east of the Montmorenci. It would seem that he had offered Montcalm a marvelous opportunity to overwhelm any one of these divided forces and to gobble up the English Army piecemeal. However, Wolfe was confident that the English fleet could rapidly concentrate his separated army at any given point. Thus, having lured Montcalm out into the open, he could bring him to decisive battle.

Montcalm, however, refused the bait. He did not fear Wolfe's army as much as the one General Amherst was leading against Ticonderoga. If Amherst could come up Lake Champlain, he might capture Montreal and threaten Montcalm's rear. Montcalm was delighted to have two-thirds of Wolfe's army bogged down among the mosquitoes and skulking Indians of the woods across the river.

"While they are there they cannot do much harm," he said. "So let them amuse themselves."[41]

On the night of July 12 a rocket exploded above the river between Quebec and Point Lévi and Monckton's cannon roared into life.

Both the first and the second salvos fell into the river, and cries of derision rose from the French. But the English gunners eventually found the range. Shells began bursting among the wharves and

streets of the Lower Town and some even shook the walls of the
Upper Town itself. Soon the French batteries were belching back.
A furious artillery duel raged throughout the night, and it continued
to roar intermittently for the next two months.

On the night of July 15 an English shell set fire to a building in
the Upper Town. High winds carried the fire to the cathedral, which
burned to the ground within an hour. A week later another fierce
fire all but demolished the Lower Town. Soon the Lower Town was
a shambles and the crowded streets of the Upper Town were not
safe for passage. One by one, sometimes in family groups, the residents of the crumbling city began to flee to the sanctuary of the
countryside.

Meanwhile, the siege continued. Wolfe's batteries on the Montmorenci made life unpleasant for the troops on Montcalm's left flank,
and Montcalm's sharpshooters cut down the rashly curious English
who visited the gorge of the river to marvel at its cataract. Both sides
languished in an alternating ordeal of heat and rain, both sides
skirmished and both sides took scalps. The American Rangers and
soon the British regulars became as proficient in this grisly art as the
opposing Indians and *coureurs de bois* until Wolfe had to issue an
order prohibiting "the inhuman practice of scalping, except when the
enemy are Indians or Canadians dressed like Indians."

Wolfe's brigadiers had repeatedly advised him to try forcing the
northern shore above Quebec, but the general had just as frequently
declined; and on July 23 he proposed to storm the very heart of the
enemy line.

In front of the gorge of the Montmorenci there was a ford during
the hours of low tide. Townshend was to cross here with 2,000 men.
Meanwhile, another 2,000 would be embarked up the St. Lawrence
and brought downstream opposite Beauport to make a feint there.
Wolfe's true object was the camp of Lévis on the Montmorenci.

In midmorning of July 31, the 64-gun frigate *Centurion* sailed
downriver and anchored off Lévis's camp, while a pair of 14-gun
catamarans worked in close to the shore. It was now high tide and
the river flowed full against the sandy beach beneath the cliffs. *Centurion* and her tiny twins opened up, battering the French redoubts
on the beaches. From Wolfe's camp east of the Montmorenci and
Monckton's batteries to the west at Point Lévi came an artillery cross-

fire aimed at the clifftops. For two hours the thunder of the cannonade continued, and the basin of Quebec echoed and re-echoed once more to the thump of discharging guns and the crash of exploding shells. Yet Lévis with about 11,000 men carefully concentrated underground was barely scratched, demonstrating the imperishable truth that when artillery fires at positions built to deflect it, its bark is worse than its bite.

Montcalm, however, was momentarily perplexed by the boated British force rowing back and forth opposite Beauport. But as the promenade became prolonged, he became convinced that the assault would come against Lévis, and he rode down to the Montmorenci through ranks of cheering, white-coated men crying, *"Vive notre général!"*

In the afternoon the tide turned to the ebb. Gradually the dark sedge of the mud flats became visible. Wolfe, standing in an open boat, cane in hand, flushed with the exultation of battle, gave the order to attack.

As Townshend began crossing the ford, the first wave of grenadiers and Royal Americans rowed cheering for the mud flats.

But the boats were swept downstream and many of them were stranded on mud ridges. The French on the heights poured a plunging fire into them. Wolfe in his boat shouted orders to delay the assault. The tide was not low enough. The French fire continued. Three times splinters struck Wolfe and his little cane was knocked from his grasp by a round shot. At length he ordered the first wave in again. The boats beached on the broad expanse of mud. Shouting and challenging each other, the grenadiers and Royal Americans floundered forward in wild disorder. The French in the redoubt on the sand fled at their approach. The English seized the redoubt, but then the French on the heights delivered a heavy fire among the redcoats milling about below.

To the rear, all was confusion. Monckton's men were ashore and Townshend's troops were already over the ford. Boats were piling up, and no one seemed to know what to do. At that moment, without orders from Wolfe or even from their own officers, the grenadiers took the battle into their own hands.

They went storming up the heights to get at their tormentors above them. Thick scattered raindrops had begun to fall and the heat was oppressive as the English swarmed up the slopes. French fire scourged them. Their breath came faster. Sweat stained their uniforms, and the ground beneath their boots became a slippery morass. Straining for handholds, using their muskets as crutches, rolling downhill to be stopped by a bush or a fallen comrade, they continued their ascent into the very throats of the twinkling, flashing muskets of the French. And then the skies darkened, the clouds opened up and a torrent of rain fell on all that wild scene.

It squelched the battle. Wolfe sounded the retreat, and as the last of the living grenadiers and Americans came sliding downhill again, while the entire assault force withdrew in good order to their boats, the rain stopped and the Indians on the heights drew their scalping knives and came clambering down among the fallen.

Wolfe had lost 443 men killed and wounded without harming a single Frenchman in an aborted battle that should never have been begun. His plan of attack upon the heart of a fixed position was not only scatterbrained in its conception but also blundering in nearly every detail of execution down to the boating of troops at flood tide in the morning for an assault to be launched at dusk and on the ebb. By the defeat of the Montmorenci, Wolfe lost the respect of almost all his staff officers, including the heretofore intensely loyal Monckton.

Townshend was particularly savage in his criticism and even the fire-breathing Murray regarded the entire affair as stupid and foolhardy. Admiral Saunders was also alienated after Wolfe sent him a copy of the draft of his ambiguous despatch to Pitt. Saunders accused Wolfe of giving the navy an unfair share of the blame, and Wolfe meekly promised to remove the objectionable parts of the letter. Meanwhile, Wolfe, his health failing every day, vented his rage upon other victims. First, the grenadiers were excoriated in a scathing General Order, and next the Canadians on the south banks of the St. Lawrence were informed that because of "the most unchristian barbarities against his troops on all occasions he could no longer refrain from chastising them as they deserved."[42]

East and west, parties were sent forth to scourge the Canadian *"canaille."* Night after night the residents of Quebec could see the glow of burning villages. Montcalm also watched this savaging of his countrymen, but with no intention of ending it. He would not be drawn into open battle under any circumstances, and thus the tormented Canadians were caught between two fires. Where Wolfe was wasting the countryside in an effort to starve Quebec and force the militia to desert to defend their homes, Montcalm kept the militia in check by threatening to turn his Indians loose on their families.

Meanwhile, Quebec was collapsing under the hammer of Monckton's artillery. Fires in the Lower Town were a daily occurrence, and in the Upper Town 167 houses were destroyed in a single dreadful night. On August 10 a shell crashing into a cellar set a vat of brandy afire and burned down many buildings, including the beautiful Notre Dame des Victoires. Most of the city fronting on the river was in ruins.

Worse, rations in the town and for the army encamped beside it were growing short. Vaudreuil's assurance that the English could not get upriver had been shattered by the audacity of the British fleet. Beginning on July 18 and with every fair wind thereafter, English ships had run the gantlet of Quebec's guns until a sizable flotilla had been assembled upstream under Vice Admiral Charles Holmes. Thus supply ships coming downriver from Montreal were frequently intercepted by Holmes's ships, while a shortage of pack animals made supply by land along the river's northern shore very difficult.

The ships, however, worried Montcalm most. Wolfe was now able to make thrusts against the northern shore to the west of Quebec. To oppose him, Montcalm sent Bougainville above the city with 1,500 men. He was to guard about 15 to 20 miles of clifftop against the English. He did, twice driving Murray off with losses. A third time, Murray landed at Deschambault and burnt a building and all the spare baggage of the regular officers. For once, Montcalm was alarmed; but then his good humor returned. He had received news indicating that General Amherst could not possibly come to Wolfe's assistance that year.

Amherst had occupied Ticonderoga and then Crown Point, after the French had blown up the first and abandoned the second. Then General Prideaux had carried out the assault on Fort Niagara. Although Prideaux was killed, the French fort had been surrendered to Sir William Johnson. Thus, with his countrymen driven from Lake Champlain and Lake Erie, it appeared to Montcalm that his right or western flank at Montreal was in extreme danger. Amherst particularly might ascend Champlain to fall on Montreal. But Amherst had dawdled at Crown Point and could not possibly assault Montreal before winter.

"Two months more," Montcalm said of the English, "and they will be gone."[43]

Toward the end of August it appeared that Montcalm was right. Wolfe's army was melting away. He had lost more than 850 men killed and wounded since June, and disease and desertions were daily reducing his strength. Worse, the general himself was gripped by an indecision nearly as destructive to discipline as his own feuding with his brigadiers. Then, on August 20, Wolfe fell ill of a fever. He lay in an upper room of a French farmhouse on the Montmorenci, his thin body racked and his white face haggard with pain. On the 25th he began to recover, and on the 29th he sent his three brigadiers a message:

"That the public service may not suffer by the General's indisposition, he begs the brigadiers will meet and consult together for the public utility and advantage, and consider of the best method to attack the enemy."[44]

Monckton, Murray and Townshend conferred. They advised Wolfe, as they had often done before, to seize a position on the north shore between Quebec and Montreal. Thus he would force upon Montcalm the choice of fighting or starving. Wolfe agreed. He not only embraced this heretofore unacceptable proposal eagerly; he went even farther. He would ascend the inaccessible heights beneath the Plains of Abraham under the very nose of Quebec. Montcalm, cut in two, would *have* to come out to fight.

Wolfe did not immediately disclose the details of his plan to his brigadiers. He divulged it only at their insistence and at the eleventh hour. Nor will history ever know how he came to adopt it, after having previously rejected all counsel to force the stream above Quebec.

It has been said that Wolfe was on the edge of despair. He had told his intimates that he would not go back defeated "to be exposed to the censure and reproach of an ignorant population." The very news that he could expect no help from Amherst might have strengthened him in that resolution so often born of desperation. Wolfe was that sort of soldier: audacious in adversity, delighted to look into the face of calamity and spit in its eye, genuinely determined to triumph or to die trying.

It has also been said that Wolfe was anxious to make one more attempt on the city before the advent of winter forced the fleet to depart. On September 10 Admiral Saunders assembled his officers and informed them that he thought the time had come to leave. Saunders had about 13,000 men under his command. With their ships they represented about a quarter of the strength of the British Navy. He could not risk being frozen into the St. Lawrence. Moreover, ice floes were already beginning to form in the Gulf of St. Lawrence. All of Saunders's officers agreed, including Holmes, but Wolfe, upon being advised of this decision, rushed to Saunders's flagship and told him of his plan. He advised the admiral that he was going to send 150 picked men up a secret path to the Plains of Abraham. If they could overpower the light guard posted there, then his main body would follow. But if they could not, then Wolfe would agree to return to England with Saunders.

Wolfe is said to have seen this secret path while studying the heights west of Quebec. Examining a little cove called the Anse-du-Foulon, he is said to have spotted outlines of a path winding up the side of the supposedly inaccessible cliff. Then, observing that there were only a few tents pitched on the clifftop, he is supposed to have concluded that the guard there was light.

This is the generally accepted explanation of why Wolfe changed his mind about the northern shore and came to choose the Anse-du-Foulon. But because it assumes too much while accepting the implausible fable of Wolfe suddenly seeing the path "through a glass darkly," and because Wolfe did deliberately destroy the September entries in his diary, it is not too much to posit the possibility of treachery.

Although history offers no incontrovertible proof of betrayal at Quebec, it does encourage a suspicion that there might have been. Montcalm himself gave the reason why. Having long ago secretly informed Paris of the corruption in Canada, as well as Vaudreuil's failure to suppress it, he had said: "Everybody appears to be in a hurry to make his fortune before the colony is lost; which event many perhaps desire as an impenetrable veil over their conduct."[45] Obviously, with Canada destroyed there would be little likelihood that the corrupt officials would be brought to book, and it would certainly be to the advantage of any or all of them to inform James Wolfe of the existence of the Anse-du-Foulon. Again, because Wolfe destroyed his September diary entries, it cannot be said definitely whether or not this happened.

However, it is known that Vaudreuil, who was constantly accompanied and advised by the false Intendant Bigot, did countermand an order of Montcalm's and left the Plains of Abraham themselves unguarded. The crack Guienne Regiment under a capable colonel was moved from the Plains back to the line of the St. Charles. Moreover, the guard of 100 men which Montcalm had placed at the top of the Anse-du-Foulon was fatally crippled.

It had been commanded by Captain St. Martin, a regular officer hand-picked for the duty by Montcalm; but Vaudreuil replaced St. Martin with the Chevalier Duchambon de Vergor, a crony of Bigot whose career as commander at Beauséjour was distinguished by corruption on one side and cowardice on the other. Where St. Martin had refused to allow the Canadians in his command to go home to help in the harvest, Vergor granted leave to 40 men on the condition that they also put in a few hours of work on Vergor's farm.

Finally, the clifftops between the Anse-du-Foulon and Cape Rouge were not even well patrolled on the night of Wolfe's attack. On that night the patrol commander, Captain de Remigny, lost his three horses. One was stolen and two were lamed.

Thus the possibility of treachery at Quebec. The facts, of course, are no more than suggestive of this possibility. Yet, even if they are not conclusive proof of it, they should not be summarily rejected in the interest of preserving the romantic idea of Wolfe on a river bank suddenly espying the chink in Montcalm's armor. Montcalm himself knew of the path, and he said to Vaudreuil: "I swear to you that a hundred men posted there would stop their whole army."[46] He was right, but there were not 100 men but only 60 under the untrustworthy Vergor, and the Guienne Regiment which was to come to their assistance had been sent away. Whether or not Wolfe knew of this belongs to the limbo of unanswerable questions. What does belong to his lasting glory, however, is the masterly preparation which he made for this attack.

First he began the difficult withdrawal from the Montmorenci. Next he made a feint at Cape Rouge held by Bougainville, and during the next few days he drove Bougainville and his men into weary distraction by having the ships of Holmes's flotilla drift upriver with the flood tide and drift downriver on the ebb, forcing the French to march and countermarch to remain abreast of the English fleet. To delude Montcalm into believing that the movement above the town was a diversion for another attack against his fortifications east of Quebec, he asked

Admiral Saunders to deploy his main fleet in a demonstration off Beauport. Finally, two deserters told Wolfe that Bougainville was sending a convoy of provisions down to Montcalm on the ebb tide on the night of September 12. Wolfe immediately saw the possibility of sending his own boats down ahead of the convoy so as to deceive the French sentinels, and he gave that order. Wolfe could not know that Bougainville had postponed the provision convoy, but neither did Bougainville inform the sentries below that the familiar store ships were not coming.

On the night of September 12 all was in readiness. The stars were visible, but there was no moon as perhaps 4,800 English began drifting upriver. Bougainville, wearied by the promenade of the past few days, was confident that they would only drift downriver again. In fact, the Sieur was going to spend the night farther west at Jacques Cartier. The desirable, and accommodating, Madame de Vienne, wife of one of Bigot's subordinates, was at Jacques Cartier. Below Quebec, Saunders was lowering boats filled with sailors and marines, his guns were thundering, and the Marquis de Montcalm was massing troops at the wrong point ten miles below the Anse-du-Foulon.

At two o'clock in the morning of September 13, 1759, the tide began to ebb. A lantern, its light shrouded from the northern shore, was hoisted to the main topgallant masthead of the *Sutherland*. It was the signal to cast off, and the boats of the English began slipping silently downstream.

General James Wolfe stood mutely in one of the foremost boats. Suddenly the general began to speak in a low voice. He was reciting Gray's "Elegy in a Country Churchyard," which he had only just memorized. His aides listened quietly. Wolfe finished, and said softly, "Gentlemen, I would rather have written those lines than take Quebec."[47] An embarrassed silence followed. No one believed him. Wolfe said no more. Perhaps he was reflecting on the prophetic line:

> The paths of glory lead but to the grave.

Unchallenged and ignored, the boats had been gliding downstream for a full two hours. Now the tide was bearing the lead craft with Wolfe's spearhead—24 volunteers who were to surprise Vergor—toward the towering shore. Suddenly there was a shout.

"Who goes there?"

No one spoke, and then Simon Fraser, a young Highland officer

who spoke French, shouted back: *"France!* And long live the King!"
"What regiment?" the sentry persisted.

"La Reine," Fraser shot back, aware that part of this unit was with Bougainville.[48]

The sentry was satisfied and the boats drifted on, one of the men giggling aloud in relief. Again the challenge. A sentry had come scrambling down the cliff face to stand at the water's edge and demand the password. Again a French-speaking Highlander, Captain Donald McDonald, gave the answer.

"Provision boats!" he hissed, deliberately disguising his accent with a hoarse whisper. "Don't make such a bloody noise! The English will hear!"[49]

The sentry waved them on. The English could see the gray of his cuff against the black of the cliff behind him.

On the boats drifted, and now the current was running strong and they had rounded the headland of the Anse-du-Foulon. The sailors broke out their oars and rowed desperately against the tide. But the spearhead boats were swept too far downstream. Undaunted, McDonald, Fraser and their men leaped out. McDonald and Captain William Delaune led the party softly up the cliff face. The figure of a sentry materialized out of the gloom above them. He shouted down at them. Still hissing his hoarse whisper, McDonald told him that he had come to relieve the post.

"I'll take care to give a good account of the English if they land!"[50]

On the shore of the cove below, General James Wolfe and two aides crouched helplessly in the dark, their ears straining for the sound of firing. It came, and Wolfe despaired.

Above, the sentry had hesitated for too long. There were 24 shadowy figures around him before he could reply, and then the English charged with blazing muskets. Captain Vergor came dashing out of his tent barefooted and nightshirted. He fired two pistols wildly into the air before he turned and sprinted for Quebec at the head of his departing troops. A musket shot pierced his heel and he fell screaming.

It was then that Wolfe's despondency changed to a fierce, wild joy for he had heard the huzzahs of his triumphant volunteers. Quickly he gave the order for the second wave to land. In came the boats, and and soon the cliff face was crawling with British soldiers. Among them was James Wolfe. Diseased, weakened by bloodletting, never strong, he was climbing on his magnificent will alone; and as he got to the top, the empty boats of the first wave were returning to the packed transports for the rest of his troops.

Now the guns at Point Levi and the Island of Orléans had joined those of Saunders firing on Beauport. Soon Beauport's batteries were thundering back, followed by those at Quebec and at Samos to the west of the Anse-du-Foulon. Wolfe immediately sent Colonel William Howe's light infantry against that battery menacing his rear, and the British silenced it.

By dawn the last of Wolfe's sweating soldiers had struggled up to the undefended Plains of Abraham. Some 4,800 soldiers began to form and to march into a north-south line parallel to and about three-quarters of a mile distant from the western walls of Quebec.

That was how the Marquis de Montcalm saw them as he rode up in a drizzling rain.

Montcalm had been completely deceived by Saunders's feint. Nevertheless, he rode over to Quebec that morning with the Chevalier Johnstone, a Scots Jacobite who had been given a commission in the French Army. En route, a messenger informed him of the British landing. Montcalm set his horse on the path to Vaudreuil's house. From there he could see clearly to those plains which had once been owned by a French pilot named Abraham Martin. He could see the red lines of British soldiers stretching from the St. Foye Road on their left—and his right—to the cliffs of the St. Lawrence. Faintly, skirling on the wind, came the wail of the Highlanders' pipes. The enemy array stood motionless, as though awaiting inspection, their regimental colors drooping in a gentle rain.

"This is serious,"[51] Montcalm said gravely, and ordered Johnstone to ask Governor Ramesay of Quebec for the garrison's 25 fieldpieces. Johnstone clattered off and Vaudreuil came out of his house. Shaken, he spoke a few words to Montcalm, and went back inside. Montcalm rode off to find his command disorganized by a welter of orders and counterorders given in an atmosphere of distrust and dislike. Ramesay would surrender only three of the 25 cannon and Vaudreuil had refused to allow the Beauport troops to move up to Quebec.

Eventually, Montcalm conferred with his officers. Should he attack now or wait until Bougainville could move on the British rear? If the French waited another hour or possibly two for Bougainville, the British could improve their position. If he attacked now, he would have to do it without Bougainville and the troops withheld by Vaudreuil, but he might also strike the British before they could dig in. His officers, afraid that Vaudreuil might appear at any moment to issue additional hamstringing orders, were for immediate attack. Montcalm agreed. He sent his troops out to the Plains of Abraham.

Out they marched to the last battle of New France. All that was French, all that Samuel de Champlain had planted 150 years before on the cliff above the river, was to be defended here this day. Golden lily and gilded cross, dream of an empire stretching to the Rockies, fervor and faith and feudalism, all that had nourished or corrupted the martial and colorful little colony along the great river was at stake on the plains beyond. Through the narrow streets they thronged, white-coated regulars in black hats and gaiters and glittering bayonets, troops of Canadians and bands of Indians in scalp locks and war paint; out of the gates they poured, the battalions of Old France and the irregulars of the New, the victors of Fort Necessity, the Monongahela, Oswego, Ticonderoga and Fort William Henry, tramping to the tap of the drum and the call of the bugle for the last time in the long war for a continent.

With them rode their general. He had never seemed more noble to his officers and men. Mounted on a dark bay horse, he was a splendid figure in his green-and-gold uniform, the Cross of St. Louis gleaming above his cuirass. "Are you tired?" he cried. "Are you ready, my children?"[52] They answered him with shouts and as he swung his sword to encourage them, the cuffs of his wide sleeves fell back to reveal the white linen of his wrist bands.

In splendid composure, the English watched the French arrive. Since dawn, when the high ground less than a mile away had become suddenly thronged with the white coats of the tardily arriving Guienne, the redcoats had been raked by Canadian and Indian sharpshooters. After Ramesay's three cannon had begun to punish them, Wolfe had ordered them to lie in the grass.

James Wolfe had put on a new uniform: scarlet coat over impeccable white breeches, silk-edged tricorne on his head. He walked gaily among his reclining men, making certain that they had loaded their muskets with an extra ball for the first volley, pausing to chat with his officers. Wolfe ignored the enemy sharpshooters and exploding shells. A captain near him fell, shot in the lung. Wolfe knelt and gently took the man's head in his arms. He thanked him for his services and told him that he would be promoted when he was well again, immediately sending off an aide .to Monckton to make sure that his promise was carried out should he be killed that day.

The desired battle had arrived, and James Wolfe was exalted. All his black moods and indecision had vanished clean away. His step was light, his voice was steady and his pale face shone with confidence. Although he did outnumber Montcalm 4,800 to 4,000, it was the quality rather than the number of his troops which gave the English general his assurance. He had trained them personally and he had taught them to stand in awesome silence until their enemy was close enough to be broken by a single volley.

Toward ten o'clock the French began coming down the hill, regulars in the center, regulars and Canadians to right and left, and Wolfe ordered his men to arise and form ranks. On came the French, shouting loudly, firing the moment they came within range, two columns inclining toward the English left, one to the right.

The English stood still.

Gradually the French lines became disordered by Canadians throwing themselves prone to reload, but they still came on, crying out and pouring a musket fire into the silent English.

"Fire!"

A single volley as loud as a cannon shot struck the French not 40 yards away. Again a volley, and then a clattering roll of muskets, and then, in the lifting smoke, the English saw the field before them littered with crumpled white coats, and the French, massed in fright, turning to flee.

"Charge!"

The British cheer and the fierce, wild yell of the Highlanders rose into the air, and the pursuit was begun. Redcoats with outthrust bayonets bounded after the fleeing enemy, Highlanders in kilts swinging broadswords overhead leaped forward to decapitate terrified fugitives with a single stroke.

James Wolfe joined the charge. He had already taken a ball in the wrist and had wrapped a handkerchief around it. Now, leading the Louisbourg grenadiers, he was wounded again. He pressed on, but a third shot pierced his breast. He sank to the ground. He was carried to the rear. He was asked if he wanted a surgeon.

"There's no need," he gasped. "It's all over with me."

He began to lose consciousness, until one of the sorrowing men around him shouted, "They run! See how they run!"

"Who run?" Wolfe cried, rousing himself.

"The enemy, sir. Egad, they give way everywhere!"

"Go one of you to Colonel Burton," Wolfe gasped, "and tell him to march Webb's regiment down to Charles River, to cut off their retreat from the bridge." Turning on his side, he murmured, "Now, God be praised, I will die in peace!" and he perished a few moments later.[53]

The Marquis de Montcalm was also stricken. His horse had been borne toward the town by the tide of fleeing French, and as he neared the walls a shot passed through his body. He slumped, but kept his seat rather than let his soldiers see him fall. Two regulars bore him up on either side. He entered the city streaming blood in full view of two horrified women.

"O mon Dieu! O mon Dieu!" one of them shrieked. "The Marquis is dead."

"It is nothing, it is nothing," Montcalm replied. "Don't be troubled for me, my good friends."[54]

But that night he was dying. His surgeon had told him that his wound was mortal. "I am glad of it," he said, and asked how much longer he had to live. "Twelve hours, more or less," was the reply. "So much the better," Montcalm murmured. "I am happy that I shall not live to see the surrender of Quebec."[55] He died peacefully at four o'clock the next morning.

Wolfe had fallen knowing that he had won an important skirmish, Montcalm perished aware that his army was routed and demoralized, but neither knew that all was won and all was lost.

Another year passed before the seal was placed on the Battle of the Plains of Abraham as the crowning victory in the 150-year war for a continent. Only a few hours after Wolfe's triumph, Bougainville appeared in the west with about 2,000 men and was repulsed by Townshend. That night, Vaudreuil panicked and abandoned Quebec, fleeing to Montreal in the van of a terrified army which had hastily quit the Beauport line leaving tents and cannon behind. Although the infuriated Levis rallied these remnants and prepared to march against the English, the town was surrendered before he could arrive. The British Army, now under Murray, passed a terrible winter in Quebec; and in the spring Lévis appeared outside its walls with a superior force. Murray rashly left the city to attack him, was driven back after losing a third of his army, and Quebec was now beseiged by the French.

By then, however, a sea battle perhaps more important than the land war in Canada had been fought between the English and the French. Admiral Sir Edward Hawke met Admiral Conflans at Quiberon Bay, decisively defeating him to break the back of French naval power and to win control of the Atlantic for England. Thus it was an English and not a French fleet which sailed up the St. Lawrence on May 16, 1760. Murray was relieved and Lévis forced to withdraw to Montreal. There, Amherst, now in command in America, applied the final blows.

Murray advanced up the St. Lawrence, Haviland ascended Lake Champlain, and Amherst descended the St. Lawrence from Lake Ontario. Trapped east, south and west, Lévis was forced to capitulate.

Canada had been conquered, and the French and Indian War was over. A few years later the Peace of Paris ended the Seven Years' War in Europe. France ceded her colony on the St. Lawrence to England, retaining in America only that vast though vaguely defined region called Louisiana. France had emerged from the conflict a wreck: only five towns in India remained to her, her navy was gone and her finances were in the ruin which was to produce the French Revolution. England and Prussia were all-powerful: the one to rule the waves, the other to rack Europe.

England had beaten France, and she had won an empire. And yet she was already in danger of losing the fairest jewel in that imperial crown. As the Count Vergennes had warned:

"Delivered from a neighbor they have always feared, your other colonies will soon discover that they stand no longer in need of your protection. You will call on them to contribute toward supporting the burden which they have helped to bring on you, they will answer you by shaking off all dependence."[56]

This they would do indeed.

PART II

The War of the Revolution

1

☆

In Boston one day in 1761 the courthouse was packed to hear the fiery James Otis attack those detested Writs of Assistance—virtual blank-check search warrants—with which Parliament hoped to crush smuggling in America. Otis was a flame of eloquence, and at one point he electrified his audience with the declaration: "Taxation without representation is tyranny!"

It was the birth cry of American freedom, and it became the rallying call of all those colonial forces whose aims were converging upon a demand for independence; but at the time it passed almost unheeded. A young lawyer, John Adams, who was in the courtroom that day, did not forget Otis's immortal challenge. Nor did his radical cousin, Samuel Adams, who swore that to have no say in how they would be taxed reduced the colonists "from the character of free subjects to the miserable condition of tributary slaves."[1] Most other colonial leaders, however, failed to second Otis's fundamental challenge to Parliament's right to make laws for the entire Empire.

Across the Atlantic, far from the towering forests and great rivers of America, King George III and his ministers heard nothing. They were too busy with the Seven Years' War. Two years later the Peace of Paris made Britain the world's foremost colonial and maritime power. King George and his ministers then turned to the task of repleting an exhausted treasury and of paying off a huge public debt of some £136,000,000. Certainly the colonists who had also profited from the four Anglo-French wars would be willing to help. Had they not been relieved of their old fear of Canada? Surely they would agree that it was expensive to maintain some 6,000 soldiers in America, troops who were even then engaged in putting down Pontiac's rising in the West.

No proposition could have been more reasonable, providing that the colonies bore the slightest resemblance to the "grateful daughters" who existed only in the mother country's imagination. Neither George nor his ministers nor most of the bribed or blindly obedient members of the King's rubber-stamp Parliament had even been to America, and they could not have known that the colonies regarded the conquest of Canada merely as having ended their need for British protection. If Britain could have appreciated the spirit of independence which frontier life and decades of self-rule had implanted in the colonial character, or realized how the colonies loathed standing armies as a threat to liberty, she would certainly have reflected before imposing taxation from London or demanding that British redcoats be quartered in private homes.

There was the tragedy. The men who ruled Britain thought that they were dealing with men like themselves, English gentlemen in the Georgian mold. But the colonists were not. They were Americans, and it would not be long before a Virginia gentleman would say: "There ought to be no New England men, no New Yorker and so on, but all of us Americans."[2] As Americans they were not yet democrats or republicans, but they were the most fiercely independent breed of men ever to tread the earth. And yet, convinced that these Americans were as submissive to Parliament as any home-grown Britisher, Britain called upon them to help pay the cost of empire.

In 1764 the Sugar Act was passed. It was intended to replace the old Molasses Act of 1733, which the colonists had either ignored or sidestepped through smuggling. It raised the import duty on sugar, imposed other levies, and cut the tax on molasses in half. It was, on the whole, a wise and sincere attempt to strike a balance between colonial planters in the West Indies and merchants in America. But the Sugar Act exploded in the colonies like a bomb.

First, the halving of the tax on molasses was an empty gesture made to conceal the very real fact that Britain intended to *collect* this duty. Smugglers and evaders accustomed to the old, unenforced Molasses Act were in for hard times. So was a colonial distilling industry so huge that in 1750 Massachusetts alone had 63 distillers. American rum—the popular drink of the ordinary man—was distilled from molasses. Obviously, both maker and drinker were opposed to price increases which would follow *any* collectable duty. They swore they would not pay the new one, and one colonial hooted that Britain's attempt to stop smuggling would be as foolish and costly as "burning a Barn to roast an Egg."[3]

In its preamble the Sugar Act stated that it was enacted to help pay the costs "of defending, protecting and securing" America. It was a *taxing* measure. This the colonists and particularly the Yankees of New England found abhorrent. A committee of the Massachusetts House of Representatives under the redoubtable Otis challenged Parliament's very *right* to tax the colonies, declaring that such measures "have a tendency to deprive the Colonies of some of their most essential Rights as British Subjects, and . . . particularly the Right of assessing their own Taxes."[4]

Where or when the colonists got this novel idea was immaterial. What mattered was that they now had a cause: taxation without representation is tyranny. Parliament, not King George, was the tyrant. The colonists were as loyal subjects of the British Crown as any Englishmen, but they, not the British Parliament, would impose their own taxes. This was the idea which such artful propagandists as Samuel Adams were spreading abroad while the colonists evaded the Sugar Act, and an attempt to enforce the long disobeyed Navigation Acts, by bringing the techniques of smuggling to a state of near-perfection.

In 1765 Britain countered with the Stamp Act. Once again Parliament thought that it was only asking the colonies to share a burden already borne at home. Englishmen had long been accustomed to buying revenue stamps to be affixed to all legal documents, commercial paper, ship charters, bills of lading, titles, and even newspapers, pamphlets and playing cards. But the Americans had not. They were infuriated to be informed that if they did not purchase stamps all their transactions would be declared illegal and their press would be closed. This, a taxing act undisguised, simply could not be accepted; and the bellow of protest which followed the Stamp Act made the uproar against the Sugar Act seem comparatively a bleat of dissent.

In Virginia, the House of Burgesses met in the lovely rose-brick-and-white town of Williamsburg to hear the fiery back-country lawyer, Patrick Henry, suggest that just as Caesar had had his Brutus and Charles I his Cromwell, some good American should stand up for his country. There was a cry of "Treason!" and Patrick Henry quickly apologized to the Speaker, vowing that he was ready to shed his last drop of blood for George III.

Still, an open defiance of the Crown had been spoken, and Patrick Henry was in the forefront of the radicals pressing for passage of the famous Virginia Resolves. Even though the most inflammatory of the Resolves were eventually killed, they were reprinted throughout the colonies as though passed in their entirety, and so increased the uproar against the Stamp Act that Massachusetts called for a congress of colonial representatives.

In October, 1765, the Stamp Act Congress convened in New York. It expressed its loyalty to the Crown and "all due subordination" to Parliament, but firmly stated that since the colonies had no representatives in Parliament they could not be taxed by that body. Only their own legislatures could tax them, the colonies continued, adding the practical argument that the stamp taxes were so heavy that they precluded the buying of English goods and would thus be harmful to English trade.

Meanwhile, up and down the coast, associations called the Sons of Liberty were formed. They were particularly powerful in Boston, where Samuel Adams had already organized the old Guy Fawkes Day brawlers into mobs responsive to his will. He turned them loose in August after one Andrew Oliver had been named Stamp Officer. Blacksmiths and cartwrights, tavernkeepers and fishermen, and some "mechanics" whose soft white hands suggested a readier acquaintance with quill and ink than with turnspit or tar, they gathered in the glare of torches and lanterns, and went roaring off to Oliver's house. They smashed his windows, shook his doors, and hanged him in effigy. Glad to get away with his life, Oliver quickly resigned his commission. That same month mobs burned the records of the Vice-Admiralty Court—destroying all evidence of smuggling tolerated in the past—and sacked the office of the Comptroller of Customs, finally moving against the fine mansion of Governor Thomas Hutchinson. In a frenzy of rage misdirected against a man who had spoken and written against the Sugar and Stamp Acts, the mob wrecked his splendid dwelling, destroyed his furniture, defaced his paintings and ruined the finest collection of books and manuscripts in America by burning most of them or scattering the pages through the streets.

Down in New York City violence erupted with the arrival of a shipment of stamped paper. Old Cadwallader Colden, the acting governor and scholarly correspondent of Linnaeus, Benjamin Franklin and Dr. Samuel Johnson, was nearly frightened out of his wits, shutting himself up in Fort George while the howling mob reduced the gilded splendor of his coach to a pile of smoking ashes. Then the mob rushed uptown to the home of the fort's commander, breaking into the wine cellar to nourish their "patriotism" before falling upon the house in a paroxysm of vandalism.

So it went from Maine to South Carolina, and as barbaric as the mobs might have been they quickly achieved their purpose of intimidation: stamp officers resigned in droves. Came November 1, 1765, the day the act was to go into effect, and the American seaboard went into mourning.

Flags flew at half-staff, minute guns were fired, and muffled bells tolled a dirge. No one bought stamps and all business was at a standstill. Political or economic death, however, was not the goal of the colonists, and soon unstamped newspapers appeared and business was resumed as usual—without stamps. The law was simply disregarded.

But it was still on Britain's books and therefore an irritant. To remove it, the colonies organized a boycott of British goods. It worked, for America was Britain's chief customer. With British factories and shops closed and thousands out of work, Britain's manufacturers and merchants petitioned Parliament to repeal the offending law. Parliament complied, although its members tried to save face by insisting that if the Stamp Act had been ill-advised, Parliament still possessed the *right* to pass it.

Nevertheless, news of the repeal brought joy to America. It was succeeded by an outburst of gratitude and loyalty lasting about a year. Then, in early 1767, Charles Townshend took over effective leadership of Britain as Chancellor of the Exchequer. No friend of America, he believed that he "understood" the colonists. They objected only to "internal taxes" such as the Stamp Act but would not oppose "external taxes" such as duties on imports. So the famous— or infamous—Townshend Acts were passed. They imposed duties on imports from England of glass, certain painters' materials and tea. Proceeds were to pay the salaries of the colonial governors and judges, who had been paid heretofore by colonial legislatures and had been therefore beholden to them. Writs of Assistance were also revived, and provisions made for a reorganized and vigorous customs service directly responsible to the British Crown.

The Townshend Acts proved how thoroughly their author misunderstood the Americans. The colonists made no fine distinctions between external and internal taxes: they hated all taxes with a fine fervor fortified by their recent "victory" over the Stamp Act. Those Writs of Assistance which had called forth Otis's immortal cry were still anathema to them, and they were not going to cooperate in the death of smuggling. From Massachusetts came a circular letter urging concerted action again. Britain responded by ordering the colonial governors to force all legislatures to drop all opposition to the Townshend Acts under pain of dissolution. Such steps were taken in half of the colonies, and only succeeded in stiffening opposition.

As practical as they were political, the Americans simply renewed the boycott of British goods. Nonimportation Agreements were made and the Sons of Liberty began roving the night streets again. In June, 1768, royal officials attempting to seize John Hancock's sloop, *Liberty,* were attacked by a Boston mob and the Commissioner of Customs was driven to the sanctuary of Castle William on an island in Boston Harbor.

Stung, Britain sent two regiments of infantry into rebellious Boston. They landed in October, 1768, and Boston coolly refused to quarter or supply them. Two more regiments arriving in later months got the same cold-treatment. Their commander found that he had to rent quarters and purchase provisions. Moreover, to their astonishment, the British redcoats found themselves vilified as "foreigners" and as "lobster-backs," a derisive reference to the British Army's custom of enforcing discipline by flogging.

Hostility degenerated into mutual hatred, with the inevitable result coming on March 5, 1770. On that day a crowd of Bostonians hurled snowballs, stones and insults at a group of British soldiers. Some of the mobsters struck at the soldiers' muskets with clubs and dared them to fire. The redcoats lost all patience and discharged a volley straight into the crowd. Eleven citizens fell, three of them instantly killed and two more mortally stricken. This became known as the "Boston Massacre."

Bells were rung and drums beat to summon militia. The whole town poured into the streets and two companies of musketmen surrounded the Town House. Rebellion, at least in Boston, might have exploded right then and there had not Governor Hutchinson quieted the crowds and had the troops withdrawn to Castle William.

Eventually, the Townshend duties were repealed, not through the belligerence of Boston but through the boycott. British exports to America had been cut in half, and in April, 1770, all of the acts but the tax on tea were abolished. With this gesture of conciliation, a period of quiescence ensued in America. Even the boycott fell into desuetude and Samuel Adams began to grieve for the slow death of the spirit of independence.

But the spirit was only sleeping, and it came awake again June 9, 1772, with the affair of the *Gaspee*. A British armed schooner of that name had run aground near Providence while pursuing a smuggler. Once more the drums beat to arms, and that night eight boatloads of volunteers boarded the *Gaspee,* wounded her commander, overpowered the crew and put the King's ship to the torch.

Britain was outraged. King George had been publicly affronted. A royal proclamation was issued offering a reward for information leading to the arrest and conviction of the *Gaspee* culprits, and a royal commission was formed to investigate the insult. But there was no one to claim the reward nor to cooperate with the royal commissioners, and Britain discreetly dropped the matter. There was no point in expanding a single incident into the *cause célèbre* which might disturb the otherwise placid colonies.

The colonies, however, had done slumbering. When Britain attempted to influence the colonial courts by paying judges out of the royal treasury, Massachusetts countered successfully with offers of higher pay. Next Samuel Adams proposed the organization of Committees of Correspondence to act as links between the various towns of Massachusetts; other colonies followed suit and an effective communications network was eventually established between them. It was now 1773, the amiable but inept Lord North was in charge of His Majesty's government, and the East India Company was frantically begging him to do something about the American refusal to buy its tea.

King George had kept the tax on tea because he believed "there must always be one tax" to maintain the right to tax. The Americans, however, thought otherwise and calmly evaded the duty by buying mostly smuggled tea. This, among other things, had brought the East India Company—in which the government had an interest—face to face with bankruptcy. A huge backlog of seventeen million pounds of tea had piled up in its warehouses in Britain. Concerned, Lord North's government agreed to reimburse the company for the import duties it had paid in England. The company was also to be allowed to export its tea directly to its own warehouses in America—thereby cutting out American importers—and to pay a duty which would still make East India tea cheaper than the smuggled brands bought by the Americans. The colonists would thus be getting tea cheaper than it could be bought in England. Surely they would be delighted.

They were infuriated.

The Tea Act threw conservative colonial merchants straight into the arms of the radical Sons of Liberty. Dealers in smuggled tea determined to prevent the introduction of a cheaper product into the colonies, and legitimate importers, enraged at the "monopoly" granted the East India Company, now flocked to the mass meetings under the Liberty Trees. Once again political and economic forces were joined, and soon American ship captains were refusing to ship East India tea aboard their vessels. The astutely agitating merchants of Philadelphia had branded anyone who approved of the Tea Act as "an Enemy to his Country,"⁵ and "the whole country was in a blaze from Maine to Georgia."⁶ Like the stamp agents before them, the new tea agents hastily resigned rather than risk tar and feathers and a ride out of town on a rail.

Now it remained to prevent receipt of the tea. In Charleston no consignee being bold enough to step forward to claim the cargo, it was seized by customs officers and left to rest for three years until the new state of South Carolina could make use of it. At Philadelphia and New York the captains of the tea ships saw fit to carry their cargoes back to England. And in Boston a group of Samuel Adams's "Mohawks"—Sons of Liberty disguised as Indians—climbed aboard three tea ships on the night of December 16, 1773, broke open the tea chests and threw the contents in the harbor.

The Boston Tea Party enraged King George. Boston, that "sad nest," that hotbed of treason, and Massachusetts, that schoolhouse for rebellion, were to be brought to heel. Boston itself was to be closed as a port, leaving Marblehead and Salem the only Massachusetts ports. Massachusetts was to suffer in its charter: its Assembly was to continue to function but its upper chamber, the Council, was to be appointed by the King. Lesser judges, sheriffs and other officials were to be appointed by the Governor, the King's man. Town meetings, the heart of self-rule in the colony, were to be held only once a year to elect officers, and otherwise only by permission of the Governor. Anyone indicted for a capital offense connected with a riot or revenue laws was to be tried either in England or in another colony, and, finally, troops were to be quartered in Boston.

These were the four Coercive Acts, which the now-seething colonies decried as the "Intolerable Acts." Not every Englishman approved them, nor were they passed by a unanimous Parliament. One by one the Coercive Acts were opposed and denounced in the Commons by such eloquent pleaders for a policy of conciliation as Burke, Barre, Conway and Charles James Fox, and in the House of Lords by William Pitt, now Lord Chatham, who was rapidly losing his faculties as well as his influence. In each case, it was the royal will that prevailed. The rod was out and the colonies were to be chastised, much as the Whigs of the opposition might argue that such a course would only provoke American confederation and rebellion, perhaps even American independence.

2

☆

A cold rain fell from a codfish sky on that momentous May 17, 1774, when Lieutenant General Thomas Gage arrived in Boston to take command of His Majesty's troops in America and to assume office as Governor of the Province of Massachusetts Bay.

The enforcer of the Coercive Acts—for Gage's two hats, or sticks, had been given him to beat both port and province to their knees—met with a mixed reception. Those patriots who greeted him with chill propriety remembered that it was Gage's troops who had perpetrated the Boston Massacre, and they deduced grimly that he was come again to destroy their liberties. Those Loyalists who welcomed

him warmly recalled Gage's service with Braddock at the Monongahela, with Abercrombie at Ticonderoga, and as the American commander in chief whose troops put down Pontiac, and they rejoiced
to receive just the man who would make Yankee Doodle dance.

It was not long, however, before this handsome, dignified and
dedicated soldier discovered that Yankee Doodle preferred to call
the tunes himself. For weeks after Gage's arrival church bells tolled
dolefully, prayer and fasting were proclaimed and mourning badges
displayed. Gage's answer was to put the Boston Port Act into effect
on June 1 with a sweeping totality that left the town paralyzed.

"Did a lighter attempt to land hay from the islands, or a boat to
bring in sand from the neighboring hills, or a scow to freight to it
lumber or iron, or a float to land sheep, or a farmer to carry market-
ing over in the ferry-boats, the argus-eyed fleet was ready to see it,
and prompt to capture or destroy it."[7]

Such Draconian thoroughness succeeded only in making a martyr
of Boston. Though many abruptly unemployed people fled to the
countryside, most of Boston's 20,000 inhabitants remained within
the city. And they did not starve, for the rest of the colonies rallied
to Boston's side. Flour, cattle, fish and other foods came pouring
into the blockaded city from all over New England. From the
distant Carolinas came supplies of rice, from Delaware money—and
even Quebec sent a thousand bushels of wheat. Boston was abjured
to stand firm, to refuse to ransom her economic life by paying for
the destroyed tea.

Boston did not waver, and on June 17 the General Assembly of
Massachusetts met in Salem to protest removal of the capital to that
place. Gage sent an order dissolving the Assembly, but the doors
were locked against his emissary. Inside, the aroused Assembly made
its historic proposal for a Continental Congress of the colonies and
elected delegates to represent Massachusetts.

Shortly thereafter Gage's task of subduing these stiff-necked Yankees was made even more difficult. The Quebec Act had been passed
by Parliament and signed into law by King George. It was probably
the most statesmanlike measure of George's stormy reign, and yet
it came at absolutely the wrong moment for the American colonies.
Extending the Province of Quebec to include those French-speaking
settlements in the valley of the Ohio and the Illinois country, the law
also recognized French civil law and the Roman Catholic Church in

Canada. Thus the abhorred religion was to be guaranteed in the North and a fresh obstacle to colonial expansion was erected in the West. It was as though Canada had never been conquered, and the colonies saw red. Meanwhile, the Continental Congress met in Philadelphia.

No new nation a-borning was ever blessed with as many able political midwives as those who gathered in Philadelphia on September 5, 1774, to attend at the birth of American freedom. Nor was this a "vagrant Congress," a motley assembly of a "rabble in arms." Few delegates were as radical as Sam Adams or Patrick Henry or Richard Henry Lee of Virginia. Many of them were conservatives such as wealthy Joseph Galloway of Pennsylvania, Charles Carroll of Maryland, or the Rutledges of South Carolina who feared "the low Cunning, and those levelling principles" of New England. Most of the delegates were moderates like John Jay or James Duane of New York, John Adams of Massachusetts—probably the most respected man at the Congress—and, of course, George Washington of Virginia, tall, wide-hipped, narrow-chested, still the most imposing figure in the Congress, but now, after his marriage to the wealthy widow Martha Custis, more renowned for his social position and vast plantations than for his military talent.

Did these men intend to break with Britain? Did they seek independence? "There is no man among us," said John Adams, "that would not be happy to see accommodation with Britain."[8] The fiery, radical ideas revolving in the great, palsied, shaking head of Sam Adams were not shared by this assembly. But then Paul Revere galloped into town, his saddlebags bulging with news from the north. Massachusetts had defied General Gage and set up its own Provincial Congress. The explosive Suffolk Resolves had been passed. They were read out before a hushed and thrilled Continental Congress: the Coercive Acts were "the arbitrary will of a licentious minister"; they were "murderous law," and because of them the streets of Boston were "thronged with military executioners";[9] the Quebec Act was "dangerous to an extreme degree to the protestant religion and to the civil rights and liberties of all America."[10] Therefore the Suffolk Resolves advised that Massachusetts form its own government to collect taxes and withhold them from the royal government until the Coercive Acts were nullified. The people of the colony were to arm and form their own militia. The most severe economic sanctions must be brought to bear on Britain.

The hearts of the radicals lifted. The standard of implacable opposition was at last being raised. Moderates also were carried away. Swarms of shouting delegates engulfed the men from Massachusetts. Without changing a comma, the Congress adopted the Suffolk Resolves. Then, calling for the third and most stringent boycott of British goods, it served notice on Parliament that the colonies were no longer bound by its laws outside purely commercial regulations. The King was politely informed that his prerogatives must conform to the Americans' ideas of their liberties and his authority.

No one had yet spoken of rebellion or independence or an appeal to arms. But the American Revolution had begun.

In Boston the war which was fought to preserve that revolt was beginning to sputter.

General Gage had been steadily accumulating troops. He called for workmen to build barracks. None came forward. Though unemployed, no one cared or dared to work for the "lobster-backs." Gage sent to New York and Halifax for workmen, and the Bostonians began a campaign of sabotage. Brick barges were sunk, straw for soldiers' beds was burned, and wagons were overturned. Enraged, Gage countered by sending soldiers over to Charlestown and Cambridge to seize colonial powder and cannon. The troops carried out his orders, but their little foray gave Massachusetts an opportunity to carry out a dress rehearsal for the later reality of mobilization.

News of the seizure spread swiftly throughout the province. Details of the coup were so magnified that the Continental Congress heard the absurd news that Gage had bombarded Boston. Nevertheless, by the day following the seizure some 4,000 armed and angry men had come crowding into Cambridge, while all over New England other men were on the march. Gage blinked and took note. Now he began to fortify the narrow neck of land linking Boston to the mainland. The Provincial Congress replied by appropriating the huge sum of £15,627 to purchase military supplies. It called for the organization of "minutemen," named three generals to command its militia, set up a Committee of Safety under Dr. Joseph Warren to take over its own duties once it had ceased to exist, and then, on December 10, having set up all the apparatus for rebellion, dissolved itself.

Gage too late proclaimed all the acts of the vanished Provincial Congress as treasonable. His attempts to undo its mischief were like the sound of a cannon trying to overtake the flash. Everywhere in New England men were drilling on the green. Guns and powder were being stolen from British forts. Colonial supplies were increasing. To counter American thefts of munitions Gage sent a British expedition to Salem on February 26, 1775. It met colonial militia under Colonel Timothy Pickering at an open bridge.

Pickering refused to obey the British demand to lower the drawbridge. Finally, a Salem clergyman intervened. He persuaded the militia to lower the bridge on the British promise to march only thirty rods into the town and return. This was done, but the redcoats discovered nothing but the Yankee willingness to fight.

Marching home they passed through the town of Northfields, where a nurse named Sarah Tarrant called to them from an open window: "Go home and tell your master he has sent you on a fool's errand and broken the peace of our Sabbath. What, do you think we were born in the woods, to be frightened by owls?"

Stung, one of the soldiers pointed his gun at her, and Nurse Tarrant scoffed: "Fire, if you have the courage—but I doubt it."[11]

A month later the fierce spirit of resistance sweeping through America had caught fire in Virginia. There, Patrick Henry arose in the House of Burgesses to declare:

"There is no retreat but in submission and slavery! Our chains are forged. Their clanking may be heard on the plains of Boston! The war is inevitable—and let it come! I repeat it, sir, let it come!

"It is in vain, sir, to extenuate the matter. Gentlemen may cry, 'Peace! Peace!'—but there is no peace. The war is actually begun! The next gale that sweeps down from the north will bring to our ears the clash of resounding arms! Our brethren are already in the field! Why stand we here idle? What is it that gentlemen wish? What would they have? Is life so dear, or peace so sweet, as to be purchased at the price of chains and slavery? Forbid it, Almighty God! I know not what course others may take; but as for me, give me liberty or give me death!"[12]

The choice was not a month away, and the gale from the North ringing with the clash of arms was already making up on the road from Lexington to Concord.

3

☆

King George and Parliament, ignoring the petitions of the Continental Congress, had moved to subdue that "most daring spirit of resistance and disobedience"[13] existing in the colonies. More oppressive measures were passed, capped by the Fishery Act forbidding New Englanders to trade with Great Britain, Ireland and the West Indies and banning them from the Newfoundland fisheries.

Angered beyond restraint by this dreadful blow at its economy, Massachusetts replied by reviving the Provincial Congress. The members of that body, seated in chambers so cold that many of them kept their hats on, placed the province on a virtual war footing. Then, once more turning the military apparatus over to Dr. Warren and the Committee of Safety, the Congress adjourned.

That was on April 15, the day after General Gage received his "get-tough" orders. Force was to be quickly applied before the rebellion could spread, Gage was told, and the leaders of the Provincial Congress were to be arrested. Gage, a practical soldier, realized that the latter instruction was not possible. Although Dr. Warren was known to be in Boston, Sam Adams and John Hancock were out in the vicinity of Concord and John Adams was still farther away. At Concord, however, lay the Committee of Safety's arsenal. Gage had been kept minutely informed of its growth by none other than Dr. Benjamin Church. This urbane grandson of the old Indian fighter of the same name had fallen hopelessly in love with a lady, and because he needed money to keep her, he betrayed the Committee's secrets to Gage.

Resolved to seize the stores of arms at Concord, Gage collected his best troops—the grenadier and light infantry companies—and placed them "off all duties 'till further orders" to learn "new evolutions." The patriot spies, however, knew what Gage hoped to "evolve." Boston patrolmen under Paul Revere had seen the transports hauling up their whaleboats for repairs. They guessed correctly that an expedition was being prepared to go by boat from Boston to Cambridge and thence take the road to Concord about 20 miles away.

Next morning Warren sent Revere riding to Lexington to warn John Hancock and Sam Adams to be ready to flee. Revere returned that night and arranged "that if the British went out by water we would show two lanterns in the North Church steeple; and if by land, one."[14] This is the famous "one if by land, two if by sea" of Longfellow's poem, but Revere did not intend that "I on the opposite shore will be." The lanterns were to rouse the Charlestown countryside.

During daylight of April 18 Gage sent mounted officers out to patrol the Concord road and to keep it free of rebel couriers. That night his elite troops—from 600 to 800 men—were awakened by sergeants shaking them and whispering to them. Startled, unaware of their destination, knowing only that their packs were full for a march, they slipped out of the barracks unknown to their sleeping comrades. Having stolen away from their own quarters, they marched openly to Boston Common where they formed ranks under the lackluster eyes of their commander, fat, slow-thinking Lieutenant Colonel Francis Smith. Fortunately for Smith, Major John Pitcairn of the Royal Marines was also coming along. Although Pitcairn has gone into some American histories as a profane and bloodthirsty boor, he was actually a gallant gentleman and a fine officer. At half-past ten the British were ready to move, and by then Dr. Warren had sent William Dawes and Paul Revere flying from Boston to warn the countryside.

Dawes took the longer land route over Boston Neck to Cambridge and thence to Menotomy (now Arlington) and the road west to Lexington and Concord. Revere, booted and swathed in a greatcoat, had himself rowed over to Charlestown. At eleven o'clock he sprang onto a waiting horse and clattered off.

Behind him two lanterns began to glow in the steeple of old North Church.

"The regulars are out!" Paul Revere cried, his excited voice rising above the hoofbeats of his horse. "The regulars are out!"

He was, with Dawes, warning every "Middlesex village and farm," cupping his hands to his lips to shout at lighted windows, tossing

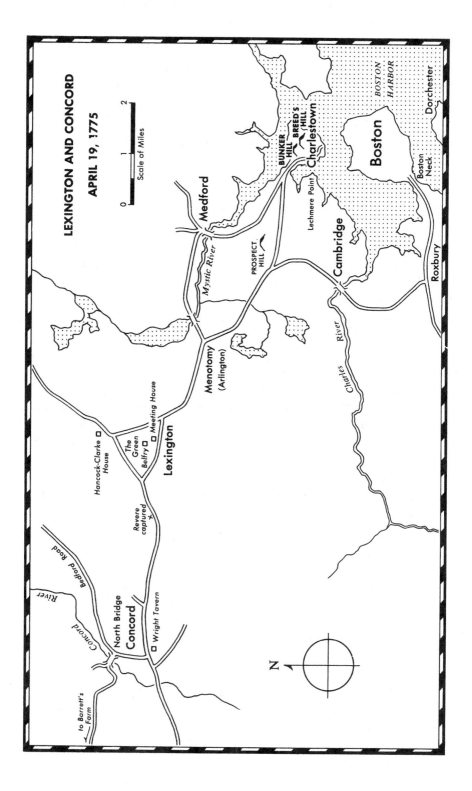

LEXINGTON AND CONCORD
APRIL 19, 1775

Scale of Miles
0   1   2

N

BOSTON HARBOR

Boston
Dorchester
Boston Neck
Roxbury
BUNKER HILL
BREED'S HILL
Charlestown
Lechmere Point
Cambridge
PROSPECT HILL
Medford
Mystic River
Charles River
Menotomy (Arlington)
Meeting House
The Green
Belfry
Lexington
Hancock-Clarke House
Revere captured
Concord River
Bedford Road
North Bridge
Concord
Wright Tavern
to Barrett's Farm

gravel at darkened ones, then riding on, his mount's hooves ringing boldly in the still darkness, the sweat on its hide forming puffs of foam.

At Lexington, Revere rode up to the home of Parson Jonas Clark. Sam Adams and Clark's cousin, John Hancock, were staying there. Revere shouted to the guard to let him in, and the guard yelled at him to stop making so much noise or he'd wake the family.

"Noise!" Revere roared. "You'll have noise enough before long. The regulars are coming out!"[15]

Adams and Hancock were awakened. They dressed and fled. It was then after midnight, and as they crossed a meadow Adams said to Hancock: "What a glorious morning this is!" Seeing his friend puzzled, Adams added: "I mean for America."[16]

It was not such a glorious morning for Paul Revere. After Dawes arrived in Lexington an hour later, the two set out for Concord. They were joined by young Dr. Samuel Prescott, who was returning home from a long evening of courting. The three rode on, spreading the alarm. Halfway between towns they were intercepted by Gage's outriders. They scattered. Revere rode into a pasture, where he was cornered and captured. Dawes wheeled and galloped back to Lexington. Dr. Prescott jumped a low stone wall and went clattering off for Concord, where he roused the militia.

The countryside had been warned, and back on the road from Charlestown the clear cold dawn of April 19 fell on the long columns of British redcoats marching into Lexington.

Colonel Francis Smith's soldiers were fuming. It was bad enough being perpetually damp from the waist down because of that moist white paste called pipe clay with which they were supposed to keep their breeches impeccably white, but now those same pants were stained with mud and the men were sopping from the chest down.

The whaleboats had put them ashore at Lechmere Point in knee-deep water. Then, after their fathead colonel had kept them waiting two hours for rations, he had led them into a backwater of the Charles in which they had been forced to wade up to their chests. No sooner had they begun squishing and squelching away for the Yankee lair at Concord than shots and ringing bells and scampering feet to either side of the road made it clear that there was to be no surprise. The only surprise that day would be if any of the officers knew any of the men they commanded. Their own officers were sick or on detached service. In their place were volunteers, thrill-seekers and smooth-chinned subalterns out for a lark. Some of them did not even come from the crack "flank" companies but wore the silly cocked hat of the line.

At Menotomy there was a surprise. Alarmed by outriders' reports that the rebels had been warned, perhaps prompted by Major Pitcairn, Colonel Smith made a wise decision: he sent an express rider back to Boston with a request for reinforcements. It was then about three o'clock in the morning. The men had been on their feet for five hours, and they continued to slosh forward, burdened by perhaps sixty pounds of equipment—packs, belts, bayonet scabbards and cartridge boxes—hampered by stiff and awkward clothing, and still clutching their ten-pound muskets, the famous Brown Bess of England.

But the guns' barrels and metal fittings were no longer brown but brightly burnished like the socket bayonets fitted to their muzzles, and these rows of gleaming barrels and glittering blades were visible from afar to the handful of patriots drawn up on Lexington Green.

Captain Jonas Parker and about 70 men had formed on the green. They stood inside a triangle formed by three roads. The road to Concord was at its base. Parker's men stood about a hundred yards above it, and they could clearly see the steady, awesome approach of the British advance guard under Major Pitcairn.

"There are so few of us," one man said, "it is folly to stand here."

"The first man who offers to run shall be shot down," Parker warned.[17]

Major Pitcairn ordered his men into line of battle. The rear ranks ran forward at the double to line up with the others and form two sections three men deep. They shouted and cheered as they ran.

"Stand your ground!" Parker ordered. "Don't fire unless fired upon. But if they want to have a war, let it begin here!"[18] Some men shook their heads and drifted away.

Pitcairn rode forward crying, "Lay down your arms, you damned rebels, and disperse!"[19]

Parker finally saw that this situation was impossible. He ordered his men to disband, taking their weapons with them. Pitcairn called repeatedly to them to lay down their arms. Shots crashed out (from the British on the road or from patriots behind a wall, history will never know), a British soldier was wounded and two balls grazed Pitcairn's horse.

"Fire, by God, fire!" a British officer cried, and a volley of British ball tore through the Americans. "Soldiers!" Pitcairn called. "Soldiers, don't fire! Keep your ranks. Form and surround them."[20] But the regulars, taunted for months in the Boston prison cage, driven mad by their frustrating march, were not to be checked. Pitcairn swung his sword downward as the signal to cease fire, but they replied with another crash of musketry, and then, after the rebels fired a ragged return, they cheered and charged with the bayonet.

The militia fled. Brave Jonas Parker stood alone. He had fired once and been wounded. He stood like a stricken bull in the arena, reloading to fire again—and British bayonets cut him down.

Eight Americans lay dead on the Green and ten more had been wounded. Only that single British soldier had been hurt—and that was all that there was to the Battle of Lexington. The British officers re-formed their exultant men, Colonel Smith came up with the main body, and then, with drums beating and fifes squealing, the redcoats swung west on the last six miles to Concord.

The alarm bell rung in Concord after the arrival of young Dr. Prescott had brought three companies of minutemen and one alarm company of old men and boys tumbling into town. Many of them joined Colonel James Barrett hurrying over the North Bridge that crossed the Concord River on the road west to Barrett's house, where most of the province's munitions were stored.

Much of these had been sent farther west the day before, but the minutemen still had to lug barrels of musket balls, flints and cartridges into the attic and cover them with feathers. Powder was hauled into the woods and a plowman dug furrows in which muskets and light cannon were laid while the earth from other furrows covered them over.

Meanwhile, other militia companies from other towns and villages were arriving in Concord. Eventually they numbered about 400 men under the nominal command of Colonel Barrett. Most of these men were stationed on a ridge overlooking North Bridge from Barrett's side of the river. They stayed there, watching, while the British marched into town unhindered.

Colonel Smith and his staff went to a tavern to refresh themselves, carefullly paying for all that they ordered, while four companies of light infantry crossed North Bridge and went up the road to Barrett's house. Behind them, three other companies of light infantry guarded the bridge, fanning out on both sides of the river. Inside Concord, the grenadiers, with a courtesy that should make the twentieth century blush, began searching houses. One huge grenadier retreated, red-faced, before a determined old lady brandishing a mop, and a grenadier officer in another house politely accepted the falsehood that a locked room was occupied by an invalid when it actually contained military stores. Still, they found 100 barrels of flour and sent them splashing into a millpond, followed by 500 pounds of bullets. But the flour barrels were not stove in and the bullet sacks were not slashed, and almost all of these supplies were salvaged. However, gun carriages found in the Town House were set afire, and then put out after the grenadiers realized that they might also set the Town House blazing. Dragged outside, they were relighted—and that column of smoke spiraling lazily into the sky above Concord's elms and oaks was seen by Colonel Barrett's men on the hill.

"Will you let them burn the town down?"[21] an officer asked Barrett, and Barrett replied by ordering the militia to march to the defense of the town and not to fire unless fired upon. In column of twos they came down, these "embattled farmers" of history, marching silently to the beat of drummer boy Abner Hosmer with Captain Isaac Davis, the Acton gunsmith, at their head.

At North Bridge Captain Laurie of the light infantry watched their approach in surprise. He sent back to town for reinforcements. Colonel Smith ordered a few companies of grenadiers forward, "but put himself at their head by which means he stopt 'em from being [in] time enough, for being a very fat heavy Man he wou'd not have reached the Bridge in a half hour tho it was not half a mile to it."[22]

Suddenly Laurie was nervous. The long column of Americans was coming straight down the steep hill to the bridge. His own men were uneasy. There were no better troops in the world, but today they were strangely unruly. Unfamiliar officers were having trouble forming them after Laurie pulled his outposts back to the Concord side of the bridge. Laurie wanted the front-rank men to fire, peel off and run to the rear to reload, thus exposing the second-rank men who would do the same and so on. Smartly executed, it was a fine maneuver designed to rake the approaching Yankees with a steady fire. But it was done clumsily that day. The first British shots fell short in the

river. One of them whistled by the ear of Captain Timothy Brown.
"God damn it, they are firing ball!" Brown exclaimed.[23]
They were indeed, and now they had the range. Captain Isaac
Davis was knocked down dead. Little Abner Hosmer toppled beside
him with a ball through the brain. Two other Americans were
wounded.

"Fire, fellow soldiers!" an American officer pleaded. "For God's
sake, fire!"[24]

The first full American volley of the Revolutionary War crashed
forth. Three redcoats—the first Britishers to die in that war—fell
lifeless, and nine more were wounded. Then the Americans cheered,
for the British were withdrawing! Leaving their dead and one wounded
man lying on the road, they rushed back to town in disorder. They
met and mingled with Smith's tardy grenadiers and were finally re-
formed and faced toward the Americans.

But the undisciplined Yankees pursued for only a few yards before
breaking ranks. Some went back across the bridge to carry off the
bodies of Davis and the little drummer boy, but most of them returned
to the ridge. Perhaps they were amazed by their own "victory" over
the regulars. Perhaps also they did not want to be caught between
Smith's force and the four companies of light infantry who might return
from Barrett's house any minute.

Silence came over North Bridge. The Yankees stared at the
crumpled red-and-white forms of the fallen foe. They saw a gangly
farmer come over the bridge. He had an ax in his hand. One of the
sprawled soldiers stirred. The farmer panicked, struck at him with his
ax and ran off. The soldier sank back onto the road.

Now came the tread of marching feet. The light infantry was returning from Barrett's house. They had found nothing. They were
disgruntled, then frightened to see their dead comrades and the
"scalped" soldier. Their step quickened. They began running. They
went tearing around the bend on the double, and the Americans on
the hill to the left let them pass without firing a shot.

It was now ten o'clock, and in Concord Colonel Smith was preparing
to leave. He hired carriages to carry his wounded and at noon the
silent columns trudged back the way they came.

> Yankee Doodle went to town
> Ariding on a pony,
> Stuck a feather in his cap
> And called it macaroni.

Earl Percy was marching to Colonel Smith's rescue with a force of 1,000 men and two cannon, and his fifes and drums were derisively playing "Yankee Doodle" as they struck confidently over Boston Neck. Passing through Roxbury a schoolboy is supposed to have laughed so hard at the tune that Percy asked him why. The boy replied with a mocking reference to a ballad that went:

> To drive the deer with hound and horne
> Erle Percy took his way.
> The child may rue that is unborne
> The hunting of that day!

On every side of the British column the Americans were gathering. Towns and hamlets too far away to fight at Lexington or Concord had sent militia hurrying to the scene. Some dispatched only a few dozen and others as many as 300 men. In all, perhaps 4,000 Americans were gathering along that 16-mile gantlet running back to Charlestown.

They fired from behind stone walls or from trees. They took long-range pot shots from houses or rushed boldly to within a few yards of the line of march and blazed away. Redcoat after redcoat slumped into the dust. Smith's hired carriages were piled high with wounded. But the patriots did not escape unscathed. Smith sent his light infantry out on the flanks. They surprised groups of militia in the hollows and put them to rout. They doubled back on themselves and took the unsuspecting Americans in the rear. They cornered them in houses and shot them down or drove their slender bayonets into them. And because they had taken as much as men can be expected to endure, they set fire to the houses or wrecked them.

But the militia were hydra-headed. Each time an American was killed or put to flight or merely quit the battle, two more arrived to take his place. And the galling fire from both sides of the road continued.

It not only tore British flesh; it fragmented British discipline. Smith's column became a disorderly crowd of men. Soldiers broke ranks to ransack roadside houses or taverns for food and whatever they could carry off. Nearing Lexington, Smith halted and ordered Pitcairn to hold off the Americans while he re-formed his ranks. The Americans swarmed around Pitcairn's rear guard and opened fire. Riflemen lying behind a pile of rails blazed at Pitcairn, conspicuous on an elegant horse. The horse plunged, threw Pitcairn, and ran into the American lines, carrying off Pitcairn's set of fine horse pistols. The rear guard was driven in and Smith was forced to renew the retreat.

Now the dreadful pace was killing. Men who had been on their feet for more than 20 hours were wilting. The light infantry were exhausted from the ordeal of covering the flanks. Some soldiers were breaking ranks in a stumbling run. Men continued to fall—from American musket balls or fatigue—and the redcoats' ammunition was running out. Entering Lexington the British were on the verge of breaking into a rout. Officers had to stagger around their hurrying men to confront them with bayonets and warn them to slow down or die. And then, at three o'clock in the afternoon, they beheld the black hats and scarlet coats and white breeches of Percy's brigade formed in a hollow square. Too tired to cheer, they passed through their saviors' ranks and sank to the ground, "their tongues hanging from their mouths, like those of dogs after a chase."[25] Percy's pair of 6-pound cannon kept the Americans at a respectful distance while Smith's exhausted men rested.

Meanwhile, American reinforcements were arriving. General William Heath came out to Lexington and so did Dr. Joseph Warren. Neither man saw the opportunity lying at hand. If a force could have been sent downroad while the redcoats rested, Percy's retreat could have been sealed off. A party of axmen could have been formed to fell trees across the British path. Neither tactic was adopted, although it must be said that the Yankee "army" was actually only a great crowd of armed and angry farmers, each fighting individually and entering or leaving the fight at his whim. Nor were they the crack shots of legend, either. When Percy resumed the retreat some time after three o'clock, the Americans again buzzed about his flanks like swarms of bees. The finest of targets lay under the muzzles of their muskets, and even though that weapon's projectile falls harmlessly to the ground after 125 yards, they still should have been able to slaughter the defenseless enemy.

Still, they continued to torment them all the way to Charlestown. And the British fought back. They were burning and ransacking every roadside house now, and at one point the flankers drove a party of patriots into a house and bayoneted 12 of them to death. At Menotomy 40 Americans and 40 British fell. At Cambridge a mile and a half of continuous battle was begun. Redcoats and men in homespun fought each other at close quarters, with bayonets and clubbed muskets.

Again and again Percy halted his column and unlimbered his little cannon. They spat, drove the Americans off, the gunners limbered up again, and the guns and carriages became covered with the scarlet coats of the wounded and fatigued. At last Percy's battered force crossed Charlestown Neck into Charlestown under the protecting muzzles of the British ships. The Americans fell back, darkness came, and the bloody retreat from Concord was over.

British casualties were 73 killed, 26 missing and probably dead, and 174 wounded, a total of 273 out of about 1,800 men engaged. The Americans lost 49 killed, 5 missing, and 41 wounded, a total of 93. If a battle's importance were to be measured by its casualties, Concord and Lexington would have been trifling indeed. But the shots "heard round the world" had been fired, and the Revolutionary War—one of the most momentous in history—had been started.

Next day, Percy's troops were hardly safely across the Charles before the vanguard of thousands of armed New Englanders rushed into Cambridge. Works were thrown up outside the city, an army arose on the plain and the siege of Boston was begun.

4

☆

The day after Lexington and Concord a British ship arrived in Boston Harbor with Lord North's "peace proposal." The King's minister, realizing that he had been too harsh to the Americans, offered not to tax those colonies which voluntarily paid their share of the cost of empire.

His Lordship, however, was too late with much too little. Americans were generally too enraged even to consider this evasion of the issue of the *right* to tax, and one of them exclaimed: "An armed robber who demands my money might as well pretend he makes a concession by suffering me to take it out of my own pocket, rather than search there for it himself."[26]

Meanwhile, couriers from the Committee of Safety had gone galloping north and south ever since the first American perished at Lexington. At ten o'clock that fateful morning, Israel Bissell went pounding
out of Watertown bound for points south. Two hours later the horse
beneath him fell dead, but Bissell mounted a fresh horse and clattered
on: New York . . . New Brunswick . . . Princeton . . . Philadelphia.
Other express riders carried the news farther south, and before the
month of April was out it had spread across Virginia and was en route
to South Carolina.

In Virginia a British major named Horatio Gates knew that Lexington meant war. Like Thomas Gage now commanding in Boston,
Gates had been wounded at the Monongahela. Gates, however, had left
the service to become an American planter. He was definitely on the
colonial side. So was another former British soldier, General Charles
Lee. Thin, ugly and irascible, fonder of dogs than of men, this soldier
of fortune was considered by many Americans to be the ablest military
man in America. Charles Lee was certainly—as he would personally
insist—more experienced than that Colonel George Washington whom
he had just visited at Mount Vernon.

Washington also heard the news from the North, and it so affected
him that he packed the old red-and-blue uniform he had worn under
Braddock and took it to Philadelphia with him for the second session
of the Continental Congress.

The Congress was due to convene on May 10.

Dawn of May 10 crept across Lake Champlain and the stone walls
of Fort Ticonderoga. Ethan Allen realized that the fort would have
to be rushed immediately if surprise were not to be lost. Turning to
address his Green Mountain Boys, he stood just a bit forward of
Benedict Arnold at his side to make it clear that he, Ethan Allen,
by orders of the Connecticut Assembly, not Arnold, representing
Massachusetts, was in command of the expedition.

"I now propose," Ethan Allen said, "to advance before you and in
person to conduct you through the wicket-gate. For we must this
morning quit our pretensions to valor, or possess ourselves of this
fortress in a few minutes. Inasmuch as it is a desperate attempt—
which none but the bravest of men dare undertake—I do not urge it
on any contrary to his will." He paused. His great figure was growing

more distinct in the half-light, and he seemed to dwarf the short, stocky Arnold. "You that will undertake," Ethan Allen called, "poise your firelocks!"[27]

All obeyed, and they marched off three ranks deep toward the fort on a venture that was not actually that "desperate." Ticonderoga was held by only 40-odd British soldiers—most of them unfit for service—under Captain William Delaplace and Lieutenant Jocelyn Feltham. Still, neither Allen nor Arnold nor their 83 men knew this as they went charging toward the wicket.

A sentry saw them, pointed his musket and pulled the trigger, but it flashed in the pan, and the sentry ran back into the fort to sound the alarm. The Americans pursued, crying, "No quarter! No quarter!" Another sentry slightly wounded one of Allen's officers with a bayonet, and huge Ethan Allen lifted his sword to cut him down. Taking pity, he softened his blow to a saber cut on the face and went on up a staircase with Arnold.

At the top of the stairs stood Lieutenant Feltham clutching his breeches.

"Come out of there, you damned old rat!"[28] Allen roared, and the astonished officer asked by what authority these men had intruded on the King's domain.

"In the name of the Great Jehovah and the Continental Congress!"[29] Allen bellowed, waving his sword over Feltham's head. Then, demanding "the Fort and all the effects of George the Third" upon pain of a general massacre, Allen brought Captain Delaplace hurrying down the stairs. Delaplace promptly handed over his sword and Fort Ticonderoga.

The gateway to Canada, with all its priceless artillery, was in American hands.

The capture of Ticonderoga startled Congress. Many of the delegates there had comforted themselves with the argument that the "ministerial troops," as the King's soldiers were called, were to blame for Lexington and Concord. But now colonials had attacked and captured a royal fort. The fact that they were openly opposing King George III sank deeper into the minds of the delegates as debate began over such matters as general defense, although the possibility of reconciliation with Britain was also discussed.

Colonel Washington, in charge of a committee "to consider ways and means to supply these Colonies with ammunition and military stores," was delighted to hear that Ticonderoga had yielded about 60 cannon and mortars. Washington, appearing daily in his uniform now, was also pleased with accounts of the fighting in Massachusetts. He assured John Adams and other powerful delegates that Americans could stand up to British regulars. Still, the prospect of fratricidal war oppressed him, and he wrote to a friend:

"Unhappy it is, though, to reflect that a brother's sword has been sheathed in a brother's breast and that the once-happy and peaceful plains of America are either to be drenched with blood or inhabited by slaves. Sad alternative! But can a virtuous man hesitate in his choice?"[30]

On May 25 King George's unhesitating choice of "sad alternative" arrived in Boston Harbor aboard the frigate *Cerberus*. A "triumvirate of reputation," Major General William Howe, Major General Henry Clinton and Major General John Burgoyne had come to America to give aid and advice to the faltering General Gage, already earmarked for recall.

William Howe was probably the most outstanding of this trio of hand-picked generals. It was Howe who had led his light infantry up the slopes of the Anse-du-Foulon to the Plains of Abraham. Now, 46 years old and grown heavier through indulgence in food and drink, he was still handsome in the florid fashion of the period. Like his older brother, Admiral Lord Richard ("Black Dick") Howe, who soon joined him in America, he was of very dark complexion. He was also, like his brother, a strange choice to subdue the colonists: both Howes were grateful to the Americans for having placed in Westminster a statue of their oldest brother, Lord George Augustus Howe, the beloved leader killed at Ticonderoga in 1758. They had agreed to serve against the colonies only on direct orders from the King.

Henry Clinton needed no such urging. A colorless career soldier, he was the only son of an admiral and former governor of New York. His military career began at 13, when he purchased a lieutenant's commission. At 20 he was a lieutenant colonel and a major general at 34. Three years later he boarded the *Cerberus,* chosen for his reputation as a planner.

"Gentleman Johnny" Burgoyne's reputation was of a different order. Wit, playwright, member of Parliament and *bon vivant,* he shared

William Howe's passion for the pleasures of the gaming table and the boudoir. Yet Gentleman Johnny seems also to have been a good soldier. He had not only astounded his officers by insisting that they read or learn something of mathematics, but also shocked them by treating soldiers as human beings who were not to be trained "like spaniels by the stick." Unfortunately for Burgoyne, his sharp tongue got him into trouble before he arrived.

Hearing that 5,000 British regulars were being cooped up by a force of raw colonial militia only twice their number, he exclaimed: "What! Well, let *us* get in and we'll soon find elbow-room."[31] Stepping ashore May 25, Burgoyne heard himself hailed as "General Elbow-Room."

The truth of the situation was exactly as Gage had been describing it for London. Yankee Doodle would not dance until more troops were sent to America. Even then, subduing the colonials would be difficult. First, the countryside was hostile: there were many loyal Tories but they so feared the Sons of Liberty that they would only be good for acclaiming a victorious army. As a result the problem of a supply line 3,000 miles long was magnified. Next, the road networks were poor and the ruggedness of the countryside, with its multiplicity of rivers, made battle in the accepted European style unlikely. Third, even though British sea power gave Gage the advantage of being able to move anywhere against these coastal colonies, there was no single centralized capital the capture of which might bring capitulation. There were, in effect, 13 different subcapitals.

All London's witty contempt for the Yankee "cowards," now being so drolly relayed by Gentleman Johnny Burgoyne, would not raise the siege of Boston. A criminal amnesty from King George would not make the "army of thieves and vagrants" melt away. Generals such as James Grant might taunt Benjamin Franklin with the remark that, given a thousand grenadiers, "he would undertake to go from one end of America to the other and geld all the males,"[32] but even Grant would have to admit the impossibility of transporting just a thousand men from one end of this wild continent to the other. Bombs, not bombast, were needed—to say nothing of a little fresh beef.

By June the British in Boston were on lean rations. "However we block up their port, the rebels certainly block up our town, and have cut off our good beef and mutton," one of Gage's officers wrote home. "At present we are . . . subsisting almost on salt provision."[33]

Outside Boston, the colonial army under General Artemas Ward had problems of its own. Ward at 48 was himself sick of "the stone," and he was having difficulty disciplining his militia. Ward dared not try to take the town. He had no siege guns to batter it, nor enough troops to storm it. The seacoast towns of the four New England provinces had withheld their militia against the possibility of invasion by the ever-present British fleet.

So as the Army of Massachusetts, or, more properly, of New England, sat down before Boston and waited for something to happen, the Continental Congress down in Philadelphia soberly began debating whether or not impetuous New England was dragging the whole continent into war.

Benjamin Franklin had written from London that war must be the unanimous will of all 13 colonies. Not all of them, however, particularly those of the South, were anxious to take up arms. Many conservative delegates such as Duane and Farmer John Dickinson of Pennsylvania had revived the spirit of conciliating the Crown.

Then, from the Massachusetts Committee of Safety came a petition for Congress to adopt the Boston army as its own. Many delegates recoiled. Even George Washington was not now sure that war was inevitable. But John Adams, now the spokesman for New England, was determined not to allow the other nine colonies to split away from the Northern four. He arose in Congress to make clear the common danger. Let New England fall and the other colonies, one by one, beginning with New York, would feel the rod. John Adams spoke of an American army recruited from all the colonies. He had already decided who should command it. Not a professional such as British-born Charles Lee, general by grace of the King of Poland, but rather a native-born American. Should he be from the North which had fielded the army before Boston, or from the middle or Southern colonies which seemed to be wavering?

On June 14, with John Hancock in the president's chair, John Adams began describing the man he wished to nominate as the American commander in chief. John Hancock listened hopefully.

"A gentleman whose skill as an officer, whose independent fortune, great talents, and universal character would command the respect of America and unite the *full* exertions of the colonies—"

John Hancock's face fell. A Northern man had been ruled out.

"—a gentleman from Virginia who is among us here, and who is—"

There was a stir. The tall man in uniform had risen quickly to his feet and bolted for the library.

"—George Washington of Virginia."[34]

There was a swelling hum of voices, raised first in surprise, as well as, from New Englanders, some resentment. John Hancock's face fell farther when his old friend, Sam Adams, arose to second his cousin's motion. Washington, in the library, might have been a bit chagrined to hear Edmund Pendleton of Virginia say that although the colonel was a decent man, he had lost every big battle he'd been in.

Debate continued until the next day, June 15, when Washington appeared and heard Hancock say: "The President [of Congress] has the order of Congress to inform George Washington, Esquire, of the unanimous vote in choosing him to be General and Commander-in-Chief of the forces raised and to be raised in defense of American liberty. The Congress hopes the gentleman will accept."[35]

The gentleman would, but with the modesty which was one of his finest traits:

"Mr. President . . . I . . . declare with the utmost sincerity, I do not think myself equal to the command I am honored with. As to pay, Sir, I beg leave to assure the Congress that as no pecuniary consideration could have tempted me to have accepted this arduous employment at the expense of my domestic ease and happiness, I do not wish to make any profit from it."[36]

He would keep an account of his expenses, and this was all he asked Congress to pay.

After selection of the leader came the choice of his lieutenants. Artemas Ward, of course, was the first of them as a major general; then Charles Lee; Philip Schuyler, the wealthy Hudson River patroon who was so influential in New York; Israel Putnam to satisfy Connecticut; and finally, as a skilled professional adjutant to handle Washington's staff work, his neighbor from Virginia, Horatio Gates.

Appointments of brigadiers followed as Congress quibbled over questions of priority or tried to assuage wounded provincial pride. In the meantime, General George Washington prepared to take command of the army which had preceded him to battle. Before he could, a fresh gale, clamorous with the clash of arms, blew down from the north.

5

☆

To beat General Gage to the high ground above Boston the Committee of Safety directed its army to seize and fortify Bunker Hill.

General Artemas Ward called a council of war at which both he and Dr. Warren expressed their reluctance to move. Ammunition was low and there were only 11 barrels of powder in the entire American camp. Moreover, Bunker Hill out on Charlestown Peninsula between the Charles and Mystic rivers was exposed to the guns of the British fleet and could be easily cut off at the rear on Charlestown Neck, an isthmus so narrow that it was flooded at high tide.

Such considerations did not deter Major General Israel Putnam, who assured the council: "The Americans are not at all afraid of their heads, though very much afraid of their legs. If you cover these, they will fight forever."[37] The council agreed, so completely, it appears, that no one bothered to ask Putnam how troops were to "fight forever" after their ammunition ran out. But then, it was not customary to challenge "Old Put."

At 57 years of age, Putnam was still an imposing figure with his bear's body, his bull's voice and his great round owlish head. He was also a legend. He had been with Lord Howe on that fatal patrol at Ticonderoga, he had narrowly missed being burned at the stake by Indians, he had been a prisoner of the French at Montreal and had been shipwrecked while leading an expedition against Havana. Such was his great courage and capacity for inspiring men that no one dared to suggest that Old Put seemed to excel at narrow escapes from avoidable traps. On the night of June 16 he led about 1,200 men into a fresh cul-de-sac.

Dressed mostly in homespun dyed the colors of the colony's oak and sumach bark, wearing broad-brimmed hats and clutching old Brown Bess muskets from the colonial wars, with here and there an

ancient Spanish fusee, they marched across Charlestown Neck in the
darkness. Ahead of them was Old Put riding a fine horse, his saddle
holsters stuffed with the splendid pistols once owned by Major Pitcairn of the Royal Marines. Beside Putnam was Colonel William
Prescott, another colonial veteran but a man as practical as Old Put
was impetuous.

Prescott sent a patrol into Charlestown to watch the enemy while
his main body marched to Bunker Hill and then along a ridge leading
east to Breed's Hill, which was closer to Boston. For a time Prescott,
Putnam and others argued about whether it was best to fortify Breed's
or Bunker. Colonel Richard Gridley, an excellent engineer, cut them
short with the warning that they were wasting precious time. So they
agreed to place the main works on Breed's while fortifying Bunker Hill
to cover any retreat. Then Gridley marked out the lines of a redoubt,
and the tall lean Prescott gave his iron-armed citizen-soldiers a single
order: "Dig!"

They did, and with such astonishing fury that a marine sentry aboard
the *Lively* staring through the dissolving mists of the hot moist dawn
of June 17 started in disbelief at the sight of the red raw earth
of the Yankee positions. *Lively* almost immediately opened fire, but
an angry order from Admiral Samuel Graves silenced her guns. Soon,
however, the entire fleet was booming away, while the surprised
British commanders gathered in a council of war.

Henry Clinton proposed that the British attack across Charlestown
Neck in the rebel rear. But Gage and William Howe, who was to
command the expedition, decided rather to land on the peninsula and
march around the Mystic River side of the redoubt to get in the
American rear. It was a good plan, although Clinton's, being based
on the obvious fact of British sea power, was probably better. However, the tide was against the British. Before Howe could begin landing
at the appointed place, six precious hours had been granted the
Americans.

Putnam and Prescott took every advantage of the respite. Prescott
drove his men relentlessly. They were thirsty and hungry and wilting
in the heat, but he insisted that they build a breastwork from the redoubt down the Mystic side of the hill. Cannon balls smashed among
them. One of them tore off the head of happy young Asa Pollard,

leaving his torso a spouting stump. Prescott saw his horrified men faltering and he jumped up on the parapet of the redoubt, striding back and forth to prove that the shot had been a lucky one.

On Bunker Hill to the rear, Old Put was in a rage of command. He was everywhere along the line, putting units into place, stiffening the spines of the unvaliant, trying but failing to get cannon out to Prescott's redoubt. Twice Putnam rode his horse across shot-swept Charlestown Neck to ask for reinforcements, and twice Ward refused him. Eventually, at the urging of the Committee of Safety, Ward sent out the New Hampshire regiments of John Stark and James Reed.

Colonel John Stark was the true commander of this force of about 1,200 frontiersmen. Though they were splendid sharpshooters, they had no ammunition. On the spot in Cambridge they were issued two flints apiece, a gill of powder and a pound of lead cut from the organs of a Cambridge church. Stark sent them back to quarters where they made up fifteen cartridges apiece. Men with bullet molds made musket balls, men without them hammered out slugs of lead.

Leading his men on the four-mile march to the front, Stark took them through enemy naval shelling at such a deliberate pace that young Captain Henry Dearborn of the leading company suggested that he rush the cadence.

"Dearborn," Stark said calmly, "one fresh man in action is worth ten fatigued men."[38]

At Bunker Hill Stark paused to survey the battle front.

At one o'clock in the afternoon, with raving fifes and rattling drums, some 2,300 British redcoats came ashore at Moulton's Point. General Howe immediately began studying the American position. He saw at once that he could not turn Prescott's left so easily. The Yankee commander had built a breastwork out in that direction. Moreover, Howe saw numerous bodies of men farther back on Bunker Hill and mistook them for an American reserve. Then he saw a column of men —Stark's sharpshooters—come marching along the ridge to Breed's Hill, and decided to call for reinforcements of his own.

In that second delay, Prescott again improved his position. The sight of the British forming on Moulton's Hill made it clear to him that there was still a gap yawning between his breastwork on the left and the Mystic River. So he sent some Connecticut troops and two cannon back to a stone-and-rail fence about 200 yards to the left rear of the breastwork. The fence ran down to the Mystic bank, and it seemed good enough to block Howe's flanking attempt.

Colonel Stark did not agree. Coming up to the rail fence Stark saw that it ended on the bank of the river, but that beneath it was a narrow strip of open beach along which four men might pass abreast. Taking his best shots, Stark put them on the beach behind a barricade built of stones. Then he posted the rest of his force along the rail fence. Now Prescott had about 1,400 men holding positions: the redoubt, the breastwork, the rail fence and the beach wall. Suddenly, to his surprise, Prescott saw Dr. Warren enter the redoubt.

Warren was a dashing sight in his white satin breeches, his pale blue waistcoat laced with silver and his carefully combed blond hair. Because he had just been appointed a major general, Colonel Prescott saluted him and offered him command.

"I shall take no command here," Warren said. "I came as a volunteer with my musket to serve under you."[39]

The fiery young revolutionary mounted the firing platform alongside the men who had flocked to his standard of rebellion.

Howe was ready.

He had about 2,500 men evenly divided between himself on the right at Moulton's Hill and Brigadier General Sir Robert Pigot on the left in the town of Charlestown. Pigot was to take the redoubt, Howe would attack the breastwork and rail fence. Howe drew up his men in three ranks and told them he expected them to "behave like Englishmen and as becometh good soliders," adding: "I shall not desire any one of you to go a step further than where I go myself at your head."[40]

Howe ordered his artillery to commence firing. It did, and suddenly fell silent. The guns' side boxes contained 12-pound balls instead of 6-pounders. Howe's fieldpieces were useless.

On the British left, American snipers in the houses of Charleston began whittling the redcoats. General Pigot complained to Admiral Graves, who sent orders to burn the town.

Ships in the harbor and batteries planted on Copp's Hill in Boston began showering Charlestown with red-hot ball and "carcasses," hollow iron balls pierced with holes and filled with pitch. Within a few moments Charlestown caught fire, to the great delight of Gentleman Johnny Burgoyne, who stood on Copp's Hill watching the scene with Henry Clinton.

Charlestown was one great blaze. Whole streets of houses collapsed against each other in walls of flame, ships on the stocks began burning, the high steeples of the churches were like great flaming spears, and everywhere was the hiss of flames and the crash of timbers.

On the British right, Howe was changing his formations. He drew off his light infantry and put them in columns of four along the Mystic beach. There were about 350 of them, and they were to storm the Yankee beach wall at bayonet point.

Opposite Howe's main body behind the breastwork and the rail fence, burly Israel Putnam rode up and down the lines roaring the immortal words: "Don't fire until you see the whites of their eyes! Then, fire low."[41]

Behind the Mystic wall Colonel Stark went Putnam one better, dashing out about 40 yards to nail a stake into the ground. "Not a man is to fire until the first regular crosses the stake," he yelled.[42]

The attack commenced.

Pigot's men climbed steadily toward the redoubt. Some nervous Americans opened fire before they were in range. Prescott swore he would kill the next man who fired. A young Yankee officer ran along the parapet kicking up the leveled muskets. Pigot's redcoats came steadily up the slope.

On the right Howe's men marched down Moulton's Hill, across a lowland, and up the slopes of Breed's against the silent breastwork and rail fence. It was hot. Neither the tall bearskins of the grenadiers nor the cocked hats of the line had brims to keep the sun out of a man's eyes. The regulars stumbled in thick grass reaching to their knees. A brick kiln and adjacent ponds broke their ranks and they had to re-form. Sweat began to darken the armpits of their scarlet coats. Men began to gasp beneath burdens of 60 pounds and more. Still they came on.

Along Mystic beach the light infantry—Howe's favorite troops—were trotting to the attack with outthrust bayonets. In the front were the dreaded Welsh Fusiliers.

Now all was thunder and flash and flame, Charlestown blazing, batteries crashing, naval guns roaring, echo and reverberation rolling over water and earth, while overhead, now exposing, now concealing, drifted the billowing white clouds of gun smoke.

The light infantry were running now.

The Welsh Fusiliers went slanting past Stark's stake, and the little wall ahead of them exploded in a crash of musketry.

The Fusiliers swayed and went down. Great rents were torn in the attacking column, but the King's Own Regiment swept forward to fill them. They ran on, while behind the fence the Yankee sharpshooters with empty muskets gave way to men with loaded ones.

Another dreadful volley crashed out, and the King's· Own went down in heaps.

Now the picked flank troops of the 10th Regiment were called upon. Officers ran among the reluctant, beating them with swords. Surely it would not be possible for the rebels to fire a *third* volley in so short a time. Once again the lines of scarlet and sun-tipped steel slanted forward, and there *was* a third volley—and that was all on Mystic beach.

Ninety-six dead redcoats had been left sprawled upon its blood-clotted sands, and even though his plan was wrecked at the pivotal point, Howe pressed his charge forward. Two ranks of men, grenadiers in front, came at the breastwork and the rail fence. Flame and smoke belched forth and tightly dressed ranks of red and white were instantly transformed into little packs of stunned and stricken men. Again and again the American weapons spoke, and men spun and toppled or went staggering away streaming blood. Every man in Howe's personal staff was either killed or wounded. It was a wonder that the general himself, in the forefront as he had promised, was not scratched. But he was mortified to see his vaunted regulars sprawling in heaps under the guns of ignorant peasants, and then, when he heard that Pigot was also thrown back in what was little more than a feint against the redoubt, there came upon the heretofore invincible William Howe, as he was to write later: *"A moment that I never felt before."*[43]

He recalled his troops, sent for more reinforcements and began reforming.

The Americans were exultant. They had met and beaten the finest troops in the world with but little cost to themselves. Colonel Prescott went among them, praising them and reminding them that the battle was not over. He encouraged them to stand fast, keeping to himself the fact that a steady trickle of desertions had drained his forces like a leaking pipe. The redoubt was down to 150 men.

There were many more men to be had back on Bunker Hill, but they refused to come forward. Putnam stormed among them, sometimes beating reluctant soldiers with the flat of his sword, but he only got a few to follow him back to Breed's.

Worse, he got no ammunition.

A quarter-hour after his first bloody repulse, Howe was attacking again.

His plan now was to avoid the beach wall. The light infantry had rejoined Howe's main body. They were to attack the rail fence while Pigot and Howe threw all that they had against the redoubt and the breastwork.

On the left, Pigot depended chiefly on John Pitcairn and his marines. They got to within a hundred feet of the silent Yankee fort, and then the wall of flame gushed forth again. Pitcairn sank to the ground mortally wounded. His son, also wounded, held his dying father in his arms. "I have lost my father!" he cried in anguish, whereupon the marines are said to have echoed: "We have lost our father!"[44]

On the right before the breastwork, the regulars there were also being sickled to the reddening earth, and the shaken Howe called for a bayonet charge. An incessant stream of fire poured from the American lines. The British light infantry was riddled. Some 38-men companies had only eight or nine men left. A few had only four or five. On the left Pigot was staggered and actually retreated. For the second time, Howe withdrew.

Reinforcing regiments had been sent to Prescott, but Putnam found the men of one of them scattered on the safe side of Bunker Hill. Fat Colonel Samuel Gerrish lay flat on the ground. He told the livid Putnam that he was "completely exhausted." Old Put snarled that he was, rather, completely cowardly—and ran among Gerrish's shrinking violets knocking some of them to the ground with his sword.

Two companies, however, did arrive in time to give some comfort to Prescott. But for every man he got, he lost three. Whenever a wounded man had been taken to safety, there were, in a cowardly dodge as old as arms, as many as twenty "volunteers" to carry him.

Most men had enough ball to repulse a third assault, but there was precious little powder. Cannon cartridges had to be broken open and their contents distributed.

Re-forming below Prescott, the British had reinforcements and all the necessary ammunition. Four hundred marines and regulars had responded to Howe's call for fresh men. Henry Clinton had crossed the river to collect all the guards and walking wounded he could find and join Pigot's force. Cannon were brought into play. A demonstration was made against the rail fence while Howe hurled himself against the breastwork in the center and Pigot-Clinton struck at the redoubt on the left.

"As soon as the rebels perceived this," Lord Francis Rawdon wrote to his uncle, the Earl of Huntingdon, "they rose up and poured in so heavy a fire upon us that the oldest officers say they never saw a sharper action. They kept up this fire till we were within ten yards of them. They even knocked down my captain, close beside me, after we had got into the ditch of their entrenchment."[45]

But the redcoats had reached the ditch, and after the American fire "went out like a spent candle," they leaped down from the parapet into the open redoubt. From three sides they came. Little General Pigot, too small to leap into the fray, climbed a tree outside and swung himself into it.

Still the Americans fought, most of them without bayonets of their own.

"Twitch their guns away!" Prescott roared. "Use your guns for clubs."[46]

Barehanded or with clubbed muskets the Americans actually tore guns out of the hands of the regulars. But more and more redcoats were pouring over the walls, and Prescott shouted: "Give way, men! Save yourselves!"[47]

Prescott fought on himself, his sword clanging against bayonets and gun barrels. His loose linen coat probably saved him. The bayonets cut it into tatters, but missed his flesh. Prescott was finally borne out of the rear gateway on the tide of retreating Americans. As he left, he passed a figure in a blue waistcoat steadily directing a covering action for the withdrawal. Outside, Prescott joined Putnam in directing a running fight from one fence or wall to another, until their force had crossed Bunker Hill and gone across Charlestown Neck onto the mainland.

Nevertheless, it was in this retreat that Americans suffered most of their casualties. One of them was found at the redoubt exit. The body had been stripped of its waistcoat, but from the quality of the blood-stained ruffled shirt it was obvious that the dead man had been a person of importance. A British officer rolled the body over and gasped in surprise.

Dr. Joseph Warren was dead.

6

☆

British casualties in the Battle of Bunker Hill had been staggering. Of 2,400 engaged, 1,054 had been shot, of whom 226 were killed. It is doubtful if British regulars had ever before suffered in such proportions, and this at the hands of a rabble in arms.

Although William Howe was not a physical casualty, he was certainly a spiritual one. Howe never forgot that moment he had never felt before. The curtain never came down upon that bloody tableau at the back of his brain, and William Howe, having formed his military character upon the ardor and daring of his mentor, James Wolfe, now turned slow and cautious.

American casualties totaled about 450—most of them suffered during the retreat—of which about 140 were killed. Unfortunately, once the Americans came to realize that they had won a victory, the indestructible myth of the invincible minuteman was born. Raw and ragged militia had given more than they got to the world's finest troops; therefore all Yankee Doodle need ever do was to get his dander up and grab his musket. This fallacy had happily overlooked the fact that the Americans were behind fortifications while the redcoats were in the open, and was based on the assumption that the great carnage among the British was due to Yankee marksmanship. There had been some sharpshooters at Bunker Hill, especially among Stark's frontiersmen, but the most nearsighted neophyte could hardly have missed packed scarlet ranks at 50 feet. No, the New England militiaman was never a crack shot. He was a plowboy or a mechanic and he was too far away from the wilderness to develop prowess with firearms.

He was also, from the standpoint of discipline, a very poor soldier, and once the ennobling fervor of battle had deserted him, he slipped back into his old slothful ways. What George Washington always excoriated as the New England "leveling principle"—that every man is as good as the next one and maybe even a little better—made it almost impossible to enforce discipline. Privates who had "listed" in the cause of freedom would not be regulated by officers whom they had helped to elect. Officers so chosen did not dare to push their constituents about, and it was not uncommon in the American camp to find a captain shaving a private or a lieutenant fixing a corporal's musket, both officers being anxious to please old customers. The camp itself was a huge, smoking, filthy hobo jungle in which each man cooked his own mess and latrines ("necessary houses") were built cheek by jowl with sleeping quarters. On one occasion a colonel who was the army's chief engineer was seen carrying his ration of beef to his tent, where he intended to cook it himself "to set the officers a good example." The Reverend William Emerson, grandfather of Ralph Waldo Emerson, has described that scene:

> Some [tents] are made of boards, some of sailcloth, and some partly of one and partly of ye other. Others are made of stone and turf, and others again of birch and other brush. Some are thrown up in a hurry and look as if they could not help it—mere necessity—others are curiously wrought with doors and windows done with wreaths and withes in ye manner of a basket.[48]

The reverend thought the camp's variety a beauty, but General Washington, who took command in Cambridge on July 3, considered it a most unmilitary mess.

Washington was already depressed to learn that he had only 14,500 men to command, few trained engineers, a dearth of artillery, no war chest and only enough powder to issue his men nine cartridges apiece in case of British attack.

Discipline, however, was the chief problem. It became Washington's chief duty to make these liberty-loving individualists understand that in armies which fight for freedom, liberty must give way to regulation. He began by insisting upon respect for authority and the display of rank ranging from his own blue chest riband to the stripe of green cloth on a corporal's left shoulder. Where Washington could not persuade, he punished.

Although the American commander seems to have discouraged some of the more barbarous punishments then in vogue, he was not loath to use the whip. Once he asked Congress to increase the number of allowable lashes from the Biblical 39 to 500. Congress wisely refused, while sympathizing with its military chieftain's enormous problems in trying to form an army on the very field of battle.

Washington was especially anxious to cashier cowardly or conniving officers, and in August he reported:

> I have made a pretty good slam among such kind of officers as the Massachusetts government abound in . . . having broke one Colonel and two Captains for cowardly behavior in the action on Bunker Hill—two Captains for drawing more provisions and pay than they had men in their company—and one for being absent from his post when the enemy appeared there and burnt a house just by it. Besides these, I have at this time one Colonel, one Major, one Captain and two Subalterns under arrest for trial.[49]

Gradually, the inflexible and sometimes irascible gentleman from Virginia produced a measure of cleanliness and order in the camp. Old latrines were filled up and new ones dug. Offal and carrion were burned. Company messes were set up and inspected regularly, loose women were run out of camp, and drunken soldiers were flogged. Although there were never enough blankets or muskets, and the men were still generally clad in homespun, a kind of military organization was developed.

A 720-man regiment of the "line" was formed consisting of 8 companies, each company having 1 captain, 2 lieutenants, 1 ensign, 4 sergeants, 4 corporals, 2 "Drums and Fifes," and 76 privates. These were new regiments, of course, for the marvel of forming an army on the battlefield was to be surpassed by the miracle of recruiting a new one to replace it.

Constant recruitment was necessary because the American soldiers believed in going home after the battle. Their enlistments expired January 1, 1776—some said December 1, 1775—and they had withstood every attempt to make them re-enlist. Thus General Washington had to face the melancholy fact that the army he was molding would melt away at year's end. He had also to contend with the fact that each of the colonies, in effect, was fielding armies of its own, often offering higher bounties than Continental Army recruiters, as well as the reluctance of the more Southern colonies such as Georgia and South Carolina to contribute troops to the Continental Army at all.

On the other hand, Maryland, Virginia and Pennsylvania came through splendidly. From the western wildernesses of these colonies came about 1,500 backwoodsmen, "remarkably stout and hardy men: many of them exceeding six feet in height." They had to march from 400 to 700 miles to reach the camp. Old Daniel Morgan, still bearing the scars of the flogging he had received under Braddock, put his men on horses and rode them 600 miles in 21 days. Not a man was lost by sickness on the way.

These men in leather hunting shirts and moccasins carried a new weapon: the Kentucky rifle. This was the long, slender and graceful gun which German and Swiss gunsmiths in Pennsylvania had designed for the American frontier. Whereas a musketman rarely could hit a man beyond 60 yards, a rifleman could put ball after ball into a seven-inch target at the range of 250 yards.

If the rifle had not been so slow-loading and if it could have been fitted with a bayonet and placed in the hands of a marksman who would accept discipline, the American arsenal would have been augmented in truly splendid style. However, the endless pop-popping of unruly frontiersmen at British redcoats far out of range drove George Washington to distraction, to say nothing of the rifleman's custom of freeing any of their comrades confined in the guardhouse for misdemeanors. They were of use later on in the Revolutionary War, but not at Boston, and Washington wished that they had never come.

Negro soldiers presented another problem. There were quite a few Negroes, both slave and free, in the New England army. One of them, Salem Poor, fought with great bravery at Bunker Hill. Crispus Attucks, one of the first American martyrs in the Boston Massacre, was a Negro slave. Actually, the problem was not Washington's but Congress's. At first, Congress decreed that no Negroes be re-enlisted in the Continental Army. But then Washington reported that "discarded" Negroes were discontented and might join "the Ministerial Army" opposing him and that he was therefore re-enlisting Negroes. Congress aquiesced, but insisted that only freedmen were acceptable.

The problem—like Washington's annual headache of forming a new army—lasted throughout the war. Southern colonies were not eager to imperil their "peculiar institution" of slavery by placing muskets in the hands of slaves. Yet the British were promising freedom to those slaves who would fight for the King against their former masters. Many slaveowners, especially in the Northern and middle states, were only too pleased to send a slave to war as substitutes for themselves. Finally, if it was embarrassing that the fight for freedom might also preserve the institution of slavery, it was equally shameful to raise an army of slaves under the flag of liberty. There was never any real solution to this complex problem. As might have been expected, the colonies most dependent upon slavery put no Negroes in the field, while the others, to the degree of their freedom from this evil, enlisted slaves and gave them, in the phrase of Alexander Hamilton, "their freedom with their muskets."

Hamilton, incidentally, was himself typical of the higher type of patriot flocking to the American standard. This bold and brilliant young captain of New York artillery eventually became one of Washington's most trusted aides. Another able officer whom the commander in chief first met in Boston, was his chief of artillery, Henry Knox. Fat, amiable and forceful, Knox had kept a bookstore in Boston and had read enough about guns to amaze the British professionals who came to his shop. Knox's friend, Nathanael Greene of Rhode Island, a handsome man who limped and was asthmatic, also emerged as a top commander as well as one of Washington's most intimate advisers.

General Charles Lee was also in Boston, followed, as ever, by a pack of yapping hounds, and surrounded by a circle of admiring yokels listening to him speak with easy expertise of such esoteric things as redans or flèches or chevaux-de-frise.

In the meantime, William Howe took command of the British Army, poor "blundering Tommy" Gage having been recalled. Howe, however, showed himself no more aggressive than his predecessor. Rather than sally forth to assault George Washington, a general as helpless as a man standing on one foot, he preferred to dally with lovely Mrs. Joshua Loring while Mrs. Loring's husband merrily seized the property and possessions of Boston's patriots and fed them to his accomplices at rigged auctions.

With the arrival of winter, both armies postponed hostilities.

Congress had taken charge in America. Although there was as yet no true American government, and the Continental Congress had no legal foundation for its actions, it had assumed responsibility for conducting the war. It had adopted the New England army, appointed its officers, drawn up a military code, set up a Postal Service under

Benjamin Franklin, named commissioners to deal with the Western Indians, issued paper currency, and, finally, found itself incapable of resisting the Canadian magnet.

At first, Congress attempted to coax Canada into joining the rebellion, but after the Canadians refused they decided to conquer her instead. Those two incompatible comrades of Ticonderoga—Ethan Allen and Benedict Arnold—had already been to Philadelphia to offer their services for a Canadian expedition, but the delegates, while generally adopting their advice and plans, chose General Philip Schuyler as the leader.

It was a bad choice. An able aristocrat and an ardent patriot, Schuyler was better fitted to counsel than to command. Fortunately, he had a fine deputy in Brigadier Richard Montgomery. Like Horatio Gates, Montgomery had fought in the French and Indian War as a British officer, later leaving the service to settle in the colonies and marry an American of wealth and family. Montgomery urged the dilatory Schuyler again and again to move quickly down the lake-and-river chain against Montreal. At last, on August 28, 1775, he took the bit in his own teeth and embarked a force of about 1,000 men on Lake Champlain.

With him was Ethan Allen. The tiger of Ticonderoga had promised to lead his Green Mountain Boys on the expedition, but the Boys had "diselected" him and Allen appeared at Ticonderoga as a regiment of one. Major John Brown, a polished and urbane lawyer with a surprising aptitude for war and the woods, was also present.

Sailing down the Richelieu on September 5, Montgomery's lookouts could see smoke rising from the British fort of St. John's. Here Montgomery began his siege, stationing his gunboats in the river to protect his own rear and sending Ethan Allen and John Brown around the British flanks—Allen to take charge of a body of rebellious Canadian volunteers waiting downriver, Brown to strike at the enemy supply line.

While the siege of St. John's was slowed down by cold and rain and sickness, these two daring spirits met in the enemy rear and decided to take Montreal by themselves. Brown had about 200 men, Allen about 100. Brown would attack above the town, Allen from below. But Brown failed to make an appearance. Allen, nevertheless, decided to go it alone. News that "Ethan Allen, the Notorious New

Hampshire Incendiary" was outside the gates threw the town "into the utmost Confusion."

Sir Guy Carleton, commanding there, remained calm. He sent a mixed force of about 250 regulars, volunteers and Indians out the Quebec Gate to attack the American. Seeing their approach, the men on Allen's flanks fled into the woods. Allen began a fighting retreat, but was surrounded and forced to surrender.

Allen's capture failed to discourage Montgomery. Eager to conquer St. John's before winter closed in, the American commander floated gun batteries past the fort to force the surrender of Chambly in its rear. Then he stepped up his attacks on St. John's until, on November 3, the fort surrendered.

Ten days later the swift-moving Montgomery received the surrender of Montreal; too late, however, to prevent Carleton's escape. A few days after that he received word from Benedict Arnold to join him at Quebec.

Arnold had come to Washington at Boston an angry and frustrated man. His great scheme had been given to Schuyler, and his personal honesty in his military accounts had been questioned. Washington, who appreciated Arnold's dash and daring, soothed him with command of a second invasion of Canada.

He was to go up the Kennebec River and then down the Chaudière to assault the old fortress of Quebec while Montgomery engaged Carleton at Montreal. Hundreds of musketmen and riflemen bored with the siege of Boston volunteered for the expedition. Altogether Arnold had about a thousand men, among them 19-year-old Aaron Burr and Captain Daniel Morgan, when he began, in late September, a march that ranks as an epic ordeal in American history.

First, the bateaux which were to carry them up the Kennebee from Fort Western (present-day Augusta) were made of green wood and badly built. They came apart. Often they had to be carried or hauled upriver against boiling rapids. Going down the swift-running Chaudière some smashed into rocks and the men aboard were lost. Floundering, stumbling against one another, the men waded for days over one stretch of nearly 180 miles.

After provisions gave out, the Americans ate soap and hair grease. They boiled and roasted their bullet pouches, moccasins and old leather breeches and devoured them. They killed and ate the dogs that accompanied them. There were dropouts and slow death and mass defections along the way. At one point Lieutenant Colonel Roger Enos refused to go on and withdrew his division of 300 men. Undaunted, Arnold pressed forward. On November 9 his ragged band burst from snow-cloaked forests onto the south bank of the St. Lawrence. They marched upriver to Point Lévi on the Isle of Orléans. They were ragged and bearded. Their feet were shod in raw skins. Their clothes hung in tatters over bodies that were but bags of sticks. There were only 600 of them. They had taken 45 days, not the estimated 20, to cover 350, not 180, miles. But they had arrived, and they were going to attack Quebec.

For all his doggedness, events were thwarting Arnold. He had collected canoes and dugouts to make a night crossing of the St. Lawrence and ascend the cliffs to the Plains of Abraham as James Wolfe had done. Quebec was held by a mere handful of marines and regulars and a weak body of about 500 militia. Arnold was certain he could not fail. But for two straight nights the winds blew so strongly that he could not cross. In the meantime, Lieutenant Colonel Allen Maclean had arrived in Quebec with about 100 veteran soldiers. Their coming heartened Quebec's defenders and raised their number to about 1,200.

Arnold still thought that in a stand-up fight his hardy band could scatter the militia and overwhelm the remaining regulars. At nine o'clock on the black night of November 13, the first detachments began crossing to the Anse-du-Foulon, now Wolfe's Cove. They landed and kindled a fire to revive a lieutenant who had fallen overboard and been towed through the ice-cold river. The rest of the Americans crossed on the following night.

Now Arnold led his men up to the Plains of Abraham, routing a force of militia there. He sent a flag of truce to Quebec to demand its surrender. His emissaries were routed by cannon ball. Then Arnold was driven off as the frigate *Lizard* sailed upriver to cut off his rear and Maclean prepared to attack with 800 men.

Miserable again, with many of their number barefoot, the invaders retreated to Pointe aux Trembles. Here, on December 2, they saw with elation the topsails of a schooner coming downriver. It was Montgomery with reinforcements of 300 men.

Montgomery had brought with him captured British clothing: great white blanket-coats with caped hoods, heavy blue overalls, sealskin moccasins and fur-tailed caps. Arnold's freezing men joyfully damned them for their tardiness and donned the winter clothes. Then, about a thousand men strong, the hardy little American army marched back to Quebec.

Once there, it became plain to Montgomery and Arnold that they could not conduct a siege. They had no heavy guns to batter Quebec's walls, they could not possibly endure an entire Canadian winter encamped outside the city's gates, smallpox had broken out, food was short, and, worst of all, the enlistment of Arnold's New Englanders expired at year's end. They decided to attack, even though Sir Guy Carleton had entered the town and raised the number of its defenders to 1,800 men. On the first snowy night they would storm the Lower Town, Arnold attacking from the north, Montgomery from the south.

The afternoon of Saturday December 30 snow began falling. It thickened. The wind rose. By early morning of the 31st a blizzard was howling about Quebec. Snow mixed with hail whistled into the faces of the Americans moving to their positions. They ducked their heads and shielded their firelocks with their coats. At some time after four o'clock, signal rockets burst red in the blackness above them and the Americans began marching.

Within Quebec drums began beating and bells tolled. Officers ran through the streets shouting, "Turn out! Turn out!" Guy Carleton's formidable barricades in the Lower Town were quickly manned.

On the left of the American pincers, Montgomery's division was slipping and sliding down the slopes toward the road from Wolfe's Cove to Cape Diamond. Men carrying unwieldy scaling ladders could barely struggle through drifts six feet deep.

On the right Arnold's force of 600 men left the suburb of St. Roche and stole silently past the Palace Gate. They veered right and a sudden blaze of musketry from the ramparts above raked them. Men fell. They moved on, Arnold leading an advance party of about 25 men, including Daniel Morgan. Behind them came 40 artillerists dragging a 6-pounder on a sled, and behind them came the main body.

Arnold and Morgan came to a narrow street blocked by a barricade. They called for the 6-pounder. It had been abandoned. A gun in the barricade fired but did no damage. Arnold called for a charge.

Out of the snow they came, yelling, rushing to the barrier, and firing through its gun ports. The British fired back. Arnold fell with a ball in his leg. Bleeding freely, he was helped away while huge Daniel Morgan took command. The Old Wagoner mounted a ladder set against the barrier, calling upon his men to follow. A blaze of fire tumbled him back into the snow. He had a bullet through his cap and another through his beard. Shaking himself, Morgan leaped erect, climbed the ladder again and jumped over the parapet. Others followed. The defenders fled. The Americans were inside the Lower Town. Another barrier lay ahead, but the Americans did not attack it. Instead, they decided to halt to await the arrival of Montgomery.

Richard Montgomery's force had also come to a barricade. Soldiers began sawing at it. Montgomery and his officers tore at half-sawed posts with their hands. They pulled it down and passed on, no more than 60 or 70 of them, the remainder of the division having been disorganized and scattered by the storm.

Now a blockhouse confronted them. Inside were about 50 men and four little 3-pounders charged with grape. The British blew on their slow matches and awaited the American approach. Montgomery came on. His men faltered. He called to them through the storm, "Come on, my good soldiers, your General calls you to come on."[50]

Montgomery, Aaron Burr, a few other officers and about a dozen men rushed forward. They were within a few paces of the blockhouse when a sheet of flame and a hail of grape and musket balls raked them. Another burst, and it was all over.

Montgomery lay dead. So did most of his officers. Only Burr and a few men got away.

To the north, inside the Lower Town, the Americans under Morgan were fighting desperately. Carleton had sent a force of 200 men and cannon out the Palace Gate to take them in the rear. Morgan's men were trapped. They began to surrender. Morgan fought on. He set his back against a wall. Tears of rage and despair flowed down his face as he stood there, his sword uplifted for his last blows. His men implored him to give up. He shook his head. Then Morgan saw a clergyman in the crowd and called: "Are you a priest?" The man nodded, and Morgan handed him his blade with the words: "Then I give my sword to you. But not a scoundrel of these cowards shall take it out of my hands."[51]

Two bursts of gunfire, an able maneuver by Carleton, and the attempt to storm Quebec had been repulsed. More and more troops were to be fed into the project, but Carleton was not to be dislodged. In the spring, as in the days of James Wolfe, a British fleet came up the St. Lawrence to raise the siege.

The American army had to retreat, Montreal had to be abandoned, and in July of 1776 the demoralized wreck of Montgomery's once proud little army washed back upon the shores of Lake Champlain. The attempt to conquer Canada, the most ambitious American expedition of the Revolutionary War, had ended in humiliating defeat.

7

☆

By New Year's Day of 1776, General Washington's army had melted away to about 10,500 men.

A month previous the Connecticut regulars had set the example of homegoing, insisting that their enlistments were up on December 1. All attempts to dissuade them had failed, most notably the perverse performance of General Charles Lee.

"Men," Lee roared, after "entreating" them with curses and insults, "I don't know what to call you. You are the worst of all creatures."[52]

The troops merely laughed, and at the appointed time they marched home, ignoring the hisses and groans of the comrades they left behind, the showers of stones and the mocking blandishments of the women of the camp. Even Washington lost his temper and wrote of the "dirty, mercenary spirit" of the men "upon whom I reckoned" and who now had "basely deserted the Cause of their Country."

In fairness to these men, however, it must be made clear that they *had* enlisted for eight months only, that the practice of enlisting for specified short terms—for the "campaign," as it was called—was customary, and that very few ranking officers, the wealthy Washington in particular, were called upon to make sacrifices comparable to those demanded of most of the junior officers and all the enlisted men.

While they served, their farms went uncared for or their trades were gobbled up by stay-at-homes. They had served long enough, they argued, and now it was someone else's turn.

Fortunately for Washington, thousands of men in the Massachusetts and New Hampshire militias decided that it was their turn. They poured into Washington's camp while the time-expired regulars jeered at them as "Long-faced People," and marched home. The new arrivals did not intend to stay long, either, but they at least gave Washington a respite in which to recruit men and rebuild his army, and they were numerous enough to keep Howe contained in winter quarters.

Actually, Washington might well have attacked at this time, and he regretted not having done so. The British Army was in frightful condition. Smallpox was at work and food was short. Howe tried desperately to maintain order and discipline, but not so desperately as to forgo the charms of blonde Betsey Loring. His officers also amused themselves. The Old South Church was turned into a riding academy, and dramatic plays—heretofore banned in Boston—were performed in Faneuil Hall. *The Blockade of Boston* was a burlesque of Washington and his ragtag army and Washington was invited to attend for the pleasure of being hanged. The American replied by raiding Bunker Hill on opening night. British officers dressing up as women heard the alarm and rushed off to battle in petticoats.

British and Tory hopes that the patriots might be quitting were momentarily raised at the sight of a red flag flying in present-day Somerville. The familiar combined crosses of St. George and St. Andrew were visible. But they were only in one corner, and the rest of the flag was covered with 13 alternate stripes of red and white. It was the first American flag, and as it was flung to the breeze the booming of a 13-gun salute celebrated the birthday of the Continental Army.

The Americans were not quitting, they were getting bolder—and soon in that eventful month of January, 1776, Tom Paine would teach them to regard even the King as their enemy.

"How impious," Tom Paine wrote in the pamphlet *Common Sense,* *"is the title of Sacred Majesty applied to a worm, who in the midst of his splendor is crumbling into dust! . . .*

"Of more worth is one honest man to society, and in the sight of

God, than all of the crowned ruffians that ever lived."

Having had at King George III—the "royal brute"—Tom swung hard at the arguments for reconciliation.

"To be always running three or four thousand miles with a tale or a petition, waiting four or five months for an answer, which, when obtained, requires five or six more to explain it in, will in a few years be looked upon as folly and childishness."

And then came the ringing call for freedom which was to electrify the colonies and to bring thousands of waverers to the side of the rebellion:

"O ye that love mankind! Ye that dare oppose not only the tyranny but the tyrant, stand forth! Every spot of the old world is overrun with oppression. Freedom hath been hunted around the globe. Asia and Africa have long expelled her. Europe regards her as a stranger, and England hath given her warning to depart. O receive the fugitive, and prepare in time an asylum for mankind!"

Such were the logic and the rhetoric which inspired the men of Washington's new Continental Army as they toiled frantically to install the guns which Colonel Henry Knox had brought from Ticonderoga.

Even the ordeal of Arnold's march to Quebec hardly surpassed the feat of bringing those heavy guns down from the mountains of the northern lakes in the dead of an American winter. They were loaded on barges, but the barges sank and Knox calmly had the guns grubbed up. They went on sleds to cross frozen lakes and rivers, and sometimes the ice broke and the cannon sank and had to be recovered again. Snow fell and the roads froze and Knox's "noble train of artillery" was packed on sledges. Up and down the Taconics the column toiled, over the Berkshires, men shouting warnings as the sledges began to gather momentum down the snowy slopes, horses and oxen panting and wheezing as they hauled the guns across the valley floor and up the next hill. Sometimes the poor beasts perished in the traces, but there were always replacements, and on January 18 the convoy at last lurched into Framingham.

Eventually all 59 pieces of ordnance—from 24-pound cannon to stubby little cohorns or mortars—would go into Washington's 14-mile line around Boston. On the nights of March 2 and 3 the regulars began mounting the biggest guns on Dorchester Heights below the city. They built forts. So great was the surprise of the British who beheld them in the morning that one officer said they were made by "the Genii belonging to Aladdin's Wonder Lamp."[53]

The guns and works on Dorchester were even more serious than those which had menaced Boston from Bunker Hill, and Howe immediately called a council of war. It was decided to evacuate the city.

On March 17 the last of Howe's soldiers and 1,000 Tories sailed from Boston Harbor for Nantasket Harbor. Ten days later this woebegone fleet of perhaps 170 vessels set sail for Halifax.

Triumphant, the patriots rushed into the city that had been the center and the symbol of the rebellion. Now it was Tory property that went under the auctioneer's hammer. Now it was Tory homes that sometimes went up in flames while the owners were stripped, tarred, feathered and ridden out of town on a rail. No one hates more than hostile brothers, and even the British themselves were not hated so venomously as were those Loyalists whom Howe was forced to leave behind.

From Maine to South Carolina they were lashed through the streets, pelted with rotten eggs or forced to go down on their knees to damn the King and his ministers. One Tory is on record with the quaint lament that he had "had the misfortune to affront one of the Committee men, by not giving his Daughter a kiss when I was introduced to her. This has offended the old man so much, that . . . he has several spys to watch my actions. Sorry I did not give the ugly Jade a kiss." Washington himself wanted the more notorious Tories hung as an example to the rest, and Governor Livingston of New Jersey said: "A Tory is an incorrigible Animal: And nothing but the Extinction of Life will extinguish his malevolence against liberty."[54] Before the war was over the patriots were forcing all secret Tories to declare themselves by imposing oaths of loyalty to the United States. Those who refused were fined, imprisoned, deprived of civil rights or, as the new states seized upon this handy means of raising revenue, dispossessed.

Witch hunt though this was (although it never led to stake or gallows), it is difficult to see how the patriots could have acted otherwise. The Tories were a dangerous fifth column. They were nearly as numerous and fully as able as the patriots, and they were so inimical to the revolution that the man who conducted the war from England always believed that it would be won by a Tory uprising.

Lord George Sackville had been convicted of cowardice at the Battle of Minden in 1759 and adjudged "unfit to serve His Majesty in any Military Capacity whatever." Yet King George III began 1776 by making Lord George Secretary of State for the American Colonies. With his name changed by an inheritance to Lord George Germain, *"that man,"* as he was described by indignant accusers, undertook "to engage the people of America in support of a cause which is equally their own and ours."

Germain's "people of America"—Tories—were numerous in the colonies south of Virginia. It was believed that the appearance of a British force there would bring thousands of Loyalists rallying to the old red flag. Germain thus approved a Southern expedition already planned. Henry Clinton was to command the troops, with young Lord Charles Cornwallis as a second. The fleet would be under Admiral Sir Peter Parker.

The British counted on the fierce Scottish immigrant Highlanders of the North Carolina interior, who hated the seaboard aristocracy, to seize Carolina ports. But then trouble in Ireland and contrary winds delayed the fleet's departure—while in Carolina the kilts came out on schedule.

In February of 1776 the clans began gathering. With the skirl of the pipes on the wind, with knives tucked into tartan hose, swords at the belt and muskets on their shoulders, all of the McDonalds and McDowells, the Campbells and Camerons of the North Carolina west were marching behind General Donald McDonald toward the port city of Wilmington on the coast.

There were about 1,500 of them, and out to meet them came 1,000 patriots under Colonels Richard Caswell and John Lillington. The patriots came to Moore's Creek Bridge and crossed it. They began to dig in, until their leaders realized that it was not wise to fight with their backs to water. They returned to the other side of the stream and dug in afresh.

In the soft daylight of February 27, General McDonald's Highlanders came to Moore's Creek Bridge. They saw the empty trenches and concluded that the patriots had fled. They rushed the bridge, and a single crashing volley of musketry smashed them to the ground. Up from their trenches rose the patriots to counterattack, to shatter the kilted ranks and slaughter them in a merciless pursuit.

Moore's Creek Bridge was a Tory disaster. North Carolina stayed firmly in the rebel camp, Georgia and South Carolina stiffened against the King, and Henry Clinton and Sir Peter Parker found no Loyalist enclave awaiting them when they joined forces off the Carolina sand bars.

So they hoisted anchor and sailed for Charleston farther south.

During that balmy May while the British fleet plunged south toward Charleston, two gentlemen met in Paris. The Comte de Vergennes had recently become Foreign Minister of France, and he saw in the American Revolution the opportunity to avenge his nation upon the detestable English. Pierre Augustin Caron de Beaumarchais, famous for his play, *The Barber of Seville,** was a passionate lover of liberty and avowed friend of the Americans.

Vergennes did not yet dare to make war upon Britain. He could, however, simply assist her enemies, the colonies. Vergennes invited Spain to do likewise, and was accepted. A secret fund of one million livres was set up. A dummy trading company to purchase munitions "privately" was created.

In May the firm of Hortalez et Cie., under the amiable management of Caron de Beaumarchais, began "acting" for the Americans. During the year 1776-77 as much as 80 percent of the Continental Army's powder would come through Hortalez and Beaumarchais. It was very good powder, made by a scientist named Lavoisier.

Charleston was the most important American port south of Philadelphia. It was also the most heavily defended.

Throughout the month of May reinforcements from Virginia and North Carolina had been hurrying to Charleston. None other than Charles Lee came down to take command. By dawn of June 4, when the horizon bristled with the masts and sun-gilded sails of the British fleet, there were some 6,000 men holding a series of fine fortifications.

To the south of the harbor lay James Island with Fort Johnson. Across the harbor mouth was a sand bar, and inside of it on the main-

---

* And later *The Marriage of Figaro.*

land and guarding the city were batteries at Haddrell's Point. To the north of the harbor was Sullivan's Island with the redoubt of palmetto logs which was to bear the name of its builder, Colonel William Moultrie. Farther north across a narrow strip of water called The Breach lay Long Island, unoccupied and undefended.

The fort on Sullivan's Island was obviously the key to Charleston. Colonel Moultrie had confidence in its walls of palmetto logs enclosing a fill of earth 16 feet thick. Moultrie believed that they would soak up British cannon balls like a sponge. Moreover, the fort had 30 guns, though very little powder, and the garrison of about 450 men was confident and actually eager for action. Moultrie improved his position while the British wasted time sounding for a channel across the bar. By June 7 they began entering the harbor. On June 9 Clinton put 500 of his 2,500 men ashore there. His plan was to cross The Breach to Sullivan's Island and attack the fort from the north while Parker's ships battered it from the south. Lee sent a force of about 800 men to Long Island to counterattack, but then recalled it and placed the troops at the northern tip of Sullivan's Island. In the meanwhile, Clinton put the remainder of his force ashore on Long Island. The two armies confronted one another across The Breach while Admiral Parker's ships consumed another two weeks working their way over the bar.

On June 28, as the British ships roared a thunderous cannonade, Clinton's grenadiers and light infantry jumped into The Breach. Many of them vanished in holes seven feet deep and Clinton called for boats. But many of these ran aground in shallows a foot and a half deep. Once it was seen that The Breach was an impassable moat of deeps and shallows, Clinton's regulars could do no more than growl at the Americans across the water while the battle for Charleston became a fight between a fleet and a fort.

The bomb ketch, *Thunder,* began the British fleet's attack by hurling shells at the fort. Then the rest of Parker's fleet sailed to battle stations. Close inshore of the fort were *Active,* 28 guns; Parker's flagship *Bristol,* 50; *Experiment,* 50; and *Solebay,* 28. Stretched farther offshore away eastward were *Actaeon,* 28; *Sphynx,* 20; *Syren,* 28; *Thunder* and the armed ship *Friendship* with 28 guns.

The British were highly confident. The wind was right, it was a clear day, and the fort seemed to be answering weakly. Then *Thunder* realized that her bombs were falling short. Rather than come in closer and perhaps foul the other ships, she increased the powder charges in her mortars. The first supercharged shots broke the mortar beds and *Thunder* was of no further use.

Now the American guns were replying with a slow and awful accuracy. *Bristol*'s cable was shot away. She lay end-on to the fort and was raked horribly. Twice her quarterdeck was cleared of every person except Parker, and Sir Peter, to his lasting mortificiation, had the seat of his trousers shot off and his behind singed. *Experiment* suffered just as badly.

Within the fort, sweat-drenched Americans were scorched by a hot southern sun and sometimes by the muzzle flashes from 30 cannon in continual blaze. Colonel Moultrie cheered his gunners on, while men with fire buckets full of grog darted along the fire platforms to refresh the thirsty. Gradually the artillery duel rose to such a frightful roar that even the veteran General Lee, who had come over to the island, was astonished. Once a combination of three or four British broadsides struck the fort with such force that Moultrie feared another such salvo would shake it down.

Then the fort's flag disappeared. British sailors cheered while American onlookers in Charleston groaned. They believed the fort was surrendering. Inside the redoubt, Sergeant Jasper cried to Moultrie: "Colonel, don't let us fight without our flag!"

"What can you do?" Moultrie replied. "The staff is broke."[55]

Jasper's reply was to run outside the fort, seize the flag, and then, fixing it on a sponge staff, set it upright again while British shot and shell crashed all around him. A cheer arose from Charleston as the blue flag with its white crescent and the word "Liberty" whipped in the breeze again.

Now three of the British second line of ships upped anchor and tried to move around the western end of the island. They wanted to batter the fort on its flank and bring their guns to bear on a plank bridge behind the island. All three ships ran aground. *Actaeon* and *Sphynx* fouled each other, *Sphynx* losing her bowsprit. Eventually, two worked free, but *Actaeon* was immovable.

As night fell the jubilant Americans could hear their shots crashing into her, and eventuall; she was set afire.

Night also marked the end of the battle. At eleven o'clock, horrified at the carnage aboard their ships, mortified at having been so mauled by the tiny American fort, the British slipped their cables and stole off into the night.

Charleston had held, the glory of Fort Moultrie had entered American history, and it was two years before the British would think again of "the people of America" who dwelt in the South.

8

☆

Parliament had voted to raise an army of 55,000 men to crush the rebellion, but the King's subjects did not rally to his cause.

Among the officer class there was much sympathy for the colonists, while the English yeoman had never been keen on the poor pay and brutal discipline of British Army ranks. Press gangs, judges and tavernkeepers had always been the King's chief recruiters, and so, faced with a spectacular lack of enthusiasm in his own people, King George went looking for hirelings.

He found them in the principalities of Germany: Brunswick, Waldeck, Anhalt-Zerbst, Anspach-Beyreuth, Hesse-Hanau, Hesse-Cassel. Eventually some 30,000 German mercenaries were hired for the American war, and because more than half of these were supplied by the Landgrave of Hesse-Cassel, all were called Hessians.

Britain promised to pay all expenses of the soldiers, as well as $35 for each soldier killed, $12 for each one wounded, and over $500,000 annually to the Hessian Landgrave alone. Thus the subjects, rather the human chattels of the German princelings, were often worth more slaughtered than on the hoof.

The decision to send them against Britain's descendants in America was the last of George's fatal blunders, He had rejected the colonies' Olive Branch Petition asking for a peaceful reconciliation, he had used harsh language in proclaiming the colonies in a state of rebellion, his Navy had wantonly burnt Falmouth, and now the King was sending mercenaries against the colonies, just as he did against foreign foes.

Americans were now convinced that there was nothing left to do but break the last ties that bound them to him.

In the fateful summer of 1776 Thomas Jefferson told John Adams that he ought to make a draft of a declaration of independence. Adams declined, and Jefferson, pressing him, asked: "What can be your reasons?"

"Reason first," Adams replied, "you are a Virginian, and a Virginian ought to appear at the head of this business. Reason second, I am obnoxious, suspected and unpopular. You are very much otherwise. Reason third, you can write ten times better than I can."

"Well," Jefferson said, "if you are decided, I will do as well as I can."[56]

Jefferson did draw up a declaration, after which Congress, much to the anguish of its redheaded author, toned down its language and cut out about a quarter of it. Jefferson's impassioned attack on slavery, which he blamed on the King, although he was himself a large slaveholder, did not get past his Southern colleagues. The vituperation poured out on King George personally—language which Jefferson may or may not have had from his friend, Tom Paine—was also deleted. On July 4, after much debate, the Declaration of Independence was adopted.

John Hancock signed first, with a great bold flourish, and said: "There, I guess King George will be able to read that!"[57]

One by one, the others signed, radicals, moderates and conservatives, all united now in their determination to be "Absolved from all Allegiance to the British Crown." There were the Adamses of Massachusetts, openly jubilant that "the river is passed, and the bridge cut away"; there was the wealthy Marylander, Charles Carroll of Carrollton, a Catholic island in a Protestant sea, signing because "I had in view not only our independence of England, but the toleration of all sects professing the Christian religion."[58] The Lees of Virginia signed, one before and one behind a beaming Thomas Jefferson. So too did Benjamin Franklin, his wise eyes still twinkling over his quip. "We must all hang together, or assuredly we shall all hang separately." After the Pennsylvanians came Caesar Rodney of Delaware. No odder-looking man ever lived than this bold bantam with a face hardly larger than an oversize apple. But Caesar Rodney had ridden 80 miles through a storm-tossed night to put Delaware on the side of the declaration and swing the Congress toward independence. Now all argument was done. All signed, 56 delegates from 13 colonies, pledging to each other "our Lives, our Fortunes, and our sacred Honor." Four days later—July 8—the Declaration of Independence was published. Philadelphia heard for the first time those noble ideals and ringing phrases which still have the power to move hearts.

When in the Course of human events . . .
We hold these truths to be self-evident, that all men are created equal,
that they are endowed by their Creator with certain unalienable Rights,
that among these are Life, Liberty and the pursuit of Happiness. . . .

Philadelphia took the news calmly. After all, the debate had been common knowledge. But it was different elsewhere in this new-born "country." Bells tolled and bonfires burned up and down the coast. Savannah burned King George in effigy. New York pulled down his statue and Connecticut melted it down for bullets, while Boston tore George's arms from the State House and burnt them along with every other vestige of His Majesty that could be found.

Thus it was an exultant and defiant United States of America, not 13 cowed and submissive colonies, which greeted Admiral "Black Dick" Howe when he arrived in New York Harbor empowered to talk of peace.

Lord Howe's "peace" overtures began with a letter to "Mr." Washington, which the American commander coldly refused to accept. Next General Howe sent a letter to "George Washington, Esquire," as well as an emissary who claimed that both Howes had been specially nominated as peace commissioners by the King. Washington received the emissary but discovered that all that the Howes had power to do was to grant pardons. Since no fault had been committed, Washington said, no pardon was needed—and he coolly dismissed his guest.

After this exchange, the Howes decided to attack New York. The general had come down from Halifax to Staten Island with a large body of regulars, the admiral had come from Britain with the Hessians, and Henry Clinton and Sir Peter Parker soon came limping up from Charleston with their men and ships. General Howe now had an army of 32,000 superbly armed and equipped troops to hurl against 19,000 ragged, untrained Americans in New York. His

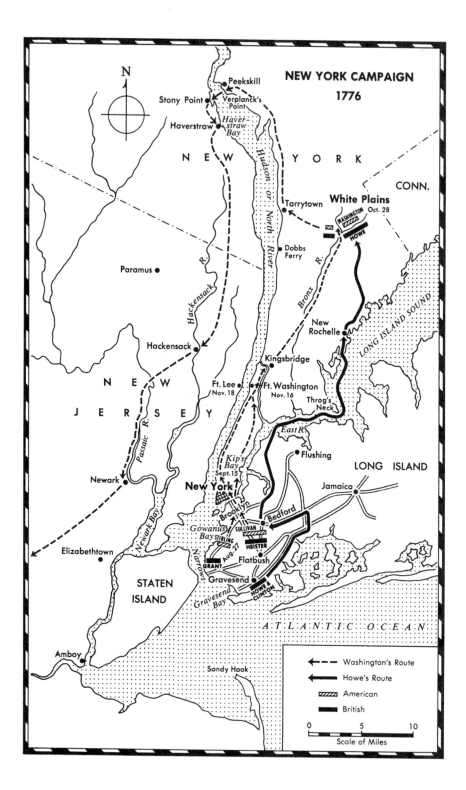

NEW YORK CAMPAIGN
1776

brother led a fleet of ten ships of the line, 20 frigates mounting 1,200 guns and hundreds of transports. Britain had never before sent out such an armada. She had spent the staggering sum of £850,000 to organize and supply it.

On August 22 the troops began landing on Long Island.

Washington clearly understood the importance of New York. "It is the Place that we must use every Endeavour to keep from them,"[59] he wrote to its commander, Brigadier General Lord Stirling.* Control of New York City meant command of the Hudson and access to the lake-and-river chain to Canada. If the British held it, they could cut off New York City and New England from the rest of the colonies.

But Washington did not yet appreciate British sea power. He believed New York could be held against it, when, actually, Manhattan Island and the other islands clustering around it were highly vulnerable to amphibious attack.

To defend it Washington divided his force into five divisions under Putnam, Greene, William Heath, Joseph Spencer and the garrulous John Sullivan of New Hampshire. One division held the northern end of Manhattan Island where Kingsbridge linked it with the mainland, three held the southern end where the mile-square town of New York was located, and the fifth under Greene was across the East River on Long Island.

Greene built works on Brooklyn Heights, which rose 100 feet above water and commanded New York. But then he came down with malaria, and was evacuated to New York. Command passed to John Sullivan, who was in charge when Howe began landing 20,000 troops at Gravesend Bay.

Great white sails flooded the bay. Longboats, galleys and flatboats crowded with scarlet coats and green-clad Hessian Jaegers rowed away from them toward shore. The sun made a million points of light on bayonets and burnished buckles, on flashing white oars and on the instruments of the bands playing lively marches to spur on "Black Dick" Howe's bluejackets. By noon Howe had 15,000 men ashore—a feat which modern amphibious commanders with motor-

---

* William Alexander, "Lord Stirling," is probably the only peer in American history, although his claim to the Earldom of Stirling was rejected by the House of Lords.

powered ships might well admire. Three days later he received another 5,000. By then Israel Putnam had replaced Sullivan as the Long Island commander.

Putnam knew nothing of Long Island's terrain or its troops. He continued Sullivan's dispositions. On the American right were about 1,700 men under Stirling. On the left was the main body under Sullivan. To the rear guarding Brooklyn were works held by Putnam's reserve. In all, say 5,000 men held Long Island. Unfortunately, although Putnam had posted troops to watch the roads, he had neglected to cover the vital Jamaica Pass opening on the Jamaica Road to Sullivan's rear.

William Howe knew of both pass and road and was planning to pivot a turning movement on them.

Howe's left under the American-hating Major General James Grant was to attack Stirling and hold him in place. The center composed of Hessians under General Philip de Heister was to strike at Sullivan and the American main body. Meanwhile, Howe's main body would slip through the Jamaica Pass and follow the Jamaica Road into Sullivan's rear.

At nine o'clock the night of August 26, Howe's main body under Clinton, Percy and Cornwallis began moving out. Tories led them to the pass. At dawn the British stole through and turned left down the road to Sullivan's rear.

To the left, Grant had begun attacking Stirling, who had reminded his men that the general opposing them had boasted he could geld every male in America. Stirling's men fought valiantly. They not only repulsed Grant's regulars but also tried to seize a British-held height. Grant, however, was content with keeping the Americans engaged.

So was Heister with the Hessians in the center. He waited until two cannon shots signaled the successful turning of Sullivan's position. They came, and the Hessians lunged forward, bands playing, some of them singing hymns. The Americans met them with the oaths and profanity characteristic of all English-speaking troops since the "Goddams" who fought Joan of Arc. Resistance was fierce, at first. But then came reports that Howe's main body was in the American rear, and Sullivan's troops panicked and ran.

The Hessians moved among them mercilessly. They had been told by their English officers that the Americans gave no quarter, and they spitted many of the ragged rebels on trees or slaughtered entire groups of men who had laid down their arms.

Caught between two fires, the American main body was completely routed, and Sullivan himself was captured trying to rally his troops in a cornfield.

On the right, Stirling's men fought on. They were now surrounded on three sides. Lord Cornwallis had come down the road to attack their rear, Grant charged them on the right, and the Hessians hit them in the front. Too late, Stirling ordered a retreat. Many of his men trying to escape through the Gowanus marshes were drowned in the attempt. The rest broke and scattered through the woods. Stirling himself then deliberately surrendered to the Hessians rather than to the detestable Grant.

Long Island was a decisive British victory, and it could have been a greater one if William Howe had consented to his subordinates' pleas to storm the American redoubts at Brooklyn. Some British officers were livid with rage when Howe ordered their eager troops to retire. But those crumpled redcoats of Bunker Hill still lay in heaps at the back of Howe's brain, and he would not again assault Americans behind fixed positions. Instead, he decided to take Brooklyn by regular approaches, thus missing an opportunity to end the war with one blow, for Washington was at Brooklyn and had brought over reinforcements.

Troubled and heart-sore, Washington saw, next day, the first of the British trenches begun. On the following day he held a council of war and decided to evacuate Long Island.

To do it he relied upon luck, darkness and John Glover's regiment from Marblehead.

They were called infantry, these men of Marblehead, but they had the look of men of the sea. They marched with a sailor's rolling gait. They wore cocked hats of the line, but also the short blue jackets and loose white trousers of the sailor. Their faces were grizzled from salt and their hands curled from oar and line. They spoke a language of their own: a stern man was "hord-horted," a barrel of tar was a "tor-borrl" and a useless man was a "froach." Their colonel, stocky John Glover, was a soldier happier to obey than command when he was on land, but on this dark night of August 29 he and his men were on water.

With similar men of the Salem regiment they took charge of the small boats which Washington had wisely collected in advance. They brought them bobbing up to the Brooklyn ferry landing. Men bent beneath loads of baggage and equipment came marching silently down to the waiting boats. No lights were shown. No words but softly whispered commands were spoken. Then the wind blew northeast against the Americans. The ebb tide ran so strong that even the Marbleheaders could not make the crossing. Suddenly, the wind veered to the southwest, lessened and subsided. All seemed well.

But all was not well. At two in the morning Major Alexander Scammel, Washington's aide, told General Thomas Mifflin that his boats were waiting and he must march at once. Mifflin objected. His was the covering party. He had stationed sentries and advanced posts close to the British to observe their movements. He *couldn't* leave. Scammel, however, insisted—and Mifflin pulled his men out.

On the way to the ferry landing Washington came riding up on his gray horse. He reined in in astonishment and halted the column.

"Good God!" Washington exclaimed. "General Mifflin, I am afraid you have ruined us by unseasonably withdrawing the troops from the lines."

Mifflin retorted angrily that he had only obeyed orders. Washington said he had not, and Mifflin burst out: "By God, I did! Did Scammel act as an aide-de-camp for the day, or did he not?" Washington admitted that he had, and Mifflin snapped: "Then I had orders through him."[60]

Composed now, Washington told Mifflin that it had all been a dreadful mistake, and requested him to return to his covering position. Mifflin obeyed, and the evacuation continued.

Toward morning and the daylight that would reveal the boats to the guns of the British fleet, a fog set in. It enabled Mifflin's covering force to be withdrawn without mishap. Not until then did the British take note of the strangely silent Yankee trenches. When they opened fire and charged, they found them empty.

Out on the water a young Connecticut lieutenant named Benjamin Tallmadge peered through the swirling mists of the fog and saw the last man step down the slippery steps of the landing into a boat. He was very tall and wore a blue sash across his breast.

9

☆

Washington had saved his army by perhaps the most brilliant feat of his career. But it was still a retreat, and his star would seldom sink lower than during those doleful days following the evacuation from Long Island.

John Haslet, the capable colonel of the Delaware Regiment, wrote to Caesar Rodney: "Would to heaven General Lee were here is the language of officers and men."[61] Worse, Washington did not seem to know what to do about New York itself.

Nathanael Greene, recovered from malaria, had wisely recommended burning the city and withdrawing. The British would take it; anyway it was two-thirds Tory—so why not spoil the prize? Congress, however, instructed Washington not to harm the city, and he decided to defend it as well.

Meanwhile, the Howes, jubilant over the Long Island victory, aware of the deteriorating morale in the American camp, decided to have another try at talking peace. Congress was approached, and John Adams, Edward Rutledge and Benjamin Franklin were chosen to confer with Admiral Lord Richard Howe. They met aboard his flagship on September 11.

Once again, the admiral was forced to confess that he could only grant pardons. Only after the colonies had surrendered would the mother country consent to discuss peace terms. He told them that he could not even receive them as members of Congress, since King George recognized no such body. John Adams replied that the Americans were perfectly willing to be received "in any capacity his Lordship pleased, except in that of *British subjects.*"

Shaken, Lord Howe said that if America fell he would lament "as for the loss of a brother," whereupon Franklin put in gently: "My Lord, we will do our utmost endeavors to save your lordship that mortification."[62]

The meeting ended with Lord Howe's affection for America severely strained, and four days later his brother began attacking New York.

British warships in the East River opened fire on American fortifications at Kip's Bay in the area of present-day 34th Street. British and Hessian troops began crossing the river in flatboats, and the Americans rose and fled before the enemy put foot on New York soil.

Washington rode to Kip's Bay in a fury. "Take the walls!" he cried to his fleeing troops. "Take the cornfield!" But only a few obeyed. In a paroxysm of rage, Washington dashed his hat on the ground and bellowed: "Are these the men with whom I am to defend America?"[63] He snapped his pistol at them, he beat them with his cane—privates, officers, even a colonel and brigadier general. But they kept on running, flinging away muskets, knapsacks, even their coats and hats—anything that could slow down their flight from troops they had not even seen.

Washington sat his horse blinded with rage or despair. He paid no attention to a party of Hessians within 80 yards of him. He would have been killed or captured had not an aide seized his bridle and hurried him away.

Howe now had another opportunity. He might cut off Israel Putnam and 4,000 men to the south if he plunged straight across the island. But he moved slowly again, not, as a charming legend suggests, because Mrs. Robert Murray beguiled him and his officers with cakes and wine while Putnam made his escape, but because he had obtained his first day's objective and was satisfied.

Next day his forces turned north or right toward the Americans' entrenchments in Harlem. They moved swiftly. A British bugler began to taunt the patriots with the notes of the fox chase. Stung, Washington sent out troops to nip off the British detachment. Then, seeing an opportunity to inflict real damage on the enemy, Washington fed in more units. So did the British. A two-hour bullet-for-bullet battle began raging. Finally, about 1,800 Americans under Greene, Putnam and George Clinton sent the Anglo-German army backpedaling through an orchard. In high spirits, the Americans had to be restrained from charging full tilt into a large body of British reinforcements pushing north under Cornwallis.

The engagement brought drooping American heads high. More important, it was a national victory. Troops from all the colonies behaved bravely, and for once the Southerners and Pennsylvanians left off sneering at the "dastardly, cowardly" New England troops.

After that action, Howe, still neglecting the opportunity to get onto the mainland and cut off Washington's escape, contented himself with accepting the acclaim of New York's grateful Tories.

The moment the redcoats marched into the town at the foot of Manhattan Island, they were overwhelmed by throngs of weeping, shouting Loyalists. Women as well as men carried British officers around on their shoulders. The rebel standard was torn down and trampled under foot and the King's hoisted in its place.

Then the witch hunt began. Rebels or suspected rebels were rounded up, especially those who had been overheard to vow that they would set fire to the town rather than allow the British to occupy it.

In the early morning of September 21, by accident or design— history does not know—New York *was* burning. By the time the alarm was given the fire was out of control. Whipped by high winds, flames believed to have begun in a shed near Whitehall Slip howled through street after street. Hovels went up, fine mansions, Dutch houses dating back to Peter Stuyvesant, wharves, churches—all were collapsed and consumed. Frenzied women and children were driven from house after house, until finally they could only lie down on the common, mingling their screams and shrieks with the cries and curses of the citizens and soldiers who had spilled outdoors to fight the blaze. But buckets were few and the supply of water was scanty, and the holocaust continued to spread, engulfing Trinity Church. Soon the church's steeple was "a lofty Pyramid of fire." Flames ate away the outer shingles, exposing timbers which quickly began burning themselves. Finally, with a great hissing roar and a shower of sparks, the entire structure came crashing down.

Meanwhile, mob frenzy had overcome the Tories. They seized suspects and strung them up without trial. Some were even thrown screaming into the flames.

At last, the wind changed and the fire was brought under control. What Nathanael Greene had wished and Congress had forbidden had come to pass. New York was gutted and of very little use to William Howe. Next day the angry general confronted an American officer accused of being a spy. He had been captured on Long Island the night of the fire. His name was Nathan Hale. He was about 24, well educated and completely composed as he admitted to Howe that he had been observing British troop movements for General Washington.

Howe curtly ordered him hanged without the grace of a trial. Hale asked for a clergyman. He was refused. He requested a Bible. He was turned down. A gallows was erected at what is now 52nd Street a bit east of First Avenue. The noose was slipped around Nathan Hale's neck. He stood there calmly, his light blue eyes betraying no inner fear, and he said: "I only regret that I have but one life to lose for my country."

Then the noose tightened and life passed from the body of the first martyr of American arms.

Far to the north, Benedict Arnold was headed for battle again. General Horatio Gates had placed Arnold in charge of a rickety, makeshift fleet with which the Americans hoped to hold Lake Champlain against the ships and soldiers of Sir Guy Carleton, issuing south from Canada.

Arnold had once cruised his own ships in the West Indies, and knew something of the water. He was also spoiling for a fight, having been humiliated at Quebec and still being harassed by government bodies demanding an accounting of public funds in his care. In such mood, he helped direct construction of galleys and gundalows made of wood as green as the amateur sailors whom Gates had recruited from his regiments. Jerry-built as they were, the boats would float and the guns would fire. Arnold sailed down the lake and took position off Valcour Island about 50 miles north of Ticonderoga.

Up the lake came Carleton with gunboats of seasoned wood prefabricated in Britain, a huge raft called the *Thunderer* mounting heavy guns poked through thick wooden walls, and about 9,000 infantry. On October 11 Carleton's superior force passed Arnold's hidden fleet at Valcour, spotted it, and doubled back into the battle.

It was fought at almost musket range. Americans and British poured shot and shell into each other while Carleton's Indians on shore raked the rebels with small-arms fire. Arnold himself aimed the guns of his flagship, *Congress,* until that rickety craft was riddled and aflame and had to be abandoned. Eventually, British superiority told. One by one Arnold's ships were hunted down and sunk. Only six survived, limping back to Crown Point where they were burnt. Arnold and his men took to the woods to return to Ticonderoga. Yet, though the British had won a tactical victory, they suffered a strategic loss. Carleton did not press on to Ticonderoga as he might have done. He did not even tarry at Crown Point and thus hold an advanced base for a fresh expedition in the spring of 1777. Instead, wary of the approaching winter, he withdrew to Montreal.

Benedict Arnold's desperate delaying action had prevented a fatal link-up between Carleton and General Howe, now moving north from New York.

Just as the Battle of Valcour Island was ending, the deliberate William Howe at last began to move. He had dawdled for nearly a month in New York. Then, on October 9, British warships sailed up the Hudson between the batteries at Fort Lee in New Jersey on their left and those of Fort Washington in Manhattan on their right. Sunken hulks in the river, a famous network of chains and booms, had failed to stop them from getting into Washington's right rear.

Howe now moved to get into Washington's left rear. He took his main body up the East River and through Hell Gate to land at Throg's Neck, and then still higher on the mainland at New Rochelle.

To forestall this double envelopment, Washington left 2,000 men in Fort Washington and 4,000 under Greene in Fort Lee and quit Manhattan to build a strong camp at White Plains in Westchester County. On October 28 Howe attacked Washington's right flank at Chatterton's Hill.

British and Hessians struck at the hill frontally while Colonel Johann Rall moved to hit the American right flank. But Rall did not get into position in time, and the Americans on Chatterton's Hill were able to pour a heavy fire into the frontal attack. The British withdrew and re-formed, Rall got into place on the flank, and the attack went forward again, forcing the Americans to abandon the hill.

General William Howe had another chance to destroy Washington. He was in position on his flank and could roll him up. But he did not move. Questioned later by the House of Commons on this decision, he refused to answer "for political reasons." Cornwallis, a Whig like himself, supported his silence. Whatever the reason—a hope that mild means would end the rebellion, perhaps even desire to vindicate Whig predictions of American independence—the lost opportunity did not reappear. Heavy rains prevented a renewal of the attack, and on the dark night of November 1 Washington marched from his lines into a new and stronger position at North Castle behind the Croton River.

Washington now expected Howe to move higher up the Hudson or cross into New Jersey. Instead, the British chief struck at Fort Washington on Manhattan.

On November 16 Howe called upon the fort to surrender or have its garrison put to the sword. Colonel Robert Magaw, the commander, swore to fight to the end. The next day, floating batteries in the Harlem River and the guns of a man-of-war in the Hudson burst into a roaring barrage, and the attack surged forward.

Howe had about 13,000 men divided into four columns converging on the fort from every side. Colonel Magaw had nearly 3,000 men, actually far too many for such a constricted position. At first, the Americans fought valiantly. They took an especially dreadful toll among the Hessians attacking from the north. But the Germans came on through the redoubts and masses of felled trees. General William von Knyphausen, their commander, tore at the branches with his hands. Drums began to beat, oboes blew, and lines of music-loving Hessians in tall brass miters swept on toward the fort.

They drove the Americans ahead of them. Fort Washington filled with swarms of beaten men. It became a slaughter pen exposed to British cannon, and Colonel Magaw surrendered it. Still the Hessians came on with their bayonets, angered because they had borne the brunt of British losses. They had to be restrained from bayoneting prisoners. Even some of Howe's officers thought that their general should have slaughtered the garrison as he had threatened. They said that he would not have been held accountable by the rules of war then prevailing, and that he "would have struck such a panic as would have prevented the Congress from ever being able to raise another Army."[64]

That army was fast vanishing. Howe, moving quickly for once, sent Cornwallis across the Hudson against Fort Lee, forcing Nathanael Greene to decamp hastily without his guns and supplies. Greene joined Washington at Hackensack. Cornwallis pursued.

Slowly, slogging over roads that fall rains had turned into a slop of mud, Washington began his miserable retreat across New Jersey. Again and again he got off dispatches to Lee in North Castle urging him to join him with the main body. Desertions were melting his force like powder in the rain. He was down to barely 3,000 men. If Lee could come down and gather up intervening units, Washington might have 10,000 men—at least on paper. But Lee, for reasons of his own, did not move.

Onward, in alternating fury and despair, Washington led his wretched scarecrows. With the oncoming raw cold of a Northern winter they suffered more. Through the Watchung Mountains they trudged, into Newark, out of it . . . into New Brunswick, and away again with Cornwallis nipping at their heels. Behind them, the numerous Tories of New Jersey were breaking out their British flags and welcoming their "saviors" in red coats. Into Trenton the rebels dragged their long tail of retreat. Washington began collecting all the boats on the Delaware, even as Congress prepared to flee from Philadelphia to Baltimore.

It was Howe who was on Washington's heels now, and he was dallying as usual. He might have gotten to the Delaware ahead of Washington, but his men did not enter Trenton until the last of the Americans were crossing the river.

Safe on the other side, George Washington fired off letter after imploring letter to Charles Lee. All depended on his bringing his troops south from New York. In another few weeks enlistments in the Continental Army would expire. The outlook was at its darkest. Pennsylvania had sent him only a few thousand men and New Jersey almost none. If the army was not quickly replenished, the general wrote to his cousin Lund Washington, "I think the game will be pretty well up. . . ."[65]

10

☆

On the morning of December 13 General Charles Lee finished his breakfast and began to write a letter to General Horatio Gates. Lee was in a tavern in Basking Ridge, New Jersey. He had finally departed North Castle on December 2 with the bulk of Washington's army. Two days' march from Pennsylvania the army had halted to make camp, while General Lee rode to the tavern four miles away.

Lee's aide, James Wilkinson, stood at the window listening to the scratching of the general's pen as he wrote:

"The ingenius maneouvre of Fort Washington has unhinged the goodly fabrick we had been building. There never was so damned a stroke. *Entre nous,* a certain great man is most damnably deficient. . . ."[66]

Lee ended his letter with another blast at Washington and a forecast of doom. He was just about to sign it when Wilkinson cried: "Here, sir, are the British cavalry!"

"*Where?*" Lee cried in incredulity.

"Around the house," Wilkinson yelled, watching with horror as about 30 dragoons under Colonel William Harcourt neatly opened files and went galloping around the tavern to surround it. Lee jumped up in alarm.

"Where is the guard?" he shouted. "Damn the guard, why don't they fire?"[67]

Wilkinson caught up his pistols, thrust Lee's letter into his pocket and ran outside to look for the guard. Behind him, Lee was coldly rejecting a maid's suggestion that he hide himself in a bed. Outside, Wilkinson saw the British dragoons chasing Lee's guard away from the tavern. Shots were fired at him, and he ducked back inside.

Then he heard Harcourt's voice saying, "*If the general does not surrender in five minutes, I will set fire to the house.*" There was a pause, and the threat was repeated. Two minutes later Wilkinson heard a voice say, "*Here is the general. He has surrendered.*"[68] There was a loud shout of triumph, the trumpet sounded the assembly, and Lee was mounted on Wilkinson's horse standing saddled at the door. He was bareheaded, in slippers and blanket coat with his collar open. He was not happy to find himself captive in the hands of his old regiment.

With a clatter of hoofs the jubilant Harcourt bore off the prize which was to bring him his own general's star.

Many Americans were as dismayed by Lee's capture as by the loss of New York. Even Washington, aware of Lee's criticism of him, continued to overvalue the general's abilities. He, too, was crushed

—although the arrival of Lee's troops softened the blow.

But only temporarily. In two weeks' time most of Washington's 6,000 men would be leaving. Very few of them were re-enlisting. Fewer were willing to join the Continental Army. General Howe— now Sir William as a reward for his summer victories—thought so little of this rag, tag and bobtail, about-to-vanish army that he had withdrawn into winter quarters in New York, leaving a chain of posts to hold New Jersey. The cause of the revolution was at its nadir, and Washington had to move swiftly lest it collapse and fall apart.

He had already conceived his counterstroke, but first he must rally his men. On December 23 he had them formed in ranks to have Tom Paine's first issue of *The Crisis* read to them:

"These are the times that try men's souls. The summer soldier and the sunshine patriot will, in this crisis, shrink from the service of their country; but he that stands it now, deserves the love and thanks of man and woman."

Words do not often inspire beaten soldiers, especially men who are threadbare and hungry and cold. But these words did. A thrill of patriotism and purpose ran through Washington's ragged ranks. They were ready for their general's great scheme, and that was simply to attack.

He *had* to attack. He had to forestall the enemy before the Delaware froze and became passable, and he had to rally the dying rebel cause. Across the river from him lay about 3,000 Hessians under Colonel Carl von Donop. They held a six-mile line from Bordentown up to Trenton. About half of them were at Trenton, and Washington proposed to strike them with three forces.

Brigadier General John Cadwalader would cross downriver with about 2,000 men to engage von Donop's Bordentown force and prevent reinforcements being sent north to Trenton.

Brigadier General James Ewing would cross opposite Trenton with about 900 men to capture a bridge and seal off the Hessian escape route south to Bordentown.

Washington himself would make the main attack with about 2,400 men. He would cross the Delaware above Trenton on Christmas Night and march downriver to make a surprise assault an hour before dawn.

As the daylight of Christmas, 1776, began fading into a storm-tossed night, the American troops under Washington began to move toward McKonkey's Ferry. Here were gathered the boats Washington had collected, and at their oars were John Glover's blue-coated Marbleheaders. Snow mixed with sleet blew into the faces of the men.

Near the ferry, General Washington was preparing to mount his horse. Major Wilkinson presented himself with a letter from General Horatio Gates. "By General Gates?" Washington asked, astonished to hear that his Northern commander was in the vicinity. "Where is he?"

"I left him this morning in Philadelphia."

"What was he doing *there?*"

"I understood him that he was on his way to Congress."

"On his way to Congress!" Washington repeated.[69] Without asking leave, the confidant of Charles Lee had gone hurrahing off to Baltimore to bask in the admiration of certain Congressmen who might also agree that "a certain great man is damnably deficient." Lee a captive, and Gates . . . what? Without a word, Washington rode off to join his troops.

Colonel Johann Rall, the hero of Fort Washington, commanded at Trenton. Rall had contempt for the Americans. He agreed with General Grant at New Brunswick that he could "keep the peace in New Jersey with a corporal's guard." Fine fighter that he was, Rall believed that when a soldier went into winter quarters he should address himself to women and wine. He had built no redoubts around Trenton as Colonel von Donop had ordered. He had only a few pickets stationed along the roads.

On Christmas Day Johann Rall awoke with the customary hangover. He dressed leisurely, listening to the serenade played by shivering Hessian bandsmen standing outside his window. He prepared to celebrate the Nativity in the hearty German manner.

At night, after the festivity, there was a minor scare when a roving American patrol shot up the picket guard. The troops were called to arms, but very soon returned to quarters. Colonel Rall dropped in on a supper party at the home of a wealthy Trenton merchant. There were wine and cards. Near the middle of the night there was a knock on the door. A Tory had come with information for the colonel. Rall would not see him. The man wrote a note informing Rall that the American army was on the march. A servant delivered it. Rall stuck it into his pocket, unread. Eventually, his heart gladdened with wine, Colonel Rall went home to bed.

Outside his window the storm mounted in fury.

The Americans had been enjoined to silence. No soldier was to break ranks under pain of death. They stood huddled by the ferry landing, ducking their heads into their collars against the rising howl of the storm. Their firelocks were hopelessly wet, but Colonel Knox's artillerymen had kept the cannon touchholes dry.

The men entered the boats. Thin, jagged cakes of ice came floating downriver to strike the boats so hard that Glover's Marbleheaders had difficulty keeping afloat. Washington had hoped to have his troops on the Jersey shore by midnight, but it was not until after three o'clock that Knox's booming voice announced that the crossing was completed.

Washington formed his forces into two divisions. John Sullivan would take his division—which included John Stark's sharpshooters—down the river road. Nathanael Greene's division, accompanied by Washington, would march on Trenton along a road two miles farther inland. Sullivan would hit the bottom of the town, Greene the top. The Americans began marching. The roads were slippery. Cruel ice cut through flimsy footwear and drew blood. In the morning, Major Wilkinson could follow the route by the bloodstains in the snow.

But down the roads they marched, steadily slipping up on the still-sleeping enemy. With daylight, just before eight o'clock in the morning, both columns reached their destination—and both flushed Hessian pickets and drove them in.

"*Der feind! Heraus! Heraus!*" the pickets shouted. "The enemy! Turn out! Turn out!"[70]

Lieutenant Jacob Piel heard the shouts and rushed to alert Colonel Rall. He hammered on his door. Rall, in his nightclothes, poked his head out the window. Piel told him he had heard firing. Rall withdrew his head and a few minutes later came rushing downstairs in full uniform. He formed his own blue-coated regiment on King Street. The scarlet-coated Lossbergs marched to the right to take over Queen Street parallel with King, while the black-coated Knyphausen Regiment made up the reserve. But at the top of both King and Queen streets stood the American artillery.

Two guns to a street, but would they fire? Captain Alexander Hamilton's gunners stuck their matches in the touchholes. The cannon roared and shook. American cheers mingled with the shrieks of Hessian soldiers stricken by grapeshot. Rall's regiment was fragmented and driven back. The other brace of cannon cleared Queen Street, but the Lossbergs mounted their own cannon and fired back. The Americans charged. Captain William Washington and Lieutenant James Monroe led their men right into the cannon's mouth. They captured them, although both were wounded—a liability which eventually would be a political asset to President James Monroe.

Sullivan's men at the bottom of the town were attacking from the west. Green's division extended its right flank to join Sullivan, while more of Greene's units worked around to the rear or the east of the town. If General Ewing had crossed to hold the bridge over Assunpink Creek, the Hessians were caught in a box.

Ewing had not crossed. The bridge lay open, and perhaps 400 Hessians were escaping over it. The remainder, however, could not get away. Even with wet firelocks the Americans fought with conquering fury. "Use the bayonet," Washington ordered. "I am determined to take Trenton."[71] Some Americans ran inside the houses to dry their pieces or pick the touchholes clear. They acted as snipers when Rall re-formed his shattered troops and tried to counterattack, and they sent two bullets into Rall's body. The Hessian commander fell from his horse, fatally stricken, and that was about the end of the battle.

Sullivan's troops now held the bridge, and the escape gap was plugged. One by one the Hessian regiments surrendered. In all, about 920 Hessians had been captured, about 25 were killed and 90 wounded. Two Americans had been frozen to death on the march, but not one was killed in the battle: two officers and two privates were wounded.

General George Washington stood radiant on the field. When Major Wilkinson rode up to him to announce that the last enemy regiment had grounded arms, his face actually shone and he extended his hand in thanks.

"Major Wilkinson," Washington said, "this is a glorious day for our country."[72]

11

☆

It had been a glorious day. From the depths of despair the American people rose to the heights of exultation. Sir William Howe was staggered. He could not believe that "three old established regiments of a people who made war a profession should lay down their arms to a ragged and undisciplined militia."[73]

Howe stopped Cornwallis from sailing home to Britain and sent him out to take command in New Jersey, while he gathered reinforcements and prepared to join him.

Washington, meanwhile, was hailed as a military genius. His reputation, tarnished by defeat and retreat, glittered as never before. A grateful Congress voted him powers that made him a virtual military dictator, and the general was quick to use them in forming a new Continental Army. While battalions of militia inspired by the Trenton victory were marching to his side, Washington persuaded his regulars to re-enlist for six weeks for a bounty of $10. He ordered his forces in New York to march to winter quarters in Morristown, New Jersey, and told Cadwalader and Ewing, who had belatedly crossed the Delaware, to join him in Trenton. Then he himself went back across the river to renew the offensive.

To Washington's surprise, Cornwallis, unlike Howe, moved rapidly to meet him. On January 2, 1777, Cornwallis marched from Princeton toward Trenton with a force of about 5,500 men, the flower of the British Army. A brigade of about 1,200 was left behind as a rear guard under Lieutenant Colonel Charles Mawhood. They would rejoin Cornwallis the next day.

Cornwallis and his main body came up with Washington on a ridge in the late afternoon. The American pickets were driven in. Washington, with his back to the Delaware, was in a bad position. Cornwallis's officers urged him to attack then and there. Sir William Erskine is supposed to have said: "If Washington is the general I take him to be, he will not be found there in the morning."⁷⁴ Cornwallis replied that the men were tired from marching all day. He would "bag the old fox" in the morning.

That night Washington's officers held a council of war. They knew that their situation was desperate. Highhearted as the Continentals might now be, they could not hope to repulse a superior force. British batteries, British bayonets, British discipline had to prevail. Then someone, perhaps Washington himself, made an audacious proposal: why stay on the defensive when the offensive beckoned? Why not steal away from Trenton and attack Princeton in Cornwallis's rear? Farther back lay New Brunswick with the British war chest of £70,000. It was agreed, even though a thaw had made a muck of the only known road. Then the weather changed. The road froze. A party of 400 men was detailed to work loudly with pick and shovel within earshot of the British. Baggage and guns were sent on ahead. Wheels were wrapped in rags to muffle their noise. At one o'clock in the morning of January 3, leaving his campfires burning brightly, "the old fox" led his men softly into the enemy rear.

It was, again, a nightmare march. But dawn of January 3 came at last, bright and frosty, as the Americans neared Stony Brook two miles outside the town. Washington sent General Hugh Mercer's brigade to hold the bridge while Sullivan with three brigades took a road to the right into Princeton.

Marching out of Princeton, meanwhile, came Colonel Mawhood and his regulars.

Mounted on a little brown pony, Mawhood clattered over Stony Brook bridge ahead of his men. Suddenly, to his left he caught the flash of arms. Yankee rebels were emerging from a wood. They were Hugh Mercer's advance guard, but Mawhood thought that they were the backwash of the American army "defeated" at Trenton. He sent mounted officers to intercept them while pulling his brigade back over the bridge. Then he led them on the double for an orchard on that side of Stony Brook. The Americans raced him for it and beat him. They quickly fortified a hedge and a gun duel ensued. Mawhood called for the bayonet, and the sight of British steel broke the American ranks.

General Mercer and Colonel Haslet tried to rally the men. But the bayonets overtook Mercer. A rifle butt drove him to the earth. He arose brandishing his sword, but seven bayonets drove into his body, and he fell dying. Haslet was shot through the head, and Mercer's brigade fled.

They poured back over the road and washed around the tall man on the big white horse, leading the main body toward the sounds of battle. He waved his hat and cried, "Parade with us, my brave fellows!"[75] and galloped down the road to within 30 yards of Mawhood's advancing regulars. The redcoats were astonished. They raised their muskets. One of Washington's aides covered his eyes in dread. A volley crashed out and smoke concealed Washington from all eyes, but when it parted he was still there, erect and valiant, calling his men forward.

They did not come. But then troops from Sullivan's division came hurrying to the rescue. Mercer's men were re-formed. Yelling battle cries, they charged the British and forced them to retreat down the road to Trenton. Washington led the pursuit, crying, "It's a fine fox chase, my boys!"[76] But the British dragoons successfully covered Mawhood's withdrawal.

In Princeton, meanwhile, Sullivan's troops had successfully stormed the town. About 200 British were cornered in Nassau Hall. Captain Alexander Hamilton's gunners put one ball into the building, and they surrendered.

Far away in Trenton, Lord Charles Cornwallis heard the distant sound of guns and guessed that the vanished old fox had bared his fangs again.

Washington's men were simply too tired to march the mere 18 miles to New Brunswick. Holding a council of war on horseback, Washington decided to leave Princeton immediately and make for Morristown. There he could rest within a defensive position from which he could attack Howe's flank should he move against Philadelphia or up the Hudson.

It was a heart-breaking decision. As the general later wrote to Congress: "Six or seven hundred fresh troops, upon a forced march, would have destroyed all their stores and magazines" at New Brunswick, "taken . . . their military chest . . . and put an end to the war."[77] But there were no such men, and the exhausted Americans straggled wearily out of town.

With the British Army's treasury threatened, Cornwallis made directly for New Brunswick and allowed Washington to escape to Morristown. It was the only course to follow, but as his Lordship was to write ruefully to Lord George Germain: "The unlucky affair of Rall's brigade has given me a winter campaign."[78]

That "campaign," it would seem, was waged against the helpless New Jersey countryside. Stung by the upstart Yankees, claiming the miserable eighteenth-century soldier's privilege of pillage and plunder, the British and Hessian regulars burned and looted and raped the winter away. In Princeton they maliciously burned all the firewood available to inhabitants whose own homes and orchards had also been burned, slaughtered and carried off cattle and destroyed mills.

The Hessians were the more proficient at plunder, which they regarded as the means of making their fortunes. Wherever they passed, anything movable was carefully piled up on wagons and carried away. Friend or foe, it made no difference. No Jaeger sergeant could read Sir William Howe's writs of immunity, and he would not have heeded them if he could: booty was booty.

To Britain's dishonor, the treatment of prisoners was something far more cruel and without any plea of custom or "uncontrollable soldiery" to excuse it. British prison ships were floating horrors in which men fought for food or for air, "some swearing and blaspheming, some crying, praying and wringing their hands and stalking about like ghosts and apparitions; others delirious . . . raving and storming; some groaning and dying—all panting for breath; some dead and corrupting."[79] One prisoner wrote: "The air was so foul at times that a lamp could not be kept burning, by reason of which three boys were not missed until they had been dead ten days."[80]

Lord Francis Rawdon believed it was necessary to ravage the countryside to teach "these infatuated wretches" a lesson. His Lordship also found the ravishing of American women highly entertaining, writing:

> The fair nymphs of this isle [Staten Island] were in wonderful tribulation, as the fresh meat our men have got here has made them riotous as satyrs. A girl cannot step into the bushes to pluck a rose without running the most imminent risk of being ravished, and they are so little accustomed to these vigorous methods that they don't bear them with the proper resignation, and of consequence we have most entertaining court-martials every day.[81]

"Of consequence" also: the Tories began turning patriot, and the atrocities of Lord Cornwallis's "winter campaign" helped to guarantee the safety of Washington's army in its hill fastness at Morristown.

12

☆

Washington had intended to stay in Morristown only a few days, but he was forced to remain there nearly five months.

It was a cruel sojourn. On March 14, 1777, Washington reported that he had less than 3,000 starved and freezing scarecrows to command. In desperation, he used his dictatorial powers to commandeer provisions. But he could not outlaw smallpox, which ravaged the camp.

At last the patriot cause brightened. About 22,000 muskets and other supplies arrived through the good offices of M. de Beaumarchais. Eventually men to shoulder them also began to arrive, not in a trickle or a flood, but in a steady small stream that was to be characteristic of Continental Army recruiting. Washington now had a force of about 9,000 soldiers, not including the Northern army with which General Horatio Gates was guarding the lake-and-river chain.

That summer two notable recruits appeared: one a huge self-styled baron, a German-turned-Frenchman named Jean de Kalb, the other a slender youth who was truly both French and noble and whose name was the Marquis de Lafayette.

Lafayette joined Washington's staff or "family," and was with him when he marched to intercept Sir William Howe's attack on Philadelphia.

The British plan of campaign for 1777 was for General John Burgoyne to lead a large force from Canada down to Albany, where he would make junction with General Sir William Howe moving up the Hudson.

Howe, however, decided to move into Pennsylvania first. He informed Lord George Germain that numerous Loyalists there would rally to his standard. Howe also believed that by drawing Washington into Pennsylvania he would make Burgoyne's invasion of New York State easier. Finally, the British commander was confident that he could finish off Pennsylvania and Washington in time to return to New York to help Burgoyne.

On July 23, after an unsuccessful attempt to trap Washington in New Jersey, Howe sailed for the mouth of the Delaware River with 260 ships and about 15,000 soldiers. He did not, as he had intended, sail up the river to take Philadelphia. Reports that the Delaware was too difficult to navigate and too well fortified to storm decided him in favor of sailing up the Chesapeake Bay instead.

On August 14 he began landing at Head of Elk in Maryland. Fifty miles away to the northeast lay Philadelphia, the "capital" of the rebellion. Howe began marching toward it. Hearing of his movement, Washington moved to head him off—and on September 11, 1777, the armies collided at Brandywine Creek.

The Brandywine is marked by numerous shallow crossings or fords. Washington, holding the east bank of the stream, chose to guard most of them. His left rested on Pyle's Ford, his center at Chad's Ford, while his right held Painter's and Brinton's. Smaller forces watched other crossings higher up, but Trimble's Ford seven miles north of Chad's was neglected.

And Howe was making for Trimble's.

Howe was duplicating his turning movement of Long Island. Von Knyphausen had been sent against Chad's Ford to hold the Americans in place while Howe with Cornwallis and the main body secretly crossed the Brandywine above them, swung south and came down on the American right rear.

Washington sat calmly still for the knockout blow. As on Long Island, he braced himself for a frontal assault. And then, in the forenoon, came two messages warning him of Howe's march to Trimble's Ford. Washington was amazed. The enemy had divided his forces! Eager to take advantage of Howe's "blunder," Washington divided his own and ordered the parts to cross the creek and attack.

Just as the movement began, a message came from Sullivan on the right advising Washington that there was no enemy on the road to Trimble's Ford. The American commander relaxed, until a hatless, coatless, bare-legged farmer named Thomas Cheyney was brought to his headquarters. The British were across the Brandywine, Cheyney shouted. He had seen them and they had fired on him and chased him. Washington's staff smiled superior smiles. Obviously the man was a Tory out to deceive them. Cheyney turned on them wrathfully. "I'd have you know I have this day's work as much at heart as e'er a blood of ye!" he yelled.[82]

Cheyney dropped to his knee and drew a map in the dust, marking the exact place where he had seen the British. Washington shook his head in disbelief.

"You're mistaken, General!" the farmer cried. "My life for it you're mistaken. By hell, it's so! Put me under guard till you find out it's so!"[83]

Washington hesitated, torn by doubts. But then a courier arrived from John Sullivan reporting that the British were in the rear of his right and were coming down. Stunned, Washington ordered Sullivan to march to Birmingham Meeting House a mile to his right rear and halt the British there. Sullivan obeyed. He occupied a hill in the enemy's path, but by then it was too late.

British bayonets again broke the Yankee ranks. The entire left of Sullivan's new line was swept away. Down at Chad's Ford, Knyphausen began attacking the Americans under Mad Anthony Wayne.

Washington was no longer deceived. He realized that the sound of cannon booming up at Birmingham Meeting House signaled the main attack. Hesitating no longer, he at once ordered Greene to march to the rescue.

Meanwhile, the Americans under Sullivan were rallying and fighting desperately. Young Lafayette, ardent for battle, had galloped up from Chad's and was with them. Five times the Americans were driven off their hill, and five times they returned to drive the enemy off. But the issue was not in doubt. A force twice their number backed up by four 12-pounders could not be denied.

Still, Greene was hurrying north. Washington was with him, goading on a reluctant old man who had been forced aboard a horse to act as guide. "Push along, old man!" Washington roared. "Push along!"[84] Above him, the Americans were giving way. British and Hessian soldiers brandishing bloody bayonets were turning an orderly withdrawal into a stampede. All seemed lost for the American army and the American nation.

And that was when the vanguard of Greene's column arrived, opening its ranks to allow the terrified fugitives to pass through and re-form, and then closing firm again to halt the onrushing British. Below, at Chad's Ford, Knyphausen's attack had broken through. But the Americans were retiring in good order. Eventually darkness came and the Battle of the Brandywine was over.

Howe had again outmaneuvered and defeated Washington. Nevertheless, the American had again managed to save his army. Nor were his men downcast. Some of them, as they retreated to Chester and thence to Germantown, were actually proud of how they had held off the regulars in a stand-up fight. Many of them were actually saying, "Come, boys, we shall do better another time."[85]

Actually, they did worse. In the early morning of September 21, British forces under Major General Charles Grey surprised Anthony Wayne's division at Paoli's Tavern. Grey had ordered his men to march with unloaded muskets, removing their flints to guard against accidental discharges. "No-Flint" Grey's men caught the Americans silhouetted by the light of their own campfires and routed them with a fierce bayonet charge. Some 300 Americans were killed or wounded, 100 more were captured, and reports of so-called "atrocities" at the "Paoli Massacre" caused fleeing Congressmen to dig their spurs into the hides of horses carrying them from threatened Philadelphia to the safety of York, Pennsylvania.

On September 26 Howe entered Philadelphia. He received a liberator's reception and he became convinced that he had come at last to the Land of the Tories. Notifying Mrs. Loring to join him —escorted by her husband, of course—Howe relaxed his vigilance. He divided his army, keeping one force in Philadelphia and a larger one in the unguarded suburb of Germantown.

Washington, seeing his chance, attacked.

From Washington's position roughly north of Germantown four roads ran down into the British camp. Washington proposed to follow all of them. He had been reinforced, and now possessed about 9,000 Continentals and about 3,000 militia. Howe in Germantown had about 9,000 regulars.

On the night of October 3 four American columns struck south for Germantown. On the right were militia, then Sullivan, then Greene, then more militia. Sullivan and Greene in the center, of course, packed the main punch. After they attacked the British, the militia to either side would hit Howe's flanks and crumple them. It was an elaborate plan, nothing less than that classical "double envelopment" so fatally attractive to commanders since Hannibal had first made it work at Cannae 2,000 years previously.

Hannibal, however, had never had Washington's problems. The American proposed to send untrained officers and men on a 16-mile night march over four widely separated roads, and then launch them in a single coordinated stroke that would surround the world's finest troops under the command of an able tactician. Yet he almost pulled it off.

Sullivan's column caught the British by surprise. They drove the vaunted light infantry back. Astonished, Howe leaped on his horse and rode to the front to rally his old outfit.

"For shame, light infantry!" he cried. "I never saw you retreat before. Form! Form! It's only a scouting party."[86]

To give him the lie, and to warm the hearts of the men he had scolded, the "scouting party" exploded a charge of grape over Howe's startled head—and the Americans came charging forward.

"Have at the bloodhounds!" they cried. "Revenge the Paoli Massacre!"[87]

Wayne's soldiers killed British troops even after they had laid down their arms. Their officers could not restrain them, and the butchery continued even though "many of the poor wretches . . . were crying for mercy."[88] Then, for the first time in the war, British bugles sounded the retreat. Fighting doggedly, the red lines fell back—and the ragged Americans pursued.

Gradually pursued and pursuer lost sight of each other in a fog which mingled with the smoke of battle. Under cover of it, a party of about 120 British slipped into a large stone house owned by Justice Benjamin Chew. The Chew House lay directly in the American path. It could have been by-passed while a small rear guard contained its garrison, but Henry Knox, fighting by the book, insisted on reducing it with artillery. Washington agreed, and precious time was lost in futile battering at a "fort" that refused to fall. At last, Washington ordered his troops on. But where was Greene?

Nathanael Greene with two-thirds of the American army had not yet appeared. Misled by a guide, he came up an hour late. Still, his men were able to drive back the British on Wayne's left as planned.

But then one of Greene's divisions blundered in the smoke and fog into Wayne's rear. At that moment Wayne became convinced that the blasting at the Chew House behind him meant that Sullivan was in trouble back there. He wheeled his division around—and ran into the lost division. Both American forces fired on each other and fled, and the departure of Wayne left Sullivan's left flank completely exposed.

Already striking at Sullivan's right and front, the British sent a counterattack roaring into the gap on his left—and with that the tide turned. Sullivan gave way. His men panicked. Soon the entire American army panicked. Washington again tried to rally them by exposing himself to the hottest fire, but it was of no avail. Many of the men were out of ammunition. Running past Washington they held up empty cartridge boxes. "We ran from Victory,"[89] Anthony Wayne wrote bitterly afterward, but these men had marched all night and fought all morning, and been undone chiefly by the blunders of their commanders.

And so Washington, with the tents of the enemy and victory within his sight, was born off into darkness and defeat on the crest of a flood of cursing, jostling, frightened soldiers. He had fought Sir William Howe for the fifth time and had lost again. But once again he had not lost his army. Undaunted, rocklike, he reformed his shattered remnants and led them off to the gloomy hills of Valley Forge.

13

☆

Early in 1777 a new betting book was opened at the exclusive Brooks's Club in London, and the first entry was made by a handsome dandified man who wrote: "John Burgoyne wagers Charles (James) Fox one pony* that he will be home victorious from America by Christmas Day, 1777."[90]

* Fifty guineas or 52½ pounds.

It was thus that Gentleman Johnny Burgoyne set out to execute his scheme for humbling the colonies. Burgoyne was to lead a large Anglo-Hessian force down the lake-and-river chain from Canada to Albany. A second smaller force under Lieutenant Colonel Barry St. Leger was to advance east on Albany from Oswego. Once both forces were joined, communications would be established along the Hudson linking Albany with New York.

Burgoyne arrived in Canada in May and found the troops in good condition after a mild winter. He had about 7,200 regulars, half British and half German, about 400 Indians and perhaps 250 Canadians and Tories. He also had three excellent lieutenants, Major General William Phillips, a veteran and skilled artillerist; Major General Baron von Riedesel commanding the Hessians; and Brigadier General Simon Fraser, the Highlander who had beguiled the French sentries for Wolfe at the Anse-du-Foulon.

In June, with a huge artillery section of 138 guns, with an enormous baggage train equipped to serve Burgoyne's elegant table, as well as to provide amenities for such women of the expedition as the blonde Baroness von Riedesel, her three little daughters and Burgoyne's mistress, the expedition set out for Ticonderoga.

The fort itself had been strengthened by the Polish engineer Kosciusko, but the American northern army had been weakened by quarrels between Generals Schuyler and Gates. As a result, there were only about 2,500 Americans under Major General Arthur St. Clair. Worse, Gates had positively forbidden the fortifying of Sugar Loaf Hill to the southwest of the fort. It completely commanded the American position, but Gates insisted the steep hill was inaccessible. Game-legged Benedict Arnold climbed it himself to disprove Gates, but the general would not budge.

There it stood, inviting, when scarlet coats again became visible through Ticonderoga's leaves, and it was not missed by General Phillips. He consulted his Swiss aide, Lieutenant Twiss, who told him that by using ropes wound around trees and calling forth much sweat the guns could be hauled up Sugar Loaf.

They were, even as a furious exchange of musketry and artillery began between besieger and besieged, but once the guns were emplaced, the battle was over. St. Clair saw the British looking down his throat, and he discretely abandoned Fort Ticonderoga.

Burgoyne at once ordered a pursuit. The British were momentarily delayed at Hubbardton, where the Americans fought a stubborn delaying action, but von Riedesel saved the day by placing himself at the head of a company of Jaegers and marching through the forest to the rescue with his band playing his country's battle hymns. Elated, Burgoyne pushed on to Skenesboro; but St. Clair eventually eluded him and reached Fort Edward in safety with most of his troops.

Now Burgoyne had to choose one of two ways of continuing his southward march. He could return to Ticonderoga and move across Lake George and so on to the Hudson, or he could strike out overland from Skenesboro toward Fort Edward. The second way was the most difficult through terrain he had himself called "impassable." Yet he chose it. It is said he was persuaded to choose it by the Loyalist Major Philip Skene, founder of Skenesboro, who stood to profit by a new road cut from his colony to the Hudson. But Burgoyne himself feared to encourage the patriots by a "retrograde motion."

Whatever the reason, Schuyler skillfully took advantage of Burgoyne's blunder. He sent a thousand axmen to make Burgoyne's straight way crooked. They felled huge trees "as plenty as lamp-posts upon a highway about London."[91]

They destroyed every bridge and multiplied the area's numerous water obstacles by digging ditches. Schuyler sent out couriers to warn the inhabitants to drive off their cattle, and even induced them to burn their unharvested grain. He made a labyrinthine hell and a scorched earth of Burgoyne's southward path, and then, as the toiling British inched their way toward him, he withdrew from Fort Edward to Stillwater on the Hudson.

On July 29, three weeks from the day he had landed at Skenesboro, Burgoyne reached Fort Edward. It had taken him three weeks to advance 23 miles, seven of which had been over uncontested water. Exhausted, Burgoyne rested—while his Indians began exploring the surrounding countryside. One small but fateful band captured a young American woman named Jane McCrea.

Beautiful Jane McCrea was in love with her former neighbor, David Jones. But Jones was a Loyalist serving with Burgoyne. To be near him, Jane came to live with her patriot brother near Fort Edward. Hungering for news of the man she hoped to marry, Jane often visited the cabin of fat Mrs. McNeil, a cousin of the British General, Simon Fraser.

Because of these connections with Burgoyne, neither woman feared death or violence when Burgoyne's painted Indians broke into Mrs. McNeil's cabin. They were afraid, of course, but not for their lives. So Jane was placed on a horse and taken away to Burgoyne's camp, while other Indians struggled with the difficulty of getting her obese friend mounted. At last Mrs. McNeil went swaying off, clad in her chemise.

To her surprise, she arrived at Burgoyne's camp first. She was taken to Fraser. Red-faced, the general rushed to cover his huge cousin with his greatcoat. Then Jane's captors appeared.

They were trailing a scalp of long silken hair.

They had quarreled over Jane and had settled their dispute by killing her.

John Burgoyne was shocked. He had already been ridiculed for the high-flown speech in which he had enjoined tenderness upon his savages. He resolved to execute Jane's killer. But his officers, like generations of French and English officers before him, pointed out that to do so would alienate his Indians. Burgoyne reluctantly agreed, and the story of the brutal murder of Jane McCrea—embellished and magnified by patriot propagandists—soon enflamed the countryside with patriotic anger.

It was white-hot in the hearts of militia gathering across the border in New Hampshire and Vermont.

"I have three thousand dollars in hard money," Speaker John Langdon is supposed to have told the General Court of New Hampshire. "I will pledge my plate for three thousand more. I have seventy hogsheads of Tobago rum, which shall be sold for the most it will bring. These are at the service of the State. If we succeed in defending our homes, I may be remunerated. If we do not, the property will be of no value to me. Our old friend Stark, who so nobly sustained the honor of our State at Bunker's Hill, may be safely entrusted with the conduct of the enterprise, and we will check the progress of Burgoyne."[92]

General Stark said he would lead the brigade. But it would be a New Hampshire Brigade only. He wanted no truck with that Congress which had snubbed John Stark (as it had snubbed Benedict Arnold) by promoting green and untried junior colonels over his head. So Stark gathered nearly 1,500 men and marched them toward Manchester in Vermont 20 miles north of Bennington.

Here, General Schuyler ordered Stark to join him in the south at Stillwater. Stark refused. He took his orders from the New Hampshire General Court and no one else. Major General Benjamin Lincoln rebuked Stark, and so too did Congress later on, but John Stark had already decided that Bennington was the place to be. He marched his men south, leaving word for Colonel Seth Warner and the Green Mountain Boys to join him at Bennington.

Baron von Riedesel did not believe that his Brunswick Dragoons could take the American wilderness much longer. They needed horses. They were ridiculous on foot. Wearing enormous 12-pound jack boots, they were constantly tripping over the long broadswords trailing from their hips, and their short heavy carbines were not made for forest warfare. Men in great cocked hats with long white plumes might be the envy of the Indians, but they were also unenviable targets as they stumbled along in tight, thick coats, stiff leather breeches and huge gauntlets nearly elbow length. No, the Brunswickers needed mounts. Riedesel told Burgoyne so, and the British commander, now also in need of cattle for his hungry men, as well as horses to replace those hundreds which had perished in this sweltering green hell of a province, decided to send out a foraging expedition to the Connecticut River valley.

A force of about 500 men under Lieutenant Colonel Friedrich Baum was to secure these badly needed supplies. Their expedition was to be a secret one, and therefore, in the curious custom of the day, a German band was going along, plus 150 of those blundering Brunswickers.

The target for the raid was Bennington.

Colonel Baum's "stealthy" advance was so harassed by militia hanging on his front like a swarm of bees that he became uneasy and sent back to Burgoyne for reinforcements.

Lieutenant Colonel von Breymann was quickly dispatched with about 650 men and two guns. Using parade-ground formations in the woods, Breymann hurried to the rescue at the rate of about one mile an hour.

On August 15, a rainy day, Baum's force nearly collided with Stark's brigade marching down from Bennington along Walloomsack Creek. Baum immediately took a position on high ground and dug in. Next day Stark attacked.

He did not launch a headlong frontal assault. Instead, he sent knots of men in shirt sleeves idling forward. They wore the Loyalist white paper badge in their hats. Major Skene, who had accompanied Baum, told him they were Tories. Baum allowed the men to get onto his flank and rear. It was then that Stark is supposed to have uttered his famous battle cry:

"There, my boys, are your enemies. You must beat them, or Molly Stark is a widow tonight!"[93]

Baum's Indians and Tories quickly fled, but his regulars fought on until their ammunition was exhausted. The Brunswickers drew their swords and tried to cut their way out. But the enraged Yankees herded them back into the slaughter pen. Baum fell dying and only nine of his 374 Germans escaped death or capture. At noon it was all over, which was just when Breymann arrived with reinforcements.

So, too, did Seth Warner with reinforcements for Stark. Between them they fell on Breymann so ferociously that they sent him thrashing backward with casualties of about 230 dead, wounded and captured. Stark lost only 30 killed and 40 wounded during both actions.

General Burgoyne, who seemed to have forgotten Bunker Hill, was stunned. Once again, like William Howe, he had underestimated the American capacity for rising to crisis. But the Battle of Bennington was only the first—though perhaps the heaviest—of the blows that fell on Burgoyne's head. Far to the west, a second was also being delivered.

Barry St. Leger had moved with his mixed force of Tories, Indians and regulars from Oswego on Lake Ontario toward Albany, where he planned to make juncture with Burgoyne. Between him and the Mohawk River, however, stood Fort Stanwix with about 750 men under Colonel Peter Gansevoort and Lieutenant Colonel Marinus Willet. On August 3 St. Leger confidently invested the fort.

Once again the Americans rose to the occasion. Eight hundred New York militia flocked to the standard of General Nicholas Herkimer, and marched to relieve Stanwix. Molly Brant, the Mohawk widow of Sir William Johnson, notified St. Leger of their approach, and Joseph Brant, her brother, laid an ambush in a wooded ravine near Oriskany. Herkimer blundered into it. A dreadful fire swept his ranks, and yet the Americans refused to panic. They had seen the faces of their despised Tory neighbors in the woods around them, and they fought back in a vicious, bullet-for-bullet, knife-for-knife melee.

Herkimer, mortally wounded, lay with his back against a tree, pipe in mouth, giving his orders. As the battle continued, Willet in Fort Stanwix led a sally against the weakened British camp. He captured and sacked it. Hearing of the enemy in their rear, the Indians and Loyalists fled and Herkimer's force withdrew.

St. Leger, however, rallied his men and reinvested the fort. During a howling night storm, Willet crept through enemy lines to reach Schuyler's camp at Stillwater and plead for relief. Schuyler consented, and was at once assailed by his critics for "weakening" the northern army. Enraged, the "damned Dutchman" bit his pipe stem in two and called for a volunteer brigadier to command the expedition. None stepped forward.

Benedict Arnold, at last a major general, eagerly took command. With a thousand volunteers he moved toward Stanwix. Arnold's plan was to frighten the enemy by a ruse revolving around a half-crazy prisoner named Hon-Yost Schuyler. Arnold told the man's mother he was going to hang Hon-Yost unless he returned to St. Leger with a report that the Americans were coming in overwhelming strength. The woman persuaded her half-wit son to agree. Holding her other son as a hostage, Arnold had Hon-Yost's coat shot full of holes and set him hurrying to St. Leger. Next, he dispatched a friendly Oneida Indian to confirm the half-wit's tale.

Hon-Yost arrived in St. Leger's camp. The Indians asked him how many men Arnold had. Hon-Yost pointed to the leaves of the trees, at which point the Oneida Indian arrived to support him. That was enough for St. Leger's red allies. Seizing supplies of rum and clothing, they fled. The Loyalists followed, and St. Leger quickly withdrew to Oswego, leaving his tents behind him.

He would not make rendezvous with Burgoyne that fall.

Burgoyne now knew that his situation was desperate. He could expect no help from Howe. The very day that St. Leger had invested Stanwix, he had received a letter from Sir William saying: "My intention is for Pennsylvania, where I expect to meet Washington, but if he goes to the northward and you can keep him at bay, be assured I shall soon be after him to relieve you. After your arrival at Albany, the movements of the enemy will guide yours."[94]

If Burgoyne had ever expected to effect a juncture with the main British Army, it must have been clear to him then that it was now out of the question. He had to push on to Albany. And yet the Americans between him and that city were growing stronger daily.

Horatio Gates now commanded the Americans. Congress, searching for a scapegoat for Ticonderoga, had removed Schuyler on August 4. But by August 19, the date of Gates's arrival at the American works at Stillwater, the "damned Dutchman" had all but reversed the situation. Nevertheless, the northern army belonged to Gates, and it was growing into a force between 6,000 and 9,000 men. Burgoyne could not sit still while his enemy swelled into an over-powering force. On September 13, 1777, he crossed the Hudson and began pushing south.

Six miles north of Stillwater was the rolling ground known as Bemis Heights. The Americans had fortified this ground. But they had neglected a height on the far left. Burgoyne saw it. Possession of it would command the American positions just as Sugar Loaf had been the key to Ticonderoga. Burgoyne ordered Reidesel to move against the American right along the Hudson River, he himself would strike the patriot center at a place called Freeman's Farm, and Fraser would swing wide to the right to take the hill.

On September 19, a cool, clear day with the grass bright with frost, the assault began. Almost immediately Americans in the treetops spotted the movement of scarlet coats and flashing steel. Headquarters was notified. Arnold, who commanded the American left, wanted to attack at once at Freeman's Farm. Gates demurred. He wanted the British to come to him. Meanwhile, the British drove in the patriot pickets at Freeman's. Arnold again expostulated, and Gates reluctantly gave him Morgan's riflemen and Henry Dearborn's New Hampshire Regiment. They were too successful. Morgan's sharpshooters all but annihilated Fraser's advance guard, but then, pressing the pursuit too eagerly, they too were routed. Morgan stood almost alone, tears of chagrin coursing down his seamed face, while he sounded his famous turkey call to rally his men to him. They returned, and Arnold, having checked Fraser on his left, began probing for the British weak spot.

He found it between Fraser and Burgoyne at Freeman's Farm. Here he eagerly fed in fresh regiments. A pitched battle ensued. Now the Americans drove the British back and seized their guns. But they could not fire them because the gunners had carried off all the linstocks holding the slow matches. When the Americans attempted to haul the guns away, the British came charging back with the bayonet.

American riflemen in the trees then trained their sights on British officers and gunners. They scourged them. General Phillips riding up to see to the guns found every artillery officer save one shot down and 36 out of 48 artillerymen stricken. Phillips called for four more guns and got them, but they soon ran out of ammunition. Again and again the British tried to carry the day with their favorite weapon, the bayonet. But the Americans repulsed them.

Now Arnold saw his chance. The British center under Burgoyne was faltering. He needed only a few more men to strike the knockout blow. He appealed to Gates and was refused. Late in the afternoon Gates changed his mind, but he sent the reinforcement to the left rather than the center. The golden opportunity had passed, and Baron von Riedesel was already marching up from the British right to stiffen Burgoyne. The Americans retreated, and as night fell the Battle of Freeman's Farm came to an end.

The British occupied the field and were the technical victors. However, they had lost between 500 and 600 men and the Americans only slightly more than 300. Burgoyne was weakened for the next round, and even as it was preparing, the Americans were busy in his rear, recapturing almost all of the lost positions around Ticonderoga and threatening to sever his line of communications.

Burgoyne *had* to try again, or else retreat ignominiously into Canada. Henry Clinton in New York with Howe's rear guard had promised help, but Clinton was moving slowly. He did not move against the patriot forts on the Hudson until October 3. He stormed them successfully, after some bitter fighting, and wrote cheerfully to Burgoyne: "*Nous y voici,* and now nothing between us but Gates. I sincerely hope this little success of ours may facilitate your operations."[95] Unfortunately, the courier whom Clinton sent north was captured by the Americans and forced to vomit up the silver bullet containing the message.

A few days later one of Burgoyne's couriers finally reached Clinton, and the alarmed general immediately sent a fleet upriver to burn Kingston while he hastened back to New York to collect reinforcements. By then, however, Burgoyne was attacking at Bemis Heights.

Three months in the American wilderness had so frazzled Burgoyne's troops that they were little better than animated bags of bones. Yet, in spite of this, perhaps because of this, Burgoyne resolved on a last desperate fling. Over the objections of some of his generals, he called for another swing at the American left. About 1,500 men would attempt to turn it. If they were successful, more would be fed in. Unknown to Burgoyne, the chances of success were higher than usual, for Horatio Gates had relieved Benedict Arnold of command.

Gates's reports of Freeman's Farm had ignored Arnold's leading role. Arnold angrily challenged Gates on the issue and then demanded a pass to Washington. Gates was only too eager to comply, but then Arnold's officers persuaded him not to leave. Nevertheless, Gates took over the left wing while Benjamin Lincoln held the right. Thus, when the British scarlet was again sighted through the trees on the left, it was Gates who ordered Daniel Morgan "to begin the game."

It was not long after Gates's holding action began, however, before a short stocky man on a big brown horse came sweeping onto the field. Cheer after cheer and man after man followed Arnold as he led a headlong charge against the British center. With his unerring eye, Arnold had found the soft spot, and an entire German unit collapsed. Now Arnold saw that Simon Fraser was skillfully rallying the enemy. He turned to Morgan and asked him to bring Fraser down. Morgan called for Tim Murphy, a legendary Indian fighter and rifleman. Murphy climbed a tree and aimed his double-barreled rifle.

His first shot creased the crupper of Fraser's horse. The second parted the horse's mane. Alarmed, Fraser's officers tried to draw him away. Fraser refused, and Murphy's next shot killed him.

With his fall, the last hope of British success perished. They withdrew to the shelter of earthworks, and it was then that Arnold called for the crusher. Spurring his horse, he rode against the left of the position. He and his men were repulsed. Riding madly across the line of battle, Arnold commandeered another general's brigade and sent it smashing into the earthworks and swept the enemy clean away.

Now a redoubt on the British right held by Breymann was exposed. Collecting two more regiments, Arnold came riding down on it. Breymann was mortally wounded, but Arnold was also shot—in the same leg that had been hit at Quebec. It was then, with the redoubt carried, with Burgoyne's main position open on his right and rear, that an officer sent by Gates came up to Arnold with orders to return to quarters before he did something rash.

Arnold returned on a litter and the battle quietly fizzled out. Burgoyne had lost 600 men, the Americans 150, and the Battle of Bemis Heights had been the last nail in the coffin of Burgoyne's army.

Leaving 500 sick and wounded, Burgoyne withdrew to Saratoga. Gates quickly built entrenchments across the Hudson. By October 11 he had Burgoyne completely surrounded. Gentleman Johnny called four despairing councils of war. At length he accepted black reality: surrender.

Even so, he asked for terms; and Gates, fearing that Clinton might come up in his rear, allowed Burgoyne to name his own. But then Burgoyne, also aware of Clinton's approach, began to stall for time. Gates threatened to renew hostilities and Burgoyne signed the famous "Convention" of Saratoga whereby his exhausted little army of less than 5,000 men laid down its arms on October 17.

Ticonderoga, Bennington, Stanwix, Oriskany, Freeman's Farm, Bemis Heights, Saratoga—all those separate actions which, woven together, form the single tapestry called the Battle of Saratoga—had culminated in one of the most decisive victories in the history of mankind.

Saratoga's effects were immediate and enormous. It spurred Congress to adopt the Articles of Confederation and send them to the separate states for ratification. More immediately important, the American victory at Saratoga brought the Bourbons into the war against England. France, watching warily, threw off all pretense of "neutrality" once Burgoyne's defeat and the surrender of a British army became known. On December 12 the Count Vergennes met with the American commissioners in Paris. Two months later he signed an alliance with the United States and after that declared war on Britain. Spain followed suit in 1779, then came Holland, ordering her Dutch West Indies to increase their aid to the Americans. Catherine of Russia followed, organizing a League of Armed Neutrality which deterred British trade. There was no longer any need of Beaumarchais and his little deception at Hortalez et Cie. Now ships and soldiers and supplies in great quantities came flowing out to America from France.

Back across the Atlantic sailed Gentleman Johnny Burgoyne. Perhaps he remembered what Charles James Fox had said to him after he had recorded that wager for victory in the betting book at Brooks's:

"Be not oversanguine in your expectations. I believe when next you return to England you will be a prisoner on parole."[96]

And he was.

14

☆

The good news from Saratoga came to Washington adulterated with the sour taste of the so-called Conway Cabal.

General Thomas Conway was an Irish-born officer of the French Army. It is his name that describes a "plot" that was actually not a plot but a haphazard coalescing of Washington's numerous critics. Among these were Samuel Adams, John Adams occasionally, Richard Henry Lee and other powerful Congressmen. They wished to replace Washington with the popular Gates.

The glory of Saratoga had served to exaggerate the shame of Germantown and the Brandywine, and since Gates had been careful to claim credit for that victory it was he who was named president of the revived Board of War. Technically, he became Washington's superior. Next, Congress named Conway as Inspector General, much to the indignation of Washington, who held Conway in contempt.

Actually Conway was a competent professional, but his tongue was unfortunately as sharp as his sword. He had already written Congress criticizing the drinking habits of Lord Stirling, after which he wrote a letter of high praise to Gates and asked if he might serve under him. In that letter, Conway was critical of Washington.

Major James Wilkinson, Gates's aide, saw Conway's letter. He mentioned it to a friend who was Lord Stirling's adjutant. Stirling was informed, and with happy malice passed the information along to Washington. Now Washington, probably using the pen of Alexander Hamilton, wrote a stinging rebuke to Conway, who denied all criticism. Gates heard of this and dashed off an angry letter to Washington protesting his innocence of disloyalty and demanding to know who was spying on his correspondence.

Washington named Wilkinson. Gates turned on his aide so furiously that Wilkinson challenged him to a duel. Gates declined the honor. But Conway did not decline when General John Cadwalader later challenged *him* to a duel, and he was so badly wounded in it that, believing himself near death, he wrote a letter of apology to Washington. Conway eventually recovered and returned to France

Before he did, however, Gates made a grievous error. He and his Board of War proposed an "irruption" into Canada. When it became clear to Congress that such an expedition was foredoomed to bloody humiliation, Gates's popularity declined and the Board of War's prestige sank to a low from which it never recovered.

Thus the Conway Cabal, and if history has shown that Gates probably did not desire Washington's hat, the fact remains that Washington and his officers thought that he did, and that criticisms raised by Congressmen safe in their snuggery at York were heard by men passing through the ordeal of that dreadful winter at Valley Forge.

It was not the cold (actually it was a mild winter) that made the Continentals suffer so, but rather a bungling quartermaster department and the selfish avarice of American farmers and merchants. Soldiers at Valley Forge went hungry because nearby farmers preferred to sell to the British in Philadelphia for hard cash, because New York's grain surplus was diverted to New England civilians and the British in New York City, and because Connecticut farmers refused to sell beef cattle at ceiling prices imposed by the state. Soldiers went half-naked because merchants in Boston would not move government clothing off their shelves at anything less than profits ranging from 1,000 to 1,800 percent. Everywhere in America there was a spirit of profiteering and a habit of graft that made Washington grind his teeth in helpless fury. In response to his appeals, Congress passed the buck by authorizing him to commandeer supplies. This he was reluctant to do among a people supposed to be trying to throw off the yoke of a tyrant. When he was forced to do it, the results confirmed his fears.

And so every night for too many weeks sticklike soldiers stuck their heads out of their smoky huts to cry, "No meat! No meat!" Firecake and water was their food, bloody footprints in the snow their sign. Their clothes were so ragged and blankets were so scarce that they often sat up all night rather than fall asleep and freeze to death. Although they had little sustenance themselves, body lice managed to feed on them. Lafayette was horrified to see soldiers whose legs had frozen black and who had to be carted off to hospitals that were little better than death terminals to have their limbs amputated. One bitter Continental wrote: "Poor food—hard lodging—Cold Weather—fatigue—Nasty Cloaths—nasty Cookery—Vomit half my time—smoak'd out of my senses—the Devil's in it—I can't Endure it—Why are we sent here to starve and freeze . . . ?"[97]

Officers fared hardly better, and the sight of them wrapped in filthy blankets astonished Lieutenant General the Baron von Steuben, former aide to the King of Prussia, upon his arrival at Valley Forge.

He had not been a lieutenant general for very long, he was not a real baron, his service with King Frederick had been very brief, and his last rank in the Prussian Army had been that of captain. However, a wise French minister of war, recognizing both Steuben's abilities and the fact that he needed some fancy titles to impress the Americans, had invested him with a counterfeit nobility. Eventually the Americans became aware of the deception, but by then they could not have cared less.

Steuben was the father of the American Army. Seeing what he saw at Valley Forge, he told Washington that no European army could ever have endured such hardship, and then set himself to give the hardy Continentals the discipline and uniformity that they so grievously lacked. He established his own system of drill, adapting the Prussian method to American conditions, and substituted it for the differing drills of the various states. Then, having endeared himself to the officers by holding a party at which no man with a whole pair of breeches might attend, he horrified them by insisting that they drill their men in person.

In this republican army the officers let the sergeants handle drill, some of the higher ranks lived in comfortable houses far away from the rows of filthy huts, and others made servants of their soldiers. Steuben, the Prussian, changed all this—and he did it by example.

Here was a lieutenant general standing in the mud or snow waving his arms and howling in German, French and bastard English at privates who thought a bayonet was for roasting meat over a fire. And the troops loved him. He made them obey, but he also made them laugh. Shrewd showman that he was, Steuben let them. Once, having blown up at a particularly slow company, he turned to a young officer named Benjamin Walker and gasped:

"*Viens, Valkaire, mon ami, mon bon ami! Sacré!* Goddam de *gaucheries* of dese *badauds. Je ne puis plus.* I can curse dem no more."98

By spring Washington had an army that could march and maneuver, and he was eager to use it against the British departing Philadelphia.

When Benjamin Franklin was informed that Howe had captured Philadelphia, he shook his head and said, "No, Philadelphia has captured Howe!"99 Franklin was right. Howe and his officers gave themselves over to balls, theatrics, horse racing and wine, much to the despair of the Tories, who wanted the British to go out and destroy the Yankee vermin in their nest at Valley Forge. Howe's dalliance with blonde Betsey Loring so exasperated the Tories that one of them wrote:

> Awake, arouse, Sir Billy,
> There's forage on the plain,
> Ah, leave your little filly,
> And open the campaign.100

Howe, however, would open no more campaigns. He had asked Lord George Germain to relieve him from "this very painful service," and in May of 1778 he handed over the American command to Sir Henry Clinton, now also a Knight of the Bath. Before Howe departed, he was honored at an extravagant pageant called the "Mischianza."

It was organized by the dashing Captain John André, who had passed the winter courting the lovely Peggy Shippen, daughter of a wealthy Philadelphian. Peggy did not attend the Mischianza, because her father would not permit her to wear Turkish bloomers like the other beautiful young Loyalists for whose smiles British officers, mounted as knights of old, shivered lances and crossed swords until the small hours of the morning of May 19.

As the Mischianza was breaking up, Howe was informed that Lafayette was in the vicinity with a large force. Actually, the young marquis was only on an armed reconnaissance. But Howe scented a last opportunity and tried to trap "the boy." It was then that von Steuben's value to the American cause became evident. Feinting and maneuvering precisely with disciplined troops, Lafayette made his escape.

On May 24 Howe sailed for home, having advised the Loyalists to make their peace with the patriots. Tory consternation turned to despair after Sir Henry Clinton announced that he was moving to New York. Clinton was acting on Germain's orders.

Germain knew that a large French fleet under Comte Charles d'Estaing was sailing for America. The French could bottle up Lord Howe's ships in the Delaware and catch Clinton's troops between themselves and Washington. So Clinton was making for New York, and he chose to go overland rather than give Washington the chance to make a cross-Jersey dash into the city before he could arrive by sea.

Clinton placed 3,000 grieving Tories aboard Admiral Lord Howe's ships, as well as two Hessian regiments of whose loyalty he was not sure, and then, as the ships dropped down the Delaware, he and Lord Cornwallis led the British Army across the river into New Jersey.

On June 27, with his forces strung out for a dozen miles along the road to Sandy Hook, he stopped to bivouac for the night at Monmouth Court House.

Washington's plan was to attack Clinton's rear guard at Monmouth, and the man who was eventually to lead the operation was General Charles Lee.

Lee had been exchanged. He had also been changed. He had spent his captivity advising his captors how to crush the Americans, and he had returned to his old comrades convinced that they could not win. Lee scoffed at Steuben's drill and swore that the Americans could never hope to meet European troops on even terms. During the council of war called by Washington after he had caught up to Clinton it was Lee who argued most vehemently against attack. When Washington decided otherwise and offered Lee the command of the advanced corps which was to strike Clinton, Lee refused it. But then, seeing the corps grow to a force of about 5,000 men, he changed his mind and rode forward to supersede Lafayette.

Clinton had started out on the road to Sandy Hook at about eight in the morning of June 28, 1778. He left behind a covering force of about 1,500 or 2,000 men. Lee proposed to cut off and destroy this force. But he had no definite plan of battle, his commanders had no idea of what to do, and the Americans moving along the road toward the British at Monmouth became an uncoordinated mass. Individual unit fights began. Clinton, hearing them, turned about to come to the rescue of his rear guard. He placed his troops on the east side of the road facing the Americans on the west side.

Lee ordered Lafayette to attack the British left. Lafayette did not believe he was in position to attack. He moved to a different position, unmasking the other divisions, which quickly began falling back. Soon all the units were pulling back, Lafayette among them, and then Lee gave the order for retreat.

Whether or not Lee had actually averted a crushing blow by Clinton, as his defenders later maintained, whether or not he had led the withdrawal with a smug spirit of I-told-you-so, the fact is that Washington did not want a retreat. He was coming east along the road with his main body. When he rode up on the great white horse presented to him that day by Governor Livingston of New Jersey and found himself surrounded by streams of backpedaling soldiers, he lost his temper in the most spectacular outburst of his career.

His face livid, sitting his horse like the splendid equestrian figure he was, Washington came galloping down on Charles Lee with all the wrath of the God of Battles. What he actually called him is not certainly known. There are many versions, but the best description came from General Charles Scott, who was there and later recalled: "Yes, sir, he swore that day till the leaves shook on the trees. Charming! Delightful! Never have I enjoyed such swearing before or since. Sir, on that memorable day, he swore like an angel from heaven!"[101].

Ordering Lee to the rear, Washington stopped the retreat. He stopped it by his magnificent presence, riding easily among the men, re-forming them, inspiring them by his calm courage. Galloping down the road to Monmouth, he halted two retreating regiments, and ordered them to hold the advancing British until he could re-form the American line behind them. Choosing high ground just west of a ravine, Washington put Greene on the right, himself in the center, and Stirling on the left. Behind him Lafayette commanded the second line, while Wayne held an outpost in Washington's front.

Cheering and charging with typical fury, the British struck first at Stirling's men on the left. A desperate hour-long battle punctuated by an artillery duel ensued. Men fought each other in sweltering 100-degree heat. Everywhere soldiers were fainting from fatigue. And here, as Steuben watched with satisfaction, Washington was at last able to maneuver like an eighteenth-century general. Stirling's position was saved when American regiments wheeled into line under fire and worked around the British right flank, forcing them to retire.

Clinton next hurled his finest troops against Greene on the right. Cornwallis personally led the assault. But volley after volley of American musketry, thickened by the shot of an artillery crossfire, repulsed the British.

Meanwhile, Wayne in the front-center was also under attack by a force led by Lieutenant Colonel Henry Monckton. "Forward to the charge, my brave grenadiers!" Monckton cried, and the scarlet waves surged forward. "Steady, steady!" Wayne cautioned his men. "Wait for the word, then pick out the king-birds!"[102] Wayne gave the word at 40 yards, and the volley that crashed out was so devastating that it broke the attack. Monckton fell so close to the Americans that they leaped out to seize his body and his battalion colors.

Wayne then withdrew, outflanked on either side by a fourth British line—but by then the battle was over. Both sides occupied the field that night. Washington lay under an oak tree with Lafayette beside him. At midnight, however, Clinton arose and led his men quietly away. He had saved his rear guard and thus, if there was any victor, it was he. Washington had not accomplished much in a military way, but his men had fought the British regulars to a standstill in open battle. A new spirit now informed a new American army.

Meanwhile, an old war dog was snapping his last. Outraged, Charles Lee demanded a court-martial. He was found guilty of disobedience, of making "an unnecessary and, in some few instances, a disorderly retreat," and of disrespect of his commander in chief. Lee was sentenced to a year's suspension from the service and Congress approved the sentence. Hearing his fate, Lee is reported to have cried: "O that I were a dog, that I might not call man my brother."[103] Later he wrote an insulting letter to Congress which boomeranged with his dismissal from the service.

And so Washington's chief military critic had passed from the scene. After Monmouth Washington's position as commander in chief was secure. After Monmouth also the two main armies did not meet again. The War of the Revolution was fought by detachments and subordinate units, while the old golden lilies of France, once detested in America, reappeared beside that new standard of "thirteen stripes alternate red and white, [with] thirteen stars white in a blue field."

15

☆

The Comte d'Estaing had taken too long crossing the Atlantic. He had held practice maneuvers en route and he arrived off the Delaware capes on July 8, 1778, ten days too late to intercept Admiral Howe's vulnerable transports.

Howe had also ferried Clinton's troops across the Lower Harbor into Manhattan, after which he put about to block d'Estaing's entry into the port. Here, the new Franco-American alliance met its first test. Would d'Estaing, with a fleet nearly double the strength of Howe's, risk crossing the bar at Sandy Hook to close with the British? The answer was no.

The French admiral spent ten days cautiously taking soundings. His best chance came on July 22 when wind and a high tide raised 30 feet of water over the bar, but d'Estaing bowed to the warnings of his pilots and stood away to the south.

New York, the very hub of British power in America, had been spared. Perhaps it had been spared because the French admiral was not too eager to end the war with a single blow and thus free Britain to turn all her power against his own country. History does not say, but the fact remains that the Franco-American alliance was, at its outset, put to a severe strain.

Washington was disappointed at the missed opportunity, and within the next few days reports of British-led Indian massacres of western settlers increased his dismay. On July 4—to mock American independence—Colonel Sir John Butler struck at the Wyoming Valley in Pennsylvania. Hundreds perished. Men were burnt at the stake or thrown on beds of coals and held down with pitchforks while their horrified families were forced to witness their torment. Others were placed in a circle while a half-breed squaw called Queen Esther danced chanting around them to chop off their heads. Soon the entire frontier was in flames, with Washington unable to come to its rescue.

All the commander in chief's resources were at that moment directed toward recovering Newport from the British. Sullivan with about 10,000 men divided between Greene and Lafayette had marched north of the vital port city to make rendezvous with d'Estaing's 4,000 French soldiers. But Clinton and "Black Dick" Howe acted quickly to discomfit them. Clinton collected a force of 5,000 to come to the aid of General Pigot, who held Newport with about 3,000 troops, while Howe, now reinforced, crowded on all sail for Rhode Island.

Hearing of Howe's approach, d'Estaing re-embarked his troops and sailed out to meet Howe. Sullivan was furious, but the Frenchman would not change his mind. On the night of August 11 the ships of both fleets were scattered by a violent storm, and both had to sail away for repairs—Howe to New York and d'Estaing to Boston.

In the meantime, the French withdrawal had so disgusted Sullivan's militia that more than 5,000 of them went home. Sullivan had to backpedal furiously away from the eagerly pursuing Pigot, and the Newport expedition ended in a fiasco. Sullivan was openly critical of his allies, and there were some tense moments in Boston after a French officer was killed during riots between sailors and soldiers of both nations—but tempers eventually cooled, especially after d'Estaing sailed away for Martinique on November 4.

A week later Walter ("Hellhound") Butler, the bloodier son of Sir John Butler, ravaged the patriot settlement of Cherry Valley in western New York. Assisted by Joseph Brant, Butler put the town to the torch. Then, with the American frontier being pushed back and ravaged, the British moved south.

In November of 1778 Clinton sent about 3,500 regulars and Tories under Lieutenant Colonel Archibald Campbell against Savannah, a port which not only offered entrance into the most southern colonies but also linked them with the West Indies. Campbell was to be assisted by General Augustine Prevost, marching up from St. Augustine in Florida.

Opposing them was Major General Robert Howe with about 1,000 Georgia and South Carolina militia. Howe took position to the east of Savannah with his right resting on a swamp and his left on rice paddies. Campbell feinted through the paddies while another column, led by a Negro slave, slipped through the swamp and turned the Americans' right. At that juncture Campbell converted his feint into a strike and both columns closed on the patriots, putting them to rout and inflicting about 500 casualties against a handful of their own lost.

The date of Savannah's fall was December 29, and after that the British, now under Prevost, set about clearing Georgia.

Up north, both Washington and Clinton had gone into winter quarters, the British in and around New York, Washington in a great arc beginning in Middletown, New Jersey, not far from Monmouth and stretching on through West Point and Fishkill in New York and thence east to Danbury, Connecticut.

It was a mild winter and the troops were relatively comfortable, a small blessing for which the harried Washington found it difficult to be thankful after having seen the campaign of 1778 begin so brightly only to fizzle out in the end.

16

☆

While the chief commanders and their armies wintered in the North, fighting flared in the South and on the western border. In Georgia, capture of Savannah had been tantamount to conquest of the state. After the arrival of General Prevost the state was once more subjected to the Crown, and as 1779 began, Georgia's inhabitants "flocked by hundreds to the King's officers, and made their peace at the expense of their patriotism."[104]

Soon Prevost moved against South Carolina, where he was opposed by Benjamin Lincoln commanding about 3,000 ragged Continentals and untrained militia. There ensued a series of marches and countermarches, skirmishes and small pitched battles, clashes between Tories and patriots marked by brutality and depredations on both sides, and although the British regulars certainly could claim most of the victories, the net result of the campaign was that Prevost withdrew to Georgia, and South Carolina remained in the rebel camp.

In the West a dashing frontiersman named George Rogers Clark struck a sharp blow at the British. Acting for Virginia, which was anxious to nail down its old claims to the Northwest, Clark had begun clearing the Illinois country during the previous summer by capturing posts at Kaskaskia and Vincennes. But then the British under the unsavory Colonel Henry Hamilton—the "Hair-buyer," as he was known to the settlers—recaptured Vincennes. Hearing of this, Clark rushed to Kaskaskia about 150 miles to the southwest. In early February he led a tiny force of 130 men, half of them French, against Vincennes. Few marches in American history equal the ordeal which awaited Clark's men. Torrential rains and floods barred their path. Much of the time they floundered through icy water up to their chests. Men who sank beneath the surface were fished up and placed in canoes. But Clark urged them on, ever onward, until at last they debouched before Vincennes. Here Clark deceived Hamilton's superior force by marching his little band back and forth to create the impression of a thousand men approaching. That was enough for Hamilton's Indians. Then, after Clark's sharpshooters began picking off the fort's defenders, Hamilton asked for talks. To make up Hamilton's mind, Clark had five Indians, who had been captured with scalps in their possession, tomahawked in full view of the garrison. Hamilton surrendered Vincennes.

Although Clark had given British power north of the Ohio a severe check, he had not destroyed it—if only because he could not capture Fort Detroit. As a result, warfare of the savage border kind was to be renewed in the Illinois country.

Meanwhile, with the advent of summer, General Washington moved to retaliate against the British and Indians who had ravaged the Wyoming and Cherry valleys the year before. He sent General Sullivan and about 5,000 men to destroy Iroquois towns and to capture Fort Niagara, the base for their raids. Niagara, however, was not taken, although the Indians were severely scourged by Sullivan leading one column up the Susquehanna from the Wyoming Valley and General James Clinton pushing up the Mohawk Valley with another. No less than 40 Iroquois towns were destroyed and the people of the Long House were struck a blow from which they never completely recovered. Standing crops were ruined, granaries burned and orchards cut down. In the cruel winter of 1779-80 which followed, hundreds of Indian families starved to death. Still, the British and Indians were not completely suppressed, and it remained for the kingdom of Spain to deal Britain her most severe blow in that summer of 1779.

On June 16, 1779, Spain declared war on Britain, and at once seriously complicated the problem of subduing the American colonies.

The British fleet, already spread thin over the vast new empire, now found it necessary to reinforce Gibraltar and Minorca. The West Indies came under the threat of a Spanish fleet at Havana and a French fleet and army at Santo Domingo. D'Estaing began to take island after island away from Britain, with the result that Sir Henry Clinton had to send 8,000 regulars from New York to the West Indies.

Clinton was so gravely weakened that he began considering the evacuation of New York. This was not done, but Newport, which had resisted both the French and the Americans the year before, was abandoned without a shot.

Then, in August, the mother country herself came under the guns of a Franco-Spanish fleet. For the first time since the Spanish Armada was routed in 1588, the "island set in a silver sea" was threatened with invasion. In his alarm, King George III tried to rally the people by reminding them how valiantly the subjects of Queen Elizabeth had met the same threat two centuries previously. His oratory was not needed, however, for the vast enemy fleet turned out to be only a "huge mob of ships." On August 16 as the combined fleets came in sight of Plymouth a storm drove them out of the Channel never to return. The Bourbons "talked big, threatened a great deal, did nothing, and retired."[105]

The only sailor who really twisted the British lion's tail in that year of 1779 was a renegade Scots captain named John Paul Jones.

British atrocities in America had so enraged the leaders of the Revolution that at one point Benjamin Franklin proposed the burning of English and Scottish cities in retaliation, and Congress authorized expeditions to set fire to London and burn the Royal Palace to the ground.

In the first years of the war, however, no daring firebrands volunteered to carry the torch across the sea. Most American sea captains were too busy taking profits as privateers. Armed with letters of marque authorizing them to take enemy ships as prizes—that is, to wage war for private profit—they took to the sea in such numbers and with such success that in 1777 Benjamin Franklin could declare that American shipping had grown richer by privateering than it had by commerce. Gradually, however, British privateers evened the score. The British Navy bottled up the Continental Navy in home ports, and it did not appear likely that Franklin's schemes of retaliation would ever be realized—until John Paul Jones stepped forward.

Born plain John Paul, Jones had knocked about the world as a cabin boy, ship's mate and finally a captain. Charged with murder in the West Indies, he proved his innocence but then faced a second charge of cruelty to his crew. With that, he changed his name and came to live in America. There, like many other British liberals, he became convinced that the Americans were upholding the rights of mankind against the forces of repression.

In 1778, in command of the *Ranger,* Jones attacked the English town of Whitehaven and burned ships in port. He also invaded Scottish soil, and soon he had so terrified the British coast that Lord North planned to send a special squadron against him as soon as Britain was free of the fear of Franco-Spanish invasion. Then, in September, 1779, Jones put out from France with his flagship *Bonhomme Richard,* 42 guns; the 32-gun frigates *Alliance* and *Pallas,* and the brigantine *Vengeance,* 12. At dusk of the 23rd, off the coast of northeast England, they sighted a British convoy escorted by *Serapis,* 50 guns, and *Countess of Scarborough,* 20.

Jones at once signaled his ships to form line while he made for *Serapis* in *Bonhomme Richard.* For some reason, *Alliance* stood off at a safe distance, while *Pallas* went after *Countess of Scarborough,* eventually capturing her. Undismayed at this lack of support, Jones engaged the heavier *Serapis.*

Richard's first broadside resulted in disaster: two of the three heavy guns on her engaged side burst, killing the crews and blowing up the deck above them. For fear of a repetition, the third gun was abandoned. Still undaunted, Jones put himself alongside *Serapis* and lashed both ships together. There they lay in the moonlight for two and a half hours, pounding each other at point-blank range.

At first it seemed that *Serapis* would prevail. Her guns splintered *Richard*'s rotten timbers and sent them flying. She scored numerous water-line hits and set *Richard* to leaking badly. And one by one she knocked out Jones's main battery of 28 12-pounders. Jones had only three 9-pounders left. All around him fires were breaking out and the pumps were falling behind the leaks. Still, he fought on. When one of his gunners called out to *Serapis* for quarter, he broke the man's skull with his pistol. When the captain of *Serapis* shouted for verification of the gunner's appeal, Jones bellowed back: "I have not yet begun to fight."[106] And when the British attempted to board him, he led the fight that repulsed them.

Yet, as badly as *Richard* had been hurt below, she had begun to conquer aloft. Under the direction of American officers, French marines in *Richard*'s fighting tops had cleared the enemy rigging of British seamen and had begun to pour a heavy fire into *Serapis.* Sniping, hurling grenades and combustibles, they cleared the Britisher's upper decks. Then a grenade thrown into a pile of cartridges on a lower deck set off a chain of explosions that racked *Serapis* from bow to stern. A half-hour later *Alliance* appeared and took up a raking position off the Britisher's bow. Some of *Alliance*'s shells struck *Richard* by mistake, but enough of them landed on *Serapis* to force the British captain to strike his colors.

By then *Bonhomme Richard* was a floating wreck, and Jones was compelled to transfer to *Serapis*. Nevertheless, he had won. By his refusal to submit, the indomitable John Paul Jones had humbled British naval pride, given the Continental Navy its greatest victory and bequeathed to the United States Navy one of its most cherished traditions. After his triumph, however, except for privateering and a few sea skirmishes, the American battle for freedom was fought exclusively on land.

The most that Sir Henry Clinton had been able to do in the North was to launch a series of destructive raids into Connecticut and to seize the Hudson River forts at Verplanck's Point and Stony Point. His objective in Connecticut was to lure Washington out of his new headquarters at West Point. But Washington, though angered by the frightfulness of the British raids, refused to budge. Instead, he sent Mad Anthony Wayne out to retake Stony Point.

Wayne led about 1,200 men of the American Light Infantry, the Continental Army's new elite. Remembering what "No-Flint" Grey had done to his own troops at Paoli's Tavern, he ordered most of his men to attack with bayonets only. On the night of July 15 all the inhabitants in the Stony Point area were taken into custody. Dogs on the line of march were destroyed to prevent their barking.

Moving along the river bank, wading through two feet of water, Wayne's men moved out silently. Just after midnight, under the guns of the fort, they parted into three columns and moved to the attack.

British sentries spotted Wayne's column on the right and opened fire. Wayne fell, stunned by a ball that grazed his skull. He got up on one knee and shouted to his men to go forward. Angered by his fall, the American light infantrymen went yelling against the fort. They overwhelmed it, and had to be restrained from using the bayonet to avenge Paoli.

It was a perfect little victory. Against American losses of 15 killed and 83 wounded, the British suffered 63 killed, about 70 wounded and 543 men captured. Only one man got away, and Wayne's triumph —even though Washington eventually evacuated Stony Point—forced Clinton to abandon his intention of a campaign in New Jersey.

Instead, he too evacuated Stony Point, and Verplanck's as well, sending the garrisons south to help defend Savannah against the French.

Washington hoped that Count d'Estaing would help him capture New York, and he daily awaited word that the French fleet had been sighted off the Delaware capes. But d'Estaing thought differently. Turning from his West Indies plunder, spurning the most valued prize, Jamaica, he sailed with his troops to recover Savannah from the British.

On September 12 about 3,500 French soldiers sailed up the Savannah River, came ashore and took up position south of the town. Three days later they were joined by Count Casimir Pulaski's mounted legion of 200 horsemen. On the 16th Benjamin Lincoln appeared with 600 Continentals and 750 militia. D'Estaing now had about 5,000 men against about 2,400 British, of whom the vast majority were Tories. If he attacked immediately he would undoubtedly overwhelm Prevost. Instead, he tried to take Savannah by summons. The wily Prevost asked for a truce, which he used to strengthen his position and await the arrival of Lieutenant Colonel Maitland from Port Royal to the north.

Maitland's march seemed hopeless. The French held the sea and Lincoln's army blocked him by land. Still, though ill of malaria himself, he led 800 regulars through a swamp, crossing the Savannah River under cover of a fog to make a most welcome addition to Prevost's fighting force. And then d'Estaing delayed further, deciding to try to take the town by regular approaches.

The first trenches were opened September 23, and on October 3 nearly 50 land guns, plus those of three ships in the river, began battering the city. Its fall seemed inevitable, and yet d'Estaing could not wait for it. Reports that Admiral "Foul-Weather Jack" Byron* was en route to Savannah with a British squadron made him fear for his ships. Storms of the season might scatter them. So he decided to attack Savannah.

* Grandfather of the poet.

Three columns were formed. One under General Count Dillon was to march to the British right rear and try to enter the town through the Sailor's Gate. A second under General Isaac Huger was to make a feint at the British left, while a third, the main blow, struck at the British right on the Spring Hill Redoubt.

Unfortunately for the Franco-Americans, Sergeant Major James Curry of the Charleston Grenadiers overheard the plan and revealed it to the British after he deserted. Prevost at once sent Maitland and a force of regulars to strengthen the Spring Hill Redoubt.

Early in the morning of October 9 Dillon's men began moving toward the Sailor's Gate. They blundered into a swamp, came out into the open and were repulsed by British fire. Dillon ordered a retreat. On the British left Huger made his appointed feint and Prevost calmly ignored it. Thus when d'Estaing and Lincoln sent the main body hurtling toward the Spring Hill Redoubt, the British were braced to receive them.

This they did with a dreadful hail of musketry and interlocking artillery fire which tumbled the American spearheads in heaps. On came the South Carolina Continentals led by the "Swamp Fox," Lieutenant Colonel Francis Marion. They reached the redoubt's parapet. Two officers raised their flag and were shot down. Another officer met a similar fate, and Sergeant Jaspar, who had bravely rescued the flag at Fort Moultrie, attempted it again at Savannah and was killed.

With Americans and French now milling wildly about outside the redoubt, Maitland launched a counterattack. The redcoats rushed from their fort and fell upon the enemy with fury. But they could not break them. A savage hand-to-hand fight raged for an hour, until the allies were finally driven back.

On their left, Count Pulaski and his legion tried to save the day with a cavalry charge. But a crossfire broke them up and the gallant Polish nobleman was himself killed. That was the end of the attempt to storm Savannah. D'Estaing refused Lincoln's plea to continue the siege operations. Stunned by losses of about 250 dead and 600 wounded, against British casualties of about 150, he re-embarked his troops and sailed away.

The French had failed a second time, to' the great delight of the British and growing numbers of Southern Tories, and to the deep dismay of Washington entering winter quarters at Morristown for a second time.

Nothing in the history of the trials of the Continental Army, not even the ordeal of Valley Forge, compares to the cold white crucible of that second winter at Morristown. It was so cold that New York Harbor froze over. Howling blizzards lashed Morristown. Often officers as well as men were buried beneath deep drifts after the wind had blown their pitiful ragged tents away. Other soldiers without tents or blankets, barefoot and half-naked, struggled to build rude huts out of the oak and maple trees around them.

"We have never experienced a like extremity at any period of the war," Washington wrote, and soon he was complaining that his men lived off "every kind of horse food but hay." Another day he wrote: "We have not at this day one ounce of meat, fresh or salt, in the magazine."[107]

Food supplies grew scantier rather than more abundant. And once again, while the Continentals suffered and died, the countryside waxed fat and flourished. Washington's only choice was to commandeer supplies, and just as he feared, he was hated for it. The situation was summed up by Alexander Hamilton, who wrote: "We begin to hate the country for its neglect of us. The country begin to hate us for our oppressions of them."[108]

As the Continentals suffered, Congress struggled with the evil which was the chief cause of their misery: runaway inflation.

On the one hand there was a shortage of goods because of the British naval blockade and a boycott of British manufactures. On the other there was a demand aggravated by the requirements of the armed forces. Into this situation came unscrupulous merchants and speculators: the one raising prices again and again, the other "cornering" articles in short supply and controlling the market for them. Washington hated these wreckers of the American economy with a white-hot ferocity and he once wrote: "I would to God that one of the most attrocious of each State was hung in Gibbets upon a gallows five times as high as the one prepared by Haman. No punishment in my opinion is too great for the man who can build his greatness upon his Country's ruin."[109] But there was no way that Congress could check profiteers from amassing huge private fortunes. In rage, the Continentals blinked at the opulence of bloated rich men; starving, they heard of dinners in Philadelphia at which as many as 169 different dishes were served. Paid in Continental dollars, the army might have found it cheaper to wear or eat that nearworthless paper.

Paper currency was perhaps the chief cause of inflation. Not only Congress but every one of the 13 states had its own issue. The states refused Congress's plea to cease printing, and some even passed laws protecting their paper money. As a result, the paper printed by Congress became less and less acceptable. Congress had to print more and more currency in larger and larger denominations. Because there was little gold to back up this paper blizzard, the value of the Continental dollar fell. In 1776 four Continental dollars were worth one in gold, but by the end of 1779 the ratio was as high as 100 to one, and the phrase "not worth a Continental" was born.

In desperation, Congress repudiated the dollar, declaring on March 15, 1780, that 40 Continental dollars equaled one in gold. By this step Congress wiped out $200 million in debt, but it worsened the plight of the small wage-earner and the Continental soldier, who was paid in Continental paper.

If he had unwisely hoarded his meager pay, he was ruined. If he tried to buy anything with such money, he was rebuffed by farmers and merchants who demanded hard coin, or else twice as much as he thought his money was worth. Thus, as Washington wrote, "The long and great sufferings of this army is unexampled in history,"[110] and a Loyalist poet could confidently predict:

> Mock-money and mock-states shall melt away,
> And the mock troops disband for want of pay.[111]

As the campaign of 1780 opened, he looked like a true prophet.

17

☆

As the year 1780 began, Sir Henry Clinton moved to subjugate the South.

He still believed, with Lord Germain, that the South was Toryland. With Georgia now restored to the Crown, using Savannah as a base, he planned to conquer the Carolinas, then Virginia, after which, with his army augmented by a huge influx of Tories, he would reduce the Northern provinces. If he could not conquer the North, he could at least save the South for the Crown.

To begin, Clinton chose Charleston where he had begun before and failed. He arrived there on February 11 with 6,000 regulars and his second-in-command, Lord Cornwallis. Clinton moved slowly. Not until March 7 did he begin to erect batteries on the west bank of the Ashley River opposite the town.

Clinton's delay seemed a godsend to his opponent, Benjamin Lincoln. He began drawing all available troops into Charleston. Even the reinforcements sent south by Washington were quartered there. In the end this was a disastrous decision. About 5,000 men representing the American Army in South Carolina had been placed inside a noose.

Clinton, whose strength had risen to 10,000 men, began drawing the noose tight. Holding the Ashley River south of the town, he extended his line to the Cooper north of it. Then he moved to cut off communications by sea and by land. By sea, the British fleet took advantage of a thunderstorm to run past the once fearful batteries on Fort Moultrie; by land, the bold and brutal cavalry leader, Colonel Banastre Tarleton, routed a small force of American horse and militia which held Lincoln's communications open 30 miles up the Cooper. With his siege works inching ever closer to Charleston, Clinton at last began raining cannon balls and red-hot shot on the city. Haddrell's Point on the waterfront was carried on April 18 and the invincible Fort Moultrie fell on May 6. On May 8 Clinton called upon Lincoln to surrender. He refused, and Clinton's batteries began taking Charleston apart preparatory to an all-out assault. On May 12 Lincoln surrendered.

It was a dreadful defeat, a mass surrender of some 5,500 men, not to be equaled in the history of United States arms until the capitulation on Bataan in 1942.

Clinton made wise use of his victory. He turned a deaf ear to the clamoring of Tories eager for rebel blood and turned to the wholesale granting of pardons and paroles. His policy was so successful that more than 2,000 men volunteered to fight for the King, provided they served against Frenchmen or Spaniards, and a British officer observed: "The most violent Rebels are candid enough to allow the game is up."[112] And then Colonel Tarleton delivered what appeared to be the knockout blow.

His American legion of mounted Tories defeated a force of American cavalry under Colonel Abraham Buford. After the Americans were driven together in a mass, with white flag flying and arms grounded, the Tories fell upon them with sword and bayonet. That was "Tarleton's Quarter," a byword for the slaughter of surrendered men; yet it seemed to have stamped out the last sparks of opposition.

Sir Henry Clinton sailed back to New York leaving Cornwallis in charge. His Lordship took objective after objective at his leisure. He drove the patriots underground and Marion and Thomas Sumter into the swamps. South Carolina seemed a sure quarry, until the Tories got out of hand.

They started taking revenge for years of ill treatment, and because the state's Loyalists and patriots were evenly divided, nothing less than a civil war began in South Carolina. Men shot at each other in the woods and on the streets of towns. It was death by ambush, not face-to-face confrontations. Long after the war a magistrate boasted that he had shot down 99 Tories in cold blood and regretted that peace had prevented him from rounding out the score. And as Cornwallis's campaign began running into difficulty, word was received that the unabashed rebels were hurrying a force south to contest him.

At first it was the huge, ascetic Baron de Kalb who galloped south to collect and rally the scattered Americans. But because he was a foreigner who had no influential friends in Congress, someone else was sought as over-all commander in the South. Washington preferred Nathanael Greene, but Congress chose Horatio Gates.

Gates took over from de Kalb supremely confident. Fortune did seem to be smiling upon him. First, 3,000 Southern militia had swelled his command to 5,000 men, more than twice the number Cornwallis led. Second, as he advanced south rebels-turned-Tory turned rebel again. Third, he had heard that Cornwallis had returned to Charleston leaving Lord Rawdon in command at Camden. Gates decided to force a battle at Camden. His force was to begin marching to the attack at ten o'clock on the night of August 15. Before they did, they dined on half-cooked meat and half-baked bread with a dessert made of corn meal mush mixed with a medicinal molasses that turned out to be a physic. "Instead of enlivening our spirits," said Sergeant Major Seymour, it "served to purge us as well as if we had taken jallap."[113] So they moved out on a sullen sultry moonless night, the men constantly breaking ranks to relieve themselves. Before they met the enemy, they were sick and weary.

Cornwallis, who had returned to Camden, was also moving—toward Gates. The two forces met in an open pine forest between two swamps. Tarleton's Tories charged the American cavalry and drove them back, only to be repulsed themselves. Both sides awaited daylight. With it, the British light infantry assaulted the American left. It was the scarlet regular with his bayonet against the ragged militiaman with his musket, and the militia broke and ran.

They unmasked the left flank of de Kalb's Continentals on the American right, and the huzzaing British poured through the hole and struck de Kalb's rear. No braver fight was ever fought by the Continentals. Men from Maryland and Delaware rallied around their gigantic leader. De Kalb's horse was shot from under him, and he fought on foot. A saber laid his head open; he fought on.

As he did, Gates tried to rally the militia running away without their weapons. He failed, and fled himself. De Kalb battled on, still confident of victory. Cornwallis hurled his entire force of about 2,000 against this valiant band of 600. De Kalb called for a bayonet charge. Cheering, the Americans nearly burst the wall of scarlet surrounding them. Ball after ball staggered de Kalb. With his last stroke he cut down a British soldier, and then fell dying from 11 wounds.

That was the end at Camden, and it was also the end of the American Army career of General Horatio Gates. Before Gates stopped flying he had reached Hillsboro, North Carolina, 240 miles from the battlefield. No general ever fled his army more precipitately. "It does admirable credit to the activity of a man at his time of life,"[114] Alexander Hamilton jeered.   To the British victories at Charleston and Camden was added Tarleton's resounding defeat of General Sumter two days later. The South appeared lost to the rebel cause, and as the year 1780 turned toward fall, Benedict Arnold in the North was preparing to sell the Hudson River to the enemy.

Benedict Arnold loved money. He also loved beautiful Peggy Shippen, the fair friend of Captain John André and other British officers. Unlike some of her friends, Peggy had escaped ostracism when the patriots returned to Philadelphia in 1778. Because Peggy's father would not let her wear Turkish bloomers she had missed the Mischianza, and since nonattendance at that gala farewell to Sir William Howe had been made the test of loyalty, Peggy was acceptable to the Americans.

Above all to Major General Arnold, now in command in Philadelphia. On April 8, 1779, Arnold married Peggy and brought her to live with him in the Penn house surrounded by elegance and a staff of liveried servants. Such opulence was beyond a general's salary, and Arnold was already accused of using his position to make money. He was also awaiting court-martial on those old charges of misuse of public funds. Moreover, Arnold, probably the most capable field commander on the American side, had been repeatedly passed over for promotion and had been personally snubbed by Washington for having the effrontery to hold a lavish party at Valley Forge.

To a man of Arnold's hot and haughty temperament insults and snubs always rankled. Moreover, he liked money and he needed it to keep his Peggy happy, and in May of 1779 he asked a china dealer named Joseph Stansbury to visit his house. Stansbury, though a political trimmer, was secretly sympathetic to the Crown. Stansbury, anticipating a profitable sale to Mrs. Arnold, was astonished when "General Arnold . . . communicated to me, under solemn obligation of secrecy, his intention of offering his services to the commander in chief of the British forces."[115]

Stansbury went to New York and got in touch with none other than John André, now a major and chief of British intelligence. André opened correspondence with Arnold and found, to his dismay, that the American general was no high-minded idealist ready to betray rather than see his country fall under French influence, but rather a hardheaded haggler who wanted his 30 pieces of silver to be very large indeed. André dropped the correspondence.

In 1780 a court-martial found Arnold guilty on two counts and sentenced him to be reprimanded by Washington. Congress confirmed the sentence and Washington carried it out. In May of that year Arnold reopened his correspondence with André. This time he baited the hook with secret documents. André and Clinton, who had returned from Charleston, were impressed. They were delighted when Arnold succeeded in waggling command of West Point from Washington, and they settled down to arrange that vital fort's betrayal to them.

Arnold bargained like a fishwife. He wanted so much per head for every soldier he surrendered to the British. In all, £10,000 and a general's commission would do. Clinton agreed. He sent André to confer with Arnold on the details. André sailed up the Hudson on the sloop-of-war *Vulture* and met Arnold on the west shore below Haverstraw on the night of September 21. Before André could return to the *Vulture,* fire from American batteries drove the sloop downstream.

André, disregarding Clinton's instructions, decided to return to New York by land. He put on civilian clothes and put the documents that would damn Arnold inside his stockings. On September 23 he was captured in Tarrytown. Warned by a bungling though innocent American officer, Arnold left his wife and child and rode breakneck to his barge on the Hudson. He was rowed to the *Vulture,* to whose skipper he surrendered his enraged rowers.

Washington arrived at Arnold's headquarters a bare hour after the traitor's flight. In rage and in sorrow, he was able to take the precautions guaranteeing West Point. He tried to capture Arnold, but failed. So he ordered Major André hanged.

Clinton tried to dissuade him. André was the only officer for whom this cold commander had any affection, and he made every effort to save him. But Washington was adamant. He could not forget what had happened to Nathan Hale, and André went to his death with great composure.

The British kept their part of the bargain. They made Arnold a brigadier general, awarded him £6,315 even though he had failed to deliver the fort, plus a yearly pension of £500 for his wife, £100 for each of his children, and in 1798, after service against the French, 13,000 acres of land in Upper Canada (the Ontario Peninsula).

Arnold served his new masters well, even though he was never popular with them. They had bought an able traitor, but they felt uneasy about breaking bread with him.

18

☆

There was one ray of light during that dark summer of 1780, although some patriots found it too painfully bright.

The Count Vergennes, evidently convinced that the Americans could not beat Britain by themselves, sent the patriots one form of assistance that they did not desire: troops. Some 5,000 soldiers under the veteran Comte de Rochambeau began landing at Newport on July 12, and many patriots who had hoped to win their freedom themselves felt rebuked by the presence of white-coated Bourbon soldiers on American soil.

"I am fond of an alliance," said General Nathanael Greene, "but I wish for the honor of America that liberty may effect her own deliverance. I should like supplies from our friends, but wish to fight all the battles ourselves."[116]

In truth, this was just what the Americans could not do. Washington's own army had not only melted away again; it was living on short rations hardly better than the winter fare at Morristown. An acute shortage of horses and wagons made it impossible for him to do anything but stand on the defensive, while Congress itself was near bankrupt and the country was sunk deep in lethargy. Thus the arrival of the French encouraged the commander in chief, even if he too was reluctant to have a foreigner take Columbia's other hand. Washington hoped that the states would now give him the men and means to strike a knockout blow. But they did not. By the middle of July only about 1,000 men had rallied to the colors. It was not possible to reopen the campaign, and even the ever-hopeful Washington lamented: "I have almost ceased to hope."[117]

The British Navy put a period to that remark. Though it had not been able to intercept the French fleet, it arrived off Newport in numbers sufficient to bottle up the French ships and to render Rochambeau's army inactive for the rest of the year. British warships also blockaded another French fleet and 5,000 more troops in the harbor at Brest.

So the dark summer passed, to be succeeded by a fall made blacker by the treachery of Benedict Arnold, and then the rebel sun rose high again over a Southern eminence called King's Mountain.

After Cornwallis had routed Gates he moved north from Camden to enter North Carolina. Before he left he detached Major Patrick Ferguson to cover his left or inland flank. Ferguson was a remarkable soldier. He had invented a breech-loading rifle which could be fired five or six times a minute, and he was a campaigner fully as arduous and as thorough as the more famous Banastre Tarleton.

However, Ferguson's merciless pillaging of the Carolinas enraged a breed of hardy Scots-Irish frontiersmen dwelling west of the mountains in what is now Tennessee. Hunters and Indian fighters, crackshots with their long-barreled rifles, these horsemen could go on campaign with a blanket, a knife and a bag of parched corn mixed with maple syrup. They were not rebels, but they hated Ferguson, and they were enraged when he told them to cease their opposition lest he cross the mountains to destroy them.

Rather than await their own ruin, they went to meet him. Their numbers swelled to 1,000 by men of similar breed from Virginia and the Carolinas, led by Colonels Isaac Shelley, John Sevier, William Campbell, Charles McDowell and Benjamin Cleveland, they caught up with Ferguson at King's Mountain.

Ferguson had about 1,200 men, all Tories. In fact, Ferguson was the only Britisher present. He believed that he held a strong position atop King's Mountain. It was a level summit about 500 yards long and 70 to 80 yards wide, broadening to 120 yards at its northeast end. Here Ferguson established his camp, defying "God Almighty and all the rebels out of Hell to overcome him."[118]

Up they came, climbing the mountain's steeps in nine parties forming a long narrow horseshoe enclosing Ferguson. "Here they are, boys!" Colonel Campbell shouted at his men at one end of the horseshoe. "Shout like hell, and fight like devils!"[119] The Tories shoved plug bayonets into their musket muzzles and routed Campbell's men with a charge. But the Americans took to the trees and began firing up the slope with deadly accuracy.

So it went: as each American corps burst in upon Ferguson's men to be driven away with bayonets, another struck him elsewhere, and all the while a deadly fire came crackling from the treetops ringing him round. Soon the Tory position was hopeless. Even so, Ferguson would not surrender. Twice he cut down white flags raised into the air, and at last, trying to cut his way out, he was shot from his horse and died with one foot caught in the stirrup.

Now the rebels turned to butchery. They could recognize their enemies—some of them neighbors or relatives—among the Tories, and they called out by name those men known to have killed or plundered patriots. Shouting, "Buford! Buford! Tarleton's Quarter!"[120] they herded the terrified Tories into a knot and scourged them with bullets and bayonets. Campbell rode among them crying, "For God's sake, quit! It's murder to shoot any more!"[121] They were finally restrained, before the victory of King's Mountain was turned into a shameful slaughter.

It was a fine victory. Only 200 Tories sent out earlier on a foraging expedition were able to escape. Hearing of Ferguson's defeat, Cornwallis began backpedaling into South Carolina.

The tide of the war was turning in the South.

19

☆

On New Year's Day 1781 the men of the Pennsylvania Line mutinied at Morristown, killed one of their officers, and began marching on Congress in Philadelphia.

They had not been paid for a year, they were half-naked and starving, and many of them claimed that they had enlisted for three years, not the duration. They were also high on holiday rum.

Anthony Wayne cut short his own New Year's celebration to ride into the Morristown encampment to quell the mutiny. The men told him their quarrel was with Congress. When he persisted, they fired shots over his head. Wayne retorted by tearing his coat open in anguish and daring them to kill him. They replied that they had no desire to hurt any of the Line's officers, and they marched off toward Princeton with guns and baggage.

They were orderly, and they even seized two spies sent into their midst by Clinton and handed them over for trial and execution. From Princeton the mutineers marched to Trenton, where they were met by Joseph Reed, president of the Pennsylvania Council.

Washington, meanwhile, was faced with an agonizing decision. He did not want the mutiny to spread, but he feared that if he used force to halt it—as he wished to do—he might provoke an unfavorable reaction among the rest of the Continental Army units. In the end, by promising part of the back pay and discharging many of the men who claimed three-year enlistments, the problem was settled.

And then the smaller New Jersey Line quartered at Pompton mutinied over similar grievances. This time Washington used force, rather than risk losing his whole army. General Robert Howe and a strong force of New England Continentals surrounded the Jersey mutineers in their huts, paraded them without arms, and singled out the ringleaders. Then twelve of the most guilty mutineers were forced to shoot two of the ringleaders, and the mutiny was quelled.

That was how the New Year began for General Washington, and then, as had happened the previous black fall, there was good news from the South.

Nathanael Greene took command of the ragged Southern army in Charlotte, and promptly broke the biggest rule of the art of war: he divided his forces in the face of a superior foe. By all the accepted maxims this meant that he had given Cornwallis the chance to destroy him in detail, to devour the parts one by one. Greene, however, had the insight to see that classic precepts presume normal situations, and the situation in North Carolina was far from normal.

Greene knew that his tatterdemalions could not meet Cornwallis's regulars, who outnumbered them 4,000 to 3,000. Yet he could not risk a demoralizing retreat. Better, then, to divide his army in two and send each part to operate against the British flanks while irregulars such as Marion and Sumter struck his rear. Thus divided they could live off the country and be mobile enough to elude the equipment-heavy British.

One detachment under Daniel Morgan was to move west from Charlotte while the other under Isaac Huger, accompanied by Greene, would move east. If Cornwallis in the center lunged to his right, he would unmask Camden and the town of Ninety Six to Morgan on his left. If he struck at Morgan on his left, Greene could dash downcoast to Charleston. Cornwallis saw this, and he realized that he too must divide his forces. Banastre Tarleton with about 1,100 men went galloping west to dispose of Morgan, and on January 17, 1781, the two small armies collided at Cowpens.

Daniel Morgan chose to fight in what looked like a trap. He held a plain dotted with widely spaced trees in which Tarleton's superior horsemen could easily maneuver, and he had his back to the Broad River. But the Old Wagoner knew his men. If he secured his wings on swamps, as he said later, his militia would have vanished through the bogs, and if he crossed the river, half of them would abandon him. He wanted no hope of retreat, so that his men would fight the dreaded Tarleton with the desperation of the doomed, and he was certain that his dashing enemy would charge straight ahead rather than nibble at his exposed wings.

So Morgan put about 150 picked riflemen forward in a skirmish line. About 150 yards behind them were about 300 militia under Andrew Pickens, and back another 150 yards on the crest of a hill was his main line of about 400 Continentals under John Howard. Again to the rear, behind another hill, were about 100 horse under the fat but capable William Washington, the cavalryman who had been wounded at Trenton.

The sharpshooters in front were not to open fire until the enemy was within 50 yards, and then they were to aim at "the men with the epaulets." They were to deliver two volleys, and then fall back on Pickens's militia. The militia were then to fire only two volleys, before retiring around the American left to the rear of the main line on the hill, there to re-form as a reserve. Morgan promised them they would be perfectly safe. He also informed every man of his plan so that no one would be alarmed at the withdrawals.

Tarleton came on. His legion cavalry rode at the sharpshooters. A scathing fire sent 15 riderless horses off the field, and the Tory cavalry fled, never to be induced to re-enter the battle. Now the main British line moved forward, dragoons on either wing. Here was the crux of battle. If the militia showed their customary reaction to bared British steel, they would flee. But Pickens's men stayed, firing and loading and firing again to send two volleys into the scarlet line. Then they began running to the left as planned, to get behind the Continentals on the hill. The militia on the right had the farthest to go, and the British dragoons came thundering down on them.

Suddenly out of the American right rear Washington's horsemen came riding. They fell upon the astonished dragoons with whistling sabers, routing and pursuing them while all Pickens's men gained the rear and re-formed.

But the impetuous British had taken Pickens's retirement to mean the start of the customary retreat, and they came shouting against the main line of Howard's Continentals. Kneeling on the hill, the Americans poured a plunging fire into the enemy. Still, the British advanced. Tarleton put his Highlanders on his left. They stretched beyond the American right. Howard saw that he was being outflanked. He called for his right-hand company to face about. Then they were to wheel and form a right angle to the main line and face about again to blunt the British flanking movement.

But they faced about and marched to the rear, and the whole line followed suit.

Morgan came rushing up to Howard, shouting, "What is this retreat?"

"A change of position to save my right flank," Howard replied.

"Are you beaten?" the Old Wagoner yelled, and Howard shot back scornfully: "Do men who march like that look as though they were beaten?"[122] Morgan nodded, and dashed off to find Howard's men a second position between the two hills.

Tarleton, sensing victory, pursued. His men broke ranks and rushed forward. William Washington, whose pursuit of the dragoons had carried him ahead of the American lines, saw the British confusion. He sent word to Morgan: "They're coming on like a mob. Give them one fire, and I'll charge them."[123] Morgan gave the order to the Continentals; they faced about and blazed away from the hip. The scarlet line crumpled and Howard cried: "Give them the bayonet!"[124] So it was that an American cheer and American blades went forward, just as Washington's cavalry burst upon the enemy flank and rear like a tornado. After that Pickens's re-formed militia struck the Highlanders down, and the Battle of Cowpens was over but for an individual and inconclusive mounted skirmish between Tarleton and Washington.

Banastre Tarleton himself rode off, his brilliant plumed helmet drooping in a defeat that was nearly total: nine-tenths of his force had been killed or captured, against only 12 Americans killed and 60 wounded.

Cowpens was the American Cannae, it was the glittering small gem of the Revolution, and it was brought off by an American backwoodsman who, like the great Hannibal himself, was merely adapting himself to men and terrain. Moreover, Cowpens made the way of the wary Nathanael Greene easier as he waged his war of attrition against Cornwallis. No one described the war he fought better than

So it went, as the American Army moved like an infuriating wraith before the pursuing Cornwallis. First, the enraged earl tried to catch Morgan, but the Old Wagoner rejoined Greene. Together, they withdrew into Virginia. Nearly exhausted, his little army dwindled to 1,900 men, Cornwallis gave chase. Greene recrossed the border, gathering forces until he had 4,400 men under his command. On March 15 Greene met Cornwallis at Guilford Courthouse, employing a line of battle similar to Morgan's at the Cowpens. British bravery and skill routed Greene's militia and broke his first two lines, and Greene wisely withdrew, having so badly mauled Cornwallis that he was compelled to fall back on Wilmington 200 miles south.

Lord Rawdon now took up the pursuit of Greene. He caught him, beat him but could not crush him at Hobkirk's Hill on April 25. Rawdon also was forced to withdraw after Marion cut his line of communications, and Greene took his army to the High Hills of Santee to pass the dreadful Carolina summer in comparatively cool surroundings. Then, on September 8, he met the British again at Eutaw Springs in South Carolina. The Americans had the battle won, and would have won it had they not fallen upon supplies of rum in the camp of the routed British. Re-forming, the British snatched the victory out of Greene's fingers.

But they had not beaten him. Greene had suffered tactical loss after tactical loss but had carried out his strategy. He had actually forced Cornwallis to abandon South Carolina and to march into Virginia instead, where he joined forces with Benedict Arnold and Phillips.

Thus was laid the foundation for the conclusive victory of the Revolution. Lord Cornwallis, steadily gathering his Virginia forces until they numbered 7,200 men, eventually led them into a little tobacco-trading port named Yorktown.

20

☆

On May 21, 1781, General Washington and Count Rochambeau met in Wethersfield, Connecticut, to plan a summer campaign.

They knew that the French West Indian fleet under Admiral de Grasse was going to be available, and Washington wished to use these ships for an assault upon New York. It was agreed that the Continental and French armies would join above the city to await the fleet's arrival, and a frigate was sent to Haiti to inform de Grasse of this plan.

Unknown to Washington, Rochambeau had privately advised de Grasse that he preferred Chesapeake Bay as an area of operations. To a sailor the Chesapeake was more attractive because it was closer and deeper, and de Grasse agreed with Rochambeau.

Thereafter de Grasse acted with a vigor and vision not always characteristic of a French admiral. He sent the frigate dashing back with word of his own intentions, he procured 3,000 regulars from the island governor, he raised from the governor of Havana the money needed by the Americans, and he took aboard American coast pilots that he had long ago requested from Rochambeau.

De Grasse also did what no British admiral answerable to a mercantile nation would have dared to do: he allowed French merchant ships to sail home unprotected and ordered about 200 others to mark time in Haiti until his return. Then, with his entire fleet of 28 ships of the line, sailing an indirect and less frequented route, he made for the Chesapeake.

In New York, Sir Henry Clinton had intercepted a number of letters from Washington and Rochambeau. From them he learned of the action concerted against New York. Alarmed, he sent to Lord Cornwallis in Virginia for 3,000 troops—and so set in motion the final event of the British campaign in the South.

Between Clinton and Cornwallis there had been almost nothing but dispute since Cornwallis, cheered on by Lord George Germain, had begun acting independently of his superior in New York. The basic difference was that Clinton wanted to campaign in Pennsylvania and Cornwallis preferred Virginia.

After Nathanael Greene and a fratricidal countryside disabused Cornwallis of his hopes of victory in the Carolinas, the earl had hurried to Virginia. There he joined Phillips and Arnold, who had been busy ravaging the Virginia country around the Chesapeake.

Then, after he received Clinton's call for reinforcements, Cornwallis began marching for Portsmouth as the point to embark them. Lafayette, then in Virginia trying to capture Arnold, struck at Cornwallis on July 6 at Green Spring. Cornwallis, always eager to catch "the boy," very nearly did. But darkness saved Lafayette, and the disgruntled earl moved on.

Thereafter he received from Clinton a welter of conflicting orders: first, to send the troops not to New York but to Philadelphia; second, to send them to New York after all; third, to retire to Yorktown on the peninsula between the James and York rivers; fourth, to go to Old Point Comfort instead, but also to fortify Yorktown if necessary; fifth and finally, to keep all the troops himself if he thought that he needed them, but to hurry to New York whatever he could spare.

Cornwallis inspected Old Point Comfort and decided against it in favor of Yorktown, and he went there in August.

Cornwallis considered himself secure so long as Britain controlled the sea. British ships entering Chesapeake Bay had easy access to Yorktown. They could supply him, reinforce him or evacuate him. French ships, of course, could seal off the mouth of the Chesapeake and thus make Yorktown very vulnerable to siege by land. But neither Cornwallis nor Sir Henry Clinton believed this to be likely.

After the French and Continental armies—each about 5,000 strong —had met in July, Washington and Rochambeau made an armed reconnaissance of New York. Washington was dismayed. Clinton's works, defended by 14,000 troops, were far too strong. The American began to think of campaigning in the South. And then, on August 14, came the wonderful news that de Grasse was en route to the Chesapeake with 28 big ships and 3,000 men!

Washington at once fell in with the Chesapeake plan. He dashed off orders to Lafayette to keep Cornwallis cornered in Yorktown. The French squadron in Newport under Admiral de Barras was ordered to the Chesapeake with Rochambeau's siege artillery. It left on August 27, making a wide circuit to avoid the British.

Next, efforts were made to convince Clinton that New York was still the allied objective. Staten Island was made to appear the staging area for an assault. Roads toward it were improved. A party of French in nearby Chatham, New Jersey, began making bake ovens as though for a siege. Leaving 3,000 men above New York, Washington sent 2,000 across the Hudson into New Jersey. The French followed. A leisurely march toward Chatham began. On August 29 the troops were making for Morristown–New Brunswick, and Clinton still believed them bound for Chatham.

But on the next day the Americans and French began marching briskly south toward Chesapeake Bay and Yorktown.

The British knew of de Grasse's departure for the Chesapeake, and the formidable Admiral Sir Samuel Hood had sailed from the West Indies with 14 "liners" to intercept him. Hood took the direct route, and arrived at the bay three days ahead of de Grasse. Poking inside, seeing nothing, Hood withdrew and made for New York, where he joined Admiral Samuel Graves with five liners. Graves, still the indecisive leader he had been at Boston six years ago, was senior to Hood and he took command. He sailed on August 31 for the Chesapeake, hoping to prevent de Barras with Rochambeau's guns from joining de Grasse.

Two days later, Sir Henry Clinton realized with horror that Washington and Rochambeau were after Cornwallis. He could not overtake them by land, and he dared not try the sea without the protection of Admiral Graves.

That commander, meanwhile, was dumfounded to find de Grasse's fleet inside the Chesapeake. Seeing his enemy, de Grasse immediately slipped his cables and stood seaward for battle—parading his ships with slow majesty to impress his strength upon the enemy. With only 19 sail and 1,400 guns against 24 ships and 1,700 guns, Graves knew himself to be overmatched. Still, with the aggressiveness typical of the British Navy, he seized the advantage of being windward of the French, and gave battle.

Graves's directions, however, were as confused as the seamanship of some of his captains, and de Grasse quickly brought his superior firepower to bear. The French mauled five British ships so badly that Graves hauled off. De Grasse kept to sea for five more days, deliberately luring Graves away from the Chesapeake so that de Barras might slip inside. De Barras did, de Grasse joined him, and the British, more badly outnumbered than before, sailed sadly north for New York.

All the way down to the Head of Elk, where Lord Howe had landed four years previously, George Washington had chewed on the question: Where is de Grasse? He had not heard of him since receipt of that letter in mid-August. On September 2 Washington had written Lafayette: ". . . my dear Marquis, I am distressed beyond expression, to know what is become of the Count de Grasse, and for fear the English Fleet, by occupying the Chesapeake . . . should frustrate all our flattering prospects in that quarter."[126]

He still had no word as his Continentals reached Head of Elk and began embarking in boats for Williamsburg on the James. The French, still elated from their wild reception in Philadelphia, followed. As Rochambeau and his elegant aides neared the landing on the Virginia shore they saw a straight tall figure in blue and buff waving his hat wildly, almost capering for joy.

Rochambeau stepped ashore and a beaming Washington rushed up to embrace him. Then French hats went soaring into the air, for Washington had informed them that de Grasse held the Chesapeake, Cornwallis was cut off, 3,000 French reinforcements were already ashore and, in the words of another Virginia general, "we have got him handsomely in a pudding bag."[127]

Without help from the sea, Cornwallis was caught—and he knew it. He had about 700 men across the York River in Gloucester, but they were cooped up and would remain cooped up by a Franco-American force three times their number.

The remaining 6,500 men held a series of fortifications curving around Yorktown on its landward side. On the morning of September 30, to the great surprise of the allies, Cornwallis abandoned his outer redoubts. His reason was that Clinton had written him promising ships to break the blockade and 5,000 troops as reinforcements. Cornwallis thought he could hold out better by concentrating his forces.

The allies, however, quickly occupied the redoubts, and then on October 6 work was begun on the first parallel about 600 yards from the lower end of the town. The trench was to run down to the water's edge. Diggers toiled throughout the night, sweating profusely in that moist heat which had already spread sickness through both camps. Heavy guns were dragged into place, and on October 9 a French battery on the left opened up. Then the American battery on the right began blasting, with Washington firing the first shot, and a British frigate on the York was driven to the Gloucester shore.

On the next night two bigger batteries began roaring. The French set another frigate hopelessly afire, and two transports were destroyed. In all, 52 guns were battering the town, and Cornwallis wrote ominously to Clinton: "We have lost about seventy of our men and many of our works are considerably damaged; with such works on disadvantageous ground, against so powerful an attack we cannot hope to make a very long resistance. P.S. 5 P.M. Since my letter was written (at 12 M.) we have lost thirty men. . . . We continue to lose men very fast."[128]

Clinton and the admirals, meanwhile, had only belatedly begun a rescue operation. But the limitations of New York's dockyards made the work of refitting proceed with agonizing slowness. It was hoped to be ready by October 5, then the 8th . . . the 12th . . . But the 12th passed and the fleet still had not sailed. Clinton was beside himself. At last, on October 17, 7,000 troops were embarked and the ships began dropping down Sandy Hook—only to be forced to wait two more days for favorable winds and tides. In the meantime, some 16,000 French and Americans drew ever closer to Cornwallis's beleaguered 7,000, and a second parallel only 300 yards away from Yorktown was begun by Steuben and his engineers.

As the trench approached the river edge, its builders were raked by fire from two British redoubts close to the water. Washington decided to storm them. The French took the left in a stirring charge, climbing the parapet with cries of *"Vive le Roi!"* and forcing its garrison of Hessians and British to throw down their arms.

Alexander Hamilton led the Americans against the one on the right. Now grown fond of the bayonet, the patriots went at it with unloaded muskets, clawing their way through the abatis, crossing the ditch and leaping over the parapets. From all the British lines came a storm of shells and musket balls. Washington, watching the assault, was cautioned by his aide: "Sir, you are too much exposed here. Had you not better step a little back?"

"Colonel Cobb," Washington replied gravely, "if you are afraid, you have liberty to step back."[129]

And so both redoubts were won, the second parallel was extended down to the river and the second nail driven into the British coffin. On the morning of October 16, Cornwallis sent out a force of 350 men to capture and destroy the batteries in the second parallel. In a brave charge, the British succeeded in entering both positions and in spiking some guns, but they were eventually driven back and the guns restored to service.

So desperate now that he was losing his judgment, Cornwallis attempted a wild escape across the river through Gloucester. He expected to burst through the Franco-American force there and proceed to New York by forced marches. That same midnight he began embarking his troops, but a violent storm broke upon him and forced him back into Yorktown.

That was the end.

In the morning of the 17th, two days before Clinton's relief force made the open sea, the allies opened on the town with a dreadful cannonade. One by one the British works collapsed. There was no answering fire, for the British had exhausted their ammunition. Soon a redcoated drummer boy strode onto a parapet and began to beat a parley. He could not be heard in all that thunder, but he was seen. The guns fell silent and a British officer advanced to be blindfolded and led to Washington.

He asked for a 24-hour armistice. Washington granted him two hours. He returned with Cornwallis's surrender terms, including a condition that his army be paroled to Britain. Washington insisted that the enemy surrender as prisoners of war, and Cornwallis submitted.

At noon of October 19, 1781, the gay military music of the French sang out, and for the last time the vivacious white-coated soldiers of France went into line on American soil. Into line opposite them, moving proudly across trampled fields to the Celtic lilt of fifes and drums, went the tall Americans in brown or hunting shirts and here and there in blue and buff. George Washington rode up on a great bay horse and stood at their right. Across from him Rochambeau and Admiral de Barras sat their horses. To the right of them Yorktown's main sally port was flung open. Faint on the wind came the mournful beat of drums and the melancholy squeal of fifes. Out rode Brigadier General Charles O'Hara. With stupefying bad grace, Cornwallis, pleading illness, had sent a deputy to surrender for him.

Bewildered, O'Hara rode first toward Rochambeau. But the count, by a gracious inclination of the eyes, directed him to Washington. Slightly flustered, O'Hara approached the tall Virginian. Washington indicated General Benjamin Lincoln. Deputy must surrender to deputy, and O'Hara handed over Cornwallis's sword. Lincoln returned it, and called for the surrender to begin.

Out they came, the scarlet-coated British and their Hessian allies brilliant in blue and green. Out came the German mercenaries, striding briskly, stacking their arms neatly, then the British, moving along slowly, their faces sullen, some of them already weeping. Down went their arms in a disorderly crash. Drummer boys stove in their drums, infantrymen smashed their musket butts and stomped on their cartridge cases. Officers pouting like schoolboys avoided the eyes of their captors.

Above the clatter of grounded arms and the hoarse cursing of broken-hearted soldiers rose the music of the British bands bringing the War of the American Revolution to its effective close with the prophetic notes of "The World Turned Upside Down."

PART III

The War of 1812

1

☆

When the news of Yorktown reached Lord North in London, he shuddered as though shot, threw his arms wide and cried: "O God, it is all over!"[1]

It was indeed, although fighting sputtered on for another year, chiefly on the western borders. On March 20, 1782, North's ministry fell, to be replaced by a Whig government eager to end the war. Even though the British naval victory in the Battle of the Saints in the following April served to retrieve British prestige, while weakening Franco-American bargaining power, the Whigs still sought peace at almost any price.

On January 20, 1783, hostilities ceased between Great Britain and the United States. In Paris, meanwhile, peace commissioners worked out an agreement to restore Minorca and the Floridas to Spain, cede Tobago in the West Indies and Senegal in Africa to France, and leave the United States free west to the Mississippi, north to Canada and south to the Floridas. On September 3, 1783, the Peace of Paris formally brought the War of the Revolution to an end, and on November 23 the British Army sailed home from New York.

To the astonishment of the world, Britain's upstart daughter had humbled her powerful mother. But now, confident in its knowledge of the natural history of revolutions, the world settled down in supercilious expectation of Yankee collapse. If the Confederation did not go the dissolving way of all unions pasted together by the mere exigencies of war, then some man on horseback—General Washington, perhaps?—would certainly establish a military dictatorship.

But General Washington had already squelched the one occasion in American history on which the military acted as though it sought political power. That had been in the winter of 1782-83, when the officers of the Continental Army encamped at Newburgh, New York, asked Congress for what was actually the barest relief of financial distress caused by war service and inflation. Congress refused, and the officers flew into a rage. There appeared two inflammatory papers known as the Newburgh Addresses and believed to have been written by Major John Armstrong, an aide of General Gates and a close friend of the ubiquitous Major James Wilkinson.

The Newburgh Addresses told the officers "that the slightest mark of indignity from Congress now must operate like the grave and part you forever; that, in any political event, the army has its alternative."[2] Should peaceful measures fail, the author continued, the army could march to the west and defy Congress.

To Washington this was at best mutiny, at worst insurrection. He met the challenge by making a surprise personal appearance in the hall where the angry officers had gathered. He appealed to their patriotism and explained the difficulties in which Congress found itself. Then, with a deft, sure touch characteristic of the leader who had guided this ragtail army through eight despairing years, he began to read a letter, paused—and drew a pair of spectacles from his pocket. The officers were surprised. They had not known that Washington's sight was failing. "Gentlemen," he explained, "you will permit me to put on my spectacles, for I have not only grown gray, but almost blind, in the service of my country."[3] Overcome, with many of them openly weeping, the officers voted to leave their problems in Washington's hands. Eventually he persuaded Congress to grant pensions acceptable to officers and men alike.

At the outset, then, the danger of military despotism was avoided and the new American nation was saved by the one man who could have killed it. The second danger—that the jealous bickering of 13 sovereign states would tear the fabric of Confederation apart—was less immediate though probably more grave.

Through the Articles of Confederation and the fact that Congress had simply seized the reins of government, the United States had been able to wage successful war. But the problems of government remained, chief among them the question of how to induce the states to surrender enough of their sovereignty so that all might be served by a single national government. The Articles did not supply the answer. They denied Congress the vital taxing power and they could not be amended without unanimous consent. In a union already divided by the sectionalism of North versus South and beset by the mutual distrust of large and small states, unanimity was not possible. Congress, being a new government, overawed no one. In fact, it was held in wide contempt. Driven from Philadelphia in June, 1783, by mutineers of the Pennsylvania Line, it wandered like a waif from Princeton to Annapolis to Trenton and finally, in 1785, to New York. Two years later Congress's basic weakness was laid bare by the rising of Massachusetts farmers known as Shays' Rebellion.

A sound money policy supported by heavy taxes had left the Bay State's farmers destitute. Farms and cattle were sold to satisfy court judgments for taxes or debts. The farmers tried to stop the courts from sitting, and they set up committees of correspondence, just as the leaders of the Revolution had acted against Parliament. But now these leaders were conducting the state government and they threatened the farmers with the gallows. The farmers paid no heed. They grew stronger and more aggressive and they called upon Daniel Shays, a distinguished soldier of the Revolution, to lead them. Shays tried to prevent the Supreme Court from sitting at Springfield, and it was here that his attack on both the courthouse and the Confederation arsenal was shattered by artillery fired by loyal state militia. After a few more, lesser defeats, Shays fled to Vermont. Massachusetts wisely treated his followers with clemency, and a newly elected legislature moved to alleviate their hardships.

Nevertheless, Shays' Rebellion alarmed the nation, delighting those Tories who saw in it the first crack in the American façade. Massachusetts had appealed to Congress for help, and Congress had been able to do nothing. Even those Americans who had feared the formation of a strong national government now favored revision of the Articles of Confederation. On May 25, 1787, the Constitutional or Federal Convention convened in Philadelphia for this "sole and express purpose."

The Founding Fathers of the United States (only four of fifty-five Convention delegates were sixty or over) did not so much revise the old Articles as devise an entirely new government as set forth in the Constitution. Congress received taxing and other important powers and was expanded from a single chamber into a House of Representatives elected by the people and a Senate selected by the more conservative state legislatures. A strong executive power vested in a President was also provided, as well as a Supreme Court.

Thus was born the American system of the division of powers—legislative, executive and judicial—acting as checks and balances on each other. In Congress the people as manifested by the popularly elected House was balanced against property as expressed by the Senate. Civilian control of the military was guaranteed by making the President commander in chief, and the President in turn was checked by giving the House the power to determine the size of the armed forces. Finally, excesses by either legislative or executive powers could be checked by a Supreme Court empowered to interpret the Constitution.

In four months, then, these political carpenters raised a stout roof over the new nation. They wrote a Constitution which, intended to serve 4 million people and 13 states for a generation, still guides 249 million Americans and 50 states while remaining, after the tests of nearly two centuries, one of the triumphs of practical politics. Above all, these men were practical. They were not doctrinaires, like the French and Russian revolutionaries who eventually replaced old tyrannies with new ones. They were experienced in the arts of self-rule. "Experience must be our only guide," John Dickinson told the Convention, "reason may mislead us."[4] And so these supreme realists proclaimed the rule of law, making no attempt to reconcile such irreconcilables as freedom and authority, populace and property, but rather balancing the one against the other so that neither might gain a clear ascendancy to establish either extreme of anarchy or oligarchy.

The Constitution was adopted, and on September 13, 1788, the Continental Congress passed the resolution ending its own life and putting the new govenment into operation. The First Congress was chosen, and then the presidential electors who made George Washington their unanimous choice. On April 30, 1789, Washington was inaugurated in New York.

The form of government which, in all its fundamental characteristics still governs the United States of America, had entered history.

The new government began life without money or an administrative system, with no navy or marine corps, an army down to 672 officers and men—and with war clouds still hovering over the horizon.

Britain had not withdrawn from her seven northwest posts as she had promised. Rather, after dividing Canada into the provinces of Lower and Upper Canada* (modern Quebec and Ontario), she planted Upper Canada's seat of government at Fort Niagara on the American side of the border. Britain also continued to sell arms to those Indians who were one of the young Republic's chief enemies.

To counteract British influence in the Northwest, the United States proposed to build a fort on the Maumee River. In 1791 about 2,000 men—the entire American Army—marched toward the Maumee under General Arthur St. Clair. The Indians, believing the fort aimed at them, prepared an ambush. St. Clair blundered into it and was put to rout with casualties of more than 900 men.

Elated, the Indians boasted that they would drive the "long knives" back across the Ohio. Britain encouraged them, for Britain hoped to block American expansion with an Indian buffer state. In the meantime, while the House of Representatives began an investigation which ended in placing the blame for the defeat on no one, the United States began to suffer at sea.

Without a navy to protect them, American merchant ships in the Mediterranean had fallen prey to the pirates of the Barbary Coast. Captured American seamen were held for ransom. Until it was paid they languished in prisons or toiled in chains at the oars of Algerian war galleys. Congress, forced to choose between war or tribute, talked belligerently of reviving the Navy but actually did nothing. Then it appropriated $54,000 to ransom the sailors at $2,000 a head and appointed John Paul Jones to negotiate a treaty of tribute with the Dey of Algiers. Fortunately for Jones's honor, he died before he could complete his ignominious mission; unfortunately for the seamen, they were to suffer many more years in captivity before the Republic at last faced up to the war-or-tribute decision.

Meanwhile, the first ripples of the tidal wave unleashed by the French Revolution of 1789 were lapping at American shores. American sympathy for their republican brothers in France rose to near-hysterical devotion after the French decreed "a war of all peoples against all kings." That was in 1793, the same year in which Britain and the French Republic went to war. Love for France thereupon

* "Upper" or "Lower" Canada then did not relate to north or south but "up" or "down" the St. Lawrence and the Great Lakes chain. Thus "upper" was actually western and "lower" was eastern.

became synonymous with hatred for England, especially after British naval vessels began seizing American ships with cargoes bound for France. Britain claimed that any enemy property was good prize, whether or not it was carried in a neutral ship. The Americans countered with the principle, "Free ships make free goods." Actually, the debate was academic; Britain had no intention of allowing America to supply her French enemy, and she had the ships to prevent it.

A war clamor arose in America. Washington, determined to avoid foreign entanglement, sent John Jay to Britain to prevent war, and also to persuade the British to evacuate the Northwest forts. In the meantime, however, Upper Canada had built a new fort on the Maumee in what is now northwest Ohio. Indians, grown confident since their defeat of St. Clair, were encouraged to attack American settlements. They did, and Washington called on Anthony Wayne to restrain them.

Wayne spent the winter of 1793-94 at Greenville, Ohio, which he had named for his old friend, Nathanael Greene. In the spring of 1794 he moved out with a force of perhaps 2,500 men, regulars whom he had personally trained, as well as a few hundred mounted Kentucky riflemen. The Indians, between 1,500 and 2,000 from a half-dozen different tribes, retreated back toward the Canadian fort. They turned to fight at Fallen Timbers, a wide swath which a tornado had cut in the woods northwest of present-day Defiance. Hidden among twisted trunks and branches, the savages were all but invisible. But the Americans in four columns marked by the white, red, yellow or green plumes of their officers' hats were unmistakable targets.

On August 20 the battle began with a charge of American dragoons against the Indian left. White horsehair plumes flying, sabers glittering, the mounted Americans galloped through an intense fire, leaped the timber barricades and fell upon the enemy with flashing steel. On the right, infantry and riflemen fired one volley and charged with the bayonet. It was over in less than an hour. The Indians, as they admitted later, "could not stand up against the sharp ends of the guns."[5]

Thus the critical year of 1794 was crowned with American military success. The prestige of the national government rose higher in 1795 as the Indians ceded the southeastern corner of the Northwest Territory, together with Vincennes, Detroit and the site of Chicago; it soared again in 1796 when the British withdrew from the Northwest forts.

Federalism, however, had reached its high-water mark. The rival theories of Alexander Hamilton and Thomas Jefferson had come out into the open and clashed, and in that collision political parties and the American two-party system were born. Hamilton's Federalists believed in an industrial America run by men of wealth and talent, while Jefferson's Republicans rallied under the standard of agrarianism and democracy. It was rule-by-the-best versus rule-by-the-most. The Federalists, political parents of today's Republicans, were realist and empiricist and they mistrusted the people; the Republicans, from whom the modern Democrats have descended, were idealist and rationalist and they trusted the people too much. Actually, the differences between the parties were never so distinct, shaded as they were by local rivalries and religious, racial and social disparities. But they were crystallized in 1794 when the war between Britain and France found the Federalists opting for Britain's conservative society and the Republicans backing republican France.

That war had repercussions in America, after John Adams became President by a narrow margin and took office in 1797. By then the French Revolution had been drowned in the blood bath of the Reign of Terror and the French Directory had become the arrogant afflictor of the Western world. Its armies, led by that very Napoleon Bonaparte who eventually destroyed the Directory and made France his own, had been victorious everywhere. Of all the Western nations, only Britain, Russia and the United States had not come to terms with France. Cheered on by the Republicans, the French fell upon the American merchant fleet with a ferocity that made previous British spoliations seem comparatively gentle. Distressed, Adams sent a mission to Paris.

It was received coldly. Foreign Minister Talleyrand sent a trio of minor officials (identified only as Monsieurs X, Y and Z) to inform the Americans that negotations would only be opened after a $250,-000 bribe had been paid to Talleyrand, and a $10 million loan be granted to France. News of the XYZ Affair enraged America and rocked the Republicans; the rallying cry of "Millions for defense but not one cent for tribute" provided support for President Adams's policy of armed neutrality.

The policy actually was nothing less than declaration of a naval war with France. Congress revived the Navy and Marine Corps, expanded the Army, and sent such famous ships as the *United States, Constellation* and *Constitution* swaying down the ways. These and other warships were authorized to capture French armed vessels wherever they might be found, and in actual battle they gave far more than they got. Meanwhile, the Army prepared to repulse an anticipated French invasion of America. George Washington put on his sword again to command this force of 3,000 men, which he found to be a distasteful motley of "the riff-raff of the country and the scape-gallows of the large cities." Fortunately, the British Navy bottled up Napoleon in Egypt and there was no French invasion. In 1799 the French government turned conciliatory and the Naval War with France quietly entered history.

The following year the Federalists lost power, never to regain it. Federalist intolerance as exemplified by the Alien and Sedition Acts —attempts to persecute the foreign-born and curb criticism—helped to establish Thomas Jefferson and his Republicans in office.

In Jefferson, the United States got a President eager to save money by cutting back the armed forces, although it was he who founded the Military Academy at West Point and although within a few months of his inauguration the U.S. Navy had found its true battle birth in the wars with the Barbary pirates.

By 1801 the United States had paid Morocco, Algiers, Tunis and Tripoli—the Moslem states of the Barbary Coast—$2 million in ransom for captured seamen and in tribute to allow American ships to sail the Mediterranean unharmed. In May of that year the Pasha of Tripoli declared war on America in an attempt to squeeze more tribute money out of her.

To everyone's surprise the pacifist Jefferson responded by rebuilding the Navy which had done so well in the Naval War with France and which he had almost personally scrapped. It did not immediately spring into being, but by 1804 Commodore Edward Preble was able to appear off Tripoli with a task force built around the *Constitution*. Preble shelled the Pasha's fortress. Unfortunately, the frigate *Philadelphia* was grounded on a reef off Tripoli. The Pasha imprisoned its crew, and floated the frigate free preparatory to making use of it himself.

It was then that young Stephen Decatur slipped into the harbor at night, boarding and capturing the *Philadelphia* and setting her hopelessly afire. And as the Pasha's naval ambitions went up in flames, he was assailed on his landward flank by one of the most implacable haters in American history.

William Eaton, the American consul at Tunis, writhed under the shame of the tribute. The author of perhaps the angriest and most anguished reports in State Department annals, he could write: ". . . recall me, and send a *slave* accustomed to abasement to represent the nation."[6] Convinced that the French consul in Tunis was in cahoots with the Bey "to milk the United States of every pailful of tribute the docile republic might yield,"[7] he denounced him in the presence of the consuls of Sweden and Great Britain and then publicly horsewhipped him in a Tunis street.

Eaton also hated the Pasha of Tripoli, who had usurped his brother on the throne, and he proposed to put the brother, Hamet, back in power on condition of his friendship for the United States.

Hamet agreed, and Eaton with the approval of the American naval commander in the Mediterranean station began rounding up his "army." It was commanded by Lieutenant Presley O'Bannon of the Marines and included 6 or 7 other marines, a naval midshipman, 40 Greeks, 100 of the flotsam of Europe and Asia coughed up on the shores of the Levant, a squadron of mounted Arabs under Hamet Pasha and a fleet of camels. Eaton's plan was to march from Alexandria to Derna 500 miles away, and then to advance on Tripoli another 500 miles westward. On March 6, 1805, the march began. It was a dreadful ordeal: burning sands and brazen sun by day, cold and sometimes mutiny by night. Eaton and O'Bannon drove their motley forward. On April 27 they attacked Derna. Three American brigs bombarded the city from the sea, while O'Bannon led a charge on the fort. It fell, and for the first time Old Glory flew over an Old World fortress.

But the formidable Eaton was not to complete his design. A highly chastened Pasha had requested peace and been granted generous terms. His captives were ransomed, his tribute was continued and his city of Derna evacuated. Chagrined and embittered, Eaton resigned from the service of his country. Yet the War with Tripoli had taught the Barbary powers to respect the U.S. Navy and the American flag. Perhaps more important in a military way, the exploits of Eaton and O'Bannon lived on in the annals of the Marine Corps. O'Bannon's charge on the shores of Tripoli was commemorated in the first stanza of the Marines' hymn, as well as in the hilt and blade of a Marine officer's sword, and it embarked his Corps on its long career of victory and valor.

The war, then, was a success, even if the Barbary bribery was to continue until 1816; and to this military achievement the unmilitary Mr. Jefferson, who also detested the shifting diplomacies of Europe, was to add in 1803 the diplomatic coup of the Louisiana Purchase. Derided as it was at the time, the purchase of the Louisiana Territory for $15 million from Napoleon (who had secretly recovered it from Spain) was a stupendous event which advanced the American frontier to the Rocky Mountains. Out of this huge province came four new states and parts of nine others, and with the Union already expanded to 17 states through admission of Vermont, Kentucky, Tennessee and Ohio, the continental expansion of the United States was already in full career not 15 years after Washington had taken his first oath of office. In 1805 its advance parties penetrated to the Western Ocean, when Captain Meriwether Lewis and Lieutenant William Clark made their overland expedition to and from the Pacific.

So much territory, as loosely defended as it was loosely defined, naturally attracted the attention of adventurers—chief among them former Vice President Aaron Burr. After the Republicans had dropped him in the election of 1804, Burr had entered into a conspiracy with some New England Federalists who hoped to secede from the Union and form a Northern Confederacy. New York State was to be the keystone of this Federalist arch, and Burr tried to capture its governorship. He was defeated, mainly by the efforts of Alexander Hamilton. Enraged, Burr seized upon a pretext—a reported slur on his character—to challenge Hamilton to a duel. Hamilton, who had no need to prove his courage, unwisely accepted. The two met at Weehawken across the Hudson from New York. Hamilton missed deliberately, but Burr took careful aim and sent a ball into Hamilton's abdomen. So perished, after 30 hours of intense pain, one of the great men of American history. Even more than Washington he was the true soldier-statesman, able to write as well as fight, to execute as well as propose.

Indicted for murder, Burr fled into hiding off the Georgia coast. When Congress reconvened in 1804, he calmly resumed his duties as Vice President until his term expired in March, 1805, after which he went west to organize what seems to have been nothing less than a conspiracy to make himself emperor of Mexico and to set up an independent republic in Louisiana. Yet if plots and conspiracies came naturally to this bold bantam and ruthless charmer, they were also common to the age. Districts run by sturdy and honest men who went "up west" out of disgust with the fumbling Confederation had already flirted with Spain, while Nolichucky Jack Sevier's fiercely republican State of Franklin often acted as though it had seceded from the Union. Nor were the Creoles of Louisiana happy when the Stars and Stripes were unfurled at New Orleans and the notes of "Yankee Doodle" came squealing into their cultivated ears. Therefore it was not surprising that Burr should win the friendship of such men as Andrew Jackson of Tennessee, that filibusterers should flock to his cause or that the Catholic Bishop of New Orleans should give him his blessing. In such times also it was almost automatic that Burr should find an accomplice in James Wilkinson, then commanding general of the American Army, federal governor of the Louisiana Territory—and Spy No. 13 in the pay of Spain. The conspiracy might very well have succeeded had not Wilkinson—finding even his duplicity unequal to the challenge of remaining a loyal conspirator, citizen and spy at one and the same time—decided to betray Burr.

Burr was taken in disguise within a few miles of Spanish Florida and brought to trial for treason. Much to the consternation of Jefferson, and to the credit of American jurisprudence, he was acquitted on strict adherence to the constitutional definition of treason. Indicted again for high misdemeanor, he fled to Europe.

By then, 1807, the threat to American security—or at least to national honor—was external again. Britain and France were locked in the duel-to-the-death known as the Napoleonic Wars, and once again America was to find her own destiny yoked to the fortunes of Anglo-French conflict.

2

☆

The magnetic chain of events drawing the United States into her second war with Great Britain began in 1805. In that year Napoleon stood poised to invade England. However, Lord Nelson won the great sea battle of Trafalgar, reasserting British supremacy at sea and ending Napoleon's hopes of invasion. Instead, like Louis XIV before him, the Corsican conqueror turned inward on Europe. After a series of lightning conquests he was supreme there.

Once again France, all-conquering on land, confronted Britain, invincible at sea.

Both sides tried to strangle each other economically. Britain issued Orders in Council proclaiming a blockade of Europe and the right to capture ships which did not submit to her regulations, while Napoleon countered with decrees closing European ports to Britain and stating his right to seize any ship dealing with the British.

The United States, largest neutral carrier in the world, was caught in an economic crossfire. But she suffered more at the hands of the British, who sailed right up to the shores of America to enforce their blockade, seizing ships and impressing American seamen. Britain claimed that the impressed sailors were deserters from the Royal Navy. Actually, most of them were. They had fled the poor pay, rotten food and brutal discipline of the British Navy, and many of them had signed on American vessels where life was far more pleasant. A few of them had become naturalized American citizens, although most merely obtained "protection" papers which could be purchased for as little as one dollar. Britain, intent only on maintaining the force of 150,00 seamen required to keep the Navy operative (she impressed her own subjects as well), proclaimed the principle: "Once an Englishman, always an Englishman." She recognized no naturalization process (neither did the U.S.), and especially not those spurious protection papers. However, British captains who stopped and searched American vessels were often arrogant. They also equated ability to speak English with proof of English birth, particularly if it was spoken by powerful or agile men, and so, many an American sailor was dragged off to serve under the detested Union Jack.

Impressment, more than anything else, outraged that growing sense of "national honor" which America, like all young nations, possessed in supersensitive degree; the inevitable blow-off came in the "*Chesapeake* incident" of June 22, 1807.

With guns unprepared for action, the U.S. Navy frigate *Chesapeake* had been only ten minutes out of Norfolk when the British frigate *Leopard* hailed her and claimed the right to examine her crew. *Chesapeake* refused. *Leopard* promptly poured three broadsides into her, sent officers aboard and carried off four seamen. One of these sailors might have been British, but the other three were an American Negro, an American Indian and a native of Maryland—and all four were not mere merchant seamen but sailors of the U.S. Navy.

National indignation nearly catapulted the United States into war with Britain. Jefferson, however, thought that he had a substitute for war. He would teach both contending powers, and especially Britain, the lesson of "peaceable coercion." Britain's chief customer was the United States, which was in turn the largest neutral carrier of goods to England. If he could cut off Britain's market and reduce the flow of her imports, Britain would be brought to terms. Thus in December of 1807 Congress by a close vote passed the Embargo Act. It forbade any U.S. ship to sail from a U.S. port for any foreign port.

This was Jefferson's noble experiment, and it was a notable failure. It did not humble Britain, but rather enriched British shipping at the expense of American, played into Napoleon's hands, nearly wrecked the American economy and came close to provoking the secession of mercantile New England. It was repealed on March 1, 1809, three days before Jefferson handed over his office to his protégé, James Madison.

Madison, a superb scholar and statesman but a shy and inept politician, sincerely sought an understanding with Britain. Unfortunately, his efforts were torpedoed by George Canning, the British Foreign Secretary. Madison's next move made him a foil for Napoleon. Congress had offered to resume trade with whichever belligerent removed its restrictions. Napoleon pretended to revoke his decrees. Madison, led to believe in his sincerity, tried to persuade the British to make some concessions too—which was exactly what Napoleon wanted. The British, however, were not deceived. They demanded evidence of Napoleon's sincerity. America could produce none simply because Napoleon's agents were still confiscating American ships.

The situation worsened. National honor became more and more outraged with each new offense. There were not only exponents of war with Britain, but also advocates of war with France—to say nothing of those Republicans who, eager to escape the imputation of Francophilism, proposed a "triangular war" with both.

Such a course was lunacy undiluted, and if it was never really seriously proposed, it does indicate that there was ample cause for war with either power. But Britain was the primary target of rage simply because she was the chief maritime offender and because the practice of impressment was so irritating. And Britain was also very vulnerable in her province of Canada.

The elections of 1810-11 brought the "war hawks" to Congress. Young men impatient with the slow processes of diplomacy, many of them Westerners who blamed Britain for the Indian border menace, they were hot for war and they seized control of the House by electing the eloquent and militant Henry Clay as Speaker. After Clay packed the important committees with war hawks like himself, war with Britain was advanced another giant step. There also began a debate which might have been comic were its consequences not so tragic. Westerners and Southerners who had never smelled salt water thundered for war for "Free Trade and Sailors' Rights," while those shippers and sailors who presumably should have been the first to fight for freedom of the seas swore that they would never lift a finger against Britain.

In truth, both sides had ulterior motives. The shippers had been growing rich under a British licensing system which allowed them to evade the blockade, and the sailors were delighted to see impressment put an end to competition from British deserters who would work for less money. Among the war hawks the maritime grievance was only a cover for their real purpose: the acquisition of more land. Not only the fertile woods of Upper Canada beckoned, but also the lands of the Indians as well as those of Spanish America. Napoleon's invasion of the Spanish homeland had set the disintegration of the Spanish Empire in motion; President Madison had already confirmed the seizure of most of West Florida by American adventurers, and now East Florida lay ripe for the plucking. On one score only were the war hawks trumpeting the truth: their hatred of Canada as the source of British support for the Northwestern Indians.

Already, by the spring of 1810, the great Shawnee chieftain, Tecumseh, had begun his desperate defiance of white imperialism. With his brother, a reformed drunkard called the Prophet who claimed supernatural powers, Tecumseh had traveled from tribe to tribe, binding his Indian federation together. Tecumseh taught renunciation of the white man and all his works, not only his dreadful firewater which drove the Indians insane,* but even his productive tools and skills. Tecumseh wished the Indians to remain hunters. To do so they had to fight for their Great Lakes hunting grounds. In 1810 they began the battle by attacking outlying white settlements. In the following year William Henry Harrison moved against them.

Harrison, a thin, wiry man whose frugal habits made him as tough as a squirrel, was not exactly a typical frontier leader. Devoted to the Roman classics, he had also aspired to study medicine, but finally turned to the army, much to the delight of his father-in-law, who said: "He can neither bleed, plead nor preach, and if he could plow I would be satisfied. His best prospect is in the army; he has talents, and if he can dodge well a few years, it is probable that he may become conspicuous."8

Harrison had become conspicuous enough to be appointed Governor of Indiana Territory, and in 1811 he led just over 900 regulars and militia into northern Indiana. It was not Tecumseh, but his brother the Prophet, who opposed him. On November 6 Harrison encamped outside the Prophet's town near Tippecanoe Creek. He expected a conference with the Indians in the morning. The Prophet, however, had brewed a "hell broth" which told him to attack the white men. More magician than military man, he turned the unplanned assault over to other chiefs and retired to a hill to chant those incantations which were to seal Harrison's doom.

In the dark and rain-swept cold of the morning of November 7, 1811, the Indians attacked with a yell and a rattle of musketry. Harrison, asleep, jumped to his feet, mounted an aide's bay staked outside his tent by mistake, and rode off in darkness toward the battle. His aide, singled out on Harrison's gray mare, was killed. Three times the Indians attacked, and each time they were driven back with losses. In the end they fled, and Harrison burned the Prophet's town to the ground.

Although the fame of the Battle of Tippecanoe eventually made Harrison an American President, and also deluded the war hawks into thinking that American militia were enough to lay Canada at the feet of Congress, defeat did not restrain Tecumseh. It merely threw him more firmly into the British camp; and after bitterly re-

* Unlike the white man, who usually drank to relax or be merry, Indians drank to get drunk. If there was not enough firewater for all, then a few were chosen to fulfill the purpose of drink: intoxication.

buking his brother for the folly of his attack, he turned once again to savaging the American frontier.

Thus the war hawks, surer than ever that Britain was supplying Tecumseh and hounding him on, rattled the saber louder. National honor had now been outraged on the landward flank, and Americans were reminded how the unholy alliance of redskin and redcoat had bloodied the American frontier during the Revolution.

To these three causes of war—maritime insult, Indian outrage, lust for land—was added a fourth when the British blockade began to produce a depression in the South and West, the centers of anti-British feeling. Ironically, American boycott of Britain had also produced economic distress in England. Receipts of American food crops had fallen to a trickle, exports to America had dried up, and the harsh winter of 1811-12 was made more unbearable by the failure of English crops. Starved and jobless English workmen began to riot while merchants and manufacturers beseeched the government to rescind the Orders in Council and reopen American trade.

It took that event unique in British history—the assassination of a prime minister, Spencer Perceval—to place in power a ministry willing to make the change. On June 16, 1812, London announced that the Orders in Council had been suspended.

However, while Parliament had hesitated, Congress had acted. The House voted 79 to 49 in favor of war with Britain, and the Senate by 19 to 13. On June 18, two days after Britain had removed the chief cause for war, President Madison signed the declaration which began the War of 1812.

3

☆

If it is true that the War of 1812 was begun for the covetous purpose of conquering Canada, then much as its proponents might be criticized for their greed, they cannot be blamed for their timing. Canada was defenseless. Britain, engaged against Napoleon in Spain, could spare only about 4,000 regulars—reinforced by about 3,000 trustworthy Canadians—to defend an open border running about 1,700 miles. Moreover, British North America numbered less than 500,000 souls, many of whom were French-Canadians indifferent to the cause of British arms, as opposed to about 7,500,000 Americans. If ever the time for attack was ripe, this was it.

America, however, was incredibly unprepared. Her Navy was in comparatively good shape, but her ground forces were a marching mockery of the war whoops raised by Henry Clay and his war hawks the day war began. There were less than 7,000 men in the regular Army. True, Congress had voted an increase of 50,000 men, but in the first six months of hostilities only 5,000 men volunteered to serve in "Mr. Madison's War." To this could be added about 50,000 militia, available for use only as the loyalty and politics of the state governors might dictate.

Commanding this force were ranking officers who seemed to be prodigies of senility or incompetence.

Henry Dearborn, the senior major general, had fought with John Stark at Bunker Hill and marched to Quebec with Benedict Arnold. He had also served as Secretary of War, in which office he distinguished himself for his reluctance to apprehend Aaron Burr. Latterly whatever ardor he possessed had been smothered in the soft life of the Boston customhouse. Taking the field again at the age of 61, he was nicknamed "Granny" by his troops.

Thomas Pinckney, another Revolutionary War veteran, was 62, and, in the words of a ranking Congressman, "as fit for his place as the Indian Prophet would be for Emperor of Europe."[9]

The senior brigadier was James Wilkinson: Wilkinson of the Conway Cabal, the friend of the author of the Newburgh Addresses, secret agent of Spain, treacherous accomplice of Aaron Burr, and, at the age of 55, an officer renowned for never having won a battle or lost a court-martial. After Wilkinson came four more brigadiers about 60 years of age, all sharing the distinction of never having commanded a regiment in battle, and chosen on the basis of family, wealth, politics or service in the Revolution. These were the top commanders who, together with officers of field rank whom young Captain Winfield Scott scorned as drunkards or drones, were to lead the lightning war envisioned by President Madison and his penny-pinching Secretary of War, William Eustis.

Eustis had been a military surgeon during the Revolution. After Benedict Arnold's flight from West Point, he administered restoratives to the shocked Peggy Shippen Arnold. He switched to politics after Shays' Rebellion and was later rewarded with the War Department,

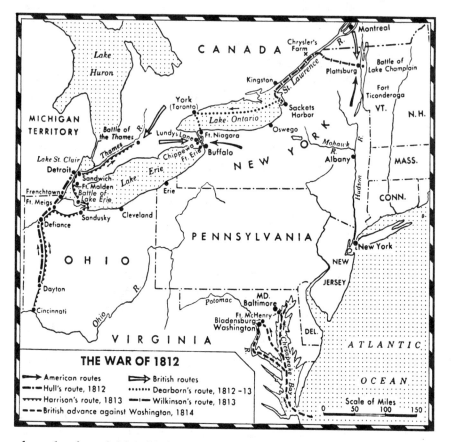

THE WAR OF 1812

American routes
Hull's route, 1812
Harrison's route, 1813
British advance against Washington, 1814

British routes
Dearborn's route, 1812-13
Wilkinson's route, 1813

where he found his chief delight in writing advertisements for bids on Army supplies detailed down to the last biscuit. Eustis probably knew less about war than the shy, scholarly Madison, and between them they dribbled along a series of "proposals" for the conquest of Canada which, in retrospect, appear to be the negation of prudence erected into a plan.

Detroit, in the heart of hostile Indian country, and menaced by the British across the Detroit River in Fort Malden, was vital to the defense of the Northwest Territory. In February of 1812, four months before the declaration of war, William Hull, the Governor of Michigan Territory, came to Washington to discuss Detroit's defenses. So did General Dearborn. Both Hull and Dearborn insisted that the key to the Northwest was naval control of the Great Lakes. At the time, this was possessed by the British. Britain also, according to the pessimistic Hull, possessed in her regulars and Indian allies the power to subdue the Northwest. The problem, then, was whether or not there was time to build a Great Lakes fleet before the British moved. And then the gloomy Hull made an enigmatic about-face.

He assured Eustis that the British could be forced to abandon Upper Canada merely by menacing them with an army placed in Detroit. British ships on Lake Erie would then fall into American hands and the nation would be spared the expense of building a Great Lakes fleet. From what depth of fatuous optimism Hull dredged up this fantastic proposal is not known, but the prospect of getting a vast province and a lakes fleet free-for-nothing was certainly appealing, especially to the parsimonious Eustis. Madison, accordingly, made no provisions for building an American fleet. Worse, out of these purely defensive considerations came the "plan" for Canadian conquest.

Madison approved Dearborn's proposal to launch a major operation down Lake Champlain against Montreal while supporting thrusts were made into Upper Canada from Sackets Harbor, Niagara and Detroit. Thus an army was not merely to garrison Detroit; it was to move across the river into Canadian territory. And Hull would command it, though reluctantly. Silver-haired and venerable at 60, "a short, corpulent, good-natured old gentleman who bore the marks of good eating and drinking,"[10] Hull had insisted that a younger man should lead. But Madison persuaded him to accept the rank of brigadier general, and in April he went out to Ohio to take command. Dearborn went to Albany to prepare for the Montreal operation.

There was no detailed plan for either Hull or Dearborn. There could not be any time set for coordinated attacks, as such a plan required, because Congress had not yet declared war. Democracies, unlike dictatorships, cannot set invasion dates beforehand and then calmly go about faking "incidents" to justify them. Democracies are given to that debate which precludes timetables and guarantees late starts. They are not always united, either, as President Madison found out when, on April 15, he asked for the Massachusetts militia for use against Montreal.

Massachusetts refused. Governor Caleb Strong coldly informed

Madison that militia were for federal use only, to suppress insurrection or repel invasion, and since neither exigency was imminent, Yankee Doodle was staying home. So were the Connecticut militia, and the message to Madison was clear: Westerners wanted this war, let them fight it. Westerners, however, were too far from the Lake Champlain region to be of immediate use, as were the regular troops scattered in garrisons across the country. Therefore the major stroke against Montreal was blunted at the outset.

Meanwhile, William Hull was marching toward Detroit serenely confident that General Dearborn was organizing the Montreal and Niagara expeditions which were to coincide with his. Hull had taken command of about 1,200 Ohio volunteers on May 25. He introduced himself with an eloquent speech which fired every breast. On June 1 the march began. On June 10 Hull was reinforced by a regiment of regulars, and eventually his army numbered about 2,000 men.

War had not yet been declared, nor had Hull been authorized to invade Canada, but he certainly must have expected orders to do so. As he marched, he drew farther and farther out of reach. Thus he had no way of knowing how hopeless the situation on his eastern or right flank had become. The Montreal operation was not only definitely bogged down, but the assault from Niagara was already a travesty. Only a handful of New York militia had gathered along the Niagara frontier, where they milled around leaderless, waiting for Granny Dearborn to appoint their commander.

Hull plodded on. His men cut such a clean slice through the forest that parts of it were still visible as late as the Civil War. At the end of June, Hull reached the Maumee or Miami River. To his delight he found the schooner *Cuyahoga* there. He decided to load it with his heavy equipment and send it up to Detroit, freeing himself for faster movement. Unfortunately, he also put aboard a trunk containing his instructions and his army muster rolls. As *Cuyahoga* set sail for Lake Erie, Hull hurried through the forests, eagerly awaiting those dispatches from Eustis which would inform him that the nation was at war. He did not receive word until July 2, four days after the British had been alerted, and then only by ordinary mail which a conscientious postmaster had forwarded from Cleveland. On the same day the British captured *Cuyahoga* as it attempted to slip past Fort Malden and enter Detroit.

Hull's mission and strength were now known to the enemy.

Major General Isaac Brock was the Governor General of Upper Canada. He was a superb soldier, decisive, energetic—and an aggressive foil to his cautious superior, Lieutenant General Sir George Prevost. Prevost, Governor in Chief of all Provinces, was impressed with the weakness of his position, and on July 10 he warned the impetuous Brock not to attempt any stroke that might unite the bickering American states. Brock was to remain on the defensive.

Brock, however, had different ideas. He had long ago realized the importance of naval power and built the ships which gave him command of Lake Erie. He knew that neither his Indians nor his militia were reliable unless he immediately took them on the offensive, and he was prepared to order them out against Detroit and Fort Michilimackinac once war began. However, Brock was also certain that the main American blow would fall on the 40-mile Niagara frontier between Lake Erie and Lake Ontario, and here he waited on the defensive while Hull moved against Detroit far to the west.

Hull reached Detroit on July 5. It was then a community of about 800 souls, including Hull's own daughter and grandchildren. The fort was a square enclosure of about two acres which was within gunshot of the British shore, but did not itself command the Detroit River. Hull might well have considered himself in a trap, for he was 200 miles above his base, and his line of communications, running 60 miles along the edge of Lake Erie, was menaced from the water by British ships and on land by hostile Indians. Moreover, he was responsible for the welfare of perhaps 5,000 American civilians in the area.

Hull did not act confidently. His troops, eager to win the war in time to be home for summer harvesting, chafed at the delay in attacking British and Canadians clearly visible across the river at Sandwich (part of present-day Windsor). Hull, however, told his importunate officers on July 9 that he had no authority to enter Canada. But that same night orders to that effect were received, and two days later his army began marching downstream as though to cross the river at Fort Malden 12 miles below Sandwich. The British immediately gathered their men inside Fort Malden, and at daybreak of the following day, July 12, Hull's army crossed at Sandwich without opposition.

News of Hull's bloodless coup filled the nation with rejoicing. But on July 16 Hull began to take counsel from his fears. On that day

Colonel Lewis Cass found a lightly guarded bridge only about four miles above Malden. He attacked and seized it. Aware that he had exceeded orders, he asked for permission to hold this vital crossing. Hull vacillated. Instead of seeing that Cass had penetrated the enemy's defenses, he preferred to believe that Cass had needlessly exposed his rear. Finally, he left the decision up to Cass, and that worthy officer —who came very close to becoming an American Vice President— retired in disgust.

The golden chance had been muffed. Along all the British frontier from Sandwich down to Malden there were not 500 men, of whom only 100 were regulars. Now was the time to storm Malden, but Hull timidly marked time. He sent off letters to Governor Meigs of Ohio pleading for supplies, and the British intercepted them and blocked the supply train. He pleaded again and again for a diversion out of Niagara, but Granny Dearborn was dragging his feet. On August 6 Hull mustered his courage and ordered an attack on Malden. Next day he canceled it, turned around, recrossed the river and took up a defensive stance in Detroit. The crossing at Sandwich had been the high point of the campaign.

Meanwhile, the resourceful Isaac Brock was already flying to the relief of Malden.

General Brock heard of Hull's entry into Canada on July 20. He immediately sent Colonel Henry Proctor and 60 regulars to reinforce Malden, called a special session of the provincial legislature to vote supplies, and then dismissed its members after they refused to suspend the Habeas Corpus Act. Certain now that Niagara was not the critical point, he embarked a force of 240 militia and 40 regulars on Lake Erie and crowded on all sail for Malden.

The value of control of the lakes was now apparent, yet not a single American hand was lifted to detain Brock as he sped toward Malden. He arrived there on August 13, and soon met Tecumseh, who had also arrived with 600 warriors. Having read the captured *Cuyahoga* papers, as well as other intercepted American documents, Brock judged that his enemy, though more numerous than he, was very low on morale. He proposed an immediate attack. Delighted, Tecumseh drew his knife and cut a map of the area on a roll of birch bark.

On August 14, while Brock made his preparations, Hull sent a relief expedition south in a last desperate attempt to bring supplies into Detroit. Making a wide circle to avoid ambush, the column became lost in the woods. Next day Brock took his regulars and militia across the river three miles below the fort. Playing on Hull's fears, he sent him a surrender demand, warning of what might happen if his Indians became angered by a prolonged siege. Hull had the wit to reject it, and Brock promptly ordered his shore batteries and two gunboats into action. Cannon shot shook the American fort, and Hull's guns began to reply—but faintly. Next Brock planted a document alluding to "5,000 Indians" in Hull's hands and dressed his untrained militia in the scarlet coats of British regulars. That night Hull learned that Tecumseh and his warriors had crossed the river below Brock and had moved inland to cut off the return of his relief column. Fatigued and exhausted, his spirit began to sink under the weight of multiplying fears.

As daylight of August 16 came, William Hull began to fall apart in the presence of his men. He sat on an old tent with his back against the rampart. His voice trembled. He avoided the contemptuous eyes of those officers who wanted to fight. In his agitation he stuffed quid after quid of chewing tobacco into his mouth until the brown spittle began to spill out and run down his beard and vest. Hull could think of nothing but the safety of the cut-off relief column or of an Indian massacre that would include his own daughter and grandchildren. Cannon shot still shook his fort, four men fell, the militia began to desert, and so William Hull sent his son to signal the surrender.

For the first and only time an American city unfurled a white flag to a foreign foe, and it was seen with incredulous delight by Isaac Brock and his soldiers as they came marching up the hill.

The surrender of Detroit was not only the most disgraceful episode in the annals of American arms; it was the first of a series of Western defeats sufficient to shake even Henry Clay's faith in the invincibility of Western frontiersmen. Hull, stunned by the news of the fall of Fort Michilimackinac, had sent orders for the evacuation of Fort Dearborn, the site of modern Chicago. Captain William Wells arrived with these instructions on August 12. However, a friendly Indian chief warned the Americans not to leave the safety of the fort, explaining that "leaden birds had been singing in his ears." He was ignored. The soldiers with their women and children left the fort on August 15. Less than an hour later they were overwhelmed by 500 red men who killed half of them and imprisoned the others.

Captain Wells was beheaded, after which the Indians cut out his heart and ate it.

Now, with the entire frontier laid open to Indian incursion, 2,000 Kentucky militia were called out to punish Indians in the Illinois country. With typical bombast their general, Congressman Samuel Hopkins, described his army as the best he had seen "in the western country or anywhere else." The closer Hopkins's army came to the Indians, however, the more unruly it became. After the red men set the prairies on fire, the "flower of Kentucky" wilted and went home.

The Northwest frontier now lay wide open to invasion, the British were over the border at Detroit, and hundreds of frightened Western settlers began leaving their homes.

America's military weaknesses and internal divisions were never so naked as during the storm of reproach and recrimination which followed the Northwest disasters. Federalists could not conceal their delight at the dismay of the war hawks, while these thwarted conquerers screamed in concert for the head of William Hull.* Even Thomas Jefferson went so far as to say: "The treachery of Hull, like that of Arnold, cannot be a matter of blame for our government."[11] However, as Henry Adams has observed, if any man was responsible for Hull's failure it was Thomas Jefferson, whose unyielding pacifism excluded military efficiency and unity from the American system. Even then, while Jefferson's protégé Madison yearned for the military victory which might retrieve his political fortunes in the election of 1812, the American military posture was a chaos of conflicts and confusions.

Madison wanted to raise a second Northwestern Army to retake Detroit. He thought of naming James Monroe, his Secretary of State, to command this and all other northern armies. But the people of the West took the matter out of his hands. They thought of William Henry Harrison, the 39-year-old hero of Tippecanoe, and a Kentucky caucus elected Harrison major general of militia.

Harrison hastened toward Fort Wayne, then besieged by Indians. Meanwhile, the federal government decided to make him a brigadier

* Two years later a court-martial convicted Hull of cowardice and sentenced him to dismissal and death, but President Madison spared Hull's life.

general junior to James Winchester, who, at 61, seemed to satisfy the Federal preference for silver hair. But Winchester was a Tennessee aristocrat who was not loved in the West, as Harrison informed Madison. And so, under pressure of a state's action, Madison on September 17 gave Harrison the Northwestern command.

Harrison was to have an army of 10,000 men and to recapture Detroit in a rapid autumn campaign. But he could not traverse the road cut by Hull's army because his own force was five times as big and the autumn rains had made an impassable quagmire of it. So Harrison decided to wait until winter had frozen the lakes and rivers and made them passable. Winter, however, was slow in arriving that year, and Harrison was frustrated in his hopes of striking at Detroit before 1813.

In the meantime, the focus of the fighting shifted to the Northeastern front.

After the fall of Detroit, General Brock hastened back to the Niagara frontier. En route, he discovered that Prevost and Dearborn had agreed to an armistice! Prevost, hearing of the suspension of the Orders in Council, had at once sent an emissary to Dearborn in Albany. Dearborn, distracted and disorganized, looked upon a truce as a godsend. Although the armistice did not include Detroit, Dearborn assured Eustis that "it will not probably have any effect on General Hull or his movements." In other words, the left arm did not need the right arm. Madison angrily repudiated the agreement, but not before Brock had had the time to organize his meager force of 1,600 soldiers and 300 Indians in mutually supporting positions along the 40-mile Niagara River.

By October some 6,000 Americans had gathered across the Niagara from Brock's 2,000. Most of them were militia, undisciplined, poorly fed and supplied. But they had at last received a commander, General Stephen Van Rensselaer, a distinguished Federalist whom the Republicans appointed.to give the campaign a nonpartisan coloring. Unfortunately, he had no military experience whatsoever. To compensate for this deficiency, Colonel Solomon Van Rensselaer, a relative and a Revolutionary War veteran, was named as his aide.

The new general's militiamen were eager to fight, threatening to go home unless the shooting started soon. So General Van Rensselaer drew up a plan for a double crossing of the Niagara. General Alexander Smyth with 1,650 regulars was supposed to move out onto Lake Ontario and come in on the rear of Fort George, located at the point where the river empties into Ontario. Van Rensselaer's own force would cross opposite Queenston, about ten miles upriver.

Smyth, however, did not wish to cross the river below Niagara Falls. He wanted to cross above the cataract at a point in the neighborhood of Buffalo, at the southern end of the Niagara, where he was based. Smyth, therefore, sat still.

Van Rensselaer went ahead. On the morning of October 11 all was in readiness—except that an American officer, either from ignorance or treachery, rowed across the river in a boat containing all the oars and left it there. Undaunted, Van Rensselaer made another attempt on the rain-swept night of October 12-13.

Colonel Van Rensselaer led about 200 men across the river. They landed successfully, but were discovered about four o'clock in the morning. The British-Canadians opened fire, and the Americans charged and scattered them. Down at Fort George, General Brock was awakened in surprise. He had expected the main blow to come from Fort Niagara almost directly opposite George. Instructing his gunners to open a restraining fire on Niagara, he hurried upriver to Queenston.

There the Americans had ascended the heights under Captain John Wool, who took charge after Van Rensselaer was severely wounded. And as Brock hurried to the battle scene, Lieutenant Colonel Winfield Scott, 26 years old and 6 feet 4 inches of muscle and righteous insubordination, came galloping down from Buffalo without so much as a by-your-leave from the uncooperative General Smyth.

Brock, meanwhile, had reached Queenston just as the Americans on the heights began firing down on a British gun. Charging down the hill, the Americans took the piece. Brock led a countercharge and was shot in the breast and killed.

Now, at about two o'clock in the afternoon, the towering Scott had come over to Queenston and taken command from Wool. He had between 700 and 800 Americans to hold off a British force which had swelled to about 1,000. Brock's system of supporting positions had gone rapidly into effect. Obviously, the Americans needed reinforcements.

But not a man of the militia so bold to fight would come to the side of their embattled comrades. They said there were no boats, but only half had been swamped or carried off by the Niagara's swift currents. They were asked to cross in detachments, but they still refused. The distraught General Van Rensselaer rode among them and pleaded with them to cross. One well-equipped militia company consented, but just as the men began stepping into the boats the sound of firing was heard from Queenston Heights and they changed their minds.

Not a soldier crossed the river, and Scott's outnumbered force braced for the enemy's assault. It was begun by the Indians, who charged splendidly. Then the British-Canadians crashed out a single volley and followed with the bayonet. The Americans gave way and broke. Many of them tried to hide along the steep banks of the river, but they were caught and killed. Others attempted to swim the turbulent Niagara and were drowned. Most of them surrendered, including Colonel Scott.

Once again a small but able British force had humbled an American military mob; but this time, with the death of General Brock, the Crown had won a Pyrrhic victory. No soldier of Brock's stature appeared on the British side for the remainder of the war. Meanwhile, the American cause passed from the tragicomedy of Queenston Heights to the travesty of Black Rock.

Alexander Smyth had replaced Van Rensselaer, who had resigned in chagrin. Smyth, more writer than fighter, spent much of his time composing ringing declarations. "Friends of your country!" he told his soldiers. "Ye who have 'the will to do, the heart to dare!' the moment ye have wished for has arrived! Think on your country's honors torn! Her rights trampled on! Her sons enslaved! Her infants perishing by the hatchet! Be strong! Be brave! And let the ruffian power of the British king cease on this continent!"[12]

Thus, hurling his exclamation points like spears, Smyth rallied a force once again grown to 6,000 men for another assault on Canada. In the early morning of November 28 a small advance guard crossed the river from the vicinity of Black Rock. The Americans seized two enemy batteries near Red House. As daylight approached, 2,000 men climbed into waiting boats. Barely out on the river, Smyth suddenly and unaccountably called off the entire expedition.

Smyth's soldiers were so enraged, however, that their general was forced to reschedule the assault for December 1. Before that date Smyth told his troops: "The general will be on board. Neither rain, snow or frost will prevent the embarkation. . . . While embarking the music will play martial airs. *Yankee Doodle* will be the signal to get under way." The general's officers, however, objected to sending Yankee Doodle across a river in broad daylight into the mouths of enemy guns. General Smyth promptly called a council of war at which his officers vetoed his proposal. Seeing a chance to get off the hook, General Smyth agreed and climbed down.

Now his men were so infuriated that they began shooting off their muskets, some of them in the general direction of General Smyth's tent. And that was the end of the Niagara fiasco.

Meanwhile, at Sackets Harbor on the eastern end of Lake Ontario there was simply no invasion whatever.

At Lake Champlain, General Dearborn had at last moved north, taking some 6,000 or 8,000 men up to Plattsburg on the lake. The Canadians countered by sending 1,900 men south from Montreal. On the night of November 19 the Americans and Canadians collided in a skirmish on the Lacolle River. The Americans captured a blockhouse, the Canadians fled, and then the Americans got lost and began firing on each other. After his militia suddenly remembered their constitutional rights and refused to cross the border, General Dearborn went into winter quarters.

Disgrace at Detroit, ignominy at Niagara, a blank at Sackets Harbor and a fizzle on Lake Champlain: thus had the 1812 campaign to conquer Canada concluded in the most inglorious chapter in American military history.

4

☆

Because of its reliance on unruly militia and white-haired generals the United States had failed shamefully in that Canadian conquest which was the true object of this war for "Free Trade and Sailors' Rights." But at sea, where battle was almost an afterthought, the brash young American Navy sailed forth to astonish the old queen of the waves.

Britain then was a sea monster of 600 ships, of which 120 were ships of the line and 116 were frigates. Roughly corresponding to a modern battleship, a ship of the line usually mounted 74 or more guns, although some carried as few as 50. Frigates—equal to a modern cruiser—were armed with 32 to 44 guns.

At the outbreak of hostilities, Britain had only one 64-gun ship of the line and seven frigates near the American coast. To oppose them, the United States had 16 seagoing vessels and about 200 gunboats. The gunboats, imposed on the protesting Navy by Jefferson in his belief that they were a cheap solution to coastal defense, were widely scattered and in varying stages of disrepair. Even in the best condition, gunboats were of use only inside harbors and not out on the stormy ocean where sea power holds sway. Only 12 of the seagoing ships were of value, but of these the seven frigates were superb.

They had been built by the Federalists when the Naval War with France threatened, and they might have had sister ships of the line had not the Jeffersonian Republicans worked their "chaste reformation" of the armed forces. Now they were the delight of the Madisonian Republicans: sturdy, swift ships heavily timbered and planked to repel enemy shot, able to throw heavier broadsides than the British frigates; and yet, with their clean lines and great spread of sail, capable of outrunning anything afloat.

This small navy was also well trained and efficient. Most of its captains were veterans of the French and Tripolitan fighting. They were eager to clash with the British, those doughty though arrogant sea dogs who looked upon all other sailors with disdain and contempt.

The *Constitution* had been called "Old Ironsides" because her live-oak planks had been forcefully bent into place without benefit of that steaming process which was believed to weaken wood. She was commanded by Captain Isaac Hull, the nephew and adopted son of William Hull. On the morning of July 18, 1812, just as his unfortunate uncle began to falter at Fort Malden, Hull fell in with four British frigates: *Shannon,* 38 guns; *Belvidera,* 36; *Aeolus,* 32; and *Guerrière,* 38. Following them but out of sight was the battleship *Africa,* 64.

Constitution, rated at 44 guns but actually carrying 54, could outfight any single frigate but not four of them. As the British quartet began closing in, Hull prepared for a fighting withdrawal.

He cut away part of his stern rail and mounted a long 18- and 24-pounder aft. He widened his cabin portholes and poked 24s through them, and because it was a windless day he put out his boats to try to drag himself out of range. So did the British, putting all their boats at *Shannon*'s disposal. Finding himself in fairly shallow water, Hull stopped towing and began to kedge. That is, a cutter carried a small anchor forward and dropped it so that all hands might tug on the attached cable and thus haul the ship ahead. Kedging laboriously, *Constitution* began to crawl away from her pursuers. Then *Shannon* began to work two kedges, drawing closer until *Constitution*'s stern guns spoke and forced *Shannon*'s cutters to keep a wary distance. So it went throughout the day, while the sweating, cursing sailors of both nations alternately rowed or dragged their ships through a glassy sea. Night gave them respite, but in the morning Hull saw that *Africa* had joined his pursuers.

Towing and kedging were renewed until noon, when a breeze sprang up. Quickly Hull ordered his tired sailors to swarm up the rigging and saturate the sails. He began to empty his ship of ten tons of drinking water to lessen her draft by one inch. Still the lighter British craft came closer.

Hull had a set of skysails made and set. All other sails were set and trimmed to the greatest advantage, close by the wind—and with the freshening of the wind at noon the beautiful American ship began to draw away from her pursuers. Two hours later she was plunging toward Boston at nearly 13 knots and the British were dwindling specks to her stern.

Rotund little Isaac Hull was not content with having taught the British a lesson in seamanship. He wanted battle with them, especially with Captain James Dacres of the *Guerrière,* who had repeatedly challenged the Americans to come out and fight him. Reconditioning his ship, Hull sailed from Boston on August 2. On August 19, three days after his uncle's surrender at Detroit, about 750 miles east of Boston, Hull's lookouts sighted the sails of *Guerrière*.

Both ships immediately began maneuvering for "the weather gauge," that is, to get to the windward of the enemy. Each wanted to be able to rake the other without being raked. But Hull and Dacres maneuvered with such skill that neither could gain the advantage. *Guerrière* opened fire at long range, blasting away in a starboard broadside that fell short. Dacres next wore ship, that is, turned in a half-circle so as to bring his portside guns to bear. This time his cannon balls went shrieking high over *Constitution*'s topsails.

Suddenly Hull set extra sail and closed quickly on the surprised Dacres. Hull waited until he was within half-pistol shot—50 feet—and then cried to his crew: "Now, boys, pour it into them!"[13]

Old Ironsides's forward guns, double shotted with grape, roared and flamed. They riddled *Guerrière*'s rigging, ripped her sails and reddened her decks with blood. Hull leaned over the rail, eager for a closer look, and split his tight buff breeches down the rear seam. His men shouted with laughter, and bent to the guns.

Running before the wind, nearly abreast of each other, both ships exchanged fire. Gradually the superior American guns and gunnery began to tell. After a quarter-hour *Guerrière* was a cripple. Her rear mast fell overboard just as her main yard gave way in the middle. Slowing with reduced sail power, she allowed Old Ironsides to steer across her bow into the coveted raking position. *Guerrière* now could fire only a few forward guns, while *Constitution* could bring all guns to bear to blast the Britisher lengthwise. Hull seized the opportunity. He raked Dacres with his starboard guns, wore ship, and raked him with the port battery. Marine sharpshooters in Old Ironsides's tops poured musket fire into *Guerrière*'s decks. Now the ships swung close and the Britisher's bowsprit caught in *Constitution*'s rigging. Both captains cried: "Boarders away!"

Marine Lieutenant William Bush leaped to the rail to lead his men aboard the enemy. He was shot through the head, falling back on *Constitution*'s deck just as the wind filled her sails and broke her free of *Guerrière*. Now Ironsides's sharpshooters took a toll of British seamen clearly visible on the enemy's decks. American gunfire cut away the Britisher's foremast and then the mainmast. Dacres, streaming blood, gallantly ran up a new Union Jack on his stump of foremast—but the battle was over. Her decks slippery with blood, her hull riddled, her masts and canvas gone and her rigging shredded, *Guerrière* was a helpless hulk dipping and rolling in the sea. Dacres fired a surrender shot to leeward and pulled down his flag.

Although Hull was forced to burn his prize, his victory was indestructible. It shone like a lone beacon of hope throughout the military eclipse of the Northern campaign. In one half-hour, says Henry Adams, Hull and his men had raised the United States to the rank of a first-class power. Never before had a British frigate struck to an American, and in Britain the *Times of London* reported: "The loss of the *Guerrière* spread a degree of gloom through the town which it was painful to observe."[14] The *Times* observed that *Guerrière* had fallen to "a new enemy, an enemy unaccustomed to such triumphs, and likely to be rendered insolent and confident by them."[15]

True enough, for even the Federalists of New England joined the general rejoicing, and even "the cautious Madison was dragged by the public excitement upon the element he most heartily disliked."[16]

Tasting blood and eager for more, the Navy's fiery young captains were granted a freedom of action rare in the usages of warfare, and they quickly put to sea in three squadrons of three ships apiece. As they did, the *Times of London* thundered: "But above all, there is one object to which our most strenuous efforts should be directed —the entire annihilation of the American Navy."[17]

The Thunderer of Fleet Street was disappointed. On October 18 the American sloop *Wasp,* 18 guns, Master Commandant Jacob Jones, came upon the British sloop *Frolic,* 19, Captain Thomas Whinyates, as she escorted a convoy of six merchantmen from Honduras to England. The seas ran high, and the merchants ships made safely off while the two sloops closed for broadside battle.

In such seas one ship would be now above the other on the crest of a wave, now below in a trough, and serving the guns was a difficult feat. Yet the Americans firing their port guns were able to catch *Frolic*'s starboard rising on the roll of the waves and put holes in her hull. *Frolic*'s starboard battery, fired on the roll as *Wasp* dipped into the trough, went screaming over the American's head or through her rigging. Thus *Wasp* quickly gained the advantage. As the ships drew closer, an American seaman named Jack Lang leaped to the rail waving a cutlass and jumped down on *Frolic*'s deck. Lang had been an impressed seaman, he was thirsting for revenge, and his impetuous action touched off an American boarding rush which brought *Frolic*'s colors fluttering down.

Once again the Americans had shown their superiority with guns, although their exultation was to be short-lived. While they struggled to bring *Frolic* home as a prize, the big 74-gun ship of the line *Poictiers* came up to free *Frolic* and take *Wasp* as prize. Nevertheless, *Wasp* had won another American victory, and 12 days later Captain Stephen Decatur made a third British warship dip her colors to Old Glory.

The hero of Tripoli commanded the *United States,* sister to Old Ironsides. Off Madeira on October 25 he fell in with the 38-gun *Macedonian.* The British ship, though fleet, was heavily outgunned, especially in long-range pieces. Decatur stood off at a distance and pot-shotted *Macedonian* to death. His highly trained crew loaded and fired with such speed that they outshot the British two to one, and Captain John Carden struck his colors. Although the British ship was a floating wreck, Decatur managed to bring her back to Newport, the only British frigate ever brought into a United States port as a prize.

And so the glorious six months passed, capped on December 29 by *Constitution*'s toe-to-toe slugging victory over the evenly matched British frigate *Java.* True, the Americans had only won a handful of single-ship victories and had not even challenged a ship of the line. Yet the Yankee seamen with their beautiful swift ships had shown the world that they could sail at least as well as and certainly shoot better than the old sea dogs of Britain. More, they had forced the *Times* to ask the incredible question: "What is wrong with British sea power?"[18]

5

☆

Re-elected for a second term and heartened by a glittering string of naval victories, President Madison began 1813 looking hopefully toward the Northwest, where William Henry Harrison stood poised to redeem American military fortunes.

Harrison's army had entered on the cruel ordeal of the Northern winter. It had dwindled to 6,500 men. Some of them were mutinous, especially the fiercely independent Kentucky long knives who held down the army's left wing at Fort Defiance under General Winchester. Nevertheless, Harrison decided to get closer to Detroit. He ordered Winchester to move from Defiance up to the Maumee Rapids. In early January, at the head of about 1,200 men, Winchester moved out.

His soldiers marched through snow two feet deep, harnessing themselves to sledges to pull their gear. At the front of the column men floundering through the drifts gradually packed them smooth, so that men at the rear slipped and fell or flailed their arms to keep their balance. Then the temperature rose and it began to rain. The soldiers slogged through slush and mud or splashed through water floating atop the rotten ice of thawing streams and ponds. Living on half-rations, soaked, their teeth chattering, lacking axes to fell firewood or utensils to cook with, they plodded on—reaching the rapids on January 10.

Winchester had begun building a fortified camp and gathering supplies, when he received an appeal from American settlers at Frenchtown (now Monroe, Michigan) on the River Raisin. The Americans said their lives were endangered by 100 Indians who were inside the town with about 50 Canadian militia. Frenchtown was 35 miles north of the rapids, 100 miles away from Harrison's main body and only 18 miles south of Fort Malden. Thus it was within easy reach of the British. Nevertheless, Winchester decided to succor Frenchtown, persuaded, perhaps, by the fact that his men had reached that point of exasperation where they were eager to fight anyone.

On January 17 Colonel William Lewis and 550 men began marching north over frozen terrain and in bitter cold. On the next day they reached the little settlement of 30 families and attacked the Indians and Canadians. After a two-hour fight the Americans cleared the village. Two days later, General Winchester came up from the rapids with 300 additional men. He set up a camp that was an invitation to disaster, leaving most of his force stationed on the north bank of the River Raisin while he himself set up headquarters a half-mile south of the river. The sight and smell of his ragged and half-mutinous long knives were too much for Winchester's elegant senses. And so, to the folly of placing men with their backs to a stream, and then trying to command them from the other side, Winchester added the dereliction of ordering no night pickets or night patrols.

Up in Fort Malden, meanwhile, it was clear to General Henry Proctor, the successor to the fallen Brock, that the Americans were incredibly far off base—although he could never have imagined that they were also off their guard. Taking about 1,200 men—half of them Indians under Roundhead and Walk-in-the-Water—he began stealing south. On the night of January 21, under cover of a raging snow-storm, he came within reach of the Americans. He put his artillery and his regulars in his center and his Indians and militia on his right and left flanks. Opposite him the American left was protected by a picket fence, while the right was only partially guarded by a crude rail fence.

Two hours before daylight of January 22, 1813, with the snow still falling, Frenchtown was suddenly shaken by artillery fire and the rattle of musketry. War whoops were heard. Almost at once the American right was overwhelmed. Within a few minutes 100 soldiers were scalped by Indians who had gotten into the rear. General Winchester, blundering to the front to rally his men, was taken prisoner.

On the left, however, about 400 men under Major George Madison fought with bravery and skill. They repulsed charge after charge. Came a lull in the battle and they saw a white flag approaching. Their hearts soared, for they thought that it was a flag of truce. But it was rather a British officer bringing a message from Winchester to the effect that he had surrendered his entire army, themselves included.

Chagrined, Madison sent back the reply: "It has been customary for the Indians to massacre the wounded and prisoners after a sur-render. I shall not agree to any capitulation which General Winchester may direct, unless the safety and protection of all the prisoners shall be stipulated."[19] Proctor raged that he would not accept dicta-tion, but in the end he agreed and Madison surrendered.

Proctor kept his word by stripping his prisoners of some of their clothing, robbing them of their money and forcing them to drag his sleds to rest his horses. His wounded prisoners were left behind without guards. An American who had asked for help for the wounded was told: "The Indians are excellent doctors."[20] So Proctor deserted them on the grounds that he wished to flee the area before Harrison could come up and attack him. As soon as he departed, the Indians became drunk and began scalping the wounded. They set fire to one houseful of them, and as those able to rise rushed to the windows to escape, they beat them back into the flames with tomahawks.

Thus the allies of the noble Proctor, and as Proctor hurried north to regain the safety of Fort Malden, Harrison, from whom he fled, was also burning Winchester's post at the Maumee Rapids and hastening south. Thirty-six hours after the Battle of Frenchtown the two enemies were 60 miles apart. A week later Harrison returned to the rapids with 2,000 men. He built a fortified camp on its south bank and named it Fort Meigs after the Governor of Ohio. Ordering up all troops in his rear, he collected a force of 4,000 men which he planned to hurl against Malden. February 11 was fixed as the day of advance, but on that day the roads were sheeted with ice and impassable, and the expedition to Malden was canceled.

So ended, in defeat, massacre and disgrace, the Western movement against Upper Canada. Although his contemporaries were kinder to Harrison than to Hull, and would one day make him President, the fact is that William Henry Harrison had done less with more. He had not even gotten across the Maumee River. The men whom he led, and in whom he had great faith, were obviously superior to those who had followed Hull into Canada. A British officer has left a description of them:

> Their appearance was miserable to the last degree. They had the air of men to whom cleanliness was a virtue unknown. . . . It was the depth of winter; but scarcely an individual was in possession of a great coat or cloak. . . . They still retained their summer dress, consisting of cotton stuff of various colors shaped into frocks, and descending to the knee. Their trousers were of the same material. They were covered with slouched hats, worn bare by constant use, beneath which their long hair fell matted and uncombed over their cheeks; and these, together with the dirty blankets wrapped round their loins to protect them against the inclemency of the season, and fastened by broad leathern belts into which were thrust axes and knives of an enormous length, gave them an air of wilderness and savageness.[21]

They were neither pretty nor perfumed, but hard with the lean toughness of adversity, and such men, given the leader to inspire and organize them, have always been invincible. However, America had yet to find its leaders. The penny-pinching William Eustis had done his country the great kindness of resigning, but Madison had replaced him in the War Department with John Armstrong, a leading Republican politician from New York who was also the author of the mutinous Newburgh Addresses as well as the crony of the treacherous James Wilkinson.

Despite his record, Armstrong was not disloyal—just personally ambitious. Nor did he fail to see, as Hull and Harrison had also seen before closing their eyes to the fact, that naval control of the Great Lakes was the key to the Western campaign. But as Armstrong assumed office on February 5, 1813, the lakes were still frozen—and out on the open Atlantic the British Navy was demonstrating the risks that are taken when a young nation with a small navy and a long coastline defies the greatest sea power in the world.

Although the American single-ship victories continued into 1813 —notably when the 18-gun *Hornet* under the gallant James Lawrence defeated the 16-gun *Peacock* in February—they could at best only scratch the iron façade of British sea power. Unshaken, the Admiralty paid the Americans the ultimate compliment of ordering heavy frigates the equal of *Constitution* and her sister furies to be built, instructed its captains to be more respectful of Yankee fighting abilities and called for improvements in gunnery training. It also began to enforce a blockade of the exits of the Delaware and Chesapeake.

The blockade was ordered after Britain realized that suspension of the Orders in Council had not brought peace. President Madison still insisted that the British stop impressing seamen, and this, of course, Britannia would never do. So the blockade was begun, and later extended north to Long Island and south to the Mississippi, carefully excluding New England for the purpose of encouraging antiwar sentiment there.

Vice Admiral John Borlase Warren was charged with enforcing the blockade and by February, 1813, he had at his disposal 17 ships of the line, two 50-gunners, 27 frigates and about 50 smaller vessels. With the years, as his fleet grew steadily larger, he turned the screws of the blockade tighter and tighter. The American economy was strangled. Exports, which had been as high as $130 million in 1807, fell to $25 million in 1813 and to $7 million the following year. Import duties, which had yielded $413 million in 1811, fell to less than half that amount in 1814.

The blockade also bottled up coastal shipping, with the result that a dreadful burden was placed on land transportation. It took 46 days for a wagon to move from South Carolina to Philadelphia, and the poor roads were so thronged with wagons that on one occasion, no less than 800 of them were counted waiting in line before a Pennsylvania ferry. Prices soared. Sugar quoted at $9 a hundredweight in New Orleans sold for $21 in New York in August, 1813, and by December had risen to $40. A hundredweight of rice that sold for $3 in Savannah brought $12 in Philadelphia.

Not content with strangling the American economy, the Admiralty ordered Admiral Warren to bring the war home to the Americans in the Delaware-Chesapeake area. Warren thereupon sent Captain John Beresford in the 74-gun *Poictiers* to the Delaware. Beresford appeared before Lewes, Delaware, and shelled the town after its inhabitants stubbornly refused to hand over 25 live bullocks as he demanded. Lewes fought back with old Revolutionary War cannon, and in so doing launched the famous du Pont powder dynasty.

Pierre du Pont de Nemours, a French intellectual who might have lost his head to the French Revolution's guillotine had not it first cut off Robespierre's, came to America with his two sons. Although he returned to France, the sons remained and built a powder factory. When Lewes came under attack, the du Ponts rushed powder there, and the militia, who had provided themselves with cannon balls by "capturing" British ones that missed their mark, actually disabled a British boat and drove Beresford off. But the British returned, and this time Admiral Warren teamed up with his second-in-command, Admiral Sir George Cockburn.

No better team for chastising civilians could have been chosen. Warren, a religious man who had once wavered between the quarterdeck and the cloth, and was now vice president of the Halifax Bible Society, was as quick with a torch as with a text. Cockburn was simply a crusty old salt who delighted in the discomfiture of landlubbers, especially those who were enemies of the Crown.

Cockburn entered the Chesapeake in the early spring of 1813, engaging first in cleaning out the hen roosts and pigsties in the area around Lynnhaven Bay. Next he ravaged Frenchtown, Maryland, put Havre de Grace to the torch and sailed up the Susquehanna 60 miles to destroy a cannon foundry. Carrying plunder and pillage to other areas in the upper Chesapeake, he turned south in June to join Warren and 3,000 regulars in an attack on Norfolk.

There were two objectives: the frigate *Constellation,* anchored near the town, and the Portsmouth Navy Yard. But an amphibious assault on Craney Island which guarded Norfolk was hurled back on June 20 by Americans fighting coolly and shooting accurately under the command of Brigadier General Robert Taylor. Frustrated,

Warren and Cockburn vented their spite on the little village of Hampton. Here the British lost all restraint. As one officer who was later to command the British Army in India noted in his diary: "Every horror was perpetrated with impunity—rape, murder, pillage—*and not a man was punished.*"[22] Warren tried to place all the blame for Hampton on a unit of French prisoners who had elected to serve with the British rather than languish in prisons, but the vice president of the Halifax Bible Society deceived no one.

Nor was Warren able to destroy the Chesapeake's privateering sanctuaries. Before the war ended there were 526 Yankee privateers swarming out of American coastal cities to strike British commercial shipping and take a total of 1,334 prizes. Even more effective were the U.S. Navy's fighting ships: 22 of them captured 165 British vessels.

Warren's fleet was eager to bottle up those fighting ships which had been caught in port. Among these was *Chesapeake,* the frigate already famous—or notorious—for its humiliation by *Leopard* in the impressment incident of 1807. *Chesapeake*'s new commander, Captain James Lawrence, did not value such celebrity. He was eager to prove that his victory over *Peacock* at the helm of *Hornet* had been no happy fluke. He was, in fact, too eager, for his crew was not yet properly trained, and the ship then watching Boston was the formidable *Shannon,* the frigate which had nearly caught *Constitution* the preceding August.

Like *Chesapeake, Shannon* was rated at 38 guns but actually carried more: 52 to the American's 50. She was commanded by Captain Philip Broke, a British sailor who did not neglect his guns. Broke had personally seen to the mounting of his ordnance and had daily drilled his men in their use. He sent Lawrence a challenge to meet him "ship to ship, to try the fortunes of our respective flags."

Lawrence sailed from Boston on June 1. Broke awaited him at sea between Cape Ann and Cape Cod. Without preliminary maneuver both ships closed to half-pistol shot and began battering each other with broadsides. Cannon roared mouth to mouth. Grapeshot swept the decks, iron balls burst wooden walls, shells exploded, canister flamed with spreading death, and marines of both sides swayed in the rigging while pouring musket shot into the enemy below. Soon both ships were floating charnel houses. But within 15 minutes

Shannon's better-trained gunners had exerted their superiority over *Chesapeake*'s mixed crew. Still, the Americans fought on, especially after Lawrence received his death wound. As he was being carried below, he uttered the famous command that became the motto of the United States Navy.

"Don't give up the ship," he gasped. "Fight her till she sinks."[23]

They did not give up until the cutlasses and grenades of a British boarding party made all further resistance madness. But her flag was never struck by an American hand.

Nevertheless, *Shannon*'s triumph had restored British naval pride, and was also the beginning of the end for America's deep-water fleet. Only two more victories remained for the graceful ships which were the precursors of the beautiful Yankee clippers, and then, one by one, the others were taken or bottled up in port until, in 1814, even the far-ranging *Essex* was caught and destroyed on a Pacific reef.

It was not, however, the end of the U.S. Navy. Far away westward on the warming water of Lake Erie the words of the dying Lawrence echoed in the heart of a young sailor named Oliver Hazard Perry.

Master Commandant Perry had gone to sea at the age of 11, and had fought in the wars with the Barbary pirates. In 1812 he wrote to Commodore Isaac Chauncey, commander of the budding Great Lakes fleet, applying for command of the Lake Erie flotilla being built at Erie, Pennsylvania. Chauncey replied, "You are just the man I have been looking for,"[24] and in March of 1813, at the age of 28, Perry arrived on the shores of Lake Erie.

He hurled himself into the task of building his flotilla and training the men to sail and fight it. He beat the bushes for carpenters, combed the wilderness for blacksmiths, scavenged for scrap iron to make the mounts for his guns, went to the foundries to observe the casting of his shot, and sailed downriver to Pittsburgh to set up a supply line. By the end of May two 20-gun brigs were launched. Soon a trio of gunboats followed. Five ships, however, were not enough to wrest control of Lake Erie from British hands. If only the young commander could free five other ships then stationed at Black Rock on the Niagara River. Unfortunately, the enemy in Fort Erie stood between them and Perry.

Then there began a chain of events in which Perry not only participated but of which he became the chief beneficiary.

Soon after John Armstrong assumed office as Secretary of War he proposed a Northeastern campaign aimed at Montreal. Yet when the orders were received by General Dearborn, Montreal, which was certainly his true objective, was not mentioned. Dearborn was told to take Kingston at the western end of the St. Lawrence River with alternate objectives at York (present-day Toronto) or Forts George and Erie.

Dearborn consulted with Chauncey and after both men grossly overestimated enemy strength at Kingston, that project was dropped and the Northeastern campaign faced farther away westward to York and Fort George.

York was assaulted on April 27 when Chauncey's Ontario ships put ashore 1,600 men under the capable Brigadier General Zebulon Pike.* Pike's soldiers drove off a small force of British regulars and Canadians, and seized the harbor batteries and magazines. They burned a half-built, 30-gun frigate which would have been a valuable addition to the British Ontario fleet, and destroyed naval supplies destined for Lake Erie. And then one of the magazines blew up with a tremendous explosion, raising a deadly shower of stones, one of which crushed the life out of General Pike. In all, 53 Americans were killed and 150 wounded, while 40 Canadians perished and 23 were wounded. The cause of the explosion was not known, but some of the Americans began to think that it was an enemy trick. They thought angrily of "retaliation," ignoring the fact of the Canadian deaths and their own status of invaders, and they began to plunder and loot. They carried off the mace and royal standard of Parliament, and then set fire to the Parliament buildings; and in so doing, even though they might have been aided by capricious Canadians, they created in Canadian hearts a thirst for retaliation in kind which would be satisfied all too soon. That was all there was to York: the wanton burning of the capitol of Upper Canada, the more profitable burning of a ship and naval stores.

At Fort George there was even less military profit. Here, General Dearborn had about 4,000 men against 1,300 under the command of Brigadier General John Vincent. His spearhead troops were led by Winfield Scott, who had been exchanged and promoted to colonel. On May 27 ships commanded by Oliver Hazard Perry bombarded the fort's crumbling wall while his seamen rowed Scott's spearheaders

* He was also the explorer for whom Pike's Peak was named.

through a wild surf. Reaching the beaches, the Americans were momentarily checked by a handful of defenders. But then, gathering force, they burst through. Bringing artillery ashore, Scott put the fort under fire, and Vincent abandoned it.

Vincent's garrison, not moldering old Fort George, was the true objective. But the British got away, chiefly because Scott was wounded and could not pursue, and the vacillating Dearborn was not ashore to give the order. Vincent ordered his garrisons at Fort Erie, Queenston and Chippewa to join him, and withdrew westward along the lake to Burlington Heights.

Two days later the British struck at the American rear. General Sir George Prevost with 800 men appeared at Sackets Harbor and forced a landing, only to be repulsed by the resolute defense maintained by Brigadier General Jacob Brown. With his line of communications thus guaranteed, Dearborn tardily turned to the pursuit of the retreating Vincent.

About 3,000 men under Brigadier Generals William Winder and John Chandler tried to catch Vincent with 1,600. On the night of June 5 the Americans set up camp at Stony Creek, ten miles from Vincent's bivouac. Early the following morning, 750 British regulars struck them in a surprise attack, scattered them and took Winder and Chandler prisoner. Next a force of 600 Americans under Lieutenant Colonel Charles Boerstler surrendered to 400 Indians and 50 regulars.

With this freshest of fiascoes along the Niagara frontier, the fumbling career of Granny Dearborn came to an end. President Madison requested, and received, his resignation. And yet out of Dearborn's mismanagement had come an indirect but enormous advantage. Merely by acting, he had forced Vincent to withdraw his garrison from Fort Erie, thus freeing Perry's ships at Black Rock to sail up the Niagara into Lake Erie.

Perry harnessed the vessels to oxen to tow them through the Niagara's swift current. Reaching the open waters of the lake, they spread sail and made for the sheltering long arm of land that formed the harbor at Erie. Now there were ten ships in Perry's flotilla, and the youthful commander was elated.

On July 12, however, he was saddened to hear of the death of James Lawrence, an officer whom he much admired. In tribute to the *Chesapeake*'s fallen captain, he named his own flagship *Lawrence*. Her sister ship was called *Niagara*.

Now Perry's problems were of a different order. He needed men. Again and again he wrote to Chauncey back at Sackets Harbor, imploring him to send men. Even as Chauncey procrastinated, or sent him the raked-over leavings of his own command, the Navy Department ordered Perry to do battle on the lake. Stung, Perry wrote Chauncey: "For God's sake, and yours and mine, send me men."[25] Chauncey sent him 60 sickly sailors, and Perry turned to recruiting his own crews by offering farmers and woodsmen the princely pay of $10 monthly for four months' service or the duration of a battle, whichever was shorter.

Even so, by mid-July he had only 300 men, and Perry was as nearly frantic as a man of his stability might become; for continued delay gave the enemy time to finish the powerful brig *Detroit,* still on the stocks near Fort Malden. And as the American waited for more reinforcements, warfare flared afresh in the Northwest.

With the coming of the spring of 1813 General Harrison's force in Fort Meigs had dwindled down to about 1,000 men. Harrison appealed to Governor Shelby of Kentucky, who sent forward about 1,200 men under General Green Clay. As the relief force approached Meigs, General Proctor moved out of Malden with 500 regulars, 500 militia and 1,200 Indians under Tecumseh and Roundhead.

The British force reached Fort Meigs on May 1, set up batteries on both sides of the Maumee River and attempted to pound the fort into submission. Just before midnight of May 4, Harrison received word that Clay's relief force was coming down the Maumee on flatboats only two hours away. Harrison decided on a daring plan to raise the siege of Meigs.

Clay's troops were to destroy the British artillery on the north side of the river while Harrison's sallied out of Meigs to take the guns on the south side. About 800 of Clay's men were to land on the north bank, spike the cannon, and then fall back into their boats before the British could get into action. Then these men would join Clay, who with the remaining 400 soldiers was to land on the south bank to cut his way into the fort.

On the south bank the plan worked to perfection. Harrison's men rushed out of Meigs to take the south battery and General Clay got safely into the fort with his 400. On the north bank 800 men under Lieutenant Colonel William Dudley quickly carried the enemy battery and spiked the guns. But then too little leadership and too much zeal betrayed the American cause. One of Dudley's details had wandered off and became engaged with Indians. Instead of falling back to the boats as planned, Dudley went to the aid of the detail. His men charged the Indians, broke them and pursued them through the woods up to the British camp. With this the British counterattacked the American front while more Indians struck the flanks. About 600 men were killed or captured. Dudley was taken and tomahawked as the Indians began to renew the horrors of the River Raisin while Proctor looked on indifferently.

But this time Tecumseh was present. He rushed in among his murdering warriors, who had already taken twenty scalps. He knocked one down with the flat of his sword, seized another by the throat and swung at a third. "Are there no men here?" he roared, and the slaughter stopped. Enraged, Tecumseh ran to Proctor to demand to know why his Indians had been allowed to kill prisoners. Proctor said, "Your Indians cannot be controlled. They cannot be commanded." Tecumseh's face twisted in contempt. "You are unfit to command," he told Proctor. "Go and put on petticoats!"[26]

Despite the Dudley disaster, Fort Meigs had been saved. On May 9, with his Indians deserting and his militia clamoring to go home to plant crops, Proctor raised the siege and returned to Malden.

Two months later he came back, and failed again. Disgruntled, he dropped down the Maumee, reached Lake Erie and coasted east to the Sandusky River. He went up the Sandusky determined to take Fort Stephenson, an American outpost so vulnerable that Harrison ordered it abandoned. Its commander, Major George Croghan, thought otherwise. "We have determined to maintain this place, and by Heaven we will," he told Harrison.[27] He did. As the British and Indians charged they were mowed down by his Kentucky sharpshooters and a single cannon called "Old Betsey" spewing out grape and nails. Proctor thought that Groghan's fire was the severest he had ever seen, and he gave up his offensive to return to Malden.

The date was August 1, one day before Commodore Perry began taking his flotilla over the bar at Erie.

Perry used "camels" to float his ships over the bar. Floats were placed on either side of a ship, filled with water and sunk to a depth just below the ship's portholes. Then timbers were run through the portholes, coming to rest on the decks of the camels to either side, after which the water was pumped out of the camels and as they rose they lifted the ship with them and floated over the bar.

By August 5 Perry had his fleet out in open water, and he began searching the lake for the British. But the enemy fleet was still in Malden under Captain Robert Barclay, a veteran sailor who had lost an arm at Trafalgar. Perry returned to Erie, where he resumed his demands for more men. On August 10 he got 90 of them, headed by young Lieutenant Jesse Elliott, whom he placed in command of *Niagara*. Perry still needed marines, however, and this shortage was eliminated when General Harrison sent him 100 Kentucky marksmen. With their easy discipline, these sailors in buckskin might have turned out to be a new trial, but they turned to like old salts after Perry explained the demands of shipboard life. Now all that the eager American commander needed was a battle, and he got it on the morning of September 10, 1813, when the one-armed Barclay brought the British fleet to Perry's new base at Put-in-Bay.

Because of so many variables in guns, number and tonnage, it is almost impossible to estimate which was the stronger fleet. Suffice it to say that Perry, with nine ships to Barclay's six, held a slight edge. Otherwise they were evenly matched, Barclay possessing superior long-range artillery, Perry being stronger at close range. Barclay planned to fight at a distance and defeat his enemy ships in detail; Perry was eager to close to bring his carronades into action.

Perry's plan was to sail his own ship, *Lawrence,* supported by *Caledonia, Scorpion* and *Ariel,* against Barclay in *Detroit*—most powerful ship on the lake—and *Hunter* and tiny *Chippewa.* Elliott with *Niagara* would fight Barclay's second ship, *Queen Charlotte,* to which she was superior, while *Somers, Porcupine, Tigress* and *Trippe* took on *Lady Prevost* and *Little Belt.*

Slowly the American ships beat their way out of the harbor. Their decks were strewn with sand to prevent them from becoming slippery with blood. Outside stood the British ships, freshly calked and painted, with their red hulls gleaming and their polished brass glittering in the autumn sun. At first the weather favored the British, but then the wind changed and Perry held the weather gauge. Suddenly an American cheer rolled toward the British ships. Perry had unfurled his standard, a nine-foot square of blue on which white letters a foot high proclaimed the words of the dying Lawrence: "DON'T GIVE UP THE SHIP." Then the British cheered. Their bands had begun to play

"Rule, Britannia"—and out of the mouths of *Detroit*'s cannon came the first shots of the battle.

Lawrence was *Detroit*'s target. She took a punishing fire as she sailed down the British line in an effort to reach her adversary. Then *Queen Charlotte* joined *Detroit,* and *Lawrence*'s ordeal was nearly redoubled. *Charlotte* was free to pound Perry's flagship because Elliott in *Niagara* was not closing as ordered. Elliott stood off at a distance firing only a few long-range guns.

For two hours the British pair blasted away at *Lawrence.* They took her apart, cannon by carronade, spar by sail, brace by bowline, and they shot her hull into a sieve. Undaunted, Perry fought on alone. Of 103 men who began the fight, 83 were either killed or wounded. Perry stood upon the blood-clotted sand and cried: "Can any of the wounded pull a rope?"[28] A few crawled to his side to help put a dismounted gun in place. It was *Lawrence*'s last gun, and Perry fired it to let the fleet know that he was still in action. But Elliott in *Niagara* still stood at a distance. All seemed to be lost, except for Perry.

The American knew that he had given as well as taken punishment. He knew that with a fresh ship he could turn the tide of battle. Hauling down his blue banner, he leaped into a boat with his 13-year-old brother, Alexander, and four seamen. They began rowing toward *Niagara.* Perry stood in the stern until the seamen pushed him down. A British broadside went over their heads. The water around them was dimpled with musket shot, but the little boat passed miraculously through. Coming aboard *Niagara*, Perry took command. He ordered Elliott to bring up the three schooners which had also lagged behind. *Lawrence* was now drifting out of control, her flag pulled down, but before the British could move to possess her, Perry returned to the fight.

Swift and straight, *Niagara* burst the British line. On the port side her batteries battered *Chippewa, Little Belt* and *Lady Prevost*; on the starboard they thundered and flamed at *Detroit* and *Queen Charlotte. Detroit* tried to turn, and fouled *Queen Charlotte.* Perry's gunners took aim at the tangled ships and shot them both to pieces. With the first- and second-in-command on each of his vessels either killed or wounded, with his remaining arm shattered, Barclay surrendered *Detroit.* Eventually his other ships were overcome, and the battle was over before dusk.

Now the battered *Lawrence* had run up her flag again, and a feeble cheer rose from the living and wounded men aboard her who still had breath to spare. Aboard *Niagara,* Oliver Hazard Perry took an old envelope from his pocket. He held it against a navy cap and penciled a message to General Harrison, waiting anxiously ashore. Perry wrote: "We have met the enemy and they are ours."[29]

Barclay's defeat unmasked Proctor at Fort Malden, and that jittery general, fearing American revenge for the River Raisin massacre, quickly prepared to flee. Tecumseh soon realized that Proctor was about to withdraw and leave the Indians to shift for themselves. He confronted him and said: "We must compare our Father's conduct to a fat dog that carries its tail upon its back, but when affrightened drops it between its legs and runs off."[30]

Nevertheless, Proctor would not stay, as he had promised the Indians, and Tecumseh realized that he would have to go with him. "We are now going to follow the British," he told his people glumly, "and I feel certain that we shall never return."[31]

As Proctor began withdrawing, William Henry Harrison moved to the attack. Governor Shelby had come to Lake Erie with 3,000 Kentucky volunteers. Harrison also had the services of Congressman Richard Mentor Johnson with 1,000 mounted volunteers. But Proctor got away. Harrison found Fort Malden and the nearby town of Amherstburg still burning. On September 26 Detroit was reoccupied, after which the pursuit of Proctor began.

Johnson's horsemen crossed the Detroit River and gave chase by land while Perry's ships tried to sail through the river into Lake St. Clair in an effort to cut off Proctor's rear. Neither was quick enough, for Proctor had reached the Thames River and was moving up its banks. On the night of October 4 he halted at the modern town of Thamesville and prepared for battle. Tecumseh gathered his warriors. He took off the sword denoting his rank as a brigadier general in the British Army and said, "When my son becomes a noted warrior, give him this."[32] He forecast his own death, just as his elder brother Cheeseekau had done in the Carolinas when Tecumseh was a young boy. "Brother warriors," he said, "we are about to enter an engagement from which I shall not return. My body will remain on the field of battle."[33]

In the morning Tecumseh was more cheerful. He hunted up

Proctor and spoke to him in a forgiving mood. "Father, have a big heart! Tell your young men to be firm and all will be well."[34] Proctor's conduct, however, was not likely to make many men stand firm. His army was aware that he was giving battle reluctantly, that he preferred flight to fighting. Yet his battle position was fairly strong.

It lay between the river on the left and a large swamp on the right. In its middle was a smaller swamp. Most of the British troops were between the river and the small swamp. Indians under Tecumseh were between the small and large swamp.

Harrison planned to make an infantry frontal assault against the British, but then, learning that the enemy regulars were drawn up in open rather than close order, he called on Richard Mentor Johnson's mounted Kentuckians. Just before the attack, Johnson decided on his own that the space was too narrow for 1,000 horsemen. He divided his regiment in two, one battalion under his brother James to ride at the British, the other under himself to charge Tecumseh's Indians between the swamps. The bugle sounded and the homespun dragoons on their ragged mounts swept forward crying, "Remember the Raisin! Remember the River Raisin!"

On the American right James Johnson's cavalrymen burst the British line. Leaning from their saddles, the Americans swung their tomahawks and scattered the regulars in terror. General Henry Proctor became so frightened that he jumped into his carriage and clattered away from the battlefield. The Americans pursued in delight. They did not catch Proctor, but they took hundreds of prisoners and captured about $1 million in supplies, including guns taken from Burgoyne in 1777, then lost at Detroit by Hull in 1812.

On the American left, Tecumseh's warriors waited until the American horsemen were within a few paces before pouring a heavy fire into them. Perhaps 20 saddles were emptied. Richard Johnson was among the wounded, but he stayed with his men as they seized their rifles and leaped from their horses to engage the Indians on foot. American infantry hurried forward in support, and the Indians charged.

One of them came at 64-year-old Colonel William Whitley. Both men fired and both fell dead. Another Indian rushed with upraised tomahawk at the bleeding Johnson. Johnson shot him through the head and fell down unconscious. In one of these two encounters—probably the first—the gallant Tecumseh was killed. His fall did not decide the Battle of the Thames, for British defeat was already guaranteed with the American charge and Proctor's flight. But the death of this noble Indian leader was also the death of his vision of a confederacy of Indians hunting, as their fathers had hunted, across vast and untroubled stretches of American plains and forest. Tecumseh's body was never found. It was believed to have been borne off in the night by his sorrowing warriors, and his final resting place remains as much a mystery as the name of the man who killed him. Richard Johnson never claimed the credit, although his followers claimed it for him during the election of 1836 which made Johnson Vice President. What is known, however, is that vengeful frontiersmen as barbarous as the butchers of the River Raisin stripped the skin from a body mistakenly believed to have been Tecumseh's and cut it into razor strops. "Tecumseh razor strops" eventually appeared in fashionable Washington.

Harrison's victory had ended British power in Upper Canada, crushed the Indians and redeemed the Northwest Territory. All this had been made possible by the earlier and more important victory which Perry had won on Lake Erie. Together the two battles raised the American flag for good over northern Ohio, Indiana and Illinois, and over the territory out of which Michigan, Minnesota and Wisconsin were formed—in other words, most of the modern Midwest, that rich, thriving, clanging, fertile territory which is at once the breadbasket and the toolshop of America and the iron heart of the continent.

And the Midwest was won for America chiefly because an ardent young captain would not give up his ship.

6

☆

Upon the resignation of Henry Dearborn, command in the Northeast passed to Major General James Wilkinson, and thus, in Ganoe's phrase, "age and infirmity gave place to age and fatuity."[35]

"The selection of this unprincipled imbecile was not the blunder of Secretary Armstrong,"[36] Winfield Scott claimed long afterward; but the fact is that Armstrong, though aware of Wilkinson's shortcomings, had no wish to offend his old comrade in arms from the Battle of Saratoga. So he was merely going to make him Dearborn's chief of staff!

"Come to the North, and come quickly!" Armstrong wrote to Wilkinson in New Orleans. "If our cards be well played, we may renew the scene of Saratoga."[37]

Few men could answer an urgent summons more slowly than Wilkinson. He received the letter on May 19 and arrived in Washington on July 31. By that time Dearborn had resigned and Wilkinson by virtue of his seniority became the ranking general. No choice, however automatic, could have been more odious. Even though Wilkinson's occupation of Mobile while he commanded the Southern Department turned out to be the only American acquisition of territory during the war, his rise disgusted every decent officer in the service. Armstrong compounded this repugnance by placing Wilkinson over Major General Wade Hampton, his archenemy. For years these two men had led rival factions in the Army. To exalt one over the other would be certain to divide the service, but to prefer the scheming and unscrupulous Wilkinson to the honorable though harsh Hampton was to give a kiss to vice and a kick to virtue.

At the outset Hampton refused to command at Lake Champlain unless his orders came directly from the War Department. Only when his and Wilkinson's commands were combined would he take orders from the crony of Aaron Burr. Armstrong agreed. Wilkinson, however, did not. He wrote Armstrong: ". . . if I am authorized to command he is bound to obey; and if he will not respect the obligation, he should be turned out of the service."[38] Armstrong did not agree with this, but neither did he tell Wilkinson that he did not.

Thus another American attempt on Montreal was begun with its two chief commanders cooperating like a mongoose and a cobra, after which the Secretary of War made his contribution to unity by getting into a wrangle over strategy with his own general in chief.

Armstrong had moved the War Department to Wilkinson's base at Sackets Harbor! It is said that he did so to slip the tight reins held on him by Madison. It is also said that he wanted to ride herd on Wilkinson. Whatever the cause for this unusual move on the part of a civilian war chief, Armstrong quickly found that Wilkinson was already unfit to command. By October he had fallen ill of fever. "He was so much indisposed in mind and body," according to General John Boyd, "that in any other service he would have perhaps been superseded in his command."[39] But Wilkinson was never so sick as to stop giving orders or to forbear from quarreling with Armstrong.

Wilkinson, apparently thinking little of Harrison, had originally wanted to clean out the Niagara frontier and attack Malden. Armstrong vetoed this with the remark that a movement west "but wounds the tail of the beast." Montreal was the beast's true heart. But the louder Armstrong spoke for Montreal, the more Wilkinson veered toward Kingston. In the end Wilkinson demanded written directions to abandon Kingston, and it was agreed to take Montreal first and *then* come back and seize Kingston: in other words, the beast's heart first and then its hindquarters.

Actually, neither man expected to capture either Kingston or Montreal. Wilkinson went so far as to ask for authorization to surrender should disaster threaten, and Armstrong secretly ordered Hampton to provide winter quarters for the army at a point 80 miles short of Montreal. In other words, he intended no serious movement on Montreal.

Unfortunately for some 10,000 Americans who had put their trust in this perfidious pair, the farce was to be played out. Wilkinson with about 6,000 men was to descend the St. Lawrence, where he was to meet Hampton with about 4,000 men, and together they would move on to Montreal. As was the custom set by their colonial forebears of a century before, the Americans did not get started until autumn plumed the woods in red and gold and the nights were chill with the breath of approaching winter. On October 17 about 300 boats carrying Wilkinson's men sailed north for the mouth of the St. Lawrence. Heavy gales scattered them, and it was not until November 5 that they had regrouped and begun sailing downriver. Behind them Commodore Chauncey's gunboats bottled up Kingston to prevent the British from following on Wilkinson's rear. To the left of the American flotilla, British guns on the northern bank made their passage difficult. But they faltered on, and as they did, Secretary Armstrong returned to Washington.

Meanwhile, Hampton had begun moving westward from his base at Lake Champlain. He reached Four Corners (New York) on the Chateaugay River and took up a position from which he could either join Wilkinson, cut the British communications to Upper Canada or move against Montreal. Appreciating this, Sir George Prevost sent about 1,500 French-Canadians against Hampton. Prevost had not always been sure of the loyalty of these Gallic troops, but in the Battle of Chateaugay on October 25-26 they fought Hampton's men with enough enthusiasm to dispel Prevost's doubts and to force Hampton to fall back. It was then that Hampton received Armstrong's orders to build winter quarters for the army. "This paper sank my hopes,"[40] said the disillusioned Hampton.

As Hampton's part in the camaign came to an end, about 1,000 boated British troops slipped out of Kingston to follow Wilkinson's flotilla. They snapped at his heels, even as the artillery on the river banks struck his left flank. At last General Jacob Brown was landed with an advance guard to clear the north bank of the St. Lawrence and a flanking movement was ordered. But the rear was left open until, on November 11, 1813, General Boyd took 2,000 men ashore and deployed them at a place known as Chrysler's Farm.

Here, in alternating snow and drizzle, while his troops attacked bravely across a field of mud and slush, Boyd attempted to crush the British force from Kingston. But he was defeated, and that was the end of the campaign. Wilkinson, learning that Hampton was not moving to meet him, flew into a rage and ordered Hampton's arrest. Then he changed his mind and decided to throw the responsibility on Armstrong. In the meantime he turned south, ascended the Salmon River and went into winter quarters in New York.

Never again did American arms menace Montreal, if, indeed, this monstrously mismanaged expedition actually ever had endangered the city. Why, it may be asked, was it ordered? Did Armstrong, as Wilkinson and Hampton both insisted, deliberately order an impossible campaign so as to bring the blame of failure on their heads? History does not know, although it has been maintained that Armstrong's motive was to rid himself of his decrepit generals so as to take the field himself as the American general in chief. If he did—and it is difficult to place any other interpretation upon his actions—then he was eminently successful, for the Montreal fiasco disposed of the last of the graybeards: Wilkinson, Hampton and Morgan Lewis. But field command never did devolve upon John Armstrong. He was already in odium in the White House, and by stripping the entire Northern border of troops so that not a regiment stood guard between Detroit and Sackets Harbor, he invited disaster along the Niagara frontier.

The British did not have to fight to recover Fort George, held by about 500 men under the militia general, George McClure. Most of McClure's men were near the expiration of their enlistments, and as the holiday season neared they began going home. McClure could neither restrain them nor persuade them to re-enlist, and so he moved his remaining force of 100 men across the river to Fort Niagara. But before he did he wantonly burnt the town of Newark, leaving its residents homeless in the frightful Northern winter. McClure said he wanted to deny the British winter quarters, but the truth was that the only building left standing was the army barracks.

Retaliation for this American atrocity, together with the burning of the capitol at York, was quick and dreadful. As the Americans in Niagara prepared to observe Christmas, a British force including 600 Indians slipped across the river. Someone had left Fort Niagara's front gate open. Yelling for revenge, the British stormed inside and bayoneted 67 Americans dead before they accepted a surrender.

Then the Indians were turned loose. By New Year's Day of 1814 Buffalo was a cinder smoking in the snow and Black Rock, Lewiston, Youngstown, Manchester, Schlosser and Tuscarora village were black heaps of rubbish. An area 12 miles wide and 36 miles long had been devastated, and as the cold and hungry survivors mourned their slain, the country was treated to the spectacle of Wilkinson and Armstrong engaged in public acrimony which ended with Wilkinson making his customary demand for a court-martial that would fix the blame elsewhere.

It would have been hard for Wilkinson to find a clean scapegoat. At the time, a New York newspaper printed the names of 13 discredited generals, headed by Granny Dearborn, along with a refrain which became popular during the court-martial of General Hull:

> Pray, General Dearborn, be impartial,
> When President of a Court-Martial;
> Since Canada has not been taken,
> Say General Hull was much mistaken.
> Dearborn himself, as records say,
> Mistaken was the self-same way.

And Wilkinson, and Hampton, too.
And Harrison, and all the crew.
Strange to relate, the self-same way
Have all mist-taken Canaday.[41]

Only one general of reputation remained. He was in the South, and his name was Andrew Jackson.

7

☆

Andrew Jackson had already run afoul of Wilkinson and Armstrong. During Burr's trial he had denounced Wilkinson to his face as a "double traitor," and sneered: "Pity the sword that dangles from his felon's belt, for it is doubtless of honest steel!"[42] Even so, at the end of 1812 Jackson, a major general of militia, had not hesitated to lead 2,000 Tennessee volunteers south to support Brigadier General Wilkinson in New Orleans.

But Wilkinson had no intention of allowing a detested militia officer of superior rank to enter New Orleans. He directed Jackson to halt near Natchez in present-day Mississippi. Throughout January of 1813 the highhearted Tennessee troops cooled their heels, and then were coldly dismissed from service by John Armstrong two days after he took office as Secretary of War.

Jackson, never a man to hold his temper long, flew into a fury. He refused to disband his men 1,000 miles from home and personally led them back to Tennessee, gaining, en route, his famous nickname of "Old Hickory." Even so, the patriotic Jackson still offered to take these self-same repudiated troops up north. "I have a few standards wearing the American eagle," he wrote to Armstrong, "that I should be happy to place upon the ramparts of Malden."[43] The offer was ignored, and Jackson dismissed his men in Nashville in May of 1813.

That same month Jackson acted as second for his friend William Carroll in a duel with Jesse Benton, younger brother of Thomas Hart Benton, later a Senator from Missouri. Young Benton fired first, missed and panicked. Turning, he doubled up and offered Carroll the seat of his pants. Taking deliberate aim, Carroll fired a ball into Benton's behind. The injury done to Jesse Benton's body was superficial, but the wound in his pride was deep. He became the butt of Tennessee's broad humor, and eventually, with his brother, he magnified Jackson's part in the affair and blamed him for the indignity.

On September 4, 1813, the Bentons came into Nashville wearing two pistols each. They went to the City Hotel. Jackson and his close friend, the gigantic John Coffee, went there also. Both were armed, and Jackson carried a whip. Seeing Thomas Benton in a doorway, Jackson brandished the whip and roared: "Now, defend yourself, you damned rascal."⁴⁴ Benton reached for his pistol, but before he could draw, Jackson's gun was at his breast. Step by step, Jackson backed Benton through a corridor. Suddenly, Jesse Benton came up behind him, drew and fired. Jackson pitched forward, firing as he fell. His powder merely burned Thomas Benton's sleeve, but blood was streaming from Jackson's left side. More shots were fired, blades were drawn, and the huge John Coffee entered the fight—but out of the smoke and shouting emerged one clear fact: General Jackson was badly wounded.

Jackson barely understood the doctors asking permission to amputate his arm, but when he did, he muttered, "I'll keep my arm."⁴⁵ He lay in great pain in his bed in the Hermitage, and he was still there when news of the Creek rising reached Tennessee.

It was the dream of Tecumseh that sent the peaceful Creeks on their nightmare war against the United States. Tecumseh hoped to bring the Southern Indians into his confederacy, and in 1811 he visited the Creek country in present-day Alabama. He taught the young and more warlike braves the dance of the Indians of the lakes, which became their symbol, and the sorcerers he brought with him infected the Creeks with a religious fanaticism which compensated for Creek deficiencies in firearms and fighting confidence. Tecumseh made a deep impression upon the half-breed Billy Weatherford, a bold and intelligent leader who boasted of French, Scottish, Spanish and Creek ancestors but "not one drop of Yankee blood." Weatherford became Tecumseh's lieutenant in the South.

Not all the Creek chiefs were persuaded by Tecumseh. Big Warrior did not hesitate to denounce him. Tecumseh told Big Warrior that he would feel the stamp of his foot as he entered Detroit. After his departure and the elapse of about the time required for his homeward journey, an earthquake shook Alabama. Tecumseh won many converts.

Returning in 1812, he won many more, for he brought the exhilarating news of the British-Indian victory at Detroit. He promised the Southern Indians aid from both the British in the North and the Spanish in the South. His influence spread, and then, late in 1812, Chief Little Warrior led a band of warlike Creeks all the way to Canada. They participated in the River Raisin massacre, and on the way home they slaughtered two white families living at the mouth of the Ohio.

The American government demanded that the Creeks hand over Little Warrior and his companions. In council, the elders under Big Warrior's lead decided to execute the murderers themselves. Little Warrior and his followers were hunted down and killed, and this act precipitated nothing less than a civil war among the Creeks.

The Upper Creeks, living in the higher valleys of the Gulf Coast streams, wanted Little Warrior avenged. The Lower Creeks, living along the lower Chattahoochee and Apalachicola rivers, feared war with the whites and tried to stay aloof. When Big Warrior sent a message calling for an end to "fooleries" among the Upper Creeks, the messenger was killed and a general uprising began. All Little Warrior's executioners were either driven into the forests or killed, and 29 of 34 Upper Creek towns declared for war. The warriors seized the crimson war clubs from which they took their name of Red Clubs or Red Sticks, and they swung them in wrath against every vestige of the white man's civilization as well as those kinsmen who refused to do the same.

In July of 1813 the half-breed chief Peter McQueen led a party of warlike Creeks into Pensacola. They brought war booty to exchange for provisions as well as a letter to the Spanish governor from the British authorities at Malden. The governor gave the Indians powder and bullets, merely for "hunting purposes," he said. American settlers already under attack could guess who the hunted might be, and they intercepted McQueen's party at a place called Burnt Corn, capturing some of the pack mules carrying the ammunition.

Two half-breeds, Major Daniel Beasley and Captain Dixon Bailey, had been among the Americans who ambushed the ammunition train, and now the Creek civil war became also a half-breed war. Hatred fed upon hatred as Billy Weatherford and Peter McQueen rallied 800 braves to avenge themselves upon the lovers of white men. They marched for Fort Mims, a stockade about 40 miles north of Mobile held by the detestable Beasley and Bailey and crowded with 550 refugees from the Red Stick uprising. Beasley commanded this motley of whites, half-breeds, Indians and Negroes, old and young, women and men, of whom perhaps 175 were armed militia. On August 30, 1813, Beasley wrote that he could "maintain the post against any number of Indians," but on noon of that day when the drum beat for dinner there were no patrols out, the gates were open, and the eastern gate, blocked by a mound of drifted sand, could not be quickly closed.

Suddenly there were whooping Indians swarming toward the fort. Beasley rushed for the gates, reached them, was tomahawked on the spot, and the yelling Indians rushed through to begin the butchery. Fifteen persons escaped, and most of the Negroes were spared for slaves, but everyone else in Fort Mims was cut down.

It was of this massacre that Andrew Jackson was informed by a committee of public safety hastening to the sick room in the Hermitage. Some 250 white scalps—a grisly harvest rare in the annals of Indians north or south—had excited the ferocity of the Creeks. And here lay Old Hickory, conscious "that he had squandered in a paltry, puerile, private contest, the strength he needed for the defense of his country."[46] Yet, without hesitation, he immediately ordered volunteers to rendezvous at Fayetteville on October 4. Propped against a pillow, he wrote:

"The health of your general is restored. He will command in person."[47]

The Creeks were not a formidable military force. At most there were about 4,000 Red Stick warriors, of whom never more than 1,000 could be assembled for a single battle. They had no artillery, and the men who did have muskets fired them only at the outset of combat, after which they relied upon bows and arrows, toma- hawks and clubs. Yet they defied the United States for a year, and that was because the difficulty was not in fighting them but in reaching them. They dwelt within inaccessible strongholds. The heart of the Creek country, the sacred Hickory Ground at the forks of the Coosa and Tallapoosa, was 150 miles away from the nearest American base.

Major General Thomas Pinckney, commanding the Southern Department, discovered these problems in wilderness logistics after two columns—one moving from Georgia, the other from Mobile—failed to accomplish much. Yet these two forces passed over easier routes than the 2,500 men whom Tennessee sent south under Andrew Jackson.

The difference was Jackson. Haggard, his arm in a sling, Benton's bullet still lodged in his shoulder to make him wary of those sudden movements which sent a thrill of agony twanging through his body, Old Hickory took command of his infantrymen on October 7. Many of them were the volunteers who had marched to Natchez and back. Among them were Ensign Sam Houston and that legendary frontiersman Davy Crockett, "the merriest of the merry, keeping the camp alive with his quaint conceits and marvelous narratives."[48] John Coffee, Jackson's closest friend and ablest lieutenant, had already advanced with the cavalry.

Coffee may have been a better general than Jackson; he was at least an instinctively superior tactician. He gave Jackson his first victory at Tallushatchee on November 3, 1813. Like Daniel Morgan before him, Coffee executed a Cannae in miniature. He placed his men in a semicircle and sent forward a small body to lure the Indians into it. As the Red Sticks attacked, the advance force retreated, the end of the semicircle swung shut—and over 180 Creeks were killed. Coffee lost 5 dead and 14 wounded. Six days later Jackson tried the same tactic, but his lines failed to hold and 400 of 700 Creeks escaped. Jackson's losses were 15 killed and 85 wounded.

Had Old Hickory been able to follow up these strokes, he might have ended the Creek War there and then. But he, too, was having his supply problems. As the year came to an end, the old American difficulty of short-term enlistments arose to plague him.

The men who had been to Natchez believed that their time expired December 10, 1813. They counted the months they had spent at home between Natchez and the Creek War as served time. Jackson disagreed. One stubborn company began marching home. Jackson, still unable to lift a musket because of the bullet in his back, rested his gun across the neck of his horse and threatened to shoot the first man who moved. The militiamen stood sullenly, glaring at him, but no man moved.

To everyone but Jackson the Creek War appeared hopeless. Governor Willie Blount wrote to him recommending a retreat. Jackson, who had dined on acorns at least once, flew into his customary passion at the perfidy of politicans. He composed a long letter to Blount, reminding him that he had "bawled aloud for permission to exterminate the Creeks," and asking: "And are you my Dear friend sitting with yr. arms folded . . . recommending me to retrograde to please the whims of the populace? . . . Let me tell you it imperiously lies upon both you and me to do our duty regardless of consequences or the opinion [of] these fireside patriots."[49] Angrily sketching the consequences of a retreat that would send thousands of hitherto friendly but wavering Creeks, Choctaws and Cherokees flocking to the Red Stick cause, he concluded:

Arouse from yr. lethargy—despite fawning smiles or snarling frowns— with energy exercise yr. functions—the campaign must rapidly progress or . . . yr. country ruined. Call out the full quota—execute the orders of the Secy of War, arrest the officer who omits his duty . . . and let popularity perish for the present. . . . What, retrograde under these circumstances? I will perish first.[50]

The letter together with a supporting thrust from the War Department stiffened Blount's spine. More troops came south. Although they were only 60-day men, Jackson made good use of them in a pair of sharp but indecisive engagements at Emuckfaw and Enotachopco creeks. In February of 1812 Jackson's army rose to 5,000 men, and the arrival of the 39th U.S. Infantry and the execution of a rebellious militiaman put steel into hitherto slouching ranks. Then Jackson learned that some 800 Red Sticks had fortified a position at Horseshoe Bend on the Tallapoosa River. They awaited all-or-nothing battle, and Old Hickory marched at the head of 2,000 men to give it to them.

The Horseshoe was a peninsula of about 100 acres of brush and small timber furrowed by gullies. Across its neck the Indians had built a zigzag row of logs pierced with double gun ports. At its rear they had drawn up hundreds of canoes in the event they were forced to flee. Jackson arrayed his main body and artillery opposite the log breastwork, and sent Coffee's cavalry across the river to cut off retreat.

Coffee's Cherokee scouts swam the river and stole the Creek canoes. Then the impetuous Coffee used them to cross and attack the Indian rear. To the front, Jackson's artillery plunged harmlessly into the breastwork's soft pine logs. Old Hickory called for a frontal assault.

Major Lemuel Montgomery, a relative of General Montgomery who was killed with Arnold at Quebec in 1775, was the first on the works. The Red Sticks shot him dead. Next came tall Sam Houston, leaping onto the breastwork, waving his sword and jumping down. A fierce fight at the rampart followed. Gradually, the Red Sticks were pressed back. They fought on bravely. Their prophets had told them that the Great Spirit promised victory. The sign would be a cloud in the heavens, said the priests, moving among them, chanting their incantations, falling as the warriors fell.

In the middle of the afternoon the cloud appeared—just as Jackson's messenger arrived offering pardon to all who surrendered. The aroused Creeks nearly killed the messenger, and the battle was renewed with redoubled ferocity. At dusk one band held out in a fortress at the bottom of the ravine. Jackson called for volunteers to take it. Sam Houston stepped forward, and was hit by two musket balls before he was carried from the field. After Jackson set the fort afire with flaming arrows the battle came to an end. More than 550 Indians had fallen on the field, and perhaps 200 more had perished in the river. Jackson's losses were 49 killed and 157 wounded.

With the Battle of Horseshoe Bend the Creek War came to an end. Led by Billy Weatherford the Red Sticks made their peace. Jackson summoned all the chiefs to the fort he had built at the confluence of the Coosa and Tallapoosa. They came, the friendly Creeks expecting rewards, the hostiles anticipating harsh punishment from "Sharp Knife," but none dreaming of such brutal terms as Jackson offered. Half of the Creek country, 23 million acres comprising three-fifths of Alabama and one-fifth of Georgia, were to be ceded to the United States. The Creeks protested, and Jackson replied that through this territory led "the path that Tecumseh trod. That path must be stopped. Until this is done your nation cannot expect happiness, mine security."[51]

On August 9, 1814, the sorrowing Creeks signed the Treaty of

Fort Jackson. Andrew Jackson wrote to his wife Rachel back in the Hermitage that the "disagreeable business" was done and "I know you humanity would feel for" a fallen nation robbed of half its patrimony.[52]

8

☆

It is to John Armstrong's credit that in 1814 the graybeard generals at last gave way to young and vigorous men. Whereas in 1812 there had been eight top generals averaging 60 years of age, in 1814 the ranking nine averaged only 36.

Among these was Major General Jacob Brown, the commander who had repulsed Prevost at Sackets Harbor the year before. Brown was ordered to make a new invasion of Upper Canada, aiming at Burlington Heights on Lake Ontario.

Speed was to be the essence of this campaign, for Britain had brought the Napoleonic Wars to a triumphant conclusion. In April of 1814 Napoleon abdicated as emperor, and at least 14 of Wellington's veteran regiments were free for service in America. By June Brown was ready with about 3,500 men.

Opposing them was the energetic Lieutenant General Sir Gordon Drummond with about an equal number. But Drummond's force was spread thin over a vast frontier. About 1,000 men were kept in York to be rushed to any threatened point, while another 2,600 were strung out along the Niagara under Major General Phineas Riall. Obviously, to respond quickly to American movements would require hard marching from the British. However, the British had little fear of the Americans.

But this was a different Yankee army. Its soldiers saluted smartly and took pride in their uniforms, and its brigade commanders were Winfield Scott; Peter B. Porter, the aggressive war hawk Congressman; and Eleazer Wheelock Ripley, one of many New Englanders whose loyalty during the war preserved their region's honor. Scott the scientific had been particularly active drilling his troops. He put them in neat uniforms, albeit of militia gray, for Scott could not obtain cloth for regulars' blue.

On July 3, 1814, General Brown threw this force across the river and invested Fort Erie. It was surrendered in the afternoon, and Brown spent the Fourth of July moving north along the Niagara.

Riall, however, had moved swiftly. Gathering his garrisons, he came south with about 2,000 men, halting at Chippewa 18 miles above Fort Erie. Here, the next day, he attacked the American camp.

Porter's militia-Indian brigade drove off a Canadian force, but the British regulars routed Porter in turn. General Brown ordered Scott's brigade, fortunately already drawn up for evening parade, to give battle. With American and British guns already dueling counter-battery, Scott led his men over a creek and deployed. Marching steadily, tall in their trim gray uniforms and high hats, Scott's soldiers spread out in a concave line to put a converging fire into the redcoated British drawn up in column, two regiments abreast. The British opened fire. Americans toppled. But the gaps were quickly closed and the long gray line came on. Seventy yards apart the two forces halted and fired. Now there were gaps in the British line, and the Americans charged with the bayonet to break and rout Riall's redcoats.

British losses in the Battle of Chippewa were 500 men, while the Americans lost 300. It was not an important victory, but its psychological effects were stunning and enduring. For the first and only time in the war regulars of both sides had met and maneuvered on an open plain, and the Americans had won. At Chippewa the *esprit* of the United States Army was born, and the battle is commemorated in the gray uniforms worn by cadets at the U. S. Military Academy.

Brown followed up Scott's victory by pressing the British back to Fort George and Burlington Heights. Encamping at Queenston, he awaited the heavy guns needed to reduce the enemy forts. They were slow in coming from Chauncey at Sackets Harbor, and Brown was forced to return to Chippewa on July 24.

In the interval, General Drummond had hurried to the Niagara from Kingston. He now ordered his 3,000-man force out in pursuit of the Americans. While Riall followed Brown, another force crossed the river to menace Brown's supplies. Brown became worried. He sent Winfield Scott down the Canadian side of the river in hopes of forcing the enemy to recall his troops from the American side. Scott came upon Riall at Lundy's Lane, a point a mile below the falls, and immediately attacked.

Such was Scott's audacity that Riall was forced to retire. But just then Drummond came up with the rest of his army, ordering the cross-river detachment to rejoin him. Drummond put his artillery on a hill, with his infantry in line slightly to the rear.

Scott attacked again, directing his brigade against the British center and left. On the left, the Americans temporarily turned the British flank, capturing the wounded Riall while doing so. But the British eventually recovered there, while in the center they hurled back charge after charge. Still Scott hung on, until, at about five o'clock, Brown arrived with the rest of his army.

Brown ordered another attack. The lines swept forward in a darkness shimmering with the flashes of the British guns, but they could not seize the hill and the British battery blazed on. Brown ordered Colonel James Miller of the 21st Infantry to take the British works. While the enemy guns thundered at an American column moving along the river, Miller's regulars slipped forward through the darkened scrub. Coming to within a dozen yards of the enemy, they crashed out a close volley, charged with the bayonet and seized both hill and battery. Now Brown brought his entire army up to the hill, and the astonished Drummond counterattacked.

Three times the dark silhouettes of the British regulars swept upward, and three times the muzzles of American muskets and the captured guns flickered and flamed to drive them back again. Brown and Scott were both hit and evacuated. Around midnight, Brown ordered Ripley, now commanding on the hill, to withdraw for water and ammunition. He did, but he also left some of the enemy guns behind. With daylight Drummond quickly reoccupied the height and turned the guns around—restoring the situation of the preceding day except that both sides were battered and bleeding and each minus about 900 men.

In the Battle of Lundy's Lane the Americans might just possibly have won a tactical victory, but they suffered strategic defeat. Lundy's Lane put out the ardent flame enkindled by Chippewa and forced Brown to abandon all hope of conquering Upper Canada. He withdrew into Fort Erie. The energetic Drummond assaulted him there on August 15, but the Americans repulsed him. On September 17 Brown led a sally out of the fort to seize and spike the British guns. No less than 500 men fell on both sides during this bitter flare-up, and now both Brown's and Drummond's armies were exhausted remnants. Drummond issued orders proclaiming a victory, and then fell back to Chippewa. Less than two months later the Americans acknowledged the futility of fighting on the Niagara frontier by blowing up Fort Erie and recrossing the river to American soil.

All had not been in vain, however, if only for the gleam which Chippewa, Lundy's Lane and Fort Erie gave to a young but thus far lusterless military tradition. The cost had been high. James Miller, the hero of Lundy's Lane, wrote a friend: "Since I came into Canada this time every major save one, every lieutenant-colonel, every colonel that was here when I came and has remained here has been killed or wounded, and I am now the only general officer out of seven that has escaped."[53]

But now the guns fell forever silent along the 40-mile strait separating New York and Ontario. For the focus of the war had long ago shifted east, where the weight of British arms flowing to the United States from victorious European battlefields was bearing the fledgling American eagle to the earth.

9

☆

By the summer of 1814 military defeat, blockade, internal dissension, a near-empty treasury and the prospect of British invasion coupled with no real confidence in Brown's expedition into Canada had brought the United States to the point where peace talk would have been sweet indeed. But by then it was too late.

America's first chance had come in 1812 when the British suspended the Orders in Council and ordered Admiral Warren to attempt to negotiate a cease-fire. At that time Secretary of State

Monroe bluntly informed Warren that the outrageous practice of impressment must be dropped first, and that, of course, was not possible.

Another opportunity appeared in March of 1813 when John Quincy Adams, U.S. Minister to Russia, transmitted Czar Alexander's offer to mediate the Anglo-American dispute. By then, Canadian defeats had chastened the Americans, and Madison, without waiting for British reaction to the Czar's offer, appointed Albert Gallatin, his capable Secretary of the Treasury, and James Bayard, a Federalist, as peace commissioners. Journeying to St. Petersburg, Gallatin and Bayard, together with Adams, were to conclude a peace which would still insist upon the end of impressment. Then, as American arms won victories at York and on the Niagara frontier, Monroe wrote to Gallatin: "These successes ought to have a salutary influence on your negotiations, [and] it might be worthwhile to bring to view the advantage to both countries which is to be promised by a transfer of the upper parts and even the whole of Canada to the U.S."[54]

Bumptiously confident as Mr. Monroe might have been, the commissioners soon found the realities to be that the Czar was out of town fighting Napoleon and the British were not interested in mediation of what, so far as impressment was concerned, was to them a domestic question. Yet Britain held the door open for direct negotiation, and Madison added Jonathan Russell and Henry Clay to the delegation. Gallatin and Bayard, meanwhile, left St. Petersburg, bumped around Europe for a bit, and entered England in April—just as Napoleon fell from his imperial throne. Bayard wrote home: "The whole nation is delirious with joy, which was not indulged without bitter invectives against their remaining enemies: the Americans. They consider [the war] as an aid given to their great enemy at a moment when his power was most gigantic. . . . They thirst for a great revenge and the nation will not be satisfied without it."[55] Gallatin wrote: "To use their own language, they mean to inflict on America a chastisement which will teach her that war is not to be declared against Great Britain with impunity."[56] Gallatin urgently advised Madison to drop the impressment issue.

Madison did. While war hawks still muttered darkly about maritime grievances and banners proclaiming "FREE TRADE AND SAILORS' RIGHTS" still fluttered from the masts of American ships, the issue which had called forth all the blood and bullets was quietly dropped in a Cabinet meeting of June 27. Instructions to that effect were sent to the peace commissioners gathered in the (now Belgian) city of Ghent to await the pleasure of their British counterparts. And while the Americans cooled their heels, Mother England raised the rod which was to despoil, as well as discipline, her runaway, impudent daughter.

If carried out, Britain's strategy probably would have left her in possession of New England, part of New York, the Great Lakes and the Louisiana Territory. Then she would have been able to bargain at Ghent on the basis of "the state of possession" at the close of hostilities.

Three expeditions were to achieve this position. The first and major force would invade New York at Lake Champlain. In support, to divert the Americans from Champlain, an army-navy team would attack American coastal cities. Finally, a third force would seize New Orleans.

In none of these plans was there a word about revenge or reprisals, and yet the first force to move, the army-navy team under Vice Admiral Sir Alexander Cochrane, went into action with retaliation as an objective.

In July of 1814 Cochrane in Bermuda received a letter from Sir George Prevost reporting that American troops had pillaged Canadian communities on Lake Erie. The raid was unauthorized, but Prevost, without waiting for the explanations and reparations which actually did follow, asked Cochrane to "assist in inflicting that measure of retaliation which shall deter the enemy from a repetition of similar outrages."[57] On July 18 Cochrane informed his squadrons: "You are hereby required and directed to destroy and lay waste such towns and districts upon the coasts as you may find assailable."[58]

A few weeks later Cochrane sailed for Chesapeake Bay at the head of 4 ships of the line, 20 frigates and sloops and more than 20 transports carrying 4,000 regulars. Major General Robert Ross commanded the troops. He was one of Wellington's finest professionals and a gentlman renowned for his "easy and beautiful manners." Reaching the bay, Cochrane and Ross conferred with a less cultivated commander, the irascible despoiler of the Chesapeake, Rear Admiral Sir George Cockburn.

Cockburn's temper had not been softened by the invective poured upon his name in the American press, and he had a particularly active hatred for the Washington newspaper, the *National Intelligencer*. It was not surprising, then, that Cockburn should propose the American capital as the first object of retaliation. Cochrane, however, wished to move first against an American gunboat flotilla commanded by the aggressive Commodore Joshua Barney. After that, a choice would be made between Washington and Baltimore.

On August 18 the British fleet began sailing up the Patuxent River with Barney's gunboats fleeing before it. Next day General Ross's soldiers and marines began going ashore. A column was formed to march parallel with the ships in pursuit of the gunboats. On August 22, finding himself trapped, Barney blew up his boats. The British were now free to punish either Washington or Baltimore, and on the night of the 23rd Ross chose the American capital.

For five days an enemy army had marched and countermarched around the capital without a finger raised against it. Few nations have submitted to insult so spinelessly, and yet few nations have been served in their peril by leaders such as John Armstrong and James Madison.

Armstrong, with his eyes fixed on Canada, had done next to nothing about Washington's defenses. He had no plan, very few regulars, and depended upon militia requisitioned from the neighboring states. Moreover, Armstrong was certain that Washington would not be attacked. "Baltimore is the place, sir," he told a militia general. "That is of so much more consequence."[59] He was right, but just because he had left America's front door open, he had invited Ross to swerve toward Washington.

At last Madison, who lacked the courage to dismiss Armstrong, placed defense of the capital in the hands of Brigadier General William Winder. A lawyer whose chief military distinction was his disgraceful capture at Stony Point the year before, Winder was chosen because he was the cousin of Levin Winder, the Federalist Governor of Maryland upon whom most of the requisitions for militia would fall. At the outset, however, General Winder found that the states were willing to defend themselves but not the capital. He called for 3,000 men and got not 300. He asked for more, but Armstrong refused to approve his call. Winder, it appeared, commanded only himself and his horse—and he nearly killed that poor beast when, starting on July 5, he rode for nearly a month over the terrain he was to defend, returning to Washington on August 1 to proclaim the obvious: Washington was poorly defended.

Its only regular force was a half-trained District Brigade. At Bladensburg on the Washington road, the obvious point to stop Ross and his 4,000, there were only 450 troops holding entrenchments voluntarily dug by the exasperated citizens of the capital. Alarmed at last, President Madison issued a call for more militia, and Brigadier General Tobias Stansbury began marching down from Baltimore to Bladensburg with about 2,000 militia. As they did, Washington flew into a first-class flap.

Citizens and clerks fought each other for wagons to carry off private or governmental valuables. Families boarded up their homes and buried the silver under the shrubs. Dolley Madison, the President's charming and saucy wife, left off scolding her neighbors for foolish talk about evacuation and busied herself moving things from the residence of her friends, the Gallatins. And as General Winder rode everywhere at breakneck speed, Secretary of War Monroe, the only official who had constantly feared an attack on Washington, mounted his horse to ride to Benedict, where he spent two days personally scouting the enemy's movements.

On August 21 both Winder and Monroe joined the District Brigade camped at the Woodyard roughly midway between Bladensburg in the north and Benedict in the south. On August 22, the day Barney blew up his boats, Winder and his cavalry rode south toward the British at Nottingham. They came upon the enemy moving north to Upper Marlboro. For perhaps an hour the Americans sat their horses watching the perspiring redcoats marching through the fields. Then they galloped back to the Woodyard and the entire force retreated out of Ross's way to Oldfields (now Forestville, Maryland). They were now about ten miles below Bladensburg. About half that distance east lay the British at Upper Marlboro. At Oldfields, meanwhile, Winder was joined by Barney with about 500 sailors and 150 marines under Captain Samuel Miller. That evening President Madison and his Cabinet rode out from Washington.

In the morning of August 23 the President reviewed Winder's troops, and rode back to Washington. After he left, Winder rode north to Bladensburg. He had not gone far before a messenger overtook him to inform him that the British were marching on the army he had left. Wheeling, Winder galloped back to Oldfields in time to see Ross's columns approaching and to give the order for retreat.

It was not an orderly withdrawal. Winder's army simply turned tail and ran west to the capital. Ross, perhaps startled by his enemy's sudden disappearance, did not pursue. Instead, he marched south to the Woodyard, and it was there that he decided to attack Washington on the following day.

Winder's retreat to Washington had brought him to the Navy Yard on the east branch of the Potomac. He came there, he said, because he believed the enemy might move on the city by the river. Winder had no thought of Bladensburg, the true avenue of approach. Neither, apparently, did Bladensburg's defender: General Tobias Stansbury. As the hot sun of August 24, 1814, rose in the Maryland sky, Stansbury pulled his troops out of that vital little village and began marching to join Winder at the Navy Yard.

President Madison and his Cabinet had already reached Winder's camp. They spoke for fruitless hours with the distracted general, until, at ten o'clock, a scout came clattering over the bridge with news that the British had been marching for Bladensburg since dawn and were nearly halfway there.

Secretary of State James Monroe immediately mounted his horse and rode hard for Bladensburg, seven miles away. After him streamed President Madison and the rest of the Cabinet, then Winder and his army, and then, after blowing the Navy Yard Bridge, came the resolute Barney with his sailors and big naval cannon.

Fortunately, the retiring General Stansbury was also alerted to the British approach. He turned and hastened back to block the Washington road west of Bladensburg. That road ran out from the town, crossed a bridge over the eastern branch, ran level through a marsh and gradually ascended rolling hills. Stansbury certainly had time to destroy the bridge, but he did not. Instead, he placed artillery and about 500 men in a position overlooking it. His main body was placed west of the marsh.

At about eleven o'clock Monroe came galloping down the hill. Without consulting Stansbury, he altered the general's dispositions— to their ultimate disadvantage. Some Maryland militia arrived at about the same time. Next came Madison and his Cabinet, Secretary Armstrong repeatedly asking for command and being just as frequently refused. The President jogged through Stansbury's lines toward the bridge and inevitable capture, until a scout headed him off. Then Winder came puffing up, placing his men on a ridge too far behind Stansbury to assist him. Thus there were three lines consisting of perhaps 6,000 men to oppose Ross's 4,000. But there was no real organization. The units had no understanding of their relations to each other, some were in excellent position to fire on their comrades, and everyone was exhausted and confused by the marching of the past few days.

At one o'clock British scarlet streamed into Bladensburg and Stansbury's artillery opened fire. Then the British light brigade rushed the bridge. Immediately, Stansbury's sharpshooters opened up. Redcoats fell, but most of them got across. Tearing off their knapsacks and tossing them into squad piles, the British formed files of skirmishers ten paces apart. They came on at the trot, and it was then that there was a gurgle, a screech and a whoosh overhead.

Ross had fired his Congreve rockets at Stansbury's second line. The first few sputtered harmlessly overhead. Then their trajectories were flattened out and the American men and mules were seized with a mad, superstitious fright. There was little to be feared from the Congreves, a weapon so innocuous that it soon ceased to frighten even savage tribes. They were all bark and no bite, yet, without a single one falling among the Americans, they put Stansbury's left and center to rout. Soldiers threw away their guns and fled, and the only casualty was a captain who ran himself to death.

Not all the Americans fled so quickly. At one point, some of them even forced the redcoats back to the cover of the river bank. But then Ross fed another regiment into the battle, and after this unit forded the stream and threatened to turn the American left, the rout became complete. The battle had not lasted a quarter-hour. President Madison, watching the stampede from a hill, suggested to Secretary Armstrong that it would be wise "to take a position less exposed." Whereupon the American Cabinet joined the American Army in a flight that did not stop until it was at least 16 miles beyond Washington.

Startled once again by his enemy's trick of vanishing, Ross regrouped and began marching west to Washington—and ran into Commodore Barney's sailors and marines.

Barney had arrived on the field as Winder was being swept away. He set up his cannon and put his men into line about a mile west of Bladensburg. By his own account:

At length the enemy made his appearance on the main road in force and in front of my battery, and on seeing us made a halt. I reserved our fire. In a few minutes the enemy again advanced, when I ordered an 18-pounder to be fired, which completely cleared the road. Shortly after, a second and a third attempt was made by the enemy to come forward, but all were destroyed. They then crossed over into an open field, and attempted to flank our right. He was met there by three 12-pounders, and marines under Captain Miller, and my men acting as infantry, and again was totally cut up. By this time not a vestige of the American army remained, except a body of five or six hundred posted on a height on my right, from which I expected much support from their fine situation.[60]

But Barney got no such support. Even though his men actually counterattacked, crying "Board 'em! Board 'em!" to drive the world's finest troops before them, the militia on the height to his right broke and quit the field. Now the British got into Barney's rear. Barney was himself wounded. Even so, his men fought on. Some of them were bayoneted at their guns with fuses still in their hands. They would have stayed until the end had not Barney, lying in a pool of his own blood, ordered them to retreat.

It was a magnificent stand, and it cost Ross about 250 casualties against Barney's 26 killed and 51 wounded. The slightest follow-up of Barney's counterattack might have produced an American victory. As it was, the road to Washington now lay open, and Ross, accompanied by Admiral Cockburn, led two tired regiments down it into the heart of the American capital.

It was dark as Ross and Cockburn and their troops entered the deserted city. Yet bullets flew at them from the house once occupied by Gallatin, and Ross's horse fell dead beneath him. Angered, the perfect gentleman had the house burned. Under the urging of Cockburn, he next sent troops to the Capitol. Using gunpowder and rockets, the British set the symbol of American sovereignty blazing in the blackness. Now Ross and Cockburn and 200 men marched through the eerily silent darkness to the White House. No one was inside. Dolley Madison had long since fled with most of the plate and valuables, although the table was set for dinner for forty. Decanters of wine stood on the sideboards, and in the kitchen, spits loaded with joints were turning before the fire, and the pots were filled with sauces and vegetables. Subaltern George Glieg, who was present, has written: "You will readily imagine that these preparations were beheld by a party of hungry soldiers with no indifferent eye. An elegant dinner . . . was a luxury to which few of them . . . had been accustomed."[61] So they ate it, after which they disposed of the immemorial problem of cleaning up by setting fire to the White House. Meanwhile, the Navy Yard and all the vessels in the eastern branch were put to the torch, along with the War and Treasury buildings. Before midnight the blazing city cast flickering red light over those Virginia and Maryland hills into which the American government and its army had crept. Then a violent thunderstorm sprang up to quench the flames and all fell dark again.

In the morning Dolley Madison hurried to meet her husband 16 miles up the Potomac. En route she stopped off at what appeared to be a friendly farmhouse. She went upstairs while her attendants announced her presence to the housewife. Enraged, the woman ran to the stairs and shouted up them: "Mrs. Madison, if that is you, come down and get out. Your husband has got mine out fighting, and damn you, you shan't stay in my house! So get out!"[62] Dolley went, her humiliation symbolizing the low estate into which the American presidency had fallen.

In Washington, meanwhile, the firebrands were up early to rekindle the dampened ruins, making certain this time that the Library of Congress inside the Capitol was also destroyed. Admiral Cockburn was delighted. Riding an uncurried white brood mare with a black foal trotting by her side, he made for the office of the *National Intelligencer*. He ordered the newspaper's library heaped in the street and lent his own hands to the burning of the books. Then he ordered his men to scatter the type, shouting gleefully, "Be sure that all the C's are destroyed so that the rascals cannot any longer abuse my name!"[63]

At noon the sky darkened and a rare tornado struck the city with a dreadful howl. It increased the havoc, but it also put out the fires. Shortly afterward an explosion at the Navy Yard injured many of Ross's redcoats and placed a final check on "retaliation." At about nine o'clock that night, leaving their campfires burning and marching in extreme silence, the British departed the dishonored capital.

10

☆

In its psychological consequences the burning of Washington first appalled and then angered and briefly united the American nation, but diplomatically it was of no consequence whatever. News of the event simply came too late to influence the peace commissioners of either side then meeting in Ghent. If the Americans had known that their capital had been contemptuously burnt like any stinking pirate's lair, they might not have been so firm in rejecting Britain's demand; but as it was, on August 24, the very date of the "Bladensburg Races," they flatly rejected them.

Britain had asked for an Indian buffer state to include one-third of Ohio, two-thirds of Indiana, and nearly the entire area from which Illinois, Wisconsin and Michigan were formed. They also demanded parts of Maine, control of the Great Lakes, forfeiture of American fishing rights in the North and other exactions equally humiliating. Asked what would be done with about 100,000 Americans then living within the area of the buffer state, the British shrugged and said that they would have to shift for themselves. So the Americans bluntly stated that the demands were inadmissible, and declared: "A treaty concluded on such terms would be but an armistice."[64]

The American reply jolted the British. Lord Liverpool, the Prime Minister, was afraid that if negotiations were broken off the British would be blamed and the war would become popular in America and unpopular in Britain. He wrote to the Duke of Wellington: "It is very material to throw the rupture of the negotiation, if it is to take place, upon the Americans."[65] So the British, who had also not yet heard of Washington, retreated from their dictatorial stand. They did not change their demands, but neither did they reiterate them as *sine qua nons*. They also sought to adjourn rather than break off the negotiations. In the meantime, British arms would bring the "impudent" Yankees to heel. "If our commander does his duty," Liverpool wrote, "I am persuaded we shall have acquired by our arms every point on the Canadian frontier which we ought to insist on keeping."[66]

Liverpool's policy of writing the peace with the point of a sword got off to an excellent start on September 1, when a British fleet entered Penobscot Bay and took Castine. At the cost of one man killed and eight wounded all of Maine east of the Penobscot River gradually fell into British hands. One hundred miles of seacoast was restored to the dominion of the King of England, while all its male inhabitants meekly, often eagerly, took an oath of allegiance to him. To nail down these acquisitions and to tidy up the Canadian frontier in a southern direction, Sir George Prevost began moving down Lake Champlain.

Sir George's army was the most splendid ever sent by Britain to America. In all of Canada he commanded some 29,000 regulars, and for the Lake Champlain expedition alone he had about 18,000 redcoats, not counting Canadian militia. The problem of feeding this host might have been insuperable but for some of Prevost's friendly enemies to the south. "Two thirds of the army are supplied with beef by American contractors, principally of Vermont and New York,"[67] Prevost reported. One commissary official noted on June 19, 1814: "I have contracted with a Yankee magistrate to furnish this post with fresh beef. A major came with him to make the agreement; but, as he was foreman of the grand jury of the court in which the Government prosecutes the magistrates for high treason and smuggling, he turned his back and would not see the paper signed."[68] Major General George Izard, commanding at Plattsburg, reported: "On the eastern side of Lake Champlain the high roads are insufficient for the cattle pouring into Canada. Like herds of buffaloes they press through the forests, making paths for themselves. . . . Were it not for these supplies, the British forces in Canada would soon be suffering from famine."[69]

Such complicity made it difficult for Prevost to decide whether to attack down the New York or Vermont side of Champlain. But then Vermont's ardor in its enemy's cause won him over, and he wrote: "Vermont has shown a disinclination to the war, and as it is sending in specie and provisions, I will confine offensive operations to the west side of Lake Champlain."[70]

On August 31, leaving behind a rear guard of about 5,000 men, Prevost led 11,000 across the border into New York. On his eastern or left flank sailed a fleet which, headed by the 36-gun *Confiance,* was nearly as formidable as his army. And in Washington far below him he possessed in the person of John Armstrong an unwitting ally perhaps the equal of either.

Although the Washington fiasco had forced Armstrong to resign (Madison still had not the courage to dismiss him), before he did so he stripped the land defenses of Lake Champlain nearly naked by ordering General Izard to take 4,000 men from Plattsburg to the Niagara frontier. Izard obeyed, while protesting that Plattsburg on Champlain was the enemy's objective. So Brigadier General Alexander Macomb was left to man Plattsburg's forts with about 1,500 effectives. Fortunately for America, Prevost was as dilatory as Armstrong was devious, and even more happily there had come to Lake Champlain a sailor in the mold of Lawrence and Oliver Hazard Perry.

Lieutenant Thomas Macdonough had been born in Delaware, the son of a physician in the Revolutionary Army. He had helped Decatur burn the *Philadelphia* at Tripoli. Before the outbreak of war he had been one of those commanders who refused to allow British captains to impress their seamen. He was handsome, devout, self-disciplined— and very thorough.

As Prevost and his veterans moved south on Plattsburg, Macdonough brought his squadron into tiny Plattsburg Bay. He realized that he could not hope to meet Captain George Downie's British fleet in long-range battle out in the open water. He hoped, rather, to lure Downie into a close-up fight fought at anchor. So he anchored his biggest ships—flagship *Saratoga, Eagle, Ticonderoga* and *Preble* —across Plattsburg Bay and put his gunboats behind him to fill the gaps. Next he carefully rigged his ships for battle at anchor, using kedges and hawsers so that he might at any time "wind" them around to bring unused broadsides to bear. This, in effect, gave him double the firepower of his 86 guns against the British 90. For Downie to enter Plattsburg Bay against such precautions was for a bowman to enter an alley full of knives with one arm in a sling. Yet he did enter— because Sir George Prevost insisted upon it.

Prevost did not understand the niceties of naval warfare, and therefore he insisted that Downie put to sea even though his flagship, 36-gun *Confiance,* was not ready to sail. So *Confiance* came down the lake with riggers and carpenters still at work on her decks, in the company of the big *Linnet,* two sloops *Chub* and *Finch,* and a dozen gunboats and row galleys. As they did, the Americans harassed Prevost's advance.

Having gathered his detachments, and been reinforced by about 800 New York militia, Macomb had about 4,000 men holding Plattsburg. They dismantled both bridges over the Saranac River and fell back south of the stream into three well-built forts. On September 6 the British probed briefly at these defenses, after which Prevost decided to sit back and await the arrival of Captain Downie.

He marked time for five days, and then he ordered a land-sea assault! America had already given pathetic demonstration of what happens to armies when civilians play soldier, and Prevost was about to show that there is something even worse: the civilian-soldier playing sailor. Prevost possessed the strength to storm the American positions, after which he could turn the captured guns on Macdonough's ships and drive them out into the unequal combat of the open lake. Macdonough had prepared well, but he had also offered Prevost the opportunity of defeating himself and Macomb in detail. But Prevost did not see it. He only saw that as he crossed the Saranac his left flank would be exposed to the fire of the American gunboats, and so he ordered Downie to sail into Macdonough's ambush.

At eight o'clock in the morning of September 11, 1814, the British fleet rounded Cumberland Head. The wind turned foul, as Macdonough had hoped, and *Confiance, Linnet, Chub* and *Finch* crept toward their anchorages with limp and flapping sails. The Americans opened fire.

Downie, disregarding his long-range superiority, had intended to lay *Confiance* alongside *Saratoga.* But now the raking fire of Macdonough's carronades forced him to anchor 300 yards away, or about 50 yards beyond the point-blank range of a carronade. Then *Confiance's* gun ports blazed and half of Macdonough's crew was felled on *Saratoga's* decks. Soon the battle became general and scattered. *Linnet* battled *Eagle, Chub* was sent drifting out of control among the American gunboats where she struck, and *Ticonderoga* and *Preble* fought what appeared to be a losing battle with *Finch* and the British gunboats. All depended now on the dreadful duel between *Confiance* and *Saratoga.* At first it went poorly for the British. Captain Downie was killed when an American gun sent a shot plunging into his groin. Then the British long-range superiority began to tell. The American left was turned when *Linnet* drove *Eagle* to refuge between *Saratoga* and *Ticonderoga,* and joined *Confiance* in battering *Saratoga.* By then *Saratoga* could not work a gun on her starboard side.

Now Macdonough's forethought came into the scales. Ignoring the battle, he directed the winding of his ship. Slowly, one by one, *Saratoga*'s port guns were unmasked and Macdonough fired on *Confiance* with one gun after another as *Saratoga* bore around. *Confiance* tried desperately to wind ship herself. Failing, she struck her colors— and her three smaller sisters were forced to surrender, although the gunboats escaped.

In the meantime, Prevost's redcoats had gotten over the Saranac at an upper ford. They were coming down on the forts when American shouts running upriver like a jubliant powder train proclaimed Downie's defeat. Prevost all but panicked. He could have, in the words of a subordinate, gone on to take Plattsburg in 20 minutes. But the news of the lake reverse so distressed him, as he explained later, that he decided to retire to the border to see what use the Americans would make of their naval superiority. Once launched on the retrograde, however, he did not stop until the last of his splendid troops crossed into Canada. Meanwhile, Thomas Macdonough reported to the Secretary of the Navy:

"Sir: The Almighty has been pleased to grant us a signal victory on Lake Champlain. . . ."[71]

It was indeed more significant than Macdonough might imagine, and two days later an event more memorable though less momentous in American history was to be written in the red glare of rockets bursting over Fort McHenry.

11

☆

In that September of 1814 mannerly Robert Ross and George Cockburn with 4,000 redcoats sailed up the Chesapeake toward Baltimore, intending to launch a demonstration which, if successful, could be converted into all-out assault upon that wealthy "nest of pirates."

At the same time General William Winder rode north from Washington expecting to take command of Baltimore's defenses. He was rebuffed, however, by Senator Samuel Smith, a militia major general who had no intention of placing the city's fate in the hands of the starter of the Bladensburg Races. Smith was a rarity: he was 61 and a Revolutionary War veteran, but he had not forgotten his military lessons and he still wanted to fight.

Because the vengeful Cockburn had diverted Ross to Washington, Baltimore, the true object of the expedition, had been granted time to prepare its fortifications. They were built by the citizens themselves, and held by as many as 16,000 men under General Smith. Baltimore's harbor, a busy privateering base, was protected by Fort McHenry.

The British plan was to bombard McHenry into submission while Ross advanced overland against the city. On September 12 the fleet anchored off North Point at the tip of the peninsula between the Back and Patapsco rivers and Ross's impatient redcoats went ashore.

Ross was confident and in high spirits. Breakfasting with Cockburn at a Maryland farmhouse, he toyed with the idea of making Baltimore his winter quarters. As he departed, the farmer asked him if he would be back for supper.

"No," Ross said, "I'll have supper tonight in Baltimore," and then, in afterthought, "or in Hell."[72]

The first conjecture seemed more likely as Ross's eager redcoats swept briskly up the peninsula. But then his scouts ran into a force of riflemen sent forward by Brigadier General John Stricker, who had marched out from Baltimore with about 3,200 raw militia. Shots were fired, the British spread out, flanked the Americans and drove them off.

General Ross hurried up with his advance guard. Two American marksmen who had not fled—Daniel Wells and Harry McComas—fired their last shots. One bullet hit Ross. He lurched back into the arms of his aide, calling his wife's name, and then he spoke no more. His body was laid under an oak tree, and the troops moving up to the attack saw it as they passed. "A groan came from the column," according to Subaltern Glieg, and it was obvious after Colonel Arthur Brooke took command that "the army had lost its mainspring."[73]

The Americans under Stricker made an unusually firm stand at

Godly Wood. Musket fire blazed out from both lines in a battle which brought death to Wells and McComas, the men who shot at Ross, and which eventually ended in a British victory. But British casualties were 300 against 200 for the Americans, and on the next day, after Brooke saw the formidable entrenchments in front of Baltimore, he stopped short to await support from the fleet.

By then, midday of September 13, 1814, Admiral Cochrane's bombardment ships were at work battering Fort McHenry. For 25 hours the British ships rained shells and Congreve rockets upon the sturdy little bastion. The Americans fired back briefly, but could not make the range. Luckily, neither could the bigger British vessels because of a barrier of sunken ships. Some 1,800 projectiles fell upon the Americans, but they could not bring about the fort's submission.

Ashore Brooke feinted twice to no avail and a British landing party was driven away from Fort Covington. McHenry had held, along with the Baltimore defenses, and the British fleet eventually sailed back to Halifax and the troops returned to Jamaica.

Such was the British failure at Baltimore, and it might not have merited more than a passing notice in the annals of American arms had not a Washington lawyer named Francis Scott Key watched the bombardment of Fort McHenry from a British cartel boat.

At one time a pacifist so fierce that he would write in 1812 of his willingness to accept "any disgrace or defeat," Key had changed his attitude and was now on a patriotic mission to obtain the release of Dr. William Beanes, a Maryland physician whom the British had caught in the act of imprisoning redcoats straggling out of Washington. Even the just General Ross had been intent upon seeing the elderly Dr. Beanes hanged in Halifax, but Key's diplomacy, together with reports that Beanes had been kind to British wounded, changed his mind. He granted the old man's release.

Throughout the night of September 13-14 Beanes and Key stood on the deck of the enemy ship watching British rockets and shells bursting over and upon the ramparts of Fort McHenry. Even at that distance Key could see the fort's huge flag illuminated again and again by the explosion flashes, and he began to jot down his impressions on the back of a letter. But old Dr. Beanes could not see so well. As dawn began to break, and the British bombardment subsided, he kept asking anxiously: "Is the flag still there?"[74]

The question triggered in Key's mind the theme of a poem, and he began to expand his jotting into verses. After he and Dr. Beanes were allowed to go ashore, he revised and expanded them and then took the completed poem to his brother-in-law, Judge J. H. Nicholson. The judge had been in Fort McHenry during those dreadful 25 hours. He had seen "the rockets' red glare" and had had his stomach squeezed by the shock of "bombs bursting in air." He had lived Key's poem, and he saw at once that it could be sung to the melody of a popular drinking song called "Anacreon in Heaven." Nicholson suggested immediate publication, and a young printer's devil named Samuel Sands set it in type and it came forth anonymously in a hand-bill entitled "Defence of Fort M'Henry." It was published on September 20 in the Baltimore *Patriot;* soon soldiers began singing it, and it spread gradually—though not suddenly—across the country. But not until March 3, 1931, did the United States Congress adopt "The Star-Spangled Banner" as the American national anthem.

If the War of 1812 had not given Americans much to brag about, it had at least given them a song to sing.

12

☆

Toward the end of October, 1814, news of the repulse at Baltimore and the Battle of Plattsburg reached London. The British were badly shaken, although they did not abandon their demand that negotiations at Ghent be conducted on the basis of "the state of possession" at the end of hostilities.

The Americans, who had already firmly rejected that demand, felt their own insistence on the *status quo ante bellum* fortified by news so stimulating that John Adams at first refused to believe it. Only a few months before, the London *Times,* reminding Lord Liverpool of his sacred duty to punish the Americans, had solemnly adjured him: ". . . oh may no false liberality, no mistaken lenity, no weak and cowardly policy, interpose to save them from the blow! Strike! Chastise the savages, for such they are!"[75] On October 19, printing the news of

Plattsburg, the *Times* observed gloomily: "This is a lamentable event to the civilized world."[76] Lord Liverpool could not agree more, for that "civilized world" was in distress both at home and abroad.

At home the loss of the American market caused by the blockade was already being severely felt, and the success of American privateers in the Irish Sea had made shipping insurance rates three times higher than they were during the war with Napoleon. Prevost's defeat meant that the war would have to be continued another year, at an estimated cost of £10 million. To raise such a sum meant extension of the detested property tax, then due to expire in a few months. Liverpool knew that his ministry could not survive, much less obtain, continuation of a tax "for the purpose of securing a better frontier for Canada."

Abroad the coalition which had conquered Napoleon was coming apart at the seams. Western Europe not only was troubled by the perils of reconstruction, but was also menaced by the new power of Russia. Diplomats at the Congress of Vienna, no longer impressed by British talk of the "contemptible Americans," would not fail to take note of the fact that some of Britain's finest regiments were beyond reach in far-off America. Czar Alexander's battalions were very close indeed.

Still, Liverpool faced up to the fact that the unpopular and unpleasant American war could yet be settled by a military decision. He asked the Duke of Wellington to assume command. Napoleon's nemesis replied: "That which appears to me to be wanting in America is not a general, or a general officer and troops, but a naval superiority on the Lakes."[77] On the diplomatic side, Wellington said: "In regard to your negotiation, I confess that I think you have no right, from the state of the war, to demand any concession of territory. . . . Why stipulate for the *uti possidetis?* You can get no territory; indeed the state of your military operations, however creditable, does not entitle you to any."[78]

The first soldier of Britain was not alone in his pessimism: all around Liverpool the country was giving way to a war weariness which quickly changed to outright opposition after the Americans cleverly made public Britain's outrageous territorial demands. Even the London *Times* was displeased, and liberals in Parliament bitterly castigated the Tory government for making demands it had no power to enforce. Recognizing reality, Liverpool moved to bring the distasteful war to a close, almost at the very moment when the dearest objects of British policy—American economic collapse and rupture of the American union—seemed to be taking place.

By the fall of 1814 it appeared that the federal government had run out of both men and money.

All attempts to establish a dependable regular army seemed to have failed. Although the paper strength of the U.S. Army was raised to 62,000 men, by the end of September the actual strength was only 34,000 men.

Secretary of State Monroe, who had taken over the War Department, boldly recommended conscription; but Congress had not the courage to give the nation its first draft. Instead, it raised the land bounty for enlistments, thereby encouraging desertion for the purpose of re-enlisting under another name to claim the bounty. At the end of 1814 the country staggered along with 34,000 regulars and the six-month militia of the various states.

By then, however, even the despised militia could not be counted upon to take the field, let alone remain there in the face of an enemy. Led by Massachusetts—possessor of the finest militia, which she would use only for her own defense—Connecticut, Pennsylvania, Maryland, Virginia, South Carolina and Kentucky began to form or to plan the formation of state armies.

Even more deplorable was the federal government's financial position, which was, in that fall of 1814, probably at its lowest point in the history of the nation. Although Congress had doubled imports at the outset of the war, while reviving some excise taxes and imposing direct taxes on dwellings and slaves, it proposed to finance the war by borrowing money. After the first year of defeat and retreat the only way the Treasury could borrow money was by selling its stock at greater and greater discounts. It has been estimated that of $80 million borrowed between 1812 and 1816, the government actually received only $34 million in specie value.

While the national debt rose, a Congress afraid to draft soldiers was also too timid to levy the taxes that would cover expenditures. Moreover, the Treasury had no national administrative system. It was not even able to transfer its deposits from one section of the country to another. Millions of banknotes collected in Middle and Southern banks had to be left on deposit there while debts in Boston and New York remained unpaid.

Finally, the section of the country which had the most cash was the center of opposition to the war. A variety of factors—not all of them so obvious or so culpable as the practice of playing quartermaster to the enemy—had enriched New England. Specie holdings in Massachusetts alone jumped from $1,709,000 in June of 1811 to $7,326,000 in June of 1814. Massachusetts, unalterably opposed to the war from the beginning, hoped to end it by withholding financial support.

When her war profits were shut off and British fleets menaced her shores, she called that quasi-secessionist assembly known as the Hartford Convention.

It is not fair to blame New England alone for the national government's shortages in men and money. Except New York, Kentucky, Tennessee, and perhaps Ohio, no state gave the war its full and earnest cooperation. Moreover, many patriots from New England volunteered for the regular Army and some of its finest regiments were recruited there. Nevertheless, the conduct of the Federalists who controlled New England is not to be admired. They gave the war the least support and took the largest profits. Shippers took advantage of Britain's licensing system to supply Britain and her allies in the Peninsular War against Napoleon, who, if he was not an American ally, was at least fighting the American enemy. Although these same ships later turned privateer to attack British shipping, their purpose was prizes not patriotism. Because of New England's antiwar spirit Britain had at first excluded her coasts from the blockade, enabling her to gain a monopoly of the import trade. Finally, New England so openly and effectively supplied the enemy in Canada that Congress had to pass a law forbidding the coastal trade.

Outraged, New England came to a boil of town meetings, just as in the days of King George, only now it was the Republican "Jacobins" and "that little man in the Palace" who were denounced. Profiteering and smuggling were cloaked in the righteous mantle of assistance to the Lord's anointed—Britain—standing at Armageddon against the Napoleonic antichrist. However, after the devil incarnate had been defeated and exiled to Elba, there was still no lessening of opposition to the war. Even after Britain extended the blockade to New England—thereby cutting war profits—the Federalists could describe the British peace terms as "moderate" and recommend relying upon British magnanimity. But then, in September of 1814, those merciful cousins from across the sea seized 100 miles of Maine seacoast and a British fleet prepared to descend upon Boston.

Massachusetts was not only dumbfounded but left to her own resources. Two years before, Governor Caleb Strong had refused to put the state militia under the War Department. Now, as the national government offered to maintain the militia so long as it was commanded by regular Army officers, Strong replied that he would call out the militia only *to defend Boston,* providing the state retained control and the United States paid the bills. The answer, of course, was no. And so Massachusetts sent out an invitation to other New England states to confer at Hartford upon "their public grievances and concerns" and to concert plans for interstate defense.

The Hartford Convention met in secret session from December 15, 1814, to January 5, 1815. Delegates from Massachusetts, Connecticut and Rhode Island attended, with only a scattering from Vermont and New Hampshire. At the outset the moderates gained control, and the issues of secession or a separate peace were almost at once ruled out. Nevertheless, the Hartford Convention pointed a pistol at the heart of the Union. In simplest terms, New England proposed to defend herself with her own forces financed by federal tax monies collected within her borders. As the Federalists well knew, what New England could do the other sections might also do, and that would be the end of *"e pluribus unum."* If Congress did not accept this and other proposals, New England would then hold another convention at which, it was safe to infer, the final step of secession would be taken.

In the minds of many Federalists there was no doubt that secession was the ultimate solution, and there were many Republicans who despaired of any means of preserving the Union. The news of the gradual softening of the British position at Ghent had not yet been received in America. What was known, as the Hartford Convention's three "ambassadors" rode off to Washington to inform Congress of New England's pleasure, was that a large British force had invested New Orleans. Even Thomas Jefferson expected that city to fall and to be held indefinitely by the British. And if New Orleans fell, then a federal government unable to pay its army or its navy or even the interest on its national debt could certainly be expected to topple too.

Britain sought New Orleans first to command the mouth of the Mississippi and to deprive the American West of its outlet to the sea, and second as a prize either valuable in itself or as a counterweight at the peace table. Some 10,000 soldiers eventually were gathered for an army to be commanded by Robert Ross, but after his death command passed to Sir Edward Pakenham, the brother-in-law of the Duke of Wellington.

To defend against this most formidable British armada to sail against a New World city, the United States had a few regiments of regulars, the Western and Southern militia and Major General Andrew Jackson. Jackson took command at his headquarters in Mobile on August 15, 1814, and promptly looked eastward away from New Orleans toward Pensacola in Spanish East Florida. Here a small British force had seized the fortifications, and Jackson, immediately calling for 2,500 Tennessee militia, proposed to expel them. Before he could, the British forces there moved against Mobile—only to be repulsed by the gallant stand of Fort Bowyer. Incensed, still looking away from New Orleans, ignoring a petition from its citizens imploring him to come there, and without authority to invade Spanish possessions, Old Hickory attacked and seized Pensacola. That was on November 7, 1814, after which he returned to Mobile.

Jackson simply could not believe that anyone would be foolish enough to mount an amphibious assault directly against New Orleans. He set this conviction down on paper, writing: "A real military man, with full knowledge of the geography of this country, would first possess himself of [Mobile], draw to his standard the Indians, and march direct to the Walnut Hills [present-day Vicksburg] . . . and being able to forage on the country, support himself, cut off all supplies from above and make this country an easy conquest."[79] Old Hickory was right. New Orleans could be defended easily against amphibious invasion, but it could not survive if its communications with the back country were cut off by a strong army above the city. However, Old Hickory probably was not aware of how powerfully the lust for prize money could influence the counsels of British admirals. It was Cochrane who decided to attack New Orleans directly, and inasmuch as he knew that the city was crammed with the produce of the American West valued at £4 million, and because he did include barges in his fleet, it is not too much to suggest that considerations of private gain as well as of public glory helped to make up the admiral's mind. On November 26, without waiting for Pakenham and with Major General John Keane commanding the troops, Cochrane sailed from Jamaica for New Orleans.

Four days before that Andrew Jackson had at last begun moving west. Big John Coffee went riding on ahead to Baton Rouge with 2,000 mounted riflemen; another 1,000 troops were left in Mobile; and with 2,000 under his own command, Old Hickory marched for New Orleans 130 miles away. On December 1 he was received outside the city by a New Orleans merchant who, together with the cultivated Creole lady who prepared his house for the reception, seems to have been surprised to observe: "A tall, gaunt man, very erect . . . with a countenance furrowed by care and anxiety. A small leather cap protected his head, and a short blue Spanish cloak his body, whilst his . . . high boots [were] long innocent of polish or blacking. . . . His complexion was sallow, and unhealthy; his hair iron grey, and his body thin and emaciated like that of one who had just recovered from a lingering sickness. . . . But a fierce glare [lighted] his bright and hawk-like eye."[80] The Creole lady complained: "Ah! Mr. Smith . . . you asked me to . . . receive a great General. I make your house *comme il faut,* and prepare a splendid *déjeuner* . . . all for . . . an ugly old Kaintuck flat-boatman."[81]

It was Jackson's energy and determination, not his unkempt appearance, which impressed the mostly French population of New Orleans after he entered the city next day to throw himself headlong into organizing its defenses. Forts protecting the city were strengthened, bayous leading into it were blocked by felled trees or filled with mud, and troops were placed in positions so that they might be concentrated at the first alarm. On December 18 Jackson put on a new uniform, mounted a splendid horse and rode out to review his colorful army of regulars, militia, free Negroes, gaudy Creoles, painted Choctaws and fierce Baratarian pirates. The last, headed by the audacious and charming Jean Laffite, had been among the most enthusiastic volunteers to Jackson's standards, but they had not been readily accepted. Jackson bluntly rejected these "hellish banditti" until Laffite personally confronted him and offered his services. Fiction has made much of this meeting, but all that is known is that Jackson, unable to resist a man who had his own habit of looking another squarely in the eye, found that Laffite's trained gunners "could not fail of being very useful." On December 20 John Coffee's dragoons clattered in from Baton Rouge, and a few hours later 3,000 Tennessee volunteers under William Carroll came floating down the yellowish broad river on flatboats. By December 23 Jackson could write home: "All well." He did not seem to be upset by the British capture of five gunboats on Lake Borgne, the watery link between the Gulf and the left bank of the Mississippi just below New Orleans. Jackson was confident that every bayou from Borgne to the river bank was blocked and guarded.

Shortly after noon a young Creole named Augustin Rousseau flung himself from his lathered horse outside Jackson's headquarters and burst upon the general with the report that the British were inside his defenses. It was incredible. As Jackson retired to his sofa to ponder such astounding news, a sentry rapped at his door to announce three gentlemen having "important intelligence." They rushed in, breathless and mud-stained. From the lips of Major Gabriel Villere fell a torrent of French. From the lips of an interpreter, Jackson heard: "The British have arrived at Villere's plantation! Major Villere was captured by them and has escaped!"[82]

Jackson listened in astonishment. Unseen, the British had landed on the western shore of Lake Borgne. They had found the thing Jackson believed to be nonexistent—an unblocked and unguarded bayou—and had passed through five miles of swamp to appear in force only seven miles below the city. Eyes flashing, Jackson sprang from his sofa, struck the table with his fist and cried: "By the Eternal, they shall not sleep on our soil!"[83]

Suddenly calm again, he gave his visitors wine to sip, called his aides and announced: "Gentlemen, the British are below. We must fight them tonight."[84]

If it is difficult to forgive Jackson for having allowed himself to be so completely surprised, as it certainly is, then it is also just to praise his quick and decisive reaction. To surprise he was offering counter surprise. He could not know that General Keane had rejected advice to push on immediately to New Orleans with his vanguard of 2,400 men. But he did accurately surmise that the British would pause, and he decided to strike them suddenly and at night when British discipline operated at least advantage.

Jackson had about 4,000 men available, as well as the schooner

Carolina. He had helped himself plentifully to Jean Laffite's guns and gunners, and the weight of *Carolina*'s broadsides forced her low in the water. In the gathering dusk, *Carolina*'s shadowy bulk began sliding gently downstream toward Villere plantation on her left. Captain Daniel Patterson would not need to search for targets. The British, drenched for days like swamp rats, had been busily gathering wood and lighting fires which blazed cheerfully in the darkness fallen on the Villere flats. Patterson was to open fire at 7:30; a half-hour later, giving the enemy enough time to conclude that the main assault would come from the river, Jackson would attack.

A cold fog rising from the river closed in on *Carolina* as she floated away on the current. Mist dimmed the moon and enshrouded the enemy campfires. Suddenly, a great glob of red glowed through the fog, followed by the muted roar of *Carolina*'s guns. For a moment, Britain's veterans came close to panic as the earth bucked and roared and men screamed. Some of them tried to douse their fires, but most ran for the cover of the Mississippi levee. *Carolina* roared on, and then, at eight o'clock exactly, the Americans attacked.

The higher voice of American 6-pounders joined the deeper-throated chorus of *Carolina*'s guns downstream. Then *Carolina* fell silent, not wishing to catch friend and foe alike in her raking fire. The Americans stumbled on against an enemy who had turned to fight, and the battle became a lieutenant's melee: squad by squad, platoon by platoon, men seeking each other in the darkness with clutching fingers or drawn knife, rifles twinkling and cannon muzzles gushing flame, and the cries of men mingling with the neighing of Coffee's horses. At one point the British threatened to capture the American 6-pounders. Jackson rushed into the fight, shouting, "Save the guns!"[85]

Marines and a company of the 7th Infantry rallied around Jackson and saved the cannon.

"Charge! Charge!" yelled the Americans, and the Creoles cried, *"A la baïonnette!"*[86]

At midnight the black battlefield became suddenly silent. Jackson, correctly suspecting that the enemy was being reinforced, decided to withdraw. Unknown to himself, he had dealt the British a blow from which they never completely recovered. British casualties of 46 killed, 167 wounded and 64 captured did not seem very heavy, even though they exceeded American losses of 24 killed, 115 wounded and 74 captured, but the very audacity of the American assault had shaken the redcoats' conviction that "the Dirty Shirts" at New Orleans would run just as fast as their Bladensburg brothers. And so, as the dawn of December 24, 1814, disclosed his assault force safely drawn up behind the dry Rodriguez Canal, Old Hickory sent into the city for those lowly shovels which, more than rifles, bayonet or cannon, are the soul of every defensive stand.

In Ghent that night the British and American negotiators signed the Peace of Christmas Eve. On November 18 Liverpool had dropped his policy of continuing the war to gain territory. Opposition in Parliament, financial strain, the difficulty of extending the property tax, unrest in the interior of France, the lack of progress at the Congress of Vienna, and, perhaps most important of all, the attitude of the Duke of Wellington had all conspired to make him change his mind. In the following month, America's astute diplomats led by Gallatin slowly forced the British away from their position of "the state of possession," until both sides finally agreed to the *status quo ante bellum.*

The Treaty of Ghent was a simple cessation of hostilities. Every principle or issue for which the War of 1812 was fought was ignored. The rights of neutrals and impressments, American fishery or British navigation rights, questions of boundaries or armaments on the lakes, all were referred to commissions for future settlements. All, in effect, was left to the healing power of time; and that was a wise decision. Henry Clay may have called the agreement "a damned bad treaty," but it has been one of the most enduring in history. Unfortunately for the men still confronting one another in this wretched, futile war, it was weeks before news of the Peace of Christmas Eve reached American shores.

Christmas Day in New Orleans began with a salvo of artillery from the British camp. Americans building their mud rampart behind the canal dropped their spades, seized their rifles and jumped to the firing platforms. Then they relaxed. The salvo was only a salute to Sir Edward Pakenham, who had arrived to take command from Keane.

Pakenham's presence gave a lift to his bedraggled redcoats. The boyish, brilliant hero of Salamanca was popular with the army. Moreover, he was confident and eager for a victory that would make him the royal governor of Louisiana with an earldom to match. His wife waited at sea, as did many other ladies accompanying a force "prepared to take over the civil administration of New Orleans, with appointments from tide-waiter to collector of customs already designated."[87] Sir Edward apparently wanted to withdraw from the present poor position and land elsewhere. But he was overwhelmed by the scorn of Admiral Cochrane, who vowed that his sailors alone could defeat the Dirty Shirts and "The soldiers could then bring up the baggage."[88] So Pakenham agreed to attack Jackson's fortifications.

On December 27 the British batteries opened on the American ships *Louisiana* and *Carolina*. *Louisiana* narrowly escaped but *Carolina* blew up with a roar that rattled windows in New Orleans. On the same day the Americans dragged their own artillery into position while Jackson began construction of a second line of defense two miles behind the first. Next day the British showered the American lines with rockets and sent two columns forward in assault.

On the American left, the redcoats came very close to turning the sector held by Coffee's and Carroll's men standing almost waist-deep in the swamp. On the right, the enemy column moving along the river bank was raked dreadfully by the guns of *Louisiana*. Rampart guns, manned chiefly by Laffite's red-shirted pirates, thickened the fire from *Louisiana* and the assault on the American right was dealt a bloody repulse. As it halted, so too did the threat to the left flank— and Pakenham's first attempt failed. Although he tried to excuse it as a "reconnaissance in force," one of his aides wrote later: "In spite of our sanguine expectations of sleeping that night in New Orleans, evening found us occupying our negro huts at Villere's, nor was I sorry that the shades of night concealed our mortification from the prisoners and slaves."[89]

The last three days of 1814 were ones of back-breaking toil on both sides. The Americans fortified the other side of the river with three batteries of naval guns and the mud line's cannon rose from five to twelve. Cotton bales were sunk into the mud flats and wooden platforms placed over them. The faces of the gun embrasures were protected by cotton bales stiffened with dried mud. As Jackson's defenses grew, he continued to send "hunting parties" into the British lines every night. His men lay still in the cane stubble between the lines, rising suddenly to shoot or tomahawk a careless sentry.

On the British side Cochrane's sailors had brought off an incredible feat of labor, bringing forward naval guns from the fleet 70 miles away. On New Year's Eve, a black and foggy night, these big pieces of ordnance were put into position 700 yards away from the Americans. Protected by mounds of earth and hogsheads of sugar, the British guns were to silence the American artillery and blast a breach in the rampart through which the redcoats, their bellies now pinched by hunger, might stream to victory.

New Year's Day, 1815, was still foggy. Nevertheless, General Andrew Jackson persisted in his intention to review his troops. Visitors from the city, among them ladies, streamed into the camp. A band played. Troops assigned to parade had cleaned up their uniforms. Suddenly the fog became suffused with scarlet, there came a thunder that was not the roll of drums, and as the mist became slashed with showers of rockets and civilians went scurrying frantically cityward while soldiers sprinted for the ramparts, the British bombardment began to work over the American camp.

One hundred balls struck and shattered Jackson's headquarters, a supply boat was crippled, cotton bales on the ramparts were set ablaze, a gun carriage was shattered, a 32- and a 12-pounder were knocked out, and a caisson loaded with ammunition was blown up. With that, the British infantry waiting to attack sent up a cheer and their gunners, satisfied that they had silenced the enemy, suspended fire. To their astonishment, through clouds of billowing, pungent smoke that blotted out everything, came the American answering fire.

It began faintly at first and then rose with a gradually ascending roar. Converging from Jackson's line and the batteries across the river, 15 guns in all answered Britain's 24, and Subaltern Glieg has described their effect:

> The enemy's shot penetrated these sugar-hogsheads as if they had been so many empty casks, dismounting our guns and killing our artillery-men in the very centre of their works. There could be small doubt, as soon as these facts were established, how the cannonading would end. Our fire slackened every moment; that of the Americans became every moment more terrible, till at length, after not more than two hours and a half of firing, our batteries were all silenced. The American works, on the other hand, remained as little injured as ever, and we were completely foiled.[90]

The Dirty Shirts had slugged toe to toe with the pride of the fleet and driven them to cover, and Andrew Jackson jubilantly wished his troops a Happy New Year with the message: "Watch Word: Fight On—The Contractor will issue half a gill of whiskey around."[91]

A week passed during which both sides were reinforced: a brigade for the British, 2,400 Kentuckians for the Americans. Pakenham now had about 8,000 men and Jackson 5,700, although Old Hickory was startled to hear that most of his Kentuckians were unarmed.

"I don't believe it," he exclaimed. "I have never seen a Kentuckian without a gun and a pack of cards and a bottle of whiskey in my life."[92]

Nevertheless, only one man in three had a firearm, so Jackson sent about 500 of them across the river to act as reserve for the 550 Louisiana militia who defended Patterson's batteries there under Brigadier General David Morgan. For a while Jackson was undecided about where to expect the enemy's next attack. News that the British were dragging boats from Lake Borgne to the Mississippi suggested that they might cross the river to strike Morgan. But then the sight of redcoats bundling cane stalks into fascines and making ladders made it clear that the enemy might try to cross the canal and scale the rampart of Jackson's main position.

In truth, Pakenham meant to do both. The boats were for Colonel William Thornton, the officer who led the charge at Bladensburg, to take 1,400 men across the river to overwhelm Morgan, seize the guns and turn them on Jackson's rear. Meanwhile, three columns would hit the canal and rampart: General Keane on the British left by the river, Major General Sir Samuel Gibbs on the right by the swamp, and Major General John Lambert in the center to be rushed wherever needed. It was a good plan, especially the cross-river thrust for the American guns. Artillery playing on Jackson's rear could be decisive. However, British fear of Dirty Shirt marksmanship had dictated that the assault take place in the confusion of darkness.

At the outset Thornton got only half of his men into boats on time and was quickly swept downriver below his landing place. Then Gibbs on the right discovered that his men had forgotten their fascines and ladders. Before dawn broke, only Keane on the left was ready. Nevertheless, Pakenham fired a rocket, that *"fatal ever fatal rocket"* signaling the attack of January 8.

Andrew Jackson and his aides had been up since one o'clock in the morning inspecting the lines. They came to the battery commanded by the fierce and dandified little pirate captain, Dominique You. Dominique's red-shirts were cooking coffee and Jackson said, "That smells like better coffee than we can get." He turned to Dominique. "Smuggle it?"

"Mebbe so, General," the little captain grunted, filling a cup for his commander.

"I wish I had five hundred such devils in the butts,"[93] Jackson muttered, passing on until he came to his Tennesseans under Coffee and Carroll on the left. He was there, standing on the parapet, when Pakenham's rocket burst in a bluish-silver shower overhead. Another from Keane answered from the river bank, and Jackson peered intently into the opaque wall of mist before him. Then a providential breeze sprang up, opening patches in the fog through which Jackson could now see the British advancing.

They were coming through a cane stubble silvery with frost. They came on bravely, cross-belts forming a white X on scarlet tunics, and Jackson issued the order: ". . . . aim above the cross plates."[94]

American cannon spoke first, then the British answered, and the fog again glowed red. Soon smoke spoiled the aim of the American riflemen, and Jackson ordered two leftward batteries to cease firing. The air cleared and the British could be seen coming at a run 300 yards away. American cannon to Jackson's right angled a scything fire into the British ranks. The red ranks shuddered, closed up and came on. Now the gleaming cross plates were just a hair above the sights of American rifles.

"*Fire!*"

Flame and flash and single crack, and the first rank of riflemen stepped down to reload while the second took its place.

"*Fire!*"

The second rank gave way to the third.

"*Fire!*"[95]

Scarlet coats lay crumpled among the stubble. Gibbs's oncoming column had been splayed out into skirmish line as though a giant hand had slapped it. Again and again the American fire ripped into them, until the foreranks turned to the rear. "Never before had British veterans quailed," an English officer wrote later. "The leaden torrent no man on earth could face."[96]

Sir Edward Pakenham came galloping up to his shattered right flank, had his horse shot dead beneath him and flung himself upon his aide's black pony. A second assault was formed, led by a "praying regiment" of Highlanders, every man six feet tall—coming on with swinging kilts, and going down among the silver stubble. Perhaps 70 of these brave men gained the bank of the canal, perhaps 30 got across it and clambered up the parapet. But none of them survived.

That was the end of Gibbs's attack. Gibbs himself was dying, Keane had been shot through the neck, and Pakenham had received his third and mortal wound. On the British left a splendid charge had carried through an American bastion, but penetrated no farther. In the center, General Lambert ignored Pakenham's dying orders to throw in the reserve and began withdrawing the stricken British Army from the field.

In all, the British had suffered more than 2,000 casualties against only eight Americans killed and 13 wounded. At half-past eight it was all over at the Rodriguez Canal. "I never had so grand and awful an idea of the resurrection," said General Jackson, "as . . . [when] I saw . . . more than five hundred Britons emerging from the heaps of their dead comrades, all over the plain rising up, and . . . coming forward . . . as prisoners."[97]

The battle was not entirely over. Across the river, Colonel Thornton drove steadily through Morgan's militia. Jackson's elation over the British failure at his main position changed to alarm as he saw the Americans across the river give way completely. Cross-river cannon fire still raking the British in front of Jackson suddenly ceased. Captain Patterson was spiking his guns. Night came and Jackson still held his breath. He had moved too late to counter Thornton, and now the British held an advantage which might easily be exploited. But in the morning Lambert recalled Thornton to the east bank. On the night of January 18, leaving their campfires burning, the British returned the way they had come. Ahead of them went the body of General Pakenham "in a casket of rum to be taken to London. What a sight for his wife who is aboard and who had hoped to be Governess of Louisiana."[98]

Three days later the majestic notes of the *Te Deum* reverberated around the stone walls of the cathedral in New Orleans.

News of the deliverance of New Orleans traveled even slower than news of the Treaty of Ghent. Up North, the "ambassadors" of the Hartford Convention were still supremely confident of American defeat as they rode toward Washington. They still intended to speak plainly to Mr. Madison. Three black crows preceded their coach into Washington, but the ambassadors remained unshaken, for Puritans took no stock in the "auguries" of a superstitious past. At Baltimore, however, they heard of the victory at New Orleans. Though shaken, they rode on to Washington. On February 13, 1815, news of the Treaty of Ghent was received in the capital. Stunned, the Hartford emissaries hung around Washington for about a week, after which, no longer able to sit still as the butt of war hawk barb and caricature, they rode back to New England.

On February 17, 1815, President Madison declared the War of 1812 at an end.

PART ☆ IV

The War with Mexico

1

☆

In February of 1815, a week after the War of 1812 came to an end, Napoleon Bonaparte escaped from Elba. Four months later he met the Duke of Wellington at Waterloo and went down to his last defeat.

Thus ended the Anglo-French duel which had extended over nearly two centuries. Six times—four times with the British, twice against them—the Americans had been drawn into that world-wide conflict; but now this new nation, hating war yet born and bred to battle, was at last free of "the broils of Europe."

America was free because Waterloo had conferred upon Britain an immense, world-wide prestige and had ushered in the *Pax Britannica,* that relatively peaceful century during which Britain "controlled extra-European events and localized European wars."[1] It is one of the great paradoxes of American history that the British Navy which had so insulted America by its insistence on the right to impress her seamen would now by its mastery of the seas enable the United States to embark unmolested upon an era of territorial expansion and internal development.

The year 1815, then, was a great turning point. Relations with Great Britain became friendly, and the so-called Era of Good Feeling commenced with the election of James Monroe as President in 1816. So also began a spirit of nationalism, which seems to have sprung from the common experience through which Americans had just passed as well as from a reaction against the selfish sectional strife which had characterized the war. Albert Gallatin, returning from Ghent, said this of his countrymen: "They are more American; they feel and act more like a nation; and I hope that the permanency of the Union is thereby better secured."[2]

Nationalism buried the states' rights Federalists in the grave dug by the Hartford Convention. Once nationalism had been the very soul of Federalism, as it was the *bête noire* of Republicanism, but the Federalists had since shifted to states' rights, and the Republicans, observing to what depth their rivals had been interred, quickly switched to nationalism. The movement's leaders, John C. Calhoun and Henry Clay, had a formula called "the American system," which included a protective tariff for the manufacturing industry developed during the war, a home market for national products and improved transportation.

Good transportation was vital to the new westward surge begun when American settlers flowed into the lands taken from Tecumseh and the Creeks. Four new states—Indiana (1816), Mississippi (1817), Illinois (1818) and Alabama (1819)—were admitted to the union. Unfortunately, territorial expansion raised the ghost of slavery extension. An even balance between slave and free states had been maintained by alternately admitting slave-soil and free-soil territories. After Alabama's entry there were 11 each. But then, in 1819, Missouri sought admission as a slave state, and this most divisive of sectional issues came alive with an acrimonious vigor which threatened to shatter the nationalist honeymoon.

Outraged Northerners insisted that the entry of Missouri, which lay north of the line then dividing slavery and freedom, was a Southern attempt to increase its voting power. Southerners, who had not yet come to defending slavery on moral grounds, claimed that they had the right to take their property, i.e., slaves, into Missouri. Both sides talked secession. Eventually the Missouri Compromise was agreed upon. Under its terms, Missouri was admitted as a slave-holding state, while Maine, which had detached itself from Massachusetts, was admitted as a free state. More important, slavery was prohibited in unorganized territory north of Missouri's southern boundary of 36°36′. Thus the South provided for the eventual admission of Florida and Arkansas as slave states, while the North guaranteed freedom in the huge unsettled stretches of U.S. territory.

Whatever the Missouri Compromise may have done in restoring a fatally deceptive tranquillity to the Era of Good Feeling, it had also driven home for the first time the fact that the question of slavery was not a political or economic problem but a moral one. Thomas Jefferson saw this, and wrote: "This momentous question, like a fire bell in the night, awakened and filled me with terror. I considered it at once as the knell of the Union."³ John Quincy Adams, now Secretary of State, informed his diary: "I take it for granted that the present question is a mere preamble—a title page to a great, tragic volume."⁴ Much of the dreadfully involved wrangle over Missouri was actually a struggle to control the trans-Mississippi West, an area finally delineated by Adams after Jackson tore Florida out of the hands of Spain.

In the fall of 1817 the first of the wars with the Seminole Indians broke out, and Andrew Jackson marched to battle again at the head of about 2,500 Tennessee militia. Breaking the power of the Seminoles, he kept marching south until he had taken Pensacola and ejected its Spanish governor, after which he went back to Tennessee a hero. In Washington, however, there were powerful men who remembered Julius Caesar and wished to have Jackson disgraced or at least reprimanded.

Adams was not one of them. He stood behind Old Hickory, insisting that Spain had long ago shown her inability to govern Florida. Spain seemed to agree, for negotiations to sell the troublesome province were begun. They concluded in the Transcontinental Treaty of February, 1819, under which, in return for $5 million, Spain ceded all her lands east of the Mississippi together with her claims to the Oregon territory. The treaty also traced the boundary between the United States and Mexico, and because it recognized an American line to the Pacific running west from the Rockies along the 42nd parallel, it made the United States of America a continental power. Mexico, however, the last Spanish province in North America, remained enormous. It included not only its present-day lands but the modern American states of California, Nevada, Utah, Arizona, New Mexico, Texas and parts of Wyoming and Colorado. Mexico was roughly equal in size to the United States itself—bigger if the Oregon territory which America jointly claimed with Britain was excluded —and Mexico a few years later was herself a free republic.

Mexican independence climaxed a seven-year eruption of revolutions which convulsed Latin America after the fall of Napoleon. One by one, under the leadership of José de San Martín, Simon Bolívar and Bernardo O'Higgins, Spain's colonies in the New World renounced allegiance to the mother country and set themselves up as free republics. Unfortunately, they did not unite as the North American colonies had. Such a multipilicity of young and unsteady republics, all open to the intrigues as well as the commerce of the older powers, created a dangerously unstable situation. Britain took the lead in attempting to stabilize it by asking the United States to join her in a declaration barring France from South America. But the Americans went Mother England one better. They decided to bar *everyone* from South America, and on December 2, 1823, in his annual message to Congress, President Monroe laid down the Monroe Doctrine warning all European powers against attempting to interfere with nations in the "Western Hemisphere." The United States, of course, had no power to enforce such a declaration. Only British sea power was capable of patrolling the shores of both continents. Yet Britain was at that moment deeply interested in preserving the peace in South America, just as she was not interested in expanding at the expense of the new Latin republics. So the Monroe Doctrine stood up—propped up, as it were, by the British Navy—gradually solidifying into one of the pillars of American foreign policy as the nation itself grew in power and prestige.

On this note, the Era of Good Feeling came to an end.

2

☆

Mexico and the United States were sister republics in name only. A better term is neighboring republics: they bordered each other from the Pacific to the Gulf, that was all.

One spoke English, the other Spanish; one was Protestant, the other Catholic; one, colonized on British lines, was organized by a strong federal government, was energetic, proliferating and expanding; and the other, colonized in the Roman way, had little unity, was torpid, thinly populated, and already weakened by an oppressive clergy and upper class and by the immemorial Latin custom of celebrating today's revolution by toasting tomorrow's. Such differences were not disputes, and none was a valid reason for going to war. But the two republics were neighbors—one strong, the other weak—and it is only in recent times, under the Sign of the Mushroom Cloud, that strong neighbors have acted as though they thought they should feed rather than eat the weak. In a sense, Mexico was to America what Ireland was to England. Again, it was a geographical fact, sheer proximity; Americans had yearned for Canada, and now, in the two decades (1825-45) following Monroe's administration, they turned their eyes from their northeastern border to the southwestern one.

This desire was never so conscious or deliberate as that illustrated by the war hawk raid on Upper Canada. Nor was the American government—at least not before President Polk—its instrument. Its agents—it might almost be said its advance guard or fifth column— were the pioneers and the backwoodsmen who crossed the Mississippi and came upon the northern outposts of Mexico.

The provinces of Upper California (the modern state of California), New Mexico and Texas were sparsely populated and bound to the parent government in the city of Mexico by the weakest of ties. Neither California nor New Mexico welcomed Americans, but in Texas they were not only welcomed but actually imported. Why, is difficult to answer. Even if it was imperative that Mexico should encourage migration to people her huge unsettled lands, it is inexplicable why she chose Americans. Europeans, especially from countries more nearly Mexican in customs, race and religion, would have been far safer. But only a few Germans were so encouraged; in the main it was *los Yanquis* who poured into Texas.

Their leaders were the *empresarios* to whom Mexico granted great tracts of land for settlement. By 1834 one such colony organized by Stephen Austin numbered 20,000 whites and 2,000 slaves and out-numbered the native Mexicans four to one. Few of these pioneers be-came Catholics as they had promised to do, and none heeded Mexican laws abolishing slavery; and as much as they might try to adhere to the laws of their adopted land, they found them forever changing in the wake of the latest revolution. As much as they might admire, say, the horsemanship of their adopted countrymen, they had the Anglo-Saxon's deep-seated faith in the superiority of the fair-skinned and soon came to despise the "greasers" as a lazy, superstitious lot. In turn, the Mexicans came to resent *los gringos* with their cold, con-descending, acquisitive ways. They were *los hereticos,* and thus it might have been New France and New England colliding again beneath a sunnier sky.

Within the United States, especially in the Mississippi Valley, there were many Americans who believed their nation had a claim to Texas. After John Quincy Adams was elected President in 1824 he offered to buy the province. So did Andrew Jackson following his election in 1828. Both times the Mexicans angrily refused. But then the peaceful pioneers were joined by their less savory migratory twins, the hard-fighting, hard-drinking, straight-shooting frontiersmen, those "ring-tailed roarers, half-horse and half-alligator" who lived on "whiskey and bear's meat salted in a hailstorm, peppered with buckshot, and broiled in a flash of forked lightning."⁵ Davy Crockett was one of them and so were the Bowie brothers of Louisiana, famous for slave-smuggling and the long knife—or short sword—that they had designed. Such men could not fail to fan the flames of hatred between Mexicans and Texans.

By 1836 there were 30,000 Americans in Texas, and Mexico, at last awake to the danger, sought to stem the onrushing tide of frontiersmen. By then the fiery and energetic revolutionary, General Antonio López de Santa Anna, had become virtual dictator of Mexico. He proclaimed a constitution which swept away states' rights and imposed an iron control on the Yankees north of the Rio Grande. The Texans replied by declaring their independence on March 2, 1836. They set up a provisional government under the Lone Star flag and expelled the Mexican garrison from San Antonio de Bexar.

Santa Anna promptly collected an army of 3,000 men and marched on San Antonio. There, less than 200 Texans took refuge in an abandoned adobe mission called the Alamo. Among them were Crockett and Jim Bowie. Their leader was Colonel William Travis. In his last message addressed "To the People of Texas and all Americans in the world," Travis declared: "I shall never surrender or retreat. . . . I am determined to sustain myself as long as possible and die like a soldier who never forgets what is due to his own honor and that of his country —VICTORY OR DEATH."⁶

For ten days the heroic men of the Alamo held off the Mexicans. Santa Anna's losses were frightful, but he pressed the assault. In the gray dawn of March 6, 1836, his entire remaining force swept forward with wild yells. Twice more they were beaten back. But on the third charge they swarmed over the Alamo's walls and fell upon its handful of survivors. Step by step, with knife and clubbed rifles, the Texans fought them off. In the end, not one of the Alamo's defenders was left alive. Colonel Travis had chosen victory or death, but he had been given both: less than 200 Texans had killed 1,544 Mexicans to turn Santa Anna's laurels into thorns, and the rallying cry of "Remember the Alamo!" that thrilled all Texas was at the least a moral victory. Three weeks later, after the Mexicans cold-bloodedly shot down 350 Texan prisoners at Goliad, all Texas burned with a thirst for revenge.

That desire was to be slaked by Sam Houston, the valiant giant who had led Andrew Jackson's charge at Horseshoe Bend. Putting himself at the head of the tiny Texas army, Houston awaited Santa Anna in a grove of live oak near the San Jacinto River. Here, on April 21, 1836, shouting "Remember the Alamo!" the Texas cavalry charged and broke Santa Anna's line and the Texas infantry put the Mexicans to rout. Santa Anna was captured and forced to sign treaties (which he did not intend to honor) by which he agreed to evacuate Texas and use his influence to obtain Mexican recognition of an independent Texas with a southern boundary at the Rio Grande. Mexico, of course, refused to recognize these claims.

In the meanwhile, the new republic elected Sam Houston as its first president, legalized slavery and sent an emissary to Washington to ask for recognition or annexation to the United States. It was a delicate question, and Old Hickory in the White House moved cautiously.

First, John Quincy Adams with the help of Henry Clay and Daniel Webster had formed the Whig Party now supplanting the old Republicans. The Whigs opposed recognition of Texas, and Northern abolitionists were crying that the Texas revolt was a plot to extend the area of slavery. By then Arkansas and Michigan had been admitted to the union, making 13 slave and 13 free states. But Florida was the last slave state remaining to the South, and there were three free territories —Wisconsin, Iowa and Minnesota—awaiting their turn. Obviously, the South would soon be outnumbered, and so Southern leaders such as Calhoun began thundering for outright annexation of Texas.

In such a situation Old Hickory was careful not to do anything to harm the chances of Vice President Martin Van Buren, his hand-picked presidental candidate. So Jackson waited until after "Little Van" was elected in 1836, and then, on March 3, 1837, his last day in office, he recognized the Lone Star Republic.

Van Buren did little about Texas, and his successor, William Henry Harrison, had no time to do much about anything. With John Tyler of Virginia as his running mate ("Tippecanoe and Tyler, too!"), the old Whig general had defeated Van Buren in 1840, but one month after

"Tip and Ty" took office, Tip was dead of a cold caught at his inauguration and Ty, a slave-holding man who was no friend of the Whigs, was the President. Tyler wanted Texas, but, like Jackson, he had to wait until his last day in office before he could inform San Houston that Texas had been admitted to the Union by a joint resolution of Congress.

Next day, March 4, 1845, James K. Polk came into the White House. And Polk not only wanted Texas; he wanted California, too.

James Polk was the first "dark horse" presidential candidate in American history. He was a protégé of Andrew Jackson's, he had been in Congress and been Governor of Tennessee—but he was still, in 1844, a colorless gray squirrel of a man alongside the sleek, beaverish Van Buren or the leonine Henry Clay. Yet the dispute over Texas killed off both Van Buren and Clay.

Van Buren, confident of the Democratic nomination, had proposed to Clay, who was certain of the Whig choice, that they should make public their opposition to the annexation of Texas on the ground that it would mean war with Mexico. There was no doubt that Mexico would so react to annexation; to keep the peace, Clay agreed. But neither man had accurately gauged the extent of expansionist sentiment in the country. Van Buren felt its strength first at the Democratic Convention when Polk the unknown was given the nomination chiefly because he was an annexationist. Clay was bowled over next when Polk won the election by a close vote aided by antislavery Whigs voting for an abolitionist candidate.

The White House has had few occupants as cheerless and friendless as James K. Polk. Yet, for whatever he may have lacked in charm, wit, good health or brilliance, he was nonetheless courageous, tenacious and purposeful. He knew what he wanted and he knew how to get it. Chief among his desires was California, and he yearned to acquire it before France or Britain obtained it from Mexico. Above all he hoped to obtain it by peaceful purchase; but this, for the simple reason that Mexico had no wish to sell, was not to be.

Mexico was so offended by the American offer to annex Texas that she broke off diplomatic relations with the United States shortly after Polk took office. After Texas did join the Union, Mexico resounded to cries for war with the United States. Polk replied by ordering General Zachary Taylor to a position "on or near" the Rio Grande to repel invasion. Taylor took station at Corpus Christi, on the south side of the Nueces River. Thus he highlighted the continuing Texas-Mexico border controversy.

Texas claimed the Rio Grande as her southern boundary. But Mexico, still claiming Texas, insisted that the southeastern limit of Texas had always been the Nueces River farther to the north. As a Mexican department, Texas had never extended beyond the Nueces. Land south and west of that river had belonged to the department of Tamaulipas. At the very best Texas had a highly doubtful claim to territory below the Nueces, yet here was an American army encamped there—much as if a Canadian army had crossed the Niagara River into New York to "defend" Ontario.

It was against this background, and even using the border dispute as a lever, that President Polk made his second, most persistent effort to buy off Mexico's northern outposts.

Recent civil wars in Mexico had, among other things, resulted in the ouster of Santa Anna as well as property damage to American nationals estimated at about $4.5 million. In 1845 Polk offered to assume that debt if Mexico would be willing to recognize the Rio Grande as the southern boundary of Texas. Another $5 million would be offered for New Mexico, and for California "money would be no object." Polk's minister to Mexico, John Slidell, was instructed to be tactful with Mexico's feeble and distracted government. So Slidell left for Mexico City in November of 1845, and when he arrived he found the nation so aroused by the Texas affair that posters were appearing charging that he had come to buy Texas and California and that any negotiation with him would be treason.

In the meantime, expansionist fever over what was known as "Manifest Destiny" had seized and inflamed the American imagination. In December of 1845 the editor of the New York *Morning News,* John O'Sullivan, wrote of "our manifest destiny to overspread and to possess the whole of the continent which Providence has given us for the development of the great experiment of liberty and federated self-government."[7]

Manifest destiny! It had a Godly as well as a golden ring to it. Not only was wealth to be had in California but the will of God was to be executed there by His newly Chosen. Here once again was the crusading spirit which had energized the colonials against their French and Indian foes. Here was "the right of our manifest destiny,"[8] as one Congressman put it, and even abolitionists, regarding expansion as a Southern plot to erect a new "slavocracy" in the Southwest, could not resist the lure of that magical, mystical phrase. By the end of 1845 the *American Whig Review* could ask: "Why not extend the 'area of freedom' by the annexation of California? Why not plant the banner of liberty there?"⁹

The answer to that question was that in Mexico City the latest government was fruitlessly appealing to France and Britain for assistance, for it did not dare receive Minister Slidell. To do so would have meant its downfall. Even so, it did topple—on the ground that it was treating treasonably with the United States! Into the office strode General Mariano Paredes. He promised no concessions to America and he proceeded to whip Mexico into a hate-America frenzy.

In Washington, hearing of Slidell's rebuff, President Polk ordered General Taylor to move his little army down to the left bank of the Rio Grande. Taylor, mistakenly believing that torrential rains barred his path, did not move south until two months later. On March 24, 1846, he reached a point on the Rio Grande opposite Matamoros and 33 miles inland from Port Isabel. Taylor assured the Mexicans that he had come only to protect American property. They replied that he was on Mexican soil, a fact which automatically created a state of war. General Pedro de Ampudia demanded that Taylor withdraw to the Nueces. Taylor refused, building a fort, training his guns on Matamoros and blockading the mouth of the Rio Grande to cut off Mexican supplies.

Thus was the powder keg built and stuffed. Texas had seceded from Mexico, making very doubtful claim to a southern boundary at the Rio Grande. Mexico recognized neither secession nor claim, and was enraged by American annexation of Texas and infuriated by attempts to buy New Mexico and California. Yet American troops now stood on soil which Mexico believed belonged to her. Opposing those Americans were Mexican soldiers. All that was needed now to explode the powder keg was the spark of war: blood.

No one appreciated this better than James K. Polk. On May 8 he had been informed by Slidell that force was now the only expedient left to the United States. Next day Polk met with his Cabinet. He found all but one in favor of his proposal to ask Congress for a declaration of war. Some, Polk included, would have liked it better if Mexico had committed some act of aggression. That very night the President learned that the Mexicans had, if one can be an "aggressor" on soil considered to be one's own.

On April 24 General Mariano Arista took command in Matamoros and promptly sent a force across the Rio Grande above Taylor's camp. Next day the Mexicans ambushed 63 American dragoons under Captain Seth Thornton, killing 11, wounding others and capturing most of the rest. On April 26, 1846, General Taylor informed Washington that "hostilities may now be considered as commenced," and called upon Texas and Louisiana for volunteers.

Taylor's 11th-hour message was a *casus belli* far superior to Mexico's failure to pay American claims or to receive Slidell, and on May 10, a Sunday, Polk worked on his war message before and after church, regretting "the necessity . . . for me to spend the Sabbath in the manner I have."[10] The following day he told Congress: "The cup of forbearance has been exhausted. After reiterated menaces, Mexico has passed the boundary of the United States, has invaded our territory and shed American blood upon the American soil."[11] Congress then declared that "by the act of the Republic of Mexico, a state of war exists between that government and the United States," authorized Polk to accept 50,000 volunteers and appropriated $10 million for war purposes. The vote was 174 to 14 in the House, 40 to 2 in the Senate. On May 13, 1846, Polk signed the war bill into law.

Five days earlier, however, Mexican and American soldiers north of the Rio Grande had made the war a flaming fact.

3

☆

Outnumbered by the United States—20 million to 7 million—Mexico nonetheless was supremely confident of victory.

Her generals, chief among them Dictator Paredes, shared the general European contempt for American military prowess. That was why Paredes, who had come to power promising to chastise the gringos, had ordered Arista to gain the victory over Taylor that would strengthen his hold on the nation.

Paredes was not being vainglorious; he merely mistook size for strength. In 1845 the Mexican Army included about 30,000 men against less than 5,500 effectives in the American establishment. However, much of Mexico's artillery was outmoded, command of her rank-heavy units* was held by officers exalted by their dexterity in changing sides rather than diligence in matters military, and the men themselves, though brave and very hardy, were poorly trained. Mexican soldiers usually shot from the hip to avoid the recoil of muskets so overcharged with powder that they generally fired high. These defects, of course, were of the hidden kind that only become apparent during the stress of battle. Thus, having heard that Taylor's troops were a rabble of undisciplined foreigners, it was no wonder that one of Arista's generals could say, "Those adventurers cannot withstand the bayonet charge of our foot, nor a cavalry charge with the lance."[12]

In truth, 47 percent of the regulars in Taylor's army of 4,000 men were foreigners. Irish alone made up 24 percent of his force, 10 percent were Germans, 6 percent English, 3 percent Scots and a scattered 4 percent were from Canada and Western Europe. But they were far from being without discipline. While at Corpus Christi, Taylor had hammered them into an efficient fighting force. A young lieutenant named Ulysses S. Grant could write home that "a better army, man for man, probably never faced an enemy."[13] Taylor's flying artillery composed of 12 horse-drawn 6-pounders under the innovating Major Samuel Ringgold was a daringly modern weapon. Moreover, the entire U.S. Army—now commanded by tall Winfield Scott, the hero of Lundy's Lane—was fortunate in possessing what was and still is the finest group of young officers in the nation's history. Most of them had been trained at West Point, and to read their names is to call the roll of generals in the Civil War. Grant is one of them, and Robert E. Lee, Thomas, Beauregard, Hooker, J. E. Johnston and Albert Sidney Johnston, Burnside and Bragg, Kearny, Pope, Meade, McClellan, McDowell, Stonewall Jackson and Jefferson Davis, Longstreet, Pickett, Armistead, Hebert, Pemberton, Simon Bolivar Buckner,

* At one time in her history, Mexico had 24,000 officers commanding 20,000 men.

Sherman and Halleck, both Hills, Reynolds, Hancock, Buell and Ewell and Jubal Early—and among the admirals Du Pont, Buchanan and David Glasgow Farragut. Not all of these men were still in service or with Taylor, but many of them were—and some of them were troubled by what Sam Grant called the "unholy" character of their mission. One considered the march to Matamoros to be "of itself an act of hostility." He saw no Texans or Americans south of the Nueces. "All were Mexicans, acknowledging none but Mexican laws. Yet we . . . drove those poor people away from their farms, and seized their custom-house at Point Isabel."[14]

The march itself was a grueling ordeal of 150 miles beneath a blazing sun which "streamed upon us like a living fire."[15] The light blue jackets and trousers of the infantrymen became caked with soft white powdery dust, and soon those stiff-necked cavalrymen who rode above the choking clouds were calling the foot-sloggers "adobies" after the white Mexican huts along the river. It was a short step to "dobies" and after this to "doughboys," and thus the immortal nickname was born. And the floury dust that had christened the doughboys also coated their tongues and clogged their nostrils to aggravate a thirst that was terrible for both men and animals. A whole day's march often lay between ponds of potable water, and yet even the agony of thirst and sunburn might be forgotten in the universal delight to behold the wide blue sky filled with "mirages": ships and islands reflected from the Gulf 60 or more miles away.

It was on this march that Zachary Taylor endeared himself to his troops. "Old Rough and Ready" made no attempt to avoid the hardships suffered by his men. His hawkish nose was also white and peeling beneath his old straw hat, and he rode along on Old Whitey, often with one leg nonchalantly slung over the pommel, looking as military as a mounted sack of flour. One day his slouching body was clothed in a blue-checked gingham coat, another in a dusty green coat, then an old brown coat or a linen waistcoat or yet again a soldier's light blue overalls.

At last, on March 23, Taylor's suffering doughboys formed into columns four abreast and went marching through a prairie now thick with grass and red and gold with blossoming cactus. On March 28 they saw the blue mists of the Rio Grande ahead of them. At ten-thirty that morning they came to the river bank and stared across the water at Matamoros.

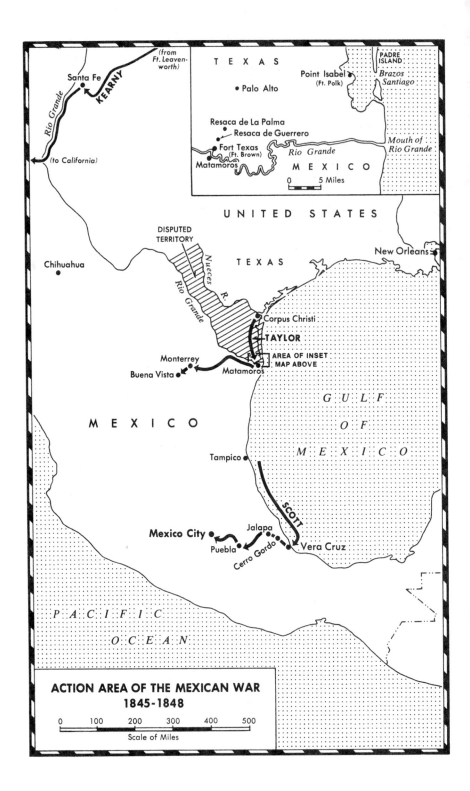

Inset map:

(from Ft. Leavenworth)

T E X A S

KEARNY

Santa Fe

Point Isabel (Ft. Polk)

PADRE ISLAND

Brazos Santiago

Rio Grande

Palo Alto

(to California)

Resaca de La Palma
Resaca de Guerrero

Fort Texas (Ft. Brown)

Matamoros

Rio Grande

M E X I C O

Mouth of Rio Grande

0   5 Miles

Main map:

U N I T E D   S T A T E S

DISPUTED TERRITORY

Chihuahua

Nueces R.

Rio Grande

T E X A S

New Orleans

Corpus Christi

TAYLOR

AREA OF INSET MAP ABOVE

Monterrey

Matamoros

Buena Vista

M E X I C O

G U L F

O F

M E X I C O

Tampico

SCOTT

Mexico City

Jalapa

Puebla   Cerro Gordo   Vera Cruz

P A C I F I C

O C E A N

ACTION AREA OF THE MEXICAN WAR
1845-1848

0   100   200   300   400   500

Scale of Miles

They saw Mexicans standing in curious throngs atop the town's tiled rooftops. They saw red roses climbing snow-white walls. They heard bands blaring, bugles pealing, dogs barking and church bells ringing in a medley counterpointed by the liquid Spanish of excited civilians and drilling soldiers—but most of all they saw the cool blue waters of the Rio Grande and many of them stripped and went bathing in it.

That was when they saw the Mexican girls come laughing down to the opposite bank to step out of their skirts and chemises and go naked in the water, and with that a difficulty unforeseen by Zachary Taylor had begun.

"Efforts are continually [being made] to entice our men to desert," Taylor reported on April 6, "and, I regret to say, [they] have met with considerable success."[16]

By then, 30 of Taylor's soldiers had crossed to Matamoros. Naked Mexican lasses splashing in the water had not been the only attraction, nor had the girls been official sirens but only local maidens following a Matamoros custom which happened to coincide with Mexican policy. The Mexicans had guessed that many of the foreigners in Taylor's army were Roman Catholics, and they made a powerful appeal to their religious loyalties. Nearly every day Matamoros celebrated a saint's day with masses, music and processions. Taylor's troops were encouraged to desert to claim bounties starting at 320 acres. Old World allure was also complemented by the contempt and cruelty which too many American officers visited upon their foreign soldiers. And so, as sex, saints and sadism began to whittle the army he had worked so hard to build, Old Rough and Ready acted. He got tough and began shooting soldiers trying to desert, starting with a Frenchman and a Swiss. Such draconic measures—taken, incidentally, before the state of war which justifies such executions had begun—plugged the leak at last. But desertions among regulars was a continuing problem for Taylor, and those who turned their coats at Matamoros were to form the nucleus of that San Patricio or Saint Patrick's Battalion which turned out to be Mexico's finest fighting unit.

In the meantime, both sides crowned the Rio Grande with fortifications, General Arista arrived to take command, to order the ambush which provided President Polk with his *casus belli,* and to cross the river downstream to cut Taylor's communications with Port Isabel.

On May 1 Taylor received word that Arista was beginning to cross the river downstream. Alarmed for the safety of his supply line, Taylor immediately struck camp and began marching for Port Isabel. Left behind in Fort Texas were about 500 men under Major Jacob Brown.

Fortunately for Taylor, Arista did not have enough boats to get his force quickly across the river. Before he could intercept Taylor the American led his exhausted command into Port Isabel. There he began filling 250 empty wagons with supplies needed to maintain his position at Matamoros, and there on the morning of May 3 he heard the dull booming of cannon from the direction of Fort Texas. The Mexicans were bombarding Major Brown's little garrison. Down at Port Isabel, some of Taylor's young officers swallowed nervously to hear their first hostile cannon. Sam Grant later admitted: "I felt sorry that I had enlisted."[17]

General Taylor was not concerned. Scouts had returned with assurances from Major Brown that the fort could hold out. So Taylor ignored the pleas of commanders wild to march to the fort's relief and continued to load his wagons while strengthening the defenses of Port Isabel. On May 6 the first recruits from New Orleans arrived, together with 500 sailors and marines from Commodore David Conner's blockading squadron. That morning Brown received his mortal wound at the position which was henceforth to bear his name and become the city of Brownsville, Texas. Defense of Fort Brown continued under Captain Edgar Hawkins, who rejected a Mexican surrender demand by explaining that he could not speak Spanish, "But if I have understood you correctly, my reply is that I must respectfully decline to surrender."[18]

At three o'clock that afternoon Taylor was ready to march. There was a moment of comedy when old Colonel William Whistler wrathfully rounded upon "a young officer of literary tastes" who had dared to put a case of books into a wagon.

"That will never do, Mr. Graham," he snapped. "We can't encumber our train with such rubbish as books."

At this point Lieutenant Charles Hoskins nervously admitted that, not being well, he had taken the liberty of inserting a keg of whiskey in the wagon, and the old colonel murmured: "Oh, that's all right, Mr. Hoskins. Anything in reason. But Graham wanted to carry a case of *books!*"[19]

With the recruits and the seamen left behind to guard the base, whips snapped, pennants fluttered, wheels turned, feet fell—and wagons and men went swishing through waist-high grass. Throughout that day and the next the Americans saw no Mexicans. Then, through the shimmering heat of noon of May 8, 1846, they saw the enemy. At first they were only a line of gleaming metal drawn up on the plain of Palo Alto, the "Tall Timbers" which rose dramatically behind them. Then they were distinguishable: the sun danced on the needle points of lances in the grasp of mounted men, it burnished the brass of cannon drawn up between masses of tall-hatted infantrymen. They seemed an enormous host, but actually, having raised the siege of Fort Brown, General Arista had little more than 4,000 men on the field.

Old Rough and Ready commanded less than 3,000. But these men had an unshakable faith in their indomitable old general, sitting there on Old Whitey with his leg hooked around the pommel while he waited for his wagon train to close up. Then he advanced to within half a mile of the Mexicans, where he halted and ordered a platoon from each company to stack arms and collect their comrades' canteens and fill them from a nearby pond. The men relaxed and forgot their tension.

Opposite them, General Arista rode across his lines waving his sword. The men shouted *"Viva!"* and lifted their banners. At three o'clock in the afternoon, the Mexican cannon began firing. At first the round brass balls came bounding through the tall grass so slowly that they could be easily sidestepped. As the Americans continued to advance, however, the missiles came faster and thicker. Lieutenant Grant gasped to see a ball knock off the under jaw of a captain standing next to him. Then General Taylor halted his advance and sent his own artillery into action.

Major Ringgold's battery went flying to the right, Captain James Duncan took his galloping to the left, and into the center went two bulky 18-pounders, each towed into place by ten yoke of oxen. Now the Americans had the range and their fire was devastating. Again and again American shot cut a swath through the massed Mexican infantrymen, and each time the enemy ranks closed up bravely. But the field artillery, which the Americans were using with a precision unrivaled since the time of Napoleon, prevented almost every Mexican effort to advance. The only attempt was a cavalry charge at the American right.

A thousand lancers with two guns came sweeping through the grass, but Taylor's flank regiments rapidly formed a square and cut the Mexican riders down with musket fire while Lieutenant Randolph Ridgeley led a section of Ringgold's battery to the rescue on the run, unlimbering and blasting the Mexican guns before they could fire a shot.

Palo Alto had become strictly an artillery duel, with the Americans holding the upper hand. American doughboys who had expected to charge with the bayonet merely stood at order arms, cheering as their artillery tore gaps in the enemy lines, or carefully watching for the Mexican solid shot so as to step out of its way. Then smoke obscured the battle. A flaming wad from one of Duncan's guns had set the grass on fire, and the breeze from the Gulf swept the choking smoke toward the Mexican line. Under cover of the prairie fire, Taylor advanced his right. But Arista threw his own right forward, so that the relative position of the lines was little changed. However, Duncan's battery had also moved under cover of the smoke, swinging out to the left to take the enemy right under an enfilading fire.

It was the moment for the American foot soldiers to press forward with the bayonet, but the opportunity had come too late. Darkness veiled the field of Palo Alto, and both sides withdrew. Nine Americans had been killed—among them the invaluable Major Ringgold—and 44 had been wounded. But Mexican losses had totaled 250, and in the early morning darkness of May 9 Taylor gathered his leaders in a council of war and asked them if he should press the attack.

It is in councils of war that the cautious are most aggressive, and this one was no exception: seven of ten officers wanted to wait for reinforcements. But then Captain Duncan rode past, and Taylor called to him to ask his opinion.

"We whipped 'em today and we can whip 'em tomorrow!" Duncan snapped, and Taylor said, "That is my opinion, Captain Duncan. Gentlemen, you will prepare your commands to move forward. The council is dissolved."[20]

The Mexican withdrawal from the field of Palo Alto began at sunup. Taylor did not pursue until he had arranged for the protection of his precious—and distracting—wagon train. At noon his men plunged into the gloomy chaparral which had masked Arista's retreat. Here the terrain differed sharply from the level plain of Palo Alto. Here were dense thickets broken by resacas, or remnants of river beds. Some were sunken lagoons and others were dry trenches, and as such they were excellent for defense. Two of them, the Resaca de la Palma across which the American attack was launched, and the Resaca de Guerrero inside which the Mexicans made their defense, have given their names to the same battle of May 9, 1846.

The Resaca de Guerrero which Arista occupied extended east and west across the road to Matamoros. It was about 200 feet wide and of a depth of three to four feet at the banks. Within it were a few narrow ponds surrounded with bushes and small trees. To either flank and to its rear it was protected by thick chaparral. Arista put his infantry on each side of the road behind the resaca. To his right or east of the road he stationed three or four guns. Then the Mexican general went back to his headquarters tent to attend to paper work. He did not believe the Americans would attack.

They did, however, coming chiefly against the Mexican artillery. Here Taylor, slouching on his horse, was delighted by the spectacle of Lieutenant Ridgeley, now commanding Ringgold's battery, charging down the road with horse-drawn guns unprotected by infantry. Ridgeley deliberately drew the fire of Mexican infantry and artillery, blasting back at their smoke. Meanwhile, the battle had become a sergeant's war. Small parties of men stumbled through the chaparral and tore at each other shot for shot and blade for blade. The Americans went forward yelling like fiends, and the Mexicans—who had not eaten for 24 hours—fought them off bravely.

In all, however, possession of Arista's guns was to mean victory or defeat. Sensing this, Taylor called upon Charles May, a dashing captain of dragoons, to lead his squadron down the road. May went trotting off to form his troopers, but he soon found that the enemy artillery was better emplaced than he had thought. He rode back to General Taylor and asked for new orders.

"Charge, Captain!" Taylor roared. "Charge, *nolens volens!*"[21]

May dashed off, his long black beard streaming in the wind. Ridgeley called to him: "Hold on a minute, Charley, till I draw their fire!"[22] Again Ridgeley lured the Mexicans into giveaway fire, and May's dragoons, observing their position, went sweeping forward in four columns.

Down the road they clattered, down into the resaca, up its opposite bank, over the guns and beyond them—too far beyond them. Before they could stop their hard-bitted horses, the Mexican gunners came swarming out of the chaparral to reclaim their pieces and to cut up May's squadron as it returned to the American lines.

Taylor was furious. He called his infantry forward and roared: "Take those guns, and by God keep them!"[23] Bayonets leveled, the infantry obeyed orders. Ridgeley's gunners followed in behind them to turn the captured cannon on the Mexicans—and it was then, with its flanks slowly giving way to stubborn Americans clawing through the chaparral and its center cracking, that the Mexican line broke. It snapped and flew backward like a broken bow. Even General Arista's tent and possessions were abandoned in the mad rush to the rear. En route to the Rio Grande and Matamoros, the fleeing Mexicans were taken under a bloody enfilade by the guns of Fort Brown. Within the river itself many of them drowned. A priest named Father Leary tried to calm a crowd of crazed fugitives aboard a big flatboat, but then a party of fleeing lancers spurred their horses aboard the boat and swamped it. The last sight the pursuing Americans saw was the priest's upheld crucifix slowly sinking beneath the water.

Now was the time for Taylor to cross the river and to crush the enemy army. He might have ended the war then and there. But Old Rough and Ready was old in his ways. He told his younger officers that the enemy had taken all the boats to the other side, and because he was an "old 'un" he had little time for engineers clamoring for permission to build new ones. No, Zachary Taylor had won two fine fights. His casualties for both totaled 48 dead and 128 wounded, perhaps not one-sixth of Arista's losses. And so, on the evening of May 9, he retired to his tent to write his report.

Even as President Polk far to the northeast was working on his war message, Taylor set down the concluding words: "The enemy has recrossed the river, and I am sure will not again molest us on this bank."[24] Arista not only failed to molest Taylor again; he eventually gave up Matamoros without a fight.

4

☆

The long-range effect of Zachary Taylor's victories at Palo Alto and Resaca de la Palma was to give to American arms a tradition of offensive success which has lasted to this day. Up until May of 1846, American troops had seldom sought and defeated an organized foe. Excepting Trenton, which was hardly more than a raid, and Yorktown, which could not have been won without the French, American victories had been gained in defensive stands or in retreats which averted disaster. But now Americans were attacking and winning, and the American nation, no less than the French placing the laurels on Napoleon's brow, was quick to idolize Old Rough and Ready.

Cities and towns across the nation passed resolutions nominating Zachary Taylor for President. Toasts were raised everywhere to "Old Zack," and the fact that he had no known political preferences meant nothing to those delirious Whigs who at once embraced him as their own. No result could have been more abhorrent to James K. Polk. He realized immediately that he, a Democrat, might be waging war to make a Whig President. But there was nothing Polk could do. Even if he had wanted to recall Taylor, he could not have dared it, for it would have made Old Zack a martyr. And with whom would he replace Taylor? Certainly not Winfield Scott, with whom Polk had already quarreled and whom he had removed from field command, for Scott was an active Whig who had once tried to obtain his party's nomination. And so, in this era of extreme partisanship when a political general was a commonplace, Polk turned to making Democratic generals in the faint hope that one of them might outshine Old Rough and Ready.

Meanwhile, a tidal wave of enthusiasm rolled across the country. Everywhere except in New England, where the annexation of Texas was still resented, volunteers rushed to the colors in the tens of thousands. In New York City walls were plastered with placards proclaiming "Mexico or Death" or "Ho, for the Halls of the Montezumas!" America's streets reverberated to the roll of drums and squeal of fife and the tramp of marching men roaring out such songs as:

> Come all ye gallant volunteers
> Who fear not life to lose,
> The martial drum invites ye come
> And join the Hickory Blues.[25]

In Indianapolis Lew Wallace raised a company in three days by parading the street with a four-sided sign inscribed: "For Mexico: Fall In!" Ohio, unhappy with both annexation and the war itself, nonetheless sent 3,000 of her sons to war in less than two weeks. Illinois volunteered 14 regiments instead of four, North Carolina tripled her quota and Tennessee gained her nickname of "Volunteer State" after 30,000 men responded to a call for 2,800 and the rejects angrily tried to buy their way in.

It was not only patriotism or a sense of Manifest Destiny that solved the manpower problem. Privately recruiters excited almost every passion with promises of "roast beef, two dollars a day, plenty of whiskey, golden Jesuses, and pretty Mexican girls."[26] The charming customs of the maids of Matamoros were presumably not excluded from such recitals. And so the highways were black with thousands hurrying off to the Halls of the Montezumas where life was lazy, lush and golden, and dark-eyed señoritas were obliging.

This time, however, the men were not diverted into those state militias which had been Washington's bane and Madison's mortification. This time the federal government avoided collisions with state authority by enlisting men in volunteer units separate from the regular Army but still liable to foreign service. They were as yet untrained and still given to the pernicious practice of electing their own officers. A soldier in the Alton (Illinois) Guards has described how one such candidate for command recommended himself to the men:

Fellow Citizens! I am Peter Goff, the Butcher of Middletown! I am! I am the man that shot that sneaking, white-livered Yankee abolitionist son of a bitch, Lovejoy! I did! I want to be your Captain, I do; and I will serve the yellow-bellied Mexicans the same, I will! I have treated you to fifty dollars worth of whiskey, I have, and when elected Captain I will spend fifty more, I will![27]

He was elected, he was—even as President Polk made another attempt to satisfy his territorial desires by peaceful means.

Polk planned to smuggle the exiled General Santa Anna into Mexico on his promise to deal with the United States. On August 4, 1846—the day on which General Paredes fell from power, and while Santa Anna was still in Havana—Polk asked Congress for a secret appropriation of $2 million to be used as an advance payment in bribing Santa Anna to cede California. In the House an obscure representative from Pennsylvania named David Wilmot attached to the measure a prohibition against slavery in any lands acquired from Mexico. This was the famous Wilmot Proviso, another "fire bell in the night" such as the Missouri Compromise had been, and though it would clang wildly during the clamorous debate which, a decade later, nearly rang out the Union, its net effect in August of 1846 was to torpedo Polk's plan. Although the House eventually approved the Wilmot Proviso, the whole appropriation measure was filibustered to death after it went to the Senate.

Polk was furious. He had no doubt that he might have stopped the war and gained California with the money, which would have gone toward supporting Santa Anna's army against a public uproar likely to follow such a deal with Uncle Sam. So ended whatever chance there might have been to end the war by peaceful means. In the meantime, the Stars and Stripes were already waving over California—and over the Oregon Territory as well.

One reason Mexico went to war with the United States was because the Mexicans hoped to have British support, if not directly, at least in an Anglo-American war which would draw off Yankee power to the Oregon Territory.

Since 1818 both Britain and the United States had jointly occupied this vast area. But then the British made the same mistake as the Mexicans: they encouraged settlements in the area of their trading posts, and the emigrants, of course, were hardy Yankees, traveling northwestward this time over the rugged Oregon Trail. In the 1840s the Manifest Destiny fever also inflamed these people, and a clamor arose for the assertion of American claims as far north as Russia's southern limit at the Alaskan Panhandle. This was the line 54°40′ which gave rise to the slogan: "Fifty-four forty or fight!"

James Polk did not want to fight, but he still believed that "the only way to treat John Bull is to look him straight in the eye."[28] Thus, after Britain rejected his offer to accept the 49th parallel as a compromise line, Polk returned to the 54-40 claim and served notice of his intention to terminate joint occupation. John Bull, however, stared straight back. Aware that war between Mexico and the United States was imminent, conscious that Polk's extreme position might split his party, the British rattled the saber. Polk naturally did not want war on two fronts, and so he renewed his 49th parallel offer and a conciliatory British government decided that this was an honorable compromise after all. On June 15, 1846, the Senate ratified the Oregon Treaty whereby the future states of Washington, Oregon and Idaho, as well as part of Montana and Wyoming, became American territory. Except for minor revisions made later on, the 49th parallel became the permanent dividing line between the United States and Canada west of the Lake of the Woods.

A few months later both California and New Mexico were in American hands. The first fell on August 7 when Commodore John Sloat merely raised Old Glory over the customhouse at the capital of Monterey. However, the Californians later rose in revolt, only to be put down by the timely appearance of Colonel Stephen Kearny and 150 dragoons.

Kearny had earlier invaded New Mexico by marching with a much larger force from Fort Leavenworth over the Santa Fe Trail. Having annexed the lonely province by proclamation of August 15, he sent out expeditions against the Navajos and into Chihuahua while setting out for San Diego himself. He arrived there after an epic and grueling trek, was worsted by the Californians in a skirmish at San Pasqual, but nevertheless managed to join forces with Commodore Robert Stockton, the new Pacific naval commander. Between them Kearny and Stockton ended the revolt by defeating the Californians at the Battle of the San Gabriel River on January 8, 1847.

Before that date, however, the province was all but subdued. And Mexico, shaken by the march of American victories, was by then in the hands of the returned Santa Anna.

Between his defeat at San Jacinto in 1836 and his return to power, Antonio López de Santa Anna had lost a leg. He lost it in 1839 to French gunners when France, angered by Mexico's failure to pay claims similar to those American ones which had helped provoke the present war, sent a squadron to bombard the fort at Vera Cruz. The event made a national hero of Santa Anna, although it could not prevent his eviction from his country in December of 1845.

During his exile in Havana he was able to convince President Polk that if he were allowed to steal back into Mexico he would seize power and sign the sort of treaty Polk wanted. And so, still vigorous at 52, limping on his peg leg, accompanied by his 17-year-old second wife, General Santa Anna went aboard the British steamer *Arab* in Havana Harbor on the night of August 8, 1846.

As instructed, the American blockading squadron allowed *Arab* to slip through its line into Vera Cruz Harbor. Santa Anna went ashore to be greeted by a carefully staged military celebration in which "not one *viva* was heard."[29] Next he issued a proclamation which made it clear that for once the calculating James Polk had miscalculated:

"Mexicans! There was once a day, and my heart dilates with the remembrance, when . . . you saluted me with the enviable title of Soldier of the People. Allow me again to take it, never more to be given up, and to devote myself, until death, to the defense of the liberty and independence of the republic."[30]

Then Santa Anna retired with his young wife to his enormous estates, while in Mexico City the way was cleared for his return to power and along the Rio Grande Old Rough and Ready Taylor made ready to strike still deeper into Mexico.

Zachary Taylor had been swamped by volunteers. They came in a steamboat flood down the Mississippi, out onto the Gulf and across to Port Isabel and thence up the Rio Grande to Matamoros or Taylor's advanced base at Camargo about 70 air miles farther west. The first arrivals were useless. They had been enlisted for six- or three-month terms, and by the time most of them arrived it was time for them to go home. Then, in July and August, 1846, the 12-monthers came whooping into camp.

They murdered; they raped, robbed and rioted. A Texas colonel thought the Tennessee men were worse than Russian Cossacks; Taylor himself thought the Texans "were too licentious to do much good"; testy little Lieutenant George Meade considered all volunteers to be "full of mutiny"; and the Mexican priests called them "Vandals vomited from Hell."[31] When they did not attack Mexican civilians or fight each other, they fought the regulars. They defied their officers and helped their comrades to escape from the guardhouse. They dressed as they pleased. The "Volunteers of Kentucky" wore full beards, three-cornered hats and hip boots faced with red morocco. Elsewhere the various "Guards," "Rifles," "Killers," "Gunmen," "Blues" and "Grays" who came crowding in on the long-suffering Taylor appeared in colors ranging through gray, green, blue and white with trimmings of red, yellow and pink. When their gorgeous going-away raiment wore out, they objected to putting on regulation blue. "Let 'em go to hell with their sky blue," swore an Indiana soldier. "I'll be blowed if they make a regular out of me."[32] Volunteers who were slaveholders expected the despised "foreigners" among the regulars to wait on them, and many of them, bitter because they did not get more than regular pay of seven dollars a month, cursed themselves as "seven-dollar targets." Gradually, in the immemorial way of indisciplined troops, they fell sick.

Camargo, at which some 15,000 American troops were assembled by August, came to be known as a "Yawning Grave Yard." It was too far from the Gulf to be cooled by sea breezes, and the rocks rimming the encampment round made it a caldron in which men were baked and boiled to death. All day long the troops heard the crashing of three volleys over the grave of some soldier, and as one officer said: "The Dead March was played so often on the Rio Grande that the very birds knew it."[33]

With the volunteers there arrived those "Democratic generals" appointed by Polk in his peeve against Winfield Scott and his fellow Whigs. One of them arrived in a fancy buggy which he expected to use in the campaign, and Polk's former law partner, Brigadier General Gideon Pillow—"Polk's spy," as he was sometimes called—provoked a howl of derision among the regulars when he built an entrenchment with the parapet on the wrong side of the ditch.

Such trials were suffered by Taylor with the outward calm which was his chief characteristic. Inwardly, he was a disturbed man: he had orders to move deeper into Mexico, and he not only had military misgivings about such a move; he also believed that his sudden popularity had given rise to an "intention to break me down." Nevertheless by mid-August he was ready to attack Monterrey, the capital of Nuevo León. His army numbered 6,000 men, half of them regulars commanded by bull-necked, big-voiced Brigadier General David Twiggs and the valorous though erratic Brigadier General William Worth; the other half volunteer horse and foot under Major General Pinckney Henderson and William Butler, a pair of part-time soldiers who out-ranked the professional Twiggs and Worth on the strength of their party loyalty. On August 18 the move to Monterrey began, and on September 19 the little army was in camp at Walnut Springs three miles outside the city.

Monterrey was as near a fortress city as might be found in Mexico. Its stone-walled houses stood on high ground forward of the little Santa Catarina River, which effectively guarded its rear. Most of the houses were loopholed and the streets were barricaded. Forts and redoubts covered the city's northern front and eastern flank, while to the west were two fortified heights between which ran the road from Saltillo. General Pedro de Ampudia, who had replaced the disgraced Arista, commanded at Monterrey; and he had 7,000 men and 40 guns to defend his fortifications. Thus the city was a very tough nut to be cracked by only 6,000 Americans without any proper siege train.

Zachary Taylor, however, now that he had reached his objective, was as confident as though he were still fighting Seminoles. In Win-field Scott's belief "few men ever had a more comfortable, labor-saving contempt for learning of every kind"[34] than Old Rough and Ready. But if his igorance was invincible, his courage was indom-itable, and thus, relying on the bayonet, as always, and dividing his command, as always, he prepared simultaneous assaults on the city's eastern and western flanks.

On September 20 Worth took 2,000 regulars and Texas cavalry on a long swing north to come in on the two fortified hills to the west. Running into difficult going, the column could make only five miles in the first four hours, and at nightfall the men encamped in the hills northwest of the city. Taylor's force was now split and separated, vul-nerable to defeat in detail; but Ampudia, who had seen his precious opportunity, made no move to sally from the city.

Next morning, September 21, 1846, the Battle of Monterrey began in earnest. Worth in the west repulsed a determined charge of Mexican lancers and began attacking Federation Hill on the southern side of the Saltillo road. By nightfall the position was taken with a loss of less than 20 men, and the Mexican guns were turned against Independence Hill across the road. In the east, however, the Americans were not so fortunate.

Here the city was guarded by the bastioned Black Fort 1,000 yards to its northern front and on the fort's east by a series of redoubts chief of which was Fort Tenería, or the Tannery. Here red-necked Dave Twiggs's regulars were to charge almost without artillery preparation. But Twiggs was not with them. He was sick, and command passed to Lieutenant Colonel John Garland.

Garland was to create a diversion for Worth engaged to the west. Whatever the purpose, the regulars pressed forward bravely—bayonets against bastions—and they were scourged from the Black Fort on the right, the Tannery on their left and loopholes and housetops in front of them. Americans flew into the air or stumbled and fell to pour out their blood on the hot earth. Scurrying low, the broken Americans sought shelter where they could find it, until, unit by unit, they could withdraw. One small unit which had gotten into a building behind the Tannery remained to pour musketry into that redoubt.

A second charge surged forward and was also broken in blood. Mexican marksmen picked off the Yankee officers with dreadful accuracy. Lieutenant Hoskins, he whose keg of whiskey had once won transportation priority over a case of books, came gasping up to Lieutenant Grant to borrow his horse. Minutes later he was shot dead from the back of the beast. Now, as the second line withdrew, General Twiggs came onto the field in "very unmilitary garb" to explain why he arrived late.

"I expected a battle today," he said, "but didn't think it would come off so soon, and took a dose of medicine last night as I always do before a battle so as to loosen my bowels. A bullet striking the belly when the bowels are loose might pass through the intestines without cutting them."[35]

No one then appreciated the humor of the situation, for a third attempt, at a fortified bridge farther to the right, had also been hurled back. Now Taylor turned to his volunteers. Brigadier General John Quitman sent the Tennessee and Mississippi regiments through a canefield which shielded them from enemy fire until the final dash at the Tannery. The moment they became visible, the Mexican guns roared. One solid shot killed seven volunteers and wounded others. One of the wounded clutched his rent abdomen while he crawled onto a rock, crouching there to sing a death psalm as he held in his intestines. But now the regulars behind the Tannery were picking off the Mexican gunners while the volunteers charged.

"Now is the time!" Jefferson Davis roared at his men. "Great God! If I had 30 men with knives I could take the fort!"[36]

It was taken with a final rush, Tennesseans and Mississippians tumbling in together. They would quarrel for a decade over who had been the first inside. Now the field artillery came flying into the suburban streets, one battery becoming caught and rendered useless, another driving off Mexican lancers who rode over the field spearing American wounded and killing medical attendants. And then it was night, and Taylor, who had won a little fort at the cost of nearly 400 casualties, ordered everyone back to camp except the troops holding the Tannery.

Before daylight, the attack was resumed. Worth's men, who had gone for two days without food and who had crouched all the rainy night at the base of Independence Hill, began crawling softly up its slopes. With dawn they charged and drove the Mexicans off its summit.

To the east there was no action, except that General Ampudia, having lost his western outposts, decided to abandon all his fortifications except the Black Fort and to concentrate his defense in the blocks of stone houses surrounding the Plaza. On September 23 the Americans renewed the assault on the east.

They did not move through shot-swept streets, but instead had their artillery shoot down them while doughboys armed with picks and crowbars burrowed through the walls of the houses. Worth, meanwhile, hearing the firing and having no orders, pressed in from the west and began shelling the Plaza. Caught between two fires, General Ampudia next day offered to surrender.

After a day of haggling over terms, Taylor accepted. His conditions —allowing the Mexican Army to withdraw intact with its arms, even agreeing to an armistice of eight weeks—were more than generous, and the armistice itself was angrily rejected by President Polk. But as much as Taylor was criticized, he could hardly have done better. His little army was down to 5,000 effectives, he was running short of supplies and ammunition, he was deep in enemy country, and if renewed assaults against a still superior enemy should fail, he would run the dreadful risk of retreating through a jubilant and vengeful countryside. If anyone was to be censured, it was Ampudia for giving up so readily.

And so, on September 25 the Mexican flag over Monterrey came down and Old Glory went up. The Mexican soldiers, neat in trim uniforms and freshly pipe-clayed belts, came marching out; and the Americans, "as dirty as they could be without becoming real estate,"[37] went marching in to the tune of "Yankee Doodle."

5

☆

Although Taylor's victory at Monterrey exalted him politically, it did not set the nation exulting as had his earlier triumphs.

Monterrey made it plain that Mexico was not going to be defeated easily. Bereft of Texas, shorn of New Mexico and California, and now menaced by American arms south of the Rio Grande, Mexico took courage from the wrathful oratory of General Santa Anna, spurning all offers to negotiate and swearing to fight on.

Thus the United States gradually became disenchanted with the war. Even Taylor privately proposed a defensive stance, holding just enough Mexican territory to force payment of claims. The idea was popular enough to attract Polk, who feared what an extended war might cost in men and money; if, indeed, he could persuade the nation to support it. But then it also became clear that to surrender the initiative to Mexico would incur a great loss in trade, prestige and national honor. Seizing a neighbor's provinces and holding them for ransom might strike the world as piracy. And so Polk and his advisers—who had begun the war with no real plan—at last decided on the obvious step of striking at the enemy's heart in Mexico City.

From the outset it was obvious that the route from the Rio Grande, an advance across 800 rugged miles, was out of the question. The best approach was from Vera Cruz on the Gulf. Cortez himself had followed this route in his campaign against the Aztecs. It had been recommended to Polk by no less a person than General Santa Anna in the days when the new Mexican commander in chief was talking treason. Taylor was for it, and so were Winfield Scott and the powerful Senator Thomas Hart Benton. But it took a Whig victory in the Congressional elections of 1846 to make Polk realize, at the repeated urgings of Senator Benton, that "a rapid crushing movement" was necessary to win the war and retrieve Democratic political fortunes.

Next came the question of a commander. Again in the partisan spirit of his times, Polk looked around for a trustworthy Democrat. But there was no such general acceptable to the Army. There were only Taylor and Scott, and because Taylor was in the habit of criticizing Polk's administration, and because Scott, clearly Taylor's superior in generalship, was also now considered politically harmless, it was Scott who received the command.

Certainly there were considerations of a nobler cast motivating Polk's decision, chief among them the fact that Scott still outranked Taylor, together with Taylor's belief that the season of the yellow fever—*el vómito*—was too near to make an attempt on Vera Cruz. Nevertheless, Scott had inadvertently qualified by committing political suicide during his dispute with Polk the preceding spring.

Polk had then ordered Scott to take command on the Rio Grande. Scott intended to obey, but about that time the alarmed Polk was also preparing to name a half-dozen Democratic generals. Scott thought he "smelt the rat" and bluntly told Secretary of War Marcy that he saw "the double trick, to supersede me, and, at the end of the war . . . disband every general who would not place Democracy above God's country."[38] Next Scott explained his failure to move quickly to the Rio Grande by informing the Secretary: "I do not desire to place myself in the most perilous of all positions:—*a fire upon my rear, from Washington, and the fire, in front, from the Mexicans.*"[39] That ended Scott's brief career as field commander, for the infuriated Polk directed him to remain in Washington. Scott's political career was concluded by his next epistolary indiscretion. He explained to Marcy that he had not been in his office to receive him one day because he had stepped outside "to take a hasty plate of soup."[40] The remark tickled the country and Scott, in a pun upon the name of the great French soldier, Marshall Turenne, became known as "Marshal Tureen." As the Boston *Courier* announced, Scott had "committed suicide with a goose-quill."[41] Still, Scott endured these professional and political setbacks with an admirable dignity. He remained devoted to his task of organizing and directing the expanding army. He might have been too fond of plans and calculations, as his nickname "Old Fuss 'n' Feathers" suggests; he may actually have been so prim and prissy that, as one general's wife disdainfully observed, you could cover his mouth with a button; but he was nevertheless the most professional and scientific soldier the United States had yet produced—and without him there might not have been much of an army.

So Scott hurled himself into the Vera Cruz expedition. On November 14 the Navy presented him a splendid gift: the port of Tampico, which would make an excellent staging area for America's first joint amphibious operation. On November 24 Scott departed for the Rio Grande and a hoped-for conference with Taylor at Camargo.

He had not been long gone before President Polk had reservations about appointing him. He still did not like him, and he liked less the prospect of seeing a second Whig trailing clouds of martial glory. Polk was not himself seeking re-election, yet he naturally wanted a Democrat to succeed him. And so it occurred to him to ask Congress to create the post of lieutenant general for Senator Benton, who would then supersede Scott. Congress, however, refused. The harsh, domineering Benton had made too many enemies among his own party, and no Whig would desert Scott.

This "vile intrigue," as Scott called it, so infuriated Old Fuss 'n' Feathers that he was later to write: "A grosser abuse of human confidence is nowhere recorded."[42] So the Polk-Scott rift widened, even as a Scott-Taylor quarrel began developing.

Scott had written to Taylor of his intention to come to Camargo. But his letters either went astray—one was intercepted by Santa Anna—or arrived after Scott did. In the meanwhile, General Taylor had slanted off on a southwestern excursion against Victoria, the capital of Tamaulipas. Why, is not clear. Inland Victoria was of no use to Taylor. To march on it was only to weaken his position on the Monterrey-Saltillo-Parras line. Yet the march did have the effect of taking him away from Camargo, and Scott on his arrival there was unable to inform Taylor personally of the disagreeable truth that he needed his troops. Instead, he had to tell him by letter that he was taking most of Taylor's regulars and half his volunteers for the Vera Cruz–Mexico City operation, and that Taylor would have to act "for a time" on the "strict defensive."

Taylor blew up. He was not only a general being stripped of his troops and stopped in his tracks; he was also a candidate halted in mid-career. Full of wrath, he accused Scott of "worming himself" into the chief command by promising to kill him off as a presidential candidate. He said he was being sacrificed to the ambition of others, meaning the partisan Polk and the sly Scott, and although Taylor was himself on record as believing that Vera Cruz required 25,000 men, 10,000 of them regulars, this was but a puny piece of logic which would not even scratch the gorgeous campaign theme of "The Martyrdom of Old Zack." So if Taylor did lose half an army, he did advance another giant step toward the White House—even as Santa Anna began advancing north against him with a brand-new army.

Antonio López de Santa Anna had been elected President of Mexico. Technically, however, he was not free to exercise both political and military command, and so executive power had passed to Vice President Gómez Farias while Santa Anna, the self-styled Liberator of Mexico, took the field with a brand-new army.

Santa Anna had no fears about the side door at Vera Cruz, for he seems to have believed that the season of the yellow fever would arrive there before the Americans could. Rather, he fixed his eyes on the front door in the north. Here he hoped to gain a single, smashing victory, after which he would bar the road while worrying the "war-weary" Americans to such an extent that they would be crying for peace before the winter of 1846-47 was over. For Santa Anna, like many other Mexicans, had listened at long distance to the rising clamor of antiwar sentiment in America and concluded that his enemy was faltering.

Opposition to the war in America, forced underground by Taylor's victories, had erupted after the Whig Congressional triumph, and its leaders included Northern Democrats as well. As in 1812, New England was the center of the movement, where it had powerful support from influential religious sects such as the Quakers, Congregationalists and Unitarians. Unitarian William Henry Channing went so far as to say that if he served in this "damnable war" he would be on the side of Mexico.[43] Once again the cry of a "slavocracy plot" was raised, and the poet James Russell Lowell warned his Yankee neighbors:

> They jest want this Californy
> So's to lug new slave-states in
> To abuse ye, an' to scorn ye,
> An' to plunder ye like sin.[44]

Less restrained were the remarks of Senator Tom Corwin of Ohio, who declared: "If I were a Mexican, I would tell you, 'Have you not room in your own country to bury your dead men? If you come into mine, we will meet you with bloody hands, and welcome you to hospitable graves.' "[45]

Outraged American soldiers might hang "Black Tom" Corwin in effigy, but the net effect of his speeches—and those of Daniel Webster—was to create in Mexico the expectation of a joint pronunciamento from Whigs and Northern Democrats forcing the American government to withdraw its troops. Meanwhile, Santa Anna was busily trying to raise his army, and in this he was again aided by the activity of his enemy.

This time it was the volunteers, more ferocious at Monterrey than they had been at Matomoros. Their severest critic, Lieutenant Meade, wrote home of them:

They are sufficiently well-drilled for practical purposes, and are, I believe, brave, and will fight as gallantly as any men. But they are a set of Goths and Vandals, without discipline, laying waste the country wherever we go, making us a terror to innocent people. . . . They cannot take care of themselves; the hospitals are crowded with them, they die like sheep; they waste their provisions, requiring twice as much to supply them as regulars do. They plunder the poor inhabitants of everything they can lay their hands on, and shoot them when they remonstrate, and if one of their number happens to get into a drunken brawl and is killed, they run over the country, killing all the poor innocent people they find in their way, to avenge, as they say, the murder of their brother.[46]

The cause, Meade said, "was the utter incapacity of their officers to control them or command respect."[47] and the cause of this was the old evil root of elected officers: men simply will not curb men who were once their civilian equals, their clients and their customers, and who will soon be so again. So the volunteers remained rapacious, making it easier for Santa Anna to recruit troops among the northern Mexicans they had ravaged.

Even so, the Liberator had to struggle against the hatred of those northern states which remembered him as their old oppressor. They refused him men and money, and even tried to combine against him. In San Luis Potosí members of a secret society called the Red Comet swore: "Nobody is bound to obey one who has no right to command."[48] For a time even the federal government seemed powerless to help him. The treasury was empty, and the Liberator was forced to the final expedient: seizure of Church property. As might be expected, such a measure raised little funds while alienating the Church and setting the old anticlerical fires blazing. And yet, by forced loans, seizures, remittances from state and federal governments and his personal credit, Santa Anna raised enough money to support an army of 20,000 men. Few generals in history have possessed the Liberator's capacity for making an army stand where none had stood before, even if, like the soldiers of Ivan the Fool, many of its men were made of straw. On January 27, 1847, then, Santa Anna's army started marching north from San Luis Potosí.

"Let them come," General Taylor said of the Mexicans. "Damned if they don't go back a good deal faster than they came."[49] But it was Taylor who went back, once his scouts reported Santa Anna to his front. Fearing that the Liberator might outflank him and strike Saltillo in his rear, Taylor withdrew ten miles to an excellent defensive position at the Buena Vista ranch about eight miles south of Saltillo. Actually he was a mile and a half below Buena Vista, at a place called La Angostura or "The Narrows." Here the Saltillo road became a narrow defile passing through a ravine-slashed plateau on the east, or Taylor's left, and a maze of gullies fronting a mountain on the west, or right. Because the right was considered impassable, it was the left that was fortified.

The road itself was barred at the Narrows, after which infantry and artillery stretched away east on the plateau in a rough arrowhead pointing south. The left or eastern side of this arrowhead was more vulnerable because there were not enough units to form a continuous line there. Still, it was a strong position; the ravines would nearly paralyze the Mexican cavalry and artillery and hamper their infantry. Thus, thought Taylor, Santa Anna's numerical superiority of about 15,000 to 5,000 would be largely discounted. Santa Anna, however, did not agree. He warned Taylor that he was surrounded by 20,000 men and would meet catastrophe unless he surrendered. His letter was carried under a flag of truce by a German surgeon, and after it was interpreted, Old Zack snorted, "Tell Santa Anna to go to hell!"[50] Turning to his chief of staff, he said, "Major Bliss, put that in Spanish and send it back by this damned Dutchman."[51] It was done, with considerably more courtesy, and in late afternoon of Washington's Birthday, 1847, Santa Anna attacked.

His artillery began roving over the American lines while his right, under General Ampudia, tried to gain the slopes of a mountain above the lightly held American left. Both sides skirmished until after dark, when the Americans withdrew to the valley.

That night Taylor returned to Saltillo with an infantry regiment and a squadron of dragoons. He feared that the Mexicans might have flanked him and be moving on the city. Finding himself in error, he started back toward Buena Vista next day—February 23—just as the Mexicans gained the summit of the mountain and opened on the American left with long-range artillery. Brigadier General John Wool at once began shifting his troops to the threatened left. Volunteer riflemen and a battery of artillery under Lieutenant John Paul Jones O'Brien rushed toward the left-center where two Mexican divisions were coming up a slope. O'Brien's trio of guns dashed forward to within musket range of the Mexicans, unlimbered and began battering the enemy. In turn, a Mexican battery on his flank struck at O'Brien. To his rear, the American riflemen had quit the field—most of them retreating all the way back to Buena Vista ranch. O'Brien and his gunners stayed on, stemming the Mexican tide until he had no more cannoneers. Then, leaving one gun behind among its dead gunners and horses, he pulled the other two out.

But now there was a break in the American left-center, and the Mexicans quickly began driving in the entire Yankee left. Only the right continued to face south, both center and left being bent back to face east. Masses of Mexican cavalry and infantry were moving along the base of the mountain to strike at Buena Vista in the American rear. At this moment, Taylor trotted up on Old Whitey. He went directly to the center of the line to direct the battle, and also, by his calm presence, to steady his men. Meanwhile, the riflemen he brought back with him checked the Mexicans in the center, while a composite command of horse, foot and guns was rushed to the rear to block the Mexican cavalry moving on Buena Vista.

With a gathering gallop, the Mexican lancers came charging forward. The Americans countercharged and split the enemy column in two. From American sharpshooters on Buena Vista's rooftops and behind her walls came a withering small-arms fire that emptied Mexican saddles and sent one wing of the broken column flying back the way it came, and the other fleeing west to make a complete circuit around the American position.

Now a second, more serious threat developed. A column of lancers prepared to charge the American infantry forward of Buena Vista. For a time Captain Braxton Bragg's guns broke up the enemy formation, but eventually it came on. At once two regiments of volunteers formed a V with the open end to the enemy. Into those yawning jaws came the lancers, at first at a trot, and then slowing to a walk, and the storm of fire that came from each side of the V of Buena Vista annihilated the head of the enemy column and broke the tail in a dozen pieces.

With its cavalry repulsed, the Mexican infantry withdrew. The tide of battle had flowed to the Americans, but then, for reasons never made known, a flag of truce passed between both armies and firing ceased. In that interval, Santa Anna prepared his last stroke. It came against what had been the American center and was now the left, and it fell just as three volunteer regiments were deploying. Once again, it was the guns of Lieutenant O'Brien, together with one gun under Lieutenant George Thomas (not yet "The Rock of Chickamauga"), which flew into the breach. With blown horses and weary men, the American artillerists drove forward to a position from which they could rake the enemy rear. After volunteer units came running forward to plug the gap, the Mexican tide halted and flowed back again.

The Battle of Buena Vista was over. A handful of artillerists backed up by volunteers fighting bravely when bravely led had repulsed a superior force executing a well-conceived and well-nigh successful turning movement. Taylor's losses were high—746 killed, wounded and missing—but Santa Anna's were five times higher. And on the morning of February 24 he turned his troops and began his horrible retreat to San Luis, arriving there with half of the force he had led north and with the next best thing to victory: the announcement of one.

As might have been expected, those materialist critics who always overlook the moral factor of war thought Taylor never should have fought Santa Anna. But Buena Vista denied the Liberator that single smashing victory which he desired so desperately, while reviving the drooping spirits of the American nation. That new determination to go on with the war and win it was solemnized by the poet Theodore O'Hara, celebrating Buena Vista in the lines:

> On Fame's eternal camping-ground
> Their silent tents are spread,
> And Glory guards, with solemn round,
> The bivouac of the dead.

After Buena Vista the Mexican War shifted to the side door at Vera Cruz, and Zachary Taylor, who had fought his last battle, raised his sights still higher on the presidency. To the newspapers who rebuked his partisans for their unseemly haste in discussing Old Zack's candidacy before the Whig National Convention, one Kentucky volunteer replied: "National convention be damned! I tell ye, General Taylor is going to be elected by spontaneous combustion!"

6

☆

On February 21, 1847—the day on which Taylor's scouts sighted Santa Anna's banners below Buena Vista—General Scott reached his staging area at Lobos Island about 50 miles south of Tampico.

Here Scott found nothing like the 20,000 troops he had been promised, but only a few thin formations of volunteers already ravaged by smallpox. Although he had organized his campaign against Vera Cruz and Mexico City down to such thoughtful details as special landing boats built to fit inside one another in "nests" of three, the inevitable delays attendant upon this first amphibious operation in American history were unraveling all his finely spun plans. Meanwhile, Scott was frantic to be off to Vera Cruz before the season of *el vómito* should arrive to turn the city into a pesthouse.

Gradually his troops arrived. Worth and Twiggs came to Lobos in transports loaded with their regulars. There was another volunteer division under Major General Robert Patterson, a wealthy Democrat to whom Polk at one time wanted to give the chief command. There were also the volunteer brigades of Quitman, Pillow and Shields. Scott had culled the cream of the West Point corps for his command. His most valued officers were the engineers, men such as the stocky, aristocratic Lieutenant P. G. T. Beauregard or testy George Meade, but most of all the splendid Captains Joe Johnston and Robert E. Lee, two old friends who were both 40 and who bunked together aboard Scott's flagship, the steamer *Massachusetts*. Crusty Jubal Early was at Lobos, too, along with Sam Grant and the tall young artillerist, Lieutenant Tom Jackson. The future would bestow the nickname of "Stonewall" on Jackson; now he was known for a painful reserve broken only by such terse remarks as: "I should like to be in one battle."[52] Tom Ewell was Jackson's exact opposite. He liked to laugh, and he was convulsed at a camp along the Rio Grande one day when Old Fuss 'n' Feathers rode up to praise the "scouts" he had seen "peering at him from behind every bush." Ewell knew that the men were not on duty but rather doing their duty, for, as he wrote home: "The water here . . . opens the bowels like a melting tar."[53]

At last some 10,000 men and about 80 ships were assembled, and on March 2 the fleet of paddle-wheelers and sailing ships—plus one queer steamer driven silently through the sea by an underwater propeller—upped anchors and made away for Vera Cruz about 200 miles south. On March 5 the vanguard ships began arriving at Antón Lizardo, 12 miles below the target city. Two days later Commodore Conner took Scott and his general and engineers aboard the little steamer *Secretary* to reconnoiter Vera Cruz and its huge stone fortress of San Juan de Ulúa on a reef across the bay. This was the 128-gun fort which British naval officers swore could "sink all the ships in the world," yet little *Secretary* slipped in close until Ulúa began to puff and roar and raise splashes all around her, whereupon she turned and sped for safety. Back on his flagship, Scott announced that he would land his army on beaches a few miles southeast of Vera Cruz and out of Ulúa's range.

March 9, 1847, was a glittering blue day. Far away west the snowy peak of Mount Orizaba glistened like a noble beacon for the soldiers and sailors of the American fleet moving north for the landing beach. Off Vera Cruz men with glasses swarmed through the rigging of the foreign war vessels while ladies twirling parasols crowded the rails. At one o'clock in the afternoon Conner's bombardment ships with double-shotted cannon were in place offshore. In closer were seven gunboats armed with grape. Now 4,500 regulars led by Worth began clambering over the sides of their steamboats into 65 of Scott's surfboats. Ashore, a few hundred Mexican lancers cantered nervously along the beach. In Vera Cruz, housetops and walls were black with humanity. All American eyes turned toward Orizaba. The moment the setting sun touched the mountain's peak the assault would commence. It happened: red ball met white mountain, from *Massachusetts* came the flash of a signal gun, from Vera Cruz and Ulúa came the roar of cannon making futile dimples on the silken sheen of the Gulf, from the American ships came the thunder of guns driving off the Mexican cavalry, and as cheer after cheer and the crashing of bands bursting into "The Star-Spangled Banner" chased the sound of the cannon across the water, the American soldiers ducked their heads beneath their gleaming bayonets while the sailors bent to their oars.

Men and officers still aboard ship watched anxiously as oars bit and flashed and the line of boats caught the swell of the Gulf. "Why don't they hit us?" a salty old sailor muttered. "If we don't have a big butcher's bill, there's no use in coming here."[54]

But the enemy beach was silent. Suddenly, the boat carrying Worth shot out in the lead. It grounded with a lurch and the impetuous general leaped out, followed by his officers. Now the Americans were jumping into the surf, holding muskets and cartridge boxes high overhead. They waded in, sprinted up the sand to the crest of the first dune, raised their standards and burst into cheers. From the fleet offshore came answering huzzas, and as the bay reverberated to the triumphant cries and music of the Americans, Conner's bluejackets rapidly brought another 5,500 troops ashore.

By midnight Vera Cruz was invested without the loss of a single man and 10,000 Americans were eating pork and biscuit in the sand. It was a splendid feat, so dazzling that General Scott could scarcely believe that he had been able to bring it off unopposed.

The first American D-Day had been a stupendous success simply because Santa Anna had chosen to fight Taylor elsewhere and because

Mexico had been shaken by the *"Polko* Rebellion."

This complicated conflict was in essence a struggle between the *"Puros,"* those doctrinaire democrats who, coming to power under Acting President Farias, "passed sentence of death" on Mexican society, and the equally fanatic *"Polkos,"* conservative merchants, professional men, craftsmen, clerks and, chief of all, the clergy. The *Polkos* got their names from the polka music played by the bands of the four independent battalions they had formed, as they said, to defend private property against the designs of the *Puros.* Actually, the *Polkos* were clericals and the *Puros* anticlericals, and the *Puros-Polkos* duel was in many ways an adumbration of the bloody factional strife of the Spanish Civil War as well as the dualism which still divides Latin America.

The apple of discord was Church property. The Mexican government, inept as well as corrupt, and so eaten by loan sharks that in 1845 it was entitled to only 13 percent of the money entering its treasury, was at last bankrupt. But the Church was still wealthy, and even other parties such as the *Moderados* regarded her property as the solution to the problem. The thinking of many Mexican leaders, not only the ferociously anticlerical Farias, who would just as soon cripple the Church as defeat the invaders, was best expressed by the Congressman who said: "If the Yankee triumphs, what ecclesiastical property or what religion will be left us?"[55]

But the Church could not agree, and so, after Congress passed laws levying on her estates, she secured the allegiance of the *Polko* battalions. This was in February of 1847, by which time all of Mexico was aware of the impending American invasion of Vera Cruz. Farias, not daring to disarm the *Polkos,* decided to get rid of them by ordering them to march to the defense of the imperiled city. The *Polkos* refused. When Farias and the *Puros* attempted to disarm them, the *Polkos* took to the barricades. Bloodcurdling cries arose from either side, there was much firing back and forth, but, as had happened so often in Mexican uprisings, most of the casualties were among innocent civilians.

President Santa Anna, meanwhile, refrained from taking sides openly. Secretly, however, he worked for the downfall of Farias and toward a *rapprochement* with the Church. Although the hierarchy distrusted him, he was obviously a lesser evil than Farias; and the *Moderados,* believing in his "victory" at Buena Vista, also rallied to his support. And so President Santa Anna came to Mexico City, a *Te Deum* was sung to celebrate his defeat of the Americans, and on March 23, 1847, he formally superseded Farias in office.

Thus the penultimate result of the tragicomic *Polko* Rebellion. The last step completed the farce: to get rid of Farias the office of Vice President was abolished, and a *Moderado* "substitute president" was appointed while Santa Anna again put aside the politician's coat-and-collar to vest himself in "glory and the robes of war." But before he could march to the rescue of Vera Cruz, American cannon were already smashing at the city's walls.

Winfield Scott had all but placed the siege of Vera Cruz in the hands of his engineers. Day after day they went out—Lee, Johnston, Beauregard, George McClellan and the others—to study the city's defenses and terrain and to site gun emplacements. Sometimes Sam Grant of the infantry went along to watch them work. Once Grant and Beauregard were inside an adobe hut when a Mexican shell slammed into it and exploded. They were only stunned, for Mexican shells were notoriously weak.

Gradually, American soldiers, toiling in sweat and ankle-deep sand, built an investing line in the sand hills behind Vera Cruz, while others cut the city's water supply or dragged artillery into position. Many of Scott's officers fretted at the delay. The idea of a siege bored them and they were impetuous for a charge.

"Ugh," General Twiggs snorted, "my boys'll have to take it yet with their bayonets."[56]

But Scott still wanted to take Vera Cruz "by headwork, the slow, scientific process."[57] He did not want to lose more than 100 men, and said: "For every one over that number I shall regard myself as his murderer."[58]

On March 22, with his cannon emplaced, Scott summoned Vera Cruz to surrender. The Mexicans refused and the American siege artillery opened with a rising roar. Yankee gunboats began bombarding the city from the water, running in so close that Ulúa began growling again. Commodore Matthew Perry—the younger brother of Perry of Lake Erie—had relieved Conner the day before, and he at once recalled his overbold gamecocks. Soon heavier naval cannon were brought ashore, and Perry's sailors, trained in the naval way not to flinch at the flash of cannon, eventually learned that on land it was no disgrace to take cover: one day four sailors standing erect in the open had the tops of their heads blown off.

Night and day the guns roared until the artillery load rose to 180 shells an hour and there were fires burning throughout the city. On March 26 a white flag fluttered at Vera Cruz. Scott sent Generals Worth and Pillow to meet the Mexican commissioners. Worth came back grumbling: "General, they're only trying to gain time—they don't mean to surrender. They evidently expect forces from the interior to come to their aid and compel us to raise the siege, or else to keep up dilly-dallying until the yellow fever does it for them. You'll have to assault the town, and I'm ready to do it with my division."[59]

Scott thanked Worth, took from him the Mexican note and called for interpreters with the remark: "Now, let's hear the English of what these Mexican generals have to say."[60] To his annoyance, but not entirely his surprise, Scott heard language indicating that the Mexicans merely wanted to save face. He at once dictated acceptable terms, and on March 29, 1847, both the city of Vera Cruz and the fort at San Juan de Ulúa surrendered.

Scott the scientific had been better than his word. He had lost only 67 killed and wounded against what were at first reported as enemy losses of 400 soldiers and 500 to 600 civilians. He was criticized, of course, particularly in the foreign press, for his "inhumanity" in bombarding the city into submission. His traducers, ignoring the plain fact that Vera Cruz was a fortified city which had refused to surrender, presumably wanted Scott to take it by syllogism. They certainly could not have wanted him to storm it, for to have done so would have been to guarantee a frightful slaughter. Actually, the British naval commander on the scene estimated that the Mexican Army lost 80 men killed and that civilian deaths numbered about 100.

Few shooting sieges have been less bloody, and yet Scott was soon to learn that the America of his day really loved a big butcher's bill. Upon the announcement of the capture of Vera Cruz in New Orleans, a man in the crowd called out: "How many men has Scott lost?" The reply was: "Less than a hundred," and the man cried: "That won't do. Taylor always loses thousands. He is the man for my money."[61]

7

☆

    While Winfield Scott exercised his formidable organizing skills to turn Vera Cruz into a base of operations against Mexico City, President Polk in Washington decided that there should be a peace commissioner attached to Scott's army.

The man chosen was Nicholas Trist, whose title of chief clerk made him the second in rank in the State Department. Trist departed for Vera Cruz on April 16, convinced, apparently, that although he had never met General Scott he disliked him most heartily.

Scott, meanwhile, was in a rage to get his army out of the coastal flats and into the highlands before the dread *vómito* arrived in mid-April. His immediate objective was Jalapa, 75 miles away and 4,000 feet above sea level, but his immediate difficulty was in obtaining animal transport. Washington had failed to forward 500 draft horses needed to pull the siege guns, and so, as a poor substitute, Mexican mustangs were rounded up. On April 8 Twigg's division stepped out on the march to Mexico City, 260 miles west.

"Old Davy" Twiggs, a man with an oxen back and matching brain, "led" his foot soldiers on horseback. Paced by a horse, floundering in sand, broiling in a brazen sun and ravaged by diarrhea, the men simply melted away. By the end of the first day's march a third of the division was missing, and the route was strewn with abandoned equipment. On the second day the Americans came to the national highway, the way of Cortez, which the Spaniards had graded, paved and guttered and used for three centuries. Now, however, it was in disrepair; but it was nevertheless a better road than most of the Yankee soldiers had seen. To either side of it, all the way from Vera Cruz to Jalapa, were the estates of Santa Anna. Here the going was not only easier but also gorgeous, and the step of the soldiers quickened and their eyes brightened to behold the birds and flowers and trees of the exotic paradise through which they tramped. On April 11 they crossed a stone bridge into the village of Plan del Río, where the road winds and begins to climb the highlands. Here the Americans sighted Mexican lancers. Next day, Captain Joe Johnston and his engineers went scouting. Johnston came back with bullet holes in his right thigh and arm and the report that Santa Anna was at the pass of Cerro Gordo.

Limping on his wooden leg, the Liberator had left the capital on April 2, and by April 5 had reached Jalapa. Here he took command of about 6,000 men, most of them the veterans of his northern campaign, and led them about 20 miles east to the point where Cerro Gordo—the "Big Hill"—guards the brow of the cordillera. Here he expected to bar the American advance and keep the invaders so far down the slopes that they would be within reach of the *vómito.*

Santa Anna's position was a good one. To the right or south of the road was a heavily fortified ridge. To the left or north was Cerro Gordo itself, also fortified, and a half-mile to the northeast was another fortified hill, Atalaya. Thus the Americans trying to climb the road would be caught between two plunging fires. They could not get behind the fortified ridge on the south for its rear was guarded by a canyon and the Plan del Río. And Santa Anna thought the north flank was protected by terrain so impenetrable that a rabbit could not get through it.

Although the Americans were much bigger than cottontails, they were also a bit more rational. Since General Scott had arrived at Cerro Gordo his engineers—Lieutenants Beauregard and Zebulon Tower the first among them—had been probing the Mexican front in the region Santa Anna thought impassable for rabbits. On April 15 Captain Robert E. Lee continued the reconnoiter.

Lee probed far to his right, slowly working his way up the ravines. He came to a spring and a well-trampled path leading from the south. He heard voices speaking Spanish and saw a party of Mexican soldiers approaching the spring. Silently, he dropped to the ground behind a log. The voices grew louder. There were more of them. Lee lay still in the moist heat while insects whirred in his ears and stung his flesh. Suddenly a Mexican sat on the log. Then another.

Their backs were not three feet from the American. Then they arose and walked away. But more soldiers came and went and Captain Lee lay still until dark. Then he lifted his stiffened limbs and crept away. Down the treacherous ravine he went, moving stealthily with that intuitive feel for ground which is among the greatest of soldierly qualities. At last he reached headquarters and reported: it seemed possible that the Mexican left could be turned.

Encouraged, Scott ordered Lee to reconnoiter the area again on the 16th. He did, using a party of pioneers to cut a path still farther to the right. Next day he began to guide Twigg's division around the enemy left.

Sweating soldiers in light blue toiled up and down chasms so steep that animals could not climb them. Artillery was let down the steeps by rope and hauled up the same way. Suddenly, at noon, the Americans were discovered by Mexicans on Atalaya. A sharp fight for the hilltop began. Both sides fed in forces, until Colonel William Harney, a man as fiery in color as a red fox, led a charge over and around Atalaya. In fact, the charge was too impetuous. It carried forward to the slopes of Cerro Gordo, where the Americans were pinned down and picked off until light artillery from Atalaya enabled them to break off and withdraw.

Now Scott reinforced Twiggs with Shields's volunteer brigade. Under Lee's direction, they dragged three 24-pounders onto Atalaya's crest. That night Scott issued his battle orders: Twiggs was "to move forward before daylight, and take up position across the national road in the enemy's rear, so as to cut off a retreat towards Jalapa."[62] Pillow's brigade was to attack the Mexican right on the fortified ridge. Worth's division was to follow Twiggs and Shields.

On April 18 the attack began. Twiggs sent the brigades of Shields and Colonel Bennett Riley on a swing right to get at the Mexican camp in the rear of Cerro Gordo and Atalaya. Shields moved directly on target, but Riley veered to his left and struck the western flank of Cerro Gordo. As both brigades moved, Colonel Harney's regulars went yelling down Atalaya, swept across the intervening hollow, and charged up Cerro Gordo's slopes. Within 100 yards of the crest, they threw themselves down to catch their breath, jumped erect and followed the shouting Harney over the enemy's breastworks.

As the Mexicans fled, Captain John Magruder turned their abandoned guns on them. At this moment, Shields's troops burst upon the Mexican camp. A blast of grapeshot carried clear through Shields's body to deal him a wound that was miraculously not mortal; but his men rallied and routed the startled enemy. At the same time, Pillow's brigade, delayed in its advance to a jumping-off point, fell upon the Mexican right. Here the Americans suffered their severest losses, and Pillow was himself wounded in the arm. But once the Mexicans here realized that they were cut off to the rear, they surrendered.

By noon the Battle of Cerro Gordo was all over. Scott lost 63 killed and 337 wounded, but half of Santa Anna's army was captured and many others must have fallen. The Liberator did not wait to tally his losses. He fled toward Jalapa leaving his baggage wagon behind. Inside it the Americans found his military chest containing coin to pay his soldiers, cooked chicken and—most precious prize of all—Santa Anna's spare wooden leg. Soon, in the tradition of the more grisly "Tecumseh razor strops," "Santa Anna legs" became fashionable in the States.

And within a few days Winfield Scott's triumphant little army was safely inside Jalapa. Behind the Americans lay the *vómito* and before them the exposed capital of a stunned nation.

8

☆

Scott was eager to pursue the retreating Santa Anna, but before he could leave Jalapa he had to reorganize and eliminate shortages which had begun to afflict his army.

The first was in troops. On April 27 he was informed that the "new" regulars recruited under the Ten-Regiment Bill were being diverted to Taylor on the Rio Grande. Next his 12-month volunteers began clamoring to go home. Most of them had only a month or six weeks left to serve, and they objected that if they waited until their discharge date they would have to leave the country through Vera Cruz just when the yellow fever was raging strongest. General

Scott accepted the force of this argument, and on May 4 about 3,000 men, the remnant of seven volunteer regiments, left Jalapa for the Gulf.

Scott's next shortage was in ready money with which to pay his troops and to purchase supplies. He also lacked cavalry and did not have enough teamsters and wagon masters, specialists who in those days were hired civilians rather than soldiers trained for the task. But even such serious problems as these were as nothing to the one raised with the arrival in Jalapa of a communication from Polk's peace commissioner, Nicholas Trist.

The Honorable Mr. Trist seems—with ample cause—to have become convinced of the magnitude of his mission and the importance of his person. He had been given the grandiloquent title of "Commissioner Plenipotentiary," he had been taken into the confidence of President Polk—where he was informed that General Pillow, not Scott, was the man to trust—and it had been intimated to him by Secretary Buchanan that if he was successful in concluding a peace with Mexico he might become the next Democratic candidate for President. Upon his arrival in Vera Cruz, therefore, Trist did not go forward to Scott's headquarters as instructed. Instead, he wrote him a letter which may stand as a model of how a civilian may harry an already harassed soldier into apoplexy.

Trist told Scott that he, Trist, "was clothed with such diplomatic powers as will authorize him to enter into arrangements with the government of Mexico *for the suspension of hostilities.*"[63] With this he sent a *sealed* letter for Scott to forward to the Mexican minister.

Scott flew into a rage. A rash letter-writer himself, he dashed off a reply stating that the "Secretary of War proposes to degrade me, by requiring that I, the commander of this army, shall defer to you, the chief clerk of the Department of State, the question of continuing or discontinuing hostilities."[64] The sealed letter, which was nothing more than a refusal of earlier Mexican demands, together with a notice that a peace commissioner was now with the American Army, was disdainfully returned.

It was all a dreadful misunderstanding, chiefly due to Trist's preconceived notion that he disliked Scott and his inflated sense of his own importance. If he had met the general personally and shown him the confidential papers in his care, as he was instructed to do, he would not have provoked a rancorous quarrel which bid fair to have most destructive consequences for the government they both sincerely served. But after Trist's first letter, all was cross-purposes. Scott, already aggrieved by the diversion of the "new" regulars to Taylor, became, like Taylor, convinced that all Whig generals were to be crucified. He wrote to Secretary Marcy and asked to be recalled, and at one point he wrote to Trist: "The Jacobin convention of France never sent to one of its armies in the field a more amiable and accomplished instrument. If you were armed with an ambulatory guillotine you would be the personification of Danton, Marat, and St. Just, all in one."[65]

Fortunately, the good offices of the British minister in Mexico helped to heal the rift. Scott and Trist met, found that they liked each other, and then, after Trist fell ill and Scott sent him a peace offering in the form of guava marmalade, they became close friends.

By then, mid-June, Scott had lost the friendship of his old comrade-in-arms, William Worth. After the army had advanced to Puebla, about 150 miles west of Vera Cruz, Worth issued an ill-founded warning to his men that the Mexicans were mixing poison with the food they sold them. Scott ordered Worth to recall his circular, and Worth demanded a court of inquiry to judge his action. The court found him in error and subject to reprimand, and although Scott sought to soften the censure, Worth could not forgive him. Nor could he abide the fact that John Quitman and Gideon Pillow had been breveted to major generals senior to him.

Such difficulties made it ever more plain to Scott that he dared not tarry much longer at Puebla. He had already written to Secretary Marcy: "Like Cortez, finding myself isolated and abandoned, and again like him, always afraid that the next ship or messenger might recall or further cripple me, I resolved no longer to depend on Vera Cruz, or home, but to render my little army a self-sustaining machine."[66] Like Cortez, he was burning his boats. He had received enough volunteer reinforcements, among them a brigade under Brigadier General Franklin Pierce, one of the few Easterners to lead combat troops in "Mr. Polk's War." He had now about 10,500 effectives to march against an enemy city of 200,000 persons defended by a force he believed to be three times his own.

On August 7, 1847, the drums beat, bugles blew and the long lines of men in faded blue went swinging away to the Halls of Montezuma. In Europe the Duke of Wellington said: "Scott is lost. He cannot capture the city, and he cannot fall back upon his base."[67]

The Mexican government had passed through another convulsion, only to lay quiescent once more beneath Santa Anna. The Liberator had outmaneuvered his numerous enemies by offering his resignation as a "sacrifice," after which, gratified by the public protest, he made the second sacrifice of withdrawing it. "What a life of sacrifice is the General's," a Mexican newspaper sneered. " A sacrifice to take the power, to resign, to resume; ultimate sacrifice; ultimate final; ultimate more final; ultimate most final; ultimate the very finalest."[68]

Amid such dissension, Santa Anna prepared his defense of the capital. He did not have 30,000 men, as Scott thought, but rather about 25,000. Nevertheless, he disposed them artfully in a system of defenses—both natural and artificial—which made the hearts of the Americans sink as they marched down the road into the magnificent Valley of Mexico in which lay the capital city of their desires.

Scott's engineers could give him nothing but discouraging reports on the screen of lakes and marshes guarding Mexico City. Passage between the lakes was possible only on causeways raised above the marshes, and most of these were heavily guarded. Santa Anna had been careful to fortify the area around Lake Texcoco and the hill El Peñon in the north, for he expected Scott to come in here from the east. But Scott saw clearly that such an attempt would mean frightful losses. He ordered reconnaissances south of Lakes Chalco and Xochimilco. Here a rough but passable road was discovered, and on August 15 the army began movement to the village of San Agustín, modern Tlalpan, nine miles south of the city.

Here also the Americans seemed stymied. A few miles ahead of them was the well-fortified hacienda of San Antonio, and two miles farther north a fortified bridge over the canalized Río Churubusco. Supporting the bridge was the thick-walled convent of San Mateo, inside which were the deserters of the San Patricio Battalion—excellent gunners who would lovingly blast away at their former tormentors of the parade ground. The route north, then, seemed barred. Could it be turned? Not on the right or east where Xochimilco lay, nor, it seemed, on the left through the Pedregal, a great gray field of lava looking like a storm-tossed sea of stone. What about the other side of the Pedregal? There was a road there—the San Angel road —but there also seemed no way across the Pedregal.

Scott kept probing, however. On August 18 a party of engineers under Captain Lee entered the Pedregal, while others pushed north toward San Antonio escorted by dragoons under Captain Seth Thornton, the man whose ambush on the Rio Grande a year ago had touched off the war. From the hacienda came cannon fire, and the first shot cut Thornton in two. As the Mexican cannonade continued, the Americans withdrew.

Captain Lee, meanwhile, had found a tiny track in the Pedregal. Following it, he came to a piled-up mass of volcanic rock called Zacatepec. He climbed it and saw the San Angel road to the west. There were enemy troops on the slope of the hill at the village of Padierna to his left. Suddenly Lee heard firing. His escort had met a Mexican picket and exchanged shots. Realizing that these men had come from the San Angel road, Lee concluded that he could get there too, and that was the gist of his report to General Scott.

That night Scott decided to try to improve the Pedregal track so that guns and wagons might move over it. Early in the morning of August 19 working parties were sent out, and by one o'clock in the afternoon a road had been brought to within range of Padierna. But then enemy soldiers were met once more and cannon shot fell among the Americans. Padierna, it was seen, was now held in force by the Mexicans.

They were there because of the insubordination of General Gabriel Valencia, commander of the army of the north. After Santa Anna had seen that Scott was not going to attack in the north, he had sent Valencia south to block the western road at San Angel. Valencia, however, had his own ideas and his own pretensions to glory. On August 18 he moved south from San Angel to the slope at Padierna, refusing, that night, to obey Santa Anna's orders to return to San Angel. By the afternoon of August 19 he was emplaced on the hill in full view of American officers standing atop Zacatepec.

To these officers it seemed that Valencia's left could be turned. General Pillow gave the word to Riley to take his brigade to the right, cross the San Angel road and cut off Valencia's retreat to Mexico City. Then he ordered Brigadier General George Cadwalader to follow Riley, after which Brigadier General Persifor Smith, moving on his own initiative, took his brigade along the same route. By late afternoon all three units—about 3,500 men in all—were safely across the San Angel road. By then General Scott had come out to Zacatepec to approve what had been done, and also to see about 3,000 Mexican reinforcements start coming south from Coyoacán to take up station at San Angel.

The Americans west of the San Angel road were now caught between Valencia to their left or south and the reinforcements on the north. But neither Scott nor Persifor Smith, who had taken command west of the road, appeared to be concerned. Scott merely sent Captain Lee to Smith and calmly awaited developments.

They began after dark when Smith told Lee that he was going to move around Padierna during the night and attack it from the rear before daybreak. He told Lee that he would like a diversionary attack to be launched in front of Padierna, and Lee volunteered to carry that request to Scott. In rain and lightning, Lee crossed the road and began working east across the Pedregal. As he did, Santa Anna sent orders to Valencia to spike his guns and return to San Angel in darkness before an American attack in the morning should cut him off. Valencia, certain that he won a "victory" that afternoon, scornfully disobeyed the order.

On the rain-swept Pedregal, meanwhile, Captain Lee and a few men picked their way among lava rocks and chasms, leaping across fissures when they saw them outlined in fitful flashes of lightning, guiding on the gloomy bulk of Zacatepec when it, too, was thrown into relief. Lee's greatest fear was of blundering into a trigger-happy American sentry. Once, hearing the tramp of feet ahead of him, he paused, and saw in a glare of lightning that they were the men of General Shields moving to reinforce Smith. Detailing a man to guide them, Lee plunged on. At last he came to Zacatepec. But Scott was not there. Weary and bruised, soaked to the skin, Lee pressed on to San Agustín, where he found his general.

Scott approved Smith's plan and ordered Franklin Pierce's troops to make diversion in front of Padierna. Pierce himself was injured, and command passed to Colonel Trueman Ransom. Lee found Ransom's men bivouacked on the Padierna and guided them into position.

West of the road, the arrival of Shields raised the American strength to 4,000 men. At three o'clock in the morning, of August 20, 1847, the rain-plastered Yankee soldiers began moving out. Once again those invaluable engineers showed them the way. Slipping and stumbling on the slippery track, they stole into Valencia's rear.

In front of Valencia, Ransom's men opened up. Valencia's soldiers returned the fire. Suddenly, they heard wild yelling to their rear. A tide of blue was flowing down the hill toward them, led by the huge Riley. Firing as they came, the Americans rushed headlong into the Mexican position. For a while the Mexican gunners worked wildly to reverse their guns. But then they broke and ran, joining the infantry already being trampled by fleeing Mexican horse. In 17 minutes the battle was over. Day had hardly dawned before the San Angel road was black with Mexican soldiers streaming north. Among them somewhere was General Valencia, who had disappeared at the commencement of the battle. Left behind were 700 dead, more than 800 prisoners and a great store of military supplies.

The Americans had lost less than 60 killed and wounded, and now General Scott was free to push up the San Angel road to come down upon San Antonio in the rear.

General Santa Anna did not sit still for his envelopment at San Antonio. Instead, learning of Valencia's defeat, he abandoned the position and ordered its troops to withdraw to inner defenses behind the Churubusco River. Other soldiers moved into those *garita,* or gates, which guarded the heads of the causeways and which were actually fortified stone buildings used as police and customs stations. It was at the Churubusco bridgehead-and-convent complex, however, that the main defense was concentrated, and here the pursuing Americans smacked "butt-end first" into the stubborn enemy.

Worth's division took the San Antonio road: Garland's brigade moving through a cornfield to the right of the road, Colonel Newman Clarke's men advancing up the road itself. On the left of the road was Cadwalader's brigade, trying to punch between bridgehead and convent. Cadwalader could not, and his men finally crossed the road into the cornfield. Farther left, Smith's brigade struck at San Mateo, while still farther left Riley hit the convent in flank.

Across the Churubusco Franklin Pierce, barely able to keep to his saddle, faced his brigade east and tried to cut the Mexican line of retreat. Pierce was eventually reinforced by Shields, and by riflemen and dragoons guided into battle by Captain Lee.

Santa Anna was now engaged across his entire front, and he fought back skillfully, rapidly countering Scott's cross-river attempts to turn him. For three hours the battle raged. From San Mateo, where the deserters were "fighting with a halter around their necks,"[69] came a dreadful drumfire. The hoarse cries of stricken men were counter-pointed by the mad screaming of horses and mules. Smoke drifted everywhere, and in the cornfield the sound of bullets popping stalks was counterpointed by the uglier one of lead smacking flesh. Across the river Franklin Pierce was down again with a twisted knee, but he urged his men on until consciousness left him.

By three o'clock in the afternoon Scott had shot his bolt. All his available men were engaged—6,000 against 18,000—they were falling by the hundreds, and they seemed stopped. One officer near Scott said to himself, "We must succeed or the army is lost."[70]

But the Mexicans were low on ammunition, and the Americans had worked their way into position for the final heave. Almost at once, they arose on three fronts and charged—and they were irresistible. Only at San Mateo did the fight continue, and here the deserters fought with clubbed muskets until at last there were only 80 of them alive to be taken prisoner. With his bridgehead gone, the convent fallen and his line of retreat threatened, Santa Anna ordered another with-drawal.

Mexican soldiers went streaming north for the safety of the San Antonio Gate, and the American infantry let them go. Suddenly bugles blew a charge and a squadron of American dragoons under hawk-nosed Captain Philip Kearny, nephew of the conqueror of New Mexico, went clattering up the road in full pursuit. They were a stirring sight, matched iron-grays moving nose to tail with their riders ramrod-straight and grasping gleaming sabers that rested, blade up, against their right shoulders. On toward the gate they charged, into a storm of enemy fire, with Kearny unaware that behind him Colonel Harney had blown recall and his rear horsemen were dropping off by fours.

Kearny had only Richard Ewell and a handful of troopers with him when he reached the gate, dismounted and tried to force it on foot. But the Americans were fighting at the cannon's mouth. Blast after blast cut them to the ground. They withdrew, with Kearny clinging to his mount with the one arm that was to remain to him and Ewell escaping on his third horse.

Perhaps the chance to enter the San Antonio Gate and drive straight into the city of Mexico had been missed. At any rate, the Battle of Churubusco was over. Chiefly because of the dreadful fire of the San

Patricios, it had been far more costly than Padierna: about 1,000 casualties in all. Santa Anna's losses for the day were about 3,200 soldiers captured, among them eight generals, and 4,000 killed and wounded, plus a paralyzing loss of arms and ammunition.

Winfield Scott, convinced that he had "overwhelmed the enemy," did not occupy the capital, as he might easily have done. Instead, he agreed to a cessation of hostilities during which Nicholas Trist and his Mexican counterparts might negotiate a peace. But the armistice lasted only two weeks. Trist's territorial demands provoked the Mexicans into advancing unacceptable terms of their own, and on September 7, learning that Santa Anna had used the truce as a breather in which to refresh his forces, Scott brought the armistice to an end.

The Molino del Rey, or "King's Mill," was part of the bastion of Chapultepec which guarded the western approaches to Mexico City. Chapultepec Castle itself stood on the brow of a hill about 200 feet high. To its west was a park and then the massive Molino del Rey built in a north-south line. About 500 yards west of the Molino lay another strong building, the Casa Mata. Between the two was an artillery battery supported by infantry. Perhaps 8,000 Mexicans held the entire position.

Scott decided that he must have this most formidable strong point after observing Mexican troop movements in that direction and hearing that Santa Anna was using the Molino as a foundry in which to cast cannon out of church bells. So he ordered General Worth to take it and destroy its contents.

Worth had a force of about 3,250 men, nearly half the 7,000 soldiers to which Scott's army had been reduced. He also had nine guns, but Worth, perhaps even more than Twiggs, scorned artillery when bayonets could be used. Cold steel, not exploding shells, was Worth's solution to stone walls. Thus the Americans jumped off in the morning of September 8, 1847, with the barest bombardment. As Molino's walls glowed white in the dawning day, two 24-pounders barked ten times apiece—and then the blue lines swept forward.

The entire Mexican front blazed with musketry and cannon. The blue lines were riddled and ripped apart. In the center, 11 of 14 officers were struck down and the ranks suffered in proportion. On the left at the Casa Mata two commanding officers fell, followed by a third. Broken, the left rallied—just as swarms of Mexican cavalry appeared across a ravine on the left. If the Mexican horse could get across the ravine under cover of Casa Mata's guns, they could charge the American left and perhaps roll up the entire line.

American bugles blew and 250 dragoons swept toward the enemy lancers. Galling fire from Casa Mata and a battery to their right emptied 40 American saddles, but still the dragoons rode on, bluffing and outmaneuvering the more numerous Mexicans.

On the right, at the southern end of the Molino, battle was confused, with units advancing independently and fighting other units in the swirl of smoke. Finally a gate was battered in and shouting Americans went pouring into the murk of the Molino. They chased the enemy up on the roofs of the buildings.

Up on the left, even as the reinforced center was returning to the attack, the enemy was also cracking. Mexican guns unwisely left outside the Casa Mata were captured and turned against the enemy. Still fighting stubbornly, the Mexicans twice mounted counterattacks. Beaten back, they began retreating east from the Casa Mata to Chapultepec.

The position was now completely in American hands, and Worth, scenting total victory and glory, asked permission to press on to Chapultepec itself. Scott refused, repeating his order to destroy the enemy "cannon" and withdraw. But there were no newly cast cannon, not even any old church bells. And the Mexican church bells which caroled away joyously in the mistaken belief that an all-out assault on Chapultepec had been repulsed seemed to mock Scott's decision to launch the attack at all.

Even though the enemy lost 680 prisoners and between 1,000 and 2,000 casualties, Worth's losses were close to 800 men, or a quarter of his attacking force and nearly an eighth of Scott's army. As one of Scott's officers wrote in his diary: "We were like Pyrrhus after the fight with Fabricius—and a few more such victories and this army would be destroyed."[71]

One result of the "victory" at Molino del Rey was that some of the men who had fought most gallantly decided to desert. They thought the American position was desperate, they had no wish to scratch stone walls with bayonets again, and they stole away even in the face of the example made of the San Patricio deserters.

A general court-martial on September 8 found 80 Patricios guilty of desertion and sentenced 54 to death by hanging, while the rest, men who had deserted before war was declared, were ordered to be flogged, branded on the cheek with the letter D and imprisoned at hard labor until the end of the war.

The first 18 to be hanged were brought by wagon to scaffolds erected outside the beautiful church of San Angel. Their necks were noosed, a drum was tapped, and the wagons rolled away. The fall, however, was not great enough to break their necks, and the condemned men choked and squirmed to death. Next came the lighter punishment. Captain Thomas Riley, chief of the deserters, was given 50 lashes, the others 25. Hot irons were pressed into their cheeks. Because Riley's D was burned in upside down, he was given a second.

Thus the examples set at San Angel, and they outraged the enemy's sensitivities and stiffened his spine. However just the sentences, however normal the punishments for the armies of that day, to have carried them out so ineptly in front of a church and in the eyes of a people who regarded hanging as a profanation of the crucified Christ was a vengeful and thoughtless variation from the considerate and humane face which Scott had tried to show the Mexicans since he landed at Vera Cruz.

The executions continued, however, while the American command considered where to deliver the next blow.

Winfield Scott had to attack. His position, if not desperate, was at least sobering. Here were the Americans, down to 7,000 men and at the end of a 250-mile supply line whose base at Vera Cruz was useless until the *vómito* vanished in November. Before Santa Anna became alive to the possibilities of this vulnerable line, Scott had to seize the enemy capital. The question at the conference of September 9, then, was not when to attack but where.

The volunteer generals and Captain Lee favored the southern approaches, but the regular generals and Lieutenant Beauregard preferred Chapultepec in the west. Beauregard argued forcefully that the fall of Chapultepec would unmask two easily traversed causeways into the city. Hearing him, Franklin Pierce changed his vote to Chapultepec and Scott declared: "Gentlemen, we shall attack by the western gates."[72]

On the morning of September 12 American soldiers seized the vacant Molino del Rey and Casa Mata on the western end of the

Chapultepec complex. With daylight, American artillery roared, battering Chapultepec's buildings and walls in the fiercest bombardment
of the war. Inside, General Nicolas Bravo called for reinforcements.
But Santa Anna had no wish to feed more troops into what might
become a slaughter pen. He kept some 4,000 troops available on the
western causeways, but they did not enter Chapultepec. Santa Anna's
eyes were fixed south, where a convincing diversion by Twiggs had
deceived him as to the American intent. So Bravo had to hold with
less than 1,000 men, of whom 100 were cadets quartered at the Military College in Chapultepec.

Against them came Pillow's division issuing out of the Molino and
Quitman's division moving north from Tacubaya against Chapultepec's
eastern end. On the west the Americans met a withering fire as they
dashed whooping through a grove of giant cypresses. Here Pillow was
wounded, and his men were brought to a cowering halt in a ditch beneath the castle, and here it was found that the storming party had
forgotten to bring scaling ladders. In desperation Pillow called for
Worth to bring up his division before all was lost. But then the scaling
ladders arrived, and the Americans leaped into the ditch, swung the
ladders against the stone wall and went swarming up them.

Lieutenant James Longstreet, rushing up with a flag in his hand,
fell to the ground wounded, and the colors were caught up and carried
forward by Lieutenant George Pickett.

On the left of Pillow's advance, Mexican musketry had cut down
the men following Lieutenant Tom Jackson as he tried to manhandle
a single gun forward. Alone among dead gunners and kicking horses,
the tall young officer called to his vanished troops: "There's no danger!
See, I'm not hit!"[73] But his gunners heard the peening of the enemy
bullets and they returned only after more guns and a column of
regulars appeared.

On the east, Quitman was attacking and taking heavy casualties.
Colonel Ransom died, so did Major Levi Twiggs of the Marines. The
fight was hand to hand, with crossed swords and clubbed muskets,
and the Mexicans stood firm for a time. But then all gave way.

All but the cadets of the Mexican Military College, many of whom
fought on to the death and entered Mexican history as *"Los Niños."*
Six of them, aged 13 to 19, gave up their lives rather than surrender.
One of these, 18-year-old Agustín Melgar, battled the Americans
step by step, dueling with them up the stairways until he reached the

roof of the college where American bayonets ended his gallant young life. Over his prostrate form stepped Lieutenant Pickett to haul down the green-red-and-white Mexican tricolor and run up the Red, White and Blue.

The men on the rooftop cheered. Below them other Americans already advancing along the causeways toward Mexico City also burst into huzzas. And from the plain of Mixcoac, some two miles to the south, came other cheers—not audible to these men but still memorable in history.

There at Mixcoac the last 29 of the condemned Patricios stood upon the hanging wagons. Red-faced Colonel Harney, the sworn enemy of deserters, had saved them for the moment when the American flag should fly over Chapultepec. They had stood in the hot September sun with their eyes riveted to the distant rooftops. Then there flashed that tiny square of Red, White and Blue, and the wagoners and the drummer boys burst into cheers. So did the Patricios, loudest of all. Their hands and feet were bound but their throats were free, and they freely saluted the victorious banner of the country they had abandoned.

Then the drums tapped, the wagons lurched, and the last of these brave but bitter men paid the price of their delusion.

The battle was now a race for Mexico City, Quitman versus Worth. Quitman had the closer route, for he moved along the causeway running directly east to the Belén Gate. Worth had to follow one causeway north before turning hard east to drive on the San Cosmé Gate. General Scott had sent both generals reinforcements, personally joining Worth, accompanied by Captain Lee. But Captain Lee, on his feet or in the saddle for nearly three days without respite, suddenly fell from his horse exhausted and unconscious.

Both of the causeways the Americans followed carried an arched aqueduct down their middles while roadways ran to either side. Both were barricaded and covered with troops and artillery. Nevertheless, the Americans slugged ahead. At 1:20 P.M. Quitman's troops crashed through the Belén Gate into the city's outskirts. The Mexicans fought back from the massive Citadel and Belén Prison. They were led by Santa Anna, who had hurried north from his fruitless vigil in front of Twiggs. At Belén the Americans hung on desperately against mounting casualties.

Worth also took losses as he slugged north and then swung east. Once again the Americans began burrowing through houses with picks and crowbars. They drove up to the San Cosmé Gate. Alarmed, Santa Anna rushed to San Cosmé, but his presence made no difference. The Americans burst the barrier and kept on fighting after nightfall.

Aware, now, that Mexico City's defenses had been breached, Santa Anna returned to the Citadel at Belén. Here, in a council of war, he decided to evacuate the city. He still had 5,000 infantry and 400 cavalry, but he chose to move north to Guadalupe Hidalgo. Before he did, some 2,000 convicts were "liberated" to prey upon the invading gringos.

In the morning of September 14, 1847, General John Quitman prepared for a stiff fight at the Citadel. His left foot bare from the stress of the previous day's fighting, he was sending his units forward when a flag of truce appeared with notice of Santa Anna's flight. Quitman quickly took possession of the Citadel, and then, hearing that the freed prisoners were plundering the city, the half-shod Quitman put himself at the head of his men and marched into the Grand Plaza. He formed them on the great square in the shadow of the Cathedral and gave to the Marines the mission of cleaning the National Palace of thieves and vagabonds.

Atop the Palace itself, the legendary "Halls of Montezuma," Marine Lieutenant A. S. Nicholson cut down the Mexican flag and ran up the Stars and Stripes, unwittingly giving to his famous Corps the first line of its hymn. And then at eight o'clock in the morning there came the sound of bugles, the rising clatter of horses' hooves. General Winfield Scott, superbly mounted and splendidly uniformed, swept into the Plaza escorted by dragoons with bared sabers. His officers followed, his bands played, his soldiers presented arms and whooped, and even his Mexican audience waved handkerchiefs.

It was the high point of a great career, and Scott had earned it. He had led one of the most momentous fighting marches in all history. Cortez may have conquered Mexico City for Spain, but the Mexican nation is no longer Spanish; whereas Winfield Scott in conquering the same capital was the chief instrument in adding 1,193,061 square miles of territory—an area more than five times the size of France—to the national domain of the United States.

That area was ceded after Nicholas Trist negotiated the Treaty of Guadalupe Hidalgo, signed on February 2, 1848. Trist had been recalled by Polk, but after Santa Anna abdicated, Trist saw his opportunity and deliberately disobeyed orders. In return for the ceded land, the United States agreed to assume the unpaid claims and pay Mexico $15 million.

All this was achieved by a repudiated diplomat and a discredited general, for Polk the superb expansionist soon became "Little Jimmy Polk" the petty politician: he relieved Scott with a Democratic general and dismissed Trist from the State Department.

Nevertheless, except for Alaska the area of the continental United States was now rounded out. Now the "firebell in the night" could clang anew over whether the new lands should be slave or free. Almost all of the great protagonists in the dreadful debate lying ahead—especially the generals trained in the Mexican War—were on the scene. They were already taking sides and even changing tunes. One young Whig Congressman, in criticizing "Mr. Polk's War" as unconstitutional, discussed the right to revolt in terms that could never have fallen from his lips a decade later.

"Any people anywhere," he said, "being inclined and having the power have the right to rise up and shake off the existing government, and form a new one that suits them better. . . . Any portion of such people that can may revolutionize and make their own of so much of the territory as they inhabit."[74]

The name of the speaker was Abraham Lincoln.

PART V

The Civil War

1

☆

True to his word, President Polk did not seek re-election in 1848. In his place the Democrats nominated Lewis Cass of Michigan, an old soldier who had been with Hull at Detroit in 1812 and was then a veteran politician enrolled in that numerous company of Northerners with Southern sympathies. The Whigs, remembering their success with Tippecanoe, passed over Henry Clay once again and named Zachary Taylor.

Old Rough and Ready swept to victory assisted by a third party of Free-Soilers. Led by Martin van Buren, this coalition of antislavery Whigs and Democrats took enough New York votes away from Cass to give that vital state to Taylor. Thus, for the fourth time in its 60-year history, the antimilitarist American nation had bestowed its highest office on a military hero.

Taylor's inauguration in 1849 seemed to open what was literally an American Golden Age, for gold had already been discovered in California and hordes of fortune-hunting "forty-niners" were converging on the Sacramento Valley. It was glamorous with the gleaming white sails of the Yankee clipper ships, then the admiration of every sea, and it was bright with the hope rising in the breasts of thousands of Old World immigrants following new roads and railways west to fill up the vast and empty empire taken from Mexico and the Indians. The nation was prospering, too: in the North the Industrial Revolution gave manufactures a golden shove, while Europe's insatiable hunger for cotton crowned that staple king of the South. Eli Whitney's invention of the cotton gin seemed to have guaranteed that the South should have economic as well as political dominance over the North, and none but a few thoughtful Southerners noticed that it had also rescued the institution of slavery from the slow death they had desired for it. Nor had Manifest Destiny perished. It had yet another decade of bumptious life, calling itself Young America while its prophets cast covetous eyes on Cuba or lectured kings and emperors on their duty to abdicate in favor of the common man.

In truth, the common man in America seemed then to be the envy of the world. He was in fact what he has since become in legend: an independent small farmer dwelling in rural order and blissful plenty. He lived better than his father had and he confidently expected his son to live even better. In the old way, of course, because most Americans then expected the old ways to continue. They did not know—few Americans did—that new winds were blowing over the world and breaking up the old ways; nor could they have suspected that the fruits of the Mexican victory were already sour with sectional discord.

To organize the new territory was to reopen the old question of slavery expansion. The South, led by Calhoun, had long ago declared that the Missouri Compromise of 1820 prohibiting slavery in territories north of 36°30' was unconstitutional. Congress, said Calhoun, not only had not the right to restrict slavery, it had the positive duty to protect it. Slaves were property, just like cattle, and a slaveowner had the right to take this property into any corner of the Union and to expect it to be protected there. Slavery, then, followed the flag.

Such was the Southern position, and although it begged the question of the morality of slavery, it was allowed to do so simply because both sides were engaged in a political-economic power struggle. First, the South feared to lose control of the government. There had been a time when the South hoped to continue in the ascendancy by gaining the allegiance of the new states now known as the Midwest through trade up and down the Mississippi River. But then the new railroads began tying the Midwest to Eastern ports. Calhoun saw clearly that the North, that is to say the Midwestern and Eastern states, was becoming stronger. Its population was skyrocketing: immigrants did not go south to compete with slave labor but stayed east or went west. If slavery were to be prohibited in the new territory north of the Missouri Compromise line, the ranks of the free-soil states would be swelled and the North would become invincibly powerful.

Thus the virus of sectionalism, which had weakened the United

States since colonial times. North and South were as different as people sharing the same language and generally the same religion and ancestry can be. The South was agricultural, the North industrial. The North wanted high import tariffs to protect its products against cheap European imports, while the South sought low tariffs or none at all so that it might import European goods in exchange for its cotton. Moreover, the South also planted crops with money borrowed in the North. Finally and most important, the agrarian debtor of the South employed slave labor while the capitalist creditor of the North hired free men. It may be, as the South came to maintain, that the wage-earner of the North often was little better than an industrial serf. He certainly had little bargaining power. But what he did have dignified him, it gave him political power at the ballot box, and the last thing he desired was to have this smallest corner of economic freedom threatened by the introduction of slave labor into the North.

Such differences were extreme enough, but they were eventually to be made even sharper and irreconcilable by the gradual shift of argument from an economic to a moral plane. Down deep the problem was moral. If slaves *were* property, then a slaveholder did have the right to take his slaves into any corner of the Union and expect the government to protect him in his possession of them there. But if it was wrong to make chattels of human beings, then at the very least the nation could not permit this evil to spread. Outright abolition, of course, was hardly even discussed by those Northern leaders who wished to preserve the Union. The South had some $2 billion invested in slaves and followed a way of life which despised labor as fit only for bondmen. Southerners considered their society superior to the North's, and it is highly doubtful that they would have accepted even compensatory emancipation—that is, to have the government repay them at the "market value" of their freed Negroes. To remove the "peculiar institution" from the fabric of Southern society was just not possible, because that fabric was woven with the thread of slavery. Northern leaders, then, recognized this seemingly ineluctable fact, just as they preferred to ignore or remain indifferent to the question of the morality of slavery.

The abolitionists of the North were not indifferent. At first they were temperate in their criticism of slavery. They considered it an incongruity in a free society and resented the fact that much of the South's political power sprang from the fact that three-fifths of the slave population was counted in apportioning slave-state representation. Gradually, however, the moderates gave way to extremists such as William Lloyd Garrison, who founded his antislave newspaper in 1831 with the declaration: "On this subject I do not wish to think, or speak, or write, with moderation. . . . I will be harsh as truth and as uncompromising as justice. . . . I am in earnest—I will not equivocate—I will not excuse—I will not retreat a single inch. AND I WILL BE HEARD."[1]

He was heard, and eventually the South began censoring abolitionist literature pouring through the mails and proposed a gag on antislavery petitions in Congress. But the abolitionist movement grew, and as it did it grew less temperate. In ever more strident tones its disciples denounced slavery as a crime and a curse and quoted the Bible as well as the Declaration of Independence to prove that all men were created equal. They harried the slave-catchers who were sent north by the masters of escaped slaves (and who sometimes also kidnaped free Negroes under the pretext that they were fugitives), and they organized the famous Underground Railroad by which escaped Negroes were passed from house to house at night until they reached some far Northern sanctuary or even crossed into Canada. They were not always popular in the North, these crusaders burning with a thirst for justice, and Ralph Waldo Emerson once advised them to love their neighbors a little more and their Negro brethren less. But they would not leave their more apathetic neighbors alone so long as slavery flourished in the United States. Hating bondage with such a fierce, deep hatred that they sometimes seemed just a little hateful themselves, disdaining compromise and ready to accept even disunion as a consequence of their goal of abolition, these fanatics nevertheless made more and more Americans realize that slavery was both a social injustice and a dreadful moral evil; and if they rubbed some delicate natures the wrong way, they also kept the public conscience awake.

They also drove the South to the position of defending slavery as a moral right and a social good. The glories of those ancient civilizations which had rested on slavery were extolled, while the Bible was quoted not only to sanction bondage but to demonstrate that God had deliberately created inferior races such as the Negroes to be the servants of superior people such as the white "cavaliers" of the South. In the South the wants of the Negroes were more than cared for, it was argued, while in the hypocritic North a wage-earner was rarely paid enough to purchase the necessities of life.

So the gap widened. More and more Southerners became willing to pick up the gauntlet of disunion thrown down by the abolitionists, and the South began to dream of a great slaveholding republic stretching from sea to sea. Then, in 1849, California decided to skip the territorial phase of organization and requested admission to the Union as a free-soil state with a constitution prohibiting slavery— and with that the South talked openly of secession.

Henry Clay, the "Great Pacificator" who had brought off the Missouri Compromise, came forward once again to preserve the Union. Clay realized that the Union was not yet ready to deal with secession. In January of 1850 he proposed a set of this-for-that compromises which touched off one of those great debates which have been characteristic of American history from the time of the Federalists to the Truman-MacArthur controversy during the Korean War.

It took place in the Senate, among the old lions—Clay, Calhoun, Webster—and such rising young leaders as Jefferson Davis of Mississippi, Stephen Douglas of Illinois, William Seward of New York and Salmon P. Chase of Ohio.

With all his conciliatory skill, Clay pleaded with the North not to insist on the Wilmot Proviso prohibiting slavery in the new territories, and to return fugitive slaves. He told the South that secession was not constitutional and would not be tolerated.

After Clay spoke, Calhoun's ultimatum was issued. "T have, Senators, believed from the first that the agitation of the subject of slavery would, if not prevented by some timely and effective measure, end in disunion."[2] The words were spoken by Calhoun's friend, Senator Mason of Virginia. Calhoun himself sat silent, wrapped in his cloak like a ghostly hawk, dying of catarrh. But his words were a clarion to the South: the North must "cease the agitation of the slave question."

Now it was the turn of Daniel Webster. It was his last great appearance. He spoke once again with that marathon grandiloquence which was typical of his time, with all his old oratorical skill: the thunderous voice and the imposing figure and massive head, the pointing finger and the questioning eye. "I wish to speak today," he began, "not as a Massachusetts man, not as a Northern man, but as an American. . . . I speak today for the preservation of the Union. 'Hear me for my cause.' "[3] Webster supported Clay's compromise proposals, even a more stringent Fugitive Slave Law, repugnant as it was to him. And he warned the South that it could not expect secession without strife. "Sir, your eyes and mine are never destined to see that miracle! . . . There can be no such thing as a peaceable secession."[4]

Senator Seward, a spokesman for the antislavery faction, and a leader-to-be of the yet unborn Republican Party, opposed the compromise and appealed to "a higher law than the Constitution." Seward's appeal to the Almighty—which disgusted Webster—had little effect on the debate. Webster's masterly speech and the powerful support of Douglas of Illinois carried the day for what has been called the Compromise of 1850.

Resolutions was adopted providing (1) admission of California as a free-soil state; (2) organization of the territories of New Mexico (including Arizona) and Utah without reference to slavery; (3) a new and stringent fugitive slave law; (4) abolition of the slave trade in the District of Columbia.

President Taylor did not like the Compromise, and might have vetoed it—except that as the debate raged he fell victim to a combination of Fourth of July oratory and medical exuberance. After listening to a two-hour speech in the boiling sun, Old Zack tried to cool off with large helpings of cucumbers washed down with cold milk. He became ill with acute gastroenteritis, from which he might have recovered had not his doctors sprung to his side to stuff him full of calomel, opium, ipecac and quinine, after which they bled and blistered him until, on July 9, 1850, the Angel of Death came to his rescue.

His successor, Vice President Millard Fillmore of Buffalo, was a man more friendly to compromise. He was also the perfection of mediocrity. The measure of his outlook and insight was his expressed hope that the slavery question had reached its "final settlement."

Although the new Fugitive Slave Law all but silenced secessionist talk in the South, it stuck in Northern throats. "This filthy enactment," Emerson called it, and declared: "I will not obey it, by God."[5] Actually the law defeated the purpose of the Compromise. In placating the South it infuriated the North, and thus guaranteed that "agitation of the slave question" would not cease—as the South demanded as the price of Union—but would increase. And then, in 1852, Harriet Beecher Stowe published *Uncle Tom's Cabin.*

No book written in America has even approached *Uncle Tom's Cabin* in its influence on American history.* Serialized in a magazine at first, each installment was eagerly awaited by millions of readers. In book form it sold 300,000 copies in less than a year, and eight presses were kept busy day and night catching up with the demand. *Uncle Tom* was also translated across the world, and plays based upon it gave additional millions the opportunity to hear Mrs. Stowe's message. Slavery, she said, debases all: master as well as slave and the society that permits it. She said this in a style that was ordinary, and through characters who were crude caricatures of the good and gentle Negro or the cruel, crass master, yet her theme erupted in the American conscience with titanic force; and after it was published it was no longer possible for Northerners to remain indifferent to slavery or for Southerners to pretend that the problem had been settled.

Alarmed and angered as the South was, it still kept its political head. In 1852, the year of *Uncle Tom's* publication, the all-powerful Democratic Party bowed to Southern wishes and nominated Franklin Pierce for President. Although Pierce was from New Hampshire, he was regarded as a "doughface," a Northern man with Southern principles. His opponent was his old military chief from Mexico City days, General Winfield Scott. The Whigs, torn by factions, had decided to go with the old war-hero formula again. But Franklin Pierce won by a margin wide enough to contain the corpse of the expiring Whig Party, and Scott's defeat—his second—seems to have demonstrated that except for the unique George Washington generals seeking to be President had better be rough-and-ready rather than full of fuss-and-feathers.

Pierce was the third mediocre President in a row. Without real convictions of his own and always persuaded by the last man to talk to him, especially if it was Secretary of War Jefferson Davis, he was the butt of friend and foe alike. Yet his was one of the stormiest of administrations, chiefly because Stephen Douglas, the Senator from Illinois who had once hailed the Missouri Compromise as a "sacred

* When Mrs. Stowe visited the White House during the Civil War, Lincoln greeted her with the remark: "So this is the little lady who made this big war."[6]

thing, which no ruthless hand would ever be reckless enough to disturb,"[7] lifted his own to kill it.

Stephen Arnold Douglas, the "Little Giant" from Illinois, five feet of plump bounce and brilliance, was a heavy speculator in Western lands and a presidential aspirant. On the first count he wanted the transcontinental railway to follow the central route from Chicago, and on the second he sought an explosive political issue for 1856.

To gain approval of the central railway route he needed the support of Southern Senators. So in a bill to divide the territory through which the railroad would pass into the future states of Kansas and Nebraska, he introduced the idea of "popular sovereignty." This meant that local residents could decide whether or not their regions would be free- or slave-soil. However, Nebraska and Kansas lay north of that Missouri Compromise line and were thus "forever" closed to slavery. In order to open them to that possibility, the "sacred" Missouri Compromise would have to be repealed. Douglas wanted this done by implication, but the Southern Senators whose support he needed for the central railway route insisted that it be repealed outright. Douglas consented, and when he did he got a political issue explosive enough to blast the Union in two.

Pride and passion, the twin terrors of human nature, were newly roused by the proposal to repeal the Missouri Compromise. This was the one agreement which had kept the peace between the sections for a generation. To attempt to overturn it, even to touch it, as Douglas seems to have known before he became blinded by ambition, was to break that peace. And it was broken: Southern pride now demanding that slavery follow the flag further inflamed Northern passion already aroused by the Fugitive Slave Act.

Yet Democratic party discipline pushed the Kansas-Nebraska Act through Congress, and the Compromise was repealed.

Next day in Boston an angry mob tried to prevent the return of a fugitive slave. A battalion of artillery, four platoons of marines and 22 companies of militia were required to get the runaway down to the ship. Thousands of civilians lined the streets, hissing and groaning and crying, "Kidnapers! Kidnapers!" Buildings were hung with crepe and church bells tolled—tolled the death of the Fugitive Slave Act, for henceforth in the hardening antislavery North a man felt it was his duty not to obey that law but to violate it.

Douglas's moral obtuseness had another result. On February 28, 1854, antislavery forces had met in a schoolhouse at Ripon, Wisconsin, to recommend formation of a "Republican party." On July 6, 1854, that party was formally organized at Jackson, Michigan. Beneath its standard were gathered Whigs, Free-Soilers and anti-Nebraska Democrats. That very fall these new Republicans gained a majority in the House, an astonishingly rapid victory that was in great part due to the scandal of "bleeding Kansas."

Even before the Kansas-Nebraska bill became law, proslavery groups had moved into Kansas from Missouri and antislavery colonists began preparing to enter the territory. Both sides sent representatives to Congress, both sides drew up constitutions and awaited admission to the Union—and both sides were armed. Civil war was the result: a small-scale dress rehearsal for the titanic conflict that was to convulse the nation. On balance, the proslavery "border ruffians," as the Free-Soilers called them, seemed to have been guilty of more violence; although the antislavery settlers from the Ohio Valley were far from adverse to squeezing the triggers of the new and accurate breech-loading Sharpe's rifles they carried. "Popular sovereignty" had become not a matter of voting slavery in or out by ballot but of shooting it either way by bullet. In Washington a Northern Senator placed the blame for this tragedy squarely on the shoulders of the South.

Senator Charles Sumner of Massachusetts made the accusation on May 19, 1856, in his sensational speech, "The Crime Against Kansas." Sumner sought to prevent the admission of Kansas as a slave state. As insensitive and insulting as he was eloquent and erudite, Sumner excoriated the "Slave Power" and directly impugned Douglas and Senator Butler of South Carolina. A few days later Butler's nephew, Representative Preston Brooks, walked up to Sumner in the Senate Chamber and caned him into bloody insensibility.

Now the North erupted in wrathful indignation again. Its passion had already been inflamed by the news that on May 21 a proslavery mob had sacked the antislavery settlement of Lawrence, Kansas, and on May 24 its own answer of violence was given by a lantern-jawed egomaniac named John Brown. His was an Old Testament creed of an eye-for-an-eye, a tooth-for-a-tooth, and after the Lawrence bloodletting he told his four sons and three other followers that "something must be done to show these barbarians that we too have rights."[8]

Then, presumably in the name of the civilized and righteous, these eight men lifted old artillery broadswords and stole off to a proslavery settlement at Pottawatomie Creek where they hacked to death five innocent men who had actually come to Kansas to get away from slavery.

Now it was the South that seethed with rage. The name John Brown was uttered like an epithet, just as "damn-Yankee" became a single word and a curse. The gulf between the sections widened: Southerners traveling in the North felt uneasy, Northerners visiting the South sensed hostility. In the South especially there developed a rising current of nationalism. Students enrolled in Northern schools came home to study, the myth of the "Cavalier" South and the peasant or plebeian North was extended and exaggerated, and Southerners were exhorted to eschew all that was not of Southern origin. In effect, two distinct nations were beginning to emerge within the boundaries of the United States. The North would not—could not—cease agitating the slavery question; and the South, driven back on herself, grew ever more rigid and inflexible in slavery's defense. The cleavage even cut the Baptist and Methodist churches into Northern and Southern branches. Even had a conciliator such as Henry Clay been alive, a reconciliation would have been impossible.

Yet the sectional showdown was avoided for another four years because the Democrats gave the South another "doughface" for President. This time it was James Buchanan of Pennsylvania, for neither Franklin Pierce nor his party desired his renomination. The "black Republicans" named John Charles Frémont, a national idol whose sobriquet of "Pathfinder" has been modified by modern historians to "Pathmarker." Frémont's campaign slogan was: "Free speech, free soil and Frémont." If he had won, the South probably would have seceded then and there. But victory went to the ponderously vacillating Buchanan, the fourth successive mediocrity to occupy the White House and the one who, having done most to get there, did least after his arrival. Nevertheless, the sectional storms were also to howl around his ears—and this was because even before his inauguration he connived at the Dred Scott decision.

Dred Scott was a Negro slave whose master took him from Missouri to Illinois and Minnesota Territory for two years. Upon his return, Scott sued for liberty in the Missouri courts on the ground that residence in a free state and a territory north of the Missouri

Compromise line automatically conferred freedom on him. The case reached the U.S. Supreme Court, and Buchanan and Chief Justice Taney with four Southern justices saw in it the opportunity to extend slavery throughout the nation. In a decision announced March 6, 1857, only a few days after Buchanan took office, the Court denied Dred Scott's claim on three grounds: (1) Negroes could not be United States citizens, therefore they could not sue in federal courts; (2) the laws of Illinois could not affect him in Missouri, where he now lived; (3) his residence in Minnesota Territory north of the Missouri Compromise line could not confer freedom because the Compromise was unconstitutional.

The Dred Scott decision shook the North like a thunderclap, and the area simply refused to be guided by it. Legislatures repudiated it and New York proclaimed the freedom of any slave who reached its precincts and promised up to ten years in prison to anyone who even passed through the state attended by a slave. To the young Republican Party the decision brought another increase of power, while to the South it brought determination to ram Kansas into the Union as a slave state.

In that year of 1857 the free-soil residents of Kansas outnumbered the proslavery settlers by nearly ten to one. Yet the Senate had rejected an antislavery constitution for the state-to-be and accepted one permitting bondage. Here Stephen Douglas, who had done so much to unsettle the Union, rose to the heights to preserve it. He led the fight to allow the people of Kansas the right to vote on the proslavery constitution, and when they rejected it by a margin of six to one they fulfilled the Little Giant's prediction: "Kansas is to be a free State."[9] For his stand on principle, Douglas became known as "a traitor to the South." In the following year, 1858, Douglas ran for re-election to the Senate against the surprisingly strong opposition of a rising Republican lawyer named Abraham Lincoln.

But for his gangly tall frame and his uncommonly homely face, Abraham Lincoln might have been just another prairie lawyer-politician. He was a Whig who had been to the Illinois legislature and been to Congress, where his opposition to the Mexican War cost him his seat in the House. He looked upon slavery as an evil, but he also regarded abolitionist agitation as harmful to the Union. The South could have its institution, Lincoln thought, but it should not be allowed to extend it. Holding this conviction, common enough among Whig Free-Soilers, Lincoln retired from politics in 1849.

In 1854 the Kansas-Nebraska Act brought him back, and he was a different man. Now he was attacking the morality of slavery itself: "Slavery is founded on the selfishness of man's nature—opposition to it in his love of justice. These principles are in eternal antagonism, and when brought into collision so fiercely as slavery extension brings them, shocks and throes and convulsions must ceaselessly follow."[10] Three years later, as a Republican, Lincoln attacked the Dred Scott decision as a reversal of the principles of the Declaration of Independence, and then, on June 16, 1858, he said:

" 'A house divided against itself cannot stand.'

"I believe this government cannot endure permanently half slave and half free.

"I do not expect the Union to be dissolved—I do not expect the house to fall—but I do expect it will cease to be divided.

"It will become all one thing or all the other.

"Either the opponents of slavery will arrest the further spread of it and place it where the public mind shall rest in the belief that it is in the course of ultimate extinction; or its advocates will push it forward until it shall become alike lawful in all the States, old as well as new, North as well as South."[11]

With this speech Lincoln became the Republican candidate challenging the Democrat, Douglas. Eventually the two agreed to discuss the issues in a series of debates across the state. Famous for their cogency, the Lincoln-Douglas Debates might be equally celebrated for the contrasts in the debaters. Here was Douglas, a bristling bulldog dressed in fine clothes, the man of power and position riding into town on a special train and very likely firing off signal cannon to herald his arrival. There was Lincoln, six feet four inches tall, his big bony hands and feet sticking out from his ill-fitting trousers as he awkwardly rides a horse toward the platform. If anyone impresses, it is Douglas, with his powerful bark and sure movements of the hands; but then, as one observer reported, Lincoln speaks and "his eye glows and sparkles, every lineament, now so ill-formed, grows brilliant and expressive, and you have before you a man of rare power and of strong magnetic influence."[12] His rough good humor softens the bite but not the point of his logic and he "*takes* the people every time."[13]

The outstanding meeting was at Freeport, where 15,000 people heard Lincoln ask Douglas how he could square his doctrine of popular sovereignty with the Dred Scott decision that slavery follows the flag. Douglas replied that residents of a Territory had it in their power to prevent or protect slavery by local police regulations. This was the "Freeport Doctrine" by means of which Douglas sidestepped the moral issue of the right or wrong of slavery. It guaranteed his reelection, but also so mortally offended the South that he lost all chance of gaining the Democratic presidential nomination in 1860.

In the intervening period, the North continued to agitate and the South to protest until fanatical old John Brown ended all hope of moderation.

"Caution, sir!" John Brown had growled before his Pottawatomie Massacre. "I am eternally tired of hearing that word caution. It is nothing but the word of cowardice."[14]

Coward he was not, maniac he was—and on the night of October 16, 1859, he and his followers again lifted their avenging swords and attacked and seized the federal arsenal at Harpers Ferry, Virginia. Their hope was to take the captured arms southward to stir up a revolt of Negro slaves, but the reality was that Colonel Robert E. Lee and a company of marines rushed to Harpers Ferry to overwhelm Brown and take him prisoner.

Within two weeks John Brown was brought to trial and convicted of insurrection, murder and treason. On December 2, 1859, content "to die for God's eternal truth," he was hanged.

In John Brown the Northern extremists saw a noble martyr while their Southern counterparts saw the embodiment of all their fears. "He wanted to arm the slaves!" secessionists said, in effect, to moderates and Unionists. "That's what the North *really* wants." It made no difference that most Northern newspapers and leaders from Douglas to Lincoln denounced Brown's acts as lawless; the voices that the South heard were those of the firebrands shouting that John Brown had been sacrificed on the altar of slavery. Not many Northerners seem to have understood the full extent of Brown's plans to raise the slaves. His earlier murders at Pottawatomie were either forgotten or ignored. Even so serene a sage as Emerson lost his customary balance long enough to hail "that new saint . . . [who] will make the gallows glorious like the cross."[15]

But John Brown left no legacy of love; rather he put hatred in the saddle and sent it galloping wildly across the land. In the South the radicals had complete control when the Democratic Party held its convention in April, 1860. They tried to "stop" Douglas, and failed; tried to get a proslavery platform adopted, and failed—and then, as had been concerted beforehand, eight Southern delegations walked out. Douglas was easily nominated, but the renegade Southerners countered by nominating their own candidate, John C. Breckenridge of Kentucky. A more moderate group named John Bell of Tennessee.

Ironically, the Southern radicals, dreading the triumph of the antislavery Republicans, had guaranteed their victory. They knew as well as Douglas that a divided Democratic Party had no chance. Yet they split it. Why? Probably because the Southerners believed that their backs were to the wall and that now it was a case of rule or ruin. It has been said that the South hoped that a "deadlock" in the Electoral College might throw the decision into Congress where Southern parliamentary skill would produce a proslavery President. But this was truly a hopeless hope. More likely the South believed that the gauntlet had to be thrown down and for the last time.

In May of 1860 the Republican Party named Abraham Lincoln of Illinois as its candidate. Seward of New York had come to the convention confident of victory, but Lincoln and his managers cleverly trotted out "Honest Abe" in the homey garb of "the rail-splitter" while making the customary behind-the-scenes political deals to gain real support. Lincoln won on the third ballot, and some Southern states announced that his election would be tantamount to secession.

Lincoln was elected. On December 20, 1860, South Carolina seceded from the Union. A few weeks later she was followed out by Mississippi, Alabama, Georgia, Florida, Louisiana and Texas. On February 8, 1861, delegates from the seven seceded states met in Montgomery, Alabama, to form the Confederate States of America and to name Jefferson Davis as its first President.

It had come. Innate differences dividing Northern and Southern societies from their very beginnings had pushed the two sections farther and farther apart until at last Southern pride and Northern passion had cut the last remaining bonds. As Mrs. Mary Chesnut of South Carolina was to say: ". . . we are divorced, North from South, because we have hated each other so."[16]

2

☆

Secession was a fact; the question now was: Would there be war?

In the new Confederacy war was not desired. The South wished to be free to consolidate and to gain recognition and allies among those European nations who were both dependent on her cotton and eager to see the American experiment in self-rule come to a ruinous end.

In the North the Federal government floundered because of the deficiencies of President Buchanan and a system which placed four long months between a President's election and his inauguration.* Lincoln could do nothing until March 4, 1861, and Buchanan—beguiled by the Southerners in his Cabinet—did next to nothing until then because he also feared to provoke powerful Virginia into joining the Confederacy.

There were, of course, movements toward reconciliation, but these were torpedoed by hotheads and even the famous Crittenden Proposals were unacceptable to Lincoln because they included the extension of slavery to the Pacific. In the meantime, the governors of seceded states seized Federal mints, forts, shipyards, customhouses and other installations. In Texas, "Old Davey" Twiggs ignominiously handed over all his posts with their men and equipment without firing a shot and while still wearing the sash of a United States general. Eventually the South held all but three of the Federal forts in the Confederacy—and one of these three was Sumter off the Charleston coast.

Fort Sumter was still in Union hands while Abraham Lincoln traveled slowly from Illinois to Washington to take possession of his House Divided. He had been advised to crush the Confederacy or to let "our erring sisters depart in peace," and the New York *Herald*

* March 4 remained the inauguration date until Franklin Roosevelt began his second term on January 20, 1936.

had also advised him to resign in favor of a more "acceptable" man or else "totter into a dishonored grave . . . leaving behind him a memory more execrable than that of [Benedict] Arnold."[17] In the South similar voices of sweet reason were shouting: "Resistance to Abraham Lincoln is obedience to God."[18] So the cleft nation, its eyes on Sumter, awaited Lincoln's speech for omens of war or peace. Lincoln clearly stated that he intended to preserve the Union, but he also told the South:

> In your hands, my dissatisfied fellow-countrymen, and not in mine, is the momentous issue of civil war. The government will not assail you. You can have no conflict without yourself being the aggressors. You have no oath registered in heaven to destroy the government, while I shall have the most solemn one to "preserve, protect, and defend" it.[19]

Having uttered these magnificent words, Lincoln did little to back them up. For weeks he vacillated nearly as badly as Buchanan. But then he made up his mind to hold the Federal forts and especially Sumter. Troops and provisions were collected for Sumter's relief. Yet Lincoln was careful to inform the South that no troops would land unless provisioning was resisted or the fort was fired upon. Clearly, the new President was adhering to the American principle of allowing the other side to strike the first blow.

The South, also loath to be the aggressor, hesitated. But the South had Virginia and other wavering slave states to be considered. Strike a blow, some men urged, fire a shot—and Virginia and the rest will be inside the Confederacy within an hour. On April 10, Jefferson Davis ordered General P. G. T. BEAUREGARD*—the old campaigner from Mexico City—to demand Sumter's surrender and to seize it should he be refused. He was refused, by Major Robert Anderson of Kentucky, who loved both North and South and had no heart to see them fight. However, Anderson also admitted that his lack of supplies would soon force him to capitulate, and BEAUREGARD telegraphed this information to the Confederate government. Still reluctant to start a civil war, the South now instructed BEAUREGARD to hold off the bombardment if Anderson would specify at what date he would evacuate the fort.

Anderson replied to this by saying that he could not hold out past

---

* For clarity, the names of Confederate leaders henceforth will be printed in capitals and small capitals.

April 15 unless he received prior instructions from his government or additional supplies. The men who heard this answer were young fire-brands, empowered to determine whether or not it was satisfactory. They decided that it was not and so informed Anderson. He told them courteously that if he did not see them again in this world he hoped to meet them in Heaven, and they returned to Charleston.

At 4:30 A.M. in the morning of April 12, 1861, a red speck rose from a mortar on the Charleston shore. It could be clearly seen de-scribing its fiery loop, going up and over, coming down with a whoosh and exploding over Fort Sumter.

The Civil War had begun.

The shots fired at Sumter—and the fort's fall the following day—-outraged and unified the North. The flag had been fired upon, that was treason, and now the cry arose: "The Union forever!" The issue of slavery was all but forgotten as the drums beat the patriotic pulse higher and young men rushed to answer Lincoln's call for 75,000 90-day volunteers.

Sumter also electrified the South, and there was a surge of Southern youth to fulfill President DAVIS's earlier call for 100,000 men. As expected, Sumter brought Virginia into the Confederacy, followed by Arkansas, North Carolina and Tennessee. But then there was a secession in reverse: the non-slaveholders of Virginia's western moun-tains, long resentful of slaveholder domination, organized their ter-ritory into a loyal section that was admitted to the Union in 1863 as the state of West Virginia.

Like the North, the South ignored the slavery issue. "States' rights!" was her rallying cry. The Union was merely a loose compact of states with nothing sacred about it, any member of which had the right to secede. To prevent secession was unjust, it was an invasion of the South. Thus both sides unconsciously sidestepped the very issue which had divided them. In the South it was probably easier to get men to fight for "our rights" rather than for the institution many of them in-stinctively despised, and in the North most of the abolitionists were cheerleaders at heart and the true fighting men would rather risk their flesh for the sacred Union than for distant Negroes whom they loved as little as their Southern opponents. This is not to mock the motives of the men of the Civil War armies. No soldiers were ever more noble or idealistic; but Johnny Reb did not put on Confederate gray or butternut to fight for Southern chivalry any more than Billy Yank vested himself in Union blue to stamp out slavery.

But with what a mixture of highhearted gaiety and religious fervor did they go to war! Farmer's sons, most of them, with a generous leaven of Germans and Irish—especially in the North—they cheered and sang and swore such mild oaths as "dang" and "durn," carrying their Bibles in breast pockets to ward off enemy bullets and attending daily services where they prayed—especially in the South—with a fervor unequaled since the Puritans of Oliver Cromwell.

In them aristocratic paternalism was meeting democratic nationalism, and if most of them found this conflict difficult to grasp, all of them regarded their own cause as sacred. In the North fathers presented swords to their sons with the command to bring them back stained to the hilt, while kneeling officers wept to receive regimental colors from the hands of little girls garlanded with flowers. In the South "gentlemen privates" enrolled themselves and their horses beneath the new nation's bold red banner—the colorful Stars and Bars, as pretty a flag as ever caught the wind—and a man's capacity to command was measured by the number of bales of cotton stacked on his wharf. Dixie, it would seem, had little need for the first conscription law in American history: the Southern woman was the Confederacy's recruiting sergeant. Mother, wife, sister, sweetheart, "she was the South's incarnate pride,"[20] and it was her smile the soldier sought, her stony contempt the slacker feared.

Once again regiments of "Guards" and "Zouaves" and "Tigers" and "Invincibles" in colorful uniforms followed the tap of the drum and the squeal of the fife into camp, but now they were peeling off into rival armies, flocking to state capitals above and below the Mason-Dixie Line, surrounding Washington and the new Confederate capital of Richmond 100 miles south with serried rows of tents. On both sides the armies were raised by calling upon the states to furnish militia to be enrolled in Federal or Confederate service. As is customary in American military history, both sides envisioned a short spectacular land war (although the Union Navy did possess 40 seagoing ships, on the strength of which President Lincoln proclaimed a blockade), and both sides thought themselves prepared.

They were not, of course. Until March, 1861, the South had no army; and the Federal Army was a splendid 16,000 strong, barely enough to police the frontier and man the coastal guns. Each side also thought itself superior, blinding itself to the other's advantages. In fairness, it is hard to blame the North for her confidence. After all, in 19 Northern states lived nearly 19 million people, compared to 9 million in 11 Confederate states. In the North were nine-tenths of the nation's industrial power, two-thirds of its rails with most of its rail manufacturing capacity, most of its mineral resources, and a growing surplus of foodstuffs which, through Northern sea power, could be exported to Europe just as surely as the Southern exportation of cotton could be cut off. In the end, finding the right combination of political and military genius, such advantages had to be overwhelming. But in the beginning they blunted political and military judgment and were also offset by certain Southern superiorities either unseen or unsuspected.

Foremost were Southern courage and zeal. Next came its feudal society, which by its very structure, like the French Canada of Frontenac and Montcalm, lent itself to the martial spirit and rapid mobilization. Then, much as the proportion of slave population might seem to reduce the South's actual strength in fighting men, it also produced a stable labor force while freeing almost every white male between 16 and 60 for duty in the field. Another hidden advantage was that the South would be fighting a defensive war, thus requiring the North to mass a larger army and risk the higher casualties which usually befall the invader. The North, of course, *had* to attack. Lincoln desired to preserve the Union and to do this he had to crush the Confederacy. The South was fighting to defend herself until that magic moment in history when King Cotton—as JEFFERSON DAVIS so fondly and foolishly kept on hoping—would force the nations of Europe to intervene on her side. In this defensive war, then, the South possessed the advantage of interior lines and terrain which the god of war had made for defensive fighting. It was in this very crosshatch of hills and gullies, of swamps and forests and mountains laced with curling, racing rivers, that Nathanael Greene had taught Lord Cornwallis the lesson of his military life. To defend such eminently defensible terrain the South possessed commanders of a quality equal to Greene. Chief among them was ROBERT E. LEE. One of the heroes of the Mexican War, LEE had refused command of the Northern armies proffered him by his old chief, General Winfield Scott, with the remark that he would only draw his sword in defense of his native Virginia. After that state seceded, LEE became a Confederate general, joining the distinguished company of BEAUREGARD, the two JOHNSTONS, both HILLS, LONGSTREET, STONEWALL JACKSON and many others. Never, before or since, has a nascent nation possessed such swords with which to cut its course in history; and yet they had once been Federal officers!

The U.S. Army, while compelling its enlisted men to remain loyal, had permitted its officers to resign, and about 270 of 900 followed their conscience South. Moderns might well gasp at such a mad and noble gesture, for no modern government would do less than imprison commanders of such proven worth and plain disloyalty. But this was the last of the gentlemanly wars, and the Union, recognizing that a man's first loyalty was to his conscience and his God, not yet committed to the brutal logic of total war, permitted them to go. Thus, at garrisons across the nation, men in the same uniform exchanged toasts of farewell and wrung each other's hands while their wives exchanged misty-eyed kisses, all knowing that the next meeting would be on the battlefield with unsheathed swords. Thus the South gained one of its greatest assets, and the Civil War one of its chief characteristics: the commanders frequently knew each other and made moves based on that knowledge.

Another Confederate asset seemed to be its President, JEFFERSON DAVIS. He, too, was a military man, a West Pointer, veteran of Mexico, and Secretary of War under Franklin Pierce. Tall, thin, handsome in an ascetic way, he was a man carved of stone, a creature who might be broken but never bent, and he was the apotheosis of mansion and magnolia just as Abraham Lincoln was the embodiment of prairie and melting pot. Like Lincoln he had been born in Kentucky, and at about the same time that the child Abraham was being taken North to become the leader of the new nationalism, the child JEFFERSON was being taken South to become the spokesman of embattled aristocracy. But DAVIS was not the military asset he was thought to be: he treated his Secretary of War as a clerk, quarreled with such capable officers as JOE JOHNSTON and BEAUREGARD, and kept the military reins so tightly in his own hands that it was not until the war's end that LEE received the powers of general in chief. DAVIS's grand strategy was also errant in imposing an embargo on cotton exports in the belief that this would create such a demand that England, at least, would go to war on the Confederate side just to get cotton. But the fact was that Europe had built up a backlog of cotton supplies and later found new sources in India and Egypt. If the Confederacy had rushed her bumper crops to Europe in 1861, she might have obtained the money to buy badly needed munitions. But she did not, nor did the timid Confederate Congress levy any taxes that year; and here was another unseen Southern weakness.

States' rights, the very cause, would help to kill the Confederacy. By what right, stormed a Governor BROWN of Georgia or a Governor VANCE of North Carolina, did the central government presume to seize state supplies or enforce taxes? DAVIS, agreeing with them in principle, could only answer: none. He was so much the man of abstract conviction, of high unbending principle, that he could not see that the revolution he was leading required revolutionary tactics. States' rights could only be protected by insisting on a temporary cession of them. This, however, DAVIS refused to accept; and as the South's chief executive remained forbearing, its Congress stayed timid.

Thus, as Southern terrain, tacticians and society offset Northern industrialism, population and resources, so the lack of cohesion in the Confederacy was the equal of Lincoln's own struggles with Peace Democrats and radical, antislavery Republicans. But there was one other Southern disadvantage, and that was the South's complete contempt for the North's fighting prowess. To too many Southern commanders the "damn-Yankees" were a crowd of cunning rabbits who could not and would not fight. Probably the most perfect expression of this foaming contempt was the "Southern Series" of mathematical problems worked out by the educator-general, D. H. HILL. For example: "A Yankee mixes a certain quantity of wooden nutmegs, which cost him one-fourth cent apiece, with a quantity of real nutmegs, worth four cents apiece . . ."; or "Buena Vista is six and a half miles from Saltillo. Two Indiana volunteers ran away from the field of battle at the same time. . . ."[21] Such a habit of mind—the eternal autocrat despising the "frivolity" of free men—is bound to cripple judgment, and it did.

Fervor, hatred and overconfidence, then, were the hallmarks of the Civil War then beginning in April of 1861. Because of these it became the most ferocious and bloody war in American history: 540,000 deaths out of a total white population of 25 million. Yet it might have been worse had it been a true civil war in which the entire population, civil as well as military, rends itself. In most civil wars the strife is internal as the factions seize or hold regions from which they seek to extend their influence. It is not only brother against brother but neighbor against neighbor. The American Civil War, however, was unique in that not only two different forms of society but two separate nations fought each other. Each was a geographical entity and each had sufficient resources to make war. True enough, in this war fathers fought sons and brothers split off into rival camps, but not to any degree comparable to, say, the Spanish Civil War. In America no city or region divided into factions, each bathing the other in blood. South and North were both solid, with every state, city and town remaining loyal; and although spies proliferated on both sides, there were no governors or generals standing ready to betray.

Only in the border states was there the possibility of internal strife.

No single factor in the Civil War was more determining than possession of the slaveholding border states of Maryland, Kentucky and Missouri. When war broke out, their allegiance was divided: some people were strong for secession, others for Union. How they swung was vital. If it was South, then the Confederacy's frontiers would be advanced to the Ohio River, the Northwest would be menaced and the Federal capital at Washington would become a Northern island in a Southern sea. If they went North, then they aimed a Union dagger at the heart of the Confederacy.

Maryland forced the issue when, on April 19, a mob of Southern sympathizers collided with a Massachusetts militia regiment marching crosstown through Baltimore to change trains for Washington. Bricks and paving stones were hurled at the startled soldiers. Pistols were fired at them. They answered with muskets. Four soldiers and 12 civilians were killed. On to Washington moved the Northern troops, the bodies of their fallen packed in ice for martyrs' burial at home; and after they departed, pro-South mobs blew the railroad bridges linking Washington and the North and cut the telegraph. Washington was isolated. There were rumors that BEAUREGARD was marching on the capital at the head of 100,000 men. There was even talk among the fainthearted of replacing the "feeble" Lincoln with a dictator. Lincoln, however, could play that hard-handed role himself.

He sent troops under Major General Benjamin Butler, a devious, cross-eyed Bay State politician-turned-soldier, into Baltimore. Butler restored the bridges and arrested the mayor, 19 state legislators and numerous other secession-minded Marylanders and threw them into jail. When Chief Justice Taney issued a writ of habeas corpus for one of these improperly imprisoned men, Lincoln merely ignored it. Bullets, not legal briefs, were now defending the Constitution; and by this and other dictatorial moves Lincoln kept Maryland firmly in the Federal camp.

West Virginia was kept there, too, after the young and brilliant Major General George McClellan defeated a Confederate force which had come there to reclaim it for the South. Though minor, this action was decisive—and in McClellan's Napoleonic prose it became a major victory.

Farther west, the Union moved softly. Kentucky was Unionist both in its people and its legislature, but secessionist Governor MAGOFFIN tried to hold off the North by issuing a proclamation of neutrality. Lincoln did move against MAGOFFIN because Kentucky would probably go as Missouri went, and there the Union cause was progressing.

Secessionist Governor CLAIBORNE JACKSON and Captain Nathaniel Lyon were the antagonists in Missouri. Lyon, a pugnacious little redhead and a born revolutionary, had not the rank to match JACKSON. That belonged to General William Harney, the bluff, red-necked old cavalryman who had hung the Patricios at Mexico City. But Harney could not believe that Governor JACKSON coveted the Federal arsenal as a means of controlling the state. Captain Lyon did, and so did his associate, Frank Blair, whose brother sat in Lincoln's Cabinet. Through Blair's influence, General Harney was called out of St. Louis so that Captain Lyon might confront Governor JACKSON.

JACKSON began the struggle by calling out about 700 Missouri militia and putting them into camp near St. Louis on the pretext of drilling them. Captain Lyon concluded otherwise. He disguised himself as a woman and clattered into camp in a carriage, a basket of eggs on his lap and beneath the eggs a half-dozen loaded revolvers. Lyon saw enough to convince him that JACKSON was preparing to seize the arsenal and take Missouri out of the Union. Returning to St. Louis, he began swearing the city's numerous Germans into the Federal service. With them, and with a few companies of regulars, he surrounded the militia and forced them to surrender.

All went peacefully enough, until Lyon attempted to march his prisoners into town through gathering crowds of angry secessionists. As in Baltimore, civilian pistols were fired, then military muskets—

and before nightfall the cobblestones of St. Louis were stained with the lifeblood of 28 Americans. Still, Lyon had kept the Federal arsenal in Federal hands, and by the middle of June he had driven Governor JACKSON out of the state capital and placed Missouri temporarily, if not firmly, in the Federal camp.

The struggle for the border states was not fully appreciated by either side. In the South sectional pride exaggerated the importance of the Confederate victory at Big Bethel, Virginia, in the first skirmish of the war, and the North did the same with McClellan's triumph in West Virginia. Both sides were also mesmerized by the cries of "On to Richmond!" or "Forward to Washington!" They believed that capture of the enemy's capital, not destruction of his army or his will to fight, would end the war.

Winfield Scott was not so misled. Still general in chief at a dropsical 75, Scott advised Lincoln that "300,000 men under an able general might carry the business through in two or three years."[22] Scott's plan was to seize New Orleans while sealing up the Southern ports, after which one large army would move down the Mississippi and cut the Confederacy in two while another menaced Richmond and so contained the Southern forces in Virginia. This, in effect, is the plan that was eventually adopted. It provided for nothing less than strangulation of the enemy economy, but because this took time, men and money, Lincoln would have none of it. After it was made public, the same press that had howled at Winfield Scott as "Marshal Tureen" derided his "Anaconda Plan." For some reason—perhaps because he sat too tall in the saddle—Winfied Scott's countrymen found him uproariously funny. So the nation clamored for immediate action, and on July 4 the New York *Tribune* thundered: "Forward to Richmond! Forward to Richmond! The Rebel Congress must not be allowed to meet there on the 20th of July! By that date the place must be held by the National Army!"[23]

Lincoln the politician had to heed such voices. Moreover, his own capital seemed to be threatened by the force gathering in Virginia under BEAUREGARD. So he directed Brigadier General Irvin McDowell to move quickly against the Confederates.

Irvin McDowell was no better and no worse than the run of generals available to the Union cause that summer of 1861. Tall and

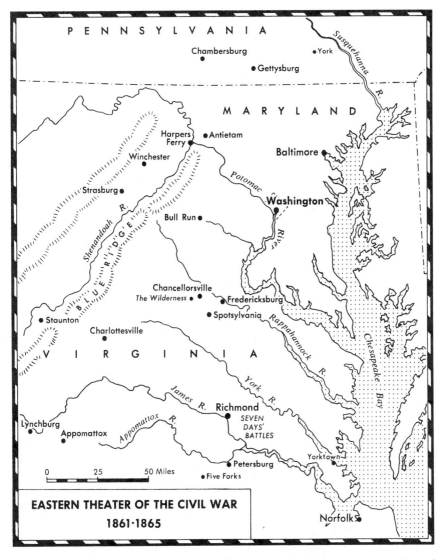

EASTERN THEATER OF THE CIVIL WAR
1861-1865

handsome, tailor-made for statues, he was a bluff, hearty man famed for his gargantuan appetite. (He once polished off a huge meal by consuming an entire watermelon that he found "Monstrous fine!") Like every Civil War leader save Winfield Scott, he had never commanded large bodies of troops. Still, he was a fighter, and he ordered his 35,000-man army to move south on July 16.

It was a parade of amateurs, this gaudy, straggling procession of half-trained 90-day men. It was American innocence marching to its grave. Here were Zouaves in baggy red breeches, short blue coats and yellow or scarlet sashes, veritable peacocks strutting to the target area. With them marched volunteers in gray to be shot at by their own men. Bands played, regimental flags of varicolored silk waved, dogs and little boys skipped alongside the troops, and the soldiers themselves broke ranks to pick blackberries, beg a glass of lemonade or take a breather in the shade. It was hot that July, and clouds of dust settled on the marchers and clogged the nostrils of sweating mules and horses dragging the wagons of McDowell's enormous baggage train stretching out behind his infantry like a great scraggly tail. A few days later the elite of Washington came out to watch the fun. By gig and on horseback, in linen cuffs and crinoline, carrying hampers stuffed with delicacies and bottles of fine wine, they followed their warriors to the battlefield to witness the whipping of the upstart Rebels.

Below them at Manassas Junction, the Confederate Army under BEAUREGARD was only hardly less naïve. But "Old Bory," as this broad-shouldered soldier with the imperial mustache was called, was a little less green than McDowell. BEAUREGARD had 20,000 men holding a ten-mile line behind a stream known as Bull Run. About 40 miles to the northwest in the Shenandoah Valley were another 12,000 Rebels under JOE JOHNSTON. A railroad linked the two forces. Mc-Dowell, aware of this, had instructed Major General Robert Patterson with 18,000 Federals to keep the pressure on JOHNSTON to prevent him from joining BEAUREGARD. But the aging Patterson allowed JOHNSTON to bluff him with a few menacing gestures. He went on the defensive, while JOHNSTON went slipping southeast.

McDowell arrived at Centreville a few miles above BEAUREGARD on July 18. If he had attacked then, he would have had the advantage of numbers. But he frittered away two days while JOHNSTON reinforced BEAUREGARD. When he did attack, on July 21, 1861, the two forces were nearly even.

Both commanders planned to strike each other's left, and it was the Federals who got there first. Hours late, two Union infantry divisions with artillery and a handful of cavalry crossed Bull Run above BEAUREGARD's lightly held left and began to roll it back.

They came out of the trees, the Federals, advancing bravely for raw troops who had been blundering through the woods for five hours on a hot day. For such an army, not too many men hid in the woods, but neither did too many keep order. It was difficult for the officers to maintain discipline with the complicated maneuvers of those days. Opposing them was a fragmented Rebel brigade under Colonel NATHAN EVANS, who had observed the Union turning movement, wheeled left and gone rushing into the breech.

Far to the right, BEAUREGARD heard the rising clamor of battle to his left and saw clouds of gunsmoke drifting skyward. Alongside him was JOHNSTON, who urged him to forget about his own turning movement and to reinforce his left. "The battle is there," JOHNSTON said. "I am going!"[24] BEAUREGARD hurriedly checked movements which had been going forward with even less precision than McDowell's. Columns of men in gray wheeled about and began marching toward the sound of battle. Among them was THOMAS JACKSON's brigade.

Fortunately for the Rebel commander, his subordinates had acted with rare initiative. Brigadier General BARNARD BEE and Colonel FRANCIS BARTOW went hurrying to the assistance of EVANS, whom the hurrahing Federals had been pressing steadily back. They formed in line on his right, but they too were driven backward. Then a Union brigade under Colonel William Tecumseh Sherman crossed Bull Run on their right and struck them hard. They were in danger of being routed. The Union cause appeared triumphant, and the Rebels began falling back on Henry House Hill where JACKSON had taken position with his infantry and a battery of artillery.

Resolute, not at all the "panic-stricken Unionists" of the school history books, the Federals pursued through the smoke and keening bullets. The Rebel lines were being whittled. BEE rode up to JACKSON, who was struck twice that day, and cried, "General, they are beating us back!" JACKSON replied, "Sir, we'll give them the bayonet," and BEE tried to rally his remnant with the shout: "There is JACKSON standing like a stone wall. Let us determine to die here, and we will conquer."[25] BEE did die that day, after conferring the undying nickname of "Stonewall" on THOMAS JACKSON.* Many more Confederates fell as the Rebel forces drew still farther back, and then two Union batteries—11 guns—came out of the smoke at a splendid gallop,

* D. H. HILL, JACKSON's brother-in-law, called this account, printed in the Charleston *Mercury,* "sheer fabrication." But it has been generally accepted in history, and HILL may have resented a nickname which he considered least suitable to the swift, tigerish JACKSON.

rolled up the Henry House slope, unlimbered and began battering the Rebel artillery.

Union infantry support was slow in forming to the right of its guns and was driven off by cavalry led by Colonel J. E. B. STUART. Still, the Union guns roared—apparently swinging the tide of battle.

It was then that a line of blue came out of the smoke toward them. But these men were Rebels, still dressed in blue uniforms, and the Union officers allowed them to get close enough to shoot down every gunner and drive off supporting marines and Zouaves. Still, the Federals rallied and retook the lost position, and the critical moment of the battle approached.

BEAUREGARD had received more reinforcements in Brigadier General KIRBY SMITH's brigade, which had arrived at Manassas by train from Winchester and had immediately marched to the battlefield. Even so, at four o'clock in the afternoon the Confederate left still seemed in danger of giving way. BEAUREGARD looked anxiously to his left. Through his glass he could see a column of marching men. But whose? A courier rode up with a report that it was Patterson's Federals believed to have followed JOHNSTON from Winchester. BEAUREGARD's heart sank. He started to give the orders to break off the action and await nightfall when he might reorganize his lines. Still, he kept his eyes on that column to his left. Suddenly he called to his messenger: "Let us wait a few minutes to confirm our suspicions before resolving to yield the field."[26] It was then that the wind caught and spread the red Confederate banner below him, and BEAUREGARD realized that Colonel JUBAL EARLY had arrived with the reserve.

All along that line rose the high shrill call of the fox hunter— the famous Rebel yell—and as these fresh troops and a battery of guns rolled around the Union right, BEAUREGARD pressed the Union front. The Federals broke. Again, they did not panic. They had merely fought themselves into exhaustion and were not in the mood for further battle. They just quit the field and recrossed Bull Run and were going down the Warrenton Turnpike toward Centreville when a Confederate battery ranged in on a bridge between them and their base. Then a wagon was upset on the bridge, blocking it—and panic did begin.

Congressmen and gentlemen and ladies who had flocked gaily to the "fun" were caught and entangled in that milling mass of fleeing soldiers. Knapsacks, guns and canteens fell among hampers and cushions abandoned along the roadway. Foot soldiers cut mules and draft horses out of their traces and rode away with the harness clinging to the heels of their mounts. Negro servants fled on their masters' chargers. Unwounded soldiers crowded into ambulances or swarmed aboard wagons which they had emptied of their contents. Animals and vehicles, all went churning and rolling through a shouting, cursing stream of frightened human beings on foot; and every time it appeared that a quiet had come upon this flood of frightened humanity, the cry arose, "The cavalry! The cavalry are coming!" and it was convulsed by a fresh tremor of terror.

McDowell's broken army did not stop until it straggled into Washington the next day under a drenching rain. And Washington itself might have fallen, if STONEWALL JACKSON had had his way. "Give me 5,000 fresh men, and I will be in Washington City tomorrow morning,"[27] he cried to President DAVIS, who had arrived on the battlefield. But DAVIS demurred, and BEAUREGARD, his own army disorganized and his judgment unsettled by false alarms, decided not to pursue.

Thus, with 2,900 Union casualties against 2,000 for the Confederates, ended the first real battle of the Civil War: the one the North mourned as Bull Run and the South celebrated as Manassas.

3

☆

The effects of Bull Run were immediate and enormous. The South's triumph impressed Europe and confirmed the Confederacy not only in its confidence but in its contempt for Northern arms. It thus tended to give the South a sense of false security.

Not so in the North, where national pride had been scorched by the humiliating retreat to Washington. Bull Run awakened the Union to the reality of a long and dreadful war, and the day after it was fought Lincoln called upon George McClellan—the hero of West Virginia—to take command of an enlarging army of long-term volunteers and regulars. Reliance on short-term militia and carefree soldiers in baggy red pants had been buried deep in the grave of American innocence.

That was the deeper significance of Bull Run: it ended the era of romantic war, or at least a romantic attitude toward war, and introduced modern warfare. War had already been democratized by the American and French revolutions. France's famous *levée en masse* commanding the hands, hearts and heads of every French man, woman and child had regimented liberty in a soldier's suit, and the huge armies of Napoleon were a result of this. But the Napoleonic Wars were fought before the Industrial Revolution made it possible for large armies to devour each other with the swift and horrible efficiency now open to both North and South. Steel and steam were to make monster killing machines of massive national armies, and the telegraph, the steamboat and the railroad were to mobilize them and get them at each other's throats more rapidly.

So now, as Northern industry cranked up and the South began its herculean struggle to build a war plant while making war, both sides drew deeper on their manpower reserves. The North voted an army of 500,000 men and the South one of 400,000. At one time or another some 900,000 men would wear Confederate gray, while 1,500,-000 put on Union blue. In the South there was as yet no single general in chief to direct this growing host. PIERRE BEAUREGARD, by his impolitic propensity for bombarding his War Department with strategic proposals, which, though sound, were also infuriating to the despotic DAVIS, gradually fell from favor.

In time, he went west to assist ALBERT SIDNEY JOHNSTON, and to be replaced in Virginia by JOE JOHNSTON.

In the North there was a new and dashing young general in chief, after the aging Winfield Scott resigned to make room for George McClellan.

George Brinton McClellan—"Little Mac" to his adoring Army of the Potomac—probably wrote the epitaph of his own military career when he said: "It probably would have been better for me personally had my promotion been delayed a year or more."[28] Perhaps it was a case of too much too soon, obtained at too little cost.

A veteran of Mexico, an American observer of the Crimean War and a successful railroad president, McClellan at 35 had brought off those West Virginia successes which catapulted him into national prominence. He had arrived in Washington hailed as the savior who would redeem all, and he wrote to his wife: "I find myself in a new and strange position here: President, cabinet, Gen. Scott and all deferring to me. By some strange operation of magic I seem to have become the power of the land."[29] There was so little humility in McClellan that he was not above snubbing Lincoln, and yet he did have organizing ability.

Camps were organized around Washington, the service of supply was made efficient, and the men were drilled daily. At intervals McClellan held huge reviews, with the newly formed brigades and divisions all drawn up with glittering bayonets and gleaming brass and waving flags—all breathlessly awaiting the arrival of "Little Mac." Suddenly he would appear, and they would cheer, as they had been trained to do; and he would ride down the line, this dapper little general on the big black horse, gazing fiercely at them as though looking each and every man straight in the eye—and they cheered and hurrahed themselves hoarse. They loved Little Mac. He had made soldiers of them and given them back their self-respect. He was the very soul and spirit of that Army of the Potomac that he was creating.

But the soul had hidden self-doubts and the spirit was one of caution. Loath to recognize this, Lincoln was at first patient. "Never mind," he told aides angered by Little Mac's hauteur, "I will hold General McClellan's horse if he will only bring us success."[30] But then December came, and McClellan was still "getting ready," and because of a minor Union debacle at Ball's Bluff the hair shirt of the radical and inquisitorial Committee on the Conduct of the War was hung around Lincoln's neck. Exasperated at last, Lincoln said, "If General McClellan does not want to use the army, I would like to borrow it."[31]

When 1862 arrived, McClellan was still marking time, and it was in the West that battle was resumed.

Command of Union forces in the West was held by Major General John Charles Frémont, the glamorous pathfinder who had been the Republican Party's first presidential candidate. Frémont took charge on the day of Bull Run, just before the South opened its western offensive.

On August 10, 1861, resurgent Confederates in Missouri met a

Union army under Nathaniel Lyon at Wilson's Creek, defeating the army and killing Lyon. The following month the Rebels seized Columbus, Kentucky, and ended that state's neutrality. Frémont's task, then, was to seize the Mississippi, stabilize Missouri and wrest Kentucky and Tennessee from the Confederate grasp. And he was not up to it.

Frémont was not a trained military commander like his capable opponent, ALBERT SIDNEY JOHNSTON. He was not adept at handling large bodies of troops and he was one of those men who dream of great, bloodless victories gained by outmaneuvering some pliant enemy who does just what the plans call for. Frémont's down-to-earth Midwesterners did not like the gold-braided European revolutionaries who crowded around the general in a babble of broken English. The Southerners considered Frémont's incompetence "a guarantee against immediate peril," but, fortunately for the North, his fondness for sending bold words ringing down the wind removed him from command.

On August 30, 1861, General Frémont proclaimed martial law in Missouri and ordered confiscation of the slaves and property of all Confederates. This was too much for Lincoln, who realized that shooting civilians would only bring Southern reprisals and that to free the slaves would erase all Union sentiment along the border. Slavery was still a very delicate issue. As Lincoln was to write to Horace Greeley a year later: "My paramount object in this struggle is to save the Union, and is not either to save or destroy slavery."[32] So Frémont was asked to modify his proclamations, and when he refused, a coldly furious Lincoln replaced him with Major General Henry Halleck.

At about the same time the Department of Ohio was created and given to Don Carlos Buell. So two Union forces now menaced General JOHNSTON in the west. One under Halleck at St. Louis was poised opposite JOHNSTON's left flank along the Mississippi, and the other under Buell headquartered at Louisville menaced JOHNSTON's right anchored far away in the Cumberlands. The right cracked first, after George Thomas, acting on Buell's orders, defeated the Confederates at Mill Springs, Kentucky, on January 19, 1862. And then in February an unknown Union general named Ulysses S. Grant began moving against the Rebel left.

When the Civil War began, General RICHARD EWELL of the Confederacy said to a friend: "There is one West Pointer, I think in Missouri, little known, and whom I hope the Northern people will not find out. I mean Sam Grant. I knew him well at the Academy and in Mexico. I should fear him more than any of their officers I have yet heard of. He is not a man of genius, but he is clear-headed, quick and daring."[33]

The Union very nearly did not "find out" about Sam Grant. Bored by the peacetime garrison life that followed the glory of Mexico City, Grant had begun to drink and had been forced out of the Army rather than face a court-martial for drunkenness. Next he failed as a farmer on "Hardscrabble Farm" in Missouri, failed at selling real estate, was a down-and-outer selling firewood in St. Louis, and drifted toward the brink of despair as a despised clerk in the family harness shop in Galena, Illinois. No one thought much of Grant except when horses were to be gentled or an armed customer to be subdued, for his was one of those natures that fade like a dying ember in periods of calm only to be blown glowing and ablaze by the winds of adversity. Grant was also the very opposite of the self-confident McClellan. After Sumter, he told a friend: "To tell you the truth, I would rather like a regiment, yet there are few men really competent to command a thousand men, and I doubt whether I am one of them."[34] Such doubts were not shared by Governor Yates of Illinois, who made Grant a colonel of volunteers at 39.

But Colonel Grant's men had their doubts when their commander arrived in camp dressed in an old civilian coat worn out at the elbows and wearing a ragged hat. "What a colonel!" they howled, but they, too, were brought to observe Grant's straight hard line of mouth, his calm glance and the amazing clarity of both his voice and his orders.

Yet Grant still had doubts as he led his regiment against a Rebel force in Missouri under a Colonel HARRIS. As he neared HARRIS's camp, he became afraid. But he kept on, and then, to his surprise, found that his enemy had fled his approach. "It occurred to me at once," Grant wrote later, "that Harris had been as much afraid of me as I had been of him. This was a view of the question I had never taken before; but it was one I never forgot afterwards."[35]

This bloodless victory earned Grant a brigadier's commission, and in the fall of 1861 he was assigned to Cairo, Illinois, at the vital junction of the Mississippi and Ohio rivers. From Cairo, Grant saw the importance of Paducah, Kentucky, which lay 25 miles eastward up the Ohio and controlled the exits of the Tennessee and Cumberland as they flowed into that river. On his own initiative, Grant seized Paducah. Now he was in position to pierce the heart of the Confederacy, for the Tennessee was navigable as far south as Alabama and the Cumberland could be ascended into east Tennessee.

The Rebels, aware of this, had built forts to guard these rivers: Fort Henry on the Tennessee and Fort Donelson on the Cumberland, about ten miles distant from each other. Grant asked General Halleck for permission to attack these forts, and it was granted.

The Army-Navy teamwork which had already distinguished Union arms during the attack upon Hatteras Inlet in North Carolina the previous summer was continued in the west under Grant and Commodore Andrew Foote. The general and the commodore liked and respected each other, and were in complete harmony when, on February 2, 1862, the Union fleet of gunboats and transports shuttling 15,000 men moved up the Tennessee. On February 5 they were in position to attack Fort Henry, and Foote invited Grant and his generals aboard his flagship *Cincinnati* to inspect the fort's defenses.

The river was full of floating mines—torpedoes, as they were called then—and Foote's sailors had brought one aboard. An armorer began disassembling it, and it suddenly began to hiss ominously. In an instant the deck was cleared, Grant and Foote racing each other for the ladder topside. Reaching the upper deck and realizing that the mine was not going to explode, the general and the commodore exchanged sheepish glances while Foote said, "General, why this haste?"

"That the Navy may not get ahead of us,"[36] Grant replied.

Next day the assault began, with Grant moving his troops ashore while Foote's armored gunboats laid down a preliminary bombardment. Fort Henry boomed back in defiance, and a ship-to-shore gun duel began. But the Rebel commander, wisely judging Fort Henry indefensible, had already sent most of his men back to Fort Donelson ten miles east, and he surrendered Henry to Foote after a token defense.

Elated, Grant notified Halleck of his victory and began moving his men overland to take Fort Donelson. Here, as he knew, he had a far harder nut than Henry to crack. ALBERT SIDNEY JOHNSTON, aware of the danger to his left flank, had sent 12,000 reinforcements to Donelson so that the fort was defended by about 15,000 men against Grant's 15,000.

Commodore Foote had gone back to Cairo. Then he took his

ironclads up the Ohio to the Cumberland, swung right and ascended that river to bombard Donelson. But Donelson was on high ground with well-mounted and well-manned guns, and Foote bored in too close. If he had kept off and slugged it out at long range, he might have battered the fort's flag down. But, like commanders everywhere, he fought this new battle with the successful tactics of the last one, and he closed to point-blank range as at Henry.

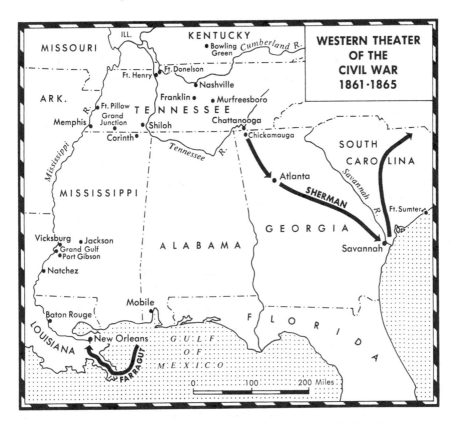

As a result, his gunners overshot, sending their shells howling harmlessly over the fort while the Confederates took deadly aim and sent theirs plunging into the ironclads. Two of Foote's six gunboats were forced out of action, the others were damaged. Foote himself was badly wounded, and as the gunboats withdrew, Grant settled down to a siege.

Though disappointed, he was not disheartened. He knew his opponents. JOHN FLOYD, the commander, had been Secretary of War under Buchanan, and gray-whiskered GIDEON PILLOW, of course, had been "Polk's spy" in Mexico. "I had known General PILLOW in Mexico," Grant said, "and judged that with any force, no matter how small, I could march up to within gunshot of any entrenchments he was given to hold. . . . I knew that FLOYD was in command, but he was no soldier, and I judged that he would yield to PILLOW's pretensions."[37]

Grant was right. With the fort pinned down in front by Union naval forces still commanding the river, he did march up to within gunshot of Donelson and surround its landward rear and flanks. On the right was a division under the politician-general John McClernand, in the center was a division under Lew Wallace of Mexico fame, and on the left was a third under salty old C. F. Smith, a ramrod regular with flowing white mustaches who had been commandant of cadets at West Point when Grant was a student there.

Inside Donelson on that bitter cold night, while the Union Army lay shivering on its arms, General FLOYD called a counsel of war and heard General PILLOW recommend breakout and escape. FLOYD, fearing capture by a Union which detested him for having weakened the Federal striking force while he was Secretary of War, agreed.

Next morning, February 15, 1862, while Grant was downstream conferring with the wounded Foote, a Confederate column sallied out of Donelson's entrenchment and struck hard at McClernand on Grant's right. The Federals were driven back, especially after Rebel cavalry under the redoubtable NATHAN BEDFORD FORREST rode down their flank. After two hours of hard fighting an escape route between McClernand and the river had been opened. A Rebel brigade under SIMON BOLIVAR BUCKNER swept into a rear-guard position to protect the getaway.

Hurrying upriver to Donelson, Grant was met by a staff officer "white with fear." He saw at once the disaster threatening his right wing in this, his first major action. He flushed slightly. Suddenly crushing the papers he held in his hand, his face cleared and he spoke quietly to McClernand and Wallace. "Gentlemen, the position on the right must be retaken."[38] Then he rode to his left toward Smith, shouting to his bewildered soldiers: "Fill your cartridge-boxes, quick, and get into line! The enemy is trying to escape; he must not be permitted to do so."[39]

While Wallace's men rushed to help McClernand's division swing the escape door shut, Grant ordered Smith to attack. Smith put his regiments in line and rode ahead of them, crying, "Damn you, gentlemen, I see skulkers! I'll have none here. Come on, you volunteers, come on! This is your chance. You volunteered to be killed for love of country, and now you can be. You damned volunteers—I'm only a soldier and I don't want to be killed, but you came to be killed and now you can be!"[40]

Taunting them, shaming them into battle, riding forward with his hat on his sword point, Smith led his men into the tangle of trees felled by the Confederates—and at this point General FLOYD faltered. Seeing the Union troops shutting his escape route, unsettled by Smith's attack, and aware that Grant had been reinforced to the strength of 25,000 men, he ordered his men back into the Donelson position. That night, another ordeal of cold for the Union soldiers, FLOYD and PILLOW made their own escape. So did NATHAN BEDFORD FORREST, but this hard and hardy guerrilla genius took his troopers with him, leading them to safety through an icy, waist-deep backwater. Thereafter FORREST and his cavalry raiders taught Grant many a lesson in the perils of an exposed line of communications.

A little past midnight, Grant, in a small cabin he shared with General Smith, received a note from General BUCKNER asking surrender terms. "What answer shall I send to this, General Smith?" he asked his old instructor, and Smith barked, "No terms to the damned Rebels!"[41] Grant chuckled and sat down to write: "No terms except an unconditional and immediate surrender can be accepted. I propose to move immediately upon your works."[42]

Protesting against Grant's "ungenerous and unchivalrous terms," BUCKNER next morning surrendered the fort and 11,500 men with all their equipment.

One of the most damaging blows of the war had been struck against the Confederacy. The Rebel front in the West had been burst asunder, the road to Vicksburg and control of the Mississippi opened, and the defense of New Orleans weakened by drawing Confederate forces north.

A thrill of hope ran through a Union accustomed to defeat and retreat. U. S. Grant became a national hero, and because "unconditional surrender" fitted his initials, he received that nickname. The phrase had a hard edge to it, and it cut deep into the mind of Abraham Lincoln.

Grant's fame was wormwood to Henry Halleck. An ambitious, bookish soldier known irreverently as "Old Brains," and also well described as "a large emptiness surrounded by an education,"[43] Halleck seems not to have trusted Grant from the start; and because he, Halleck, had already failed to wangle over-all command in the West, he was now at pains to remove a rival for that honor from the field. St. Louis was rife with rumors that Grant was drinking heavily. Halleck himself told McClellan that "General Grant had resumed his former bad habits,"[44] and was disobeying orders. After Halleck removed Grant from his command, however, President Lincoln entered the controversy by ordering Halleck to make specific charges. Unable to do so, Halleck quickly smoothed the matter over and returned Grant's army to him with the exhortation to "lead it on to new victories."[45]

Grant's next move was against JOHNSTON's army in Corinth, Mississippi. Sending his advance guard to Pittsburg Landing on the Tennessee 20 miles north of Corinth, Grant set up his own head-quarters in Savannah about ten miles farther north. He was waiting for Buell to join him, after which they would move down to Corinth to crush JOHNSTON.

The Confederate commander, however, was not sitting still for his destruction. BEAUREGARD had convinced him that Rebel fortunes might be retrieved by a signal victory. Grant was the target because he was well forward of his base, was unsupported and had divided his forces. On April 3 JOHNSTON put his 40,000-man army on the road for Pittsburg Landing.

It was a disorganized movement, made with the carefree, whooping, straggling indiscipline typical of a Rebel army on the march. It took so long that the day of battle had to be postponed from April 4 to the 5th and then the 6th—and BEAUREGARD, who had proposed the attack, now wanted to call it off on the ground that the enemy could not help but be forewarned. JOHNSTON disagreed, and said: "I would fight them if they were a million."[46]

They were actually about 33,000, and their defenses were even sloppier than the Confederate approach had been. Between Shiloh Church and Pittsburg Landing two miles to the northeast Grant had stationed five divisions. A sixth under Lew Wallace was at Crump's Landing five miles north.

Most of the regiments in the Shiloh-Pittsburg force were green and knew little about scouting and outpost duty. As a result, JOHNSTON's noisy army was able to bivouac two miles to their front without being detected. Worse, neither William Tecumseh Sherman at Shiloh nor Grant himself back at Savannah anticipated a Rebel attack. Both were overconfident, and Grant wrote to Halleck on the night of April 5: "I have scarcely the faintest idea of an attack (general one) being made upon us, but will be prepared should such a thing take place."[47]

April 6, 1862, was a Sunday, but there were no services in Shiloh Church, standing empty and silent on a hillside near the banks of the Tennessee. Around its bleak log walls were serried the white tents of the Union Army, neat, in a dreadfully prophetic way, as gravestones in a cemetery. Similar encampments lay to the rear of Shiloh or stretched eastward to the river. In all of them men in blue were cooking breakfast or cleaning equipment for Sunday morning inspection. Birds sang, for it was a bright clear day with the sun glistening on grass wet with the previous night's rain.

Near Shiloh, a suddenly anxious Sherman had sent patrols probing to his front. They blundered into Confederate pickets, exchanged shots, and came running back to announce an enemy attack. At once, Sherman formed his regiments in front of the tents, with his guns on higher ground. Far to his left, however, the Union men thought the gunfire was from green troops shooting at shadows or firing off muskets to see if the rain had dampened their powder. But then came the hollow baying of artillery, and on the hillsides at Shiloh the men in blue felt the enemy's shells crash among them and saw the Confederates approaching in two long lines of butternut.

JOHNSTON had not achieved complete surprise, as he had hoped, but the momentum was his. His troops smashed into Sherman's left-flank units around Shiloh Church and broke them. Whole regiments fled the field. One colonel called, "Fall back and save yourselves,"[48] before dashing to the rear. Many of these men came back to fight, as their cowardly officers did not, but at the first impact they gave way so completely that Sherman was forced to call upon McClernand to plug his collapsing left.

Ten miles downstream, Grant at breakfast heard the gunfire. Getting painfully to his feet (his horse had fallen on him two days ago), he hobbled down to the river and boarded a steamboat. Before leaving Savannah, he had directed one of Buell's divisions to move to a point opposite Pittsburg Landing, and now, reaching Crump's

Landing, he paused to notify Lew Wallace to stand by for battle. Then he hastened upriver, reaching the battlefield at 8:30 A.M., two hours after the fighting began.

By then the fury of the Confederate assault had driven the Union soldiers back from their camps. Jubilant Rebels pursued them, running into the tent streets and stopping there to loot and eat. In that interval, the Union divisions reorganized. In the center of the line a division under Benjamin Prentiss fell back through a peach orchard to a sunken road about two feet deep, taking position in this ready-made trench.

In the Union rear, however, all was chaos. The roads running back to the river landing were a tangle of terrified soldiers and wagons, guns, horses and ambulances. Into this backwash of near-disaster rode U. S. Grant moments after he reached the landing, and he set out at once to form a straggler line and return his demoralized remnants to battle, organizing a line of guns on high ground to protect the landing— where he expected to receive reinforcements—and sending orders to Lew Wallace and Buell's troops to hurry to the rescue.

Meanwhile the lines of gray and butternut flowed into those of blue again. Cannon boomed, canister spewed their shrieking shot, bullets whizzed or made that ugly smacking sound of lead striking flesh, while the screams of stricken horses and men mingled with the high fierce cry of the Rebel yell or the hurrahing of the Northerners. Shiloh was one of the fiercest battles in the war, and it was also battle at its most uncontrolled. Both sides green as well as gallant, the two armies struggled back and forth like two great "fighting swarms." Control was all but lost at the regimental level. Colonels fought on foot like privates and privates led companies. Units were cut off and captured only to be freed after their captors blundered into captivity. Only the battle flags fluttering in and out of drifting clouds of dirty white smoke gave the commanders any sense of unity.

Gradually, however, the Confederates drove the Federals back again—except for Prentiss at the sunken road. Here the Union troops held an excellent position and had been ordered to hold at all costs. Grant needed time to straighten out his battle line, to receive reinforcements, and Prentiss and his men gave it to him. The Rebels, instead of pinning down and by-passing the sunken road—or "Hornet's Nest," as they called it—were diverted by it. Some 60 guns collected in the peach orchard thundered at the Hornet's Nest, and 12 separate attacks—one led by JOHNSTON himself—were hurled against it. But

Prentiss fought on, "as cool as if expecting victory,"[49] and it was not until 5:30 P.M. that he surrendered.

By then JOHNSTON had died of wounds, to be replaced by BEAUREGARD, and the Rebels had missed the opportunity for victory. At one point they had turned Grant's left and had Pittsburg Landing within their grasp. Seizing this, they could have prevented reinforcements from reaching Grant and might have pressed the Union Army back against two creeks. But BEAUREGARD had no reserve available and some of his units were out of ammunition. Before nightfall, a gallant Rebel bayonet charge against the landing was repulsed, and that was the end of battle.

As night closed in, Lew Wallace finally arrived (he had taken the wrong road), and Buell's advance guard reached the landing. Niether force was in time to change the course of battle, but they would be of use when it was resumed in the morning.

That night the rain fell in torrents, aggravating the agony of the wounded and magnifying the ordeal of stretcher bearers and surgeons. General Grant made his headquarters under a tree a few hundred yards from the river. But the rain, the throbbing of his swollen ankle and the booming of the gunboats *Tyler* and *Lexington* firing down the length of the Confederate line made it impossible to sleep. So the general moved back to the shelter of a log house which had been taken as a hospital. Here, the cries of the wounded and of men undergoing amputation seemed to Grant "more unendurable than encountering the enemy's fire,"[50] and he returned to his tree in the rain.

In the morning, with General Buell and two more divisions arrived on the field, the Union Army attacked. BEAUREGARD was surprised. He had already informed Richmond of a great victory and had passed the night in Sherman's captured tent. But here were the Federals rolling toward Shiloh, and the second day of battle around that historic little meetinghouse was nearly as bloody as the first.

By midafternoon the tide turned against the Confederates. BEAUREGARD's army was exhausted and outnumbered. "General," an aide asked BEAUREGARD, "do you not think our troops are very much in the condition of a lump of sugar thoroughly soaked with water, but yet preserving its original shape, though ready to dissolve?"[51] BEAUREGARD agreed, and began his retreat to Corinth.

Grant let him go. His own army was fought out, and as Sherman later said: ". . . we had quite enough of their society for two whole days, and were only too glad to be rid of them on any terms."[52]

At Shiloh were fought two of the bloodiest days in Civil War history. Union losses were 13,700, Confederate 10,700. Tactically, Shiloh was a standoff; strategically it was a Union victory: the Rebels had been forced to withdraw with a shattered army and the way was clear for a larger Union army to pursue.

Henry Halleck led that "pursuit." Having treated Grant shabbily after Donelson, he did the same after Shiloh, taking personal command at Pittsburg Landing and advancing on Corinth with such pick-and-shovel caution that his troops swore he was trying to get there by burrowing. On May 30 Halleck arrived in Corinth to find the town evacuated. He had taken 31 days to march 20 miles!

Grant, meanwhile, found himself once more under fire. It was said that he had been drunk at Shiloh and he was described as a heartless butcher who sacrificed men to redeem his own errors. One high-placed Republican came to Lincoln to obtain Grant's dismissal. He spoke at length on the general's faults. After he had finished, Lincoln sank into prolonged silence. Suddenly he looked up, and cried: "I can't spare this man—he fights!"[53]

4

☆

In the summer of August, 1861, a Swedish inventor named John Ericsson wrote to President Lincoln offering to design and build an ironclad warship capable of wrecking the Rebel fleet in Norfolk.

In time, Ericsson's offer was accepted, although some naval officers scoffed at his plan for a ship with but two guns mounted in a revolving turret and a water line so low that it seemed any passing wave might sink her. One officer said that to worship Ericsson's model of his *Monitor* could not possibly be idolatry "because it was in the image of nothing in the heaven above or in the earth beneath or in the waters under the earth."[54] Lincoln himself held the model in his hand and said: "All I have to say is what the girl said when she put her foot into the stocking. It strikes me there's something in it."[55]

Before Ericsson went to work on the *Monitor,* however, the Confederate Navy had raised the sunken 40-gun U.S. frigate *Merrimac,* covered her with 4-inch iron plates and fitted her prow with a formidable cast-iron ram. It did not seem that Ericsson's bizarre little toy could possibly oppose this big ironclad, and even as a tugboat began towing *Monitor* south from New York in March of 1862, *Merrimac* moved out of Norfolk against the wooden Union warships *Congress* and *Cumberland,* blasting and battering them into floating wrecks. *Minnesota,* also wooden, was forced aground. Next day she too would be smashed and the Rebel ironclad would be free to move on Washington.

Terrified Federal authorities nearly panicked, and no one was more frightened than Secretary of War Edward Stanton. Now everyone in authority lamented the time and money wasted in the crack-brained *Monitor* experiment. Moreover, they asked, where *is* the *Monitor?*

She was limping south, storm-tossed. One fierce blow had sent black waves breaking over her low decks. Water tumbled down her blowers to swamp the engines, and Lieutenant John Worden and his crew hurriedly rigged hand pumps. Then a second storm threatened to part her towline. But at last *Monitor* made Hampton Roads and came to the side of stranded *Minnesota.* At dawn of March 9, 1862, *Merrimac* came out to finish *Minnesota,* and tiny *Monitor* sailed straight toward her.

Federal troops at Newport News cheered when the little raftlike Union vessel came at the big roof-shaped Confederate. Rebel sailors in the harbor laughed in astonishment at this upstart "cheesebox on a raft" this "tin can on a shingle," this David challenging Goliath two guns to ten. Lieutenant CATESBY JONES, acting captain of *Merrimac,* ordered broadside after broadside hurled at the little Yankee —but most of the Rebel shot screamed harmlessly over her low silhouette, or rattled off her turret like pebbles.

Inside that turret the Union sailors heard a monster metallic clanging, and some were stunned by the impact of the enemy shells. But they kept on firing their brace of 11-inchers. Each time the guns were withdrawn into the turret for recharging, metal stoppers were swung into place to seal the gun ports. Each time the turret began to revolve, the guns were fired "on the fly" for it was not possible to stop or reverse the turret once started.

Although the battle began at a mile range, the two ironclads gradually closed the distance until they were 100 yards apart, sometimes scraping up against each other. Once the *Merrimac* tried to ram. But her iron beak had been twisted off the day before, and she struck only a glancing blow which started a leak in her own armor. Next the audacious little *Monitor* tried to ram *Merrimac!* But she missed.

After four hours of inconclusive thundering, the two ships drew away. History's first contest between ironclad battleships had ended in a draw, although both sides claimed a victory. In a sense, the Union cause had been better served, for the menace of the *Merrimac* had been ended for good and the Federal Navy now had the time in which to build a fleet of ironclads.

Eventually the Confederacy was forced to blow up *Merrimac,* and with her passing the South's chief threat to Union naval supremacy came to an end. One day after Shiloh, Island Number 10 in the Mississippi River was surrendered to Union gunboats and General John Pope, and the Rebels' river defense was forced back on Memphis. After Union gunboats and rams wrecked a makeshift Confederate fleet off Memphis, the defense fell back farther to Vicksburg.

And then the very mouth of the Mississippi fell into Union hands when Admiral Farragut made a nighttime assault on the forts guarding New Orleans and compelled the city to surrender. New Orleans, the great port that was to send out cotton and take in guns, was in Federal hands by the end of April.

Throughout that black-bordered spring of 1862, the South felt the North's amphibious whip strip her of positions on the Atlantic coast. For a time, much was hoped from the Confederate raider *Alabama* which put to sea from Liverpool, England, on July 29, 1862. *Alabama* was a veritable sea scourge, but one ship could not win a war, and even this gallant vessel went to her doom under the guns of the *Kearsage* two years later. And when the Confederates attempted to have other ships built in France and huge rams constructed in Scotland, Yankee diplomacy ruined both ventures.

By the summer of 1862, then, it was plain that the Union held a clear-cut naval superiority. Even with her enormous coastline, the South had never had the sense of sail possessed by the Middle and New England states. She had always let the British or the Yankees carry her cotton over the seas. She had never understood sea power, and now, with the Union blockade drawing the economic noose ever tighter around her throat, with her very life depending upon control of the Mississippi, she was beginning to pay a fearful price for that mistake.

5

☆

It had not been a pleasant winter for George McClellan. True, there had been the pleasure of seeing the entire Union Army expand and improve under his own hand. But he had also been harried by a revival of the cry, "On to Richmond!" as well as by Radical Republicans who did not scruple to suggest that Little Mac deliberately dragged his feet to serve the South.

More by accident than design (at least at this time), McClellan had become identified with those Northern Democrats who wanted the war won only to restore the Union. But among Republicans there was a growing conviction that the secession could only be crushed by stamping out slavery. To the Democrats, this was a harsh position; to the Republicans anything less than this was soft. Thus the Republicans distrusted the Democrats, if not as outright traitors at least as fainthearted patriots or Southern sympathizers, and each new delay on the part of McClellan was looked upon as another proof of doubtful loyalty. Thus, also, the Republican government was not in harmony with its Democratic general in chief.

On March 11, in fact, McClellan was relieved of over-all command, ostensibly so that he would have more freedom for action in the field. The real reason was McClellan's refusal to move until he was ready, capped by his failure to move against JOE JOHNSTON's army while it was concentrated around the old Bull Run battlefield. On March 9 the wily JOHNSTON pulled his 40,000-man force back behind the Rappahannock River. Union soldiers entering his abandoned trenches and log-hut encampments found evidence that McClellan's army had been more than twice as big as JOHNSTON's, and that cautious Little

Mac had been bluffed by dozens of dummy wooden cannon—"Quaker guns," as they were called. Lincoln, who had taken to complaining, "He has got the slows,"[56] was now exasperated. Unfortunately, no new general in chief was appointed for four months, and the military reins remained firmly in the hands of the President.

One result of this was a clumsy command setup. Between them two political generals, Nathaniel Banks and John Charles Frémont, had about 28,000 troops in the Shenandoah Valley and West Virginia. Both men were coequal to McClellan and any coordination of their movements had to come from Washington. This was to work to McClellan's disadvantage, as was the fact that Lincoln and Secretary of War Stanton, being politicians first and military men second, were both unduly concerned with the defense of Washington. Stanton, a fierce man outwardly who was constantly threatening generals with dismissal, was inwardly timid. The slightest Confederate gesture toward Washington brought him close to panic.

Thus STONEWALL JACKSON was able to do McClellan a great disservice when he tangled with a Union force under James Shields at Kernstown in the Shenandoah Valley. JACKSON was defeated, but his presence in the valley so upset Lincoln and Stanton that when McClellan finally did begin moving south, they withheld 35,000 troops under Irwin McDowell to stand guard in upper Virginia.

McClellan, disappointed in his hopes to drive overland against the Confederate capital, had decided to steam down to Fortress Monroe on the tip of the York Peninsula. Landing not far from the site of Washington's victory at Yorktown, he would march quickly up the peninsula between the York and the James rivers and so take Richmond from the side door. The Union Navy, meanwhile, would guard his flanks.

It was a pretty plan, except that the *Merrimac* still barred the James, and Rebel batteries inside the York were too strong to pass. The Navy could offer McClellan only token support, and it could not get around Yorktown, the anchor for a line of fortifications stretching across the peninsula to the James. McClellan would have to breach this line, and on April 4, 1862, he ordered an advance. Next day, he changed his mind.

There were only 15,000 men in the Rebel line, opposing 53,000 under McClellan, but they were commanded by that consummate actor, JOHN BANKHEAD MAGRUDER. McClellan might well have remembered "PRINCE JOHN's" penchant for theatricals, and might have regarded the constant marching and countermarching of the Rebel Army as a stage production. Instead, he was deceived into thinking MAGRUDER led a large force, and he at once settled down to siege warfare. No less than 150 huge mortars, among other big guns, were mounted in the Union lines opposite MAGRUDER; and no less than a solid month was lost, during which JOHNSTON gathered his forces and placed them between Richmond and the Army of the Potomac. In joyous amazement, JOHNSTON told LEE, "No one but McClellan could have hesitated to attack."[57] On May 4, when Little Mac finally did give the order to bombard the line he considered "one of the most extensive known to modern times,"[58] his shells fell into empty trenches. JOHNSTON had waited until the last moment, and then, on the preceding night, had quietly fallen back on Richmond.

McClellan now ordered a pursuit, while preparing an amphibious force to sail up the York and cut off JOHNSTON's retreat. But he was too slow in getting his enveloping movement water-borne, and JOHNSTON, anticipating him, defeated his forces when they attempted to land at West Point. On land, the pursuing Federals ran into a Rebel rear guard under JAMES LONGSTREET near Williamsburg. LONGSTREET, wounded 15 years before while carrying the colors at the Molino del Rey, was at once attacked by a division led by Joseph Hooker, who had earned his "Fighting Joe" nickname in Mexico. LONGSTREET hurled Hooker back, and then, counterpuncher that he was, attacked himself—and that was when a third hero of the Mexican War came galloping up the muddy road.

Fiery Phil Kearny had fought for the French in Africa and Italy since he lost his left arm at the San Antonio Gate. Fierce as ever, sword in hand and reins in his teeth, he led his division to Hooker's rescue—and found the road blocked by wagons mired in the mud. "Tip those wagons out of my way!"[59] he roared, and when an officer tried to explain that the wagons were stuck, he bellowed: "Move them, I say—or I'll put the torch to them!"[60] The wagons were dragged aside, and Kearny's men sloshed forward to see their general go dashing across the Confederate line like a flame in the saddle and deliberately draw the fire that gave away the enemy positions. At that juncture, the Yankee-hating D. H. HILL—who had helped storm the heights of Chapultepec—brought his division to LONGSTREET's side. The battle raged on inconclusively, until Winfield Scott Hancock

—who had been with HILL at Chapultepec—took his Union division wide to the right and found an opening on LONGSTREET's flank and rear. Under cover of darkness, the Confederates withdrew.

Tactically, the battle had been a Confederate victory, for LONGSTREET had held off the Federals long enough to cover the withdrawal of JOHNSTON's precious supply trains. Measured by Civil War standards, however, Williamsburg had not been a major battle. Yet in miniature it possessed all those elements which were to be characteristic of the dreadful, three-year struggle between the Army of the Potomac and the force that LEE named the Army of Northern Virginia. Bull Run had shown what the war was not to be like, Williamsburg showed what it would be. At Williamsburg men who had fought together in Mexico as lieutenants and captains now fought each other as generals, and they commanded troops whose fighting qualities probably have never been surpassed. Because both sides now realized that the enemy was in earnest, because both had a supply of trained commanders who wanted passionately to win and a reservoir of men who wanted fiercely to kill, the battles in the East —like those already fought in the West—were to be to the finish. Very few commanders were going to be bluffed or maneuvered off the field. Most of them were going to stay until beaten. And that, of course, meant a blood bath of three years' duration.

Williamsburg, a delaying action, was therefore only a smaller blood bath. But the Federals occupying the field that night were nevertheless horrified by the black and bloated dead, as well as by the cries of the wounded and the sound of surgeons sawing off limbs whose bones had been shattered beyond repair by the huge bullets of .58 caliber and more fired by both sides. There was also the customary horror of battlefield theft. In the morning the pockets of friend and foe alike had been turned inside out, and even the buttons cut from their uniforms. Such ghouls and scavengers have marched with every army since Agamemnon's, and the men of the Army of the Potomac were only being introduced to another of the ancient horrors of war when they heard a swag-stuffed Union soldier simper: "I wish there was a battle every week."[61]

McClellan now had another chance. He had broken through the defenses of Yorktown and forced the evacuation of Norfolk, which opened the James River to him. With Norfolk gone, *Merrimac* had no home. The big ironclad's draught was too deep for her to flee up the James, and so, at the end of an eventful two-month career, she had to be blown up. But then the Union Navy was dealt one of its rare reverses. Attempting to reduce the Rebel forts at Drewry's Bluff seven miles out of Richmond, its ships were driven off. For nearly three years the river approach to Richmond was to remain in Rebel hands, and McClellan was thus denied that convenient avenue to the capital.

Yet McClellan had 105,000 men against JOHNSTON's 60,000, and he still did not move until another month elapsed. Depending on intelligence reports supplied by the woefully inept private detective, Allan Pinkerton, he believed that JOHNSTON's strength was double his own. Perhaps he unconsciously wanted to believe Pinkerton. He certainly accepted the detective's incredible calculations without a murmur of surprise, and he failed to question methods that may have been fine for catching bank robbers but which were dreadful for counting enemy heads. Throughout the Civil War there was never a time when any single army in the field numbered as many as 150,000 men; in fact, the peak strength of the entire Confederate Army, reached in June, 1863, was only 261,000 men. Yet in May of 1862 McClellan believed or preferred to believe that JOHNSTON alone commanded from 250,000 to 300,000 soldiers.

That was the tragedy of McClellan. Personally, of course, he was brave. But if he could organize and train a great army, even get it to the battlefield, he would not risk it. Defeat was worse than death to him. Vain rather than proud, with his Napoleonic prose and imperial mustache, he resembled the great Corsican in mere physical size only. He was truly a little man on a big horse. Night after night in letters dramatically dated "Midnight" or "1 A.M.," he writes to tell his young wife how firm he is, how resolved, how inexorable—and then some self-pitying bleat escapes him: ". . . the necessity for delay has not been my fault. I have a set of men to deal with unscrupulous and false."[62] He is like a man who lifts one hand to strike and with the other points out the reasons why he cannot.

Yet McClellan did have some excuses. First, the weather was wretched, making movement difficult and his men miserable. Second, he was thwarted in his desire to have McDowell's force of 40,000 sent south to join him in front of Richmond. In this the villain was again General STONEWALL JACKSON.

TOM JACKSON had thought of living in Mexico for a while, but then, deciding that "Spanish was meant for lovers,"[63] he came home, resigned from the army, and began teaching at Virginia Military Institute. His students thought him a dullard who taught from the book and they called him "Tom Fool." But JACKSON was strange rather than foolish, a silent awkward figure forever sucking a lemon, riding his shambling sorrel horse with his big clumsy feet turned out in the stirrups, only the lemon and his brown beard visible beneath a mangy forage cap pulled down so that the broken visor concealed the cold blue eyes of the killer.

During battle, those icy eyes gleamed with an intense light, the fire of the burning bush, for STONEWALL JACKSON was a warrior out of the Old Testament. He was a pious soldier who could spend hours on his knees praying to the God of Battles, or write a clergyman in lengthy explanation of why he fought on the Sabbath. He was also brutal, as successful soldiers must be, and when an officer protested that his men would be annihilated if they obeyed an order of JACKSON's, STONEWALL replied: "General, I always endeavour to take care of my wounded and to bury my dead. You have heard my order—obey it!"[64] In his soft, gentle voice, Jackson could call a colonel a "wicked fellow" for swearing at his men, or murmur to an officer who regretted having to kill brave Federals: "No, shoot them all, I do not wish them to be brave."[65] Such a man, fierce, swift and relentless, was just the commander to carry out ROBERT E. LEE's plan to prevent McDowell from joining McClellan.

LEE, now a full general, was military adviser to President DAVIS. LEE knew that a juncture of the Union armies in front of Richmond could prove fatal to the Confederacy. So he decided to play on Northern fears for the safety of Washington by sending STONEWALL JACKSON into the Shenandoah Valley to make a bloody diversion.

Moving with a celerity which was to make his troops famous as "JACKSON's foot cavalry," STONEWALL led a small force west to the Alleghenies, where he jumped the unsuspecting Frémont. Then, turning his back, reinforced to a total of 15,000 men, he swept toward the lower valley and practically annihilated Banks's flank guard at Front Royal, ripped up his rear guard at Winchester, and drove the Union general clear back to the northern side of the Potomac.

Once again, Washington was in a state of near-panic. It was rumored that JACKSON was going to invade the North. Frantic telegrams went out alerting Northern governors to the danger, and McDowell, Frémont and Banks were ordered to converge on JACKSON.

By then STONEWALL was heading home, his mission accomplished.

He had lowered Northern morale and had moved Lincoln to cancel McDowell's orders to join McClellan. Instead, that vital reinforcement went into the valley.

As a second result of JACKSON's famous Valley Campaign, McClellan was caught astride the flooding Chickahominy River.

Little Mac had sent one part of his army south of the Chickahominy to hold a bridgehead, while keeping the larger part on the north bank to protect his base. After McDowell arrived, he would move the entire army across the river. That was all right. But then McDowell was diverted to the valley, and McClellan still clung to this vulnerable position. So General JOHNSTON decided to try to wipe out the small Union force south of the river before the larger force north of it could come to the rescue.

Heavy spring rains worked to JOHNSTON's advantage. They turned the Chickahominy into a raging torrent that threatened to sweep away the bridges built by McClellan's engineers. Confederate staff work, however, redounded to JOHNSTON's disadvantage. LONGSTREET, in charge of the main attack, took the wrong road and fed in his units piecemeal.

The battle began on May 31, 1862, and ended the next day. It was fought over and around a railroad station known as Fair Oaks and a farm called Seven Pines, and bears both those names. In the end, the Rebels got so thoroughly in each other's way that they were too late to stop Union reinforcements from rushing over bridges which did hold, despite the flood. Fair Oaks–Seven Pines was as bloody as it was confused and inconclusive: some 5,700 Rebels dead or wounded, some 4,400 Union casualties. One of these Confederate casualties was the oft-wounded JOE JOHNSTON himself. And that was a great calamity for the North, because command of the Army of Northern Virginia then passed to ROBERT E. LEE.

"Army of Northern Virginia, fabulous army," sang Stephen Vincent Benét, and now it was LEE who led these gaunt and dauntless Rebels, this "army of planters' sons and rusty poor-whites";[66] it was ROBERT EDWARD LEE, the flower of Southern chivalry and the last White Knight of the battlefield. In the words of Winfield Scott he was the hero of the Mexican War and "the greatest military genius in America";[67] in the eyes of his brother officers he had been "the handsomest man in the Army";[68] in the affections of his men he was

"Marse Robert"—but when he rode among them on his great gray stallion Traveler, they did not whoop and cheer but rather stood in awe or removed their slouch hats while gazing reverently at this tall, white-bearded patriarch of a soldier. "I've heard of God," one Confederate lady said, "but I've *seen* General LEE." In LEE's own eyes he was perhaps the earthly representative of George Washington: LEE's father, Light-Horse Harry Lee, had been one of Washington's intimates, and LEE's wife, Mary Randolph Custis, was the great-granddaughter of Washington's wife. Washington had been a Virginian, and LEE was first and foremost a Virginian. Hating slavery, he had drawn his sword not to defend that detestable institution but in the service of the beloved soil that made him.

LEE had seen his duty, and to LEE duty was paramount—above all duty to the will of God. Not since the Middle Ages, when reference to God was often as perfunctory as a genuflection, have the orders of a chief been so full of supplication to the will of God. They are like a litany: God gives victory or defeat, and if it is success He is to be praised, and if failure the Army of Northern Virginia is exhorted to search its soul to see where it has sinned. In this, there are a fatalism and submission that are perhaps not good for a commander of armies.

There were also in LEE a strange gentleness and a compassion alien to the field of combat. He was more at ease in the company of women, delighting especially in the gentleness of young girls, and those women whom he scrupulously honored felt toward him a reticence as cool and proper as an outstretched hand. "LEE was a great soldier and a good man," Mary Chesnut wrote, "but I never wanted to put my arms around his neck, as I used to want to do to JOE JOHNSTON."[69] If STONEWALL JACKSON was the avenging sword of the Old Testament, then ROBERT E. LEE was the warrior of the New.

JACKSON might mutter, "No quarter!"—as he did—but LEE could take the hand of a wounded but defiant Union soldier, look lovingly into his eyes and say, "My son, I hope you will soon be well."[70] Some of JACKSON's hardness, however, might have made LEE an even greater commander. In his very real humility, he deferred almost without deviation to JEFFERSON DAVIS. In his gentleness, he could not be severe, and therefore found it difficult to dismiss incompetent officers or to settle disputes over authority or to discipline those magnificent scarecrows whom he loved to the depths of his being. And in his simplicity, in his very desire to live no better than any private soldier, he was sometimes unapproachable. Too many Confederates thought of ROBERT E. LEE as a saint, and because human beings, prone to mistake goodness for saintliness, are also afraid of sanctity, they kept away from him.

Such were the virtues that sometimes tended to become defects when mounted in the saddle of the commander in chief, and they are detailed here only because the personality of ROBERT E. LEE seems to be buried beneath an avalanche of bronze statues, LEE memorial days and the uncritical adulation of worshipful biographers. LEE the man is frozen inside a marble myth. Great soldier that he was, he was not matchless; and he might have been even greater had his idealism been tempered with an understanding of the holes in human nature. Nevertheless, his nobility of character made him the soul of his army. No commander ever possessed a greater capacity for inspiring troops, for electrifying them by his very presence on the field of battle. Nor was any commander more masterful in defense, in devising fortification—or more audacious in attack.

McClellan, still convinced that he was outnumbered, made no offensive moves after Fair Oaks. He seems to have been preparing to take Richmond by siege operations. But LEE was busy, building fortifications with that energy and skill that caused his men to call him the "King of Spades," and drawing up a plan to strike McClellan.

First he needed to know McClellan's exact position, and for this information he called upon JEB STUART. A man of great physical strength and presence whose West Point nickname of "Beauty" was in joking reference to his homely face and big bold nose, JEB STUART was the Southern cavalier par excellence. For all his homeliness and huge brown beard curling down below his breastbone he was the darling of the Southern ladies, whose delight it was to garland his bridle with roses or to make some contribution to a costume that made the hussar getup of the flamboyant Federal cavalryman, George Custer, seem funereal garb indeed. Beneath a broad gray hat looped with a gold star and adorned with a plume, STUART wore a short gray jacket bright with buttons and braid. A gray cavalry cape trailed from his shoulder, around his waist was an ornate and tasseled yellow sash from which a light French saber hung, great leather gauntlets reached almost to his elbows, on his legs were enormous jack boots with gold spurs, while his saddle held a pistol and a bright red blanket. When

STUART gave commands, it was in a voice that carried like a bugle call, and he was in good voice, singing "Kathleen Mavourneen," as he led some 1,200 horsemen in a spectacular ride around McClellan's entire army. Upon his return from this 150-mile circuit he brought the information LEE required, although he also developed a taste for the sensational which was to prove harmful in the future.

Nevertheless, LEE now knew that McClellan had moved most of his army south of the Chickahominy but had left one corps under Fitz-John Porter on the north bank at Mechanicsville. LEE decided to have 25,000 men under the actor JOHN MAGRUDER hold down McClellan's main body of 60,000, while hurling 65,000 men against Porter's 30,000. To do this he ordered JACKSON to march down from the valley and hit Porter's right flank. As he did, A. P. HILL would cross the river at Mechanicsville to clear the town. After this, LONGSTREET and D. H. HILL, across the river above the town, were to come in behind JACKSON and A. P. HILL in support. Together, the four commanders would roll Porter down the river bank before McClellan could come to his rescue.

It was a fine plan, but as had happened to JOHNSTON, it went awry. JACKSON was slow in arriving and did not get his men into action. A. P. HILL, despairing of JACKSON's arrival, went rushing across the river without orders and charged smack into the formidable Union line. The result was miniature disaster. The Battle of Mechanicsville ended in 1,500 Confederate casualties against 250 for the Union.

LEE was annoyed but not dismayed. MAGRUDER had succeeded in deceiving McClellan again, and the bulk of the Rebel Army was north of the river in position to crush Porter. Next day, June 27, 1862, at Gaines's Mill, the attack was renewed. Again and again the Confederates charged the Union line, only to be repulsed each time. Artillery thundered throughout the day, and Union guns south of the Chickahominy reversed aim to hurl shells into the onrushing Rebels. Rifle fire was so thick that the brush and saplings were cut down as though scythed.

Just before sunset there was a lull. Weary Union soldiers thought the battle had ended in a Rebel defeat. But LEE, across the river, had assembled every available man for a general assault. Behind a sudden crash of artillery, screeching the Rebel yell, they came running forward—and this time the Federals broke and ran.

Gaines's Mill was a victory for LEE, but it had cost another 8,750 casualties against 4,000 for the Union. Yet, if Porter had not been crushed, as expected, then McClellan had been cowed. South of the river that night, where he had held his main body inactive all day, McClellan ordered a retreat to the James River.

Once again MAGRUDER had fooled him with one of his typical productions—marching men in full view, sending out patrols and skirmishers, firing off cannon—but he had not beguiled Hooker or Kearny, who knew PRINCE JOHN too well. These two division commanders had the audacity to burst into McClellan's headquarters, and when Little Mac curtly demanded the reason for such behavior, Kearny burst out: "The enemy lines around Richmond are thin. They can and must be broken. An order to retreat is wrong! Wrong, sir! I ask permission to attack MAGRUDER at once."

"Denied," McClellan snapped, and after Kearny renewed his arguments, he said: "Nothing has changed, General. The retreat will be made on schedule." With that, according to General Hiram Berry, who was present: "Phil unloosed a broadside. He pitched into McClelland with language so strong that all who heard it expected he would be placed under arrest until a general court-martial could be held."[71]

McClellan, however, merely allowed Kearny to calm down, and let him go without a word. That night, the supply trains of the Army of the Potomac began the retreat.

One of ROBERT E. LEE's favorite maneuvers was to strike the flanks of a moving enemy, and he tried it repeatedly against the retiring Federals. Once, at Frayser's Farm, there was an opportunity to gain a splendid victory. But for the fourth time since LEE began his campaign STONEWALL JACKSON was slow in moving. Throughout June 29, he stayed in his camp and wrote a letter to his wife telling her how much to contribute to their church. That night he fell asleep while eating, and when he did move out the following day the opportunity was lost. Either because he thought the enemy's position too strong, or because he had lost too much of the sleep his frail physique required, STONEWALL had failed the leader whom he idolized as "the only man whom I would follow blindfold."[72]

LEE never got over the missed opportunity at Frayser's Farm, and when JUBAL EARLY expressed concern that McClellan was escaping, he lost his habitual self-control and snapped: "Yes, he will get away because I cannot have my orders carried out."[73]

McClellan did make it safely to Harrison's Landing on the James.

Here his supply line was safely in the hands of the Union navy, and his front was guarded by Malvern Hill, blocking the road to the James.

Malvern Hill was a natural fortress. With his fine engineer's eye, LEE saw this at once as he rode forward to sweep the position with his glasses. Still, he thought so little of McClellan that he believed one more blow might crumple the enemy. He became more confident after LONGSTREET reported that a Confederate crossfire could silence the Union artillery so that the butternuts could charge the Federals off their 150-foot hilltop. D. H. HILL disagreed, saying, "If General McClellan is there in strength, we had better let him alone."[74]

He was there in strength. Massed infantry held every strongpoint, and there were divisions in reserve. Artillery was abundant, with some 100 fieldpieces parked hub to hub to blast any Confederate assault. Still, on July 1, 1862, LEE attacked—and it was the Confederate artillery, not the Union, that was knocked out. Throughout the war, Union artillery was to dominate the Confederate, and Malvern Hill was probably its finest hour. One by one, the Southern fieldpieces were silenced. And when the gallant gray lines surged forward, the Union guns shredded them, maimed them, pulped them—and then a storm of rifle fire broke them in blood. Some 5,500 Rebels fell in those dreadful wasting attacks, and next day a horrified Federal officer looked down the slopes and saw: "A third of them were dead or dying, but enough of them were alive and moving to give the field a singular crawling effect."[75] Long afterward, D. H. HILL wrote of Malvern Hill: "It was not war, it was murder."[76]

6

☆

General HILL was right, but the great tragedy of the Civil War was that neither he nor General LEE nor U. S. Grant nor any other high commander ever came to realize why it was that war had become "murder," or, in the phrase of William Tecumseh Sherman, "all hell."

The rifle bullet was the reason. The bullet had given the advantage to the defense. It had dethroned the bayonet, the shock weapon of the assault, and together with its handmaidens, the ax and the spade, had made the defense just about invincible.

The point that had been missed was that the bullet ended the era of headlong assault. In the days of edged or pointed weapons— the sword, the battleax and the lance—the assault was the ultimate tactic because all fighting was hand to hand. An attacker had little difficulty in approaching his enemy. This situation might have been ended by the bow and arrow, except that the invention of gunpowder came so close upon perfection of the English longbow that the possibilities of this silent missile were not fully realized.* But after muskets appeared the bullet was subordinated to the bayonet.

This was because the effective range of the smooth-bore flintlock was only from 30 to 100 yards. It was not accurate, and it took so long to load and fire that most commanders regarded it as a noise-and-smoke-making machine. The first volley would both frighten the enemy and produce a smoke screen under cover of which the assaulters could charge, risking at most a single volley from the defense before achieving "the bayonet clinch, the flash of steel, the stab and the yell of victory."[77]

Shock tactics made rapid decisions possible. The bayonet did not so much kill men as make men run. But the slaughter of Wellington's finest, the red-coated conquerors of Napoleon, at the Battle of New Orleans was a dreadful adumbration of the inevitable outcome when bayonets charge entrenched rifles. The lesson was ignored, however, and even the battles of the Mexican War were fought with the shock tactics of the past. One reason for this was the difficulty of making a satisfactory bullet for long-range muzzle-loading rifles.

A muzzle-loader bullet had to be small enough to permit it to be dropped down the bore and rammed home. The problem, then, was to design a bullet which would expand into the bore's grooves and utilize the power of the powder gases forming behind it. This was solved by the Minié ball named for the Frenchman who designed it, and when it was, the bullet's effective range rose from 100 to 500 yards. With the killing zone extended five times, the defense was five times more effective and the assault five times more dangerous. When to this were added trenches and rifle pits and all the other

* Kit Carson once said that he never fully realized what a weapon the bow was until he had arrows fired at him in the dark.

products of ax and spade, the assault was penalized further. All of the attacker's body was exposed as compared to about a fifth of the defender's. More, improved rifles could fire at a rate of three times a minute, and toward the end of the war, breechloaders even faster. This also favored the defense; *any* increase in range or firepower *had* to favor the defense simply because the defender was underground and the attacker aboveground. Obviously, then, the bayonet charge was a bloody anachronism. Civil War soldiers sensed this, derisively describing their blades as "candlesticks" (when thrust into the ground the bayonet's upturned socket was just the right size to hold a candle). Civil War generals, however, did not realize that the bullet had ushered in the horrible era of trench warfare, that all shock tactics, including cavalry charges, were actually a thing of the past. Even artillery was being chased off to a respectful distance by the bullet's increasing range, while its effect was being reduced by the spade's increasing protection.

What was needed were new weapons and tactics whereby the defense could be pinned down in its entrenchments while its flanks were turned, or the attack might advance to within assault range at a minimum risk. These were not developed, and it would be far from fair to fault either LEE or Grant for failing to understand the revolution worked by the bullet. It was not understood in the West as late as World War I and beyond, when automatic weapons and barbed wire made the power of defense even greater, and the famous "*banzai* charges" of the Japanese during World War II were even bloodier repetitions of the shock tactics which reddened the slopes of Malvern Hill.

LEE's explanation for these assaults was that he believed the enemy to be demoralized. Granting him the universal failure to grasp the limitations now imposed upon the attack, his judgment must be upheld. During the Seven Days' Battles begun at Mechanicsville and ended at Malvern, LEE had suffered 20,000 casualties against 16,000 Union losses, and yet it was McClellan, not LEE, who was backing off.

He ordered a general retreat to Harrison's Landing on the James. His decision enraged many of his officers, none more than Phil Kearny, who slammed his famous kepi into the mud, and roared: "I, Philip Kearny, an old soldier, protest this order for retreat. We ought, instead of retreating, to follow up the enemy and take Richmond. And in full view of all the responsibility of such a declaration, I say to you all, such an order can only be prompted by cowardice or treason."[78]

Neither accusation, of course, was true. Phil Kearny was one of those fighting generals who walk in a two-tone world and whose contempt for politics often conceals an inability or reluctance to swim in those conflicting currents. McClellan missed his great chance because he was still adding up the disadvantages and therefore submitting to the moral mastery of ROBERT E. LEE. Besides, he was playing politics.

Not long after the withdrawal, President Lincoln came down to Harrison's Landing and McClellan gave him a letter which was nothing less than a blueprint for running the war. In effect, he advocated those very policies which Republicans detested as "soft" and intimated that his army, McClellan's army, the fighting force molded by McClellan in McClellan's image, would not fight to destroy slavery. Lincoln, who was already coming to the conclusion that some form of emancipation was necessary, read the letter in McClellan's presence and put it in his pocket without a word. He never replied to it, masterpiece of self-important insolence that it was, and a few days later he lifted Henry Halleck out of the West and brought him to Washington as general in chief. Halleck assumed command of all the armies on July 11, 1862. In Virginia he confronted this situation.

On June 26, because of failures in the valley and command complications there, Lincoln had created the Army of Virginia under General John Pope. Pope had a threefold mission: to protect Washington, to guarantee the safety of the valley, and, by threatening LEE's rail communications, to draw troops off from Richmond and thus make McClellan's task easier. McClellan, however, continued to mark time at Harrison's Landing, and so Halleck went down to see him.

Once again, Little Mac wildly overestimated his enemy's strength, claiming that LEE had 200,000 men when he actually had fewer than McClellan's own 90,000. He asked for 30,000 more men, but Halleck told him he could have only 20,000 and would that be enough to take Richmond. McClellan answered modestly that there was a "chance." Halleck at once concluded that if LEE's army was so big it would be madness to allow him to sit between McClellan's and Pope's divided forces. So he ordered McClellan to return to his Washington base and then unite with Pope.

That, of course, meant an ignominious end to George McClellan's Peninsular Campaign, and a victory for ROBERT E. LEE. And as the Army of the Potomac began its ponderous slow movement north, the audacious LEE moved at once to strike at Pope.

John Pope had become famous for his victory at Island Number 10 on the Mississippi. He was a dashing figure, especially on horseback. He was also given to bluster, and he did not make the men of the Army of Virginia love him when he issued the order: "I have come to you from the West, where we have always seen the back of our enemies. . . ."[79] His reported remark, that his headquarters would be "in the saddle," left the salty Confederate soldiers, even, it is said, ROBERT E. LEE, shaking with laughter at the general who had his headquarters where his hindquarters ought to be.

Otherwise, General LEE did not find General Pope comic. Pope's harsh orders regulating Confederate civilians within the Union lines angered LEE, and he observed that Pope would have to be "suppressed." To do this, even before McClellan began retiring from the James, LEE sent STONEWALL JACKSON north.

JACKSON began the business on August 9, 1862, at Cedar Mountain. Here he met Pope's advance guard under Nathaniel Banks and was rocked back on his heels by a fierce Federal rush against his left flank. The Confederates were on the verge of being routed when A. P. HILL's division arrived, after which JACKSON mounted a counterattack to drive off the outnumbered Banks. Next day Pope's main body came up and JACKSON drew off to await the arrival of LEE.

LEE was quick in coming. As soon as McClellan's withdrawal from Harrison's Landing began, leaving only two brigades behind, he hurried to join STONEWALL with the rest of his army in hopes of carrying out the "suppression" before Pope could be joined by McClellan.

LEE, however, was surprised to find Pope countering all his own maneuvering skill with an equal mastery. Marching and countermarching was wearying LEE's troops and would soon wear down their fighting edge. Something had to be done, and that something was triggered in LEE's mind by one of JEB STUART's typical exploits.

LEE's cavalry leader had been piqued at the loss of his famous red-lined cape and plumed hat to the Federals. In retaliation, he raided Pope's headquarters and there found not only the Union general's dress coat but also many of his papers and a dispatch book. From these LEE learned that overpowering reinforcements were en route to Pope, who even then outnumbered LEE 75,000 to 55,000. If LEE was to move, it must be quickly. So he called STONEWALL JACKSON to his headquarters and ordered him to take 25,000 men on a wide sweep around Pope's right flank to get in his rear, and to cut his communications to Washington.

No more daring move could have been devised. Even today there are critics who say it was foolhardy to violate the sacred canon of concentration of forces by committing the cardinal sin of dividing them in the face of a superior foe. But the audacious LEE was a gambler. Throughout his leadership of the Army of Northern Virginia he was guided by the principle that he must take long chances to offset an enemy superior in men and munitions. He was not, however, contemptuous of Pope, as has also been said. He was merely trying to make him retreat by getting on his line of communications in his rear. He did not then intend to give battle. Only after the grasp of the situation slipped suddenly from Pope's fingers did he move to strike.

JACKSON worked that change. After a two-day march his "foot cavalry" came out of the Bull Run mountains to fall upon Pope's supply base at Manassas Junction. With glad yells and shouts of famished glee, they gorged and looted, and then they filled their wagon trains with ammunition and rations, put the torch to the rest, cut the railroad—and vanished. Pope sought them frantically. In the interval JACKSON took a strong position on Stony Ridge overlooking the old Bull Run battleground while LEE hurried to his side with LONGSTREET and 30,000 veterans.

On August 29 Pope found JACKSON and began battering him with steady, heavy attacks. He also finally began to think about the rest of LEE's army and sent a force to hold them off while he disposed of JACKSON. But he had not sent enough, and before the first day of battle had ended, LONGSTREET was in position on JACKSON's right. That was the moment for LEE to swing hard at Pope's unsuspecting left. Three times LEE declared to LONGSTREET that the magic moment had come, and three times the solid but slow "Old Pete" declared against it. Because the gentle LEE could not bring himself to order

LONGSTREET forward, the moment passed—and JACKSON spent the day fighting for his life against determined Federal attacks.

That night Pope became convinced that the Confederates were withdrawing. He jubilantly telegraphed Washington that the Rebels were in retreat, and next day he ordered a pursuit. But when the "pursuing" Federals came up against JACKSON's right wing, LONGSTREET's artillery came plunging among them and broke them. LEE, seeing his opportunity reappear, did not delay this time. He at once ordered LONGSTREET forward, and the gray lines smashed Pope's left flank so thoroughly that his entire army was broken and sent reeling back on Henry House Hill, the place where STONEWALL JACKSON had won his nickname the previous year.

This time there was no Federal panic, and next day Pope began an orderly withdrawal. Hoping to strike at his rear again, LEE sent JACKSON on another sweep. But the Federals were prepared, and on September 1, 1862, a savage battle was fought at Chantilly mansion. As a storm-tossed night closed in, Confederate riflemen under A. P. HILL heard a horse galloping toward them. A flash of lightning illuminated a Federal officer. The Rebels opened fire, the horseman turned—and then fell with a bullet in his spine. HILL ran to the fallen man and peered at him by the light of a lantern.

"You've killed Phil Kearny," he gasped. "He deserved a better fate than to die in the mud."[80]

7

☆

LEE had won a fine victory. If Second Bull Run (Manassas) had not been decisive, it had at least cleared most of Virginia of the locust-like Federals and had again demoralized Union forces in the East. The question was: What now?

LEE did not think he could wait and thus surrender initiative to the enemy. If he did, a larger Army of the Potomac might move south again. No, LEE decided, the thing to do is to invade the North.

His reasons seemed cogent. First, by entering Maryland and Pennsylvania the enemy could be drawn away from his Washington defenses. With Maryland held by the South, no Federal army based on Washington would would dare move against Richmond again and Virginia would be free.

Lee also believed that most Marylanders were sympathetic to the Southern cause and would flock to his standards. He was convinced that an invasion of the North would widen the gulf between the Peace Democrats and Republicans, and, most of all, bring to fulfillment that fondest dream of Confederate diplomacy: friendly intervention by France and England.

So far, the two chief powers of Europe had sat on the fence. Neither King Cotton nor Southern diplomacy had budged them. The nearest thing to a break had occurred in the fall of 1861 during the celebrated Mason-Slidell affair.

JOHN SLIDELL, who had been President Polk's emissary to Mexico, and JAMES MASON had been appointed to represent the Confederacy abroad. Slipping out of Charleston on a blockade-runner, they reached Havana, where they took passage on the British mail steamer *Trent*. On November 8, 1861, the U.S. frigate *San Jacinto*, Captain Charles Wilkes, fired a pair of shots across *Trent*'s bow, sent a crew aboard, and bore off Messrs. MASON and SLIDELL to the United States.

Britain became enraged. The fleet was put on a war footing and 11,000 troops were rushed to Canada. In the North there was many a firebrand who was willing to take on the British, but Abraham Lincoln had a cooler mind, and he apologized to the British and released MASON and SLIDELL. It was a wise move, for neither MASON in Britain nor SLIDELL in France was able to gain recognition for their country.

Except for Queen Victoria, who favored the North, the effective rulers of both nations were sympathetic to the South, if only to see America permanently divided. While detesting slavery, the aristocracies of both nations felt a kinship for the genteel South, especially the English, who scorned the Yankee North as a rude polyglot and looked upon the Confederate cavaliers as true-blooded English. But the middle and lower classes, again especially the English, were solidly for the North.

However, not many Englishmen believed that the North could subdue the South. In August of 1862, during and after Second Bull

Run, England and France were considering a proposal to effect a peace based on the independence of the Confederacy. A successful invasion of the North, then, could not fail to give impetus to such a movement, and that is why President DAVIS gave tacit approval to LEE's plan.

LEE knew that there were risks involved. For one thing, if he had just inflicted 14,500 casualties on the Federals, he had lost 9,500 himself. He was short on rations, thousands of his men were shoeless and many of his horses were worn out. Nevertheless, on September 5, only three days after Chantilly, LEE's sunburned, tobacco-chewing scarecrows went splashing across the Potomac singing, "Maryland, My Maryland."

They received a frosty reception. Secessionist sentiment had had 17 months to cool in Maryland, and even those who still sympathized with the South were repelled by the sight of these ragged and ravenous "liberators." In Frederick City, Dame Barbara Fritchie, nearly 100 years old, remembering the Revolution, is supposed to have leaned from her window to shake the Stars and Stripes at STONEWALL JACKSON's troops. Whittier immortalized her with the lines: " 'Shoot if you must this old gray head, but spare your country's flag,' she said." As Carl Sandburg has observed, no Confederate poet has done the same for the woman who stood on her doorstep with tears in her eyes, crying, "The Lord bless your dirty ragged souls!"[81]

But there were not many like her, and ROBERT E. LEE was dismayed. He pressed on, however, full of confidence in himself and contempt for George McClellan.

Little Mac was back. He had never really been removed from command, although his command had been taken from him bit by bit and fed to John Pope. After Pope was discredited, however, McClellan was reinstated, and the beaten men of the Army of the Potomac shuffling north from Chantilly shouted and cheered and threw their hats and their knapsacks into the air when they heard a general call out, "Boys, McClellan is in command of the army again! Three cheers!"[82] Throughout that night of defeat and retreat they straightened their backs and cheered themselves hoarse as the magical little man on the big black horse rode among them. Incredible as it may seem, these men actually did love this simulacrum of a general, this splendid hesitator. They knew nothing of his failings;

they knew only that he had once made soldiers of them when they were men of straw, and here he was to do it again when they were straws of shame. McClellan understood this and he returned their affection, saying, "We are wedded and should not be separated."[83] Thus, for all of his shortcomings in the field, McClellan had twice saved the Union Army from despair. Soon he had again effected its rejuvenation, and then, with 95,000 men, he marched northwest from Washington in search of General LEE.

They did not find him, at first, but two of McClellan's soldiers— Corporal Barton Mitchell and First Sergeant John Bloss—made a find of their own in the sleepy town of Frederick. It was a prize, three cigars wrapped in a paper, and that meant a smoke apiece with perhaps a flip for the odd one. Then Corporal Mitchell noticed the paper, smoothed it out and began to read:

SPECIAL ORDERS NO. 191

Headquarters, Army of Northern Virginia,

September 9, 1862

The army will resume its march tomorrow, taking the Hagerstown road. General Jackson's command will . . .

There were other generals mentioned—LONGSTREET, STUART, D. H. HILL—and the two soldiers jumped to their feet in excitement and ran for the captain. The captain dashed for the colonel, the colonel jumped on his horse and clattered away for the general, and thus, with a speed not always characteristic of the Army of the Potomac, the deployment ordered by ROBERT E. LEE was very shortly known to George Brinton McClellan.

LEE had again divided his forces. Confident that McClellan was still marking time around Washington, and anxious to protect his line of communications to Virginia, LEE had ordered STONEWALL JACKSON to capture Harpers Ferry and then rejoin him at Hagerstown before McClellan could move. McClellan, at Frederick, read of this deployment with rising jubilation. Here was a heaven-sent opportunity to destroy LEE's army in detail. LEE was not only fragmented, but the fragments were closer to McClellan than they were to each other! Waving the captured order, McClellan cried: "Here is a paper with which, if I cannot whip Bobbie Lee, I will be willing to go home."[84]

Resolving to strike at the Hagerstown fragment, McClellan began to move with what he probably considered to be speed. But it was not quick enough. Although he did break through South Mountain in a savage fight, he could not prevent LEE from withdrawing to Sharpsburg on the Potomac. Nor could he stop JACKSON from taking Harpers Ferry and rejoining LEE at Sharpsburg. Thus the great opportunity was lost. Knowledge of LEE's deployment had enabled McClellan to wreck LEE's invasion, but a 16-hour delay in attacking had ruined his own chance to destroy Marse Robert.

Nevertheless, McClellan with some 70,000 troops followed LEE to Sharpsburg. There he found him with 39,000 men, the Potomac to his back and across his front a sluggish creek called the Antietam.

As at Shiloh, there was a little church at Antietam. It was a Dunker church, standing white and peaceful along a road with a wood to its rear and across the road a cornfield and another wood. Here, on the morning of September 17, 1862, McClellan attempted to break LEE's left wing under STONEWALL JACKSON.

Fighting Joe Hooker led off for the Federals. Three dozen guns cleared the cornfield and cut it to the ground, after which a full corps swept furiously up to the little church. But then JACKSON fed in reinforcements and the Union troops were driven back to their starting point. Now another corps, under red-faced, white-haired Joseph Mansfield, came swinging into the battle—and after Mansfield was killed and Hooker wounded, these men also failed. Still neglecting to concentrate, still feeding in his units piecemeal, McClellan ordered in Edwin Sumner's corps. For a time, old Bull Sumner seemed to have gained possession of the church, but once again JACKSON hurled in fresh troops. They struck Sumner's flank and rear and rolled him back. Now, with the cornfield cut down, the wood lots riddled, the rail fence along the road draped with corpses, Sumner shifted his attack farther left toward a sunken lane held by the Confederates. And so another sunken lane entered Civil War history, this one to be known as Bloody Lane, for after it was taken by Sumner's men it was found to be stuffed with bodies.

Everywhere, now, the cooling autumn earth was warmed and soaked with blood and the air was vile with the reek of death. In the cornfield were so many dead that one soldier said it was possible to walk from one end to the other without touching the ground. Wounded men who had crawled from the battle to take refuge under haystacks were burned alive when the hay caught fire. The body of one Confederate soldier hanging over a fence in Bloody Lane contained no less than 57 bullets, and the Hagerstown road in front of the church was so horribly cluttered with carcasses and corpses that a colonel riding through it next day observed how his horse "trembled in every limb with fright and was wet with perspiration."[85]

Yet the battle raged on, and LEE's center grew weaker and weaker. The lines there were so thin that LONGSTREET and his staff were firing guns and D. H. HILL seized a musket to lead a counterattack. If McClellan hurled in fresh troops, he might burst through. But he hesitated, and the roar of battle began to shift gradually from the center of LEE's line to his right, where Ambrose Burnside with four divisions was trying to force the Antietam crossings.

Burnside also committed his divisions one at a time, and they met four bloody repulses. Still, Burnside pressed the attack, crossed the river and by two o'clock in the afternoon ROBERT E. LEE faced disaster. JACKSON on the left could do nothing against the Federals, his center was nailed down and his right was crumbling under steadily rising Union blows. He had no reserves. He had only the hope that A. P. HILL might arrive in time from Harpers Ferry, 17 miles away. Then, at 2:30, a courier galloped up breathless with the news that HILL's men were only an hour off. Could the butternuts hold?

It did not seem so. At three o'clock a fresh Federal assault broke with a roar against LEE's right. Standing in the high echoing streets of Sharpsburg, LEE could see the Federal columns plunging forward under a pall of smoke. He pointed to a distant column and asked a lieutenant named JOHN RAMSAY, "What troops are those?" RAMSAY focused his telescope and replied: "They are flying the United States flag." LEE pointed to another column on his right and repeated the question. RAMSAY answered: "They are flying the Virginia and Confederate flags." LEE, his breast swelling with a vast thanksgiving, said quietly: "It is A. P. HILL from Harpers Ferry."[86]

It was only half of HILL's division, for the other half was strewn along the roadside half-dead from the man-killing pace of the march. But there were enough men to turn the tide, to flow straight into battle and to strike Burnside in the flank, forcing him to halt, to withdraw and call for reinforcements that never came. Thus in the high drama of a roaring and critical twilight, the Battle of Antietam, the bloodiest single day in the Civil War, came to its close.

LEE had suffered 13,700 casualties against 12,350 Union losses, and that night LONGSTREET and other generals came to LEE and urged him to withdraw. "Gentlemen," he said calmly, "we will not cross the Potomac tonight. . . . If McClellan wants to fight in the morning, I will give him battle again. Go!"[87] It was the White Knight of the Confederacy who spoke; it might have been another Roland preparing another Roncesvalles, except that ROBERT E. LEE knew his man. McClellan did not give battle again. Next day he had it within his power to overwhelm LEE's exhausted and riddled Army of Northern Virginia, but something in those calm and reorganized lines awaiting him across the debris and stench of no-man's land unsettled his nerves. He did not see LEE with his back to a river but only LEE with his face to the front, and that night the Confederate Army slipped across the Potomac and returned to Virginia.

Antietam (Sharpsburg) was not so much a Union victory as a Confederate defeat, but however it may be described its effects were more far-reaching than those of any other battle in the war. First, by forcing LEE to withdraw from Maryland, it caused Britain and France to postpone a decision on intervention. Second, it called forth the Emancipation Proclamation.

Since the war began Abraham Lincoln had moved cautiously on the slavery issue. The loyal slave states of Maryland, Delaware, Kentucky, Missouri and West Virginia were highly sensitive on the question, and they had blocked Lincoln's cherished proposal for compensated emancipation. In some ways, the Negroes themselves were forcing Lincoln closer and closer to a major decision. Whenever Union arms entered Confederate territory, the Negroes flocked to the Stars and Stripes, thus enraging their masters and embarrassing Federal commanders. For a time this problem seemed solved when Ben Butler used his lawyer's mind to classify the slaves as "contraband of war," and the "contrabands" were organized into labor battalions.

Such a legalism might have been a good joke on the South, but it resembled a solution to the slavery problem about as much as a cough resembles an earthquake. And Abraham Lincoln had come to realize that only the cataclysm would do. He had asked himself: Of what avail to restore the Union without destroying the slavery that divided the House? His answer was: "The moment came when I felt that slavery must die that the nation might live."[88]

On July 22, 1862, Lincoln informed his Cabinet that he intended to free the slaves effective next New Year's Day. After Secretary of State Seward pointed out that to make such a declaration on the heels of defeat would sound like the "last shriek of the retreat"[89] from Richmond. Lincoln then decided to wait until the Union had won a victory. Antietam was that victory, and on September 22, 1862, President Lincoln issued the Emancipation Proclamation proclaiming that as of January 1, 1863, all slaves held in any state then in rebellion would be "then, thenceforward and forever free."

The proclamation did not free a single slave, simply because they were all in Rebel hands; it was of doubtful legality under the President's vague "war powers"; and if abolitionists thought it was not strong enough, the loyal slave states and the Northern Democrats thought it went too far. Yet the Emancipation Proclamation is among the most profound and revolutionary events in history. It opened the world-wide struggle for racial equality, and it opened it within the one country which, possessing in miniature all those colors and creeds, prejudices and fears which divide humanity, had it therefore in its power to produce the model solution.

In its immediate effects, the proclamation isolated the Confederacy. No foreign power responsible to public opinion dared enter the war against a nation now dedicated to the destruction of slavery, and henceforth all the South received from abroad was sympathy. Henceforth, also, the Civil War was a war to the death.

In the South, Emancipation Proclamation was spelled *Unconditional Surrender*. A wave of fury swept the Confederacy. Lincoln was accused of violating the sacred rights of property, of encouraging Negroes to rise in murder and rapine. Members of the Confederate Congress talked wildly of running up the black flag and killing all enemy wounded and prisoners. In effect, the Southern spine was stiffened to fight to the end.

So was the North's. Abraham Lincoln had lifted the North's purpose from the cause of Union to the high call of the crusade to crush slavery. Soldiers in blue now marched to a nobler end than the cry of "Home and Rights" which drew the butternuts into the field. And they also sang a nobler marching song. It had been "John Brown's Body" until Julia Ward Howe replaced that monotonous litany to a murderer with her magnificent "Battle Hymn of the Republic."

> Mine eyes have seen the glory of the coming of the Lord:
> He is trampling out the vintage where the grapes of wrath
>   are stored;
> He hath loosed the fateful lightning of his terrible
>   swift sword:
>   His truth is marching on.

Only the men of the Civil War could have sung such a song. Only the sons of a nation just shedding its innocence could have been exalted, rather than embarrassed, to cry aloud: "Oh! be swift, my soul, to answer Him! be jubilant, my feet!" or to attest in song that they were where Abraham Lincoln always said he wanted to be: on the side of the Lord. So they went down the lanes on that crusade and singing that song; and if ROBERT E. LEE was the last of the generals to enter battle submissive to the will of God, then the Union soldiers were the last to march to it with His name on their lips.

Abraham Lincoln had strummed a mystic chord within the nation's soul. He had truly "sounded forth the trumpet that shall never call retreat."

Unfortunately for Lincoln, he possessed no trumpet which could call George McClellan into battle again. Having permitted LEE to depart Antietam unmolested, McClellan allowed six weeks of splendid autumn marching weather to slip by before crossing the Potomac in pursuit. Even then, he was annoyed by Lincoln's importunate messages to get going. "I feel that I have done all that can be asked in twice saving the country,"[90] he wrote to his wife after Antietam.

Abraham Lincoln could not agree, and in his mind he prepared a test for McClellan. If Little Mac should permit LEE to cross the Blue Ridge and interpose his army between Richmond and the Army of the Potomac, George Brinton McClellan would be through. That happened, and on the night of November 7, 1862, two men stumbled through a driving snowstorm to reach General McClellan's tent near Rectortown.

One of the men was General Burnside and the other was Adjutant General C. P. Buckingham. Burnside seemed nervous and embarrassed. McClellan understood why after Buckingham handed him a message relieving him of command and ordering him to turn his army over to Burnside.

8

☆

Where, it has often been asked, did Abraham Lincoln find Ambrose Everett Burnside? The answer is that he had been around all the time. All the other generals of reputation—McDowell, McClelland and Pope—had failed, Grant seems to have been still beneath the cloud of Shiloh and Henry Halleck had no intention of crossing swords in the field with ROBERT EDWARD LEE.

Lincoln may have been impressed with Burnside's record as an independent commander of a successful amphibious operation along the North Carolina coast, and at Antietam he had done at least as well as any other corps commander. Yet Burnside had never shown any capacity for high command, and he knew very well himself that a good corps commander does not always make a good leader of armies.

Twice Burnside told Lincoln that he was "not competent to command so large an army,"[91] and he was so shocked by the President's final order that he had to be talked into obeying it by George McClellan himself.

Perhaps it was Burnside's very candor and modesty that impressed Lincoln. Certainly Burnside had much to be modest about. As a young officer in Mexico and against the Indians he was renowned for his poor skill at cards; he had had the unique experience of leading a young lady to the altar only to have her decline at the last moment with a loud and ringing "No!"; and as a civilian he went broke trying to manufacture a breech-loading rifle he had invented. George McClellan, then a railroad president, rescued him from the last misfortune, and Burnside was treasurer of McClellan's road when war broke out.

Burnside was a strong, handsome man, although completely bald at 39. His face, however, was not hairless, and even in this most mustachioed and bearded of wars' he possessed facial foliage and was also unique. It was neither beard nor mustache but a growth that began beneath his nose and spread back to either ear in two great bushy loops. The style was named "the burnsides" in his honor, and has since flip-flopped into the dictionary as "sideburns." In dress, Burnside wore a high, well-crowned hat and a musty frock coat that made him appear, in modern eyes, the prototype of the Keystone Cop. Even in those days there must have been something faintly ridiculous about Ambrose Burnside, something that might have been slapstick, had not the lives of 113,000 men been in his keeping.

Burnside's plan was to threaten Richmond directly by crossing the Rappahannock River at Fredericksburg. After Halleck sidestepped the responsibility of deciding on this proposal, Lincoln gave it his reluctant approval with the words, "It will succeed if you move very rapidly, otherwise not."[92] Burnside did move fast, at first. By November 17 his advance guard under Sumner was on the Rappahannock opposite Fredericksburg. Old Bull Sumner wanted to ford the river at once, brush aside the handful of Rebels in the town and seize the high ground to its rear. Burnside hesitated. Heavy rains were falling and the pontoon train he needed to bridge the stream had gone astray. He decided to wait for the pontoons, and thus became the fourth Federal commander to sit unwisely still in front of LEE.

LEE quickly gathered his forces in Fredericksburg. He probably would have preferred to oppose Burnside farther back, where there was room for maneuver, but JEFFERSON DAVIS was as insistent upon the distant defense of Richmond as Abraham Lincoln was eager for its quick capture. So LEE mustered 75,000 veterans, the peak strength of the Army of Northern Virginia, under JACKSON and LONGSTREET. He watched the Federals build their bridges over the Rappahannock and allowed them to cross into the little city without much more than token opposition from sharpshooters and a few cannon. LEE knew his position was secure, and he could hardly believe that Burnside would actually attack the heights which he held behind the town.

On his right flank was JACKSON with A. P. HILL's massed artillery, and it was here that LEE expected the brunt of the Federal attack. He could not conceive that anyone would dare LONGSTREET on the left. Here was a death trap, here was another sunken road, even deeper than those at Shiloh or Antietam. The side facing the Federals was lined with a stone wall four feet high forming a perfect parapet for the Rebel riflemen. Behind the road rose Marye's Heights, crowned by LONGSTREET's artillery. To approach this position the Federals had to cross open, uphill country. It was no wonder one of LONGSTREET's artillerists said to him: "General, we cover that ground now so well that we comb it as with a fine-tooth comb. A chicken could not live in that field when we open on it!"[93]

LONGSTREET laughed, just as he had chuckled when STONEWALL JACKSON appeared that day wearing a handsome new gold-braided dress coat. "Old Jack's" men whooped and hollered at the sight: "Come here, boys! STONEWALL has drawed his bounty and has bought himself some new clothes."[94] Watching the midmorning sun burn off the mists above Fredericksburg, seeing the steeples appear and the streets filled with marching Federals, LONGSTREET jokingly asked JACKSON if he was not afraid of all those Yankees. No man for a joke, JACKSON growled: "Wait till they come a little nearer, and they shall either scare me or I'll scare them."[95] One of STONEWALL's aides thought the general was allowing the enemy to get too close, but JACKSON said: "Major, my men have sometimes failed to *take* a position, but to *defend* one—never!"[96]

Burnside had two grand divisions, one under Hooker which was to attack LONGSTREET, and the other under William Franklin, which was to strike JACKSON. Franklin moved first, plastering JACKSON with artillery before his blue files began skirmishing. But JACKSON's answering artillery broke up the Federals.

It was then that Hooker's divisions swept toward LONGSTREET holding the sunken road and Marye's Heights. From the stone parapet came a crash and a flash of flame, from the hill behind it a roar of artillery—and the carnage was begun. Again and again these gallant Union soldiers obeyed those remorseless, heartless, mindless orders to conquer a very hell of flame and steel. They were like lead soldiers storming a stove. They had only their blouses between their hearts and the bullets of the entrenched Rebels, yet onward they came, flesh flowing against lead, brigade after blue brigade, and the Rebels standing four deep behind the stone wall loaded and fired, loaded and fired, shattering the blue lines into fragments, scattering them across the frozen mud.

Such was the charge at Marye's Heights, a tragedy of high courage at the abuse of high incapacity. Even the Rebels were thrilled by the bravery of their enemy, and GEORGE PICKETT later wrote his wife: "The brilliant assault . . . of their Irish brigade was beyond description. Why, my darling, we forgot they were fighting us, and cheer after cheer at their fearlessness went up all along the line."[97] Fearlessness, however, cannot conquer entrenched rifles, and some 7,000 Federals fell before Marye's Heights.

On LEE's right, more Yankees were falling as Franklin renewed his assault on JACKSON. Here a Confederate counterattack was launched, and LEE, standing on a hill, heard the weird high cry of the Rebel yell and saw a line of ragged butternuts come running out of a wood in pursuit of a body of fleeing Federals. LEE's eyes flashed, but then the gentler, truer side of his nature came uppermost and he murmured: "It is well that war is so terrible—we should grow too fond of it!"[98]

On that cold, clear night the aurora borealis blazed in white splendor upon horrors which a Confederate soldier on burial detail described two days later as:

Eleven hundred dead bodies—perfectly naked—swollen to twice the natural size—black as Negroes in most cases—lying in every conceivable posture—some on their backs with gaping jaws—some with eyes large as walnuts, protruding with glassy stare—some doubled up like a contortionist—here one without a head—there one without legs—yonder a head and legs, without a trunk—everywhere horrible expressions—fear, rage, agony, madness, torture—lying in pools of blood—lying with heads half buried in mud—with fragments of shell sticking in the oozing brain —with bullet holes all over the puffed limbs.[99]

Many more than 1,100 were buried during the truce LEE granted for such purposes. In all, Union casualties were 12,600 against Rebel losses of 5,300. The Army of the Potomac was so stunned that LEE might have counterattacked and broken it that very night, or at least the next morning. JACKSON is said to have counseled a night attack, with the Rebels stripping naked so as to avoid confusion in the dark. LEE, however, perhaps overwary of the Union artillery across the river, did not move—thus missing the same opportunity that McClellan failed to grasp after Antietam.

Burnside, who had shed real tears of grief at the slaughter of his soldiers, wanted to lead a fresh attack personally the next day, but his generals dissuaded him from this possibly expiatory course. Suddenly turning tenacious, he decided to move farther up the Rappahannock and get around LEE's left. On January 20, 1863, his army started to march, just as three days of icy, pouring rain began. Wagons, horses and soldiers sank into the bottomless mud of the Virginia roads. The impossibility of movement was described by the officer who requested "50 men, 25 feet high to work in mud 18 feet deep."[100]

Drenched and dispirited, the Army of the Potomac slogged back into camp, and with the ludicrous "Mud March" to cap the holocaust of Fredericksburg, Ambrose Burnside was relieved of his command.

9

☆

The Union defeat at Fredericksburg brought the Lincoln administration close to disaster. The fall elections had already gone against the Republicans, the Peace Democrats were gaining strength, and in the Northwest war weariness was so great that Lincoln was told he must open the Mississippi or face a demand for a negotiated peace.

It was to the West, then, that the eyes of the Union turned. Here, Grant with his Army of the Tennessee was poised to move against Vicksburg on the Mississippi in the campaign that would open the great river to New Orleans and cut the Confederacy in two. Just below Nashville, Tennessee, was the Army of the Cumberland, now commanded by William Rosecrans.

Rosecrans had replaced Buell after that general had failed to pursue BRAGG on his retreat from Kentucky. Red-faced, heavy, excitable and devout, "Old Rosy" was a favorite with the men. He liked to drill them personally and to offer such gems of battlefield advice as: "Never turn your backs to the foe; cowards are sure to get shot." "When you meet the enemy, fire low."[101] Rosecrans was also a fighter, and in December he began moving down into central Tennessee to get at BRAXTON BRAGG's army based at Murfreesboro.

JEFFERSON DAVIS was in Murfreesboro at the time, savoring the good news from Fredericksburg as a vindication of his defensive strategy. The Confederate President was also enjoying a gay Christmas season in Murfreesboro, a red-hot Rebel town where gallant soldiers and charming girls sang songs such as "The Bonny Blue Flag" or danced to the sentimental strains of "Lorena." The highlight of the season was the wedding of 37-year-old JOHN MORGAN, the fabled leader of Rebel cavalry, to young Martha Ready, daughter of a Tennessee member of the Confederate Congress and also a determined young lady who had resolved to marry MORGAN before setting eyes on him. The marriage was sanctified by portly General LEONIDAS POLK, who was also an Episcopal bishop. After the wedding, in that cavalier abuse of cavalry characteristic of both sides, MORGAN was allowed to gallop off on another flamboyantly useless raid and leave BRAGG without scouts or the services of 4,000 proven fighters. In all, BRAGG had about 38,000 men and Rosecrans 45,000, when, on December 31, 1862, the two armies collided at Stones River a few miles west of the town.

Both generals planned to swing their left flank, a situation which would give the advantage to the first to strike. In this case, it was BRAGG. His butternuts drove into Rosecrans's right wing and might have crushed it but for the battle put up by a division under a cocky young general named Philip Sheridan. One by one, Sheridan's brigade commanders were killed, and yet his division responded to his orders "as if on parade."[102] Still, Rosecrans was forced to retire his right to re-form it and he was able to do so while George Thomas, the stolid general from Virginia, held steady in the center.

It was a bloody day, this final 24 hours of 1862, and at one point the thunder of guns and muskets was so great that Rebels charging through a cotton field stopped to pick the raw cotton and stuff it in their ears. Night fell with the Union Army badly bent and seemingly beaten. BRAGG did proclaim a great victory, but found the stubborn Rosecrans still on the field on New Year's Day. BRAGG neglected to strike until January 2, 1863, after which, having been repulsed, he abandoned both the field and Murfreesboro to the enemy.

It is difficult to say what was achieved by the slaughter at Murfreesboro (Stones River). Losses were equal, both armies suffering about 12,000 casualties, yet Rosecrans might have been the technical victor because he occupied the field. Otherwise nothing substantial was gained. Both armies went into winter quarters and BRAGG's army still blocked Rosecrans's objective at Chattanooga. Meanwhile, the war shifted farther west to Vicksburg.

Vicksburg was the key to the Mississippi, if not to the entire war. If it fell, the great waterway would be in Union hands, but if it held out, as Abraham Lincoln said: "We may take all the northern ports of the Confederacy and they can still defy us from Vicksburg. It means hog and hominy without limit, fresh troops from all the States of the far South, and a cotton country where they can raise the staple without interference."[103] Vicksburg, however, was a very tough nut, especially from the water. It stood on high bluffs on the eastern bank commanding a great bend in the river, while on its eastern or landward side it was protected by the valley of the Yazoo, a watery labyrinth of swamps and bayous.

Eager to get at Vicksburg, U. S. Grant finally received word from Halleck: "Fight the enemy when you please."[104] However, as he made ready to move his Army of the Tennessee into an overland assault, his problem was complicated by an intrigue behind his back.

The political general John McClernand, a faithful War Democrat high in Lincoln's favor, had gone to Washington to ask the President to place him in command of a force to sail straight down the Mississippi and capture Vicksburg. McClernand told Lincoln that unless the great river was opened soon, the Northwest would drop out of the war. Eager for a victory, Lincoln consented—although he did not give McClernand exactly the carte blanche command he desired.

Grant learned of this design through newspaper rumors, and found himself forced to put his Vicksburg plans into premature operation. First, he ordered Sherman to sail downriver from Memphis before McClernand could arrive to supersede him. Then he began advancing into Mississippi with the intention of drawing JOHN PEMBERTON, the Confederate commander, away from Vicksburg and thus weaken the city for Sherman's assault. However, by then an alarmed JEFFERSON DAVIS had appointed JOE JOHNSTON to over-all command in the West. JOHNSTON wisely ordered his cavalry into action against Grant's rear, capturing both his supply base and wrecking his communications. Out of touch with Sherman, Grant was unable to inform him of what had happened, and on December 29 the far-from-weakened Confederates dealt Sherman a bloody repulse at the Battle of Chickasaw Bluffs.

Grant's plans were now completely upset. Moreover, he could see that political considerations had ruled out the easier overland approach in favor of the more difficult river route. Thus, doubting Mc-Clernand's competence to command, he requested and received permission to take charge on the Mississippi himself. On January 30, 1863, he arrived at Young's Point, about 20 miles above Vicksburg on the western bank.

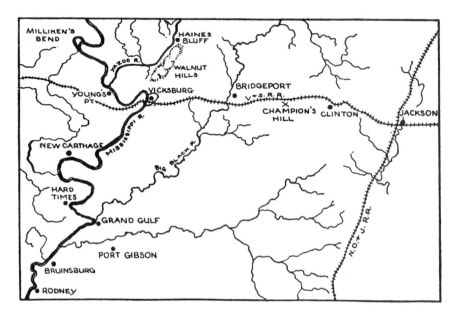

THE VICKSBURG CAMPAIGN

Few generals have faced a more bleak outlook than Grant at that moment. JEFFERSON DAVIS had already hailed the defeat at Chickasaw Bluffs as proof that Grant would slink back to Memphis. Grant was himself still under the stigma of Shiloh, still rumored to be a drunkard, and still the object of infamous attack in the Eastern press. Moreover, unable to turn back from the river approach, he could neither storm Vicksburg frontally nor establish a base below the city until the spring rains ceased. Least of all, he could not sit still for four or five months to give his enemies proof of his "timidity" or to allow his army of 45,000 men to fall apart. Thus, to keep his men occupied, to perplex PEMBERTON in Vicksburg, and also just on the chance of finding a chink in the city's armor, he made four flanking attempts.

Opposite Vicksburg was a peninsula formed by the river's great hairpin bend. It seemed that if a canal were cut across its base the river might flow into it and thus by-pass the city. However, after the channel was dug, the Father of Waters refused to enter it. Next, Grant tried to deepen and connect a chain of lakes and streams which wound west from Lake Providence above the city to a re-entry point in the river 150 miles below it. Here, two months of hard work ended in failure. So did two similar attempts undertaken in the labyrinthine Yazoo above the city to the east. So the outcry against Grant continued. He was "pronounced utterly destitute of genius or energy; his repeatedly baffled schemes [were] declared to emanate from a brain utterly unfitted for such trials; his persistency was dogged obstinacy, his patience was sluggish dullness."[105]

During this ordeal of frustration, however, Grant had come to suspect that the country might be prosperous enough to support his army on the march, and this fact was at the back of his mind when he proposed to march his troops down the river's western bank to a point below Vicksburg where a crossing to the eastern bank might be made. Grant's top generals, especially William Tecumseh Sherman, objected to such an advance. Sherman insisted that the only way to take Vicksburg was to return to Memphis and follow the line of the Mississippi Central Railroad. But Grant was not to be dissuaded, and so, to confuse PEMBERTON, he ordered Sherman to make a diversion north of Vicksburg, while 1,700 cavalry under Colonel Benjamin Grierson went on a raid through central Mississippi, tearing up railroads and upsetting PEMBERTON's troop deployments. In the meantime, the bulk of the army slipped down the western river bank to Bruinsburg. Here Grant awaited the arrival of the Union fleet which was to run the gantlet of Vicksburg's guns so that it might carry his army to the eastern bank. On the night of April 16-17, 1863, the fleet under Admiral David Dixon Porter made its move.

With lights dowsed and engines silent, the ships began floating downstream. The dark, wooded shores of the peninsula were on their right as they headed for the end of the hairpin turn. Reaching it, the Union fleet suddenly found itself illuminated by the flickering light of a house set ablaze on the peninsula and a calcium fire lighted on a Vicksburg hill. Stealth was not possible now, and Vicksburg's batteries were already booming. Thundering back with their own guns, the Yankees cracked on steam. One by one—armored gunboats, turtle-backed rams and steamboats belching fire and smoke from their tall funnels—the Union ships swept through the Rebel shot and shell. Soon the cotton bales which served as "armor" for some of the transports caught fire, and as the stricken *Henry Clay* staggered downstream she trailed a wake of fiery bunches of cotton that made Admiral Porter think "a thousand steamers were coming down."[106] But all the other ships had come safely through, and on April 30 the crossing of the Mississippi was begun. "When this was effected," Grant wrote, "I felt a degree of relief scarcely ever equalled since. . . . I was on dry ground on the same side of the river with the enemy. All that campaigns, labors, hardships and exposures from the month of December previous to this time that had been made and endured, were for the accomplishment of this purpose."[107]

Now Grant's clear-sightedness and daring came into play. Although he had about 33,000 men against PEMBERTON's 23,000, the enemy army in Vicksburg was linked to the interior by rail and could be easily reinforced or supplied. Grant decided to attack the city's rear, its supply base to the east in Jackson, then held by JOE JOHNSTON with about 6,000 men. The Union chief proposed one of the most audacious moves in history: to cut loose from his base, seize Jackson, and then, still living off the land, turn west to invest Vicksburg. Thus, as Grant moved east toward Jackson, the bewildered PEMBERTON sallied from Vicksburg to "cut" the nonexistent Yankee supply line. In the meantime, Sherman's corps went crashing into Jackson, JOE JOHNSTON went dashing out, and on the night of May 14 Grant slept in the room which JOHNSTON had occupied the night before.

About-facing, posting a sizable force in his own rear to block JOHNSTON should he attempt to return, Grant moved on Vicksburg. On May 16 PEMBERTON tried to halt him at a place called Champion's Hill, but the Confederate commander was hurled back and finally driven inside his defenses at Vicksburg. On May 18 Grant stood on the Walnut Hills overlooking Vicksburg. Beside him an admiring Sherman cried: "Until this moment I never thought your expedition a success. I never could see the end clearly, until now. But this is a campaign; this is a success, if we never take the town."[108]

Next day Grant ordered a full-scale assault, which failed completely. Unfortunately, Grant also failed to learn the lesson of the new invincibility of the entrenched defense, and he ordered a second, bloodier assault on the 22nd. This also failed, after which the Union commander settled down to siege warfare.

Vicksburg was caught in a noose. On the river, gunboats kept up a steady slow shelling of the city; on land, the Union trenches spread their strangling arms wider, and gun batteries wormed their way ever closer. Within the city, the garrison and the people lived like cave-dwellers. Cave-digging became a regular business, and a woman wrote: "The hills are so honey-combed with caves that the streets look like the avenues in a cemetery."[109] Clothes and shoes wore out, and were replaced with homemade ones of rags. There was little to eat but corn bread and mule meat. Soldiers lived on spoiled bacon and bread made of pea flour. Those with hardy stomachs trapped and ate rats, comparing their flesh to spring chicken. When the tobacco gave out, they smoked sumac leaves. Throughout it all, there was hardly a glimmer of hope: the Union fleet held the river and Grant held the land. No reinforcements or supplies could possibly get through, and on July 4, 1863, PEMBERTON finally surrendered.

Not many campaigns in history can compare to Grant's capture of Vicksburg. His losses were 9,400 compared to Rebel losses of 10,000 dead and wounded and 31,000 prisoners, including 15 generals. Within 18 days of his Mississippi crossing he had fought and won five battles and marched 200 miles with but five days' rations. He had cared promptly for the wounded on both sides, and treated Confederate prisoners with a compassionate understanding which gives the lie to that still-undying legend of Grant "the brutal butcher."

But most of all, he had cut the Confederacy cleanly in two. Not long after Vicksburg fell, the fortress of Port Hudson to the south also surrendered, and Abraham Lincoln could say with deep satisfaction: "The Father of Waters again goes unvexed to the sea."[110]

10

☆

On January 26, 1863, the Army of the Potomac came under the command of Fighting Joe Hooker. A hard-drinking, profane driver, Hooker was also easily the most handsome general in the Union Army, a square-shouldered Adonis with his curling blond hair and clean-shaven face of a complexion "as delicate and silken as a woman's."[111]

Abraham Lincoln had his good reasons for making Hooker his fifth choice in his search for the soldier who would lay the prize of Richmond at the Union's feet, but Lincoln was also aware of some of Hooker's defects, and he did not hesitate to detail them in writing what must certainly be among the most extraordinary letters of promotion ever composed by a commander in chief:

> I have placed you at the head of the Army of the Potomac. Of course I have done this upon what appears to me to be sufficient reasons, and yet I think it best for you to know that there are some things in regard to which I am not quite satisfied with you. I believe you to be a brave and skillful soldier, which, of course, I like. I also believe you do not mix politics with your profession, in which you are right. You have confidence in yourself, which is a valuable, if not an indispensable, quality. You are ambitious, which, within reasonable bounds, does good rather than harm; but I think that during General Burnside's command of the army you have taken counsel of your ambition, and thwarted him as much as you could, in which you did a great wrong to the country and to a most meritorious and honorable brother officer. I have heard, in such a way as to believe it, of your recently saying that both the Army and the Government needed a dictator. Of course, it was not for this, but in spite of it, that I have given you the command. Only those generals who gain successes can set up dictators. What I now ask of you is military success, and I will risk the dictatorship. The Government will support you to the utmost of its ability, which is neither more nor less than it has done or will do for all commanders. I much fear that the spirit which you have aided to infuse into the army, of criticizing their commander and withholding confidence from him, will now turn upon you. I shall assist you as far as I can to put it down. Neither you nor Napoleon, if he were alive again, could get any good out of an army while such a spirit prevails in it. And now beware of rashness. Beware of rashness, but with energy and sleepless vigilance go forward and give us victories.[112]

To Lincoln's gratified surprise, Hooker proved himself an unusually able organizer. He raised his army's drooping spirits and halted a disastrous flow of desertions by introducing a system of furloughs and improving the food, living conditions and hospitals. Scrapping Burnside's unwieldy "grand divisions," he reorganized the army into seven infantry and one cavalry corps, and by thus concentrating his mounted strength he made better use of it than those predecessors who had dissipated it by attaching it to the infantry. However, Hooker did decentralize his artillery to his later disadvantage.

All in all, the Army of the Potomac was a fine striking force of 94,000 effectives when, in April of 1863, it moved against Richmond again. In the Army of Northern Virginia, still concentrated along the Rappahannock near Fredericksburg, there were only 53,000 effectives, for LEE had found it necessary to send LONGSTREET south to guard the Virginia-Carolina coast.

Hooker's basic plan was to draw LEE out of his fortified defenses. John Sedgwick with 40,000 men was to demonstrate in front of Fredericksburg and hold LEE there while Hooker took the remaining 54,000 men up the Rappahannock to cross and come down on LEE's left. If LEE retreated, he would make, in effect, a flank march across Hooker's front and could be struck and annihilated. Joe Hooker had already announced that it was up to God to have mercy on the Confederates, because he would have none, and now he prepared his own superior brand of fire and brimstone.

At first, Hooker's maneuver was carried out with such skill and speed that he had three full corps over the river and advancing on LEE's left rear before the Southern chief realized what had happened. On April 29 Hooker was in Chancellorsville, a place which was hardly more than a long name for a little lone brick house at a tiny crossroads within a murky tangle of forest called "the Wilderness." Here, stands of second-growth oak and pine were choked with underbrush and laced with narrow, swampy streams, and here visibility was very poor and movement most difficult for large bodies of troops. Here, also, Hooker made the mistake of pausing, while the restless LEE gradually saw through Sedgwick's sound and fury at Fredericksburg. Realizing that his left rear was imperiled, LEE left 10,000 men under JUBAL EARLY to contain Sedgwick and hurried to halt Hooker with the rest of his army.

LEE did not, however, move fast enough. His advance units were pushed back by the Federals, and his right flank was gravely menaced by an entire corps under George Gordon Meade. The usually irascible Meade was so overjoyed that he cried: "Hurrah for old Joe! We're on LEE's flank, and he doesn't know it!"[113] Even better, Hooker's observation balloons had detected how weakly JUBAL EARLY was holding Fredericksburg. Here was the golden moment of Joseph Hooker's career. On his own front he had LEE outflanked and outnumbered, at Fredericksburg he had 40,000 men who could easily brush EARLY aside and crash into LEE's rear. What did he do? He let Sedgwick sit still and he ordered his own troops back to Chancellorsville.

Long ago in California an officer had noticed how "Hooker could play the best game of poker I ever saw until it came to the point where he should go a thousand better, and then he would flunk."[114] Hooker had flunked at Chancellorsville. He might say, with an outward assurance, "The enemy is in my power, and God Almighty cannot deprive me of them,"[115] but some of his indignant generals were already convinced that this was the bluster of the beaten man.

LEE was not yet convinced, although STONEWALL JACKSON was. Slowly, gradually, suspecting such an easy victory, LEE followed Hooker to Chancellorsville. By sunset of May 1, however, he had changed his mind.

No mere card-player who risks only money on the turn of a pasteboard, but a gambler willing to hazard armies and his own life and reputation on the bold move that can change the destiny of nations, LEE was again dividing his forces! JUBAL EARLY had 10,000 at Fredericksburg, LEE would keep another 14,000 at Chancellorsville in front of Hooker, while STONEWALL JACKSON took 28,000 on a sweep around the Union right flank to strike Hooker in the rear. To separate his force into three parts, none of which was superior in numbers to any enemy force, was audacious even for ROBERT E. LEE; yet LEE had inexhaustible faith in JACKSON, as JACKSON had in LEE, and between the one to conceive and the other to execute there has never existed a more perfect command collaboration in history.

On the morning of May 2, 1863, as JACKSON's corps began the long turning movement, the two men met briefly at a crossroads. JACKSON's Sorrel shambled forward toward LEE mounted on Traveler. JACKSON pointed ahead. LEE nodded, and JACKSON rode off. Throughout the day, JACKSON's butternuts marched across the Union front. They were detected by both scouts and observation balloons, yet Hooker did little to strengthen his right flank held by the one-armed Oliver Howard. It seemed that the very terrain there was too difficult for an enemy to penetrate. Hooker himself was extremely confident, touring his lines and repeatedly murmuring, "How strong! How strong!"[116] It was his expressed hope that the Confederates would attack him; and yet, as dusk began to gather, there had appeared no move.

The sun was low on the Union right. Soldiers who had stacked arms to eat dinner might have noticed, as they squatted on their knapsacks, how the blue of their uniforms grew less vivid. Suddenly groups of deer came running out of the woods to their right. The soldiers whooped and cheered, never bothering to wonder what had frightened the deer. Then came a riffle of rifle shots, the spine-chilling keen of the Rebel yell, thick rolling volleys of musketry, the boom of cannon —and into their midst came the first waves of a butternut flood.

With one great smashing blow, Jackson shattered the Union right. An entire Federal corps was sent reeling back, and as it did, Lee, far to the east, pressed forward to hold Hooker's left. It might have been complete disaster for Hooker, except that night soon fell, the Confederates became disorganized, Stonewall Jackson was wounded by the fire of his own men, A. P. Hill was also wounded, and Federal artillery massed in the Union center struck viciously at the Confederates throughout the night.

In the morning Jackson's attack was resumed under Jeb Stuart. Hooker, stunned by a falling pillar in the Chancellorsville mansion, failed to grasp the fact that his bigger army lay between Lee's fragments and that he could turn defeat into victory. Instead, his lines were bent back into a horseshoe holding his bridgeheads over the Rappahannock. He was so obviously eager to escape that when Sedgwick burst through Early at Fredericksburg on May 3, Lee calmly turned his back on him and went east to hurl Sedgwick back over the river. Turning again, he marched up to Hooker's horseshoe to complete the rout of the Army of the Potomac. But Fighting Joe Hooker had had enough of Marse Robert. He got his divisions safely across the Rappahannock, returning to the roost opposite Fredericksburg and there allowing the campaign which was to make the Lord blush for his mercy dwindle away to ignominious failure.

Federal losses at Chancellorsville were 17,000, compared to 13,000 for the Confederates. Yet Lee was soon to suffer an irreparable loss. At first it had seemed that the wounded Jackson would quickly recover from his wounds. However, word soon came to Lee that Jackson's left arm had been amputated and that he had displayed signs of pneumonia. Grieving, Lee told Jackson's chaplain: "Give my affectionate regards, and tell him to make haste and get well, and come back to me as soon as he can. He has lost his left arm, but I have lost my right."[117] Inside the little cottage where he lay, Stonewall Jackson worsened, drifting in and out of delirium. May 10,

1863, arrived and JACKSON whispered: "It is the Lord's day. . . . My wish is fulfilled. I have always desired to die on Sunday."[118] He sank back into unconsciousness. Suddenly, clearly, softly, his voice rose from the bed: "Let us cross over the river, and rest under the shade of the trees."[119]

He did cross, and LEE the Jove of war had lost his thunderbolt.

Chancellorsville has been called the high noon of the Confederacy. Actually, in retrospect it may be seen that there never was a Confederate high noon. Southern victory had followed Southern victory, but none had been decisive, each had merely postponed the inevitable and thus prolonged the war. ROBERT E. LEE, splendid commander that he was, had not struck that shattering blow that annihilates armies and which can be marked by the wholesale surrender or desertion of enemy soldiers. ROBERT E. LEE has been compared to Hannibal, to whom a Carthaginian general said on the morrow of Cannae: "You know how to gain victory, but not how to use it."[120]

It may be that LEE, having drawn his sword for Virginia, could not see that the Confederacy was then, in that May of 1863, in serious trouble. The noose of the Federal blockade was slowly strangling the Southern economy and seaport after seaport was falling to the Union. In the central theater, Rosecrans and BRAGG neutralized each other, but along the Mississippi Grant had driven PEMBERTON into his corner at Vicksburg and slammed the door. LEE, of course, was not responsible for all this, because he was not the general in chief. Yet LONGSTREET did not hesitate to advise the Confederacy to rescue the Mississippi by taking advantage of its interior lines. Troops could be shifted from place to place by rail faster than the Federals could counter, he said. LEE should use two corps in Virginia to contain Hooker, and send all other troops west to help crush Rosecrans. Such a victory would stun the North and force the withdrawal of Grant from Vicksburg, argued LONGSTREET. The proposal was reasonable, although it overrated the capacity of the Confederacy's "worn-out" railroads.

LEE, however, preferred to defend the Confederacy in Virginia rather than on the Mississippi. To do this, he proposed to invade Pennsylvania, believing, as he had in 1862 when he invaded Maryland, that his movement north would draw the Federals away from Richmond. LEE was also convinced that the growing peace movement

in the North would be strengthened, perhaps decisively, by a successful invasion. Moreover, he simply could not feed his army on the
Rappahannock. He had to enter the North for provisions, if nothing
else; and there, beyond doubt, is the proof that the "high noon" is a
midday mirage. An army which invades to ease its hunger does not
march under the banner of a prospering cause. Yet JEFFERSON DAVIS,
troubled at the time by calls for troops at Vicksburg, also favored
another invasion. The only officer of rank who opposed it was, again,
JAMES LONGSTREET.

It is possible that LONGSTREET had grasped the enormous advantage
which the bullet and the spade had conferred on the defense. When
he rejoined LEE after Chancellorsville, he argued that the invasion
of the North should be offensive in strategy and defensive in tactics.
As he wrote later:

> I suggested that, after piercing Pennsylvania and menacing Washington,
> we should choose a strong position, and force the Federals to attack us,
> observing that the popular clamor throughout the North 'would speedily
> force the Federal general to attempt to drive us out. I recalled to [LEE]
> the battle of Fredericksburg as an instance of a defensive battle; when,
> with a few thousand men, we hurled the whole Federal army back, crip-
> pling and demoralizing it, with trifling loss to our own troops.[121]

LEE listened, but was not persuaded. Unfortunately, for both men
and the cause they served, LEE did not directly refuse the advice.
LONGSTREET, in his vanity, mistook courtesy for consent—and left
the interview convinced that the invasion would be conducted along
the lines he had recommended.

Meanwhile, LEE reorganized his army into three infantry corps
under LONGSTREET and A. P. HILL and one of JACKSON's old division
commanders: RICHARD STODDART EWELL.

Bald-headed, long-nosed, pop-eyed and shrill-voiced, DICK EWELL
had lost a leg at Second Manassas to complete his appearance as one
of nature's jokes. Yet he was a fighting soldier whose perverse humor
and sulphurous tongue made him a favorite with the men. "Old
Baldhead," they called him, laughing at the thought that if he had
lost a leg he had, in the period of his convalescence, gained a wife.
However, EWELL, like A. P. HILL, was better with a division than a
corps, although he led LEE's invasion off well enough by defeating
the Federals at Winchester and clearing the way for an advance to
the Potomac.

To the rear at Brandy Station, JEB STUART was to have screened LEE's right flank with his cavalry. But on June 9 STUART was surprised by a strong Union force of cavalry under Alfred Pleasonton. The biggest cavalry battle ever fought on the American continent began, 10,000 sabers to a side hacking at one another and firing pistols point-blank from heaving saddles. Gradually, STUART gained the upper hand; but he did not pursue Pleasonton, and the result was that Brandy Station burnished the tarnished pride of the Union horsemen and so stung STUART's vanity that he eventually took off on one of those sweeping "ride-arounds" he enjoyed so much. He did not screen LEE's flank; in fact, he allowed the Union Army to get *between him and Lee.*

Deprived of the eyes of his army, LEE entered Pennsylvania as though blindfolded and under the optimistic assumption that the Army of the Potomac was still sitting still on the south side of the Potomac.

On the night of June 28, however, a spy reached him with the news that the enemy army was across the Potomac around Frederick, squarely on LEE's flank, and that it had a new commander.

Like McClellan, Fighting Joe Hooker had been a casualty of Henry Halleck's fixation on Harpers Ferry. Halleck wanted to hold it, Hooker wanted to abandon it as indefensible and use the troops elsewhere. Actually, Hooker had been getting a little frantic about troops, complaining that LEE's army of 76,000 men outnumbered his own force of 115,000 men. Thus, when Hooker hotly sent off a telegram of resignation, it was quickly accepted. In the black early morning of June 28, 1863, an official from the War Department went to George Meade's tent and awakened that sleeping soldier. Meade thought he was being placed under arrest and tried to think of what he could have done wrong. It was only after a while that he realized he had been placed in command of the Army of the Potomac.

Like Burnside, he tried to decline, only to be informed that he could not disobey orders. So it was that this tall, hawk-nosed, hot-tempered, modest and competent general became the sixth man to command in the East. He was taking charge at a difficult time, on the eve of impending battle and with his army loosely scattered. Such difficulties were well appreciated by ROBERT E. LEE when he heard that night of his old comrade's promotion. Yet he could say: "General

Meade will commit no blunder in my front, and if I make one he will make haste to take advantage of it."[122]

Thus, on the following day, LEE hastened to concentrate his own forces. In the afternoon he spoke quietly to his officers: "Tomorrow, gentlemen, we will not move to Harrisburg, as we expected, but will go over to Gettysburg and see what General Meade is after."

General Meade was after General LEE. He was cautiously poking north from Maryland into Pennsylvania, with two corps moving toward Gettysburg. On June 30 two blue brigades of cavalry under John Buford rode into the town. A few leading riders clattered west of it on the Chambersburg Pike.

East along the dusty pike came the butternuts of A. P. HILL's corps, lean, bearded, sunburned men in mismatching shirts and pants, some without hats, others without shoes. They were after shoes, these men of JAMES PETTIGREW's brigade in HARRY HETH's division. They had heard that there was a big store of shoes in Gettysburg. Outside the town, however, they ran into Buford's outriders and were driven back. PETTIGREW reported the skirmish to HETH, and HETH received HILL's permission to take his entire division to Gettysburg the following day to "get those shoes."

Meanwhile, dismounted Union cavalrymen carrying breech-loading carbines were fanning out in a heavy picket holding the Chambersburg Pike. From his headquarters in a theological seminary, John Buford messaged General Meade that he had found enemy infantry and that he thought there might be trouble at Gettysburg the next day.

Buford's troopers were up early on July 1. Part of them patrolled roads north of Gettysburg, but most of them held the ridges west of town. Here one man in four stood 50 yards to the rear holding the horses, while the others took cover. There were not many of them, but their stubby new breechloaders would enable them to fire faster than the enemy, and because they need not make telltale motions of the arm ramming bullets home as was necessary with muzzle-loaders, they could remain concealed. They also had artillery, six guns in the center of their line.

It grew light and breezy, and the Federals saw the enemy column approaching. Ahead of it were skirmishers fanned out to both sides of the road and coming three deep through the fields. One of the Union guns was aimed at a group of mounted officers three-quarters of a mile off. The gunner pulled his lanyard, there was a flash and a bucking roar—and the Battle of Gettysburg was joined.

Soon Confederate guns began baying. ROBERT E. LEE, riding into Cashtown about six miles west, heard that distant grumble. Artillery! Leaving LONGSTREET behind, he urged Traveler forward into Cashtown. There he found A. P. HILL, pale and sick that day, who told him only that HETH had gone ahead under instructions not to bring on battle until the rest of the army came up. LEE's forces were scattered: LONGSTREET to the rear, HILL at Cashtown, and EWELL north of Gettysburg. Fearing an escalating fight, a "meeting engagement" for which he was not prepared, LEE galloped toward the sound of the guns.

On and on he rode, "like a blinded giant,"[123] absolutely in the dark about where the Federals were or what his own forces were doing. Louder rose the sound of the guns, counterpointed now by the roll of musketry and the sharp spatting of the Yankee carbines.

South of Gettysburg, couriers from Buford brought the news of battle to John Reynolds. He, too, galloped toward the sound of guns, ordering his corps to follow. He rode toward the seminary. Buford saw him from the belfry. "There's the devil to pay!"[124] he yelled, and clattered down the stairs. Reynolds took charge. His soldiers went into line with Buford's troopers on Seminary Ridge west of the town. He called for help from General Howard and his corps, and messaged Meade that the enemy was attacking Gettysburg but "I will fight him inch by inch. . . ."[125]

Reynolds's units arrived just in time, just as the butternuts drove back Buford's exhausted troopers. Counterattacking savagely, the blue-clad infantrymen wrecked two Confederate brigades. Then a Rebel sharpshooter killed the gallant Reynolds, but then also, at noon, Howard arrived with his corps to block the northern road down which EWELL had begun to advance.

Below Seminary Ridge, ROBERT E. LEE had reached the battlefield. He could learn nothing except that two of HETH's brigades had been shattered. Then, to the left of HETH's lines, LEE saw a long gray column emerge from a wood. It was one of EWELL's divisions, forming on HETH's left. It could not have happened better if LEE had planned it. Still, he hesitated.

"No," he told an eager general, "I am not prepared to bring on a general engagement today—LONGSTREET is not up."[126]

It was then that LEE saw, still farther left, another of EWELL's divisions form up, and he hesitated no longer. With a yell and a roll of musketry, the gray lines swept forward, and the blue ranks were broken and forced into a stubborn retreat through Gettysburg to Cemetery Hill south of town.

LEE saw that if he could take Cemetery Hill he would control the entire position. A. P. HILL, however, said that his men were too exhausted to fight. LEE asked EWELL to make the attack, and then LONGSTREET rode up and LEE showed him Cemetery Hill where blue columns were massing. Studying the height through glasses, LONGSTREET said: "All we have to do is to throw our army around by their left, and we shall interpose between the Federal army and Washington."[127] Obviously, LONGSTREET still clung to his theory of offensive strategy and defensive tactics, but LEE answered him at once: "If the enemy is there, we must attack him."[128]

There was no further action that day, however, because EWELL had delayed and LONGSTREET's corps was still marching toward the battlefield. Meanwhile, two more Federal corps had arrived, together with Winfield Scott Hancock whom Meade had sent forward to take command. Howard objected. He had been distinguished that day, riding over the field with a battle flag stuck under his stump of right arm, and he was senior to Hancock. At length, the two generals agreed to cooperate in organizing the position. Culp's Hill to the right of Cemetery Hill was fortified, and so was Cemetery Ridge to the left.

At midnight George Meade arrived. Somewhat regretfully, he decided to accept the fight forced upon him. The successful holding action begun by Buford and continued by Reynolds and Howard had given him time to bring more of his forces forward. LEE's numerical superiority had been whittled and Meade now held a slight edge. LEE realized this. He, too, had accepted battle reluctantly, if he was not actually forced into it by eager subordinates.

Neither EWELL nor HILL had served LEE particularly well that day, and he was beginning to doubt LONGSTREET to the extent that for once a cry of complaint escaped him: "LONGSTREET is a very good fighter when he gets in position, but he is so slow!"[129] Even if LONGSTREET had been right about getting around the Federal left and standing on the defensive there, LEE, with only a few thousand cavalry, knew so little about Meade that he could not be sure that such a maneuver might not end in disaster. No, there was nothing for LEE to do next day but strike with all his strength before the entire Federal Army arrived on his front.

That night a full moon shone upon the armies massed opposite each other. It illuminated the dreadful debris of battle and shone palely on the sign at the graveyard gate warning that a five-dollar fine would be imposed on anyone caught discharging a firearm in the cemetery.

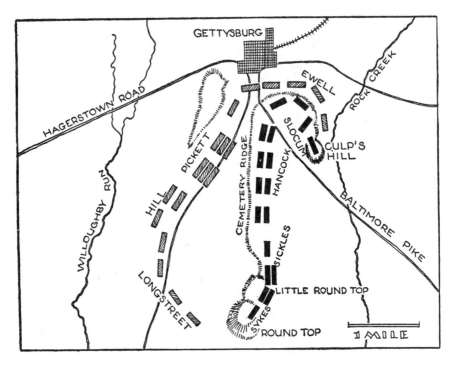

BATTLE OF GETTYSBURG

July 2 came in hot. Sweat stained the armpits of Federals putting the finishing touches on their log breastworks, and darkened the homespun shirts of Confederate soldiers marching over dusty roads or into sultry fields where the sunlight hung heavy in suffocating folds. Any way the Rebels looked at it, either from their left where EWELL's men were going at Culp's Hill and Cemetery Hill, or from their right where LONGSTREET was to storm Cemetery Ridge, the advance was going to be uphill over rocky slopes and into massed guns.

It did not, however, begin on time. LONGSTREET was again late. When he did arrive, he renewed his argument for the turning movement around the Yankee left. LEE, who wanted to attack first thing in the morning, was still for immediate battle. After LEE left him, LONGSTREET said to General JOHN HOOD: "The General is a little nervous this morning. He wishes me to attack. I do not wish to do so without PICKETT. I never go into battle with one boot off."[130]

LONGSTREET's other boot was not on until three o'clock in the afternoon, when his artillery began firing. An hour later his men swept forward, coming against a peach orchard and high ground which extended the Yankee flank farther left.

Here was a corps under the legendary Dan Sickles, a duelist and political general who also had his own ideas of how a battle should be fought. On his own initiative Sickles had occupied this new ground with its apex in a peach orchard. The position was too extensive to be defended by a single corps, and because of its wedge shape it could be struck on either side by Rebel artillery. An infuriated George Meade snapped all these defects into Sickles's teeth after the rumble of LONGSTREET's guns brought the Union commander galloping to his embattled left. By then it was too late to withdraw. The Confederate bombardment was rising in fury, taking off one of Sickles's legs and beheading the little peach trees. Federal guns bellowed back, and then the Confederates charged.

Back and forth swayed the battle, through the splintered peach orchard, into a wheat field, around a jumble of boulders to be known as the Devil's Den. Men and horses dashed in and out of choking blue clouds of powder smoke. Confederate and Federal knelt to blast away at each other at point-blank range. Officers peered anxiously into the smoke, trying to follow the course of the battle by a glimpse of battle flags. Everywhere was the deafening and dreadful clamor of combat, the crash of gun and shell, the hoarse high cries of men or the terrible screaming of stricken horses; and everywhere also the varied voices of invisible death: the keen of the bullet, the wail of the shell and the shrieking of shards of stone. At first the Federals were forced back. Reinforced, the blue lines regained the lost ground, only to be thrown back again by a furious Confederate counterattack. Now a great hole gaped in Meade's left, until another Federal corps rushed forward to plug the gap.

On Meade's right, EWELL's attack did not spring forward until shortly before dark. The Rebels came struggling up smoke-drifted hills, and were spun and scythed to the earth or toppled and sent rolling down the slopes. At one point, the Confederates seized a foothold; but they could not hold it, and when night fell only their fallen remained on Cemetery Hill.

That night JEB STUART's weary horsemen at last rode into the Confederate camp, and the fresh troops of GEORGE PICKETT's division also arrived. With these reinforcements, LEE resolved on a supreme effort to crush the Army of the Potomac. STUART was to take all the cavalry and strike the Union rear while LONGSTREET hurled himself once more upon the Federal left. Again, on that fateful morning of July 3, 1863, JAMES LONGSTREET protested—and for the same reasons. LEE, however, was determined; but because of LONGSTREET's reluctance he shifted that general's attack to the Federal center. And so, as JEB STUART and his veteran troops rode off to an inconclusive saddle-to-saddle joust with Federal cavalry in Meade's rear, LONGSTREET began massing 160 guns and 15,000 infantry opposite the Yankee center on Cemetery Ridge. Objective for both men and guns was a grove of umbrella-shaped chestnuts: the center of the center which, if it gave, would break Meade's army in half.

Noon came, and all was in readiness on Seminary Ridge where the Confederates had massed. A mile away, across a little valley, the Federals waited, sweating under the same sun, their own cannon massed, their eyes fixed on the ranked red battle flags. The moment had arrived for the boom of artillery and the long quavering yell, but it was slow in coming because JAMES LONGSTREET could not bring himself to give the final order for the charge. To his artillery chief, EDWARD ALEXANDER, he wrote: "If the artillery does not have the effect to drive off the enemy or greatly demoralize him, so as to make our effort pretty certain, I would prefer that you should not advise PICKETT to make the charge."[131] ALEXANDER, loath to accept his general's responsibility, demurred. There was an exchange of notes, until ALEXANDER finally wrote: "General: when our fire is at its best, I will advise General PICKETT to advance."[132]

At 1 P.M. the Rebel guns began bellowing. A mile away, Union cannoneers ran to their pieces. The mightiest bombardment of the war was under way, a monstrous metallic clanging that filled the little valley with the fog of war and spread death and destruction on both ridges. Twenty minutes after it began, ALEXANDER notified PICKETT: "If you are to advance at all, you must come at once or we will not be able to support you as we ought. But the enemy's fire has not slackened materially and there are still 18 guns firing from the cemetery."[133] A few minutes later, through a rent in the smoke, ALEXANDER saw the Federal batteries withdrawing from the chestnut grove, and he wrote to PICKETT: "For God's sake come quick. The 18 guns have gone. Come quick or my ammunition will not let me support you properly."[134]

PICKETT was standing beside LONGSTREET when he received ALEXANDER's first note. He handed it to the general. LONGSTREET read it without a word, and PICKETT asked: "General, shall I advance?"[135] LONGSTREET glanced away, turned back and slowly nodded his head. PICKETT saluted. "I am going to lead my division forward, sir,"[136] he said, and galloped away. LONGSTREET walked back to a fence and sat on it to watch the battle which had commenced against his wishes and without his having spoken a single word of command. At one point, learning that ALEXANDER was low on ammunition, he thought of halting PICKETT. "I don't want to make this charge," LONGSTREET said. "I don't see how it can succeed. I would stop PICKETT now but General LEE has ordered it and is expecting it."[137]

So PICKETT was not detained, and he rode among his butternuts shaking his long hair and crying, "Up men, and to your posts!"[138] Seizing their muskets, the Confederates walked through their now silent gun batteries and began dressing ranks. The time had come.

Across the valley, the Federals sensed it. Their guns, too, had fallen still; not because they had been silenced or withdrawn, as ALEXANDER thought, but because the Union gunners wanted to conserve ammunition until the moment when the Confederate lines were caught helplessly out in the valley. Now the Rebel skirmishers could be seen emerging from the woods of Seminary Ridge. Now the whole line was visible, dressing almost perfectly . . . coming on, a moving forest of steel, bayonets glittering in the sunlight. Now there was a gap between right-flank units, but still they came on . . . 100 yards they came . . . 200 yards . . . not quite 300—

With a dreadful roar the full fury of massed Union guns struck that gallant host. Flags went down, men sank to the ground, horses fell or galloped riderless over the field, but PICKETT's charge pressed forward. Because they were coming at the Union center, the Rebels could be enfiladed from both sides, and the Union guns savaged them mercilessly. Their lines broken and ragged, with units forward and back, they stopped to redress once again, and kept on. Then they were at the hill beneath a stone fence and charging up it. There was a twinkling of flame from the wall and the men in butternut were toppled and spun. From the remnant came a ragged Rebel yell, and LEWIS ARMISTEAD put his hat on his sword, cried, "Follow me!" and leaped the stone wall to die with his hand on a Union cannon. But few followed him.

PICKETT's charge had been broken by Union artillery and long-range musketry before it could even gain momentum. Only the great bravery of such soldiers and the gallantry of such officers could have brought it so far as the stone wall on Cemetery Ridge. Now, however, the broken bits of regiments and brigades were washing back down the valley. Now there was the opportunity for a Federal counterattack. LEE, sensing this, rushed to meet PICKETT to tell him to put his division behind a hill and prepare for a Federal sally. "General LEE, I have no division now," PICKETT said sadly, "ARMISTEAD is down, GARNETT is down, and KEMPER is mortally wounded."[139]

"Come, General PICKETT," said LEE, "this has been my fight and upon my shoulders rests the blame."[140] Still preparing for the Federal thrust, LEE rode among the returning butternuts, crying to them, rallying them, and whenever he met a man only lightly wounded, calling to him, "Bind up your hurts and take a musket."[141]

General Meade, however, was content with his defensive victory, and he remained in position. That night LEE prepared to retreat to Virginia. His second attempt at invasion had ended more disastrously than the first. As a rainy night fell upon the bloodiest battlefield in American history, the exhausted LEE walked Traveler through the silent tents of his sleeping army. Reaching his headquarters, he suddenly burst into a cry of admiration: "I never saw troops behave more magnificently than PICKETT's division of Virginians did today in that grand charge upon the enemy! And if they had been supported as they were to have been—but for some reason not yet fully explained to me, were not—we would have held the position and the day would have been ours." LEE paused, and then, in a loud and agonized voice, he cried: "Too bad! *Too bad!* OH, TOO BAD!"[142]

11

☆

    Gettysburg remains the most famous battle in the Civil War, chiefly because of the immortal Gettysburg Address delivered there by Abraham Lincoln on November 19, 1863, and because it was such a dreadful blood bath. Union losses totaled 23,000, while the Confederates, reporting 20,400, probably suffered closer to 28,-000. That was no less than one-third of LEE's force, and if Meade had pursued vigorously he might have made Gettysburg a truly decisive victory.

    Meade, however, followed so cautiously that LEE got safely back to Virginia. "We had them within our grasp," Lincoln lamented. "We had only to stretch forth our hands and they were ours. And nothing I could say or do could make the Army move."[148] Gettysburg, then, merely ended for all time Southern hopes for that victory on Northern soil which would bring help from abroad. It was Vicksburg, which fell the day after PICKETT's charge, that gave the Confederacy its mortal wound. Lincoln was aware of this when, on August 26, he wrote of the great event with such sprightly jubilation:

    Thanks to the great Northwest for [Vicksburg]. Nor yet wholly to them. Three hundred miles up they met New England, Empire, Keystone, and Jersey, hewing their way right and left. The sunny South, too, in more colors than one, also lent a hand. On the spot, their part of the history was jotted down in black and white. The job was a great national one; and let none be banned who bore an honorable part in it. And while those who have cleared the great river may well be proud, even that is not all. It is hard to say that anything has been more bravely and well done than at Antietam, Murfreesboro, Gettysburg, and on many fields of lesser note. Nor must Uncle Sam's web-feet be forgotten. At all the watery margins they have been present. Not only on the deep sea, the broad bay and the rapid river, but also up the narrow muddy bayou, and wherever the ground was a little damp, they have been, and made their tracks. Thanks to all. For the great republic—for the principle it lives by, and keeps alive—for man's vast future—thanks to all.[144]

Lincoln's elation over Vicksburg, however, was tempered considerably by the realization that Meade's failure to destroy LEE's army had prolonged a war growing ever more unpopular in the North. Only the previous July a mob howling "To hell with the draft and the war!"[145] had terrorized New York City for three wild and bloody days. Burning homes, public buildings, churches, police stations, stores, factories, saloons, even an orphanage, murdering Negroes and battling police and soldiers hand to hand in the streets or from behind barricades, driving draft officials from their offices and wrecking draft apparatus, the rioters exploded in a fury of resentment against "a rich man's war and a poor man's fight." In the end, the draft was suspended in New York and regiments from the Army of the Potomac marched into the city to quell the mob. But not before 400 persons had been killed or wounded and $5 million lost in property damage.

In truth the rioters, incited by antiadministration newspapers as well as by such personages as Franklin Pierce and Governor Horatio Seymour, had much to resent in a draft law that permitted anyone to buy an exemption for $300 or to hire a substitute to go in his place. Obviously the law was designed for well-heeled lip-servers of the Union cause, most notable among them being Grover Cleveland, who hired a substitute to fight his fight for the nation which he was twice to lead as President. In New York City some $5 million was siphoned from the city treasury for draft-evasion purposes, the money going to politicians, lawyers, examining physicians, fixers and other patriotic types who would thus see to it that the "right people" would be deferred. Thus, of 292,441 men called in New York, 39,877 failed to report, 164,394 were exempted, 52,288 bought exemption for $300 apiece and 26,002 hired substitutes. Only 9,880 men—about one out of 30—who either lacked political pull or possessed true patriotism went off to fight. No wonder the mob rose in fury! No wonder there were similar though not nearly so violent protests throughout the North, especially in New England where sanctimonious "blue noses" often bought exemption and then, once the war was over, piously prevailed upon local legislatures to repay them for this patriotic outlay. The humorist Artemus Ward ridiculed such coat-holders with the remark: "I have already given two cousins to the war, & I stand reddy to sacrifiss my wife's brother, ruthurn'n not see the rebellion krusht. And if wuss comes to wuss, I'll shed every drop of blood my able-bodied relations has got to prosekoot the war."[146] So it was the farmers, the wage hands, and especially the immigrants, who arrived in the North to the number of 800,000 during the war years, who shouldered the Union muskets.

Meanwhile, enormous profits were being made by war contractors. Among those famous fortunes founded during the Civil War were Armour in meat-packing, Borden in dairy products, Carnegie in iron and steel, Marshall Field in merchandise, Huntington in merchandise and railroads, Remington in guns, Rockefeller in oil and Weyerhaeuser in lumber. Profiteering naturally contributed to inflation, and wages, without benefit of organized unions, trailed far behind skyrocketing prices. In purse as well as in person, then, it was "a rich man's war and a poor man's fight."

Among Lincoln's other difficulties in that summer of 1863 was the intrusion of France into Mexico, where Napoleon III hoped to set up a puppet government with the young Austrian Archduke Maximilian as his emperor. Little Napoleon had flagrantly violated the Monroe Doctrine, but there was not very much that Lincoln could do about it until after the war. Nor was there much that either Lincoln or JEFFERSON DAVIS could do about the defeatism and disloyalty which grew stronger in each camp with every passing month.

Some of the opposition to both Presidents was provoked by the ruthlessness with which they enforced conscription. Some of it came from persons honestly convinced that peace could be achieved by negotiation, and some from those fainthearted or selfish persons for whom plotting or treason always has seemed the way of safety or profit. Thus both sides organized secret societies. In the Northwest the "Knights of the Golden Circle" terrorized loyalists with midnight raids or met with Southern spies to plot fifth-column uprisings for which they really had no stomach, and in the South the "Heroes of America" gave more surreptitious aid and comfort to the North. On both sides, opposition was too formidable for either President to move against it.

DAVIS's chief difficulties came from states' rights governors such as JOSEPH BROWN of Georgia, who suspended the draft and raised a militia of 10,000 men to defend his state alone. Governor VANCE of North Carolina was only less obstructionist, and he acted in that fashion because his state was so full of antiwar sentiment that at one point there was open talk of seceding from the Confederacy. Much as the gentlewoman had been the South's chief recruiter, too many beloveds had been coming home in coffins. Mrs. Chesnut wrote: "Is anything worth it—this fearful sacrifice; this awful penalty we pay for war?"[147] Another wife of a Confederate officer wrote: "I am for a tidal wave of peace—and I am not alone."[148]

The North's peace movement was more open and better organized. In the Northwest, where intense patriotism and open treason flourished side by side, it was led by those antiwar Democrats called Copperheads from their lapel insignia of an Indian head carved from a copper penny. A former Ohio Congressman named Clement Vallandigham was the Copperhead leader. While in Congress the proslavery Vallandigham had taunted Republicans with the remark: "War for the Union was abandoned; war for the Negro openly begun, and with stronger battalions than before."[149] While campaigning for governor of Ohio in 1863 he had characterized the war as being fought "for the purpose of crushing out liberty and erecting a despotism."[150] Lincoln would have been content to let Vallandigham talk himself out, rather than make a martyr of him; however, the blunt General Burnside was now in command in Ohio and he had Vallandigham arrested, tried by a military court and sentenced to jail for the rest of the war. With keen good humor, Lincoln changed the sentence to banishment within the Confederacy. The Copperheads replied with a 40,000-member mass meeting in Lincoln's home town where they resolved "that a further offensive prosecution of this war tends to subvert the Constitution and the Government."[151] They also assailed Lincoln's treatment of Vallandigham, to which he gave the grim answer: "Must I shoot a simple-minded soldier boy who deserts and not touch a hair of the wily agitator who induces him to desert?"[152]

By then the North was shooting deserters a half-dozen at a time, and with such solemnity and deliberation as would strike fear into the hearts of soldiers massed to witness the executions. Desertion was a problem for both sides—one out of nine enlistments in the South deserted, one out of seven in the North—but the Union Army had to deal with defeatists who systematically encouraged soldiers to desert and mailed them packages containing the civilian clothes and railroad tickets which would facilitate their disappearance. Most despised deserters of all were the bounty jumpers, men who enlisted in one state or locality to claim a bounty, and then deserted to claim another one in a different place.

The bounty system was another Union headache. To reduce the number of men needed to be drafted from any state or city, bounties were paid to men who would volunteer. However, the bounties rose to as high as $1,000 per man after reluctant draftees began to bid against states and cities for the services of a substitute. Next there entered the inevitable middleman, the sly, grasping bounty broker who for a fee would find a man willing to enlist. Too often the broker operated like a waterfront crimp, getting his man drunk and inducing him to sign away his bounty rights for a pittance and then rushing him through the enlistment process. Some did not scruple to scour the slums of Europe for recruits. As a result, the dregs of society were often draped in Federal blue, to the indignation of one recruiting officer who protested against putting the uniform "upon branded felons; upon blotched and bloated libertines and pimps; upon thieves, burglars and vagabonds; upon the riff-raff of corruption and scoundrelism of every shade and degree of infamy which can be swept into the insatiable clutches of the vampires who fatten upon the profits of the execrable business."[153] Naturally, the chief concern of such "soldiers" was how best to avoid fighting and how quickly to get out of uniform; and so, as the war grew older, they were treated with increasing harshness by a government which still had not the moral courage to draft outright all those shrinking, perfumed patriots who had purchased their own safety with these decrepit or debased human beings.

Although the South was not so hypocritical in waging "a rich man's war and a poor man's fight," it nevertheless did discriminate to a lesser degree. Substitute-buying, though not as widespread, was permitted; and to the numerous exempt classes was added that of the plantation overseer at the rate of one to every 20 Negro slaves. This was the infamous "20-nigger law" which enraged the poorer whites, and helped to raise the rate of deserters and men absent without leave. In June of 1863 the proportion of absentees from the Confederate Army was nearing one-third, and President DAVIS proclaimed an amnesty for all who would return to their units. Few, however, came back; nor did many respond after Gettysburg evoked a repetition of the offer. Confederate arms, then, appeared to be in desperate straits when Union forces in the West began driving for Chattanooga.

Chattanooga was one of the South's vital east-west railroad junctions, it was the gateway to Georgia, and possession of it by the North would liberate pro-Union populations in east Tennessee and northern Georgia. Chattanooga was the objective of William Rosecrans, as its defense was the mission of Braxton Bragg. Since the Battle of Murfreesboro, however, Old Rosy and his Federals had built what appeared to be a permanent camp around the town while Bragg and his Rebels had gone into similiar hibernation at Tullahoma 20 miles to the south.

On June 23, 1863, after months of inaction, Rosecrans and his Army of the Cumberland began moving toward Bragg and Chattanooga. As they did, they were swamped by torrential rains. "No Presbyterian rain, either," a soldier said, "but a genuine Baptist downpour."[154] Yet the army stumbled on, and Rosecrans, maneuvering with rare skill, was able to threaten Bragg's rear and force him to retreat all the way to Chattanooga.

Old Rosy, however, wasted the next two weeks at Tullahoma, bickering by long-distance telegraph with General Halleck over reinforcements. Curtly ordered to resume his advance, he moved out on August 16. Again he maneuvered deftly, getting his army across the Tennessee by demonstrating above Chattanooga while his main body crossed the river below the town. Bragg, again fearing for his rear, evacuated Chattanooga and fell back into Georgia.

To Rosecrans, this withdrawal looked like a retreat. He resolved on headlong pursuit to catch and crush Bragg, and because the terrain below Chattanooga was a most difficult land of huge ridges offering few passes, he divided his forces to facilitate their movement. But Bragg was not retreating. He was actually concentrating his army for battle, receiving reinforcements being rushed to him from Kentucky and Mississippi. Far away in Virginia, President Davis, at last conceding the importance of the West, had put James Longstreet and most of his corps aboard rickety trains and sent them by a roundabout route to Bragg's side. When they arrived in September, Bragg outnumbered Rosecrans by 70,000 to 60,000; and he saw that the Federal commander's rash dispersion was his own opportunity.

The battleground was to be in the valley of Chickamauga Creek. Here, Bragg first struck at the separated Union right under George Thomas and Alexander McCook. But the Confederate commanders, unaccustomed to any celerity from Bragg, moved with the usual deliberation and failed. Their failure alerted Rosecrans, who began frantically pulling his forces together on his left a few miles south of Chattanooga. BRAGG evolved another plan: swing hard against the Union left before it could concentrate, driving it away from Chattanooga into a jumbled wilderness where it could be fragmented and beaten to death by bits.

BRAGG as usual delayed, and Rosecrans rapidly moved Thomas's corps into position on the left of Thomas Crittenden's. So the Army of the Cumberland seemed prepared when BRAGG began attacking on September 19, and the opening Confederate blows were blunted. Next morning the Rebels struck again, the right under the battling bishop LEONIDAS POLK coming against Thomas with crushing fury. Fighting desperately, the Federals held. But Thomas was hurt and he kept calling for reinforcements. Rosecrans tried to feed him a division from his quiet right flank, but the unit went astray and never reached Thomas. Thomas, however, renewed his pleas for help, giving Rosecrans the impression that a Confederate tidal wave was rolling against his left. In fact, POLK had been beaten back, and it was Rosecrans's *right* that was endangered.

Here JAMES LONGSTREET had prepared his customary set-piece haymaker. Under cover of woods, he had formed his troops in a column of brigades. When they hit, they would hit in a series of hammer blows. And now, opposite LONGSTREET, chance was entering the battle.

Rosecrans had received an erroneous report that there was a gap to the right of his center. He ordered one division to "close up" on another to plug the gap, but the division commander, knowing that there was no gap, construed the "close-up" order to mean he should get *behind* the other division. So he pulled out of the line, leaving a gaping void, and as he did LONGSTREET's brigades came rolling into the hole.

They struck Union brigades as they were leaving the line, Union brigades as they were entering, and they came yelling against them on their flanks. The result was sheer catastrophe. The Union right was swept away. Rosecrans, his staff, even Assistant Secretary of War Charles Dana were jostled off toward Chattanooga on a struggling flood of soldiers, ambulances, baggage wagons and artillery. When Dana saw the devout Rosecrans crossing himself in supplication, he concluded that all was lost.

But all was not lost. George Thomas, the solid general from Virginia, was hanging on. While LONGSTREET and POLK eagerly closed around him, he reorganized around Horseshoe Ridge. LONG-STREET might cry jubilantly, "They have fought their last man and *he* is running,"[155] but the fact was that the Federals were rallying, tightening their lines beneath the smoke, waving their flags defiantly at the oncoming Rebels. In the hollow of a hill, Thomas stood feeding his horse corn, impassively following the battle. At one point Thomas told a colonel that his hill must be held at all costs, and the colonel replied: "We'll hold it, General, or we'll go to heaven from it."[156]

The hill held, Thomas held—like a rock, to receive the immortal nickname of "the Rock of Chickamauga"—and the Army of the Cumberland was saved from destruction. That night Thomas retired, and the Confederates failed to pursue. Nevertheless, the South was thrilled to hear of BRAGG's great victory at the Battle of Chickamauga. It seemed that he had turned the tide in the West, and even the price of 18,450 Confederate casualties as against 16,170 Union losses seemed not too high to pay for such a great reversal of fortunes. Moreover, BRAGG had Rosecrans's army penned up in Chattanooga, and it seemed only a matter of time before the Federals capitulated.

Unfortunately for the South, BRAGG had also succeeded in bringing U. S. Grant into the field against him.

News of the defeat at Chickamauga and fears for the safety of the Army of the Cumberland all but panicked the Washington government. Two full army corps were immediately detached from Meade and sent west under Joe Hooker, while Sherman was ordered east from Memphis with part of the Army of the Tennessee. Finally, Lincoln named Grant chief of all Union forces between the Allegheny Mountains and the Mississippi,* with the option of choosing Rosecrans or Thomas to command at Chattanooga. Grant chose Thomas, until, on October 23, he arrived there himself.

Grant found the Union forces caught in a trap and in danger of being starved into surrender. A vast Confederate semicircle enclosed the Federals. It ran around Chattanooga from the Tennessee upstream, following the heights of Missionary Ridge south and then swinging west again to Lookout Mountain and a bit beyond to the Tennessee. To the north of the Union rear ran wild, mountainous country

* Except for the force in New Orleans under Banks.

penetrated only by a single cart track. Thus there was no way out if a retreat were contemplated, and no way in for supplies.

The situation could hardly have been worse, and for Grant, whose spirit thrived on adversity, that was tantamount to never being better. Almost at once he determined to open a supply line. On the night of October 26 about 1,500 Federals surprised a Rebel force at Brown's Ferry to the west, seized a beachhead and threw a pontoon bridge over the river. From here, Joe Hooker led a march overland to Bridgeport, the Union supply depot on the Tennessee. Thus was opened the famous "cracker line" over which troops and supplies came into Chattanooga. BRAGG, failing to grasp the importance of this breach in his investing line, did little to retake Brown's Ferry. Instead, he detached LONGSTREET and 15,000 badly needed veterans, sending them 150 miles east to attack General Burnside in Knoxville, Kentucky.

Now Washington actually did panic, bombarding Grant with shrill requests to do something to relieve Burnside. On November 7 Grant asked Thomas to attack BRAGG's right flank so as to compel him to recall LONGSTREET. Thomas, however, grimly alluded to the fact that he had not enough mules or horses (10,000 of them had died during the siege) to draw a single piece of artillery. Grant agreed to wait until Sherman arrived. Once Sherman was on the scene, Grant began attacking.

His plan, which evolved as the situation changed, was to bring off a double envelopment. Hooker was to strike the Confederate left at Lookout Mountain while Sherman hurled himself at the Rebel right on the upper end of Missionary Ridge. In the meantime, Thomas's men were to put the pressure on the center at Missionary Ridge to prevent BRAGG from reinforcing his flanks.

The battle began November 24, 1863, with Hooker meeting immediate and spectacular success. His men outnumbered the Rebels by five or six to one, and they swarmed up Lookout Mountain's rocky slopes and meadows to drive the defenders off the summit. Below them, war correspondents gazed in enchantment at the mountaintop alive with the winking of thousands of deadly fireflies, and then after a fog drifted in between valley and crest, giving Lookout a circlet of smoke infused with flame, the phrase "battle fought above the clouds" was born.[157] Actually, Hooker had not done much more than knock BRAGG's left anchor loose.

Meanwhile on the right, BRAGG's men were breaking Sherman's attack into fragments. Here, there was not one continuous ridge as Grant and Sherman believed, but a jumble of separated small hills. The Rebels fought from behind excellent fortifications, sometimes rolling big boulders down upon their luckless attackers. With nightfall, Sherman had not made much of a dent in BRAGG's right.

Next day, November 25, the double assault was renewed. This time Hooker's men descended the other side of Lookout Mountain and blundered into futility on a wooded plain, while Sherman once again could get nowhere on the right. In fact, Sherman was so convinced that BRAGG was reinforcing from his center that he asked Grant for help. Grant's reply was to order Thomas to press forward against the Rebel center on Missionary Ridge.

Here were bristling lines at the foot of the 500-foot hill and on its crest. Thomas had some doubts about taking even the rifle pits at the bottom, but Grant prodded him forward. Standing on a hill smoking a cigar, Grant watched Thomas's men start for the blazing pits. Into a tangle of felled trees they poured, 20,000 strong, breaking through in several places to strike the dismayed Rebels on opened flanks and exposed rear. In an instant, the Confederates broke and fled up the ridge. Into the abandoned pits jumped the aroused Federals, men of the Army of the Cumberland who had fought hard at Chickamauga only to find themselves the butt of endless needling by the unbeaten dandies of Sherman's and Hooker's units. Now they looked eagerly up the ridge to the Confederate guns.

Cocky little Phil Sheridan, resplendent in dress uniform, sat his horse and looked at the guns. He drew a flask from his pocket and toasted a group of Confederate officers above him, crying, "Here's at you!"[158] At once, the Rebel guns roared at Sheridan, striking close enough to shower him and his officers with dirt. Sheridan's face darkened. "I'll take those guns for that!"[159]

And then, suddenly and in a rush, the Federals went charging up the ridge, straight into a storm of enemy fire, and right before the incredulous eyes of U. S. Grant on his hilltop. Wheeling in anger, Grant snapped: "Thomas, who ordered those men up the ridge?"

"I don't know," Thomas replied slowly, and then, addressing one of his corps commanders, Gordon Granger: "Did you order them up, Granger?"[160] Slowly at first came the answer, "No, they started up without orders," and then, with a flash of pride: "When those fellows get started all hell can't stop them!"[161]

Growling something to the effect that someone would suffer if the
attack failed, Grant turned to watch the charging Cumberlands, and
saw to his delight that all hell indeed could not stop them. The great
battle line was now a series of V's struggling upward behind fluttering
battle flags, for the regiments were racing each other for the crest. On
through the Rebel fire and smoke they came, sometimes pausing for
breath, but sweeping inexorably closer until Confederate astonishment
turned to alarm, then to fear—and they broke and ran. Jubilant
Federals chased them, beckoning their comrades forward and calling,
"My God! Come and see them run!"[162]

Butternuts had never before been routed like this, but they had
been through much, these weary fighters of BRAGG's army. So they
gave completely away, a two-mile hole was punched in BRAGG's
center, and the Battle of Chattanooga ended with BRAGG retreating
into Georgia and the Union forces in full possession of the West.

Chattanooga, with 5,820 Union casualties and 6,600 Confederate,
also placed the reputation of U. S. Grant beyond reach of his numerous
traducers. Abraham Lincoln had already suggested that perhaps those
timid generals who deplored "Grant's drinking" might do well to try
Grant's brand of whiskey. After the winter of 1863-64 passed without
another Union success, the President called Grant to Washington and
placed him in command of all the armies.

12

☆

On March 9, 1864, Ulysses S. Grant received the revived
rank of lieutenant general and took command of all the Union armies.
After four years of fruitless searching, Abraham Lincoln had at last
found *his* general: a man of single purpose and ruthless driving energy
who would ignore politics and concentrate upon destroying the Confederate Army.

Under Grant there was to be a common plan, with all forces acting
in concert, and armies, not cities, were to be the objective. These
targets were the Army of Northern Virginia with 60,000 men under

LEE and the Army of Tennessee with about the same number now under JOE JOHNSTON, who had replaced the feckless BRAXTON BRAGG. William Tecumseh Sherman with 100,000 men in Chattanooga was to go for JOHNSTON while Grant with 120,000 in Virginia went for LEE. In effect, Grant would hold LEE by constant attack while Sherman maneuvered against his rear by pushing JOHNSTON back toward Atlanta. Thus neither Confederate force could help the other; each would be worn down until one or the other was crushed, and then both Union forces would unite to destroy the survivor. Thus, also, the Confederacy would be forced to contend with those high casualties which were its daily dread.

Actually, George Meade still led the Army of the Potomac; however, inasmuch as Grant had decided to accompany this force in the field, it came to be known as Grant's army and by his continued presence often did come under his direct control. Grant was always the general in chief. The plan was his; the war, in effect, was his; and to make it total he ordered Ben Butler to take the Army of the James against Richmond and a Shenandoah army under Franz Sigel to move on Staunton and threaten LEE's railroads. Phil Sheridan was also brought east to command Grant's cavalry. In the simplest terms, the pressure was to be applied everywhere and made unbearable. LEE would not be permitted to maneuver, and he would be thrown on the defensive with the inevitable results.

In eight weeks, then, U. S. Grant put together his war machine, oiled and geared it, and on May 4, 1864, he sent it clanking toward the foe.

LEE's army had passed a frightful winter. The men were in rags, half-starved and freezing in their miserable huts along the Rapidan. Food was so scarce that when LEE had guests one day he could serve nothing but stringy bacon and cabbage. Because there was obviously not enough bacon to go around, the diners politely declined it. Next day there was even less to eat. Lee, remembering the untouched bacon, asked his steward about it and was told that it had been borrowed in the first place and had already been returned to its hungry owner.

Shortages in hay and fodder also caused the death of thousands of horses. When LONGSTREET left for Georgia, he was not able to take his guns, and half the animals in JEB STUART's horse artillery were dead.

Unbelievable as it may seem, this incredible army had not yet lost its fighting spirit. Nor had its commander, when, on April 6, he successfully divined Grant's plans. Immediately, LEE ordered BEAUREGARD to defend Richmond against Butler and scraped together a scratch force to hold off Sigel in the valley. He would attend to Grant himself, letting him cross the Rapidan and then hitting him in the flanks as his ponderous slow army struggled through the steaming tangle of the Wilderness.

As Grant moved, LEE moved, and on May 5 they collided.

Only a year ago the armies of LEE and Hooker had swirled through this maze of swamp and swale, leaving it a monster burial ground. Here eyeless sockets stared from the bleached skulls of men and horses, there a skeletal hand or leg rose from a half-finished grave; every thicket was strewn with rusty guns and canteens and every bush seemed to blossom with rotten bits of bloodstained clothing. Even the bullet-nicked trees bore mute testimony to the savagery of Chancellorsville, and the entire scene startled the Federals of Gouverneur Kemble Warren's corps as that unit came poking south from the Rapidan. They quickly recovered from their horror, however, when they blundered into the butternuts of DICK EWELL's corps who had come marching east along a turnpike. Gradually this chance encounter built up into full-scale conflict, the opening notes of the Battle of the Wilderness, and within a few hours it had become a blind, black struggle over which neither commander exercised much control.

In a field near Wilderness Tavern, U. S. Grant sat on a stump, smoking a cigar and whittling on a stick, issuing the orders that fed more and more soldiers into the fight. In the Confederate rear, ROBERT E. LEE calmly rode with A. P. HILL as that general's corps came rushing up on EWELL's right. LEE also sent orders for LONGSTREET to hurry up from Gordonsville, 42 miles away. So the battle grew and grew, the Rebels trying to get around the Union Army, the Federals building up their left flank to contain them. Soon rolling clouds of smoke intensified the forest gloom. Now soldiers merely fired blindly into the smoke and murk, others groped their way forward or crawled on their bellies. A horizontal rain of bullets three feet high swept the battlefield. Then the woods took fire, and the crackle of flames mingled with the wild screams of men and animals being burned alive.

By midafternoon Grant had the corps of Sedgwick, Warren and Hancock, right to left, opposed to EWELL and HILL. He resolved to crush the Confederate right under HILL and sent Hancock crashing forward. Once again, the Wilderness was the Rebel ally. It quickly fragmented solid formations into bits, while the outnumbered Confederates, better woodsmen who knew every path and fastness by heart, riddled the Union attack. By nightfall, however, two of HILL's divisions were badly battered.

That night LEE realized that he had met his most aggressive adversary. All day long the Federals had attacked, attacked, attacked; never surrendering the initiative and never once giving LEE the opportunity to maneuver. He had been held in place as never before, and now his right flank was badly damaged. Still, he hoped that LONGSTREET would arrive next day in time to turn the tide. Early on May 7, however, the roar of enemy guns told LEE that HILL's weakened divisions were once again being assaulted.

LEE mounted Traveler and rode toward the guns. He rode through stragglers, and then, to his mounting alarm, through a butternut flood pouring away westward. LEE's right was shattered. Not since Antietam had he faced such a crisis. LEE rode back to consult A. P. HILL and to look anxiously for LONGSTREET. HILL shouted at his artillery to fire off 12 loaded guns before withdrawing the pieces from danger. The guns bucked and roared and hurled shells into the woods and the approaching Federals only 200 yards away. Smoke swirled around LEE. The Federals came on, and then, through the smoke behind him, LEE saw a score of ragged soldiers dash forward with muskets in their hands.

They were Texans. Texans! That meant they were from JOHN B. HOOD's famous brigade in LONGSTREET's corps. LONGSTREET had arrived! In rare excitement ROBERT E. LEE spurred Traveler forward through the gun pits. He came up with his advancing reinforcements as though to lead them forward. "Go back, General LEE, go back!" they cried. He ignored them, and they shouted: "We won't go on unless you go back!"[163]

Persuaded at last, LEE reined in Traveler, waved his hat at the onrushing Texans, and rode back to see LONGSTREET. That stolid general bluntly told LEE to go farther behind the lines, and then came forward himself to stop the Yankee attack—and to be wounded badly by the fire of his own men.

So the Battle of the Wilderness ended as Antietam had ended, with the eleventh-hour arrival of reinforcements to save LEE's crumbling right. Would it also end as had all other drives on Richmond? Would the Army of the Potomac turn north, recross the river and regain Washington to refit and regroup before shuffling south again? It seemed so to many of the Union soldiers lying weary and heart-broken in the darkness. When they were ordered to take the road, it seemed only that the command to retire had come sooner than usual. It was another Chancellorsville, they told each other. Then they came to a crossroads. If they turned left, they would be retreating again. They turned right, and suddenly those tired men lifted their heads and a great cheer rose in the night. They capered in the dust and tossed their caps in the dark and shouted with a wild fierce joy until U. S. Grant reined in his great war horse Cincinnati and told his staff to tell the men to stop cheering or else the enemy would realize that the Army of the Potomac was slipping away south.

Neither LEE nor Grant had fought with distinction, only with determination; and if casualties measure victories, then LEE had won: Union losses were between 15,000 and 18,000, Confederate estimated at between 7,750 and 11,400. Casualties, however, measure only the costs of battle. It was Grant who was the victor. He had achieved his objective: he had held LEE, had fixed him, had thrown him on the defensive. All LEE's moves hereafter were to be in response to Grant's. Yet Grant the slugger was stalking LEE the boxer and must inevitably become bruised and lacerated, while the very success of Grant's policy was to call forth from LEE all that mastery of defensive warfare which was uniquely his. A field engineer by education, LEE had spent decades building forts and dredging rivers. He had a marvelous feel for terrain and here, in the Wilderness, he was fortifying his own back yard. "When our line advances," an aide of Grant's wrote, "there is the line of the enemy, nothing showing but the bayonets, and the battle-flags stuck on top of the works. It is a rule that when the Rebels halt, the first day gives them a good rifle pit; the second a regular infantry parapet with artillery in position; and the third a parapet with an abattis in front and entrenched batteries behind. Sometimes they put this three days' work into the first twenty-four hours."[164] Thus did the "King of Spades" make bloody woe of Grant's progress south, and on that very night that the Union chief sideslipped left to come up under LEE's right at Spotsylvania Court House, LEE shifted right to race him for that position. The Confederate commander won, and on May 8 Grant found his path once again blocked.

It was blocked because the Confederate advance guard had marched with lightning speed and because the Union cavalry had dawdled clearing the road through Spotsylvania. Meade blamed this failure on Sheridan, and when the little cavalry chief appeared at his headquarters the towering commander of the Army of the Potomac lost his temper with a roar that could be heard by every orderly with a pretext for being within hearing distance. Black-eyed Phil Sheridan, five foot three inches of pure pugnacity, yelled back with an insubordinate vigor that rattled the chain of command and warmed the orderlies' hearts. It was Meade's fault, Sheridan shouted, because Meade countermanded his orders and used his cavalry as scouts and errand boys rather than as a fighting corps. What Sheridan wanted, Sheridan shouted, was to go out and whip JEB STUART clear out of his saddle. Somewhat startled, Meade took the dispute to Grant and Grant said: "Did Sheridan say that? Well, he generally knows what he is talking about. Let him start right out and do it."[165] So Grant ordered Sheridan to "cut loose from the Army of the Potomac, pass around the left of LEE's army and attack his cavalry."[166] He was also to cut LEE's communications. Thus, shortly after noon of May 8, Sheridan led more than 10,000 troopers on a jingling swing around the Union right and then made due south as though bound for Richmond.

In the meantime, the Battle of Spotsylvania was swelling from an advance-guard encounter into a rolling, roaring eight-day battle which eventually embroiled both armies. While the conflict developed, LEE skillfully entrenched himself between the Po and Ny rivers in a line roughly resembling an inverted V. This enabled him to put most of his troops on the line and to move them to and from either face of the upside-down V as the situation required. Trees and underbrush concealed most of his works, and his skirmish line was pushed far enough forward to prevent Union scouts and officers from reconnoitering it. This made it difficult for Grant to gauge the extent of the opposition, and with Sheridan's cavalry gone he was, like LEE at Gettysburg, fighting nearly blindfolded.

Confederate sharpshooters also kept Federal artillery at a respectful distance, or pinned down those gunners rash enough to drag their pieces within sniping range. On May 9 John Sedgwick tried to rally his nervous artillerists by standing erect among the pinging bullets and crying, "Don't duck, they couldn't hit an elephant at this distance!"[167] A minute later Sedgwick was down and dying with a sniper's bullet under his left eye. Command of his corps passed to Horatio Wright, and it was Wright who seems to have decided that the weakest point of LEE's heretofore impregnable line was the west face of the V, or "the Mule Shoe," as the Rebels called it. Although the works there were strong, they could be enfiladed by Union artillery, and there was a stand of trees that would enable a Federal force to come within 200 yards of the works undetected. It seemed to Wright that the Mule Shoe could be taken by a sudden, silent rush, and he organized a special force of 12 regiments under an intense young colonel named Emory Upton.

Upton was among the most professional commanders in the Union Army. Free to criticize, he was himself very hard to fault because of his capacity for taking pains. He planned his assault carefully, taking his commanders forward to study the ground, organizing four lines of three regiments each. The first line was to pierce the outermost Confederate line and widen the gap so that a second line could rush through to assault the second Rebel position. The last two lines were to form a reserve, lying down beneath the Confederate breastworks until called for.

Late in the afternoon of May 10, 1864, Union artillery began pounding the Rebel positions. At 6:15 P.M., Upton's blue lines charged and drove straight through as planned. But then the Rebel guns scattered the Union reserve, which had formed in the open contrary to orders, and Upton was left isolated inside the Confederate position. He hung on until nightfall, assisted by another attack on the Federal right, and then withdrew. Yet he had proved that the salient at the Mule Shoe could be penetrated. Obviously, a larger force might break it and split LEE's army in two. That was what U. S. Grant meant when he said to Meade: "A brigade today—we'll try a corps tomorrow."[168]

It was two days later and with two full corps that Grant attacked the Mule Shoe. Hancock's corps came straight down against the tip of the V while Wright's hammered away at the western face, and throughout that day and night of May 12, 1864, there raged probably the most vicious battle ever fought on American soil, and possibly one of the most ferocious fought anywhere. It was worst on Wright's front, "the Bloody Angle," as it was called. It was hand to hand. Men fired muskets muzzle to muzzle, and struck at each other with battle flags. The Rebels ran their guns right up to the parapets and sprayed double canister shot into rank after falling rank of Yankees. Fence rails and logs in the breastworks were actually splintered by the hail of Minié balls, and trees over a foot and a half in diameter were cut in two by them. Skulls were smashed with clubbed muskets, men were stabbed to death by swords and bayonets thrust between the logs of the parapets separating the forces, and the wounded were entombed alive by the crush of dead bodies toppling upon their wriggling, helpless forms. Night fell and a fierce rainstorm broke, and still the struggle convulsed the Bloody Angle until at last, at midnight, both sides sank on their arms in exhaustion.

At the point of the V, meanwhile, it appeared that Hancock's massed Federals had won the day. They bore straight down on the Mule Shoe, broke it, captured artillery pieces and took prisoners and swept on until momentarily checked by an incomplete line of breastworks. Here ROBERT E. LEE came riding on Traveler, faced once again with disaster. He rode straight to the center of the division commanded by JOHN GORDON, and GORDON thought that "LEE looked a very god of war."[169] Then LEE turned his horse's head as though to lead the desperation charge needed to shatter Hancock's advancing front.

At once GORDON spurred his horse across Traveler's front and grasped LEE's bridle. Lifting his voice deliberately so that his men might hear, GORDON said: "General LEE, you shall not lead my men in a charge. No man can do that, sir." Turning to his men, GORDON asked if they would fail LEE. "No, no, no!" they roared back, "We'll not fail him!" Turning back to LEE, GORDON shouted: "You must go to the rear," and his men echoed him with a thundering shout: "General LEE to the rear, General LEE to the rear!"[170] Crowding around the beloved Marse Robert, some clutching his bridle, others holding his stirrups, they forced Traveler around with such vehemence that GORDON believed that if LEE had resisted they would have carried both horse and rider to the rear. But LEE submitted to their pressure, and GORDON's division rolled forward with cyclonic force to shiver Hancock's lines and eventually force the Federals out of most of the Mule Shoe.

In the meantime, while attacks by Warren on the Federal right and Burnside on the left were also repulsed, LEE hurried construction of a new line at the base of the Mule Shoe. By nightfall the Confederate position was out of danger.

By then also JEB STUART had overtaken Sheridan's cavalry at Yellow Tavern about ten miles above Richmond. Outnumbered two to one, STUART tried to hold off the Union horse until infantry reinforcements could arrive from Richmond. But the Federals were too strong, they were scattering the Rebels aside, and STUART personally led a mounted countercharge. As he did, a dismounted Yankee trooper ran past him, fired his pistol at him and vanished. STUART slumped in the saddle, gravely wounded.

That had been on May 11, and Sheridan's cavalry had broken through, riding through Richmond's outer defenses and eventually making a complete circuit of LEE's army. On the night of the 12th while the Mule Shoe battle still raged, LEE learned that STUART was dying. LEE's voice was trembling when he told his staff: "He never brought me a piece of false information."[171] Later, he was told that STUART had died. Grief-stricken, LEE retired to his tent with the remark: "I can scarcely think of him without weeping."[172] It was a black night for ROBERT E. LEE, who had lost his right arm, JACKSON, a year ago and tonight "the eyes of the army." JACKSON dead, STUART dead, LONGSTREET wounded, A. P. HILL sick and EWELL weakening. All the old faces were vanishing. Two of his corps were in the hands of men as yet untried to high command: RICHARD ANDERSON and JUBAL EARLY. Yet LEE must hang on—and he did, assisted by four days of rain that enmired Grant's subsequent attempts to burst the Rebel line.

Nevertheless, Ulysses S. Grant had not given up. His casualties at Spotsylvania totaled between 17,000 and 18,000, against between 9,000 and 10,000 for LEE. Yet on May 19 he sat down to write his famous report: "I purpose to fight it out on this line if it takes all summer."[173]

On the following night he sideslipped left again in another attempt to draw the King of Spades outside his invincible earthworks.

Although Grant was successfully holding LEE while Sherman in Georgia had begun to drive JOHNSTON before him, Union movements elsewhere were being decisively defeated. Ben Butler's advance on Richmond was blocked by BEAUREGARD at Bermuda Hundred, after which Butler allowed himself to be trapped on the Bermuda Hundred peninsula, corked up neatly in a bottle, as Grant phrased it, thus releasing troops to LEE. In the Shenandoah Valley, Franz Sigel, a Union general by virtue of his abhorrence of slavery, had met JOHN BRECKINRIDGE at Newmarket and been defeated in a battle distinguished by the fighting of a corps of cadets from Virginia Military Institute. It was now up to Grant alone to keep the pressure on his opponent. He did, compelling LEE, in fact, to follow him; yet never succeeding in drawing Marse Robert out into the open.

LEE's counter to Grant's second sideslip was to move into another V-shaped position prepared the previous winter inside the steep-banked North Anna River. Again LEE was able to move troops from face to face of the V, making such clever use of the terrain that if Grant tried to move from flank to flank he would have to cross the river twice. Grant had no desire to be so discomfited, and after a few days of light skirmishing he sideslipped left again. Skirmishing once more to Totopotomoy Creek, he stepped left a fourth time and finally came up against LEE at a place called Cold Harbor.

Here Grant came to the conclusion that because LEE had not attempted an offensive he was beaten. The time had come for the crusher, Grant thought, and he ordered an all-out frontal assault. However, he had failed to reconnoiter LEE's lines, and had given LEE an extra day in which to fortify. Now he attacked *all along the line* rather than massing at a single point. No less than LEE at Gettysburg or Burnside at Fredericksburg, Grant had failed to grasp the new and awesome power of the defense. As a result, the Battle of Cold Harbor fought on June 3, 1864, was a Federal butchery.

Charge after charge was broken up, some in less than a quarter-hour. In one sector an outraged company commander, believing that his men had basely taken cover, ran over the field indignantly prodding them with his sword only to discover that they were all dead. Taken in their flank by enemy fire, some Union lines collapsed one upon the other like toppling dominoes. Across their entire front all the Federals could see were the black slouch hats of the Rebels and the flash of their muzzles. In less than an hour Grant lost 7,000 men against 1,500 for the Confederates, and he finally called off the assault.

It was an incredible defeat, made more doleful next day by the cries of "Water, water, for God's sake, water!"[174] breaking from the agonized lips of Grant's wounded outside the Confederate lines. LEE did not attack over this ground, but neither did Grant ask for a truce until June 6, and it was not until the night of June 7 that one was agreed upon. By then those wounded who had not been rescued by their comrades were all dead.

Cold Harbor closed a month of battle such as neither the Army of Northern Virginia nor the Army of the Potomac had ever before experienced. Many Union soldiers and some officers saw nothing but senseless slaughter. "For thirty days it has been one funeral procession past me," cried the sensitive General Warren, "and it is too much!"[175] It was not too much for U. S. Grant. True enough, he would one day write: "I have always regretted that the last assault at Cold Harbor was ever made."[176] Though shaken, he was not dismayed, and he saw in his defeat proof that frontal assault against LEE would never succeed. Instead, he decided to attack LEE's rear, to move all the way down to the south bank of the James River and cut off LEE's source of supply.

Here was an audacity worthy of ROBERT E. LEE. Grant was going to break contact with the watchful LEE and march undetected into LEE's rear, moving through LEE's own country swarming with LEE's own spies. To do this he must march 50 miles through swamps and across two rivers—including the half-mile-wide tidal James—always risking attack from that masterly commander whose favorite tactic was to strike an army on the move. Yet Grant had confidence in himself and his men, and he believed that the Rebel Army was no longer capable of those lightning adjustments which once had been its specialty. Whittling his sticks, gazing throughtfully through clouds of cigar smoke, Grant formulated his plans.

First, a force under Sheridan went into the Shenandoah Valley to disrupt LEE's supply lines there. Next, Meade prepared a second line of entrenchments to the rear of Cold Harbor under cover of which the army might slip away. Then William ("Baldy") Smith was ordered to take his corps by water up the James to seize Petersburg, holding it until Grant arrived with his main body.

Petersburg was the key to Grant's scheme. It was a vital rail junction lying 20-odd miles south of Richmond. If it fell and the Shenandoah line was blocked, Richmond could not be held and the specter of starvation would drive LEE's army into the open for a finish fight.

On the night of June 12 the Army of the Potomac began slipping away, moving as much like clockwork as is possible for 100,000 human beings. Every crossroad was strongly held to screen the army's movements. The James was spanned by one of the greatest military bridges in history, a pontoon crossing 2,100 feet long built to resist a strong tidal current and to adjust to a four-foot tidal rise and fall. Even Confederate gunboats on the upper James were contained. It was truly a magnificent maneuver, and LEE was left in the dark.

On the morning of June 13 his scouts reported the enemy trenches at Cold Harbor were empty. LEE did not know exactly where to look for Grant's vanished army. He had already moved to check the Union build-up in the Shenandoah, and he had also sent JUBAL EARLY there to threaten Washington and play the old game of panicking the North. Thus LEE was looking north while Grant was moving south, and he had weakened himself at a time when he needed to be strongest.

BEAUREGARD, holding the Petersburg defenses, had divined Grant's intentions and had pointed out that Petersburg was in great danger. Eventually LEE came to realize this, and when he did he began rushing reinforcements south in a race against time.

From the Union viewpoint, all depended now on Baldy Smith. He arrived with his corps by water at Bermuda Hundred on July 14 and was reinforced by a division of Negro troops and one of cavalry. He had about 10,000 men, but BEAUREGARD had only about 2,200 holding Petersburg. If Smith moved swiftly, he could crack BEAUREGARD's thinly held defenses and walk into the city. But it was not until 4 P.M. of July 15 that he ordered his attack. Then it was discovered that the artillery horses had been sent to water, and another two hours passed before the supporting guns could be hauled into position. Finally, with a division of Rebels marching madly to BEAUREGARD's rescue, with Hancock's corps coming toward Smith, the Federal assault began.

The Rebels were overrun, and the Negro troops were so jubilant that they danced in triumph around their captured cannon. Petersburg was Smith's for the taking, but he decided to hold what he had and wait for Hancock. When Hancock did arrive, Smith advised him not to attack, and so these fresh, eager soldiers merely relieved

Smith's weary men. They had marched toward Petersburg crying, "We'll end this damned rebellion tonight!"[177] but after they realized that the golden chance had gone glimmering and that tonight's weak enemy would be tomorrow's strong foe, they cursed and ground their teeth in anguish. "The rage of the enlisted men was devilish," a soldier wrote. "The most bloodcurdling blasphemy I ever listened to I heard that night, uttered by men who knew they were to be sacrificed on the morrow."[178]

With the eternally true instincts of cannon fodder, the men were right. During the night BEAUREGARD moved all his troops from Bermuda Hundred across the Appomattox River to reinforce Petersburg. This unbottled Butler, who could have placed himself between Richmond and Petersburg and perhaps, like Baldy Smith, won the war. But Butler only justified BEAUREGARD's contempt for him, making a few token moves before retiring in the face of reinforcements from LEE. In the meantime, BEAUREGARD's butternuts held off three entire Federal corps the next day, the 16th. They did the same on the 17th. On the 18th BEAUREGARD pulled back and the Union assault struck thin air. By the time the Federals regrouped, LEE had arrived with more reinforcements and Petersburg was too tough to storm.

Thwarted by his subordinates, baffled by BEAUREGARD, Grant settled down to a siege.

13

☆

A siege, ROBERT E. LEE had said, would make it "a mere question of time"[179] for the Army of Northern Virginia. Yet time was exactly what the Army of the Potomac was not supposed to grant the enemy.

Abraham Lincoln needed a quick victory, one that would come soon enough to influence the presidential election. Not only Lincoln's office was at stake on November 8 but the very fate of the nation as well: the election would also be a vote for or against continuing the war, and if the North said no to the war, that meant that the Union stood dissolved, perhaps permanently.

Discontent and disenchantment were spreading, and for different reasons. On the one hand were those radical Republicans who thought the war was not being fought hard enough, and they had already nominated John Charles Frémont as their own candidate for President. Such a splinter party could not fail to hurt Lincoln, who had been nominated by the so-called Union Party and had chosen a War Democrat, Andrew Johnson of Tennessee, as his running mate. On the other hand were those Peace Democrats, Copperheads, strict Constitutionalists and others who thought the war ought to be waged less harshly or else abandoned outright. Then there was the great bulk of the people who favored prosecution of the war but were dismayed by the sight of so many limbless veterans and the sound of so many funeral bells, and were wondering if the South was not actually unconquerable.

The Confederacy did seem unshaken in the summer of 1864. It was in truth a hollow shell, its insides eaten away by economic ills, but most people only saw that hard outer rind. Grant may have done exactly what he had proposed to do in fixing LEE on the defensive, but to many Northerners it appeared that he had only advanced to the James at the cost of a stunning butcher's bill of 60,000 men. Nor did Sherman seem to have done much better against JOHNSTON.

True, Sherman did not suffer so many losses and he had driven JOHNSTON deeper and deeper into Georgia. Yet JOHNSTON's army, his true objective, remained undefeated; and because the Rebels gathered in reinforcements as they retreated, it had grown even stronger. By the middle of July, 1864, Sherman had reached the outskirts of Atlanta, but he seemed to be stalled there.

At the same time, JUBAL EARLY came bursting out of the Shenandoah to menace Washington. This, of course, turned out to be only a passing scare. "Old Jube" knew very well that if he took his men into Washington he probably would never come out again, and after Grant calmly sent a corps north by water to attack him, EARLY quickly turned about and headed for home. Still, this last play of ROBERT E. LEE's capital card had not helped Northern war nerves. Nor were they eased when Grant made his last attempt to take Petersburg by literally blasting his way in.

A regiment of miners had dug a 500-foot tunnel under the Confederate lines and had planted four tons of gunpowder beneath the enemy's works. At dawn of July 30 the mine went up with a dreadful roar. Bodies, dirt and guns flew into the air. A huge crater was opened in the Confederate lines and defenders to either side of it fled in terror. Once again, the North had a chance to walk into Petersburg. However, instead of going around the crater, the troops went into it and found a 30-foot bank at the end. They could not climb it, they had no ladders, and as they milled around in confusion more and more troops were jammed into the pit, two of the Federal commanders took drunken refuge in a bombproof to the rear—and the Confederates rallied to counterattack. Before the Battle of the Crater was over the Federals had lost another 4,400 men, and Northern resolve to continue the war received another blow.

Such defeats nourished defeatism to the extent that the Radical Republican editor Horace Greeley could announce flatly: "Mr. Lincoln is already beaten. He cannot be re-elected."[180] Lincoln himself was deeply pessimistic. On August 23 he mystified his Cabinet by asking its members to sign a folded paper which would probably have flabbergasted them had they read it. It said:

This morning, as for some days past, it seems exceedingly probable that this administration will not be re-elected. Then it will be my duty to so co-operate with the President-elect as to save the Union between the election and the inauguration; as he will have secured his election on such ground that he cannot possibly save it afterward.[181]

In effect, "such ground" was virtual Copperhead control of the Democratic Convention gathered at Chicago that month. Led by Clement Vallandigham, who had slipped back into the North, the Peace Democrats denounced the war in the most violent terms and poured personal vituperation on the head of Lincoln. In the immemorial American way delegates took the convention floor to shout that free speech had been suppressed, and one of them avowed that his right to speak his mind openly had been denied on "the infamous orders of the gorilla tyrant that usurped the Presidential chair."[182] In the end George Brinton McClellan was nominated on a peace platform. McClellan did not actually accept that platform, however, only the support of those who formulated it. And as August ended it appeared that universal war weariness would put Little Mac in the White House.

With hindsight it can be seen that the flood of Federal misfortune —rather of apparent misfortune—had turned to the ebb long before Vallandigham and his bellicose pacifists made common cause with the pacific warrior McClellan. As the month of August began, the Southern façade began to crack and bulge under the strain of inexorable Federal pressure, and the first fissure appeared at Mobile.

Mobile had always seemed to Ulysses S. Grant one of the cornerstones of Confederate power. In 1863 he had told Halleck that an expedition from Mobile could detach Mississippi, Alabama and most of Georgia from the Confederacy. After he took command on March 9, 1864, Grant had wanted to seize Mobile so as to threaten JOHNSTON in his rear while Sherman pressed him on the front. The troops for such an expedition were then on the Red River Campaign under Nathaniel Banks. Their mission was to invade Texas for the sake of cotton and of frightening Napoleon III out of Mexico. However, they were defeated by the Rebels at Sabine Crossroads, Louisiana, on April 8, 1864, and Grant thereafter changed his plan.

Mobile, meanwhile, became an objective of the Union Navy. It was the Confederacy's last port on the Gulf of Mexico and it sheltered a Rebel gunboat flotilla and the big ironclad ram *Tennessee*. On August 5 a Federal fleet of wooden sloops, monitors and gunboats under Admiral Farragut entered Mobile Bay.

Farragut had climbed into the rigging of his flagship *Hartford* for a better view, and the ship's skipper, remembering the admiral's attacks of dizziness, had had him lashed there as a precaution. From the leading ship, *Brooklyn,* came a warning that the bay was filled with mines (torpedoes they were called then), and from Farragut came the famous reply: "Damn the torpedoes! Four bells! Captain Drayton, go ahead! Jouett, full speed!"[183] One by one the Rebel gunboats were sunk, the ram *Tennessee* was crippled and captured, and on August 23, the day of Lincoln's deepest pessimism, Fort Morgan was taken by assault.

The Confederacy, severed east from west by Union possession of the Mississippi, was now nearly shut off from the sea. As the month ended, William Tecumseh Sherman tried to cut it again, north from south.

". . . Mr. DAVIS had an exalted opinion of his own military genius," U. S. Grant was to write. "On several occasions during the war he came to the relief of the Union army by means of his *superior military genius.*[184]

One of these occasions came that July, when DAVIS angrily relieved JOE JOHNSTON of command of the Army of Tennessee and replaced him with JOHN B. HOOD. The Confederate President could not see that JOHNSTON had been skillfully fighting the only kind of campaign possible, which was to refuse to attack Sherman until he had him at a disadvantage. DAVIS wanted action, for he, too, was in political trouble, and HOOD was the kind of man who would give it to him.

Sherman was delighted. HOOD was a valiant fighter who had lost a leg and had an arm crippled in the forefront of battle, but he was also reputed to be rash and reckless. Sherman hoped that he would attack him as JOHNSTON had not, and HOOD did.

Three times within a week—July 20 to July 28, 1864—the Confederates struck at the Federals, hitting them hard north, east and west of Atlanta. Each time they were repulsed, and HOOD was forced to fall back on Atlanta. Sherman followed him and opened a siege, subjecting the city to heavy bombardment. Refusing to assault the Rebel works, Sherman drew his noose tighter and tighter. At the end of August he moved south and southwest to sever HOOD's communications, and with that the Confederate commander evacuated the city. On September 2 jubilant Federals marched into a city half-wrecked by Union guns and retiring Rebel dynamiters, and a few days later Sherman made his report beginning: "So Atlanta is ours, and fairly won."[185]

News of the capture of Atlanta electrified the North. It stunned the soft-war forces which had rallied around McClellan and silenced the plotters in Lincoln's own party who had been secretly preparing to repudiate the President in favor of "some candidate who commands the confidence of the country."[186] Down at Petersburg, an overjoyed U. S. Grant ordered a loaded 100-gun salute fired at the Rebel batteries.

Obviously, the Union's pressure on the Confederacy was becoming unbearable, and before the month was over it had opened another seam in the beautiful and prosperous Shenandoah Valley.

Here was one of the South's great assets. It not only provided food and forage for LEE's army but aimed a dagger at the Federal heart in Washington. Because the valley ran southwest to northeast, a

Confederate army marching down it would be moving directly toward the Union capital; but a Union army ascending the Shenandoah would only be going farther away from Richmond. Again and again LEE had taken advantage of this geographical accident. STONEWALL JACKSON and others had gone repeatedly into the valley to frighten Washington and draw Union troops away from Richmond for the Northern capital's defense. It might almost be said that LEE defended Richmond in the valley, just as he also supplied his army from there.

Of these facts U. S. Grant was well aware. He wanted the valley cleared of Rebels and an army of hungry Federals to "eat out Virginia clear and clean as far as they go, so that crows flying over it for the balance of the season will have to carry their provender with them."[187] The man eventually selected to carry out this mission was Philip Sheridan.

At first Grant had ordered that no houses were to be burned and that the valley's inhabitants—many of them pacifists with a religious horror of war—though notified to move, were to be treated justly. Sheridan echoed these instructions. However, such compassionate reservations are not possible to an army ordered to make "a desert" of a lush and smiling garden, and it is difficult not to suspect that they were advance disclaimers for the excesses that both Grant and Sheridan must have known were inevitable.

One reason that excesses were inevitable was that by the summer of 1864 the American Civil War had followed the logic of warfare, which argues that when the enemy does not quickly submit, then more and more brutal means must be brought to bear to compel his submission. A thickening fog of hatred had also descended upon both camps, especially after both sides learned of the horrible treatment of their captured soldiers. The South's infamous camp at Andersonville, where 10,000 Yankee prisoners died in seven months, was probably the most notorious of these dreadful pestholes; yet there were places in the North such as the camp at Elmira which were only a bit less miserable. There were also atrocities committed by both sides, and again the South led the way with the burning of Lawrence, Kansas, by Colonel WILLIAM QUANTRILL's raiders and the massacre of the Union garrison at Fort Pillow carried out by NATHAN BEDFORD FORREST. Many of these soldiers were Negroes, and FORREST reported: "The river was dyed with the blood of the slaughtered for two hundred yards. . . . It is hoped that these facts will demonstrate to the Northern people that negro soldiers cannot cope with Southerners."[188] Irregular bands such as QUANTRILL's were another reason that the soldiers of Sheridan's Army of the Shenandoah were not going to fill the hypocritical bill of a gentle desolation. Many of these guerrillas operating in the Shenandoah were little better than outlaws. Deserters and desperadoes, they had no stomach for the battle line but preferred the sudden midnight swoop and the quick getaway; and they were detested as much by Confederate commanders as they were dreaded by Federal soldiers. The fires of hatred, then, had crept into that last calm crevice of war: the breast of the common soldier. Johnny Reb and Billy Yank had openly fraternized from Vicksburg to Petersburg, swapping jokes and comic taunts and trading Confederate tobacco for Yankee newspapers and coffee. But now they hated, if not each other, at least the other side; and in this growing mood of savagery the Union picked up the red-hot iron of total war and pressed it down hard on the Shenandoah.

The results were red and smoking scars. From mountain to mountain billowing clouds of smoke shut out the sun by day, and by night the shadows danced and flickered in the light of glowing bonfires. Stacks of hay and straw were burned, barns filled with harvested crops were set blazing, all supplies of use to man or beast were set afire and all cattle were driven off. Everywhere that Sheridan's troops lifted the torch they were met by throngs of weeping old men, women and children, but the work of scorching the enemy's earth went on inexorably. As a Union chaplain wrote: "The time had fully come to peel this land and put an end to the long strife for its possession."[189]

The strife, however, was not yet over. Alarmed, LEE sent JUBAL EARLY to drive Sheridan out of the valley. Tall, thin, twisted, with a rasping wit to give bite to his misanthropic jibes, "Old Jube" had begun to distinguish himself as one of the ablest of that able company of lieutenants who served ROBERT E. LEE. Above all, EARLY was impetuous, and he did not hesitate to hurl his 15,000 lean veterans against Sheridan's 45,000.

The two forces met at Winchester, where EARLY caught Sheridan's advance guard and drove it back. Riding forward on his great black horse Rienzi, Sheridan built up his battle line and pressed the Rebels back. Not since the days of Fighting Phil Kearny had Federal soldiers seen a Union general so far forward. Waving his little flat hat, crying out, "Come on, boys, come on," disdaining enemy fire, laughing when a shell burst directly overhead, the fiery little general on the big horse infused his army with a dash and daring hitherto unknown among the Federals of the Shenandoah. Just before dusk, a splendid Union cavalry charge struck the Confederates in their left flank and rear to roll them back—and Winchester was another Union victory to lift Lincoln's reviving political stock still higher. Three days later, on September 22, Frémont withdrew from the presidential race.

Sheridan pursued EARLY up the valley, still spreading devastation as he moved, and still harassed by the attacks on his supply line made by the masterful Confederate partisan chieftain JOHN MOSBY.

MOSBY played on Sheridan's line like a virtuoso, forcing the Union general to detach large bodies of troops to protect his rear.

By mid-October Sheridan's army was encamped at Cedar Creek 20 miles south of Winchester. Sheridan had gone to Washington for a brief visit. He did not think that the twice-beaten EARLY would dare attack his powerful army. On the night of October 18, Sheridan was back in Winchester—and the daring EARLY had already made up his mind to strike the Union left at Cedar Creek the next morning. Out of the misty dawn the Confederates poured on that memorable October 19, 1864, rolling back the surprised Federals and threatening to rout Sheridan's entire army. Up in Winchester, an officer awakened Sheridan and told him he had heard artillery. "It's all right," Sheridan said, explaining that a scouting force was "merely feeling the enemy."[190] Two and a half hours passed before Sheridan was mounted on Rienzi, and it was then that he heard the roar of artillery to the south. Leaning forward in his saddle, he heard it grow at a rate indicating that his own army must be falling back. He had heard:

> The terrible rumble, grumble and roar
> Telling the battle was on once more—
> And Sheridan twenty miles away![191]

Sheridan did not go galloping wildly all the way down that road, as Read's poem says, but he did urge his horse forward into the frantic backwash of a beaten army. Wagon trains, sutlers and camp followers, walking wounded and artillery wagons, stragglers and skulkers, all flowed back toward Winchester, their hurry and their fright eloquent of a disaster at the front. Sheridan rode faster, now, coming at a gallop in front of some 50 mounted men. Now he saw real soldiers retreating, and he drew rein to shout at them: "Turn back! Face the other way! If I had been here with you this morning this wouldn't have happened."[192] On he rode, crying, "Turn back! Turn Back!" swinging his little cap and calling for more and more speed from the tireless Rienzi. Then he fell silent, his face setting into stone while his piercing black eyes took on the dull red stubborn glint of a spirit defiant in defeat.

Suddenly, Sheridan had reached the battlefield. Across the battle line he galloped while a thunderous great cheer broke from the throats of his army. "Sheridan! Sheridan!" his soldiers shouted, as though the mere repetition of his name would avert disaster. Such emotional outbursts rarely occur on modern battlefields, but there were men there who swore that Sheridan's presence meant: "No more doubt or chance for doubt existed; we were safe, perfectly and unconditionally safe, and every man knew it."[193]

Regrouped, revitalized, the Union Army swept forward; and it was irresistible. The redoubtable JUBAL EARLY and his veterans could not contain such furious waves of blue, and the fact of Sheridan's ride was thus equal to the legend: by his sudden appearance the Union general turned defeat into victory and closed the Shenandoah to the South forever.

Mobile, Atlanta, the Shenandoah, they were names that stuck in the minds of Northern voters going to the polls on that fateful November 8, 1864. There, with ballots not bullets, the real battle was being fought. There, in an event unique in history, a democracy engaged in a dreadful civil war was electing a President. At Washington on that rain-swept night Abraham Lincoln awaited the result in the war telegraph office. He was confident. He told of another rainy election night, when he had lost to Stephen Douglas. Walking home on a slippery hogback, "my foot slipped from under me, knocking the other one out of the way, but I recovered myself and lit square, and I said to myself: 'It's a slip and not a fall.' "[194] Toward midnight Abraham Lincoln knew that he had been re-elected. Well-wishers besieged the telegraph office with a brass band and demands for a speech.

"It is no pleasure to me to triumph over any one," Abraham Lincoln said, "but I give thanks to the Almighty for this evidence of the people's resolution to stand by free government and the rights of humanity."[195]

14

☆

As the year 1864 came to a close the Civil War possessed all those hideous features that make the Medusa of modern war. It had begun with gay flags and blaring bands and pink-cheeked farm boys in baggy red pants, and it was ending with sabered pigs and burnt barns and weeping women shoved rudely aside by gaunt men with hollows in the cheeks where innocence had bloomed.

Along the way the Civil War had introduced the breech-loading rifle, barbed wire, hand grenades, winged grenades, wooden wirebound mortars, rockets and even booby traps. Magazine rifles were invented and also the Requa machine gun. At Mobile the Confederacy had built a submarine, the 35-foot *R. L. Hunley* which was propelled by a screw worked from the inside by eight men, and on February 17, 1864, the *Hunley* torpedoed and sank the U.S.S. *Housatonic* and went down with her. The first battle of ironclads had been fought between *Monitor* and *Merrimac*, while on land there were armored trains as well as land mines. Trench warfare as grim and dirty as any in World War I had already started outside Petersburg, and poison gas was foreshadowed by the Confederate officer who toyed with the notion of a stink-shell to give off "offensive gases" and cause "suffocating effect." Flag and lamp signaling also was used, as well as field telegraph, while both sides maintained observation balloons. In fact, "the meanest trick of the war" occurred when the North captured a Rebel balloon made of silk dresses donated by patriotic ladies. Finally, the restless mind of Ben Butler had come up with the forerunner of the flame-thrower, a "small garden engine" squirting Greek fire. "Also he is going to get a gun that shoots seven miles and, taking direction by compass, burn the city of Richmond with shells of Greek fire."[196] In this, the concepts of Big Bertha and of fire-bombing are rolled into one, and Butler may have been unique in thinking of constructing an auger to bore a tunnel five feet in diameter and thus dig his way into Richmond. Except for tanks, airplanes and atomic bombs, then, the foundations for the arsenal of modern warfare had been laid; and a week after Lincoln was re-elected the very tactics of frightfulness which moderns condemned as evil incarnate when they were used in the service of Nazi Germany were being put into effect by Sherman in the state of Georgia.

Of all the remarkable leaders of the Civil War the most original was William Tecumseh Sherman. Many military historians acclaim him as the first of the modern strategists. Certainly he was the first to see that industrialized war shifted the target from the military to the economic and moral. A nation must be struck in its capacity to fight and its will to fight, Sherman reasoned. This meant by-passing its armies and attacking its industrial potential and its population; this meant nothing less than deliberate desolation and demoralization: this was blitzkrieg.

The man who conceived this strategy was not, as the descendants of his Southern victims maintain, the reincarnation of Attila the Hun. He was rather an unusually perceptive, gifted and complicated human being, in whose character and career can be found perhaps more marks of genius than in those of any other American commander before or since. Chief of all, he cared nothing for human respect. He wore rumpled, muddy, mismatching uniforms; he conceded a russet beard to the chin fashions of the day but kept it close-cut; he was tall, lanky, awkward, given to shoving his hands into his pockets or rubbing up his thatch of coarse red hair; his face was wrinkled, his nose pointed and red, and his little eyes black and sharp. "Uncle Billy," as the soldiers called Sherman, talked rapidly in a high voice about a host of subjects, his features often all but obscured by clouds of "segar" smoke and his clothing covered by a fine film of cigar ash. One young lieutenant who met him thought him the "ideal Yankee," while admitting that he had "experienced almost an exhaustion from the excitement of his vigorous presence."[197]

In Sherman were combined so many seemingly conflicting qualities that he would seem to have been crippled by that inconsistency which is "the hobgoblin of little minds." Actually he was balanced: quick in thought and careful in detail, visionary in planning and practical in execution, dynamic yet reflective, warmhearted but coolheaded, Sherman was one of those unique double personalities who are at once the man who thinks and the man who feels. Neither gained the ascendancy, but such a struggle between head and heart must necessarily carry a man very close to insanity, and so it was no wonder that he was often thought "crazy" or that he, too, was touched with that divine discontent which sank him deep in despondency or sent him soaring to the heights of inspiration. "A dead cock in a pit," he called himself before the war, although he had already been reared in the household of the famous Senator Ewing of Ohio, educated at West Point, trained in the law, soldier in Mexico, voyager around the Horn, Indian fighter, banker, battler for law and order in lawless San Francisco, and, finally, president of a military academy in Louisiana. After Louisiana seceded, Sherman remained loyal; and Lincoln liked him because he said he did not want appointment to high rank, preferring instead to work his way up while he learned the art of war.

By the fall of 1864 he knew it well enough to make one of the boldest gambles in military history. By then, Hood had shown that he could prevent Sherman from destroying his army. By then also, Sherman had learned that his long supply line back to Louisville was becoming a costly nuisance. First Nathan Bedford Forrest had gone into Tennessee to tear up railroads and cause enough trouble to compel Sherman to send Thomas and 30,000 men back to Nashville to contain him. Then Hood himself had begun to maneuver against the Union supply line north of Atlanta, hoping to draw Sherman north. Hood did not hurt the supply line much, but neither did Sherman ever catch Hood in a finish fight. Finally, with the boldness born of desperation, Hood began marching his entire army toward Tennessee in the belief that Sherman would now have to abandon Atlanta and come after him.

Sherman's response to Hood's gamble was an even bolder decision. He proposed to ignore the enemy army and attack instead the spirit of the South. He decided to abandon his supply line and lead some 60,000 men from Atlanta to Savannah and the sea. An army of human locusts would devour the food so badly needed by Lee's hungry soldiers in Petersburg and then destroy what they could not eat or carry off. They would make the people of Georgia feel the harsh hand of war in their very homes, and they would make the entire South feel helpless at the sight of a Union army moving unchecked through its heartland. "I can make the march, and make Georgia howl!"[198] Sherman told Grant, and eventually both Grant and Lincoln agreed.

On November 15, then, as HOOD marched north toward Tennessee, Sherman set his face in the opposite direction: the seacoast. First, however, he burned Atlanta. It is said that Sherman only intended to wreck and burn railroad installations and factories, that he wanted to spare shops and stores and private homes. Nevertheless, as the South still maintains with much justice, Sherman's soldiers were "a mite careless with powder and fire," and most of Atlanta went up in flames.

Nor were Sherman's soldiers very careful about property rights as they moved on a 60-mile front through a rich land where the harvest was in, the barns were stuffed with corn and forage, smokehouses bulged with hams and bacon, and the fields were full of cattle. Each morning each brigade detached a forage company of about 50 men to comb the countryside a few miles to either side of the brigade's line of march. Seizing farm wagons and carriages, they loaded them with bacon, eggs, cornmeal, chickens, turkeys and ducks, sweet potatoes— whatever could be carried off—and delivered their loads to the brigade commissaries at the end of each day. Meanwhile, other units drove off livestock. What they could not take, they killed. To save ammunition, they sabered pigs and poleaxed horses and mules between the ears. From sunup to sundown lean veterans accustomed to hardtack and salt pork gorged themselves on ham and yams and fresh beef, and as they advanced across the state they grew fat and sleek. So did the Negroes to whom they gave the plantation masters' food, and who frolicked on the heels of the advancing host in the living embodiment of the famous ditty:

> Say Darkies has you seen old Massa
> Wid de muffstache on his face
> Go long de road sometime dis mornin'
> Like he gwine to leave de place?
>
> De massa run, ha-ha!
> De darkey stay, ho-ho!
> I tink it must be Kingdom Coming
> And de year ob Jubilo.

It was indeed the Year of Jubilo for the Negroes, just as for Sherman's laughing veterans the march had become a picnic promenade, but to the South it seemed a wanton and barbaric ruin that cried out to heaven for vengeance. From wing to wing 60 miles apart there rose columns of smoke as the advancing army trailed its own somber clouds of destruction. Warehouses, bridges, barns, machine shops, depots and factories were burned. Not even houses were spared, especially not by the "bummers," those deserters, desperadoes and looters, North and South, who were drawn to the march for the sake of loot. These were the men who forced old men and helpless women to divulge the secret places where silver, jewelry and money were hidden. They danced with muddy, hobnailed boots on snow-white linen or gleaming table tops, smashing furniture with gun butts, slashing feather beds with sabers and shattering windows and mirrors with empty bottles. Sherman, who might have restrained them, did little to stop them. "War is cruelty, and you cannot refine it,"[199] he had told the people of Atlanta, and it was his intention to demonstrate that the Confederacy was powerless to protect its people against it.

Railroad-wrecking was another object of the march, and to this, Sherman wrote, "I gave my personal attention."[200] After the rails had been pried up they were heated over bonfires of crossties and then twisted around trees to be left useless, and the countryside was festooned with "Sherman hairpins" or "JEFF DAVIS neckties." Thus like a flow of molten lava 60 miles wide and 300 miles long, the Union Army marched to the sea.

Meanwhile, General HOOD had begun a successful drive into Tennessee. On November 29-30 near Franklin he nearly trapped a Federal army under John Schofield, but the Federals eventually escaped after savage fighting which caused the death of five Confederate generals. HOOD pursued toward Nashville, where Thomas blocked his path. Thomas, in fact, was in position to destroy HOOD; and a jittery U. S. Grant ordered him to do so before the Rebel Army could by-pass Nashville and invade the North. Such a maneuver might upset all Grant's plans and thus prolong a war which seemed on the verge of being won. But the stolid Thomas moved in his own good time, so slowly, in fact, that Grant resolved to relieve him. On December 15, however, Thomas struck HOOD with such fury that the Confederate Army was sent south in headlong retreat. That was the South's last gasp in the West, and six days later, when Sherman's sleek tatterdemalions poured jubilantly into Savannah, the death rattle of the Confederacy was clearly audible on both sides of the Mason-Dixon Line.

JEFFERSON DAVIS was not the man to listen to his own death rattle. Unbending die-hard or eleventh-hour savior, he would not in either case be conscious of impending defeat. As the year 1864 came to a close the Confederacy had shrunk to the Carolinas and Virginia, HOOD's army was a wreck, Sherman was poised to march north to join Grant's swelling Army of the Potomac, and Sheridan was ready to ride down to Petersburg with all his immense and veteran horsemen. Surely the South, for all its splendid fighting spirit, should fight no longer. Its economy was crippled, and its government so powerless to wage war that even the gentle ROBERT E. LEE raged against Congressmen who "do not seem to be able to do anything except to eat peanuts and chew tobacco, while my army is starving."[201] LEE's army was also cold and poorly clothed, and its ranks were dwindling. Desertions were now at their height, because when Sherman menaced a hearth in Georgia or the Carolinas he twisted a heart at Petersburg. Moreover, as Grant inexorably extended his lines to his left, the outnumbered LEE had to move right to contain him, and this thinned his lines. Yet JEFFERSON DAVIS had no thought of capitulation, not even after the Union seized Fort Fisher on January 15, 1865, and thus sealed off Wilmington, North Carolina, the Confederacy's last major port.

The Confederate President, a son of the eighteenth century, if not an earlier age, still saw the war as a contest between armies, soldier to soldier, not as a conflict between nations in which capacity to fight is paramount, or a war between democracies in which the will to fight is major. Attrition and blockade had scuttled the Confederate capacity, while hunger, defeat and calculated frightfulness had worn down the will. Southern morale had also been weakened by disputes over DAVIS's frequent suspensions of the writ of habeas corpus, and many a brave butternut left the trenches and headed home after being informed that the Confederate commissary was stripping his farm of food and animals. Under these conditions a peace movement was begun under the leadership of DAVIS's archfoe and obstructionist, Vice President ALEXANDER STEPHENS. DAVIS agreed to ask for a peace conference, but actually only in the hope of provoking a harsh statement of Union war aims that would stiffen the Southern spine.

On February 3, 1865, STEPHENS and two others met Lincoln and Seward on the *River Queen* in Hampton Roads. STEPHENS proposed that the two camps make peace to join in evicting the French from Mexico in defense of the Monroe Doctrine. Lincoln replied that he could not enter negotiations unless the Confederacy agreed to return to the Union and abolish slavery. Such proposals, of course, could not even be considered by the Confederates—and the war went on.

It continued with JOHNSTON recalled to block Sherman's northward march through the Carolinas, and with ROBERT E. LEE at last the Confederate commander in chief. Popular resentment against DAVIS's conduct of the war had led to creation of this position, but the gesture came as the hands of the clock neared midnight. LEE knew that the Confederacy was teetering on the edge of disaster. Desertions had so drained his armies that the Confederacy passed a law conscripting slaves. With splendid irony the South offered Negroes the equal opportunity of fighting shoulder to shoulder with whites in a war begun to preserve their own enslavement.

Nevertheless, JEFFERSON DAVIS was determined to go down to utter defeat rather than accept any terms that did not recognize Southern independence, and because it was not LEE's habit to challenge the President on matters of policy, LEE also decided to fight on. Ever the gambler, he resolved on a last, desperate chance: a breakout from Petersburg followed by a lightning march south to join JOHNSTON and overwhelm Sherman, after which both armies would return north to defeat Grant. General JOHN GORDON, the hero of Spotsylvania, was ordered to lead the assault on Union-held Fort Stedman directly east of Petersburg. An hour before daylight on March 25, 1865, the Rebels attacked.

They went in with a silent rush, surprising and seizing Stedman and sending a spearhead ahead to pierce the Federal secondary line. If they could widen their breakthrough and hold it, LEE's army could pour through the breach and get clean away to North Carolina. But the Federals rallied. Forts to either side of Stedman refused to fall, a counterattack was launched on Stedman, and Union artillery shattered the Rebel front. By midmorning LEE's last sally had been broken and hurled back with losses of 5,000 men. Now it was the turn of U. S. Grant.

Before GORDON's attack Grant had seen that he must crush LEE's right flank, seizing the roads and railways by which the Confederates might escape south. Heavy rains had delayed putting his plan into operation, but after Philip Sheridan arrived at Petersburg with all his cavalry Grant began to move swiftly.

On March 29 a full corps began striking LEE's right, while Sheridan led a corps of cavalry and one of infantry in a wide sweep toward Five Forks still farther to the Rebel right. If he could get in behind LEE, he would cut off the Confederate escape and practically guarantee LEE's defeat. LEE reacted swiftly, sending PICKETT to oppose him. On March 31 the Confederates halted Sheridan's forces short of Five Forks at a place called Dinwiddie Court House. But the little Union general was not defeated. He had wisely retired to await reinforcements, and Grant sent him Warren's corps.

Next day Sheridan chafed at Warren's delay. Sheridan smelled victory, he could win the war that day, and he cried aloud: "This battle must be fought and won before the sun goes down!"[202] In simple terms, Sheridan wanted to crush and scatter PICKETT's force and seize the Southside Railway to his rear. If this was done, it was all over with LEE and probably for the Confederacy.

At last Warren's veterans began moving into line. Sheridan was everywhere among them. When one of his skirmish lines was staggered and seemed ready to fall back, he galloped toward his faltering soldiers, shouting, "Come on—go at 'em—move on with a clean jump or you'll not catch one of them!"[203] A soldier beside him was hit in the throat. "I'm killed!" he cried, blood spurting thickly from his jugular vein. "You're not hurt a bit!" Sheridan roared. "Pick up your gun, man, and move right on!"[204] Obediently, the soldier trotted forward—and fell dead. Now the battle line was formed, and Sheridan shouted: "Where's my battle flag?"[205] It was brought forward, and the general raised his little swallow-tailed red-and-white banner high over his head and rode black Rienzi up and down the line.

A bullet pierced the flag, and the sergeant who had brought it fell. Sheridan rode forward, spurring his horse toward the Rebel earthworks. After him came the yelling Federal infantry. Sheridan put Rienzi over the works in a splendid leap, and his infantry swarmed in after him. Now a perfect rage of battle had come over Sheridan, in the midst of which he relieved the unfortunate Warren of his command. It was brutal, it was probably not just, but Sheridan realized with Grant that the end of the war was within the Union grasp, and a general should be ready to press forward as obediently as the private whose lifeblood poured from his throat.

"What I want is that Southern Railway," Sheridan roared repeatedly. "I want you men to understand we have a record to make before the sun goes down that will make Hell tremble!"[206]

Capture of the vital railway that day was not to be. Yet PICKETT's force had been completely shattered and Five Forks fell to Sheridan. A jubilant Grant cabled the information to Lincoln, who relayed the information to the press. For the next few days an eager North read with drawn breath of the progress of that single win-the-war battle that had eluded the nation for four years.

Next day, April 2, Grant attacked all along the line. Row upon row of Federal gun batteries began baying in a voice of rolling thunder, hurling a dreadful weight of death and destruction upon the Rebel positions. Then came silence. Thousands upon thousands of Federal soldiers moved forward. Slowly, with a gathering rush, they struck the Confederate lines, and in the weakened center they tore them apart. One by one clusters of Rebel muskets winked out in that predawn darkness, and black gaps opened in the Southern line. Into the open spaces rushed the Federals, widening them, and a quarter-hour after Wright's corps attacked in the center a decisive breakthrough was achieved.

To the rear A. P. HILL heard of the penetration while discussing the battle with LEE. He rode forward, to receive a bullet in the heart and strip from LEE yet another of his great lieutenants. Tears in his eyes, LEE called upon LONGSTREET. But "Old Pete" and his valiant men could not stem the rising Federal tide.

As the Sunday of April 2, 1865, grew lighter, LEE prepared to abandon Petersburg. He still hoped to join JOHNSTON. It was a forlorn hope, and LEE doubtless knew it, yet his sense of duty kept him loyal to President DAVIS's designs. As 30,000 red-eyed and starving survivors of the Army of Northern Virginia began streaming west, LEE dictated the long-dreaded telegraph to the War Department.

Meticulously dressed in gray, cold as a marble statue, JEFFERSON DAVIS sat in the family pew at St. Paul's Episcopal Church. Surrounded mostly by women, many dressed in black, DAVIS heard the preacher say: "The Lord is in His holy temple; let all the earth keep silence before Him."[207] Into that churchly silence there crept the tinkle of spurs. An officer holding his saber came striding down the aisle. He handed DAVIS a paper. The President unfolded it and read: "I advise that all preparation be made for leaving Richmond tonight. I will advise you later, according to circumstances."[208]

    With tight-lipped calm, DAVIS pocketed LEE's message of doom and walked majestically from the church. Going to the War Department, he telegraphed LEE that to move the Confederate government that night would "involve the loss of many valuables." LEE received the protest in the field, and angrily tore it to bits with the remark: "I am sure I gave him sufficient notice."[209] Regaining his composure, he notified DAVIS that it was "absolutely necessary" to move that night.

    Richmond learned swiftly that the government was fleeing. Throughout that Passion Sunday civilians fought government clerks for possession of carts and wagons, carriages and gigs, while crowded streets echoed to rolling wheels or the rumbling of departing trains. The Confederate treasury—less than a half-million dollars in bullion—was placed in charge of a battalion of naval cadets. Civilians able to flee joined the government exodus. Those who could not, locked their doors and closed their shutters and sat down in despair to await the Yankee invasion. Night fell and the city began to tremble to the detonation of bridges and arsenals.

    Soon the city was afire. So was neighboring Manchester. They blazed like beacons in the dark while the James lay glittering between them. Inevitably, those people of Richmond whom inflation and food shortages had transformed into wild, half-starved creatures turned to looting. Commissary depots were full of supplies never delivered to LEE's hungry army, and now that they were left unguarded they were broken into and plundered. Barrels of whiskey were also found, and soon there were drunks capering in the reflected flames of burning cotton or tobacco warehouses. Then the mob began breaking into shops and storehouses, sotted women fought each other for ostrich plumes, drunken men shot each other over boots and sashes. So the flames and the frenzy spread, and soon the only safe place in Richmond was in the green hills of Capitol Square. Here women in shawls clasped frightened children to their bosoms, and here, while the night winds whipped the fires, as tall flames roared and drunken revelers shrieked, like a shower of sparks from a falling building, the capital of the Confederacy collapsed.

ROBERT E. LEE had a headstart of one day in his race against the tenacious Grant. With this advantage, LEE believed he could get his army to Danville, the pleasant little city on the Dan River to which JEFFERSON DAVIS had already moved the government. Here he could be joined by JOHNSTON.

On April 3 it did not seem to LEE that Grant was pursuing too rapidly. That night his ragged veterans staggered into Amelia Court House, 21 miles west of Petersburg. There, to his dismay, LEE found not a single ration to feed 30,000 agonizingly hungry men. He had no recourse but to halt next day while forage wagons searched the countryside for food. In the meantime, the day's headstart was lost. Federal cavalry were everywhere. Close behind them hurried three eager corps of Union infantry, marching a few miles south of LEE on a straighter, parallel route. That night of April 4 some of Sheridan's riders menaced Amelia.

On the morning of April 5 the forage wagons came in, and LEE saw with concealed despair that they were nearly empty. His men must march now on their nerves alone, their hearts nourished by LEE's spirit but their bellies empty and growling with hunger. Another delay ensued: EWELL and ANDERSON were slow in closing up. Finally, the army moved south from Amelia Court House—and found Federal infantry and cavalry barring the way.

There was nothing left to do but to shift west toward Farmville, where there was hope of receiving rations from Lynchburg. This meant a night march that killed a good part of LEE's army. It was a slow stumble over crowded roads made by men with leaden limbs, men who moved like sleepwalkers. Many fell out never to return. Many were captured by Federal cavalry, which never left off nipping at LEE's heels. Grant was clinging to LEE's army, and he would not let go.

Still, LEE pressed on. On April 6 the Federals caught up at a place called Sailor's Creek. Here they overwhelmed GORDON, who was covering the Confederate trains, capturing the greater part of LEE's wagons, and here, as LEE watched in agony, they broke EWELL's and ANDERSON's corps. Sitting on Traveler and holding a red battle flag, LEE saw the wreck of shattered regiments come backwashing toward him, and he cried aloud: "My God, has the Army been dissolved?"[210] That day LEE lost between 7,000 and 8,000 men. That night LEE's army was down to 15,000 muskets and sabers to oppose 80,000 Federal infantry and cavalry. On April 7, however, his pale and pinched veterans struggled into Farmville, where they received their first rations since the retreat began. From Farmville, LEE continued his withdrawal. He got safely across the Appomattox River and burned the bridges behind him. Some of them were saved by the Federals, however, and once more Union cavalry began to bite on LEE's rear. That night LEE received Grant's invitation to surrender. He handed it to LONGSTREET, who replied: "Not yet."[211]

There was still hope. If LEE could get to a place called Appomattox Station, he could feed his men from four trains of food from Lynchburg, and then swing south to safety at Danville.

On April 8 LEE was forced to fight another rear-guard action to save his remaining wagons. As he did, Sheridan's cavalry and infantry under E. O. C. Ord swept past his southern flank and drove into Appomattox Station. They captured LEE's ration trains and put themselves across his line of march. That night LEE's army reached Appomattox Court House. Below them, across their path, lay Sheridan's force. If it was only cavalry, it might be brushed aside and the army yet saved. But if infantry was there in force, the Army of Northern Virginia was doomed.

April 9, 1865, was a Palm Sunday. Very early that morning ROBERT EDWARD LEE put on a new gray uniform, a sash of deep red silk, the jeweled sword given him by ladies in England, beautiful red-stitched spurred boots and long gray gauntlets. An officer expressed surprise, and Lee said: "I have probably to be General Grant's prisoner and thought I must make my best appearance."[212]

To the east, riding anxiously toward Appomattox over sloppy roads came a slender brown-bearded man wearing a mud-spattered private's blouse. His face was strained, for he had a bad headache and had been up all night bathing his feet in hot water and applying mustard plasters to his neck and wrists. Still, Ulysses S. Grant was hopeful that today would see an end to four years of blood and agony.

Yet Palm Sunday was beginning with the roar of guns. Down from Appomattox Court House charged the butternuts under General GORDON. They brushed aside the Federal outriders, and saw a solid blue phalanx of glittering bayonets to the rear. The Army of Northern Virginia had come to the end of the road. Back to LEE went GORDON's message that he could do nothing without reinforcements. "Then," said ROBERT E. LEE calmly, "there is nothing left for me to do but to go and see General Grant, and I would rather die a thousand deaths!"[213]

It was the end. With cries of anguish, protesting men and officers clustered around LEE. One general proposed that the army disperse and turn to guerrilla warfare. LEE replied that to do so would make mere marauders of his soldiers and inflict anarchy upon the South. He was prepared to sacrifice his own invincible pride for the safety of his country, and as the messages went out to Grant, Phil Sheridan opposite LEE grew impatient. He had massed both his men and horse with the passionate cry: "Now smash 'em, I tell you, smash 'em!"[214] Now his bugles blew and his blue lines leaned forward, and out from those pitiful gray ranks huddled beneath a host of battle flags a lone rider galloped. He carried a flag of truce and he told Sheridan that LEE was waiting to see Grant in the McLean House.

Skeptical at first, Sheridan finally ordered a cease-fire. Dazed, the two armies sat down and contemplated each other. In the spring stillness they suddenly heard bird song rather than bullets. Then General Grant rode up to Sheridan. He inclined his head toward the village and asked, "Is General LEE up there?" Sheridan said, "Yes," and Grant said, "Well, then, let's go up."[215]

They "went up" to that McLean House which, ironically, had brought the war full circle. It was at the home of Wilmer McLean that BEAUREGARD made his headquarters during the First Battle of Bull Run. To get away from the war, McLean sold out and moved to Appomattox. Now it was in McLean's front parlor that Grant met LEE.

Grant came in alone and saw LEE with two aides. Taking off his yellow thread gloves, Grant stepped forward to shake LEE's hand. He was aware of his own mud-stained appearance and LEE's splendor, but he gave no sign of it. Both men sat at tables while a half-dozen of Grant's generals entered with tinkling spurs and clanking sabers to stand behind their chief. LEE gave no sign of disapproval of their presence.

Grant spoke: "I met you once before, General LEE, while we were serving in Mexico, when you came over from General Scott's headquarters to visit Garland's brigade, to which I then belonged. I have always remembered your appearance, and I think I should have recognized you anywhere."

"Yes," Lee said, "I know I met you on that occasion, and I have often thought of it and tried to recollect how you looked, but I have never been able to recall a single feature."[216]

Grant talked eagerly of Mexico, perhaps to soften the impact of the request that he must make, and LEE, probably anxious to be done with the ordeal of surrender, brought him back gently with the words: "I suppose, General Grant, that the object of our present meeting is fully understood. I asked to see you to ascertain upon what terms you would receive the surrender of my army."[217]

Without changing countenance, with not a hint of exultation or gloating in his voice, Grant quickly outlined his terms: ". . . the officers and men surrendered to be paroled and disqualified from taking up arms again until properly exchanged, and all arms, ammunition and supplies to be delivered up as captured property."[218]

Next Grant set down his terms in writing. LEE read them, courteously corrected an unintentional oversight, and agreed. There was, however, the matter of the horses, which were the private property of his cavalrymen and artillerists. Would the men be permitted to retain them? At first Grant said that the terms allowed only officers to keep private property, but then, seeing how much this request meant to LEE, he promised "to let all the men who claim to own a horse or mule take the animals home with them to work their little farms."[219]

LEE was relieved and grateful. "This will have the best possible effect on the men," he said. "It will be very gratifying and will do much toward conciliating our people."[220] In Grant's generosity LEE saw not a vindictive but a compassionate conquerer.

ROBERT E. LEE knew then that the South had fallen. Even though the army which he formally surrendered a few minutes later was only his own, even though combat might sputter on until May 26, the fighting soul of the South died with LEE's signature on that Palm Sunday of 1865.

After he signed, LEE arose and shook hands with Grant. He bowed to the others in the room and strode silently out the door. On the porch of the McLean House he paused to draw on his gauntlets. He gazed sadly toward the hillside where his little army lay, faithful and fearless to the last. Twice, with slow and savage ruefulness, LEE drove his fist into his palm. Then, crying for Traveler in a hoarse and choking voice, he mounted and rode out of sight.

PART VI

Indian Wars,
the Spanish-American War
and the Philippine Insurrection

1

☆

What was to be done with the fallen South?

She had been crushed. She had gone down before the North's superior firepower, manpower and industrial power, and now she lay prostrate. In those areas where the armies of both sides had fought and marched, her railroads were demolished, her cities devastated and her countryside ravaged. Her warrior pride had been humbled and her manhood mutilated. Her economy was wrecked: land values had collapsed, the currency was worthless and some 3.5 million slaves "valued" at $2 billion had been freed without compensation for their "owners."

Empty warehouses and rusting river boats, rotten wharves and deserted plantations, these were what remained to the land of cotton; and while former Confederate generals plowed their own fields or hawked homemade pies along grass-grown streets, many of the emancipated Negroes loafed in their cabins or roamed the roads in enjoyment of their new-found freedom. Who could blame them? The defeat of the Confederacy had struck away their chains, and to them this meant only that they would no longer have to work. An idle labor force, however, meant that the land lay barren, and soon hunger followed poverty in the wake of ruin.

Politically, what was to be done with the South? Military victory had in no way solved the problem of states' rights. It had only quelled rebellion. But were the Rebels to be punished? Had the Confederate states actually left the Union and thus forfeited statehood? Were they to be treated as conquered territories or as errant equals? Above all, what of the Negroes: they were free, but were they to be the white man's social and political peers?

To all these questions Abraham Lincoln hoped to give a compassionate answer. There had been enough bloodshed: at least 540,000 dead in battle, in prisons and in hospitals. The legacy of hate —useless, festering hate—was large enough, and Lincoln would not add to it. Again and again he had advised his generals, "Let 'em up easy," and in his second inaugural address he had said: "With malice toward none; with charity for all; with firmness in the right, as God gives us to see the right, let us drive on to finish the work we are in; to bind up the nation's wounds; to care for him who shall have borne the battle; and for his widow, and his orphan—to do all which may achieve and cherish a just and lasting peace among ourselves, and with all nations."[1] On the night of April 11 Lincoln stood on the White House balcony to announce the most merciful terms granted by any victor. The rebellion was to be forgotten and every Southern state was to be readmitted to full privileges in the Union after 10 percent of its electorate took an oath of allegiance and organized a state government. Of Negro suffrage Lincoln said that he preferred to confer the vote at that time only on the "very intelligent" and those who had served as Union soldiers.

On the 14th, Good Friday of 1865, Lincoln told his friends of having had the same dream which had preceded some of the great battles of the war. An unfamiliar ship seemed to be carrying him toward an unknown shore. That night, with his wife and two friends, the President went to Ford's Theater to see the play *Our American Cousin*. He entered the presidential box and sank into an upholstered rocking chair. Although the door to the box was closed, the President's guard left his post there to watch the play.

At half-past nine the actor John Wilkes Booth entered Ford's Theater. He slipped along a back corridor to the presidential box. Stooping, he peered through a tiny hole he had previously drilled in the door and saw the President in his chair. Entering silently he aimed his six-inch brass derringer at the back of Lincoln's head and fired.

Lincoln slumped forward. Booth leaped to the stage below, breaking his leg. In an instant he was up, brandishing his pistol and shouting, "*Sic semper tyrannis!*" and before the stunned audience could move he had rushed through a rear exit and made his escape by horseback.

Unconscious, Lincoln was carried across the street to a lodging house. He lay diagonally across a bed that was too short for him, breathing with slow full breaths, his pale gaunt features calm and striking. At 7:22 A.M. April 15 he breathed his last. "Now he belongs to the ages,"[2] said Secretary Stanton, while in the South a

Confederate leader heard the news and cried aloud: "God help us if that is true."[3]

No event could have been more inimical to Southern recovery or national harmony than the assassination of Abraham Lincoln. His murder not only deprived the Union of the one man whose rare combination of vision, common sense and compassion might have led the nation through the difficult period of Reconstruction, but also unleashed those very forces of hatred and vengeance which he alone might have restrained.

For three weeks following his death Secretary Stanton conducted a spiteful little reign of terror. The North was provoked into crying for the blood of the captured Jefferson Davis and other "conspirators" such as Robert E. Lee. Not until John Wilkes Booth was killed resisting capture and three of his accomplices were executed, along with the unfortunate woman who harbored them, did the hysteria subside. Davis, meanwhile, was imprisoned in Fortress Monroe, where he spent two unrepentant years before his release. The only Southern war criminal executed was Captain Henry Wirz for his cruelties at Andersonville.

Nevertheless, hatred for the South still lingered, and nowhere did it rankle more than in the breasts of the Radical Republicans. These were the men who were determined upon a harsh peace. They sought equal rights for Negroes as well as almost unlimited power for themselves. Even today historians have difficulty separating their sincere aspirations from their selfish ambition, and this is probably because the one served the other. Negro suffrage meant that the Negroes would certainly vote for the Republicans who had enfranchised them, and never again would the Democrats of the South join their Northern colleagues to control Congress.

Such, simplified, was their policy; and just because these political split personalities pursued it so often in the language of hatred, the face that has come down to posterity is that of a hideous political Mr. Hyde, who wanted to crucify the South, rather than that of a humanitarian Dr. Jekyll, who wanted to give the Negroes free schools, free homesteads and the vote. In their defense, it should be remembered that the times were full of hate. The war had ended with a shriek of hatred—though not among the generals—for Lincoln had been felled by a mad dog, and the North was now engulfed by a flood of loathsome literature full of false tales of Southern atrocities.

Emerson thought that "General Grant's terms look a little too easy,"[4] while the House heard George Washington Julian of Indiana declare: "As for Jeff Davis, I would indict him, I would convict him and hang him in the name of God; as for Robert E. Lee, unmolested in Virginia, hang him too. And stop there? Not at all. I would hang liberally while I had my hand in."[5] True, noncombatant politicians are often quick to call upon God to help tie the hangman's knot, yet the sober *New York Times* did not hesitate to say of the starving South: ". . . if we should feed them, we would make them insolent and they might think it unreasonable in us to stick bayonets in them afterwards in order to make them sincerely sorry for their rebellion."[6] Eventually, it did come to bayonets, but not until after President Andrew Johnson clashed with the Radical leaders, Sumner of Massachusetts and Stevens of Pennsylvania.

It was Charles Sumner whose vituperative speech, "The Crime Against Kansas," had fanned the flames of sectional hatred in 1856 and led to his being caned into insensibility by a Southerner on the Senate floor. It was more than three years before Sumner recovered from that attack, and now, the most powerful man in the Senate, he was his old moralistic and dogmatic self, pursuing his humanitarian ideals under the impression that debate means monologue and that "There is no other side."[7] Even more powerful, even more vitriolic, was Representative Thaddeus Stevens. Tall and bent by his 74 years, his white face a death mask beneath his dark brown wig, trailing the club foot that seems to have envenomed him since birth, Thad Stevens had none of Sumner's idealism. Although his concern for the Negro was genuine, it could also be traced to the fact that his closest companion for most of his bachelor life was a handsome Negro woman, while his hatred for the South might have sprung from the destruction of his Chambersburg property by Lee's soldiers in 1863. When Thad Stevens fought for Negro rights, then, it was not only to secure justice for a downtrodden people whom he actually did love, but also to avenge himself upon a section that had injured him; and the certainty that both of these objectives converged in guaranteeing "perpetual ascendancy to the party of the Union,"[8] i.e., the Republicans, only made their attainment that much more desirable. So the scornful Sumner and the harsh Stevens prepared their prescription for Southern political impotence, and at first it seemed that they had the President's approval of it.

Andrew Johnson, the self-taught tailor from Tennessee, had succeeded to the presidency because Lincoln had wanted a loyal Democrat as his running mate. Johnson's reputation as Vice President had been that of an honest, forthright and courageous public servant. He was an ardent Unionist whose constantly repeated remark, "Treason is a crime and must be made odious,"⁹ had an ominous ring for the South. In fact, when the Radicals first conferred with Johnson, Senator Ben Wade exclaimed: "Johnson, we have faith in you. By the gods, there will be no trouble running the government."¹⁰ But there was trouble. The Radicals were mistaken in their conviction that Johnson's hatred for the Southern aristocracy would lead him to support their program of Negro suffrage. As a Southerner, Johnson had no desire to destroy white man's rule and he favored only a limited suffrage for Negroes. Moreover, he was convinced that the Radicals meant to hobble the white South to protect Northern industrialists, and he had no more love for tycoons than for planters. Finally, Johnson sincerely believed that the Radicals' civil rights program was unconstitutional. He felt that such matters were the concern of the state governments. Thus Andrew Johnson gradually came to embrace the lenient policy laid down by Abraham Lincoln, and after he did there was joined a political battle unrivaled in American history.

The conflict began when the Radical-dominated Congress refused to seat members from Southern states recognized by Johnson. In essence, Congress specified that no Southern state would be readmitted until it had guaranteed civil rights and the vote for Negroes, while disqualifying many ex-Confederates and repudiating the Confederate war debt. In the fall of 1866 the battle between the presidential veto and Congressional majorities shifted to the ballot box, and it was here that the Radicals were aided by the ineffable stupidity of the "Bourbon South."

Moderates such as Wade Hampton of South Carolina and General Beauregard of Louisiana had counseled the South to confer the vote upon its educated freedmen, of whom there were about a half-million employed as farmers, barbers, mechanics or small business men. This cadre could then be used to educate the great mass of newly freed but illiterate slaves. Such a gesture might also go a long way toward placating the North. But, no, the Bourbon reply was the infamous Ku Klux Klan by which the Negro was frightened away from the polls, and the Black Codes by which the Negro, valuable for his labor, was permitted to stay in the South—if he was not actually compelled to—but prevented from becoming "uppity," that is, attempting to better himself.

Black Codes were most severe in states such as Mississippi, South Carolina and Louisiana, where Negroes outnumbered whites. In Mississippi, Negroes were required to sign contracts binding them to service with their employer for a full year, and the law stated: "Every civil officer shall, and every person may, arrest and carry back to his or her legal employer any freedman, free Negro or mulatto who shall have quit the service of his or her employer before the expiration of his or her term of service without good cause. . . ."[11] This was not slavery, merely involuntary servitude, and to the Radicals it was proof positive of the South's intentions to replace bondage with legal serfdom. "We tell the white men of Mississippi," the Chicago *Tribune* trumpeted, "that the men of the North will convert the State of Mississippi into a frog pond before they will allow such laws to disgrace one foot of soil in which the bones of our soldiers sleep and over which the flag of freedom waves."[12]

The Black Codes, as well as Southern race riots in which hundreds of Negroes were murdered, swung Northern sentiment solidly toward the Radical Republicans. Johnson supported the Democrats, many of whom had been Copperheads, and the astute Radicals, temporarily soft-pedaling the issue of Negro suffrage, made the issue one of "patriotism" versus "rebellion." They attacked Johnson with a vigor which exhausted the art of invective. He was a drunkard and a traitor, they cried, and Charles Sumner declared: "Jefferson Davis is in the casement at Fortress Monroe, but Andrew Johnson is doing his work."[13] Enraged, the President struck back. "If I have played the Judas," he cried, "who has been my Christ that I have played the Judas with? Was it Thad Stevens? Was it Charles Sumner?"[14] Such unbridled language did not fall gracefully from the lips of an American President, and bluff, tactless Andrew Johnson, never a man to charm an electorate, was roundly repudiated. The election gave the Radicals enough votes to override the President on any issue, and the new Congress had not been long in session before they had need of all of them.

In March of 1867 Congress passed the first Reconstruction Act carving the South into five military districts commanded by Federal generals. Johnson at once took up the challenge. Four times he vetoed Reconstruction Acts, and four times the defiant Radicals overrode him. They also began a campaign to strip the presidency of much of its power, even reaching out to control his own Cabinet by a Tenure of Office Act making dismissal of Cabinet officers subject to approval of the Senate. Stubborn bulldog that he was, Johnson fought back—and in 1868 the Radicals picked up the ultimate weapon: impeachment.

The pretext for impeaching Johnson was his dismissal of Secretary of War Stanton, who had constantly betrayed Cabinet secrets to the Radicals. Before the bar of the Senate it was charged that Johnson had broken the new Tenure of Office Act. There were other trumped-up charges, but this was the main accusation. Johnson's reply was that the act was unconstitutional, a position later upheld by the Supreme Court. The Radicals, however, were not interested in legality, only in bringing down the presidency and making it subservient to Congress. Once again, they covered Johnson with shameless and lying invective. Their position was best expressed by the credo of Thad Stevens: "Throw conscience to the Devil and stand by your party."[15] In the end, that was what it came down to: party loyalty versus conscience. In the end, seven courageous Republican Senators sacrificed their political careers on the altar of truth and voted for acquittal. One more vote for conviction, and Johnson would have been removed from office. A precedent would have been set by which any future Congress differing from the President might move to impeach and silence him.

Unfortunately for President Johnson's own peace of mind, it was many years before he was vindicated by some of the very men who had impeached him; and by then Radical Reconstruction had been fixed upon the South at the point of the bayonet.

Each of the South's five military districts was held by an army of occupation and commanded by a general with full responsibility for law and order. Moving swiftly, the generals removed six of the state governors, dismissed thousands of local officials and purged legislatures of those conservative members who might block the policies of the Radicals. New state governments were elected with the Negroes voting, and by 1870 all 11 states of the old Confederacy were regulated by such governments.

With these developments, and the disfranchising of many ex-Confederates, power was transferred from the old aristocracy to the new triumvirate of Negro, "carpetbagger" and "scalawag." A carpetbagger was one of those Northern opportunists who had come swarming South with their possessions supposedly crammed inside a single carpetbag, and a scalawag was a white Southerner who made common cause with the Radicals. Between them they often controlled the more numerous, but politically inexperienced Negroes, and the results were frequently scandalous. Spoilsmen and profiteers were allowed to debauch the state treasuries. They played upon the Negro legislators' very human desire to make the most of their new-found prestige. A Negro majority in the South Carolina legislature kept a fancy restaurant and bar open from 8 A.M. to 2 A.M. at a cost of $125,000 for a single session. They voted themselves free wine, whiskey and food, fine furniture, gold watches and perfume. They refurbished the state capital at a cost of $200,000, but after they were replaced by a conservative legislature the state's property was valued at a total of $17,000.

Such were the extravagances and corruptions that have made Reconstruction a nightmare memory in the mind of the white South; and yet much good was accomplished by Reconstruction governments. The new state constitutions abolished property qualifications for holding office, reapportioned legislatures on more equitable lines and established free public education for all children. The new governments also repaired war damage, built railroads—a chief source of graft—constructed roads, softened harsh penal codes and undertook public works. If the carpetbaggers and the scalawags stole, such was the public morality of the times, and they could not equal Boss Tweed of Tammany Hall who stole more than $100 million from New York City alone.

Nevertheless, the Reconstruction governments were anathema to most of the white South. Inevitably, a counterattack was launched. The objective was the voting Negro who gave the carpetbag governments their power, the tactics were pure terror, and the troops were the white-sheeted night riders of the Ku Klux Klan. They kidnapped, horse-whipped or hanged Negroes who clung to their rights. Eventually, the Klan's "lynch law" became so widespread that the South recoiled and the Klan was officially disbanded in 1869. But it continued unofficially on its career of terror, doing as much if not more to restore white supremacy than the devices of poll taxes and literacy tests which also kept the Negroes away from the voting booths. As Negro suffrage became a mockery, factional fights among the Radicals further weakened their hold upon the legislatures.

By 1872 the North had wearied of its attempt to impose its will on the South. By then also Ulysses S. Grant was in the White House. In 1868, backed by his "Boys in Blue" and the Negro vote, Grant had defeated his Democratic opponent, Horace Greeley, to become the fifth war hero in 80 years to receive the "peace-loving" American nation's highest office. Grant was to prove himself among the weakest of Presidents, yet he understood that the public was tired of Reconstruction. In 1872 he ordered the occupation troops not to interfere in Southern politics. Without Northern support, the Radicals were swept away by the resurgent Democrats of the South. By 1876 only three states remained under Radical control.

These also went Democratic after the disgraceful—or at least dubious—election of 1876. In this, the Democratic candidate Samuel J. Tilden of New York appeared to have defeated the Republican, Rutherford B. Hayes of Ohio. Prematurely, the Democrats rejoiced. But then the votes of the three remaining carpetbag states, South Carolina, Florida and Louisiana (together with Oregon), were called into question because of returns from rival election boards. Without these disputed states, Tilden had only 184 votes in the Electoral College. With them, Hayes had 185. The Republicans immediately declared that they had won and telegraphed their election boards to hold the line.

Now the election was thrown into Congress, where a special electoral commission made up of five Senators, five Representatives and five justices of the Supreme Court was appointed to study the disputed votes. Dividing on exact party lines, the commission voted 8 to 7 in favor of Hayes. For a time the Democrats refused to accept the verdict. There was talk of insurrection, and it was then that the Southern Democrats parted company with their Northern colleagues. They agreed to support Hayes at the price of a more generous policy toward the South. This ultimately resulted in the expulsion of the Radicals from the last three carpetbag states and creation of the so-called "Solid South" with all its political implications for the Negro and the nation. It was not until 1890, and after, that "Jim Crow" made the social suppression of the Negro complete. Long before then, in 1877, President Hayes kept his word by recalling the last of the Federal troops from the South.

They were needed to help suppress the Indians.

2

☆

Two and a half centuries had passed since Samuel Champlain fired those fatal shots on the shore of the lake that bears his name. It was in the flash of his firelocks and the fall of the painted Iroquois that the wars of America had begun, and now, eight wars later,* the clash of two incompatible civilizations was at last coming to its conclusion.

It had been an unequal struggle. From the outset the white man had been better organized and better equipped, possessing all the advantages of a superior civilization. In the days when he had been outnumbered, his discipline had enabled him to cling to his toeholds, his "beachheads," in effect, on the red man's continent. Thereafter, Indian indiscipline had led to the red man's defeat in detail. Tribe by tribe, outpost by outpost, the dispersed Indians went down before the concentrated white men. It never occurred to Indians of the interior that the tribes of the East Coast were fighting their battle, that they were resisting the white invasion "at the water's edge." No, they went their own way until the white tide flowed over the mountain barriers and engulfed them, too. So each tribe or confederation fought the white man alone, and each time they were conquered the white man expanded his beachhead, that is, he advanced his frontier farther westward and received more "reinforcements," i.e., immigrants from the Old World and his own progeny.

Such reinforcements swelled the white man's forces while the treaties of peace were in effect, and in retrospect it can be seen that the In-

* King William's, Queen Anne's, King George's, French-and-Indian, Revolutionary, 1812, Mexican and Civil.

dians never should have granted a single treaty. It was not so much that they would be dishonored—that was inevitable, granting the white man's purpose of conquest—it was that they gave the white man time to dig deeper, to consolidate and expand, until at last he had transformed his tenuous beachhead into a secure base.

After that happened, the outcome was foreordained. French in the North, English in the center, Spaniards in the South, the white men began the inexorable process of eviction and extermination. Of the three, the English and their American descendants were the most savage and successful. Seeking the land for itself, rather than for its gold or furs, they were more prone to evict than to exploit. And when the evicted resisted and struck back, extermination followed. The Iroquois and King Philip, Pontiac and Tecumseh, Creek and Seminole, all these and more had fallen victim to this insatiable lust for land, and as the Civil War was succeeded by the last and largest westward movement, this hunger began to feed on the tribes of the Great Plains.

There were some 200,000 of these Indians, the Sioux, Northern Cheyenne and Arapaho in the North, the Comanche, Southern Cheyenne, Kiowa and Apache in the South. Peerless horsemen, excellent shots, hardy and brave, they may have been the finest light cavalry in history. Mounted on fast ponies, they swept down upon settlements or mining camps, loosed their flights of arrows and then were gone before the whites could strike back. If they had had a Genghis Khan to organize them, they might have blocked or at least long delayed the American westward expansion. But at the time of their wars with the United States, they had only good tactical captains to follow, no unifying, visionary chief such as Tecumseh.

Up until 1861 the Plains tribes had been relatively peaceful, but in that year the appearance of settlers on the upper Mississippi and Missouri and the entry of miners into Colorado resulted in open warfare. In 1862 the Sioux of the Dakotas took to the warpath, ravaged the Minnesota frontier and had to be put down by a Union army under John Pope. For the next quarter-century Indian warfare raged practically unabated. Both sides fought ferociously, and both sides committed atrocities. In 1866 a force of 80 soldiers was massacred at Fort Phil Kearny, Wyoming, by Indians under Red Cloud, and even veteran Indian fighters found that the mutilations inflicted on the fallen were indescribable. So too did a force of Colorado militia treacherously destroy a band of Indians while peace negotiations were under way. A white man who witnessed the carnage reported: "They [the Indians] were scalped, their brains were knocked out; the men used their knives, ripped open women, clubbed little children, knocked them in the head with their guns, beat their brains out, mutilated their bodies in every sense of the word."[16]

Such reports enraged the American public, particularly in the distant East. Reformers and churchmen demanded a more humane policy toward the Indians, and in the midst of the uproar the mistake of rapid demobilization went unnoticed. An army of 25,000 men was hardly able to occupy the South and cope with the intrepid Plains Indians, who were made even more formidable by the modern breech-loading, magazine rifles sold to them by Western carpetbaggers and even Indian agents themselves. All the sympathy, however, was for the red men; and the ill-paid, sometimes unpaid American regular with his converted muzzle-loader struggled through what has been called "the dark ages" of the U.S. Army.

In the meantime, attempts were made to clear the main line of Western advance by taking the Plains Indians away from the roads and settling them on reserved lands in the Black Hills of Dakota and in Oklahoma. The Indians, however, refused to step aside. They preferred roaming the prairie to settling down on a reservation. On the open plains they could hunt the buffalo which provided them with food, clothing, weapons and even fuel. Unfortunately, the buffalo was vanishing at a rate accelerated by the appearance of railroad interests in the Plains. Railroad gangs joined hunters and miners in the slaughter of the herds, all but depriving the red men of their means of subsistence.

In 1875 prospectors discovered gold in the Black Hills. Here was the holy ground of the Sioux which the U.S. government had promised to hold inviolate. But no government in Washington, no puny, scattered army could restrain the rush of greedy miners into the Indian lands. With this, the Sioux lifted the hatchet again and went on the warpath under Crazy Horse and Sitting Bull. General Phil Sheridan, then commanding the army, organized a force to destroy them.

On June 17, 1876, 1,000 regulars and 250 friendly Indians under George Crook, probably the greatest of all Indian fighters, caught up with Crazy Horse and 6,000 Sioux and Cheyenne at the Rosebud River in Montana. The Indians were driven off, and their retreat took them across the path of other American columns. One of these was commanded by the young and vainglorious Colonel George Custer. Custer's orders were to get behind Crazy Horse and await the arrival of the main body. However, on June 25, 1876, having found the enemy, with a force of only 212 men at his own disposal, Custer rashly attacked Crazy Horse at the Little Big Horn. The result was the annihilation known as "Custer's Last Stand."

Not an American survived, but neither did Crazy Horse's army long survive this famous victory. In January of 1877 the regulars defeated him and his war came to an end. That same year discovery of gold on the Salmon River brought a characteristic rush of miners into the western Idaho lands held by the peaceful Nez Percé.

Led by the noble and eloquent Chief Joseph, the Nez Percé struck back. But they were defeated, after which Chief Joseph led his people on a masterful fighting retreat over 1,500 miles of mountain, plain and river. Just short of sanctuary in Canada, he was overtaken and compelled to surrender on October 5, 1877. His farewell was memorable: "Hear me, my chiefs, I am tired; my heart is sick and sad. From where the sun now stands, I will fight no more forever."[17]

In the meantime, the Southwest had become inflamed by the Apache uprising under the legendary Geronimo. Once again it was the redoubtable Crook, together with the capable Nelson Miles, who brought the Apache to submission. In 1886 Geronimo surrendered, but border warfare blazed fitfully until 1890. In that year, Sioux under Sitting Bull danced "the ghost dance" and put on the "ghost shirts" which they believed would protect them against white men's bullets. Orders went out to arrest Sitting Bull, but the old medicine man resisted and was killed. With that, his Sioux broke out of their Dakota reservation, only to be brought to bay at a place called Wounded Knee. There, in December of 1890, 300 Indian men, women and children were slaughtered by machine guns in the hands of the regulars.

As it had begun nearly three centuries before, so had it ended: from firelock to machine gun, the Indian fought a hopeless fight. He had been brave, but courage cannot master technocracy. He went down—he had to go down—because his indolent civilization could not possibly coexist beside the most dynamic in history. He had been too content, too conservative, satisfied for centuries with his continental Eden. It may be that the white man played the very devil in driving the Indians from their virgin paradise—certainly the ruthlessness of the Indian conquest remains the blackest page in American annals—yet only a sentimental romantic could maintain that the passing of this primitive society was not inevitable.

So the long, long battle between the hunter and the settler, between communal land and private property, had ended in the utter defeat of the hunter. When it did, so also ended the period in which American wars were fought on American soil.

3

☆

With the end of the Civil War on May 26, 1865—the date of the Confederate surrender west of the Mississippi—the nations of Europe expected the United States to turn upon France or Britain.

The triumphant Union had scores of able generals, millions of trained soldiers, almost unlimited reserves of the most modern weapons and a gigantic new munitions industry. With such a war machine, Europe reasoned, President Johnson would certainly seize Canada in retaliation for official British sympathy for the Confederacy and in compensation for shipping losses inflicted by Confederate raiders built in Britain. But Johnson did not move against Canada, and the shipping claims were amicably settled with an award of $15.5 million.

Neither did Johnson order an invasion of Mexico to evict the French and their puppet emperor, Maximilian. Instead, Phil Sheridan and 50,000 men marched to the Rio Grande as a reminder that the Monroe Doctrine was still in force. France took the hint, withdrawing her troops and abandoning Maximilian to the Mexican republicans, who had him shot to death.

Instead of foreign adventure, then, the triumphant Union quickly disarmed. There were a million men under arms at the Appomattox surrender, but there were only 183,000 seven months later—and by the end of 1866 the United States Army was down to 25,000 men, and the Navy was reduced to a few wooden sloops of war and ironclad monitors. Europe was astonished. Her own nations embarked upon a great imperialist scramble for colonies in Asia and Africa, she could not understand why the United States did not make similar acquisitions. Nor could she understand—as modern despotisms still do not understand—that a nation may be martial without being militarist. The fact was that the United States was sick of war and was looking inward. Manifest Destiny, although not dead, was at least asleep. Secretary of State Seward discovered this after he made his singlehanded deal to purchase Alaska from Russia for what would today be considered a paltry $7.2 million. The howl of derision at "Seward's Folly" forced the imperialistic Secretary to abandon schemes to annex Hawaii, the Danish West Indies and even Santo Domingo. Foreign adventures, then, were anathema in America. Foreign policy was so little respected that the New York *Sun* advocated abolition of the diplomatic service. "It is a costly humbug and sham," the paper said. "It is a nurse of snobs. It spoils a few Americans every year, and does no good to anybody."[18]

Isolation, George Washington's injunction to beware of the broils of Europe, was still the American watchword. Isolation had enabled the American nation to throw down political roots, to expand at the expense of Mexico and the Indians and to pass through a terrible Civil War without outside interference. Now isolation would continue so that the Midwest could become a global breadbasket, the two oceans might be linked by transcontinental railroads and a new-born industrial giant could be nursed to mammoth manhood.

There was, unfortunately, very little to admire morally about the new colossus. Where railroad magnates openly bought legislatures like penny candy, industrialists herded millions of migrants to the Land of Opportunity into dreadful mines and mills and there sweated their labor out of them for a dollar a 14-hour day. These were the days of the gilded tycoon and bloated robber baron. Because the notions of Darwin expressed by the phrase "survival of the fittest" had been applied to the world of business and there given free rein, it was thought proper that the men who built the railroads and created the nation's industrial plant should do so by ruthless suppression of competition and methods of corruption that would shame a pirate. "Nothing is lost save honor!"[19] cried big Jim Fisk at the conclusion of one particularly shameful railroad deal. Yet the nation did grow mighty under the guidance of such men, and historians are still divided over whether it could have done so in any other way, whether the bitter dregs of wholesale corruption and widespread waste and extravagance had not to be taken with the sweet tonic of a powerful industrial system.

Closer scrutiny from the White House and more responsibility in the Congress probably would have made the history of postwar internal development less of a stench in the nostrils of posterity, but, as Henry Adams observed: "No period so thoroughly ordinary had been known in American politics since Christopher Columbus first disturbed the balance of American society."[20] With the possible exception of Grover Cleveland, the Presidents from Grant through McKinley passed over the sands of American political history like men without feet. All Republicans, they allowed the Republican Party of such noble origin to become the complete captive of big business.

Grant was so indifferent toward the scandals that shook his two terms in office that the word "Grantism" has gone into the political lexicon as the ultimate in permissiveness. Hayes also cultivated the hands-off attitude, as did his successor, James A. Garfield, and Chester A. Arthur, who stepped up to the presidency after Garfield was assassinated by a disgruntled office-seeker. Cleveland's opposition to the tariff alienated big business and brought about his defeat by Benjamin Harrison, the grandson of old Tippecanoe; although Cleveland did manage to "make a comeback" and defeat Harrison next time to become the only President to succeed his successor. Laissez-faire in their domestic policy, then, all these men were naturally isolationist in foreign policy. Cleveland also avoided foreign commitments, and in his first inaugural he declared for "the policy of neutrality, rejecting any share in foreign broils and ambitions upon other continents and repelling their intrusion here. It is the policy of Monroe and of Washington and Jefferson—'Peace, commerce and honest friendship with all nations; entangling alliances with none.' "[21]

Yet, even as Cleveland charted this uncompromising isolationist course, a nascent imperialism was gaining converts in America, and five years later the disappearance of the frontier produced a profound change in the nation's attitude.

In 1890, just as the Indian war whoop and the peal of cavalry bugles subsided into history, the director of the census announced that the frontier had ceased to exist. Probably the Indian conquest and the closing of the frontier were associated, for each new westward thrust had had to contend with hostile Indians. Now, with the Indians gone, settlement had reached clear to the Western ocean and the land frontier had vanished. But the expansionist spirit did not disappear. The itch to move on, to grow, to settle new lands was far too deeply ingrained in the American character to perish merely upon the exhaustion of the supply of free land. Instead, expansionism changed its name to imperialism and began to wonder if new lands might not be found beyond the ocean barriers. Captain Alfred Thayer Mahan, the naval strategist and exponent of sea power, declared openly: "Whether they will or no, Americans must now begin to look outward."[22] Gradually, business leaders began to accept Mahan's doctrines. The enormous growth of American industry suggested the need for foreign markets to absorb the surplus from the nations' farms, mines and factories. Naturally this did not mean that foreign markets could not be acquired through normal economic or diplomatic processes rather than through conquest or seizure, but the fact was that the imperialists of Europe were already using the force of arms to exploit Asia and Africa, and it was argued that if the United States did not join the ranks of the aggressors she would be left far behind. Eventually, and inevitably, a divine mandate was invoked for imperialism. The American sense of crusade which had carried the colonists of Boston to the cliffs of Quebec two centuries before was revived, together with the jingoist cant of Anglo-Saxon supremacy. The Congregationalist minister Josiah Strong wrote: "This race of unequalled energy, with all the majesty of wealth and numbers behind it—the representative, let us hope, of the largest liberty, the purest Christianity, the highest civilization—having developed peculiarly aggressive traits calculated to impress its institutions upon mankind, will spread itself over the earth."[23] Specifically, Strong charted a course to "move down upon Mexico, down upon Central and South America, out upon the islands of the seas, over upon Africa and beyond."[24] Finally, the internal discontent of the 1890s was another powerful force making for imperialism. Ill-paid industrial workers and farmers scourged by dust storms, insect plagues and falling grain prices found that looking outward could be a form of escapism, just as the leaders who were unable to satisfy demands for reform found the golden dream of imperialism a convenient diversion.

In 1893, with Benjamin Harrison in the White House, imperialism reached out toward Hawaii. There a group of powerful Americans revolted against Queen Liliuokalani and seized power. Their chief motive was annexation to the United States in order to escape the import duties on sugar. President Harrison appeared to favor annexation, but he was a lame duck defeated the previous year by Grover Cleveland. The new President was still a moderate in foreign policy, and he believed that the dispatch of American Marines to Hawaii during the revolt had been a wrongful intervention in the affairs of a foreign state. So he withdrew the treaty of annexation, merely recognizing the new Republic of Hawaii organized by the revolutionaries.

Mild and restrained in 1893, Cleveland was a fire-breathing jingoist two years later after Great Britain rejected his attempt to mediate her dispute with Venezuela over the boundaries between that nation and British Guiana. American "mediation" consisted of a reminder that the Monroe Doctrine was still in force and that Britain actually had no right to colonies in Latin America. "Today the United States is practically sovereign on this continent," the British Foreign Office was bluntly informed, "and its fiat is law upon the subjects to which it confines its interposition. . . . Its infinite resources combined with its isolated position render it master of the situation and practically invulnerable as against any or all other powers."[25]

Britain, however, replied that the Monroe Doctrine had nothing to do with the border dispute, and an angry Cleveland called upon Congress to vote funds for a commission to determine the boundary line of British Guiana. The President declared that the nation must be ready to prevent Britain from ruling any territory that "we have determined of right belongs to Venezuela."[26] Cleveland's challenge, for such it was, was ignored by a Britain too deeply involved elsewhere in the world, and perhaps also too deeply aware of the new and powerful navy at Cleveland's back, and as the clamor for war in America gradually subsided, the dispute was submitted to arbitration. Nevertheless, the crisis had been significant and prophetic. Captain Mahan said: "It indicates as I believe and hope, the awakening of our countrymen to the fact that we must come out of our isolation, which a hundred years ago was wise and imperative, and take our share in the turmoil of the world."[27]

To enter that turmoil the United States need look no farther than Cuba, where a revolt against Spanish rule had begun.

Cuba had been among the first of the Spanish colonies in the New World. She had been discovered by Columbus in 1492, and Spain had been in "the pearl of the Antilles" since 1511. But the once proud Spanish empire deteriorated; Spain's South American colonies dropped away from her one by one. Cuba, taking note, wished to do the same. Her people arose in 1868, only to be put down in a bloody ten years' war. Thereafter Spanish rule grew more oppressive. Taxation maintained a corrupt bureaucracy and an occupying army, while a blind colonial policy imposed strangling commercial regulations. From America came relief in the form of a tariff admitting raw sugar duty-free. Then a tariff in 1894 imposed a heavy duty on sugar. Since four-fifths of the wealth of Cuba was invested in sugar production, this action by her chief customer provoked a severe depression. This, together with Spanish misrule, brought on the revolution of 1895.

Americans at once sympathized with the revolutionaries. Cuban patriots centered in New York played skillfully upon this sympathy. They spread stories of Spanish atrocities and successfully appealed for funds. They also threatened to destroy American property in Cuba unless its owners contributed to the rebel cause, and they launched filibustering expeditions from American shores. Thus they early involved the American people, if not their government, in the Cuban Revolution.

In Cuba itself, a cruel war was being fought. The policy of the rebels was to wreck the economy to cripple Spanish resources, force the unemployed into the ranks of the revolution and starve the Spanish garrison. In reply, General Valeriano Weyler, the Spanish Governor General, adopted a policy of "reconcentration." The Cuban people were ordered to come to the towns occupied by the Spanish troops or else face trial as rebels. When the poor uprooted peasantry obeyed, it was found that the Spanish could not feed them. There was much suffering, and yet the policy of reconcentration was hardly crueler than the rebels' program of merciless ruin. However, the Cuban patriots in the States were careful to see that only the stories of Spanish barbarity were circulated.

Pro-Cuban sentiment grew strong enough to demand direct intervention, but Grover Cleveland had by then recovered his balance and he ignored the jingos. Interest in the Cuban Revolution also waned during the famous election of 1896 in which the silver-tongued William Jennings Bryan, the Democrat, stumped the country crying that mankind would not be crucified "upon a cross of gold," while the Republican, William McKinley, sat on his front porch in Ohio to chat with carefully screened delegations from across the nation. McKinley won, and promptly declared that there would be "no jingo nonsense" in his administration. However, McKinley did not reckon upon the influence of such stout expansionists as the powerful Senator Henry Cabot Lodge or the bellicose Theodore Roosevelt, and especially not upon America's "yellow press."

Though a new factor in world affairs, the popular press had already shown its power to detonate a political powder keg by its part in triggering the Franco-Prussian War of 1870. By the end of the nineteenth century its standards of accuracy and decency were decidedly lower than those of today, and in America no newspaper was more shamelessly sensational than Joseph Pulitzer's New York *World* or the New York *Journal* of William Randolph Hearst. Both Pulitzer and Hearst were locked in a bitter circulation battle, and they found the Cuban Revolution a source of the sensational kind of news that would sell newspapers. They seized upon "every incident calculated to shock, horrify, titillate, or disgust their readers and blew it up to fantastic proportions."[28] Out of history's dust bin came the Anglo-Saxon caricature of the Spaniard—swarthy, leering, cruel and cowardly— and his atrocities were detailed with a lip-smacking sense of outrage that was not deterred by the realization that many of them had been fabricated by the Cuban revolutionaries. Pulitzer and Hearst were absolutely without conscience. To an artist who cabled from Cuba, "There is no trouble here. There will be no war. I wish to return," Hearst issued his famous reply: "Please remain. You furnish the pictures and I'll furnish the war."[29]

Thus, while Hearst's *Journal* described the Spanish commander as "Butcher" Weyler, "the devastator of Haciendas, the destroyer of families and the outrager of women," Pulitzer's *World* printed such "reports" as this:

The horrors of a barbarous struggle for the extermination of the native population are witnessed in all parts of the country. Blood on the roadsides, blood on the fields, blood on the doorsteps, blood, blood, blood! The old, the young, the weak, the crippled—all are butchered without mercy. There is scarcely a hamlet that has not witnessed the dreadful work. Is there no nation wise enough, brave enough to aid this blood-smitten land?[30]

Certainly not all of the American press was so irresponsible, yet the fact remained that the warmongering *World* and *Journal* had a combined circulation of 1,560,000 against 225,000 for the total anti-war press based in New York, and because most of the nation's newspapers took their editorial leads from New York, the result was that the screams of the war hawks drowned out the cooing of the doves. In such an atmosphere it was impossible for the American people to maintain a calm, detached judgment, nor was the situation improved after Hearst triumphantly printed a letter of the Spanish Ambassador's which criticized President McKinley as "weak and a bidder for the admiration of the crowd."[31]

By then, February of 1898, the American nation was on the brink of war, brought there by the jingo press, the evangelical zeal of Josiah Strong, Captain Mahan's dreams of world power, Senator Lodge's political aspirations and Theodore Roosevelt's love of adventure. Moreover, the American people were eager for a diversion which might efface the memory of a recent depression and the ugly class conflict which arose during the election of 1896. Agrarian reformers who had followed Bryan to defeat at the hands of Eastern capital welcomed the prospect of a fresh crusade against a foreign foe. Nevertheless, not one or all of these reasons combined was enough to push America into another war. Neither Hearst nor Pulitzer had been able to demonstrate that the United States was in any way endangered by the Cuban Revolution, and sympathy for the Cuban people was just not enough to detonate a war. What was needed was that extraneous spark that comes flashing out of nowhere.

Spain did not seem likely to provide it. She had hardly protested after McKinley sent the battleship *Maine* into Havana Harbor during a riot there. The Spanish authorities thought that the *Maine*'s presence in Cuban waters might result in an incident that could cause war. "We are trying to avoid it at any cost,"[32] they told McKinley. Then, on the night of February 15, 1898, a terrific explosion shook the *Maine* and sent her to the bottom with 250 men. Back in New York William Randolph Hearst heard the news, and told his editor: "This means war."[33]

It did indeed, even though it is still not known who sank the *Maine*. Theodore Roosevelt said, "The *Maine* was sunk by an act of dirty treachery on the part of the Spaniards,"[34] a charge which, without a shred of evidence, was echoed and embellished upon by the press. But the fact is that the *Maine* could have been sunk by an internal accident, by Cubans eager to draw America into their failing fight, by some misguided, bumbling Spanish "sympathizer," or—least of all, probably not at all—by Spain herself. The last thing that decrepit old Spain wanted was war with powerful young America, yet this was the first thing guaranteed by the sinking of the *Maine*. Spain might immediately express regrets and condolences, even allow the American dead to be buried in Cuban soil, but nothing would now placate those Americans who, motivated either by ulterior purpose or a belief in comic-strip causality, were bellowing that the national honor must be avenged.

Diplomacy was useless. By April 9 Spain had acceded to every American request except Cuban independence: she had released every American prisoner, recalled General Weyler, recalled her offending ambassador, revoked the reconcentration order, agreed to furnish food for Cuba and finally granted an armistice. Still the press and the imperialists thundered on, and the Congressional mail reeked of sulphur. McKinley had not the strength to resist the tide making for war. On April 11 he asked Congress for authority to use force to intervene in Cuba. On April 19, 1898, Congress jointly declared Cuba free and independent, demanded Spanish withdrawal from the island, and granted McKinley the power to secure both objectives. On April 21 Spain broke off diplomatic relations with the United States, and on April 25 Congress declared that a state of war had existed since that day.

4

☆

A war for an island by contending offshore powers has to become a naval war, or at least be decided by sea power. Because part of the Spanish fleet was halfway around the world in the Philippines—where a native insurrection was also in progress—the Spanish-American War became a two-ocean naval war.

For once America was prepared. Her Navy was three times as large as Spain's and was far more efficient. The American Navy had four first-class battleships and one second-class one, against a single

Spanish first-class battleship, which, laid up for repairs, never saw service. American cruisers and other warships were vastly better equipped and served than those of the Spanish Navy. Never before or since has the American Navy sailed to battle with such superiority, and much of this was due to the theories of Captain Mahan and the driving energy of Theodore Roosevelt.

Mahan, of course, persuaded many influential Americans to adopt his theories of imperialism backed up by a powerful navy. Roosevelt, whom McKinley made Assistant Secretary of the Navy in 1897, was his chief convert. Proud, energetic and brilliant, warm and outgoing by nature, "Teddy" Roosevelt had struggled for years to overcome the handicap of a frail body and a weak constitution. By the strength of his will and his devotion to the "strenuous life" he had so changed his physical appearance that many of his contemporaries regarded him as the epitome of the clean-living American. Others saw in Teddy's buck-toothed grin, walrus mustache and bright eyes twinkling behind little glasses the features of "perpetual adolescence." Yet even his detractors would grant Roosevelt's driving energy and his leading role in preparing the American Navy for war.

Actually, it was Roosevelt who put part of it on a war footing two months before hostilities commenced. On February 25, 1898, shortly after the *Maine* was sunk, while Secretary John Long was away, Roosevelt ordered Commodore George Dewey to take the Asiatic Squadron to Hong Kong and there stand by to attack the Spanish squadron in the Philippines. It has been charged that Roosevelt's unauthorized action is proof of an imperialist clique's plot to annex the Philippines. In fact, Secretary Long, though infuriated to discover Roosevelt's cable, did not rescind it. By then the entire American government was resigned to war—and Commodore Dewey quickly cleared his decks for battle.

His white ships—cruisers *Olympia, Boston, Raleigh* and *Concord,* gunboat *Petrel*—were painted battle gray. Coal colliers were purchased from Britain and arrangements were made for an emergency base off the south China coast. The cutter *McCulloch* arrived April 17 and was also painted. Meanwhile, Dewey waited impatiently for the arrival of cruiser *Baltimore* with a load of ammunition. If she did not appear before war was declared, the neutral British authorities in Hong Kong would order him to sea without her. On April 22 *Baltimore* arrived from Yokohama, and in 48 hours she was docked, scraped, repaired, painted, coaled and provisioned—to the astonishment of the British.

Even so, the British did not believe that Yankee energy was enough to humble Spain. It was hard for Europe to forget the noble naval history of the voyaging Iberians, and Dewey himself wrote: "In the Hong Kong Club it was not possible to get bets, even at heavy odds, that our expedition would be a success, and this in spite of a friendly predilection among the British in our favor."[35] On April 24 Dewey cleared Hong Kong. A few more days were spent off the Chinese coast. Ammunition was distributed. Spars, chests, hatch covers and other flammables of wood were sent to the colliers. On April 27 the U.S. Asiatic Squadron sailed for the Philippines.

Rear Admiral Patricio Montojo y Pasaron, commander of the Spanish squadron in Manila Bay, was like most Spanish naval officers: utterly brave and utterly defeatist. He knew that he served but the shell of an empire, and that his seven ships—flagship *Reina Cristina, Castilla, Don Juan de Austria, Don Antonio de Ulloa, Luzon, Cuba* and *Duero*—were no match for Dewey's six. Yet he was prepared to go down fighting. To prevent the bombardment of Manila, he stationed his ships in the shallow but unprotected waters off Cavite, a few miles away. There, in gloomy resolution, he awaited the Americans.

Commodore Dewey had looked into Subic Bay. Finding it empty, he made for Manila—arriving off the city on the last night of April. The moon was up, drifting through light clouds; nevertheless Dewey decided to run the channel. Just before midnight the mouth of the bay was sighted. It yawned darkly between two dark headlands. Corregidor Island's grim bulk loomed farther back in the space between. Flagship *Olympia* leading, the American ships steered straight in. Sailors who had been called stealthily to their stations by word of mouth rather than blaring bugles steeled themselves for the sound of gunfire. Suddenly, the soot in *McCulloch's* funnel caught fire. Flames shot up, died down, shot up again. . . . Still, no enemy gun spoke until well after midnight. The shells did no damage, the Spaniards stopped firing, and by daybreak the American squadron had safely sailed the 23 miles to Manila.

The seven Spanish ships were in line. American sailors heard cheers rising from the enemy decks and saw Spain's historic red-and-orange battle flags catch the wind. The Spanish fired first: wild and high. A shell burst above *Olympia,* and the ship's crew cried: "Remember the *Maine!*" Commodore Dewey spoke to *Olympia*'s captain: "You may fire when ready, Gridley."[36] At a distance of 5,500 yards *Olympia*'s starboard 8-incher belched smoke and flame. Soon all the American ships were firing. Deliberately and with slow majesty, Dewey paraded his bellowing ships before the Spanish ships. Five times they promenaded, three times west and twice east, until the smoke of battle obscured the stricken enemy. As Dewey broke off the action for breakfast, an excited *Olympia* gun captain cried: "For God's sake, captain, don't let us stop now! To hell with breakfast!"[37]

Nevertheless, the respite was taken, and at 11:16 A.M. Dewey stood in to renew battle. By then the Spanish fleet was dying. *Cristina* was a blazing shambles, *Castilla* had to be abandoned and *Ulloa* soon went down with colors flying. After the Sangley Point batteries above Cavite were knocked out, light-draft *Petrel* ran boldly into the inner harbor to complete the enemy's destruction.

Petrel found most of the Spanish ships abandoned or sunk. Her crew set fire to those ships beyond hope of salvage, and her 6-inch guns quickly brought the Spanish flag fluttering down the pole at Cavite Navy Yard. Upon threat of bombardment of the city, the Spaniards agreed to silence their shore batteries.

It was all over. Dewey's squadron took up unchallenged command of the bay, masters of Manila and of the entire Philippine archipelago as well. In seven hours, with not a man killed and only eight lightly wounded, the United States had become a world power and had embarked on her Asiatic career.

5

☆

America went wild over Dewey's victory at Manila Bay. North and South, coast to coast, there was a rush to join the colors. Old soldiers who had fought each other in the Civil War were reunited in regulation blue. Once again there were tootling bands and emotional farewells. Women adorned departing troop trains with sheaves of lilies and bouquets of daffodils, while perspiring young men in hot woolen uniforms bought kisses with brass buttons cut from their tunics.

Camping grounds blossomed at state capitals across the nation. Such was the invincible innocence of this post-Civil War generation that one governor opposed letting his militia camp in the field with the question: "But what if it rains?"[38] Inclement weather could not dampen the ardor of William Jennings Bryan, who took well-publicized command of a Nebraska "silver" regiment which the government discreetly kept far away from any headline-harvesting field of battle. Theodore Roosevelt quickly resigned from the Navy Department and telegraphed Brooks Brothers in New York for a "blue cravenette regular Lieutenant-Colonel's uniform without yellow on the collar and with leggings."[39] Then Teddy joined a regiment of volunteer cavalry which was commanded by the competent Colonel Leonard Wood but which was forever known as Roosevelt's Rough Riders. After drilling one of the squadrons on a hot afternoon at San Antonio, Teddy, who liked his wars jolly or "bully," bought beer for the men—and that night the irate and professional Colonel Wood made Roosevelt's conduct the subject of a lecture on discipline. If the abashed Roosevelt could apologize, however, there was very little the Army as a whole could do to escape the coils of confusion wound around it by such enthusiastic amateurism.

Unlike the Navy, the Army was unprepared. Kept to 25,000 men throughout the Indian Wars, after the *Maine* was sunk it had been raised to a paper strength of 28,000, not a formidable force to oppose 155,000 better-trained and better-equipped Spanish troops in Cuba. After war broke out, the regular Army was expanded to 61,000 men, and President McKinley called for 125,000 volunteers and again for 75,000. Before the end of November, 1898, more than 223,000 men had enlisted. Once again the volunteer system with all the mistakes of the Mexican and Civil Wars was put into service. Instead of using the regulars as cadres around whom the volunteers could be formed into new units, the regular formations were left intact and the volunteers were assembled in huge camps of instruction. Without the regulars to temper them, to impart to them something of their own toughness and respect for the soldier's hard calling, the volunteers counted themselves veterans the moment they put on those romantic broad-brimmed campaign hats or those prosaic suspenders and leggings.

Confused as such a call-up would have been under any circumstances, it became chaotic under the genial misrule of the politician who ran the War Department. Russell Alger seems to have been the sort of man who meets a problem in logistics with a cheerful smile. Under him an Army shrunken by neglect was racked by growing pains. There was not enough of anything, especially of the new Krag-Jorgensen magazine rifles which fired a .308 caliber bullet using smokeless powder. The food was so bad that the soldiers swore they were fed "embalmed beef," and because of inadequate sanitary and medical facilities disease carried off 2,565 men, more than seven times the 345 men who died in battle. Volunteers arrived at the camps without arms, blankets or tents, while heavy equipment disassembled and packed in unmarked boxes was scattered in hundreds of railroad cars parked on quiet spurs and side tracks.

Still, the Army had a plan. Havana, the seat of Spanish authority, was to be the objective. The regulars were to be assembled at New Orleans, Mobile and Tampa while the volunteers were being trained. A detachment of about 5,000 regulars under Major General William Shafter was to sail from Tampa for Cuba to make a reconnaissance in force and bring supplies to the Cuban rebels. In the meantime, the powerful Atlantic fleet at Key West was to blockade Cuba and seize control of the sea. After this happened, a huge expeditionary force would embark for Cuba.

That was the original plan, changed, of course, by events on the sea.

Spain had two fleets in the Atlantic, the smaller one in home waters, and the larger one in the Cape Verde Islands under Admiral Pascual Cervera. On May 29 Admiral Cervera sailed from St. Vincent with four cruisers and three torpedo boats. His mission was to break the American blockade of Cuba. Opposing him was Rear Admiral William Sampson at Key West with a powerful fleet of three battleships, two cruisers and numerous smaller vessels. Eventually, Sampson's strength would be augmented by the mighty new battleship *Oregon*, just launched at Bremerton, Washington, and then steaming around the Horn at flank speed.

Unfortunately for Sampson, the public and the jingo press became so jittery over rumors that the Spaniards were sailing to attack the East Coast that he was forced to detach a powerful "Flying Squadron" from his fleet and send it north on patrol duty off Hampton Roads, Virginia. Still, he searched the Caribbean for Cervera. The Spaniard hoped to refuel at San Juan, Puerto Rico, but after he arrived at Martinique he learned that there was no coal there. Cervera decided to make for Curaçao, where he expected to find coal colliers, but when he arrived the colliers were not there. In despair, in great need of fuel, he sailed for Santiago de Cuba, the only open port in which he might obtain coal, and after he entered the harbor on May 19 the American fleet under Sampson found him there and bottled him up.

Now the American plan of campaign was changed. Sampson dared not risk forcing the harbor to get at Cervera's squadron. Even though many of Santiago's land batteries were obsolete, the Spaniards still possessed a few modern guns, the narrow channel was sown with mines and Cervera's ships might be able to "cross the T," that is, put themselves broadside to the Americans advancing in column and concentrate all their firepower upon them. Finally, American relations with foreign powers were so strained at that time that the United States could not afford to lose a single ship. Sampson had special instructions not to risk the fire of land batteries.

At first, he tried long-range bombardment of the shore positions, but without success. Next, facing a prolonged blockade, he moved to establish a coaling base on Cuban soil. Marines were sent to seize Guantánamo Bay, about 40 miles east of Santiago. They succeeded, and drove off a Spanish counterattack in the first land battle between the two nations. Yet, even before this happened, it had become clear to U.S. authorities that a continued blockade would not solve the problem. Inside the harbor at Santiago, Cervera was being supplied from the interior. He could hold out indefinitely, immobilizing Sampson and thus blocking the entire American expedition to Cuba.

What was needed now was an attack on Santiago from the landward side. On May 30, 1898, instructions went south from Washington to General Shafter at Tampa: "You are directed to take your command on transports . . . to the vicinity of Santiago de Cuba . . . to capture or destroy the garrison there; and . . . with the aid of the navy capture or destroy the Spanish fleet. When will you sail?"[40]

General Shafter blithely informed Secretary Alger that he could sail in three days, after which he took personal charge of efforts to unravel the logistics tangle at Tampa. He moved his headquarters to the pier at Port Tampa, where a packing case served him as a desk and two boxes supported his 300-pound bulk. There he sat, his huge stomach hanging between his legs, gasping like a beached whale in the hot Florida sun, while the process of "mounting out" America's greatest military expedition went forward with a chaos born of Shafter's confidence that his colonels could each get his own men and animals, guns and supplies, aboard his own ship in his own way.

Here was the antithesis of Winfield Scott with his minute preparations for Vera Cruz. Though a brave and determined officer, Shafter was an old frontier fighter whose experience with small units and local actions had ill prepared him for the complexities of a large amphibious operation. Shafter left the embarkation up to the colonels, and they, discovering that the ships would carry only 18,000 out of Tampa's 20,000 men, immediately raced each other for the transports. Tents were struck, camps were policed, and tired, hungry men with bedding rolls slung over their shoulders were marched off to the railroad stations. Only a few regiments found trains waiting for them; one marched to an appointed track, found no train, marched to another track, again found nothing and finally commandeered a coal train; another seized a cattle train and sent its soldiers rolling to the docks ankle deep in soft stinking filth. At the water's edge the rush to commandeer ships began. There were no assigned transports, merely a process of first-come-first-served, and Theodore Roosevelt took a squad of Rough Riders to hold the gangplank of the *Yucatan* against another regiment. So it took eight days, not three, to sail; but on June 8 with all his ships loaded and moving down the bay, Shafter was notified by Alger to wait for further orders.

The ships were recalled, while the Navy searched for two Spanish ships reported in waters between Florida and Cuba. They were not there, in fact they did not exist, and while the "Phantom Fleet" was thus pursued, Shafter's soldiers sweltered and sickened in their hot, airless holds. On June 14, with the false alarm over, General Shafter and a force of 17,000 men in 32 transports steamed south.

The vessels formed in three long lines, escorted by battleship *Indiana* and other warships, but they soon were spread out over 30 or 40 miles. After five and a half days of uneventful sailing beneath

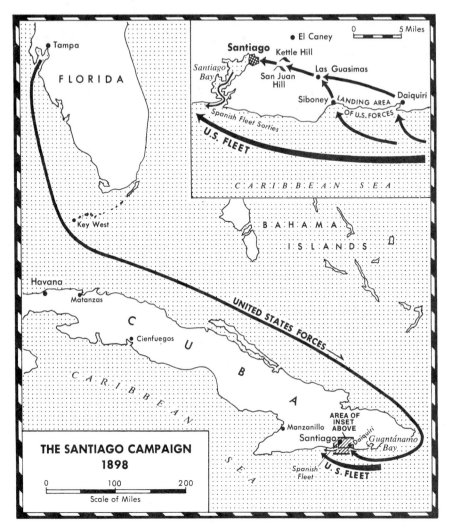

THE SANTIAGO CAMPAIGN
1898

0   100   200

Scale of Miles

bright suns and starry skies and over a glassy sea, they joined Admiral Sampson's fleet off Santiago. Here Sampson came aboard Shafter's ship and sailed with him 18 miles west to a rendezvous with General Calixto García, the Cuban rebel leader. At a council of war held in a palm-frond hut, Sampson suggested that Shafter land his men on both sides of the entrance to Santiago Harbor. The doughboys would then charge up steep slopes to capture Morro Castle and the sister forts at Socapa.

General Shafter demurred. En route to Cuba he had read an account of a disastrous British expedition to Santiago in the eighteenth century. He had no wish to repeat the bloody mistake of charging a stone fort perched atop a 230-foot cliff. Instead, he would land 15 miles east of the city at Daiquirí, and advance overland on Santiago. He would have to strike quickly, before the yellow fever arrived, and he would have to land over open beaches beneath high, fortified bluffs. Still, General García had informed Shafter that there were only 300 men at Daiquirí and that his own rebels could drive them off. It was agreed then to land at Daiquirí, while the Navy distracted the Spanish by bombarding other points along the coast and one of Shafter's two divisions feinted a landing west of Santiago.

On June 22, 1898, the landings began.

Lieutenant General Arsenio Linares, commanding in Santiago Province, had 36,500 troops distributed throughout the area. Of these, 12,000 were in the city of Santiago itself, with some 5,000 stationed between the town and Daiquirí. If General Linares had ordered this latter force to oppose the American landing, he might have dealt the *Yanquis* one of the bloodiest defeats in their history. Even 300 men fighting from the fortified stone bluffs above the Daiquirí beaches could have raked and ripped the go-as-you-please amphibious assault launched on that sparkling, sunlit morning. Yet Linares had chosen to withdraw even that bare garrison, to fight only delaying actions while he concentrated most of his forces around the city for a major defense closer in.

So the American naval guns belched smoke and gouts of orange flame and sent huge red blobs screaming into the Cuban hillside, uprooting trees and smashing cliffs—but hitting no military objectives —while boatloads of men in blue raced through the swells without one Spanish bullet to dig up a spurt in the sea.

The sprint for shore became anticlimactic after a Cuban ran out on the iron pier at Daiquirí to wave a white flag in signal that the Spanish had fled. The swarm of correspondents present, who would eventually write more words on the campaign that was then beginning than there were bullets fired in it, were disappointed. Not so the soldiers who jumped safely onto the iron pier or leaped into the surf of the Daiquirí beaches, setting up a wild cheer that was picked up by every ship in the fleet and carried for miles out on the ocean. Meanwhile, the horses were "unloaded" by throwing them into the water, where boatmen seized their halters to lead them ashore. When a group of cavalry horses began swimming out to sea, buglers on the beach blew the calls that turned them in the right direction. Before nightfall, the Navy had put 6,000 troops ashore with most of their equipment at a loss of only five horses drowned.

On the two days following the landing, the Spaniards continued to fall back on Santiago, while the Americans pushed forward to Siboney to set up their base. The road they followed was a rut in the jungle, passable only two abreast and so densely overgrown to either side that it was not possible to put out scout flankers. Two weeks of shipboard life had already weakened the Americans, and as the moist, oozing tropic heat drenched them in their own sweat and drew upon them the stinging torments of clouds of mosquitoes, their pace slowed perceptibly so that the long blue line snaking back through the brush became an easy target for Spanish ambuscade. The Spanish, however, were interested only in a delaying action while the entrenchments around Santiago were strengthened.

To delay the invaders, a force of about 2,000 men held the height of Las Guasimas about five miles inland from Siboney and astride the road to Santiago. General Shafter had no desire to attack Las Guasimas. He wanted his advance division to halt at Siboney and hold it until enough supplies were built up for the push to Santiago. However, Brigadier General Joseph Wheeler thought otherwise. Wheeler was a veteran Confederate commander of cavalry who had shared prison life with Jefferson Davis, and he gloried in the nickname of "Fighting Joe." Thus, early in the morning of June 24, 1898, the old Rebel led a division of dismounted cavalry northwestward from Siboney and ran into the Spanish at Las Guasimas.

Wheeler sent one column up against the Spanish front while another tried to get around the enemy's right flank. The Spaniards fought back grimly. A blind, hot, wearisome fight ensued. American soldiers and artillery mules thrashed through tangles of creeper, fern and vine while Spanish bullets clipped the branches overhead. Before it was over, Wheeler called for reinforcements, but by then the Spaniards were retreating.

"We've got the damned Yankees on the run!"[41] Wheeler yelled, momentarily forgetting his new allegiance, while mistaking the Spaniards' motive. They were only carrying out an orderly fallback to prepared positions.

Nevertheless, a wild outburst of overheated press copy celebrated

Las Guasimas as a splendid American victory, although American casualties of 16 killed and 52 wounded, against Spanish losses of 10 dead and 18 wounded, certainly do not suggest anything but a skirmish. Yet the fighting did teach the Yankee invaders that "the Dons" were willing fighters indeed, while restraining the impetuous Wheeler long enough for Shafter to come ashore and take command. So Las Guasimas, probably the most formidable of all the excellent positions which General Linares was so easily relinquishing, was occupied by the Americans while Siboney grew as a base.

As it did, the Americans began to lose some of their enthusiasm for their Cuban companions in arms. At the Daiquirí landing, the two races had exchanged glad cries of *"Viva Cuba libre"* and *"Viva los Americanos."* The Yankee deliverers did all they could to help ease the misery of these ragged, barefoot, hungry *amigos.* But at Siboney they began to resent them, because, as a British correspondent wrote: ". . . the Cuban insurgent regarded every American as a kind of charitable institution, and expected him to disgorge on every occasion. The Cuban was continually pointing to the American's shirt, coat, or trousers, and then pointing to himself, meaning that he desired a transfer of property."[42]

Meanwhile, there was a halt at Siboney. It was probably due to Shafter's illness. He was not only prostrated by the heat, but suffered so from the gout that he moved about with his foot in a gunny sack and was unable to get his great bulk aboard a horse. In the interval, General Linares opened a series of rifle pits on San Juan Heights about a half-dozen miles from Shafter's advanced base at Sevilla, and also fortified the little village of El Caney to the left or north of San Juan. A few miles behind these positions lay Santiago.

Shafter's plan was to take El Caney with Henry Lawton's division, and then, two hours later, to move against San Juan Heights with the rest of the command. In the meantime, General García and his Cubans would block the road west from Santiago to prevent the arrival of Spanish reinforcements. By these movements, Shafter hoped to penetrate Santiago's outer defenses and the city would be cut off from its water supply.

Shafter's plan was limited in seeking only the enemy's outer works, and unwise in assigning nearly half of his force to securing his right flank at El Caney. As Shafter knew, the village was held by fewer than 600 men. Instead of sending Lawton's entire division to storm it, he could have contained it while using most of Lawton's men as a reserve to crash straight into Santiago once San Juan was reduced. As it turned out, the men at El Caney under the gallant Joaquín del Rey held off Lawton's division for most of the day. The slender little Spaniards in straw sombreros and blue coats fought with stubborn bravery, especially at a small stone fort south of the town. An American artillery battery of four 3.2-inch guns tried to batter the fort down, but without success. Marking the smoke rising from some Americans firing old-fashioned black-powder cartridges, the Spaniards opened up with their smokeless Mausers and drove a regiment back. At ten o'clock General Lawton gave his exhausted doughboys a rest. Three hours later he renewed the assault, and once again the Spaniards repulsed them.

To the south, meanwhile, the assault on San Juan was stalled awaiting news that El Caney had fallen and that the American right flank was secure. Alarmed, Shafter notified Lawton to leave El Caney and join the main attack. By then, however, Lawton's force was too deeply engaged to withdraw.

Still, the Americans closed in on the El Caney blockhouse. About 150 yards from the fort orders were issued for only marksmen and sharpshooters to fire. Thirty or 40 of them crept forward to fire at every rifle pit, window, door and gun port in sight. Some Spaniards threw down their rifles and ran. An American sergeant bellowed, "Remember the *Maine!*" Four Spaniards were shot down at the door of the fort. Another waving a white flag ran out and was felled. A second seized the flag and was also shot. Then, suddenly, there was a silence.

The fort had fallen. A half-hour later El Caney surrendered. Only a little thatched-roof fort west of the town held out under General del Rey. Here the Spaniards fought heroically, until del Rey was killed, after which all resistance at El Caney came to an end.

To the south, a division of American infantry under Jacob Kent moved against San Juan Hill on the left while a division of dismounted cavalry under Samuel Sumner went up against Kettle Hill on the right. This was the San Juan Heights complex, and the Americans approached it in a slow and confused advance. First, an observation balloon towed along the ground made an excellent aiming point for Spanish artillery, which had already registered on the existing roads. Next, American artillery firing in support sent up clouds of giveaway smoke from black-powder ammunition and was quickly silenced by the Spanish. Finally, the entire assault was delayed by difficult terrain and the unexpected stubbornness of the Spaniards at El Caney. It did not actually begin until ten o'clock in the morning, when the Spaniards shot down the observation balloon.

It sank into the treetops on the left near the ford of the San Juan River. The Spaniards, aware that American troops must be near it, aimed a converging fire at it and panicked an entire volunteer regiment. Regulars were sent to push through the demoralized volunteers. The point of a regiment of dismounted Negro cavalrymen came up, led by a hard-bitten lieutenant named John J. Pershing. Then came the Rough Riders. The panicked volunteers cheered at the sight of Theodore Roosevelt, now in command, but Teddy replied tartly: "Don't cheer, but fight. Now's the time to fight."[43]

Once across the river, the units of troopers were shifted to the right until they were directly in front of Kettle Hill. At about one o'clock, Sumner ordered them up.

Roosevelt, splendidly mounted on his horse Little Texas, paraded in front of his dismounted troopers. Joined by other regiments of cavalry, Negro as well as white, the Rough Riders went up Kettle Hill with a rising cheer. They quickly drove the Spaniards from the ranch buildings at the summit, and seized the heights of San Juan beyond. But on their left, at San Juan Hill, the Americans were in trouble.

Here an open plain led up to San Juan's steep slopes, and three batteries of American artillery had failed to silence the Spanish riflemen and gunners who made it a no-man's land of shot and shell. A blockhouse crowning the hill also survived the bombardment. To cross the plain and charge the hill appeared to be a suicidal assignment, until a battery of three Gatling machine guns under Lieutenant John Parker swept daringly forward. Firing at ranges of from 600 to 800 yards the famous "coffee grinders" began to drive the Spaniards out of their trenches. With that, the American infantry broke from cover and began the ascent famous in history as "The Charge at San Juan Hill."

It was not, however, a charge—rather a creeping ascent in the face of steady enemy fire, and therefore even more dangerous. Foreign military attachés present were astonished. "It is very gallant, but very foolish,"[44] one of them cried. But the blue lines went forward, the soldiers holding their rifles across their chests and climbing heavily. In the forefront were just a few, spread out like a fan, then came the more regular lines. Slipping and stumbling in the smooth high grass, while the hillside and hilltop flashed with flame, they crept upward. Some fell, sinking suddenly from sight or rolling downhill, but not as many as might have been expected, for the Spaniards, rattled by the Gatlings and shaken by the Americans' silent, inexorable ascent, were firing high. Suddenly, nearing the summit, the blue fragments joined and gained momentum, and the Spaniards fired a final volley and fled.

At nightfall, with Lawton moving down from El Caney to hold the American right, all of San Juan Heights was in American hands and the road to Santiago appeared open. In the morning, however, General Shafter discovered that the inner defenses prepared by General Linares appeared to be very strong. On June 2, while Shafter extended his lines almost to Santiago Bay and thus surrounded the city on its landward side, there was more fighting. Casualties rose to 143 killed and 1,010 wounded. By July 3, still sick himself, fearing the advent of the yellow-fever season, Shafter was so dispirited that he considered withdrawing for five miles. Yet on that same day he called upon the Spanish to surrender, just as Admiral Cervera's squadron sortied from the harbor in a desperate dash for freedom.

Admiral Cervera had hoped to escape from Santiago by night, until Admiral Sampson began to illuminate the harbor mouth with floodlights. Upon the arrival of the American Army, however, Governor General Blanco in Havana urged Cervera to leave lest Santiago fall and the squadron be included in the surrender. On July 2, alarmed by the American victory at San Juan, Blanco bluntly ordered Cervera to depart—and the admiral sailed the following morning.

No one in the American blockading fleet expected Cervera to come out. Sampson certainly did not. He had sent battleship *Massachusetts* and smaller *Suwanee* to Guantánamo for fueling, and on July 3 he sailed east with flagship *New York* and two smaller ships to confer with Shafter. Nevertheless, Commodore Winfield Scott Schley still commanded a formidable force: battleships *Iowa, Indiana, Oregon* and *Texas,* his own flag cruiser *Brooklyn* and the armed yachts *Vixen* and *Gloucester.* At 9:35 in the morning, the Spanish ships began coming out. Flagship *Maria Teresa* led, followed by the cruisers *Vizcaya, Cristóbal Colón* and *Oquendo,* and destroyers *Pluton* and *Furor.* Because of the shallow, narrow channel, partially blocked by the sunken American collier *Merrimac,* the Spaniards came out slowly, one at a time, at intervals of about ten minutes. *Iowa* was the first to sight *Maria Teresa* rounding Smith Cay, her magnificent battle flag flying in the wind. *Iowa* closed and began firing while the other startled American ships got their engines turning and sounded general quarters.

Aboard *Teresa,* Captain Victor Concas ordered the bugles blown for battle. "Poor Spain!" he murmured to Admiral Cervera beside him, and the admiral looked away in agony, aware, as Concas said later, that he was hearing the last echo of the bugles sounded at the fall of Granada four centuries ago, and that Spain "was becoming a nation of the fourth class."[45]

Almost immediately, Americans shells began to rack *Teresa.* Cervera's flag cruiser shuddered, and there were dead on her decks as she swung to her right or westward. She made directly for *Brooklyn,* the westernmost American. Cervera hoped to knock out *Brooklyn* and open a gap through which his squadron might escape to Cienfuegos halfway down the island or perhaps even around to Havana on the opposite coast.

For ten minutes gallant *Teresa* was alone beneath the concentrated fire of the American fleet, able to fight back with only two of her guns. Five miles to the east, Admiral Sampson heard the thunder and turned *New York* around. Before he could come up, *Teresa* had been knocked out of action, deliberately beached on Cervera's orders. Meantime, *Vizcaya* and *Colón* had come out and had taken advantage of the attention paid to *Teresa,* gaining a good lead under cover of the gun smoke. Not so the unfortunate *Oquendo,* sortying just as the Americans finished *Teresa* and looked for new targets. Battered and smashed like the flagship, *Oquendo* was forced to run ashore only a half-mile beyond *Teresa.*

By then mighty *Oregon* had shown surprising speed, forging well ahead of *Texas* and keeping pace with the swift *Brooklyn.* These three Americans pursued escaping *Vizcaya* and *Colón.* At the harbor mouth now, little destroyers *Pluton* and *Furor* poked out, and fell victim to a dreadful converging fire. Salvo after salvo from *Texas, Iowa* and *Indiana,* even from distant *Oregon* and the fast-arriving *New York,* fell upon them, while *Gloucester* came boldly close to finish them off.

Within a few minutes *Pluton* was forced onto the rocks, where she blew up, and the riddled *Furor,* almost cut in two by a shell from *Iowa,* sank beneath the surface.

To the west, the running fight continued, the Americans gaining and scoring hits, the Spaniards firing high. Smoke was everywhere across the American path, smoke from funnels, from guns' muzzles, from explosions. It got into the sailors' ears and noses, choked them, blinded them, but the pursuit was pressed. *Vizcaya* was dropping behind. Soon she was crippled, and at eleven o'clock she staggered inshore and was grounded.

Iowa went in to watch her, *Indiana* sailed back to guard the harbor mouth, and *Oregon, Brooklyn* and *Texas* with *New York* coming hard concentrated on the fleeing *Colón.* Soon *Colón* was out of range of *Brooklyn*'s 8-inchers. But mighty *Oregon* was armed with huge 13-inchers firing an 1,100-pound shell. Just before one o'clock *Oregon*'s forward turrets bellowed. On her sixth shot, at a range of five miles, a huge geyser of water rose just ahead of *Colón,* and with that near-miss as a hint of more accurate fire to come, *Colón* turned and headed for shore. A few minutes later another 13-incher struck under *Colón*'s stern, and her colors dropped in a heap.

Cheer after cheer rose from the American ships and the bands began playing the "Star-Spangled Banner"; but aboard *Texas* a compassionate Captain John Philip cried: "Don't cheer, men—the poor fellows are dying."[46] Soon the Americans who had just been killing Spaniards were rushing to their rescue, taking them off their stricken ships. Of 2,200 Spanish seamen, 323 Spaniards died, 151 were wounded, and most of the rest were taken prisoner. American losses were one killed and one wounded. Jubilant, ignoring Schley's role in the battle, Sampson telegraphed Washington: "The fleet under my command offers the nation, as a Fourth of July present, the whole of Cervera's fleet."[47] And while America rejoiced at the death of the Spanish Navy, the dubious General Shafter took heart and messaged Secretary Alger: "I shall hold my present position."[48]

Day by day, Shafter extended his lines around Santiago. More and more guns pointed at the city, more and more troops filled the American rifle pits, while Santiago's supplies and strength sank lower and lower. From this position, Shafter began to negotiate for Santiago's surrender, dealing with General José Toral, who had replaced the wounded Linares.

At first, a truce was arranged for the exchange of prisoners and it appeared that the Spanish were willing to surrender. However, Spanish law did not permit a commander to capitulate as long as he had ammunition and food, both of which Toral possessed. Moreover, he was to uphold the honor of Spanish arms. Gradually, however, the hopelessness of the situation was borne in upon the Spanish, especially after American field and naval artillery bombarded the city on July 10-11. From his sickbed General Linares appealed to Madrid for permission to surrender. The arrival of Major General Nelson Miles, the Army's commanding general, with a brigade of reinforcements also helped make up the Spanish mind. At last, after more delays and misunderstandings, General Toral agreed to lay down his arms.

On July 17, 1898, Shafter, now able to mount a horse, rode with a troop of cavalry to a field outside Santiago. He met Toral with a company of 100 men. The Spaniards presented arms, and the Spanish flag which had floated over the ancient New World city for 382 years was hauled down and furled.

6

☆

There was no more fighting in Cuba. Yellow fever was the new enemy, and as the Americans sickened and died in their camps, fear of a yellow-fever epidemic forced the withdrawal of Shafter's men. They were replaced by the "Immune Regiments," so called because they were composed of Southerners believed to be immune to the disease.

Meantime, General Miles had taken his command to Puerto Rico, which he occupied in an almost bloodless operation, and on July 26, 1898, Spain made overtures for peace through the French Ambassador. On August 12 preliminary arrangements were completed, and on the same day—August 13 on the other side of the International Date Line—Manila fell to the Americans.

Here there had been difficulties of a different nature. Ships of all nations had scrupulously observed Dewey's blockade, except for a German squadron of five ships under Vice Admiral Otto von Diederichs. The German commander openly communicated with the Spanish and Filipinos ashore without consulting Dewey. Annoyed, Dewey told a German officer: "Does Admiral von Diederichs think he commands here, or do I? Tell your Admiral if he wants war I am ready."[49]

Although the Germans were as powerful as Dewey, they did not want war—only a few choice scraps from Spain's crumbling Pacific empire. But the presence of a British squadron prevented this, and Dewey was left to deal with the other problem of the Filipino *insurrectos*.

The American admiral had already brought Emilio Aguinaldo, the insurgent leader, to Manila from Hong Kong. Once ashore, Aguinaldo gathered his Filipino forces, capturing towns and proclaiming a republic with himself as president. Aguinaldo was anxious for Dewey to make an alliance or an agreement which would recognize Filipino freedom. This Dewey carefully avoided, until American ground troops at a strength of 8,500 arrived under Major General Wesley Merritt. The fact was that if the United States was planning to make Cuba *libre,* she was also preparing to keep the Philippines for herself. Hawaii had already been annexed in July of that year, Guam had fallen without a fight, and America was fairly embarked on a career of imperialism.

Yet, if Aguinaldo and his 10,000 insurgents were a hindrance to Dewey and Merritt, they also turned out to be a help in bringing about Manila's fall. The Spaniards knew that the oppressed Filipinos were eager to sack the city. Therefore, they preferred to surrender to the Americans, saving, of course, their military honor.

This was spared by the shots fired at Fort San Antonio Abad by Dewey's ships, operating on the left or water flank of Merritt's columns as they drove northward into Manila. The Americans met only token opposition, quickly capturing the city and successfully preventing Aguinaldo's men from entering it on its eastern side.

Gradually, however, the Filipinos pressed in upon the Americans. They demanded joint occupation of the city. They began to rob, beat and burn. The American Army of 8,500 men found itself in the position of having to guard 13,000 Spanish prisoners while 10,-

ooo infuriated Filipinos gradually penetrated their lines and clamored for Spanish spoils. At last, General Merritt ordered Aguinaldo to withdraw his army. Angered, but helpless against the guns of Dewey's squadron, the Filipino President moved his government to Malolos. He was not cowed, however, but merely making a prudent retirement while awaiting the outcome of the peace talks between America and Spain. Neither Aguinaldo nor his countrymen had any intention of exchanging the despotism of the Spanish oppressor for the paternalism of the American liberator. Even silken chains form a yoke, and they wanted a freedom as complete as Cuba's. Unfortunately for them, the new American imperialist party had grown too powerful.

American isolation died with the annexation of Hawaii. It did not perish, however, without a fight from the anti-imperialists who pleaded with McKinley and Congress to heed the advice of Washington and Jefferson and remain within the ocean barriers. McKinley's reply was: "We need Hawaii just as much and a good deal more than we did California. It is Manifest Destiny."[50] It was argued that acquisition of the islands would not only advance Mahan's program for American control of the Pacific but also promote trade and commerce. In reply, the opposition charged that the true motive was the old "unconquerable Anglo-Saxon lust for land," and Manifest Destiny was described as "the specious plea for every robber and freebooter since the world began."[51] Nevertheless, on July 7, 1898, Hawaii was annexed.

Armed with this precedent, the imperialists opened the struggle for the annexation of the Philippines. Gradually, they won over business interests heretofore reluctant, convincing them that the European powers were trying to close the door to American trade in China, and that possession of the Philippines would give America a base in eastern Asia.

Another new ally was Albert Beveridge, soon to be elected Senator from Indiana, who declared: "It is God's great purpose made manifest in the instincts of our race, whose present phase is our personal profit, but whose far-off end is the redemption of the world and the Christianization of mankind."[52] Religious leaders echoed the cry of Christianizing the Filipino, ignoring the fact that the Roman Catholicism professed by almost all of them was a fairly well-known form of that faith. McKinley was also persuaded. The man who had once wanted "no jingo nonsense" could not resist the imperialist tide, the public clamor to obey Rudyard Kipling's injunction to "take up the white man's burden."

McKinley's own description of his conversion to imperialism was given a few years later to a group of visiting clergymen:

> I thought first we would take only Manila; then Luzon; then other islands, perhaps, also. I walked the floor of the White House night after night until midnight; and I am not ashamed to tell you, gentlemen, that I went down on my knees and prayed Almighty God for light and guidance more than one night. And one night it came to me this way—I don't know how it was, but it came: (1) That we could not give them back to Spain—that would be cowardly and dishonorable; (2) that we could not turn them over to France or Germany—our commercial rivals in the Orient—that would be bad business and discreditable; (3) that we could not leave them to themselves—they were unfit for self-government —and they would soon have anarchy and misrule over there worse than Spain's was; and (4) that there was nothing left for us to do but to take them all, and to educate the Filipinos, and uplift and civilize and Christianize them, and by God's grace to do the best we could by them. . . . And then I went to bed, and went to sleep, and slept soundly.[53]

After this memorable night of illumination, McKinley did indeed "take them all," and Spain reluctantly agreed to terms by which Cuba became free, and Guam, Puerto Rico and the Philippines were ceded to the United States for $20 million. In signing, Spain observed sorrowfully, "This demand strips us of the very last memory of a glorious past and expels us . . . from the Western Hemisphere, which became peopled and civilized through the proud deeds of our ancestors."[54]

The treaty was not ratified without a bitter battle, however. An Anti-Imperialist League was organized by Americans such as Grover Cleveland and William Jennings Bryan, steel tycoon Andrew Carnegie, labor leader Samuel Gompers, and many leading educators and writers such as Mark Twain and William James. Like Rome before her, these men argued, America was embarking on the road to ruin. Imperialism was not only unconstitutional; it was certain to require an expensive army and navy to maintain it. From William Vaughn Moody came the haunting lines:

Tempt not our weakness, our cupidity!
For save we let the island men go free
Those baffled and dislaureled ghosts
Will curse us from the lamentable coasts
Where walk the frustrate dead. . . .
O ye who lead,
Take heed!
Blindness we may forgive, but baseness we will smite.

The imperialist reply was made by Senator Beveridge in his maiden Senate speech. Maintaining that the Pacific would be paramount in the twentieth century, he said: "The power that rules the Pacific, therefore, is the Power that rules the world. And, with the Philippines, that Power is and will forever be the American Republic."[55] But it was politics, not oratory, that decided the issue: the defection of the Democrat, Bryan, to the ranks of the imperialists. Bryan urged Democratic Congressmen not to oppose annexation, and on February 6, 1899, the Treaty of Paris was ratified and the Spanish-American War formally came to an end.

"It has been a splendid little war,"[56] John Hay wrote, but most of the world seemed to prefer the observation of Bismarck: that there was a special Providence for drunkards, fools and the United States of America. Yet both Hay and Bismarck were wrong. The splendid little war just ended was among the most expensive in American history, for hundreds of thousands of veterans needlessly mobilized and never sent into action have drawn pensions valued at close to $5 billion, and 60 years later there were still 10,000 of them receiving a total of $150 million annually. Nor was Bismarck's special Providence at work then; on the very eve of the war's end, the longer and bloodier Philippine Insurrection began.

Major General Ewell Otis commanded in Manila. Tall, bulky, wearing sideburns, the tedious Otis knew less about the Philippines than he did about controlling them. He had the faculty of alienating people, including the homeward-bound Admiral Dewey who called him a pincushion of an old woman; and his brilliant but arrogant division commander, Arthur MacArthur, who said that Otis resembled an upside-down locomotive. Still, Otis was determined to keep the peace in the islands, and he had the Navy and 21,000 troops to back him up. About 14,000 of these soldiers formed two divisions under MacArthur and Thomas Anderson. Armed with artillery and those detested .45 caliber Springfields that kicked like a mule, as well as with modern Gatling and Hotchkiss machine guns, these two formations held Manila.

Opposed to them was Aguinaldo's army of 80,000 Filipinos, of whom 30,000 surrounded Manila in a four-mile arc that had its north and south terminals on the bay. This force possessed a few Krupp guns, but a third of the men were without rifles. They carried machetes or bolo knives and wooden spears. Of the riflemen not many knew how to shoot. Some of them threw away their rear sights as a nuisance. Thus they would inevitably fire high. Yet they were confident. They assured themselves that they had defeated the Spaniards and that they would have no difficulty with the Americans. On the night of February 4 they attacked.

There was very little method in the assault. The insurgents merely sallied from their trenches and blockhouses to make random thrusts at the Americans, while the Sandatahan or fifth column created panic inside the capital. Only two concerted rushes were made, and they were shattered as the hard-kicking Springfields spewed bullets of such dreadful shocking power that they tore huge holes in the Filipinos' bodies and nearly tore off their heads. Meanwhile, the Sandatahan uprising also failed, and in the morning the Americans counterattacked.

The *insurrectos* were astonished. During the centuries that they had fought the Spaniards, all combat had taken place in the cool of the night, with both sides retiring at daybreak to avoid the heat of the day. Yet the *Americanos* were advancing by daylight behind an artillery barrage. Shattered as well as startled, the Filipinos on the northern half of the line fled. MacArthur's division pursued them into the hills and captured the reservoir. On the northern sector, General Anderson's division was even more successful, and the Filipinos learned the dreadful folly of anchoring a flank on water patrolled by a hostile navy. The ironclad *Monadnock* and smaller ships shelled positions ahead of the American line, which was marked by a red flag. Aiming through new telescopic sights, *Monadnock*'s gunners sent 500-pound shells screeching in upon the *insurrectos,* driving them out of their trenches and barricades so that the pursuing Americans could pour rifle fire into their backs.

The Filipinos were utterly crushed. Their casualties were probably five times higher than American losses of 59 killed and 278 wounded.

In this second battle of Manila it was clear that the insurgent army could never fight the Americans in orthodox wars of maneuver and massed assault, a fact which became plainer on February 10 after MacArthur took the rail center of Caloocan several miles north of the city. South and east there were also easy victories. It seemed certain that the insurrection was on the verge of collapse.

Actually, as the Spaniards might have told the Americans, it had only begun. Since 1551 Spaniards had been beating the Filipinos in open battle, but had never crushed them. To the elusive and hardy *insurrectos* formal defeat was merely the signal to begin guerrilla warfare, to fragment their forces, vanish into the wild interior, and conduct a hide-and-seek, hit-and-run harassment designed to exhaust American patience. Such warfare naturally depended upon a loyal populace, and the Filipinos were loyal to the insurrection; almost fanatically faithful to the revered Emilio Aguinaldo, who was himself an adept in the art of irregular war. No, the Spaniards might have said, "You will not stamp out the insurrection so soon; you will have no great and decisive blaze of battle but hundreds of small brush fires flaming up all over the islands."

General Otis, however, did not ask for Spanish advice but pursued the Filipinos with confidence in orthodox warfare. On Luzon, the rebel capital at Malolos was seized and burnt, but the government escaped to San Isidro. On the other islands capitals were also occupied, but the insurgents faded into the mountains. Sometimes the Filipinos turned and gave battle, and then there were American casualties. By June 10, 1899, losses were nearly 2,000. Not counting the sick and the dead of disease, this was more than the entire Cuban campaign.

American sick lists were appalling. After the doughboys entered San Fernando in May it was found that of 4,800 combat troops in the area 2,160 were on sick report. One regiment had 70 percent of its men in the hospital. The heat, the bad food, the endless exertion of chasing a tireless, indomitable enemy, all wore upon the will of the Americans. Then, in June, the rains came. From May to October no less than 70 inches fell. Roads were washed out, bridges collapsed, low-lying lands and rice paddies became temporary lakes and where the ground was not under water, it was often an impassable paste of mud. In such weather operations broke down, men sickened and soldiers who were well turned sullen. Now the Americans hated the Filipinos with a fierce black hatred. They killed all they found, frequently failing to distinguish between soldier and civilian. In truth, it was hard to do so. The *insurrectos* no longer wore their gingham uniforms. At one moment a Filipino might be an enemy insurgent aiming his Mauser out of the bush; at the next, hiding his rifle, he might be a friendly civilian with a smile on his face, welcoming the Americans with cries of, *"Amigo! Amigo!"* So the Americans decided: "There are no more *amigos*."[57]

Sometimes the doughboys entered villages where their comrades had been held captive, only to find tortured bodies booed to pieces. Their reply was to burn the village and slaughter its men, women and children.

They became what they fought. The Filipinos were fighting the kind of war that is based on terror; the Americans fought back just as cruelly. They developed a "water torture" that made even the Spanish cringe. If a captured Filipino refused to divulge military information, four or five gallons of water were forced down his throat until his body became "an object frightful to contemplate."[58] Then the water was forced out by kneeling on his stomach. The treatment was repeated until the prisoner talked or died. Almost all of them talked. Thus did the Americans civilize their "little brown brothers," and as one historian of the insurrection has observed: "What Otis was now doing to the Filipinos was almost what 'Butcher' Weyler had done to the Cubans; and the paradox was all the greater since we had gone to war with Spain to put an end to such abominations."[59]

Yet the Filipinos still resisted, and as the dry season set in General MacArthur went smashing through the central Luzon plain in an attempt to crush them. In November of 1899 the latest insurgent capital at Tarlac fell and MacArthur wired Otis: "The so-called Filipino Republic is destroyed."[60] But it was not, and the vanished Aguinaldo's army continued to raid American camps, tear up railroads, steal supplies and slaughter surprised American garrisons in the little outpost towns. By the spring of 1900, Filipino casualties were up around 17,000, but American losses were at least one-fifth of that, and as the war that was "won" continued without respite, reports of American suffering and of American brutality began to slip through the strict censorship imposed by General Otis.

A good part of the country was dismayed. Even the jingo *World* turned anti-imperialist and parodied Kipling's injunction with the lines:

We've taken up the white man's burden
Of ebony and brown;
Now will you tell us, Rudyard,
How we may put it down?[61]

Tales of torture, looting, wanton destruction of property and the summary execution of Filipinos by drumhead courts shocked the national pride and so disturbed President McKinley that he looked around for a civil governor to take control of the islands out of the hard hands of the generals. His choice fell upon Judge William Howard Taft, an elephantine man of more than 300 pounds and a reputation for largeness of mind and heart as well. Like Otis and the others, Taft knew nothing of the Philippines. Nor did he want the job. But McKinley prevailed upon him to accept. In April, 1900, at the head of a five-man commission, Taft sailed for Manila. In May the mortified Otis offered a resignation which was speedily accepted.

MacArthur succeeded Otis in his military duties, and was very much annoyed when Taft arrived armed with not only civil power but the right of financial control over the military. Although the two men never did get along, Taft was able to organize a model administration. Schools were constructed, public works begun, graft was abolished, and Filipinos who took the oath of allegiance began to participate in the government. Such benign tactics, it would seem, were bound to disarm the insurrection.

Yet this could not be, not for as long as the vanished Aguinaldo remained free. In his breast the fires of freedom burned strongest, and in his brain was the capacity to organize and direct the fight for it. So the guerrilla war continued without letup, while Aguinaldo based his hopes on a Democratic victory in the American presidential election of 1900.

Opposition to the war in the Philippines was carried on chiefly by the Democrats, who again nominated Bryan for the presidency, joined by the Anti-Imperialist League. Bryan, who had again changed his mind, went so far as to demand the military defeat of his own country, while the Anti-Imperialists stated flatly: "We demand the immediate cessation of the war against liberty, begun by Spain and continued by us. . . . We propose to contribute to the defeat of any person or party that stands for the forcible subjugation of any people."[62] They bombarded soldiers in the Philippines with leaflets, advising them: "Boys, don't re-enlist. Insist [upon] immediate discharge."[63]

The flaming Anti-Imperialist Edward Atkinson published a series of pamphlets describing the war as criminal, quoting American soldiers as saying that the Spaniards were appalled by Yankee cruelty, predicting that 8,000 American soldiers would die in the first year and that in two years the country would be bankrupt, and quoting a mother's description of McKinley as an unadulterated murderer. Atkinson tried to ship his pamphlets to the troops in the Philippines, but the War Department intercepted them. Indignant, Atkinson cried that free speech was being suppressed, and once again an American nation at war was faced with the problem of discovering at what point criticism ceases to be such and becomes treason.

Bryan and Atkinson and the other Anti-Imperialists were aware that the insurgents constantly quoted their remarks to encourage the Filipinos to fight on. In effect, they gave aid and comfort to the enemy Even if they were sincerely convinced that the war was wicked, to continue to say so cost more American lives. Thus the problem of conscience versus country, one which always haunts a divided democracy at war. Insoluble in 1812, 1847 and during the Civil War, the dilemma remained unsolved in 1900.

McKinley's reply in the fall campaign was to stress America's new prestige, the victory over Spain, prosperity and the pretext that the Philippine situation was well in hand. With some very handsome assistance from his highly popular running mate, the ebullient Teddy Roosevelt, who stumped the country in his Rough Rider hat, McKinley was easily re-elected, and with the defeat of Bryan the insurrection began to lose heart.

Although the insurrection had begun to falter, Aguinaldo was still at large. Unless he were captured or killed, the guerrilla war, though dwindling, might drag on for years and some new spark might set all the old fires blazing again. Yet no one knew of Aguinaldo's whereabouts. By February of 1901, after two years of insurrection, the Americans had not been able to find a single traitor among eight million Filipinos. But then one of Aguinaldo's couriers was captured. His name was Cecilio Segismundo, and it was he who revealed the hideout of his chief.

Aguinaldo later charged that Segismundo did not talk until after he had been given the water cure twice, but American officers insisted that he gave his cooperation voluntarily. However that may be, a daring scheme began to evolve in the romantic mind of Frederick Funston, a short, red-haired and muscular brigadier general of volunteers. From the dispatches taken from Segismundo, Funston learned that Aguinaldo was expecting guerrilla reinforcement at his headquarters at Palinan in northeastern Luzon. Funston would provide them.

His Maccabebe Scouts, a tribe of bloodthirsty mercenaries who had fought their brother Filipinos for Spain and now served America, were dressed as *insurrectos*. Their leaders were Segismundo, Hilario Tal Placido, a renegade insurgent, and a disguised Spanish secret service officer named Lazaro Segovia. Into their custody went Funston and four other American officers playing the part of "prisoners." With MacArthur's approval, on February 6, 1901, this bogus band set sail for lonely Casiguran Bay. Just after midnight of February 14, they were set ashore, to begin a 100-mile, five-week trek through the unknown wilds of Aguinaldo's own country.

Passing from village to village, often hailed as heroes, sometimes received with brass bands and full municipal honors, but never suspected, the guerrillas moved on Palinan. Word was sent ahead to Aguinaldo that his reinforcements were arriving with American prisoners. At once the wily Aguinaldo, fearing that the Americans might learn of his whereabouts, dispatched a force of his followers to take charge of them. With this, the Maccabebes hid Funston and his friends in the bush and told the loyalists that the Americans were back in Casiguran. The loyalists pressed on to Casiguran, while Funston's pretenders pushed on to Palinan.

Here Aguinaldo sat in a room on the second floor of a little house overlooking the village square. Two bodyguards were with him. Below, in the square, was a group of armed loyalists. As the Maccabebes came up they faced the loyalists with lowered rifles while Segismundo, Placido and Segovia walked boldly into the house. In a moment, Segismundo came out and departed. On the second floor, Placido told stories and cracked jokes while Segovia stood at the window watching the Maccabebes maneuver into position around the loyalists. Segovia nodded, and the Maccabebes opened fire. Annoyed, thinking his men were firing their weapons to welcome the reinforcements,

Aguinaldo walked to the window and shouted: "Stop that foolishness. Don't waste your ammunition."[64] With that, the burly Placido hurled himself on the slender Aguinaldo, while Segovia began shooting at the bodyguards. One fell wounded and the other fled. Aguinaldo was thrown to the floor. Placido sat on him until Funston came running upstairs to inform him that he was a captive.

Almost with relief, Aguinaldo gave himself up. On March 28 he was brought to Manila in triumph, and on April 19, 1901, finally coming to see the futility of fighting on, he took the oath of allegiance to the American government and called upon his followers to lay down their arms.

Still, the fires of insurrection once lighted are not quenched with a word. Although Luzon became quiet, resistance moved to the southern islands, especially among the fierce Mohammedan Moros. Inevitably, Moro massacres were succeeded by American reprisals every bit as ferocious. "Kill and burn" were the orders for Samar, and the ordeal of battle there was so intense that for years veterans of it were introduced at officers' mess with the salute: "Stand, gentlemen, he served on Samar."

At length, after 4,230 Americans had died, with hundreds more later dying of disease, and more than 20,000 Filipinos had perished, the Philippine Insurrection was ended by presidential proclamation on July 4, 1902. The proclamation did not instantly end the shooting, nor had it the power to prevent an *insurrecto* from shooting a campaign hat off the head of General MacArthur's dashing young son, Lieutenant Douglas MacArthur. Yet it remains the official date of the end of the Philippine Insurrection.

The President who issued it was named Theodore Roosevelt. On September 6, 1901, William McKinley was assassinated in Buffalo by an anarchist fanatic, and Roosevelt became the fourth Vice President and the sixth war hero to move into the White House. With his assumption of the presidency the new imperialism was confirmed with all of 43-year-old TR's free-swinging vigor. Some Republicans were appalled. They had believed that when troublesome Teddy accepted the empty office of Vice President he had taken the political veil.

"Now look!" one of them cried. "That damned cowboy is President of the United States!"[65]

PART VII

World War I

1

☆

The "splendid little war" and its Philippine corollary was one of the major turning points in American history. It made America a colonial power and a Far Eastern power, and because it involved her in the rivalries of European nations in Asia it inevitably drew her into the complex of European power politics.

Even before the guns in the Philippines fell silent, the United States had made a fateful intervention in the Far East. Fearing that the European powers and Japan would carve weak China into private pieces from which American trade would be excluded, the United States in 1899 asked the powers to agree to an "Open Door" policy of free trade within those "spheres of influence" which they had extorted from the helpless Celestial Empire. The powers' replies were ambiguous, yet Secretary of State Hay managed to interpret them as complete acceptance of the Open Door.

A year later came the Boxer Rebellion. A Chinese secret society called the "Patriotic Harmonious Fists" arose to drive out the "foreign devils" occupying their country. Europeans were massacred and the foreign legations in Peking were besieged. Enraged, the powers prepared to use the Boxer uprising as a pretext for further demands upon China. An international relief force was formed, and it included American soldiers and Marines. With them, however, went Hay's announcement that America intended to support Chinese territorial integrity. Thus a second Open Door pronouncement. Like the first, it did little to guarantee Chinese independence; that was preserved by the powers' own inability to agree on how to divide the country among them. Still, the Open Door was a statement of American foreign policy second only to the Monroe Doctrine, even though it lacked the military power required to back it up. First Russia and then Japan forced the United States to retreat from it. But the position was never abandoned, and if, 41 years later, the American guarantee of Chinese independence was to lead to Pearl Harbor, it was also, in 1900, to enmesh America most deeply in the affairs of a Europe going gradually mad with militarism.

In 1861, the second year of the American Civil War, King William I of Prussia announced: "The Prussian Army will, in the future, also be the Prussian Nation in Arms."[1] The remark was ominous for the peace of Europe, for it signaled nothing less than the rebirth of the Prussian spirit of militarism. Eventually compulsory conscription would provide Prussia with a huge standing army backed up by a reservoir of trained reservists and territorials.* In the hands of Otto von Bismarck, the superb Iron Chancellor, this force became the big stick backing up the carrots of Prussian diplomatic policy. It was used to humble Austria, after which, combined with diplomacy, it helped unify Germany under Prussian leadership. For the first time all those fragmented kingdoms and dukedoms, petty states, principalities and free cities which spoke German and thought of themselves as being German were given political cohesion. A united Germany, however, was not enough for Prussia. Germany must become the First Power of Europe.

Thus, in 1870, Bismarck skillfully and deliberately goaded France into declaring war on Germany. The Franco-Prussian War which ensued drew the German states ever closer around Prussia and resulted in the complete defeat of France. In January, 1871, in the Hall of Mirrors at Versailles, King William I of Prussia was proclaimed Emperor of Germany. Almost at the same time, because of the withdrawal of French support, the Papal mercenaries in Italy surrendered to Victor Emmanuel and the new Italian nation was born.

Few wars have been more influential than this one. First, mighty France had been humiliated and Germany was lord of the Continent. Second, French enmity was guaranteed by German annexation of the French provinces of Alsace and Lorraine. Third, the rise of Germany as First Power of Europe forced Britain to end her ancient quarrel

---

* Territorials are older reservists, usually between 35 and 45, who have fulfilled their obligations in the regulars and the reserves but are still liable to service. They are comparable to the Home Guard, and their chief value, except in times of desperation, was that they relieved younger troops for duty on the fighting fronts.

with France in order to redress the balance of power on the Continent. Since Tudor times, Britain's policy had been to keep the Continental powers divided so that she would hold the balance of power between them; i.e., whichever side she took automatically became the stronger. Now Imperial Germany had become the successor to Hapsburg Austria and Spain and Bourbon and Napoleonic France as dominant power. And as her industrial strength grew, Germany later challenged Britain for world markets. Although Anglo-German commercial rivalry was to become the deepest root of world-wide conflict, it did not develop until a few decades after the Franco-Prussian War.

What did immediately set in was widespread infatuation with Prussian militarism. Bismarck's little lightning wars—against Denmark in 1864, Austria in 1866, France in 1870—were the admiration of chancelleries and military headquarters everywhere. They had been made possible, it was seen, by (1) universal conscription, (2) massed artillery and the increasing use of railroads for military transportation, and (3) the meticulous planning of the Prussian Great General Staff.

The first, of course, was nothing less than the Democratic Revolution, derived from the French *levée en masse,* and the second from the military uses of the Industrial Revolution. They had been joined before, most notably, at least to those few students who had bothered to examine them, in the campaigns of the American Civil War. But the third was new; it was the application of commercial business management to the business of war. It was the advent of the Managerial Revolution, the scientific training of officers to form an administrative organization through which the supreme commander might mass and move his armies. Men who understood metallurgy or engineering or ballistics or transportation problems now found themselves more in demand than those who could lead a charge or wear a family crest or discourse knowingly on Jomini or Clausewitz. The age of the adventurer, the fire-breather and the titled dilettante was ending—at least on the higher levels. Promotion was now to be found in staff offices rather than in the field, and a general in the saddle would soon be more ludicrous than a general in an armchair.

Business efficiency methods gradually induced commanders to become more and more detached from the human quotient of war, to regard the exploding armies and arsenals of Europe as so many ciphers to be expended or husbanded as the fortunes of war might dictate. Such an impersonal attitude is bound to wall a general's heart within a vault of staff reports. Yet to deplore this is only to deplore the impersonal attitude, which is the vice of the virtue of efficiency. War has as much right to efficiency as peace has. It is only because the mistakes of war are measured in blood and ruin and the fate of nations that they seem more hideous than those of peace; which, after all, are the ones that lead to war. In war are met all the problems of peace, but with the utmost urgency because of the consequences of delay, in every kind of weather or terrain, and, most unsettling of all, while under fire. Therefore, efficiency in military matters would seem even more desirable, and the wonder about the Managerial Revolution in war is that it took so long in coming.

Its overriding effect, then, was not that it made the generals less personal but that it made them more perfect. They became so expert in the new, scientific war that unschooled diplomats and civilian leaders were less inclined to restrain their rampant militarism. Modern armies on the Prussian model sprang up everywhere across Europe. Clausewitz had said, "War is a continuation of State policy by other means," and thus the capacity to make war or peace had always been kept in the hands of the makers of policy. But now war became the exclusive province of the general staff, peace that of the diplomats and civilians. "But what could civilians and diplomats do," asked the writer Guglielmo Ferrero,

when the old rules of the art of making peace were made inoperative by the new methods of making war? The soldiers perfected the technique of war; the diplomats lost the art of making peace. . . . Being unable to make peace, the diplomats in their turn began to prepare the way for war by making and unmaking alliances. Two Powers had signed the armistice of 1871, but when it was repudiated in 1914 it was two formidable groups of Powers that confronted one another, armed to the teeth.[2]

Here was another legacy of the Franco-Prussian War: the end of wars between nations and the beginning of wars between giant coalitions. Henceforth no one nation, not even sea-ruling Britain, would possess enough resources to make war without an ally.

Such, then, were the forces making for mass slaughter when, as the nineteenth century came to a close, the commercial rivalry between the empires of Europe became more intense, and the United States of America, the newest empire, stepped from the warm incubator of isolationism into the blustery cold world of international life.

Four men thrown up by the Spanish-American War made America eligible for the dawning century of coalition carnage. They did not, of course, force the nation into the Great War then preparing, nor were they the causes of its entry; but they were the chief authors of the profound psychological, political and military changes that made it possible for America to intervene as deeply and as effectively as she did. These men were Theodore Roosevelt, Elihu Root, Leonard Wood and Alfred Mahan.

Few occupants of the White House have been as contradictory in their character or in the passions they inspired in their contemporaries as Theodore Roosevelt. Here he was, an Eastern patrician, privately tutored and educated at Harvard, wealthy, erudite, sensitive to the new problems presented by the rise of industry and the cities, and yet a self-made Midwestern millionaire of plebeian origins and plutocratic convictions called him a "damn cowboy." Beloved by the people generally as "Teddy" or "TR," he was detested by his own class which he often excoriated as "malefactors of great wealth." To his admirers he was pure act, to his detractors pure noise; one visiting Englishman considered that he was, with Niagara Falls, one of the two natural marvels of America, while another derided him as one of the world's "masters of the obvious." Like many great and controversial men there were enough quirks and qualities in TR to justify both camps, but among all his traits one characteristic stood preeminent: his worship of power.

He idolized it because he believed that the judicious use of power would both protect his country and preserve world peace, and he was morally certain that both he and his nation were fit to exercise it. In fact, TR never had much difficulty in convincing himself of the righteousness of any policy that attracted him. It was the young TR who had calmly issued to Commodore Dewey those unauthorized battle orders which led to the annexation of the Philippines and American entry into world politics, and it was only a slightly older Teddy who said, in his brief inaugural address as Vice President: "We stand supreme in a continent, in a hemisphere. East and West we look across two great oceans toward the larger world life, in which, whether we will or not, we must take an ever-increasing share."[3] Six months later an assassin's bullet fired at Buffalo put Roosevelt into the paramount position from which the new American world power might be asserted.

The adage "Speak softly and carry a big stick" symbolized his foreign policy, and he fought successfully to obtain the big Navy to back it up. However, there was no soft voice but only a big stick evident when TR all but ripped the Panama Canal Zone out of the hands of Colombia in 1903. Colombia had balked at American terms for the right to build and control a canal across her Isthmus of Panama, whereupon insurgent Panamanians arose in revolt. It may not be true that Roosevelt encouraged them, but it is true that Washington made haste to recognize the new Republic of Panama and American naval forces prevented Colombia from putting down the rebellion. Roosevelt himself said later: "I took the Canal Zone and let Congress debate, and while the debate goes on the Canal does also."[4]

Doubtless to link the Atlantic and the Pacific was a great service not only to America but also to the maritime world, yet such high-handedness gave birth to a tradition of arrogant intervention in the Caribbean and Latin America. If Teddy got his Canal, his country was bequeathed a lasting legacy of Latin hatred which remains a heavy handicap to those who battle in today's Cold War for the minds of men.

In Asia, TR was inclined to speak more softly in attempting to uphold the Open Door policy. He also succeeded in mediating the Russo-Japanese War by the Treaty of Portsmouth signed September 5, 1905. In retrospect, it appears that Roosevelt may have saved Japan from ultimate defeat, yet the Japanese government informed its people that TR's big stick had beat them out of vast territorial acquisitions. A year later racist discrimination against Japanese in California brought the United States and Japan to the brink of war. Still speaking softly, TR negotiated the "gentlemen's agreement" of 1907 whereby Japan agreed to ameliorate the problem by discouraging further emigration to the United States. Another year, and the big stick was out again: in 1908 the "Great White Fleet" began its 14-month cruise around the world. It was described as a "friendship voyage," and it was at least non-warlike, but after the Japanese had counted 16 modern battleships in the harbor at Yokohama they concluded that the United States did possess the power to support its new position in world affairs.

The most astonishing departure from traditional isolationist policy came in 1906, when Roosevelt sent a representative to the Algeciras Conference called to mediate conflicting French and German claims in Morocco. Never before had the United States intervened in European affairs.

Perhaps more important, or more significant, than these and other gambits on the international chess board was TR's *rapprochement* with Great Britain. Before he became President Roosevelt had concluded that in the interplay of world politics American interests coincided most nearly with those of Britain, and he gave this conviction force when he entered the White House. TR also preferred France to Germany. After American influence at Algeciras brought a decision thwarting Germany, Roosevelt chortled that he had stood the Kaiser "on his head with great decision."[5]

Algeciras, however, was merely a temporary truce between the emerging European power blocs. American intervention there was still unthinkable of course, yet the historian Henry Adams could write with great prescience: "We have got to support France against Germany and fortify the Atlantic System beyond attack; for if Germany breaks down England or France, she becomes the center of a military world, and we are lost."[6]

But if Roosevelt could personally come closer to Britain, and if he could walk with confidence in the labyrinth of power politics, he could not persuade the bulk of his countrymen to follow him. The American government might understand the realities and responsibilities of empire, but the American people buried their heads in the isolationist sands and pretended that there were no problems. They could not understand that to "have" the Philippines and naval bases across the Pacific, to compete for trade in the Far East or to guarantee the independence of distant China, and to exert generally a moral influence on world affairs, America must participate in power politics.

Perhaps the American people, accustomed to inveighing against the crimes of the empires, sensed that to enter the world arena was to expose their own snow-white escutcheon to smear and stain. It may be that they recoiled from the thought of any repetition of the barbarities which American soldiers had committed in the Philippines beneath the banner of imperialism. Yet they did not reject their new-found empire, only its obligations. It was as though Americans wanted to end world injustice by preaching against it. But wrestle with the Devil? No. So they entered the pit pretending that they had not entered the pit, adopting an ambivalent attitude which, if it was not to have immediate effects, was to bear fearful fruit in the decades of the twenties and the thirties.

Yet, even if Roosevelt himself could not persuade the American people to accept their international obligations, he at least induced them to acknowledge the possibility of their existence. There was no Anglo-American alliance, but there was enough debate about it to suggest that those "entangling alliances" which were the anathema of Washington and Jefferson were now debatable. This was Roosevelt's achievement, to plant the ground with the seeds of change. After Roosevelt, then, the possibility of intervening somewhere on someone's side was a fact of national life, just as after Elihu Root it would be possible to intervene in strength.

Elihu Root may be justly called the father of the modern American Army, for it was he who introduced American arms to the Managerial Revolution. Oddly enough, this immensely able and profoundly perceptive man spent a good part of his life earnestly working for peace. Like the bellicose Theodore Roosevelt, he was a recipient of the famous Nobel Peace Prize founded by the inventor of dynamite, yet it was he who infected his country with the disease of militarism.

Root became Secretary of War under McKinley, replacing the inept Russell Alger. With his breadth of mind he saw at once that the Army's problem was not only in the Philippines, but rather a universal one. "Two propositions" struck him as being "fundamental": "First, the real object of having an army is to provide for war. Second, that the regular establishment of the United States will probably never be by itself the whole machine with which any war is fought."[7] In this, whether he realized it or not, Root was concluding with Emperor Wilhelm I that the national army must be the nation in arms. He might begin with only the best features of the Prussian model, as he did, but he would have to end with the worst: universal conscription. This is not to indict Elihu Root. Given the attitudes and convictions of his day, to have done other than he did would have been dereliction of duty. Moreover, he was continued in office by a President whose slogan was, "Speak softly, and carry a big stick." It was Root's assignment to make the stick hard as well as big, and he did it well.

In 1901 the Army War College was founded, and in 1903, through Root's efforts, the strength of the peacetime army was quadrupled to 100,000 men, the general staff system was introduced and the unwieldy office of commanding general was replaced by the far more efficient and powerful one of chief of staff. Root had also hoped to give his new model army an effective reserve by incorporating the state National Guards under federal control. Here he was defeated by the state interests. The Guards remained voluntary and state-controlled, although they were to be organized, trained and equipped by the federal Army. Nevertheless, Root's revolution was a highly respectable one. He killed off the "old Army" of the little wars and frontier garrisons, and brought into being the apparatus for a modern war machine. It was lacking only in the universal conscription characterizing the cadre armies of Europe, and this omission was to be remedied in a psychological way by General Leonard Wood.

Wood had been Roosevelt's chief with the Rough Riders in Cuba, and in 1910 he became Chief of Staff under TR's hand-picked successor, President William Howard Taft. It was Wood who made the new staff system stick, and it was he who preached, in and out of the Army, the new military gospel of a cadre army. He did not get one, of course—"Big Bill" Taft was too much of a pacifist and too beset by domestic difficulties to encourage Wood in this ambition—nor was there the tiniest enemy on the horizon to persuade the American people to abandon their traditional abhorrence of peacetime conscription. Yet, as Walter Millis says of Wood: "His name is associated with few contributions to military strategy or technology, but is imperishably linked with the great campaign for preparedness which was to convert the American people from their free-born, insouciant ways to acceptance of the conscript army and the rudiments of the garrison state."[8] Wood, then, gave to America her first force in readiness, one trained for no specific war but theoretically able to meet any emergency which might arise. In this, he was the Army's counterpart to the Navy's great theorist and the fourth man to prepare the United States for mass warfare: Captain Alfred Thayer Mahan.

Captain Mahan, the seagoing son of West Point's famous "old Dennis," was the first president of the Naval War College. It was his theories on sea power which captivated the mind of Theodore Roosevelt and the other imperialists who fought for annexation of the Philippines. It was not so much his powerful advocacy of the importance of sea power in war which shook the naval world, but his argument for a big peacetime navy. Mahan argued for a "fleet-in-being," much like Wood's later force-in-readiness, if it was not the genesis of it. However, Mahan's fleet-in-being required colonies for bases and coaling stations to maintain the world-ranging fleet which was to command the seas, as well as a large peacetime merchant marine to trade with the colonies and a huge shipbuilding industry.

In war, the merchant marine would provide troop transports and cadres of trained seamen for a navy expanding from existing shipyards.

Again to quote Millis: "The whole wrapped up amazingly into one glorious package of power, protection and profits. A big Navy would 'pay,' even in peace."⁹

It would be difficult to underestimate the influence of Mahan's first book, *The Influence of Sea Power on History, 1660-1783.* Long before Mahan's book became the naval bible at home, it was being devoured in Europe, and by no one more avidly than young Kaiser Wilhelm II of Germany.

The German Emperor whom American doughboys were one day to deride as "Kaiser Bill" ascended the throne in 1888. Pious and patriotic, quick-witted but superficial, he was nonetheless a hysterical swaggerer whose habitual blustering was to make him, in J. F. C. Fuller's phrase, "the Spanish fly of international politics."¹⁰ "There is only one master in the country, and I am he,"¹¹ the Kaiser said, and in the following year he made his boast a fact by dismissing Chancellor Bismarck, the one man able to restrain him.

Thereafter the rattling of the young Kaiser's saber disturbed friend and foe alike. "Cousin Nicky," the Czar Nicholas II of Russia, became so upset that he eventually formed an alliance with France. The French, rearming, burning with a "sacred anger" over the loss of Alsace-Lorraine, needed a partner who could supply the manpower deficiencies caused by a declining birth rate. Thus was born the Double Entente, and the very fact that republican France could make common cause with the "insane regime" of reactionary, Czarist Russia is a measure of the fears which Wilhelm's inflammatory oratory could arouse. Germany, meanwhile, continued with Austria-Hungary in the Double Alliance which had become the Triple Alliance after Italy joined to allay her fears of France.

Before the turn of the century, then, the alliances had shifted. Yet Britain remained aloof from both camps, and so long as she preserved the balance of power it did not appear that the peace of Europe would be disturbed. But then the rapid industrialization of Germany catapulted the Germans into competition with Britain for world markets. As the last decade of the 1800s began, Kaiser Wilhelm, undoubtedly influenced by Mahan, launched a program of naval expansion. He began to expand his empire. His merchant fleet grew great enough to challenge the maritime supremacy of Britain. He boasted openly of building a navy equal to the British mammoth, and in 1904 he publicly styled himself Admiral of the Atlantic Ocean.

The great tragedy of this mushrooming Anglo-German rivalry was that Germany and her Kaiser were extravagant admirers of the British. The Germans considered the Anglo-Saxons to be true Teutonic cousins, while Wilhelm was the grandson of Queen Victoria. Germany aspired to be Britain's trade partner, not her rival; and this she might very well have been had the Kaiser accepted Bismarck's advice to content himself with land power, had the Kaiser not trumpeted his mad naval challenge across the North Sea.

It was insane because its consequences could be foreseen: rather than surrender her supremacy, which meant accepting a lower standard of living, Britain picked up the gauntlet and a furious ship-building race was begun. The malediction of militarism was now compounded by the curse of navalism, and two international peace conferences called at The Hague were unable to bring either to a halt. Actually, the shipbuilding race was accelerated after Britain introduced the all-big-gun, "dreadnought" class of battleship.

Formerly, capital ships carried complements of, say, 12-inch and 8-inch guns, because the inaccuracy of the long-range weapons could be offset by the rapidity of the short-range ones. However, the Spanish-American naval battle of Santiago had been distinguished by the inaccuracy of all calibers, especially on the Spanish ships, and so the British Admiralty began to improve its gunnery. Once long-range guns were made to be accurate, it was concluded that the smaller calibers were useless: 12-inchers could knock out enemy vessels before the 8-inchers came within range. In 1906, when H.M.S. *Dreadnought* took to the sea, she carried nothing but big guns and just enough smaller ones to beat off close-in torpedo attacks. The moment her bow plunged into the waves she made every other battleship in the world obsolete. This included America's handsome post-Spanish War fleet, as well as Kaiser Wilhelm's new armada. So the naval race became a mad sprint to replace the outmoded battleships with new heavyweights of the dreadnought class.

Meanwhile, Britain had entered into secret negotiations with France. In 1904, through the *entente cordiale,* she became semi-attached to the French-Russian bloc, although her obligation was kept secret.

Then, in 1905, the world was stunned by the Japanese defeat of Russia. Well might it be stupefied, for Japan's conquest of Russian troops at Port Arthur, and destruction of the Russian fleet in the Straits of Tsushima, were events of incalculable consequences that remain with us today. First, these victories helped to provoke the Russian Revolution of 1905, which, though ruthlessly suppressed, was an ominous earnest of the future, as well as the impulse for revolutions in the Turkish Empire. Second, throughout darkest Africa was heard the electrifying news that the invincible white men had been worsted by a small, unknown non-European race; across the Asian land mass from Persia to India to vast China there ran a thrill of racial pride, as though Asia had done dreaming of past glories, of the days of the Great King or the hordes that rode into Russia, and was at last stirring from her sleep of centuries. Japan's triumph sounded the death knell of colonialism, even though Japan herself had now emerged as a colonial power. Witness after witness has corroborated the impact of the Japanese victory on the non-Caucasian mind, and it is not too much to suggest that the Afro-Asian nationalism which is one of the chief characteristics of modern international life may be traced to it.

More immediately, little Japan had demonstrated that Russia was a giant with spindly legs. France and Britain were dismayed, Germany and Austria-Hungary were delighted. Finding herself liberated from concern with her eastern border, Germany concentrated on the western frontier with France, thus driving the British into closer cooperation with the French and Russians. Now the coalitions were firm, now they confronted each other like two giants armed to the teeth in a Europe which historically has never been large enough for two great powers; and yet from time to time the partners paused to glance nervously behind their backs to see what the Socialists at home were up to.

The growing Socialist International was a new, explosive and untested force in European life. Here was the ghost of 1848, the phoenix risen from the ashes of the Paris Commune of 1871, a spirit stalking the world full of an old and vigorous hatred for the established order. As long ago as 1847 the Communist League had been founded in London, and Karl Marx and Friedrich Engels had concluded the *Communist Manifesto* with the celebrated exhortation: "The proletarians have nothing to lose but their chains. They have a world to win. Workingmen of all countries, unite!"[12] They had united, to the extent that by the close of the first decade of the twentieth century socialists, syndicalists and anarchists were gathering annually at Socialist International Congresses to tell the workingman in all the tongues of Europe that he had no country to defend, that he must not shoot at his class brothers across the borders, that his real enemy was his wealthy exploiter at home, and that the only true and holy war was the class war which would strike the capitalist chains from the workers of the world. Every government had to contend in some degree with the Socialists, who would one day change their name to Communists, every government had its lists of Socialist agitators to be imprisoned upon the moment the mobilization orders were issued, and all, with the possible exception of Britain, might wonder if the class brothers actually would refuse to shoot each other down, or whether their brethren in the factories would paralyze the war effort with strikes.

Even Czarist Russia could not pretend that the suppression of the Russian Revolution of 1905 had eliminated the radicals. It had merely scattered them. One group of ultraextremists preaching the destruction of all existing institutions had gathered in Zurich around a newspaper, *The Social Democrat,* edited by one V. I. Ulyanov and his wife. Ulyanov signed his articles "N. [for nothing] Lenin." Lenin was the leader of the "Bolsheviks," or majority group of Socialists, who had split off from the "Mensheviks," or minority. Another Bolshevik named Lev Davidovich Bronstein had escaped from exile in Siberia and gone to Vienna, where he wrote articles under the name of Trotsky.

Not even conservative America, cut off from the ferment of Europe, remained untouched by Socialism. In the election of 1912 some 900,000 Americans voted Socialist, and the violent Industrial Workers of the World had already rung out their manifesto: "Abolition of the wage system. It is the historic mission of the working class to do away with capitalism."[13] The "Wobblies" of the I.W.W. were never very numerous, yet they were savagely socialistic and their predilection for violence and sabotage was one of the domestic problems which drew President Taft farther and farther away from the exuberant internationalism of his predecessor. Taft also drew farther away from Roosevelt personally, and eventually these old friends became enemies.

After the Republican Convention of 1912 nominated Taft, Roosevelt and his followers broke away to form the Progressive Party, and to insure, in effect, a Democratic victory. When the votes were counted that fall, the American nation had conferred its highest office upon a novelty in American life: a professor in politics.

For different reasons, Thomas Woodrow Wilson, the 28th President of the United States, was a person as complex in his character as Theodore Roosevelt. Where TR was a volcano needing to be cooled, Woodrow Wilson was an iceberg needing to be warmed. An eloquent scholar whose deep Christian faith, moral fervor and sincere dedication could sway the masses, he could not lead men. Wilson said of himself: "I have a sense of power in dealing with men collectively, which I do not feel aways in dealing with them singly."[14] Wilson loved humanity as an abstraction. He was a "man-ist," from the calm of his study contemplating "man" triumphant or "man" enchained, as though mankind were some sort of deity symbolized by the kind of heroic-size murals found in post office lobbies. Only his family and a few intimates saw Wilson gay and playful, using his waspish wit to poke fun at himself. The remainder of his associates saw only the cold eyes behind the pince-nez, the prim mouth and the stubborn lantern jaw.

Aloof, he sought little advice. Because his mind was intuitive rather than analytical, he was able to make a judgment without facts; and because it was *he* who had made it, he wanted not information but confirmation. Yet, in spite of this, or perhaps because of this, Wilson became a strong President. In 1914, however, Wilson was a comparative unknown. Only a few liberals among the Democrats seemed aware of this former Princeton president, who, as a reform governor of New Jersey, had calmly demolished the state Democratic machine which put him in office. And Wilson's nomination, which did not come until the 46th ballot, was actually the gift of a hopeless deadlock among the favorites. The Taft-Roosevelt rift was another stroke of fortune. Yet this comparative unknown walked into the White House with the assurance of a man going up his own front steps. Although an internationalist, or at least an ardent advocate of a comity of nations, Wilson spent his first few years in office concentrating on the economic and labor reforms for which he is justly hailed. Then, in early 1914, his first major action in international affairs ended in an impasse.

In 1911 a revolution in Mexico replaced the iron-fisted dictator, Porfirio Díaz, with Francesco Madero, an ineffectual dreamer, who could not contain hungry, landless peasants suddenly liberated from 35 years of oppression. When Wilson became President in 1913, chaos reigned in Mexico and attacks upon American lives and property provoked a mounting clamor for intervention. Wilson prudently adopted a course of "watchful waiting." Then, after Madero was overturned and assassinated in a revolt led by General Victoriano Huerta, Wilson repudiated a government installed by bloodshed. He threw his support to a rival of Huerta, Venustiano Carranza. By doing so, Wilson fanned Mexico's factional flames hotter, and as fighting increased, American interests were placed in greater jeopardy. Still, the President stayed his hand. He deplored intervention, even though he had in fact intervened by supporting Carranza against Huerta.

Crisis came on April 9, 1914, when Huerta's forces seized a boatload of sailors who had come ashore at Tampico from an American ship. Huerta promptly released the Americans and apologized. But he refused to deliver the salute to the American flag demanded by the naval officer in command. The United States became enraged. "I'd make them salute the flag if we had to blow up the whole place!"[15] roared an American Senator. Wilson hesitated, until he received reports of a shipload of German munitions approaching Vera Cruz. With that, he ordered the occupation of that city.

On April 21, 1914, 77 years after Winfield Scott's invasion fleet sailed south to Vera Cruz, a second American "D-Day" was staged beneath the snow-capped peaks of Mount Orizaba. Marines stormed ashore, seized the city in a brief, brisk fight, and held it until Army reinforcements arrived under the command of that Frederick Funston who had captured Aguinaldo. The moment of military glory, however, was not worth the embarrassment it ultimately caused President Wilson.

The cool, detached professor in politics had lost his balance in a fit of "national honor." He had resorted to the use of force which he had condemned in Huerta. And, anyway, what did he want with Vera Cruz? Certainly, in view of the explosive state of affairs in Europe and his own convictions, he had no intention of deeper intervention. But how was he to get out of Vera Cruz? Happily, he was lifted off the dilemma by an offer of mediation from Argentina, Brazil and Chile. He promptly accepted, and then, in August, Huerta was forced to resign and Carranza took his place with Wilson's blessing.

This episode behind him, Wilson looked from his own hemisphere to Europe and was shaken by what he saw. At his inaugural he had prophesied an "age of settled peace and good will" among the nations. Now he saw a primed powder keg waiting for the charge. Britain had moved closer toward the Franco-Russian bloc, thereby almost guaranteeing war with Germany, and Russia had reacted from her defeat in the Far East in a fashion which promised conflict with Germany's ally, Austria-Hungary.

Turning from Asia, Russia concentrated on her European borders. She cast her eyes south, toward the Slavic races which had traditional ties with Russia but were now part of the Austro-Hungarian Empire. She looked toward Turkey, where control of the Dardanelles would give her an outlet to the Mediterranean. That was why Russia was elated to see Turkey all but driven from Europe during the two Balkan Wars of 1912-13. That was why Russia assured little Serbia on the borders of Austria-Hungary that she would never abandon her. That was why, in the spring of 1914, Wilson's roving Ambassador, Colonel Edward House, could report from Germany: "Everybody's nerves are tense. It only requires a spark to set the whole thing off."[16]

Who would strike the spark? Would it come from the Kaiser's fatal fondness for playing Bismarck? What about France? She had been riven by the hatreds boiling out of the Dreyfus affair, and now Frenchmen were again happily hating one another over the scandalous acquittal of Madame Caillaux, the minister's wife who had defended her tarnished "honor" by shooting a newspaper editor dead. Russia, rocked by bitter strikes, remained a "tangle of cowardice, blindness, craftiness and stupidity,"[17] whose feckless Czar protected the evil monk Rasputin, the corrupter of his court and also, it was said, the seducer of his daughter. Even England was unsteady. Civil war appeared imminent in Ireland, and the British government was an uneasy coalition. Sir Edward Grey, the Foreign Minister, never could be sure that either his government or Parliament would back him in standing by France in the event of war. All that Grey could do was to give France the assurance that Britain would fight Germany if the Germans violated the neutrality of Belgium.

Actually, none of these powers or persons wanted war, and neither did doughty old Emperor Francis Joseph of Austria-Hungary. He was military-minded and a Spartan, at 84 years of age still devoted to cold baths and long gallops, but he did not want war. What about the Balkan States? Here was the "powder keg of Europe," here was the seething cockpit of national animosities which Bismarck had said was not worth the bones of a single German grenadier.

Here the ambitions of Austria and Russia clashed. Here Austria in 1908 suddenly annexed Bosnia and Herzegovina. Austria had in fact been administering them for 30 years as nominal Turkish provinces confided to her charge, but to annex them outright outraged neighboring Serbia and nearly provoked war with Serbia's friend and ally, Russia. It was here that Austria hoped to expand her empire at the expense of Serbia, thus drawing closer to the Dardanelles coveted by Russia, and it was here that the Serbs, encouraged by Russia, hoped to bind Bosnia and other Slavic states into a Greater Serbia at the expense of Austria.

Here also, on June 28, 1914, came Archduke Francis Ferdinand of Austria. With his wife Sophie, the archduke rode in an open automobile through the streets of Sarajevo, the capital of the Austrian province of Bosnia. From neighboring Serbia came seven fanatical young men with bombs and pistols hidden on their persons. They thought of themselves as Serbian patriots, and they hated Archduke Ferdinand because the empire which he symbolized had thwarted a Greater Serbia. They had come to kill him. One of them threw a bomb that missed, five others lost their nerve. But the seventh, a fanatical young consumptive named Gavrilo Princip, did not falter. He stood in a street with drawn pistol and by one of the great small blunders of history, the Archduke's chauffeur made a wrong turning and drove the open limousine to within five feet of Princip.

Twice, his little pistol snapped. One bullet struck Archduke Ferdinand in the neck, the other pierced Sophie's stomach. Blood spurted from Ferdinand's mouth, and as his wife screamed and fainted, he gasped: "Sophie dear, Sophie dear, don't die! Live for our children!"[18] Sophie did not live, nor did the Archduke Ferdinand, and with their deaths the sparks went flashing into the powder keg.

2

☆

From the vantage of half a century it appears inevitable that there would have been an explosion. Too many forces were on collision course. What is most tragic, however, is that the war was not localized, and that, through mismanagement and misunderstanding, the first fires should have blazed up uncontrollably and engulfed the world.

One major misunderstanding was Britain's secret attachment to the Triple Entente. To the very end, Germany expected Britain to remain neutral; so did many leading Britons, who were unaware, as Parliament was unaware, of their government's secret obligations to France and Russia. Even so, the British attitude would never have been called into question had not the German Kaiser been so incredibly irresponsible as to the intentions of his partner, Austria, and had not the Austrian Foreign Minister been so intent upon punishing Serbia.

Certainly Count Leopold von Berchtold was no sinister misanthrope bent upon convulsing the world. Yet he might have foreseen that Russia would not allow him to harm Serbia. As a diplomat, Berchtold had a high reputation; personally, he was regarded as a luxury-loving lady's man. As such, he may stand as history's archetype of the bellicose sybarite who sends peaceful men into stinking trenches with orders issued from a scented boudoir. He was also known to be lazy, although he worked very hard at intimidating Serbia.

Berchtold wanted to invade Serbia immediately, but was restrained by Count Tisza, the Hungarian Prime Minister, who urged leniency, and by General Conrad von Hötzendorf, the chief of staff, who protested that it would take Austria 16 days to mobilize. Mobilize first, then send Serbia your ultimatum, Conrad counseled. Instead, Berchtold played a cleverer game.

He sent an emissary to Berlin to ask the Kaiser's advice. In the meantime he pocketed Count Tisza's letters urging Emperor Francis Joseph to be moderate and brought Tisza to his side by assuring him that no territorial demand would be made upon Serbia. This was a lie: Berchtold was already planning the partition of Serbia.

In Berlin, Kaiser Wilhelm, bound for a holiday cruise to Norway, blithely gave Austria a carte blanche. Berchtold's emissary was told that Austria must decide for herself what was to be done, but that in any event Germany would stand behind her. Even among allies, such unquestioning loyalty is unheard of in international life. History still stands dumfounded before it. Even if Germany believed, as has been said, that Austria must have satisfaction from Serbia rather than risk a humiliation which would encourage Balkan nationalism, "satisfaction" need not have been the extreme of war, and the Kaiser need not have pledged himself in advance with a blank check. But he did, and when Emperor Francis Joseph was told that the Kaiser backed him all the way, he said sadly: "Now we can no longer hold back. It will be a terrible war."[19]

Immediately, Berchtold prepared his ultimatum to Serbia. He gave the little kingdom 48 hours to comply with demands which no self-respecting nation could possibly accept. Sir Edward Grey in London read a copy of the ultimatum and described it as the strongest demand ever made by one state on another. The Kaiser, idling aboard the yacht *Hohenzollern* off Norway, commented to his naval aide: "A spirited note, what?"[20] In Belgrade a Serbian minister read the note and shrugged: "Well, there is nothing to do but die fighting."[21] Yet, even as Russia was called upon for help, Serbia managed to compose a most conciliatory reply. Even Berchtold was astonished at its meekness.

Unfortunately, almost at the moment the pacific note was being delivered, Serbia ordered mobilization for war. It was a disastrous decision, made, it appears, for political considerations. Premier Pašić of Serbia faced an election amid a mounting clamor for war from Serbian officers, many of whom were associated with the very Black Hand society which had masterminded the assassination of Archduke Ferdinand. The officers were powerful politically. To placate them and ensure their support, Pašić made this warlike gesture which would make his meek note more palatable at home. It was, of course, a move made strictly for home consumption, but it played right into Berchtold's hands.

Yet at that moment a general war was not inevitable. Even if Russia moved to defend Serbia, it would be with that ponderous slowness characteristic of the so-called Russian "steamroller." By then it might be all over. France had no intention of fighting for Serbia, but would fulfill her obligations to Russia; that is, move to her side if she became engaged with Austria. Germany was holding off, because to do so would keep France inactive and because, with her marvelous railway system, she could mobilize the most rapidly. Britain, the least committed of the Triple Entente, moved to keep the peace. Probably, if she had immediately informed Germany that she stood by France, there would have been no general conflagration—at least not then.

However, Sir Edward Grey was still in the service of a shaky coalition faced with ugly trouble in Ireland, and now was not the time to shock Parliament with the announcement that Britain was in fact obligated on the Continent. Instead, Grey attempted to persuade Chancellor Theobald von Bethmann-Hollweg of Germany to "mediate" the crisis. Bethmann-Hollweg agreed, and did nothing. To him "mediation" meant "localizing" the war; that is, to keep all the powers quiet while Austria raped Serbia. Thus, while Grey mistakenly thought that mediation was being urged upon Austria by Germany, nothing of the sort was being done.

At last Bethmann-Hollweg awoke to the danger of Great Power war. He had been informed that the British Grand Fleet was steaming to battle stations, and Italy had already notified him that, since Austria had not consulted her as an ally prior to declaring war on Serbia, Italy "could not consider herself bound" by the Triple Alliance. Shorn of an ally on one side, beginning to suspect that Britain might not, after all, be neutral, the Chancellor wired Count Berchtold asking him to consider Grey's proposal and to accept the Serbian reply as a basis for further discussion.

That was done on July 27, 1914. Even by then, Bethmann-Hollweg thought there was still time. He did not believe Austria's 16-day requirement for mobilization would allow her to attack before August 12. But he had failed to reckon with the headstrong Berchtold. Austria's declaration of war was already completed. On July 28 the climactic lie was told by Berchtold. Serbia is attacking, he informed Emperor Francis Joseph, and the old man signed the document.

July 28, 1914, one month after the murders at Sarajevo, Austria-Hungary declared war on Serbia.

Two days later, July 30, 1914, Russia began mobilizing. On July 31 Germany called upon her to stop, Russia refused, and Germany and Russia were at war.

On August 1 France and Germany mobilized.

On August 2 Italy declared herself neutral.

Thus the great Powers were arrayed, France and Russia confronting Germany and Austria sandwiched between them. The next question was: What would Britain do?

Britain, to her very real sorrow, had no choice. She was not only secretly attached to France and Russia, she was by virtue of her commercial and maritime supremacy opposed to the rise of Imperial Germany. Nevertheless, at the outset she did no more than to promise

France to protect her coasts against German attack. Whether or not she would do more depended on one crucial question: Would Germany respect the neutrality of Belgium?

The answer to that had been given a decade ago.

In 1905 Count Alfred von Schlieffen, then Chief of the German General Staff, drew up his famous plan for two-front war against France and Russia. Some historians still prattle about the Schlieffen Plan as the masterpiece of a military mastermind, but neither the concept nor the conceiver were exceptional. Schlieffen was no genius, but rather almost a caricature of the typical cold, colorless Prussian officer, a man so inhuman in his dedication that he could, every Christmas Eve, present a difficult logistics problem to one of his married officers with orders to produce a written solution next day. His plan merely recognized two facts of European history and geography: first, that Russia was always slow to mobilize; second, that Belgium was the gateway to France.

Schlieffen proposed to hurl his main body upon France while containing slow-moving Russia with a smaller force, after which all his force could be combined to crush the Czar. To do this Germany could not attack through the rugged terrain of the Franco-German border. That would take too long: before Paris could be reached, the Russian steamroller would be rolling across Germany's eastern frontier. No, the quick route was across the Belgian lowlands into northern France. It was longer in distance—250 air miles as opposed to 180—but it was shorter in time.

So the Schlieffen Plan was approved, even though Germany was well aware of Belgium's neutral status. Along with Britain and the other Powers, Germany had guaranteed Belgian neutrality after the little kingdom between France and Holland was created by the treaties of 1831 and 1839. To violate her, however, was considered "a military necessity" by Schlieffen and the other German war lords who succeeded him. That was the only thing exceptional about the Schlieffen Plan: military necessity had imposed its will upon the German diplomats. Force and persuasion, the twin servants of foreign policy, had been thrown out of balance with the final result that the Kaiser spoke to the world with a pistol.

Of course, having lost this battle, the German Foreign Office was quick to pretend that it did not matter: effete, libertarian Britain would not fight, it was maintained, she would not be so unrealistic as to enter the war merely to keep a promise.

But Britain would. On August 3, after Germany shocked the world by demanding free passage across Belgium, the British responded to the German ultimatum by demanding that the invasion of Belgium be halted.

Germany seethed with rage. Newspapers screamed that Britain had betrayed her cousin. Bethmann-Hollweg summoned the British Ambassador and stormed, "Just for a scrap of paper, Great Britain is going to make war on a kindred race."[22] At midnight of August 4 Britain did declare war on Germany.

One by one the other Powers exchanged formal declarations of war. Stiffly, stiltedly, like puppets jerking across a stage, powerless to stay the forces that guided them, they began the war that nobody wanted. In chancelleries across the face of Europe there were emotional farewells between old friends who would henceforth be implacable enemies. Ambassadors asked for their passports in choking voices. All knew that catastrophe had befallen the old order, but the most skilled diplomatist did not know how. "Oh, if only I knew!"[23] Bethmann-Hollweg lamented.

In London on that fateful evening of August 4, 1914, Sir Edward Grey stood at a window with a friend, watching as the lamps were being lighted in the street below. Sir Edward's gentle bird-watcher's eyes were sad as he turned to say: "The lamps are going out all over Europe."[24]

3

☆

The outbreak in Europe of the spreading conflagration at first known as the Great War and now called World War I shocked the American public as had no event since the firing upon Fort Sumter.

Horrified as Americans were, they were also determined to stay out of it. On August 4 President Wilson proclaimed American neutrality and later told the nation: "We must be impartial in thought as well as in action, must put a curb upon our sentiments."[25] Even Theodore Roosevelt wrote, "I am not now taking sides," and declared that it would be "folly to jump into the war."[26]

To be impartial in thought was not possible. This was Europe blazing, and Americans were Europeans transplanted. Those who lived on both coasts and in the South, mindful of their British blood and culture, still cherishing an affection for France born of the Revolution and lately brought to that *rapprochement* with Britain, favored the Allied cause. True, the despotic Czar was on the Allied side, but they closed their minds to this. Others who were of German descent naturally echoed the Kaiser's cry that Germany must have her place in the sun, while those of Irish blood, remembering Albion's crimes against Erin, prayed to see her humbled. The heartland of America, meanwhile, the home of isolationism and of the Progressive movement, raised the banners of strict neutrality. Among Progressives, pacifism or at least an abhorrence of war as a cruel waste and a roadblock on the path to social justice was an article of faith. Immigrants to America, many of whom could be justly described as refugees from European militarism, turned their backs with a scornful "plague on both your houses," while Socialists and their sympathizers frankly rejoiced in the *Götterdämmerung* of the dynasties, the last of the capitalist wars which was to pull down the entire rotten edifice and make way for the new order of the proletariat.

In all, the great bulk of the American people, especially the working men, were neutral or pacifist; and even those who did favor this or that bloc did not wish their nation to become a combatant. Except for some youths who joined the British Army or flew for the Lafayette Escadrille in France, America was to be a spectator to the agony of Europe.

Some six million men were deployed across the face of Europe in that awful August of 1914. Germany confronted France with 1,500,-000 soldiers and placed 500,000 more opposite Russia. Austria wheeled another 500,000 into place against Serbia and Russia.

Against these troops of the Central Powers, France mustered about 1,600,000 men—to be supplemented by another 100,000 from Britain and Belgium—and Russia called up 1,400,000 more.

These were the early dispositions. Eventually, Britain went far beyond her original contribution, the Russian mobilization alone placed 12 million men in the field, Germany's rose to 11 million, and by the time the war had spread and become truly world-wide there were more than 65 million men under arms. As events were to show, not many nations were as fortunate as America in her size and the two oceans which guarded her like moats. This was a war between empires, especially after Turkey followed Bulgaria into the camp of the Central Powers and Italy and Japan joined the Allies. Except for North and South America, the empires encompassed the globe. There was not a place at sea and scarcely a spot on land where one enemy could not strike at the other.

Because a consumptive madman had fired two shots in Bosnia, men of every color and creed were to kill each other from Eurasia to Africa, innocent women and children were to sink to the bottom of the Irish Sea, both coasts of South America were to rumble with the sounds of the sea cannonade, and Japan would go scavenging among the Kaiser's unprotected Pacific possessions. Gavrilo Princip was too young to be executed for his crimes, but he was older than some of the Turkish soldiers who froze to death in the Russian Caucasus or the Australian and New Zealand riflemen who died of dysentery or malaria on the waterless slopes of the Dardanelles. From every clime and continent they came, these devoted, often blindly obedient masses of the empires. Canadians of both French and British blood at last had found a unifying cause after three centuries of bloody war and bickering peace. Cockneys from London and Irishmen who had "taken the King's shilling" fought beside phlegmatic Breton fishermen, solid Belgians or vivacious Parisians in the battle against the Kaiser's "Huns"—brawny peasant lads from Pomerania or factory workers from Düsseldorf under the command of corseted Prussian Junkers. Out of the welter of the Austro-Hungarian Empire, that "melting pot on a cold fire," came unwilling warriors from eight nations and 17 countries, of whom not one soldier in four spoke the German language of the empire they detested. Serbs and Montenegrins, Rumanians, Portuguese and kilted Greeks, all the Slavic and Oriental races of the vast sprawling giant called Russia came serried to the roll of the drum; British bugles summoned all the warlike tribes of India; Arabs, Jews, Anatolians and Persians fought for or against the Ottoman Empire; and out of Africa, not knowing or caring why, marched Senegalese, Congolese, Kikuyu and one miserable outcast little tribe called Bastards.

It was to become truly a world convulsed, a time of dreadful upheaval in which the ramshackle old empires were to come crashing down and even those of Britain and France were to crack and sag. Yet few men on either side suspected the nature of the catastrophe at hand. On both sides mobilizations were gay and carefree. "You will be home before the leaves have fallen from the trees,"[27] the Kaiser told his troops. It was generally believed on both sides that a prolonged war was economically impossible, and both sides were confident of quick victory.

Among the French generals there existed an almost mystical devotion to what has been called the School of the Attack. Studying the Franco-Prussian War to learn the reason for France's humiliation, the French General Staff made the astounding discovery that their enemies had based their strategy on the campaigns of Napoleon. Delighted, the French began restudying their own great captain. From him they came upon the secret of success: the offensive! *L'attaque,* always the attack, shock, penetration, the bayonet charge, this would restore to France her martial glory.

Like all other European staffs, the French had disdained to study the American Civil War, in which diametrically opposite conclusions had been given bloody proof. They were not aware that the defense was king of the battlefield, a far bloodier sovereign now, with improved artillery, machine guns and barbed wire at his command. No, the French took their lessons from the Crimean War, in which the old shock tactics of the bayonet charge seemed to have been effective; and to this they joined their love affair with the Napoleonic past.

Inexorably, the School of the Attack captivated all but a few French military minds, and its devotees became strong enough to blight the career of an obdurate major named Henri Philippe Pétain, and to pull down the French Commander in Chief (*Grand Quartier Général*) himself. In his place went General Joseph Jacques Joffre, an imposing man whose large paunch and huge white mustache seemed to emphasize the air of monumental calm which was his chief characteristic, and also, his traducers say, his single military attribute. In post-Dreyfus, republican France a nonaristocratic general of obviously indifferent Catholicism was eminently acceptable to French politicians. To the General Staff, the ponderous Joffre seemed "a solid shield behind which subtler brains could direct French military policy."[28] Knowing to whom he owed his promotion, "Papa" Joffre accepted *l'attaque.* He also accepted Plan XVII calling for an audacious French drive out of their border fortresses into the lost provinces of Alsace and Lorraine. And that, except for a change in the German command, might have been exactly what the Schlieffen Plan had ordered.

General Helmuth von Moltke in some ways resembled Joffre. He also was fat, slow-moving and aging—at 66 only four years older than the Frenchman. Prussian officers did not exactly admire Moltke for frequently falling off his horse on maneuvers, nor were they especially impressed by the fact that he painted, played the cello, read poetry and professed an interest in odd religious cults. Nevertheless, Moltke was a nephew of the great Helmuth von Moltke, the soldier who had conquered France in 1870, and he was also a favorite of the Kaiser's. For these reasons he succeeded Schlieffen as Chief of Staff, after which he began to make drastic revisions in the Schlieffen Plan.

The original proposal was to send a powerful right wing through Belgium and down into France while luring the French into Germany with a weak left wing. Then the left wing would halt to block the French attack while the right wing came around Paris to smash into the French rear. It has been said that Schlieffen's dying words were: "It must come to a fight. Only make the right wing strong."[29] This Moltke did not do. He weakened the right wing while strengthening the left. As a result, when the French divisions rushed forward they were not allowed to blunder into difficult terrain where they were eventually to be held and crushed between two fires. They were hurled back into France. Even so, their repulse was a dreadful defeat.

French soldiers in bright red pants and horizon-blue coats were marshaled in fields and along roads in plain view of German artillery observers or machine gunners invisible in their field gray. Bands played the "Marseillaise." Flags waved. Officers wearing white gloves stood 20 paces in front of the troops. They had been taught that *cran* and *élan,* pluck and verve, would beat the detestable Boche. *"En avant!"* they cried. *"A la baïonnette!"* Bugles blew, the bright lines swept boldly forward, and the result was reported by a British observer:

Whenever the French infantry advance, their whole front is at once regularly covered with shrapnel and the unfortunate men are knocked over like rabbits. They are very brave and advance time after time to the charge through appalling fire, but so far it has been of no avail. No one could live through the fire that is concentrated on them. The officers are splendid . . . but so far I have not seen one of them get more than fifty yards without being knocked over.[30]

So died the School of the Attack: riddled by stuttering bursts of machine-gun fire, shredded by deadly showers of shrapnel, fallen among silent bugles and muddy flags and windrows of bloody blue coats. With dawning horror, the French generals came to realize that they had grasped not the pistol grip of military fortune but the muzzle. Yet by this very repulse in the Battle of the Frontiers France was actually saved. One mistake was canceling out the other: the alteration of the Schlieffen Plan countered the miscalculations of *l'attaque,* so that the French troops were back in their fortresses and available as reserves when Papa Joffre at last realized that the German smash into neutral Belgium was no mere grab for land.

The Belgians had fought bravely, but they had not upset the German timetable. Probably they had done something far more consequential. By resisting, King Albert's troops evoked the admiration of the world and emphasized the injustice of the German invasion. Subsequent German atrocities only swung the pendulum of world public opinion farther away from the Central Powers. In a military sense, however, even the Belgian stand at Liége did not long delay Moltke's field-gray hordes. Huge German howitzers, among them the famous Big Bertha, a 16.5-inch mammoth able to hurl an 1,800-pound shell a distance of nine miles, simply blasted the Liége forts into rubble. Eventually five full German armies, perhaps as many as two million men, were charging down on Paris.

Ahead of them they drove the French Army, the tiny British Expeditionary Force which the Germans called "the contemptible little army," and masses of terrified French, civilians fleeing the Boche advance. When these fear-mad fugitives erupted into the Allied positions, they snarled communications and multiplied the problems of resistance. Still, the Allies fought desperately, especially the soldiers of the B.E.F. who now proudly called themselves "the Old Contemptibles." But as August neared its end, the fall of Paris appeared inevitable, and with it France and the Allied cause.

At that point, the Schlieffen Plan was weakened again. Far to the east the gigantic Battle of Tannenberg was raging between Germany's small holding force and a huge Russian army. At first it appeared that the Russians, holding a two-to-one superiority, would crush the Germans. But then the stolid General Paul von Hindenburg, assisted by his brilliant deputy, General Erich von Ludendorff, the hero of Liége, arrived on the Eastern front.

Hindenburg and Ludendorff brought off nothing less than a double envelopment, a magnificent maneuver worthy of Hannibal at Cannae, which struck the Russians a stunning blow. Before they did this, however, a German staff officer on the Western front, mistakenly concluding that the Allies were defeated, took two German corps and sent them rolling east. They were never needed in the east, but their departure again weakened the right wing which Schlieffen wished to be made strong. The necessity of posting guards in captured cities to the rear, as well as protecting the lengthening line of communications, had also weakened that flank. Worst of all for General von Moltke, the detachments were taken from the two armies on his own right or western flank, the ones that had to make the farthest turn in the swing around Paris and which therefore needed the most men.

These were the First Army under General Alexander von Kluck and the Second under General Karl von Bülow. Kluck was on the right or seaward flank, Bülow to his left or east. It was Kluck who was to make the swing around Paris and lead the drive into the French rear.

On August 24, as the Germans neared Paris, General Joffre paced the garden of his headquarters in solitary silence. Hands clasped behind his back, his cherubic pink-and-white features expressionless, the bulky old man walked for more than an hour. At last he raised his head. He knew now. The reports had convinced him. Plan XVII had been a bloody delusion. It had already cost 300,000 men. On his left, there was the peril! Paris, that was the enemy's objective!

Next day, to help defend the capital, Joffre formed the Sixth Army under General Michel Joseph Maunoury. On that same day, however,

Sir John French notified Lord Kitchener in London that he intended to withdraw to the southwest. In effect, the B.E.F. was leaving the war.

Even so, at almost the same time, the Germans began to make blunders of their own. The outside armies under Kluck and Bülow were exhausted from more than two weeks of fighting and marching. There were gaps between them. Kluck, convinced that he had beaten the British and that the French were fleeing, decided he would come closer to Bülow. This meant that instead of keeping to the west of Paris, and then wheeling east *below* the city to scoop it into the German net, he was turning east *above* it. He was going to slide by Paris. For the last and most fateful time, the Schlieffen Plan was changed.

Kluck made his fatal turn on August 31. It was observed and reported by a British aviator, but Joffre did not react as yet. Two days later he advised the Ministry of War: "All our hopes are defeated. We are in full retreat all along the line. Maunoury's army is falling back on Paris."[31] The government fled. General Joseph Simon Gallieni, Commander of Paris, prepared for battle, determined to hold out if it meant reducing beautiful Paris to rubble. In the meantime, Lord Kitchener had rushed across the Channel to confront Sir John French in a painful interview and order him back into action.

That night in General Gallieni's headquarters, as France seemed to lie hushed and huddled beneath the enemy's descending hammer, additional reports of Kluck's eastward turn were pinned up on a map. Two French colonels observed the maneuver and cried joyously: "They offer us their flank! They offer us their flank!"[32] It was true. By turning to his left Kluck had exposed the German right wing. Moreover, unknown to the Allies, his army was about played out. "Our men are done up," one of Kluck's officers wrote in his diary that day. "They stagger forward, their faces coated with dust, their uniforms in rags. They look like scarecrows."[33]

Sensing the golden opportunity, Gallieni informed Joffre and persuaded him that the time had come to turn and fight. If he held all along the line, he could swing his left around the German right. All depended on the French Sixth Army on the far left and its right-hand neighbor, Sir John French and the B.E.F.

Joffre ordered the Sixth Army into action and called upon Sir

John, of whose intentions he was still not certain. He begged him to cooperate. *"Monsieur le maréchal,"* he said, "it is France who beseeches you." Unable to stammer his reply in French, Sir John turned to an aide and said: "Dammit, I can't explain! Tell him that all that men can do our fellows will do."[34]

Thus was begun the Battle of the Marne. It raged for seven days on a broad front from Verdun in the east to Meaux in the west, a furious, bloody and confused compound of large actions and small skirmishes, of heroism and stupidity, of lightning thrusts and lost opportunities. At one point, the French Sixth Army was in danger of being destroyed as it floundered around Kluck's right. In Paris, Gallieni loaded a relief force into 1,200 taxicabs and sent this famous "Taxicab Army" rattling to the rescue.

In the center Louis Franchet d'Esperey had taken command of the French Fifth Army. When one of his corps commanders called to plead for relief of his tired troops, Franchet d'Esperey cut him off with the remark: "There is to be no more discussion. You will march—march or drop dead!"[35] Thereafter the Fifth's poilus—"hairy ones"—fought Bülow's army to a standstill.

On the right, General Ferdinand Foch entered history. At the head of the new Ninth Army formed by Joffre, Foch counterattacked the German Ninth Army into exhaustion. It was here that Foch was supposed to have signaled Joffre: "My right gives. My center yields. Situation excellent. I shall attack!"[36] This, of course, is apocryphal. What actually happened was that the bandy-legged little Frenchman had deduced that in attacking the French flanks the German commander had weakened his center. Plunging straight ahead, therefore, Foch's soldiers broke the German middle.

Now the goddess of war beckoned to Sir John French. Now there was a widening gap opened between Kluck and Bülow and opposite Sir John. If he sent his B.E.F. plunging into the hole, he might break through and split the enemy in two; but Sir John hesitated, and by the time Joffre had persuaded him to strike, the gap had closed.

Yet the Battle of the Marne turned against the Germans. Far away in his Luxembourg headquarters, Helmuth von Moltke, the general whom the Kaiser had always teased as "Gloomy Gus," sank deeper into despair. At last he granted a staff colonel the power to do what he dared not do: sound the retreat. Back to the Aisne River went the stunned and thwarted Germans. Back to Paris came the sheepish French government. Papa Joffre and "the Miracle of the Marne" had saved France.

The Marne was the decisive battle of World War I, and also one of the most decisive battles in history. No matter that it occurred within only the first of 51 months of war, or that it was not a stunning tactical triumph like Tannenburg. The Marne denied to Germany her only chance to destroy France, drive Britain into the sea and then defeat Russia at leisure. Germany had planned and played for this one chance, and when she lost it, she lost all.

True enough, Germany still held the initiative, and she continued to score victories over the Russians and to redeem the failures of her overzealous but ineffectual Austrian ally. But after the Marne there was no more chance of maneuver in the West. Mobile warfare gradually degenerated into siege warfare of the most hideous character, and the very outcome of the war passed from the battlefield to the factories.

Immediately, the defeat at the Marne ended the career of Helmuth von Moltke. He was succeeded by General Erich von Falkenhayn, an energetic driver who immediately attempted to get around the Allied left flank. Joffre countered by attempting to turn the German right. Thus both armies made sideways lunges in the same direction, and began the Race to the Sea. As they did, King Albert was driven out of his last stronghold at Antwerp, retreating to the little town of Nieuport on the North Sea. There he linked up with Anglo-French forces on his right. Soon afterward the pursuing forces came to a halt opposite him, and the Race to the Sea had ended in a tie. The German right and the Allied left were firmly anchored on the water while at the other end of the front the opposing flanks rested on the mountains of neutral Switzerland.

To escape each other's artillery, both armies dug in. They constructed those elaborate systems of trenches which, often only a few hundred yards apart, eventually traced a 400-mile zigzag scar from the North Sea down through a corner of Belgium across France to the Swiss border. It was now a war without flanks. It was no longer possible to get around the opposing army to strike its rear, and the only maneuver possible—or so all the generals thought—was to effect a "penetration" by straight-ahead assault.

The Germans tried this first. On October 20, 1914, they began the

First Battle of Ypres, which raged until snuffed out by howling November blizzards. The Allies also attempted to break through, and were halted by a German counterattack. The casualties: a quarter-million men. Ypres, a lovely little Gothic jewel, was broken into shards. Thus, at the moment static, position warfare began, it showed its hideous features: an appalling loss of life and wanton destruction of property.

To the generals, however, the remedy for stalemate was more munitions. Within a year, Britain increased her production of shells from 30,000 monthly to 1,200,000 a month, with a corresponding rise in artillery production. Germany and France ordered similar speed-ups. More guns, however, could not break the deadlock. They intensified it. They either bombarded the enemy's positions, forcing both sides to build ever-deeper, ever-wider trench networks, or they multiplied the casualties. Artillery barrages were laid down in front of infantry assaults. They tore up the middle ground between the armies, creating that famous no-man's land of shell-pocked mud, but they did not knock down the enemy's barbed wire or silence his artillery. Troops stumbling through no-man's land were struck by enemy shellfire the moment their own barrage lifted. If they made it to the enemy's barbed wire, they were riddled by interlocking machine-gun fire.

It was the machine gun that froze the front. What the rifle had been to the American Civil War, the machine gun was to World War I. True, artillery probably killed more men, as it always does, but the machine gun killed the offensive. It was light, it fired lightweight ammunition at a dreadful 450 rounds a minute, and it could be hidden underground during artillery barrages and then quickly carried into position once the enemy assault began. The machine gun, then, magnified the problem of the attack.

Since the introduction of firearms, the attack's problem had always been how to advance exposed firepower against entrenched firepower. The answer, of course, was the tank, which is nothing less than an armored mobile gun. Its armor plate gives the attacking soldiers inside it the same protection which forts and trenches give to soldiers on defense. Moreover, because it is mobile as well as armored, its advance, short of a direct hit, is *inexorable*. Its moral power is thus immense: it terrifies the defense, and since battles are not won by killing men but by making them run, the tank had shocking power to smash the defense. However, tanks were not yet developed, and the airplane, another weapon able to break the deadlock, was being used only for scouting or minor harassment.

In a way, World War I was a technological tragedy. It caught the nations at a period in history when the Industrial Revolution was advanced only far enough to turn out the simpler weapons of defense. The more complicated ones favoring the attack—tanks, airplanes, motor transport, all thé weapons of mobility—did not appear except in their primitive stages or in ineffectual small quantities. So the factories continued to turn out the guns that canceled each other out and the machine guns that forbade a decision, and the war went on for four years with neither side able to move forward more than a few miles. "Penetration," that Medusan muse which held the generals spellbound, was not possible to unprotected foot soldiers. No matter how massive the million-man assaults or the thousand-gun artillery barrages, the spearhead troops simply could not move fast enough to achieve a decisive breakthrough. The enemy fell back, trench by trench, then turned to pin down the exhausted spearheads while his artillery broke up the oncoming reserves. Then he began hammering on the shoulders of the salient in an effort to cut off the spearheads. So the spearheads had to withdraw. Slaughtered on their way into these shallow salients, they were butchered on the way out.

It is not necessary here to recite the catalogue of inconclusive battles which, in the 32 months between the outbreak of the war and American intervention, soaked the soil of Europe in the blood of its finest. On the Eastern front, casualties were even more appalling. Here, massed battalions of Russian soldiers, led by probably the worst officers in the war, attacked machine guns across open fields. They knew little or nothing of the techniques of cover or squad rushes developed in the no-man's lands of the West, and a shocked and bleeding Russia said with awful truth that the Czar's only weapon was the living breasts of his soldiers.

Yet the wasting attacks continued on the orders of generals often too far behind the lines in comfortable châteaux to know what was going on. They cared, of course, but chiefly for their reputations. Very few, if any, at a level less than corps command suffered so much as a smidgen of mud on their spotless riding breeches or stepped from a staff car into the "cold" without a batman waiting with outstretched cape. They were like coldly efficient corporation executives, entertaining each other with regimental bands and excellent meals, while conferring on mutual problems and studying statistics which too often meant that the loss of so many battalions, that is, so many thousands of flesh-and-blood human beings, must be "accepted" in the next futile attempt to bludgeon a path through the enemy's front. Joffre, who went to bed punctually each night at ten o'clock, after nourishing his huge paunch from an epicurean mess table, did not endear himself to the world or his poilus when he justified his own wasting attacks with the phrase: "I am nibbling them."[37] While Joffre nibbled, Falkenhayn gnawed; and the contribution of Sir Douglas Haig, the picture-book soldier who eventually replaced Sir John French as the British commander, was to cling to the conviction that cavalry could conquer the meat grinder.

General-baiting, of course, is always tempting sport, and yet it is hard not to despise these generals. After their vaunted military scientism had brought the world to a bloody bind, they refused to admit to anyone, especially themselves, that the old methods of fighting were a murderous anachronism. Neither did they accept the truth that an infantry war without flanks has to become an attrition war, and therefore, at least on the Allied side, settle down to a strong defensive posture while the British blockade strangled Germany. And was it a war without flanks? Could not Britain, the mistress of the seas, have turned the Germans on their seaward flank? Or does the answer to that so far unanswered question lie in the melancholy truth that by fielding her own mass, conscript army on the Continent of Europe, Britain degraded her Navy to the rank of a subsidiary service and thus lost her old flair for amphibious distraction. However that may be, the generals continued their wasting attacks, each stuffing the other's trenches with their own dead in stupid attempts to force steel with flesh. Again, it is not easy to find excuses for such hidebound commanders, especially when they took such uncommon good care of their own comforts and clothing while their men munched hardtack in the mud.

Cold weather brought no relief to these millions of human moles. Again because of technological advances, the supply systems made it possible for the men to remain in their mud tunnels rather than go into winter quarters. Actually, all was not misery and death. By mutual agreement certain parts of the front, usually those southeast of Verdun toward the Swiss border, became "quiet" sectors. Here green troops were introduced to trench warfare and battered divisions from the "noisy" sectors could be brought to rest, to gorge themselves on cheese, sausage, fresh bread and low-priced wines, and to try to forget the nightmare of battle.

Rotation had also been begun whereby fresh or rested units would relieve exhausted ones. The relieved men would be sent back to quiet villages beyond the range of the guns. Here they would pass through delousing stations while their clothes were cleaned in a steam chamber. One day after they returned to the squalor of the front, however, they were once more infested with "seam squirrels." Once again they would struggle through knee-deep mud while frogs and huge rats bloated with human flesh splashed through the trenches, and in the no-man's land between the armies the snows of winter shaped the corpses into soft white mounds.

4

☆

In the spring of 1915 widespread fighting recommenced with the use of poison gas by the German Army.

On April 22, 1915, Allied troops in front of Ypres were basking in a mild spring sun. In late afternoon they heard the rumble of German mortars and then a strange hissing sound. Suddenly two great greenish-yellow clouds appeared in the sky. They merged and came rolling low like a glistening fog over five miles of front, swirling over the Allied soldiers in their trenches, engulfing them, choking them, inflicting upon them slow death or disability, and provoking a panic which left a wide gap in the Allied line.

Eventually the hole was closed, chiefly because of the courage of a Canadian division and the reluctance of the. German commanders to follow too closely upon those killing clouds. Nevertheless, the lid of Pandora's box had been lifted higher. In self-defense the Allies also resorted to gas attacks, more and more deadly mixtures were developed, and martial moles already heavy with helmets, rifles, packs, canteens, entrenching tools and ammunition belts were to be made heavier and uglier with the universal issue of gas masks. In the meantime, Allied wasting attacks went forward in Artois and Champagne, while Britain became bogged down in her ill-fated expedition to the Turkish Straits.

The Turkish Straits were once called the Hellespont, and then renamed the Dardanelles after the fortifications at their mouth. They link the Black Sea with the Mediterranean and in 1915 they were the most vital narrow waters in the world. At the urging of Winston Churchill, then First Lord of the Admiralty, Britain concluded that command of the Dardanelles would wrest Constantinople and its munitions factory away from Turkey, give Russia access to the Mediterranean and open a path through the Balkans to attack Germany.

Entering the Dardanelles, on the right hand lies Asiatic Turkey, or what is also known as Asia Minor. On the left lies European Turkey and the long strip of land called the Gallipoli Peninsula. On Gallipoli had been built the forts commanding the straits. Here, in early 1915, an Anglo-French naval force attempted to force the straits, succeeding only in losing three capital ships and so alerting the enemy that Gallipoli was at once strengthened and reinforced. After Allied assault troops landed on Gallipoli in April of 1915, their beachheads were turned into slaughter pens.

Gallipoli may have been the most mismanaged Allied debacle of the war. The British historian J. F. C. Fuller has called it the greatest disaster to befall British arms since Saratoga. It forced Churchill out of office, and of a half-million Allied troops sent to Gallipoli, half of them became casualties. Although Turkish losses were only slightly less, Turkey still held the vital passage to Russia and the Black Sea.

On May 23, 1915, Allied fortunes appeared to be on the rise again with Italy's declaration of war on her neighbor and former ally, Austria-Hungary. Italy's motive was Austrian booty, which she hoped to wrest from an Austrian Army already battered by Russia and humbled by Serbia. However, a combination of Austrian arms and treacherous terrain proved too much for Italy.

In 1915 four huge Italian offensives were broken in blood on the Isonzo River. Italy never achieved its objective of seizing a bridgehead across the river and so piercing the famous Ljubljana Gap opening on the Balkans. A quarter of a million Italians were killed in that quartet of disastrous attacks, and yet the Italian Army persisted with its Isonzo fixation. So it went on: Fifth Battle of the Isonzo . . . Seventh . . . Ninth . . . Eleventh. In all, an army of a million men was thrown away in a vain and vapid attempt to force a howling wilderness bristling with stones and bayonets. The Isonzo battles were nearly the whole war for Italy, and the humiliation was barely redeemed in 1918 by the defeat of punch-drunk Austria at the Battle of Vittorio Veneto.

For the Allies, Italy's entry into the war did little more than to draw the Austrian Army away from Russia. But Russia, by the end of 1915, was very nearly beyond help; but by then, also, the course of events had drawn the United States away from her policy of strict neutrality and made of her, in effect, an Allied arsenal.

The sea war made strict neutrality impossible. Nothing short of a Jeffersonian embargo forbidding any U.S. ship to sail from a U.S. port for a foreign port would have made it work; and since such a drastic measure was not even considered, America was caught in the crossfire between Britain's blockade and Germany's undersea warfare. The situation was strikingly similar to 1812, when Britain's war with Napoleonic France led to the impressment of American seamen and detonated the second Anglo-American war. This time it was the Germans, by reason of their submarine attacks on neutral ships and Allied passenger liners, who outraged American public opinion.

If Germany had possessed a fleet to rival the power of the combined Anglo-French fleets, she might not have resorted to unrestricted submarine warfare. She might have chosen to challenge the blockade above the waves. But Germany had no such fleet, and so she moved to counter the British surface blockade with a submarine blockade of her own. Unfortunately, by its very nature the submarine commits its advocates to a policy of shotgun warfare against enemies and neutrals alike. This is because submarines must strike suddenly and unseen, like a snake. Indeed, like the snake, they strike without warning out of fear. Thin-skinned and slow, armed with a single puny deck gun, they cannot risk surfacing to hail a ship and inspect her, like the big-gunned, armored warships of the British fleet. A seemingly innocent ship seen imperfectly through a periscope might actually be a disguised raider, or be armed with guns big enough to sink the submarine—or turn out to be a warship. So the undersea boat stays hidden and shoots her torpedoes without warning. She does not even surface to pick up survivors, because her quarters are unbelievably cramped, and to take enemy civilians aboard, if it does not expose the commander to the danger of seizure of his ship, certainly dictates turning around for home port. Even if the sunken enemy vessel happens to be a passenger liner, the chances are good that it is covertly carrying some form of contraband, and if it is flying a neutral flag, well, the record is full of reports of British ships flying neutral flags. So the torpedo tubes are opened and the steel fish go flashing toward the target, and if the stricken ship carries innocent women and children to the bottom, the German answer is a shrug implying, "This is war," and the question: What about the women and children starved to death by the British blockade?

There was the rub. Gradually, beginning in 1915 and reaching its full impact by 1917, the British blockade was to introduce famine into Germany. It has been claimed that as many as 750,000 Germans starved to death because of the blockade. Such estimates are often inflated and are never susceptible to proof; but even if this figure were cut in half, it would still stand as fifty times greater than the number of persons who lost their lives on Allied ships as a result of Germany's submarine warfare.

The truth is that Germany had to fight against the blockade in some way or else go under. Because the submarine, an unrivaled commerce-destroyer, is cheap and quickly built, the Kaiser reached for this weapon. He never seems to have realized that in the world's eyes he was wielding not a sword but a snake. Moreover, he was too hasty, too prone to bow to the heartless scientism of his simplicist generals. Britain's absolute blockade had already angered the neutrals, especially the United States. He might have marked time until this resentment rose to a point where it might force the British to accept some restrictions on the blockade that was strangling him. However, it is probably too much to ask that the man who consented to the violation of Belgian neutrality and the use of poison gas would show a decent respect for world opinion.

So the events began. By 1915 the British blockade had reduced neutral munitions shipments to Germany to a trickle. Germany retaliated by announcing that she would consider all grain and flour as contraband. Contraband consists of either equipment for war or foodstuffs for armies. To classify *all* shipments of a certain kind of foodstuff as contraband was to widen the definition.

Britain seized upon this departure as an excuse to seize a neutral ship docked at Falmouth with a food cargo bound for Germany. The Kaiser's response? *All* goods of whatever character moving toward Britain were to be contraband. After February 18, 1915, he stated, the waters around Britain were to be considered a combat zone. Enemy merchant ships found within them "would be destroyed without it always being possible to warn the crews and passengers."[38] Britain struck back by proclaiming that henceforth no neutral ship would be allowed to leave or enter a German port no matter what it carried.

In this savage exchange of retaliation and reprisal the neutral nations were bound to suffer. Yet the British brand of blockade was the least reprehensible: neutral cargoes which were seized were always paid for at war price, and not a single citizen of a neutral nation lost his life to the British blockade. Germany, however, sank neutral ships without recompense and caused hundreds of neutral citizens to lose their lives. Some 200 Americans alone perished in submarine attacks.

Even before the Kaiser's all-out U-boat warfare began, President Wilson informed the German government that he would hold it to "a strict accountability" for "property endangered or lives lost." The test of "strict accountability" came on March 28, 1915, when a German submarine sank the British steamer *Falaba* without giving the passengers and crew time to escape. One American, Leon C. Thrasher, was drowned.

At once Wilson's administration became divided over how to handle the Thrasher case. One side, led by Secretary of State William Jennings Bryan, argued that Thrasher's death was incidental to the destruction of *Falaba*. Under international law, therefore, the United States was justified only in requesting pecuniary damages. The other side, to which Wilson appeared to incline, insisted that the *Falaba* sinking was such a flagrant violation of international law that the United States must ask Germany to disavow the crime, punish the U-boat commander and pay damages. Such a drastic attitude was almost certain to lead to war, and because of this, Wilson, even then attempting to restore the peace of Europe, gradually veered toward a policy of ignoring the Thrasher incident entirely. But then on May 7, 1915, another German U-boat torpedoed the British liner

Lusitania. The great ship went to the bottom within 18 minutes, taking with her 1,198 persons, most of them civilians, of whom 128 were American citizens.

America rocked with rage, and in the heat of her anger strict neutrality evaporated. It made no difference that the German Embassy had warned Americans not to take passage on the ship, or that the *Lusitania* was carrying arms for the Allies. Americans could only see with horror that nearly 1,200 noncombatants had been brutally murdered. Bellicose interventionists clamored for war and the press took up the cry. Actually, it is now clear that May, 1915, was the right time for the United States to have intervened. If she had, her immense power might have begun to have a decisive effect as early as 1916, thereby saving an untold number of lives and perhaps delaying, if not preventing, the Russian Revolution and the rise of the ruthless "-isms." However, even though the sinking of the *Lusitania* made the American people firmly pro-British or anti-German, it did not make them eager to intervene. When Wilson said, "There is such a thing as a man being too proud to fight,"[39] he reflected, however ignobly, a general reluctance for war.

Nevertheless, the *Lusitania* was a turning point, and not even the invasion of Belgium surpasses it as a German blunder. "Only to these two grand crimes and blunders of history," Winston Churchill wrote, "was her undoing and our salvation due."[40] After it, Germany and America were on collision course. Secretary Bryan was aware of this when he resigned rather than sign Wilson's note to Germany denying the legality of a "war zone" and declaring: "The lives of non-combatants cannot lawfully or rightfully be put in jeopardy by the capture or destruction of an unresisting merchant-man."[41] To accept this doctrine, Germany would have had to renounce submarine warfare—which she did not. Bryan's solution to the problem was to disclaim responsibility for the life of any American taking passage on a belligerent ship, declaring: "Germany has a right to prevent contraband from going to the Allies, and a ship carrying contraband should not rely upon passengers to protect her from an attack—it would be like putting women and children in front of an army."[42]

After his resignation, Bryan toured the country preaching pacifism; but his was not the voice of the hour, rather it came from those calling for "preparedness." Ostensibly, "preparedness" was to keep America out of war, yet it was advocated by those who, after the *Lusitania,* openly called for intervention on the side of the Allies. Among them was General Leonard Wood, who organized the first Plattsburg training camp at which volunteers paying for their own food, equipment and expenses were given the instruction in military art which would qualify them for commissions in an expanding army. Here were the beginnings of Wood's coveted cadre army.

Meanwhile, a few months after the *Lusitania* went down, an attaché of the German Embassy unwisely left his briefcase on a New York elevated train. It was picked up by the Secret Service and found to contain documents detailing the subsidization of American newspapers, motion pictures and lecturers, as well as the bribing of labor leaders to foment strikes and to agitate for a general arms embargo. Once again the American nation was furious. Here was direct German interference in the life of the nation, and it did little good for the pro-Germans to protest that British propaganda was also at work in the States. As Secretary of the Treasury William McAdoo said later: "I am morally convinced that the British were doing the same thing, but we had no documentary proof."[43]

The British also outmaneuvered the Germans in placating Southern cotton interests angered by Britain's suppression of the cotton trade to Central Europe. After placing cotton on the contraband list, Britain began buying the staple in secret, thus stabilizing the price and avoiding Southern agitation for an arms embargo. Then, in August, 1915, the State Department raised no objection to an Anglo-French commission's negotiation of a $500 million loan among New York bankers. Much of this huge sum, of course, was to be spent in America on munitions orders. Industry, therefore, had no desire to kill the golden goose with an arms embargo, and the financial interests which floated this and other loans now had a heavy stake in an Allied victory. With this, all talk of neutrality was either born of ignorance or a hypocritical desire to conceal the truth: America, in effect, was now an ally of the Allies.

By the fall of 1915 the Anglo-French were in dire need of an ally, indirect or otherwise, for they were getting little help from two shaky partners in the East. First, the little Serbian Army which had humbled Austria in 1914 was caught in a vise between an Austro-German army in the north, and a Bulgarian force on the east. Greece, pledged to help Serbia, asked the Allies for assistance. By October 2 the vanguard of an Allied force began landing at the little Greek port of Salonika. But they were too late to prevent the Serbian Army from being driven all the way west to the Adriatic. More Allied troops came in to form the Army of the Orient, but when they tried to march north to Serbia's rescue, they were driven back to Salonika. Eventually some 600,000 men—chiefly British and French with some Greek, Serbian, Albanian, Italian and Montenegrin units—formed the Army of the Orient. Its disease-ridden quarters were derided by the Central Powers as the Allied concentration camp, and it was not to have any effect on the war until 1918, when it crushed the Bulgars.

In the meantime, two Austro-German offensives in the East struck hammer blows at Russian arms and unwittingly began the slow unraveling of the rotten fabric of Czarist Russian society. In all, the Austro-German forces advanced 300 miles, captured 3,000 guns and inflicted a staggering two million casualties on the Russian armies under Grand Duke Nicholas. So dreadful were the Russian losses that the Czar virtually banished Nicholas and placed himself at the head of his own armies.

Czar Nicholas took this action, as often, upon the urging of the Czarina, who remained, as always, under the baleful influence of the monk Rasputin. However, the Czar was no commander, and his assumption of military command merely signified to the Germans that Russia would not negotiate a separate peace, while failing to rally a nation shocked by the mass slaughter of its soldiery and the loss of 100 miles of Russian territory.

A tide of terrified refugees flowing back from the occupied border towns with tales of criminal negligence (e.g., unarmed soldiers waiting in line for their comrades to be shot so that they might seize their rifles) helped to scatter the seeds of discontent across Russia. The Dumas, a rudimentary parliament with very few real powers, had met in August to make perfunctory declaration of its defiance of Germany and then go home. Instead, it remained in session to rock Russia with charges that German capital controlled Russian banks, and that German interests in the favor of the court were sabotaging Russia. Frightened but furious, Nicholas ordered the Dumas prorogued, but his order ending the session boomeranged: there was mass rioting in the cities and munition plants were struck. Eventually, the Czar met with leaders of the Dumas and agreed to allow it to remain in session.

So the crisis passed. But the Czar had been defied without bloody repression and the effects of German military blows had been measured, like shock waves on a seismograph. Neither lesson was lost upon Nikolai Lenin in Switzerland nor upon the German General Staff.

5

☆

The year 1916 was the year of the great bloodletting. Three rivers of blood flowing from the Carpathians to Picardy snuffed out perhaps a million lives, bored deeper into the foundations of the empires and swept away the brightest military reputations. The first of these was at Verdun.

Verdun is perhaps the classic and most revolting example of what happens when a scientific general comes to regard his human statistics as cannon fodder. Erich von Falkenhayn was such a general. By 1916 he had concluded that if he could destroy the French Army he would force Britain to withdraw from the Continent. But how destroy the French? Not by frontal attack, Falkenhayn reasoned, for he at least had perceived the futility of attempts at penetration. The defense merely withdrew, selling ground so dearly that the offense finally became exhausted. The answer, then, was to find a place from which the French would not retreat, and there to launch a massive, killing assault.

That place was Verdun, the fortress city sacred to the soul of France, the place once burned by Attila the Hun and the spot upon which the heirs of Charlemagne had divided the Frankish empire. Verdun was the Citadel of France, an Allied bulge menacing the Germans midway in the Western front. France would never surrender Verdun. On this anvil, Falkenhayn reasoned, she would be broken by the hammer of German arms.

On February 21, 1916, the Germans began the battle with the

most shattering bombardment in the history of warfare. Three days later the fortress was tottering, and the French picked up the gauntlet. On February 25, Joffre ordered Henri Philippe Pétain to take charge of its defense.

Now there entered history the tall, icy, methodical soldier who had once dared to oppose the School of the Attack. Here was the careful infantry officer chary with the blood of his soldiers, the born defensive fighter coming to the right place at the right time. "They shall not pass!" Pétain cried, and inflamed France with his resolve. To this he fused driving energy and tactical skill. Verdun was reinforced with men and arms. French counterbattery fire broke up the German gun concentrations. Lost forts were reoccupied. Most important, the service of supply was reorganized. Bridges were built, light new railway nets were laid down and the congested road to Bar-le-Duc in the rear was turned into *la Voie Sacrée*—the Sacred Way—over which 3,000 trucks rode back and forth, night and day, to create a huge conveyor belt feeding the battle. For the first time in military history motor transport was used to supply a fighting front.

"Courage, we will get them yet!"[44] Pétain cried to his dogged poilus, and the French hung on. Then Falkenhayn was hoist with his own petard: victory at Verdun became almost as important to the German nation as to the French, and as spring turned into summer, Falkenhayn was forced to feed the best German troops into the battle. By June the tide was beginning to turn, and by December Verdun was firmly in French hands.

Because of the confusion and the length of this battle, it is difficult to determine the casualties. Yet even the most sober estimates place the total in the neighborhood of 700,000, with the French losing roughly four-sevenths of that figure. Other sources put French losses at half a million men and German at 400,000. Meanwhile, the second blood bath had already begun at the Somme.

It is not true that the Battle of the Somme was fought to relieve the pressure on Verdun. It came to that eventually, of course, but even before Falkenhayn struck in February, Joffre and Sir Douglas Haig had agreed that a big battle must be fought on the Allied left flank. Haig actually believed that he would split the German lines in two within a single day. Then he would wheel and roll up the exposed German flanks while his beloved cavalry went galloping through the gap into the enemy rear.

Actually, Haig's Big Push was aimed at the strongest field fortifications yet built. On the day it began, July 1, 1916, the British lost 60,000 men—the blackest single day in the annals of British arms. At this juncture Sir Douglas should have ended the carnage. But he persisted throughout the summer. On September 15 he introduced Britain's secret weapon: the tank. Some three dozen of these "land battleships," British armor plate joined to American caterpillar tracks, went rumbling toward the enemy. They gained a mile and a half, they terrified the Germans and heartened the British, but they eventually broke down. The Somme's churned-up earth was no place for rudimentary tanks. Nor were the crews properly trained or the commanders wise in the use of this new weapon. The debut of the tank, like that of poison gas at Ypres, was a flop. At last torrential rains turned the battleground into a miserable mire where wounded men drowned in shellholes; and on November 18 the Battle of the Somme ended with each side suffering about 600,000 casualties, and nothing achieved in a military way.

In all, the Anglo-French lost about 1,200,000 men in killed, wounded and captured on the Western front in 1916, while German losses were 800,000. Such shocking exercises in bloody futility had powerful repercussions in Allied capitals: David Lloyd George became the British Prime Minister and Georges Clemenceau moved a step closer toward the French premiership. Papa Joffre was discreetly kicked upstairs, awarded a field marshal's baton to wave over airy nothing while actual command of the French armies passed to Robert Nivelle, one of the heroes of Verdun. For some inexplicable reason, perhaps his unrivaled skill at composing dispatches turning defeat into victory, Haig was also made a marshal and allowed to remain in command.

Von Falkenhayn also lost his post. Snubbed by the Kaiser, he resigned as chief of staff and was replaced by von Hindenburg and Ludendorff. Here was the team which was to run the German Army and eventually the country: Hindenburg the stolid Junker of the awesome command presence, practically dictating to the Kaiser with words and ideas supplied him by his brilliant, dynamic second. Verdun-Somme, having buried whole armies, had also shaken the command structures, while in the East the Czar was being staggered by his only success.

This was the third blood bath: the Brusilov Offensive. It was named after the capable Russian general, Alexey Brusilov. Nearly bursting through the Carpathian passes into Austria itself, the Russian assault cost the Central Powers 600,000 men, including 400,000 Austrian prisoners. It relieved the pressure on the Western front and also brought Rumania into the war on the side of the Allies. Like Italy, Rumania sought Hapsburg booty, but Rumania was to regret reneging on her alliance with Austria. German-Austrian-Turkish forces under General August von Mackensen, and the still capable though demoted Falkenhayn, shredded the Rumanian Army and captured all the country but Moldavia in the north.

In the meantime, the Brusilov Offensive ran itself into exhaustion and cost the Czar a million men. With this, the Russian Army became an incubator for revolutionaries. Both Romanov and Hapsburg, dynasts of Russia and Austria, were now withered blind giants groping toward the graveyard. In Vienna old Francis Joseph gave up the ghost at the age of 86 and after a reign of 67 years. He was succeeded by his great-nephew, Charles, who was eager to put out the war the old Emperor had started.

In Petrograd the end came for Rasputin and with him the Romanovs. On the night of December 29 two avengers of Russian honor —Prince Yusupov and Grand Duke Dmitri Pavlovich—invited this evil, reeking spellbinder to "dinner." They plied him with vodka laced with cyanide. He kept on drinking. They emptied a pistol into him. He still lived. Then these inept assassins dragged Rasputin to the frozen Neva River and dropped him through a hole in the ice. That ended the career of the Mad Monk who had never been ordained, and it was the first act in the Russian Revolution.

Rasputin's executioners openly boasted of their deed, defying the Czar and the wrath of the vengeful Czarina. From then onward Imperial Russia sank into chaos. Rioting broke out in the streets of the capital in late February, 1917. In March hungry rioters sacked the city's bakery shops. Three days later, troops were called out to quell the riots, but instead they shot their officers and joined the mob. Next day all the 190,000 soldiers stationed in Petrograd joined the mutiny. The Winter Palace was invaded, public buildings were set afire and the fortress of Sts. Peter and Paul stormed and the prisoners set free. The revolt spread, engulfing city after city. Behind each blaze of rebellion was the guiding hand of the Councils of Workmen's and Soldiers' Delegates (the Soviets). Eventually, the Soviets controlled Russia and Czar Nicholas II was forced to abdicate. In his place a Provisional Government began to rule with Prince Georgi Lvov as its Prime Minister. Ultimately, leadership went to the eloquent Socialist, Alexander Kerenski.

Thus the year 1917 began with what appeared to be the triumph of democracy in despotic Russia. It was hoped that a revitalized Russia would now go forward to ultimate triumph against a Germany beginning to suffer from the effects of the British blockade.

Although great wars are usually fought and won on land, they are often decided at sea. This is in some ways true of the naval Battle of Jutland fought on May 31–June 1, 1916, between the British Grand Fleet and the German High Seas Fleet off the coast of Denmark.

The British under Admiral Sir John Jellicoe had 149 ships to 99 for the Germans under Admiral Reinhard Scheer. Moreover, Jellicoe had more dreadnoughts and more big guns. At Jutland, however, Jellicoe was a cautious admiral. He knew that, in Churchill's phrase, he was "the only man who could lose the war in an afternoon."[45] On his fleet depended the British Empire. Rather than risk the destruction of it, he did not pursue the battered Germans fleeing his ships into their own mine fields. So Jutland became a German moral victory: with a smaller force, but with better maneuvering and marksmanship, they had sunk 117,025 tons of British warships while losing only 61,180 tons themselves. But if Jutland was a German tactical victory, it was a British strategic triumph. The German High Seas Fleet was chased into home port to stay.

That is the significance of Jutland, the last great naval battle fought solely on the surface. Because of it, Germany saw its only salvation in the U-boat, and by so doing she brought about American intervention.

Germany did not immediately take this drastic step, but only ultimately, under pressure of the gradually tightening blockade. Before Jutland was fought, in fact, she had soft-pedaled the U-boat war. This was because of the furious American reaction to the submarine attack on the unarmed Channel steamer *Sussex* on March 24. From President

Wilson the following month there came the ultimatum: if Germany did not abandon submarine warfare against passenger and freight-carrying vessels, the United States would sever diplomatic relations. Although Wilson's note infuriated the German people, who believed that the American President was trying to wrest from their grasp the one weapon which could give them victory, the German government was not yet at the point where it wished to risk retaliation. In reply, Germany reaffirmed earlier pledges that submarines would not attack merchantmen without warning, and promised to do all possible to insure the safety of passengers and crew. However, Germany also declared, in effect, that if the United States did not compel Britain to end her blockade, she would reserve the right to renew the U-boat warfare. This was an astute twist. It got Germany off the hook and hung Britain in her place.

Many Americans agreed with Germany that the British blockade violated "the laws of humanity," and many others were angered by British economic warfare against anyone who traded with Germany. But worst of all was Britain's ruthless suppression of the Easter Rebellion which erupted in Ireland on April 24, 1916. With savage folly, Britain executed the leaders and then hung Sir Roger Casement, the Irish nationalist who had come from Germany to lead the revolt. Treason or no, not only Americans of Irish descent were enraged by these executions. The U.S. Senate, which had formally appealed to Britain for clemency, was largely embittered, and the *New Republic* declared: "The Dublin executions have done more to drive America back to isolation than any other event since the war began."[46] It was not toward isolation but rather toward intervention in Germany's favor that America appeared to be driven after both the British and French seized and examined parcels in the American mails, and after Britain published a "blacklist" of 87 American and 350 Latin-American firms with whom British subjects were forbidden to deal.

Wilson immediately retaliated by obtaining laws empowering the President to refuse clearance to any ship refusing the freight of a blacklisted American citizen, and to deny the ports to any vessels of any nation discriminating against Americans. By the autumn of 1916 Wilson's attitude toward the Allies had so hardened that his pro-British Secretary of State, Robert Lansing, shuddered to think that he might be asked to negotiate a German-American alliance. And it is safe to say that Wilson might have made swift use of his retaliatory powers had he not by then been fighting on one hand for his political life, and on the other trying to avert a war with Mexico.

Relations with Mexico had appeared to be friendly after the United States recognized the new Carranza government. But then one of Carranza's lieutenants, the wily Francisco (Pancho) Villa turned on his chief. To draw the United States into Mexico, and therefore discredit Carranza, Villa began the systematic murder of American citizens. On January 11, 1916, he stopped a Mexican train, removed 17 Americans and shot 16 of them on the spot. After Wilson refused to be stampeded into intervention, Villa struck again: on March 9 he and 1,500 Villistas rode into Columbus, New Mexico, setting the town on fire and killing 19 more Americans.

Now it was not possible for Wilson to refuse demands for reprisal. Carranza agreed to a protocol allowing either nation to pursue bandits across the borders, and the Punitive Expedition under Brigadier General John J. Pershing crossed into Mexico in pursuit of Villa. Pershing never caught the elusive bandit chief, but because he took 6,600 men 300 miles deep into Mexican territory he alarmed Carranza to the extent that at one point a second war with Mexico seemed imminent. Carranza had never expected such a large, prolonged expedition to evolve out of an agreement to facilitate bandit-chasing. His followers angrily demanded eviction of the *Yanquis*. His prestige was at stake, just as Villa had hoped. Again and again, Carranzistas and American soldiers clashed in bloody skirmishes. America quivered with cries for war. The newly federalized National Guard was swiftly mobilized and the Mexican border bristled with *Yanqui* arms. At one point Wilson was prepared to ask a joint session of Congress for powers which could have led to nothing less than a second war with Mexico. But Wilson kept his head, and so did Carranza, until tempers eventually cooled and the Punitive Expedition was withdrawn.

Mexico may have been only a passing call to arms, yet its effects were great and lasting. First, it made the reputation of "Black Jack" Pershing, but far more important the successful mobilization of the National Guards in the federal service finally killed off the old militia and volunteer systems, while providing a dress rehearsal for the mass mobilization of 1917. Moreover, Mexico impelled Congress to begin sweeping military reorganization under the 1916 Defense Act, and it conditioned the American people to unprotesting acceptance of universal conscription. After Mexico, General Hugh Scott, the Army Chief of Staff, could announce to the nation which once abhorred large peacetime armies: "Universal military service has been the cornerstone upon which has been built every Republic in the history of the world."[47] The general could state that without challenge, when history shouts the very opposite: that free republics which begin by adopting conscript armies in self-defense usually end as regimented democracies maintaining them for every external purpose from conquest to the "containment" of the present day. To this degree, then, had Mexico inflamed the national militarist fever which Elihu Root had transmitted from Europe.

Mexico also dovetailed with the "preparedness" movement, which had grown from Leonard Wood's pygmy of the previous year into a loud-mouthed and hysterical giant. It was never clear for what the nation was preparing. Pro-Allied leaders wanted to prepare for intervention against Germany, others feared a Teutonic invasion of the Western Hemisphere following a German victory, and still others wanted America to be strong in the postwar world or to command the strength to support its fight for freedom of the seas.

Woodrow Wilson was among the last group, and he led a spirited fight for preparedness against the onslaught of those infuriated Progressive pacifists who accused him of "sowing the seeds of militarism, raising up a military and naval caste."[48] It was a sharp, stiff fight. Wilson did not get all that he wanted, but Congress gave him enough to make possible the massive intervention of 1917. On the other hand, the Progressives, acting on the premise that preparedness favored the rich, triumphantly passed legislation doubling the income tax or making other assessments frankly geared to a program of taxing the wealthy. "What has become of the dollar patriots?" one of them taunted. "Where are the members of the Preparedness league and the Navy league? Is the counting room hollering loud and long because they find that incomes must bear a portion of the burden they had hoped to unload upon the farmer and the steel worker?"[49] Out of preparedness, then, and the steady steer toward war, came the drive to redistribute wealth which is now known as "soaking the rich."

Even though preparedness cost Wilson the support of Progressives and other pacifists who had helped elect him in 1912, he removed some of the sting by adopting "He kept us out of war" as his campaign slogan for 1916. It was effective, especially in contrast to the vague and tepid "America first and America efficient" which was adopted by the Republican standard-bearer, Justice Charles Evans Hughes of the U.S. Supreme Court. Hughes and the Republicans were just as vague in their criticism of Wilson's policies in Mexico or vis-à-vis the European powers. Nevertheless, preparedness hurt. When Wilson went to bed on election night, he was prepared to move out of the White House. Morning newspapers proclaimed a victory for Hughes. But the late-coming returns from California tipped the scales in Wilson's favor, and gave him a popular-vote margin of 594,000 votes out of 17,662,000 cast. By that slim verdict the man who had kept America out of war retained the power to take her in.

With all the passion of a sincere heart, Woodrow Wilson still desired peace. Through his close friend and confidant, Colonel Edward House, he had tried to mediate peace in 1915 and again in early 1916. After his re-election, he was anxious to try again. Unfortunately, there was a streak of ivory-tower naïveté in Wilson. He could not see that hate had taken hold of the combatants, just as it had envenomed the North and the South in the last months of the Civil War, and that a negotiated peace was now almost impossible. The man in the street who was now the man in the trenches was snarling, "Kill them! Victory!" and no statesman in Europe would ignore him. Sincere, then, but also starry-eyed, Wilson bit hard on a large piece of German peace bait.

On December 12, 1916, Germany announced that she was ready to negotiate with the Allies. This she was, but only from her present position of strength. She wanted Wilson to bring the Allies to the conference table while the Central Powers still occupied Belgium and large portions of Italy, Russia and France, and before the British blockade brought her to her knees. Moreover, a deal had been made between Chancellor Bethmann-Hollweg and the German war lords: Bethmann-Hollweg might now move for the peace talks he so ardently desired, but if he failed, Germany would resort to unrestricted submarine warfare as its last hope of breaking down Britain.

Much to the consternation of his pro-Ally advisers, Wilson issued identical notes to both sides suggesting immediate negotiations. The Allies saw the trap and refused, while stating· clearly that nothing would satisfy them short of complete restitution and reparation. The German reply was evasive. Bethmann-Hollweg had failed.

Still, Wilson made one more attempt. In a speech before the Senate on January 22, 1917, Wilson pleaded for "peace without victory," for only a "peace among equals" could last. "I would fain believe," he concluded, "that I am speaking for the silent mass of mankind."[50] What he said was noble and true, but it ignored human nature. Much of the silent mass of mankind was grinding its teeth and wanted only victory.

A few days later Wilson received final proof of German duplicity. On January 9, 1917, while the German Chancellery still talked peace, the Kaiser had signaled his ships: "I order that unrestricted submarine warfare be launched with the greatest vigor on February 1."[51] Two days after that date, Wilson severed diplomatic relations with Germany. In that same month Britain informed him of the famous "Zimmermann telegram" which the German Foreign Minister had sent to the German Ambassador in Mexico. It said:

WE INTEND TO BEGIN UNRESTRICTED SUBMARINE WARFARE. WE SHALL ENDEAVOR TO KEEP THE UNITED STATES NEUTRAL. IN THE EVENT OF THIS NOT SUCCEEDING, WE MAKE MEXICO A PROPOSAL OF ALLIANCE ON THE FOLLOWING BASIS: MAKE WAR TOGETHER, MAKE PEACE TOGETHER, GENEROUS FINANCIAL SUPPORT, AND AN UNDERSTANDING ON OUR PART THAT MEXICO IS TO RECONQUER THE LOST TERRITORY IN TEXAS, NEW MEXICO AND ARIZONA.[52]

It was a ridiculous proposal, it was a cornered lion calling to a rabbit for help. Mexico had no military power and was still on the verge of anarchy. Nevertheless, the Zimmermann telegram capped the climax. Americans became enraged, Theodore Roosevelt thundered: "Germany is already at war with us!"[53] The same persons who had joined Preparedness Parades now marched for war with Germany. On March 16 the American ships *City of Memphis* and *Illinois* were torpedoed by German submarines, and that was the end of American neutrality.

Woodrow Wilson had fought nobly and courageously for peace. He had sincerely striven to keep his nation neutral. All along, he had known that once America took up arms the world would be on a war footing, that the one powerful neutral with the strength to command respect and the impartiality to make reasonable judgments would be herself a combatant. "It means," Wilson told Frank Cobb of the New York *World* one anguished night in the White House, "an attempt to reconstruct a peacetime civilization with war standards, and at the end of the war there will be no bystanders with sufficient peace standards left to work with. . . . Once lead this people into war, and they'll forget there ever was such a thing as tolerance. To fight you must be brutal and ruthless, and the spirit of ruthless brutality will enter into every fibre of our national life, infecting Congress, the courts, the policeman on his beat, the man in the street."[54] Conformity, Wilson said, would be the only virtue.

Thus sorrowing, on April 2, 1917, Wilson asked Congress for a declaration of war. *"The world must be made safe for democracy,"* he told his audience, many of whom were overcome with emotion, and concluded: "It is a fearful thing to lead this great peaceful people into war, into the most terrible and disastrous of all wars, civilization itself seeming to be in the balance. But the right is more precious than peace . . . the day has come when America is privileged to spend her blood and her might for the principles that gave her birth and happiness and the peace which she has treasured. God helping her, she can do no other."[55]

On April 6, 1917, Congress declared war on Germany.

6

☆

It has been said that not since Varus lost his legions in the year A.D. 9 was there an event as portentous in European life as the entry of America into World War I.[56] Yet, even as the Americans mobilized, there began in far-off Russia an ideological revolution of a power unrivaled since the day in 622 when a camel driver named Mohammed fled his native Mecca for Medina.

To the Allies, and America as well, it had seemed that the Russian Revolution ousting the Czar would culminate in a democracy on the Western pattern. Had not the mutinous sailors and the rioting workers sung the "Marseillaise," the great rallying song of liberty, equality and fraternity? Like their French brethren of 1789, having killed autocracy they would shortly erect democracy in its place. Unfortunately, just like the French with Napoleon, the Russian Revolution had its own killer waiting in the wings.

Nikolai Lenin in Zurich had already telegraphed his Bolshevik followers in the Petrograd Soviet: "Our tactics—no support, complete contempt. Armed proletariat, only guarantee."[57] Thus Lenin, the ruthless disciple of Karl Marx, was already plotting the overthrow of the Provisional Government. But how was he, a Bolshevik undesirable, to return to Russia? Lenin's answer was characteristic: with the help of Germany. Through an emissary, he suggested to the German Supreme Command that one sure way to get Russia out of the war was to send him, Lenin, to Petrograd to undermine the government. The war lords agreed. A special train was furnished Lenin and his followers.

Much has been made in history of the "sealed train" which carried the germs of Communism to Russia, but the fact is simply that Lenin, not wishing to be molested by German officials en route, and also determined not to have any of his followers desert, had requested that no one board the train as it passed through Germany or German-held territory, and no one be permitted to get off. The request was granted. On April 9, 1917, the train left Zurich. On April 16 Lenin arrived in Petrograd.

There he made it clear that he desired complete power. Such Bolshevik deputies as Josef Vissarionovich Dzhugashvili, called Stalin in the underground, might think that this was a bit less than possible, but Lenin knew his own mind. Only by destroying all could he begin to build his Communist state. When Lenin ordered the Bolsheviks to "negotiate," he meant not to give and take but only to take; when he told them to join a movement or a committee, it was not to work with it but to control it or destroy it. Such were Lenin's basic tactics of takeover then; so they remain among his orthodox followers today.

Night after night this stocky Slav of the large head and luminous eyes harangued the Petrograd crowds. "What do you get from war?" he shouted. "Only wounds, starvation, and death!"[58] Meanwhile, Russian soldiers everywhere were throwing down their arms and heading home. Gradually, Russian battlefield defeats eroded the prestige of the government, and as Kerenski's power waned, Lenin's grew. Eventually, Lenin controlled the Petrograd Soviet and his lieutenant, Leon Trotsky, controlled the one in Moscow.

Now Lenin summoned an All-Russian Congress of Soviets to assemble in Petrograd the first week in November. Before it did, the army regiments in Petrograd passed the resolution: "We no longer recognize the Provisional Government. The Petrograd Soviet is our Government."[59] Here was the bugle blast of Communism, and Lenin, hearing it, immediately ordered full-scale revolt. Within 48 hours which were almost devoid of either drama or battle, the Provisional Government fell, Kerenski fled, and the Communist Revolution was complete. With it, Russia's departure from the war was all but guaranteed. Lenin, appearing before the Soviet Congress, read a decree calling for a "just and democratic peace."

"The war is ended!" cried the delegates. "The war is ended!"[60]

Elsewhere in Europe, two attempts to end the war had failed. Austria, operating behind her German partner's back, attempted to make a separate peace with France and Britain. But none of the terms Austria offered was acceptable to Italy, and the war went on. It also continued after a plea for peace by Pope Benedict XV fell on stony ground.

In America the war began with the nation probably better prepared than at any other time previously. Much has been made of American unreadiness in 1917, and if the comparison is to be the unfair one between a distant democracy and the mass armies of a Europe either autocratic or afraid of autocracy, then the United States was not prepared. Yet an opposite conclusion may be made from the facts that the nation enthusiastically accepted its first military draft in history, and that an army of 200,000 men out of a nation of 100 million people is roughly six times greater than the little army of 25,000 men serving some 70 million at the outbreak of war with Spain. Moreover, the Army still had veterans of that war and the Philippines, the Marine Corps had veterans of the "Banana Wars" resulting from American intervention in Haiti and the Dominican Republic in 1915, and there were thousands of cadre officers trained during preparedness. The Punitive Expedition also had taught lessons in logistics and command to such career officers as a dashing young cavalryman named George Patton, who was already wondering if motor vehicles would not soon supplant horses, and the War Department staffs were served by men such as George Catlett Marshall and Douglas MacArthur, by then a veteran of the Philippines and Vera Cruz.

It is true that aircraft and aviators were practically nonexistent and that in the obsolete American arsenal there reposed not a single weapon up to European standards, and it is just there—in equipment and the ability to make rapid changeover from peacetime to war industry—that America was ill-prepared. Almost to the end of the war American soldiers used British rifles and French artillery. Yet it is often forgotten that in early 1917 the British and the French were not looking to America for immediate help on land. They eagerly anticipated the masses that would eventually be "coming over," but at that moment they had great offensives of their own planned. What the Allies looked for then was help on the sea.

Three days after the American declaration, Rear Admiral William S. Sims of the U.S. Navy called on Sir John Jellicoe in London. With hardly a word, Jellicoe handed Sims a paper detailing Allied shipping losses. Sims was "fairly astounded."

"It looks as if the Germans are winning the war," Sims said.

"They will unless we can stop those losses,"[61] Jellicoe replied.

Jellicoe told Sims that he saw no solution to the German submarine attacks. At the start of the war, the Allies had had about 21 million tons of shipping available. Of this some 15 million tons were considered absolutely necessary to continue the war, and the remaining 6 million provided a "cushion" against losses. But by the time Sims arrived in London, the U-boats had devoured one-third of the cushion and April's shipping losses were expected to be a staggering 900,000 tons. Shipbuilding, meanwhile, had fallen far behind losses. At this rate, then, the cushion would be gone by fall and the submarines would be gnawing on the "vital" 15 million tons. If that happened, the Allies were lost.

Fortunately, no better liaison officer than Sims could have been sent to the British Admiralty. Able and energetic, as well as perceptive enough to have been an all-big-gun advocate before *Dreadnought,* Sims was also a friendly man whose warmth and sincerity quickly won the confidence of the British. Sims rapidly came to the conclusion that the convoy system proposed by Commander Reginald Henderson was the answer to submarine warfare. Merchant ships assembled in convoys could be protected by escorting warships, chiefly destroyers. The beauty of this plan was that it was defensive-offensive. If the protecting warships scared the submarines away, then the convoy crossed in safety. But the fact was that the submarines *had* to attack the convoys, and when they did, they were exposed to the counter-attacks of the destroyers, swift and maneuverable vessels especially designed for such work. Thus the attrition war was turned against the undersea craft themselves, and it was this simple plan which was to win the war.

Nor is it too much to say that the influence of Admiral Sims was the chief factor in persuading the British to adopt the convoy system. Moreover, Sims almost immediately enlisted the U.S. Navy in this new warfare. On May 4 six ships of an American destroyer division under Captain J. K. Taussig arrived in Queenstown (modern Cóbh), Ireland. "At what time will your vessels be ready for sea?" a British admiral asked Taussig, and the American replied: "I shall be ready when fueled."[62]

With such wholeheartedness did the U.S. Navy commence its fight in World War I, and within another three months there was a total of 47 American ships based in European waters. As the American contribution grew in size, so also did German submarine warfare diminish in vigor. By December of 1917 sinkings were down to less than 400,000 tons monthly. Never again did they approach the peak losses of 881,000 tons for that April, and long before then Allied vessels had confidently begun the mission of transporting the American Expeditionary Force to France.

"Black Jack" Pershing commanded the A.E.F. He was already famous, if not in some quarters notorious, because of his Punitive Expedition which failed to catch Pancho Villa. But Pershing had known in advance that this expedition might be a face-losing mission, and he had carried it out well enough to impress Wilson and his able Secretary of War, Newton D. Baker. Nor was Pershing's ambition exactly thwarted by the fact that his father-in-law, Senator Francis Warren, was chairman of the Senate Military Affairs Committee. So Pershing was chosen.

Even today John J. Pershing remains a sphinxlike figure. What was the secret of his enormous prestige? He was not a simple, insightful soldier like Grant, a daring gambler and inspiring leader like Lee, or a whirlwind fighter like Stonewall Jackson. His qualities were more akin to immobility, like the marble in the monuments he resembled. He was almost inhumanly controlled, this Iron Commander of the thin, set lips, flinty gray mustache, impeccable uniform and cold, colorless voice. Those who knew him said that he was changeless: when he received word in 1915 that his wife and three small daughters had perished in a fire, it was said that his only visible reaction was to grow gradually grayer. Black Jack had earned his nickname in Cuba with a regiment of Negro cavalry, but his habits of mind were from West Point and the frontier army in which batmen burnished the captain's buttons and enlisted men spoke to officers in the third person: "Begging the lieutenant's pardon, sir, but the sergeant begs to report . . ." As such, Pershing was a strange man indeed to lead this rollicking, boisterous American Army of lighthearted civilian-soldiers; and although he always commanded respect, he never inspired devotion.

Yet no soldier since Washington so thoroughly dominated an American war as did John J. Pershing. Superficially, one reason for this might be the strict censorship which Pershing invoked in France, thereby killing off, as it were, any rival for renown. Actually, the chief reasons were Pershing's unshakable faith in the fighting qualities of the American doughboys and his invincible refusal to allow American battalions to be fed into British or French armies like so much imported cannon fodder. By these stands, Pershing compelled Europe to admit the equality of American arms.

Pershing was implacable at the outset. In May, before he embarked for Europe, Allied missions in Washington were already asking for American reinforcements, and Pershing refused. "The French," he wrote, "really wanted us to send small, untrained units for incorporation into their divisions."[63] By then, the Iron Commander had given the U.S. Army the beginnings of its present divisional system by forming the 1st Infantry Division out of four infantry regiments and one of artillery.* Eventually, American infantry divisions were to be composed of four foot regiments, an artillery brigade, one engineer regiment and various attached specialists. As such, they were huge unwieldy formations 28,000 strong and double the size of Allied or enemy divisions.

The 1st was the first to embark for France, and Pershing was there to greet them when they arrived. On the Fourth of July, 1917,

---

* Until now, the author has refrained from identifying units because, with the regimental system and the multitudinous "Guards," "Zouaves" or "Blues" of the militia and the volunteers, there were simply too many.

a battalion of doughboys paraded in Paris. There were not very many of them, but they were *there;* and as these young and clean-cut regulars looking ten feet tall in their high campaign hats went swinging along the historic avenues of the City of Light, all Paris took them to their hearts.

Laughing, weeping, shouting, the French swept the astonished doughboys off their feet. They pelted them with flowers, drenched them with scent and smeared them with lipstick. Pershing himself wrote: "With wreaths about their necks and bouquets in their hats and rifles, the column looked like a moving flower garden."[64] It was not possible for the Yanks to remain in formation during the five-mile march from the Tomb of Napoleon to the Tomb of Lafayette. There, standing beneath the statue of the French nobleman who had symbolized France's support for the Revolution, Pershing was expected to speak. Black Jack, however, was no orator, and in his place he sent his friend, Colonel Charles E. Stanton. Stepping forward, Stanton saluted and cried: "Lafayette, we are here!"[65]

It was a happy phrase, and it delighted the history-minded French, but it was also something of an exaggeration. *We,* as Pershing well knew, were far from being there. American shipping was nearly nil, shipbuilding was only beginning to expand, and the Allies could not spare many vessels to transport the vanguards of the half-million men inducted in the States during 1917. Still, Pershing did not scruple to cable Washington, "Plans should contemplate sending over at least 1,000,000 men by next May," and to add on July 11: "Plans for the future should be based, especially in reference to the manufacture, etc., of artillery, aviation, and other material, on three times this force—*i.e.,* at least 3,000,000 men."[66]

Possibly, Pershing might have been led to increase even this estimate had Marshal Henri Pétain, now commander in chief of France, given him the details of a mutiny which had nearly destroyed the French Army. It began after the ill-fated offensive launched by Robert Nivelle, successor to Joffre. Nivelle was a vain optimist who assumed that his small-scale storming successes at Verdun could be expanded into one gigantic offensive that would crush the Germans. He was also a charmer whose glib assurance captivated both the British and French premiers. Thus the Nivelle Offensive was given the green light. Actually, it never had a chance of success. The Germans

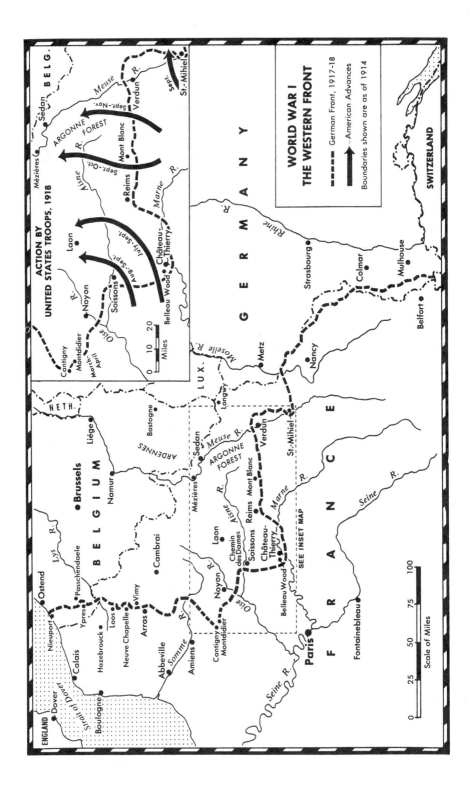

WORLD WAR I
THE WESTERN FRONT

- - - - German Front, 1917–18

American Advances

Boundaries shown are as of 1914

ACTION BY
UNITED STATES TROOPS, 1918

Miles
0   10   20

Sedan   BELG.
Mézières
Meuse R.
ARGONNE
FOREST
Sept.-Nov.
Verdun
Sept.
St.-Mihiel
Mont Blanc
Aisne R.
Reims
Sept.-Oct.
Marne R.
Laon
July-Sept.
Château-Thierry
Aug.-Sept.
Soissons
Belleau Wood
Noyon
Oise R.
Cantigny
Montdidier
March-April

GERMANY

Rhine R.

Strasbourg
Colmar
Mulhouse
Belfort

SWITZERLAND

ENGLAND
Dover
Strait of Dover
Calais
Boulogne
Nieuport
Ostend
Lys R.
Passchendaele
Ypres
Loos
Neuve Chapelle
Hazebrouck
Arras
Vimy
Abbeville
Somme R.
Amiens

BELGIUM
Brussels
Liège
Namur
Cambrai

NETH.
Bastogne
ARDENNES
Sedan
Mézières
Meuse R.
Liège

LUX.
Longwy

Moselle R.
Metz
Nancy
Verdun
St.-Mihiel
ARGONNE
FOREST
Mont Blanc
Reims
Chemin des Dames
Soissons
Laon
Aisne R.
Noyon
Oise R.
Cantigny
Montdidier
Château-Thierry
Belleau Wood
Marne R.

SEE INSET MAP

FRANCE
Paris
Seine R.
Fontainebleau

Scale of Miles
0   25   50   75   100

discovered Nivelle's plans in advance and simply withdrew from the salient which he had hoped to pinch off. Thus, when the French rushed forward, they struck at thin air. Moreover, they floundered in a smoking desert deliberately desolated by the withdrawing Germans. Although Nivelle had promised to call off the offensive if it did not succeed on the first day, when he must have known that great battles cannot be turned on and off like a faucet, this one raged for ten days and cost France 187,000 men.

That was the end of Nivelle and also nearly the end of the French Army. Bled white, the weary poilus refused to venture into any more sausage machines. On April 29 one regiment mutinied and the movement swept through the Army like an epidemic. Whole battalions refused to march, threw down their arms, got drunk or ran off into the forests to live lives of defiant seclusion. Others set up noncommissioned officers' committees to replace their officers. They never injured the officers, however. "We will not harm you," one poilu with 32 months of battle duty told a lieutenant. "You have been abused as much as we have. But we will not obey you. The war must end."[67] Into this situation fraught with disaster strode Pétain, and the Savior of Verdun here performed an even greater service for his nation. A soldier's general, he understood the grievances of the men; and he restored order by assuring them that there would be no more blood baths, by improving the food and granting more furloughs. Where he had to be, Pétain was stern. In all, however, only 55 ringleaders were executed; although this figure probably does not take into account the number of men shot on the spot by drumhead courts.

Thus, when Pershing and the A.E.F. arrived, the mutiny was over. But the French Army was still weakened, and it was feared that at any moment the Germans might learn of its disability and destroy it. It was for this reason, among others, that the French Army was so eager for American levies. The British, staggered by losses in the battles of Arras (158,000), of Third Ypres (380,000) and Messines (108,000), were also understandably anxious for Yankee replacements. Both nations wanted to brigade American regiments with British and French formations in the weakening Allied line. Pershing remained obdurate: *he* wanted an *American* army.

By fall there were more than 100,000 men in the A.E.F. in France. And there was nothing like them. America had not yet shed its innocence, had not yet been sobered by the weight of world responsibility, and so the heart was still above the head. As a result, the A.E.F. ranks among the merriest armies that ever marched. Trudging over the dusty roads of France, or slogging through the mud of the autumn rains, these exuberant doughboys bawled out their lilting war ballads and ditties, charming the French populace with their warmth and their boyishness, complaining very little about being sent 3,000 miles to risk their flesh in a foreign land in a war that was, in some vague way, to make "the world safe for democracy." Of course, they griped. All good soldiers do. The food was a tasteless swill and the tight-fitting uniforms they wore seemed to have been designed by Procrustes to cut off circulation. Yet, when they went into battle, the doughboys whooped and hollered as though entering a football game, and the first ones to do so were the men who had made that memorable march in Paris.

In late October the 1st Division took over a quiet sector near the Swiss border. Here, the poilus and the Boches sunned themselves, hung out their underwear or smoked their pipes, exchanging each evening a barrage of shells carefully aimed at open fields. Only a visit from some officious brass hat from headquarters was likely to disturb the tranquillity of these trenches, until *les Americains* came bursting among them with all their brash and upsetting notions about warfare. On October 23, 1917, an artillery sergeant named Alex Arch sent the first Yankee shell screaming toward the enemy. It struck not an empty lot but a crowded trench. Startled, the Germans decided to humiliate the new arrivals.

An assault company specializing in hit-and-run raids was brought up, and on the morning of November 3 a box barrage fell upon a company of doughboys. It isolated them in a wall of flashing steel. It shrank to enclose a platoon. The German elite troops came forward, 100 men against 40. Bangalore torpedoes blasted a hole in the American wire. Now the side of the box nearest the Germans vanished. With Lugers, knives and grenades, the assaulters came yelling out of the dark. They leaped upon the surprised Americans in the trenches. Expecting their enemy to flee, they were themselves surprised when the Yanks stood and fought. In three minutes it was all over. The assaulters withdrew, dragging 11 stunned Americans with them, leaving three of their own dead behind. In the trenches there also lay three dead doughboys. James B. Gresham, Thomas F. Enright and Merle D. Hay were the first Americans to give their lives in World War I. And in this first test of battle the Americans had shown that they would fight.

Meanwhile, in Italy the Italian Army had been all but destroyed at the Battle of Caporetto. Some 305,000 Italians were lost, and a mob of retreating soldiers and terrified civilians fled the Austro-German advance into Italy itself. British and French divisions had to be rushed to Italy to help keep this faltering ally in the war, and as the fortunate onset of an early winter forced Ludendorff to recall his German divisions from Italy to the Western front, the Allied ministers met at Rapallo to form the Supreme War Council to direct the war. Shortly afterward, Georges Clemenceau emerged as the new Premier of France.

Here was "the Tiger of France," short, aging, bald, his eyelids drooping sleepily over coal-black eyes, his voice harsh and rasping, his whole being energized by hatred. For years the Chamber of Deputies had stood in terror of Georges Clemenceau. He was the wrecker of governments, and on November 16, 1917, he was told by President Poincare: "You have made it impossible for anyone else to form a cabinet; now see what you can do."[68] Clemenceau took hold as a virtual dictator. "But I, Messieurs," he told the deputies, *"I wage war!* . . . In domestic policies, I wage war. In foreign policies, I wage war. Always, everywhere, *I wage war!"*[69]

With Clemenceau's rise to power, the figure of Ferdinand Foch drew closer to chief military command, and as a new will for battle seized the French nation, the new weapon of the tank was given a second try at the Battle of Cambrai.

Here, the British massed more than 300 tanks and sent them lumbering toward the Germans as a steel spearhead for 12 infantry divisions. Moving over a firm chalky plain, carrying fascines or bundles of sticks and dropping them in German trenches to form makeshift bridges, the tanks at Cambrai revolutionized modern warfare. Mobile and armored firepower in the mass had solved the problem of advancing guns. More ground was won at Cambrai in one day than in the four bloody months of Third Ypres, and with only 4,000 casualties. Eventually, the Germans rallied and broke down the shoulders of the British salient, forcing them to withdraw. Nevertheless, the tanks at Cambrai had shown the way. Only the generals of both sides refused to follow. J. F. C. Fuller, second-in-command of the British Tanks Corps, understood the lessons of that day. So did a tall and very serious young French Army captain named Charles de Gaulle. But it remained for another world war and another German Army to take up the doctrines laid down by these two perceptive soldiers. In the meantime the snows of the winter of 1917-18 made more soft mounds of more corpses sprawled across the face of Europe.

7

☆

When its wars were limited, America had been free to permit dissent, to ignore indifference and to make generous interpretations of its laws on treason. But now war was unlimited, it was for annihilation, and it became the unpleasant duty of the professor in politics to suppress dissent, to dragoon the indifferent and to stuff the nation's prisons with men and women convicted of "disloyalty" by hysterical and hate-mad juries.

Socialists, Wobblies, anarchists, pacifists, every sort of nonconformist who, either by strikes, antiwar agitation or protests against conscription, was considered to be giving aid and comfort to the enemy was rounded up and given short shrift. In all, 1,500 were arrested for disloyalty, and among those who went to jail were the Socialist presidential candidate Eugene Debs, the Socialist Congressman Victor Berger, anarchists Emma Goldman and Alexander Berkman and "Big Bill" Haywood of the Wobblies. Meanwhile, newspapers from Ireland were banned for slurs upon the British ally, German- or Slavic-language newspapers were carefully scrutinized, magazines of dissent closed up shop and a motion picture called *The Spirit of 1776* was forbidden the screen because of a scene in which British redcoats committed atrocities upon American soil. It was a case of, "Welcome, old buddy, formerly British bully," and America rapidly began to resemble medieval Japan in which the emperor instructed his samurai to kill anyone they saw doing anything different.

Worse, the general public joined the hue and cry of the spy hunt. Little old ladies of both sexes found a potential saboteur in every stranger with a foreign accent or a draft dodger inside every civilian suit. Americans of German blood, who supported the war as much as anyone else, were the special target for the ire of the superpatriot. It was not enough to dismiss them or refuse them employment; some states had to pass laws forbidding German to be taught in schools or colleges, German books were thrown out of public libraries and the persecution of German and Austrian artists ended with the arrest of Dr. Carl Muck, once the revered conductor of the Boston Symphony Orchestra. Then, as though to mock Yankee doughboys accustomed to treat the captive enemy with civility, the nation stopped eating sausage, called sauerkraut "liberty cabbage" and refused to listen to the insidious music of Mozart and Beethoven.

Obviously, America had gone a little mad with hatred. Day after day, organized by a committee on public information, every outlet of communication poured out a torrent of invective on Germany. There were few radios then, but there were 75,000 "four-minute men" trained to spew out hatred at movie houses and public gatherings across the country. Motion pictures and periodicals detailed the atrocities of the "Hun," while thousands of canned editorials told the mass man that he should hate a race that had always been depraved. Here, like a scene from George Orwell's *1984,* is one observer's report of the mass mania which swept the nation:

> We hated with a common hate that was exhilarating. The writer of this review remembers attending a great meeting in New England, held under the auspices of a Christian Church—God save the mark! A speaker demanded that the Kaiser, when captured, be boiled in oil, and the entire audience stood on chairs to scream its hysterical approval.[70]

However, it was not hatred but charity and a spirit of sacrifice that led the American people to help feed the Allies by curtailing their own consumption of food. This was done by observing wheatless Mondays or meatless Tuesdays. Under the slogan "Food Will Win the War," the Food Administration headed by Herbert Hoover preached the "Gospel of the Clean Plate" clear across the country. Americans also experimented with culinary horrors such as dog fish, vegetable lamb, sugarless candy, whale meat and horse steak. As a result, America in 1918 was able to export three times her normal quota of meat, sugar and breadstuffs.

Meanwhile, organized labor agreed upon a no-strike pledge in exchange for a promise that its rights would be recognized, and the nation was startled by the presence of women on factory production lines. A quarter-century later there would be nothing surprising in women taking the place of men called into uniform, but in 1917-18 the American woman was still a Victorian who could not vote, who wore long skirts and whose place was in the home.

In addition to Hoover's Food Administration, there was a War Industries Board to supervise purchases, a Railroad Administration to run the railways the President found it necessary to seize, a Fuel Administration which introduced daylight saving and gasless days and otherwise conserved fuel, a Labor Administration to coordinate capital and labor, a War Trade Board to license foreign trade and blacklist firms suspected of dealing with the enemy, a Shipping Board to provide the vessels to transport men and munitions overseas and a War Finance Corporation to float the loans financing a war that was to cost $35 billion before it ended. In the throes of total war, the Managerial Revolution had overtaken government. All power—political, economic, military or ideological—was now concentrated in Washington. The apparatus with which Big Brother keeps strict watch over his slaves had to be assembled by the home of the free to defend democracy.

In the meantime, Wilson, conscious that his country was slipping into a state of "wardom," sorrowfully aware that hatred was melting his hopes for a just and lasting peace, made one last effort to end hostilities. On January 8, 1918, he laid down his famous Fourteen Points for peace. In summary, they called for freedom of the seas, the removal of economic barriers, reduction of armaments, evacuation and restoration of all conquered territory, the impartial adjustment of colonial claims, self-rule for the peoples of the Austrian Empire, and the creation of an independent Poland. Last of all was a call for a League of Nations to keep the world peace.

Reluctantly, and with reservations, the Allies accepted the Fourteen Points. The Central Powers praised all but the points calling for evacuation and restoration. Actually, the Fourteen Points had no effect on the progress of the war. While a sincere expression of Wilson's vision of a peaceful world, they had also been a propaganda attempt to break down German resistance and prevent Russia from leaving the war. On both these counts, the last Wilson peace drive was a failure.

By early 1918 Erich von Ludendorff had become the virtual dictator of Germany. Through Hindenburg, the First Quartermaster

General dominated both the Kaiser and the High Command, and it was his insatiable lust for land which eventually compelled Russia to sign the humiliating Treaty of Brest-Litovsk on March 3, 1918. By its terms, Russia yielded to Germany 34 percent of her population, 32 percent of her farmland, 50 percent of her industrial holdings and 90 percent of her coal mines. Cowed by German arms, the Communists had had no other choice. "This is a peace which Russia, grinding her teeth, is forced to accept,"[71] said Leon Trotsky.

For Germany it was a foolishly gluttonous peace, and a mirage. Great nations are never so completely humbled, or at least not for long. By trading space for time, Trotsky was able to build the Red Army which eventually recovered the lost land and beat off the Allies' feeble postwar attempt to destroy Communism.

Ludendorff was determined to risk all in 1918. Victory had to come before the British blockade starved Germany into submission, and before American intervention could be decisive. It would come, he believed, by overwhelming the British in the north with the new tactic of "infiltration." This was forest warfare on a grand scale. Instead of striking strong points, the troops probed for soft spots through which they could speed to the enemy's rear while following divisions contained or reduced the strong points. In this way, Ludendorff planned to punch a hole between the French and the British, rolling the British back to the North Sea while the French fell back on Paris. After disposing of the British, he would turn and destroy the French. The first blow fell on March 21 on the British in front of Amiens.

It began with the bellowing of 6,000 massed German guns dueling 2,500 British cannon. Five hours later the guns fell silent and the German hordes rushed forward through a fog streaked with billowing clouds of brown smoke and green gas. Assisted by the fog and that dreadful artillery barrage, the Germans broke through. For the first time penetration had been achieved. Yet the British hung on doggedly, while Marshal Haig appealed to Pétain for French reserves. Pétain, however, held back; he believed the blow at Amiens was a feint preparatory to the true attack on the French to the south.

In such a dilemma, with victory or defeat hanging in the balance, it became necessary for the Anglo-French to pick a single supreme commander. On March 26 most of the Allied leaders met in the town hall of Doullens. All were grave. Outside, they could hear the shuffling tread of thousands of retreating soldiers. Pointing to Haig, Pétain drew Clemenceau aside and said: "There is a man who will be obliged to capitulate in the open field within a forthnight, and we shall be lucky if we are not obliged to do the same."[72] Clemenceau, who had come to Doullens prepared to insist that Pétain be made the Allied chief, was shaken. Then Ferdinand Foch spoke. "You aren't fighting?" he rasped. "I would fight without a break. I would fight in front of Amiens. I would fight in Amiens. I would fight behind Amiens. I would fight all the time. I would never surrender!"[73] With that, Foch gained Clemenceau's support and became the Allied Generalissimo.

A few days later, Foch received a visit from General Pershing. To his delighted surprise this obstinate American who had resisted all pressures to break up his army had come to place all that he had at Foch's service during the crisis. "All that I have" then consisted of about 325,000 men forming four divisions which were the equivalent of eight or nine French ones. Foch, deeply touched, immediately accepted—although the doughboy divisions did not get into the fighting which blunted the first blow in Ludendorff's spring offensive. By April 5 the Germans before Amiens had spent themselves and Ludendorff halted the battle.

A week later he hurled another thunderbolt across the old blood-stained, mud-churned battlefield of Ypres. Once again he hoped to press the British back against the Channel and to seize the Channel ports. His onrushing spearheads came so close to success that on April 12 Marshal Haig issued his famous Order of the Day telling his embattled troops: "There is no other course open to us but to fight it out. Every position must be held to the last man. There must be no retirement. With our backs to the wall and believing in the justice of our cause, each one of us must fight to the end."[74] Stiffening after Foch threw seven divisions into battle, the B.E.F. held—and the Battle of the Lys ended on April 29 short of Ludendorff's objective.

By then two American divisions were in the battle line, the 26th at Seicheprey near Toul in the south, and the 1st farther north at Cantigny in the vicinity of Amiens. Both saw action and held their own with the Germans, although the 1st at Cantigny was deliberately drenched with shellfire and gas on Ludendorff's orders to bear down hard on the untested Yankee divisions. Ludendorff also wanted to delude Foch into believing that he intended to strike near Amiens again. Actually, still confident of victory, Ludendorff was aiming a blow farther south.

This was in the Chemin des Dames sector north of the Aisne River and above Paris. Ludendorff's purpose here was to strike the French such a blow that they could not again come to the aid of the British, whom he still reserved for destruction.

Opposite Ludendorff's 42 divisions in the Chemin des Dames were but 16 Allied divisions, of whom five were battle-weary British units brought south for a "rest." On May 27, behind a thundering artillery barrage, the Germans crashed into these outnumbered, poorly positioned troops and tore a gaping hole in their center. Jubilant, the Germans poured through. Nothing like this had ever happened before on the Western front. The fleeing Allies had even left the bridges over the Aisne intact, and the Germans went streaming across them in an unchecked gray tide. On they rolled, until they came to the Vesle River 80 miles from Paris. Now it was up to Ludendorff. Should the Germans stop? After all, the Aisne Offensive was but a diversion to draw Allied strength away from the B.E.F. in the north. Moreover, the salient had not been widened. The penetration just kept getting deeper, and therefore narrower; and yet Paris was only 80 miles away!

Ludendorff could not resist, the gray ranks swept forward . . . five miles . . . ten miles . . . miles! miles on the Western front! On June 3 the Germans were once more on the Marne. They were east of a place called Château-Thierry, and Paris was only 56 miles away.

Once again the French government prepared to flee. Again the roads were clogged with the backwash of defeat. Peasant farmers drove carts heaped high with household goods or crates of chickens. Some led cows on leashes. Women wheeled babies in perambulators. Dusty poilus stumbled along, sometimes stopping to loot abandoned farmhouses. The sick lay gasping along the roadside. Terror stalked the Paris road, until, up the road toward the sound of the guns, a brigade of American Marines came marching.

Two of the five divisions Pershing placed at Foch's disposal were the 2nd and 3rd. Foch moved both of them toward the Chemin des Dames in an effort to plug the gap in the collapsing center. The 3rd went the farthest to the right, or east, and stopped the Germans in a brief fight at Château-Thierry. The main effort, however, was farther to the west, at a place called Belleau Wood.

Here the 2nd Division brought its two brigades, one of doughboys and the other of Marines commanded by a tough and intelligent soldier, Brigadier General James G. Harbord. Here, also, in this insignificant little hunting preserve, a historyless mile square in the middle of a rectangle formed by four tiny French villages, the arms of Germany and America were to clash. Here also, as S. L. A. Marshall says, the German commander was to risk all "in a local dogfight: and he had picked on the wrong people. The Marine Brigade because it was unique—a little raft of sea soldiers in an ocean of Army—was without doubt the most aggressive body of die-hards on the Western Front."[75]

Those die-hards marched out the Paris road on June 1. That night Harbord was told by the French commander: "Have your men prepare entrenchments some hundreds of yards to rearward." Harbord passed the word along to his men with the comment: "We dig no trenches to fall back on. The Marines will hold where they stand."[76] They did. With poilus telling them that the war was lost, they checked the German advance. "Retreat, hell, we just got here!"[77] Captain Lloyd Williams told a French major imploring him to withdraw. Then they went into that stinking, gas-drenched patch of woods and boulders, some of them through a green wheat field waving and rippled with machine-gun bullets, "C'mon you sonsabitches, do you want to live forever?"[78] old Sergeant Dan Daly roared at his faltering men, and they came on and many did not live. With losses of 55 percent, and with help from the Doughboy Brigade of the 2nd Division, they took Belleau Wood. Paris was saved, the cutting edge of Ludendorff's third offensive was blunted, and the flagging spirits of the French soared to learn that there were Americans fighting along the Marne.

Almost all of those Americans were doughboys, and they fought with the ferocity of soldiers robbed of their glory. Because of a slip in Pershing's iron censorship, the Marine brigade had been identified. It was the only unit so identified throughout the war, and, as it happens when the press knows no other name, too often the glories of the doughboys were pinned on the breasts of the Marines. The Marines did not seek this distinction, although it helped to make the reputation of their Corps, but the doughboys thought that they did. Thus the 2nd's infuriated soldiers took it out on the Germans dug in at Vaux on the right flank of Belleau Wood. They drove them out, and the first messenger of victory was a gigantic doughboy captain carried into a forward hospital with his legs in bloody splints. Sitting erect on his stretcher, groggy with ether, he cried out exultantly: "Oh, the goddam sonsabitches! The headline-hunting bastards! We showed the sonsabitches _how to do it!_"[79]

The captain was not referring to the defeated German enemy.

8

☆

Belleau Wood may not have won the war, but it compelled Erich von Ludendorff to revise his earlier poor opinion of American soldiers. "Personnel must be called excellent," wrote the First Quartermaster General. "Spirit of troops is high. Moral effect of our fire does not materially check the advance of the infantry. Nerves of the Americans are still unshaken."[80]

Ludendorff's nerves were also steady, and he decided to take one more bite at the French Army before hurling Operation Hagen at the British in the north. On June 9 a fourth German offensive was launched south of the Amiens bulge. It was broken by a French counterattack. So a fifth blow was struck farther south in Champagne, and here the German formations streaming south of the Marne swirled around the 38th Infantry of the U.S. 3rd Division.

"The time may come when Americans may have to give ground," Colonel Ulysses Grant McAlexander told the 38th's young officers. "But right now our job is so to impress Germans with our willingness to fight that their morale will be destroyed."[81] Holding fast, the 38th earned the nickname "Rock of the Marne." To its left, however, the Germans poured across the Marne en masse. Undismayed, Foch calmly loosed a prearranged counterbarrage of artillery and bombs, and counterattacked with a pick-up army. Its spearhead was a French Moroccan division in the center and the U.S. 1st and 2nd on either flank. Again, the Americans rushed into battle as though to a carnival, moving well ahead of the Moroccans. They broke the German drive. Farther south, at Château-Thierry, French and American troops pursued retiring Germans across the Marne.

Now was begun the great German retreat. Operation Hagen was suspended and then canceled, and as the Germans backpedaled from the Marne for the last time, the Kaiser's armies were placed on the defensive for good.

Elated with the Second Marne, Foch accepted and improved upon Haig's proposal to strike a massive blow at the Germans in the Amiens bulge, assigning Sir Douglas the French First and Third Armies. On the left of these forces Haig had the British Fourth Army, with its splendid Canadians and Australians and the U.S. 33rd Division. Leading them were some 400 tanks, for Amiens was to be another Cambrai on a much larger scale.

Amiens also began with a single, sudden, smothering blast of artillery, and Amiens also broke the German front. Before daylight of August 8, 1918, had arrived, the British Fourth Army had swept past the critical point at which so many other offensives had been halted and broken. Then the French heaved forward. They surprised the Germans, who had been shifting to their right to hold the British. Collapsing right and left, the Germans began to break. A solid penetration was achieved, and Ludendorff called August 8, 1918, "the black day of the German Army in the history of this war."[82] Three days later, Amiens came to an end. Casualties were not high by existing standards: 46,000 for the Allies, 75,000 for the Germans, plus 30,000 prisoners. But if the tide ever turned in this war that was never really fought to a conclusion, it turned at Amiens. Here was capped a series of German failures stretching back over a five-month period. Ludendorff had never been in the position to deliver a knockout blow. His numerical superiority had been slight, his reserve was depleted, his supply system was awry and his fuel stocks were down. Ignoring this, he had launched his win-the-war offensive which, without reserves to reinforce critical areas, gradually degenerated into a series of uncoordinated wild swings. Now, after Amiens, he acknowledged reality. On August 11, he informed the Kaiser: "It is no longer possible to make the enemy sue for peace by an offensive. The defensive alone cannot achieve that object. Termination of the war must be brought about by diplomacy."[83]

The Allies, however, had different plans.

Before the Battle of Amiens, the A.E.F. had reached a strength of one million men, and a quarter-million more were beginning to arrive in France each month. They were eager and gay, these boyish Doughboys of Black Jack Pershing. They came to France as though setting out on high adventure, like so many Tom Sawyers in flat-brimmed steel helmets. Many were also imbued with a high-minded spirit of idealism: at Woodrow Wilson's behest they had come to make the world safe for democracy.

And they sang. Few armies in history—not even the vocal Rebels and Federals of the Civil War—have sung as much as the A.E.F. Mostly their ballads were gay: "Oh, How I Hate to Get Up in the Morning," "Madelon" and "Mademoiselle from Armentières." In "Over There" they sang of what they intended to do. But this happy army was also a homesick one, and as the doughboys tramped over the dusty roads of France they sang sentimental songs such as "There's a Long, Long Trail," "It's a Long Way to Tipperary," or "K-K-K-Katy, Beautiful Katy," who was the only g-g-g-girl that they adored. The French were enchanted. These highhearted, apple-cheeked warriors, in tightfitting khaki were like nothing in their experience. They loved them like sons, and they grieved for them. "We cried more over the Americans leaving for the front than over our own men," said one French peasant woman. "They were so young and looked so innocent and were so far from home."[84]

When the doughboys did enter battle, their exuberance was irrepressible. Such dash impressed both friend and foe alike, and General Pershing was most anxious to see what his Americans could do on their own. After Amiens, he recalled the divisions which he had loaned to Foch and incorporated them with seven others into a separate American Army. Some 665,000 strong, he aimed it toward the Saint-Mihiel salient.

Saint-Mihiel, about a third of the way up the front from the Swiss border, was the last German bulge in the Allied line. Pershing's plan was to strike it from both sides. Before he did, however, he called upon the second weapon developed during World War I: the airplane.

It was not until late in World War I that the generals realized the possibilities of air power. Early in the war the Germans had bombarded British cities from the big dirigibles called Zeppelins, but these huge, sausage-shaped airships filled with gas were highly vulnerable to ground fire and were rapidly blasted out of the history of warfare. Meanwhile, most generals regarded their aircraft as scouts, the "eyes" of their army. Aviators flew over enemy territory to observe enemy activity or to direct artillery fire. The airplane seemed not so much a weapon as a useful means of transportation, like a horse or a truck.

However, as it became clear that something had to be done to prevent aerial scouting, and that ground fire rarely brought down an observation plane, both sides turned to developing a fighter or interceptor. The problem here was one of firepower: how to shoot from speedy, maneuverable aircraft. At first, aviators shot at each other with rifles, and then machine guns were mounted on the topmost wing of biplanes. Neither method was satisfactory, and in 1915, the great Dutch designer, Anthony Fokker, produced a swift monoplane with machine guns synchronized to fire through its propeller.

Thereafter the deadly Fokkers ruled the skies for Germany, until one of them was shot down and its secret discovered. With that, the Allies began to produce their own rapid-firing fighters. French Spads and Nieuports and British Sopwith Camels and de Havilland IIs engaged the Fokkers and later the Albatrosses on even terms. Dogfights over the Western front became common, and a new type of warrior hero—the fighter pilot, glamorous in helmet, goggles and silk scarf—was born. His ambition was to become an "ace" by shooting down at least five enemy aircraft. Early in the war there were American aces, men of the Lafayette Escadrille such as the famous Raoul Lufbery. In all, the Lafayette Escadrille claimed 199 German aircraft destroyed against 51 of their own pilots killed.

When America entered the war, the Lafayette Escadrille was disbanded, and its pilots joined the new American Air Service units being formed. One of these was the 94th ("Hat in the Ring") Pursuit Squadron, which scored the first American aerial victory on April 14, 1918, over Toul. Captain Eddie Rickenbacker flew for the 94th, and with 26 kills he became the outstanding American fighter pilot of World War I.

Meanwhile, the rival air forces had moved from development of the relatively small fighter to production of big aircraft able to carry a load of explosives. The Germans had bombers able to deliver bombs weighing up to 660 pounds, and before the war was over the British had developed a bomb weighing 1,650 pounds. The British under Major General Sir Hugh Trenchard had also developed a theory of air power which captivated a dashing young American colonel named Billy Mitchell. Eventually, Mitchell was to become convinced that air power alone could win a war, but at the time of Pershing's Saint-Mihiel offensive he was content with maintaining that massed bombing could break the Western stalemate. Under Pershing's orders, Mitchell assembled what was then a truly tremendous aerial armada: no less than 1,481 planes, of which 609 were American and the rest French and British with a sprinkling of Italian and Portuguese. Like the American infantry preparing to hit both sides of the Saint-Mihiel salient, Mitchell led this bombardment force against the German flanks.

Unfortunately, the weather was unfavorable for bombing, and although exaggerated claims were made for this first massive use of tactical air power, it does not seem to have been unusually effective. Nor was the artillery bombardment delivered later by 3,200 massed guns. What was effective was that when the doughboys struck in the drizzling early-morning dark of September 12, 1918, they caught the enemy on one foot.

Even as the Americans attacked, the Germans were withdrawing, and when the Germans turned to fight, they were at a distinct disadvantage. Some strong points fought fiercely, of course, but within 48 hours Saint-Mihiel was in the hands of the American First Army. In a military sense, it was not a striking victory: the Germans had been preparing to evacuate the salient and most of their troops were not of first-rate quality. Yet, as Pershing wrote: "The St. Mihiel victory probably did more than any single operation of the war to encourage the tired Allies."[85] Some Americans thought it might have done immeasurably more had Pershing been permitted to push on toward Metz. That fortress city of Lorraine was temporarily defenseless. The Americans might have seized it and so pierced the Hindenburg Line, thereby shortening the war. Pershing thought this was possible. So did Douglas MacArthur, who was there with his 42nd Division, and who wrote long afterward that the failure to take Metz was "one of the great mistakes of the war."[86] It is a moot point, especially since Pershing had already consented to fight his Yanks in the murky maze of the Meuse-Argonne.

Like most Allied leaders, Ferdinand Foch had expected the war to continue into 1919. But then, at the end of July, he asked himself:

"What am I risking, after all? You can prepare for the worst and another year of fighting, but there is no crime in hoping for the best—decisive victory within a few months."[87] German defeats, the performance of the Americans and the steady swelling of the A.E.F. made the bandy-legged marshal still more buoyant. By the end of September there were 39 U.S. divisions in France, together with 102 French, 60 British, 12 Belgian, 2 Italian and 2 Portuguese. Thus a total of 217 Allied divisions* faced 193 German and 4 Austrian, and when it is considered that the huge American divisions were nearly twice the size of the British, more than twice the French and four times the size of some of the whittled German divisions, as well as filled with fresh, physically strong and ardent troops, it is no wonder that Foch at the end of August was crying: *"Tout le monde à la bataille!* Everyone to the battle!"[88]

That was Foch's master plan: everyone was to strike the groggy Germans on a massive front from Verdun to the North Sea. The Americans, except for six divisions serving with the Anglo-French, were to drive the Germans from the terrain immediately west of Verdun. This was the belt between the Argonne Forest on the west or left and the Meuse River on the right. It was also the nastiest stretch of fighting country on the Western front.

The Germans had held the Argonne since 1914. Using steel, concrete, barbed wire and artfully sited machine guns, they had turned a natural labyrinth into a wicked meat grinder. Because the terrain was so easily defended, and had been so well fortified over four years, the French had never dared to attack it. Why Pershing accepted the Meuse-Argonne is not exactly clear, although he may have had to agree as the final concession in his fight for a separate American army. He had always told Foch that he would fight anywhere, anytime, as long as it was under his own colors. Certainly, he did not demur; and he may have been delighted to draw the sector where the Americans could win the war.

The Argonne was the pivot of the Hindenburg Line. Smash it, and the entire front as far as the North Sea would become unhinged. Take it, and the two great German rail centers at Sedan and Mézières would become unmasked; and in Foch's great offensive not only the enemy armies but the railroads which supplied them were the ob-

* The United States was not, properly speaking, one of the Allies but was rather an "associated" power.

jective. Control of the railways certainly would mean a German retreat and probably a defeat. So the American First Army was hastily shifted west from Saint-Mihiel. Superb staff work directed by Colonel George Marshall reconcentrated the divisions in time for the opening of the assault on September 26.

On the first day, because the Germans had been deceived into drawing off strength elsewhere, the Americans made three miles against light opposition. But then reinforcements came in, the terrain splintered the American attack, and the Yanks were stalled. Thereafter, the Meuse-Argonne seemed to demonstrate the truth of Pétain's observation: "The Americans are good. Their soldiers have great dash. But the higher staffs and command are not only untried; their whole organization is clumsy."[89] Such awkwardness was at once apparent as the battle degenerated into a blind, shot-for-shot, trench-by-trench stumble. Moving over a thousand separate lanes through a tangle of wood and hill, the big Yankee divisions so capable of powerful blows had their strength fragmented. There was little of the teamwork required in a point-by-point advance, and poor staff work compounded the confusion. Yet there was much heroism. Acting Captain Samuel Woodfill personally wiped out four enemy machine-gun nests, and then, running out of ammunition, stormed a fifth with a pickax. Sergeant Alvin York saved an American platoon from destruction by picking off machine gunners with his rifle, after which, having halted an enemy charge, he picked up a pistol and captured 132 prisoners. And the "Lost Battalion" of the 77th Division refused to surrender after it had been cut off, holding out until relieved.

Savage fighting also characterized the German defense. Troops supposedly ready to throw down their arms fought with a ferocity that mocked the faintheartedness of their First Quartermaster General. Two days after the battle began, Ludendorff called a staff meeting within the safety of his faraway headquarters at Spa. Beginning to review the situation, he suddenly burst into an impassioned defense of his own actions. Here was born the "stab-in-the-back" fiction by which Ludendorff and the other Junkers of the German General Staff were to blame everyone but themselves for their own failures. Here, Ludendorff stormed at his own officers as cowards, charged the Navy with treachery and the German people with cowardice, and called the Kaiser a weakling. As he raged, the veins stood out on his forehead like purple ropes. His words became thick, his mouth frothy, and he sank to the floor in a convulsive fit. Revived but still trembling, Ludendorff visited Hindenburg that night to tell him that all was lost, that Germany must surrender all her conquered territory and attempt to negotiate a peace based on President Wilson's Fourteen Points.

Next day Kaiser Wilhelm and his entourage arrived at Spa. Wilhelm was also pale and trembling, for the Communists had only lately killed his cousin, Czar Nicholas II, and his entire family. Moreover, Germany quivered like an awakening volcano. Anarchists were calling for revolution, Socialists were pleading for defeat, the people were starving and fresh troops arriving at the front were taunted by near-mutinous soldiers with the cry: "Blacklegs, you are prolonging the war!"[90] Eager for peace now, the Kaiser summoned Prince Max of Baden to the Chancellery and requested him to end hostilities. Not until October 4, 1918, however, did Max obey, and it was not until the following day that he cabled Wilson: "To avoid further bloodshed, the German Government requests the President to arrange the immediate conclusion of an armistice on land, by sea, and in the air."[91]

At this juncture, with the Meuse-Argonne in full deadly swing and men still dying from France to Africa, the American President not only did not consult either Clemenceau or Lloyd George or any of his own military leaders; he also delayed three days himself before asking Prince Max if he accepted the Fourteen Points. Before Max could reply, German atrocities in the Argonne and the sinking of two passenger ships by German submarines so inflamed the Allied world that Wilson abruptly notified Max that there could be no discussions with such an enemy: the Allies would set the terms for an armistice.

Now Wilson informed his associates of the secret correspondence, and although Clemenceau and Lloyd George were solidly behind Wilson, they never forgot his failure to consult them at the outset. Meanwhile, Allied arms were answering all outstanding questions. In Palestine, General Edmund Allenby's colorful, polyglot army vanquished the Turks, and at Salonika the Army of the Orient under Franchet d'Esperey at last crushed the Bulgars. On the Western front the Americans smashed the Meuse-Argonne pivot, while the British, French and Belgians began breaking through all along the line. On October 23, after Wilson hinted that the Allies might talk to a Germany devoid of its militarists, the Kaiser dismissed Ludendorff. Exchanging his baton for dark glasses and a fake beard, the First Quartermaster General went slinking away to neutral Sweden. On

October 30 Turkey surrendered. Four days later the British broke through the Germans in Belgium and began striking at their rear. On that same November 3 Admiral Scheer ordered the High Seas Fleet out of port. He intended to give battle and go down with colors flying, but his sailors had opposite designs. They mutinied, killed some of their officers, and sailed back into port flying the red flags of revolution.

On November 6 the Americans broke through the Meuse-Argonne and looked down upon the spires of Sedan. On November 7, with the German volcano about to erupt, a German Armistice Commission confronted Marshal Ferdinand Foch inside a railway car run up on a gun spur in the Forest of Compiegne. "What is your purpose?" Foch snapped. "What do you want of me?"[92] Matthias Erzberger, the commission chairman, murmured that he had come to hear the Allied armistice "proposals." But Foch had no proposals, only terms. They included among other conditions not only the return of all conquered territory, together with Alsace-Lorraine, but the surrender of all submarines, large stocks of war material and evacuation of the left bank of the Rhine. Erzberger hedged, although it is now known that he had been instructed to sign, and that the terms seemed to him more generous than he had expected. While he delayed, a German republic was proclaimed in Berlin on November 9 with a Socialist for its first chancellor; and on November 10 Kaiser Wilhelm stepped aboard his cream-and-gold Imperial train and went rolling out of history and into the sanctuary of neutral Holland. Next day the Armistice was signed.

At eleven o'clock in the morning of this 11th day of the 11th month of the year 1918, the guns began to fall silent; and the great cataclysm which had convulsed the world came shuddering to a stop.

PART VIII

World War II

1

☆

On December 4, 1918, President Woodrow Wilson sailed for the peace conference at Paris. He sailed with high hopes for a peace between equals and a League of Nations to keep that peace. In this he seems to have had with him the aspirations of mankind, for wherever he appeared in Europe he was hailed as a savior.

"No one has heard such cheers," one observer wrote. "I, who heard them in the streets of Paris, can never forget them in all my life. I saw Foch pass, Clemenceau pass, Lloyd George, generals, returning troops, banners, but Wilson heard from his carriage something different, inhuman or superhuman."[1]

But they were only cheers, the plaudits of war-weary Europeans hopeful that peace would come enduringly upon their tortured Europe. They did not represent the considered purposes of Wilson's colleagues of the Big Four—Clemenceau, Lloyd George and Premier Orlando of Italy—and if Wilson had read the signs right, he might have foreseen that he was to become a party to no peace between equals but a vengeful ultimatum imposed by the victor upon the vanquished.

First, the conference itself had been delayed while David Lloyd George, taking advantage of a rise in popularity gained by the Armistice, successfully campaigned for re-election on such merciful slogans as "Hang the Kaiser!" or "Make 'Em Pay!" Second, the blockade of Germany, which had caused the deaths of 800,000 German noncombatants in its last two years, was not to be lifted until the treaty was signed and the Allies had gained a head start in the postwar trade race. Third, the Allies, miffed at Wilson's high-handed lone hand during the German capitulation, had already negotiated secret treaties providing for a traditional sharing out of the spoils of war not exactly in accordance with the principles of the Fourteen

Points. Fourth, the defeated nations were to be excluded from the conference, the clearest sign of all that the "peace" was to be an ultimatum, and the smaller Allied nations, for whose rights the war supposedly had been fought, were relegated to the sidelines. Fifth, Premier Georges Clemenceau and the French nation burned for a hard peace that would humble and hobble Germany for good and all, and the very fact that the conference was to convene in Paris was proof enough that they intended to get it.

Yet it is difficult not to sympathize with the French. Twice within Clemenceau's lifetime the Germans had hurled themselves upon his country. In the war just ended no nation had suffered like the French. Her manhood had been bled white and much of her countryside had been ruined. France's railroads were worn out, her ports were taxed beyond endurance, and the spiteful Ludendorff, having seen in 1918 that he could not win, had deliberately wrecked France's vital northern mines in order to cripple a trade rival. This Clemenceau could neither forgive nor forget, and Wilson's refusal to visit the mines (so as not to prejudice himself, his aides explained) only infuriated the Tiger of France further and convinced him that he was dealing with an idealistic visionary who thought that he was the second Messiah. "Mr. Wilson bores me with his Fourteen Points," Clemenceau snapped. "Why, God Almighty has only ten!"[2]

Mr. Wilson, however, was not quite so starry-eyed. He understood the difficulties of redrawing the map of Europe as well as his colleagues, some of whom were learning their geography at the conference table. Wilson's mistake was not so much in fancying himself the Prince of Peace reincarnate as in his willingness to sacrifice many of his points in the interests of obtaining a League of Nations. Many of his concessions were justified in his mind because one of the League's functions was to review the decisions made at Paris. Yet, if he had stood up for his principles at the outset, with the weight of world public opinion on his side he might have been able to block the Carthaginian peace which Clemenceau was preparing.

In fairness to Wilson, however, he could not have appeared to be too solicitous for the late enemy at a time when the common man everywhere was calling for the enemy's scalp, nor could he have risked bolting the conference and thus leaving Europe open to the menace of Bolshevism. Nor was Mr. Wilson entirely to blame for the futile attempt to settle Europe's problems on the basis of national self-determination. Even before the war, Norman Angell had written: "Political nationalism has become, for the European of our age, the most important thing in the world, more important than civilization, humanity, decency, kindness, pity; more important than life itself."[3] Believing in this new religion, the powers thought it would be a great good to break up the multinational Austrian Empire into separate national states.

They set up the separate states of Austria and Hungary, a new republic of Czechoslovakia, and, by joining some Slavic areas to Serbia, the new state of Yugoslavia. Poland was revived as an independent state and given a corridor to the Baltic, and Rumania was all but doubled in size at the expense of Hungary. These new national boundaries, however, did not coincide with those of population or of language, and where once there had been a common market of Middle Europe there were now trade barriers erected by each of the new succession states. Each new state also included minorities quick to demand their own self-determination, or included minorities such as the German-speaking peoples of Czechoslovakia and Poland who had allegiance elsewhere. Thus strategically vital Middle Europe was transformed into a congeries of squabbling states powerless to make common cause together; and Austria, once the central nervous system, was left a weakling without ports or markets whose only salvation would be in union with Germany. This, of course, was not to be permitted.

Germany also was to be kept weak. She was to lose all her overseas colonies, to acknowledge war guilt as a basis for reparation to be determined later, to give up land for the "Polish Corridor" and the other "buffer states" ringing her round, to allow demilitarization of her territory west of the Rhine, and to be disarmed of all but enough troops to police her interior. True enough, the terms were probably not so harsh as those a triumphant Germany might have dictated to the Allies; but they were none the less Carthaginian, certain, as Germany's own severe Treaty of Versailles had been certain, to produce another war. Worst of all, they ignored the economic problems which had caused the conflict.

One of Wilson's points had been to call for removal of all economic barriers, but he and his colleagues ignored this completely. "The fundamental economic problems of a Europe starving and disintegrating before their eyes was the one question on which it was impossible to arouse the interest of the Four,"[4] the British economist, John Maynard Keynes, observed. He went on:

The future life of Europe was not their concern; its means of livelihood was not their anxiety. Their preoccupations, good and bad alike, related to frontiers and nationalities, to the balance of power, to imperial aggrandisements, to the future enfeeblement of a strong and dangerous enemy, to revenge, and to the shifting by the victors of their unbearable financial burdens on to the shoulders of the defeated.[5]

Eventually, Lloyd George awoke to the danger. On March 25, 1919, he circulated a memorandum stating:

You may strip Germany of her colonies, reduce her armaments to a mere police force and her navy to that of a fifth-rate power; all the same, in the end, if she feels that she has been unjustly treated in the peace of 1919, she will find means of exacting retribution from her conquerors. The maintenance of peace will . . . depend upon there being no causes of exasperation constantly stirring up the spirit of patriotism, of justice or of fair play to achieve redress. . . . For these reasons I am, therefore, strongly averse to transferring more Germans from German rule to the rule of some other nation than can possibly be helped. I cannot conceive any greater cause of future war than that the German people, who have certainly proved themselves one of the most vigorous and powerful nations in the world, should be surrounded by a number of small states, many of them consisting of people who have never previously set up a stable government for themselves, but each of them containing large masses of Germans clamouring for reunion with their native land.[6]

It would be difficult to discover a more accurate forecast of the nationalist discontent which was to undergird the vengeance even then being vowed by a valorous but fanatic German corporal named Adolf Hitler. Nevertheless, Lloyd George's advice was not heeded.

On May 7, 1919, a German delegation headed by Count Ulrich von Brockdorff-Rantzau was led into the Trianon to hear the terms. Brockdorff bitterly assailed the Allies for continuing the blockade and declared that the Fourteen Points were binding on all who signed the Armistice. Then he refused to sign the treaty. In the meantime, the German press published the terms. Germany was stunned. A clamor against the treaty arose. In Paris one of those who was shocked by the terms was Herbert Hoover, the American engineer who had made himself famous by feeding war victims. Rushing outside his hotel before dawn, Hoover walked the dark streets in dismay. Later he wrote: "It seemed to me the economic consequences alone would pull down all Europe and thus injure the United States."[7]

The Allies, however, were adamant. Germany must sign. Germany knew that she must, for the blockade was killing her and the Bolshevik yeast was fermenting. On Saturday, June 28, 1919, a new German delegation arrived at the Palace of Versailles. They waited outside the great doorway into the Hall of Mirrors, the same glittering room in which France had been humbled in 1871. Inside, the Allied leaders were seated at a long table. Clemenceau, hunched like a small, yellowish gnome, was at the center.

"Faites entrer les Allemands," he rasped. "Show in the Germans!"

At the door soldiers in the gorgeous uniforms of the Garde Républicaine lowered their sabers into their scabbards with a flash and a click. In came the Germans; silently they signed the treaty lying on a small table. Outside, a crash of guns signaled Paris that the second Treaty of Versailles had been signed. Now the Allies signed . . . Wilson, Lloyd George, finally Clemenceau. Turning, the Tiger found his arms seized by former Premier Paul Painlevé, who congratulated him.

"Yes," he murmured, his black eyes brimming with tears, "it is a beautiful day."[8]

2

☆

The Treaty of Versailles capped the climax of the most momentous of the wars which have by turns unified or divided the West since Europe emerged from the Dark Ages.

Because of the war and its treaty all European balance was destroyed, and because Europe was the center of world trade as well as the headquarters for all but two of the world's empires, so also was world balance upset. Three of these empires—the German, Austrian and Turkish—disappeared. A fourth, Russia, exchanged the whip of the Czar for the goad of the Commissar, while replacing its Christian faith with the new creed of Communism. A fifth and once the most powerful, Great Britain, sank from the status of world banker to that of a debtor nation. A sixth, the French, was reduced to the status of a second-rate power and left prey to the party politicians who customarily live off the France for whom patriots have died. A seventh, the United States of America, having shown herself to be the new colossus, was already digging herself an ostrich hole. The eighth and the newest, Italy, having received the South Tyrol, Trieste, Rhodes and the Dodecanese Islands, calmly seized Fiume and then retired sulking because she could not do the same to islands off Dalmatia and Albania. Only the ninth, Japan, was satisfied. By reason of a casualty rate of .002 percent—that is, 300 dead and 907 wounded—Japan had emerged as the dominant power in the Far East and with a collection of German islands upon which to base her expanding sea power in the Western Pacific. These former German possessions, like the others awarded the Allies, were held in trust for the League of Nations under the euphemistic title of "mandates."

Of all these changes, the most significant were the Russian Revolution and the passing of the *Pax Britannica*. The first change had yet to consolidate itself, but the second was an unalterable historical fact: *Pax Britannica* was dead. By allowing herself to be drawn into a continental land war between huge conscript armies Britain had forever lost control over the balance of power by which she had prevented wars from becoming world-wide. Perhaps this was inevitable, granting the industrialization of other nations and the race for markets, and granting also the rapid acceleration of nations with land-mass-plus-population toward the rank of superpower; and perhaps the truly remarkable fact is that for the space of 100 years this seafaring island race was able even to check Europe's fratricidal tendencies. However that may be, something had to replace the *Pax Britannica*. For Woodrow Wilson, this would be the League of Nations, and he was as certain of this as he was positive that his country would ratify the treaty and thus accept the League Covenant.

Unfortunately, Wilson had neither the American people nor the Senate with him. Even before he sailed for Europe, he had alienated the Republicans by calling for an all-Democratic victory in the midterm election of 1918. Then he had neglected to name a high-ranking Republican to the peace delegation. Next, he had defied Republican Senators who opposed making the League Covenant part of the treaty. "When that treaty comes back," he had said, "gentlemen on this side will find the covenant not only in it, but so many threads of the treaty tied to the covenant that you cannot dissect the covenant from the treaty without destroying the whole vital structure."[9] That was what happened, and although to have made warp and woof of League and treaty has been hailed as Wilson's great triumph of statecraft, in fact it helped to doom them both.

Wilson mistook his countrymen's flaming enthusiasm in World War I for an eagerness to accept international responsibility. He was not aware of the speed with which they were becoming indifferent to foreign affairs. The old American illusion about war—"The game's over, we've won, let's go home!"—had taken hold. Two decades and one more horrible war had to ensue before they would even begin to admit that wars are fought for political objectives. Moreover, apathy was giving way to angry disillusion. The war fought to end war had cost 126,000 dead and 334,000 wounded, and yet there was still all this talk about "preventing future wars." Many Americans thought they had been cruelly hoaxed, others vowed that they would never again ignore Washington's admonition against involvement in the broils of Europe. To a nation devoted to the knockout punch and the home run, the wearying labyrinthine way of collective security wound up the bill of Sisyphus, and so Senator Henry Cabot Lodge of Massachusetts, the suave and powerful "scholar in politics," had no difficulty in martialing opposition to the League, this "evil thing with a holy name."[10]

Lodge hated Wilson with an implacable hatred. Even though he personally favored a world organization, he wanted none bearing the Wilsonian stamp. So Lodge moved to block the treaty by hobbling it with reservations and hamstringing it with debate. Lodge was supported not only by all that was reactionary in the nation, including the resurgent isolationists, but by many internationalists who believed that Wilson had betrayed his own principles for the League. The *New Republic* shed its old-time Wilsonian fervor with the blast: "The European politicians who with American complicity have hatched this inhuman monster, have acted either cynically, hypocritically, or vindictively, and their handiwork will breed future cynicism, hypocrisy, and vindictiveness in the minds of future generations."[11]

Shaken but still convinced of the rectitude of his cause, Wilson went to the people. In September of 1919 he began to stump the country. "I can predict with absolute certainty," he declared, "that within another generation there will be another world war if the nations of the world do not concert the method by which to prevent it."[12] Prophetic, eloquent and passionate, Wilson still spoke to a nation facing the other way. On the night of September 25 his health broke. Silently, with drawn blinds, the presidential train rolled back to Washington carrying a paralyzed President. For two months Wilson lay in the White House with no one permitted to see him except his secretary, his family and his physician. He could do no more than scrawl an indecipherable signature to the few documents brought him by his wife or by Joseph Tumulty, his secretary.

Here for the first time was the situation foreseen by the Constitution: "In the case of . . . inability to discharge the powers and duties of the said office, the same shall devolve on the Vice President." One and one only attempt to act upon this proviso received such a furious rebuff from Tumulty that it drove Secretary Robert Lansing back to the State Department. Moreover, Vice President Thomas R. Marshall, a deep thinker famous for the proverb, "What this country needs is a good five-cent cigar,"[13] was terrified at the thought that "the same should devolve" on him. Eventually, Wilson recovered his mental powers, but not his bodily health. His pride he had never lost, and when defeat of the League appeared imminent, he rejected advice to compromise with a fierce, "Let Lodge compromise! Better a thousand times to go down fighting than to dip your colors to dishonorable compromise."[14]

This, from the same man who at the peace conference had made a religion of compromise. In the end the League did go down. On November 19, 1919, it was defeated in the Senate, and an attempt to rescue it the following year was also defeated.

"We had a chance to gain the leadership of the world," Woodrow Wilson said with great sorrow. "We have lost it, and soon we shall be witnessing the tragedy of it all."[15]

3

☆

It has been maintained that American abstention wrecked the League of Nations, but the fact is that the League was already foredoomed to failure by its dependence upon the power of international law and public opinion, rather than force, to impose its decisions. It was a policeman without a pistol, a preacher, and because nations are even less willing than men to bind themselves with covenants of words, it rapidly degenerated into a noble futility.

The League did settle some minor international disputes, and it tried very hard to interest the nations in disarmament. But it had no success. Then, faced by the new breed of international gangsters spawned by the Treaty of Versailles, the League could do no more than lecture or invoke empty sanctions; going unpunished, the gangsters defiantly exploited the League's impotence.

Chief among these new apostles of power were Adolf Hitler of Germany, Benito Mussolini of Italy and the clique of militarists who had seized control of Japan. All owed their success at home to the rising spirit of nationalism which the men of Versailles had mistakenly thought was the answer to Europe's problems, and they converted—or, rather, perverted—this spirit into the movement toward authoritarian nationalism now known as Fascism.

In Japan Fascism bore a theocratic stamp. In a land nominally Buddhist, the Japanese militarists had resurrected the ancient Shinto religion of nature worship with its belief in a divine emperor as the source and fount of the race. They also revived the ancient code of the samurai class of warrior nobles. Between Shinto and samurai an entire nation was indoctrinated in the belief that the greatest good was in fighting for the emperor and the most sublime end was to die in his cause. The souls of those who did were transported to Yasakuni Shrine, a warrior paradise much like the Valhalla of the Teutons. Finally, the militarists pursued their economic ends by restoring to prominence the neglected slogan *"Hakko ichiu"*—"Bringing the eight corners of the world under one roof." That roof was intended to have a Japanese pagoda shape, and so was born the concept of the "Greater East Asia Co-Prosperity Sphere." The Rising Sun of Japan was to be the center of an economic galaxy running north-south from Manchuria to Australia and east-west from the Fiji Islands to the Bay of Bengal. All, of course, depended upon a judicious exercise of the moral authority of the divine emperor. The most recent, Hirohito, though deploring this high-handed use of his name, was powerless to halt it, for every movement made by moderates against the militarists seemed to end in failure.

In fairness to Japan, it is not easy to see how she could have followed anything other than an imperialist course. At one time she had been self-sufficient and insular, but in 1853 the American Admiral Perry opened her up to world trade, and with that event she became hopelessly smitten with the Western disease of industrialism. Worse, in the four home islands of Japan there were almost no raw materials. In this she resembled Britain; but even the British possessed much coal and iron when they launched the Industrial Revolution, and it was only after these resources became exhausted that they found it necessary to import them. But here was an agricultural race suddenly turned industrial and immediately forced to scramble for the raw materials of industry. And so, between 1875 and 1879, Japan acquired the Kurile, Bonin and Ryukyu islands, in 1891 the Volcano group, and next, in the Chinese War of 1894-95, she picked up Formosa, the Pescadores and Port Arthur. Pressure by Russia, France and Germany forced her to give up Port Arthur, but in her subsequent defeat of the Russians she regained that vital outpost, together with the southern half of the island of Sakhalin and control of Korea. In 1910 she annexed Korea outright, and then, after World War I, she obtained mandates over former German territory in the Marshall, Caroline and Marianas islands.

Like Britain, Japan was an island empire, a situation which required a strong navy. Japan built one, and then, in 1920-21, the limitations imposed by the Naval Disarmament Conference tended to make her even stronger. This conference was held in Washington after Britain and the United States had decided that a naval arms race between them was not only costly but also senseless. Japan was invited as the third major naval power, France and Italy as medium ones, and Belgium, Holland, Portugal and China as minor. At Washington it was agreed to scrap much tonnage and to limit the building of capital ships. A 5-5-3 ratio in battleship and aircraft carrier tonnage was set up among Britain, America and Japan. Because British sea power was spread over the Atlantic, Pacific and Indian oceans, the American over the first two and the Japanese only over the Pacific, this tended to make Japan supreme in the Western Pacific. Moreover, the United States pledged herself not to strengthen any bases, such as Guam or Manila, lying west of Pearl Harbor, and Britain denied herself the same privileges east of Singapore and north of Australia. Japan, of course, had every intention of fortifying the mandates she was not supposed to strengthen, and because she built up to the limit in ships, whereas Britain and America did not, she was to that degree better prepared for war. Clearly, China was her next objective. Obviously, that theater would bring her into conflict with an America committed to maintain the Open Door policy. Japan prepared herself for this possibility with great realism, while the militarists who ruled her, appealing to the national and racial pride of this energetic, warlike and conforming people, under the aegis of a divine emperor and through the use of every device of regimentation—"Thought Police," indoctrination of schoolchildren, massed marching, vowing and singing—turned the country into a modern Fascist state cloaked in the medieval mantle of a samurai.

If Fascism had a father, it was probably Benito Mussolini. An obscure editor before the Armistice, he catapulted himself into national prominence by inventing the myth of Italian "victory" in World War I. In his inimitable literary style, which emphasized every untruth with an exclamation point, he told his countrymen that "our heroic armies" had conquered those Austrian lands which actually fell to Italy under the secret agreements. In fact, except for Vittorio Veneto, Italy had been severely chastised in the war, having lost 500,000 dead and suffered a million wounded. She had also had 540,000 deserters. Nevertheless, such appeals to national and racial pride are usually irresistible, and in them Mussolini found the source of his strength.

Another source was the Communist-Socialist attempt to seize power in Italy. In 1919 the Italian people lived at starvation level. They were ripe for revolution. A wave of Communist-inspired strikes and disorders threatened anarchy, and Prime Minister Nitti, becoming afraid, allowed the Communists and Socialists a free hand. They then began those antinational excesses and brutalities which opened opportunities for Mussolini and his *Fascio di Combattimento,* the forerunner of the Fascist Party.* Fascism, then, meant authority: authoritarian nationalism locked in a duel to the death with international Communism. Fascism won. To give Mussolini his due, he was the first to halt the march of Bolshevism. Many European leaders hailed him for this feat, among them Winston Churchill who said in 1927: "If I had been an Italian, I am sure that I should have been wholeheartedly with you from the start to finish in your triumphant struggle against the bestial appetites and passions of Leninism."[16]

However, power, not merely the repulse of Communism, was Mussolini's real goal. After the Red menace faded, he kept the threat of it alive, and thus created the alliance between Fascism and the propertied classes who saw their only shield in Mussolini's black-shirted strong-arm squads. In October, 1922, Mussolini and his Black Shirts made their famous march on Rome, so cowing the King that he made Mussolini his Prime Minister. Now a second characteristic of Fascism appeared. Mussolini became *Il Duce,* the Leader, and as the sham of "office" was gradually dropped, all power was vested in him personally.

His square jaw outthrust, his massive shaven head bared, the Duce habitually harangued his people from a balcony, until at last his vision of a new Roman Empire, in which was implicit not only the ancient military glory but the old inequalities of rank and caste, came to be derided as the "Balcony Empire." Again to give Mussolini his due, he created a stable and healthy Italy at a time when even Britain had put its people on the dole to prevent revolt. He ended unemployment, chiefly by the device of putting most of the unemployed in the army, and he became famous for making the slipshod Italian railroads run on time. Yet his Fascism was a kind of building backward, an attempt to construct the future with the dimensions of the past. Fascist Italy looked toward the future through the wrong end of the telescope; it was like a Roman chariot fitted with a propeller.

* The name derives from its insignia, a Latin "fasces," the bundle of rods holding an ax which was carried before a Roman magistrate as a symbol of his authority.

It was also a war chariot. "War is to the man what maternity is to the woman," Mussolini said. "I do not believe in perpetual peace; not only do I not believe in it, but I find it depressing and a negation of all the fundamental virtues of man."[17]

So also thought the disciple who was to become his master: Adolf Hitler.

Born of Austrian parents on April 20, 1889, Hitler as a young man went to live in the capital at Vienna. Here, in this brilliant cosmopolitan city, Hitler seems to have conceived his violent hatred of Jews and other "inferior races." Here he began to drink deeply of the racist poison injected into the German cultural bloodstream by the French writer Gobineau. Here also he came under the spell of the twin giants of German philosophy and music: Friedrich Nietzsche and Richard Wagner. Hitler's intense, mystic nature was inflamed by Nietzsche's hatred for the leveling tendencies of democracy or the socialist quest for security. He, too, despised Christianity and the Christian virtues of meekness and love. In the place of the Christian saint he erected the "superman" of Nietzschean philosophy. In this, like so many disciples of this unclear prophet, Hitler was confused. Nietzsche never called for the "blond beast" of Nazi mythology, but rather for a moral giant who would redeem the world. He said that the purpose of the human race was to produce such superior types. Hitler, however, full of racist nonsense about the "pure Aryan," his soul attuned to the crash and thunder of Wagnerian opera, made his superman the warrior god of the Teutonic pantheon. A superman naturally must spring from a superrace, and this Hitler expected to find in the Germans, once they had been cleansed of "foreign elements."

These were the ideas which influenced the young Hitler. They did not yet bear the brutal stamp of the Nazi brand of Fascism. That had to await the social upheaval of World War I, which threw up the Communist reaction against capitalism and the Fascist reaction against Communism. At the age of 24, Hitler departed Vienna for Munich in Germany, not, as he said, to escape Jews but to dodge the Austrian draft. He was not a coward—he proved his courage during World War I—but he did not want to serve in a cosmopolitan army. After the war, he returned to Munich.

The rickety German republic which had succeeded the Kaiser's government was then laboring under a reparations bill of $33 billion. Its protest that this enormous and impossible indemnity was suffocating the feeble German economy met with some sympathy in Britain, but was dismissed by the French as an attempt to evade payment. The truth was that the Allies depended upon German reparations for the money to pay their American war debts, and if the United States, instead of earning Europe's opprobrium as "Uncle Shylock" insisting on his pound of flesh, had rather freed its former associates from what was also an impossible obligation, Germany and the West as well might have better withstood the strains and stresses of the post-war world. But this did not happen until it was too late, and the Germany to which Adolf Hitler returned now added the ordeal of poverty to the humiliation of Versailles. Hitler himself was, in his own phrase, "a human nothing," a down-and-outer who slept by day in beds rented from workers who could afford a room. Burning with a bitter shame, he looked around for scapegoats and found them in "the Jews," socialists, pacifists and slackers.

Hitler's hatred for such "traitors" was shared by the men of the numerous Free Corps who ranged the country as the self-appointed guardians of the law and foes of Socialism. They fancied themselves the reincarnation of the Teutonic Knights of the Middle Ages, but with no knightly vows of charity. In the main soldiers trained to the battlefield—to victory, honor and glory—they had come home to defeat and disgrace. To such simplicists the sword is the ultimate solution, and although they were of service in beating back Bolshevik encroachment on the Baltic, or in suppression of Socialist revolt at home, they eventually degenerated into bands of lawless reactionaries specializing in the murder of those who disagreed with them. Matthias Erzberger, the statesman who had gone to meet Foch in the railway car at Compiègne and who had advised Germany to sign the despised treaty, was the most famous victim of their guns.

After Hitler became the seventh man to join an obscure group called the German Workers Party, which he came to lead as the renamed National Socialist Workers Party (of which title the word "Nazi" is a contraction), he drew many of his recruits from the ranks of the Free Corps. By 1923, 70,000 armed and uniformed Nazis had rallied to the swastika standard.

By then, also, Germany was on her knees. France, angered at German failure to make reparations payment, had invaded the Ruhr, the industrial heart of Germany. In retaliation, German workers went on strike, and the result was that a stumbling economy lurched to a halt. Inflation followed. By late 1923 German currency was literally not worth the paper that it was printed on. Workers carried their salaries home in wheelbarrows. To mail a letter to the United States cost a billion marks, and a single American dollar could buy a mountain of marks measured in 13 figures.

Here was the chaos on which Fascism thrives. In Munich, Hitler gained a distinguished recruit: Erich von Ludendorff, already sunk into paganism and half-mad with worship of Thor. Hitler and Ludendorff plotted the overthrow of the Bavarian provincial government, after which they would seize power nationally. On the night of November 8, 1923, amidst a mass rally of monarchists and nationalists in the Burgerbrau beer hall, Hitler pushed the speaker from the podium, drew a pistol, fired two shots into the ceiling and shouted that the revolution had begun.

As his Nazis raced to bar the doors, Hitler drew the Bavarian leaders aside and begged them to join him. He wept as he talked, waving his pistol in one hand, a beer stein in the other. At that moment, in strode Ludendorff in full and bemedaled uniform. The Bavarians pretended to fall in with Hitler, but, during a night of wild rioting, they quietly melted away, and in the morning Hitler and his Nazis attempted the *putsch* or coup on their own.

Led by Hitler and Ludendorff, they got as far as the main square. There, massed soldiers and police opened fire. Sixteen Nazis fell dead, Hitler broke his shoulder diving for cover, and Ludendorff kept on going through a lane which the police obligingly opened so that the First Quartermaster General might march unscathed out of German history and into hilltop communion with Wotan. For his part in the abortive "Beer Hall Putsch," Hitler was sentenced to five years in the Fortress of Landsberg.

The Landsberg was Hitler's Wartburg. He served only 13 months there, but it was time enough in which to begin to set down his convictions and his course of action in the turgid and often raving work called *Mein Kampf* (*My Struggle*). Hitler repudiated both capitalism and Communism. Both had an economic base, he believed, both were the enemies of excellence, both destroyed the race. Against the common man of democracy Hitler opposed an elite, against Communism's termite man the hero. "Men do not die for business but for ideals," he wrote, and again: "The greatness of the Aryan is not based on his intellectual powers; but rather on his willingness to devote all his faculties to the service of the community. . . . The renunciation of one's own life for the sake of the community is the crowning significance of the idea of all sacrifice. . . . Posterity will not remember those who pursued only their own individual interests, but it will praise those heroes who renounced their own happiness."[18] There they were, the triple supports of the crooked black cross of Nazi Fascism: race, sacrifice and heroism. In Nazi theology, race was deified, sacrifice sanctified and heroism made holy.

Yet it would not be wise to sneer at Hitler's exaltation of sacrifice as the puerile outpourings of a hero worshiper or a cynical propaganda stunt intended to hypnotize a romantic race. Hitler's gospel appealed not only to the uprooted and the disinherited, the dim-witted and the brutal, but to much that was noble and brave. Postwar Germany was filled with despair. The surrounding world seemed devoid of value. Both Communism and capitalism alike seemed to worship at the altar of mammon, and where democracy put man in the place of God, Socialism put the body before the soul. Nationalism—the race—did seem to be worth dying for, worth sacrificing for. Unfortunately, Nazism put the race before mankind, thereby debasing all sacrifice in its name, and Hitler's hero, so far from being heroic—neither noble pagan, Hebrew prophet nor Christian saint—was actually only a battlefield berserker straight out of the crashing cymbals and horns of Richard Wagner. He was Siegfried riding along the Rhine, and he was, as Hitler might have suspected, galloping straight toward *Götterdämmerung,* the dusk of the gods.

Still, when Hitler came back from the Landsberg, his concept of an earthly Valhalla rallied to his side that band of lieutenants who were to become world-famous. There was Hermann Goering, a flying hero of the last war who would one day command the German Luftwaffe and also become the obese and gaudy swashbuckler whom the German General Staff derided as "the fat boy." There was nothing derisive about Heinrich Himmler. The Chief of the Gestapo was a neat little sparrow of a man, given to rimless glasses, plain suits and the systematic torture and murder of millions of human beings. Dr. Joseph Goebbels looked much more sinister, with his club foot, his oversize upper lip and piercing eyes staring out of his big head. Goebbels, a failure as a writer, would be minister of propaganda and would drench the world in all the Nazi nonsense of the superrace. As such, Goebbels is perhaps the apotheosis of the writer who becomes published, not through the power of his writing, but through power alone.

With this crowd at his back, Hitler, a pasty-faced, dumpy, malevolent, teetotaling and vegetarian mystic, set out to enchant and enslave the race of poets and philosophers. How was it possible? First, what Churchill has called "the prejudice of the Americans against monarchy"[19] had deprived postwar Germany of a father figure to replace the vanished Kaiser. With no experience of true representative government, the Germans erected a shaky republic which was blown upon by the evil winds of Versailles, the French invasion of the Ruhr, an inflation which wiped out the middle class, an influx of high-interest foreign loans and the Great Depression which followed the collapse of the American stock market.

Politically shrewd, Hitler rang every change on these themes. Whenever German economic fortunes rose, his political stock sank, and vice versa. In the end, the depression delivered the knockout blow. In 1932 the Nazis gained nearly 40 percent of the total popular vote, which made them the most powerful party in Germany, and they made it impossible for any other party or coalition to rule. Like the Communists, they would work with others only to undermine or take over. On January 30, 1933, the aging, senile Paul von Hindenburg, President of the republic, called on Hitler to fill the office of Chancellor.

Now the Nazis prepared to hang the republic with a rope of Nazi laws. In June of 1934 Hitler purged the party in a brutal blood bath known as "The Night of the Long Knives." Ernst Roehm, the man who had built the Storm Troops, was murdered along with hundreds of others. With Roehm out of the way, Hitler was able to assure the German General Staff that it need not worry about a second army in Germany. Hitler also ingratiated himself with the industrialists. Like Mussolini, his Fascist state seemed to be making a strong and healthy Germany, while all around her the democracies were starving weaklings. On August 2 Hindenburg died—and that was representative government's last gasp. Hitler abolished the office of president and proclaimed himself *der Führer,* the Leader of the German people.

"Ein Volk, ein Reich, ein Führer!" he cried. "One race, one realm, one leader!"

Racial unity was to be achieved, first of all, by extermination of the Jews. It began unofficially in 1933, and in 1935 it became official when a law was passed stripping Jews of all their rights. They were less than slaves. Anyone with a grievance against a Jew might take it out without fear of legal restraint. Armed with this law, Herr Himmler set to work on what eventually came to be called "the final solution of the Jewish question," and after the Nazi career of conquest was begun, "the final solution" also fell like a death sentence upon the Jewish communities in the conquered countries.

To the Nazis, merely to have been born with Jewish blood was a crime. There was no escaping it; no act of renunciation, even if desired, was possible. Perhaps the most famous demonstration of this inescapable judgment was in the case of Edith Stein, the German philosopher who became a Roman Catholic nun, took refuge in a convent in Holland, and there was hunted down, seized and taken to her death. It was genocide, the systematic murder of an entire race. Subjected to every indignity, dragged from their homes, spat upon, beaten, forced to lick the streets with their tongues, the Jews were herded into concentration camps, there to await the final end of starvation, degradation and indecent death. In all, six million Jews were sacrificed to Adolf Hitler's insane hatred.

Christianity also felt Hitler's wrath. A faith preaching the brotherhood of man under the fatherhood of God was anathema to a leader demanding faith in himself and preaching the gospel of racial supremacy. Therefore Protestants and Catholics were also persecuted, and the campaign against the Catholic clergy was distinguished for its obscene cunning. So that the soul, not the body, of Catholicism might be destroyed, priests and nuns were brought into court to answer the falsest and foulest charges, which a lackey press dutifully circulated throughout the nation. In the end, however, Hitler's anti-Christian campaign failed, and with the coming of war it disappeared.

With these persecutions, which shocked and outraged the outside world, and which drove many of the best minds and souls out of Germany, the Fuehrer strengthened his hold upon the German people. It was as though his baleful nature had entered into communion with some dark spirit slumbering beneath the veneer of civilization. His power to exalt the German masses was unbelievable. Using Wagnerian stagecraft yoked to mob psychology, Hitler emerged not only as a cherished father figure but as Herr Gott. After he had won over the German generals, he insisted upon a personal oath of loyalty which went:

"I swear before God to give my unconditional obedience to Adolf Hitler, Fuehrer of the Reich of the German People, Supreme Commander of the Wehrmacht [armed forces], and I pledge my word as a brave soldier to observe this oath always, even at peril of my life."

After this oath was administered to the generals by their inferiors, Rudolf Hess, Hitler's alter ego, informed the German nation: "By this oath we again bind our lives to a man, through whom—this is our belief—superior forces act in fulfillment of Destiny. Do not seek Adolf Hitler with your brains; all of you will find him with the strength of your hearts. Adolf Hitler is Germany and Germany is Adolf Hitler. Germany is our God on earth."[20] And in a roar of ecstasy, the masses thundered back:

"Heil Hitler!"

4

☆

While Fascism marched, democracy slept—and nowhere more soundly than in the United States of America. Having raised an army of four million men and sent half of them abroad, having accepted all forms of restraint, Americans now hastened to disarm, to throw off the wartime bonds and to have a good time.

"Back to normalcy," President Warren G. Harding called it, by which he meant back to the womb. It was a suffocating, self-indulgent womb which sheltered this decade styling itself the Torrid Twenties. Actually, the twenties were rather more tepid or terrified. Fear of Bolshevism provoked the hysteria of the "Red raids" conducted by Attorney General A. Mitchell Palmer. Radicals and aliens suspected of subversive activities were rounded up, and 150 of them were summarily deported to Russia. America, an observer reported, was "hag-ridden by the specter of Bolshevism. . . . Property was in an agony of fear, and the horrid name 'Radical' covered the most innocent departure from conventional thought with a suspicion of desperate purposes."[21]

Meanwhile, America not only turned her back on the world, but also, restricting immigration and raising tariffs, built racial and economic barriers between herself and the outside. Prohibition, that "noble experiment" which imposed a minority's moral convictions on the nation, and thereby made a public crime out of a private foible, provoked such a reaction that much of America fell over backward into a binge of bootleg booze and bathtub gin. The twenties also were characterized by the promiscuity styled the "Sexual Revolution" and by a widespread movement to "debunk" war.

The debunkers told the nation that all that mud, misery and mayhem had been in vain. But in insisting that modern war is not glorious, as William Tecumseh Sherman had made plain a half-century earlier, they also intimated that it was not efficacious. Many of these writers had fought in a bloody stalemate, and they had the idea that all wars are bloody stalemates. But war can be efficacious, and, up until World War I, in no history had it been more so than in the American. Unfortunately, Mr. Wilson's propaganda mill had ground out the monstrosity of "the war to end all wars," and his frenzy factory had made everyone believe it. Such, of course, is no more possible than a peace which makes everyone peaceful; yet the American nation had believed it down deep in their bones, and to have been thwarted in that belief left them disillusioned and eager to believe that "war is the bunk."

Under the three Presidents who held office during the Republican ascendancy of 1921-33, isolationism became so firmly imbedded in the public mind that no other attitude seemed possible. Harding had declared that the nation needed "not submergence in internationality but sustainment in triumphant nationality,"[22] and that position helped him to defeat the internationalist Democrat, James M. Cox, in 1920. Harding, incidentally, might easily challenge Millard Fillmore for the crown of presidential mediocrity. Like his "big bow-wow style of oratory," he was large, impressive and shallow. His easy morals and low tastes fairly accurately reflected national standards, and Alice Roosevelt Longworth has described how, visiting the White House once occupied by her father, she went upstairs to find that "trays with bottles containing every imaginable brand of whiskey stood about" in "a general atmosphere of waistcoat unbuttoned, feet on the desk, and spittoon alongside."[23] If she had looked downstairs, she might have found Harding's young mistress being smuggled in the back door and bundled into a cloakroom.

In 1923, alarmed by the financial scandals that shook his administration, Harding tried to recover his waning popularity with a speaking tour across the continent. En route home from Alaska, he fell painfully ill of eating tainted crabs, and on the night of August 2 he died of apoplexy.

His successor, Calvin Coolidge, became the fifth Vice President to move into the White House. Though a man of high moral integrity under whom the Harding scandals were liquidated and prosperity returned to the nation, Coolidge was a colorless small-town lawyer whose political career was "a shining example of what inertia could do for a man of patience."[24] His most famous remark was: "The business of America is business."[25] It remained that way after "Silent Cal" defeated the Democrat, John W. Davis, in 1924, and also held off a party rebellion under the Progressives of Robert La Follette. Only one ray of internationalist light ever penetrated the isolationist night of Coolidge's administration, and this was the false dawn of the Kellogg-Briand Pact. Under American initiative, eventually 62 nations (including Germany, Italy and Japan) signed this pact and thus solemnly agreed that they would not resort to war as an instrument of national policy. But Kellogg-Briand was an empty handshake. The pact bound no one, it employed no sanctions and it set up no machinery to settle international disputes. Worse, having chloroformed any remaining qualms about national responsibility, it sent the nation off to sleep happily convinced that the big bad wolf of war had at last been banished from everybody's door.

By 1928 isolationism was so automatically "American" that neither the Republican Herbert Hoover nor the Democrat Alfred E. Smith, the first Roman Catholic to receive a presidential nomination, bothered to discuss it. Instead, the campaign became disfigured by an outpouring of bigotry upon Smith and his faith, and Hoover, who would have won without the raising of the religious issue, was elected.

Herbert Hoover was a good and sincere man whose great capacities for administration were often hampered by his incapacity to harmonize conflicting interests. In other words, he was not a politician. Nor had his world travels altered an ingrained isolationism. Instead, they had convinced him that Old World and New World concepts were hopelessly hostile. Moreover, during his first year in office the stock market collapsed, the great and terrible depression began, and domestic problems became paramount. Finally, his Quaker religion disposed him to look upon all forms of violence with horror, so that, when Japan made her inevitable move against China in 1931, he ruled out any hint of the use of force to restrain her. Instead, he settled for "moral condemnation." The United States would not recognize any changes in China that conflicted with either the Open Door policy or 'the Kellogg-Briand Pact. Japan feared moral censure about as much as a wolf fears a shepherd's whistle, and since the shepherd's stick was nowhere in evidence, she continued to consolidate her position in the Chinese province of Manchuria. Disheartened, the League of Nations declined the Japanese challenge.

The defeat of Hoover in 1932 by the buoyant Franklin Delano Roosevelt did not signal the end of isolationism. Roosevelt, once a fervent internationalist, had modified his position. Indeed, economic paralysis at home had to be and was his chief concern, and it was of this only that he thought when he uttered that electric inaugural sentence: "First of all, let me assert my firm belief that the only thing we have to fear is fear itself."[26] The dictators, however, ultimately drew FDR's eyes outward.

In 1935 Italian troops invaded little Ethiopia on the east coast of Africa, as Mussolini commenced the re-evocation of the Roman Empire. Halfhearted economic sanctions by the League did nothing to deter him. That same year, the coal-rich, German-speaking Saar voted 90 percent to return to Germany, and Hitler repudiated all arms limitations imposed by Versailles and in direct violation of that treaty created the Luftwaffe. In 1936 his troops occupied the demilitarized zone of the Rhineland. Again he violated Versailles, and again the Western powers stood still. Also in 1936, General Francisco Franco raised the standard of revolt against the leftist republican government of Spain. Thus began the terrible and bloody Spanish Civil War, in which both Hitler and Mussolini, and Premier Stalin of Russia, seized the opportunity to train their armed forces in a real war. The Fascists sent arms and men to Franco, while the Communists eventually took over the Loyalist cause. Although the democracies were in the main sympathetic to the Loyalists, they did not intervene for fear that to do so would bring on World War II. They adopted a position of strict neutrality.

So did the United States, where the "revelations" of the Nye Committee had already put a neutrality law on the books. In 1934 the isolationist Senator Gerald Nye demonstrated on the basis of specious evidence that America entered World War I "to save the skins of American bankers who had bet too boldly on the outcome of the war." While this position was arguable, it was an absurd simplification. Nevertheless, the Nye report gave an official or "scientific" cast to the debunking movement and seemed to prove for all time that wars are fought to fatten profiteers and munitions-makers. Out of it was born neutrality legislation which placed an embargo on arms to all belligerents, ordered all belligerents who bought goods in America to pay for them on delivery and cart them away in their own vessels (cash-and-carry), banned loans to belligerents and forbade American citizens to travel in belligerent ships.

Such legislation, passed in 1936 and after, was eminently fitted to prevent the war of 1917. Like Prohibition with drink, it was an attempt to legislate war out of existence, and while it was being made, Franco triumphed in Spain and the Japanese moved deeper into China. Among Japan's excesses in 1937 was the infamous "rape of Nanking" during which Chinese mothers were forced to watch the beheading of their babies and then to submit to rape. Though horrified, Americans did not act. Nor did they throw off their isolationist fixation when the Japanese with contemptuous deliberation bombed and sank the American gunboat *Panay* in the Yangtze River. Not American ire, but Japanese second thoughts about American oil and scrap iron, produced an apology and an indemnity.

President Roosevelt and a few of his Cabinet members saw the danger. In 1937 Roosevelt called for a "quarantine" against aggressor nations. If international lawlessness was not checked, he warned: "Let no one imagine that America will escape, that America may expect mercy, that this Western Hemisphere will not be attacked."[27] The nation, however, was not listening.

In Europe the dictators were moving toward formation of the Axis which Japan eventually joined in a Berlin-Rome-Tokyo hookup, and Hitler, following the course forecast two decades earlier by Lloyd George, had embarked on his career of *Anschluss,* or reunion. German communities planted in the buffer states by the men of Versailles were to be the strings by which Hitler yanked these nations inside his Third Reich.

The techniques were to become familiar. Nazi agents in the target countries were to excite the Germanic aspirations of the detached communities, to undermine the government and to create the crisis which would give Hitler his pretext for a takeover. Where possible, the countries would be bullied into *Anschluss;* where not, force would be used. Since *Anschluss* included Austria, Hitler moved first against his native land. In 1938 his troops crossed the border, and in a plebiscite or free election conducted with most of the country held in the Nazi fist, Austrians voted nearly 100 percent for *Anschluss.*

Next came the German Sudetenland within the boundaries of Czechoslovakia. After Hitler announced that he intended to "protect" the Sudetan Germans against all Czech "atrocities," the governments of Britain and France rushed not to the side of the nation they had created and guaranteed but to placate Hitler. At a conference in Munich in September, 1938, all Hitler's demands were accepted by Prime Minister Neville Chamberlain of Britain and Premier Edouard Daladier of France. Hitler promised that he would make no more land grabs in Europe, and Chamberlain wrote out a pledge of Anglo-German friendship which Hitler signed with the customary fidelity which he reserved for "scraps of paper." Chamberlain waved this document in front of a cheering crowd in London, and said: "I believe it is peace for our time."[28]

To such British leaders as Winston Churchill it was rather war "for our time," and Hitler's Nazi agents were already at work manufacturing the crisis which paved the way for the ultimate takeover of Czechoslovakia. On March 15, 1939, Hitler entered Prague in triumph. A brave and vigorous nation, one of the finest small armies in Europe, and the giant Skoda arsenal were his. He had gained them without firing a shot, merely by capitalizing on the spirit of appeasement that had palsied the hand of the West; and by penetrating the Czech mountain fortress line he had secured his southeastern flank.

Looking north to the Baltic, Hitler next demanded and received the return of the port of Memel, then in Lithuanian hands. Now it was Mussolini's turn. Jealous of the Fuehrer's success, the Duce overwhelmed his little neighbor of Albania across the Adriatic Sea. Obviously, the Axis promise to seize no more land could not be taken seriously, yet from the United States came a cable from President Roosevelt asking Hitler and Mussolini to promise no more aggression for the next 10 or 25 years. Mussolini read the appeal and snapped, "A result of infantile paralysis!"[29] The remark was a scornful reference to the disease which had crippled the President, and it was typical of the Axis contempt for the democracies.

Democratic dissent and political freedom were to them the marks
of degenerate anarchy. They believed that the Allies had lost the
will to fight. Mussolini was very much impressed when British youths
of the Oxford Union passed in 1933 the shameless Joad Resolution
which resolved: "That this House will in no circumstances fight for
its King and Country."[30] Of the British nation of 1939, the Duce
said: "These men are not made of the same stuff as Francis Drake
and the other magnificent English adventurers who created the Empire. They are, after all, the tired sons of a long line of rich men."[31]
Mussolini mistakenly believed that Axis muscle had terrified the
democracies, when, in fact, they had been distracted by the depression.
France had been weakened by the recurrent crises which were endemic
to her multiple-party system, as well as her politicians' infinite capacity
for hating each other; and the eyes of Britain had been turned inward
by the abdication of King Edward VIII, in order to marry the twice-
divorced American, Mrs. Wallis Warfield Simpson., The Fuehrer
shared Mussolini's delusion, extending it to Americans with the remark: "There's nobody more stupid than the Americans. . . . I'll never
believe the American soldier can fight like a hero."[32]

In truth, there was nothing very frightening in the image America
presented to the world. The twenties had seen Americans preoccupied
with themselves, after which the depression had appeared to knock
them flat. And the spirit of isolationism had culminated, in 1938,
in the ludicrous Ludlow Amendment proposing a constitutional
change that would make any declaration of war subject to a popular
referendum! The spectacle of a menaced nation springing to the
ballot box must have seemed merry indeed to both Fuehrer and Duce,
and if the Joad Resolution was the work of foolish boys misled by
a pacifist professor, the Ludlow Amendment was the considered
wisdom of an American Congressman, and when it was returned to
committee by a House vote of 209-188, it fell only 21 votes short of
consideration by the whole Congress. So America remained isolationist, convinced that she was blessed by two oceans guarding her shores
like moats, thereby convincing the Axis that she would not again enter
a European war.

By the spring of 1939 that war became a certainty. On March 31
Britain and France guaranteed Poland and Rumania against aggression. By this act, World War II was assured. The Allies, of course,
were not to blame for it, although their timid spirit of appeasement

certainly made it inevitable. Hitler *could* have been stopped when he should have been stopped: when he reoccupied the Rhineland and began to rearm. Now Hitler was the stronger, and just as he turned upon Poland with his demand for return of the Polish Corridor, the Allies moved to stop him. They could not possibly help Poland. They were simply too far away and could only assist her with Soviet Russia as their partner. But Russia, ignored at Munich in an area vital to her security, was already moving toward a *rapprochement* with Germany.

On August 23 Stalin signed a nonaggression pact with Hitler. The free world was stupefied. Fascism and Communism—mortal enemies —had joined hands. What had happened, of course, was that Hitler and Stalin had agreed to a deal which each hoped would undo the other. Stalin would not interfere with Hitler while he plundered Poland, in return for which favor Stalin would receive half of the booty; nor would Stalin hamper Hitler when he turned from Poland to deal with Britain and France. Stalin was not so naïve as not to suspect that Hitler intended to attack him after he had disposed of the democracies. Hitler's program of *Lebensraum* required the acquisition of European Russia. Stalin was also buying time in which to rearm and to reorganize an army demoralized by a series of purges, which, for brutality and ruthlessness, were at least the equal of any conducted by Hitler. Nor would it be too much to suspect in Stalin a cynical hope that his hyena partner and the Allies might exhaust themselves in France, as in the last war, whereupon he would wolf them all down. Unfortunately for Stalin and the West, however, the Fuehrer had no intention of fighting a second World War I.

If it is true that justice frequently deserts the camp of the victor, so also does self-criticism. Having won, the victor is often content with what won for him, but the vanquished wants to know why he lost. This was true of the Allies and the Germans after World War I. France expected to fight defensive warfare and built her Maginot Line all along the Rhine. Britain anticipated a renewal of economic warfare, that is, another blockade supported by "strategic bombing" of enemy industrial centers and populations. But the Germans saw that the stalemate of trench warfare had been their undoing and they formulated the blitzkrieg or lightning war. Many ingredients went into this martial mixture: the tactics of "infiltration" which had not quite succeeded in the 1918 offensive, a study of the American Civil War with strong emphasis on the campaigns of Stonewall Jackson, and a realization that by yoking guns to internal combustion engines the mechanical revolution had conferred a great velocity upon the offensive. Finally, the Germans seized upon the very tactics which this radical change had called forth from the minds of such Allied military thinkers as Liddell Hart, Fuller, de Gaulle and Martel. This was to attack the "brains" rather than the "body" of an army. By "brains" are meant the commanding generals and staff officers in the rear areas of division, corps and army headquarters, by "body" the soldiery manning the fighting front. If the brains are destroyed, the body becomes a disorganized and demoralized mass, much like (there is no better image) a chicken with its head cut off. Moreover, as Fuller advocated to Foch in his famous "Plan 1919," the brains had to be knocked out *before* the body was attacked.

The weapon to accomplish this was the tank, the tank formed into armored divisions supported by fighters and dive bombers which were to break through the enemy front at selected points and make straight for the command posts in the rear. After them would come the slower-moving formations to mop up the leaderless and terrified foe. This, then, was the blitzkrieg of the Germans under the leadership of the new Attila, Adolf Hitler.

For all his lies, murder and hate-mad frenzies, much as some historians may dismiss him as an "uneducated paranoiac" or a "vulgarian vandal," Hitler had some exceptional military insights. "Who says I'm going to start a war like those fools in 1914?" he cried. "Are not all our efforts bent toward preventing this? Most people have no imagination. . . . They are blind to the new, the surprising things. Even the generals are sterile. They are imprisoned in the coils of their technical knowledge. The creative genius stands always outside the circle of the experts."[33] This was more than the raving of an "irrational fanatic"; rather, it reflected the convictions of a military visionary who had added to the blitzkrieg theory of striking the enemy's rear his own special concept of striking the enemy's will. Sherman had done it in Georgia, and Hitler would do it in Europe—but *before* the war began.

"The enemy people must be demoralized and ready to capitulate, driven into moral passivity, before military action can even be thought of. . . . We shall have friends who will help us in all the enemy countries. We shall know how to obtain such friends. Mental confusion, contradiction of feeling, indecisiveness, panic: these are our weapons."[34]

There it was, total, amoral war, and the world had certainly come a long way since the thirteenth century when the Lateran Council naïvely banned crossbows as being contrary to the laws of God and morality. Crossbows, of course, were used, as has been every weapon ever contrived by the mind of man; and Adolf Hitler was also going to use everything that he had. He was the only leader in Europe with a set purpose and the means to achieve it: *Lebensraum* and blitzkrieg.

So August of 1939 came to Europe as it had come during that hot and fateful August of 1914. Battle lines were drawn, armies were expanding, soldiers drilling, tanks went clanking through streets, airplanes were parked in rows on the airfields, buildings were sandbagged and trenches dug in the parks, and gas masks were issued to civilian populations. This time no spark was needed to detonate the powder keg. Hitler wanted war, and he told his generals: "I am afraid that some pig-dog will make a proposal for mediation as at Munich." Screaming at them, "Close your hearts to pity! Act brutally!" he declared: "I shall give a propagandist reason for starting the war, whether it is plausible or not. The victor will not be asked, later on, whether he told the truth or not. In starting and waging a war it is not Right that matters, but Victory."[35]

On the last night of August, acting on the Fuehrer's orders, Herr Himmler faked an "incident" on the Polish border. Next morning, the German spearheads went crashing into Poland.

5

☆

Poland possessed an army of about 1,700,000 men with which to halt about 800,000 German invaders. But she had a very small air force—about 450 airplanes to 1,400 being used by the Germans—and almost no mechanized formations. Moreover, Poland relied too much on sheer courage and the distraction of an Allied attack from the west.

Britain and France did declare war on September 3, 1939, but out of this came only a few French patrols from the Maginot Line, after which the defense-minded French retired to their forts. By then, too, nothing could be done to save Poland.

Within 48 hours the German Luftwaffe had annihilated the Polish air force. Surprised on the ground, Polish aircraft were destroyed with scarcely as much as a single air battle. Antiaircraft installations were knocked out, complete mastery of the skies fell to the Luftwaffe, and with that the German armored or Panzer divisions were free to roll without fear of air attack.

Roll they did, spearheading two huge German armies smashing into Poland from north and south. Clattering deep into the Polish rear, they overran the command posts as they were supposed to do, and they struck at Polish nerve centers: road and railway junctions, bridges, telegraph stations, tunnels and airfields. The emphasis was on penetration, the deeper the better, for with command of the air the Panzers did not fear being cut off and chopped up piecemeal. The slow-moving Polish Army, geared to the past, was literally knocked brainless within two days. Polish cavalry attacked tanks, and went down in kicking, screaming confusion. Polish soldiers fought with traditional bravery. But they were leaderless and fragmented. Powerless to form a continuous front, the roaring enemy tanks brushed them aside and left them to be destroyed or imprisoned by the German infantry and artillery following about 20 miles in the German rear.

In the Polish rear, the Luftwaffe was systematically completing destruction of Polish communications. Stuka dive bombers protected by Messerschmitt fighters struck at railroads and railway junctions, at troop columns and motor transport, rail depots and radio stations. Polish troop concentrations were broken up. Polish commanders found it impossible to make orderly troop withdrawals, or to receive reinforcements.

So efficient were the Germans that they carefully refrained from the destruction of bridges or roads that would be needed during the advance, and everywhere they went they had the assistance of some two million German civilians who lived in the battle zone and could be counted upon to give precise information on Polish positions and intentions. Polish civilians, meanwhile, were scourged by the

EUROPEAN - NORTH AFRICAN
THEATERS OF WORLD WAR II

[:::]	Allied Nations
[///]	The Axis Powers, September, 1939
[ ]	Maximum extent of Axis expansion
[\\\]	Vichy French areas occupied by the Allies in 1941-1942, and held to end of the war.
[ ]	Neutral Nations
—·—·—	National Boundaries as of September, 1939
············	Pre-Anschluss Austrian and Czechoslovakian boundaries
— — —	Boundary of Vichy France

0   100   200   300   400   500
Scale of Miles

Murmansk

Arctic   Circle

White Sea   Archangel

FINLAND   Lake Onega

Helsinki   Lake Ladoga
Gulf of Finland
Leningrad
ESTONIA   Volga R.

LATVIA   ● Moscow

LITHUANIA

U.   S.   S.   R.

Dnieper R.   Don R.   Volga R.   Aral Sea

POLAND   Kiev   Kharkov   Stalingrad
Maximum

U K R A I N E   Don R.   eastward Axis expansion

Dniester R.   Rostov

Sea of Azov   C A S P I A N   S E A

RUMANIA   CRIMEA   ● Yalta

Bucharest
Danube R.   B L A C K   S E A   Baku

BULGARIA
Sofia

Istanbul

GREECE   ● Ankara   ● Teheran
Aegean Sea
Athens   T U R K E Y   I R A N

CRETE   RHODES   Euphrates R.
CYPRUS   S Y R I A   Baghdad   Tigris R.

N   S E A   I R A Q

PERSIAN GULF

Tobruk   PALESTINE   TRANS
Alexandria   JORDAN
El Alamein   Suez Canal   S A U D I

Cairo

E G Y P T   Nile R.   A R A B I A

Red Sea

Schrecklichkeit or "frightfulness" deliberately calculated to force them onto the roads where their terrified masses would foul Polish ground movement. Stukas with whistles in their wings fell screaming on the cities, units of paratroopers were dropped into the countryside to spread sabotage and terror, and fighters flew at treetop level to machine-gun refugees on the roads.

It has been said that Poland might have defended herself more ably if she had fallen back from her long, indefensible western border to a good fighting position east of Warsaw. But the fact was that inside this Polish salient exposed to German assault from west, north and south was most of the nation's industrial plant, as well as her coal fields and oil refineries. To have surrendered these would have been to surrender her lifeblood. So Poland's fingers were pried one by one from the salient until, on September 17, the Russians delivered the decisive stab in the back. On that date, in accordance with Stalin's secret agreement with Hitler, the Soviet Army invaded Poland from the east. Caught between two fires, with no help forthcoming from her Allies, Poland was helpless. On September 27 the last resistance in Warsaw ended, and on the following day Joachim von Ribbentrop of Germany and Vyacheslav Molotov of Russia met across the butcher's table.

Germany took most of Poland's mines and factories, almost half of her 150,000 square miles and 22 of her 35 million people. Russia took the rest, together with most of Poland's oil resources. With his eastern flank now securely resting on a prostrate Poland and a friendly Russia, Hitler turned west.

After the tragedy of the blitzkrieg in Poland came the comedy of the "sitzkrieg" in France. On October 6 Hitler had asked France and Britain to end the war on the basis of his having "settled" the Polish question. The Allies refused and so began the sitzkrieg or "sitdown war," the six-month lull between the fall of Poland and Hitler's attack on Norway and Denmark in April, 1940.

It was also called the "Phony War," because the French Army and the British Expeditionary Force sat comfortably still inside the Maginot Line while the Germans opposite them did the same in the Siegfried Line. The B.E.F. did not suffer a casualty until December 9, and by Christmas the total French casualties on land, sea and air were 1,433. So far from bombing each other, the rival air forces spent their time showering enemy soldiers with propaganda leaflets. Stalemate had come again to the Western front, and most military experts predicted an Allied victory brought about by the holding action of the huge French Army and the attrition of the British blockade.

Hitler, however, was moving on schedule. His industrial mobilization had not yet achieved peak output, a condition which he deemed essential for an attack on France, and he was not only moving his formations westward at his leisure, but also training them in the successful tactics of the blitzkrieg. He wanted more and more tanks, and the artillery also needed to be motorized. Moreover, it was now Premier Stalin's turn.

Hitler had already assured Stalin that the four Baltic states of Estonia, Latvia, Lithuania and Finland should fall within the Soviet sphere of influence. By threat of naked force Stalin compelled the first three to accept treaties preparing them for outright annexation. Finland alone refused to submit, and the enraged Russian press protested that the ferocious Finns were planning to attack peace-loving Russia. This would be like a beaver assaulting a bear, for in Finland there were 4 million people to 180 million in Russia, and an army of 33,000 men with a handful of tanks and 60 aircraft opposing one of 1,500,000 men, 9,000 tanks and 10,000 aircraft. Yet, in "self-defense," Russia invaded Finland on November 30, 1939.

About 100,000 troops moving over five routes began one of the most astonishing invasions in history. Convinced by Communist propaganda that they would be welcomed as "liberators," some Russian battalions marched across the border behind brass bands. Others came laden with banners and propaganda leaflets. Certain of swift success, they wore light clothing and were thus ill-clothed for the Finnish winter, just as they were ill-equipped for fighting in the Finnish forests or around the countless Finnish lakes. Least of all were they prepared for the ferocity of the Finnish defense.

Under Field Marshal Karl von Mannerheim the Finns fell back to lure the Russian spearheads deep into snow forests or onto frozen lakes. Then they struck. They attacked first this column, then another. One Finnish force would hit and hold the Russian front while others slashed at the flanks and rear. They cut up the Russian units and devoured them piecemeal. Finnish ski troopers clad in white sped over the forest snows like wrathful wraiths, halting columns, shooting up supply columns, cutting off stragglers and sometimes so thoroughly isolating entire brigades that the Russians were forced to supply them by air.

Finnish resistance provoked world-wide admiration. For a time France and Britain considered coming to Finland's aid, and in the United States there was much righteous admiration for the only nation which had paid her war debts. This amused the Finns, although they were not amused when isolationist America refused to loan her money to buy arms in Sweden. Hitler, meanwhile, was delighted to witness the discomfiture of his ally, while Stalin was appalled. To break the will of the Finns, a redoubling of the bombing of civilians was ordered, and here came the first opportunity to test the second of two theories which had emerged from the mechanical revolution.

This was the concept of strategic bombing, which embraced not only aerial destruction of an enemy's war plant but also deliberate terrorizing of civilian populations through the bombing of cities. The latter, of course, is "frightfulness," and it is not a German idea at all. It was first formulated by the Italian General Giulio Douhet. Describing the terror which a single bombing raid might create in a single city, Douhet went on to declare that the bombardment of scores of cities could not fail to destroy order, halt production and drive a terrified populace into the countryside. Then, said Douhet: "The time would soon come when, to put an end to horror and suffering, the people themselves, driven by the instinct of self-preservation, would rise up and demand an end to the war—this before their army and navy had time to mobilize at all."[36] In other words, wars of the future were to be won by air forces alone.

In Britain the powerful allure of this idea led to the first independent flying service, the Royal Air Force, and in the United States the Army took its aircraft away from its Signal Corps and created the Army Air Corps. Proponents of strategic bombing multiplied, and the concept gained such a notable convert as Hermann Goering. However, in Poland air power was used only in the tactical sense. It was part of the blitzkrieg, it was the flying artillery that covered the Panzers. Frightfulness in the cities helped, but was far from decisive. Now, in Finland, with this redoubtable small nation refusing to collapse, the Russian Air Force had the opportunity to test air power's capacity to knock out a country from the air.

Helsinki and other Finnish cities were bombed for two weeks, but instead of breaking the Finnish will to fight, the Russian frightfulness succeeded only in strengthening it. So Russia had to resort to the conquest of Finland with an old-fashioned steamroller. Opposite the Mannerheim Line—the defensive belt built by the Finns on the Karelian Isthmus linking their country to Russia—the Communists massed 27 divisions and lined up artillery hub to hub. On February 2, 1940, after a shattering artillery bombardment, the assault began. For ten days the doughty Finns held firm, but then, three days later, the Mannerheim Line was breached, and when the Russian hordes debouched into the open plains, it was impossible for the little Finnish Army to contain them. On March 12 Finland accepted Russian terms. She had fought with consummate bravery and skill. She had lost 25,000 dead but had killed 200,000 Russians. Of more decisive importance in the history of World War II, Finland seemed to show Adolf Hitler that the Russian bear was a tame beast indeed.

There never was a Phony War at sea.

On the night of September 3, 1939—the very date that Britain and France declared war—a German U-boat rose from the black depths of the ocean about 250 miles off the coast of northwest Ireland to send a torpedo flashing into the side of the British passenger liner *Athenia*. Sinking slowly, *Athenia* was able to rescue all but 112 of the 1,417 persons aboard before she went down.

The German U-boat commander's excuse for this violation of international law was that *Athenia* was steaming without lights on a zigzag course, and he thought that she was an auxiliary cruiser. Nevertheless, world public opinion was again outraged, and nowhere more so than in the United States. Twenty-eight Americans had perished aboard *Athenia,* and Hitler, remembering the *Lusitania,* became so alarmed at American anger that submarine commanders were ordered to take no hostile action against passenger liners. In the meantime, to placate America, Goebbels declared that *Athenia* had been sunk by a bomb secretly placed aboard her on orders of Winston Churchill. Churchill, now First Lord of the Admiralty as he had been in the last war, laughed at the lie, but he could not laugh at the rising rate of British shipping losses. He feared that Hitler would do what the Kaiser had nearly done, cut off Britain from her sources of supply.

Churchill could not suspect that, even as in World War I, the German Submarine Service was commencing its operations as a Wehrmacht orphan from whom not too much was expected. In September of 1939 the Germans possessed only 56 submarines compared to the Anglo-French total of 141; and of these, only 46 were operational, with but 22 suitable for service in the Atlantic. Adolf Hitler did not begin the war relying on the U-boats to strangle Britain. Unlike the seagoing Kaiser, who was sometimes salty enough to veto the land-locked thinking of his generals, the Fuehrer had great difficulty comprehending sea power. "On land I am a hero," he said, "but on water I'm a coward."[37] Moreover, the exhausting character of under-sea attrition warfare was most unattractive to a Hitler given to blitzkriegs and intuitive, impulsive decisions. In fact, Hitler had steadfastly snubbed the Submarine Service. Two months before war broke out, Captain Karl Doenitz, its senior officer, informed Hitler that he had too few submarines for war with Britain. Hitler's reply was the bland assurance that there would be no war with Britain! So the generals and Air Marshal Goering continued to dominate Nazi strategy, and as late as 1943 the entire German Navy was restricted to allotments of less than 5 percent of German steel production. This blind spot in Hitler was to show up again and again, and it was, in the long run, one of the Allies' most valuable assets. If the Fuehrer had approved construction of only half of the 300 submarines requested by Doenitz, the history of World War II might have taken quite a different course.

As it was, with sometimes as few as five to seven U-boats operating at one time, but with this handful at the command of the resourceful Doenitz, the British Admiralty shivered for its lifelines. In the week following the sinking of *Athenia,* a dozen British ships were sent to the bottom. Then the mighty aircraft carrier *Courageous* was sunk, and Churchill, deciding not to risk any more of these valuable ships, withdrew the carriers from antisubmarine patrol and revived the convoy system. He improved it by adding aerial protection at either end. Still, the U-boats sank 67 Allied merchantmen in September-October. On a dark October night, the daring Commander Guenther Prien slipped into the great British naval base at Scapa Flow and sent the battleship *Royal Oak* to the bottom.

However, the convoy system was again killing U-boats. No less than 20 were destroyed in the September-October period. Such losses were appalling to Doenitz. He decided to attack British shipping around Gibraltar and to use the "wolf-pack" tactics evolved out of his own experience as a U-boat commander in World War I. This was to concentrate a number of U-boats in night surface attacks upon a convoy. Fortunately for the Allies, Doenitz did not get submarines in the numbers he required for such tactics, and until the spring of 1940 he had to be content with lone-wolf operations. Nevertheless, during the ensuing four months his submarines sank another 132 ships.

In the meantime, Doenitz ordered the U-boats to mine British territorial waters. British ships began to blow up as they left and entered port. Eventually, the alarmed Admiralty discovered that the Germans were using a new type of magnetic mine which was drawn to a ship's steel hull as the vessel passed over it. Not until one of these mines was recovered and disassembled did the British discover its secret. Then all ships were demagnetized by encircling them with electric cables. Gradually, shipping losses by mines diminished, but not until after 115 ships had been lost to them.

The third threat posed against British sea supremacy was the surface raiders of the German fleet. Hitler, of course, had never hoped to challenge the British Navy as the Kaiser's admirals had done at Jutland. British tonnage outweighed the German 2,000,000 to 235,-000 tons. However, the Germans possessed the pocket battleships *Deutschland, Admiral Scheer* and *Admiral Graf Spee,* as well as the battle cruisers *Scharnhorst* and *Gneisenau.* With these, the German Navy hoped to riddle the British blockading line of armed merchant cruisers. In November *Deutschland* sank one of these ships, and the British Navy gave chase. Try as they might, the British could not corner the elusive Germans. A rising volume of criticism of Churchill grew sharper after *Graf Spee* began to attack shipping off the coast of South America.

Considered one of the most beautiful ships in the world, with her strong clean lines and the unbroken sweep of her main deck, *Graf Spee* was like a wolf among sheep, bursting out of the ocean wastes with her 11-inch guns spouting doom, then vanishing over the horizon while the boiling white knuckle of water she left behind her testified to still another victim. In two months *Graf Spee* claimed nine ships.

On December 13, 1939, however, a trio of British cruisers caught up with the German raider off Rio de Janeiro. Mounting only 8-

or 6-inch guns, the gallant Britishers nevertheless gave battle. *Graf Spee's* 11-inchers knocked one of them out of action, but the other two hung on grimly, pursuing the German all the way down to Montevideo. Taking refuge in this neutral port, the German commander, Captain Hans Langsdorff, was notified that if he did not leave Uruguayan waters his ship would be interned. In the meantime, the British, reinforced by another heavy cruiser, had sealed off the mouth of the harbor. As Hitler had commanded, Langsdorff might have made a fighting breakout. But he exaggerated British strength, and he also hated Hitler. So he scuttled his great ship, and then, as a deliberate affront to the Fuehrer, he wrapped himself in the old Imperial German flag and shot himself.

With that, and with the French fleet in control of the Mediterranean, the first phase of the Battle of the Atlantic ended in favor of the Allies. It awaited the summer of 1940 and the advent of the ferocious wolf packs to begin the second phase, and in the meantime the Phony War came to an explosive end.

6

☆

As early as 1939 Hitler had ordered plans drawn up for the invasion of Norway and Denmark. He needed these countries for air and submarine bases on Norway's west coast, to control the Skagerrak passage from the Baltic into the North Sea, to lie athwart Britain's sea communications to northern Russia and to secure the Norwegian territorial waters down which vital Swedish iron ore was carried to Germany. The fact that Norway and Denmark were neutral nations was of little concern to him.

Faithful to his concept of subverting a nation's will to fight beforehand, Hitler subsidized the widespread Norwegian fifth-column*

---

* The word was coined by one of Franco's generals who said he would take Madrid with four columns of troops and a "fifth column" of Franco sympathizers within the city.

movement led by Major Vidkun Quisling. Quisling's mission was to seize Norwegian ports and airfields and hold them until German troops arrived.

On April 8, 1940, the Allies gave Hitler his pretext. They announced that on the previous night they had mined Norwegian waters to prevent the passage of German ore boats. It was a clear breach of neutrality, made with no intention of preventing German intervention in Norway, and Oslo protested. Before the Allies could reply, Hitler had moved.

On the morning of April 9, German armor rolled over the Danish border. Danes cycling to work in Copenhagen were astonished to encounter a column of steel-helmeted German soldiers marching on the Royal Palace. At first they thought that a movie was being made, until they heard the palace guard open fire and the Germans return it. That, however, was all the shooting in Denmark. Nazi agents had already cut off the kingdom from the outside world, and after the King told his guards to stop firing, Denmark was in Hitler's hands.

By nightfall of the same day Norway was on its way. Here the fifth columnists occupied the strategic port of Oslo, holding it for the arrival of airborne troops, while seaborne troops took four other important cities. At Oslo the port's harbor defenses rallied to sink the German cruiser *Blucher* and a smaller ship. But the assault from the sea went forward to put a period to the capture of the Norwegian capital.

At Narvik 800 miles to the north there was a short, sharp fight. Here the Nazis had planted a Trojan horse: ore boats secretly stuffed with soldiers left standing innocently in the harbor, until the assault force swept in behind ten destroyers and a pair of cruisers. Narvik also fell.

Meanwhile, as the Nazi troops began to move inland, Quisling seized the radio and proclaimed a government ruled by himself. His exhortations had little effect on his countrymen, who would one day execute him and make his name synonymous with the word for traitor, and many of them took up arms and fled Oslo with King Haakon to take refuge in the hills, there to fight on. Pursued by German aircraft and armored cars, they were bombed and machine-gunned while Haakon appealed to Britain for help.

With most of its ground forces committed in France, Britain could do little more than scrape together a pick-up force which was landed piecemeal in the vicinity of Trondheim. It was, unfortunately, a rash move made in the face of enemy control of the air. Under such conditions it could not be supported by the British fleet, and therefore should never have been attempted. The men who were put ashore were dumped into a miserable mire of snow and mud and systematically hacked to pieces by the Nazis. Four days after they landed, half of them were dead, and six days later the survivors were withdrawn. The only British success in the entire operation came when the battleship *Warspite* broke into the harbor at Narvik and pounded seven German destroyers beneath the waves.

In unequal exchange, however, Britain lost the aircraft carrier *Glorious* and two destroyers to the gunfire of *Scharnhorst* and *Gneisenau*. They went down on June 8, the last day of action in the Norwegian campaign. Once again, Hitler had won. Again, his blitzkrieg bore his own special stamp of precision, speed, daring and enemy demoralization. He had not only coordinated moves by land, sea and air, but by combining the concepts of Trojan horse with fifth column had shown his capacity to adopt from the past as well as adapt to the present.

Elated, Hitler had already hurled his third thunderbolt: the invasion of neutral Belgium, Holland and Luxembourg. With this, however, he brought into the field against him one of the few men in the world whom he respected, and the one he hated most: Winston Churchill. By his attacks on the Low Countries, Hitler had caused the downfall of the Chamberlain government. In its place stood Churchill, indomitable, jut-jawed and glowering, the living embodiment of embattled John Bull, and a leader who spoke of victory amid the ruins of defeat. "I have nothing to offer but blood, toil, tears, and sweat," he told Parliament on May 13. "Come, then, let us go forward with our united strength." Even at that moment, filled, as he said, "with buoyancy and hope,"[38] Churchill knew that Allied united strength was unraveling fast. Even then, as he called for victory and proclaimed a crusade against the "monstrous tyranny" of Nazism, Churchill realized that across the North Sea the Netherlands were falling.

On the night of May 9, 1940, Admiral Wilhelm Canaris, the anti-Nazi chief of German counterintelligence, informed the Dutch military attaché in Berlin that Holland was to be invaded at dawn. The message was dutifully transmitted to Amsterdam, and the Dutch considered themselves ready.

They planned to delay the Germans until help could come north from the French and British. To do this they were going to open the dikes and let the sea inundate the plains. Long ago, in the sixteenth century, the Dutch had thwarted the Spanish Duke of Alva in this fashion. Now in the twentieth century, they were going to drown the blitzkrieg by pulling a few levers, and then, after bridges were blown up, the Dutch soldiery would hold roadblocks and forts covering the vital road nets. It did not occur to the Dutch that the airplanes and parachutists of the twentieth century might move too fast for their fingers to reach the levers.

And they did. Out of the predawn darkness of the 10th of May came clouds of German paratroopers, floating to earth alongside the dikes and the canals. Some of them wore Allied uniforms, or the uniforms of Dutch policemen, postmen or railway guards. They carried machine guns and radios and rubber boats for crossing the canals. Assisted by Dutch fifth columnists, they seized the canal locks and water controls, secured the bridges, and opened to the waiting tanks the fair prospect of a dry level plain.

So the Panzer divisions went swarming over the lowlands, while above them the Luftwaffe swept the skies and added still another coat of tarnish to Hitler's green spurs by the deliberate bombing of Rotterdam, which the Dutch had declared an "open city." The Germans had stated on the 14th that unless the Dutch surrendered, Utrecht and Rotterdam would be bombed. Without waiting for a reply, they proceeded to reduce Rotterdam to ruins.

Demoralization in the Dutch Army was also being achieved by the bewildering number of enemy columns slashing for the key cities. The objective was a swift conquest which would provide the Germans with enough Dutch airfields to provide flanking air cover for the conquest of Belgium to the south. Most of the fields were taken from the air. First, bombers struck at medium levels to frighten Dutch antiaircraft gunners away from their stations. Next came dive bombers and strafing fighters to keep them underground, and finally the German paratroopers came down, "And so, when the defenders came up for air, they found themselves looking into the muzzles of tommy-guns."[39] Finally, all these gains were consolidated with the arrival of German infantry and artillery.

Although the Dutch fought bravely, Holland fell in five days, and the morgue of history prepared a slab for still another nation disarmed by its overconfidence in natural obstacles. Yet Dutch resistance lasted five times as long as the "battle" put up by tiny Luxembourg. With scarcely a platoon to defend her, Luxembourg buckled under the jack boot in a single day.

But in Belgium it seemed that the world would again witness a stirring stand the equal of King Leopold's gallant fight in World War I. Belgium held an eminently defensible position in the line of the Albert Canal, and the bridges over the canal were guarded by "invincible" Fort Eben-Emael. The Germans, however, knew all about Eben-Emael. For months, they had been training a force of just 150 men to take it. In gliders, under cover of darkness, they landed silently on the fort's roof. Throwing up a smoke screen, they set to work: exits and observations posts were blown up, big guns were destroyed by dropping explosives down their muzzles, and grenades and explosives went down ventilation shafts and gun slits and into ammunition elevators. In less than a day Eben-Emael capitulated, and the uncovered bridges over the Albert Canal were seized by glider troops before they could be blown.

To outflank the canal from the Dutch side, the Maastricht bridge was taken by guile described thus by a witness:

A plainclothes man walked over to the sentry on the bridge on the east bank and asked him, as a friend, to allow him across the bridge for a last word with a pal on the west bank. He was allowed to pass. He walked across the bridge, and after a few minutes conversation strolled back towards the sentry with his friend. This second man then, gangsterlike, shot the sentry and bolted back to the far bank, where he disconnected the wiring of the mines prepared for the destruction of the bridge. While this was being done, the first man possessed himself of the sentry's rifle and easily prevented any interference. The timing was a work of genius; within a few minutes, parachutists and gliders descended in a cloud on the top of the Dutch fortifications and the Belgian fortifications west of the bridge which is just in Dutch territory.[40]

With this, a lodgment was found across the canal, and as a Panzer division burst loose and threatened to envelop the entire Belgian position, the Belgian Army was forced to fall back upon the French and British. Supported by Polish formations which had escaped the first blitz, the Anglo-French had been moving north to the rescue. Very soon they were fighting, not to save Belgium or Holland but themselves and France.

During the period of the "Phony War," French propaganda had informed the world of the might of the French Army. Nowhere else was there such a powerful force: 800,000 front-line troops backed up by a trained reserve of 5,500,000 men. Nowhere, said General Maurice Gamelin, the French Chief of Staff, was there a soldier like the poilu. Was he not the descendant of the victors of Verdun and the Somme? Admittedly, some of the poilus had not had too much training, and quite a few had grown gray hairs. It was also true that they lacked tanks and airplanes. Yet, it was said, the poilu knew war, and when he was on the defensive there was no finer fighter in the world.

La défense. Just as French military thought had been mesmerized by *l'attaque* before the last war, so now was it hypnotized by the defensive. Its symbol was the great Maginot Line which War Minister André Maginot had begun in 1929, and which stretched from Switzerland to Longwy just below the Ardennes Forest in Belgium. It had cost a half-billion dollars, and it was a gigantic complex of great underground forts six levels deep, each containing living quarters, kitchens, ammunition dumps, telephone systems, miniature railways, power stations, hospitals, general supplies, water tanks, and bomb-proof aboveground casements with the guns sighted in the direction from which the Boches were supposed to appear.

History has asked why the Maginot Line was not continued to the sea, and the answers are that to do so would have been most costly, that it would have seemed to neighboring and neutral Belgium an unfriendly act, and that the French would not have had enough men to man such a long line and still provide a strong reserve. More important, the Maginot Line was not begun as a defensive concept. It was not to be a Chinese Wall, but a shield acting in concert with its sword, the French Army. The Maginot would shield against attack from the east, forcing the invaders out into the open north where the sword would cut them down. Yet the tragedy of the Maginot is that it did, in the minds of the French, become a Chinese Wall. The French came to feel confident in its impregnability and to adopt that habit of defensive thinking which, surrendering all initiative to the enemy, placed all faith in the shield and allowed the sword to rust.

The French Army was rotten. It had never recovered from the shock of the last war, and since 1936 it had been shabbily armed and its will to fight weakened by the indifference and pacifism of the leftist Popular Front. The French nation was also sick. France had been bled white in the last war and was further depleted by a declining birth rate. Political crisis, political scandal, strikes, the vicissitudes of bloc government, personal vendettas, the traditional French refusal to pay taxes, a literature of nihilism and despair, all these and more had conspired to demoralize France. To many Frenchmen, democracy seemed a failure, or at least it had not survived the depression as well as the dictatorships. And France was so flabby with fear of Communism that many Frenchmen were prepared to accept Fascism as the lesser of two evils.

Yet, as the French and their British allies drove north to Belgium, few persons in positions of power suspected that France was a soft ripe melon ready to burst beneath a single blow. On the 10th of May, then, the Allies held a solid broad front of 102 divisions, mostly French, from the Channel to Switzerland. On the 12th the Allied left wing heaved forward. As it did, its right flank came to rest on the Ardennes. This was the hilly wooded region just to the west of the point where the Maginot Line ended. It was held by French divisions composed, in the main, of elderly reservists who were badly trained and poorly armed. This was because the French were confident that no breakthrough could be achieved in the difficult terrain of the Ardennes. Armor would be immobilized there, and any thrust by slow-moving infantry could be easily contained. This seemed to be true. Moreover, one reason for French emphasis on the defensive was that they believed that any German attack would be based on the old Schlieffen Plan: a thrust into the Low Countries, a left wheel, and then a drive down into France. That, of course, is what the Germans wished the French to think, for they had at last thrown off their own obsession with Schlieffen and decided that armor *could* penetrate the Ardennes.

This was the conviction of a young corps commander named Fritz von Manstein. He had converted Hitler to this belief, with the result that Schlieffen at last went into the waste basket and a new "Plan Yellow" evolved. Three groups of armies were to strike. The right flank would overrun Holland and Belgium, the left flank would feint at the Maginot Line, and the center with five full Panzer divisions as its warhead would burst through the Ardennes. Thus the Germans were delighted with the Allied movement above the Ardennes. In fact, the Luftwaffe made no move to deter it, even though the roads abounded in targets.

On May 13 the German center under General Ewald von Kleist came through the Ardennes and tore a hole 50 miles wide in the Allied right flank. Through the gap sped the Panzers—tanks, armored cars, motorcycles, troop trucks—roaring away on a wild dash for the Channel coast. On the 15th the Dutch surrendered and it appeared that the Belgians were about to give up. Back in Germany, Adolf Hitler exulted at the news. "The Fuehrer is beside himself with joy,"[41] one of his generals wrote in his diary. In Paris the customary French solution of shuffling the government had put Paul Reynaud in power. On the 15th he telephoned Winston Churchill and said, "We have been defeated. We are beaten, we have lost the battle."[42] Alarmed, Churchill flew across the Channel the next day and rushed to the Quai d'Orsay. Awaiting him were Reynaud, Gamelin and Daladier, now the War Minister. "Utter dejection was written on every face,"[43] wrote Churchill.

After Gamelin had mournfully outlined the extent of the German breakthrough, Churchill asked the inevitable question: "Where is the strategic reserve?" Gamelin shook his head and said: "There isn't any."[44] Churchill was dumfounded. It was incredible that the French should have committed all their strength already, and had no reserve with which to maneuver against the invaders. Looking out the window, Churchill saw smoke curling upward from bonfires of public documents built in the square. Obviously, the flight from Paris was being prepared. He turned again to Gamelin and asked when he proposed to strike the shoulders of the German "salient," and heard him say, with an eloquent shrug: "Inferiority of numbers, inferiority of equipment, inferiority of method."[45]

At the head of his list Gamelin might have placed inferiority of leadership; and yet it is unfair to blame the French alone. Britain might have sent more of its cherished fighter squadrons across the Channel, and the British Army—the father of the revolutionary tank —had come to France *without a single armored division*. So what Churchill mistakenly called "a bulge" turned swiftly into a pair of paralyzing thrusts. The column racing west for the Channel hoped to cut off the Allies in Belgium from the greater mass in France. The second swept south on Reims to cut off the French in the Maginot Line. On the 17th a jittery Reynaud brought Marshal Henri Pétain into his government and replaced Gamelin with Maxime Weygand. The hero of Verdun was by then 84 and Weygand was 73!

On rushed the Germans, and by the 20th they had reached the Channel and cut the Allies in two. Gradually, they smashed through Belgian resistance and drove the British Expeditionary Force back toward the water. On the 28th King Leopold of Belgium capitulated, and the B.E.F., with its left and right flanks gone, had its back to the water in the little French city of Dunkirk. Cooped up in Dunkirk, scourged from the skies by the Luftwaffe, their front and flanks shrinking under German blows, it did not appear that the British could get away.

In London, Winston Churchill thought that they could. Leopold's surrender had convinced him that he could not risk the loss of the B.E.F. Dunkirk contained the flower of the British Army, the seasoned professionals who one day were to command armies and theaters and to organize the services of supply, and not the least among them were Harold Alexander and Bernard Montgomery. Churchill ordered the Admiralty to evacuate the B.E.F., and so began the "miracle of Dunkirk."

High overhead and out of sight, fighters of the R.A.F. fought with the Luftwaffe for mastery of the air, while beneath them a ragtag fleet emerged from the shadows of the white cliffs of Dover. There were 887 vessels in all, of which 655 were civilian, and they included boats of every size and shape, wind-driven, oar-driven, motor-driven. There were motorboats and fishing boats, pleasure boats and whaleboats, lifeboats and fireboats; there were yachts and yawls and channel ferries; passenger ships, tramp steamers, paddle-wheelers, French ketches, Dutch *shuits,* tugs towing barges and one car ferry making its first voyage on the open sea. They sailed for the great pall of smoke lying like a shroud over Dunkirk. Like shepherds of the sea, destroyers dashed among them, herding the larger craft offshore while smaller ships put into the beaches black with troops.

Men standing shoulder high in water were hauled aboard, the men behind in waist-deep water moved to shoulder depth, and their places were taken by men standing knee-deep. With remarkable order and calm in the midst of seeming chaos, and over the space of a week, the British saved their B.E.F. In all, about 340,000 men were evacuated, of whom 198,000 were British and the rest Polish, French and Belgian. It was an epic feat of arms, yet on June 4 Churchill warned Parliament: "Wars are not won by evacuations."[46] It was then that the British leader, remembering Ferdinand Foch's famous fighting speech in front of Amiens, delivered the peroration which was to fire the blood of his countrymen and excite the admiration of his cousins across the sea:

We shall go on to the end. We shall fight in France, we shall fight in the seas and oceans, we shall fight with growing confidence and growing strength in the air, we shall defend our Island, whatever the cost may be. We shall fight on the beaches, we shall fight on the landing-grounds, we shall fight in the fields and in the streets, we shall fight in the hills; we shall never surrender; and even if, which I do not for a moment believe, this island or a large part of it were subjugated and starving, then our Empire beyond the seas, armed and guarded by the British Fleet, would carry on the struggle, until, in God's good time, the New World, with all its power and might, steps forth to the rescue and the liberation of the Old.[47]

Having driven Britain off the Continent, the Germans next turned to the destruction of France. With lightning speed they broke through the Weygand Line in the north, and the armored columns began splitting off again, taking the roads and driving for the Seine and Paris, for the Swiss frontier and victory.

In front of them they drove a demoralized French soldiery that had utterly lost the will or the capacity to fight. *"Sauve qui peut!"* the poilus cried. "Every man for himself! Run for your lives!"[48] That was the battle cry of the "magnificent" French Army, and with it rifles and machine guns went clattering into the ditches. All across a stunned and sorrowing nation, long, ragged columns of shamefaced French soldiers shuffled off to the prison cages, while their weapons were stacked on the roads and broken into pieces by German tanks.

Who will blame them? Their leaders were powerless to lead, their skies were full of enemy airplanes and their roads swarmed with enemy tanks. They themselves were on foot holding hand guns, and as a French officer informed Paul Reynaud in a postcard: "I am killing myself, M. le Premier, to let you know that all my men were brave, but one cannot send men to fight tanks with rifles."[49] All the exhortations to remember the glory of Clovis and Charles Martel, of Charlemagne and Napoleon, would never supply such a deficiency; and once the Luftwaffe seized complete control of the skies, the collapse of the French Army was succeeded by the panic of the French people. Hundreds of thousands of terrified French civilians had already clogged the roads in mass flight from the northern battlefront; now they flowed through Paris and infected the capital with their fear. Twenty-six years earlier "the Taxicab Army" had rattled out of Paris to the Battle of the Marne, and a fighting general had vowed that he would fight until not a stone stood upon a stone in the beautiful City of Light; but now out of Paris crept a beaten citizenry led by a government fleeing to Tours.

Upon them all fell the brutal wrath of the Luftwaffe. Along roads south of Paris the Stuka's shriek, the bomb's blast and the bullet's spang were counterpointed by the wailing of women and children, the curses of men and the screams of the stricken.

At this juncture, Il Duce struck. He had already said, "I need a few thousand dead so as to be able to attend the peace conference as a belligerent,"[50] and now, seeing that "quasi-mathematical certainty of winning"[51] which he also required, he declared war on France. In America President Roosevelt said: "On this tenth day of June, 1940, the hand that held the dagger has struck it into the back of its neighbor."[52] In London Churchill heard his friend's voice over the radio and gave "a deep growl of satisfaction."[53]

Two days later Churchill flew to Tours in a last-ditch effort to plead with the French to continue to fight. But every face was gray and grim and weighted with defeat, every face except the proud and sorrowing visage of a tall colonel named Charles de Gaulle. On June 14 the Germans entered Paris, and next day they paraded in triumph on the Place de la Concorde. "All is lost," cried Premier Reynaud, desperately appealing to President Roosevelt for "clouds of airplanes."[54] It was not only impossible, it was too late. On June 16, with France doomed, Churchill made his last desperate proposal of a political union of France and Britain. But on the following day the German columns reached the Swiss frontier, boxing the French in their Maginot Line, and it was all over.

Marshal Pétain was now in power and on that 17th of June he announced to a broken nation: "It is futile to continue the struggle against an enemy superior in numbers and in arms. It is with a heavy heart that I say we must cease the fight."[55] In the soul of Henri Pétain, that dark pessimist strain had at last triumphed: he had surrendered without asking for terms.

Yet what could he have done? France was prostrate. There were many who welcomed the Nazi victory, and few who, like Charles de Gaulle, chose to flee and to rally the Free French to his side. There was certainly no possibility of recruiting and rebuilding a fresh army, not with the mines and the industry of the north in German hands, not with a populace which had lost its nerve. It may be, as has been suggested, that France could have fought on from her colonies in North Africa; and it is also highly fortunate indeed that she made no such attempt. Inevitably the Germans would have pursued the French there, would have seized all of North Africa, and with that would have cut the British lifeline through the Mediterranean.

So Pétain surrendered France. The prostrate nation was divided, the north placed in German hands and the south ruled by Pétain with a capital at Vichy. Thus was born the "Vichy Government" which was to go down into history smeared with the stain of "collaboration."

On June 21 Hitler came to the Forest of Compiègne where Germany had capitulated 22 years before. France had had her revenge for 1870, now Hitler was to have his for 1918. He danced a little jig of victory. He read the Allied War Memorial: "Here on the Eleventh of November, 1918, succumbed the criminal pride of the German Empire, vanquished by the free peoples which it tried to enslave." Hatred flashed in his eyes, to be succeeded by contempt and the gleam of triumph. Then Adolf Hitler went into the same railway car in which Foch had dictated the Armistice and heard his own terms dictated to the French.

7

☆

The outbreak of World War II did not shock America as its predecessor had done in 1914. This time Americans had seen the storm gather and break; and this time they declared: "We're staying out of it."

But Americans were far from neutral in thought as Woodrow Wilson had asked them to be in 1914. President Roosevelt was aware of this when he said: "This nation will remain a neutral nation, but I cannot ask that every American remain neutral in thought as well."[56] Like FDR, the vast majority of Americans were openly for the Allies. Pro-Fascist organizations such as the German-American Bund were few, small and ineffectual.

Yet the Americans had no intention of intervening. Again unlike 1914, this generation had had experience of European war and was not eager to renew it. A poll taken at the time showed only 2.5 percent of the nation favored intervention. The disenchanted and disillusioned remainder told the Allies, in effect: "Last time we pulled you out of a hole, and the only thanks we got was to be called 'Uncle Shylock' when we asked you to pay back the money we loaned you. Now you're in trouble again because of the mess you made at Versailles. Well, we wish you well, but we're not coming over this time." Some idealistic young men went off to Canada to train for the Royal Air Force, but the bulk of a youth fed from the cradle on the horrors of war preferred the football fields to the battlefields of Europe, and one famous coach carried this analogy to its fatuous *reductio* when he remarked: "Football is the American substitute for war."

This attitude differed vastly from the conviction of President Roosevelt, who believed that an Allied victory was essential to American security. FDR was convinced that the fate of democratic government was at stake. A German victory would leave an unarmed America alone in the world against the Axis Powers all-powerful in Europe and Asia. Fortunately for democracy, this magnetic, vigorous and bold President was uniquely fitted to convert his countrymen to his belief that the Allies must be helped. Even as late as the fall of 1939, in the seventh year of his administration, FDR was still held in high esteem by the majority of Americans. His New Deal had not ended the depression as it had promised, but it had done much to restore American self-respect. It had also revolutionized American political thought. Prior to FDR, debate focused on such matters as Prohibition, the war debt and law enforcement; after him it took up the problems of social security, labor legislation or public housing. In addition to this social revolution, Roosevelt rescued the presidency from the desuetude into which it had sunk in the hands of his three predecessors, and he not only raised it to the position of dignity and power intended for it by Washington and Jackson and Lincoln, but he also streamlined it into an instrument capable of standing the strain of modern government.

Why then, it may be asked, did not this powerful and able chief mobilize his nation's vast industrial and military resources to the point where America would dominate the world situation and bring an end to the war? The answer to that question, which might also have been asked of Woodrow Wilson, was that Roosevelt governed in a democracy. He could only lead the people as far as they wanted to be led, and his task, then, was to make them wish to advance to his own objective of a strengthened defense establishment and "all aid to the Allies short of war."

To do this, in September of 1939 he proclaimed a "limited national emergency" and immediately authorized an increase of 17,000 regulars in the Army and raised the National Guard by 35,000 to its authorized strength of 200,000. The Army Air Corps had already been authorized to expand to 6,000 aircraft and 50,000 men. By European standards, these increases were minute, but they were all that the public was then ready to accept. Roosevelt never forgot that he was dealing with a public that was largely pacifist, he was always mindful of the public opinion polls, and he never jeopardized his over-all objective by taking some indiscreet giant step that would put the isolationist hounds on his track. As it was, he was widely criticized as a hypocritical warmonger who was craftily nibbling away at American isolationist tradition, taking a nation to war against its will. Granted the isolationist-pacifist dogmas, the criticism would be correct.

FDR's next step was to call for revision of neutrality legislation, and Congress obliged in November of 1939 by repealing the arms embargo and placing the trade of all belligerents, whether for munitions or other supplies, on a cash-and-carry basis. The President told the nation that developing such a trade in munitions would help build national defense, and that by keeping it on a cash-and-carry basis the United States would avoid the kind of incidents at sea which had led to intervention in 1914. "There lies the road to peace!"[57] he exclaimed.

There, rather, lay the road to war. FDR did not think so because he still believed that the Allies were stronger than Hitler. But repeal of the arms embargo effected a deep breach in the isolationist wall, if it was not also an interventionist act. It favored the Allies because, through their control of the seas, they could buy all the war material that they needed, while Germany could not; and implicit in it was the assurance that if the Allies proved weaker than Hitler, as they were, then other radical steps would be taken to prevent their collapse.

Isolationism waxed strong again with the onset of the Phony War, and the corresponding "phony peace" in America. Presented with a war that was not a war, Americans refused to take it seriously, ignored the plight of the democracies and began to lose their temper at British interference with neutral trade. FDR's hands were so firmly tied that, in the words of his biographer Robert Sherwood, "It was the one crisis in Roosevelt's career when he was completely at a loss as to what action to take—a period of terrible, stultifying vacuum."[58]

Ironically, Hitler's blitzkrieg in the Low Countries and France freed Roosevelt's hands. On May 16, 1940, he appeared before Congress to ask for 50,000 airplanes and a defense appropriation of $900 million. He did not, however, dare to ask for peacetime conscription. This bill had to await the fall of France and be introduced on the initiative of private citizens. France's fall also startled some isolationists, who became aware that a Luftwaffe based in the French colonial port of Dakar could raid Brazil. Air power had brought the Western Hemisphere within range of the broils of Europe, and this sobering thought raised some ostrich heads from the sands.

But only a few. Such powerful isolationist groups as the America First Committee still battled on even terms with interventionists such as the Committee to Defend America by Aiding the Allies. The America Firsters maintained that the nation could best defend herself on her own shores and should make herself so strong as to discourage invasion, while their opponents argued that now was the time to intervene while Britain still held out as a free world bastion and the British fleet still controlled the sea. At no time up until Pearl Harbor was this debate ever resolved. America remained hesitant, indecisive. A poll taken at this time showed only 7.7 percent favoring intervention. A Britain alone and at bay had increased interventionist sentiment by only 5 percent!

In the meantime, Franklin Delano Roosevelt had made what has been aptly called "the great commitment." In May of 1940, using his great powers, he had begun to transfer airplanes and equipment of the U.S. Army and Navy to the Allies. With that act neutrality was fitted for a shroud, and after Italy entered the war on Hitler's side, FDR made his action public. "In our American unity," he said, "we will pursue two obvious and simultaneous courses; we will extend to the opponents of force the material resources of this nation and, at the same time, we will harness and speed up the use of those resources in order that we ourselves in the Americas may have equipment and training equal to the tasks of every emergency and every defense."[59]

In September of that year Congress passed the Selective Service Act calling for the first American peacetime draft. An Army of 1,400,000 men was to be raised, and aircraft production increased to 36,000 annually. All this, however, was strictly for "hemisphere defense," as was the mighty two-ocean Navy also authorized by Congress. Roosevelt resisted every appeal for direct intervention, and he had not been moved when, on June 15, Churchill wrote: "A declaration that the United States will if necessary enter the war might save France." FDR knew that the nation would not support such a course. Moreover, 1940 was an election year, and Roosevelt was seeking a precedent-shattering third term against the strong Republican dark-horse nominee, Wendell Willkie. He would soon be saying, "Your boys are not going to be sent into any foreign wars," and "Your President says this country is not going to war."⁶⁰ To have made Churchill's desired declaration probably would not have saved France, and it certainly would have killed off Roosevelt politically.

Nevertheless, "hemisphere defense" was going to call forth a giant war machine geared to a gargantuan war industry, and once it was in mesh, it would be able to roll in any corner of the world. This fact certainly could not have been missed by Churchill, who was already on very intimate terms with FDR. And Roosevelt? He had already said: "I have one supreme determination to do all that I can to keep war away from these shores for all time."⁶¹ *These shores?* They would be defended one day by carrying the war to Guadalcanal and North Africa.

All possible material aid, then, was as far as Roosevelt would go, and in that same fall of 1940, one year after the start of the war, he went the distance. Britain was then in need of destroyers and America had 50 overage destroyers from the last war. On the other hand, America needed bases to defend the 300-mile-wide "security zone" which she and Latin-American countries had drawn around their coasts, and these the British possessed. So Britain got the destroyers and America got the bases—leased or otherwise granted—and with this single and severely criticized presidential act, FDR secured great strategical advantages for the U.S. Navy and came to the side of beleaguered Britain during her darkest hour.

In his blitzkriegs, Adolf Hitler had been flawless. By the summer of 1940—within less than a year—the scalps of Poland, Norway, Denmark, Luxembourg, Holland, Belgium and France dangled from his war belt. He had evicted Britain from the Continent, which the Kaiser had not been able to do. But now Hitler was to make mistakes, to slip and stumble in a fashion all but foreordained by the two great errors imbedded in his policy.

The first of these was made clear when, in August, Britain refused his offer of a negotiated peace based upon recognition of his conquests. Hitler could not understand that Britain would not allow him to establish hegemony over Europe. European hegemony had been possible only to the Roman Empire, which may be said to have organized Europe. Since Rome fell, the attempts of this or that conqueror to "unify" Europe by his own arms and under his own standard had bathed that Continent in blood. It had not been and will not be possible, and Britain was the last nation to allow it.

Hitler's second error consisted of two parts. The first was the failure to realize that Britain was the center of gravity of the alliance against him; the second his inability to comprehend sea power. By overpowering all the Allies but Britain, Hitler was like a hunter who shoots the cubs before the lioness. Still unconquered, Britain was free to fight on and to recruit new allies, among them, perhaps, the United States or even Russia. Eventually, reluctantly, Hitler came to realize this and because of it he ordered the invasion of Britain. In so doing he displayed his ignorance of sea power. The way to crush Britain was not the direct route of invasion, but the indirect one of attrition at sea. Hitler had the very weapon at hand, the U-boat, then being built in numbers and beginning to sortie from submarine pens located from the Arctic Ocean to the Spanish coast.

Moreover, the French fleet was lost to Britain, and with Italy in the war against her she was denied the direct sea route to Egypt through the Mediterranean. If Egypt were taken from her, all of North Africa would be in Axis hands. Shorn of the Suez Canal, without an overseas base within striking distance of Europe, strangled by the undersea blockade, Britain's plight would indeed be desperate—so desperate that America might give up her cause as lost and Britain would be compelled to sue for peace. Then, and then only, would Hitler be free to turn on the Soviet Union to carve his *Lebensraum* out of Caucasian Russia.

That was the course to pursue against the Queen of the Waves: cut her lifelines and seize her vital overseas bases. But Hitler and his generals were land-minded rather than sea-minded, they preferred annihilation to attrition, and thus instead of undermining their chief enemy they chose to overwhelm her.

From Hitler on down, the Germans were totally unprepared for Operation Sea Lion, the code name for the invasion of Britain; and to examine the catalogue of their deficiencies is to wonder if it was not after all a gigantic bluff. First, there was no plan, and in mid-July Hitler gave proof of his monstrous ignorance of amphibious warfare by ordering one to be prepared in 30 days! Second, there were no proper landing craft, proof again that Hitler must have commenced the war without reckoning on knocking out Britain. Third, barges and river boats had to be collected and converted into tank lighters, assault boats and vehicle ferries. Fourth, no soldier in the German Army had been trained in amphibious warfare and no officer had experience of it. Fifth, apart from the very severe limitations imposed by tides and weather, the *sine qua non* of success was control of the air. Sixth, even if the Luftwaffe knocked the R.A.F. out of the sky, it probably could not prevent the mighty British Navy from attacking the invasion fleet. Seventh, to embark the first wave of about 100,000 men would require more than half of the 1,200,000 tons of shipping which Germany had available for all her needs, and it would not be possible to concentrate it all in a single staging area.

At the outset, the Army and Navy quarreled. The Navy maintained that it would have to land the first two waves two days apart, because it had not enough ships. This was utterly rejected by General von Halder, who snapped: "I might just as well put the troops that have been landed straight through the sausage machine."[62] In reply, the Naval Chief of Staff said that to attack on a broad front as the Army proposed was to invite slaughter on the passage over. In the end, it was agreed to cross the Channel at its narrowest point, with the troops sailing through a corridor formed by two thick mine fields patrolled by submarines on either side, and the Luftwaffe providing cover overhead. Such was Sea Lion, a most fantastic and improbable sea monster indeed, and because neither of the squabbling services had any real faith in it, they ended by passing the baton to Reichs Marshal Hermann Goering.

The Air Supreme Commander was delighted. Here was the opportunity at last to vindicate the Douhet theory of strategic bombing, to prove that a war could be won by aerial bombardment alone. Goering and his Luftwaffe would not only destroy the Royal Air

Force but would bomb the stubborn British into submission.

Meanwhile, the British had turned their island into a bristling hedgehog ready to repel invasion from both sea and sky. Antiaircraft guns were in position, barrage balloons floated overhead, beaches were barricaded and fortified, buildings were sandbagged and lines of fortification were dug across beautiful golf courses and gardens. Men of the B.E.F. who had lost their equipment at Dunkirk were rearmed —often with weapons of World War I vintage sent across the ocean by America—and a Civil Defense Service and a Home Defense Guard were organized. Everywhere fire-fighting squads, repair units and demolition platoons were organized, and as every person and penny in Britain were mobilized, with seemingly every man, woman and child on fire watch or air-raid alert, factories adopted round-the-clock schedules to turn out guns and airplanes. Thus that great British quality of rising to the occasion, of flourishing on adversity, had come to the fore again. Britain had not been successfully invaded since William the Conqueror came over in 1066, and in commemoration of the British determination to prevent any recurrence of that event, A. P. Herbert addressed a derisive verse to Hitler, which went:

> Napoleon tried. The Dutch were on their way,
> A Norman did it, and a Dane or two.
> Some sailor-King may follow one fine day;
> But not, I think, a low land-rat like you.[63]

Meanwhile, Churchill rallied the island race with a call to battle which concluded: "Let us therefore brace ourselves to our duties and so bear ourselves that, if the British Empire and its Commonwealth last for a thousand years, men will still say: 'This was their finest hour.' "[64]

On July 10, 1940, Goering began the aerial combat known as the Battle of Britain. He had about 2,670 front-line aircraft to hurl against the R.A.F.'s 1,475 front-line planes. His first objective was to sweep British fighter strength from the skies, pitting his Messerschmitts against Britain's Spitfires and Hurricanes. Between the rival fighters there was little to choose: the Germans were faster and had a faster rate of climb, the British more maneuverable and better armed. Goering, therefore, relied on numerical superiority. This advantage, however, was more than offset by Britain's great secret weapon of radar or radio location. Through radar, the R.A.F. could learn of the German approach, their strength and precise location, and could therefore rise to the defense well ahead of time and concentrate in the critical areas.

The Luftwaffe's first strikes were over the Channel and south of England in an effort to draw British fighters into annihilating combat. The British fliers took up the challenge with great daring and tenacity. These were the very youths of the generation which had passed the Joad Resolution. They had been disdained as effete, spineless hedonists. Nevertheless, assisted by Polish, French, Czech, Belgian and Canadian fliers, as well as some American volunteers, they fought with a bravery and skill that won the world's admiration and evoked Churchill's famous accolade: "Never in the field of human conflict was so much owed by so many to so few."[65]

Because Goering's fliers gave full rein to their disastrous habit of exaggerating their success, the marshal believed he had obliterated the Channel air defenses and moved his attacks inland. Bombers struck at British airfields and enemy fighters were again drawn into battle. Once again, the British fighters cut deep into the German numerical superiority. They were far from destroyed. Nevertheless, Goering next ordered daylight bombing of British industry.

Then, having failed to knock out Britain's fighter defenses, or to cripple her industry, he shifted his sights to the British cities. He would destroy the food stocks and the will of the people living in them, and chiefly those in London. This was the final step in the Douhet doctrine of strategic bombing, and Goering, having exceeded his original purpose of providing air cover for the invasion, was now attempting nothing less than bombing Britain into submission.

On September 7 the dreadful "London Blitz" began. For two solid months the crowded capital on the Thames felt the full fury of the Luftwaffe. The Germans attacked by day and by night. As many as 320 bombers escorted by 600 fighters struck, or as few as a half-dozen or even a lone wolf, gliding silently down to keep Londoners unnerved. Yet the British calmly dug themselves out of the ruins and doggedly went about the business of defending their island. They passed through a very great ordeal in which the fear of attack, the screaming of sirens and the relentless rhythm of recurrent crisis were often more formidable than the hideous clang and crash of death and destruction which actually engulfed them. Yet they survived it. Their will to fight not only was not weakened, it was made stronger. In the end, Goering had to give up his gorgeous dream of victory by bombardment. By October 31 it had become a nightmare. No less than 1,733 aircraft had been lost by the Luftwaffe against 915 for the R.A.F. Operation Sea Lion was postponed until the spring of 1941 and then shelved altogether. Britain had won the Battle of Britain, the giant air battle for the skies above her island. But beneath the surface of the surrounding seas she was losing the fight for her life.

8

☆

"The only thing that ever really frightened me during the war," wrote Winston Churchill, "was the U-boat peril."[66]

The fall of France had given Doenitz's submarines bases from North Cape to Bidassoa, and had thus doubled their cruising range. Moreover, Doenitz, now an admiral, had earned the admiration of Hitler and had begun to get some—but not nearly all—of the big new U-boats he requested.

From his headquarters in Lorient on the Bay of Biscay, "Papa" Doenitz formed his undersea killers into wolf packs and sent them prowling into the North and South Atlantic in fanwise groups of eight to 20. The moment any one submarine contacted a convoy, it radioed Doenitz and shadowed the enemy vessels while the admiral sent in all the other U-boats in the vicinity.

The wolves gathered at night. Rising silently to the surface, they slipped in among the ships of the convoy, fired their torpedoes, and then dove to escape the wrath of converging destroyers. Half an hour later, they might surface again to renew the attack, firing their deadly "fish" in the flickering light of burning victims. Their attacks continued throughout the night, and often during the following day from beneath the surface, and unless enemy counterattacks proved too effective, the wolf packs might hang onto a convoy for days on end.

To meet this renewal of the dreaded U-boat war, the Admiralty evolved new antisubmarine tactics and weapons. If the wolf packs launched night surface attacks, the escorting warships lighted the night with rockets, searchlights and star shells. Forced beneath the surface, the U-boats had to move more slowly and were exposed to blankets of depth charges. They could also be detected by new listening devices such as sonar, or asdic as the British called it. Equipment housed in a steel bubble beneath a ship's hull listened for a U-boat's propellers or sent out echo-ranging "pings" which bounced off a U-boat's hull and returned. In defense, the Germans invented *Pillenwerfer,* a device which shot out small gas bubbles which returned an echoing "ping" similar to those used in sonar. Thus they could confuse the sonar operators. Radar also was used in antisubmarine warfare, but only to detect surfaced submarines. "Huff-duff," a high-frequency direction finder, picked up U-boat messages to other submarines or to Doenitz, and through this information a bearing could be taken on the U-boats. Eventually, huff-duff would enable Allied aircraft to surprise surfaced submarines, sometimes catching the unfortunate crews sunning themselves on deck.

Most of these measures, of course, were the product of experience, coming only with the passage of time, and not soon enough to reduce the appalling losses which staggered Britain in the fall of 1940. Before France fell, Britain had been receiving about 1,200,000 tons of cargo a week by sea. A month later, sinkings brought this down to 750,000 tons. Within the ensuing two months losses soared far above the critical point reached during World War I. In October one wolf pack of only eight submarines caught an Atlantic convoy of 34 ships and sank 20 of them. By January of 1941 the arrival of ships in British ports was *less than half* of what it had been the previous year. During the first three months of 1941 no less than 142 ships were sunk, to say nothing of the number damaged.

Obviously, Britain was being strangled, and just as she began gasping for supplies, she found that she had no more money to buy them. Up until November, 1940, Britain had paid for everything she received from America. In all, $4.5 billion had been disbursed and Britain had but $2 billion remaining, most of which was invested. Even if she divested herself of all her gold and foreign assets, she could not hope to pay for more than one-twentieth of the war material she needed. Britain, then, faced strategic bankruptcy. To avoid it, Churchill adopted the bold course of a frank appeal to his great friend across the sea. But first he must await the result of the American elections, which he did with great anxiety. Much as he respected Wendell Willkie, and appreciated Willkie's statement, "All of us—Republicans, Democrats and Independents—believe in giving aid to the heroic British people,"[67] he still preferred to deal with a man whom he had known since the days of World War I when Roosevelt was Assistant Secretary of the Navy.

In the United States the election brought out a record 50 million voters at the conclusion of a campaign distinguished by the invective poured upon Roosevelt's head by the isolationists. However, FDR won by 3 million votes, news which Churchill received with "indescribable relief." A month later the Prime Minister sent the President a 4,000-word letter outlining Britain's plight, her shipping losses, her faltering production and her exhaustion of her dollar supply. He asked, in effect, for two things: material and the safe delivery of that material. This was nothing less than to request that American industry and the American Navy be placed at Britain's disposal, and Churchill, leaving to Roosevelt the details of how such an unprecedented course might be adopted, ended by saying: "If, as I believe, you are convinced, Mr. President, that the defeat of the Nazi and Fascist tyranny is a matter of high consequence to the people of the United States and to the Western Hemisphere, you will regard this letter not as an appeal for aid, but as a statement of the minimum action necessary to achieve our common purpose."[68]

Churchill later said this was one of the most important letters he ever wrote, and he was right. Roosevelt was so impressed that he pondered the letter for a week, gradually evolving the revolutionary concept that came to be known as Lend-Lease. He explained to the country, "Now, what I am trying to do is eliminate the dollar sign," and he gave the famous illustration:

Suppose my neighbor's house catches fire and I have a length of garden hose four or five hundred feet away. If he can take my garden hose and connect it up with his hydrant, I may help him put out the fire. Now . . . I don't say to him before that operation, "Neighbor, my hose cost me fifteen dollars; you have to pay me fifteen dollars for it." No! . . . I don't want fifteen dollars—I want my garden hose back after the fire is over.[69]

It was a homey and touching analogy, even if it did overlook the fact that the material to be lent or leased to the Allies would not, like the garden hose, be returned intact after the crisis had passed but was very likely to be destroyed in surmounting it. But the "garden hose" very neatly squelched the isolationists, even drowning the famous charge that Lend-Lease would "plow under every fourth American boy." Thus FDR received from Congress the power to lend or lease any war material to any government "whose defense the President deems vital to the defense of the United States." Ultimately, Lend-Lease would include Russia, China and the rest of the Allies, it would take 14 cents out of every dollar the United States spent to fight the war, and it would rise to a total outlay of $50 billion. Only about $8 billion came back in "reverse Lend-Lease," that is, food, equipment and services supplied by the Allies to American troops overseas. Of this, Britain contributed $2 billion and Russia nothing. The Communists claimed that they had made payment in blood, implying, therefore, that they alone had bled and suggesting that they be subsidized in defending themselves.

Still, what Churchill called "the most unsordid act in the history of any nation"[70] probably did as much as any other factor to save Britain and doom the Axis. After it was passed, FDR turned to the second part of Churchill's appeal, safe delivery of the material, and in so doing he justified many of the isolationists' charges against him, and held a wake for neutrality.

By then neutrality was hardly more than a convention. Axis consulates in America were closed down and Axis assets frozen. Now FDR began his Undeclared War against the U-boats. In April of 1941 he made an enormous expansion of the North Atlantic "security zone," advancing it roughly halfway across the ocean. West of this line, the U.S. Navy would defend American ships. They would also notify the British of any submarines they had located.

Inasmuch as Germany in 1941 could no more afford the free passage of arms across the Atlantic than she could in 1914, the Nazi government angrily protested. No matter, and soon German and American warships were shooting at one another in the "war short of war." Next, in July of 1941 American Marines took over occupation of Iceland from the British. Then, in August, FDR led his nation still closer to the Allied cause when, meeting secretly at sea with Winston Churchill, he proclaimed the Atlantic Charter and the Four Freedoms: freedom of speech, freedom of religion, freedom from want, freedom from fear. Here, in the Charter, was the cornerstone of the United Nations, an attempt to ensure peace based upon pledges of no territorial aggrandizement, respect for national self-determination, equal access to world resources, economic collaboration and abandonment of the use of force in international life. Here also was another source of aggravation to isolationists, who demanded to know how much FDR had promised to Churchill. In fact, he made no binding commitments; but in September, angered by losses of American ships, he ordered the Navy to shoot Axis vessels on sight. Shortly afterward he asked Congress for armed merchantmen to trade with belligerents. Although the isolationists fought the proposal bitterly, the sinking of the destroyer *Reuben James* by a German submarine clinched the battle against them. In November, 1941, the last of the neutrality restrictions was voted away.

The situation had now gone far beyond the delicate relationship existing between America and Germany in 1917. Now, with very little attempt at concealment, America was giving military assistance to Britain, and was preparing to arm the ships that were bringing Britain the lifeblood of war. If she was only *de facto* a British ally, she might have been *de jure* a German enemy, for it would seem that any nation using arms to help one side ought to expect the use of arms against her by the other. Yet Hitler held his hand. He had no desire to provoke the American eagle before he could dispose of the Russian bear.

The Fuehrer's war for *Lebensraum* had lost its masterly, timetable quality and had begun to become hit-and-miss and reactive. Hitler no longer controlled events but was improvising. First, his failure to invade Britain or to conquer her from the air made him lose sight of the fact that Britain was still his chief enemy. He might yet strangle her at sea or wreck her empire by evicting her from North Africa, the Middle East and East Africa. To do so probably would force Spain and Turkey into the war on the Axis side, deny Britain both the Suez and her last overseas base within striking distance of Europe, create the possibility of Asian hookup with the new Axis partner in Japan, and open up the easy southern route for the eventual invasion of Russia. Britain was very weak in these outposts, while Italian control of the Mediterranean would make possible an Italo-German concentration there. But Hitler failed to appreciate these promising possibilities. He turned away from Britain and prepared to attack Russia. It was a mistake of the first magnitude, and the pages of history show few more grave. Here was Britain still defiant and the United States manifestly preparing to come to her side, and instead of maintaining the pressure on Britain, he chose to ease up and take on an entirely new enemy. He was like a man in a street fight turning from a battered but still strong opponent to take on a spectator just as strong.

Hitler had his reasons, of course, and they must have seemed compelling. To prepare for the prolonged struggle with Britain he needed the resources of European Russia and he had to make sure of his eastern flank once and for all. Stalin had already made it plain that he would not give Hitler a free hand in the West without guarantees of Russian bases in the Balkans. This Hitler would not do. Instead, he would destroy Russia, after which the Wehrmacht would be reorganized with emphasis on the naval and air power required to subjugate Britain. Thus Hitler was running the risk of the two-front war he had sworn to avoid. He was very like "those fools of 1914," and no more than they could he escape the dilemma of German geography. She is landlocked, sandwiched between Frank and Slav. Better for her to have wooed the French than to make war on them. And so, if Hitler's great mistake was to attack Russia, a greater one was in going to war at all.

But then, just because the war had become reactive, and because his partner in Rome was growing jealous of him, he got a left-handed chance to follow the Mediterranean route he had rejected.

Mussolini had always found a victorious Hitler unbearable. When he learned of Hitler's plan to invade the Low Countries, he ordered his Foreign Minister to warn Holland and Belgium. Hitler blamed the betrayal on King Victor Emmanuel, whom he detested, but thereafter he kept his plans to himself. And so, after the Duce read in the newspapers of the German occupation of Rumania on October 7, 1940, he complained: "Hitler always faces me with a *fait accompli*. This time I am going to pay him back in his own coin. He will find out from the papers that I have occupied Greece."[71] Three weeks later Italian troops based in Albania crossed the Greek frontier, and on that same morning as Hitler stepped off a railroad train in Florence, Mussolini greeted him with the gleeful cry: "Fuehrer, we are on the march."[72]

Hitler was disturbed, especially after it developed that the Italian march was to the rear. The doughty Greeks not only halted the Italians, but threw them out of Greece and pursued them all the way into Albania. Sixteen Greek divisions chased 27 of the Duce's for 30 miles beyond the border and then penned them up in the Albanian mountains for months.

Mussolini's chagrin deepened after the British carrier *Illustrious* made a daring aerial strike on the Italian battle fleet, surprising it in the harbor at Taranto and putting it out of action for six months. Across the Mediterranean in Egypt, worse was yet to come. Here, the Italian Army had been attempting to drive the British from Egypt. But the Army of the Nile under General Sir Archibald Wavell had been reinforced with tanks and New Zealand, Australian, Polish, Indian and Free French troops. In December Wavell attacked and drove the Italians all the way back into Libya. By mid-January of 1941 Wavell had taken the coastal citadel of Tobruk, and with losses of less than 2,000 men had wrecked ten Italian divisions and taken 113,000 prisoners. Next, the British turned south to drive Italy out of Ethiopia, after which they sent a badly needed corps of troops to Greece to help defeat the Italians there.

Hitler was enraged. Like pulling a loose thread, Mussolini's precipitate action had unraveled all his war plans for 1941. First, Italian losses had encouraged the resistance movement in France and persuaded Franco to sit out the war. Second, although Hungary and Rumania were ready to join the Axis, Yugoslavia and Bulgaria had now decided to decline the invitation. That meant that Hitler might have to conquer them to secure his southern flank for the invasion of Russia. Crestfallen, Mussolini said that he was sorry that his letter to the Fuehrer had not reached him in time to obtain his advice on the Greek campaign. In fact, Mussolini had made certain that the letter would not reach him in time, and the Duce was only sorry that he had broken the military 11th Commandment: Thou shalt not lose. So Hitler was forced to come to Mussolini's assistance in Greece, and to dispatch the redoubtable General Erwin Rommel with an armored division and air support to redeem the situation in North Africa.

One of the few non-Junker generals to achieve high rank, Rommel combined daring and drive with a solid grasp of the military art. Very quickly he earned the nickname of "Desert Fox." On April 3, 1941, he launched a series of lightning thrusts which drove the British back into Egypt and once again imperiled their position in North Africa. Three days later the Nazis rolled into Yugoslavia with a juggernaut of 650,000 men covered by 1,000 aircraft. Although

Bulgaria had at last bowed to Hitler's will and joined the Axis, and for a time Yugoslavia seemed to have done the same, a rising of Yugoslav officers compelled the Fuehrer to subdue them. Still farther south, he hurled an army of 500,000 men against the Greco-British defenses and forced the British to evacuate. Eventually Greece and Yugoslavia fell and his southern flank was secure. To make doubly certain of it, on May 20, 1941, Hitler attacked Britain's vital Mediterranean outpost on the island of Crete. The first full-scale airborne assault in history was carried out by the Germans with great audacity and precision. After control of the air had been established, daily aerial reconnaissance kept the island under close surveillance, until on May 20, 1941, parachutists came gliding down from the skies and gliders crash-landed their cargoes of airborne troops. Within minutes the Germans landed 15,000 fully equipped men, and from that lodgment gradually expanded their hold until Crete fell.

The Balkans, then, had also been blitzed. Turkey, recognizing reality, would soon sign a nonaggression pact. And now the Fuehrer, still ignorant of the fact that this southern diversion had in fact placed the British windpipe under his thumbs, was intent upon going ahead with Operation Barbarossa.

Hitler persisted in his determination to invade Russia because he believed that he could conquer the Soviet Union in six months. "We have only to kick in the door," he said, "and the whole rotten structure will come crashing down."[73] Not every German commander agreed with him. Marshal Goering protested, but his loss of prestige in the Battle of Britain had weakened his standing. Grand Admiral Erich Raeder also objected, insisting that Britain should first be subjugated through the U-boat war. But his advice was rejected.

Hitler's faith in his own military genius had become so swollen by his victories that it had crowded out of his mind most other considerations. For one, the Balkan diversion, especially the resistance of the Yugoslavs, had delayed Barbarossa by four weeks, bringing it that much closer to the dread Russian winter. For another, his very career of conquest had begun to drain off divisions needed to garrison the occupied territory. Also, when he had attacked the West in 1940, his Eastern flank had been guarded by the Nonaggression Pact with Russia and only seven divisions; but in 1941 as he prepared to strike in the East, he had 49 divisions holding the Atlantic Wall. Finally, his tactics of annihilation which were ill-suited to the invasion of Britain were also ill-chosen for conquest of Russia.

Russia was simply too vast and too poorly equipped with roads for the blitz to do its work before the immobilizing snows fell. The blitz might work if it was concentrated against Moscow, the center of Russian gravity, but Hitler envisioned a broad advance from the Baltic to the Black Sea. Intuitive, blindly confident in his destiny to surpass Napoleon and Alexander, Hitler overrode his General Staff and cried: "When Barbarossa begins the world will hold its breath!"[74]

On June 22, 1941, it did begin along a front of 1,800 miles with a force of 150 Axis divisions supported by 2,400 air planes; it took the Russians completely by surprise. Both President Roosevelt and Prime Minister Churchill had attempted to warn Premier Stalin of his peril, but the Communist dictator had preferred not to trust the despised democracies.

In the north the objective was Leningrad and the Baltic, in the center White Russia and the city of Smolensk about 400 miles inside Russia, and in the south the city of Kiev and the Black Sea. Everywhere the Germans met with astonishing success. By July 2 they had knocked the Soviet Air Force from the skies and had captured 150,000 Russian soldiers, 1,200 tanks and 600 big guns. On July 3 the German Chief of Staff, General von Halder, wrote in his diary: "It is probably not an exaggeration to say that the campaign against Russia had been won in fourteen days."[75] Next day, the central force captured Smolensk, pausing to await success in the north before moving on Moscow 200 miles east.

Yet the very rapidity of this advance on a broad front had spread German strength thin and exposed it to counterattacks on the flanks. This the Russians began to do with great skill. Moreover, the Germans, who had expected to encounter only 200 divisions, were astonished to identify no less than 360 by August 17. Finally, alarmed to learn that the Red Army was concentrating between Smolensk and Moscow, the General Staff urged Hitler to place his maximum power in the center and drive for Moscow without delay. There, they said, they could break the Russians before they had time to concentrate.

Hitler refused. His eyes were north and south, on Leningrad and Stalingrad, the twin "holy cities of Communism" whose fall would cause a Russian collapse. In the south also were the industry, oil and granaries he desired. Thus Hitler's offensive had psychological and economic objectives which tended to obscure its true objective: the Red Army.

Still, the Nazi divisions pushed forward. Resistance was stiffening, and Stalin's "scorched-earth" policy was slowing them down, but they continued to advance nonetheless. In September Kiev fell with 660,000 prisoners. Hitler was overjoyed. His generals were not. They considered that the opportunity to capture Moscow had been lost. And it was then that Hitler ordered the advance on the Russian capital. As it bounded forward, covering half the distance in only two weeks, Hitler told the German nation: "I declare today—and I declare it without reservation—the enemy in the East has been struck down and will never rise again."[76] Few observers would challenge him. By October 20 the leading German columns were within 40 miles of Moscow. Hitler had already ordered 40 divisions disbanded and the men returned to industry, and his planned reshaping of the Wehrmacht was beginning.

But then came the Russian winter.

It came early, preceded by raw, drenching October rains, and it came with the German divisions all but spent. As the attack became stalled in mud, Hitler's generals wisely recommended a halt until spring. Hitler refused. The attack would go forward over frozen ground. It did. Throughout November the German columns ground slowly toward Moscow. Drenched by rain or snow, moving in falling temperatures for which they were neither clothed nor equipped, they battled their way into Moscow's western suburbs. They could see the gilded towers of the Kremlin. And the thermometer fell to zero.

Russia's traditional ally, General Winter, froze the German advance, and now the Russians rose up to counterattack. From Hitler came the order: no retreat. Haunted by the memory of Napoleon's retreat from Moscow, he commanded his men to stand their ground, even if by-passed. And that, of course, meant that they would ultimately be fragmented and forced to surrender. Eventually, the German Army was driven back 200 miles from Moscow. Never again would the swastika come so close to obliterating the hammer and sickle. Some 800,000 casualties were lost because Hitler's intuition had gained the ascendancy over the wisdom of his generals.

December 6, 1941—that was the date of the great Russian counterattack, the day upon which the Russian bear turned upon its tormentor. One day later, Japan aroused the American giant.

9

☆

Since 1931 Japan had repeatedly flouted the American Open Door policy guaranteeing the independence of China, while America averted her eyes or pronounced moral condemnations or sent the suffering Chinese heartfelt expressions of her sympathy. But then in the summer of 1940, encouraged by the successes of the German juggernaut, Japan made the moves that opened American eyes to her ambitions in Asia.

For three years Japan had been encountering stiffening resistance in a China led by Premier Chiang Kai-shek. To cut China's supply lines, the Japanese in 1940 forced the distraught Vichy government of France to allow her to occupy parts of Indo-China, and extracted from distracted Britain a promise to close the Burma Road. If successful here, she intended next to bring all resource-rich Southeast Asia under her control, together with the Philippines, the Dutch East Indies and the islands of Oceania. She would then rule perhaps the most populous and certainly the richest empire the world had ever known.

President Roosevelt replied to these steps by placing a partial embargo on exports to Japan. In July Congress passed the Two-Ocean Navy Act and FDR began imposing embargoes on some forms of scrap iron. Japan's response was to sign the Tripartite Pact with Germany and Italy. It carved up the world into spheres of interest, recognizing Japanese supremacy in East Asia. It was also aimed directly at the United States, for it stated that each ally would help the other "if attacked by a power at present not involved in the European war or in the Sino-Japanese conflict."[77]

Roosevelt now brought heavier pressure to bear on Japan. Japanese assets in America were frozen, exports of steel and scrap iron halted, and with the cooperation of the British and the Dutch shipments of oil were cut off. This was nothing less than an economic blockade of Japan. Without oil and iron, the blood and bone of war, Japan could not continue her conquest of China. By the summer of 1941, then, she had come to the crucial decision of her modern life.

Two choices were open. One was to withdraw her troops from China as America demanded and then settle back to take an economic profit from the European conflict, just as she had done in World War I. The second was to continue the war in China and risk hostilities with America, and probably Britain and the Netherlands as well. The first course was obviously more sensible, and it was the one advocated by the moderates. But to withdraw from China would be to "lose face" in Asia and to indict the policy of the militarists as a failure, and this, of course, the militarists would not allow. Gradually, using the so-called moderate Premier Prince Konoye as a foil, making their customary use of terrorist secret societies, the militarists strengthened their hold on the government. In Ocober, 1941, Konoye resigned and was replaced by General Hideki Tojo and a war Cabinet.

Tojo announced that he would pursue Konoye's policies of "continuation of conversations with the United States."[78] To Tojo "conversation" meant nothing less than assent to his diplomatic demands. What he could not get at the conference table he was prepared to take on the battlefield. Shrewd, unbending, convinced of Japan's mission in the world, Tojo did not shrink from conflict with Britain and America. Hindsight has censured him for having challenged the world's foremost industrial nations and its two leading sea powers, but in that fall of 1941 war looked like a pretty fair risk to a nation confronted with a win-all, lose-all decision.

First, the Japanese would be operating on interior lines, and would be much closer to their objectives than their enemies. Second, the enemy's garrisons in the target area were very weak and could be easily overrun. Third, the oil and mineral resources of the new empire would make Japan militarily stronger. Fourth, Japan's chief Asiatic rival, Russia, seemed on the verge of collapse; Britain was preoccupied elsewhere and America would never concentrate her strength in the Pacific while Germany remained undefeated.

Japanese strategy, then, was to seize their objectives quickly and exploit them to build a powerful empire behind the barriers of the Indian and Pacific oceans. This strategy rested on two poles: German strength and American weakness.

If Germany won, Japan was safe. If Germany did not, she at least would pin down the enemy long enough for Japan to crush China and to make her new empire invincible against counterattack. It would be impregnable because the enemy, and most of all the Americans, would never have the moral stamina required for a prolonged war across the oceans to the doorstep of Japan. Instead, the Americans would be eager to accept a negotiated peace which would leave Japan in possession of most, if not all, of her stolen empire.

The first premise, the effect of German strength, is at least pardonable, granting the inexorable German advance through Russia in that fall of 1941. But that of American weakness is not. The Japanese thought very highly of their own "spiritual power" and very little of the effete, luxury-loving Americans. They had become, in Arnold Toynbee's phrase, "enchanted with the ephemeral self." They believed their own propaganda and read it into every isolationist manifesto or pacifist bleat emanating from American shores. They saw only the Ludlow Amendment of the pacifists picketing the capitol during Lend-Lease debate, not an America gradually being converted to a wartime economy or rearming through its first peacetime draft.

Not all of Japan's military thinkers believed that America would be supine enough to allow Japan to fight the limited war she desired. Isoroku Yamamoto, the much idolized "iron admiral" of the Japanese Navy, had served in the United States as a naval attaché and knew well the power of Pittsburgh and Detroit and the inner determination of the people. Yamamoto warned that it would not be enough "to take Guam and the Philippines, not even Hawaii and San Francisco." To win it would be necessary to crush America, "to march into Washington and sign the treaty in the White House."[79] This, he implied, was not possible. But Yamamoto's advice was not heeded. A Japan which had won limited wars against a Chinese jellyfish and a Russian hollow man was quite certain it could do the same against an America which seemed to her to be a large but spineless playboy.

Acting on this miscalculation, then, Japan's strategy in the Pacific was to destroy American naval power based at Pearl Harbor, after which she would begin her timetable of conquest. By the time America recovered from the Pearl Harbor blows, the expanded empire would be safely solidified and protected by a chain of island fortresses.

Plans for the Pearl Harbor operation were formulated by Yamamoto. Six new aircraft carriers mounting 423 combat planes were gathered, together with a support force of 2 battleships, 2 cruisers and 10 or 11 smaller ships, and placed under Vice Admiral Chuichi Nagumo. To escape attention, the ships stole out of the Inland Sea by twos and threes under orders to rendezvous in lonely Tankan Bay in the Kuriles. Meanwhile, the forces for invasions of territory ranging from the Philippines to Singapore were moved into position. Like Nagumo's task force, they would strike once it became plain that all diplomatic efforts in Washington had failed.

Japan had not yet abandoned the diplomatic initiative. Throughout that summer and fall of 1941 her emissaries—Admiral Kichisaburo Nomura and later Ambassador Saburo Kurusu—conferred almost daily with Secretary of State Cordell Hull. In retrospect it may be seen that the negotiations were doomed from the outset. America would not lift the economic blockade until Japan withdrew from China and Indo-China, and this Japan would not do—could not do if she wished to remain an Asiatic power. Yet in some American quarters there persisted a faint hope that a formula might be found to avert disaster.

The Japanese had no such illusions. Their diplomats were given a pair of proposals, A and B, a stiff and a less stiff statement of the Japanese position which made no real concessions and demanded an end to the economic blockade. The diplomats were told that if these were not accepted by November 25, the issue of war would go to the Emperor. In other words, there would be war. So the negotiations began, with the Japanese unaware that their diplomatic code had been broken by a secret process known as "Magic." Thus every time the Japanese conferred with Hull the American knew their instructions in advance. He also knew of the November 25 deadline, when, on November 10, Nomura presented Proposal A. It was, of course, unacceptable; but the Americans, seeing war staring them in the face, wanted to gain time to prepare for it. So they began to stall. As the days wore on, Tokyo became frantic. On November 15 Nomura received instructions on how to destroy his code machines. A few days later Kurusu arrived in Washington and quickly learned that the United States was insisting that Japan withdraw from China and quit the Tripartite Pact. Tokyo thereupon instructed him to present Proposal B. This too was unacceptable. But now the Americans, desperate for time, considered countering with a three-month truce during which a certain amount of trade would be permitted. This, however, was torpedoed by the vociferous protest of Chiang Kai-shek in Chungking, and the proposal was not made.

Now the Americans intercepted a sobering message from Tokyo to Nomura. It agreed to extend the deadline to November 29, but added: "This time we mean it, that the deadline cannot be changed. After that, things are automatically going to happen."[80] Alarmed, President Roosevelt conferred on November 25 with his so-called "War Cabinet." According to Secretary of War Stimson, the possibility of a Japanese surprise attack was discussed, and "The question was how we should maneuver them into the position of firing the first shot without too much danger to ourselves."[81] Next day the Americans were disturbed to learn that a Japanese expeditionary force of about 50 ships had sailed south from Shanghai. They did not know that on that same day Admiral Nagumo's Pearl Harbor force had sortied from Tankan Bay.

On November 26 the United States made its proposal, asking Japanese withdrawal from China, Indo-China and the Tripartite Pact. The stunned Japanese reported home: ". . . we were both dumbfounded and said we could not even cooperate to the extent of reporting this to Tokyo. We argued back furiously, but Hull remained as solid as a rock."[82] On the 28th a message, decoded by Magic, came back from Tokyo indicating that negotiations would be broken off, but instructing Nomura and Kurusu to give the impression that they would continue. By then the Americans were certain that war was imminent, and messages had gone out to Rear Admiral Husband E. Kimmel and Major General Walter C. Short in Hawaii. Kimmel was informed, "Consider this dispatch a war warning,"[83] and Short was told that hostilities with Japan might ensue at any time.

Short's reaction was unfortunate. Warned to expect sabotage, aware that 160,000 persons of Japanese ancestry resided in the islands, he proceeded to park his planes in bunches to protect them from sabotage, thus making them highly vulnerable to air attack, and ordered most of his men into the field to repel a seaborne invasion. The Navy's mistake was to prepare for submarine rather than aerial attack, but Admiral Kimmel's decision to reinforce Wake and Midway with Marine fighter planes most fortunately took the carriers *Lexington* and *Enterprise* away from Pearl Harbor.

The last deadline had come and gone. Out in the lonely North Pacific, following a route over rough waters rarely sailed by commercial ships, Admiral Nagumo's fleet sailed steadily toward Pearl Harbor. It was a foul voyage. Mountainous black waves staggered the ships and washed men overboard. Anxiously, Nagumo awaited word from Yamamoto. On December 2,* it came: "Climb Mount Niitake." It was the code word for "Proceed to the Attack." Immediately, Nagumo swung his carriers south and sent them plunging through mounting seas toward Pearl Harbor.

In Washington the usual last-ditch efforts to avoid catastrophe, including a letter from FDR to Hirohito, had wended their futile way. The Japanese were already destroying codes and preparing to depart. On the 6th the first 13 parts of a 14-part memorandum from Tokyo began arriving. They were intercepted and decoded and delivered to President Roosevelt that night. FDR saw at once that they meant war, but he still did not consider that Japan would strike American soil. He expected fresh aggressions in Asia. On the morning of December 7 the 14th part was intercepted and decoded. It broke off negotiations. Roosevelt received it about ten o'clock that morning, or 4:30 A.M. Pearl Harbor time. Then there was another message which Magic had intercepted. It was to Kurusu and instructed him to present the Japanese reply at exactly 1 P.M. In Pearl Harbor, that would be 7:30 A.M., exactly the moment at which the Emperor's "glorious young eagles" would be swooping down on Battleship Row.

An alert naval officer quickly grasped the significance of the timing. General Marshall, taking his Sunday horseback ride across the Potomac, was called to the War Department. But his warning message to Hawaii could not be sent immediately because, as was customary for that time of day and year, the department radio was not in contact with Honolulu. It went by commercial wire and radio, and it was not received until 7:33 o'clock on the morning of December 7, 1941.

Eight battleships were neatly moored along Battleship Row, some of them side by side. They were *Nevada, Arizona, Tennessee, West Virginia, Maryland, Oklahoma, California* and *Pennsylvania.* With

---

* East Zone time, which is one day later than our own West Zone. Hawaii is in the West Zone. Henceforth all dates will be given for the zone in which the event occurs.

them were five cruisers and 26 destroyers. Fortunately the three carriers representing all the Pacific Fleet's air power were out at sea along with seven other cruisers.

It was a Sunday, and about one-third of the crews were on shore leave. Antiaircraft batteries were only partially manned. Most of the ammunition aboard ship was in padlocked steel chests. As the hour of doom approached, some of the ships were piping the men to breakfast; others were raising the flag. Ashore, two Army radar operators, one of them still in training, noticed the blips of approaching aircraft on their screen. They notified a young officer, who displayed a vast disinterest, informing the soldiers that it was probably a flight of American B-17s arriving from California. But there were no American aircraft aloft on that sunny, sparkling morning—not even patrol planes. On land, sea and air all was calm and serene. America was at peace, the church bells were beginning to chime, the messenger with General Marshall's warning was pedaling on his untroubled way to Fort Shafter, when, at five minutes before eight o'clock, the bombs came whistling down.

Forty Japanese torpedo bombers or "Kates," 51 Val dive bombers, and about 50 twin-engined Betty bombers escorted by 50 Zero fighters were in the first wave.* The Kates came skimming in low over the water to release their deadly fish, the Vals plummeted straight down to drop bombs and 16-inch armor-piercing shells designed to penetrate steel decks, and the Bettys and the Zeroes went wolfing over the airfields. *Oklahoma* was the first to die. Three torpedoes peeled her open like giant can openers. Two more ripped her, and she turned over. *Maryland,* moored alongside, fought back under protection of *Oklahoma*'s riddled hull. She escaped with only two bomb hits.

Meanwhile, Battleship Row had begun to thunder and blaze. American sailors and Marines were battering padlocks off the ready chests with ringing blows of axes and mauls. Ammunition was passed out and antiaircraft guns began to stutter at the red-balled Japanese planes flashing among the ships. Men on shore leave were racing back to the docks, jumping into small boats to come churning out to the battle. Some swam out. Already, the message had been flashed to America:

---

* Later in the war, to simplify identification, Japanese aircraft were given nicknames: male for fighters, female for all others. At that time the Zero fighter began to be called "Zeke."

"AIR RAID, PEARL HARBOR—THIS IS NO DRILL."

Tennessee and *West Virginia,* also moored together, suffered the fate of *Oklahoma* and *Maryland. West Virginia* on the outboard side took two bombs and six or seven torpedoes, went over, straightened— and sank upright. *Tennessee* was covered by her hull, but was nevertheless set afire by flaming debris from *Arizona* moored behind her. That unfortunate ship was so riddled by hits that she sank with hundreds of sailors trapped inside her. *California,* moored alone, blew up when a bomb exploded in her magazine. *Nevada,* also moored alone, was the only battleship to get under way. In a running fight with swarms of buzzing Kates, she finally ran aground. *Pennsylvania,* meanwhile, was in dry dock and put up such a cloud of AA that she escaped with one severe bomb hit. And on the airfields the American aircraft were destroyed parked wing to wing with only a few of them able to roar aloft to challenge the red-balled enemy.

A second wave from Nagumo's carriers and a third also struck at Pearl Harbor, but by midmorning the damage had been done. Seven of the Pacific fleet's eight battleships were sunk or very badly damaged, and half of the base's aircraft were destroyed.

In Washington Ambassadors Nomura and Kurusu had been much slower than the Americans in decoding their own messages. They did not arrive outside Secretary Hull's office until a little after two. As they moved into the waiting room, Hull received a telephone call from President Roosevelt.

"There's a report that the Japanese have attacked Pearl Harbor," FDR said.

"Has the report been confirmed?" Hull asked.

"No,"[84] the President said, and hung up.

In cold fury, aware both of what they had done and what they would say, Hull heard the Japanese out. Staring directly into Nomura's eyes, he said: "In all my fifty years of public service I have never seen a document that was more crowded with infamous falsehoods and distortions—infamous falsehoods and distortions on a scale so huge that I never imagined until today that any Government on this planet was capable of uttering them."[85]

Silent, heads down, the Japanese walked from his office.

10

☆

The day after the Japanese attack on Pearl Harbor, President Roosevelt addressed a joint session of Congress. "Yesterday, December 7, 1941—a date that will live in infamy," he began, and concluded by asking Congress to declare war on Japan. Congress did, with but a single dissenting vote.

Never before had Americans been so united. Isolationists and interventionists alike burned with anger at Japan's treacherous sneak punch, and only the most indiscreet of cool heads would have dared to suggest that such surprise attacks are common in warfare or that tactically Japan could have done nothing else. In truth, Japan could have done nothing worse. With one blow she had aroused and united a nation that had been dedicated to passivity and torn by dissension. Other factors might gradually have brought America to intervene against the Axis, among them disgust with the dictators, a growing sense of kinship with and admiration for Britain, propaganda from those Communist sympathizers who had remained notably silent while Stalin was Hitler's ally, the fact that Americans of Irish or German origin were now a few generations removed from hostility to Britain or loyalty to Germany, the enmity which America's articulate Jewish community bore for Hitler, and even FDR's growing association of his nation's interest with the Allied cause. Yet, if all these generally disparate and unorganized influences had spoken with a single voice, it would have been but a whisper in comparison with the concerted roar of outrage which broke from America's throat in the wake of Pearl Harbor. Washington, Madison, Polk, Lincoln, McKinley, TR, even Woodrow Wilson might well have been envious of how swiftly the problems of leading a pluralist nation at war had been simplified for Franklin Delano Roosevelt.

For Japan, retribution was to be complete. She had arrayed against her an immensely superior coalition of powers. She had foolishly believed that the United States would allow her to fight a limited war. She had misjudged the American character, and for the sake of an initial advantage had given that character greater strength and purpose. "One can search military history in vain," wrote the naval historian Samuel Eliot Morison, "for an operation more fatal to the aggressor."[86]

It was unique, then, and perhaps because the Japanese character was unique. Like their soldiers killing themselves in battle rather than accepting the disgrace of defeat or imprisonment, Japan's militarist chieftains preferred a kind of national hara-kiri to a meek and submissive return to the secondary status reserved for her by the Western powers. Nevertheless, it was a "stunned and silent nation"[87] that heard Tojo read the Imperial Rescript declaring war. Too many Japanese had relatives in America or had been there and thus knew her power. But they dared not speak, not in the presence of youths fired by Shinto and samurai, not at the risk of being overheard by agents of the Thought Police or dagger-wielding members of the secret societies.

In Germany there was also much uneasiness. Hitler may have been jubilant to hear that American naval power had been crippled, but on that December 7 his countrymen were stunned. On that day they heard that America was a belligerent and that the temperaure on the Moscow front had dropped to 40 degrees below zero. An observer reported: "Unrest grew among the people. The pessimists remembered Napoleon's war with Russia, and all the literature about *La Grande Armée* suddenly had a marked revival. . . . Even the most devoted Nazi did not want a war with America. All Germans had a high respect for her strength. Nobody could help remembering how America's intervention had decided the first world war.[88]

German gloom was matched by a boundless joy in Britain and the occupied countries, where it seemed plain that the Axis could never hope to master the British-Russian-American coalition. Yet the Fuehrer and the Duce kept faith with Japan and declared war on America, and the United States replied in kind. After Britain declared war on Japan (which Russia did not do) and Latin America came to the side of the Allies there were 35 nations, representing half of the world's population, engaged in this greatest of wars, a conflict so vast that even the unengaged half of humanity could not escape its effects.

These, then, were the results of the attack on Pearl Harbor. More immediately, this brilliant stroke (for such it was in a military sense) had achieved its purpose of immobilizing the American fleet while the tide of Japanese conquest flowed over Southeast Asia and out across the Pacific. In the Philippines American air power was destroyed on the ground, and on December 10 the first of six landings was made on the big northern island of Luzon. Steadily, the roll of Japanese conquests grew longer: they captured the American island of Guam, subdued Thailand, landed in Malaya to the rear of the great British bastion of Singapore, invaded Borneo in the Dutch East Indies, seized Hong Kong on the coast of China, invaded New Britain, New Ireland and the Solomons in the Southwest Pacific and sank the British battleship *Prince of Wales* and battle cruiser *Repulse*. With this last blow Japan made herself supreme in the Pacific and Indian oceans, and mighty Singapore, the center of British strength in the Far East, was left helpless.

Yet the island citadel with its garrison of 70,000 men did not consider itself doomed. It was believed that the Straight of Johore to the north or rear of Singapore could not be crossed and that the Malayan jungle still farther north was impenetrable. As a result, like the French with their Maginot Line, the British sighted the guns of Singapore where the enemy was expected to be, in this case to sea. But the Japanese did penetrate the jungle and did cross the strait, and then compelled a capitulation which dealt British arms its greatest check since Burgoyne surrendered at Saratoga.

Only at Wake Island did the Japanese suffer a setback. Here the garrison of 500 United States Marines hurled back an invasion attempt, the first and only time in the war that an amphibious assault failed. America was thrilled by the hope that a relief force was at sea and might yet rescue Wake, and she was electrified by the Marine battle cry: "Send us more Japs!" However, the relief force was recalled, and no one on Wake had or would have sent such a signal. The phrase was gibberish padding for a coded message. After the Marines killed 700 of the Japanese, sank a destroyer transport and damaged four other vessels, while shooting down a few dozen aircraft, all at a loss of 100 men killed and wounded, Wake hauled down the flag.

On flowed the Japanese flood. The East Indies fell after the Allied naval disaster in the Battle of the Java Sea; New Guinea was invaded;

and on April 9, 1942, the fall of Bataan heralded the end of American resistance in the Philippines.

Japan sought the Philippines as a flank guard to the East Indies and to deny them to America as a base of operations. America defended them as she did because of a naïve faith in the effectiveness of air power and the persuasive personality of Douglas MacArthur.

Up until mid-1941, military planning for these islands had called for the weak American ground and naval forces there to cling to Manila Bay until the arrival of the fleet in strength. Few planners actually believed that this was possible with existing forces, and some naval experts predicted that it would take two years for the Navy to fight its way across the Pacific. This attitude was in force when Anglo-American planners formulated "Rainbow 5," the plan for joint war against the Axis. It called for a defensive stance in the Pacific until Germany was defeated, and it implied acceptance of the loss of Guam, Wake and the Philippines.

Douglas MacArthur, however, believed that the Philippines could be held. MacArthur had retired after serving as Chief of Staff and had come to the islands to guide organization of the Philippine Army which was to defend the commonwealth after it achieved independence in 1946. In 1941, as the crisis with Japan worsened, FDR recalled him to active duty and placed him in command of U.S. Army Forces in the Far East with headquarters in Manila. It was then that MacArthur received a copy of Rainbow 5.

No man of MacArthur's ardent and optimistic nature would be likely to accept the defeat implied in this plan, and because of his great reputation and his experience in the Philippines he was able to persuade General Marshall, Chairman of the Joint Chiefs of Staff, that the entire archipelago could be defended. MacArthur's confidence sprang from a misplaced faith in the Philippine Army and his enthusiasm for the B-17 high-level bomber, the famous Flying Fortress. Marshall also believed wholeheartedly in the Flying Fort. Three weeks before Pearl Harbor, he declared that the 35 Forts based in the Philippines represented the greatest concentration of heavy bomber strength in the world! He claimed that the B-17s could defend the Philippine coastline without sea power and could counterattack by setting the "paper cities" of Japan on fire. Here was Douhet pure and unadulterated, maintained a year after its signal failure in the Battle of Britain. Actually, the B-17 had not enough range to fly to Japan and back, and throughout the war it would demonstrate its woeful inability to sink ships at sea. Horizontal bombers striking from high altitudes simply could not hit ships moving over water. Such accuracy was possible only to dive bombers swooping down almost to masthead levels or torpedo bombers boring in low beneath a ship's very gunwales.

Still, faith in the Forts remained strong and every effort was made to get more of them to MacArthur. Only the onset of bad weather, a deterrent often ignored by proponents of air power, prevented their arrival. Other reinforcements were also planned, but the attack on Pearl Harbor canceled the sailing of nine shiploads of arms and men. Nevertheless, by December of 1941 General MacArthur did command a force of about 31,000 Americans, 12,000 Filipino Scouts and 100,-000 conscripts of the Philippine Army. The naval forces assigned to him were small—1 heavy cruiser, 2 lights, 4 old destroyers, 29 submarines, 32 patrol bombers and a number of auxiliaries—but he did have those 35 B-17s based around Manila. Part of MacArthur's plan for defense of the islands called for these bombers to strike at the Japanese fields on Formosa the moment war began. Came December 8, 1941, with news of the Japanese attack on Pearl Harbor, and the Flying Forts did not attack.

Why, has never been made clear. General Richard K. Sutherland, MacArthur's chief of staff, and General Lewis Brereton, chief of his air forces, both tried to blame each other, and it is probable that the very hostility they bore one another kept the Flying Forts immobile during that moment of opportunity. Thus, the interservice friction that was to plague the American war effort did its corrosive work at the outset. Shortly before noon, after the raid on Formosa had finally been ordered, and while the B-17s were being armed and their pilots were at lunch, the Japanese struck.

They arrived almost without warning and before they departed they had destroyed the Far Eastern Air Force as an effective fighting force. Eighteen B-17s, 56 fighters, 25 other aircraft and numerous installations were knocked out. So was Cavite Navy Yard a few days later and then the patrol bombers of the Asiatic Fleet. Now the air and sea belonged to Japan, and soon northern Luzon was all but theirs when MacArthur's cherished Filipino divisions broke and ran before the onslaught of the soldiers of General Masaharu Homma's Fourteenth Army. This last blow shook MacArthur. With the resilient resourcefulness which was his greatest trait, he at once scrapped his own plan of defense and adopted the old one. On December 23, 1941, he decided to withdraw his forces from Luzon to the Bataan Peninsula, to declare Manila an open city and to move his headquarters to Corregidor in Manila Bay.

MacArthur's forces executed this double retrograde movement with masterly skill. Using swamps and rivers as shields, fighting tank actions to cover withdrawals and check the enemy's motorized advance, and holding roads and bridges until the moment they could be blown in the pursuing enemy's face, they got back to Bataan while their commander installed himself in murky Malinta Tunnel on "the Rock" of Corregidor. By this decision and movement, MacArthur averted immediate defeat, delayed the Japanese timetable by four months and tied up enemy forces which might have been used elsewhere. Nevertheless, it merely prolonged the inevitable. With the Japanese in control of the air and the sea, it was not possible to reinforce or supply the Philippines. Moreover, most of the fleet that was to fight its way west to the rescue was at the bottom of Pearl Harbor.

In America, General Marshall had called Dwight Eisenhower to Washington and ordered him to do all that was possible to save the situation. But Eisenhower, using Australia as a base, could get only a driblet of help to MacArthur. Meanwhile, MacArthur raised false hopes among his men by repeatedly assuring them that "help is on the way." On January 15, 1942, he told them: "Thousands of troops and hundreds of planes are being dispatched."[89] It was not true, and it bore no more resemblance to the truth than MacArthur's bombastic communiqués which assured America that the enemy was being beaten. Actually, Homma was steadily pressing MacArthur back down the peninsula. But the American commander was spared the ignominy of defeat. In March, deciding that MacArthur was much too valuable a soldier to lose by surrender, President Roosevelt ordered him to proceed to Australia. On March 24 four PT boats left Corregidor with 21 persons: General MacArthur, members of his staff, his wife, son and a Chinese nurse. Sailing south to Mindanao, they were flown to Australia in B-17s. Command on Bataan passed to Jonathan M. Wainwright, and with that resistance began to crumble.

Food stocks were low and the troops lived off slaughtered horses, ponies and carabao. Some dined off the flesh of lizards, others off monkeys, although one soldier observed that "monkey meat is all right until the animal's hands turn up on the plate."[90] Bitterness had begun to sour the hearts of the defenders of Bataan, and nowhere more than in their resentment against MacArthur.

Because he rarely visited the front and spent most of his time in Malinta Tunnel, MacArthur had been given the sobriquet of "Dugout Doug." As a reflection on his bravery it was unfair, for a more courageous man never lived. Yet it accurately described his indifference to his troops, as opposed to his concern for his own comforts. Although all service families had been ordered home, MacArthur had maintained his own in Manila. When he escaped to Mindanao, the necessity of taking his wife, son and his son's nurse kept three American officers out of the boat. When he arrived in Australia, he said, with customary grandiloquence: "I came through, and I shall return."[91] I, I, I. No American commander has ever used the first person singular as often as did Douglas MacArthur, and throughout the Pacific War his communiqués were to be studded with references to himself and to be issued under the highly personal dateline, "GENERAL MACARTHUR'S HEADQUARTERS." Because of this monstrous conceit which defaced the character of one of the most remarkable soldiers in American history, Douglas MacArthur came to be hated by many of the men he commanded. Perhaps his staff officers were charmed by his great courtesy, but the men in the mud eating a slop of wormy rice usually crooked their little fingers in derision and sneered: "*I* shall return."

Behind him General MacArthur also left a legacy of friction which was to overshadow the Pacific War. Under him the Army and its semi-autonomous Air Force were already at each other's throats, and the hatred of the Navy and the Marines was guaranteed when, two days before leaving for Australia, MacArthur recommended *all* units on Bataan and Corregidor for unit citations *with the exception of Marine and Navy units.* General Wainwright later corrected this deliberate slight, but he could never efface the memory of General Sutherland's pointed remark that the Marines had gotten enough glory in the last war and would get no more in this one. If Christian theology states that one of the three sins that cry out to Heaven for vengeance is to deprive a working man of his wages, what is to be said of robbing a soldier of his glory?

Still, these splendid scarecrows of Wainwright fought on. Gaunt, sour of heart and stomach, ragged and red-eyed, bombed by day and shelled by night, they fought on and sang their sardonic requiem:

> We're the Battling Bastards of Bataan;
> No mama, no papa, no Uncle Sam,
> No aunts, no uncles, no cousins, no nieces,
> No pills, no planes or artillery pieces.

From both Roosevelt and MacArthur had come orders not to surrender, and MacArthur had ordered a desperation counterattack as a last resort. Fortunately, General Edward P. King on Bataan had the moral courage to see, in Wainwright's words, that "he had either to surrender or have his people killed piecemeal."[92] King surrendered on April 9, 1942. Then there followed the infamous "Death March" in which American prisoners, without food or water, were clubbed, beaten and bayoneted on the 65-mile route from Mariveles to San Fernando. Then and thereafter, thousands of these American prisoners perished.

Corregidor still remained. Here was Wainwright with a mixed force of American soldiers and Marines. Although under steady aerial bombardment, the Rock held out for another four weeks until the Japanese succeeded in landing there. On May 6 with the Japanese within yards of Malinta Tunnel, while his men spiked guns, smashed equipment and burned codes, Jonathan Wainwright composed his last sad message to President Roosevelt.

"With broken heart and head bowed in sadness but not in shame," he began, and he ended: "With profound regret and with continued pride in my gallant men, I go to meet the Japanese commander. Good-bye, Mr. President."[93]

With the fall of the Philippines, the Japanese timetable of conquest was complete.

The ancient military disease known as "victory fever" had smitten Japan's military chiefs. A career of conquest unrivaled in modern arms, eclipsing even the triumphs of Adolf Hitler, had so exhilarated them that they decided not merely to hold what they had but to reach out for more.

Japan would seize Tulagi in the Solomons and Port Moresby in New Guinea while the Combined Fleet crossed the ocean to destroy the American fleet and capture Midway Island. Then a defense would be established down from the Aleutians in the north through Midway, Wake, and the Marshalls and Gilberts. Behind it, New Caledonia, the Fijis and Samoa would be invaded, Port Moresby and the southern Solomons seized, and Australia cut off from the world.

This decision was not reached without debate. Some sober heads saw the danger of overreaching. The Army, which had come in as a cockboat to the Navy's man-of-war during the glorious days, was especially reserved. The Army still regarded the Soviet Union as its chief enemy and was still committed in China. However, the powerful influence of Isoroku Yamamoto carried all before it. Yamamoto was convinced that Japan could not succeed in her strategy without destroying the American fleet. The invasion of Midway was intended to lure that fleet out to the battle in which it would die.

Yamamoto was after the American aircraft carriers. Japan's entire Pacific posture had been based on the fact that she possessed ten big carriers to seven for America, of which only three were in the Pacific. Unluckily for Japan, those three had not been in Pearl Harbor when Nagumo struck. He had wrecked only the American battleship fleet, and Nagumo's very successes from Pearl Harbor to Ceylon had convinced the naval world that the new queen of sea battle was the carrier. In other words, Midway was to rectify the failure of Pearl Harbor.

Although Yamamoto's proposal was accepted, some members of the high command deliberately hesitated putting it into operation, until, on April 18, 1942, Tokyo was bombed. At the very pinnacle of Japanese success explosions shook the capital in an unprecedented insult to the Emperor. To the end of the war the Japanese never quite understood how this had happened, although the explanation was simple enough. The Navy had trained Army pilots to fly medium bombers off a carrier deck. Under Admiral William F. ("Bull") Halsey, the famous "Shangri-la" task force sailed to a point within 670 miles of Tokyo, where 16 of these B-25 Mitchells led by Colonel James H. Doolittle roared aloft and struck at Japan. Then, because they could not land on carrier decks, the Mitchells flew on to China, although some crashed en route.

Yamamoto was so stunned by the raid that he put on dress whites and paid a personal call on Hirohito to offer his apologies. Thereafter there was no stopping the Midway Operation. The Americans must be driven so far back that they could never again think of desecrating the imperial capital. In May, 1942, the first part of the campaign began with invasion foces sailing to Tulagi and Port Moresby. At Tulagi there was no opposition and Japanese troops quickly seized this tiny Solomons Island outpost. But the bigger force sailing for New Guinea was intercepted by aircraft of the carriers *Lexington* and *Yorktown*. Thus was begun the Battle of the Coral Sea, the first naval battle fought by ships out of sight of each other and by naval aircraft alone.

First blood went to America. Her pilots sank the light carrier *Shoho* in ten minutes, a record for the war, and *Lexington*'s dive-bomber commander sent off the jubilant signal: "Scratch one flat-top!"[94] As a result, the invasion force had to turn back. Next day the war birds of both nations found each other's carriers. The Americans damaged big *Shokaku* and *Zuikaku* while the Japanese pounced on *Lexington* and gave "Lady Lex" her death blows. So the Battle of the Coral Sea ended in a tactical standoff and a strategic American victory. The invasion of Port Moresby was thwarted, and two big Japanese carriers were put out of action for the major strike on Midway.

Yamamoto had collected a powerful fleet of 162 ships and parceled them into larger and smaller task forces. The smaller was to invade the Aleutians in the north and draw American strength away from Midway. The larger one was for Midway, and it included transports loaded with amphibious troops. Even if the Americans did not snap at the bait in the Aleutians, the Midway force was strong enough to overwhelm them.

Opposing Yamamoto was Chester W. Nimitz. Pink-cheeked, blue-eyed, white-haired, without a shade of pretense or singularity, Nimitz was a strange officer indeed in this war of posturing, strutting commanders. He was also a fortunate choice as the successor to the discredited Admiral Kimmel. Nimitz had great organizing capacity, and he was a calm and careful leader with the courage to take risks. Although he had only 76 ships against Yamamoto's 162, Nimitz had been forewarned by Magic of the enemy's intentions. Thus he refused to take the Aleutians bait and concentrated his carriers—*Yorktown, Hornet* and *Enterprise*—northeast of Midway. Command at sea was given to Raymond Spruance, a silent, modest sailor who was in many ways Nimitz's seagoing counterpart.

Spruance's immediate antagonist was Chuichi Nagumo, the hero of Pearl Harbor, commanding a striking force of big carriers, *Akagi, Kaga, Hiryu* and *Soryu,* all veterans of Pearl. Yamamoto was to the rear with the Main Body, sailing aboard the battleship *Yamato,* the mightiest ship afloat and the very symbol of Japanese naval power. On June 4 Nagumo's combat planes were launched to bomb Midway itself. They were scourged by severe American antiaircraft fire. One-third of the attacking force was shot down, and Nagumo ordered a second strike.

That was exactly what Spruance had hoped for. His chief of staff, Captain Miles Browning, had calculated that Nagumo would continue to steam for Midway and would launch a second strike. He decided that the time to hit the Japanese would be at this moment, while they were rearming and refueling. This is when a carrier is most vulnerable, with bombs on deck and gasoline lines running. So the Americans found the Japanese sailing in box formation over a sparkling blue sea beneath a bright blue sky flecked with fleecy white clouds.

In came 15 Devastator torpedo bombers from *Hornet,* attacking without fighter cover. They were all shot down. Next came 14 Devastators from *Enterprise,* and ten of these were sent spinning into the sea. A dozen from *Yorktown* followed, and only four survived. Thus superb pilots had been sacrificed to faith in a wretched aircraft, and not a single Japanese ship had been touched. For one hundred golden moments it seemed to Chuichi Nagumo that the Japanese had won the war. But then the splendid Dauntless dive bombers came screaming down from the blue. There were 37 of them from *Enterprise,* and half of these struck at *Kaga* and half hit *Akagi.* They sank them both. After that, 17 Dauntlesses from *Yorktown* left *Soryu* a crippled wreck to be sunk later by the torpedoes of U.S.S. *Nautilus.* In six minutes, Nagumo had lost three carriers, and very soon afterward another flight of dive bombers from *Enterprise* came upon *Hiryu* and put her on the bottom. It was a stunning defeat. Not even the success of the Japanese Kates in torpedoing and sinking *Hornet* could relieve the black night of despair which engulfed the Japanese.

Far to the rear, Yamamoto ordered a general retirement. For the first time in 350 years Japan had suffered a naval reversal. In a single day's fighting all the advantages gained at Pearl Harbor had been canceled out. Parity in carrier power between the United States and

Japan had been restored at six to six. The Japanese victory flood had been checked, and the Americans were now free to go on the offensive.

Since February, 1942, Ernest J. King, Chief of Naval Operations, had been convinced that the Japanese ought not to be permitted to consolidate their conquests. This conviction, however, seemed to challenge the basic Anglo-American strategy: to contain Japan until after Germany was defeated. King accepted this strategy and was generally faithful to it, but he also saw that a purely defensive stance in the Pacific would play into Japanese hands. For this he earned the enmity of half the chiefs of the Anglo-American military alliance, beginning with Winston Churchill and ending with Secretary of War Stimson. Nevertheless, this hard and stubborn admiral insisted that limited offensives be launched against the Japanese.

Here he collided with his colleagues on the Joint Chiefs, Chairman Marshall and General H. H. Arnold of the Army Air Force. These two generals were pushing an early cross-Channel invasion of France, and were trying to block Churchill's attempt to divert this build-up to North Africa. They believed that King's proposal for a Pacific offensive was a similar diversion. Then came Midway, and King proposed an operation against Tulagi-Guadalcanal in the Solomons. The Joint Chiefs were not enthusiastic. But then the Japanese made their own reaction to Midway. They abandoned all immediate thought of seizing New Caledonia, the Fijis and Samoa and began to concentrate on the Southwest Pacific.

Port Moresby was to be invaded overland. Troops would land on the New Guinea coast in the Buna-Gona area and march across the towering Owen Stanley Mountains to come in on the port's back door. To support this operation, naval strength was built up at Rabaul, the great base on the island of New Britain across from New Guinea, and airfields were built there. Airfields were also to be built in the Solomons. Possession of Port Moresby and Solomons airfields would still allow Japan to isolate Australia and to cut her lifeline from America. So the Japanese build-up began, and when they started to construct an airfield on Guadalcanal, the Joint Chiefs, at King's behest, decided to authorize an American offensive in that area.

The next question was one of command. General MacArthur in

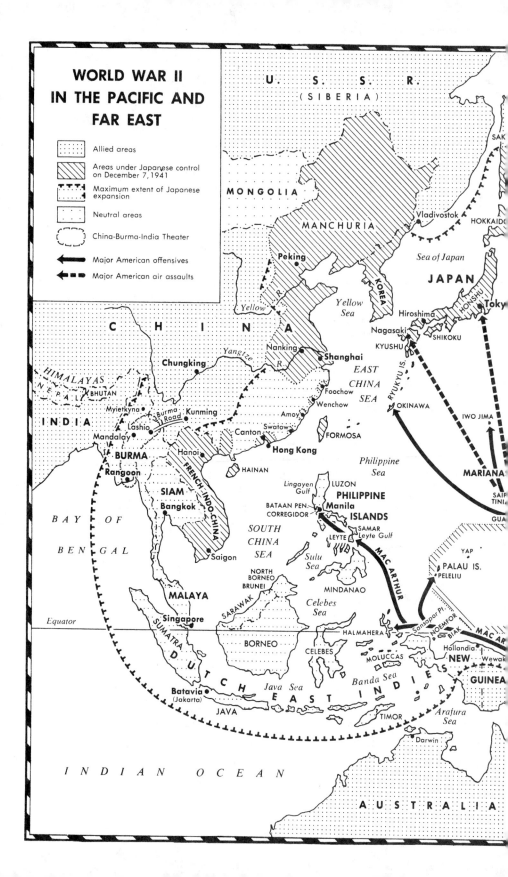

WORLD WAR II IN THE PACIFIC AND FAR EAST

Allied areas

Areas under Japanese control on December 7, 1941

Maximum extent of Japanese expansion

Neutral areas

China-Burma-India Theater

Major American offensives

Major American air assaults

U. S. S. R.
(SIBERIA)

MONGOLIA

MANCHURIA

Peking

Vladivostok

HOKKAIDO

SAK

Sea of Japan

JAPAN

KOREA

Yellow
R.

Yellow
Sea

Hiroshima

Nagasaki

KYUSHU

HONSHU

Toky

SHIKOKU

C H I N A

Chungking

Nanking

Shanghai

EAST
CHINA
SEA

RYUKYU IS.

OKINAWA

IWO JIMA

Yangtze

Foochow

Wenchow

HIMALAYAS

NEPAL

BHUTAN

Myietkyna

Lashio

Burma
Road

Kunming

Amoy

Swatow

FORMOSA

Philippine
Sea

MARIANA

INDIA

Mandalay

Canton

Hong Kong

SAIP
TINI

BURMA

Hanoi

HAINAN

Lingayen
Gulf

LUZON

PHILIPPINE

GUA

Rangoon

SIAM

Bangkok

BATAAN PEN.

CORREGIDOR

Manila

ISLANDS

SAMAR

YAP

SOUTH
CHINA
SEA

LEYTE

Leyte Gulf

PALAU IS.

PELELIU

BAY OF

FRENCH INDO-CHINA

Saigon

Sulu
Sea

MINDANAO

BEN GAL

NORTH
BORNEO

BRUNEI

MACARTHUR

Sansapor Pt.

NOEMFOR

BIAK

MAC AR

MALAYA

SARAWAK

Celebes
Sea

HALMAHERA

Hollandia

NEW

Wewak

Equator

Singapore

SUMATRA

D U T C H

BORNEO

CELEBES

MOLUCCAS

GUINEA

Batavia
(Jakarta)

Java Sea

E A S T   I N D I E S

Banda Sea

JAVA

TIMOR

Arafura
Sea

Darwin

I N D I A N   O C E A N

A U S T R A L I A

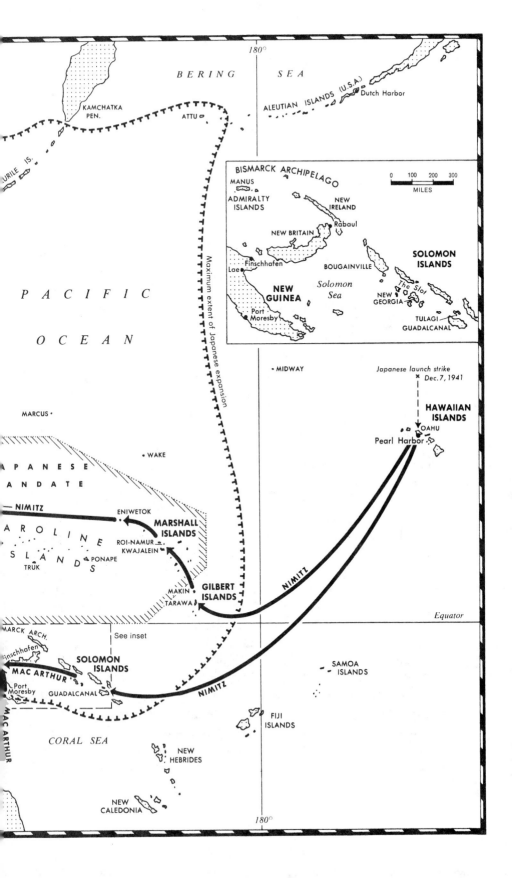

BERING SEA

KAMCHATKA PEN.

ALEUTIAN ISLANDS (U.S.A.) — Dutch Harbor

ATTU

KURILE IS.

180°

BISMARCK ARCHIPELAGO

MANUS

ADMIRALTY ISLANDS

NEW IRELAND

NEW BRITAIN

Rabaul

SOLOMON ISLANDS

Finschhafen

BOUGAINVILLE

Lae

NEW GUINEA

Solomon Sea

The Slot

NEW GEORGIA

Port Moresby

TULAGI
GUADALCANAL

0 100 200 300
MILES

PACIFIC

OCEAN

Maximum extent of Japanese expansion

MARCUS

MIDWAY

Japanese launch strike
Dec. 7, 1941

HAWAIIAN ISLANDS

OAHU

Pearl Harbor

WAKE

JAPANESE

MANDATE

NIMITZ

ENIWETOK

MARSHALL ISLANDS

ROI-NAMUR
KWAJALEIN

CAROLINE

PONAPE

ISLANDS

TRUK

MAKIN
TARAWA

GILBERT ISLANDS

NIMITZ

Equator

MARCK ARCH.

Finschhafen

See inset

SOLOMON ISLANDS

MAC ARTHUR

Port Moresby

GUADALCANAL

NIMITZ

SAMOA ISLANDS

FIJI ISLANDS

MAC ARTHUR

CORAL SEA

NEW HEBRIDES

NEW CALEDONIA

180°

Brisbane now commanded the Southwest Pacific Theater and Nimitz in Hawaii commanded the huge Pacific Ocean Area. Under Nimitz in the smaller South Pacific was Robert L. Ghormley. Even though the Solomons were in MacArthur's area, it was decided to allow Admiral Ghormley to command this first operation, after which MacArthur would lead the way up the Solomons ladder to Rabaul and thus open the road for a return to the Philippines. The troops chosen for the assault were those of the 1st Marine Division.

For 30 years the United States Marine Corps had been maintaining that a war with Japan would be an island war, a war for bases. Even if these island bases were fortified and defended, they would have to be seized. In this, the Marines rejected the dreary dictum that seemed to have been born during the British debacle at Gallipoli in 1915. This was that hostile, defended shores could not be conquered from the sea. The Marines maintained that they could be, and that it was not necessary to capture ports with all their facilities but that landings could be made across open beaches. In developing this doctrine the Marines were literally fighting for their life. Without amphibious warfare as a reason for being, they would very rapidly revert to the status of naval police. So they did evolve the weapons and the tactics of modern amphibious warfare, creating, meanwhile, a deep sense of mission and learning from the Banana Wars of the Caribbean all those lessons of jungle warfare which were to be given much wider application in the rain forests of Oceania. Service on the Navy's capital ships also instructed the Marines in the importance of sea power, while duty on China stations brought them into contact with the Japanese and taught them not to underestimate the enemy. Thus, when the island war with Japan came, the United States was in possession of a service uniquely fitted to fight it and led by tough and seasoned professionals eager to prove their theories.

One of these officers was General Alexander Archer Vandegrift, commander of the 1st Marine Division. In late June, 1942, Vandegrift had brought the vanguard of his division to Wellington, New Zealand, where he expected to begin six months of intensive training. But on June 27 he was informed by Admiral Ghormley that he was to land at Tulagi-Guadalcanal on August 1. Vandegrift was astounded. Only a few of his troops were then in New Zealand, and the rest were strung out in stations and ships from San Diego to Hawaii. He said that he could not possibly land anywhere by August 1. Ghormley agreed with him and later, after conferring with MacArthur, notified the Joint Chiefs of their strong objections to the operation. However, the Chiefs were adamant. They had learned that the Japanese airfield on Guadalcanal would be finished by August 7. Thereafter, any landing attempted in the face of land-based air power would be foredoomed to failure. So Vandegrift was given a final deadline of August 7, 1942, and told to meet it.

To his credit, Vandegrift did. He had to scramble for supplies, collect his far-flung detachments, unload and then combat-load his ships under the driving rains of the Down Under winter, and, most difficult of all, draw up a plan based on what knowledge of the target area might be gained from a short story by Jack London, a faded snapshot postcard mailed many years previously by a missionary and the imperfect recollections of Australian planters and ship captains who had lived in the Solomons. In the meantime, Admiral Richmond Kelly Turner had arrived in Wellington to take charge as amphibious force commander. In late July Vandegrift and Turner made rendezvous at sea with a two-carrier supporting force commanded by Admiral Frank Jack Fletcher. In all, 19,000 Marines and 89 ships, the largest invasion force yet assembled, had been organized for the expedition which Vandegrift's staff called "Operation Shoestring." On July 27 Turner and Vandegrift learned just how thin their shoestring was when Admiral Fletcher informed them that he would provide air support for only two days rather than the required five. Turner and Vandegrift were dumfounded. They protested heatedly, but Fletcher, who was bitterly opposed to the entire operation, would not budge. He had a deep-seated fear of the Japanese torpedo bombers and Japan's dreaded Long Lance torpedo, and he was not going to risk his valuable carriers for more than two days.

Thus, in indecision and division, in reluctance even, the Americans launched their counteroffensive against the Japanese. And yet it proceeded almost without a hitch. Aided by bad weather which grounded enemy airplanes at Rabaul, the invasion fleet approached Guadalcanal-Tulagi undetected. The Japanese were asleep in their beds when the landings began on the morning of August 7, 1942.

On the big island of Guadalcanal there was almost no opposition. On Tulagi, however, the Japanese garrison resisted fiercely until it was finally destroyed. In the meantime, Rabaul had been alerted and the

Japanese began their counterattack. A strong surface force under Admiral Gunichi Mikawa sailed down The Slot, the 500-mile corridor running between the double chain of the Solomons. In the dark early morning of August 9, the Japanese, who were superbly trained in night fighting, surprised the Americans and sank the cruisers *Quincy, Astoria* and *Vincennes* along with the Australian cruiser *Canberra*. The Japanese then turned and raced up The Slot to put distance between them and the American carrier aircraft which they expected to rise at dawn. This they need not have feared, however, for Admiral Fletcher had kept his promise and withdrawn his carrier force. Left unprotected, Admiral Turner was forced to withdraw his transports before they were half unloaded. With this, Alexander Vandegrift and his Marines were left alone to conduct probably the greatest defensive stand in the annals of American arms.

Although the strategy for Guadalcanal was offensive, the tactics were now defensive. The Americans had captured an air base, which they named Henderson Field, and the Japanese were determined to recapture it. In this, the character of the Pacific War was made evident at the outset. In each battle the Americans sought to dislodge the Japanese from one of their bases, and then to use this conquest as their own base for the next strike. It was a steppingstone war, and Guadalcanal, the first such battle in it, was exceptional in that for the first and only time the Japanese made a determined counterattack, which came very close to succeeding.

For the first three months of the campaign, the issue was always in doubt. By night the Japanese sent their reinforcements and supplies stealing down The Slot, bombarded the Americans from the sea or came howling out of the jungle in full-scale attempts to seize Henderson Field. By day the Americans patrolled the jungle, strengthened their cordon defense around the field, fought off repeated aerial attacks or launched land operations designed to improve their position or destroy enemy concentrations. It was a most savage battle. Neither side gave or asked quarter. Japanese laborers and native Melanesians as well as the Marines, soldiers, sailors and fliers of both nations, fought each other from every imaginable type of vehicle, ship or aircraft, wielding every kind of gun or knife, striking with spears and axes, clubs and fists and stones, even, and often continuing the fight within the water where shipwrecked sailors or downed airmen clawed at each other with bare hands until, sometimes, sharks brought the battle to a horrible end. And while they fought, both sides were scourged with malaria, racked by dysentery, emaciated by hunger and scorched or drenched by turns in the blistering sun and torrential rains that made their battleground a stinking, steaming, festering slime.

In the end, the Americans triumphed. On land, the Marines, later reinforced by two Army regiments, defeated Japan's unwise attempts to retake the airfield with piecemeal reinforcements. If the Japanese had been patient and had slowly built up their forces on the island for one big push, the results might have been different. But they did not, and this was chiefly because of their foolish contempt for the fighting prowess of the Americans. In the sky the pilots of Vandegrift's "Cactus Air Force" very quickly exploded the myth of the invincibility of the Zero fighter and seized control of the air. At sea the American Navy came to threaten The Slot and to dominate Iron Bottom Bay, the channel between Tulagi and Guadalcanal, which was so named for the number of ships sunk in it.

Because the aggressive William Halsey had relieved the indecisive Ghormley, the American effort was given a resolution which it had not formerly possessed. Halsey assured Vandegrift of all-out support, and while Vandegrift's men hung on, he repeatedly risked carriers and capital ships to come to their rescue. On the night of November 12-13, 1942, an outnumbered American cruiser force hurled itself upon a Japanese battleship fleet in a furious, desperate ship-to-ship, gun-for-gun melee fought over the narrow waters of the bay. The Americans suffered heavily, but they drove the enemy into flight. This exposed a Japanese troop convoy to aerial attack, and with the coming of daylight the American pilots destroyed nearly an entire enemy division at sea. On the following night, another clanging, bellowing sea fight between battleships ended in American victory, and with that the tide of battle flowed away from the Japanese.

Japan could not now reinforce or supply her troops, while the Americans steadily brought in more soldiers and Marines. Ultimately, they went on the offensive out of the Henderson bastion, and in early February, 1943, the Japanese evacuated the island. So ended the battle for Guadalcanal, the fight that turned the tide of war in the Pacific.

To the north, Japan had failed to capture Port Moresby. Marching over the Owen Stanleys from their Buna-Gona base, the Japanese had come in sight of the port city only to be driven back the way they came by the Australians. Then a combined American-Australian force fell on the Buna-Gona beachhead and drove the Japanese out of it. With this and Guadalcanal, General MacArthur's road back to the Philippines lay open. A year after the Japanese had launched their limited war, the outer defenses of the line that was to hold for years had been burst asunder. Control of air and sea, the necessary conditions of victory in amphibious war, had passed to the Americans.

Thus the chain of reverses which the Japanese suffered after overreaching at Midway; and while this swift sure breach in her line was being held open for another six months, the Allies turned upon Hitler.

11

☆

While the battle for Guadalcanal raged during that summer and fall of 1942, the Soviet Army became locked in desperate combat with the German invaders, and America, fearing that her ally might be knocked out of the war, began rushing supplies to Russia.

Three routes were chosen, the most famous and dangerous being the "Murmansk Run" along the Norwegian coast and into the Arctic Ocean to the ports of Murmansk and Archangel. Dreadful shipping losses were suffered on this route, not only from U-boats but from long-range Nazi bombers based in Norway.

Less dangerous was the "Persian Corridor." Here, convoys sailed around the Cape of Good Hope and up the Persian Gulf into ports in Iran (Persia), after which supplies were unloaded and shipped overland to Russia. Safest of all routes was through Japanese-controlled waters to Vladivostok in Siberia. Japan and Russia were still bound by a nonaggression pact, and because the supplies were carried in vessels flying the Soviet flag they were not molested by the Japanese. However, shipment from Vladivostok via the trans-Siberian Railway was a long, slow and complicated process. Nevertheless, supplies flowed steadily into Russia from the arsenal of democracy, and as they did, Stalin demanded that a second front be opened in France to draw German strength westward.

Stalin had uttered not a word of protest when Hitler closed that front with his conquest of France. But now, with Hitler at his throat, he wanted it opened. Molotov was dispatched to Britain and America to urge it, and the vocal left wings of both nations, having remained silent during the Hitler-Stalin honeymoon, were now instructed to call out loudly for "The Second Front—Now!"

This demand coincided with the American plan to build forces in Britain for an early cross-Channel invasion of the Continent. The Americans were still thinking in terms of military victory only. They had no political objectives, at least not more than those vague, idealistic proposals put forward in the Atlantic Charter. They did not see that wars are fought for political rather than military purposes. Victory is not the goal, but the means by which the true goal of political stability may be secured. Militarily, there could be no better plan than to invade France and place Hitler between the two fires that would destroy him. Politically, nothing could be more disastrous, for it would leave Stalin and Communism free to pounce upon those nations of Central and Eastern Europe which they desired no less hungrily than Hitler. Naïve as Americans then were about Stalin's intentions, it was difficult for them to realize that Communism was as much the sworn enemy of democracy as Fascism. Hitler had driven them together as temporary allies, like a cat and a rat menaced by a snake, but once the common foe was vanquished the common cause would disappear and they would be enemies again. In a warm glow of comradeship, deftly fanned by leftist opinion, Americans believed that "we're all in this together." They were, but for different purposes: Americans to win the war, Communism to win the peace. This, then, was the basic fallacy of American war planning, and it was to have tragic consequences.

Not immediately, however, for the British ally, like the Russian, also had a peace plan. It was simply to thwart Russian postwar ambitions, at least in the Balkans, and to restore if possible the balance of power lost in the last war. British political purpose was ably served by British military strategy, a revival of the traditional concept of using a large navy and a small army to strike the enemy on his flank and rear, to exhaust him by distraction, to encourage uprisings against him and to stand ready to support these risings wherever they might occur. This was the strategy which was abandoned in World War I, when Britain for the first time fielded a mass army on the Continent. That mistake might have been repeated in the present war, except for the evacuation at Dunkirk, an event which restored to Britain her traditional freedom of action. The British plan was to subject Germany to strategic bombing from the air, while the naval blockade again drew tight the noose of hunger. In May of 1942, the R.A.F. began massive night raids against German cities, leading off with the 1,000-bomber raid on Cologne.

A more immediate British argument against the cross-Channel invasion was that the forces to attempt it were not yet large enough. Three times in the war—in France, Norway and Greece—the British had been thrown off the Continent. Next time they went back, they wanted to stay. The disastrous Anglo-Canadian reconnaissance-in-force at Dieppe in August of 1942 was to convince them that it would require great force indeed to burst Hitler's Atlantic Wall. What the British wanted was to invade North Africa, evict the Axis and cross into Southern Europe.

Throughout the first six months of 1942 the Anglo-Americans argued over their opposing plans. When in June Churchill flatly informed Roosevelt that Britain could not undertake a Cross-Channel operation that year, the American chiefs became so miffed that they were ready to abandon the Germany-First strategy and concentrate on Japan. FDR, however, did not wish to turn entirely away from Europe, and with some reluctance his chiefs accepted the North African invasion. Their reluctance quickly vanished, however, after Rommel began winning the Desert War again.

Taking Tobruk, Rommel drove the British back into Egypt and threatened the loss of the one area which, short of the home island, they had to hold. To oppose him, Churchill placed Bernard L. Montgomery in command of the Eighth Army. Wiry, waspish, egotistic, this general in the tank trooper's black beret was an excellent organizer. He took over by firing the incompetents, generals as well as subalterns, and gained the confidence of his multinational army by repeated visits to the front line. At El Alamein in northern Egypt he declared, in effect: "We will fight on the ground we now hold, and if we cannot stay here alive, we will stay here dead."[95] Rommel's armor clanked forward, aiming for a breakthrough and a dash to the Suez. But the Eighth Army held, and the triumphant Montgomery began building his forces for his own breakout.

Here the British general was in his element, for few commanders in World War II could equal him in the careful preparation of a "set-piece" battle. Supplies were then coming to him in great quantities, especially from America, and every gun, every tank, every soldier and bayonet had to go into its proper place in the exact proportion of superiority desired before Montgomery would move. In this, he was the exact opposite of the daring gambler Rommel. But Rommel had fallen ill and had returned to Germany, and the Italo-German force opposing the Eighth Army was now commanded by Georg von Stumme. On October 23, 1942, Montgomery informed his command: "When I assumed command of the Eighth Army I said that the mandate was to destroy Rommel and his army, and that it would be done as soon as we were ready. We are ready *now!*"[96]

Beneath a bright moonlit night a thousand big guns bombarded the Axis positions for four hours, after which infantry and light armor cleared two corridors through the enemy mine fields. Then the heavy formations surged forward. Battle for a time was confused, until General von Stumme fell dead of a heart attack, after which the fortunes of war turned against the Axis. In Germany Hitler called upon Rommel, and the Desert Fox left his sanatorium and flew into the battle. But he could not stop the Eighth Army, and his own forces were forced back eastward along the Libyan coast, while the British Navy bombarded them from the sea and the R.A.F. struck them from the air. Then Rommel heard even more depressing news: the Americans were landing to his rear.

The expedition to North Africa inscribed the name of Dwight Eisenhower in the pages of history, and gave to American arms her first personality general. This was one of Eisenhower's greatest assets, his warm personality characterized by a wide, friendly grin and laughing blue eyes, by his amazing capacity to return a soft reply to the harsh word, and it was no small quality in an officer who commanded in a democracy. In other ways, Eisenhower epitomized the new type of general evolved by the Managerial Revolution. He had never been and never would be in battle, and it is difficult to envision him leading a charge, like Napoleon at the bridge at Lodi. He was, rather, an excellent planner and an able administrator, a wise and tactful chairman of the board. As such, he was a wonderful choice to command a coalition. Military history may be compared to a vast burial ground of Allied causes done in by difference and division. Foch

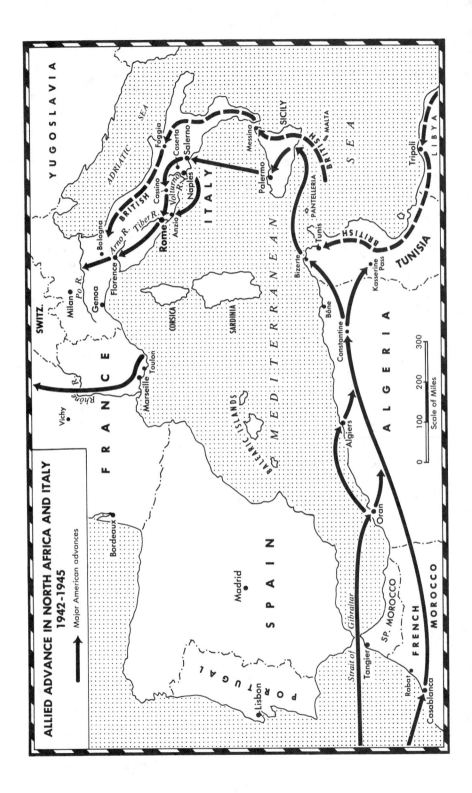

ALLIED ADVANCE IN NORTH AFRICA AND ITALY
1942-1945

→ Major American advances

Scale of Miles
0   100   200   300

YUGOSLAVIA

ADRIATIC SEA

BRITISH

ITALY

Bologna
Florence
Arno R.
Tiber R.
Rome
Anzio
Voltur. R.
Cassino
Naples
Salerno
Caserta
Foggia
Palermo
Messina
SICILY
BRITISH • MALTA

Po R.
Genoa
Milan
SWITZ.

FRANCE

Vichy

Rhône R.
Marseille
Toulon

Bordeaux

SPAIN

Madrid

PORTUGAL

Lisbon

CORSICA

SARDINIA

BALEARIC ISLANDS

MEDITERRANEAN SEA

BRITISH

Tunis
Bizerte
Bône
PANTELLERIA
Kasserine Pass
TUNISIA

Constantine

Algiers

ALGERIA

Oran

Gibraltar
Strait of Gibraltar
Tangier
SP. MOROCCO

Rabat
Casablanca
FRENCH MOROCCO

Tripoli
LIBYA

had never been free of such distraction in the last war, and the campaigns of Napoleon were always made easier because they were fought against coalitions. Eisenhower was deeply conscious of this, and all his tact and persuasiveness had gone into an effort to harmonize the Anglo-American expedition.

He was most tactful of all with the Vichy French of North Africa. First of all, he had seen that the 83,000 Americans in his force of 105,000 troops would form the spearheads. This was because the Vichy French resented the British attacks on their fleet after the fall of France. The British had also given support to the Free French strike at Dakar commanded by Charles de Gaulle. Because of this, the Vichy government had bombed British bases in Gibraltar and proclaimed the British an enemy.

Eisenhower's greatest worrry was not the U-boats or enemy air, both of which failed to harm his invasion fleet, but how the French would react to his landings at Casablanca, Oran and Algiers. He hoped that they would join the Allies, or at least not oppose them. To this end, the Combined Chiefs had cast about for a leader the French would follow.

Charles de Gaulle was not the man. De Gaulle had repudiated Pétain's capitulation and organized the Free French. Many Vichy officers accused him of being unfaithful to his soldier's oath. They also felt an implied rebuke in de Gaulle's conduct: if he was right, then they were wrong—it was that disturbingly simple.

The right man seemed to be Henri Giraud, a popular and highly esteemed general who had been captured during the Battle of France. Escaping his German captors, he was brought to Eisenhower's headquarters, and there, to the American's dismay, he made it plain that he expected to command the expedition to North Africa. After Ike explained that he only wished him to bring the French over to the Allied side, Giraud shook his head and replied: "Giraud will be a spectator in this affair."[97] Disheartened, Eisenhower went to bed; but in the morning Giraud told him he had changed his mind and would accompany the expedition.

That night Dwight Eisenhower stood with his staff on the dark headlines of Gibraltar, peering anxiously down at the hundreds of Allied ships slipping through the strait. At any moment flame and explosion might signal the advent of disaster. But there was neither, and in the morning of November 8, 1942, the landings began.

There was much confusion at all three ports, much loss of equipment—particularly of landing craft—because of inexperience. Nevertheless, there was success at the outset. At Algiers, farthest penetration inside the Mediterranean, the Americans easily captured the city in a single day. About 130 miles to the west at Oran, however, the French resisted stubbornly, and their officers showed no inclination to take orders from General Giraud. A long and bloody battle appeared certain, until Eisenhower learned that Admiral Darlan was in Algiers visiting his sick son.

If there was one man the French would obey it was Jean François Darlan, a British-hating sailor who had already been designated as Marshal Pétain's successor in Vichy. At once, General Mark Clark and Robert Murphy of the American Foreign Service went to confer with this powerful Frenchman, who was a *de facto* prisoner in his own back yard. At length, and only after he learned that Hitler had violated his word by occupying Southern France, Admiral Darlan gave the cease-fire order.

Meanwhile, there had been fierce fighting at Casablanca on the Atlantic coast. Here the French Navy had fought chiefly to defend its honor, and although it was severely pounded by the Americans, it was resolved to fight on. Here also General George S. Patton's soldiers were locked in combat with the French. Committing his tanks, Patton called for an aerial strike on the city, and Dauntlesses from the carrier *Ranger* were circling overhead when Darlan's cease-fire was received by the French. With that, hostilities ended.

Within four days Eisenhower had secured his North African bases. On November 15, 1942, he and Admiral Sir Andrew Cunningham drew up a formal accord with Darlan which made the Frenchman chief of a civil government in North Africa. Eisenhower was severely criticized for this "deal" with detestable Vichy. In fact, Eisenhower had ensured French cooperation, saved many lives, nailed down his bases and avoided the sabotage of future operations.

These operations were aimed eastward at Tunisia, to which Rommel was then retreating westward away from Montgomery. If Eisenhower arrived there first, he could put Rommel between himself and Montgomery. However, the alert Germans, already bombarding Allied shipping in the newly won ports, quickly took over Tunisia and converted it into a bastion. Eisenhower's drive eastward thereupon began to outrun its supplies and to slow down in rain and mud, and while sandstorms stopped Montgomery, Rommel's retirement was made secure by occupation of the Tunisian ports.

In January, 1943, Roosevelt and Churchill and their military chiefs met at Casablanca. Here, Anglo-American unity took a large stride forward after the British removed their objections to American exploitation of the newly won Pacific advantages, while the Americans consented to the invasion of Sicily that summer and agreed to postpone the cross-Channel operation until 1944. Here, also, Roosevelt, with Churchill's support, proclaimed the Allied policy of Unconditional Surrender.

The phrase was not included in the official agreement at Casablanca, and Roosevelt himself explained: ". . . suddenly the press conference was on, and Winston and I had had no time to prepare for it, and the thought popped into my mind that they had called Grant 'Unconditional Surrender' and the next thing I knew, I had said it."[98] So casual, so offhand, this drastic new policy ruled out any possibility of negotiation with the enemy through customary diplomatic channels, and it put the steel of desperation into the spines of the Axis war lords and thus prolonged the war and wasted many thousands of lives. By calling for a fight to the bitter end it weakened opposition to Hitler, strengthened his hold, and eventually left Germany leaderless and without a law and Russia supreme on the Continent.

It had been said that Unconditional Surrender had been offered as a sort of sop to Russia, a means of informing Stalin that the Allies would not let him down and that there would be no more "deals" as with Darlan. If so, then this mistake was the daughter of another perhaps deeper error: the fear that Stalin would make a separate peace with Hitler and quit the war. To do so, the Russian premier would have had to give up European Russia, that is, to surrender the bear's heart and head while keeping the useless big body for himself. In actual fact, Stalin criticized the concept of Unconditional Surrender. He knew that it would produce a last-ditch desperation in the enemy, and as late as May, 1945, Harry Hopkins reported that Stalin "feels that if we stick to unconditional surrender the Japs will not give up and we will have to destroy them as we did Germany."[99] Stalin certainly wished to see Hitler utterly destroyed, but he had no desire to see the German nation which he coveted wrecked by a prolonged war.

So the policy was proclaimed, and while Goebbels pounced upon it to raise the morale of the German Army, the rainy season ended in Tunisia.

Dwight Eisenhower was now in complete command in Tunisia. In the northwest his First Army under Sir Kenneth Anderson faced a German force commanded by Marshal Juergen von Arnim and in the southeast the Eighth under Montgomery was moving toward the Mareth Line held by Rommel. To Rommel's rear or north was an American force in the vicinity of Kasserine Pass. Assisted by Arnim, Rommel decided to strike the Americans before hitting Montgomery. If possible, he might effect a penetration and force an Allied withdrawal.

On February 14 the Germans fell on the inexperienced Americans at Kasserine Pass. They won a quick initial success, and in some areas the Americans panicked in their first night combat. Most of them hung on, however, and Rommel was forced to withdraw. This was the battle that blooded the American Army which fought in Europe. It had made at Kasserine the mistakes which are born of inexperience, and its complicated chain of command had permitted Rommel to pull back without hindrance. Yet the Americans learned fast. After Kasserine the American soldiers—brave and, what is sometimes better, flexible and adaptable—went on to victory after victory.

Rommel's next move was to strike at Montgomery, and he failed, after which, a sick man, he returned to Germany for good. Arnim, with whom Rommel had quarreled, was now in command. Meanwhile, Patton took over the II Corps which had fought at Kasserine. With his general's stars painted on both his helmet and his command car, his boots glistening and his pearl-handled pistol swinging from his hip, he roared into his new headquarters breathing fire. Very soon his men began calling him "Old Blood and Guts," and very quickly, because of his insistence upon discipline and soldierly pride, a demoralized corps was revitalized. For all his theatrics, most of which were put on to please his men, Patton was a solid commander with a thorough understanding of tank warfare, and he was able to distract the Germans with diversionary blows while Montgomery opened his major assault on the Mareth Line.

Bogged down at first, Montgomery changed his tactics to a maneuver reminiscent of Chancellorsville. While his main body pinned down the German left, another column turned the German right, menaced their rear and forced them to abandon the Mareth Line. Now Eisenhower relieved Patton, who was to command in Sicily, with Omar Bradley. Bradley's corps moved to the First Army's extreme left flank, and soon the battle for Tunisia became a race between Bradley's Americans and French driving down from the north and Montgomery's Eighth Army thrusting up from the south. Between them were Arnim's Italo-Germans, and with the Allies in control of the air and Montgomery alone possessing a four-to-one tank superiority, the outcome was a matter of time. On May 7 the Americans slammed into Bizerte and Tunis. All along the front Axis units were cut off and encircled and they were surrendering en masse. On May 13 the battle ended with the surrender of the Italian First Army to Montgomery. In all, 275,000 Axis soldiers were captured in the last week of fighting.

With the fall of North Africa, the Western Allies dealt Hitler his first defeat. Equally important, they had cleared the Mediterranean for their shipping and gained a great advantage in the deadly sea fight known as the Battle of the Atlantic.

Perhaps the most far-reaching decision taken at the Casablanca Conference was the agreement worded: "The defeat of the U-boat must remain a first charge on the resources of the United Nations."[100] It was made at the peak of the U-boat war, which had taken a disastrous turn in mid-January of 1942. Five weeks after Pearl Harbor, Admiral Doenitz opened a furious undersea attack on shipping off the East Coast of America. The campaign was called Operation *Paukenschlag,* or "Roll of the Drums," and it began with only six U-boats. Yet this scanty sextet of drummers did beat out a dreadful dirge for American shipping. They attacked at night, firing their torpedoes from seaward against ships boldly silhouetted by the lights of the coastal cities behind them. Not until May of that year was a blackout imposed on the coast, and in the meantime it was "business as usual," with ships sunk and sailors drowned by the light of boardwalks and ballrooms. The vessels themselves were lighted, and even the lighthouses and buoys showed lights. Thus obliged, only barely annoyed by ineffectual antisubmarine tactics, the U-boats grew so confident that they began to attack in daylight. On June 15 thousands of bathers at Virginia Beach watched in helpless horror while a German submarine torpedoed two American freighters. These were the six months of unrivaled success that U-boat crews forever afterward looked back on as "the happy times," and during them they sank no less than 568 Allied ships. Alarmed, General Marshall notified Admiral King that shipping losses in the Atlantic and Caribbean threatened the entire American war effort.

Gradually, with the introduction of the convoy system for coastal shipping and improved antisubmarine warfare, the American losses lessened. And Doenitz, resourceful as usual, began to concentrate on the Caribbean. He had by July, 1942, introduced the big new submarine tankers, "milch cows," capable of carrying 700 tons of fuel. Meeting U-boats at sea, the milch cows could feed 50 tons of fuel to a medium U-boat, thus widening its cruising range in the Caribbean, or give 90 to a big one and send it ranging as far away from base as the Cape of Good Hope. Toward the end of the year, the wolf packs returned to the North Atlantic.

Doenitz had discovered that air cover for the Allied convoys was given only at either end of a voyage. There was a wide gap in mid-ocean, and this came to be called "the black pit" after the wolf packs began massing there. Ship after ship vanished into it. Then, in November, 1942, with many of the escorting warships drawn off to the landings in North Africa, the U-boats sank 117 ships! That was the blackest month of the Battle of the Atlantic, just as 1942 became the black year.

During it the Allies lost eight million tons of shipping. U-boats sank ships faster than America could build them, and this, of course, imposed a dreadful burden on the American shipbuilding industry. First, it had to replace most Allied shipping losses, after which it was supposed to double the replacement if shipments of munitions to all the fighting fronts were to be doubled as scheduled. Finally, it had to build the warships especially designed for protecting the new merchant fleet.

The response to this dual challenge was magnificent. Newly opened shipyards on both coasts began building Liberty ships. Ugly, slow and uncomfortable for those who sailed them, the Libertys could nevertheless be built very quickly. With amazing speed, American know-how cut construction time from the 244 days required to build the first Liberty in 1941 to an average of 42 days per ship in late 1942. In all, 2,700 Liberty ships were built and they carried 75 percent of America's cargo overseas.

Meanwhile, new fleets of destroyer escorts and small escort aircraft carriers called CVEs were built. They were designed to give aerial cover across that deadly gap in mid-ocean. Each CVE carried 16 fighters and 12 torpedo bombers. Screened by the swift, sub-killing destroyer escorts, the CVEs became the scourge of the wolf packs. Their fighters could strafe surfaced subs or depth-bomb submerged ones, and their bombers struck with torpedoes. Toward the end of the war they launched the "Fido" homing torpedo. Dropped anywhere near a submarine, it would make for the U-boat's steel hull. Thus, assisted by a growing array of detection devices able to pinpoint the U-boats, the Allies became more and more expert in locating submarines.

In April of 1943 flotillas independent of escort duty were formed to hunt and kill the U-boats, now at their peak operating strength of 230. Gradually, they drove the wolf packs beneath the surface, and then they began to kill them off. In May, 30 U-boats were destroyed. By June shipping losses were at their lowest since America entered the war. Then Allied bombers entered the battle, patrolling the skies over the Bay of Biscay and helping to destroy another 37 U-boats in July.

German shipyards struggled to replace Doenitz's losses. They concentrated on producing a giant new submarine equipped with the new "schnorkel" breathing device which would enable them to travel farther and faster underwater. What the shipyards could not replace, however, were seasoned skippers and trained crews. One by one the undersea aces failed to return to port, among them Doenitz's two sons and his son-in-law. Meanwhile, Allied shipping had been granted a great breathing spell by the fall of North Africa, which cleared the Mediterranean routes and cut 45 days from schedules formerly routed around the Cape. But the biggest blow of all was struck with the Allied invasion of France in June, 1944. With this the French ports were lost to Doenitz.

Still, he did not despair. He was confident that the new boats with their increased speed and range would revolutionize warfare, and he expected to have 350 of these built during 1945. Shortages of special materials required ruined his plans, however, and in the main he was compelled to carry on with the smaller, older boats, many of which were destroyed in their pens by Allied bomber raids.

In the end, the Battle of the Atlantic was won by the Allies. Some 780 German submarines were lost, of which 632 were sunk at sea by the Allies. They had accounted for the loss of 14 million tons of Allied shipping, against the losses of 11 million inflicted by their predecessors in World I. Once again the submarine service, the poor relation of the German military family, had come very close to winning the war on its own. And not until May 28, 1945, were the United States Navy and the British Admiralty able to issue this joint announcement:

"Effective this date . . . no further trade convoys will be sailed. Merchant ships by night will burn navigation lights at full brilliancy and need not darken ship."[101]

12

☆

After the fall of Tunisia, General Eisenhower wished to invade Sicily as soon as possible, but he could not because there were not enough landing craft available. One good reason for this was that Allied production was concentrating on the weapons that would win the war against the U-boats. Another, not so good reason was that, in this greatest of amphibious wars, the advocates of strategic bombing had made their point and the factories were busier with bombers than with landing boats. Thus a two-month delay was forced upon Eisenhower, and before he invaded Sicily he struck at the island of Pantellaria.

Lying between Tunisia and Sicily, Pantellaria had an airfield from which the invasion could be menaced. It was also a tiny and impregnable rock held by 11,000 Italian soldiers whose guns were zeroed in on the one harbor through which landings could be attempted. Eisenhower, however, was convinced that "most Italians had had a stomachful of fighting and were looking for any good excuse to quit."[102] So Pantellaria was subjected to a powerful aerial pounding lasting six days and nights. On June 11, seeing the Allied invasion force approaching, the island's defenders hoisted the white flag. They and their fortifications had been hardly scratched, but the sight of men who could harm them—not the bombs—had caused them to quit without a fight.

Now Eisenhower was ready. About 180,000 Allied troops would go against the 405,000 men—315,000 Italians and 90,000 Germans —holding Sicily. Aware that the best of the German forces were concentrated in the west, Eisenhower planned to land in the south and southeast, after which the two armies would race away from each other around the coast and meet in Messina. As such, the plan was not calculated to trap the enemy forces but rather to clear them out of Sicily. In hopes of deceiving the enemy, a corpse carrying information indicating strikes at Greece and Sardinia was washed ashore in Spain. The hoax deceived only Hitler, who reinforced those areas; but the astute Albert von Kesselring, the German commander in Italy, reinforced Sicily. So the Allied fleet gathered. With a total of 1,375 ships, it was the largest amphibious force yet gathered, larger even for its first day than the Normandy operation of the following year. Some of these ships came from the United States and Britain, and because some of the smaller vessels were to put out from Tunisia, Sicily was to be a shore-to-shore as well as a ship-to-shore operation.

At Sicily also the Axis would see what had been wrought by Anglo-American naval ingenuity. Here were unveiled the 1,500-ton, 328-foot Landing Ship Tank (LST), the 550-ton, 112-foot Landing Craft Tank (LCT), and the 200-ton, 158-foot Landing Craft Infantry (LCI). The LST, which its disenchanted passengers insisted stood for "Large Stationary Target," was the work horse of amphibious warfare. It could run up on a beach, open its bow doors, and lower a ramp down which troops ran and vehicles rolled. It could also do this at sea for amphibious vehicles to go splashing into the water. When the LCIs ran ashore, gangways to either side of the bow were lowered for the troops to debark. However, the LCIs were not very seaworthy transports and eventually were converted into rocket ships. The LSTs carried the tanks and artillery which are vital in the initial hours of a landing. Troops at the water's edge are most vulnerable to counterattack, especially by tanks, and an invading force needs its own tanks and guns to repel them. Aircraft flying close-up strikes also can break up an enemy tank thrust, but the Sicilian armada was not to get the tactical air support it required. Allied aircraft became too preoccupied with trying to win the campaign by saturation bombing.

Nevertheless, on the morning of July 10, 1943, Allied soldiers went sloshing through the roaring white surf of Sicily. General Patton's Seventh Army landed on the left, Montgomery's Eighth on the right.

They were all but unopposed. Meanwhile, Allied paratroopers held up the crack Hermann Goering Division which came racing out of the west under orders to throw the invaders into the sea. The airborne troops had landed during the night, and many of them had been lost when the gliders were cut adrift too soon and high winds blew them back into the sea. Otherwise, the landings were a great success. Quickly, Montgomery's men began driving north toward Messina while Patton's split into two columns, one racing west along the coast, the other pushing straight north across the center of the island.

Eleven days after the landing, American forces cut the island in two and clattered into Palermo. "As we approached," wrote Patton, "the hills on each side were burning. We then started down a long road cut out of the side of a cliff which went through an almost continuous village. The street was full of people shouting, 'Down with Mussolini,' and 'Long live America.' "[103]

So it went as the Allies pursued the hated Germans. Flowers were strewn in the path of the liberators, and gifts of wine, lemons or melons pressed into their hands. Italian soldiers began to surrender in the thousands, and eventually both Allied armies joined flanks to present a continuous line. Nevertheless, the Germans fought stubbornly, not to hold the island but to delay its conquest and to save their men and arms. They were expert in mining roads or in sowing them with tank traps. They fought as though by timetable, carrying out skillful rear-guard actions, blowing bridges and destroying the narrow shelf roads snaking around Sicily's steep cliffs. All this was carried out with very little real interference from the dreadful weight of metal poured upon them from the skies, and it forced the Allies to press mule trains into service while their engineers, clinging to the cliff faces like human spiders, built the trestles that supported advancing spearheads. Thus the Germans were able to get across the Strait of Messina into Italy before Patton's spearheads clattered into the Sicilian capital. Nevertheless, the Allies had won Sicily, a most valuable bridgehead for invasion of Italy, the area which Winston Churchill was fond of calling "the soft underbelly of Europe." And as Sicily was falling, the father of Fascism also fell.

By the summer of 1943, Benito Mussolini had begun to lose his hold on Italy. He had led his nation into an unpopular war, and now Allied aircraft were bringing the mainland under massive bombardment. They also dropped propaganda leaflets aimed at exploiting the Italian defection. One of them, signed by Roosevelt and Churchill, concluded: "The time has now come for you, the Italian people, to consult your own self-respect and your own interests and your own desire for a restoration of national dignity, security and peace. The time has come for you to decide whether Italians shall die for Mussolini and Hitler—or live for Italy, and for civilization."[104] Such communications gave encouragement to Fascist leaders plotting the Duce's downfall. Mussolini himself rushed off to a meeting with Adolf Hitler on July 17. Hitler, however, had small comfort to give. He had already suffered his worst military disaster, the defeat at Stalingrad where an entire army of 300,000 men was destroyed. Now the Russians were counterattacking with growing strength. No, the Duce could get only homilies from Hitler, and advice to defend Italy "so that Sicily may become for the enemy what Stalingrad was for us."[105] Then an agitated Italian official interrupted with the report: "At this moment Rome is undergoing a violent enemy air bombardment."[106] Mussolini rushed back to Rome and found that opposition to him had hardened under Count Dino Grandi.

Grandi, a former Foreign Minister and Ambassador to Britain, had bitterly opposed Italian intervention. He now compelled Mussolini to call a meeting of the Fascist Grand Council, not convened since 1939. The Council met on July 24, 1943. Twenty-eight Fascist chiefs dressed in black Fascist uniforms solemnly voted on Grandi's proposal that command of the armed forces be given to the King. Nineteen voted "Yes," seven "No," and two abstained. With that, Mussolini's arrest was quietly arranged, while the outraged Duce rushed next day to confront the King.

Mussolini began to storm at the Grand Council's decision, and the King replied: "My dear Duce, it's no longer any good. Italy has gone to bits. Army morale is at rock bottom. . . . At this moment you are the most hated man in Italy."[107] The King said that he thought he would replace Mussolini with Marshal Pietro Badoglio, whereupon Mussolini thundered: "Then, according to your Majesty I ought to *resign!*"

"Yes," the king said calmly, "and I accept your resignation forthwith."

The Duce was stunned. "Then my ruin is complete,"[108] he muttered hoarsely, and tottered outside to be taken into custody. In such comic-opera style did a dictatorship of 21 years come to its end. It had had its moments of glory. It had raised Italy to a prominence that she had never held before. It had cleansed the nation of Communism. It might, with discretion and courage, have also kept out Nazism. But it had not, and as it says in the Parable, "the last state of that man becomes worse than the first."[109]

Mussolini's fall filled Dwight Eisenhower with an eagerness to invade Italy at once, preferably up high on the boot, around the shinbone, at Naples. His British colleagues were more cautious, favoring a strike at the toe. Moreover, landing craft were leaving the Mediterranean for the Pacific, and ships and aircraft and troops had been ordered to the Atlantic in the build-up for the cross-Channel operation the following year. Finally, the policy of unconditional surrender, coupled with Marshal Badoglio's timidity, gave the Germans the time to pour 13 divisions into Italy, to seize Rome and other cities, to pluck Mussolini out of the hands of his captors and install him as chief of a puppet government and to fortify the peninsula.

Badoglio has since claimed that to have proclaimed a peace would have turned Italy over to the Germans bound hand and foot. He also minimized the importance of unconditional surrender. Yet for five weeks he did haggle over the meaning of those two words, until an exasperated Eisenhower finally ordered a resumption of bombing attacks. With that Badoglio surrendered his country. The date was September 3, 1943, the same day on which two divisions of the Eighth Army crossed the strait between Messina and Reggio di Calabria on the toe of the Italian boot. Their objective was the German airfields at Foggia on the Adriatic coast. On the opposite Mediterranean coast six days later, the American Fifth Army under General Mark Clark began landing at Salerno. Clark's objective was Naples with its enormous harbor. Thus an Allied column was to advance up either coast.

At Salerno the Americans hoped for surprise, but as the assault boats neared the beaches in the early-morning darkness, a loudspeaker began crackling ashore and a German voice roared in English: "Come on in and give up. You're covered!"[110] They *were* covered, and naked as well in the eerie light of flares shooting into the sky. From front, left and right came the raking fire of German guns emplaced above the beachhead. Still, the Americans went in, gradually establishing a foothold on those pebbly beaches, and then battling inland to expand it. Four days later the Germans counterattacked, nearly hurling the Americans into the sea. Rushing to the front, Clark told his soldiers: "We don't give another inch. This is it. Don't yield anything. We're here to stay."[111]

They very nearly did not stay, after Kesselring sent his tanks clanking into the battle. They burst through the American front and began to carve out pockets in the rear. Had Kesselring massed his 600 tanks, it is likely he might have dealt the invader a death blow. But he did not, and the American soldiers at Salerno, helped by air support flying in from North Africa and Sicilian bases, held firm.

Meanwhile, Montgomery's steady drive up the Adriatic had unmasked Kesselring's left flank, forcing the German to fall back on Naples. Then the Eighth Army took the vital Foggia airfields, providing air support right on the edge of the battlefield. Kesslering retreated farther, and the Americans entered the blackened ruins called Naples. With customary thoroughness, the Germans had made a smoking desert of one of the oldest cities of Western civilization, excluding neither university nor church from their torches, throwing open the prisons, looting the hospitals, sowing the harbor with sunken ships and the streets with booby traps. Yet within a month resourceful American engineers had the harbor partially cleared and working, while civil affairs officers, a merciful new wrinkle on the ugly face of war, began to care for a hungry and horrified populace.

After Naples and Foggia, the two-pronged Allied advance began to slow down. Von Kesselring had assured Hitler that he could hold northern Italy against all comers, and to do so he threw a series of defensive lines across the peninsula. Artillery was registered on every road and trail and possible bivouac area. Mine fields and demolitions guarded every avenue of approach, and mortar and machine-gun positions were well dug in and camouflaged to blend with the countryside. The terrain was made for such warfare. It was a jumble of steep hills, laced with valleys and gorges through which raced cold swift rivers fed by Alpine lakes. The rivers twisted and turned so frequently that one American division crossed the Volturno several times during a single advance, causing a GI to burst out: "Every damn river in this fool country is named Volturno!"[112]

Winter brought torrents of rain which carried off bridges, washed out roads and turned the earth into mud. The Italian campaign had become a repetition of the position warfare of World War I. There was absolutely no room for maneuver because there was, once again, a front without flanks. Terrain made tank tactics useless, and when the weather was clear enough for the Allies to utilize their control of the air, their saturation-bombing attacks had no more power to effect a breakthrough than had the massive artillery bombardments of the last war. Why, then, did not the Allies draw their amphibious whip again and strike Kesselring's rear with landings far up the Adriatic?

Because there was simply not enough assault shipping or landing craft to do it. There would never be enough to meet the demands of two-ocean amphibious war, and most of what was then available in that winter of 1943-44 had left the Mediterranean for the Pacific.

13

☆

Early in the Pacific War Admiral Nimitz and General MacArthur concluded that it would be a costly mistake to attempt to take all or most of the island forts with which Japan proposed to defend her new empire. Instead, they decided to seize the most important and by-pass the others, leaving them to "wither on the vine." Should any of the by-passed islands menace the American line of communications, they would be "neutralized" by carrier and land-based aircraft.

This was the concept of "island-hopping" which was to speed up the island war and which, General Tojo later admitted, was one of the chief causes of Japan's defeat. In the straitened habit of thought which was another great flaw in the armor of Nippon, the Japanese believed that because they had acquired and fortified these islands one by one, the Americans would try to do the same.

Island-hopping followed two invasion routes. Nimitz's was westward through the Central Pacific and the little islands of Micronesia, before veering right or north at the Marianas and thence to Japan. MacArthur's was through the Bismarck Barrier formed by the enormous island of New Guinea on the left or south and the Solomons –New Britain–Admiralties complex on the right. Beyond the Bismarck Barrier lay other island steppingstones to the Philippines.

The conquest of Guadalcanal and the eviction of the Japanese from the northeast coast of New Guinea had begun MacArthur's march, after which he had been compelled to mark time while Allied strength was concentrated for the blows in the Mediterranean. There had been a few sideshows, however, if any operation in which men suffer and die may be so lightly described. There was one of a bloodless nature in the Russells farther up the Solomons ladder, which Marines occupied unopposed in February, 1942. The following May American infantry reclaimed the Aleutian islands off the coast of Alaska. Americans on Attu fought in deep snows and against an enemy whose blind devotion to his emperor led him to arm even his sick and wounded for a final suicidal "banzai" charge. Next the Japanese evacuated Kiska and by mid-August the entire chain was again in American hands.

Other than these actions, most of the combat during the first eight months of 1943 took place in the air. On March 1 a Japanese convoy of eight ships and eight destroyers attempting to reinforce New Guinea strong points was detected in the Bismarck Sea. It had no aerial cover, and Allied aircraft very quickly sank all the transports and half of the destroyers. In this Battle of the Bismarck Sea, the great folly of attempting to reinforce or supply without aerial support was demonstrated. Never again did the Japanese risk big ships in such attempts. Thereafter, barges were used. They moved by night, and holed up by day in the numerous coves and inlets of the islands. Eventually, the Bismarck barge traffic was also destroyed, hunted by day by American aircraft and scourged at night by torpedo boats.

Japanese aerial warfare rose to a furious crescendo during April as Admiral Yamamoto hurled a series of strikes aimed at pinning down the Americans on Guadalcanal and New Guinea while the Bismarck Barrier was being strengthened. Although outnumbered, the Americans had the advantage of being forewarned by the coast watchers.

The coast watchers were the human radar of the South and Southwest Pacific. Mostly Australians, they were planters and ship captains who had gone into the bush with the Japanese capture of New Guinea, the Bismarcks and the Solomons. From wilderness lookouts guarded by faithful Melanesian natives, they kept watch on Japanese movements and radioed this information to Allied forces. Because of the coast watchers, many a surface force stealing down The Slot had sailed straight into waiting American naval guns, and many an aerial strike was shot to ribbons by American fighters "stacked" in the clouds beforehand. Coast watchers also rescued fliers shot down in sea or jungle, as well as shipwrecked American sailors. If Japanese in similar straits were willing to surrender, they were taken prisoner; otherwise they were killed. Lieutenant John F. Kennedy, later to become President of the United States, was rescued by a coast watcher after an enemy destroyer rammed his torpedo boat and cut it in two. With such sharp-eyed allies, then, flying better aircraft and being better fliers, the Americans broke up Yamamoto's strikes and inflicted serious loss on the enemy.

However, those Japanese pilots who did get back to base reported great success. Such deception, born of the Oriental fixation on saving face, was to occur again and again in the Pacific War, to the great benefit of the Allies and the grave detriment of Japan. From the high command reporting personally to Tojo or Hirohito, down to riflemen and seamen coming back from patrol, the Japanese habitually exaggerated their successes or at least minimized their failures. In this operation, Yamamoto was so misled that he canceled future strikes and scheduled an inspection trip to the big island of Bougainville in the Upper Solomons. The Americans, again blessed by Magic, learned of the trip and immediately queried Washington on the wisdom of removing Yamamoto. After the Pentagon replied that the death of the iron admiral would be a grave loss to Japan, a "killer" band of 12 Lightning fighters was assembled. On the morning of April 18, they skimmed low up The Slot. With perfect timing, they arrived just as the transport carrying Yamamoto was dropping down for a landing. While the rest of the Lightnings tore into the admiral's cover of nine Zeros, the American trigger section, the best shots, flashed down for the kill. Captain Thomas Lamphier's guns stuttered, sawing off the transport's wings, and the aircraft crashed into the jungle carrying the Emperor's "one and only Yamamoto" to his death.

Now MacArthur began to deliver his blows against the Bismarck Barrier, striking on the left while Admiral Halsey, under his command, swung at the right. MacArthur's first three objectives were the enemy strongholds at Salamaua, Lae and Finschhafen on the Huon

Peninsula of New Guinea. He took them when and as he pleased, using his limited resources of American and Australian infantry, assisted by the Navy and the A.A.F., to baffle and blast the enemy by turns. Landings were made from both the sea and the sky, and the enemy often found himself caught between two fires front and rear or else facing in the wrong direction to receive attack. By early October MacArthur was in full possession of the Huon Peninsula. By then Halsey had commenced the right-hand advance.

Halsey's first objective was the island of New Georgia in the Central Solomons. Here the Japanese had constructed Munda Airfield, the southernmost of their air bases running down from Rabaul. The first landings were made by Marines on the island's southern tip, then soldiers occupied Rendova Island standing west of Munda, quickly emplacing artillery which began to bombard the airfield across the channel. Finally, Army infantry crossed the water to invest Munda itself. An entire corps was ultimately committed against the Japanese, who fought with customary tenacity, and it was two months before Munda fell on September 25. Next, Halsey leapfrogged Kolombangara and occupied Vella Lavella unopposed and in Nevember, 1943, Marines stormed ashore at Bougainville.

This operation was commanded by Vandegrift, who had decided to draw enemy strength to the south before landing at Cape Torokina about halfway up the 130-mile island's west coast. Then, because of the density of Bougainville's jungle, the enemy would have great difficulty collecting his forces for a counterattack. So diversionary landings were effected below the island and a feint made at its southern tip. Because of this, it was not until March of 1944 that the Japanese were able to launch their unsuccessful counterattack. In the meantime, Seabees and Army engineers had transformed a jungle swamp into Torokina Airfield and thus brought Rabaul within aircraft range. Fifth Air Force bombers and fighters based on New Guinea also struck at this central Bismarck bastion, while the Navy's fast carriers rocked it with surprise raids.

Rabaul was rapidly becoming a ghost base, and yet it was still much too powerful to take by direct assault. Instead, it was by-passed. In December, 1943, Marines seized Cape Gloucester at the western end of New Britain, 370 miles away from Rabaul; and in February, 1944, dismounted cavalrymen assaulted the Admiralties still farther west and north. This last stroke sealed Rabaul's fate and burst the

Bismarck Barrier. It was typical of MacArthur's daring and flexibility. Begun as a reconnaissance in force with MacArthur personally in command, it was quickly expanded into an occupation once it was discovered that the Japanese could be evicted. Thus the year 1944 began with Douglas MacArthur poised to take his second big step toward the Philippines. Concurrently, Admiral Nimitz had completed his first long step toward Japan.

Battle in the Central Pacific differed from fighting in the Southwest as heat-bathed coral differs from rain-drenched swamp, knockout from exhaustion and frontal assault from maneuver. From Guadalcanal to the Admiralties, Americans and their allies had fought prolonged, wearying campaigns to seize large, heavily forested islands where maneuver was always possible and on which malaria-bearing mosquitoes and monsoon rains were enemies nearly as formidable as the Japanese. In the Central Pacific they stormed small ocean forts in brief, bloody battles fought beneath a blazing sun and across featureless, shelterless coral on which maneuver was seldom possible.

The chains of the Central Pacific were formed by atolls, that is, rings of coral islets enclosing a lagoon. Not every islet in an atoll ring needed to be fortified. The Japanese chose the largest one to hold an airfield and then transformed it into a fortress. Both the seaward and lagoon waters bristled with barbed-wire barricades, mines and cement antiboat obstacles. Sometimes a sea wall four or five feet high would girdle an islet. In this were firing ports to sweep the narrow beaches, and behind it were interlocking systems of artillery, machine-gun and rifle fire. Mortars and artillery were registered on all boat approaches and the beaches. Inland were networks of pillboxes mounting antitank guns, again interlaced with small arms and automatic weapons. These positions were sometimes connected by tunnels or trenches. Inland also were the troop reserves or the tanks which were to deliver the counterblows designed to execute the Japanese battle doctrine of destroying the enemy at the water's edge. Finally, huge bombproofs, often of walls of reinforced concrete four or five feet thick, housed the fighting headquarters or coastal defense guns up to 8-inch in caliber. Obviously, such fixed positions could neither be turned, surprised nor bombarded into submission. The Japanese defending Oceania were not the defenders of Pantellaria. Like their comrades in the Southwest, they sang the ancient battle oath which was now the national anthem:

> Corpses drifting swollen in the sea depths,
> Corpses rotting in the mountain grass—
> We shall die, we shall die for the Emperor,
> We shall never look back.

Here was an army unique in history, not because it was sworn to fight to the last man, but because it very nearly did. Against such soldiers holding such positions, Nimitz relied upon the blasting power of his aerial and naval artillery and the quality of his assault troops. Fortunately, in his opening operation he found American bravery sufficient to redeem the deficiency of American bombardment.

This was in the Gilberts, 2,400 miles west of Hawaii. Here Nimitz chose to seize Makin and Tarawa atolls, and simultaneous landings were made on November 20, 1943. As expected, lightly defended Makin was quickly overrun by two regiments of infantry. Tarawa, however, was a different proposition. Here the parrot-shaped islet of Betio, 291 acres in all, had been so fortified that its commander boasted: "A million men cannot take Tarawa in a hundred years."[113] It fell to about 12,000 American Marines in four days. But they were bloody days. At Tarawa were made certain mistakes which the Americans, with their characteristic ability to learn from error, were not to repeat. Naval intelligence had correctly calculated that Betio was defended by 5,000 men. This figure was arrived at by the ingenious procedure of studying photographs of Japanese latrines, counting the number of holes, and then, aware of the Japanese ratio of behinds to holes, multiplying them by the proper number. Intelligence failed grievously in estimating the depth of water which would cover the inner or drying reef which usually lies about 500 to 1,000 yards offshore of a coral islet. Britons who had lived in the British-held Gilberts were questioned and had assured the Americans that there would be five feet of water over the reef, enough to permit the passage of landing boats. However, this assurance was based on the assumption that the Americans would attack on the flood tide, the time of year when all tides are at their highest, when, in fact, they were going in on the neap, the season of lowest tides. As a result, the water over the reef was only *three* feet, and landing boats could not cross.

The tragic consequences of this error might have been forestalled had the preinvasion bombardment fulfilled expectations. For weeks prior to the invasion little Betio was pounded from sea and sky. Before the Marines went in an admiral promised them he would obliterate the island. Three battleships and a host of cruisers and lesser ships thundered at Betio until it was obscured beneath a pall of glowing pink dust. Yet, minutes after the bombardment lifted, the Japanese had recovered from their shock and were blasting away at the Americans churning shoreward in amphibious tractors. They knocked out so many amtracks that there were not enough of them left to transport the second wave of men stalled in their landing boats on the other side of the impassable reef. Thus the Marines *had to wade in.*

Rifles high overhead, they moved a half-mile through waist-high water while all around them sang the unseen messengers of death. Some of them stumbled in potholes and sank out of sight, drowned by the weight of their equipment. The follow-up waves did get in, however, and thus turned the tide of battle; but they suffered grievously in so doing. From this bloody lesson the Americans learned that saturation or "blanket" bombardment is a misnomer. No target, not even 291-acre Betio, is small enough to be blanketed. Fire had to be directed, targets pinpointed, for both naval guns and aerial bombs, and this had to be done *on land.* Aerial photo interpretation of that time was not the marvel that it is today, and observers in the sky or on the sea were always too far away to tell whether an innocent hummock of sand was, in fact, a pillbox, or whether an obvious pillbox was actually a dummy made of sand. So the Americans developed techniques by which specially trained ground observers went in with the first wave to pinpoint targets for battleships and bombers. After Tarawa also, admirals were very cautious in gambling on tides or weather.

Tarawa had other repercussions. The nation was shocked by casualties of 1,000 dead and 2,300 wounded. Actually, as these dreadful costs are measured, the price was not too high. Amphibious assault usually accepts a three-to-one adverse casualty rate, yet the Marines in killing 4,700 Japanese had more than reversed this in men killed. Of course, American losses might have been, should have been, lower. Nevertheless, for all its failures and misconceptions, Tarawa ranks as one of the decisive actions of the Pacific War. In demonstrating that the Americans had both the weapons and the men to take Japan's ocean citadels, it foretold the doom of the island empire.

Nimitz's next strike was at Kwajalein Atoll in the middle of the Marshalls 650 miles west of Tarawa. Kwajalein was an ideal base. Its atoll ring enclosed the largest lagoon in the world. The Japanese had airfields in the twin islets of Roi-Namur in the north and Kwajalein Islet in the south. Both were subjected to intensive preinvasion bombardment characterized by a greater emphasis on individual targets. Naval gunfire was also more accurate, and was delivered at very close range by a specially trained force of bombardment ships, mainly the refitted old battleships sunk at Pearl Harbor. This time the troop transports sailed *inside* the lagoon through a passage covered by artillery sited on islands seized before the invasion. On February 1, 1944, an Army division stormed ashore at Kwajalein and a Marine division hit Roi-Namur. Roi had been utterly wrecked, but there was a fierce fight before Namur fell. On Kwajalein, half of the islet's 5,000 defenders had survived the bombardment, and they fought for four days to the bitter end.

Next, Nimitz struck at Eniwetok, the westernmost of the Marshalls. Here the *battleships* sailed inside the lagoon, and they were a terrifying sight indeed to the islet's defenders, gliding toward the pillboxes with spouting guns and swaying towers. Eniwetok fell to a Marine regiment on February 23.

Meanwhile, Nimitz had also struck hard at Truk. "The Gibraltar of the Pacific," Truk was Japan's great air-sea base in the heart of the huge Caroline Islands chain. It was a drowned mountain range encircled by a coral reef. The mountain peaks above the great anchorage that was Truk Lagoon formed the islands on which were based airfields and supply depots. American planners considered Truk impregnable to assault from the sea, and it probably was. Nimitz, however, had determined to "neutralize" it. By early 1944 he had received many of the fast new carriers which were to be decisive in the Pacific War. With these, and with such mighty new battleships as *New Jersey* and *Iowa,* he formed the magnificent Fifth Fleet under Admiral Spruance and sent it steaming toward Truk. On February 17 carrier aircraft surprised the Japanese and seized mastery of the air over Truk. Then shipping in the lagoon was bombed and torpedoed while Spruance led his big warships on a round-the-atoll prowl for escaping ships. So audacious and successful was the American assault that they actually rescued their downed airmen inside the enemy lagoon. By nightfall the Gibraltar of the Pacific was a smoking rubble which Nimitz could now safely by-pass while making his right-hand turn north to Japan.

This path led up the ladder to the Marianas Islands, the Pearl Harbor of Japan. Seizure of the Marianas would uncover Japan's inner defenses. On the large islands of Guam, Saipan and Tinian the Americans could build bases for the huge new B-29 Superfort bombers which were then coming into production, and thus bring Japan within bombing range. Finally, Nimitz hoped that a Marianas invasion fleet would lure the Japanese fleet into decisive battle.

On June 14, 1944, the American bombardment fleet ringed Saipan with bellowing guns while two Marine divisions stormed the western beaches at the southern end of the island. As at Tarawa, the Japanese artillery had registered on the boat approaches, and there were even colored flags in the water to mark the range. This time, however, the Navy's frogmen had carefully scouted the reefs and waters in advance, and the Marines, led by new amphibious tanks called "armored pigs," went roaring through the enemy's fire with a minimum of casualties. They fought off counterattacks to nail down the beachhead, and a few days later an Army division was put ashore.

It was then that the Japanese Navy bit hard on the Saipan bait. Even as the landings began, the Combined Fleet was ordered to attack and destroy the American invasion force. Saipan simply could not be lost. Admiral Spruance knew of the Japanese approach. His submarines had been shadowing the enemy. With calm fortitude he sent Turner away with the transports and supply ships, put himself and the fighting ships in a defensive position around Saipan and sent Admiral Marc Mitscher and the fast carriers racing west to intercept the enemy. Thus began the Battle of the Philippine Sea, which opened with disaster for Japan when the submarine *Cavalla* sank the big flattop *Shokaku*. Then Mitscher's war birds sank the carrier *Hiyo,* after which submarine *Albacore* sank carrier *Taiho*. In the skies above, American fliers slaughtered the enemy in what came to be known as "The Marianas Turkey Shoot." In all, Japan lost three big carriers and 476 airplanes against American losses of 130 airplanes—many of which crashed during night landings—and three ships damaged. Where Japan lost 445 fliers, the Americans lost only 76. It was perhaps the most stunning aerial victory of the war, and it marked the effective destruction of Japanese carrier power in the Pacific.

On Saipan, meanwhile, the American divisions had cleared the southern end of the island and faced about for a three-abreast, up-island drive. And here there occurred that famous squabble between the generals Smith which symbolized the interservice feuding of the Pacific War.

Howland M. ("Howlin' Mad") Smith, a Marine, had been Nimitz's ground commander throughout the Central Pacific drive. Ralph Smith, a soldier, commanded the Army division which was in the center of the American line. Because this division faltered, it frequently exposed the flanks of the Marine divisions to either side and gave the line a concave appearance. Angered at this delay, the Marines' Smith fired the Army's Smith and replaced him with another Army general. Doubtless, if both had been of the same service, nothing would have come of such an ordinary battlefield incident. Howland Smith had sufficient ground and ample authority for his action, and he was, after all, only doing what Sheridan had done to Warren at Five Forks. Yet, because the Smiths wore different uniforms, because Howland was not a discreet man and because Ralph had most respectable political connections, the incident became a *cause célèbre* and a brouhaha the echoes of which have yet to subside. It also obscured the gallantry of *all* the American foot soldiers making a grinding advance into the face of Japanese artillery used with deadly effect. Saipan held out for 25 days, during which a ghoulish banzai charge was delivered by the halt, the lame and the blind; the island commander killed himself, to be followed in ritual suicide by Chuichi Nagumo, the discredited hero of Pearl Harbor, after which the fanatic fatalism of the Japanese character was given its most gruesome expression when Japanese civilians joined the soldiery in hurling babies and children to their death over the northern cliffs and leaping into the sea after them.

Guam was next. A Marine division and brigade made the assault there on July 21. The landings were bitterly contested, but the beachheads were secured. Then the Japanese broke their own backs once again with the largest—and most drunken—nocturnal counterattack of the war. Guam apparently had been converted into the Japanese liquor locker for the Central Pacific, and the Japanese commanders drew heavily on it to fortify their men with liquid courage. Screaming, smashing empty bottles, clanging on rifle barrels with bayonets, the befuddled enemy gave away both his position and his intentions. As a result, the counterattack was broken up with great slaughter. One penetration was made by suicide troops who had strapped explosives to their bodies with the intention of hurling themselves against American tanks. However, most of these human bombs blew up when struck by bullets, and the breakthrough was contained. Once again the Americans, reinforced by an Army division, formed a broad front to clear the enemy from the island, and Guam, the first American-held territory to be reclaimed from the enemy, was pronounced "secured" on August 10.

Before Guam fell, Tinian was taken in a masterpiece of amphibious warfare. Tinian was immediately south of Saipan across a narrow strait. The Japanese had thoroughly fortified the only feasible landing beaches on the island's southwest coast. Undismayed, Harry Schmidt, the stolid Marine general who had replaced the controversial Smith, went looking for other beaches. He found them in the northwest, but they were only postage-stamp size: one 60 yards wide, the other 100. To land 20,000 men there with full fighting gear seemed the height of folly. Schmidt, however, feinted hard at the southern beaches with bombarding warships and transports carrying a full Marine division, and as the Japanese rushed to defend them, he sent another Marine division streaming across the strait and up the undefended northern beaches. It was a most successful shore-to-shore operation, carried out with hardly a casualty, and the surprised Japanese were never able to recover. The first use of napalm in the war set Tinian's cane fields afire and delayed troop movements to the threatened beaches, and after the decoy division was brought into the battle, Tinian fell on August 1.

The effects of the Marianas operations were enormous. The fall of Saipan had already brought the fall of General Tojo, who was replaced by General Kuniaki Koiso and a new Cabinet, and now, two and a half years after Pearl Harbor, the Americans stood inside the island empire's inner defenses. They no longer seemed effete to the Japanese; they were obviously determined, ingenious and, by the widespread use of such weapons as flamethrowers and napalm, bent on waging war without reservation. Soon the giant wings of the Superforts would cast long shadows across the Pacific. On November 24, 1944, the Superforts rose from Marianas airfields to stagger Tokyo with the first of many massive bombing raids. Retribution for Pearl Harbor was already at hand.

14

☆

In World War II the United States was transformed into what may be called the "warfare state," a condition which bestowed an uneasy prosperity on the great mass of the people at the expense of the sacrifice, suffering and death of a relative handful of sailors and soldiers.

This novelty was the result of accident rather than design, because the war was two-ocean and global and because internal-combustion engines had conferred upon it an amazing fluidity and variety. Thus the nation's scientific community as well as its young manhood and its industry was subjected to total mobilization. In the military no less than 16 million men wore the uniform at one time or another: 11,260,000 in the Army, 4,183,000 in the Navy and Coast Guard and 670,000 in the Marines, as well as 216,000 women in the various auxiliaries. Yet this great mass of soldiery suffered only 291,000 battle deaths. This is less than the total for the Civil War and averages out roughly as one man in 55. Such an incredibly low rate is in great part due to a determination to save lives; it is also indicative of how few men actually fought. Except for the Russian front "fewness" was a characteristic of World War II. If "so few" saved Britain, then it was again so few who fought from American tanks, ships and aircraft or on the mud or coral of the battlefields. Because rotation was not introduced until late in the war, and because seasoned soldiers are an army's backbone, it was the same few who ventured into battle again and again. The same man might also be a casualty more than once, and if the campaigns were new it was usually the same old ships and divisions that were fighting them. Because of the fluidity of this war, then, and because of the variety of weapons used in it and the vast distances covered, the ratio of combat troops to the number of men in support, training or just sitting on the sidelines was very low indeed. Thus even within its military establishment the American warfare state exposed relatively few people to the horror of war.

At home, except for the relatives of those truly engaged, the war was not malignant but benign. American cities did not quiver and burn beneath the enemy's bombers, nor was the countryside ravaged as in France, Italy or Russia. At home the war ended unemployment and broke the back of the depression. American industry performed such prodigies of production that even Joseph Stalin remarked: "Without American production the United Nations could never have won the war."[114] In 1944, the peak year, the United States turned out over 50 percent more munitions than the combined enemy, and actually produced 45 percent of the total arms of *all* belligerents. In shipping alone, 5,200 vessels totaling 53 million deadweight tons were built, and in aircraft the annual output rose from 2,100 military airplanes made in 1939 to 86,000 in 1943 to 96,359 in 1944. But this was only *half* of the national output, the other half going toward *consumer* goods. Still secure behind their ocean moats, then, the American people at war were not only prosperous but also able to buy the good things of life. New automobiles were not available, of course, and there was rationing of food, tobacco and gasoline; yet a flourishing black market made it possible for most people to eat well, to smoke and to ride in the family car to a football game or a tavern. In the services, the quip, "You never had it so good," was coined to chide the well-fed, well-clothed and well-paid noncombatants who had come from underprivileged homes, and it might also have been applied to the American people. Again, except for the few who fought, it is difficult to discover the war squeezing a single real sacrifice out of the great bulk of the population. In the name of "morale," that trenchant battle cry of the embattled merchants of trivia or pleasure, not a single lipstick was lost or baseball game canceled.

On the other hand, the phenomenal success of the war-bond sales was a tribute to the American people's faith in their country and their cause. They bought no less than $156.9 billion in war bonds, a sizable share of the total of $389 billion expended by the government between July 1, 1940, and June 30, 1946. When it is considered that 46 percent of the costs of the war were raised by taxation, and the remaining 64 percent by borrowing, it may be seen that 85 million private investors made a substantial contribution indeed. Fund-raising was also expedited by the ingenious pay-as-you-go taxation scheme proposed by the financier Beardsley Ruml. This was the beginning of the withholding tax, without which it would probably not be possible to wage the Cold War. The national debt likewise soared. It had been $43 billion on June 30, 1940, and six years later it stood at $269.4 billion. Thus the per capita debt had risen from $75 per American at the end of the Civil War to $240 in 1919 to $2,000 in 1946. All but a trickle of this had gone for defense and war, a total of $360 billion of the $389 expended.

One of the better features of the war was the restraint exercised by the various departments of the government. True, the old apparatus of alphabetical agencies which had conducted World War I was revived with such improvements as an Office of Price Administration to control prices. But there was no attempt to seize the railroads, as Wilson had done, or to prohibit strikes. Congress also resisted agitation for a bureau which would tell people where to work. Throughout the war Americans were free to work when and as long as they pleased. Nor did Congress h ng any Joint Committee to Conduct the War around Roosevelt's neck, as was done to Lincoln. Control of the war was left in the President's hands, and Senator Tom Connally of Texas declared: "I am not in favor of Congress undertaking to put on shoulder straps, epaulets, and big hats, and saying, 'We are going to run the Army: we are going to run the war.' "115

The waste, inefficiency and profiteering which would naturally be a concomitant of such a gigantic effort was subjected to the scrutiny of a special committee headed by Senator Harry S. Truman. Hard-working and scrupulously careful not to trespass upon the prerogatives of either business or the military, Truman and his "watchdog committee" were highly successful. Much of Truman's criticism of the military establishment contributed to the unification movement which followed the war.

Because the "sneak punch" at Pearl Harbor had unified the American nation as never before, dissent was not much of a problem during World War II. Moreover, it was a unique American who, for one reason or another, did not wish to see the world rid of Fascism. As a result, criticism was virtually nonexistent. There were, however, proportionately more conscientious objectors. Even so, the highest estimate of 100,000 objectors comprised only one-third of one percent of the 34 million Americans who registered for Selective Service. In the main, they were treated fairly, although some Jehovah's Witnesses went to jail because they claimed deferment on the ground that they were all ministers—a tenet of their sect—rather than on a religious horror of war, the only admissible ground. Those objectors who did not wish to serve in uniform as noncombatants were sent to camps to work on important nonmilitary projects. There they suffered much discomfort, but never in any degree comparable to the misery of a front-line soldier's life.

On one occasion only did the nation's desire to defend itself encroach upon constitutional rights. This was during the movement of 80,000 Japanese and Americans of Japanese parentage from the West Coast to inland relocation centers. The excuse for this wholesale invasion of individual freedom—the greatest in America since the abolition of slavery—was military security. In retrospect, it does not hold up: all the relocated Japanese and their children were loyal to the United States.

On the other hand, the Supreme Court displayed a strong determination to uphold the right of free speech during wartime. In one decision it refused to halt propaganda to obstruct the draft and encourage disloyalty in the armed services, and in another it threw out government prosecution of 25 German-American Bundists on the ground that by counseling refusal of military service the Bund had merely been awaiting the verdict in a test case on the matter.

America also was highly generous with her men in uniform. A private's pay was raised from $21 monthly to $60, with corresponding raises all along the line, and before the war was over Congress passed the famous "GI Bill of Rights" which provided unemployment compensation of $20 weekly for 52 weeks for returning veterans, appropriated $500 million for veterans hospitals, guaranteed half of loans up to $2,000 for veterans' homes or businesses, and gave veterans attending college $500 annually for tuition and books as well as subsistence of $50 monthly for single veterans and $75 for those who were married. The GI Bill was a benevolent and farsighted piece of legislation. It provided the means for millions of youths to make an orderly transition from war to peace, stimulated the economy and created a huge reservoir of technical and intellectual skills.

It is possible that this new American preoccupation with education sprang from an awareness of what science had done for the war effort, for it was in World War II that the fifth revolution—the Scientific—had overtaken modern war. The Democratic, Industrial, Managerial and Mechanical Revolutions had all wrought their changes on mankind's custom of trying to find a final solution in an appeal to arms, and now perhaps the most far-reaching of all was at hand. It was "the battle of the drawing boards," fought between rival scientists—designers, researchers and engineers—in a never-ending struggle to provide their armies with superior weapons. Competition was especially keen in aircraft and tank design, in the velocity of shells, destructiveness of bombs and the accuracy of fire control, guidance systems and detection devices. It grew fiercer at such an accelerating rate that toward the end of the war no new battle was won with the same weapons that won the last. God, Napoleon had said, is on the side of the big battalions, but in this war He seemed to favor the latest models. Probably it was the very fluidity of the new warfare that called forth each successive ingenuity. When General Eisenhower said that the four weapons vital to his success in Africa and Europe were the bulldozer, the jeep, the 2½-ton truck and the C-47 transport airplane, he was testifying to the fact that this was the communications war par excellence. Not one of these "weapons" had a trigger on it, yet Eisenhower believed that they did most to win the war. In this, then, the multiplication and growing sophistication of weaponry, did World War II differ from its predecessors.

New wars are generally fought with the latest weapons of the old. Thus the tank and airplane introduced but neglected in the last war came into their own during this one. But in 1939-45 the ability of the various states to mobilize their scientific and technical skills, as well as to concert them with the military, gave innovation and invention an immediate effect upon the course of battle. Information on flaws or possible advantages detected in combat could at once be routed to a laboratory and thence to the production lines. As soon as the British captured a German magnetic mine, they learned how to nullify it; when the Germans realized the effectiveness of radar, they began to jam it; and two months after the Americans became aware of the vulnerability of Flying Forts to frontal attacks they were fitting the Fort's nose with a power-driven gun turret.

Because the enemy's scientists usually were clever enough to devise a counter to or copy of any new weapon, both sides took pains to keep their inventions from falling into enemy hands. It was a long time before the Americans captured one of Japan's excellent torpedoes, and were able to remedy the deficiencies of their own wretched "fish." But the Japanese never did recover one of America's radio proximity fuses. This remarkable development detonated any anti-aircraft shell which merely came near the target, and up until the end of the war it was only fired over water to prevent recovery of a dud. For similar reasons the Americans were mum about having broken the Japanese code—affecting great surprise at the announcement of Yamamoto's death—while an elaborate secrecy cloaked the activity of both sides during the most spectacular scientific achievement of all, the race for the atomic bomb.

In this the Americans became the victors probably because they were, with their British allies, the earliest to mobilize academic as well as industrial scientists. Fascism's beastliness had already driven some of its best minds into the democracies—among them Albert Einstein of Germany and Enrico Fermi of Italy—and Hitler seems to have neglected basic research. Expecting a short war, he ignored theoretical scientists until 1942. Japan neglected hers almost entirely, chiefly because her squabbling Army and Navy could not agree on how to use them. But in America President Roosevelt had set aside funds for atomic research as early as 1939, and in June of that year had created the predecessor of the all-powerful Office of Scientific Research and Development under Dr. Vannevar Bush. This was the agency which mobilized colleges in the defense effort. Under its aegis was developed the first atomic bomb, the crown and symbol of the Scientific Revolution.

The war also gave a powerful impetus to medical research. First blood plasma and then whole blood became available on the battle-field itself, thanks to the efforts of medical science and a citizenry willing to donate 13 million pints of blood. The so-called "wonder drugs" and penicillin were brought to a high peak of development during the war, and with Japan in control of most of the world's quinine, troops in malarial regions were given such effective substitutes as Atabrine. Numerous insect repellents were produced, the most famous being DDT.

These are only a few of the effects which scientism had on modern war, but they are nevertheless indicative of the warfare state's all-encompassing mobilization of every discipline and skill within its purview. One unforeseen and unfortunate consequence, at least in America, was that as the specialist took precedence over the ordinary soldier, the soldierly virtues of obedience and fortitude were not encouraged as much as they might have been. By fortitude is meant not only valor but the capicity to endure adversity. There were not enough commanders who understood that the best training for front-line troops is long hikes and short rations. As Napoleon said: "Poverty, privation and misery are the school of the good soldier."[116] This is a hard saying, especially to young men trained to the quest for "the good things of life," but it is nevertheless true. To keep the good things a man must be prepared to put them aside for a time and take up the harsh calling of arms. There were also not enough American commanders who realized that a soldier's pride must be nourished as carefully as his belly, and that any army which snubs its soldiers in favor of its noncombatant specialists is well on the way to suicide. Japan's mistake was to exaggerate the "spiritual power" of her soldiery and to belittle the Americans. If the Americans did not underestimate the enemy, they were yet a bit too preoccupied with firepower and brain power, at the expense of the spiritual. In war there are three, heart, head and hand, and it is an error to exalt any one above the other.

Finally, the cold, impersonal character of the Scientific Revolution divested World War II of any glamour it might have had for the Americans fighting in it. Wars, of course, are never glamorous. Nor are they ever very jolly. Yet there is usually something about a war that makes it seem worthwhile: to fight for independence, in self-defense, for a cause or a crusade, even for booty. However, most American servicemen in World War II did not believe they were fighting for any of these. There were, of course, the elite of the volunteers: the Marines, the fighting ships of the Navy, the Army's fliers, paratroopers and Rangers, as well as a scattering of infantry divisions of seasoned draftees who nourished themselves on their own *esprit*. Otherwise, the American serviceman was an unwilling draftee born and bred to pacifism. World War II seemed to him to be someone else's war. In him there was little of the lighthearted altruism which sent the doughboys off to France to defend democracy. His self-imposed nickname of GI was an abbreviation of the phrase "Government Issue," and that was what he thought of the Army and the war: it was all cut-and-dried, prepackaged, by-the-numbers Government Issue. Every war but his had had a song to sing or a rallying cry. His songs were from other wars, and his battle cry of the Four Freedoms was not very compelling. Noble and idealistic as the freedoms were, they could not move the heart of a man in a foxhole. As Cardinal Newman once said, most men will die upon a dogma but few will be martyr to a conclusion.

Nevertheless the GIs neither mutinied like some of the Continentals in the Revolution nor ran away like many of the "milishy" in 1812. They fought. And by mid-1944 they fought so well that the end of this cheerless and deadly chore appeared to be in sight.

15

☆

The chief reason for the invasion of Italy was the Allied desire to draw German divisions away from the Russian front and to spring of 1944. A lesser reason was the capture of Rome. keep them preoccupied when the invasion of France began in the

The Eternal City was more of a political than a military objective. Its capture would signal the fall of the first Axis capital and herald the inexorable advance of Allied arms. It might also, as Winston Churchill constantly hoped, encourage revolt in the occupied countries. Militarily, Rome was surrounded by useful airfields and was the nerve center of the Italian communications system. However, Italian weather, Italian terrain and the artful Kesselring had so stalled the Allied drive on Rome that it was proposed to turn Kesselring's front with an amphibious hook at Anzio on the west coast of Italy.

A landing at Anzio might cut Kesselring's line of communications south of Rome, and force him to withdraw north of the city. If not, it might compel him to draw off strength from his right flank and enable Mark Clark's Fifth Army on the Allied left to break through to Rome. Winston Churchill was the most ardent advocate of this plan. General Eisenhower was never enthusiastic about it, but then, because he had been named commander of the cross-Channel invasion, he became reluctant to influence a decision in a theater he was about to leave. H. Maitland Wilson of Britain succeeded Eisenhower as Mediterranean chief, and he did not so much approve the Anzio operation as go along with Churchill's advocacy of it.

Anzio was about 60 miles above the stalled Allied left flank, and 35 miles below Rome. It had good landing beaches opening on fairly level terrain suitable for maneuver. Good roads led to the Alban Hills some 20 miles inland, and this high ground commanded the entrance into Rome. Seizure of the Alban Hills might force Kesselring to pull all the way back north of Rome. While the landings were being made at Anzio, the Fifth and Eighth Armies were to move against the Gustav Line to pin down the German troops. Clark's Fifth on the left was to prevent the Germans from reinforcing Anzio. If his soldiers made a breakthrough, they might force a German withdrawal which the Anzio landing to their rear could turn into a rout.

Eventually, a force of 110,000 troops, mostly Americans, was collected for the Anzio assault. General John P. Lucas was to command it. His orders were to land at Anzio, and if the enemy reacted in strength against him, to take the defensive. If, however, there was a chance for the offensive, he was to move rapidly on the Alban Hills. Such orders leave much to the discretion of the commander, and General Lucas does not seem to have been a very daring leader. He was a professional soldier and a meticulous planner, but he was already fatigued by mountain warfare and eight days before the operation began he turned 54. "I am afraid I feel every year of it,"[117] he wrote in his diary. Again and again Lucas confided his forebodings to his diary. At one point he writes: ". . . these 'Battles of the Little Big Horn' aren't much fun and a failure now would ruin Clark, probably kill me, and certainly prolong the war."[118] At another: ". . . the whole affair has a strong odor of Gallipoli, and apparently the same amateur is still on the coach's bench."[119] In fairness to Lucas, there were shortages of landing boats, the troops assigned to him demonstrated their inexperience during a confused rehearsal, and there was good cause to doubt the success of an operation carried out 60 miles away from support of the main body. Still, Lucas seems to have brooded more over the consequences of failure than to have exulted over the possibilites of success. "They will end up by putting me ashore with inadequate forces and get me in a serious jam," he told his diary. "Then, who will take the blame?"[120]

Yet Lucas's forces were more than adequate when the U.S. Navy began landing them on January 22, 1944. They had taken the Germans completely by surprise and were all but unopposed. An assault force of some 50,000 men and 5,200 vehicles had sailed 120 miles north from Naples and never been detected. What had happened was that Clark's assaults upon the German right flank, especially a bloody attempt to cross the Rapido River, had forced Kesselring to send his reserves south. Lucas had the golden chance to deliver the stroke that might capture Rome. But he did not take it.

Instead of launching a strong offensive toward the Alban Hills, Lucas busied himself building up his beachhead. He feared that if he moved immediately on the hill mass, he might overextend himself and be chopped up piecemeal. But while Lucas waited to grow stronger, Kesselring was recovering from his surprise and organizing a powerful counterattack. Thus began the bitter, seesaw battle of Anzio. Kesselring hurled some 90,000 men, of whom 30,000 were noncombatant troops, against Lucas's 100,000. The German also introduced one of Hitler's secret weapons: a miniature tank called the Goliath. About the size of a big dog, the Goliath was stuffed with explosives and operated by remote control. It was a failure as colossal as its namesake, and the factor that told at Anzio was the dogged valor of Lucas's men, clinging stubbornly to their toehold while naval gunfire in the roadstead behind them scourged the Germans. In this battle also, some of Kesselring's troops behaved badly, one so-called crack regiment of unblooded soldiers actually fleeing in panic to prove, once again, that there are no "crack" units of rookies.

In the end, the Anzio gamble did not succeed. Kesselring's swift reaction had put the Americans there on the defensive, and Anzio contained was of little use to Clark contained. It was still up to the Allied main body battering bloodily against the Gustav Line. Here the Americans made another mistake. Held up by the Germans concentrated around the ancient Abbey of St. Benedict on Monte Cassino, General Clark gave orders to bomb the abbey. Leaflets were dropped warning the monks to take cover. However, there were no monks inside Monte Cassino, nor were there any Germans, and all that was accomplished by destroying one of Western civilization's most cherished landmarks was to create a maze of rubble from which the Germans were able to fight a successful delaying action. Not until May 18, 1944, was Monte Cassino in Allied hands. By then massive Allied assault had finally burst the Gustav Line. Not only Anglo-Americans, but French, Poles, Anzacs, Brazilians and Italians participated in this attack. The French and Poles fought with notable bravery, as Kesselring was forced to retreat all the way up the Italian boot to prepared positions in the Apennines 175 miles north of Rome. Meanwhile, the Americans broke out of Anzio and went clattering up the road to Rome. On June 3 they brushed aside the last German defenses and on the following day entered the Eternal City; and with the liberation of Rome, Italy became a theater secondary to the great Channel crossing already being prepared by furious Allied aerial onslaught.

It was the British, not the Germans, as is popularly supposed, who were the first to resort to strategic bombing in World War II. The first British bombs were dropped on Freiburg in Baden on May 11, 1940, three months before Hitler opened the Battle of Britain. Thereafter, the R.A.F. steadily increased the tempo of its blitz on German industry. Actually, after the fall of France there was very little else that the British could do. Apart from their abortive expedition to Greece, it was three years before they returned to the Continent and in that long interval they had no intention of allowing the enemy to consolidate and expand.

Neither Winston Churchill nor his military chiefs believed wholeheartedly in strategic bombing's power to win the war on its own. Still, as Churchill said, it was a "well worth while experiment," and Sir Arthur Harris of Bomber Command was given a green light.

In the American Army Air Forces strategic bombing was a doctrine central to its being. Most of the leaders of the A.A.F. had been the devoted followers of General Billy Mitchell during the twenties. Many of Mitchell's ideas had been picked up and systematized by Douhet. In 1921 Mitchell had struck a great propaganda blow against sea power and for air power by leading a bombing attack which sank a fleet of captured German warships. True enough, not being in motion but at anchor, having no aircraft or antiaircraft guns to defend them, the target ships were but fish in a barrel. Yet Mitchell made his point, and the Air Corps was embarked on the road to quasi independence which was reached when General Henry H. ("Hap") Arnold, Chief of the A.A.F. and the Army's deputy chief of staff for air, became a member of the Joint Chiefs of Staff.

Unlike their British colleagues, who preferred night bombing because of its relative safety, the Americans favored daylight bombing because of its accuracy; and they adopted the precise Norden bombsight and the tough, long-range Flying Fortress. Some 13,000 of these B-17's were accepted by the A.A.F. between January, 1940, and August, 1945, and after the Battle of Midway most of them were concentrated in Europe.

After the first American heavy-bomber raid—over Rouen in occupied France, August 17, 1942—the Allied air chiefs agreed that the British would continue to bomb Germany at night while the Americans would strike by day. Thus the enemy would be continuously scourged from the skies. Until 1943 most of the American raids were over France or against Doenitz's submarine pens, and the results of daylight bombing were not encouraging. The first really successful mission occurred late in January, 1943, when 53 of 91 bombers reached the target city of Wilhelmshaven and dropped their bomb loads. By that time Churchill and Roosevelt had met at Casablanca and declared the objective of the Anglo-American Strategic Air Force to be: "The destruction and dislocation of the German military, industrial and economic system and the undermining of the morale of the German people to the point where their capacity for armed resistance is fatally weakened."[121]

This was a call for all-out strategic bombing, with the German aircraft industry and the German Air Force the twin targets. The Luftwaffe rose to the challenge, attacking a flight of 60 Forts over Kiel on June 17, 1943, and shooting down 22 bombers with a loss of 39 aircraft. This was a defeat for daylight bombing. Another one occurred on August over the Rumanian oilfields at Ploesti. Flying from North African fields, a formation of 177 Liberators knocked out 42 percent of Ploesti's capacity, but also lost 54 bombers. Most of these losses occurred because the Americans had not developed long-range fighters capable of escorting the bombers to their targets and back. Without protection, the bombers—which were usually only jolted or damaged by enemy ack-ack—were exposed to the swiftly improving tactics of the Luftwaffe.

The German fighters knew where to strike the American bombers and how to attack their formations. They massed for strikes over the target area, usually ganging up on the lead bomber whose bomb drop was the signal for the others to release. The Germans armed their fighters more heavily to counter the heavy armament of the Forts, and they also tried air-to-air bombing or trailed ropes with bombs attached. Still, the daylight raids continued, and on August 17 the

A.A.F. struck a spectacular blow with 516 Flying Forts hitting the twin cities of Regensburg and Schweinfurt. Again there was violent resistance, but the strikes on the enemy's vital ball-bearing plants at Schweinfurt were continued until October 18, when a flight of 228 bombers suffered losses of 62 planes destroyed and 138 damaged. Obviously, the daylight raids were becoming prohibitive, even though the Luftwaffe was being whittled, and they were curtailed until December when the long-range P-51 Mustang fighters entered the battle. After the Mustangs came the Lightnings and P-47 Thunderbolts, and the Americans again joined the British in the aerial war on German industry.

Ranging over the Ruhr and the Rhineland, striking night and day, the Combined Air Offensive struck telling blows at German industry and particularly at fighter aircraft production. But it did not knock it out. German resilience was amazing. Light industry was dispersed into the countryside or out into East and Central Germany, while workers were housed in bombproof shelters or reinforced cellars or were sent outside the cities to live. Gradually, the Ruhr was emptied of its vitals and transformed into an industrial shell, so that many of the raids upon it did hardly more than convulse the rubble of previous raids. Heavy industry such as coal and steel was not, of course, susceptible to dispersion, and it suffered accordingly. But by September of 1944 most of the industries outside the Ruhr had been supplied with enough coal and steel to continue production. And the attempt to destroy German aircraft did not succeed. In 1944, the knockout year, German aircraft production *rose* instead of falling. The Luftwaffe accepted some 40,000 planes compared with 15,600 in 1942 and about 24,000 in 1943.

Meanwhile, the attempt to break the will of the German people was continuing à la Douhet. In the last week of July the R.A.F. raided the seaport of Hamburg six times by night and twice by day, dropping 7,500 tons of explosives. So many fire bombs fell that a dreadful firestorm sprang up and swept howling through the city. Inrushing cooler air feeding the base of a 2½-mile column of heated air sucked into it air from outside the perimeter of the fire, increasing its velocity from 11 to 33 miles per hour. Soon the temperature was so high that everything burned, and Hamburg was "burnt out." In all, 60,000 to 100,000 people were killed, 300,000 dwellings demolished and 750,000 people made homeless.

Hamburg offered showcase proof of Churchill's determination to make Germany "bleed and burn," but 60 other cities were similarly savaged with the result that 3.6 million houses representing 20 percent of Germany's total residential area were destroyed or severely damaged, 7.5 million people were made homeless, 300,000 were killed and 780,000 injured—and with what result? "The mental reaction of the German people to air attack is significant," the *United States Strategic Bombing Survey* concluded.

Under ruthless Nazi control they showed surprising resistance to the terror and hardships of repeated air attack, to the destruction of their homes and belongings, and to the conditions under which they were reduced to live. Their morale, their belief in ultimate victory or satisfactory compromise, and their confidence in their leaders declined, but they continued to work efficiently as long as the physical means of production remained. The power of a police state over its people cannot be underestimated.[122]

Nevertheless, the strategic aerial offensive did make a very solid achievement. If it did not destroy the German economy, it undermined it and prepared its eventual collapse. It also denied the enemy fighter aircraft at a time when he needed them. This was during the massive dogfight which raged from February through March of 1944, when the Luftwaffe massed its fighter strength and hurled it aloft in a desperate attempt to knock the Anglo-Americans out of the sky. The gamble failed, and the Luftwaffe, losing about 800 aircraft, ceased to be an effective fighting force.

Because of this, the Allies possessed a 30-to-1 superiority in the air when they began crossing the Channel in June of 1944.

16

☆

A massive host and a mighty armada had been assembled in Britain under the command of Dwight Eisenhower. Men by the millions, ships by the thousands and tanks and vehicles by the tens of thousands had been formed into what Eisenhower called "a great human spring, coiled for the moment when its energy should be released and it would vault the English Channel in the greatest amphibious assault ever assembled."[123]

Not all of these men and arms were to make the crossing on the first day. Most would cross after a beachhead had been seized on the French coast and the Allied armies began driving on Germany from the west, while the Russians, who had already launched their pulverizing summer offensive, struck for Berlin from the east. Eisenhower's general plan was to land on the Normandy coast from Britain while another force landed in Southern France from Mediterranean bases. Because of the shortage of landing craft, however, the invasion of Southern France had to be postponed until enough Channel shipping could be spared. Thus there would be only the Normandy landing, after which Eisenhower planned to build up his forces before breaking out of the enemy's containing armies. Then he would advance across France on a broad front with two army groups, putting emphasis on his left to capture the necessary ports and to reach the German frontier and menace the Ruhr. On the right he would link up with the force that was to invade France from the south and move on to Germany. There, with left and right again joined, he would build up his forces again, cross the Rhine and complete the conquest of Germany.

To contain Eisenhower's host southern England was transformed into a huge armed camp. No less than 1,627,000 American soldiers and 53,000 sailors were quartered there, and the roads were thronged with marching men while the air crackled and boomed to the sound of soldiers testing their weapons. At the embarkation ports, the harbors bristled with masts and the docks were piled high with supplies. Very little was neglected for this great undertaking, which was to be, in effect, nothing less than a large modern city sailing to battle. Divisions of soldiers, and tanks, trucks, guns, rations, barbed wire and medical supplies were the ordinary articles of war, but there were also assembled bulldozers, power plants, radio stations, fleets of buses, hospitals, railroad locomotives, entire telephone exchanges, bakeries and laundries and prison cages and police stations, to say nothing of huge supplies of food, clothing and gasoline and a satisfactory amount of newly printed French money. There were even portable ports called Mulberries, enormous concrete structures which looked like six-story buildings laid on their sides. Two of them, each about the size of the harbor at Dover, were constructed to be towed in sections across the Channel and sunk opposite the invasion beaches. There were also Gooseberries, to be formed by sinking sixty blockships to provide a breakwater, and a submarine pipeline to carry fuel across the Channel.

During the last ten days of preparation, a cloak of secrecy was thrown around Britain. A ten-mile strip of southern England was declared off limits to Britons, all exits to other countries were sealed off, and mail from American servicemen to the United States was held up for ten days. Still, Allied intelligence received an almost electric shock on the day that "Overlord," the code word for the invasion, appeared in a newspaper crossword puzzle. It was not, however, a signal to the enemy but only a coincidence.

For the invasion itself, Eisenhower assembled 150,000 men, 1,500 tanks, 5,300 ships and craft and 12,000 planes. The aircraft were to cripple the enemy's mobility, and thus prevent him from reinforcing the critical area. As early as 60 days before the invasion date, that is D-Day-minus-60, aircraft were demolishing French and Belgian railways, on D-minus-46 they began destroying bridges in northwestern France and on D-minus-2 they started knocking out airfields within a 130-mile radius of the landing beaches.

While the aerial barrage rose in thunder, Eisenhower took great pains to deceive his rival, Marshal Gerd von Rundstedt. Eisenhower had chosen to land in Normandy because he knew that Rundstedt expected him to take the narrower Dover-to-Calais route. With about 50 infantry and 10 Panzer divisions to defend Fortress Europe from Holland to the Bay of Biscay, Rundstedt had concentrated 19 in the Calais area and had placed only ten in Normandy. Eisenhower desired to preserve that imbalance. An elaborate dummy "Headquarters" was built at Dover across from Calais. Divisions not to be used in the first days of the invasion were quartered there. Details of the "Calais Invasion" were deliberately leaked to known German agents, and for every scouting mission flown over Normandy another was flown over Calais, while that area was worked over from the air nearly as thoroughly as Normandy.

Rundstedt was completely deceived. From his headquarters in Paris he made no effort to change his dispositions. Meanwhile, he quarreled with Erwin Rommel, who had been sent west to hold the Atlantic Wall under Rundstedt's command. Rommel wanted to fight on the beaches, which meant concentrating close up, but Rundstedt favored allowing the enemy to land and then hitting him before he could consolidate, and that required holding the bulk of the forces in the rear. In the end, they made the usual bad compromise: infantry forward, armor back—and no coordination between.

Nevertheless, Rommel organized the coastal defenses with customary thoroughness. Mine fields, barbed wire, dragon's teeth, hedgehogs and other obstacles were planted on the beaches and offshore, and the very stretch of Normandy coastline on which Eisenhower intended to land received particular care. Rommel had not actually abandoned his plan to fight at the water's edge. "The war will be won or lost on the beaches," he told his aide, Captain Hellmuth Lang. "We'll have only one chance to stop the enemy and that's while he's in the water . . . struggling to get ashore. Reserves will never get up to the point of attack and it's foolish to consider them. . . . Believe me, Lang, the first 24 hours will be decisive . . . for the Allies, as well as Germany, it will be the longest day."[124]

Weather would dictate the date of that day. The sea had to be calm for the invasion ships, the tides high for the landing boats and the moon bright for the paratroopers who would jump the preceding night. Only a few days in June appeared likely to fulfill these conditions, and Eisenhower chose June 4, 1944. On that day, however, gray clouds scudded low over Normandy, strong winds heaped the waves high and a wild surf pounded the beaches. It was not possible to land or provide air cover, and Eisenhower postponed the invasion.

Eisenhower literally looked desperately for a hole in the storm. Early next morning, he and his staff attended another weather conference. A near-hurricane wind howled around the building. With grave visage, Eisenhower heard Captain J. M. Stagg, the chief meteorologist, report: "I think we have found a gleam of hope for you, sir. The mass of weather fronts coming in from the Atlantic is moving faster than we anticipated. We predict there will be rather fair conditions beginning late on June 5 and lasting until the next morning, June 6, with a drop in wind velocity and some break in the clouds."[125] Eisenhower now faced the decision of his career. He had been told, in effect, that he could expect a 36-hour interval between the end of the present storm and the arrival of another. Should he

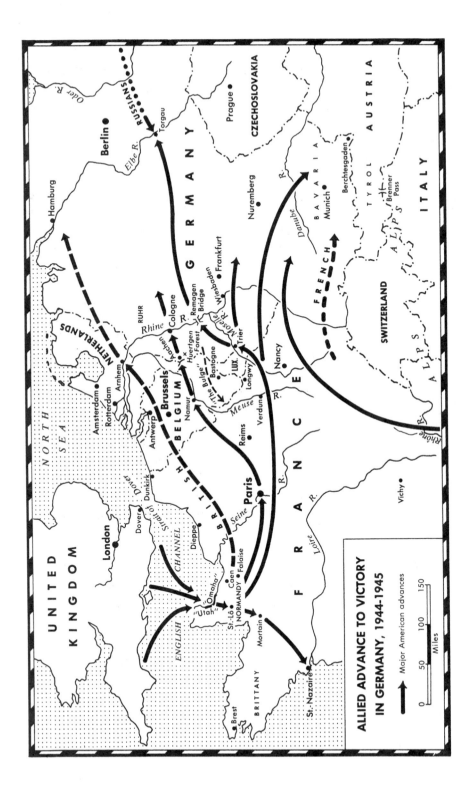

**ALLIED ADVANCE TO VICTORY
IN GERMANY, 1944-1945**

→ Major American advances

Miles
0   50   100   150

risk it? If he did not, he would have to wait two weeks for the tides to turn, and there might be another storm then. That could mean a month's delay. One lost month had been fatal to Hitler in Russia, and 30 days lost to the Allies could mean winter on the Siegfried Line instead of an autumn push through it. For five minutes Eisenhower sat silently on a sofa, tensely weighing the chances. Then he looked up, tension gone from his face.

"Okay," he said briskly. "We'll go."[126]

By nightfall of June 5 the great invasion fleet of some 2,700 ships was on its way, converging on the Normandy coast from British ports stretching from Wales to the North Sea. Five assault divisions were sailing to the battle. One Canadian and two British were to land on the left, and two American would hit Omaha and Utah beaches on the right. Overhead thundered the transport planes carrying three airborne divisions whose men were to jump behind German lines and seal off the beachheads. One British division was to secure the Anglo-Canadian left flank, and the two American units were to seize a wide lagoon behind the American beaches. If the Germans held the causeways across the lagoon, they could easily contain the American beachhead and turn it into a slaughter pen. Much depended on this operation, and there had been strong objection to it on the ground that the American airborne troops would be cut to pieces before their feet touched the ground. Eisenhower, however, had held firmly to it—and at a little after midnight the paratroopers began jumping and the gliders began lettting down for their crash landings.

On the left, the British air troops achieved complete surprise and 5,300 of them came safely to ground. On the right, many of the Americans jumped in high winds and misty clouds. Some fell as much as 35 miles from their targets, others were caught in treetops and still more, weighted with their equipment or tangled in their harness, drowned in swamps only three feet deep. Some were taken prisoner because their own signaling device was used against them. Each man carried a dime-store cricket with which a single *click-clack* squeeze was answered by two: *click-clack, click-clack.* The Germans took these from their first prisoners and used them extensively to trick more into their cages. Yet, gathering forces, the Americans knocked out the German guns and seized the causeways. Now there would be safe exits from the beaches.

Offshore, Allied battleships and cruisers stood well out to shoot at selected targets. Graceful destroyers sped inshore to fire at pill-boxes, rocket ships loosed their missiles like flights of arrows visible in the sky, and while mine sweepers swept the offshore waters frog-men in green rubber suits leaped into closer depths to blow up obstacles and clear a path for the assault boats.

From the Allied air forces came a massive air umbrella composed of thousands upon thousands of fighters and medium bombers rang-ing over the French interior or strafing and bombing the invasion beaches. During the night a thousand British heavy bombers bombed the coastal defenses, and just before the landings at Omaha began another thousand Americans roared overhead to deliver the final blow: a blanket of 13,000 bombs. However, almost all of these went cascading harmlessly into the empty hedgerows three miles inland. Fearing to bomb through the smoke and overcast, and perhaps hit the assault boats below them, air had delayed the drop and thereby canceled out its contribution. Now, as always in an invasion, it was up to the foot soldier with the hand gun who can neither sail away nor fly away. In they came, and the Germans, like the Japanese before them, quickly recovered and began shooting at them.

It had been the Americans' bad luck to hit Omaha just when an excellent German division was on maneuvers there. By its quick counterattack from the bluffs above the beach, this unit transformed Omaha into a smoking graveyard of wrecked boats, drowned vehicles and burned-out tanks, among which were sprawled the bodies of the dead, the dying, the stricken and the terrified. Offshore, aboard cruiser *Augusta,* General Omar Bradley listened gravely to frag-ments of reports indicating disaster for his command. But then the Americans rose up to attack. Courageous captains and lieutenants led the soldiers forward, and as unit after unit knocked out enemy positions one by one, the whole effort gradually coalesced and surged ahead. At 1:30 P.M. Bradley heard the message: "Troops formerly pinned down on beaches Easy Red, Easy Green, Fox Red advancing up heights behind beaches."[127] To the right at Utah, the landings had also begun badly, after the spearhead regiment was put ashore 2,000 yards off course. However, the Americans rapidly corrected the situation, and Utah was also seized. On the left flank, the Anglo-Canadians under General Montgomery received a far less bloody reception and moved swiftly inland toward Caen, making penetrations of as much as seven miles.

By nightfall of June 6, 1944, Marshal Erwin Rommel's "longest day" had lasted just long enough for the Allies to come back to France.

Rommel had not been present to direct the German defense on that fateful sixth of June. Confident that the Americans would not attack during such foul weather, on June 4 he had gone back to Germany to celebrate his wife's birthday and also to call on Hitler to ask for reinforcements. As soon as he learned of the invasion, he rushed back to the front, but by then it was too late. Other German generals in the area had also been absent from their posts, having gone inland to participate in a war game based on the possibility of Allied landings in France! Rundstedt, still positive that Eisenhower would strike at Calais, brushed the Normandy landings aside as a feint or a diversion. Meanwhile, the two Panzer divisions which might have ground the Allies into the beaches could not be brought forward without Hitler's permission, and the Fuehrer was sunk deep in his customary drugged and inviolate sleep. Hitler did not hear the details of the invasion until midafternoon, and then he dismissed the operation as a mere raid and turned to "more important" matters.

One of these was the progress of his new "wonder weapons," the V-1 and V-2 rockets. A week after D-Day the first V-1s fell on London. They were small, pilotless, jet-propelled bombs which the British nicknamed "buzz-bombs" or "doodle-bugs." But there was nothing funny about their successors, the one-ton V-2s which buried themselves deep in the ground before exploding. Flying at 3,000 miles an hour, the V-2 could not be heard approaching and the only warning was the sound of its explosion. In all, the V-2s killed 8,000 British, nearly as many as the entire blitz of 1940. Only the capture of the launching sites ended this new threat to Britain, and once again Eisenhower's decision to chance the break in the weather was fruitful for the Allied cause.

Meanwhile, by daring, deception, luck and the brilliant coordination of forces, the Supreme Commander had achieved complete tactical surprise. It was mid-June before either Hitler or Rundstedt realized that the true invasion had been at Normandy. By then

Eisenhower had about a million men and a hundred thousand vehicles ashore. However, the Allied advance was slowing down. On the left, Montgomery's forces were halted above Caen, and on the right Bradley's was fighting the bitter "Battle of the Hedgerows." The specter of containment, of a front grinding to a halt and a resumption of the position warfare of World War I haunted the Allied command. But then, on July 17, the organizing brain behind the German defense was removed from the scene: an American fighter plane caught Marshal Rommel's staff car on an open road, fired a cannon into it and seriously wounded the Desert Fox. A few days later Rommel's career was permanently ended by the failure to assassinate Hitler.

Opposition to Hitler was centered around General Ludwig Beck, former chief of the General Staff. Beck's most notable recruit was Erwin Rommel, although the idolized German marshal may not have known that Beck intended to get rid of Hitler by killing him. Rommel was certainly not aware that he had been chosen as Hitler's successor. Beck's most active recruit was Colonel Count Claus Schenck von Stauffenberg, chief of staff of the Reserve Army. A handsome and charming young Junker, Stauffenberg had suffered horribly during the Tunisian campaign, losing his left eye, his right hand, two fingers of his left hand and much of the muscle power in both legs. During his convalesence he had become convinced, like Rommel and other Germans in or out of uniform, that Hitler was a mad dog who had disgraced Germany and would not hesitate to sacrifice the entire nation on the altar of his vanity. Hitler must be killed and this senseless war ended, he believed. Under Beck's orders, Stauffenberg searched for an assassin and the right moment to kill the Fuehrer. After two attempts by others were aborted by mischance, Stauffenberg resolved to do the job himself.

It was his duty to report regularly to Hitler at the "Wolf's Lair" in East Prussia, and on July 20, 1944, Stauffenberg arrived there carrying a bomb concealed in his briefcase. It had been his intention to sacrifice his own life, if necessary, to make sure the bomb killed Hitler. But his co-conspirators persuaded him that it was more vital for him to live and to sound the tocsin of Hitler's demise. Therefore, after he entered the conference room and casually placed the lethal briefcase under a large oaken table close to Hitler, he did not stay there to make certain that it was not moved, but rather mumbled an excuse and left the room. Another officer, finding the briefcase in his way, then moved it away from Hitler and placed it on the other side of a strong table support.

The bomb exploded, blowing out all windows, collapsing the roof and blasting a hole in the floor. "Murder! Murder!" an officer screamed. "Where is the Fuehrer?" He was on the floor, pinned beneath a fallen beam, but still alive. Four men had been killed instantly, 20 others were wounded, but Hitler suffered only temporary paralysis of his right arm and the puncture of his eardrums. He had been saved by the tabletop and the support, both the allies of chance, that ageless nemesis of the incomplete plotter. And his fury was fiendish. One by one the conspirators were rounded up, tortured and executed. Stauffenberg was mercifully shot by a firing squad before he could be held for the Fuehrer's feast of revenge. Eight other leaders, not so fortunate, were stripped naked and hung from meat hooks by piano wire while cameras recorded their prolonged, writhing agony. The movies were then rushed to Rastenberg for the edification of the Fuehrer and selected guests.

And Rommel? He had been removed to his home to recuperate. In October SS guards surrounded his house while a pair of toady generals went inside to inform Rommel that he had been implicated in the conspiracy. To save his family, Rommel killed himself by taking poison. So ended the plot of the 20th of July. Thereafter Hitler became more than ever convinced of his destiny. No one dared to oppose his will. Between the Fuehrer's paranoia and the policy of Unconditional Surrender, the German nation which had once been driven by whips was henceforth scourged with scorpions.

Five days after the plot failed, the Americans attempted to break out of Normandy behind the most massive tactical bombing strike in history. Some 2,000 bombers unloaded 12,000 tons of explosives, 5,000 of them within 45 minutes, stunning the enemy and knocking out his communications long enough for tanks and infantry to burst through his defenses at Saint-Lô. After the breakout, Bradley committed the Third Army under Patton, and the "cowboy General" sent his armored spearheads clattering south into Brittany, before splitting off and wheeling west and east. Meanwhile, the First Army under Courtney Hodges continued to drive south before swinging east.

With his rear menaced, the enemy obviously would have to withdraw from Normandy toward Paris. But Hitler's orders had been: "It is forbidden to shorten the front. It is not permitted to maneuver."[128] Therefore the Germans massed their armor and struck west at Mortain in a counterattack aimed at cutting the Americans in two. Penetrations were achieved and the maneuver seemed successful, until Bradley boldly turned it into disaster. Coordinating his moves with Montgomery, he wheeled his forces north while the Briton sent his driving south. With any speed they could meet to the rear of the German Seventh Army and complete its encirclement. But Montgomery's formations moved a bit too slowly and the frantically back-pedaling Germans were able to hold open an exit at Falaise through which most of their armor escaped.

Even so, the Germans passing through the Falaise gap were exposed to a dreadful ordeal from the air. The roads and the countryside were littered with wrecked German equipment and dead German soldiers. "Forty-eight hours after the closing of the gap," Eisenhower wrote, "I was conducted through it on foot, to encounter scenes that could be described only by Dante. It was literally possible to walk for hundreds of yards at a time, stepping on nothing but dead and decaying flesh."[129] Even though more than a third of the Seventh Army escaped the trap, the disaster in Normandy was the worst German defeat since Stalingrad. With it, the liberation of France was guaranteed; and as the jubilant Allies took up the pursuit of the fleeing enemy, the invasion of Southern France was begun.

The American Seventh Army and parts of the French First under Alexander Patch hit French ports in the Mediterranean on August 15 and began driving north to join Bradley's eastward-racing armies. This was exactly what Eisenhower had planned, and also exactly what Premier Stalin desired. With this, Anglo-American armies were kept out of Central Europe and Communist domination of the heart of the Continent was assured. Again and again the Americans had been warned of this eventuality by Winston Churchill and his generals. Repeatedly, the British had attempted to divert the forces for the invasion of Southern France to an amphibious assault in the Trieste-Fiume area on the Adriatic. Here, the Germans in Italy could be taken on the flank and the Anglo-Americans could pour through the Ljubljana Gap into the Austro-Hungarian plain. And there they could make sure that the rampaging Russian armies which had already won Eastern Europe for the hammer and the sickle would not do the same to the Balkans. But it was not to be. The Americans were bent only on winning the war.

President Roosevelt had made this clear at the Teheran Conference during December, 1943. Teheran was the first summit conference among the three Allied chieftains, and where Churchill and Stalin acted like men who knew exactly what they wanted from the war, and Roosevelt acted like a man who wanted only to win it. Thus Stalin's insistence upon keeping the Anglo-Americans in the West of Europe carried the day, and all Churchill's efforts thereafter, his desperate end run at Anzio and his eloquent appeals to the American chiefs, were not able to alter that fatal decision. The expedition into Southern France went forward, and because it was militarily much sounder than the political thrust into the Balkans, it very quickly gave Eisenhower vital southern ports and accelerated the German withdrawal from France.

Giving swift chase, Patton had already by-passed Paris in his eagerness to put himself across the Seine. But on August 19 the French underground in Paris leaped to arms against the German garrison, and Eisenhower despatched the French 2nd Armored Division to their assistance. On August 25, 1944, the Germans surrendered. Charles de Gaulle walked down the Champs Elysées. Throughout the dark night of France's travail, he alone among her leaders had upheld her honor and preserved her world interests, and a delirious Paris gave a weeping welcome to that tall, stern figure. They also gave a wild reception to American troops, but this time the Yanks were not marching through Paris on a morale-building parade but moving grimly to the front. Now, again as Eisenhower had planned, two army groups were thrusting toward Germany. On the left was the 21st under Montgomery, on the right the 12th under Bradley. As planned, another, the 6th under Jacob L. Devers, was coming up from Marseille to join Bradley. But now an unplanned, unforeseen obstacle had been reached: a shortage of supply.

When Eisenhower decided to follow up on the Saint-Lô breakthrough, he also decided to abandon scheduled seizure of the Brittany ports. This left him dependent upon the beaches, the Mulberries and the port of Cherbourg for his supplies. Within three months, in a triumph of logistics, the forces under Eisenhower had poured two million men and 3½ million tons of supplies into France. Unfortunately, all these men ate up all those supplies, and the very speed of Eisenhower's huge thrusting spearheads consumed the vast quantities of the gasoline which is the lifeblood of modern war. With every mile of advance, the supply situation grew more critical. One answer was the "Red Ball Express," an enormous, circular, one-way trucking route running from Normandy to the front and back. But it was not enough. Gasoline stocks dwindled, threatening to stall the advance, and with this Eisenhower faced a great decision.

He *did* have enough supplies and fuel to hurl *one* army group into Germany and thus perhaps crush the enemy before he could turn and recover. Naturally enough, both army group commanders saw this and each advocated that he be chosen to strike the knockout blow. Each wanted the other to mark time on short rations while he struck for victory with all the resources of the Allied forces at his back. Montgomery's plan was to take the northern route across the Rhine between Holland and Germany, and then come down the northern German plains through the industrial Ruhr and into Hitler's heart at Berlin. Bradley's was to drive straight eastward across the waist of Germany, cut the country in two and perhaps come up on Berlin from the south. Either plan might have won the war quickly, Montgomery's probably the sooner because it was the bolder, followed a quicker route and also would unmask vital Antwerp—the third largest port in the world—to Allied arms. Unfortunately, Eisenhower chose neither and adhered to his original plan of advancing on a broad front. Many historians have taxed him with timidity for this decision, and with much justification. The Germans were at that moment punch-drunk and a single daring blow might have knocked them out. General Eisenhower, however, was not audacious. His were the great organizing and harmonizing skills which had brought the mighty Anglo-American coalition over the Channel and across France within a scant two months. But the very defect of these virtues was the lack of forcefulness required to order either of his strong-willed group commanders to sit still for the other. Instead, he adhered to his original plan of the broad axis, and ordered his armies to line up along the Rhine "in order to complete our front from Switzerland to the North Sea."[130]

So the golden moment was lost. Yet, in Eisenhower's defense, it should be remembered that his plan had been thus far productive of spectacular results, and it ultimately achieved its ends. Moreover, what-might-have-been is a frail stick indeed with which to beat success. And if the bold stroke was not in Dwight Eisenhower, neither was it in Bernard Montgomery. His forte was the set piece backed by overwhelming superiority, not the single rapid thrust he was proposing; and Eisenhower, who sometimes complained that Montgomery was always stopping "to draw up his administrative tail," might have had this consideration in mind. Still, he did accede to a modification of Montgomery's plan. This was an airborne operation into Holland designed to cut off an entire German army in western Holland, and to turn the right flank of the Siegfried Line. Known as "Operation Market-Garden," it began on September 17.

Twenty thousand glider troops and paratroopers from one British and two American divisions were dropped. At first, the operation was successful. At Eindhoven and Nijmegen the Americans beat down German resistance and seized bridges, clinging to them until ground forces came to their relief. Farther north, however, 8,000 British "Red Devils," so called for their red berets, passed through a nine-day ordeal at Arnhem. Their mission was also to seize bridges and hold them until ground forces fought through to them. But here the Germans reacted so strongly that the infantry could not get through, and when the valiant Red Devils were at last withdrawn there were only 2,000 of them left.

Frustrated here, Montgomery turned to capturing the port of Antwerp. Canadian troops cleared the Scheldt Estuary in a grim and grinding series of amphibious operations, and by November 26 the great port was open to Allied shipping. With this, the supply pinch was eventually eased, but not soon enough for a thrust across the Rhine in 1944. Having outrun their supplies, the Allies sat down to refresh and regroup.

17

☆

Although the Americans had very early in the war burst through Japan's island defenses in the Pacific, it was not until late in the conflict that any major Allied efforts were directed against the Japanese in the China-Burma-India Theater.

In 1942 the Japanese wrested Burma from the British and cut

the Burma Road linking India and China. Holding Burma, the Japanese could menace India in the west and strangle Chiang Kai-shek in China to the east. The problem then facing the Allied command was to defend India on the one hand and supply China on the other, meanwhile weakening the Japanese hold on Burma.

Inside India itself there were serious nationalist disturbances with the result that Viceroy Sir Archibald Wavell imprisoned Mahatma Gandhi, Jawaharlal Nehru and other leaders. He then reorganized the Anglo-Indian forces while Chinese troops flown into India were being trained by the American General Joseph W. ("Vinegar Joe") Stilwell. Meanwhile, supply of China was begun by air, and American transport pilots based in India began flying supplies "over the Hump," a 17,000-foot Himalayan Mountain range, into China. This flow of supplies was just enough to keep Chiang alive, but was never sufficient to be decisive. To bring more supplies to the Chinese leader, General Stilwell conceived the idea of the Ledo Road. It was to run 478 miles from Ledo in India down into north Burma, and it would link up with the Burma Road once the Japanese were ousted from Burma. Construction, however, was literally a matter of building by inches, with American engineers supervising hordes of Chinese coolies working with hand tools and hand baskets. As it inched toward Myitkyina in the south, it became necessary for Stilwell to cover it from enemy attack.

Under the over-all command of Admiral Lord Louis Mountbatten, chief of Allied Forces in Southeast Asia, Stilwell opened his Myitkyina drive in early 1944.

But as Stilwell drove south, the Japanese came thrusting north in an offensive of their own. In the ensuing fight, Allied air superiority made the difference, and Myitkyina fell to Stilwell in August. The Japanese tried one more blow, hurling 80,000 men at Imphal just across the Indian border. But the Allies struck them head on and shattered them. Thereafter the Japanese were driven steadily back, until, in early 1945, they were completely evicted from Burma.

Now, with supplies again flowing freely into China, it would seem that Chiang would be able to rise up and strike the Japanese tormentor. However, the chief of the Nationalist Chinese government based in Chungking was fighting a war within a war: the first against the Chinese Communists based at Yenan in the north, and the second against the Japanese invader. Much of Chiang's supplies were siphoned off by his feudalistic war lords who hoarded the loot in their own "godowns" either for personal use or sale to the Communists. Chiang also quarreled repeatedly with Stilwell, who had become his chief of staff and adviser. Vinegar Joe had been well named, and his advice to let the Communists alone and concentrate on the Japanese was couched in such acid phrases that the "Peanut," as Stilwell contemptuously called Chiang, at last demanded his recall to the United States. It was not until the spring of 1945, when the Japanese were reeling badly, that the Nationalist Chinese under Chiang finally took the offensive. And throughout the war, action in China-Burma-India—savage, dripping warfare that it was—remained a sideshow to the main theater of conflict in the Pacific.

After the brilliant stroke at the Admiralties in March of 1944 had sealed off Rabaul and burst the Bismarck Barrier, MacArthur went leapfrogging westward along the New Guinea coast. His strategy was to make "kangaroo jumps" of about 200 miles each, the distance usually governed by the range of land-based fighters. For larger leaps, he would require carrier-based aircraft for support, and his next jump was a 600-mile westward vault into Hollandia. It took place on April 22, it was a model of the coordinated use of the triphibious whip —land, sea and air—and it carried MacArthur clear over the strong Japanese garrison at Wewak. Now the Southwest Pacific commander was in position for four more jumps.

In mid-May the island of Wake was occupied, and then the island of Biak. At Biak the Japanese commander surprised the Americans by conducting a new type of defensive battle. Throwing away the old Japanese dogma of destruction at the water's edge, he organized a defense in depth. There were no more stupid banzai charges. Instead, the Japanese holed up in caves and dugouts and they made the American infantry fight very hard indeed for possession of the island's airfields. Next, MacArthur's troops seized Noemfoor. There was little resistance, and the actual capture of the island was a letdown to the soldiers who had sailed 700 miles to the battle in open boats. The fourth strike was at Sansapor on the northwest point of New Guinea's Vogelkop Peninsula. Here the Japanese garrison was so completely surprised that it was quickly overwhelmed. In three months MacArthur had leapfrogged 550 miles west from Hollandia. There remained the last jump to Morotai, the northernmost island in the Halmaheras group. Once again, the cool and daring MacArthur completely outmaneuvered the Japanese. They had expected him to go for the main island of Halmahera with its powerful garrison of 30,000 men, but instead MacArthur went for Morotai with less than 500 men, and he took it with five casualties. Now the American commander could fix his unobstructed gaze upon the southern Philippines across the Celebes Sea. And as he did, Nimitz came up on his right flank by taking the Palau Islands. Here a force of Marines hit Peleliu and fought the fiercest single-division battle of the war. At Peleliu the Japanese brought to perfection the tactics first used at Biak, and because this spit of coral was actually an undersea reef heaved above the sea by a submarine volcano, it was, with its steel-doored caves and caverns housing 10,000 men, ideal for defensive warfare. Peleliu held out for a month and did not fall until after an Army regiment entered the battle.

On September 11, 1944, four days before Peleliu was assaulted, Roosevelt, Churchill and the Combined Chiefs met in Quebec to concert, among other things, a timetable for the Pacific. It was agreed that MacArthur would land in Mindanao in the southern Philippines during November, and that in the following month MacArthur and Nimitz together would invade Leyte in the central Philippines. While the conference continued, Admiral Halsey reported that his carrier aircraft had found Japanese air defenses in the archipelago suprisingly weak. Halsey recommended the invasion of Leyte in October. MacArthur agreed and the Combined Chiefs made the authorization. Thus, in a remarkable demonstration of service cooperation and flexibility at the summit, the schedule was advanced two months and the sights raised higher.

It was a bold and brilliant decision. By attacking the center of the archipelago the Americans would split the 250,000 Japanese there, giving MacArthur the opportunity to defeat them in detail: first on Leyte, then on Luzon and finally on Mindanao. This was the kind of maneuvering at which MacArthur excelled; and if the Japanese attempted to re-establish a continuous front, they would have to commit their fleet—an eventuality dear to the heart of Admiral Nimitz. So the return to the Philippines was begun early in October when Halsey took his Third Fleet ranging against Formosa, Okinawa and Luzon, destroying enemy ships and installations and knocking out upwards of 700 aircraft that might be used to defend Leyte. Although the Japanese only damaged a few of Halsey's ships, they broadcast total destruction of his fleet, and the exuberant admiral signaled

Nimitz: "All Third Fleet ships reported by Tokyo as sunk have now been salvaged and are retiring at full speed in the direction of the enemy."[131]

Next, Halsey joined with Admiral Thomas C. Kinkaid's Seventh Fleet in escorting the Sixth Army under General Walter Krueger to Leyte. A Japanese scout plane sighted this vast armada and flashed the word to Admiral Soemu Toyoda, chief of the Combined Fleet. Toyoda at once committed his fleet. From ports in Singapore, Japan and the Pescadores, the Japanese Navy came sailing out to all-or-nothing battle. Meanwhile, on October 20, four infantry divisions began landing on Leyte. They took the Japanese by surprise and quickly seized a pair of beachheads. A few hours later MacArthur waded ashore. Standing atop a radio truck, he declared: "People of the Philippines: I have returned! By the grace of Almighty God our forces stand again on Philippine soil—soil consecrated in the blood of our two peoples." Calling for an uprising all over the islands, he cried: "Rally to me!"[132]

The Japanese, however, reacted swiftly. A cloud of aircraft tried to sink the invasion fleet, actually regaining control of the air for a few hours on October 24, before losing it for good. Meanwhile, General Tomoyuki Yamashita, landed 45,000 men on the opposite coast. And then the Battle of Leyte Gulf, the greatest naval battle in the history of warfare, began.

Toyoda had divided his fleet into three groups: A Northern Group under Admiral Jisaburo Ozawa built around four carriers; a Center Force of battleships and cruisers, including superbattleships *Musashi* and *Yamato,* under Admiral Takeo Kurita, and a similiar Southern Force under Admiral Shoji Nishimura. Ozawa's Northern Group was to act as bait and decoy Halsey's Third Fleet away from Leyte Gulf. Then Kurita's Center Force would slip through San Bernardino Strait and come down on the unprotected American invasion fleet from the north while Nishimura's Southern Force passed through Surigao Strait and came up on it from the south. After sinking the invasion fleet and again stranding an American army in the Philippines, the three forces would turn on Halsey and destroy him, and with this Japan would win the war.

At first, all the hard knocks were delivered by the Americans. Submarines sank two Japanese cruisers and reported the enemy's location. Halsey then hurled his war birds against Kurita's Center Force, sinking mighty *Musashi* and damaging other ships. Dismayed, Kurita turned around and sailed back the way he had come. The Americans, however, lost light carrier *Princeton* to land-based dive bombers. Even so, Halsey was jubilant. He believed Kurita had been beaten, and he bit hard on the northern bait being offered him by Ozawa and those four tempting carriers.

Like Jellicoe at Jutland, Bull Halsey was an admiral who could lose the war in an afternoon; unlike the overcautious Jellicoe, he was a bit too audacious and he went tearing north on what is now known as "Bull's Run." To the south, meanwhile, Admiral Jesse B. Oldendorf awaited the enemy Southern Force stealing up Surigao Strait. Oldendorf had six battleships, eight cruisers and a host of destroyers and torpedo boats against Nishimura's two battleships, four cruisers and eight destroyers. The American placed his heavies in battle line, put his destroyers in front and sent the PTs down the strait on patrol duty. It was a trap, and in the pitch-black early morning of October 25, Nishimura sailed into it.

First, the American PTs struck at him with torpedoes and missed, and then the American destroyers attacked. Squadron after squadron hit Nishimura, and by the time he had reached Oldendorf's battle line he had only one battleship, one cruiser and one destroyer left. Oldendorf's heavies began bellowing in what a destroyer captain called: "[the] most beautiful sight I have ever witnessed. The arched line of tracers in the darkness looked like a continual stream of lighted railroad cars going over a hill."[133] When the guns stopped, battleship *Yamashiro* was sinking with Nishimura aboard, and the age of the battleship had come to an end. For nearly 300 years action at sea had been fought by great ships-of-the-battle-line maneuvering on the surface and shooting at each other with cannon. Those three centuries of naval warfare had been concurrent with the rise of the American nation, and now as the mighty descendant of those little maritime republics emerged as the most powerful nation afloat, it was her guns which roared a requiem for the ships and the tactics of the battle line.

With dawn of October 25, however, it appeared that battleships might yet write new pages of history. Admiral Kurita had turned again, had stolen through San Bernardino Strait with 22 ships of the Center Force, and was steaming south toward the unprotected and thin-skinned American invasion fleet. Between Kurita and his prey stood only three small forces of baby carriers known as Taffy One, Taffy Two and Taffy Three. Yet these gallant ships flew off their aircraft to attack Kurita and began a zigzagging withdrawal while their destroyers and destroyer escorts struck boldly at the Japanese. One destroyer launched a spread of torpedoes at *Yamato* and forced the mightiest warship afloat to retire temporarily from the battle. Then the Japanese gunners began to make hits, and to the amazement of the Americans the enemy's armor-piercing shells went right through and out of the little flattops' thin armor without exploding. Yet carrier *Gambier Bay* was sunk as well as two destroyers and a smaller vessel, and Kurita seemed certain to burst in among the American transports like a wolf among sheep. And then a sailor aboard *Fanshaw Bay* cried, "Goddammit, boys, they're getting *away!*"[134] It was true, Kurita had turned a third time, and although the cocky American bluejacket's assessment of the maneuver was not quite correct tactically, it did give eloquent testimony to the spirit which had redeemed Halsey's near-fatal miscalculation in the Battle of Leyte Gulf.

Halsey, meanwhile, had begun to devour the bait which had drawn him north. Eventually, his ships and aircraft sank all of Ozawa's four carriers along with a cruiser and three destroyers. With these blows, the Japanese Navy ceased to be an effective fighting force. Effort after effort was made to reinforce Yamashita's embattled forces on Leyte, but to no avail. By mid-December the Japanese abandoned all efforts, and their troops in the Philippines were now in the same position that the Americans had been in three years previously.

By then General Krueger's troops had battled their way inland during torrential rains and against spirited resistance. On December 7 an infantry division landed on the southern end of the island, and before the year was out Leyte had fallen to the Americans. Now MacArthur moved against Luzon, calling his shots in advance like a true master of amphibious warfare. "With my Eighth Army off the southern coast of Luzon," he told his aides,

. . . I will threaten landings at . . . southern ports and draw the bulk of the Japanese into the south. This done, I will land the Sixth Army in an amphibious enveloping movement on the exposed northern shore, thus cutting off the enemy's supplies from Japan. This will draw the enemy back to the north, leaving the Eighth Army to land against only weak opposition on the south coast in another amphibious movement. Both forces ashore, with but minor loss, will then close like a vise on the enemy deprived of supplies and destroy him.[135]

This is exactly what was done during January, 1945. Ably served by the Navy, supported by Army and Marine air flying off newly built Leyte fields, MacArthur's soldiers caught the enemy between two fires. By skillful use of guerrillas and aircraft, the Americans disrupted Japanese communications so badly that Yamashita was forced to commit his forces piecemeal. MacArthur's amphibious hooks next proceeded to cut off the Bataan Peninsula and prevent Yamashita from retiring into it as MacArthur had done, and sent two forces driving on Manila from north and south. A bitter battle was fought in Manila and that once beautiful city reminiscent of old Spain was tumbled into ruins before it fell. Meanwhile, from the liberated prison hells of Luzon came a stream of emaciated wrecks who had once been American soldiers. Details of the Death March became known, and a mounting documentation of Japanese brutality against both the prisoners committed to her care and the population she had subdued demonstrated that the eastern end of the Berlin-Rome-Tokyo axis, though possibly less refined and purposeful in its cruelty, was the beastly equal of the western.

The last blows were struck in February when American paratroopers and amphibious troops landed on Corregidor and compelled the garrison there to blow up their installations and themselves. Mac-Arthur came to the Rock in March. "Hoist the colors," he ordered his victorious troops, "and let no enemy ever haul them down."[136] In the same month landings were made in Mindanao, and the isolated enemy there was fragmented and chopped up or forced to conduct irregular warfare from mountain hideouts. On July 5, 1945, MacArthur declared that the Philippines had been reconquered.

18

☆

In the fall of 1944 the Third Reich which Adolf Hitler had built to last a thousand years was already crumbling. In the East the Soviets had swept up to the gates of Warsaw; they stood within reach of the German homeland and they had occupied Rumania and

Bulgaria in the Balkans and were advancing on Hungary. In the West the Anglo-Americans had liberated Belgium, Luxembourg and most of France and were menacing the Ruhr. To the north Finland had capitulated to Russia and unmasked the Germans in Scandinavia, and in Italy to the south Kesselring was making his last stand on the Gothic Line. East and west, north or south, the last three months had stripped Hitler of 78 divisions and territory several times the size of Germany.

Yet, Hitler's control of the German nation remained firm. After Heinrich Himmler's peace feelers in late 1943 produced only a reiteration of Unconditional Surrender, influential Nazis realized that the issue might be victory-or-death. It was stated again after the attempt on Hitler's life in July, 1944. Then, in September, details of the "Morgenthau Plan" leaked out of the Quebec Conference. Devised by Secretary of the Treasury Henry Morgenthau, and endorsed by Churchill and Roosevelt, the plan called for a "pastoral" Germany stripped of her industry and her mineral resources. Fortunately, the Morgenthau Plan was abandoned after violent opposition from Roosevelt's Cabinet. Cordell Hull called it "a plan of blind vengeance"[137] which, by wrecking Germany, would also partially ruin Europe. But it was not jettisoned before Goebbels learned of it and began to make propaganda capital of it. The Allies, he said, wanted to turn Germany into "a potato patch." By destroying German industry, the plan would compel 50 percent of the working population to face starvation or to emigrate as working slaves. Goebbels declared: "It hardly matters whether the Bolsheviks want to destroy the Reich in one fashion and the Anglo-Saxons propose to do it in another. They both agree on their aim: they wish to get rid of thirty to forty million Germans."[138] Naturally, Herr Goebbels was under no compulsion to describe the plans for the brutal enslavement of "inferior peoples" which Hitler had already put into effect in Eastern Europe, and as he had predicted, the Quebec decision actually did redouble German resistance. Eisenhower himself appealed to the Combined Chiefs for some modification of Unconditional Surrender but was told that it could not be done. Thus the German nation was conditioned into giving unconditional obedience to a Fuehrer who had sworn never to surrender, and thus Hitler's generals were only mildly startled when he gathered them at his Eagle's Nest in Bavaria in mid-September and informed them of his plan to win the war.

He was going to counterattack through the Ardennes, split the

Allies, seize Antwerp and thus turn the tide of battle. As he talked, Hitler showed all the effects of the July bombing. He was pale, his hands trembled, his left arm twitched and he dragged his leg as he walked. Yet his eyes shone with visionary fire, for the bombing had also convinced him that "Providence" had willed it that "the greatest captain of all times" should redeem all with a single stroke. After he had seized Antwerp the Allied armies in the north would be cut off, and such a grave military crisis would so shock the West that public opinion, especially in the United States, would demand a withdrawal from Europe. In this low estimate of American staying power, the German Siegfried hardly differed from the samurai of Japan.

Marshal von Rundstedt was brought out of retirement to put the plan into operation. He was given three full armies containing most of Germany's armor, 2,000 tanks and about 2,000 planes. Under cover of darkness and bad weather that had grounded enemy reconnaissance planes, he put his forces into place within the wooded confines of the Ardennes. Eisenhower, meanwhile, having collected enough supplies to resume his advance, had ordered Bradley's 12th Army Group to attack above and below the Ardennes. Confident that the Germans would not attempt the woods and snows of the Ardennes, Bradley stood lightly on the defensive there.

With the onset of foul weather that grounded Allied aircraft, Rundstedt attacked. On December 16, 1944, a powerful artillery barrage fell upon the Americans, and the German spearheads surged forward. They broke through. They tore open a hole 45 miles wide through which armored columns poured in a pell-mell dash for the Allied supply dumps at the Meuse River and for Antwerp beyond. Yet, just as the reluctant Runstedt had predicted, they did no more than drive a deep bulge into the Allied line, giving the action the name of the Battle of the Bulge. Even though Eisenhower halted his own offensive, he was not unduly disturbed. He sent an airborne division to hold the pivotal town of Bastogne and ordered Patton to bring his armor up from the south. In Bastogne the Americans under General Anthony McAuliffe fought valiantly. Here they held a fine road center that threatened Rundstedt's rear, and their intention to keep it was manifested by McAuliffe's reply to German surrender demands. "Nuts!" he told them. On December 24 the weather cleared, and with that the Germans were doomed. Some 5,000 Allied aircraft struck at the German supply columns and all but isolated the battle-field. When Patton relieved Bastogne, the issue was no longer in doubt, and on January 1, 1945, Rundstedt was in full retreat. By the 31st the bulge was eliminated and the Allied line remained firm again.

The Battle of the Bulge had far-reaching consequences. It proved, like the breakout at Saint-Lô, that if air power is not irresistible strategically, it is tactically indispensable to either side. It also demon-strated that Eisenhower's broad front was vulnerable to counterattack. Rundstedt's blow that failed was, after all, only a repetition of the blow that succeeded against Gamelin in 1940. Fortunately for the Allies, Eisenhower in 1944-45 held such an overwhelming superiority, especially in the air, that it could not be repeated. Hitler simply would not admit this, and for the last time he proved that military mysticism does not overcome shortages. He had not had enough troops to expand the penetration or even to hold open the shoulders of the gap for the reserves to come in, and he could not match the Allies in the air. Unfortunately for European history, Hitler had also dis-astrously weakened his 1,500-mile Eastern front in order to strike hard in the Ardennes. His desperate gamble set back Eisenhower's offensive timetable and accelerated the Russian advance. When the Soviets struck on January 12, 1945, they crashed through a hollow shell. They overran Poland, captured most of East Prussia, knifed into Silesia and came sweeping into Germany at such speed that before they lost momentum they stood on the Oder only 30 miles from Berlin. In the meanwhile, Eisenhower had resumed the offen-sive.

Not since Napoleonic times had the broad German Rhine been crossed by an invader. The Germans relied upon it as one of the world's safest barriers, and Hitler had covered the approaches to it by building the Siegfried Line to the west. Yet by February 21 the forces under Eisenhower had burst these defenses, marching and fighting over roads that were little better than broad ribbons of mud, and had reached the Rhine. Here, by one of the great mischances of history, they found a bridge still standing. It was at Remagen. It was scheduled to be blown along with all other Rhine crossings, and the charge was detonated. But it did not tumble the bridge into the rushing waters below, and within 24 hours the jubilant Americans had put 8,000 men across the river to seize and hold a bridgehead while engineers repaired the bridge that was "worth its weight in gold." The Germans made every effort to destroy the unblown bridge, sending 21 of their new jet bombers against it and firing V-2 rockets at it. But the bridge was not hit, and when it did finally fall into the Rhine, it made no difference because the Americans had thrown 62 temporary bridges of all types across the river and the "impassable" Rhine had been crossed for good at Remagen.

All along the river, now, the Germans were retiring, and seven Allied armies were crossing in pursuit. They went over by every means available—by landing craft, amphibious trucks, pontoon bridge or prefabricated bridge—and they drove deep into the heartland of Germany. Eisenhower was now 300 miles from Berlin, while the Russians on the Oder were 30 miles east of it. But the Russians were exhausted and needed time to regroup for a final thrust. Once again, Churchill urged Eisenhower to concentrate behind Montgomery in a desperate dash for Berlin before the spent Russians could regain their breath and get there. Central Europe might yet be saved from Communist domination. Eisenhower, however, continued his broad-front advance. By April 12 his troops had reached the Elbe, only 100 miles from Berlin. The Russians had just begun their final offensive. There was still time. General Eisenhower, however, halted his troops on the Elbe. A week later he also halted Patton short of Prague, the capital of Czechoslovakia, and while the Russians were thus free to take the prize at Berlin they also had the honor of "liberating" Prague.

Eisenhower saw the situation in purely military terms. He was not racing the Soviet Army for booty and he had no authority to pursue political objectives. Berlin did not seem to him to have any military value, as it did not. In stopping at the Elbe, he did exactly what military considerations required. The Elbe was the point to which he was supposed to withdraw anyway, once Germany had collapsed, and to halt there would save lives and conserve forces for the Pacific War. In Czechoslovakia he curbed Patton upon the urgent request of the Soviet High Command, at that time a still friendly and powerful ally. So the Soviets went into Berlin and Prague, and Vienna as well, and it was in this way that most of Central Europe, the nerve center of the Continent, came under Communist domination.

For the last time American naïveté had made straight the way of the Reds. And on the day that the Americans reached the Elbe and halted there, the one man who could have ordered them eastward had breathed his last.

Franklin Delano Roosevelt's health had not been good since the Teheran Conference in December, 1943. Upon his return to Washington, he came down with a respiratory ailment that prevented him from concentrating fully on his duties until May, 1944. Nevertheless, FDR accepted his party's nomination for a fourth term as President. He was passionately determined to see the war through and also to win the peace that followed.

Second place on the Democratic ticket went to Senator Harry S. Truman of Missouri. Truman was not very familiar with foreign policy, but his watchdog committee had made him nationally famous and FDR hoped that he would be helpful in the Senate. Roosevelt's opponent was Governor Thomas E. Dewey of New York, who was chosen by the Republicans on the first ballot after Wendell Willkie went down to a disastrous defeat in the Wisconsin primary. Dewey was an internationalist like Roosevelt, and he had little criticism of FDR's conduct of the war. Dewey's chief issue seemed to be that Roosevelt at 62 and ailing was too old and too sick to run the country. This was all too true, but it was not enough to defeat FDR. He won an electoral landslide of 432 votes and a popular plurality of 3.5 million.

In February, 1945, Roosevelt again met with Churchill and Stalin, this time at Yalta in the Russian Crimea. At Yalta were made the concessions and agreements which enabled Stalin to place Communist puppets in power in Poland and to undermine opposition to the Red takeovers planned for Central Europe and the Balkans. Yalta also made the Soviet Union an Asiatic power at the expense of Chiang Kai-shek and prepared the way for the rise of the Chinese Communist leader, Mao Tse-tung. At Yalta President Roosevelt was a very sick man. A glance at the photographs of him offers sufficient proof of this. Here is that commanding presence, that immense vitality, shrunken to a worn and weary shadow; and his famous black boat cloak hangs from his thin shoulders like a shroud.

Upon his return to Washington FDR's pallor was evident to everyone who saw him. An anxious American public speculated on the health of the 63-year-old President. Then, in April, FDR went to

Warm Springs, Georgia, for a rest. Shortly after noon of April 12, as he sat quietly in front of a fireplace while an artist sketched his portrait, FDR exclaimed: "I have a terrific headache."[139] Those were his last words. He had felt the onset of a massive cerebral hemorrhage, and two hours later he was dead. In Washington, Harry S. Truman became the fifth Vice President to succeed to the White House on the death of his chief. Next day President Truman told the press: "I don't know if any of you fellows ever had a load of hay or a bull fall on him, but last night the whole weight of the moon and stars fell on me. I feel a tremendous responsibility. Please pray for me."[140]

Twelve days after President Roosevelt died, the first of the Allied leaders to become a casualty in the cause of freedom, a less noble end overtook the father of Fascism.

On April 25, 1945, the Allied armies in Italy were driving on Milan, the center of Benito Mussolini's puppet government. Terrified, the Duce fled. He took with him his mistress Clara Petacci, and a hoard of gold, and went into hiding in a farmhouse on Lake Como. Here he was discovered by a Communist partisan leader named Valerio. "I have come to free you," Valerio told the Duce, and as his men began to push Mussolini and his mistress out of their bedroom and into a waiting car, the Duce sensed that he was in the hands of enemies. "Let me go," he cried to Valerio, "I shall give you an empire!" Valerio said nothing, until he ordered the car halted near a wall. "Get out quickly, both of you," he said. "Stand at the corner of that wall." The Duce's mistress screamed, "You can't do that!" Valerio raised his pistol and shot them dead with the words: "I execute the will of the Italian people."[141]

Their bodies were brought to Milan and there subjected to every indignity by a mob gone hysterical with hate. Kicked and beaten to a pulp they were at last hung upside down in the public square, and even then the mob was not sated. One woman emptied a pistol into the Duce's lifeless flesh. "Five shots!" she screamed. "Five shots for my five murdered sons!"[142] At last, upon the intercession of a cardinal, the mob was quieted and Mussolini's body was cut down and given secret burial. And once again the crowd erupted, finding the unmarked grave and spitting and trampling upon it. Where once they had thundered, "Duce! Duce! Duce!" in paroxysms of national pride, the mobs that had made Mussolini could not now, in an orgiastic transferral of guilt, do enough to revile the memory of their sawdust Caesar. So ended the Duce, while in Berlin, the Fuehrer met the end by pretending it was the beginning.

One by one the Nazi leaders had slipped away from Berlin to evade the wrath of the oncoming Russians. Allied bombers had reduced the city to a blackened skeleton. It had been worked over again by Russian artillery, and in late April it had become a deadly battleground where Germans and Russians fought each other in a maze of trenches and barricades. Still Adolf Hitler remained at his post in the network of bunkers beneath the Reich Chancellery. He held daily conferences with those followers who had not deserted him. His was the deadly calm of the demented, issuing orders to vanished divisions, calling upon last-ditch defenses in areas long ago lost to the enemy, acting as though he still commanded the mighty Wehrmacht of 1940 rather than the wretched remnant which the Allies had broken to bits in 1945. Sometimes, with each new message of defeat or report of betrayal, the calm would desert Hitler and he would scream in demoniac agony.

On April 22 he received the cruelest blow from his old henchman, Hermann Goering, who wrote: "My Fuehrer: In view of your decision to remain at your post in the fortress of Berlin, do you agree that I take over immediately the total leadership of the Reich?"[143] Next came reports of Heinrich Himmler's unsuccessful attempt to negotiate a separate surrender with the Western Allies, and Hitler shouted: "Nothing now remains! Nothing is spared me. No loyalty is kept, no honor observed! There is no bitterness, no betrayal that has not yet been heaped upon me."[144] On April 29, 1945, Hitler expelled Goering and Himmler from the Nazi Party and named Admiral Doenitz as his successor. On the same day the 56-year-old Fuehrer took a wife. In a lunatic ceremony witnessed by his most loyal adherents, the Goebbelses, Hitler married Eva Braun, his devoted friend of a dozen years. Next day he had his favorite dog, Blondi, destroyed. In the afternoon he retired to his suite. There Adolf Hitler shot himself in the mouth with a pistol. Beside him lay the body of Eva Braun, who had taken poison. Then Dr. Goebbels carefully poisoned his six little children, after which he stood beside his wife while Nazi guards shot them through the head. A few days later Russian soldiers at last burst into the bunker within which the Nazi beast had died.

The death of Hitler on the last day of April in the year 1945 was the definitive end of the war in Europe. By then the German nation was beaten, beaten straight down to the ground as it had never been beaten before. Doenitz's attempt to rally the people on May 1 was tragically ludicrous. One last attempt to negotiate a separate peace with the Western Allies was scornfully spurned by Montgomery, and then, on May 7, 1945, in a dismal brick schoolhouse in Reims, France, a German delegation led by Field Marshal Alfred Jodl, chief of the German General Staff, surrendered unconditionally to the Allies.

19

☆

While Germany was collapsing, Admiral Nimitz reached out for island bases for the final assault on Japan.

The two islands finally chosen were Iwo Jima in the Volcano Group and Okinawa in the Ryukyus. Iwo Jima was to be taken first because it was believed to be easier, and because this tiny island's airfields were urgently needed to provide emergency landing fields for B-20 Superforts returning from raids on Japan. Since November 24, 1944, the Superforts had been flying from Marianas bases to attack the Japanese home islands, and they had been suffering grievous losses. Radar based on Iwo alerted enemy fighters of their approach, and many of these valuable aircraft with their invaluable crews were either shot down or so crippled that they crashed into the sea during the 1,500-mile flight back to base. Iwo, only 760 miles south of Tokyo, was the ideal halfway haven for crippled B-29s. Moreover, if Iwo was made a regular stopping point, the Superforts could carry less gas and more bombs and make more continuous attacks. Finally, possession of Iwo would knock out the enemy's warning system and provide fighter escort to the target and back.

It is not often that the value of an objective is so clearly understood beforehand, and in fact there was but one error in all the American estimates on Iwo Jima. This was that it would be easy to take. Just as, three years previously, Douglas MacArthur had delayed the Japanese timetable of conquest, so had the Japanese on Leyte and Luzon held up MacArthur's advance. As a result, the target date for Iwo was delayed a month, and in that interval the Japanese put the finishing touches on what was probably the world's most formidable fixed position.

Iwo Jima, or Sulphur Island, is only 4½ miles long and 2½ miles wide. In shape it resembles a pork chop. To the south, at the tip of the pork chop's tail, the extinct volcano Mount Suribachi rises 550 feet above sea level. To either side of the tail are the island's only landing beaches, both lashed by high surf, terraced and covered with a mixture of brown volcanic ash and black cinders finer than sand. Widening to the meat of the chop, the island ends in a plateau with rocky, inaccessible bluffs. Difficult as it was to land at Iwo, the island might indeed have been easy to take in September, 1944, when the Joint Chiefs were debating where to hit next, because by then General Tadamichi Kuribayashi had only begun the task of transforming this lonely, uninhabited cinder clog into a fortress.

Kuribayashi was a perfectionist martinet who had been impressed by the tactics of defense in depth perfected at Peleliu. He began his assignment by convincing his 21,000-man garrison that they all— each and every one—must fight to the death. Before dying, each man was to kill ten Americans. Even if the island was lost, America would pay a bloody butcher's bill which she would not readily incur again, and the enemy timetable would be delayed.

At Mount Suribachi in the south, Kuribayashi constructed a labyrinth of positions for artillery, mortars and automatic weapons. From Suribachi observers could see most of the island and signal instructions to the positions in the north. Here a system of caves even more elaborate than Peleliu housed the Japanese main body. Its characteristics were invisibility and flexibility. Positions were hidden by camouflage and usually so constructed that the guns could be fired in any direction. Finally, Kuribayashi wisely instructed his men not to return fire and give away their positions when the Americans began their preinvasion bombardments.

As a result of this, and also because of the nature of blanket bombing, the most prolonged bombardment of the war was also the most unrewarding. Some 6,800 tons of bombs and 22,000 rounds of naval shells ranging from 5-inch up to 16-inch were put on Iwo Jima, but when two Marine divisions under Harry Schmidt went churning toward the landing beach, on February 19, 1945, it was the same old story. The target was obscured beneath a cloud of dust and smoke, but under the cloud was a virtually unscathed enemy crouching safely in his bombproofs and waiting only for the bombardment to lift before rushing back to his guns. Well had a Marine chaplain issued all hands printed cards bearing Sir Jacob Astley's famous prayer before the Battle of Edgehill in 1642:

> O Lord! Thou knowest how busy I must be this day;
> If I forget thee, do not Thou forget me.

At first it seemed that bombardment had at last won an island on its own. There was only light opposition. Most of the difficulty seemed to be in Iwo's soil. Assault troops leaping out of their amtracks sank calf-deep into that loose ash and cinder in which it was impossible to run or dig. They plodded forward, leaving elephant tracks behind them. The amtracks found no traction and could not move. Nor could they penetrate the beach terraces ranging from five to 18 feet in height. Vehicles began to pile up on each other. Confusion spread, and it was then that the guns of Iwo compounded it into bloody chaos.

Kuribayashi had deliberately allowed the Americans to come ashore lightly opposed. This would grant him surcease from naval gunfire and give the enemy just time enough to become bogged down. Then he could open up with everything he had, holding the Americans in front of his fixed positions while cutting them off from their supplies so that he could defeat them at leisure. Thus after the passage of almost an hour Iwo Jima's black sands were clotted red with blood. Artillery boomed from Suribachi and the northern heights, automatic weapons spat from innocent hummocks and antitank guns whammed from underground pillboxes. Until they could take cover among the wreckage of their own vehicles or behind their own dead, the Marines on Iwo were naked to their enemies. Yet they clung to their beachhead and expanded it. Gunfire ships offshore covered their flanks or their front with rolling barrages, and after the assault signal companies came ashore to pinpoint targets, the fire became more accurate. Kuribayashi had given the Marines one hour, and it had been too much. By nightfall it was clear that they had come to Iwo to stay.

Next day a Marine regiment turned south to strike at Suribachi. Blasting and burning pillboxes, sealing up interconnected caves with flamethrowers, grenades, rockets and demolition charges, the Marines reduced Suribachi in three days. On February 23 a patrol fought its way up to the volcano's summit, and raised a flag there. But it was too small to be seen on the island, and a larger flag was brought up. It was raised by six men—one of them a Navy medical corpsman— and the event, photographed by Joe Rosenthal of the Associated Press, became the most famous picture of the war.

Meanwhile, the Marines below had pivoted north and had begun their dreadful up-island advance into Kuribayashi's meat grinder. It was not possible to turn the flanks, and to penetrate was to expose their own flanks to enemy fire. The Japanese lines had to be pulverized piece by piece, sometimes with the aid of warships or aircraft, but most usually by men on foot fighting among gullies, caverns, ledges and crevices, and using tanks or flamethrowers wherever they could. As Admiral Nimitz was to say: "Among the Americans who served on Iwo Island, uncommon valor was a common virtue."[145] Eventually, elements of a third Marine division had to be fed into the battle, and with this, and also by the impetus gained in a surprise night attack, the Japanese center was opened up and the defenses finally fragmented. Iwo was secured on March 26, but Kuribayashi had put a fearful price on the victory: ashore and in the fleet, 19,000 Americans were wounded and 7,000 killed. Among the foot Marines alone there were 5,900 dead. Yet only 200 of the enemy's 21,000 survived to be taken prisoner. As General Graves B. Erskine said in a moving speech saluting the fallen of his division: "Let the world count our crosses! Let them count them over and over. Then when they understand the significance of the fighting for Iwo Jima, let them wonder how *few* there are."[146]

Even before Iwo fell, the island had begun to pay enormous military dividends. On March 4 a B-29 running low on gasoline made a forced landing there, and before the was was over, 2,251 Superforts with 24,761 crewmen were saved by emergency landings on Iwo. Some of these had participated in the fire-bombing of Tokyo on the night of March 9-10. In this, the most horrible raid of the war, worse even than the atomic bombings that were to follow, 250,000 dwellings were burned to the ground, a million people were made homeless and nearly 84,000 persons burned to death. Yet, as the American onslaught thickened in savage fury, as it became a war of annihilation fought to fulfill the mistaken policy of Unconditional Surrender—if such a lack of program may be called a policy—the will of the Japanese people did not falter, and the second operation against Okinawa went ahead as scheduled.

Okinawa, the chief island of the Ryukyus, lies about 350 miles south of Japan. It is a slender irregular island, about 70 miles long and 18 wide at its broadest and two at its narrowest. It was defended by the Japanese Thirty-second Army of from 75,000 to 100,000 men, under General Mitsuru Ushijima. Like Kuribayashi, Ushijima was determine to fight a defense in depth. "You cannot regard the enemy as on a par with you," he told his men. "You must realize that material power usually overcomes spiritual power in the present war. The enemy is clearly our superior in machines. Do not depend on your spirits overcoming this enemy. Devise combat method based on mathematical precision—then think about displaying your spiritual power."[147]

Ushijima also decided to let the enemy land unopposed, choosing to defend only the southern half of the island, which was cut up by cliffs and pocked with limestone and coral caves, all of which, as well as the lyre-shaped tombs in which Okinawans kept the bones of their ancestors, Ushijima had carefully organized and connected. He had also collected considerable artillery. With this he would fight the kind of defensive battle which would detain the supporting American fleet and expose it to the attacks of the kamikaze.

The kamikaze was the weapon with which Japan hoped to stave off defeat. The word means "divine wind," and it celebrates an event immortal in Japanese history. In 1570, when the Emperor of China assembled a vast armada to invade unprepared Japan, the gods sent a kamikaze in the shape of a typhoon which scattered the invasion fleet. In 1945, the kamikaze were young pilots pledged to crash their bomb-laden aircraft into enemy ships. The first of the kamikaze appeared off Leyte in October, 1944, and at Iwo Jima kamikaze pilots crashed and sank the escort carrier *Bismarck Sea* and badly damaged big *Saratoga* and others. Of course, the kamikaze pilots were expendable, but such noble suicide appealed to the Japanese character, and there was no difficulty in obtaining volunteers for the Kamikaze Corps.

They would have plenty of targets to choose among an American armada of 1,300 ships under Admiral Spruance, the veteran of Saipan and Iwo Jima. Okinawa was to be the biggest battle of the Pacific, eventually involving 548,000 Americans of all services, and the greatest amphibious assault of all time. In the Tenth Army were three Marine and four Army divisions with another in reserve, comprising an assault force of 172,000 combat and 115,000 service troops. Tenth Army was commanded by General Simon Bolivar Buckner, the 59-year-old son of the Confederate general who gave Grant his unconditional surrender at Fort Donelson. On April Fool's Day, 1945, Buckner's spearheads landed on the Hagushi beaches midway on Okinawa's western coast.

Two Marine divisions went in on the left, two Army divisions on the right, while a third Marine division feinted off southern Okinawa. There was no opposition, and among the jubilant American riflemen who went vaulting over the formidable Hagushi sea wall, L-Day or Landing-Day at Okinawa became known as "Love-Day." A Marine general following his troops ashore smiled at the good news and said: "There was a lot of glory on Iwo, but I'll take it this way."[148] Before nightfall the Americans had swept inland and captured two airfields, and within three days the island was cut in two. Then the Marines wheeled left to clear the lightly occupied northern half while the soldiers pivoted right to drive into Ushijima's formidable cross-island defense. It was a grinding advance, and eventually Buckner was forced to commit five divisions, three Army on his left and two Marine on the right. Still, the Japanese resisted doggedly, demonstrating, as at Biak, Peleliu and Iwo, that they were not the invincible offensive fighters they had thought themselves to be, but rather peerless defensive soldiers movable only in death. Alarmed, the Navy urged greater speed, some critics of Buckner suggesting an amphibious hook at Ushijima's rear, but the down-island drive was continued, and as it was, the kamikaze scourged the American invasion fleet.

They came in massed attacks called *kikusui,* or "floating chrysanthemums," with sometimes as many as 350 suiciders diving out of the clouds supported by as many conventional aircraft. The only way to stop them was to blow them up before they struck or shoot them into the sea; otherwise their momentum carried them straight into their targets in a rocking, searing blast. American seamen were exposed to an ordeal thus far unsurpassed at sea, especially among the destroyers of the radar picket line. Evidently mistaking the "tin cans" for battleships and cruisers, the kamikaze made them their favorite targets. So did another type of suicider called *oka* (cherry blossom) by the Japanese and *baka* (idiot) by the Americans. Provided with rocket propulsion and a human pilot, these 4,700-pound missiles were slung beneath the belly of a twin-engined Betty bomber. Once cast off, the *bakas* swooped upon their victims at speeds up to 600 mph, so fast and so small they were very difficult to shoot down. Fortunately, the Japanese did not have many of them, and their very weight made it impossible for the Bettys to maneuver, thus leaving them easy prey to American fighters. Still, the *bakas* and the kamikaze made life on ships of the American picket line a sleepless, flaming hell. If ever an argument in support of speedy conquest of an island objective were needed, it was supplied at Okinawa, where the slowness of the advance contributed to ultimate American naval losses of 34 ships sunk and 368 damaged. Nevertheless, the kamikaze and *bakas* were complete suiciders, self-destroying in their effects, and the Okinawa campaign may be said to have broken the back of the Japanese Air Force. Some 3,400 Japanese aircraft were lost over Okinawa and the southern home island of Kyushu, and 800 more destroyed on the ground, a total of 4,200 against American losses of about 1,000. And after the Air Force committed effective hara-kiri, so did the Navy, sending a suicide battleship south to its destruction.

This was *Yamato,* the supership which might have revolutionized naval construction as had H.M.S. *Dreadnought,* had not air power doomed the big-gunned vessel. *Yamato*'s mission, with eight accompanying destroyers and cruiser *Yahagi,* was to destroy the ships the kamikaze missed. She was not expected to return, and she had only enough fuel for a one-way voyage. *Yahagi* had only enough food for five days. On April 6 the force sortied and was quickly discovered by the omnipresent American submarines. As at Saipan, Spruance calmly put a force of surface ships between the enemy and their objective and sent his fast carriers into action.

On April 7 the American war birds found *Yamato* sailing within a diamond-shaped destroyer screen with *Yahagi* following. Within easy range of her home port, the greatest fighting ship ever built had no air cover whatsoever. She was absolutely naked to attack, and with bombs and torpedoes the Americans very quickly sent her to join the mighty sister *Musashi* on the bottom of the sea. *Yahagi* also was sunk, along with four destroyers, and the four remaining destroyers were damaged and sent limping back to port. That was the end of Japan's Navy. Her carriers were gone, and she had only one battleship and a handful of smaller vessels left. Her shores were not only defenseless from the sea, she had no way in which to reinforce the Thirty-second Army on Okinawa.

There, Ushijima's defenses were crumbling. The capital at Naha fell in mid-May and on the 29th a company of Marines took shell-pocked Shuri Castle, the pivotal center of the line. On June 18 Buckner began his final offensive, and was killed by artillery fire as he watched the spearheads move out. Buckner was replaced by Roy Geiger, a Marine who had commanded Vandegrift's air on Guadalcanal. It was therefore fitting that an officer in at the start of the American counter-offensive should command at the kill. On June 22, after General Ushijima killed himself and the Japanese soldiery began to surrender for the first time in the war, Geiger proclaimed the Okinawa campaign at an end.

The day Okinawa fell, Emperor Hirohito met with his Supreme War Council and gave utterance to a belief which no one else in authority dared to utter: a way must be found to end the war. Japan was helpless. Not only her Navy was gone but her merchant fleet as well. American submarines had done to Japan what Doenitz and his U-boats could not do to Britain. They had isolated her. In all, American submarines sank 60 percent of the 2,117 Japanese vessels lost in World War II, as well as 201 warships. In June, using an electronic sonar device which could detect undersea mines, a force of nine American submarines slipped into Japan's Inland Sea and sank one enemy submarine and 28 merchant ships at a loss of one of their own boats. Here was a penetration into the very heart of Japan, much as if an enemy were to control the Great Lakes. As the submarine blockade strangled the Japanese economy, the people faced starvation and the production of war materials was being brought to a standstill.

Meanwhile, clouds of Superforts ravaged the islands. Since the Tokyo fire-bombing, whole hearts of cities had been burned out, and 33 selected cities were being subjected to regular bombardment. Offshore, the American battle fleet under Halsey paraded the Japanese coast with impunity. All that was left to Japan was a hoard of several thousand aircraft kept carefully hidden and camouflaged against the day of American invasion. Even Russia was making ominous gestures, having announced in April that she would not renew her Neutrality Pact with Japan. In May Germany surrendered, collapsing all Japanese hopes for a wonder weapon that would turn the tide, and then Okinawa, the last Japanese outpost, fell to the Americans.

Yet to carry out Hirohito's wish to end the war was not easy. The militarists favored a war to the bitter end, and negotiations would have to be carried out in secret to find some terms less odious than Unconditional Surrender. In no case would the Japanese scuttle their imperial system and expose their divine Emperor to any possible risk of trial as a war criminal. So the Japanese went to the only neutral: Russia. And the Russians stalled. They had no intention of helping Japan out of the war until they had gotten into it and picked up a little booty themselves. Thus, when the Big Three met at Potsdam, Stalin did not mention the Japanese peace feelers to Truman or Churchill. Nor did he inform Clement Atlee, the new British Prime Minister whose Labour Party had defeated Churchill and the Conservatives in the British elections held during the Potsdam Conference.

Harry Truman knew about the peace feelers, because Magic was still intercepting and decoding Japanese messages, and it was thus that Truman's undeceived common sense got an early insight into Stalin's duplicity. Thus also the Potsdam Proclamation was issued on July 26 by Britain, China and America. It specified that Unconditional Surrender was for the armed forces only; it declared that Japan would be stripped of all possessions except the four home islands, and that part of the nation would be occupied until the people could elect a new government in a free election. Unfortunately, the Potsdam Proclamation made no reference to the fate of the Emperor, the key point with the Japanese. This was because the Allies had not yet made up their minds on that point. Yet, by insisting that "stern justice will be meted out to all war criminals," the proclamation gave the war party in Japan the opportunity to interpret the omission as an ominous one. After the Potsdam Proclamation, Stalin at last informed his colleagues of the Japanese peace feelers, after which he continued to stall the Japanese while making ready his own entry into the war.

The Americans, who had just successfully exploded the world's first atomic bomb, went ahead with plans for the invasion of Japan in November, 1945. While they waited and hoped for some break in the Japanese façade, the cruiser *Indianapolis* carried an atomic bomb to Tinian in the Marianas. While the Japanese argued among themselves and the Russians stalled, the Americans at last lost patience and interpreted the Japanese silence after Potsdam as tacit rejection of the terms. On August 6 a silvery Superfort named *Enola Gay* thundered aloft from Tinian with the deadliest of eggs nestled in her belly. Flying over Hiroshima, she dropped the bomb, and in a single flash of light and ensuing fireball an entire city and 78,000 people were destroyed.

Two days later, August 8, the Russians gave the Japanese their answer: war. On the 9th a second atomic bomb was dropped over Nagasaki, with similar dreadful results. On the 10th the Russians entered Korea to plant the seeds of another war. On the same day the Third Fleet, having ridden out a typhoon, resumed its strikes against the Japanese homeland. Hammer blows were now falling upon a nation whose leaders were divided between one party vowing to fight to the death of the nation and another frantic to surrender but fearful that to do so would kill the nation's soul. On that eventful August 10 Hirohito again met with the Supreme War Council and sanctioned a proposal to accept the Potsdam Proclamation with retention of the Emperor. The United States was notified through Sweden and Switzerland, and the Allied reply as expressed by Secretary of State James F. Byrnes was: "From the moment of surrender the authority of the Emperor and the Japanese Government to rule the state shall be subject to the Supreme Commander of the Allied powers who will take such steps as he deems proper to effectuate the surrender terms."[149]

Vague as the Byrnes note might have been, it did indicate that the Japanese could keep their Emperor. The debate in Tokyo was now over whether or not to accept any diminution of imperial authority would not bring on eventual destruction of it. At last, on August 14, Hirohito rose before the Council and insisted that the terms be accepted. "We demand that you will agree to it," he said. "We see only one way left for Japan to save herself. That is the reason we have made this determination to endure the unendurable and suffer the insufferable."[150] On August 15 United States forces were ordered to cease fire. On September 2, aboard mighty battleship *Missouri* in Tokyo

Bay, in the presence of MacArthur and Nimitz and representatives of Britain, China, Russia, Australia, Canada, France, Holland and New Zealand, the Japanese signed the surrender document.

With that not only did the greatest war in history come to an end, but, under the ominous mushrooming clouds of nuclear weapons, a new era of warfare was born.

PART IX

The Korean War

1

☆

The greatest of wars had lasted six years and a day and it had taken 30 million lives among soldiers and civilians alike, maiming many millions more and filling the world with its homeless and uprooted victims. The face of Europe and much of Asia was disfigured by wreck and ruin on a scale too colossal to be calculated, and the ocean floor was littered with sunken ships stuffed with irrecoverable goods of the earth. Yet, for all of its waste, World War II seemed to have achieved its purpose, for Germany and Japan lay utterly prostrate and defeated.

But just because the purpose of war is not merely to defeat the enemy but to ensure a better and more lasting peace, the war of 1939-45 ended in tragic failure. The Allies had won not a victory but an annihilation. They had oversucceeded. Unconditional surrender had ignored the political truth that today's enemy is often tomorrow's ally. Utterly wrecked and discredited, Germany and Japan could not be immediately enlisted against Russia the moment Stalin began to make his aggressive moves to west and east. Finally, an even greater tragedy was that Russia and America, which had emerged from the war as superpowers, could not sink their differences and make common cause for world peace; for the wreckage of the German and Japanese empires had left a power vacuum into which Russia rushed and where she was finally confronted by the United States. Thus was begun the Cold War, which is now in its third decade.

This time the war was for men's minds as well as for their lands. In one sense it was the ultimate conflict with capitalism so ardently desired by Communism, and in another it was an attempt by America to prevent Russia from satisfying her age-old territorial ambitions. As the Cold War began, the advantage was very much on the side of the Russian Communists, and this for three reasons:

The first was the moral defeat which America suffered when that single blinding flash of light over Hiroshima destroyed a city at a stroke. With this, and the following atomic blast at Nagasaki, the United States lost the moral ascendancy which she had once held in the world and joined the company of Tamerlane with his towers of skulls, the Germans with their poison gas, the Japanese with their biological warfare, and the other ruthless conquerors who did not scruple to employ the foulest means to achieve their victories. In these twin holocausts the high moral principles which were the soul of Wilson's Fourteen Points and the strength of Roosevelt's proposal for a United Nations were charred as crisp and as black as the 120,000 Japanese immolated there. Henceforth, every American documentation of Russian aggression or Communist cruelty had to be read in the light of these atomic fireballs.

In defense of this decision, it has been argued that by dropping the atomic bomb President Truman shortened the war and saved hundreds of thousands of lives. This is open to most serious question, although at the time the U.S. government undoubtedly feared that the invasion of Japan would be a costly and bloody process. Actually, Japan was already beaten.

According to the U.S. Strategic Bombing Survey: "Based on a detailed investigation of surviving Japanese leaders involved, it is the Survey's opinion that certainly prior to 31st December, 1945, and in all probability prior to 1st November, 1945, Japan would have surrendered, even if the atomic bomb had not been dropped, even if Russia had not entered the war, and even if no invasion had been planned or contemplated."[1] Therefore the war, which had cooled since Okinawa and was not to resume until November 1 with the invasion of Japan, was shortened only slightly. For this the United States lost her honor, gained the enmity of most of Asia and the opprobrium of honest and compassionate men everywhere and gave to the Communists a powerful psychological stick with which to beat the free world.

Stalin also held another club, the concessions granted to him by Churchill and Roosevelt at the Yalta Conference, and here is the second reason for Communism's early advantage. At Yalta, Stalin was promised the Kurile Islands, the southern half of Sakhalin Island taken from her by Japan in 1904, privileges in Darien and Port Arthur and recognition of her "pre-eminent interests" in Manchuria. These concessions relating mainly to Chinese territory were made without consulting China, and Churchill and Roosevelt thus were in the position of a man giving away not only what is not his but what belongs to a friend and ally. Nevertheless, they promised Stalin to make Chiang accept these agreements, and Stalin in turn pledged himself to recognize Chiang's sovereignty in Manchuria. Stalin, of course, had no intention of doing any such thing, nor did he intend to honor the treaty of friendship he later signed with Chiang's Nationalist government. Finally, his pledge to set up interim, democratic governments in Eastern and Central Europe were also to be dishonored.

How did it happen? For two reasons. The first was the belief that if the Allies were "nice to Russia" the Soviets would join in the postwar task of building a free and peaceful world. Franklin Roosevelt believed that this was possible because of a naïve confidence in his ability to handle "old Uncle Joe." In fairness to FDR, he was not the only one to believe that the Communists were trustworthy. The country as a whole then admired the Kremlin, and it was not only the card-carrying Communists or their fellow travelers who sang so sweetly of Uncle Joe. Ambassador Joseph Davies said that to distrust Stalin was "bad Christianity, bad sportsmanship, bad sense,"[2] Wendell Willkie composed canticles to Soviet rule, and even Harry Truman came back from Potsdam saying, "I *like* Uncle Joe."[3] Stalin, who could be very charming and agreeable when in pursuit of his objectives, fooled them all. Perhaps he did not actually deceive Winston Churchill. Certainly the British chief understood the nature of Communism and the extent of Russian ambition. Yet he too went along with the policy of accommodation, and this may have been because Roosevelt's enthusiasm for it left him no real choice. Moreover, Churchill had already erred in the Balkans by abandoning the Yugoslav partisan leader, Mikhailovitch, in favor of Marshal Tito. There he had mistakenly concluded that British gold could control Tito, and at Yalta he may have hoped that FDR, the force of world opinion and perhaps even good faith might restrain Stalin.

The second reason for the Yalta concessions was the American fixation on drawing Soviet Russia into the Pacific War. It was believed that Japan could not be defeated without her help. Impressed by the last-man battles put up by the Japanese Army, the Joint Chiefs of Staff concluded that Japan would fight to the bitter end and advised

Roosevelt and Churchill that the Pacific War might last for 18 months after Germany fell. Thus, having underrated Japan at the start of the war, the high command now overrated her at the end. But the facts were that in February, 1945, when the Yalta Conference convened, Japan was on her last legs. A few days after the conference ended on February 11, American carrier-based aircraft were raiding the Tokyo area and American Marines were storming ashore at Iwo Jima. By then Japan had lost her navy and her merchant marine, she was beginning to feel the pinch of hunger and material shortages and her shores were open to invasion. Yet, at Yalta, and still again at Potsdam, one month *after* the Japanese on Okinawa began to surrender by the thousands, *one month before Japan did surrender,* the Americans were still intent upon getting Russia to enter the Pacific War. When she did come in, it was with a jackal's leap like Mussolini's. For a six-day war against a skeleton foe she got effective suzerainty in Manchuria and the status of a Pacific power.

True enough, if Stalin had kept his promises, the agreements made at Yalta might have worked. It is also true that by then the Soviets had the power to take what they were granted. But that was no reason to invest Communist aggression with a legal title or to throw a moral cloak over Communist subversion. And so, except for possession of the Turkish Straits, the dreams that used to sweeten the sleep of the Czars were realized by the most adroit, the most ruthlessly purposeful and the most calculating of the Commissars.

The third factor working to Communist profit was America's rush to disarm. Americans still seemed to cling to the old delusion that the big grim game was over and it was now time to celebrate the victory. The Red Army might be garrisoning half of Europe, but in America the cry was "Bring the boys back home!" They were brought home, and very speedily discharged. Within a year the number of men in uniform was down to three million and then cut again by half. Irate mothers invaded General Eisenhower's headquarters in the Pentagon to lecture him on the excesses of militarism. The mightiest navy the world had ever seen, before or since, was dismantled and put into moth balls and a drive was begun to reduce the Marines to the status of naval police. Certainly no true democracy could be expected to maintain such a huge and costly military establishment in peacetime. Nevertheless, there was quite a difference between hanging up the sword and breaking it up, as America was doing. But the country, as in 1918, was in a hurry to get "back to normalcy."

Amazingly enough, with controls suddenly lifted there was no onset of galloping inflation, and a wave of nationwide strikes called by a labor movement eager to assert its power did not more than momentarily slow the flood of automobiles, radios, refrigerators and all other kinds of consumer goods flowing from production lines so rapidly reconverted from the manufacture of munitions. Certainly the vigor of the American economy came as a shock to Stalin and the Communist economists, who for years had been predicting that another depression would finish capitalism. This, they said, was most likely to occur in the difficult period of postwar adjustment. The actuality was quite the reverse, and employment soared to the incredible high of 60 million jobs. Ironically, this very prosperity was in some ways as much an asset to Stalin as a depression. Instead of reaching for power over the body of an America prostrate, he might do so behind the back of an America preoccupied with pleasure and possessions. This, joined to the rapidity of American demobilization and disengagement, doubtless suggested that he was dealing with the same old fun-loving ostrich of the twenties and thirties.

But he was not. The Americans who went to war with Hitler and Japan may not have been as lighthearted as those who fought the Kaiser, but neither were they as naïve. Not so starry-eyed, they were not so prone to disenchantment, and thus they did not turn away in disgust when Stalin opened a new round of imperialist aggression, but instead, with the same grim though reluctant purpose which had characterized them in the war, they picked up the gauntlet and put on the mantle of free world leadership. The pursuit of pleasure was not, of course, abandoned. But isolationist self-indulgence was, and in its place America followed a policy of enlightened self-interest. It was a matter of agreeing that "When a strong man armed keepeth his palace, his goods are in peace."[4]

Much of the credit for this change in attitude is due to President Truman, and it is possible that in him Stalin may have met his match. Truman's simple courage, his undeceived good sense and his great capacity to come rapidly to the right decision were just the qualities to thwart the political genius of the astute Commissar who had aptly named himself the man of steel. Within a year of postwar "negotiation" with the former Russian ally Truman realized that the word was a misnomer when applied to Communists.

In Germany, Russia showed that she had no intention of treating that conquered nation as an economic whole. In her own occupation zone in the East she systematically stripped the territory of raw materials, dismantling industries and carting them off to Russia and refusing to cooperate with the Americans, British and French. In Poland, Russia almost at once violated the Yalta and Potsdam agreements by setting up a satellite government. In Hungary, Rumania and Bulgaria she stubbornly blocked all free elections so that her hand-picked puppet Communists, backed by the power of the Red Army, subverted and took over the governments. In Yugoslavia, Marshal Tito put his country inside the Red camp. Only Austria escaped a similar fate, and Czechoslovakia for a time.

In September of 1946 the United States called upon Russia to respect the principles of Yalta and Potsdam, especially in Germany. In reply, the Soviet Union continued to go her own way, and the Western Allies decided to merge their occupation zones regardless of what the Communists might do. With this Germany eventually became divided into a separate West Germany and East Germany. Still, the Soviet aggression continued, and Stalin finally made his move south. Guerrillas from the satellite states in the Balkans infiltrated Greece, imperiling her independence. Russia herself began to exert pressure on Turkey. Now the entire eastern Mediterranean was threatened, as Stalin sought to satisfy the old Czarist ambition to achieve hegemony there and to control the Turkish Straits. Britain, who had been so long supreme in the Mediterranean, was now powerless to thwart him. At this point, President Truman stepped into the breach.

On March 12, 1947, Truman asked Congress for $400 million in aid to Greece and Turkey. The request was approved, and eventually the Communist attempt to break into the Mediterranean was beaten back. Even more significant was President Truman's declaration: "I believe that it must be the policy of the United States to support free peoples who are resisting attempted subjugation by armed minorities or by outside pressures. . . ."[5] This was the famous Truman Doctrine whereby America undertook to confront Communist aggression all over the world; it was the policy of "containment" which vowed that not another soul or foot of free soil would pass behind the Iron Curtain. It was followed by the so-called Marshall Plan after General Marshall, now Secretary of State, discovered that as a result of economic chaos in Western Europe, especially France and Italy, Communism was making dangerous inroads.

Marshall proposed a program of European recovery based upon enormous financial assistance from the United States. It was not to be merely anti-Communist, Marshall explained: "Our policy is not directed against any country or doctrine, but is directed against hunger, poverty, desperation, and chaos. Its purpose should be the revival of a working economy in the world so as to permit the emergence of political and economic conditions in which free institutions can exist."[6] Thus Russia and the satellite states were invited to join the program, but Communism, preferring the economic chaos in which it thrives, declined the invitation.

At the end of 1947 President Truman asked Congress for an appropriation of $17 billion to support the program, and at once touched off a bitter debate. It was the internationalists and isolationists all over again, with the difference that the former emphasized the high purpose of the proposal and the latter, while agreeing that something must be done to help Europe, assailed the size of the outlay. Later the isolationists would describe the Marshall Plan as the "Great Giveaway." But Senator Vandenberg, once the leader of the isolationists and now an ardent internationalist, persuaded some of his former followers with the challenge: "The greatest nation on earth either justifies or surrenders its leadership. We must choose. . . ."[7]

Choice was made much easier when the Soviets, with characteristic bad timing, brought Czechoslovakia behind the Iron Curtain with a swift and ruthless *coup d'état*. Here was the first genuine democracy, one of the most stable governments in Europe, being subverted by the very techniques which were threatening to undermine the rest of the Continent. So the Economic Cooperation Administration, or Marshall Plan, was passed. In the end, it was even more successful than the program which saved Greece and Turkey. By 1950, as a result of very hard work on their own part and by an outlay of $12 billion by America, the nations of Western Europe were back on their feet.

Before that happened, however, Stalin made one last bid to intimidate the Allies in Germany. In the summer of 1948 he imposed the Berlin Blockade. Berlin was within the Russian occupation zone, but by agreement it was under four-power control. Unfortunately, the Western Allies had not obtained corridors of access to the city, as they should have done. They were in Berlin only on Soviet sufferance, and when this was withdrawn they were shut out of their areas of the capital, and it appeared that what is now called West Berlin would be starved into the Soviet sphere.

Once again Harry Truman refused to retreat. "We are going to stay, period,"[8] he declared, and his response to the Russian challenge was the improvised marvel of the Berlin Airlift. For 11 months the Americans, assisted by the British, flew round-the-clock flights to bring food, clothing and coal to besieged Berlin. Thwarted by this determined resistance, Stalin raised the Berlin Blockade on May 12, 1949. Even before he did, however, the free world had organized against possible further aggression. Upon American initiative, the North Atlantic Treaty was signed. For the first time in American history, the United States had entered into an alliance with other countries. Thus if the Kaiser and the Fuehrer had forced this nation to abandon isolationism, Stalin had compelled her to accept international responsibility. He also drove her back to the briefly abandoned condition of a warfare state.

One reason why Stalin did not move with naked power against Western Europe was the American monopoly in atomic weapons. Yet Europe was not the only area of Cold War confrontation. There were others in which the use of A-bombs was not practical, if indeed these weapons of annihilation were of any real political use anywhere. They might cow Communism by menacing its Russian heartland, but they could not control events, say, in Greece or Turkey or in any other theater where the techniques of the new subversive warfare were being employed. What was needed was military power, conventional military power—and this a demobilized America did not have.

What she did have in the immediate wake of the war was another interservice squabble. The Army Air Force, which had delivered the A-bombs, had captured the imagination of the people. Most Americans believed that air power alone could enforce the nation's will, a concept which, though contrary to the lessons of the war, the Air Force eagerly advanced. In many ways, the atomic bomb had become the American Maginot Line. It was widely believed that with this power in America's solitary possession no aggressor would dare move against her. Thus the Air Force held an ascendancy over the Navy and even its parent Army; and when all the services, profiting from the wartime mistakes caused by interservice squabbling, finally moved to unify the military establishment, it appeared that an air general and an air power theory of war would dominate it.

This the Army and especially the Navy could not abide, and out of the Navy's reaction came the study which led to the Unification Act of

1947. There were to be three coequal services—Army, Navy and Air Force—under a Department of Defense. Each service would have its own civilian secretary under an over-all Secretary of Defense, and each would have a representative on the Joint Chiefs of Staff.* Also, a National Security Council composed of the President and his military and civilian chiefs was created, as well as a National Resources Board which was to provide the military's needs in manpower, raw material and industrial resources.

All of this, however, was merely the bare bones of the warfare state. The flesh and blood—men and munitions—had yet to be put back on. In 1948 there were only 1,374,000 men in the armed services, of which only 671,000 were effective ground troops. Of these, 253,000 were on occupation duty. Of the entire total, many carried outmoded arms. American striking power, therefore, was not very strong. As General Marshall said: ". . . we are playing with fire while we have nothing with which to put it out."[9] In 1948 the fire came scorchingly close with the Berlin Blockade, and it was then that the Defense Department moved for a huge appropriation of $20 billion and a program of universal military training. Just like the Spartans, every young American was to learn the profession of arms. Military service would build his character, it was argued, and inculcate in him a high and noble patriotism. Such sentiments, though worthy of an Assyrian war lord, did not seem in keeping with the character of what had only recently been a pacifist nation. The Cold War, however, was changing many convictions. Then the Berlin Blockade was lifted, and as tension eased, the defense appropriation was cut to $15 billion and instead of universal military training the expired Selective Service Act was re-enacted. America was not yet a militarist nation, but it now had a military establishment and a military habit of mind which would make the aforesaid Assyrian chieftain bite his chariot in envy. Gradually, however, the old habits of economy began to reappear, and as the war machine again went into decline, the Communists, thwarted in the West, moved openly in the East.

The war had left America supreme in the Pacific. As the result of her conquests on Iwo Jima and Okinawa she continued to occupy the Bonins and Ryukyus, and held United Nations trusteeships in the

---

* Later the Commandant of the Marine Corps became an ex officio member of the Joint Chiefs, permitted to attend meetings at which matters relative to the Marines were discussed.

Carolines, Marshalls and Marianas. In Japan America was the sole occupying power under General MacArthur, and because of MacArthur's wise, skillful and compassionate direction, this nation once so militarist and totalitarian was transformed into a peace-loving, self-sufficient democracy. On the mainland of eastern Asia, however, American policy was not so well served.

China, the nation for whose sake America fought Japan, went solidly Communist. Probably, this could not have been averted. First, Stalin's duplicity at Yalta put him in the position to come to the assistance of the Communist leader, Mao Tse-tung. Second, the demand to bring the boys back home stripped the Pacific of three million Americans between September, 1945, and March, 1946, and all the available occupation troops were sent to Japan rather than to China to help Chiang. Third, Chiang himself was a most inept leader. Between runaway inflation and a corrupt officialdom, his Nationalist government was a wooden sword indeed compared with the iron discipline of the Communists who followed Mao. Fourth, high-placed officials in the Truman administration actually favored backing Mao instead of Chiang. They had been deceived by the false portrait of Mao, the simple, non-Communist "agrarian reformer," which had been painted for them by left-wing American journalists. Even General Marshall, who went to China in 1945 to prevent a civil war, employed this phrase to describe Mao and his followers. Marshall did obtain a cease-fire, but Mao granted it only to gain a breathing spell in which to build his strength with Russian aid. Although American aid to Chiang reached the figure of $2 billion, the Nationalist leader never got the direct military assistance he sought, and in 1949 the Communists under Mao forced him out of China and onto the big offshore island of Formosa. There Chiang built a new army, biding his time against a possible return to the continent, and hoping against hope that his supporters in the United States would persuade that nation to intervene in his behalf. This, however, was not to be. While Chiang marked time hopelessly on Formosa, Mao clamped the Communist hold on China tighter and tighter.

Such was the tragic outcome of the Pacific War. From the Open Door policy to the declaration of war on Japan, a century of American effort to succor the helpless Asian giant had ended in a Communist, anti-American China. It did not take Mao long to sour traditional Sino-American friendship. His Hate-America campaign convulsed

China in a frenzy. And because this outpouring of invective shocked the American public, some Americans looked around for scapegoats of their own and found them in imaginary "traitors" in the State Department. It was not treachery, however, but the duplicity of Stalin at Yalta joined to Mao's ability and Chiang's ineffectiveness that brought great China into the Communist camp. Any attempt to retrieve the situation would have required a massive American military intervention costing hundreds of thousands of lives and untold billions of dollars, the success of which could not be guaranteed and the support for which the American public most certainly would have withheld.

So China was "lost," and in that same disastrous year of 1949 the free world was shocked again by Russia's success in exploding an atomic bomb. Aided by captured German scientists, as well as by American and British traitors, the Communists had ended the American monopoly in ultimate weapons. And what was the American reaction? They built and exploded the hydrogen or "thermonuclear" superbomb. When Russia inevitably countered with one of her own, the costly and endless nuclear arms race was begun. Mankind seemed to dwell beneath the grim dark shadow of the mushroom cloud, and even an eventual agreement to suspend testing of these weapons did not dispel a universal, gnawing dread that if World War III should erupt it would mean the destruction of civilization. And then Communism and capitalism, having avoided a shooting war in Berlin, went rolling along a collision course in Korea.

It was in Korea in 1904 that Japan had humbled Russia and driven her back on Europe, and it was in Korea in 1945 that Russia returned to the Pacific. It was also in Korea in 1895 that a rising Japan had clashed with a declining China, for the central fact of Korea's unhappy history is that this little land had been for centuries a pawn in the power struggle in Asia. She has been coveted not only for her people and resources, and her warm-water ports, but also because of her strategic position. A peninsula 500 to 600 miles long jutting out from the mainland of China, Korea can be either a springboard for the invasion of Japan or a corridor for a march into Manchuria. China invaded her, and then Japan, after which Russia, feigning friendship for China, came rushing into the breach to despoil the Japanese. Japan, however, showed the most staying power, and her victory over

Russia in 1904-05 prepared Korea for eventual assimilation into the Japanese Empire. To her credit, Japan did much to improve the country she had renamed Chosen. To her discredit, her typically oppressive policies finally reduced most Koreans to the status of hewers of wood and drawers of water. Opposition to Japanese rule became a constant of Korean life. Guerrillas harried the conquerors incessantly. Among their leaders was the legendary Kim Il Sung, who died with a price on his head. Another was Kim Sung Chu, a pudgy, stone-faced officer who joined the Red Army and fought at Stalingrad. With 35 other hand-picked Koreans, Kim Sung Chu was indoctrinated in Communist doctrine and trained to take over in postwar Korea. A third enemy of Japan was Lee Sung Man, a passionate aristocrat who suffered imprisonment, torture and finally exile in his efforts to free Korea. Better known by the westernized version of his name, Syngman Rhee, he was to appear before the world as a tireless witness to the plight of Korea and became in his own mind the living embodiment of his country's cause.

In August of 1945, as Japan was collapsing, Stalin, who had agreed with the Cairo Conference declaration that "in due course Korea should be free and independent," had reaffirmed this commitment at Potsdam. It appeared that the only problem in Korea was to find a line north of which the Russians would accept the surrender of Japanese troops, south of which the Americans would do the same. It was settled when an American admiral pointed to the 38th parallel which divides the country roughly in half and said, "Why not put it there?"[10] There it went.

On August 12, two days before Japan fell, with the nearest American troops 600 miles away in Okinawa, 100,000 Russian soldiers crossed the Siberian border into northern Korea. Behind them, other Soviet troops overran Manchuria and subsequently shipped much of the province's industrial plant back to Russia. Meanwhile, some 600,000 captured Japanese soldiers in both northern Korea and Manchuria were bundled off to Siberia as slave laborers. Finally, the Russians went to work to seal off the north from the south, so that when the Americans arrived in the south nearly a month later they found the country cut in half.

The 38th parallel, an imaginary line which never had any place in Korean history, a military nightmare running over mountains and across rivers, had become the dividing line for two zones of occupation that had never been intended. The industrial north of nine million people was separated from the agricultural south of 21 million. Very rapidly, the Russians isolated the south. They shut off electric power and cut railroads. Armed guards patrolled the parallel. The exchange of goods dwindled and then dried up. A once viable economy was cut in two, the south deprived of coal and chemicals and caught in an inflationary spiral, the north crying for food. On both sides of the parallel a nation recently jubilant to feel the Japanese bonds struck from its feet now seethed with rage at the unnatural division of its country.

Most of the blame fell upon the Americans, who appeared to be occupation troops. In the north the Russians worked carefully in the background. Their hand-picked team of Koreans led by the former guerrilla chief, Kim Sung Chu, had set up an interim government. Kim made a dramatic impact on the people of the north when he presented himself to them as Kim Il Sung, the legendary leader of old. He also confiscated great estates and divided them among the peasantry. Later, after the peasants learned that they could neither sell their land nor borrow on it, after taxes disguised as "production quotas" rose to a ruinous 60 percent, the "land reform" came to be recognized as a veiled form of serfdom; but in the beginning it scored great propaganda victories for the Communists, giving the comrades in the south a handy stick with which to beat the Americans, who had neither reform nor program of any kind. Moreover, American "rule" was military, and because it did not understand Koreans or their customs, it was harsh and inept.

Against this background the United States in late 1945 persuaded the Soviets to set up a Joint Commission on Korea. This, however, the Russians proceeded to sabotage with one hand while with the other they consolidated their position in the north. The city of Pyongyang became the headquarters for an armed camp. Koreans who had fought either for Red Russia or Red China streamed across the Yalu River to join an army commanded by Nam Il, another one of the 36. Obviously, the north was to be the satellite state from which the south would either be subverted or invaded. At last, in 1947, an alarmed and frustrated America took the entire issue to the United Nations.

The world had held much hope for the United Nations, the international organization which Franklin Delano Roosevelt and Winston

Churchill had devised to keep the peace. Stronger than the old League of Nations, it was composed of a Security Council to act and a General Assembly to investigate, discuss and advise. The Security Council was composed of 11 member nations,* five of whom—Britain, France, China, the United States and the Soviet Union—were permanent members. In the General Assembly all members had a single equal vote. The Council could take action against an aggressor either by severing diplomatic relations, employing economic sanctions or by the use of "air, sea or land forces."

Unfortunately, the UN had provided a veto power through which any member of the Big Five on the Council had the power to nullify any decision. Here was the UN's basic defect, and it was not, as is popularly supposed, instituted at the behest of Russia, much as she came to abuse the privilege. It was put there because both Churchill and Roosevelt rightly concluded that their countries would not accept any diminution of their sovereignty. In fact, no country will. Closed societies such as the Communist ones, being free of any criticism, may pretend to accept it; but open societies such as the democracies, being subject to public opinion, have to face the problem honestly. And the problem of national sovereignty, of how to restrain or punish a sovereign state, is the root problem of any attempt to impose world peace through an international organization. When individual persons stopped thinking of themselves as sovereign and accepted order, there was an end to anarchy; and when nations do the same, there will be an end to war. But that, as Thomas More said of the advent of Utopia, will probably not be for some time; and in 1947 the United Nations ran straight into the problem of sovereignty when it attempted to hold free elections throughout Korea.

The Russians simply refused to allow the UN Commission north of the 38th parallel. Elections were held only in the south, where a National Assembly was chosen and Syngman Rhee was named President. A government was set up with a capital at Seoul. Thus was born the Republic of Korea, called South Korea, whose soldiers were called ROKs for its initials. In the north the Communists retaliated by proclaiming the People's Democratic Republic of Korea, with a constitution similar to that of Communist Bulgaria. Kim Il Sung was its chief.

At the end of 1948, with great fanfare, the Russians began leaving

* Originally there were only nine.

North Korea. They had done their job, leaving behind them a good modern army under Nam Il. The implication, of course, was that it was now up to the warmongering Americans to demonstrate their good faith by withdrawing. This the Americans did not do until June, 1949, handing the Reds another propaganda handle. Nor did the Americans endow Syngman Rhee with a military machine nearly the equal of Kim's. President Truman was afraid that Rhee might use force to unify the country. The fierce old patriot, broken-hearted at the division of Korea, had declared that if the Americans gave him enough gasoline and airplanes he would conquer North Korea in two weeks. And just because Rhee's tactics were hardly less high-handed than those of the Communists, the American Congress was loath to arm him. Thus American support carefully excluded tanks, big guns, combat aircraft and even large stocks of ammunition. Without these, the ROK Army was about as modern as a Minié ball.

Congress also stalled in approving Truman's requests for economic aid to South Korea, and on January 12, 1950, it appeared that this scrawny little son of the United Nations had been turned out into the cold, for on that date Secretary of State Dean Acheson declared that the American line of defense in the Pacific "runs along the Aleutians to Japan and then goes to the Ryukyus [and] from the Ryukyus to the Philippine Islands."[11] Korea had been excluded. In May Senator Tom Connally declared that Russia could seize Korea without American intervention because the peninsula was "not very greatly important."[12]

Such words and deeds certainly could not be missed by the Russians and their puppets in Pyongyang. Even though Congress eventually approved aid to Korea, even though Acheson later explained that the defense line was drawn through places where America had troops, as in Japan, and not through places where she did not, as in Korea, it would be surprising if the Communists did not conclude that America would not fight to defend South Korea. This they did conclude, and they also decided to move quickly before South Korea's reviving economy became healthy and before real military aid could come from the United States. And so, between the 15th and 24th of June, the North Korean Army cleared civilians from a belt just above the 38th parallel. Meanwhile, Pyongyang radio broadcast a "peace offer," one tailor-made for their Communist comrades in South Korea, and one bound to be rejected by Rhee, as it was. Now Kim Il Sung had his excuse for the "defensive" invasion of South Korea. On the rainy Sunday morning of June 25, 1950, the Red artillery opened a bombardment.

Along the border, ROK soldiers thought that a thunderstorm was making up, until the Communist shells began to crash among them.

2

☆

While the spearheads of some 90,000 North Korean soldiers went plunging south behind hundreds of tanks, Premier Kim Il Sung announced that his country was acting in "self-defense." The "bandit traitor Syngman Rhee" had attempted to attack the North, Kim declared, and a "righteous invasion" of South Korea had been ordered to parry Rhee's blow. Kim did not explain how it was that his "defending army" was already 10 to 20 miles inside the borders of the "invader."

The truth was that the invasion had been well planned beforehand and the Red soldiers, following five ground routes and one by sea, were moving with astonishing speed. They had little difficulty overwhelming the surprised ROKs. In some areas South Korean divisions were only at half-strength, with the rest of their men back in Seoul on weekend leave. Only one small sector in the east offered stiff resistance, and here the defending ROK division was at full strength and the NKs attacked without tanks. But wherever the big Russian-built T-34s were at work, the Red advance was irresistible.

ROK soldiers armed with 37-millimeter antitank guns or an occasional 2.36-inch rocket launcher were no match for the thick-skinned T-34s firing an 85-millimeter cannon and a pair of heavy machine guns. ROK shells flashed off the sides of the tanks like futile fireflies, and ROK roadblocks of logs and sandbags were smashed like barriers of straw. Behind the armor came the NK infantrymen, cutting down terrified ROKs flushed into view by the tanks. Some valiant South Koreans attempted to rush the tanks with satchel charges or explosive-tipped poles, and others leaped aboard them and tried to open the turrets to drop grenades inside; but all were either machine-gunned by the tanks themselves or picked off by covering infantry. Eventually, the very clank and clatter of approaching Red armor was sufficient to terrify whole battalions, and by nightfall of June 25, except for that momentary repulse in the east, the NK Army had carried out or exceeded all of its first-day missions. By then also the world seemed to teeter on the brink of World War III.

Sunday June 25 in Korea was Saturday June 24 in Washington, and it was not until 9:26 that night that the State Department received Ambassador John J. Muccio's telegram: "North Korea forces invaded Republic of Korea territory at several points this morning. . . . It would appear from the nature of the attack and the manner in which it was launched that it constitutes an all-out offensive against ROK."[13] A half-hour later the report was in the hands of Secretary Acheson, who immediately telephoned President Truman, then vacationing at his home in Independence, Missouri. At first, Truman was for flying straight back to Washington, but changed his mind after Acheson informed him that there were no details available. Instead, both men agreed to request a meeting of the United Nations Security Council.

When the request was relayed to UN Secretary General Trygve Lie of Norway, Lie burst out: "This is war against the United Nations!"[14] Indeed it was, for the Republic of Korea had been brought into being under UN auspices, and Lie very quickly scheduled a Security Council meeting for 2 P.M. the following day.

In South Korea that following day, June 26, the ROK Army made a desperate attempt to save Seoul, the ROK capital located on Korea's west coast 50 miles south of the parallel. The plan was to hold Uijongbu, a highway center 20 miles above Seoul, and thus deny an invasion corridor to the enemy tanks. Two roads led into Uijongbu. On the left or western one, a ROK division's counterattack drove the NKs back. On the right, a sullen ROK general showed his disapproval of the entire operation by sulking in his tent, and a tank-led NK division easily smashed through his imperfect defenses. This exposed the western ROK division's entire right flank, and the unit was forced to withdraw. By evening two NK divisions were safely inside Uijongbu and the straight road south to Seoul lay open.

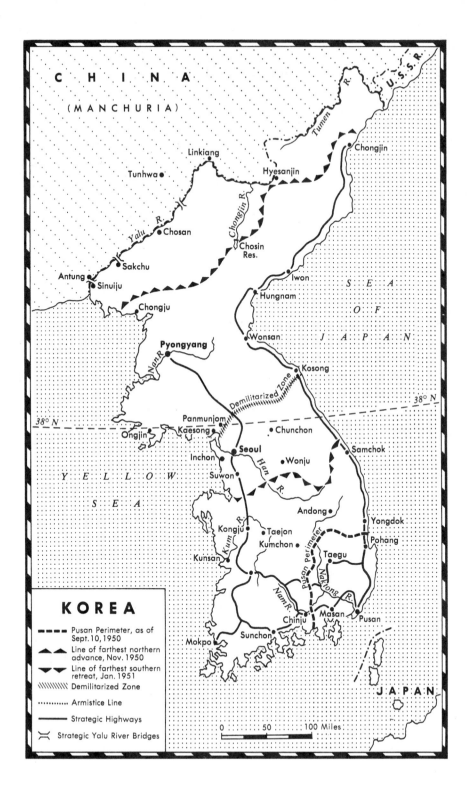

KOREA

- ▄▄▄▄ Pusan Perimeter, as of Sept. 10, 1950
- ▲▲ Line of farthest northern advance, Nov. 1950
- ▼▼ Line of farthest southern retreat, Jan. 1951
- \\\\\\\\ Demilitarized Zone
- ·········· Armistice Line
- —— Strategic Highways
- ⋊ Strategic Yalu River Bridges

A few hours earlier the Security Council convened at Lake Success, New York. Only ten members were present. The eleventh, the Soviet Union, was absent. Thwarted in her attempt to put Red China on the Council in place of Nationalist China, Russia had been boycotting the Council's meetings since January of that year. By her decision to stay away from this momentous meeting, she may have committed one of the great blunders of history, for she was therefore unable to exercise that veto power which would have made the Council powerless to act. The Council did act, and quickly, calling for a cease-fire throughout Korea and directing the North Koreans to withdraw north of the 38th parallel. A resolution to these ends was adopted by a vote of 9-0, with Communist Yugoslavia abstaining.

In the meantime, President Truman had flown back to Washington. En route, the President had reflected on the tragic rise of the dictators prior to World War II, how Hitler, Mussolini and the Japanese war lords had moved from takeover to takeover, confident that no hand would be raised against them. Now, not five years after the end of that war, Communist aggressors were resorting to the same means. Let South Korea be gobbled up, and no small nation would have the strength of will to resist a stronger Communist neighbor. South Korea must be succored, Truman decided; the policy of containment which had held Communism at bay in Europe must also block it in Asia. Accordingly, he notified Acheson to assemble the defense chiefs. They were waiting for him when he reached Blair House (the White House was then undergoing repairs), and Truman instructed them to prepare American forces for battle in the event that the United Nations should call for action against North Korea. Meanwhile, Truman instructed General MacArthur in Tokyo to send a party to South Korea to report on the best means of assisting the ROK government. MacArthur was also to send ammunition and equipment to South Korea, and to use the air and naval cover necessary to guarantee the delivery of supplies and to protect the evacuation of American dependents. Next, Truman placed the Seventh Fleet under MacArthur's command. The President's intention was to send the fleet into the strait between Chiang Kai-shek's island of Formosa and the Communist Chinese mainland, hoping thereby to forestall an aggressive move in either direction and thus prevent the war from spreading.

All these moves were preparatory. None involved America in the war. Yet all of them implied the President's willingness to intervene should the North Koreans ignore the UN call for a cease-fire and the South Koreans fail to halt the invasion.

By the morning of June 27—the third day of invasion—it became clear that the North Koreans had no intention of withdrawing and that the ROKs could not hold. By then the rumble of Red artillery could be heard in Seoul and the capital itself was in a state of panic. All day long crowds of terrified refugees streamed through the streets toward the three railroad bridges and one highway bridge across the broad Han River to the south. All that these miserable fugitives owned hung from wooden A-frames strapped to their backs or was piled high in little ox-drawn carts. Gradually, like a river passing its tributaries, the stream swelled. Leaderless and weaponless soldiers were drawn to it, and the sight of them together with the sound of the Red guns booming closer thickened the flood until, at midnight, the Han bridges were thronged with humanity. And it was then that the American military advisers to the ROK Army learned that the ROKs intended to blow the Han bridges.

Originally, the time set for destruction of the crossings was the moment that enemy tanks appeared in front of ROK Army Headquarters in Seoul. This was not likely to happen until late the following day. However, the Vice Minister of Defense had ordered them blown at 1:30 A.M. on that day. Why he did so is not known, although he may have been trying to cover the flight of the South Korean government to Taegu. Whatever the reason, the order horrified the Americans. Aware that most of the ROK Army was still north of the bridges, to say nothing of the thousands of fugitives streaming across them, the Americans rushed to ROK Headquarters and tried to have the order rescinded. Precious time was lost arguing, until a ROK general finally was ordered to drive to the highway bridge and countermand the orders of the engineers already in position south of the Han. Jumping into his jeep, the general plunged straight into the highway jam north of the bridge. With agonizing slowness, his vehicle crawled closer to the bridges. At 2:15 A.M., June 28, he was within 150 yards of the bridge telephone when the sky flashed orange, there was a terrible shattering roar, and the south end of the Han bridges tumbled into the river below.

On the highway bridge alone, between 500 and 800 persons lost their lives, while uncounted hundreds on the other crossings also perished. But far, far worse than this was the military calamity that befell the ROK Army. Most of its soldiers were north of the Han when the bridges fell. They had to abandon all their vehicles and heavy weapons, trying to rejoin their units by drifting eastward through the mountains to work their way south by the eastern coast, or else attempt to cross the river in small boats and rafts. Many were captured and others simply deserted. By the end of June the ROK Army of 98,000 men was down to 22,000. Eventually, as stragglers began to report in, this strength rose to 54,000. Nevertheless, the ROKs had lost 44,000 men as well as 30 percent of their small arms. Syngman Rhee's government, beginning to function far to the south at Taegu, did so without an army to defend it. And on June 28, while the North Korean spearheads clattered into Seoul in triumph, the Communists in Pyongyang jubilantly predicted that they would take the rest of South Korea before the United States or anyone else had time to stop them.

The day before Seoul fell, General MacArthur notified President Truman that a collapse of the ROK Army was imminent. As Truman wrote later: "There was now no doubt! The Republic of Korea needed help at once if it was not to be overrun. More seriously, a Communist success in Korea would put Red troops and planes within easy striking distance of Japan, and Okinawa and Formosa would be open to attack from two sides."[15] Accordingly, the President authorized MacArthur to use American aircraft and warships against North Koreans south of the 38th parallel and to "neutralize" the Formosa Strait by sending the Seventh Fleet there. Truman also approved strengthening of forces in the Philippines and increased aid to the French then fighting the Communist-led Vietminh in Indo-China.

It was significant that Truman did not commit American ground forces, and this was because he shared the widespread belief that air and sea power were sufficient to retrieve the situation. Moreover, he could not be sure whether or not the attack in Korea was a feint to draw off American strength from some other critical area where the main blow was to fall. Finally, he feared that if he sent in American divisions Stalin might counter with Russian divisions, and thereby touch off World War III. Thus, standing shy of the irrevocable act of committing ground troops, Truman announced his decisions to the public on June 27.

On that same day, with the Soviet Union again absent, the UN Security Council met once more. Observing that North Korea had ignored its first resolution, the Council passed another recommending "that the Members of the United Nations furnish such assistance to the Republic of Korea as may be necessary to repel the armed attack and to restore international peace and security in the area." Here, for the first time in history, a world organization was taking up arms to oppose aggression. Eleven days later, with the Russian chair still vacant, the Council authorized a United Nations Command and asked the United States to appoint its commander. Thus, by her insistence on boycotting the Council, Russia had enabled the Truman administration to bring off a brilliant diplomatic coup. Eager to help South Korea, but loath to act independently and perhaps antagonize the neutral nations of the world, Truman had wisely gone to the United Nations.

In any one of these three Security Council meetings the Soviet Union might have wrecked Truman's plans. Through use of the veto, she could have prevented the UN from intervening and thereby compelled America to take that unilateral action which world Communism might gleefully brand as "capitalist warmongering" or "imperialist aggression." But she had not, and even though the free world's effort in Korea was in the main an American one, it was nevertheless fought beneath the blue-and-white banner of the United Nations. Finally, when the Soviet Union and her satellites rejected the UN's invitation to help save South Korea, they ranged themselves against that very flag.

To this day it is not known exactly why the Soviets made this decision. They certainly could have returned to the Council just to exercise the veto on intervention, after which the boycott might have been resumed. Probably, they had no direct orders pro or con from Moscow, and since lesser Communists did not lightly alter the orders of Joseph Stalin, they probably had to stand pat. As a guess, the very speed and determination of the American reaction probably took the entire Communist world by surprise. And so 15 nations eventually joined America in history's first venture into collective security. Britain was first, placing her warships of the Far Eastern Station under American command. Then came Australia, New Zealand and Canada. France, already bleeding in Indo-China, sent a battalion commanded by Lieutenant Colonel Ralph Monclar, a gallant soldier who gave up his rank as a three-star general in order to fight in Korea. Turkey sent a brigade, and 5,000 riflemen came from the Philippines. Thailand dispatched a regiment and a ship while the Netherlands and Colombia provided a battalion apiece. Belgium and Ethiopia each contributed a battalion, little Luxembourg sent a company of soldiers, a fighter squadron came from South Africa while Greece gave an infantry battalion and an air transport squadron. From nations with a policy of neutrality there came missions of mercy: a field ambulance from India, a hospital ship from Denmark, and hospital units from Sweden, Norway and Italy.

All these contributions did not arrive at once in Korea, and most of them were only token, especially when ranged alongside the American commitment of eight big divisions which, with supporting arms and services, together with the Seventh Fleet and the Fifth Air Force, eventually totaled ten times the effort of all the others combined. Moreover, this very variety of arms, language, food, dress and customs actually complicated rather than simplified the problems of the United Nations Commander in Korea. Nevertheless, here for the first time in the history of the world were men of all colors and creeds putting aside their differences to fight for another nation's freedom. Meanwhile, one day after this force was authorized, Douglas MacArthur, the soldier Truman appointed to command it, flew to Korea from Japan to make a typical cannon's-mouth reconnaissance of the battlefield. Moving to a hill just below the Han, MacArthur stood appalled while the debris of defeat washed around him. He saw at once that the ROK Army was shattered, and that there was nothing to stop the North Korean armor from rushing down to Pusan at the southern tip of the peninsula. MacArthur wired Washington: "The only assurance for holding the present line and the ability to regain later the lost ground is through the introduction of United States ground combat forces into the Korean battle area."[16]

Truman now had no reason to withhold ground troops. He had already decided that Stalin did not intend to fight in Korea, and he was fairly sure that the Communist Chinese felt the same way. It was also obvious to Truman that the North Koreans planned a swift conquest, after which Communist-controlled elections would be held in mid-August. So he authorized MacArthur to commit ground troops, later issuing instructions which sent every arm into action and opened up all but a few military targets north of the parallel to attack by American ships and planes. Step by reluctant step, then, President Truman had come to his confrontation with Communism in Asia. Controlled by events rather than controlling them, acting *ad hoc* in the absence of any clearly enunciated policy vis-à-vis Asiatic Communism, consulting neither Congress nor the people but using the enormous accrued powers of the presidency as though he were any absolute monarch, he had put America into what was, in point of casualties, her third largest war. Again and again, Mr. Truman would say, "We are not at war," and to speak of the "war" in any executive department was to incur the presidential wrath. Always it was the Korean "Conflict," a euphemism probably coined to fob off the fiction that the United States was directing a "police action" at the behest of the United Nations. The reverse, of course, was true, and to the 33,629 Americans who died in Korea or the 103,283 who were wounded there, the war was as real as any other.

Nevertheless, it was not truly "Mr. Truman's War," as the President's Congressional critics often charged. If it was anyone's, it was Mr. Roosevelt's. For the war in Korea was the bitter fruit of the seeds sown at Yalta. Once again men had to die to redeem the mistakes of the peacemakers. Therefore President Truman's decision —hesitant, tardy and confused as it was—must stand among the noblest and most efficacious in the annals of American arms.

3

☆

General MacArthur had about 83,000 ground troops with which to save South Korea and guarantee the safety of Japan. His battle formations consisted of four understrength divisions armed with outmoded World War II weapons and in which infantry regiments functioned with two rather than three battalions, and artillery battalions fired two rather than three batteries.

The Seventh Fleet which sounded so mighty on paper actually sailed the seas with a piddling 14 ships, and Vice Admiral C. Turner

Joy's Far East Command consisted of one ship less. MacArthur's air was somewhat more formidable: 1,172 aircraft and 33,600 men making up the Far East Air Force under Major General George Stratemeyer.

With so few ground troops at his disposal, MacArthur with characteristic audacity decided to cow the enemy commander with "an arrogant display of strength." What he had would be committed to Korea as rapidly as possible, albeit piecemeal, so as to slow down the enemy advance, in the hope that the presence of American troops in the field would chill the enemy's ardor and compel him to be more cautious. In the meantime, MacArthur would build his forces until he found himself strong enough to launch a counterattack. In brief, the UN Commander was going to fight a delaying action, to buy time with blood. He ordered the 24th Division from Japan to Korea.

Major General William Dean commanded the 24th. A veteran infantry officer and a former Military Governor of South Korea, this tall, lean, crew-cut soldier was a fighter and a driver. Moving swiftly, he notified Lieutenant Colonel Charles ("Brad") Smith to get his battalion on the road to Itazuke Airfield. Mystified, remembering a similar rush order he had received on the morning of December 7, 1941, at a place called Pearl Harbor, Colonel Smith rounded up 406 of his men, put them aboard trucks and went careening through a heavy rain to Itazuke, 75 miles away. On the morning of July 1, General Dean met him there. "When you get to Pusan, head for Taejon," he told Smith. "We want to stop the North Koreans as far from Pusan as we can. Block the main road as far north as possible. . . . That's all I've got. Good luck to you, and God bless you and your men."¹⁷ With that, what was to be known as Task Force Smith boarded airplanes and climbed the dripping skies bound for Pusan.

Pusan at the southern tip of the Korean Peninsula was the Rhee government's finest port. Here, MacArthur intended to build his forces. Pusan was also the objective of the North Koreans. If they could get there before anyone could intervene in strength, they would be able to crush the Rhee government and unify Korea. Militarily, to invade hostile shores would be vastly more difficult for the Americans than to land in a friendly port. Politically, even America would be loath to attack the *fait accompli* of a Korea united under Communist banners, and her allies in the United Nations would be even more reluctant. Thus Pusan was the great prize—and the NKs sent their two finest divisions clanking south from Seoul in the final dash that would end the war. Even as Task Force Smith became airborne, these two divisions made a fighting crossing of the Han River and battled their way into the suburbs of industrial Yongdongpo. About 170 miles to the southeast of them, on July 1, the men of Task Force Smith landed at Pusan and were driven north along flag-bedecked streets lined by cheering South Koreans. On July 5 the Americans came to the town of Osan high on the Seoul-Pusan road. By then, the NKs on the east coast had been slowed down by rain, rock slides and the guns of the U.S. Navy. On the west, however, they had shattered all remaining ROK resistance. All that remained between them and Pusan was MacArthur's "arrogant display of strength": Task Force Smith, now grown from 406 to 540 men.

Smith had chosen his Osan position well. Hills to either side of the road were held by soldiers armed with rifles, machine guns, mortars, bazookas and 75-millimeter recoilless rifles. The road between them was, in effect, a pass—and they commanded it. To the left rear Smith put his lone antitank gun equipped with but a half-dozen armor-piercing shells. Still farther behind this he placed four howitzers supplied with high-explosive (H-E) shells. On the morning of July 5, while a dirty dawn crept over those dismal rain-swept hills, and while American soldiers crouching in ponchos tried to eat their cold C rations, sometimes retching in nausea at the odor of human dung wafted up to them from the pale green pools of the rice paddies, Smith's forward observers sighted the enemy approaching.

Some 10,000 soldiers came down the road behind a column of 33 tanks spearheaded by a group of eight. At 8:16 A.M. the first American shell of the war went shrieking toward the enemy. Its impact was observed, the range was adjusted, and soon many more shells were exploding among the tanks. Some made direct hits, but because they were ordinary H-E they merely jolted the tanks. And the T-34s came on.

At 700 yards, the recoilless rifles fired. They, too, scored hits, but their shells also flashed harmlessly off the enemy's armor plate. Next the 2.36-inch rocket launchers—the famous "bazookas"—began firing. Results were the same. Inexorably, ominously, all 33 of the tanks were rolling down the road, gathering speed, coming in groups of four behind the spearhead eight. The Americans hit them with all that they had, but could not deter them. At last, two spearhead tanks shot the pass and went clanking past Smith's antitank gun. Six shells howled forth, and the two tanks lurched and halted. One burst into flames. Its turret flipped open and two NK soldiers emerged, hands high. But a third popped up firing a burp gun straight into an American machine-gun position. The gunner there died—the first American to perish in the Korean War, but no one got his name. Instead, his comrades killed the North Korean who shot him, and with that the rest of the tanks shot the pass, roaring down the road fully buttoned up and firing wildly as they went.

Even though two tanks were lost eventually, the bulk of the Red armor got through. It rolled into Osan unopposed, and it cut off Task Force Smith's rear. An hour later, the enemy infantry attacked Smith's front. Momentarily repulsed by concentrated fire, they quickly seized a hill overlooking Smith's leftward position, forcing the Americans to withdraw to the right side of the road. Then they outflanked the right-hand hill and moved to encircle it. With this, Smith gave the order to withdraw, and as the Americans began to pull back the North Koreans caught them in a crossfire of automatic weapons, fragmenting them and putting them to rout.

Task Force Smith no longer existed as a fighting force. It was shattered. Small party after small party attempted to save themselves. Fleeing men climbed hills or floundered shoeless through stinking rice paddies. For the next two days American soldiers drifted into towns as far south as Taejon. Some men walked west to the Yellow Sea, others trudged east to the Sea of Japan. Of Task Force Smith's 540 men, 150 were killed, wounded or missing (probably captured). That night a North Korean private wrote in his diary: "We met vehicles and American POWs. We also saw some American dead. We found four of our destroyed tanks. Near Osan there was a great battle."[18]

At Osan the Americans and the North Koreans met for the first time and the North Koreans were victorious. As a result, the arrogant display of strength had backfired, at least temporarily. So far from being frightened upon finding Americans in the field against them, the North Koreans took heart from their victory and pressed even more eagerly down the Seoul-Pusan road.

General Dean was deeply disappointed by the defeat of Task

Force Smith. He had hoped it would hold while he came to Taejon about 60 miles south to rally the broken South Koreans and put more Americans into line. The South Korean generals, however, were of little help. They were too busy placing the blame for the debacle on each other's shoulders, shouting "Communist!" at one another or offering Dean a variety of excuses for their inability to clear vital roads of streams of refugees and straggling soldiers. Nevertheless, Dean did have two more battalions of his 34th Regiment and he placed them in a blocking position ten miles south of Osan at Pyongtaek-Ansong.

This second position was vital, for the Korean peninsula flared to the west just below Pyongtaek, offering the southward-bound invaders the opportunity of maneuver to their right. But if the Americans held at Pyongtaek-Ansong, they would confine the NKs to that single Seoul-Pusan road, corking them up in a bottle. But they did not. The battalion in the east at Ansong withdrew without orders and the battalion at Pyongtaek, with its right flank thus exposed, also withdrew.

General Dean was infuriated when he heard of the unauthorized pullback. He jumped into his jeep and drove pell-mell to the front, but by the time he located the errant battalions at Chonan, 15 miles south of Pyongtaek, it was too late to send them north again. They might run into a night ambush and be slaughtered. So he allowed them to dig in at Chonan, about 110 miles northwest of vital Pusan, and on July 8 Chonan also fell. This time, however, the Americans put up a spirited fight. Now, just as all the advantages were falling to the foe, the disadvantages were beginning to multiply against him. He had been able to launch a broad turning movement into the westward bulge below Pyongtaek, and below Chonan he found two good roads which enabled him to divide into two columns and thus compel Dean to spread his thin forces thinner across two attack routes. However, the North Koreans were now beginning to slow down. As MacArthur had hoped, the enemy commander had overestimated American strength. He had also begun to outrun his supplies, a failing which was to be chronic with the Communists throughout the war, and he could not move so openly by day beneath the scourging impact of American air. Flying from Japanese bases and from carrier decks, the Americans struck repeatedly at the enemy's columns, at his supply trains and at his precious tanks.

Still, General Dean was far from optimistic, and on July 8 he sent MacArthur an urgent request for antitank shells and immediate airlifting of 3.5-inch bazookas from the United States. Dean also told MacArthur: "I am convinced that the North Korean Army, the North Korean soldier, and his status of training and quality of equipment have been underestimated."[19] MacArthur considered the situation serious enough to use part of his heavy bomber strength in tactical bombing of the battle front and on July 9 he notified the Joint Chiefs:

> The situation in Korea is critical. . . .
> I strongly urge that in addition to those forces already requisitioned, an army of at least four divisions, with all its component services, be dispatched to this area without delay and by every means of transportation available.
> The situation has developed into a major operation.[20]

MacArthur's message shook the Pentagon. Although the UN Commander had earlier asked for a Marine brigade, which was even then taking ship from California, it was thought that this unit was to be the spearhead of MacArthur's two-division "early counter-offensive." But here was the general asking for "at least" four full divisions, 40 percent of the entire American ground strength exclusive of Japan. Though startled, the Joint Chiefs did order the 2nd Infantry Division to begin movement to Korea, while MacArthur himself, now convinced that he would have to use his entire Eighth Army if Pusan was to be saved, alerted the 1st Cavalry Division (dismounted) for movement to Korea from Japan.

But even as these reinforcements and supplies came rushing toward South Korea, the situation was still touch-and-go on that Seoul-Pusan road. As before, the enemy's central thrust had stalled in mountainous terrain, and on the east coast he was barely crawling along a narrow coastal road held by hard-fighting ROKs backed up by American naval gunfire. So the western road was still critical. To hold it, General Dean now had two more battalions of another regiment, the 21st. These units took position just below Chonan, fighting hard until they were forced back to Chochiwon about 15 miles above the hub city of Taejon. "Hold in your new position and fight like hell!"[21] Dean ordered the 21st. The 21st fought, assisted by light tanks; but the

American lights were no match for the North Korean heavies, and the 21st could not contain an enemy desperate to win the war in a single dash. On July 12 the Americans fell back once more.

Nevertheless, the North Koreans had been delayed for two more days, time enough for Dean's third and last regiment—the 19th— to arrive on the battle front, and for elements of the 25th Infantry Division to come in as reinforcements for a central sector which had begun to collapse. In the meantime, American air began to smash at the enemy in the center, the Marine Brigade was tearing at flank speed for Pusan and the 1st Cavalry Division was being hurried to Pohang on the east coast. It was up to Dean to hold for a few more days, and he attempted to defend at the point where the Kum River bent like a moat around Taejon.

Here the North Koreans struck with massed fury. Filling their depleted ranks with South Koreans drafted at gunpoint, they steadily pressed the Americans back against the Kum, and then drove them across the river into Taejon. And there the Americans turned again.

Dean had not planned to fight in that city. He was aware that with the enemy across the Kum, Taejon could be outflanked. Instead, he had planned to hold briefly in Taejon while preparing stronger defenses at Yongdong about 28 miles to the east. But then he was ordered to hold Taejon for at least two days until a cavalry regiment, just landed on the east coast, could get to Yongdong. So the 24th Division turned at Taejon. Having armed his men with the new 3.5-inch bazookas capable of killing the T-34s, Dean was confident that he could stop the Reds. But the North Koreans had brought up heavy artillery. On July 19, behind their heaviest barrage of the war, they attacked in two tank-led columns. One struck from the northwest, another from the west. Gradually a third, smaller column detached itself from the western force and swung southeast to come up through Taejon's open back door. At three o'clock in the morning of July 20, the northwest column burst through the American roadblocks and came speeding down on Taejon. At daylight the third column slipped into the city from the rear. Snipers in civilian clothes rode the tanks, dropping off to dart into deserted buildings and harry the retreating Americans.

Now Taejon was burning. Exploding shells, especially the white phosphorus kind which both sides dreaded, had set buildings on fire. Eventually a good part of the city was ablaze, and in this roaring, crackling holocaust General Dean formed truck columns full of soldiers and sent them speeding for the last escape route east. But the North Koreans held that road, too, and the Americans who followed its tree-lined curves ran a gantlet of death.

That night General Dean became a casualty. Searching for water for wounded men, he fell down a slope and was knocked unconscious. When he awoke he found his shoulder broken and his men gone. For 36 days Dean drifted through the mountains trying to rejoin his division. Down in weight from 190 pounds to 130, he was at last undone when a pair of South Korean civilians betrayed him to the enemy. Yet, even as General Dean awoke on that morning of July 21, 1950, the crisis had passed. Dean's 24th Division had delayed the enemy long enough for the 25th Division to plug the central gap and for the 1st Cavalry to go into line at Yongdongpo. With that, MacArthur's arrogant display became a success, and the vital port of Pusan was saved.

4

☆

For the second time within a decade, America had been drawn into a major foreign war—but with what a difference! This time there was no massive outburst of unifying rage such as had succeeded Pearl Harbor, but rather reluctance, bewilderment and partisan recrimination. From soldier to civilian, from the White House to the Pentagon, the heart of the American nation simply was not in the Korean War.

At the outset there was very little to cheer about. The performance of the 24th Divison during its 15-day delaying action from Osan to Taejon had not been glorious. Some men and officers did fight gallantly, but in the main the failure of the North Koreans to get into Pusan was due not to American heroism but to Communist inability to exploit the Han River crossings. Time and again the 24th's men and officers retreated against orders, threw away their rifles and helmets, abandoned equipment, refused to fight, left their wounded behind or sat down to await capture.

In so doing they were, of course, neither more nor less ungallant than the troops of any other nation who are sent into battle soft and ill-trained. These young men were for the most part garrison soldiers who had spent their service in Japan eating the fruits of the victories won by their older brothers in World War II. As General Dean was to write later, they were "soldiers who less than a month before had been fat and happy in occupation billets, complete with Japanese girl friends, plenty of beer, and servants to shine their boots."[22] Philip Deane, a British war correspondent captured along the Pusan road, has quoted one of those riflemen sent to hold it: "Gee, back in Sasebo I had a car, only a Ford, but a honey. You should have seen my little Japanese girl. Gee, she was a honey. Lived with me in my little villa. It was a honey, my little Japanese villa."[23] Colonel Roy E. Appleman, a veteran of the early fighting and also its historian, has declared: "A basic fact is that the occupation divisions were not trained, equipped or ready for battle. The great majority of the enlisted men were young and not really interested in being soldiers. The recruiting posters that had induced most of these men to enter the Army mentioned all conceivable advantages and promised many good things, but never suggested that the principal business of an army is to fight."[24]

Nor could those posters ever have conveyed the vile conditions in which Korean fighting took place. These unprepared soldiers often fought with the possibility of retreat cut off, for the favorite enemy tactic was to attack frontally to hold the Americans while other columns slipped around the flanks to cut off escape. Men who wished to avoid capture, then, were forced to drift through the mountains, or worse, through those filthy, stinking rice paddies which tormented them with myriads of stinging, disease-bearing insects and which sometimes sucked off their very boots. Always the refugees clogged the roads, which torrential three- and four-day rains turned into bogs. When the sun shone, the Korean countryside steamed and stank like a giant diaper pail. Reluctantly fighting somebody else's war in somebody else's land, where the climate was an alternating hell of heat and cold and where the people were not only generally indifferent to the outcome but also inclined to regard the American savior as more alien than the northern enemy—considering such conditions, the wonder of that 100-mile delaying action and all subsequent actions is that the Americans stayed to fight at all.

At home, the American public was not so much shamed by newspaper accounts which very often exaggerated GI shortcomings as angered by them. The people did not ask, "Why did they run?" but "Why are they there?" The answer to the last question was never convincing to Americans. Containment in Asia could not be made as clear as containment in Europe. Most Americans did not realize that Communism had spread from Europe into Asia, and perhaps had found in that despotic land a more hospitable soil. They did not understand that the contending ideologies which had collided during the Berlin Airlift were also in collision in Korea. The Korean War did not appear to be what it actually was, the application of the Truman Doctrine to Asia, but rather seemed an alien conflict. It looked more like a war fought in Asia to save one Asian nation from another, and as such it was "none of our business."

In this, the Korean War exposed a curious ambivalence in the American character. Much as Americans might decry "the broils of Europe," almost all of their wars have been intimately associated with the fate of Europe. Much as they might commit themselves in Asia, as in the Open Door policy or annexation of the Philippines, they are reluctant to fight there. It is as though Americans, most of them transplanted Europeans, like to keep the fight "in the family." Therefore, if the nation could be solidly agreed, as it was, that Europe must be saved from Communism, it had only the barest disposition to fight with or finance Chiang Kai-shek in his battle against Asiatic Communism. Therefore the war in Korea was as alien to the American experience as rice differs from wheat or chopsticks from knives and forks. It was also a war which had come upon America unawares at the instigation of unknown men. Entry into it had not even been debated. All America's wars had been preceded by debate and all but the two World Wars of this century had been characterized by continuing dissent. But in Korea no isolationist clashed with interventionist, there was no prior argument over "staying out" or "getting in." The American people, accustomed to control their own destinies, had been given little option in Korea. Completely alien, then, absolutely not of America's own doing, Korea could provoke no impassioned or patriotic response.

Finally, Korea was a limited war, and this was also a condition alien to the experience of Americans who knew only the totality of the two World Wars. Both of these had appealed to their crusading spirit, the first having been fought to save democracy, the second to rid the world of dictatorships. In both there existed that total mobilization and sense of national purpose and unity springing from the realization that "everybody's in it." Not so in Korea. The American people blocked this seeming anomaly, this limited war, out of their minds. They called it Truman's Folly, and their mood may best be described as one of sullen acquiescence when, on July 19, the President asked Congress for an end to restrictions on the size of the American armed forces, also requesting an additional $10 billion and declaring that higher taxes and limitations on consumer credit would be necessary. With these moves, it became obvious that the UN "police action" in Korea was becoming a major war to be fought and financed chiefly by Americans.

The United Nations Command in Korea consisted of the U.S. Eighth Army and attached UN units on one hand and the ROK Army on the other. The Supreme Commander was General Douglas MacArthur with headquarters in Tokyo. MacArthur's orders came from President Truman and the Joint Chiefs of Staff acting as executives for the UN Security Council, and he in turn gave orders to the Commanding General, U.S. Eighth Army, whose directives also controlled the ROKs. At this time the Eighth was commanded by Lieutenant General Walton ("Johnny") Walker, a short, powerfully built veteran of both World Wars whose outthrust jaw was suggestive of his bulldog tenacity. On July 17, 1950, when Walker first unfurled the UN flag in Korea, he had at his disposal the U.S. 25th Infantry and 1st Cavalry (dismounted) divisions with the battered 24th in reserve. The ROK Army was a few days away from completing the reorganization which would give it about 85,000 effectives divided among five divisions and a headquarters and training unit. En route to Korea were roughly another Army division and the largish Marine Brigade. Britain, Australia, Turkey, Canada and the Philippines were also sending troops to the Peninsula and the U.S. Navy was bringing 48 ships out of mothballs.

General Walker's mission was still to cling to Pusan, to fight the kind of delaying action that would trade space for time. The North Koreans, though thwarted in their first attempt to dash into Pusan, were now prepared to bludgeon their way into that vital port. They now had about a dozen divisions south of the parallel, and they sent them south along four attack routes, plus that free-wheeling movement to the west that had been begun when the bulge below Pyongtaek was left open. Still holding the initiative, the North Koreans confidently predicted that they would sweep "the American aggressors and the Syngman Rhee puppet troops" out of the peninsula by mid-August.

Their first objectives were to capture Taegu, the city housing Rhee's government and Walker's headquarters, and to cut the road to Pusan below it. To do this, they hit from the front and both sides. On the right or east, the ROKs supported by American naval bombardments were able to hold. They also held in the mountainous center. But along the same vital road running southeastward from Taejon to Taegu the Americans did not hold. Here the Communists gained 25 miles in four days. Far to the west, that turning column had gotten below Pusan and was now wheeling east to make a flanking dash on the port city. In both these critical sectors withdrawal followed withdrawal. Incensed, Walker on July 29 issued a controversial order in which he, in effect, called upon his men to stand or die. The order was widely criticized in the United States, which had been lulled into a sense of false security by MacArthur's roseate communiqués, and also by some of Walker's commanders who felt that to stand was just the wrong thing to do against an enemy whose most successful tactic was to cut off the rear.

Even so, Walker had cause for exasperation. Under the pretext of "readjusting the lines," unauthorized withdrawals were still common among some American units. "Bugging out," a phrase describing unseemly and precipitate flight, was already a battlefield cliché, and one regiment had already adopted "The Bug-Out Blues" as its "theme song." Even though Walker was already planning a general withdrawal to more defensible positions, he was absolutely right in warning his troops that any attempt to retreat to Pusan would end in "one of the greatest butcheries in history."[25] Finally, the situation could not have been more critical. The North Koreans were attacking with everything they had, and seemingly everywhere at once. General Walker was playing the role of a fire chief, shifting his most trusted units to the places where the fire blazed fiercest and hoping that the smaller fires would be contained with available forces or that no new outbursts would flare up in the uncovered gaps. By the end of July the threat to Taegu was so great that the Rhee government was preparing to flee to Pusan. Below Taegu, along the vital road to Pusan, a gap 50 miles wide lay open to that enemy column even then speeding in from the west. With this, Walker made a desperate gamble. He moved the 25th Division down from the center to this imperiled southwestern sector. By so doing he left his center perilously weak, but he also closed the gap and blunted the attempt to cut the road. In this maneuver, Walker saved his position. On August 2, with the arrival of the Marine Brigade, the UN Command began an orderly withdrawal behind the Naktong River into the position which became famous as the Pusan Perimeter.

This defensive line resembled a vertical rectangle about 80 miles deep and 60 miles wide. On its right and rear it was protected by the sea. On its front and left it followed the Naktong as it flowed west from the coastal mountains and then turned sharply south to the sea. Inside the perimeter, Walker's forces grew steadily until by August 5 he outnumbered the enemy with 92,000 combat troops —47,000 Americans and 45,000 ROKs—to about 70,000. Walker also had the advantage of interior lines, although there were so many blown bridges or roads mired in mud or clogged with refugees that the massed movement of troops rarely exceeded five miles an hour. He also had a good airfield at Taegu, so that aircraft formerly based on Japan were now available for longer periods of time. Also a battalion of tanks salvaged from old Pacific battlefields had come into Pusan, along with the new Pershing mediums, only a little smaller than the T-34s. The UN supply situation was now excellent, while the enemy's long lines of communication and supply were now exposed to the gunfire of American ships and the bombing and strafing of American aircraft. Under this interdiction, the North Koreans began supplying their units by the nocturnal movement of human and animal transport. South Koreans were impressed into service as carriers, and horse- or oxen-drawn carts plied the roads usually disguised as commercial vehicles. Even so, the North Koreans had begun to feel the pinch of hunger, their ammunition was low and their ranks were depleted. Desperate to make good on Kim Il Sung's boast that his armies would clear Korea in time for mid-August elections, they launched their August offensive.

Communist tactics were now simply a matter of conquering

firepower with manpower. Three or four waves of troops were employed. The first wave, often composed of forcibly recruited South Koreans, was compelled to attack in an effort to overwhelm the enemy by sheer numbers. If this wave was stopped, and it usually was, then second and third waves of slightly better-trained troops came forward. By then, as the North Koreans calculated, the enemy would have exhausted his ammunition and it was time for a fourth wave of veterans to go in. Frequently this was what happened, and the UN troops were forced to withdraw. Another NK tactic was the "refugee attack," in which masses of helpless civilians combed from the crowded roads would be herded toward UN positions like massive shields of living human flesh. Behind them came the North Korean regulars.

With such desperate, foul and foolish tactics, the enemy struck in the east, northwest, west and southwest. He had no real plan, but merely hoped to stumble on some soft spot which could be opened and expanded. Walker responded with his old tactics of shuttling troops back and forth to meet recurrent crises. On August 7 he launched a counterattack of his own in the southwest. At first the soldiers and Marines under Major General William Kean wilted in the heat. But then, with the Marine Brigade in the spearhead, and using carrier-based Marine aircraft in devastating close-up support, the Americans advanced 26 miles and ended forever the threat to Walker's lower left. It was then, however, that the Reds struck their hardest blows of all in the Naktong River bulge below Taegu.

Here the NK 4th Division, one of the two that had taken Seoul and tried to dash into Pusan, crossed the Naktong and was moving on the rail junction at Miryang midway along the vital Taegu-Pusan road. If the Reds took Miryang, they would isolate Taegu and force the Pusan Perimeter to shrink to slaughter-pen proportions. The 24th Division tried to contain the Reds, but a penetration was achieved at a place called Obong-ni. As the enemy began to expand it, Walker threw in the Marine Brigade. Again using aircraft dropping 500-pound bombs and napalm in close-up support, the brigade attacked twice, only to be repulsed twice; but then, on a third thrust, the Reds were driven back into the Naktong. "The enemy was killed in such numbers," the log of the carrier *Sicily* reported, "that the river was definitely discolored with blood."[26]

Such losses did not deter the Communists, who were apparently willing to accept anything short of annihilation if it would give them Taegu. Thus, while the attempt to cut the road below Taegu was halted, five NK divisions and a tank brigade continued to attack toward the provisional capital from the north and northwest. Opposing them were two American and two ROK divisions. They fought desperately, but their lines continued to contract toward Taegu. After the city was brought under Red artillery fire, Rhee and his government fled to Pusan, leading an enormous exodus of 600,000 civilians whose presence on the road again complicated the Eighth Army's communications problems. Once again, Walker looked around for a troubleshooter. He found it in the 27th Infantry (Wolfhound) Regiment of the 25th Division. Led by Colonel John ("Mike") Michaelis, the Wolfhounds were probably the finest Army outfit in Korea, and they justified Walker's faith in them by moving into and holding the precious Naktong Valley corridor running from Sangju to Taegu. Meanwhile, as the Americans and ROKs continued to counterattack, refusing to allow the Reds to consolidate any newly won ground, American artillery broke up the enemy's troop concentrations on the west bank of the Naktong. American air also ranged over the battlefield, disrupting the North Koreans' daylight movements and steadily whittling away at their tank superiority. Even big Superforts from Japan attempted tactical bombing strikes against enemy troops, although one well-advertised carpet-bombing by 100 B-29s dropping 850 tons of bombs turned out to be a loud and furious bust.

The fight for Taegu raged on until August 24, and during it the UN Command uncovered fresh evidence of Communist atrocities. On August 17 Americans who retook a lost hill found 26 of their comrades murdered. "The boys lay packed tightly, shoulder to shoulder, lying on their sides, curled like babies sleeping in the sun. Their feet, bloodied and bare, from walking on the rocks, stuck out stiffly. . . . All had hands tied behind their backs, some with cord, others with regular issue army communication wire. Only a few of the hands were clenched."[27] In their treatment of South Korean civilians the Communists had been even more ferocious, regularly shooting captured officials out of hand and, later on, herding them into jails and town halls to burn them alive. Because of the murder of the 26 GIs, General MacArthur broadcast a warning to Kim Il Sung, declaring: "I shall hold you and your commanders criminally

accountable under the rules and precedents of war."[28] In the meantime, the enemy's blows against Taegu grew weaker and weaker,
until on August 24, General Walker could say: "Taegu is certainly
saved."[29] A few days later, however, the resilient Reds were coming
again in the most furious assault of all.

By the end of August, when the North Korean People's Army
launched its Great Naktong Offensive, the United Nations Command was superior to the enemy in every way. The Reds had a force
of about 98,000 men, against Walker's army of 180,000 of whom
91,500 were ROKs and the remainder, except for 1,500 newly
arrived British soldiers, were Americans. Walker also held a five-
to-one edge in tanks, and the big new Pattons he had begun to
receive were at least a match for the T-34s. By the end of August
UN dread of enemy armor had disappeared. Walker also held control
of the sea and the air, and by August 25 the Red Ball Express
carrying his supplies from Japan was delivering 949 tons daily. Sea
power was by then a decisive factor in Walker's plans. Because
Korea was a peninsula, the U.S. Navy, assisted by a British task
force, could practically guarantee Walker's flanks with carrier-based
aircraft and such mighty gunfire ships as the battleship *Missouri*. In
this, it turned out that in any war in which the capacity to bombard
enemy coasts is a factor, the big-gun ship was not quite obsolete.
She had given way to the carrier, of course, but she still had her
uses.

Walker's recurrent refugee problem was also on the way to being
solved. After being screened—that is, merely checked to see if their
robes covered a North Korean soldier's guns—the refugees were
moved south from the combat zone to about 60 camps in the Taegu-
Pusan area. Meanwhile, between 30,000 and 60,000 South Korean
youths had been fed into depleted U.S. Army units. This was the
much-vaunted "buddy system" under which the Koreans were paired
off with Americans who were supposed to give them on-the-job
training in the soldier's craft. Because of obvious differences in
language, temperament and customs, it was never much of a success.
In all, however, the UN Command was a formidable force, and it
was not very wise of General Kim Chaik to attack it with the same
slovenly swarming tactics which had failed against every objective
since Taejon.

Once again General Kim's soldiers took all the roads to Pusan, fighting whomever they met, and once again such tactics produced a series of scattered crises which Walker was able to contain. In the north a ROK corps began to falter under sledgehammer blows, but it rallied after Walker despatched the 27th Wolfhounds up in support. In the southwest, the NKs pushed the 25th Division back to within 30 miles of Pusan, and the fighting around Battle Mountain was so fierce that that height changed hands 13 times before coming to permanent rest in UN possession. On the east coast Pohang was again lost, but then retaken by the 24th Division and a ROK corps assisted by carrier-based aircraft and gunfire ships. And from the west came another near-thing at Miryang. Four divisions swarmed across the Naktong to secure a dozen bridgeheads on the east bank. The 2nd Division was split in two as the enemy swept past No-Name Ridge and penetrated 12 miles. Here, as before, Walker threw in the Marine Brigade. The Marines counterattacked, and then, joining forces with Army units which once had fought with them 32 years before in Belleau Wood, they shattered the enemy threat.

These were the four main actions, although the Great Naktong Offensive seemed to thunder and storm everywhere along that river. Again and again, the enemy crossed to the east bank only to be forced back whence he had come. Some sectors were constantly ablaze, while others sat tight and quiet while the fighting roared and crackled around them. Always the UN troops held the edge in artillery and had the support of their ubiquitous air. With this superior armor and the advantage of interior lines and the capacity to move the right reinforcement to the right place, General Walker put out every fire as it arose.

The Communist performance was not nearly so skillful. Actually, except for the lightning stroke across the 38th parallel against a surprised and ill-equipped ROK Army, the North Korean generalship was consistently poor. The enemy erred in July when, as the audacious MacArthur had anticipated, they exaggerated his piecemeal intervention and failed to appreciate the extent of ROK demoralization. By not concentrating their forces during July and August and September they failed again. Such swarming attacks as the Reds launched were easily turned by a commander who would not lose his nerve. And once the valor of the tenacious Walker's troops began to match his own fighting spirit, the Reds were doomed. Yet, as September grew older, they continued to batter at the Pusan Perimeter. As they did, one of the great counterstrokes of history fell like a sledgehammer behind them.

5

☆

For all the petty flaws in the character of General of the Army Douglas MacArthur, it is difficult to escape the conclusion that his is the most illustrious name in American military history. Admittedly, he was much too much a walking monument. He was conceited in an almost childish way, forever posing or striking attitudes like a man perpetually on the lookout for mirrors or photographers. He could not confess himself in error or fall in with someone else's plan, and his glacial manner and aloofness from his troops, together with the purple, preening prose of his communiqués, may have been fitting in an Oriental potentate, but they were most unbecoming in a soldier who commanded in a democracy.

Yet MacArthur was also incredibly brave and impeccably moral. If his manner was lofty, his mind moved on the highest planes. As a supreme commander his record is unsurpassed, as was his grasp of his profession, and the penetration of his military insights was matched by the audacity with which he put them into execution. Finally, MacArthur's career is without parallel.

It stretched back a half-century to the Philippine Insurrection, and encompassed nearly half of the wars of America. At Vera Cruz, MacArthur very nearly won a Medal of Honor. In World War I he was the youngest and most decorated of division commanders. His academic record at West Point still stands unmatched chiefly because Douglas MacArthur, as the youngest superintendent of the Military Academy, toughened the curriculum. He was the youngest Chief of Staff and the first to serve more than one term in peacetime.

He was also the first American to command a foreign force, the Philippine Army, or to be called back to duty in World War II. His brilliant campaigns in that conflict, most of them undertaken with shoestring forces, have already been recorded, and his conduct of the occupation of Japan remains a model for proconsuls everywhere. No other American military career quite equals his, not those of Washington or Benedict Arnold, Andrew Jackson or Winfield Scott, Lee, Grant or Sherman, not MacArthur's own father or Black Jack Pershing, and finally neither Dwight Eisenhower nor George Catlett Marshall. Yet, in the fall of 1960, MacArthur was supreme commander in another major war, and he was preparing to cap this unrivaled record with the most masterful maneuver of all.

This was to cut the North Korean Army's line of supply by a daring amphibious envelopment all the way up the west coast at Seoul. It was typical of MacArthur that he conceived this single stroke for victory in the midst of defeat. On that black day in July when he made his reconnaissance up to the Han River, MacArthur decided on the delaying action which would slow the enemy advance, and then hold him in place while an amphibious action to his rear destroyed him. Returning to Tokyo, he had ordered his staff to plan the operation. But then the North Koreans showed surprising staying qualities. The 1st Cavalry Division and then the 1st Marine Brigade, both of which had been earmarked for the landing, had to be diverted into Walker's perimeter. The need for men also stripped the 7th Infantry Division of much of its troops. Nevertheless MacArthur clung to his vision of victory. To remain on the defensive was repugnant to his gambler's nature. So was a long, bloody advance up the peninsula. Therefore, on July 10, MacArthur asked the Joint Chiefs of Staff to give him the 1st Marine Division for this operation.

The request was refused. General Omar Bradley, then Chairman of the Joint Chiefs, was not a devotee of amphibious warfare or an admirer of the Marines. In 1949 he told Congress that he doubted if large-scale amphibious warfare would ever again be needed, a statement which might have been pardonable in a landlocked German or Russian general, but not in a two-ocean American. Bradley next suggested that most of the big landings of the past had been made by the Army rather than the Marines. Bradley's objections, however, did not dissuade MacArthur, and because of his repeated requests President Truman on July 19 authorized the call-up of the Marine Reserve. It was a cruel blow to these men, who, like the Army reservists later brought back to duty, were being asked to risk their flesh a second time. But because of it the Marine Division which on June 30 was down to 7,789 men was rapidly expanded to a small army of 26,000 well-armed and well-equipped troops, some of whom were veterans of as many as five amphibious assaults.

Ironically, it was from these very Marines, as well as from veteran Navy officers, that MacArthur received most of the protests against his proposal to strike at Inchon, the port for Seoul. These objections were summarized by Lieutenant Commander Arlie Capps, who said: "We drew up a list of every conceivable natural and geographic handicap, and Inchon had 'em all."[30]

First of these was Inchon's enormous tides, the second deepest in the world with an average 29-foot rise and fall of water. Some days it measured 36 feet. Inchon's numerous harbor islands not only helped to heap the tides high, but they also broke up wave action, so that, over the centuries, the vast untroubled ebb and flow of water had built great mud banks which ran out from shore as far as 6,000 yards. To clear them, the landing ships could only approach the shore on days when the tide rose to a 29-foot minimum. Only three days in every month fulfilled this condition. MacArthur had his choice of September 15, October 11 or November 3 for his D-Day, and of course he selected September 15.

Other objections were the narrowness of the channel and a swift current which would make maneuver for ships difficult, and a dearth of decent landing places. Major General Oliver P. Smith, who commanded the 1st Marine Division, did not like Inchon because its sea walls could be easily defended. Next, the tides dictated a landing at 5:30 P.M. Because sunset would come at 6:42 P.M., the Marines would have little more than an hour in which to land and consolidate before the anticipated counterattack. Nor could there be any pre-invasion bombardment, because this would rob MacArthur of the element of surprise on which he counted so heavily. Tactically, MacArthur had no way of knowing how many soldiers were defending Inchon. Strategically, he could not say how the Communist Chinese forces might react. The CCF, as they were called, were already known to be moving troops north into Manchuria across the Yalu River from North Korea. Would they allow MacArthur to land at Inchon and thus destroy the North Korean Army? Or would they strike the American invasion force while it was jammed inside Inchon's narrow, cluttered, emptying harbor?

MacArthur could not tell, but he calculated the risk and took it, along with a myriad of lesser chances. When the Joint Chiefs of Staff themselves came to Tokyo and met with him on August 23, he was still adamant against all their arguments. Even Rear Admiral James Doyle, MacArthur's amphibious commander, still had his misgivings. "General," he said, "I have not been asked nor have I volunteered my opinion about this landing. If I were asked, however, the best I can say is that Inchon is not impossible."[31] MacArthur, puffing calmly on his corncob pipe, merely nodded. Then General J. Lawton Collins, the Army Chief of Staff, argued that Inchon was too far from Pusan to have the desired effect. Collins said that to make the landing required the restoration of the 1st Marine Brigade to the 1st Marine Division, and that this would weaken Walker at Pusan. He suggested that MacArthur land at Kunsan, a port of fewer obstacles lying 100 air miles south of Inchon. Admiral Forrest Sherman, Chief of Naval Operations, seconded Collins' objections. MacArthur listened, not so much to Collins and Sherman, but to the voice of his father telling him many years before: "Doug, councils of war breed timidity and confusion."[32]

Still sitting at his desk, deliberately waiting for tension to mount in the hushed room, MacArthur the showman began to speak. His voice was casual, conversational. As he spoke, he sometimes jabbed his pipe into the air to underline a point. Once or twice his voice rose, became resonant, before dropping to a dramatic whisper. The very objections to his plan, he said, would guarantee surprise. "For the enemy commander will reason that no one would be so brash as to make such an attempt."[33] Observing that surprise was the most vital element in war, he drew an analogy between his own operation and Wolfe surprising Montcalm at Quebec. MacArthur said that the very boldness of the plan would excite the Oriental imagination and strike a great blow for freedom in Asia. The troops landed at Inchon would become the anvil upon which Walker's hammer blows could beat the enemy to pieces. Kunsan, he said, would not achieve this because, though safer, it was not far enough in the enemy's rear. "If my estimate is inaccurate," he concluded, "and I should run into a defense with which I cannot cope, I will be there personally and will immediately withdraw our forces before they are committed to a bloody setback. The only loss then will be my professional reputation." His voice sank dramatically. "But Inchon will not fail. Inchon will succeed. And it will save 100,000 lives."[34]

Six days later, after the Joint Chiefs had returned to Washington, MacArthur received from them a message beginning: "We concur . . ."

MacArthur's plan was for the 1st Marine Division to land at Inchon and capture Seoul. The 7th Infantry Division would land behind the Marines and take up a blocking position below Seoul astride the road to Pusan. These two divisions, designated X Corps under Major General Edward Almond, MacArthur's chief of staff, were to operate apart from the Eighth Army. Once the Reds' line of supply was cut, the North Koreans would have to fall back, at which point Walker's Eighth Army would pursue and turn their retreat into a rout.

On September 13 MacArthur went aboard the *Mount McKinley* at Sasebo, and almost at once the odds seemed stacked against him. A typhoon struck his invasion fleet. But then the weather cleared, and there remained only one more natural obstacle: Wolmi-do.

Wolmi-do or Moontip Island was a tiny pyramid of land inside Inchon Harbor just to the west of the city, to which it was connected by a causeway. Rising 350 feet above water, little Wolmi guarded the inner harbor. It was well fortified. Its guns could rake the Americans attempting to storm the port's sea walls to either side of it. Even at the risk of losing some of MacArthur's cherished surprise, Wolmi-do had to be bombarded beforehand, while other task forces made diversionary bombardments on both Korean coasts. In the early-morning darkness of September 15, 1950, a long column of gunfire ships slipped into Flying Fish Harbor. Behind them came a battalion of Marines aboard a landing ship dock (LSD) and three destroyer transports. At 5:40 A.M. the guns of the warships began booming. Little Wolmi was sheathed in flame. At daybreak rocket ships ran inshore to hurl 6,400 missiles into the island. Then Marine Corsairs dropped out of the skies to strafe, and at 0627 the first wave of Marine landing boots went roaring into Wolmi. Forty-seven minutes later the "yellow-legs," as the Reds called the Marines after the leggings they wore, raised the American flag over Wolmi.

There had not been a single man lost, and MacArthur, smiling with the contained elation of a man who knows he has changed history, turned to Admiral Doyle and said, "Please send this message to the fleet: 'The Navy and the Marines have never shone more brightly than this morning.' " Then he said, "Let's go down and have breakfast."[35]

The successful landing at Inchon and capture of the port was almost anticlimactic, although when the 1st Marine Division moved east upon Seoul it ran into one of the fiercest battles in its embattled history. But the Marines captured Kimpo Airfield, the biggest in Korea, and then the 7th Division came ashore unopposed to move against the air base at Suwon to the south of Seoul and cut the Pusan road. Now the X Corps was where MacArthur wanted it: formed like a giant anvil across the enemy's line of supply. Next he ordered Walker at Pusan to begin to strike his hammer blows. Walker did. For a time, the enemy resisted fiercely. But then, with his supplies gone, with command and communications cut off, he had to let go. The North Korean People's Army turned in flight. Walker broke out of Pusan after them, and the result was complete rout.

Red regiments simply melted away. Their soldiers threw down their weapons, shed their uniforms and took refuge in villages or wandered into the hills in small groups. The highways were littered with abandoned arms and equipment. Whole regiments and battalions surrendered. Within a month 130,000 prisoners were taken. And as Walker's troops pursued relentlessly, one armored group drawn from the Eighth Army sped 105 miles in three days to make a juncture below Suwon with units of the X Corps. It had taken the North Korean 2nd Division about a month to travel the same distance in the other direction, and with that link-up of Americans from north and south the destruction of the North Korean Army became complete. On that same day, September 26, MacArthur announced: "Seoul, the capital of the Republic of Korea, is again in friendly hands."

As usual, MacArthur had jumped the gun, and Marines still fighting in Seoul's barricaded, burning streets were compelled to battle for two more days before the city fell. On September 29 MacArthur flew to Kimpo to restore the ROK capital to President Rhee. He drove to Government House through a blackened desert of rubble, fire-eaten buildings and unburied dead. Splinters of glass came showering down from the shattered skylight of the Legislative

Chamber while MacArthur, standing in the presence of his generals, Rhee, ROK officials and the UN Commission, declared with unconcealed emotion: "By the grace of a merciful Providence our forces fighting under the standard of that greatest hope and inspiration of mankind, the United Nations, have liberated this ancient capital of Korea. . . ."[36] Then, having led the assembly in the recital of the Lord's Prayer, he turned to Rhee and said: "Mr. President, my officers and I will now resume our military duties and leave you and your government to the discharge of the civil responsibility."[37]

The aged Korean chieftain seized MacArthur's hands. "We admire you," he said, tears filling his eyes. "We love you as the savior of our race."[38]

6

☆

With the broken North Korean Army now fleeing for home, General MacArthur prepared to pursue, to destroy and to win the war. An advance up both coasts would be followed by a junction at the Yalu River. All that was needed to start moving was United Nations authorization to cross the 38th parallel, and while MacArthur confidently awaited this decision, the ROK Army took the bit in its teeth and went galloping into North Korea.

Syngman Rhee had already told his soldiers to clear the north of its last enemy soldier, and on October 1, while the UN was still debating the question of pursuit, the ROK I Corps began advancing up the east coast. A few days later, the ROK II Corps struck up the center of the peninsula, making for the industrial complex known as the Iron Triangle. The more spectacular gains, however, were made in the east. Here the ROKs were welcomed as saviors and their greatest difficulty was in finding NK soldiers to oppose them. Jubilant, their officers vowed, "We will wash our swords in the waters of the Yalu." On October 13 the ROKs entered the important port city of Wonsan about a 100 miles above the border.

Six days before this happened, the Eighth Army began attacking in the west. Here, too, there was unbounded confidence. In General Walker's eyes, the pursuit was now a turkey shoot. "We have flushed the covey and we are now kicking up the singles," he said. "As any quail hunter knows, it's when you're kicking up the singles that you get the most birds."³⁹ One of Walker's ROK generals happily explained that his tactics in moving on the enemy capital of Pyongyang would be: "No stop."⁴⁰ One day after the Eighth Army began moving north from Seoul, the UN General Assembly authorized the invasion of North Korea, and the Joint Chiefs' directive to MacArthur instructed him to cross the parallel to carry out "the destruction of the North Korean Armed Forces."

So the pursuit of the broken North Koreans was pressed with vigor, while MacArthur prepared to strengthen his right or eastern flank by sending X Corps around the peninsula by ship to make landings there. Meanwhile, all apprehensions over the possible intervention of Red China appeared to vanish. As late as October 14 the daily intelligence summary of MacArthur's Far Eastern Command declared: "Recent declarations by Communist Chinese leaders, threatening to enter North Korea if American forces were to cross the 38th Parallel, are probably in a category of diplomatic blackmail."⁴¹ On the following day, when General MacArthur and President Truman met in conference at Wake Island, MacArthur was asked what he thought of the possibility of Red Chinese intervention. His answer was: "Very little. Had they interfered in the first or second months it would have been decisive. . . . Now that we have bases for our Air Force in Korea, if the Chinese tried to get down to Pyongyang there would be the greatest slaughter."⁴² MacArthur was not alone in his optimism. Both the State Department and the Central Intelligence Agency had reached the same conclusion, and at Wake General Bradley went so far as to discuss the transfer of troops from the Far East to Europe and said he would like to bring two divisions home from Korea by Christmas. The very next day, October 16, 1950, the Fourth Field Army of the Chinese (Communist) People's Republic commanded by General Lin Piao began crossing the Yalu River in secret.

Because the Red Chinese intervention was to prolong the Korean War for yet another 33 months and to bring mankind to the brink of World War III, it is worthwhile to understand why it was made and why the United States refused to believe that it would be made.

Up until late August, 1950, Red China had had very little to say about Korea. All her protests had been against the presence of the U.S. Seventh Fleet in the Strait of Formosa. Evidently, the Reds had been preparing to invade Formosa to crush Chiang forever. Forestalled by the Seventh Fleet, which also prevented Chiang from invading the mainland, Red China protested angrily. But only for a time. Throughout most of August the Russians did all the Communist world's talking about Korea. Soviet Delegate Jacob Malik had returned to the Security Council to take up the presidency rotated to Russia, and to pronounce all that was done in his absence as "illegal" because of Nationalist China's "unlawful" presence on the Council. Then he proceeded to discuss Korean matters in the continued presence of this "illegal" member. Malik, of course, was not in the slightest way distressed by such a contradiction. His true purpose in the Council was to bluster, to vilify the U.S., to court the favor of neutral India and to detach a few of America's allies from the UN Command. With the possible exception of the campaign to woo India, he was not successful. But then, on August 17, U.S. Delegate Warren Austin made public the policy of "fair and free elections" for all Korea. Three days later Red China broke her silence. Foreign Minister Chou En-lai sent the UN his first cable in six weeks, declaring: "Korea is China's neighbor. The Chinese people cannot but be concerned about solution of the Korean question."[43]

Now there began a succession of bellicose, saber-rattling statements by American officials. Secretary of the Navy Matthews advocated "instituting a war to compel cooperation for peace. . . . We would become the first aggressors for peace."[44] General MacArthur spoke of Formosa as part of an island defense chain from which "we can dominate by air power every Asiatic port from Vladivostok to Singapore,"[45] and Major General Orvil Anderson, commander of the Air War College, said bluntly: "We're at war. . . . Give me the order to do it and I can break up Russia's five A-bomb nests in a week."[46] True enough, an infuriated President Truman moved quickly to suspend General Anderson, compel MacArthur to withdraw his statement and, apparently, force Matthews to resign, but even these moves and Truman's public disavowal of any designs on Formosa or anywhere else in the Far East did not dispel Red China's conviction that America was embarked on a course of aggression in Asia. Truman's denials may have seemed to them no more than a crude attempt to put the cat back in the bag.

In late September, therefore, while the Russians shifted their area of maneuver from the Security Council to the General Assembly, the Red Chinese launched a Hate-America campaign at home. Cartoons dripped with venom and editorials howled with hate. Here is one typical description of America: "This mad dog seizes Formosa between its hind legs while with its teeth it violently bites the Korean people. Now one of its forelegs has been poked into our Northeast front. Its bloodswollen eyes cast around for something further to attack. All the world is under its threat. The American imperialist mad dog is half beaten up. Before it dies, it will go on biting and tearing."[47] Then, as suddenly as it began, the Hate-America campaign subsided into silence. Red China, evidently, was awating the result of Russian diplomacy in the United Nations.

Here, Foreign Minister Andrei Vishinsky tried to prevent the UN from invading North Korea. He took the position that if UN troops crossed the parallel they would be aggressors. He ignored the fact that the North Koreans had been the first to violate the parallel and now demanded, in effect, that the culprits be given sanctuary behind it. Yet India found Vishinsky's argument appealing. Another decade would pass before New Delhi would herself feel the bite of Communist ambition in Asia, and so she clung to her delusion of peace-by-wishing and maintaining that it was lawful to defend South Korea with force but not to punish the aggressors that way. Nevertheless, most of the rest of the UN did not agree, and on October 4 the General Assembly's Political and Security Committee, by a vote of 46 to 5 with 8 abstentions, voted in effect to authorize the invasion of North Korea.

A few days earlier, Chou En-lai's last attempts to warn the UN and the United States had fallen on deaf ears. He had said Red China would not "supinely tolerate" an invasion of her neighbor, North Korea, and he had asked the Indian Ambassador, K. M. Panikkar, to inform Washington that if American troops entered North Korea Red China would enter the war. Unfortunately, Chou had given his message to an old Communist errand boy. Because of this, President Truman was inclined to take Chou's warning as a bluff. He thought Chou was trying to control the General Assembly vote by threats, and when MacArthur's intelligence report of October 14 pooh-poohed this warning as "diplomatic blackmail" it was merely echoing the conviction of official Washington. Thus, while the Eighth Army in the west and the ROKs and later the X Corps in the east began their win-the-war offensive, the vanguard of some 320,000 Red Chinese soldiers began movement to Manchuria on the North Korean border.

This, then, was the tragedy of Korea; tragedy that was, in truth, redoubled. First the Soviet Union and its North Korean satellite had mistakenly believed that the United States would not fight in Korea. Now the United States and her UN allies were making the same error with Red China. Well might the question be asked: how could such a monumental mistake be made a second time? The answer, if a clear answer can ever be made while half the evidence remains suppressed behind the Iron and Bamboo Curtains, would seem to be merely that both America and Red China mistrusted and misunderstood one another.

First of all, they did not maintain diplomatic relations; and when nations, like people, are "not speaking" to each other, when their intercourse depends upon intermediaries who might possibly have ulterior motives, it is almost certain that they will suspect one another of insincerity. Second, both powers thought of each other in preconceived, inflexible stereotypes. They believed what they wanted to believe of each other. To Peking, the Americans were always "Wall Street warmongers" or "Western imperialists." Thus the official assurances of a policy of nonaggression made by Truman and Secretary Acheson did not seem to be so much the "true voice" of America as were the unauthorized bellows of the saber-rattlers. To Washington, on the other hand, the Red Chinese were actually more Chinese than Communist; it was believed that their own national interests would lead them inevitably to oppose the Russian ambition to dominate them. Thus Mao Tse-tung would be loath to pull Stalin's chestnuts out of the fire. In fact, events subsequent to the Korean War seem to have upheld this theory. But it was not applicable in 1950. Mao was most dependent upon Stalin then. China was much like a ten-year-old Communist dominated by a 30-year-old one. Give her another ten years and she would make shocking challenges to Russia's hegemony, but right at that moment she had to do Russia's bidding. Furthermore, there were very good reasons for Red China to intervene. Chief of these was the fact that a great American victory in Korea would raise American prestige in Asia, especially among the emergent nations of Southeast Asia and in Japan, where the Americans were preparing a generous peace treaty.

This, Red China could not allow. She may have considered it imperative to demonstrate to Asia that the United States was indeed a "paper tiger." American policy-makers, therefore, might well have paid closer scrutiny to Red China's advantages in Korea, rather than to have been hypnotized by her supposed disadvantages there. However, like the Chinese, the Americans were prone to believe their own propaganda.

Finally, there is the question: why did the United States and her UN allies go rushing over the parallel into North Korea? Why were they not satisfied with having saved South Korea? After all, this was what they had set out to do. Their original purpose had not been to unify Korea by force of arms. Why, then, did they attempt it and thus provoke North Korea's powerful neighbor? The answer to this seems to be that they had a bad case of victory fever. The very brilliance of MacArthur's success at Inchon had carried them away, and they now thought that the time was propitious for solving the Korean problem for good. Even sober Britain lost her balance, and instead of cautioning her exuberant young partner as she usually did, she encouraged her to make sure, in the words of Foreign Secretary Ernest Bevin, that from now on there would be "no South Koreans, no North Koreans: just Koreans." Another reason was the belligerence of Syngman Rhee, who repeatedly announced his determination to unify his nation with or without UN assistance. On the home front, the Republicans were making great political capital of their demand for a more aggressive Far Eastern policy, and a great victory in Korea certainly would have enabled the Democrats to pull that rug out from under them before the November election. Yet none of these explanations or even all of them in combination was as influential as that sudden, sweeping surge of victory begun at Inchon. The sight of the once victorious North Korean Army washing backward in broken bits was simply too exhilarating. Phrased in its most simple and inelegant terms, the United States and her UN allies thought they could get away with it. Red China, unfortunately, thought otherwise.

It was in this way that the Korean tragedy had its encore, and military history was to receive another melancholy proof that when one side thinks the other won't fight there is always war.

In the last weeks of October it did not seem that the Korean War would last past Thanksgiving. On October 19 spearheads of the

Eighth Army entered Pyongyang to find the enemy capital abandoned. Premier Kim Il Sung had fled to the Yalu River, taking with him his Russian advisers. Behind him, he left enough stores of Russian supplies and enough pictures, busts and posters of Stalin, as well as enough streets named after him, to make it clear who was pulling the Korean puppet strings. On October 20 American paratroopers began jumping behind the enemy to seal off his escape routes, and with that the demoralized North Koreans began to surrender wholesale. By the end of October there were 135,000 of them in captivity. By then, too, the victorious UN Command uncovered still more evidence of Communist atrocity. The bodies of scores of captured American soldiers were found sprawled alongside the railway tracks in a grisly demonstration that the fleeing foe was lightening his load in the foulest way.

On the east coast, there were similar spectacular advances. The ROKs at Wonsan had resumed their northward advance to the Yalu, and on October 26, after the Navy completed the hazardous mission of clearing Wonsan Harbor of its numerous mines, the 1st Marine Division came ashore there. Its mission was to mop up the Wonsan-Hungnam area and then to take the road from Hungnam to Chosin Reservoir. From Chosin, the Marines would attack west to link up with the Eighth Army at the Yalu. Meanwhile, the 7th Infantry Division landed at Iwon 78 miles north of Wonsan and also struck out west for the Yalu. This was a broad dispersal of forces, one which General Almond freely admitted, but he was confident of swift victory. Even though the presence of the Communist Chinese Forces (CCF) in Korea was by then acknowledged by American commanders, even though on October 25 a ROK division had been attacked by a CCF division at a point 37 miles northwest of Hungnam, MacArthur's headquarters still insisted that Red China planned no massive intervention. On October 28 his intelligence summary said: "From a tactical viewpoint, with victorious U.S. Divisions in full deployment, it would appear that the auspicious time for such intervention had long since passed; it is difficult to believe that such a move, if planned, would have been postponed at a time when remnant North Korean forces have been reduced to a low point of effectiveness."[48]

True enough, by then the North Korean Army had ceased to exist as an effective fighting force. Its divisions were fragmented and many of the bits were nothing more than bands of foragers desperately trying to live off a land already turning hard and barren under the first cold breaths of a cruel winter. By October 26 a ROK regiment had reached Chosan on the Yalu. The end seemed in sight, and it was because of this that General Almond had changed his plans and flung his forces wide. Yet because the North Korean was down was no reason to count his Chinese savior out. The South Koreans had been in even worse straits before the Americans came to their rescue. However, the American military as well as political leaders insisted on believing their own propaganda. Their intelligence did not so much consider what the Communist Chinese had the capacity of doing as what it *believed* they would do. Such habits of thought have always been the undoing of armies. Finally, if the Defense Department in Washington had prepared no plan looking toward CCF intervention, the UN Command in Tokyo was similarly derelict. Yet the Red Chinese in Korea were daily growing in strength. Surely *someone* would suggest that the customary purpose of an armed enemy is to deny you the victory. But no one, at least no one in authority, seems to have done so. From President Truman to the troops in the field the Americans were bent upon celebrating the victory beforehand. Men of the 1st Cavalry Division boasted of flaunting their bright yellow scarves in a victory parade in Tokyo on Thanksgiving Day. The division even turned in some of its equipment preparatory to return to Japan. From the Far East Air Force's Bomber Command came the complaint, "We've run out of targets," and General Stratemeyer, while authorizing two bombardment groups to return to the States, ultimately suspended Bomber Command's operations.

On October 25, however, just as the ROKs in the east were being attacked by Red Chinese, a ROK battalion nearing the Yalu stumbled into a CCF roadblock and was annihilated. That roadblock, of course, was intended to bar the retreat of the very ROK regiment which was advancing to the Yalu in triumph. On October 26, the day that regiment reached the river, it turned in alarm and withdrew. It ran into the CCF roadblock. During the day American air held the regiment together. At night it fell apart. Of the regiment's 3,553 men, only 875 survived. After this action, the entire ROK II Corps began to collapse. Fear of China, that massive and often hostile neighbor north of the Yalu, is endemic to all Koreans. To know that the Chinese with all their inexhaustible legions and immemorial ambitions were in the field against them simply paralyzed the Korean will to fight. By November 1 the ROK II Corps was in full and literal flight and the entire right flank of Walker's Eighth Army lay open. On the left, NK opposition stiffened. During that same November 1 the first of the Russian-built MIG-15 jet fighters appeared over North Korea. That night the CCF was attacking the Eighth Army so savagely that the U.S. 1st Cavalry and 2nd Infantry divisions had to fight for their lives. From all along the Eighth Army front for the next few days came reports identifying CCF divisions in action. By November 5 it was clear that Red China was in the war against the United Nations. Next day MacArthur issued a special communiqué concluding:

> While the North Korean forces with which we were initially engaged have been destroyed or rendered impotent for military action, a new and fresh army faces us, backed up by a possibility of large alien reserves and adequate supplies within easy reach of the enemy but beyond the limits of our present sphere of military action. Whether and to what extent these reserves will be moved forward remains to be seen and is a matter of gravest international significance.[49]

The following day, November 7, Peking coolly announced that the "Chinese People's Volunteers," as the CCF was called with a typically transparent fiction, had come to North Korea's side in much the same noble fashion that "the progressive people of France, inspired and led by Lafayette, assisted the American people in their war of independence."[50] That same day, while the entire Communist world chuckled over the irony of this communiqué, the Korean War flip-flopped again. As quickly as they had popped up, the Red Chinese disappeared. For nearly three weeks, from November 7 to November 26, there was almost no action in North Korea. UN patrols sought the enemy in vain, and during this inexplicable lull the first snows of winter began to fall.

7

☆

Contrary to the customs of civilized nations, Red China had intervened in the Korean War without prior notice of belligerence, and this, it would seem, was done simply to set a trap for the overconfident UN Command. However, this snare was skillfully avoided. Then, in the three-week lull which came upon the battlefield, it would appear that the CCF began digging another pit.

Unfortunately, official Washington was still scrutinizing the enemy through rose-colored glasses and the lull was cheerfully taken to indicate that Red China had made a "limited intervention." This wonderfully cozy theory, bruited everywhere by Communist propaganda, declared that the CCF had merely drawn a *cordon sanitaire* across northernmost Korea in order to protect Manchuria and the Yalu River power plants as well as to provide a base for Premier Kim's fugitive government. So appealing was this argument that it was accepted by the C.I.A. and such allies as Britain and France. These two nations joined in a Security Council draft resolution offering "to hold the Chinese frontier with Korea inviolate" and to protect Peking's interests in the frontier zone if the CCF would agree to withdraw. Some nations, and some of Truman's advisers, thought that Red China would not resume the attack if the UN forces stayed where they were, or even withdrew farther south! Red China, of course, had not made a single official commitment anywhere to anyone. All the "limited intervention" talk came from Communist propaganda sources. Nevertheless, at a National Security Council meeting Secretary Acheson talked hopefully of a "buffer area" in northeast Korea or of a demilitarized zone extending ten miles on each side of the Yalu. Even though the Secretary quickly recovered his balance by declaring that nothing but the abandonment of South Korea would satisfy the Communists, President Truman still hastened to assure Red China that America never had any hostile feelings toward her. Britain also promised Peking that no invasion of her land was intended. The Security Council went so far as to invite Red China to attend a discussion of General MacArthur's report.

Red China's reply was a harsh refusal. Soon her propaganda outlets were pouring insult and invective on the UN head, and such intemperate language reminded the UN allies that this ill-tempered dragon which they sought so earnestly to mollify was in fact at war with the United Nations. They remembered also that Red China had recently begun to assist Communist forces in Indo-China and that she had invaded helpless Tibet. In late November the Red Chinese made their intransigence plain when they sent General Wu Hsiu-chuan to Lake Success* to "discuss" the Korean situation by vilifying the UN

* This village on Long Island was the site of the first UN headquarters.

while defending the right of her "People's Volunteers" to fight against UN troops. So much, then, for the "limited intervention." It had been nothing but a propaganda pitch to mask the true intention of gaining a respite in which to regroup and reinforce for a new offensive.

One of Mao Tse-tung's most cherished military theories was that a peasant army such as his must follow the policy of "luring the enemy to penetrate deep," to stretch his line of supply to the utmost before turning to fall upon him in overwhelming numbers. Such strategy would work best in a strange land during unfavorable weather, and the Korean winter was now tightening its grip upon the north. Moreover, the CCF divisions in Korea were never able to carry more than five days of supply. When this vanished, they had to stop to await resupply by a crude communications system depending upon the A-frames on the backs of forcibly conscripted Korean civilians and animal transport ranging from oxen to camels. At the time the CCF broke off contact and pulled back, the Red divisions were fought out. They needed a respite and General Peng Teh-huai, the CCF commander with headquarters in Mukden, needed time to bring up the rest of his forces. To the west, General Peng sent reinforcements to Lin Piao's Fourth Army opposing Walker. To the east against Almond's X Corps he sent the IX Army Group under General Sung Shin-lun.

All this troop movement clogged the Yalu bridges with nocturnal traffic, and MacArthur at once resolved to destroy the crossings. In doing so, he would be acting within the scope of orders issued him on September 29 when George Marshall, the new Secretary of Defense, instructed him "to feel unhampered tactically and strategically" in pursuing the enemy army. Now, however, the Joint Chiefs thought otherwise and they quickly reminded President Truman of his promise to consult Britain before taking any action against Manchuria. Truman therefore ordered MacArthur to suspend the strikes against the Yalu bridges until he could explain why such a move was necessary. MacArthur's reply was agonized. Here was a commander who had already been forbidden to harm what he called Red China's "privileged sanctuary," i.e., Manchuria, and now he must watch that same enemy pour undeterred into the field against him while he explained the "necessity" of destroying his points of entry. Yet he did, pleading for permission to launch the raid. Back came the order: bomb only the Korean side of the bridges.

When MacArthur asked General Stratemeyer if he could comply with such instructions, Stratemeyer is said to have replied: "It cannot be done—Washington must have known that it cannot be done."[51] What Stratemeyer meant was that the enemy, apparently confident that only the Korean side of the bridges would be attacked, had already built his antiaircraft defenses with the guns zeroed in on these approaches. As a result, the Superforts were forced up to altitudes of 18,000 feet, where they were buffeted by winds of up to 120 knots. Accuracy was next to impossible. They not only could not hit the Korean side of the bridges, they were also exposed to Red Chinese jets who rose from their base at Antung across the river to levels of 30,000 feet, from which they came slashing down in quick firing passes before banking to regain the "privileged sanctuary" of Manchurian air. Again agonized by the appeals of his airmen, MacArthur requested the policeman's right of "hot pursuit," so that American fighters so attacked might be granted "two or three minutes" in which to chase the enemy across the border and destroy him. This, too, was denied by Truman after consultation with his UN allies.

The President's desire to limit the war was undoubtedly sincere, and his decision not to allow himself to be drawn into a general Asiatic war so as to weaken and expose Europe to the ambitions of Russian Communism seems also to have been upheld by events subsequent to the Korean War; yet these restrictions were very hard indeed upon Douglas MacArthur. Few if any commanders in history have been so hobbled. To a soldier of MacArthur's pride and ardor they must have been doubly galling. Compelling as the political considerations might have been, they were nevertheless denying him the right to protect the lives of his soldiers and the safety of his army. Because of this, MacArthur says, he decided to request relief from his command. He was convinced that "the enemy commander must have known of this decision to protect his lines of communication into North Korea, or he never would have dared to cross those bridges in force."[52] True. But this need not suggest treachery in Washington. Over and over again, America and her allies had publicly promised to keep Chinese territory inviolate, and President Truman went so far as to rule out use of nuclear weapons, thus unwisely depriving America of even the threat of her atomic arsenal. Has any enemy ever been so sedulously assured of soft blows? General Peng need not have had any clandestine assurances from American fifth columnists; all he needed to do was to read the daily newspapers. Nevertheless, Mac-Arthur would always cling to this suspicion of betrayal or inexplicable faintheartedness; although he did allow his chief of staff to dissuade him from resigning. With great reluctance he accepted the bridle of limited war and returned to the business of winning it. Characteristically, he decided to renew the attack, and in this he might have fallen in with the CCF strategy of luring the enemy to penetrate deep.

During the three-week lull the CCF in Korea had grown to a force of 300,000 men, augmented by about 40,000 North Koreans who were now directly subordinate to the orders of General Peng. American intelligence had erroneously estimated that the "People's Volunteers" numbered only about 70,000 men. In this, they may have been deceived by the Chinese ruse of identifying full armies and divisions as "battalions" or "units." Against Eighth Army in the west the CCF had 180,000 men, with another 120,000 opposite X Corps in the east. Between these two opposing forces lay a rugged mountain range. Because of this, General Peng's plan was to swing two gates and pin both enemy armies back against the water. First, he permitted Mac-Arthur to advance.

On November 24, the day after a good Thanksgiving dinner, General Walker's troops began to strike north on a three-corps front: left to right, the U.S. I and IX and the ROK II. The men attacked behind a heavy artillery barrage, moving with the cold already at zero levels, over icy roads winding through snow-blotched brown hills and into a cruel, cutting north wind. They made good gains, quickening the spirit of confidence which had christened the advance as the "win-the-war" offensive. Next day, however, the enemy launched probing attacks. Then they began striking all along the line, hunting, as has been suggested, for South Koreans. They found them, the units of the same ROK II Corps they had battered a month ago. That night, under a cold bright moon, to the blare of bugles, the shrill of whistles and clanging of cymbals, the Chinese came swarming through the hills. They had not made these sounds, incidentally, to terrorize the enemy, as some war correspondents mistakenly reported during the war, but only to signal their formations into position. However, the clamor did have the effect of unnerving the ROKs, and thus made them vulnerable to the tactics of *Hachi Shiki*. This was a V formation with the mouth open to the enemy. When the enemy had entered the V, the sides closed around him, while other forces moved into his rear to set up roadblocks to intercept reinforcements and prevent escape. Such tactics can upset hardened veterans, and the ROKs were not quite in that category. As they began to crumble, therefore, a giant CCF counterstroke fell on their front like a sledgehammer. The ROK II Corps was broken into pieces and sent reeling backward in a leaderless stream. The Eighth Army had no right flank. It had only a gaping void 40 miles wide. Into it came the Red Chinese, hurrying to swing west and thus drive Walker's two other corps against the Yellow Sea.

These other corps were also being hit, and hit hard. All along the Chongchon River Walker's divisions were falling back. But that gaping right was critical. Here Walker fed in the Turkish Brigade and then the British Brigade and the 1st Cavalry Division. The gap could not be closed. There were too many Chinese, and they had too many targets. Southbound roads were thronged with traffic, with soldiers of all races moving to the rear. Unable to hold at the Chongchon line, Walker began a full retreat that signaled the collapse of the "win-the-war" offensive. His withdrawal was covered by the 2nd Division in the north fighting a dogged delaying action. Then, having regained the south bank of the Chongchon, the 2nd also attempted to withdraw. Some 7,000 soldiers boarded trucks to drive five miles south to Sunchon—and they drove straight into a massive ambush. An entire division of Red Chinese held that five-mile stretch. With guns sited in the hills to either side, and a roadblock at the end, they turned the road into an avenue of death. Of the 7,000 Americans who ran the gantlet, roughly 3,000 were killed or wounded and the loss in vehicles was appalling.

The 2nd's Golgotha might well have been worse, and so might the ordeal of the entire Eighth Army, had it not been for the intervention of American air. Unaccountably unmolested by MIGs, the American planes scourged the enemy and bequeathed him a scorched earth of torn-up roads and blazing supply dumps. In the west, then, Peng's attempt to pin the Eighth Army against the sea had failed. But in the east it appeared to be succeeding.

When the CCF first appeared in Korea, the X Corps included two ROK divisions and the U.S. 7th Infantry and 1st Marine divisions. The ROKs and most of the 7th were able to make an orderly withdrawal and fall back on the port of Hungnam. But the 1st Marine Division continued its advance toward Chosin Reservoir 78 miles northwest of Hungnam, and as it did the cold white claws of a beastly winter closed around its men,

The cold was not typical of Korea, but peculiar only to the high northeastern plateau up which the Americans were marching. There, the temperatures were consistently from −20° to −30° or lower during the night and rarely rose above zero during the day. In such weather, weapons froze, food froze, human flesh and blood froze, and both the Americans and the Chinese would use the frozen bodies of their comrades to barricade their positions. Such cold causes frostbite and stomach disorders born of eating frozen food, and it is as inimical to a mechanized army as any swamp or jungle. But if the cold hobbled these 20,000 Marines under Oliver Smith, it was, with its howling blizzards and overcast skies, a wonderful white cloak for the trap being set by 100,000 Chinese under the fiery Sung Shin-lun.

General Sung intended to destroy the 1st Marine Division, after which he would rush into Hungnam and drive the ROKs and the 7th Division into the Sea of Japan. He intended to wait until the Marines were well along that iron plateau before closing in on them. To this end, he slipped his IX Army Group into position around Chosin Reservoir; and to this end he was well served by the gradual fragmentation of the Marine Division. One fragment was at Chin-hung-ni, 37 miles northwest of Hungnam, another at Koto-ri ten miles farther north, a third at Hagaru-ri 11 miles higher and the fourth, the main body, was 14 miles higher still at the little town of Yudam-ni to the left or west of the reservoir. General Smith had not willingly separated his forces thus, but had been compelled to string them out because of the narrowness of the road and because of the urgency of his orders to advance to the reservoir. After the Eighth Army became imperiled in the west, he received further orders to attack in that direction to relieve the pressure on Walker.

Such a maneuver, of course, fell in deeper with General Sung's scheme of destroying the Marine Division piecemeal. He would allow the main body at Yudam-ni to advance west—into the jaws of his ten-division trap—and then destroy them. The three smaller frag-ments would then be gobbled up and the path to Hungnam would lie open. But the wary Oliver Smith had sniffed the Chosin air in suspicion and then in alarm. En route to the reservoir, his main body had repeatedly clashed with CCF divisions and had even taken Chinese prisoners. Because of this, Smith built an emergency airfield at Hagaru-ri and ordered the main body at Yudam-ni to drag its feet on the way west. These two moves probably saved his division.

On November 27, 1950, struck by Sung's spearheads while moving slowly west, the main body quickly pulled back to the Yudam-ni hills, fortified them and that night hurled back a savage Chinese attack. To the east of the reservoir, a second Chinese thrust shattered elements of the 7th Division known as Task Force Faith. Eventually, its survivors were rescued by the Marines at Hagaru-ri. However, with daylight of November 28 it was plain that Sung's divisions had outflanked the Marine Division on both sides of its long axis all the way down to Chinghung-ni. What Smith had to do now was to hold the little hill towns against repeated enemy attacks, and gather his forces. It was to be a fighting withdrawal, Yudam-ni to Hagaru-ri to Koto-ri to Chinghung-ni, and then, with his division at last concentrated, the final 43-mile thrust to Hungnam and safety. "We are not retreating," Smith said. "We are merely attacking in another direction."[53] This was exactly true, for his men took a dreadful toll of General Sung's IX Army Group. It was a war by battalions: this battalion holding this pass, this one blasting through an enemy roadblock, another climbing and storming Chinese gun positions to either side of the road, and still another holding open a bridge or at least throwing a defensive perimeter around the ruins of a destroyed one until sections of portable bridges could be air-dropped to them. Meanwhile the Marine Division's own air wing gave a devastating demonstration of what close-up air support can do for 20,000 men running a 100,000-man gauntlet. Hovering over the American column day and night, these planes and others from the Fifth Air Force were directed to enemy targets by ground observers, and they came in at treetop level to blast and burn them out of the path.

So the fragmented units drew together, fighting from town to town, swelling in strength and ardor, until at last they broke out of the trap in what was beyond question the greatest fighting withdrawal in the history of modern arms. They had suffered 7,500 casualties— of which about half were due to frostbite—and inflicted about 37,500 casualties on the enemy. They not only came out, but they brought with them all their weapons, their vehicles, their wounded and their dead. They had not only wrecked Sung's plan but ruined his IX Army Group. So X Corps also ultimately eluded the Chinese trap; it was eventually withdrawn and taken south to Pusan. The U.S. Navy not only drew off 105,000 men of X Corps, but also 91,000 Korean civilians who wanted no part of the Chinese liberator, as well as 17,500 vehicles and 350,000 tons of material. Hungnam was left a useless, smoking ruin, and well might Admiral Doyle exult: "They never laid a glove on us."[54] To President Truman the Hungnam evacuation was "the best Christmas present I ever had."[55]

8

☆

The wine of Inchon was now the hangover of Chosin and the Chongchon, and as Red China exulted and boasted of what she would do to the UN Command, a dispirited America read of impending disaster in Korea.

As usual, the press was lamenting a little too mournfully, for the CCF offensive had fallen far short of being decisive. By mid-December the Red Chinese had lost momentum and General Walker was establishing a new defensive line across the peninsula just south of the 38th parallel. It was now the Chinese who were being "lured to penetrate deep." It was their supply line which was now being extended and exposed to the interdiction of American air everywhere and to the guns of American ships along the coasts.

Nevertheless, the retreat from the Yalu was never what MacArthur and his apologists attempted to call it: a successful spoiling attack or a reconnaissance in force. Echoing his defenders, MacArthur had claimed that he deliberately "reached up" to spring the Red snare. If he did, it was not the UN Command's hand but its head and shoulders that went into the trap; and it is a strange reconnaissance in force indeed when all the forces are on reconnaissance. No, what happened was that MacArthur had failed in his attempt to win the war before the onset of winter. He failed because his heady optimism had led him to misjudge the enemy's strength and intent. Nevertheless, his command was intact, and that, of course, was chiefly due to some very hard fighting, and to the intervention of American air and sea power. It was now, as MacArthur said, a new war. Arrayed against the UN Command was the limitless manpower of the Chinese nation supported by Soviet material resources.

No one was more aware of this depressing turnabout than Harry Truman. Very quickly, the President remembered what containment had meant originally: that *nothing more* was to fall to Communism. Containment had not meant, however, that any territory the Communists possessed as of 1947 was to be taken from them by force. This was what had been attempted in the invasion of North Korea, and it would not be tried again. Rather, Mr. Truman was ready to accept the *status quo ante bellum*. To this end, the UN General Assembly on December 14 voted to seek an armistice in Korea and set up a three-man Cease-Fire Committee to approach Peking and Pyongyang.

Now it was Red China's turn to play the part of the strong boy flushed with success. Chou En-lai notified the Cease-Fire Committee that Peking would talk peace only after the UN withdrew from Korea, America withdrew her support of Formosa, the west ceased to rearm and Red China was admitted to the United Nations. Clearly, the Communist Chinese thought that they could achieve the military solution denied to the Moscow-Pyongyang and the U.S.-UN coalitions. However, Chou's harsh answer had the effect of rallying the United Nations behind the newly evolved American policy of "negotiation from strength." It was recognized that the Communist Chinese could only be brought to the conference table by force of arms, and so the UN Command in Korea was instructed to deflate Red China's military pride.

The Eighth Army began its new mission with a new commander. General Walker had been killed when an ROK truck crashed into the jeep in which he was riding. His successor was Lieutenant General Matthew Ridgway, a veteran paratroop commander and a perceptive soldier who, though not enamored of the perplexities of limited war, was in no way baffled by them. Ridgway's arrival in Korea coincided with the coming of American Sabrejets, which very rapidly re-established American aerial supremacy and began killing off enemy MIGs at an astonishing ratio of 14 to 1. The Eighth Army which Ridgway took over was by then a truly international force. Fifteen nations—the United States, Great Britain, Australia, New Zealand, India, South Africa, France, Canada, the Netherlands, the Philippines and Greece—now had units in Korea. Like Walker, Ridgway trained them in American miltary doctrine at a UN Reception Center before attaching them by battalions to the seven American divisions then deployed in Korea. Only the British Commonwealth brigades, eventually combined in the 1st Commonwealth Division, functioned autonomously.

Including the ROKs, Ridgway commanded a force of about 385,000 men. Against him were an estimated 485,000 troops now under General Lin Piao, and Lin opened the CCF's "Third Phase Offensive" on New Year's Eve by hurling the bulk of this force at the UN positions north of Seoul. Swarming over snow-covered hills and across frozen paddies, the Communist soldiers fell by the thousands, but they continued to attack until they had broken and routed two ROK divisions and driven a deep wedge in Ridgway's center. With this, Ridgway committed X Corps to his collapsing center and began a covering action while withdrawing from Seoul.

To see Seoul surrendered to the Communists a second time was indeed a psychological blow to President Rhee and the South Koreans, as well as to the anxious UN allies back at Lake Success. But Ridgway had no other alternative. Obviously, Lin had committed most of his forces. Ridgway with his smaller army could not stand and fight, especially with his back to the broad Han River, without inviting encirclement and destruction. Better to withdraw, to draw the onrushing enemy into the UN's superior air and artillery, and to fall back to previously prepared positions in the south so that the ill-supplied CCF offensive would exhaust itself in the intervening ground.

This is what Ridgway did and this was what happened. Once again Seoul's wretched residents streamed south from their native city, although this time the stoic silence of their exodus was accompanied by the whispering dry murmur of slippers on the snow. Again the capital was engulfed in flames, but this time many of the fires were set by UN soldiers putting to the torch all supplies that could not be carried away. And this time the retreat was an orderly one. Communist soldiers charging into American artillery fire failed utterly to press Ridgway's army against the river, and when they rushed into the abandoned city they were subjected to saturation aerial bombardment. And then, as Ridgway had calculated, Lin's poorly supplied divisions ground down to a halt out in the middle of nowhere. By mid-January the "Third Phase Offensive," which was to knock the UN Command out of the war, was an obvious failure, and the proud and fiery Lin, having suffered his first military defeat, immediately blamed the reversal on "the failure of the Chinese Central Government to furnish air and tank support as promised."

Unfortunately, one of the risks of a retrograde movement is that, requiring time and patience for success, it often unstrings the nerves of politicians. Thus, just as the enemy's blows began to fall fainter, America's allies in the UN began to lose heart. Because General Lin's offensive seemed to be succeeding, the General Assembly on January 13, 1951, presented Red China a new peace plan. It offered complete capitulation on the issues of Formosa and Red China's admission to the United Nations, if she would agree to a Korean settlement. The United States did not favor this proposal, but because she had pledged herself to work through the UN, and because it was clear that most of the members approved it, she voted for it.

With that a hurricane of indignation broke upon Harry Truman's head. He was accused of selling out to the appeasers. There were widespread demands that Secretary Acheson resign, even though he had in fact fought against adoption of such a fainthearted plan. Senator Taft called the Formosa and UN-membership concessions "the most complete surrender to which the United States has ever agreed." As might be expected, none of Truman's wrathful critics suggested that the U.S. go it alone in Korea, as she might have had to do if she quarreled with her allies. Fortunately, Red China again overplayed her hand. First she must be admitted to the UN, then a loaded peace conference was to be held in Peking while the war went on. In other words, the Communist Chinese would continue to make their points with a pistol. With this, the softening spines of the UN allies finally stiffened, growing so steel-like with the news of Lin Piao's failure that on February 1 the General Assembly formally branded Communist China as an aggressor in Korea.

Once again the solution was to be found in an appeal to arms.

Matthew Ridgway had planned to counterattack as soon as he had determined that the Communists had spent themselves. On January

24, 1951, in personal aerial reconnaissance north of his defensive line, he flew over land so motionless and frozen that he became convinced that "if I should order an attack, I would not be sending Eighth Army into a trap in which it could be destroyed."[56] Next day, he advanced in the west on a two-corps front. There was no opposition. Gradually, Ridgway fed more troops into the advance. Now the Chinese countered, but it was obvious that they were fighting a delaying action. Then, in the center, Lin hurled his counterstroke. Two CCF armies and one North Korean corps tried to break through Dutch, ROK and American troops. Ridgway contained this thrust with an American regiment and a French battalion, and then broke it up with the counter-attack of another American regiment. With that, Lin's main counter-stroke was blunted, as was a smaller one attempted in the east, and his armies went into full retreat. Ridgway pursued, authorizing an advance called "Operation Killer."

At once, shrill bleats of protest arose from American left-wingers who had already been offended by Ridgway's habit of wearing paratroop harness with a hand grenade at his breast. The general was too bloodthirsty. Words such as "killer" might affront the sensitive Asians and it would be more fitting if the general would find a more delicate way of expressing himself. It was thus that the exquisite souls added their own lavender patch to the crazy quilt of the Korean "conflict"; but Ridgway was undismayed by his critics, and continued as before with "Killer." He had given his soldiers back their ardor, and they now took the last of Lin Piao's footholds south of the Han away from him. Below that river, the hills and valleys were scarred with the raw red mounds of the mass graves of Lin's soldiers. They had been scourged by epidemics of typhus, by American air strikes and a cruel winter. They had slowly starved at the end of a leaky supply line running 260 miles back to the Yalu. American propaganda leaflets taunted, "Count Your Men!" and Lin Piao, counting his losses in the hundreds of thousands, was finally relieved of his command. In another 15 years, Lin was to emerge as Mao Tse-tung's second-in-command, as well as the idol of the brutal young vandals he had organized into the Red Guards, but in the spring of 1951, either because of wounds or failure, he lost his command. General Peng came down to Korea to take over, and his first order was to hold Seoul at all costs.

But the Reds could not hold Seoul, not under the onslaught of "Operation Ripper." Supported overhead and on the seaward flanks, spearheaded by tanks and backed up by artillery, the Americans and their allies drove again into the capital. For the fourth time Seoul changed hands. By the end of March, using airdrops to cut off the enemy's escape routes, Ridgway had brought the Eighth Army and the ROKs back to a line generally approximating the 38th parallel. For the second time, the war was back where it had started—this time at the expense of Red China. Once again the UN Command prepared to cross the border, not, however, to attempt to unify Korea by force of arms, but only to continue to belabor and bruise Communist China's military pride. At this point Eighth Army got its third commanding general.

On April 11, 1951, President Truman relieved General MacArthur of his command and replaced him with Ridgway.

General MacArthur's running dispute with President Truman over American foreign policy commenced shortly after the war began. In essence, it was a matter of MacArthur believing that the war against world Communism was to be fought and won in Asia, and Truman maintaining that Europe, with all its factories and shipyards and skilled workers, its universities and its scientists—in a word, its high civilization—was Stalin's true goal. Mr. Truman and his military chiefs believed that the war in Korea might be a feint to draw free world strength into Asia so that Stalin might march into Western Europe unopposed. In Washington and all the other chanceries of the free world, concern was not so much for Korea but for the possibility that mighty Russia might be preparing to march.

Thus the American remobilization which followed the Communist crossing of the parallel was not so much to save Korea as to protect Europe. In the winter of 1950-51, Congress raised military appropriations from the "maximum ceiling" of $15 billion to about $60 billion. The Navy got funds to resume building its mammoth carriers, the Air Force received money to build not only its controversial B-36 superbombers but also jet bombers, and the Army began a vast new tank production program.

But most of this was destined or designed for Europe, where the American constabulary rose from one to five divisions plus the equivalent of a large sixth in three armored regimental combat teams. Meanwhile, NATO, which had been at first a political and diplomatic alliance, was transformed into a military coalition and Dwight D.

Eisenhower was drafted from the presidency of Columbia University to become its first Supreme Commander.

Thus the concept of Europe-first which had been adopted against the Axis was being revived in the face of Communist ambition. Thus, Korea was to get, in effect, the leavings—just as the Pacific had been treated in the former war. This was indeed hard upon Douglas Mac-Arthur. In 1941-45 he had been asked to hold the Philippines on a shoestring and been given short shrift in the Southwest Pacific. In Korea, where he was already handcuffed by orders not to violate the enemy's Manchurian supply line, where he was with limited forces opposing a huge Communist army in the only shooting war that was then in progress, he was once again being compelled to defer to the priority of Europe, then at peace—and once again to defer to the requirements of Eisenhower, his old subordinate.

Against this developing background, on July 29, 1950, came Chiang Kai-shek's offer of 33,000 Nationalist Chinese troops for use in Korea. This was declined by Truman because he feared that to use Nationalist Chinese in Korea might be to offer gratuitous insult to Red China. Two days later, General MacArthur flew to Formosa to confer with Chiang. Immediately, in Congress and among the UN allies, his trip was interpreted to portend a shift in American policy from neutralization of Formosa to the active defense of that Nationalist stronghold. Truman found it necessary to explain to Congress: "Our desire is that Formosa not become embroiled in hostilities disturbing to the peace of the Pacific and that all questions affecting Formosa be settled by peaceful means as envisaged in the Charter of the United Nations."[57] Truman also sent an emissary to MacArthur to tell the general that he must not permit Chiang to be the cause of starting a war with the Communists on the Chinese mainland. MacArthur replied that, as a soldier, he would obey; and Truman himself assumed that "this would be the last of it."[58]

But then, on August 26, MacArthur in a message to the Veterans of Foreign Wars publicly challenged Truman on Formosa by declaring: "Nothing could be more fallacious than the threadbare argument by those who advocate appeasement and defeatism in the Pacific that if we defend Formosa we alienate continental Asia."[59] Although this statement was not to be read until August 28, it was given out to the press two days earlier, and by August 26 one weekly magazine carrying the full text was already in the mails. Deeply dismayed,

Truman thought of replacing MacArthur in Korea with Bradley and allowing MacArthur to continue in command of the Japanese occupation. Instead, however, he merely ordered MacArthur to withdraw the statement, a useless gesture which MacArthur, having publicly made his point, was quick to do.

There followed a respite of four months, during which Europe gradually took precedence over Korea and MacArthur was driven back from the Yalu. In late December, 1950, the Joint Chiefs suggested to MacArthur that he might be compelled to evacuate Korea and withdraw to Japan. Now MacArthur was dismayed. He composed a long reply setting down his convictions that, so far from submitting to Red Chinese force, the UN might crush the enemy by blockading the Chinese coast, bombarding and bombing his industrial capacity, using Nationalist troops against him in Korea and sending Chiang against the mainland. MacArthur said: "I understand thoroughly the demand for European security and fully concur in doing everything possible in that sector, but not to the point of accepting defeat anywhere else—an acceptance which I am sure could not fail to ensure later defeat in Europe itself."[60] In other words, Asia was first, not Europe.

Back from the Chiefs came a brusque rejection of MacArthur's suggestions for crushing Red China. Administration policy was still Europe-first. MacArthur was told that his basic mission was to protect Japan and again advised that if the safety of his command warranted it, he should withdraw to Japan. So now MacArthur's dismay was doubled. Talk of evacuation and the new emphasis placed upon defense of Japan seemed to him an attempt to put the onus for any evacuation on him. At that time, of course, withdrawal seemed likely. Ridgway's retreat had so unstrung the politicians that even Senator Taft was calling openly for withdrawal. So Douglas MacArthur angrily demanded "clarification" of the entire situation. Did the United States intend to stay in Korea? This and earlier messages drew from President Truman a long, patient and detailed explanation of American policy. Yes, aggression must be resisted in Korea, but the United States must be most prudent not to extend the area of the war there, and not to alienate allies upon whom she must also depend should Stalin move against her.

MacArthur was mollified, although it was only a few days later that the United States voted in favor of the UN's sweetheart peace offer to Red China. Although it was ultimately rejected, the fact that it was made with American support may have made MacArthur wonder if Truman really meant what he had said. In a few days, however, Lin Piao's offensive sputtered to a halt, and all talk of evacuation or appeasement vanished for good.

But then, on February 21, 1951, MacArthur requested permission to bomb Racin, an enemy supply port 35 miles below the Siberian border. It was denied on the grounds that Racin was too close to Soviet territory. Next he asked if he might bomb Red China's power plants on the Yalu, and was again refused. At this time, MacArthur's friends in Congress were attacking "Mr. Truman's War." Joseph Martin, Republican minority leader in the House, renewed a call for opening a "second front in Asia" with Chiang's troops. Three weeks later, Operation Killer began and as the UN Command very quickly pricked the bubble of Red Chinese military pride, President Truman prepared a conciliatory statement of American peace aims which it was hoped would bring the deflated Chinese to the conference table. This was on March 19, and a few days later MacArthur astounded Washington by publicly warning the enemy of impending destruction and stating that he stood ready to negotiate in the field with the enemy commander.

This "MacArthur pronunciamento," as the Norwegian Ambassador described it, was interpreted by the administration and its UN allies as an attempt to scuttle Truman's conciliatory policy. In fact, Red China very quickly rejected MacArthur's ultimatum as "a threat that the aggressors will advance on our homeland." As Truman later wrote: "By this act MacArthur left me no choice—I could no longer tolerate his insubordination."[61] Perhaps. But as titular chief of the Democratic Party, Mr. Truman would not lightly martyr a military hero with such obvious Republican connections. He would, rather, forbear—until Douglas MacArthur at last threw down the gauntlet in the very pit of American politics: the floor of the House of Representatives.

Minority Leader Martin had asked MacArthur to comment on his February 12 speech attacking the administration policy of limited war and calling for an Asian second front with Chiang's help. On April 5 Martin read MacArthur's reply in the House. The last paragraph said:

It seems strangely difficult for some to realize that here in Asia is where the Communist conspirators have elected to make their play for global conquest, and that we have joined the issue thus raised on the battlefield; that here we fight Europe's war with arms, while the diplomats there still fight it with words; that if we lose the war to Communism in Asia the fall of Europe is inevitable; win it, and Europe most probably would avoid war and yet preserve freedom. As you point out, we must win. There is no substitute for victory.[62]

Now, said Harry Truman, "The time had come to draw the line."[63] After conferring with his top advisers, he dismissed Douglas MacArthur. He did so with bad grace, telling the newspapers before he informed MacArthur. MacArthur learned of his dismissal when a staff officer in Tokyo beckoned Mrs. MacArthur away from luncheon with her husband to tell her that he had heard on the radio that the general was through. With such matchless incivility did Harry Truman bring America's greatest military career to a close. In his defense, Truman explained that a Republican newspaper had learned of the decision and was preparing to "break" the story first. To forestall this, Truman called his own press conference. Probably so, but the shabbiness of his treatment of MacArthur, whether intended or not, helped to magnify the thunder of the storm that broke upon Harry Truman's head.

It was the fight of his political life. Some Republicans called for his impeachment. He was castigated as a mean and vengeful little man, and the Red-baiting Senator Joseph McCarthy, having already accused the Democrats of "twenty years of treason," declared that Truman had fired MacArthur while "full of brandy and bourbon." MacArthur, meanwhile, was hailed as a martyr to State Department appeasement. In that spring of 1951, it is probable that MacArthur's popularity surpassed Dwight Eisenhower's in 1945, and he did have those articulate Republican friends. Thus, when he came home after an absence of 14 years, he was given the equivalent of a Roman triumph from coast to coast. So careful was the administration not to tread on his toes again that he was accorded the rare privilege of addressing a joint session of Congress. There he made an eloquent and moving speech, in which he said again: "In war, indeed, there can be no substitute for victory."[64] It was a golden phrase. It ignored the central fact that in limited wars the victory is also limited. This, of course, was what everyone was arguing about. But this, the very bone of contention, was overlooked during the Great Debate triggered by that felicitous and vote-freighted phrase.

The Great Debate raged in and outside the hearing room of the Senate Armed Services and Foreign Relations committees. More than two million words of testimony were heard there, with the unfortunate result that almost every detail of American Cold War strategy was made public for the instruction of Soviet Russia, and that Americans began to believe that the dispute was over Truman's right to dismiss MacArthur. That, of course, was beyond question, just as his provocation to do so had been beyond doubt. Once Mr. Truman very patiently made this clear, the resentment against him began to subside. It never changed to admiration or approval, however, for Mr. Truman's War still hung like a hair shirt on the body politic. Because of this, Harry Truman did not regain his countrymen's affection until he was out of office. Nor did MacArthur's popularity ever decline. His critics might grow into a veritable host, some of them mean, most of them unaware of the extent to which MacArthur's patience had been tried, and others simply partisan and unfair; but as much as they chipped or chiseled away at his reputation, they could not cut down the heroic figure which still lives in the public mind. Nor could Harry Truman ever instruct the American public in the complications or the purposes of limited war. Senator Taft may have been closer to the hearts of his countrymen when he concluded the Republican minority report on the Senate hearings with the words: "We believe a policy of victory must be announced to the American people in order to restore unity and confidence. It is too much to expect that our people will accept a limited war."[65]

So buffeted, so misunderstood, President Harry S. Truman was therefore eager to listen when the hammer blows of the Eighth Army forced Red China to cry for truce.

9

☆

While General Ridgway took over General MacArthur's duties as Supreme UN Commander, command of the Eighth Army and the ROKs passed to Lieutenant General James Van Fleet.

Van Fleet was a solid soldier. Big and strong physically, he was also a student of the art of war, a professional whose wide and varied battle experience ran back through both World Wars to the Mexican border. It was Van Fleet who rebuilt the Greek Army and directed the fight that defeated the postwar Communist guerrillas there, and his experience of peninsular warfare in Greece had trained him for similar combat in Korea.

Van Fleet took over just as General Peng was preparing to move what was now a force of 700,000 men against the UN. This time, the CCF and their North Korean allies were to have aerial support. General Liu Ya-lou, chief of the Communist Chinese Air Force, had quietly begun a build-up of air power with bases in Manchuria. Ironically, General Liu found himself handcuffed in much the same way as the enemy General MacArthur. Fearing American retaliation, Peking forbade Liu to use his Manchurian bases. Again like MacArthur, Liu complained: "The conservative policy adopted by China has apparently ensued from the high-handed policy of threats of the enemy."[66] Nevertheless, he went ahead with his build-up, repairing and constructing scores of airfields across North Korea. Meanwhile, his MIGs seized air superiority above them.

The American reaction to this threat was exemplary. Ordered by Stratemeyer to destroy the enemy bases, Brigadier General James Briggs reasoned that it would be wasteful to knock them out at once because the enemy's inexhaustible manpower would enable him to repair them quickly. Instead, he decided to hold off until just before the fields were operational and the Red spring offensive began. This he did, while Sabrejets went thundering north to "MIG Alley" to recover air supremacy. Then, between April 17-23, Superforts, Marine and naval aircraft, fighter bombers and B-26 night intruders struck with such fury that the enemy's Special Aviation Inspection Group was forced to report that it had "spent two months on the battlefield supervising the repair of 69 airfields which in the end only helped facilitate the operations of 30 planes."[67] Such expensive futility, the report said, "was far beyond the financial power of Red China."[68] General Peng, then, did not have air support when, on April 22, he launched his big push.

This time Peng collided with an Eighth Army that may have been the most professional fighting force yet fielded by the United States. It numbered about 229,000 men, one British Commonwealth and seven American divisions backed up by heavy tanks and an enormous array of artillery. It was not so much the firepower, however, but the moral power—what Napoleon called the "divine" element in war—that made the Eighth Army so formidable. These Americans and their UN allies were moved by a spirit of cockiness that was amazing to behold in men fighting what one of their comrades called "The war we can't win, we can't lose, we can't quit."[69] Their grim and sardonic toughness of mind was manifested by the rifleman's quip: "I was attacked by two hordes, sir, and I killed them both."[70] Eighth Army morale had also been improved by a rotation system which made a man eligible for return to America after one year in Korea, and by sending a man to Japan for five days of "Rest and Rehabilitation" after six months there.

Besides the 229,000-man Eighth, Van Fleet commanded 357,000 ROKs. Although the ROK Army had been revitalized, it was still weakened by staggering casualties of 170,000 men, who had then been replaced by green recruits, some of them schoolboys who arrived in camp carrying their books. The ROK divisions were lightly armed and they had no organic artillery, depending on corps artillery when they needed it. They fought well enough when opposed by CCF or NK divisions similarly armed, but when they were outgunned or outnumbered they did not. Therefore Van Fleet tried to spot them in easily defended terrain or wedged between dependable Eighth Army divisions. These were the ones Van Fleet relied on, in the main, when Peng came against him with 700,000 men.

The first of the three blows which Radio Pyongyang said would utterly destroy the UN Command came lightly in the center. Next came a stronger thrust in the east, followed by a massive stroke in the west against Seoul. Peng's plan was to retake the capital city by enveloping it on both sides. The UN held fast until the ROKs in the center cracked, after which Van Fleet ordered a general withdrawal south of Seoul. As the UN fell back, American air and artillery hammered the pursuing foe. Once again the Communist offensive literally ran out of gas, for Soviet Russia had again failed to come through with promised shells and fuel. As the enemy slowed down, Van Fleet began a limited counterattack. Then the CCF stiffened and returned to the assault. In mid-May they made their most intensive effort to destroy the UN—and they ran into the dreadful artillery concentration made famous as the "Van Fleet Load." The UN Commander had said, "We must expend steel and fire, not men. I want so many artillery holes that a man can step from one to the other."[71] Thus five times the normal output struck the enemy. One American artillery battalion alone fired 12,000 shells in a single day. The Van Fleet Load literally shredded Peng's assault, and then Van Fleet sent the UN Command surging across the parallel for the third time.

By June 16 the UN held a line beginning in the west at Munsan ten miles below the parallel and then running 40 miles northeast to the base of the Iron Triangle before running gently southeast to the east coast. By then the Communist army was beaten. In one year the North Koreans had suffered 600,000 casualties, and their army was all but destroyed. In only eight months the CCF lost a half-million men. Van Fleet, as he later testified, was ready to go with the knockout blows: amphibious landings up the east coast and a breakout drive northeast. But his request for permission to do so was denied, and that was because he had so badly battered the enemy that the Communists were asking for an armistice.

The first break came on June 23, 1951, when Jacob Malik suggested that both sides discuss an armistice. Two days later Peking seconded this proposal, and on June 29 President Truman instructed General Ridgway to broadcast the following message to the enemy: "I am informed that you may wish a meeting to discuss an armistice. . . . Upon the receipt of word from you that such a meeting is desired I shall be prepared to name my representative. I propose that such a meeting could take place aboard a Danish hospital ship (*Jutlandia*) in Wonsan Harbor."[72] The following night Premier Kim Il Sung and General Peng Teh-huai agreed to the meeting, but suggested that it be held in the town of Kaesong about a mile below the parallel and ten miles northwest of the UN western flank. Ridgway accepted this counter-offer, and the talks began.

10

☆

General Van Fleet may have been understandably dismayed at the order which halted his conquering army in its tracks, but there can be little doubt that the decision was a wise one.

If the UN had driven the CCF out of Korea, it would have succeeded only in shortening the enemy's supply line and forcing him back on his Manchurian base, where he would regroup, rearm and return. Few Americans would have approved invading Manchuria or pushing on into the bottomless pit of mainland Asia. Indubitably, there were many Americans who were by then willing to subject Red China to nuclear bombing, but such immoral incineration of millions of innocent human beings would have solved nothing and probably would have brought on Russian retaliation and therefore nuclear holocaust. To "win" in Korea was to risk winning too big. In the end, the Communists were willing to leave South Korea alone. But they would never have surrendered North Korea. For the UN to have occupied it for a time, then, would have been to provoke counterattack. It would have been to "overwin," for it should now be clear that if the free world had its policy of containment, so did the Communists.

Nevertheless it was a grave mistake on the part of the Americans to believe that the Communists sincerely wished to talk truce. All that they really wanted was relief from Van Fleet's blows. They came to the conference table to obtain what they could not get on the battlefield, and also to belittle and deride the imperialist "paper tigers." True enough, the Truman administration was under almost unbearable pressure to obtain a cease-fire, and it is difficult to see how it could have done otherwise than to trust the enemy. Yet, if each fresh proof of Communist insincerity had been followed by a few severe military knocks on the head, the truce talks might not have dragged on for two long agonizing years.

Communist duplicity was at once apparent when, on July 8, Colonel Andrew Kinney inspected "neutral" Kaesong and found it in fact an armed camp. Kinney was required to fly white flags from his jeeps so that crowds of correspondents and cameramen, carefully combed from all over the Communist world, might record the spectacle of the paper tigers crawling to Kaesong on their knees. Two days later when the talks began inside a Kaesong teahouse, Admiral C. Turner Joy, chief of the UN delegation, found the area swarming with armed and insolent Red sentries, one of whom menaced him with a burp gun. Joy's seat at the conference table was so low that he almost sank out of sight, so that little General Nam Il, seated in an unusually high chair, seemed to tower over him. This and similar contrived manifestations of Red superiority were duly photographed, and if such tactics seem childish they nonetheless added up to effective propaganda.

Although actual control of the Communist delegation seemed to be exerted by CCF General Hsieh Fang, the spokesman and nominal chief was General Nam. He began by demanding the withdrawal of all foreign troops from Korea, a condition which would restore the situation existing in June, 1950, and thus leave him free to invade South Korea again. After two weeks of angry bickering, Nam dropped this demand, and with the adoption of an agenda, he turned his tactics toward fixing a demarcation line at the 38th parallel. This would compel the UN Command to give up a fine battle position about 20 miles above the border. Also, to specify *any* line on a map *before* a cease-fire could be ordered would have the effect of freezing the battle line, thereby relieving the Communists of the military pressure still being maintained by the UN. To avoid this, the UN delegation sought to fix the principle of a truce line that would be the line of contact between belligerents *at the time the armistice was signed*. Thus either belligerent would be free to exert military pressure on the other until hostilities ceased. Military pressure, of course, was what had brought the Communists to the conference table. They were now only trying to talk themselves free of it. If a truce line on the parallel were fixed *before* the cease-fire were ordered, it would inhibit all UN offensives. Any ground won would have to be surrendered upon the signing of the armistice. Nor could Van Fleet ask his soldiers to die taking hills that they were going to have to give back anyway. At this point, it must be remembered, the war was still going on. There had been no truce. The talks at Kaesong were aimed at obtaining that truce, after which the belligerents might talk peace. For these reasons, then, Admiral Joy rejected Nam's demands, and with that the talks were deadlocked for four angry weeks of mutual insult and vituperation. At one point Nam Il responded to a proposal of Admiral Joy's with what may have been the longest cold stare in the history of nonviolent hostility: 2 hours and 11 minutes of glaring silence, only broken when Joy got up and walked out.

Unable to move the UN delegation, the Communists resorted to a propaganda campaign aimed at discrediting it. They accused the UN of bombing Kaesong and trying to murder their delegation. When Colonel Kinney, an aviator, went to the "bombed" area to investigate, he found no evidence of explosions, and the small unexploded rocket shown to him as "evidence" turned out to be of a type which had not been issued to UN fliers for nearly a year. Such reasonable refutation made no impression upon the Communists. Instead, they demanded that Colonel Kinney admit UN guilt there and then. When he refused, an obscure NK lieutenant colonel announced that the armistice conference was at an end.

What had happened was that during the truce talks, with the UN Command unwilling to make any large-scale offensive, the Reds had been able to build their forces practically unmolested. Now, unable to get what they wanted in the Talking War, they resorted to the Shooting War. However, an attempt to regain control of the air was shot to pieces, while Van Fleet's forces broke up a massive ground offensive and then went over to the attack themselves. By mid-October, 1951, they were still higher above the parallel, and the Communists, beaten again in the field, came back to the conference table.

This time it was at Panmunjom, a few miles away from the Kaesong propaganda circus. Here, in this deserted village of four mud huts, seated at a green-topped table within a simple military tent, the delegates of both sides were to sit and haggle and argue and abuse each other for another 21 months. And here the Communists renewed their attempt to talk the military pressure off their backs. Subtle this time, they dropped their demand for a truce line at the 38th parallel and agreed to the line of contact between belligerents. But they wanted this to be *permanently at the present line.* In effect, they were surrendering a few dozen miles of North Korean territory to obtain a *de facto* cease-fire, for if the truce line were to be final *before* the truce, who would try to change it? Their true objective, therefore, was to obtain the *de facto* cease-fire during which they could make their present position impregnable and also build their forces to overwhelming strength. In the meantime, they would drag out the armistice negotiations to the ultimate disillusionment of the Americans and their UN allies. In this their strategy was similar to Japan's in the previous war. Its basic assumption was that the Americans would not have the stomach for a long, costly and unpopular war. And the UN Command did make itself unpopular when Admiral Joy's delegation continued to insist upon a truce line fixed at the line of contact *at the time the armistice was signed.* The UN Command seemed to be opposing a cease-fire, the heart's desire of all the world. It was not generally realized that the cease-fire was only *de facto* and not one officially agreed upon. Nor was it realized that even an official cease-fire does not end a war but only begins a truce, which can be broken at will and under any pretext. Thus Washington had almost no other recourse than to give this *de facto* cease-fire a 30-day trial. By November 27 the line of contact was agreed upon, and there then began what is known as the Little Armistice.

The front became quiet, the world became optimistic and for the second year in a row American servicemen talked gaily of being home for Christmas. Then came the great disillusionment. December 27 passed without the slightest signs of agreement at Panmunjom, and with that the guns began to roar again and it became clear that the Communists *had* used the cease-fire to make themselves strong.

Throughout the October-November delays at Panmunjom and during the Little Armistice they had poured men and arms and materials into their positions at such a rate that they now stood 850,000 strong inside some of the finest fixed positions ever built. The key feature was a tunnel begun on the reverse side of a hill which emerged facing the American lines. The tunnel was then expanded into a honeycomb of corridors and galleries big enough for battalions and resembling in many ways the Japanese island fortresses of World War II or the trench networks of World War I. In fact, the Korean War resembled 1914-18 in many ways. It too had begun with six months of maneuver, before settling down to a prolonged period of static, position warfare. It was also a front without flanks, for the amphibious hook had been denied Van Fleet, and the mountainous terrain prohibited the use of tanks to any effective degree. The other weapon of fluidity, the airplane, was inhibited for the same reason, because the enemy was so deeply underground and because he had emerged as the world's master of repair and of camouflage.

Every attempt to isolate the battlefield, that is, to cut off the Communist front line from its source of supplies to the rear, ended in utter failure. These attempts failed even though the UN possessed clear-cut control of air and sea and used both these arms unsparingly in an all-out effort to cut the enemy's supply line. Operation Strangle was the most sensational exhibit in this melancholy catalogue of futility. For ten months, while the U.S. Navy tightened its marathon siege of Wonsan, Air Force, Navy and Marine planes struck at Communist roads, bridges, railroads, tunnels and supply depots. Even inviolate Racin was stripped of its immunity and bombed. What was the result? The Communists not only maintained their flow of supplies but actually increased it.

Having little machine power, they had limitless manpower. Coolie labor battalions were stationed all over North Korea. Using picks, axes, shovels, sandbags and wicker baskets they could fill in a road crater or clear a blocked tunnel in a matter of hours. Because the area's rivers were shallow they could be bridged rapidly. If blown railroad bridges or blocked tunnels were too difficult to replace, then the trains were shuttled: one would come down to the break and be unloaded by hand, with the supplies then carried down to another train waiting below. Mountainous North Korea's numerous tunnels were also ideal hideouts for trains which only moved at night, just as mine shafts provided similar cover for troops and labor battalions. The ingenious enemy was also able to make roads and railways that were operable at night appear to be destroyed during daytime. Just before dawn, a crane would lift a bridge section out of place and deposit it in a nearby tunnel. At dusk the section would be replaced. Railway lines were made to appear broken by strewing debris over them or having labor gangs take up sections of track and hide them in tunnels. All day long the Communists busied themselves in the arts of deception: they left hopelessly wrecked trucks or trains in plain view to invite useless aerial attacks, hid trucks in bombed-out buildings or left them parked with their hoods up or their wheels off to simulate immobility; they issued drivers oily rags to be lighted upon attack to simulate a hit; they marked their vehicles with Red Crosses or UN flags or parked them alongside churches, schools, hospitals and all other structures immune to enemy attack, and they even put their locomotives in the centers of trains rather than at the front or back. Dummies were everywhere: dummy tanks, trucks, trains, troops, even dummy UN airmen dangling from parachutes hung in trees and intended to draw curious UN aircraft into AA fire or steel cables drawn across the narrow valleys. By these and hundreds of other equally ingenious ruses and devices, the Communists thwarted the UN's superior firepower, and in so doing they worked another revolution in warfare.

Since the seventeenth century, when the wars of America began, the West had imposed its will upon the world because of its superiority in weapons and discipline. Now the masses of Asia had been disciplined under a creed which, however cruel or criminal, had been able to demonstrate that by simple ingenuity and a lavish expenditure of human life and labor it could neutralize the West's mechanical and scientific superiority. Chinese soldiers and Chinese coolies were both cheap and abundant, and because one fought hard and the other worked hard, because the men who had organized them so mercilessly were also incredibly clever in the arts of cover and camouflage, the war was now grinding down to a stalemate. There would be patrols and skirmishes, of course, and even full-scale offensives launched by one side or the other to make a point at the conference table; but the war in Korea was now as completely stalled and deadlocked as those dreadfully abusive "talks" still buzzing angrily along within the tent at Panmunjom.

The delegates had gotten nowhere on the truce line and were now discussing formation of a Neutral Nations Supervisory Commission which was to oversee the armistice. Admiral Joy proposed Sweden, Switzerland and Norway for membership, while General Nam offered Poland, Czechoslovakia and—with a straight face—the Soviet Union. Unable to believe his ears, Joy objected. He himself might as well have proposed America as a "neutral." Unfortunately, his objections could not be made on the ground that Stalin was the probable instigator of the war and the Soviets the certain supplier of the Communists. Rather, because it was feared that to denounce Russia as an aggressor might wreck the United Nations, Joy had to say that the Soviet Union was unacceptable because she was a neighbor of North Korea. Nam pounced on this transparency with great glee, endlessly baiting Joy with remarks like this: "Why do you give no logical reason for opposing the great, peace-loving U.S.S.R. as a member of the Neutral Nations? You give no reason because you have none. You are unable to deny that the U.S.S.R. is a true neutral in the Korean conflict."[73]

Eventually, the impasse was removed when the UN dropped Norway from its list and the Communists did the same with Russia, thus providing for a four- rather than a six-member Supervisory Commission. In the meantime, the Reds had turned the entire discussion into a propaganda pitch which reached the height of prevarication when Nam Il, seeking to belittle American military strength, coolly announced that in the last war Japan had been defeated by Russia!

Yet some progress was made. On February 17, 1952, the delegates agreed that after the armistice became effective the root questions of withdrawal of foreign forces from Korea and the peaceful settlement of the entire Korean problem should be made at a high-level political conference between the belligerents. Eventually it was agreed to fix a line of demarcation at roughly the point of contact at the time of the armistice. Both sides were to withdraw a distance of two kilometers to create a demilitarized zone between them. The question of repatriation of prisoners, however, was the most explosive one of all. Here, the Americans had enunciated a principle new in warfare: that a prisoner who does not wish to return to his homeland should not be forcibly repatriated. This was proclaimed to meet a situation also new in warfare: the fact that of 132,000 Chinese and North Korean prisoners in UN custody, 60,000 of them did not wish to return home.

The Communists could not or would not believe this. To accept as truth the claim that 45 percent of their captured soldiers did not wish to live under the socialist system for which they had fought would be to accept a propaganda defeat that would shake the entire Communist world. Therefore the Communists insisted that these men be forcibly repatriated—at gunpoint, if necessary—and they made this demand a *sine qua non* of any armistice agreement. In reply, President Truman said: "We will not buy an armistice by turning over human beings for slaughter and slavery."[74] To uphold this principle, he was willing to continue the Korean War, and the conflict was indeed prolonged for another 18 months. During this period the UN suffered an additional 140,000 casualties, of whom 32,000 were Americans, 9,000 of whom were killed. And as the wrangling and the mangling continued in a melancholy counterpoint of Talking War and Shooting War, the world was treated to the political phenomenon of an American nation at arms pausing to elect a President.

Harry Truman could have run for a third term, because the constitutional amendment which now limits an American to two terms in the White House was proposed during his tenure in office and thus did not apply to him. However, Harry Truman declined the honor in March, 1952. At that time, the political winds were blowing strongly against the Democrats. The Republicans made a major issue of the so-called "mess in Washington," a compound of "influence peddlers" who asked a commission of 5 percent for their services in obtaining fat government contracts, the givers and takers of bribes able to "fix" a federal case, and Mr. Truman's own complacency about the dishonesty of some of his cronies. Moreover, Senator McCarthy had been able to convince many Americans that the Democrats were guilty of his spurious charge of "twenty years of treason." Against this background Truman declined to run.

In his place, the Democrats on the third ballot chose Governor Adlai E. Stevenson of Illinois, an urbane and thoughtful man with a reputation for skillful administration. The Republicans, having been handed two fine issues by the Truman scandals and the McCarthy charges of Democratic "sellout" to the Reds, looked around for a candidate. They did not go to "Mr. Republican," Senator Robert A. Taft, a veteran politician of great integrity, political courage and a deep knowledge of government, but rather to General Eisenhower, a soldier whose political inexperience was more than offset by his enormous popularity.

Although Stevenson attracted the support of many intellectuals— the "eggheads," as Eisenhower called them—all his wit, eloquence and high-minded intelligence were of little avail against Eisenhower's wide grin and the sincerity of his promise to "clean up the mess in Washington." Eisenhower also hinted at doing something about the Korean War. When he told one of his audiences, "I will go to Korea," the delirious gathering almost tore the house down. Finally, Stevenson did not give an impression of strength and he had those Truman and McCarthy millstones around his neck. Thus on election night it was clear that America, like the jubilant Republican Party, had decided: "I like Ike." Eisenhower's plurality of 55.2 percent of the total vote was the greatest since 1936, as the war-hating Americans installed their seventh war hero in the White House.

In the meantime, the campaign had had a direct bearing on the Korean War. Eisenhower's decision to seek the Republican nomination compelled him to resign as chief of NATO, and his place as Supreme Allied Commander was taken by General Ridgway. Ridgway was succeeded as Supreme Commander, UN Command, by General Mark Clark, the tall, hawkish soldier who had participated in the North African landings and commanded the Fifth Army in Italy. Clark arrived in Tokyo on May 6, 1952, just as the Communists in Korea opened their propaganda counteroffensive.

The Communists had no intention of accepting the UN principle of "no forced repatriation," and while they prepared their propaganda counterstrokes they moved to seize secret control of the big UN prison camp on the island of Koje 20 miles southwest of Pusan.

For reasons of economy and security, the UN had assembled almost all of its POWs in this one camp. Because troops were badly needed on the battle front there were too few guards, about 25 men to each 5,000-man compound, and these were raw recruits terrified by stories of Oriental cruelty. Because the UN sought to gain face in Asia by a policy of gentleness, neither force nor disciplinary action was to be used against the prisoners. At Koje there was no roll call, no bed check, no inspection of quarters; any Communist soldier who entered Koje passed at once out of the control of his captors.

Actual control was exercised by Senior Colonel Lee Hak Koo, the former chief of staff of the NK 13th Division. Colonel Lee had surrendered on September 21, 1951, at the time of the breakout from Pusan, gently waking sleeping American soldiers to put himself in their power. Whether or not Colonel Lee deliberately planted himself to organize his countrymen then surrendering in droves is not known, but it is a matter of record that he very quickly began to do so. Gradually, the Red prisoners took secret control. They set up kangaroo courts to try fellow prisoners accused of being friendly toward the United Nations. POWs sentenced to die were executed by being beaten to death with tent poles while their comrades sang patriotic songs to drown out their screams.

Next, Colonel Lee began assembling an arsenal. Hammers, pliers and metal shears began to vanish inside the compounds. Oil drums used as garbage cans were converted into primitive forges in which crude knives, swords, hatchets and bayonets were made. Steel arch supports from GI shoes were fashioned into spearheads fitted to the tips of poles. Flails were made of strips of barbed wire cut from compound fences and fitted to wooden handles, and gunpowder was manufactured from wood ashes and crude nitrates extracted from urine.

By the end of 1951 Colonel Lee was virtually the king of Koje. Having terrified his fellow captives with torture and death, he now turned to frightening his guards. Once, as the Americans changed the guard, a terrified POW was dragged into view. "Yankees, see and beware," a Red prisoner taunted. "This is what we do to the traitors who oppose us."[75] With this, they cut off their comrade's tongue and then beat him slowly to death, jeering at the Americans, who were sickened by the sight. This was the last act before the arrival in Koje of an unkempt, slow private named Jeon Moon Il.

A few days later, shaven and sharp, he took command as Brigadier General Pak Sang Hyon, the chief of North Korea's Political Committee and one more of those 36 North Koreans whom Stalin had hand-picked and trained. Having organized Koje to their own satisfaction, the Communists in February of 1952 suddenly agreed to the screening of their prisoners to determine which ones wanted to come home.

However, when UN interrogators appeared at Koje to confront the assembled POWs, hardly a hand was lifted in response to their naïve request for a show of hands among those who refused repatriation. Lee and Pak were triumphant, and the UN now realized that they must resort to individual screening. This, of course, required control of the compounds, and when American soldiers attempted to regain it in a bloodless, predawn coup, the Reds rose in bloody riot. It was put down with American casualties of 1 dead and 39 wounded, against 75 POWs dead and 139 wounded. General Nam Il in Panmunjom now had the propaganda handle he needed. Accusing the UN of "massacring" helpless captives, he declared: "In order to cover up this fact, your side has invented the myth that our captured personnel were not willing to be repatriated."[76] Nevertheless individual screening was begun, continuing as Koje erupted in a series of riots, and ending with the announcement that only 70,000 of 132,000 prisoners wished to be repatriated. The Communists were stunned, and there was small comfort for them when this figure was raised by 5,000 after brutal control of the *anti*-Communist compounds was broken up. Like the enemy, Syngman Rhee had had his own agents at work in Koje. As a result of this count, the Communists angrily repudiated the screening agreement, even denying that it had ever been made. To placate them, Admiral Joy offered to conduct a second screening under the auspices of the International Red Cross. This also was flatly rejected, for by then, May 2, Nam Il was ready to go with another coup.

On May 7, on Nam's orders, the Koje prisoners captured the camp commandant, Brigadier General Francis Dodd. On that date the American general acceded to a request for an interview from the spokesman in Compound 76. It took place not in Dodd's office but outside the compound gate! In other words, the captor came hurrying at his captive's call, and while Dodd stood outside the gate, the Communists simply hauled him inside it. He was held for ransom, until Brigadier General Charles Colson, eager to save his friend, un-wisely signed a pledge to cease "violence and bloodshed" among the POWs. With this, Nam Il took up the cudgels again. "Is it a sign of your good faith," he asked, "to continue to slaughter war prisoners in open repudiation of the pledge of no further maltreatment or murder of war prisoners made by Colson?"[77] Now the propaganda hounds were in full voice, and the Communist delegates attended meetings only to denounce or vilify. Certain that the truce talks were doomed, Admiral Joy resigned and was relieved by Major General William Harrison. In the meantime, General Van Fleet ordered Briga-dier General Haydon Boatner to use infantry to break up the Red nests on Koje.

Boatner built smaller 500-man compounds, and after the Com-munists refused to march to them, he told his men: "Go in and roust them out." Wearing gas masks and hurling tear-gas grenades, moving behind tanks that battered down the compound fences, the Americans went in. They did not shoot until the Reds charged, and then, in a brief fight during which one American was killed and 14 wounded, against 41 dead and 274 wounded prisoners, they restored Koje to UN control. Later, when the Red compounds were searched, the skeletons of 16 prisoners executed by kangaroo courts were unearthed. The Communist press, however, did not mention these murders while redoubling their denunciation of "the American Fascists." Now, it seemed, all attempts to talk at Panmunjom were hopeless. The lan-guage of the Communist delegates grew ever more scurrilous as they attempted to fill the record with distortions and false charges. Chief of these was the "germ warfare hoax" which they temporarily suc-ceeded in foisting on the world.

On February 22, 1952, North Korea accused the United States of having used bacteriological warfare in Korea. Specifically, canisters crammed with infected insects were supposed to have been dropped from planes. With a single great shout, Communism's world-wide propaganda apparatus began to shout: "American atrocity!" Riots and demonstrations against America were staged in the free world as well as Communist countries. America quickly denied the charge and asked the International Red Cross to investigate. When this organization queried the Communists, they received no reply. Instead, the Reds brought out their propaganda masterpiece: the "confessions" of 38 captured American airmen.

Since the first year of the war, interrogators expert in the inhuman craft of wearing down the wills of helpless men had been busy "brainwashing" a selected group of 78 captured American airmen. Forty of the Americans had refused to submit; but 38 of them, after pressures varying from only a few days of threats to five months of solitary confinement in an unheated 3 x 7 hole, had signed "confessions." With these, the Communists returned to the propaganda attack, and their germ-warfare hoax had a long run until it fell apart in the United Nations, the one place where it had been expected to have the most effect.

Here, the U.S. delegate Dr. Charles Mayo described the brainwashing technique which had produced the "confessions":

> It is a method obviously calculated by the Communists to bring a man to the point where a dry crust of bread or a few hours' uninterrupted sleep is a great event in his life. . . . The total picture presented is one of human beings reduced to a status lower than that of animals, filthy, full of lice, festered wounds full of maggots, their sickness regulated to a point just short of death, unshaven, without haircuts or baths for as much as a year, men in rags, exposed to the elements, fed with carefully measured minimum quantities and the lowest quality of food and unsanitary water served often in rusty cans, isolated, faced with squads of trained interrogators, bulldozed, deprived of sleep and browbeaten with mental anguish.[78]

After this indictment, the United States proposed that the United Nations set up a commission to investigate both American charges of Communist atrocities and Communist charges of American germ warfare, and with that the Soviet Union changed the subject.

As the Talking War began to subside, the Shooting War picked up. Under General Mark Clark's orders, the UN Command stepped up its aerial onslaught, and in September-October, 1952, the Communists attempted to storm a series of hills overlooking Van Fleet's battle line about 20 miles north of the parallel. Although the Reds attacked behind surprisingly fierce artillery barrages, they were able to make no headway whatsoever, and the war sank back into a stalemate made more rigid by an iron winter. As it did, the UN delegation at Panmunjom served notice that it was adjourning the armistice talks until the Communists accepted its proposal on prisoner exchange or made a suitable counteroffer. On October 8, 1952, the Talking War came to a close, and it did not resume for six more months.

The United States had no intention of accepting the stalemate in Korea. One of the Truman administration's last acts was to warn Peking, through India, that extension of the war was inevitable unless a solution was reached soon. President Eisenhower did the same, dropping broad hints that he intended "to move decisively without inhibition in our use of weapons, and would no longer be responsible for confining hostilities to the Korean Peninsula."[79] There is no doubt that both Peking and Moscow were informed of the hardening American resolve. To what extent they were influenced by it is not known. Still, the Americans made one last effort to break the diplomatic log jam. On February 22, 1953, General Clark wrote General Peng a routine letter asking if he would be willing to exchange seriously sick and wounded prisoners under the terms of the Geneva Convention. The answer was silence. And then, on March 5, Moscow radio announced: "The heart of the comrade and inspired continuer of Lenin's will, the wise leader and teacher of the Communist Party and the Soviet people—Josef Vissarionovich Stalin—has stopped beating."

It is not known what effect the death of Stalin had upon the Communist world's attitude toward the Korean War. It may have been extensive, if only because many leading Russian Communists, and chief among them Nikita Khrushchev, had come to regard the Korean adventure as a colossal blunder which had succeeded only in uniting the West. Moreover, Mao Tse-tung was now free of a mentor to whom he had once been obliged. Mao was sick of the war. Like the Japanese war lords before him, he had found the American to be surprisingly tenacious. Therefore, even if the death of Stalin meant exactly nothing, it was still a wonderful excuse to pretend that "new days" were at hand. Whatever the reason, on March 28 Premier Kim and General Peng accepted General Clark's forgotten proposal to exchange sick and wounded prisoners. They went even further, proposing a resumption of armistice negotiations. Two days later, Chou En-lai proposed that prisoners who refused to be repatriated be handed over to a neutral state and there be exposed to "explanations" by their native government. His remarks, endorsed on April 10 by Soviet Foreign Minister Molotov, were the most encouraging yet made, and after talks were resumed the exchange of sick and wounded prisoners known as Operation Little Switch was begun on April 20, 1953. During it, the UN returned 6,670 ailing POWs, while receiving 684. Of these 149 were Americans, and from the stories they told, the American armed forces were able to confirm an unhappy suspicion that many of their men in captivity were openly collaborating with their captors.

On April 27 both sides were back at the green-topped table in the tent at Panmunjom, where it became at once apparent that the Communists were retreating from their previously stubborn stand on prisoner repatriation. Then, just as the world's hopes were raised, they were dashed once again by the revolt of Syngman Rhee.

South Korea had never been represented at Panmunjom. When armistice talks began, President Rhee sent an observer, while publicly predicting failure for the truce talks. Actually, this was what he desired. Rhee clearly perceived that a truce would end in the *status quo ante bellum:* a Korea divided North and South. This he could not abide, nor could he endure the presence of Chinese on Korean soil. Rhee realized that North Korea had undergone a change of masters, that the puppet strings in Pyongyang were no longer pulled in Moscow but in Peking. Therefore, on April 24, three days before Operation Little Switch began, his ambassador in Washington notified the American government that Rhee would withdraw the ROK Army from the UN Command if any armistice was signed permitting the CCF to remain on Korean soil.

This alarming announcement brought General Clark flying over to Seoul. Clark tried to explain the impossibility of evicting Red China from Korea by diplomacy when two and a half years of warfare had failed to force her out. Rhee made no commitments. Instead, he opened his own propaganda war against the armistice. He said that he would continue the war on his own if necessary.

Hearing this, the Communists on June 13-14 undertook to deflate some of Rhee's military pride, hurling their strongest attack in two years straight at a sector held by two ROK divisions, driving them back and demonstrating to Rhee that he had not the power to unify Korea on his own. Meanwhile, President Eisenhower had promised Rhee a mutual security pact and vast economic aid if he would not obstruct the truce talks then moving so swiftly toward success. Rhee rejected the offer. He also declined the supreme gesture of an invitation to the White House. On June 17, however, he agreed to receive an emissary from the State Department; but then, on the following day, he delivered his masterstroke against the armistice.

By his orders, ROK guards at anti-Communist prison camps in South Korea threw open the gates and allowed 27,000 North Korean prisoners to go free. It was, as General Clark said ruefully, a "dramatic, well-planned operation." Each prisoner knew where to go, what to take with him, where to get civilian clothing and where to shed and burn his prison uniform. South Korean police were instructed to help the fugitives, and Rhee's radio broadcast an appeal to the South Korean populace to take them into their homes. With this, the 27,000 NKs quite literally vanished. It was simply impossible to recover them, as an embarrassed General Clark attempted to explain to the outraged Communists at Panmunjom.

These infuriated Reds, however, would not have taken an explanation from Lenin himself. On June 20, as Rhee hoped, they broke off the armistice talks. With iron logic they asked: Can you control Rhee? Would an armistice include him? No replies were possible until the furious Americans finally convinced Rhee that however just his cause was, however correct he was in perceiving that ancient China had returned to Korea, his was a hopeless fight. All the world disagreed with him, all the world wanted an armistice, and Rhee at last agreed not to oppose the armistice.

On July 10, 1953, the second anniversary of the beginning of truce talks at the teahouse in Kaesong, the delegates returned to Panmunjom. Three days later, just to be sure that Syngman Rhee understood his weakness, five Communist Chinese armies struck fiercely at three ROK divisions. The onslaught was more furious than the June 13-14 assault, and the CCF was willing to lose 72,000 soldiers, 25,000 of them killed, to make their point.

At ten o'clock on the morning of July 27, 1953, Lieutenant General William Harrison and Lieutenant General Nam Il led silent, grim-faced delegations into a "peace pagoda" made of tar paper and straw mat. Harrison and Nam sat alone at separate tables a few feet apart. Without exchanging a word or a glance, they signed 18 copies of the agreement, nine of which were covered in United Nations blue, nine in Communist red. Ten minutes later, still haughty and silent in frozen hostility, the delegations departed.

Twelve hours later the guns fell silent.

PART X

World-wide Upheaval and the War in Vietnam

1

☆

The cessation of hostilities in Korea brought none of the rejoicing that had celebrated the end of World War II. Instead, the national mood of sullen acquiescence gave way to one of dull relief. The boys were going to come home again, and that was all there was to cheer about.

For the first time in her history, it seemed, America had gotten into a fight she had failed to finish. Matched against the "backward" Communist Chinese, the most powerful nation of all time had settled for a standoff, and this seemed to dishonor the 33,629 Americans who had been killed and the 103,283 who had been wounded in Korea. Perhaps even more humiliating were the disclosures that many captured Americans had collaborated with the enemy. In order to obtain privileged treatment, they had written for Communist publications, participated in Communist plays or oratorical contests which denounced and derided their country, or they had praised the enemy during Communist radio broadcasts or signed "peace" petitions and appeals. All of this, admittedly, had been done under duress. Collaboration had been compelled either by a milder form of the brainwashing technique used on fliers during the germ-warfare hoax, or by denying men necessities, refusing to tell their relatives that they were alive, or by attempting to exploit racial or economic discontent among American prisoners who were Negroes or the sons of the poor. Cleverly seizing upon every difference of class, color, creed or character, the Communists succeeded in inducing many of their American prisoners to betray, hate, injure and even kill one another. Moreover, the Communists so successfully dominated their American captives that few attempted to escape, and none, so far as is known, succeeded.

In defense of these unfortunate men it must be stated that none of them had been warned that the enemy might make war on their minds as well as their bodies. Moreover, many so-called collaborators merely feigned cooperation just to escape hardships; most of those who signed a peace petition or made a broadcast did so only to let their relatives know that they were alive; some elite troops such as the Marines actually refused to collaborate; and the sorry escape record may be in great part explained by the fact that for an American, white or black, to move undetected from the Yalu to the Han would have been about as easy as for a Chinese to pass unnoticed from Spain into Morocco. Yet, for all these mitigations, the truth is that only 5 percent of the captured Americans actively resisted the enemy. This was indeed gall for America to drink down on top of the wormwood of the stalemate, and when it was also learned that 75 U.S. soldiers had agreed to spy for the Communists or act as their agents after repatriation to America, and that 21 more did not want to return at all, one of the most unpopular wars in American history became also the most unpalatable.

It became even less so when it was learned that more than 6,000 American troops and 5,500 other soldiers—most of the latter ROKs —had perished after falling into Communist hands. Half of these 11,500 prisoners were deliberately murdered, while the other half died in captivity. The U.S. Army alone had proof that 1,036 American soldiers were killed in cold blood after their capture, and that 2,370 more died after reaching enemy prison camps. Many of the latter perished because they could not endure the bitter cold on the meager rations which were also their Communist captors' daily diet. Nevertheless, many others died because the Communists were either indifferent to their suffering or had deliberately withheld food or medical care in order to compel their collaboration.

Korea, then, became an unhappy memory. Even Americans who had fought there, perhaps dazzled by MacArthur's glittering half-truth that "in war there is no substitute for victory," felt cheated. So America hastened to demobilize again, "to disengage," as it was called, turning away from this exercise in frustration, this abhorrent anomaly, and thus overlooking the fact that her men had fought bravely and that Korea was in truth a victory.

First, Korea halted Communism's lunge southward and preserved the South Korean nation, which has since become stabilized. Second, it made certain that Japan would not go Communist and showed all Asia to what lengths America would go to help an ally. Third, it transformed North Korea from the status of Russian puppet to Chinese puppet and thus widened the Sino-Soviet rift. Fourth, it proved that collective security was feasible. Fifth, it dealt Communism a propaganda defeat when it became known that if 21 Americans, 1 Briton and 350 South Koreans did prefer to live in Red China, an incredible number of Red soldiers—50,000 of them—refused to return to Communism. Finally, Korea was a turning point in the Cold War.

To regard Korea as decisive, it should be understood that the Cold War, which might better be called the Confrontation, has given rise to an entirely new era of warfare. It is a time of little wars, and each of these may be regarded as a single battle or skirmish in the long, continuing struggle between the forces of Communism and the democracies. In fact, during the two decades 1945-65 there were no fewer than 40 of these little wars. Not all, of course, involved these two contending ideologies. Eight were anticolonial revolutions such as the Algerian revolt against France or the Mau Mau uprising against the British in Kenya; three were power grabs like the Indian seizure of Goa from Portugal; and six more were of the conventional neighbor-vs.-neighbor variety, as in the two Indian-Pakistani conflicts or the Israeli-Arab War. Nevertheless, 23 of these 40 wars did involve Communists and thus were bona fide "little wars" of the Confrontation; that is, they erupted on the rimland or periphery, wherever the free world and Communism were in point of contact. In the main, they have occurred in underdeveloped lands, and this illustrates another salient feature of the new kind of war.

That is the attempt by both Communism and the free world to turn the nationalist revolution each to its own account. Like the Confrontation itself, the nationalist revolution is one of the chief results of World War II. It is not only the revolt of the peoples of Asia and Africa against the British, French, Dutch, Portuguese and Belgian empires; it is also the determination of these nationalist rebels to evict all those white officials, traders, entrepreneurs and professional people who, though they might have brought law and order to the colonies, had certainly come there chiefly to exploit native resources and native labor. Thus British India was fragmented into the inde-

pendent states of India, Pakistan, Ceylon and Burma.* French Indo-
China broke up into Laos, Cambodia and North and South Vietnam.
Portugal was ousted from Goa, its enclave on the Indian coast, and
from Mozambique and Angola in Africa. The Dutch East Indies became the Republic of Indonesia, while its neighbors in the British
colonies of Malaya and Borneo formed the state of Malaysia. In Black
Africa the precipitate departure of Britain, France and Belgium left
a welter of states so shaky-new and unprepared for self-rule that
the region's political life became an alternating rhythm of coup and
countercoup. In North Africa, meanwhile, the old Barbary States of
Morocco, Tunisia and Algeria recovered their independence from
France, while a Pan-Arab movement was launched throughout the
Middle East by the Egyptian ultranationalist, Gamal Abdel Nasser.
Even the head-hunting Papuans of New Guinea turned independence-
minded, the British West Indies were transformed into a clutch of
tiny island republics, and British Cyprus became a cockpit of colliding Greco-Turkish nationalist ambitions. In Latin America, which
freed itself of Spanish dominion early in the last century, nationalism
has been not so much a revolt against an alien oppressor as the
rising discontent of the downtrodden with systems which operate for
the benefit of the favored few.

The American response to nationalism was best expressed in the
Philippines, which received the independence promised them on July
4, 1946. Elsewhere, United States policy has been to encourage nationalist aspirations and to support them in hopes that the new government will reject Communism and become an open society ordered
by democratic institutions. Communism, however, has characteristically sought to subvert and exploit nationalism. Its cadres have infiltrated many indigenous movements for the time-honored Communist
objective of taking them over. Once in control, the Communists
planned to impose some form of "socialism" with an attractive home-
grown name, after which a program of organization-slaying would so
effectively remove all opposition, political or otherwise, that the
clamps of true Communism might be screwed down tight. Where a
nationalist movement resisted the Communists, then the tactics of
disruption and subversion were applied, together with every form

* Burma had been separated from British India in 1937 and made a Crown
colony.

of propagandistic or economic pressure, in an effort to topple the new government.

Thus, because of the nationalist revolution, the American policy of containment, begun in Europe and then translated to Asia during the Korean War, had, in effect, to be broadened to include the emergent states of the world. It had now become containment-plus-prevention. Because Communism never takes its first steps except in concealment and disguise, the rub was to discover when a movement was truly native-led and when it was under Communist control. Nor was it uncommon for little states to play the giants off against each other. A state rebuffed by one camp could quickly find solace in another, as when Nasser, angered by American support of Israel, turned toward the Soviets for assistance. Finally, there were the so-called "nonaligned countries," neutral states, which believed, with varying degrees of sincerity, that they could stay out of the Confrontation. Neutralism, however, seemed only possible on sufferance, as India learned when her "friendly" neighbor in Red China came crashing across her borders.

In this way, then, the nationalist revolution broadened the scope of the Confrontation to make it very nearly global. Naturally, neither Communism nor the United States could be strong everywhere; one power could not expect to subvert the world nor the other to police it. Yet, when either made a move, each had to consider its worldwide effects; e.g., to strengthen one's position in the Far East might be to weaken it in Central America. Crisis, then, became the world norm. Only a few backwaters escaped a terrible, tightening tension, which, with the accelerating development of nuclear weapons, became almost unbearable.

After the atomic bombs dropped in Japan came the so-called hydrogen or "hell bomb," a few of which, triggered by the smaller A-bombs, would be capable of "vaporizing" great centers of population and reducing a country the size of the United States to a state of incredible chaos. Next came the guided missiles, which could be fired from land or sea and were fitted with warheads a hundred times more powerful than the bomb which had eradicated Hiroshima.

Gradually, however, both the Soviet Union and the United States came to realize that intercontinental nuclear warfare made them capable only of mutual destruction. When the United States deployed its fleet of Polaris nuclear submarines, it also became clear that this nation, at least, could destroy any other even after it had itself been devastated by surprise atomic attack. Nuclear warfare, then, was unthinkable. Yet the leaders of both superpowers talked of nothing else. It was a rare Red Army Day in Moscow or House Armed Services hearing that passed without a public and detailed pronouncement of how quickly and efficiently one side could destroy the other. It was believed that after the superpowers had destroyed each other nuclear fallout would finish off the rest of the world. As crisis piled upon crisis along the rimland of the Confrontation, the nerves of most of mankind were drawn close to the snapping point.

Actually, both giants were coming to realize that there is simply no defense against nuclear weapons. Because of this, it is likely that such weapons may never be used unless the survival of the nation possessing them is at stake; and there, of course, is the third and final feature of the Confrontation. In the age of atomic plenty, war has once again become limited, not only as to objectives but as to means. The ultimate weapon is taboo, and only limited weapons are practical.

It is against this background of the Confrontation with its characteristics of little, limited wars, the nationalist revolution and, *for the first time,* a tacit agreement to use limited weapons that the importance of the Korean War must be considered. In fact, it was in Korea that America not only learned that nuclear weapons were impractical tactically, but also by refraining from using them against Red China made it plain that she considered them "too ultimate" to serve any practical political or social end. Perhaps more important, by holding her hand America indicated that she feared Russian retaliation. In Korea, then, the nuclear stalemate began. In Korea, also, were made certain tacit agreements suggesting that both sides were willing to limit escalation of the war. When General MacArthur complained that the American decision not to bomb north of the Yalu gave the Red Chinese a "privileged sanctuary" in Manchuria, he overlooked the fact that by refraining from air attack on his bases in Japan and his carriers offshore the enemy had done the same for him. Obviously, even though the combatants were not in direct communication with each other, they had signaled by their actions that there was a line that they would not cross. Tacit agreement, then, has become another feature of the Confrontation.

But far more important than all these considerations, the Korean War may have been the turning point of the struggle. If it is accepted that this largest of the little wars so far was but one of a series of "battles" to be fought until the long convulsion is over, then Korea can be compared to the First Battle of the Marne in World War I or Guadalcanal in the Pacific War. Neither engagement ended either war, of course, but after both had been fought the war was never the same. First Marne saved France and denied quick victory to the Kaiser. Guadalcanal marked the high-water mark of Japanese aggression and doomed Japan's dream of a limited war ending in successful negotiation. It makes no difference that after First Marne and Guadalcanal the wars continued for four and three years, respectively; what matters is that after them the wars had been changed in mood, direction and tactics, and that a certain outcome altering the course of world events had been shaped.

This is true of Korea. In Korea were all the characteristics of the Confrontation. In Korea there was an aspiring nationalism befriended in the South by America and exploited in the North by Stalinist Russia. In Korea, however, the Communists did not apply the piecemeal tactics of disruption and subversion. Rather, it was believed that the South was so weak, and America so fainthearted, that outright, old-fashioned invasion would do the job more quickly. This failed, and after it did fail, Communism fell back on the more amenable tactic of the "war of national liberation."

Communists classify war into three types: general, limited and national liberation. World War II had been a successful general war in which Hitler was defeated and the Iron Curtain rung down across Europe. Korea had been an unsuccessful limited war, and Greece and Turkey had been unsuccessful "wars of national liberation," to use typically misleading Communist terminology. A better Communist phrase, however, is revolutionary guerrilla warfare.

Guerrilla warfare, of course, is not new. It may be as old as warfare itself. It is the way in which the weak may defeat the strong, wearing down his strength and his discipline with harassment, sabotage, sudden raids and the withholding or destruction of food ,and supplies. Guerrilla warfare may be patriotic, as when an aroused Russian populace scourged Napoleon's Grande Armée on the retreat from Moscow; or it can be revolutionary, as when the British regulars under Cornwallis felt the wrath of the wraithlike men of Francis Marion. True revolutionary guerrilla warfare depends upon the sympathy of the people in whose midst it occurs, and it has been the military genius of the Chinese Communists to understand this truth.

In a phrase usually attributed to Mao Tse-tung, General Chu Teh said: "The guerrilla is the fish, the peasant is the water in which he swims."[1] Bring the water to the right temperature, that is, warm and friendly, and the fish flourish. The people give the guerrilla food, sanctuary, recruits and intelligence. Enemy forces moving against him usually strike at thin air. If the guerrillas are trapped, they hide their guns and vanish among the people. To search out and destroy guerrillas among a friendly people, and in the dense uninhabited jungle in the lands where most national wars of liberation have taken place, has been compared to "finding tears in a bucket of water."[2]

The people, then, are the true objective in a war of national liberation. Whichever side wins their support will win the war. Because of this, this new kind of war is more political than military. Communist guerrillas actually are trained more in political agitation and propaganda (agitprop) than in shooting, for their most important job is to win over the people. Mao has thus reversed Clausewitz's famous dictum that war is the continuation of policy by other means. Clausewitz said this because he considered peace, during which diplomacy serves foreign policy, to be the normal condition—or at least more common than war. Mao, however, believes that war is the norm. His most famous declaration, "Political power grows out of the barrel of a gun," was followed by the declaration: "The seizure of power by armed force, the settlement of the issue by war is the central task and the highest form of revolution. This Marxist-Leninist principle holds good universally, for China and for all other countries."[3] To Mao, then, peace is only the extension of policy by other means. Peace is to be used to gain strength while the enemy relaxes and grows soft. A truce serves the same purpose, and "negotiation," as Korea so decisively demonstrated, is only the device by which "the enemy can be brought to the conference table and there defeated."[4]

With this strategy and these tactics, Mao Tse-tung hoped to make the world Communist. He advocated mobilizing, organizing and arming the peoples of Asia, Africa and Latin America to prove his famous jeer that the Americans and their allies were "paper tigers."

Thus regimented, these peoples would fight Mao's "protracted war," that is, wear down the democracies' will to fight while their own strength was growing. They would control the countryside and from it encircle and besiege the cities. As Lin Piao explained:

The countryside, and the countryside alone, can provide the revolutionary bases from which the revolutionaries can go forward to final victory. Taking the entire globe, if North America and western Europe can be called "the cities of the world," then Asia, Africa and Latin America constitute "the rural areas of the world.' . . . In a sense the contemporary world revolution also presents a picture of the encirclement of "cities" by the "rural areas." In the final analysis the whole cause of world revolution hinges on the revolutionary struggle of the Asian, African and Latin American people who make up the overwhelming majority of the world's population.[5]

Lin's statement was made in September, 1965, long after the Korean War was over, and just as it seemed that the tactic which was to win the world for Communism—the war of national liberation—was about to succeed in Vietnam.

2

☆

The "little war" in Vietnam is a successor conflict to the War in Indo-China, begun in 1946 when French attempts to reclaim their "inheritance" in Southeast Asia conflicted with the nationalist ambitions of the Vietnamese.

French Indo-China comprised roughly the eastern third of the resource-rich Southeast Asian peninsula. Taken by the French in the latter half of the last century, it was divided into Cambodia, Laos and what is now generally called Vietnam. Running for roughly 1,500 miles down the eastern coast of Southeast Asia, Vietnam is a long, narrow land of coastal lowlands, swampy river deltas, table-top plateaus and mountainous jungle. Its chief areas are the Red River Delta in the north (Tonkin) centered around Hanoi and its port of Haiphong, and the Mekong River Delta in the south (Cochin) with its city of Saigon. Between them lies the mountainous center (Annam), which has been compared to a carrying pole supporting the two "rice baskets" of the deltas at either end. After the French arrived in Indo-China they cut up Vietnam into three colonial areas: Tonkin, Annam and Cochin.

This trifurcation seemed only yet another division of a people already split by a welter of conflicting tribal, religious and regional loyalties. Yet the Vietnamese people still cherished a strong yearning for national independence while holding onto a sense of national history. They were proud of the fact that they had successfully resisted assimilation by China, their powerful and ever-encroaching neighbor to the north. China may have been the Vietnam suzerain for a thousand years, and the Vietnamese may have accepted Chinese culture practically *in toto,* yet the Vietnamese also retained their own national language while persisting in their determination to wear no other nation's collar.

This spirit remained alive under French domination. It had to be clandestine, of course, for the French could be cruel masters, and it stayed underground when the Japanese in World War II evicted the French and attempted to make Indo-China part of their Greater East Asia Co-Prosperity Sphere. During the war American policy on Indo-China was inconsistent. At one point, President Roosevelt succeeded in persuading Stalin and Chiang Kai-shek to approve a postwar trusteeship for Indo-China with eventual independence for Vietnam. Actually, it is doubtful that Chiang really was willing to surrender China's ancient irredentist claim to the "lost territories" in Vietnam, as well as portions of contemporary Russia, India and Burma. Stalin's sincerity may be judged from his performance elsewhere and the fact that Communist cadres were already at work in Vietnam under the leadership of an old-line Marxist-Leninist named Ho Chi Minh.

A man of many names and much mystery, of wide travel and a long trail of alliances and betrayals, Ho Chi Minh ("He Who Shines") was perhaps the apotheosis of the professional Communist revolutionary. Born Nguyen Van Thanh, the son of a poor prefect in Annam, Ho grew up among ardent revolutionaries, and although he received a French education and entered the French civil service, his obvious anti-French nationalism eventually cost him his position. In 1911, at the age of 21, he went to sea as a cabin boy. Thereafter he roamed the world, passing the time in port perfecting his linguistic skills, spending the long hours at sea devouring the seminal literature of mankind. In the end, as he was to say later: "I studied and chose Marx."[6] Having by 1922 seen most of the cities of Europe, as well as some of those in America, Ho made his pilgrimage to the Communist mecca at Moscow. There, as in Europe, this slight, soft-spoken, wispy-bearded Asiatic impressed everyone with a nationalist spirit that seemed unique within the internationalism of that time and place. There Ho stayed to complete his revolutionary training, after which he returned to Asia to found, among other groups, Indo-China's first Communist organization. For the next two decades Ho's life was that of a professional Comintern agent, commuting between Moscow and the Far East, dodging the "capitalist" police, spending a year in a British prison in Hong Kong, passing into the obscurity of an eight-year interregnum, and finally turning up in South China in 1941.

Shortly afterward, he was over the border into Indo-China, hunted by both the Vichy police and Japanese occupation forces. He was still inflamed with his passion for a free Vietnam, and still thinking of "freedom" in Communist terms, i.e., to replace the whip of the imperialist with the goad of the commissar. Like all successful Communists, he was tediously dogmatic and doctrinaire in all that he said, and yet immensely pragmatic and practical in all that he did. Thus, having received funds from the anti-Communist Nationalist Chinese to carry on espionage and sabotage against the Japanese in Indo-China, he actually used the money to help build his own organization. This was the Vietminh, which gained its name from a contraction of the Vietnamese words for "The League for the Independence of Vietnam."

By no means all of the groups and sects enrolled under the Vietminh banner were Communist ones. Ho, a master organizer, was especially adept at the Communist technique of gathering together all movements which, however disparate, shared the paramount objective of national independence, and then, after inviting these sheep into the fold, carefully seducing or killing off their shepherds. The rank and file of these groups might still cling to the religious, social or ethnic cause which undergirded their nationalism, but they took orders from leaders who were now either Communists or fellow travelers. Thus an organization such as the Vietminh was like a monster which fattens on its friends. Once all are "assimilated," that is, devoured and digested, the monster turns Red, as the Vietminh did openly in 1949.

One friendship which Ho sought assiduously was that of the Americans. In 1944 and 1945 he repeatedly asked Americans stationed in China for arms in exchange for sabotage against the Japanese, intelligence and continued help in rescuing Allied pilots downed in Indo-China. More often than not he was refused, either because FDR had by then adopted a "hands-off" policy toward Indo-China, or because the official on the spot regarded him as a hard-core Communist. Sometimes Ho did receive American arms, because he was, after all, fighting the same foe. But whenever he proposed to be America's man if America, so sincerely determined to grant independence to the Philippines, would persuade the French to do the same in Indo-China, the Americans weren't listening. FDR had notified the State Department that "we should do nothing in regard to resistance groups in Indo-China."[7]

There are some who maintain that here, possibly, was America's first and major mistake in Vietnam. Instead of coming to the side of French colonialism after the war was over, the United States might have earned the gratitude of all Asia had it supported Ho Chi Minh in his struggle to bring independence to Indo-China. Ho had not only made himself a symbol of anticolonialism throughout the region; he was also a genuine and masterful leader. Moreover, like all loyal Vietnamese, he feared and distrusted China—Nationalist, Communist or otherwise—and his allegiance to faraway Moscow was tenuous. Ho Chi Minh, then, the argument goes, was ready to work for the democracies.

Attractive as this argument sounds, it is nevertheless the sort of simplification that ignores the facts of history and human nature. At that time, Japanese-occupied Indo-China was but a backwash of the Pacific War, and the Free French were then allies of considerably more stature than the unknown and seemingly outlandish Vietminh. Second, to suppose that a man with a Communist pedigree as long as Ho Chi Minh's was somehow going to become a good capitalist is to indulge in the sort of wishful thinking that made "agrarian reformers" of Mao Tse-tung and Lin Piao. Third, the mood of the American people immediately after World War II would have permitted no such embroilment in a place of which they had not heard and for which they did not care. In 1945 the Truman Doctrine and the policy of containment were two long years away, Russia was still an ally and the Cold War was a term yet to be coined.

So Ho Chi Minh was rejected by America, and as the war ended and the French returned to Indo-China with the help of British and French occupation troops, he proclaimed the independent Republic of Vietnam with himself as President and his headquarters in Hanoi. In March, 1946, eager to speed the exit of profiteering Chinese occupation forces and the entry of their own troops, the French recognized Ho's republic as a free government within the framework of the Indo-Chinese Federation and the French Union.

Both these organizations were devices through which the French hoped to exercise power over their colonies. The Federation was special for Indo-China, and the French Union would control France's world-wide possessions. Both were insincere. Unlike the British Commonwealth, the French Union did not envision drawing genuinely new and native governments into an association with France. This was probably because the French, crushed so early in the war with Germany, did not really understand how the old colonial order had been overturned. Hurt in their pride, they thought that French *grandeur* might be restored by recovering their old empire. And at that time, Charles de Gaulle, the one man who could teach France that *grandeur* was not to be obtained by clinging to colonies but rather by shedding them, had gone into voluntary political exile. Nevertheless, France tried to enmesh Ho's new government in these organizations, and she also repudiated her promise to hold a referendum in the south. Instead, she created a new puppet regime in what was then Cochin and what is now, with roughly half of Annam in the center, known as South Vietnam. With this act it may be said that France set the stage for the war in Indo-China.

It did not begin, however, until December, 1946, when French customs guards at the port of Haiphong near Hanoi impounded a Chinese junk allegedly carrying illegal arms for the Vietminh. With this, the Vietminh erected roadblocks in the city. A French bulldozer crew attempting to remove a roadblock was attacked, whereupon the French shelled the city and the Vietminh responded with terrorism in Hanoi. On December 19, 1946, the Vietminh attacked French installations throughout Indo-China, and as Ho's government fled Hanoi into the jungle, the war in Indo-China began.

The year 1949 is memorable in the history of Asia. In that year Mao Tse-tung's armies defeated those of Chiang Kai-shek and China became a Communist country; at the same time the Communist takeover of the Vietminh across the border became complete and undisguised. The two events, naturally enough, were interrelated. The hard fact that the giant in the north was now a Communist was certainly enough to convince any wavering Vietminh official of the direction in which his political future lay. Very soon, the Vietminh began to receive Communist Chinese aid and were training troops at two camps in southern China.

In 1949, also, the French, shaken by the strength of the Vietminh resistance, not only in the north but in the south as well, attempted to split Ho's movement by setting up the puppet emperor, Bao Dai, as chief of a Vietnamese state, which, with Laos and Cambodia, was to become associated with the French Union. In February, 1950, both Britain and America recognized the Associated States of Laos, Cambodia and Vietnam. Although Britain was displeased with the failure to grant Vietnam real independence, America seemed content.

Here was the real American mistake. Instead of pressing the French to grant true freedom and to announce publicly that it would withdraw its troops once this had been obtained, the United States went along with the puppet regime. Because of this, the defeat of French colonialism was only made that much more certain, and the Communists were able to tar America with the same colonial brush with which they blackened France. Having repented of her single, ill-starred imperialist venture in the Philippines, having made honest and true recompense for it, America was nonetheless presented to Asia as the newest and most vicious of the "imperialists." As American aid to France, begun in that same year of 1950, became larger and larger, the invective poured on her by Communist propaganda became more and more vituperative. Much of it stuck, and some still sticks, if only because it is natural for the poor to delight in the discomfiture of the rich, no matter how palpably false the charges against them may be.

American failure here, of course, was in part due to American reluctance to press the harassed French too hard, and in part to a hope that the granting of independence was to be a continuing, step-by-step process. But Bao Dai's government was a true puppet, and by the time the Americans became unhappily aware of this, the Korean

War had broken out and America became preoccupied elsewhere. By then, also, the French were losing the war against the Vietminh.

Ho Chi Minh had not taken the field at the head of his troops. Rather, he had turned military command of the Vietminh over to Vo Nguyen Giap, a lawyer and former teacher who was to become a brilliant general. Under Giap, the Vietminh successfully hurdled the critical "first stage" of revolutionary guerrilla warfare. This is when the guerrilla is on the defensive. His only goal is survival—and winning the people. He hides more than he fights, avoiding pitched battles, hitting the enemy only in ambush, raiding him for guns and equipment—chipping away at him piecemeal while his own strength grows. This is what Giap did against the French, who, with excellent officers and a splendid soldiery, nevertheless played directly into Giap's hands. They strung their outposts out along the road and from these attempted to expand their power over the countryside. But the countryside belonged to the guerrillas, who were harmless peasants by day and armed terrorists by night.

Moreover, such strategy, later to be called the "oil slick" or "ink blot" theory, requires the deployment of as many as a million men so that the areas to be "pacified" may be occupied and held while this process is continuing. To clear the enemy from villages by day and then to return to base by night was only to invite the enemy to return to reimpose his rule and to avenge himself on the villagers who had either given him away or collaborated with the French. Yet there were never more than 190,000 troops in the French Union forces in Vietnam. For one thing, French draftees were prevented by law from serving outside metropolitan France, so that the French had to rely on regulars, volunteers and the French Foreign Legion. Pacification also requires the partnership of a vigorous, popular native army, and the South Vietnamese Army under the French, which never exceeded 150,000 men, was not especially aggressive and was officered in the main by Frenchmen. Moreover, the France–Bao Dai coalition was simply not popular. Bao Dai had been known to be a playboy emperor, and now it was believed he was a playboy puppet. The French were obviously more concerned about their own political and economic power than about Vietnamese independence, and because the Japanese had so publicly humiliated French officials during their occupation, it was now realized that the white man's feet were also made of flesh. Therefore General Giap guided his Vietminh forces successfully through the perilous first stage of the war.

The second stage may properly be called true guerrilla warfare. It is all mobility, a war of movement, and Mao has described it this way:

> . . . select the tactic of seeming to come from the east and attacking from the west; avoid the solid, attack the hollow; attack; withdraw; deliver a lightning blow, seek a lightning decision. When guerrillas engage a stronger enemy, they withdraw when he advances; harass him when he stops; strike him when he is weary; pursue him when he withdraws. In guerrilla strategy, the enemy's rear, flanks, and other vulnerable spots are his vital points, and there he must be harassed, attacked, dispersed, exhausted and annihilated.[8]

Gradually, even imperceptibly, the second stage or war of movement evolves into the third stage: conventional warfare. It is difficult to tell when this stage is reached, because it is, after all, only that point at which the guerrillas consider themselves strong enough to engage the enemy in pitched battle. General Giap thought this occurred in the fall of 1950, when he gathered 40 Vietminh battalions, armed them with mortars and artillery, and hurled them against a string of French forts on the Chinese border. Although the result was a stunning defeat for the French, Giap actually was unable to follow up this victory with the conquest of the Red River Delta, as he had planned. Instead, he was forced to fall back on Stage Two until, in December, 1953, he was ready to mount his critical offensive against the French fortified camp at Dienbienphu.

At Dienbienphu, directly west of Hanoi on the Laos border, were about 16,000 French troops. Against them Giap marshaled about 38,000 to 40,000. As numbers go, then, the fight preparing at Dienbienphu would not seem a great one. Psychologically, however, it was to be decisive.

This was because the French nation was wearying of the war and the French government was passing through one political crisis after another. Moreover, members of the French Communist and Socialist parties, some of whom had been Ho Chi Minh's teachers in 1922, organized an effective propaganda campaign against "that colonial, imperialistic war." Troops embarking for the front were jeered, families with a proud tradition of service were publicly insulted, and returning casualties were mocked as fools who deserved their wounds. Thus the men fighting in Indo-China felt deluded or betrayed, and the nation behind them was so unsteady and divided that any signal defeat might compel the French to cry for peace.

Against this background, Giap prepared his *coup de grâce*. First, Dienbienphu was chosen because it was a "sitting duck." The fortress lay in a valley floor surrounded by wooded hills giving the Vietminh both cover and complete observation of their enemy. Land routes in and out consisted of a few rough mountain trails. Far from the main French base in the Red River Delta, Dienbienphu could be supplied only by a 400-mile aerial round trip. Moreover, its single airfield was threatened by Vietminh artillery—by then numerous and various— and its own artillery was poorly sited.

The French, of course, did not expect a major blow to fall against this distant outpost. They did not simply because Giap had deliberately prepared a series of diversionary actions before hitting hard at Dienbienphu. In January, 1954, he staged attacks in northwestern and middle Laos. Then came actions in the western highlands of central Vietnam, in upper Laos and in the Red River Delta. All of these had the effect of forcing the French to disperse their troops, and to draw them away from the true objective at Dienbienphu. Wherever the Vietminh attacked, they remained only until the French poured in reinforcements, after which they departed and left only a token force behind to keep the French occupied. Thus it may be said that before a shot was fired at Dienbienphu the French were defeated. They had felt compelled to defend everywhere that the Vietminh attacked. They believed they could not afford to lose any more territory and feared the effect that any defeat in open battle by the "inferior" Vietminh might have in Paris and on the world. So they allowed the Vietminh to isolate Dienbienphu, a fortress so firmly anchored in the "water" of a hostile peasantry that the French were never able to supply it by land.

Using his artillery well while his sturdy guerrillas ringed the enemy camp in a network of trenches, Giap steadily pressed the French toward disaster. Alarmed, President Eisenhower considered direct intervention on the side of the French. Some of the military advisers urged him to step in, fearing that a Vietminh victory would encourage Mao Tse-tung to probe elsewhere. Militarily, they were probably right. Politically, they were wrong. To have helped French colonialism to crush a nationalist uprising, however Communist-controlled, would not have improved the American image in Asia. There were other considerations, however, among them the fact that the country was again cutting back military spending and the popular revulsion to the Korean War.

Extricated from "the mess in Korea" a short eight months previously, America simply would not have accepted intervention in another Asian war. According to General Ridgway, then Army Chief of Staff, to intervene directly in Vietnam would require about eight divisions of foot troops, or about as much as the maximum deployment in Korea. To President Eisenhower this was out of the question. What, then, of nuclear weapons? The answer again was that, tactically, they were impractical. Strategically, they could do nothing more than invite Russian retaliation, and politically the use of them would convince Asia that the United States was truly a racist monster. Once again the ultimate weapons were found to be "too ultimate."

So American aid, which had grown from a trickle to a torrent, was continued—but there was no direct intervention. Nor could all those American guns and gadgets do much to deter those fervent Vietminh peasant soldiers fighting their own kind of war on their own terrain. Now French diplomacy tried to save what French arms could not protect. A conference was called in Geneva to settle the problems of both Korea and Indo-China. It was attended by the foreign ministers of the powers involved—Russia and China as well as the United States, France and Britain—and even as it was convened, the Vietminh on May 7, 1954, swept victoriously over the last French barricades at Dienbienphu.

With that shock, yet another French government fell, to be replaced by one headed by Premier Pierre Mendès-France, who had publicly announced his intention to obtain a cease-fire within one month or resign. In the meantime, it had become plain at Geneva that nothing could be done about Korea. As was expected, neither side could agree on any means of unifying that divided peninsula, and so it remains divided and the military stalemate continues. A 2½-mile Demilitarized Zone still separates the hostile nations of North and South Korea, and Americans and ROKs confront North Koreans and Communist Chinese. Except that South Korea now occupies a better defensive position, nothing has been changed.

Indo-China was changed, however. Laos and Cambodia were already independent states, and now Vietnam was divided at the 17th parallel into a Communist-controlled state of North Vietnam with a (1962) population of 16 million and a non-Communist South Vietnam with a (1965) population of 16 million. As the French gradually withdrew from South Vietnam, the American influence there grew stronger. American policy was now based on a fear that if South Vietnam were to fall to Communism, the helpless neighboring states of Laos and Cambodia and perhaps all those of Southeast Asia would thereafter topple "like dominoes."

The line of the Cold War Confrontation, drawn through Germany and Berlin in Europe, drawn again at the 38th parallel in Korea, had been drawn once more at the 17th parallel in Vietnam.

3

☆

While the Geneva talks were in progress, Bao Dai remained the chief of state of South Vietnam and also its Prime Minister. However, on July 7, 1954, Ngo Dinh Diem took charge of the government.

Diem,* who had been living in the United States in self-imposed exile, was the son of an ancient mandarin family of scholar-courtiers. He had once studied for the Catholic priesthood. Abandoning this vocation (although he remained devoutly religious and seems to have made a vow of chastity), Diem was educated by the French and trained for public office in Vietnam. In 1933 Diem broke with the French over their refusal to adopt his proposed educational and financial reforms. For the next decade he remained out of politics, reading, gardening or sometimes journeying to Saigon to talk nationalism or possible revolution with intellectual friends. After the Japa-

* This is actually Ngo Dinh Diem's "first name." However, because Vietnam, like Korea, has a limited number of family names, Westerners have adopted the practice of using a man's given name to distinguish him among the veritable legions of Ngos and Nguyens, Trans and Vans.

nese came to Vietnam, Diem refused to serve them as a puppet premier. He also refused to work with Ho Chi Minh in 1946, chiefly because Ho had ordered the murder of his brother and because Ho wanted to lead Vietnam into the Communist camp. Still committed to a truly independent Vietnam, he twice refused to become Bao Dai's Premier because the French would not accede to his demand that the Vietnamese be allowed to conduct the anti-Vietminh war themselves. On the third offer, which promised him full political power, he consented.

In July of 1954 this plump, passionate, self-absorbed and aristocratic man took charge of a broken country. Almost at once he repudiated the agreements being made in Geneva, thereby laying the legal groundwork for his subsequent refusal to abide by them. Under the Geneva Accords, elections were to be held throughout Vietnam. Diem, of course, refused to hold them, correctly judging that they would be won by Hanoi. Ho was popular, and the Vietminh had been a winner, Bao Dai was discredited, and Diem himself, although admired in some quarters for his incorruptibilty, had been away from the country too long. American left-wingers and doctrinaire liberals have since made much of this "betrayal" of Ho. Having defended Kim Il Sung when he refused to permit UN-sponsored elections in North Korea, they now attacked Ngo Dinh Diem for having rejected elections provided by international agreement to which his government had not been a party.

The United States also declined to sign the Geneva Accords, merely taking note of them while declaring that it would not disturb them by the use or threat of force, but that it would regard any renewal of fighting as a danger to international peace and security. With this, America implied that she would defend South Vietnam against aggression, and drew the containment line in Southeast Asia. Shortly afterward, the United States set up the Southeast Asia Treaty Organization (SEATO), whose members—Britain, France, Pakistan, the Philippines, Thailand, New Zealand, Australia and the United States—promised to help each other against outside aggression.

SEATO was not to be as successful as NATO, simply because Britain, France and Pakistan seemed to resent being dragooned into membership. They would do very little to help South Vietnam against the aggression that was to come. In the meantime, Ngo Dinh Diem struggled to shore up a shaky government. Without a real political base to support him, he was like a man attempting to spring out of a bog. His problems were as various and as interconnected as South Vietnam's numerous sects, movements and conflicting allegiances and loyalties. Not the least of them was the fact that Bao Dai, as chief of state, was still Diem's superior and still, for instance, making appointments; that the very legality of Diem's government was under heavy Communist attack throughout the world; and that, as the French officials departed, Diem had few Vietnamese with the necessary skills to replace them. Moreover, communications were in collapse, the Vietminh having effectively sabotaged them, the South Vietnamese soldiery was deserting by the thousands, and the countryside was in such a state of anarchy that Diem's authority hardly extended beyond the precincts of Saigon.

Eventually, chaos was compounded when 860,000 Northerners came streaming south. Most of them were from the 2,000,000 Northern Catholics who had been the first to feel the clamp of Ho's Communism, and at least another 400,000 would have followed them had they not been prevented. Although this huge influx of people who knew Communist persecution was to sow South Vietnam with the seeds of resistance to it, it was also to present a drastically unsettled country with a major problem of refugee resettlement. Finally, only 30,000 to 100,000 Vietminh and their sympathizers took the opportunity to go north. Many others stayed behind, most of them Communist cadres under orders to bury their arms and to return to their villages, where they were to marry and mingle, working, meanwhile, for the allegiance of the people in the "struggle" against Diem. These underground Vietminh, always directed and organized by Ho, were to emerge later as the "indigenous" Vietcong.

These, in brief, were the problems of Ngo Dinh Diem, and because it is now clear that he was an administrator and not a politician able to persuade rival factions and persons to work together, it is obvious that they were insurmountable. Of course, Diem did begin to receive substantial American aid, but he was unable to make effective use of it. In the meantime, the American people, under pressures unprecedented in history, began to look everywhere else in the world but toward Saigon.

In January, 1954, when it became apparent that the French were losing in Indo-China, Secretary of State John Foster Dulles issued a statement warning that America possessed "a great capacity to retaliate, instantly, by means and at places of our own choosing." The warning, made two months before the climactic battle at Dienbienphu was begun, was intended for Red China, to forestall her direct intervention on the side of the Vietminh. As such, it was neither realistic nor relevant. Unfortunately, the word "capacity" was ignored and the unhappy and unintended policy of "Massive Retaliation" was born.

This infelicitous phrase restored the American public's faith in The Bomb. The Korean War came to be regarded as an anomaly, an aberration, the kind of conventional war that The Bomb was supposed to have made obsolete. In fact, said the superpatriots and simplicists, ignoring both the nature of nuclear warfare and the fact that Russia had possessed her own bomb since 1949, Korea could have been stopped before it really started if America had "had the guts" to drop The Bomb. Thus the slogan "No More Koreas" meant that next time The Bomb would be used. American military strategy was again based upon the power of this single weapon, which, both Korea and Indo-China had made plain, was of no use whatever in limited war.

The Bomb was also attractive to its proponents because it was relatively cheap to manufacture in large quantities. The idea was to "substitute machines for men," or to get "more bang for the buck." American technocracy would offset the mass armies of Asia, it was maintained, once again discounting the truth that had emerged from Korea—that the ruthlessly regimented masses of Asia could, by ingenuity and a brutally indifferent expenditure of life and labor, make mockery of western gadgetry. The Vietminh's peasant army had done the same to the road-bound, technocratic French. Nevertheless, the fixation on The Bomb and "Massive Retaliation" continued, so that each time crisis flared on the Cold War periphery, Americans caught their breath and asked themselves if this was the spark that would detonate World War III.

Thus the fifties became a time when thoughtful men could not pick up the morning newspaper without a feeling of trepidation. It was a time when any loud noise in the night might signal to some Americans that the end of the world was at hand. New homes were sometimes constructed with air-raid shelters, mountains were hollowed out as depositories for valuable records, and as the practice alerts of the air-raid sirens disturbed the tranquillity of every American city and hamlet at precisely twelve o'clock every Saturday morning, a newly created Civil Defense Corps stuffed building basements with huge barrels of water and other "survival gear," while conducting air-raid drills which occasionally caused even the man in the White House to go whirling away by helicopter to some presidential hideout.

The first of the post-Korean crises began in September of 1954 when the Communist Chinese began to bombard the Nationalist Chinese offshore islands of Quemoy and Matsu. The shelling continued throughout early 1955, and as it appeared that Mao was preparing to invade Formosa itself, the United States made it plain that it would defend Chiang and his island strongholds. With that, Mao called off the cannonade, although a similar eruption occurred three years later.

In between, while American and Communist war planes shot each other down in "incidents" around the rimland, Europe and the Middle East exploded again. On June 28, 1956, workers in Poznan, Poland, rose up against their Communist masters, and a few days later uprisings began in East Germany. Both outbursts were brutally crushed by the Russians, and then, on October 23, a widespread revolution against Red rule erupted in Hungary. This, too, was put down with great bloodshed, the Russians using tanks, aircraft and artillery to quell Central Europe's first and most serious attempt to throw off the Communist yoke. As they did, they incurred the loathing of the non-Communist world; and yet, before they were through, that revulsion had in part shifted elsewhere.

This was because on October 29, 1956, while the Hungarian uprising was in full swing, Israel, acting in conjunction with Britain and France, invaded Egypt's Sinai Peninsula as a preliminary to an Anglo-French attempt to seize the Suez Canal. Here was a crisis which was a direct consequence of the postwar spirit of nationalism. For some time, Colonel Nasser of Egypt had been maneuvering to put himself at the head of a Pan-Arab movement which, among other things, aimed at eventually destroying Israel. One of Nasser's first moves was to bar Israeli ships from the Suez Canal.

The canal itself had been built under the auspices of European nations which were shareowners in the proprietary Compagnie Universelle. By 1950 Britain was the company's largest shareholder, and, by treaty with Egypt, maintained a small military base in the canal's neutral zone. The company's record had been impeccable; it had studiously respected Egyptian sovereignty and its board of directors included five Egyptians. Its importance to world trade as a link between East and West may be judged from the fact that by the time of Nasser's action nearly 15,000 ships had passed through it in one year. By then the British had withdrawn, and Nasser, in violation of a convention holding the canal open to the ships of all nations, and in the face of a United Nations order to end his ban on Israeli ships, still denied the Suez to the Israelis.

At this point, Secretary Dulles sought to bring Nasser into line by offering to help him build the immense Aswan Dam which was to impound the waters of the Nile and irrigate millions of barren acres. Nasser seemed agreeable. Actually, he was dickering with Moscow for a better deal, and negotiating with Communist Czechoslovakia to buy arms. Learning of this, Dulles on July 19, 1956, abruptly canceled his own Aswan Dam proposal. Enraged, Nasser retaliated by seizing the Suez.

Alarmed by this threat to their economic and national security, apparently mistaking the twentieth century for the nineteenth, Britain and France urged Israel into the Sinai and then attacked the Suez itself in an old-fashioned, imperialist power play. With this, they shook the entire Western Alliance. For one thing, they had not informed America in advance of their decision, for another they made their move the day before the American presidential election, and for a third they effectively lifted Soviet Russia off the hook of a United Nations condemnation of her breach of the peace in Hungary.

Dulles was furious and Eisenhower stupefied by the Anglo-French coalition's unilateral action. The day after they landed forces in Suez, November 6, 1956, Eisenhower again decisively defeated Adlai Stevenson to win his second term in the White House, and thus, armed with another American mandate, he instructed his ambassador at the United Nations to support a Russian-inspired demand for a cease-fire in Egypt. Reluctant and bitter, France and Britain withdrew from the Suez area, Israel returned inside her borders, and a UN peace-keeping force took charge of the Canal Zone.

With this, Nasser improved his image as the leader of Arab nationalism. In the "newsspeak" and "double-think" of the day, he proclaimed a "victory," when, in fact, the Israeli Army had easily defeated his troops and only the intervention of Russia and the United States had saved him from the Anglo-French. Nasser's next move was to absorb Syria into his newly proclaimed United Arab Republic, after which he organized a *coup d'état* in Iraq which ended in the assassination of King Feisal. Jordan and Lebanon were to come next, but as Nasser's agents began to subvert Lebanon, its President appealed to the UN for help. The UN moved slowly, and Lebanon turned to Eisenhower, who on July 14, 1958, sent in Marines followed by airborne troops. In the meantime, Britain landed paratroops in Jordan, and with this Nasser's attempt to control two more Arab states was thwarted.

World tension had been far from eased, however. Russia and America may have been uneasy friends during the Suez Crisis, but they were very soon old enemies again. In 1957 the Soviets dazzled mankind by launching the world's first spacecraft, and with this Premier Nikita Khrushchev embarked upon a new Cold War offensive against the free world. Khrushchev's opening blast was an ultimatum to the West to get out of Berlin within six months or else he would turn the city over to East Germany. The West did not retreat, and then, in a surprising reversal of attitude, Khrushchev in September, 1959, came to the United States to confer with Eisenhower. Arrangements were made for the chiefs of Russia, Britain, France and America to meet at a "summit conference." Before they met, however, an American U-2 high-altitude photographic plane was shot down over Russia, and when Eisenhower admitted that such flights had been authorized to observe Russian nuclear activities, Khrushchev denounced the American President and torpedoed the summit conference.

The new Communist Cold War offensive was resumed. Moreover, the Communist Confrontation was no longer a rimland phenomenon, but was now firmly established 90 miles off the coast of Florida, threatening several Latin-American countries.

During the period when the United States granted $44.8 billion in Marshall Plan aid to Western Europe, all that its "good neighbors" in Latin America received was a paltry $6.8 billion. It was not much to shore up a congeries of independent states whose economies were based on the export of raw materials and whose tariff restrictions inhibited the development of native manufacturing. Yet it was believed in Washington that the influence of democratic institutions and the Roman Catholic Church would keep Latin America out of the Communist camp.

Unfortunately, those democratic institutions were forever being "suspended" in the name of "law and order" by the newest dictator swept into power by the latest flurry of shots fired across the capital plazas, and the discipline and dynamism marking the North American brand of Catholicism were in no way duplicated by the fainéant faith of the south. Latin America was ripe for revolt, and as early as 1954 both Moscow and Peking had made it plain, in Lin Piao's phrase, that here was another "rural area" from which to besiege the free world "cities."

The most telling charge against America was her alleged support of the dictators. Ironically, her policy of detachment was the result of American attempts to erase the memory of the Mexican War and of the interventions of Theodore Roosevelt, Wilson and Coolidge. But the result of this policy was recognition of every new regime that came to power, no matter how it did or what it did afterward.

One attempt to avoid this dilemma was U.S. membership in the self-regulating Organization of American States, formed in 1948 as the successor to the Pan American Union. Another was *sub rosa* attempts to subvert the dictators. One, against the Argentine dictator Juan Perón in 1945, backfired with Perón's re-election and a ten-year lease on power. A second, against the Communist-oriented Jacobo Arbenz of Guatemala in 1954, put arms in the hands of Guatemalan exiles, who returned to Guatemala, deposed Arbenz and set up a constitutional government.

Among the Communists who fled Guatemala was an Argentine physician named Ernesto ("Che") Guevara, who later joined forces with a bearded young Cuban revolutionary named Fidel Castro. In 1956, accompanied by about ten other bearded rebels, they landed in Cuba's Oriente Province and began to rally around them the forces that eventually overcame the cruel and corrupt Cuban dictator, Fulgencio Batista. Here in Cuba was a textbook demonstration of the tactics of the war of national liberation. Not only did the original guerrilla band of a dozen men swell into a force numbered in the thousands, but it also drew to its standard every category of Cuban malcontent. All shared a grievance against the Batista regime; many were not Communists. Yet it was Communists who controlled them and Communism for which they fought, a fact which Castro so cleverly concealed from the outside world that some American journalists hailed him as a democratic liberator, and the doctrinaires, motivated by their dogmatic belief that all uprisings represent the will of the people, invited him to the United States where he was lionized by the universities and even offered foreign aid by the State Department.

Once firmly in power, however, Castro threw off all pretense. He seized banks, sugar plantations and all major industries, jailed or executed the opposition, closed the churches and drove 250,000 of his countrymen into exile. Cuba by 1960 was a Communist state, armed and subsidized by Moscow. Revolutionary guerrilla warfare had planted a Marxist beachhead in the Western Hemisphere, and from this base in the Caribbean Castro proposed to export national wars of liberation designed to subvert the rest of Latin America. On this melancholy note, Dwight Eisenhower came to the end of his last year in the White House.

Limited by law to two terms, Eisenhower was replaced as the Republican candidate by the youthful Vice President, Richard M. Nixon. To oppose him, the Democrats chose the equally youthful, handsome and controversial Senator John F. Kennedy of Massachusetts.

Kennedy was not controversial as a politican, but because of his Catholic faith. This was probably the only real issue in a campaign distinguished by the candidates' agreement to continue containment abroad and welfare at home, as well as the fact that America was for the first time choosing a chief from between two war veterans. As in 1928, there was an outpouring of anti-Catholic bigotry, but the 1960 brand was more sophisticated than the invective directed at Alfred E. Smith. This time the appeal to prejudice was on a higher level.

It persisted throughout the campaign, much as Nixon and many Protestant leaders might deplore it. Moreover, it was also clear that many Catholics were going to vote for Kennedy just because he was a Catholic, or at least to put an end to the prejudice against having a Catholic in the White House. In the end, Kennedy won—by a narrow popular-vote margin of 100,000 votes and by an equally close 303-219 Electoral College count—and he entered office at a time when the pressures of the Confrontation had well-nigh reached the blow-off point.

4

☆

At the beginning of 1961, when John Fitzgerald Kennedy took office, it appeared that the free world was in full retreat before Communism's new Cold War offensive. Soviet spacecraft still led the way in space, while on earth the Sino-Soviet team strove with all its resources to shatter the Western Alliance, to turn the new nationalism against the free world and to seize power in the underdeveloped areas.

In West Berlin the Soviets still sought to oust the West by nuclear blackmail. In Southeast Asia, Ho Chi Minh's terrorists were working to bring down the Diem government, and the Western orientation of Laos was menaced by another Communist-led insurgency. Meanwhile, Arab nationalism was still beholden to Moscow, Indonesia was arming with Soviet weapons, India was flirting openly with her powerful Red neighbors, and in Africa the Russians and the Chinese were both competing for the allegiance of Mali, Ghana, Guinea and the revolution-torn Congo. So well did Mao's jeer of "paper tiger" seem to describe the United States that in Japan and Latin America the anti-American riot was almost a fixture of the social season. To reverse this three-year tide of defeat and retreat, President Kennedy attempted to erase the Communist beachhead in the Caribbean.

Perhaps with the success of the Guatemalan expedition in mind, some 1,500 Cuban exiles were given American arms and training, and in April, 1961, they invaded Cuba at the Bay of Pigs. It had been hoped that once this obviously tiny force came ashore, it would draw all anti-Castro forces to its standard and generate a popular uprising. However, for reasons still not known, the exiles were denied American air cover, and were thus left in the condition of lead soldiers storming a red-hot stove. Once Fidel Castro's jet trainers arrived, the Bay of Pigs invasion was completely defeated and most of the invaders captured. With this, Fidel Castro tightened his hold on Cuba and another hole appeared to have been punched in the paper tiger.

Still another appeared the following August, when, at Khrushchev's orders, the East Germans constructed a huge concrete and barbed-wire wall across Berlin and thus sealed off the city's Eastern and Western zones. The wall was built to halt the flight of Germans from Communism, and it violated prior agreements guaranteeing free access to all Berlin. It did not come down, however, for the free world, still fearing nuclear holocaust, struck at it with nothing more powerful than words of protest.

Convinced, now, of the timidity of his opponents, Khrushchev moved swiftly into Cuba to erect missile bases menacing the United States and much of Latin America. This time President Kennedy reacted boldly. With the approval of the Organization of American States, he put Cuba under a tight blockade. Ships surrounded the island and aircraft patrolled its coasts. Florida and the Gulf ports were mobilized for an invasion, the Strategic Air Command sent nuclear B-52 bombers aloft, intercontinental missiles were placed in readiness and the Polaris submarines deployed.

Here was the critical point of the Cold War. Here, for the first time, the two superpowers openly confronted each other; and here, as Russian supply ships plodded toward Cuba with American blockading vessels under orders to turn them back, was the spark that might detonate nuclear holocaust. To the astonishment not only of the Communists but also of the free world peoples, the paper tiger was snarling. Almost to a man, the American public backed President Kennedy. Khrushchev gave in; he turned back his ships and pulled his missiles out of Cuba.

The focus of the Confrontation now shifted to Asia once more, where Red China had invaded India, settling for a truce after American aid helped the Indians stem the tide, and where the Vietcong were openly in arms against South Vietnam.

It may never be possible to say exactly when the Vietcong "war" against the government of South Vietnam began. There is no definite starting point such as the customs patrol incident which touched off the Vietminh war against the French. Perhaps it "began" in 1956, when with the passing of the deadline for nationwide elections, it became clear to Ho Chi Minh that a unified, Communist state of Vietnam was now possible only through the overthrow of the government in Saigon. Certainly Ho never envisioned the permanent division of his country. Why he consented to it is not yet known, although it has been suggested that he did so at Sino-Soviet urging. The Soviets, it is said, were eager to have France scuttle a proposed European Defense Community, which she did, and were therefore intent upon pleasing the French and retaining their influence in Southeast Asia. Moreover, by their very presence at Geneva, the Communist Chinese gained considerable big-power prestige, and it might very well be that they were pleased to see Vietnam divided, so long as no really stable anti-Communist government could be erected in Saigon. Such a state of affairs would compel Hanoi to continue to rely upon Peking. Finally, it seems likely that Ho Chi Minh was persuaded to settle for half a country on the grounds that the rest would be his after the elections. When these were not held, the Communist cadres in the south began "the Struggle."

This English translation of the Vietnamese term, *dau tranh*, it has been said, "fails to convey the drama, the awesomeness, the totality of the original."[9] To a revolutionary, the Struggle was everything. It was at the heart of his being and was its purpose. The Struggle was also a two-edged sword, both political and military. Politically, it indoctrinated its own forces while using agitprop techniques to gain the allegiance of the enemy troops and enemy officials. Militarily, its "violence program" of guerrilla warfare, sabotage, kidnapings, executions, assassinations and calculated cruelty sought to do by terror what agitprop could not do by persuasion. Both activities were controlled by the National Liberation Front, which had been organized in 1960 on Ho's orders and was controlled by Communists. On the one side the NLF had its Central Committee, which was in charge of agitprop, on the other its "Liberation Army," which carried out the violence program. It was this NLF which was known as the Vietcong, from the abbreviation of *Cong-san*, the Vietnamese term for Communist.

The struggle begun by the Vietcong in South Vietnam was distinctly different from the one with which the Vietminh won North Vietnam. It was an imported war. Even though most of the Vietcong were Southerners—and not all of them Communists—the leadership and aid were not. Nor was the South Vietnamese war an anticolonial and patriotic war concerning all Vietnamese. Rather, the French were gone, the attempt to paste the colonialist label on America had largely failed, and because the South was overwhelmingly agricultural and rural, the people had little sense of national identity and therefore were not moved by the appeal for reunification. Because of this, the war in South Vietnam was far more political than its predecessor. It was a war for the people, not only for their allegiance but to impose upon them an entirely new way of life.

For the Southern people to yearn for reunification, they had to be taught to think that it would be of some benefit to them. For them to accept a socialist Vietnam, they had to be taught to scorn the old ways: "old" education, "old" religion, "old" social and economic customs, and even, if it came to that, "old" people. Finally, for them to want to fight for this unified socialist state, they had to be made to hate the "imperialist puppet" in Saigon which kept Vietnam divided. Thus the true war in the South was not the clash of armed men that made the headlines, but rather the twin pressures of agitprop and terror upon the people.

The NLF sought to organize South Vietnam into every conceivable type of Liberation Association: farmers, women, youth, workers, students, intellectuals, artists, writers and so on. The main emphasis in such a rural country was, of course, on farmers, women and youth. Villages and hamlets were the targets of the NLF's highly trained agitprop teams. Usually, these teams worked through some party member or sympathizer planted in a village. They appeared at dusk and entered the village with great fanfare, for their arrival represented a break in the monotony of village life. Having been welcomed, the agitprop leader organized a meeting at which the villagers were taught to sing beloved songs with new verses emphasizing the need to join the Struggle against the American "imperialists and their lackeys." After the first meeting, the villagers split off into smaller meetings of the various Liberation Associations. Finally, there was a general gathering in which the villagers were invited to participate. They were encouraged to complain and protest, even to accuse one another of crimes, and all their grievances—crop failure, flood or epidemic— were attributed to some phase of "imperialist" activity. From friends planted in the audience came questions seemingly critical of the NLF, but which the agitprop leader skillfully turned against the enemy. He was believed, because he was usually a man of the people, deliberately chosen because of his reputation for virtue, honesty and dedication to the cause of Vietnamese nationalism. Finally, the visit would end with some ribald skit at the expense of American soldiers in Saigon, after which the agitprop team hauled up the NLF flag, scattered leaflets and departed.

Naïve as this may seem, it was highly effective among a simple peasantry, and was no more to be scorned than the sawed-off chair that scuttled Admiral Joy at Kaesong. In the cities, of course, there was more sophistication. There, agitprop men were guided by instructions such as this:

> On a busy train, in a bar, at a private party, make the subject lively and raise the level of the class consciousness of the individuals present according to the circumstances. . . . But be careful not to reveal yourself and avoid talking too much. . . . Here is a good example: Take a newspaper that carries a story about a certain man named A who committed suicide because he was unable to find a job. Bring up the subject of the newspaper story and then lead the conversation to the general subject of jobs, unemployment, the difficulties of earning a living, etc. In this way people are invited to complain about the hardships they face. From this seek an opportunity to incriminate American aid as a source of this state of unemployment and starvation.[10]

Where agitprop failed or needed support, the violence program took over. When employed against the South Vietnamese Army the main tactic was the ambush; against a village itself it was harassment as manifested by desultory sniper fire; and against the government it was sabotage and mass terrorism, the destruction of roads, bridges, railways and telephone and telegraph facilities together with the bombing of crowded streets, cafés and theaters. When aimed against the individual, however, the violence program was at its most ruthless and brutal. Here, its victims were teachers, village chiefs, priests, government officials, farmers and all other influential persons who seemed to oppose the Struggle or whose death might serve as a warning to others. Starting in 1957, it is estimated that one civilian was murdered by the NLF every other day. By 1960 that figure was up to five a day and at the start of 1967 it was calculated that the number of civilians slaughtered by the Vietcong in one decade of "violence" was more than 15,000 counted, and thousands more uncounted, while at least 40,000 more had been kidnaped.

All these victims were from the country's elite, and it was in this way that the Vietcong sought to slay the shepherds of a society so that the leaderless sheep might then be led into their own fold. To oppose them, the South Vietnamese government, led by Ngo Dinh Diem and assisted by the Americans, began to fight a war of counterinsurgency. Diem also had to fight for the allegiance of the people, while attempting to make his own military forces strong enough to destroy the Vietcong.

Unfortunately, the drawbacks of Diem's own personality, of his family and of his people were too much to overcome.

One of Ngo Dinh Diem's chief problems was to crush three powerful sects, which, fielding private armies and flourishing in South Vietnam practically as governments within a government, siphoned off his own strength and divided the country still further. Two of these were the Hoa Hao and the Cao Dai, both bizarre amalgams of religion and politics typifying the Vietnamese passion for syncretism. The third was the Binh Xuyen, a bandit and racketeering power in control of gambling and prostitution in Cholon, the Chinese city adjacent to Saigon. To Diem's great credit, he did succeed in crushing the sects. To his discredit, he did little or nothing to enlist these smashed organizations—at least the Cao Dai and Hoa Hao—under the Saigon banner. He had to crush them, of course, for they made a travesty of his own national government. But because they represented nearly 10 percent of the population, he also needed their support. Yet, instead of waiting a decent interval before making a gesture of conciliation toward them, he continued to alienate them.

Alienation, it seems, was Diem's besetting political sin. On the one hand he might be high-minded and incorruptible, but on the other he was aloof and distrustful. He could not delegate authority and allowed his passion for doing everything himself to lead him to such ridiculous extremes as himself setting the trees in public parks. Because he was so remote and suspicious, Diem was fair game for his brother Ngo Dinh Nhu. Eventually, Nhu became his brother's Rasputin. Whether ambitious for personal power or because he wanted to make South Vietnam over in his own way, Nhu played upon Diem's suspicions of other people so that in the end he exerted a powerful and baneful influence over him.

Nhu's first success was in 1955 when he rigged the referendum through which Diem unseated Bao Dai as chief of state, becoming the first President and virtual dictator of South Vietnam. With this flagrant manipulation, Diem's public image was hurt, and the career of alienation begun with suppression of the sects gained momentum. The following year Diem alienated the countryside by canceling the village elections. Thereafter, he alienated the intellectuals by his obvious contempt for them; alienated the villagers by badly mismanaged programs of resettlement resulting in grievous hardship; angered the farmers by programs of land reform, which, however well intentioned, ended in much of the land falling back into the hands of greedy landlords or public officials in cahoots with Army officers; disgusted almost all professional politicians by arresting the lone member of the National Assembly who could have been considered in opposition to him; and, finally in 1963, with the alienation tumbrel beginning to roll downhill like a juggernaut, he rapidly alienated the Buddhists, the students and the Army.

The Buddhist revolt sealed Diem's doom. Ostensibly, it was a religious movement; actually, it was a thrust for political power. The Buddhist hierarchy sought to build a political base, and to rally the laity to their banner they raised the cry of religious persecution. It was maintained that the Catholic Diem and his family favored Catholics, who represented only 1½ million out of the country's population of 16 million. The Buddhists, claiming 11 million members, but with a real following of 4 million practicing Buddhists, maintained that this was persecution. Actually, Diem never persecuted any religion. Yet it would be hard for his government to escape an imputation of *de facto* favoritism toward Catholics. Because of the loss of administrative talent caused by the exodus of the French and the departure of the able Southerners who had joined the Vietminh, Diem was desperate for trained personnel. The only significant source was the million refugees, most of them Catholics, who had fled the North. The Catholics were also considered more reliable because of their implacable hostility to Communism. Once in positions of influence, however, they tended to favor their coreligionists. Therefore, if Diem can be acquitted of the charge of persecution, he cannot be freed of one of sectarianism. His civil service was too exclusively Catholic and Northern.

The Buddhists, however, chose to concentrate on its Catholic aspect, and in May, 1963, they began their revolt in the ancient city of Hue in northern South Vietnam. It exploded in the world consciousness when the first of seven Buddhists committed sacrificial suicide by having himself soaked in gasoline and setting himself afire at a Saigon street crossing. Americans were especially shocked, and the charge of persecution seemed valid when a frantic Diem began raiding Buddhist pagodas. The raids only served to anger South Vietnam's students to the extent that even grade-school children joined the anti-Diem movement. Finally, as Diem cracked down on the students, he alienated field-grade officers whose younger sisters and brothers were among the students arrested on charges of treason. After that, the general officers came in, and by October, 1963, national disintegration was complete.

By then it was clear to the United States that Diem had to go. By then Americans were aware of the anti-Diem coup being planned by General Duong Van Minh. And by then Nhu had learned of the coup and conceived a fantastic countercoup which gives eloquent testimony both to the conspiratorial nature of Vietnamese government and his and his brother's utter inability to recognize reality. A fake revolt was to be staged in Saigon, Nhu and Diem were to flee, "chaos" was to be manufactured by killing some Vietnamese and a few Americans —and then the brothers would return to the capital to restore "law and order." However, General Minh learned of his rival's counterplot, and he was the first to move. On the night of November 1, 1963, Minh's troops surrounded the presidential palace. Diem and Nhu inside refused to surrender. At midnight Minh's tanks arrived, and at 3:30 in the morning of November 2 a full-scale attack began.

Diem and Nhu, however, had slipped out of the palace by a tunnel. At first, they hid in a little Catholic church, from where Diem got to a telephone and informed his enemies of his willingness to surrender. An armored personnel carrier was sent to pick up Diem and Nhu. Once inside it, on whose orders no one knows, the brothers were shot in the head and then repeatedly stabbed.

Three weeks after the downfall and death of Ngo Dinh Diem, the American President was himself assassinated.

5

☆

It was under President Kennedy that the United States moved away from the policy of Massive Retaliation and the fallout-shelter panic to a program of more flexible military response. Under Kennedy the conventional forces were strengthened and streamlined to fight the little wars of the Confrontation. More important, it was chiefly through his efforts that the nuclear nations agreed to a ban on nuclear testing.

In June of 1963 President Kennedy had made his famous appeal to Americans to take a new look at the Soviet Union. He urged his countrymen to put aside the prejudices and conflicts of the Cold War, and in a famous "signal" heard as far away as the Kremlin, he said: "If we cannot now end our differences, at least we can make the world safe for diversity."[11] It was this speech which convinced Khrushchev that much was to be gained by mutual renunciation of nuclear testing, and on August 5, 1963, Russia, Britain and the United States agreed to hold no more underwater or open-air tests.

With this, Khrushchev seemed to have given the free world an earnest of his sincere intentions to pursue a program of "peaceful coexistence," even if it did mean that Communist China, now openly in schism from Communist Russia, would pillory him once again as a "revisionist." For President Kennedy the pact seemed to fulfill his inaugural promise: "Let us never negotiate out of fear, but let us never fear to negotiate."[12] Three months later, he began a political fence-mending trip through Florida and Texas. On November 22, 1963, he and his wife rode through the streets of Dallas in an open limousine. With them were Governor John Connally of Texas and Mrs. Connally. Their vehicle passed the Texas School Book Depository. At a sixth-floor window above them stood Lee Harvey Oswald, a miserable young man, a sullen expatriate and a paranoiac. Oswald aimed a rifle fitted with a telescopic sight. The rifle snapped repeatedly. Governor Connally was hit. President Kennedy slumped forward, his neck and the back of his head pierced. Rushed to a hospital, he was pronounced dead one hour after noon.

Fortunately, Vice President Lyndon B. Johnson was in the motorcade. Fearing a conspiracy against the government, Johnson insisted on accompanying the President's body by air back to Washington. Within the airplane, in the presence of Mrs. Kennedy still wearing a bloodstained raspberry-colored suit, Lyndon Baines Johnson took the oath of office as President of the United States, becoming the eighth Vice President to enter the White House through the death of his chief. Johnson signified his intention of continuing the Truman-Eisenhower-Kennedy policy in Southeast Asia with the dramatic phrase: "Let us continue!"

The stroke that had brought down Diem had been a mere *coup d'état,* yet the South Vietnamese regarded it as a "revolution." It was widely believed that new days were at hand. A people suddenly freed from oppression felt like dancing in the streets, which is what many literally did in defiance of the detested Diem blue laws, and the government went on an anti-Diem binge that resulted in the dismissal of three-fourths of the 41 provincial chiefs. There was a government of sorts, a military junta headed by General Minh sitting atop a civilian provisional body. But it seemed to be on holiday. It had no real policy or program. Now, it appeared, was the Vietcong's chance.

Ironically, the Vietcong had been hoist with its own petard. It had concentrated so completely on vilifying Ngo Dinh Diem, had so successfully personified in him all that was wrong with the country, that his death left them without a devil. The people were uninterested in the General Uprising that was to complete the Struggle. They seemed to say: "Why talk of bogeys when the bogey-man is dead?" Unable to transfer hatred to Minh and his junta, the Vietcong decided to bring him down with force, and at this point the Struggle in South Vietnam became first and foremost a military one.

There was not only a step-up in the Vietcong's armed activity, but there was also the movement of thousands of North Vietnamese regulars south. Ho Chi Minh did this for three reasons. First, the added strength of the Northerners would help deliver the knockout blow against the Saigon government. Second, the United States would be reluctant to send in large numbers of troops to fight North Vietnamese regulars. Third, the presence of Northerners below the border would forestall any separatist movement which might follow the Vietcong's seizure of power.

The grounds for this decision seem to have been the Communist belief that they stood on the brink of victory. Only one extra shove would send the Saigon government tumbling into the abyss. To their surprise, the shaky South Vietnamese Army did not crumble, even though, on January 30, 1964, the junta led by General Minh was itself toppled by a rival junta of disgruntled generals headed by General Nguyen Khanh. This stroke set unhappy South Vietnam on a teetering course of coup, countercoup and attempted coup, during which the extremely well-balanced General Khanh gave a remarkable performance of political tightrope walking. Khanh ruled practically singlehanded for almost a year, during which time both North Vietnam and the United States made the moves that involved them deeper in the conflict.

At some time in 1964, it is believed, the Communist leaders of the Vietcong and North Vietnam collided in a debate on policy. The point at issue was whether or not to escalate the Struggle, to move from Stage Two into the frontal-assault phase of Stage Three and ultimate victory. The Vietcong were in general opposed to this proposal. They believed that the Struggle still could be won by indoctrinating the people and immobilizing, but not destroying, South Vietnamese military power. The Northerners held otherwise, quoting Mao and Giap to the effect that no revolution could be won by guerrilla tactics alone but must, by an inexorable inner logic, move into Stage Three. The Northerners won the debate, and this brought on a direct military confrontation with the United States.

Up until this point, American military forces in South Vietnam had not been large, and had been there "to aid and assist" the Saigon Army, but not to become engaged against the Communists. Now, however, there were direct Communist attacks on American military installations, and on August 2, 1964, North Vietnamese motor patrol boats attacked the U.S. destroyer *Maddox* about 30 miles off the Vietnamese coast in the Gulf of Tonkin. Other attacks followed, and the American response was to send carrier-based aircraft against North Vietnamese coastal facilities and boats. More important, Congress passed a resolution authorizing President Johnson "to take all necessary steps, including the use of armed force" to help defend South Vietnam.

President Johnson did not at once act upon the Gulf of Tonkin Declaration. Running for re-election against the ultraconservative Republican, Senator Barry Goldwater of Arizona, Johnson soft-pedaled the issue of intervention. When Goldwater called for escalation of the war and attacked what he called Johnson's "no-win" policy, the Democrats accused him of being "trigger-happy." Moreover, some of Goldwater's domestic policies seemed reactionary to a nation by then thoroughly accustomed to the welfare state, and there was an immense tide of sympathy running for the successor to the martyred Kennedy. Thus, in the second straight presidential contest between war veterans, Goldwater was drowned in a Johnson flood, and "LBJ" became the fourth straight war veteran to enter the White House as well as the 16th of 36 Presidents to fit that description. Now President in his own right, Johnson began intervening in Vietnam in much the same manner advocated by his defeated opponent.

In early February, 1965, new North Vietnamese attacks on Americans had provoked fresh American aerial retaliation. On the last day of February, the United States government issued a White Paper on Vietnam. It was a 14,000-word indictment of North Vietnamese aggression against the state of South Vietnam. More than that, it was justification for the forthcoming direct intervention on the side of Saigon. On March 2, 100 American jets flew north to bomb a munitions depot. A few days later two battalions of United States Marines landed at Danang on the upper coast of South Vietnam, and it was announced that Army units would soon follow.

When, in the summer of 1964, Ho Chi Minh decided to move the war into Stage Three, he also decided to commit regular forces of the North Vietnam Army in the South.

In this, one of the key decisions of the struggle, if not the chief decision, he dramatically altered the size and purpose of the conflict. He also calmly dropped the pretext of an "internal war," which his sympathizers in Europe and the United States had echoed so faithfully, supplanting it with the new—and equally popular—line that the "American imperialists" had invaded South Vietnam.

From that moment forward, the "war of liberation" was to escalate and to become more and more openly directed from Hanoi, with the bulk of supplies coming from the Soviet Union and some material and moral support from China. Indeed, the very subordination of the Vietcong may have been one of the various reasons for Ho's momentous decision: namely, that the Vietcong had become so strong during 1963 and 1964 that they threatened to challenge Hanoi's influence, and also to thwart Ho's dream of a single Vietnam unified and controlled by him.

Although it is true that Ho did not desire two Vietnams, even if both were Communist, it is also true that at the time the Vietcong had signally failed to achieve their chief objective—the allegiance of the people—and in fact, their tactics of assassination, terrorism, taxation and gunpoint recruiting had begun to turn the countryside against

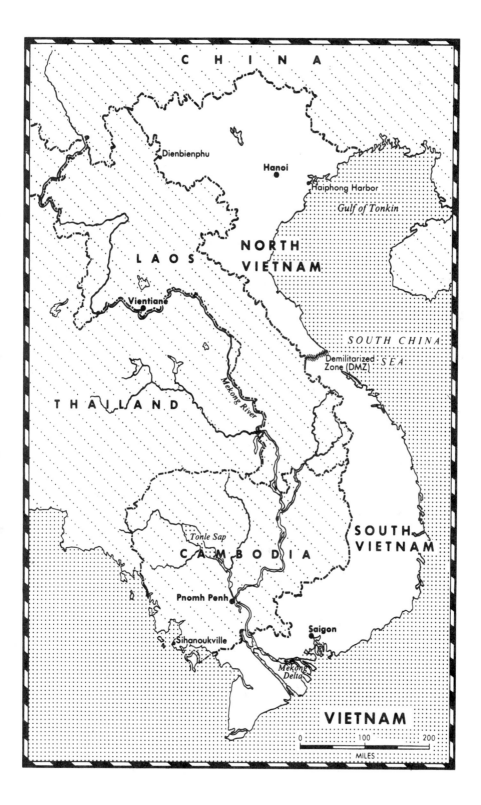

C H I N A

Dienbienphu

Hanoi

Haiphong Harbor

Gulf of Tonkin

NORTH VIETNAM

L A O S

Vientiane

SOUTH CHINA

Demilitarized Zone (DMZ)

SEA

T H A I L A N D

Mekong River

SOUTH VIETNAM

Tonle Sap

C A M B O D I A

Pnomh Penh

Saigon

Sihanoukville

Mekong Delta

VIETNAM

0   100   200

MILES

them. Thus Ho and the Politburo may actually have sent their regulars south to save the Vietcong. Moreover, they had become most apprehensive over the American intervention. American military response after the Gulf of Tonkin resolution had been swift and shocking. Into Saigon to take command of Military Assistance Command, Vietnam (MACV)—the office which actually ran the war—had come General William C. Westmoreland, a dynamic and aggressive commander in World War II and Korea, with an impressive record as a battle leader as well as an administrator and scholar. General Maxwell Taylor, a World War II hero, possessed of an astute military mind and formerly President Johnson's military adviser, had come into Saigon to replace Henry Cabot Lodge as the American ambassador. Between them, these two generals breathed a new spirit of aggressiveness into MACV and encouraged their South Vietnamese partners by the speed and size of their military commitment.

By the end of 1965 no less than 185,000 American troops had reached Vietnam, together with 15,000 South Koreans and 2,000 Australians and New Zealanders. By the end of 1967 there would be a total of 60,000 combat troops from Allied Nations other than the United States and South Vietnam, compared to the 39,000 sent by the United Nations to South Korea, and a total of 45 nations who contributed men, money or materials to the allied cause. By June, 1967, the American build-up alone would reach a total of 540,000 men, compared to the Korean peak of 327,000.

In the early years of the war these American warriors proved to be as fine fighters as any ever fielded by the United States. Better educated, more politically mature, they were aggressive and dedicated, and their grim professionalism more than compensated for whatever they may have lacked in the gay recklessness of their predecessors. Moreover, they had the advantage of knowing that their "time in hell" was limited. They were required to serve no more than 3 years and no more than 13 months overseas. Most gratifying, in the beginning, was the performance of black servicemen. They had rarely seen combat in World War II, and in Korea, probably because they were still segregated, their record was not good. In the early years in Vietnam, however, fully integrated at last into the services, they performed well.

The arrival of the Americans in 1965 also coincided fortuitously with General Giap's attempt to give Ho the knockout blow he demanded.

Giap's plan was simply to cut South Vietnam in half, to sever it at the narrow neck of the Central Highlands along a line running from Pleiku through An Khe to Qui Nhon on the sea. Giap sought a spectacular victory rivaling even Dienbienphu, calculating that it would discredit the Americans and cause a collapse of South Vietnamese resistance. Giap also strove for a quick victory, before the American build-up could get any larger. To gain it, he was confident that the superior foot mobility of his troops would tell against American technology frustrated by the mountainous, rugged, near-roadless terrain of the Central Highlands.

General Westmoreland was aware of Giap's intentions. His intelligence had accurately predicted the location and the date: October–November, 1965. Westmoreland also recognized that the key to victory lay in mobility, and he at once chose the First Cavalry Division (Airmobile) as the force with which to blunt Giap's blows.

The First Cavalry went to war on the wind, rather than on land, and for wheels and feet it substituted wings and rotors. The soul of this unique fighting force was the helicopter, of which it possessed nearly 450, 5 times as many as a normal infantry division. Everything—maneuver, supply, firepower, command and control, reconnaissance—hinged on the helicopter. Because it could fly over mountains and jungles, cross rivers and set down almost anywhere in roadless, trackless wastes, the helicopter division placed in Westmoreland's hands a technological mobility at least the equal of Giap's mobility of foot.

The celebrated Communist general was not aware of this. He had already tested the American fighting man in August, having hurled a regiment at United States Marines at Chu-lai on the coast south of Danang, with disastrous results. However, Giap reasoned, this had been against the world-famous First Marine Division, out in the open on a sandspit where superior American firepower shot his men to pieces. In the Ia Drang Valley, where Giap planned to meet the enemy, his soldiers' superior skill in the jungle would defeat the ordinary road-bound American fighting unit.

Wily as ever, a master at the feint intended to draw his enemy's strength to the wrong place, Giap intended to strike first at Plei Me, a Special Forces camp on the Laotian border about 25 miles southwest of Pleiku. It was Pleiku, the key to the Central Highlands, that he really desired. The siege of Plei Me, he reasoned, would bring a relief force from lightly held Pleiku. He would ambush it, finish off the garrison at Plei Me—and then move on Pleiku.

In the twilight of October 29, 1965, one Communist regiment began bombarding Plei Me. Another took position between the camp and Pleiku in order to ambush the expected relief force from Pleiku. But the South Vietnamese commander there did not seize the bait. He recognized this standard Communist tactic. Moreover, he knew that he did not have enough strength both to relieve Plei Me and defend Pleiku. So he waited—for developments and reinforcements.

Meanwhile the shelling of Plei Me continued. Casualties mounted. Still the defenders hung on. Now the mobility of the First Cavalry came into play. A battalion was flown to Pleiku to cover the city while the South Vietnamese sent a relief force spearheaded by armor to the relief of Plei Me. Expecting ambush—which is the surest means by which it may be thwarted—the Southerners ran into one about 5 miles above the camp and gave their Northern brethren a fierce beating. Staggered themselves, the South Vietnamese held in place, while a complete brigade of cavalrymen was flown to Pleiku. Next, helicopters brought artillery support to the South Vietnamese, and the following day they broke the week-long siege of Plei Me.

Giap's first blows had been blunted. At once Westmoreland saw the opportunity to counterattack and inflict a major defeat on him. His orders to the First Cavalry were: "Find and destroy the North Vietnamese forces." For four days reconnaissance helicopters swept low over an area roughly the size of Rhode Island, searching for the enemy hidden in a wilderness of mountain, river valley, rain forest and fields overgrown with helmet-high elephant grass. On the fourth day they spotted a complex of buildings along the Tae River. A squadron of cavalrymen was landed. Routing the area's handful of defenders, the Americans found that they had captured a field hospital. More important, on the body of a dead North Vietnamese officer they found a map showing enemy unit locations and the march routes to be used by enemy regiments.

Based on that information, the Americans were able to bring the North Vietnamese to battle beneath Chu Pong Mountain along the River Drang. Here, in a series of clashes between November 3 and November 6, the enemy suffered complete defeat. The superiority of American firepower was too much for him, and the swiftness with which American helicopters were able to move men and arms from point to point confounded all his plans. In a later battle between the Americans and North Vietnamese at "Landing Zone X-Ray" along the Drang, the same results were obtained. Thus what came to be known as the Battle of the Ia Drang Valley ended in a major defeat for General Giap. Americans had met North Vietnamese face to face on the enemy's chosen ground and had defeated him. More important, Westmoreland's brilliant spoiling attack had denied Hanoi the victory which it needed before the American build-up became too great, and it had forced the Communists to fall back on Stage Two while surrendering all hope of an immediate military victory.

President Johnson's decision to commit ground forces in Vietnam came at a time when the Saigon government was at its shakiest since the overthrow of Diem. In January, 1965, the Buddhists were again reaching for power. This time the target of their protests was Premier Tran Van Huong, whose civilian government functioned by the grace of General Khanh and the Armed Forces Council. Charging Huong with restoring Diemists to office, the Buddhists organized a student and general strike in Hue. The chief result of this move was to compel Huong to add four military men to his cabinet, among them General Nguyen Van Thieu and Air Marshal Nguyen Cao Ky.

Still not satisfied, the Buddhists went on a hunger strike and ordered an all-out anti-American campaign. In Hue a crowd of 5,000 students wrecked the U.S. Information Service Library and burned 8,000 books. In Saigon another mob demonstrated outside the U.S. Embassy. Whether by accident or design, the Buddhist outbursts dealt the South Vietnamese cause a body blow in the United States. Although the Johnson administration was certainly determined to weather this new squall, the general public was not. Americans were agonized to see their so-called allies acting like their enemies. They were bewildered by a sequence of no fewer than eight coups since Diem's fall, and they could not understand a people who insisted upon playing the conspiratorial game while they "had a war going on." As a result public opinion, never strong in support of the war in Vietnam, began to veer toward a feeling of heartsore frustration.

In Saigon the sure-footed General Khanh used the Buddhist revolt as a lever to compel the Armed Forces Council to oust the Huong government and restore himself to power. However, Khanh's footwork had by then begun to annoy the younger generals on the council—among them Thieu, Ky, and Nguyen Chanh Thi—even though Khanh had restored the facade of civilian government by making Dr. Phan Huy Quat the new Premier. On February 19, 1965, therefore, a free-wheeling coup typical of the Vietnamese passion for plotting gave the Armed Forces Council the opportunity to adopt a vote of "no confidence" in Khanh and thus end both his political and military career. Dr. Quat continued as Premier, although the real power seemed vested in General Thi, with Thieu and Ky in the shadows.

Probably there was no direct relationship between this latest shake-up and the American decision to intervene militarily. However, the first attacks on the Vietcong by planes manned by American crews, as well as the resumption of raids on "selected targets" in North Vietnam, helped to stiffen the spine of the new Saigon government, although it did not save Dr. Quat. This time the pressure came from the Catholics, assisted by some representatives of the Hoa Hao and Cao Dai sects. On June 12 Dr. Quat was forced to resign and a new National Leadership Committee was formed. Thieu, a Catholic convert and a Northerner, became its head, while Ky, a Buddhist and also a Northerner, took charge of a new Executive Council. Meanwhile the Buddhist Thi began to lose influence, and eventually Thieu became chief of state and Ky became Premier. Between them the colorless, careful Thieu and the flamboyant, impulsive Ky were to give South Vietnam a small but not unimpressive measure of political stability.

Ky, a swaggering figure in his black silk jump suit or flying his silver jet, was probably sincerely determined to stamp out corruption. Unfortunately his very power reposed on a rotten foundation of extortion and graft. He was unable to dismiss dishonest officials because they had paid for their jobs, and he could not promote the good ones because they had not. Corrupt military commanders and political chiefs ignored his orders to "clean house," unless he could convince them that to court-martial this colonel or fire this district chief was in "their own best interests." It was pathetically ironic that Ky's own Anti-Fraud and Corruption League would later be dissolved by General Thieu on the grounds that it was putrid with fraud and corruption, and that his drive against corruption, which was launched in the fall and winter of 1965-66, ended with the execution of one culprit: an unfortunate Chinese merchant delivered up to him as a scapegoat by the wealthy members of the Chinese community of Cholon. No one else was brought to book, and especially no one of Ky's official family.

Worse, Ky was an inept politician. All of the generals of South Vietnam were inept politically, and this may account for the failure of any of them to give the country the stability that the Americans kept demanding. Diem may have been tryrannical and his program may not have been a good one, but he still had a program and he knew something, at least, of the political art of getting disparate and even rival groups to work together for the good of the country. None of the generals possessed this skill. They seemed to be more concerned that military rule should continue than with building the "strong, free nation" that was the objective of American policy. In the fact that they did possess power may be discerned what was perhaps the vital difference between themselves and their enemy. Police state that North Vietnam undoubtedly was, it was run by civilian politicians. The Politburo in Hanoi seemed to share Clemenceau's belief that "War is too important to be left to the generals." All military policy and all decisions for war or peace were made by the politcians, leaving only the execution of their commands to the generals. War, Ho Chi Minh and the rest of the Politburo knew, was fought for political ends. To remind the Communist generals of this, each commander in the field was accompanied by a political commissar. Power, meanwhile, was reserved for the politicians. In Saigon, however, the junta holding power seemed to fit President Truman's gibe at General Eisenhower: "He knows as much about politics as a pig knows about Sunday."

Premier Ky's naïveté was sadly apparent in his handling of the second Buddhist crisis. The Buddhists deeply resented Ky's junta and campaigned constantly for national elections for a civil government. In March, 1966, Ky dismissed General Nguyen Chanh Thi, a Buddhist member of the junta and commander of the First Corps in Danang. Immediately, the Buddhists staged demonstrations throughout South Vietnam. In Danang, soldiers of the leaderless First Corps openly paraded with civil servants and dock workers demanding national elections and shouting anti-American as well as anti-junta slogans. Gradually other dissident groups, even the Catholics of the area, all motivated by a common hatred of the junta, joined forces with the Buddhists. For a tense month or so dismayed Americans feared that

South Vietnam might be sundered by a regional separatist movement. When Ky tried to end the revolt by personally leading a force of Marines to Danang, he found the rebelling First Corps soldiers arrayed against him in superior numbers and flew back to Saigon.

Angered by Ky's resort to force, encouraged by his reluctance to try conclusions with the rebellious First Corps soldiers, the Buddhists turned in fury upon both Ky and the Americans. Demonstrations broke out again in Saigon and the cities of the First Corps area. In Danang and the ancient capital of Hue demonstrators waved placards reading: DOWN WITH THE CIA, or: END THE FOREIGN DOMINATION OF OUR COUNTRY. Official Washington was aghast. Was the budding "strong, free nation" to be torn apart by a civil war that would leave it easy prey for the Communists?

Fortunately, General Ton That Dinh, the new commander of the First Corps (the one sent to replace Thi, who had already defected to the Buddhists), did not panic under pressure. Aware that he had no troops to carry out the junta's order, he began to negotiate with the dissidents. Order was restored to Danang. Next, President Thieu convened a National Political Congress made up of Buddhists, Catholics, the sects and other groups for the purpose of transferring power to the civilians, after which he promised elections for a constitutional assembly within the next six months.

The Buddhists, it appeared, had won a signal victory—until, a month later, Premier Ky casually announced that the only elections to be held would be for a constituent assembly. He also said that he would like to remain as Premier for another year.

Again Washington was horrified. Secretary of State Dean Rusk went on television to declare that Ky must have been misquoted. But Ky had meant what he said. A few days later he led a force of Marines against Danang, supported by a wing of fighter-bombers. They seized the airfield, the radio station and First Corps headquarters. General Ton That Dinh fled to Hue in a helicopter loaned to him by a U.S. Marine officer, refusing, meanwhile, all offers of cabinet posts or ambassadorships if he would publicly announce that he had "invited" Ky's troops to Danang. Civil war apparently was at hand. Which side should the United States support, or should it support anyone? Barricaded in their pagodas, the Danang Buddhists pleaded with President Johnson to intervene in their behalf. Secretary Rusk replied with his own plea for the Vietnamese to settle their "lesser differences" and join forces against the Communists.

In the end, Danang was subdued by force and Hue was starved into submission. Unfortunately, Washington's unswerving support of the junta put the United States in the position of supporting force and bloodshed while seemingly opposing creation of that civilian government which was the *sine qua non* of its objective. America had poured forth blood and treasure to come to the aid of her ally in South Vietnam, but henceforth she was to be hated by many of those very people for whose sake she was literally crucifying herself. Moreover those younger leaders of the revolt who were not imprisoned by the junta were left no alternative but to join the Vietcong.

One fortunate consequence of the Buddhist uprising was that free elections were, in fact, held the following September. An astonishing percentage of the adult population—a full two-thirds—was registered, despite denunciations of the elections as "fraudulent" by the National Liberation Front and a campaign of terrorism conducted by the Vietcong; and of these, an incredible 81 percent—a far greater proportion than that which turns out in the United States—actually voted. One hundred and seventeen delegates were chosen for an assembly which, with the exception of the election-boycotting Buddhists, was truly representative of the numerous political parties and minority groups making up the South Vietnamese body politic.

The Constituent Assembly convened in October, and in April, 1967, it promulgated a constitution of which the principal features were the selection of a president and vice-president running on the same ticket for four-year terms, a bicameral legislature and an independent judiciary. The president was empowered to appoint a premier and his own cabinet.

At first, it was believed that Premier Ky would be chosen as the junta's candidate for president with President Thieu as his running mate. Thieu, however, announced in May that he would run for president. Both the other generals and the Americans were equally dismayed. Both believed that rival generals would split the Army and divide the electorate and perhaps produce a civilian president. Ironically enough the Americans, still striving for that "strong, free nation" resting upon the keystone of civilian government, continued to support—however quietly and discreetly—the military. Probably the Americans were not confident that a civilian government at the moment could prosecute the war. Moreover the junta led by Ky had given some small measure of stability. Nevertheless, to many of

Saigon's intellectuals and political leaders the American position was at best contradictory, at worst hypocritical.

Thus, to both the generals and the Americans, the crisis created by Thieu's rival candidacy was real and appalling. To resolve it, all the flag officers of South Vietnam's armed forces convened in a three-day meeting, during which the generals argued and cajoled, wept and snarled, by turns threatening to kill themselves or those who disagreed with them, debating, over and over, the question of whether to allow civilians to take power or to scrap the constitution and go on ruling themselves. Both Ky and Thieu delivered affecting speeches offering to withdraw their candidacies. Finally Thieu turned the tables by appearing grim-faced at the final meeting to denounce, by chapter and verse, the corruption rampant in the national police. Inasmuch as the national police were run by General Nguyen Ngoc Loan, the officer who had brutally suppressed the revolt in Danang and who was also believed to be Nguyen Cao Ky's "gray eminence," it was obvious whom Thieu was attacking. At once General Loan rushed from the room, leaving everyone behind him to dissolve the intolerable impasse in a flood of tears. Weeping, Ky offered to resign. Instead, the generals persuaded him to accept the number two position, and the junta entered the September 1967 elections united behind a Thieu-Ky ticket.

Thieu and Ky did win, but by a surprisingly small margin. Of 5 million votes cast, they received only 1,649,561—merely 35 percent of the total. Moreover most of their support came from isolated military districts—a suspicious circumstance which was one of the chief reasons why the defeated candidates immediately raised the cry of "fraud." Banding together as the "Front for the Struggle for Democracy," six of them charged Thieu and Ky with rigging the election. A special committee of the Constituent Assembly recommended non-certification of the result because of alleged irregularities. In the end, however, the full Assembly did proclaim the election of Thieu and Ky as valid, and on October 31, 1967, Nguyen Van Thieu was sworn in as the new government's first president.

6

☆

Although the Ia Drang Valley success had demonstrated that American technological mobility was superior in pitched battle to North Vietnamese foot mobility, General Westmoreland and his commanders gradually came to the uneasy realization that it also had had the unhappy effect of surrendering the tactical initiative to the enemy.

Swiftly as the helicopters might move men and material to the point of attack, once on the ground the Americans were immobilized. They could do no more than dig in and defend. Their opponents, meanwhile, were free to attack or not to attack, to maneuver, withdraw, sideslip or break off action and fade back into the friendly jungle. They need not sit still to be pounded to pieces by American bombers and field artillery. They could choose to fight or not to fight. In this tactical advantage, which the North Vietnamese soon came to understand and to use, there was reflected on the lower level the absence of American initiative which also existed on the highest level: strategy.

For the strategical initiative was also possessed by Ho Chi Minh and his advisers in the Politburo, if only because President Lyndon Baines Johnson went to war with no strategy for winning. True, he did have an objective: to deny the Communists military victory in South Vietnam with one hand, while building "a strong, free nation" with the other. It was the Johnson administration's hope that this goal might be achieved within about three years, at which time American troops would be withdrawn.

This, however, was not strategy, but rather "grand strategy," similar to the Allied grand strategy of World War II which was to destroy the Axis first while containing Japan, after which it would be Japan's turn. To implement this policy Allied strategy had been to strike the enemy everywhere with all their might. In South Vietnam, however, Johnson took no such initiative. Apparently, the memory of Chinese intervention in Korea so haunted the White House that the United States did not go on the strategic offensive against North Vietnam. Hanoi's jugular vein was protected from the knife by America's fear of war with Red China. No attempt was made to sever the enemy's supply routes by blockade or mining of the port of Haiphong or by slashing across the southern part of North Vietnam just above the Demilitarized Zone. True enough, North Vietnam was subjected to steady aerial bombardment, but even the aerial war was so carefully circumscribed and regulated as to targets and intensity that it was to become, in the eyes of Ho and Giap, an endurable irritant. Worst of all was the prohibition against fighting beyond the borders of South Vietnam, which left General Giap free to mass and move as he pleased within his own country and within his sanctuaries in Cambodia and Laos.

These were enclaves carved out by the North Vietnamese in the two countries bordering South Vietnam's unpopulated and highly vulnerable western boundary. Two of them, the so-called Parrot's Beak and the Fishhook in Cambodia, provided the Communists with staging areas reaching to within 30 miles of Saigon. Inside them, the enemy could amass war stocks and move men, sallying forth as he pleased to strike the allies, retreating back into them confident that the Americans would not pursue. Much the same immunity was extended to the "Ho Chi Minh Trail," the network of trails running south from North Vietnam through Laos. This was the enemy's main troop infiltration route, and although it was eventually bombed, it was only once attacked on foot: a half-hearted effort by the South Vietnamese later in the war. That which is destroyed from the air may be repaired, but that which is lost to a land army can only be retrieved by counterattack—the kind of conventional stand-up warfare that the Communists knew they could not wage against the Americans.

Thus the enemy was never placed on the strategic defensive, his staging areas and his heartland were safe from total attack, and under these circumstances the only way to "defeat" him, that is to say, to deny him military victory, was to destroy his army: in a word, to kill his soldiers.

This was a war of attrition, a war without strategy. But it was forced upon Westmoreland, and was the reason why he adopted his controversial "search-and-destroy" tactics. These were massive operations in brigade or divisional strength, sometimes even multidivisional, against the enemy's numerous redoubts and strongholds throughout South Vietnam. There were about 80 major bastions and hundreds of minor ones. They were shrewdly located in inaccessible swamps, mountain heights or impenetrable jungles, always defended in depth and provided with escape routes. Some of them had tunnels dug as deep as a mile and a half below the ground. Used for refuge, rest, resupply, training or staging, even for hospitals, this was the network that maintained the Vietcong insurgency. One operation against a single one of them—the Iron Triangle—is illustrative of the difficulty of reducing these redoubts.

Less than 20 miles north of Sagion, the Iron Triangle was aimed like a dagger at the heart of South Vietnam. It was not one of the larger bases, lying like a link midway between the two superbases War Zones C and D. It was used as a stopping place for units on the march or as a staging area for major assaults against strong points around Saigon. It had been an insurgent sanctuary for 20 years, against the Japanese, the French and latterly the Americans. During that time its natural defensive features—40 square miles of jungle mountaintop bounded by rivers and rain forest—had been turned into an iron anthill, a subterranean labyrinth through which men and arms might move to or from battle. In its tunnels and chambers were housed classrooms, offices, storage areas, hospitals and printing plants. During its two decades of existence the Iron Triangle had resisted all efforts to reduce it, until General Westmoreland, acting upon the advice of a young captain, decided to burn it down.

First, aircraft burned off the jungle cover by dousing the jungle with chemical defoliants, leaving it to wither and dry under two months of intense sunlight. Then, by leaflet and loudspeaker, noncombatants were warned to leave the area. Finally, cargo aircraft dropped barrels of oil and gasoline into the area and attack airplanes ignited them with napalm and incendiary bombs. A huge fire swept howling through the Iron Triangle—and then, to the consternation of the Americans, the intense heat produced an atmospheric confluence in the humid tropical air and a giant cloudburst put out the forest fire, leaving the Vietcong sitting safe and unsinged in their tunnels.

Chagrined, Westmoreland tried again in late 1965 with a reinforced brigade of Australians, New Zealanders and Americans. Although the commander exultantly reported "the destruction" of the base, the fact was that his brigade had stayed there only 3 days, had burned down some buildings and killed 44 soldiers. It was not until January, 1967, that the Iron Triangle was truly destroyed, and it took two entire American divisions replete with armor and helicopters to do it. Moreover the enemy had fled, and even though engineers and demolition experts systematically reduced the base to uninhabitable rubble, the Communists returned to it six months later.

Obviously, the Communist commander in the Iron Triangle had decided not to fight, and his decision to flee emphasized the difficulty of annihilating—through attrition—a foe who holds that option. In a war of counterinsurgency such as Westmoreland was fighting, stalemate and time always favor the guerrilla.

Such truths, however, were not immediately apparent to the Americans, and as the war progressed the idea of surrendering tactical initiative to the enemy became enshrined in a new infantry doctrine. Because it had been quickly realized that attrition was a two-way street, commanders tried to do it as "safely" as possible, that is, with the least loss to their own troops. To search and destroy, then, actually meant to find and fix the enemy until superior American firepower could be brought to bear. This included artillery or formations of huge B-52 bombers able to fly soundlessly overhead while dropping enormous loads of explosives on the "found and fixed" enemy. Soon it became standard procedure for American units, once having located the foe, to withdraw into defensive positions while calling for fire support. Thus B-52s, which had made only 60 support sorties monthly in 1966, were making 800 a month in 1967. With these tactics it was not unusual for Americans to be able to kill as many as 300 or more enemy soldiers while losing only 11, as occurred at Loc Minh in late 1967. Such incredible casualty ratios were neither uncommon nor untrue. Nevertheless the tactical initiative still belonged to the Communists. As often as not the bombs and shells went crashing harmlessly into empty jungle vacated by a foe who had chosen to flee rather than stand. Nor was he ever pursued. The idea of bringing him to battle, of breaking his back so that he could never rise to fight again, simply did not exist in Vietnam. It was a rare commander who was tough enough to risk "unnecessary" casualties achieving such a military result, when he could safely achieve the desired statistical result. Thus, an expedient tactic forced on the military by restraints born of political considerations in Washington had unfortunately been evolved into doctrine. Such reliance on supporting fire also had the unwelcome effect of creating in the minds of many junior officers what Westmoreland called a "firebase psychosis," a defensive mentality born of almost total dependence on air or artillery.

The war of attrition, meanwhile, also led to the notorious "body count." If the purpose is to kill the enemy's soldiers until he has reached the "crossover"—that point at which his replacements are less than his losses—then it is well to know his losses to compare them to estimates of his replacements. Thus Westmoreland demanded a strict body count from his commanders. Unfortunately, if a commander's prowess is to be judged by the number of soldiers his men kill, there is probably created thereby a temptation to inflate the figure. Also all corpses, whether civilian or combatant, were sometimes considered certifiable "bodies," a practice which helped to lead, later in the war, to American attacks on South Vietnam villages. Psychologically the gruesome phrase, "body count," was not well received in the United States or among its allies, nor was the other phrase of "search-and-destroy." To many Americans, it sounded as though their troops were thrashing wildly and aimlessly around in the jungle. Nevertheless the war of attrition went on, Westmoreland continuing to press for the crossover point as he dueled Giap, while on the other hand he supported and advised the Saigon government in its older struggle against the Vietcong for the allegiance of the countryside. These were the two parallel wars which agonized South Vietnam, and to conduct them, the ingenious American arsenal brought forth an incredible complex of new weapons. They ranged from a "cluster-bomb unit" spewing out more than 800 bomblets, through lightweight automatic weapons, barracks ships, prefabricated airfields designed for specially built "short take-off" aircraft, heat-seeking missiles such as the "Sidewinder" that went after aircraft exhaust or the "Weasel" carrying helicopters to attack the enemy's very effective SAMs (surface-to-air shoulder weapons), "smart" bombs guided to their targets by laser beams, and huge blankets of herbicides which, upon being ignited from the air, destroyed and suffocated all beneath them, and giant blowers that blasted tunnels with jets of air at a temperature as high as 900°F.

Riverine warfare conducted in the Mekong Delta called forth a a variety of vessels, including armored gunboats designed to attack river redoubts, while infra-red and radar systems were used to find the foe in the night. And everywhere, doing everything, it seemed, was the ubiquitous, omnicompetent helicopter. It took men to and from battle, ferried supplies and artillery, evacuated casualties, gave the infantry close-up support with its own firepower and provided an aerial armchair for commanders. Actually, because of the helicopter, battle in Vietnam was perhaps the most supervised—or "oversupervised"—combat in history. A lowly platoon leader or company commander might well be granted his disenchantment to discover, orbiting above him, his battalion commander, brigade commander, assistant division commander and perhaps even his field force commander.

Unfortunately this technological attempt to equalize the revolutionary guerrilla's advantages of terrain and foot mobility, as well as his ability to "swim" unseen in the "water" of the populace, tended to exaggerate the defensive mentality born of the "firebase psychosis," if it was not indeed the direct cause of it. Moreover, as happened in Korea, much of the technology was canceled out by the Communist leaders' ruthless exploitation and regimentation of their manpower. Simple muscle power used on a massive scale could frustrate the sophisticated airpower of the United States in its attempts to cut the enemy's supply lines, as the story of one North Vietnamese laborer on the Ho Chi Minh Trail illustrates. It took this man two harrowing months to carry two mortar shells to the battlefront where, to his consternation, they were fired off in ten seconds. And when the mortar commander snapped, "Go back and get two more," he burst into tears. Nevertheless he did as he was told. Two manpower months per shell would seem a prohibitive price to pay for logistics, at least for modern warfare; but not, it seems, for revolutionary guerrilla warfare conducted by a police state.

Technology was also thwarted by a war that was nothing less than a war without fronts. With the possible exception of the Philippine Insurrection, it was fighting without parallel in American history. Here were the triune enemies of terrain, the Communists and a people who were, as often as not, either openly hostile or secretly sympathetic to the foe. Here, a 14-year-old boy selling soda might be a Vietcong spy sent inside an American encampment to sketch the positions. Here, a 12-year-old girl leaning a bicycle against a barracks wall might be planting a vehicle of death, its tubular frame packed with explosive. On patrol, Americans encountered booby traps set along the trails, on farmyard gates, in chicken coops and fishing nets or the very doors of schoolhouses. Mines—pressure, trip or electrically detonated—were everywhere. Trails were sown with sharpened bamboo stakes—punji sticks—which inflicted painful wounds, elephant traps were dug with the bottoms lined with such spikes and the fields were planted with long sharpened poles designed to ward off helicopters. Searching for the enemy, the Americans were like flies on a windowpane with their big bodies, big noses and white or black skins, while the little tan guerrilla "swimming" in the "water" of the people was as easy to find as a teardrop in a bucket of water. Yet, if technology was thus frustrated in the field, its miscarriage there was almost as nothing compared to its spectacular failure to bring the Communists to the negotiating table by almost three and a half years of aerial bombing.

American air strategy in Vietnam was, first, to strike the North with "a measured amount" of airpower in order to compel Hanoi to accept President Johnson's invitation to negotiate a peace, and second, to halt the flow of supplies and reinforcements to the South. Whether or not the use of nuclear weapons was considered is not known, although to have used them, obviously, would have been to risk—if not certainly provoke—nuclear war with Russia. Bombardment of the enemy's extremely vulnerable system of dikes and dams in the North, thus unleashing terrible floods on the civilian population, was discussed but rejected on the grounds of "overkill" and the probable adverse effect on American as well as world public opinion. Thus, for what appears to be judicious and humane reasons, President Johnson limited himself as to weapons and targets. Unfortunately, because 1964, the year of American intervention, was also an election year, Johnson further limited the aerial war for political reasons.

Johnson's opponent was Senator Barry Goldwater, known as the "super-hawk," who openly advocated bombing North Vietnam. Johnson, meanwhile, presented himself as the candidate of peace and humanity, portraying Goldwater as a saber-rattler who would surely provoke World War III. Once elected by a record landslide vote, Johnson promptly followed exactly the course recommended by Goldwater: he ordered an air campaign against both Laos and North Vietnam.

His delay, however, had given the enemy some time to prepare. In November, Premier Phan Van Dong of North Vietnam traveled to Moscow to request antiaircraft weapons: jet fighters, surface-to-air missiles and a sophisticated radar-control system. The Russians consented. Thus, when the bombardment did begin the following year, Hanoi was ready for it.

Now that Washington had finally decided to bomb the North, a debate developed over how and in what strength it should be conducted. Secretary of War Robert McNamara and his associates wanted to "orchestrate" it, that is, to begin gently with slowly rising volume like a symphony moving toward its conclusion. This, it was argued, would put Hanoi in a "slow squeeze." The Joint Chiefs of Staff disagreed. Emphatically, along with the Central Intelligence Agency and almost every commander of rank in all services, they opted for immediate application of major force to obtain maximum results with minimum losses. They insisted that they could destroy all of Hanoi's major airfields and petroleum reserves in three days, leaving the enemy all but powerless to wage war.

They were not heeded, perhaps because Secretary McNamara, who shared his chief's penchant for reservation, did not even bother to convey their objections to the President. Civilian analysts supported McNamara, arguing that an agricultural society such as North Vietnam was not vulnerable to bombing, a perplexing position which, by extension, seemed to suggest that the primary purpose of the bombardment—to bring Hanoi to the bargaining table—was not possible, while ignoring the military truth that it is precisely such a rural country, supplied and armed from outside by an industrial ally, which cannot endure the deprivation of its technical plant and oil (the lifeblood of modern war) or the ensuing attrition against its attempts to repair and replace them. Nevertheless the policy of "graduated response" was adopted, and an air campaign codenamed "Rolling Thunder" was begun in March, 1965.

Rolling Thunder was restricted and hamstrung in the sky perhaps even more than Westmoreland's campaign on land. No flights were permitted north of the 19th parallel; South Vietnamese aircraft had to participate in some way in each strike; no reconnaissance was allowable before a raid and seldom after it; pilots who could not zero in on their targets the first time over were not allowed to return; and homeward-bound fliers with a few shots left in their lockers were forbidden to expend them against "targets of opportunity"—that is, suddenly discovered enemy formations, vehicles or rolling stock—but rather compelled to jettison them into the South China Sea. An iron control was clamped down from Washington. It was not the air commanders in South Vietnam and later Thailand, or Admiral U. S. G. Sharp, chief of all forces in the Pacific, who chose the targets, named the strike day or specified the number of aircraft and the size of the bombs, but rather Secretary McNamara assisted by the White House.

As may be expected, this gentle warning to the North failed, and when the "orchestration" began with a bombing halt called on May 18 in expectation of the enemy's cries for peace, this also failed. As it was to do in all subsequent bombing halts until the end of 1968, Hanoi, acting with cynical shrewdness, made all the motions and hints eagerly awaited in Washington, while taking advantage of the pause to regroup and repair, to rush more men and arms south; in a word, to dig in to meet every return of Rolling Thunder with ever-increasing strength.

Vacillation in Washington also gave North Vietnam the opportunity to save its vital oil stocks, without which it probably could not have continued the war. All of Hanoi's "POL"—petroleum, oil and lubricants—had to be imported, most of it from Russia. In 1965, its stocks were concentrated in a few major storage areas and were extremely vulnerable to strategic bombing. The military asked for permission to destroy the enemy's POL capacity at once, either by destroying the major storage centers or by closing Haiphong Harbor—where Soviet tankers unloaded—or both. It was denied, and the North Vietnamese rapidly began to multiply, disperse and fortify their storage centers. When in 1966, under pressure from the Joint Chiefs, some of his White House aides and even Secretary McNamara, President Johnson finally gave his consent, it was too late to strike the single, decisive, destructive blow. Much of the enemy's POL went up in flames around Hanoi and Haiphong, but most of it was stored elsewhere. Not even a wide-ranging bombing campaign was able to locate and bomb all of it. Meanwhile the port of Haiphong remained open to Russian tankers. Although the North's vital POL stocks had been reduced, they had not been destroyed.

In fairness to Johnson and his civilian advisers, it must be remembered that, as the war went on, they were being slowly hoisted onto the horns of a dilemma. Opposition to the war grew apace with its escalation and rising casualty lists, so that Johnson must have been haunted by his campaign pledge not to bomb North Vietnam, made in August, 1964, when he also said he would not consider "committing American boys to fighting a war that I think ought to be fought by the boys of Asia to help protect their own land." Among the clergy and in Congress, the academic community and the press, the drumbeat of dissent had risen to a strident storm. Such influential senators as J. William Fulbright and Robert F. Kennedy were coming out openly against the war, if Kennedy did not actually perceive in the unpopular war the issue which would enable him to wrest the Democratic nomination away from the President. Lyndon Baines Johnson, known to the press as "the political animal," was fighting for his political life. Sincerely committed as he was to containment of Asian Communism, he apparently did not have the force of will to risk his career on it. Every roll of aerial thunder had to be muted and every blow softened to mollify or placate these dangerous critics at home. He gave Westmoreland most of the troops he requested, but limited their use; he gave Sharp the pilots and the planes, but circumscribed their sphere of operation. Such ambivalent policy is the antithesis of war, even limited wars of counterinsurgency. Limited though a nation may be in objectives and weapons, it is still at war—which is raw, brutal, bloody violence. It is cruelty, and as Sherman said, "You cannot refine it." Even when limited, it is total in its application: you must strike the enemy first, hardest, everywhere and anywhere, despite the limitations. Although Johnson had waived the use of the nuclear arsenal and the vulnerable dikes and dams as a target, he still possessed the options of an amphibious strike across the southern part of North Vietnam above the DMZ, thus cutting the enemy's line of communications—historically the way armies are defeated and wars won—or of destroying the Cambodian and Laotian sanctuaries, or of bombing and blockading the vital ports of Haiphong or Sihanoukville in Cambodia. Eighty percent of the Communists' supplies arrived by sea, and although Sihanoukville was certainly in a "neutralist" country, so were those North Vietnamese interlopers whom Prince Norodom Sihanouk and his Khmer countrymen, hating and fearing them for centuries, had always been powerless to oust. All these alternatives, then, were waived for political reasons.

Then unaccountably, in the spring of 1967, it appeared that Rolling Thunder was to be allowed to flash and rumble free of restrictions.

President Johnson gave authority to bomb areas previously proscribed, and many of the earlier shackles were removed. Throughout June, July and August the North trembled under a growing rain of bombs which shook the morale of its people and destroyed much of its war-making capacity. But then Washington eased off. "The pressure period was foreshortened," Admiral Sharp wrote bitterly, "even as the enemy began to hurt."[13]

Once again, the decision was a political one; but once again, it must be emphasized that 1967 was as difficult a year as any experienced by any American President. It was a year of "the long, hot summer," when racial rioting—in part associated with the antiwar movement—erupted in many cities, together with organized antiwar and antidraft demonstrations that brought protesters streaming into Washington by the tens of thousands. That spring, Johnson had been shocked by General Westmoreland's request for 200,000 more troops and the Joint Chiefs of Staff's demand that he call up the reserve. For Johnson to have acceded to just one of these politically explosive petitions would have been to sign his own political death warrant. The President also was torn between his military advisers pressing him to strike for the enemy's jugular vein, and civilian analysts, headed by McNamara, warning that to raise the level of the bombing would be to alienate the American people and world opinion while risking open war with Red China. Concurrently, there was a rising clamor in the press and among college and university professors for an end to the bombing. It was to these voices, not those of his military advisers who, after all, had but one vote apiece, that the President listened.

He did not, of course, immediately curtail the campaign, allowing it to continue through the extremely bad flying weather of that winter. But by the time the air war was finally launched, it called forth a massive reaction from the Communists. In 1965, they had had no missiles, no jets, less than 20 radar sets, limited airfields and a handful of obsolete antiaircraft guns. By 1967, they possessed a sophisticated defense system the equal of any in the world: 250 SAM sites, MIG-15 and MIG-17 jets, more than 100 radar stations, 5,000 antiaircraft guns and a network of modern airfields. Against this, Admiral Sharp hurled what was probably the finest air force in the world. Sorties—that is, one flight by one plane—rose to 10,000 a month in 1966 and 13,000 a month in 1967. More bombs were dropped than in World War II and twice as many as in Korea. But North Vietnam's now powerful defenses took their toll in planes and crews. Hundreds of Americans eventually became prisoners of war in the North.

Thus, because of the absence of any positive air strategy, Rolling Thunder was largely a failure. It was not completely so, if only because it did give great encouragement to the South Vietnamese, aware that their enemy brethren in the North were also suffering, and it doubtless made it much easier for General Westmoreland to fight the war. Yet the North Vietnamese were able to survive the twin onslaughts of attrition on land and thunder from the sky. At the end of 1967, although they had lost about 50,000 men, they would still send another 60,000 south.

7

☆

When, in 1966, the American expenditure in Vietnam reached the total of $2 billion a month, much of that money was being expended on the "pacification" program. Pacification was the attempt to build the "strong, free nation" that would be able to stand on its feet politically and economically, so that, when the United States eventually withdrew, South Vietnam would be able to defend itself. "Pacification" is also the general word given to the various programs which had this end in view; Strategic Hamlets, New Life Hamlets, Really New Life Hamlets, Rural Reconstruction, Revolutionary Development, and so on. In its simplest terms, pacification aimed at clearing the Vietcong from the villages, making them secure and gradually restoring them to government control.

Pacification was as old as the war itself. The French had tried *quadrillage,* a system of small "squares" of friendly enclaves in the countryside which would spread like an "oil slick." In 1962 Diem had launched his ambitious Strategic Hamlets program, designed to draw the peasants together into centralized, fortified villages. Each center was to have moats, barbed wire and trained defenders. The theory was that these friendly areas would also spread until the entire countryside was loyal to Saigon.

Although the British had been able to pursue such a policy in Malaya with great success, it did not work under Diem and the Americans. Probably it failed because the scheme was too grandiose, attempting to do too much too fast, and because, particularly on the part of the Americans, it ignored the basic character of the Vietnamese people.

Unlike the dynamic, mobile, technocratic Americans, to whom competition and change are a way of life, the traditional Vietnamese villager lived a highly circumscribed, almost changeless though rhythmic life, bound to the sacred earth of his village and its surrounding circle of rice fields. His life was a trinity of family, village and religion, if some of the syncretic sects and a way of life such as Confucianism may be described as religion. His technology had not changed in 1,000 years. He still dug and span, sowed and reaped, the way his ancestors had done. In fact, he worshiped his ancestors, in the sense that the son wanted to do exactly what his grandfather had done, that the father passed the land along to the son who would one day be a father, and that the land was not really "owned" but rather held in a kind of sacred trusteeship for each successive head of the family. The land, then, sanctified by the graves of the ancestors buried in the rice field, was sacred and inviolable. To remove someone from his land, to take him from his village, was to violate the villager in his very soul.

Nevertheless, pacification based upon moving villagers from their traditional, ancestral homes was pursued. Strategic Hamlets appeared to be getting along marvelously. Province chiefs, aware of Diem's enthusiasm for them, vied with one another in building more hamlets to "secure" more people. The statistic-minded Americans rushed to feed computers that coughed up ever more glowing evidence of progress.

In reality, Strategic Hamlets were collapsing just as surely as those showcase villages which the Vietcong, having calmly watched their well-publicized erection, carefully and joyfully destroyed. The people did not support pacification, and they continued, freely or under duress, to shelter the Vietcong guerrillas. When Lieutenant General Lewis Walt, chief of the Marine forces in Vietnam, made the remark,

"Breaking the back of the VC main force won't take long, but rooting out the VC guerrilla is a long-term task,"[14] he expressed, from a military viewpoint, the crux of the political problem. The guerrillas simply were not going to allow pacification to work.

The bureaucratic mentality, which walks on paper while the peasant walks on earth, had much to contribute to pacification's failure. Vietnamese or American, the bureaucrats who directed the program did not seem to realize that the British had succeeded in Malaya because they were fortifying Malayan villages against Chinese Communist insurgents. In Vietnam, they were fortifying Vietnamese villages against other Vietnamese who had grown up in those same villages. A guerrilla's sister or younger brother or parents might live in that hamlet, or a father's family. Moreover, to ignore the Vietnamese psychology, that almost holy attachment to land, was another typically bureaucratic error, perhaps the prime example of which occurred in the populous Mekong Delta. Here, the peasants did not live in hamlets, but rather in farms along the river or on the rim of the dikes. Nevertheless they were transported to the concentrated settlements where many of them ended up with no land of their own or else were compelled to walk considerable distances to their former fields.

Originally, pacification was to have followed in the footsteps of triumphant American arms. Westmoreland's forces were to "clear" the Vietcong from the selected areas, after which they would be defended by units of the South Vietnamese Army. Unfortunately this presumed a point-by-point operation, simply not possible in a war without fronts. Even when an area was cleared, the South Vietnamese soldiers apparently had no interest in defending strange hamlets. Too frequently, they were at least as oppressive as the Vietcong. Stories of South Vietnamese raping and robbing the villagers were all too common. One battalion camped only 10 miles from Saigon stood idly by while, 500 yards down the road, the Vietcong destroyed the village they were supposed to be protecting. In another province a South Vietnamese regiment butchered the livestock of an entire village, while raping so many of its women that the male inhabitants cut off their own trigger fingers and sent them to the government in protest.

Gradually the American forces grew disenchanted with their South Vietnamese allies and began trying both to clear and to protect the villages at the same time—a policy which placed an intolerable burden on Westmoreland's command and led, in time, to another misguided practice: that of destroying the villages in order to dry up the "water" in which the guerrilla fish "swam."

To say that pacification was a total failure would not be true. It was partially successful, and in some areas, particularly those closest to Saigon, many hamlets actually did come under government control. However, pacification never came near winning the allegiance of 67 percent of the countryside, as its proponents proudly claimed.

It was this habit of serving up impressive but misleading statistics to visiting congressmen and the media, only to admit at year's end that perhaps pacification had not been quite that efficient, which proved to be so discouraging to Americans who supported the war and so encouraging to those who opposed it. Yet each year a new try was made under a different name. Each year the newest swarm of social scientists would alight upon the unhappy country, their briefcases bulging with elaborate new schemes for building that "strong, free nation" that the Johnson administration so ardently desired. Each year another flood of bright young analysts from the consulting corporations roved the countryside to study means of "getting the peasants politically motivated" or "building a bridge" between them and Saigon. Each year the confident young Americans from the Agency for International Development (AID) sallied forth to the villages accompanied by bright young officers of the South Vietnamese Army to make this "the year" of success. And each year the cadre teams trained by the Vietnamese under the supervision of the Central Intelligence Agency were graduated from their schools with torchlight parades and speeches by General Ky or General Thieu praising them in advance for the social revolution that they were to accomplish. Assigned an appalling variety of tasks to perform, they were sent to villages where they were either murdered or intimidated by the Vietcong, or else switched so frequently from place to place that they could never even begin their mission. Gradually their enthusiasm was eroded by disillusionment. Frequently they found that the wicked village leaders whom they were supposed to eliminate were either relatives of high-placed Saigon officials or else had bought their positions. The schools or first-aid stations they hoped to erect went unbuilt because the materials had been stolen. Nevertheless each year was begun in confidence and certitude.

Each year, meanwhile, the American cornucopia poured forth its customary shower. Bulldozers and fire engines, concrete for new roads, barbed wire to protect the hamlets and corrugated tin to roof them in, surgical instruments, thousands upon thousands of tons of wheat and cooking oil, and seed for soybeans and "miracle" rice, surgical and dental instruments, copper plumbing, machine tools, trucks, compressors and calculators—in a word, all that was needed to build a village while feeding, clothing and sheltering its inhabitants—together with such primitive tools as sewing kits and such sophisticated ones as an atomic reactor. Of this constant rain of goods and products, an estimated 25 percent was stolen (not, in fact, an outrageous figure considering the pilferage percentage on, say, the docks of Boston and New York) and another 25 percent wasted (again not really so inefficient compared to the wastage figures for, say, a federal welfare agency), so that 50 percent of it did get to the villages. And yet each year a New Life Village would rise above the ruins of a Strategic Hamlet, or a Revolutionary Development Center come into being alongside the overgrown rubble of the fortified square that the French had built for the fathers of these relocated peasants two decades earlier. How was it possible for the Vietnamese villagers to have any faith in these reiterated and unfulfilled promises of a safe and happy future?

Still, the program was pursued—to the point of self-deception. Doubting dignitaries from the States were usually treated to a tour of "typical" pacification villages; typical, actually, of the kind of stage hamlets which the Russian favorite, Prince Potemkin, planted two centuries earlier along the Dnieper for the deception of the touring Empress Catherine.

The doubters were flown by helicopter to happy hamlets replete with maternity clinics, pig farms, plots of "miracle" rice and smiling children waving national flags. If they still doubted, asking questions about reports of disaster in certain provinces, then they were taken to a province "cleared" of Vietcong, but in reality one in which the Vietcong had never existed. Even if they also doubted in their own hearts, the officials from the State Department, the Army or the CIA, the civilian social scientists and analysts, all those pursuing the policy of pacification, spoke no such reservations aloud. Of course the program was succeeding! It had to succeed. This year will be better. It's amazing the progress that's already been made . . .

It was in this way that self-delusion compounded the original errors of ignoring the Vietnamese psychology and underestimating the tenacity of the Vietcong. Perhaps this was a graver mistake: for if putting forth propaganda is sometimes an error, to believe it yourself is always a disaster.

Possibly the sorriest side of the pacification debacle was the tactic of destroying villages adopted by General Westmoreland in 1965. Aware that the guerrillas still "swam" in the "water" of the people, Westmoreland resolved to "dry it up" in some areas by deliberately razing the villages. They were burned or bulldozed, while jungle cover was removed by defoliant bombing or dropping huge blankets of herbicide which, upon ignition, smothered all beneath them.

As Westmoreland had expected, the campaign created a flood of homeless refugees flowing into the government camps prepared for them. There the government was supposed to care for them: feed them, clothe them, find them jobs. Sometimes this happened, sometimes it did not—with the result that hungry, jobless people descended in hordes upon the cities.

Eventually, by the end of 1967, perhaps as many as 3 million villagers—nearly 20 percent of South Vietnam's total population of 17 million—had taken refuge in the cities, none of which had the capacity to feed and clothe them all or give a sufficient number employment. Shantytowns of tin shacks made from American beer cans, food cans and all other forms of metal containers blossomed around the outskirts of Saigon, Danang and other major cities. There the inhabitants became dependent on American aid.

Meanwhile the influx of refugees helped to turn many of the cities of the South into cesspools. By the end of the war Saigon, the "Paris of the Orient," had swollen from a city of about 1.4 million in 1962 to 4.2 million, of which probably about 1 million were prostitutes, hooligans, drug addicts or victims of venereal disease.[15] How many of these unfortunate people had once been peaceful villagers is not known, and the number can only be guessed at.

It is not unusual, of course, to discover such corruption trailing in the wake of a large army quartered in a foreign land; nor could the debauching of the South Vietnamese economy have been avoided. Such an enormous amount of money poured into what had been basically a barter economy produced a ruinous inflation which, during the two years 1965-67, reached a monstrous 170 percent before eventually "leveling off" to about 60 percent annually. A half million well-paid American soldiers with more millions to spend also helped to drive prices higher; not even the wise decision to pay them in scrip did much to arrest that upward spiral, while the Commercial Import Program, modeled on the Marshall Plan, did for Vietnam exactly the opposite of what its parent had done in Europe. Instead of useful or productive equipment, the Vietnamese importers brought into their country a flood of luxury goods—radios, televisions, motorcycles, refrigerators, watches, and the like—that they knew the chief holders of American dollars would pay for dearly. Thus most people profited not at all. Nor could most people afford to shop in the black markets flourishing near every American base.

All this money—which usually enriched only the hotel owners, black marketeers, brothel keepers, importers, diamond merchants, rice and real estate dealers, pharmacists and distributors of American luxury goods—also had the baleful effect of reversing values. Traditionally, ownership of land and government service had been the most desirable and respected callings. But in the new society created by the American billions, a taxi owner operating between American bases and the bars and brothels of the cities, a prostitute or even a respectable secretary working for the Americans could make more than a government minister, a colonel or a university professor. "We people in this society curse the Communists because we live in a free society," an embittered soldier complained. "Thus, crooks, cheats, thieves, and prostitutes are free to climb the ladder of values."[16]

Naturally enough, such corruption spread to government officials and Army officers, whose greed had also been excited by the presence of so much money, so that they too, taking advantage of their positions of power, emerged as some of the most outstanding profiteers in the business of washing the Americans' clothes, slaking their thirst or satisfying their lusts. And the probable prince of this band of bloated bandits was President Thieu himself.

Thieu, of course, was never linked directly to any of the rackets—prostitution, extortion, drug traffic and so on—which enriched so many of his appointees in the Army and the ministries. Most of the American correspondents and investigators in South Vietnam were agreed upon this point. Thieu's private preserves and those of his family circle were not quite so obvious. The President dealt in favors.

He asked no financial return or percentage of the ill-gotten gain from any of those friends and cronies he raised to positions of power: only favors. When the time came, they would do as Thieu asked; chiefly, they would look the other way.

Thieu's major source of income was smuggling, both out of and into South Vietnam. Scrap metal was the leading export, and of this brass was the most lucrative. A modern war is made to make scrap metal. A million soldiers fighting each other shoot off billions of bullets and shells, leaving small mountains of empty brass cartridges of all calibres glittering on the battlefield. Bombs and shells also make wrecks of trucks and tanks and airplanes, while all manner of vehicles, appliances and machinery wear out or are broken, and much of this junk eventually ended in the scrapyards controlled by Thieu. Such scrap metal fetches amazingly high prices in the markets of the world, especially in Japan. Thieu smuggled it out of his country to the highest bidders.

When he was ready to make a shipment, access roads to his dumps were cut off. This might and did make travel difficult for the people of the area, but it also provided the required secrecy. The scrap was loaded in canvas-covered Army trucks, which drove to the Saigon docks to be unloaded into waiting ships of Panamanian registry usually manned by South Korean crews; or the material was taken to lighters waiting on the Saigon, Dong Nai or Mekong rivers and thence to ships anchored offshore. All of this was made possible, of course, by public officials and Army officers who obligingly looked the other way while furnishing the labor and transportation necessary for the operation. Such cooperation also facilitated widespread smuggling of luxury goods into South Vietnamese black markets under the direction of Thieu's wife, the diamond-fancying Mai Anh.

Thieu's smuggling may not have been necessarily harmful to the war effort, but one of the unexpected problems caused by the profits from it most decidedly was. The Thieus had millions of piasters—the South Vietnamese currency—all of which obviously could not be spent or banked in Saigon. Piasters, however, were worth very little outside the country, until Thieu discovered a chain of banks in Hong Kong run by Communist Chinese. It was there that he "laundered" his piasters in exchange for Hong Kong or U.S. dollars, to be deposited in Swiss or other European banks. The Communists wanted the piasters for use in South Vietnam: to pay their agents and troops, to buy goods from local merchants who would accept no other currency, to buy rice and medicine for the Army or even to buy into legitimate local enterprises with the intent either to take them over or to sabotage them from the inside. In this way, Thieu had placed himself on a golden treadmill: he was battening on the war, and one of the chief effects of the battening process was to make the war continue.

Thieu's corruption was well known to American officials in South Vietnam, certainly to the Defense Department if not also to the White House. Yet to every indignant demand for his ouster came the reply that Thieu was indispensable. He was the only viable leader in Vietnam. He might be a thief indeed, but he was *our* thief.

It was with such leaders, with such corruption, such waste, such misdirected programs as pacification and with such misery that the naïve yet determined Americans pursued the dream of building "a strong, free nation" in South Vietnam.

8

☆

Although the Communists had shown themselves to be cunning and tenacious, they had nevertheless suffered military reversal during 1965-67—a fact which did not go unobserved in the rest of the world, especially in Asia. America's credibility as an ally had been enormously enhanced. In late 1967 she could now point to South Vietnam, as well as South Korea, which had just re-elected a president without a single riot, as an example of American fidelity and generosity. South Korea, meanwhile, had raised its assistance in South Vietnam to 45,000 men, and troops had also come from the Philippines and Thailand. Of America's remaining 40 allies, 32 had contributed some form of token, nonmilitary aid. Even Japan, where the anti-American riot had once been so common as to seem customary, sent economic aid; and in a 1967 poll, the Japanese people chose the United States as their favorite nation.

No longer did Red China jeer at the "paper tiger." At home, Red China was torn by incipient civil war caused by the "cultural revolution" through which Chairman Mao sought to impose a more rigorous form of Communism. Abroad, her abortive coup in Indonesia caused the destruction of the Indonesian Communist Party—third largest in the world—and made her name an odor in the nostrils of Asia; and while she lost influence in Africa, Cuba and Latin America, her continued public abuse of her former partner in Moscow widened the Sino-Soviet rift, while pushing Russia closer toward detente with the West. To say that all these Communist reverses were the result of American military intervention in South Vietnam would be absurd. Because they happened after it does not prove that they happened because of it. Yet, at the end of 1967, it seemed safe to say that Communism's new Cold War offensive launched a decade earlier had been halted and thrown back. The South Vietnamese had actually held a series of free elections during a bitter, savage war with an implacable enemy in their midst. It may have been true that the only change was from uniform to mufti; nevertheless, a start had been made. If a stable civilian government could take power in Saigon, freeing the generals for their true mission of raising and training an army strong enough to drive the invaders from the soil of South Vietnam, then, it would seem, in two or three years the American military could withdraw. "Containment" would have again succeeded in Asia, and South Korea and South Vietnam would stand as the check and checkmate of the Confrontation.

All this seemed true—until the Tet Offensive.

Thoughout the spring and summer of 1967 the Politburo in Hanoi had been divided in debate between one faction—led by General Giap—which wanted to launch a desperation, all-out-win-the-war offensive in South Vietnam, and another—headed by the theorist Truong Chinh—which held out for phasing the war back to a lower level of intensity. Basically, the argument was over the question: On whose side was time? Normally, time favored the guerrilla. This was revolutionary guerrilla warfare dogma. Truong Chinh spoke orthodox doctrine: if American might could not be outfought, then it must be outwaited.

However, from the standpoint of Giap and Ho Chi Minh, who supported his chief soldier, time had taken on a new quality of urgency. Ho was by then 76 and sickly. He had not long to live, and he did not want to close his eyes on a homeland still divided. Although Giap was only 55, he was nevertheless already suffering from that Parkinson's Disease which would eventually disable him. Moreover the crossover point had been reached. North Vietnam was now sending south fewer men than it was losing in battle. The Saigon government was showing unfortunate signs of stability. There had not been a single coup attempted in two years. Time, always the ally of the revolutionary, now seemed to favor the Americans— growing stronger daily.

Ho and Giap won the debate, and in late 1967, chubby Vo Nguyen Giap—the former history teacher who had taught himself the art of war—began to lay his plans. His model was his own political-military-psychological masterpiece: the Battle of Dienbienphu. Like France, America was showing signs of war weariness. Like France, her will was being eroded by a powerful antiwar movement. As with France at Dienbienphu, Giap would distract Westmoreland with a series of peripheral battles, drawing away his strength from the selected point at which the main blow would fall in a shattering victory that would collapse the American will to continue.

Giap made five calculations: first, he was certain that President Johnson would not raise American troop strength above the present limit: second, that he would not remove his restraints on his commanders; third, that a great Communist victory in an election year would either destroy Johnson or compel him to withdraw from Vietnam; fourth, that Saigon possessed "an army that would not fight"; and fifth, most important of all, that a Communist victory would provoke a general uprising among the people of South Vietnam.

In November and December of 1967, making skillful use of his sanctuaries in Laos and Cambodia, Giap triggered a series of bloody border clashes. They cost him dearly. His troops were mowed down by the superior firepower of the Americans and South Vietnamese. Giap was not dismayed. As he had already said publicly, the lives of hundreds of thousands of his countrymen "represents really very little." He was interested only in results, and he got them: harvests of headlines in the United States reporting heavy American casualties. He also shrewdly stirred in the minds of Westmoreland's principal officers haunting memories of the peripheral battles that had preceded Dienbienphu. They searched uneasily for another likely point where the true main blow would fall, and then, when Giap struck at Khe Sanh, they thought they had found it.

Khe Sanh was a Marine fire base sitting astride a natural invasion route from Laos westward across the populous narrow neck of South Vietnam toward Hue and Quang Tri on the coast. Two whole North Vietnamese divisions were discovered working into position to surround the camp as soon as heavy formations of artillery could be emplaced. Again, the similarity to enemy tactics at Dienbienphu. Moreover one of the divisions was discovered to be the renowned 304th—the very victor of Dienbienphu!

Once more the newspaper scareheads became thicker and the voices of the radio and TV commentators rose higher. Soon showers of artillery shells rained down on the Marine defenders. They braced, fighting off waves of attackers. General Giap gently raised the hysteria level among the American media, letting it be known—falsely—that he was in command at the siege.

Now not only General Westmoreland and the Joint Chiefs stared hard and grimly at their situation maps of Khe Sanh; but by mid-January, 1968, Lyndon Johnson had his own constructed in the war room in the basement of the White House: a huge, minutely detailed photomural showing trenches, gun positions, bunkers, ammunition dumps and the day-to-day progress of the encircling enemy, together with a detailed terrain model of the battle area. Gradually the tempo of battle rose. Both sides rushed in reinforcements. B-52 bombers struck savagely at the enemy, dropping a total of nearly 100,000 tons of bombs. Giap thickened his artillery concentration, increased his antiaircraft defenses, sent his men creeping in closer— and threatened a mass assault by moving up armor.

The critical battle, it seemed, was on: William Westmoreland slept closer to his operations center. Lyndon Johnson demanded a guarantee of victory from his Joint Chiefs. He got it, swiftly and unreservedly—for the Joint Chiefs knew that Giap could never match American firepower, nor the tactical mobility which would enable Westmoreland to move entire divisions rapidly from point to point.

So did Vo Nguyen Giap.

General Giap had indeed used the border battles to set up Khe Sanh. But he had no intention of fighting a stand-up fight against American forces that had beaten him in every battle since the Ia

Drang Valley. He was only too aware of his enemy's superiority in such combat. No, Khe Sanh was not to be another Dienbienphu. It was to be, rather, the loud noise intended to distract the Americans from the true master stroke: nothing less than large-scale assaults across the entire face of South Vietnam.

This, Giap reasoned, would bring on the uprising of the people against the "American puppets" in Saigon. It was for this—this general revolt—for which the entire "struggle" had been fought. It is difficult to underestimate the belief in a general uprising held by the Communists in Vietnam. It was an article of faith, almost a religious conviction, which has been compared to the belief in the second coming of Christ held by the early Christians. In one single, glorious moment, every hamlet and village, every city and province, would rise in righteous wrath and thrust off the tyranny that had held them in thrall.

To provoke it, Giap planned his general offensive: clandestine assaults on almost all the provincial capitals and major cities, district capitals and important hamlets—and Saigon itself. Military installations and almost every airfield were to be hit.

Surprise was to be the chief element. To obtain it, the huge feint along the borders and at Khe Sanh was intended to distract and overextend the Americans. Moreover, these clashes were to be intentionally long and bloody, thus harvesting the American headlines so necessary for Giap's campaign against the American will. They also had to be far from the centers of population and fought by Northerners whose presence in the South might discourage the people there from rising in revolt.

Local Vietcong units were to be used for the opening assaults, after which, having provoked the uprising, they would be joined by North Vietnamese (who would also make certain of Hanoi's continued control). The Vietcong units were massed close to the cities, just far enough away to escape detection. There they were drilled daily, issued new Russian AK-47 assault rifles and B-40 rockets and subjected to hourly propaganda exhortations. Supplies and stocks of ammunition were amassed. Undercover agents hidden in the infrastructure for years surfaced to join regular Vietcong units, bringing with them sheaves of death sentences and lists of "traitors." Many of these troops would infiltrate the cities beforehand so as to sabotage enemy efforts to halt the general attack which was to follow.

When it came, the Vietcong were to surge into the cities, bypassing enemy positions which might delay them, to seize all symbols of government: police stations, radio stations, administrative buildings, political headquarters and the like. There, they would announce the fall of the Saigon regime, broadcast an amnesty to South Vietnamese soldiers and call upon the people to arise.

In mid-January, Vietcong cadres and soldiers began to slip into the cities. They came in civilian clothes, joining the crowds of travelers journeying home for the approaching lunar holidays. They put on South Vietnamese uniforms and hitched rides on American trucks, or they came in buses or rode into town on motor bikes and scooters. Arms and ammunition followed them, packed in flower carts, mixed with loads of vegetables and fruit—even in caskets borne in sham funeral processions. Once safely infiltrated, they awaited the signal which was to send them into action.

And that would come on the first day of Tet.

Tet is the Vietnamese lunar holiday. Like the doctrine of the general uprising, it is difficult to overstate its sacredness in Vietnamese life. It is as though Thanksgiving, Christmas, New Year's and the Fourth of July were to be celebrated in a single week. It is a time for gaiety, for family reunion, for forgiving enemies, for facing the new year full of resolve. Although Giap intended to make it a time of terror, it had heretofore been a time of truce, when soldiers of both sides laid aside their weapons and went home to their families. In 1968 the first and most holy day of Tet was to fall on January 30, ushering in the Year of the Monkey.

In the North, Ho Chi Minh changed the first day to the 29th, ostensibly because of the position of the moon, actually to allow his people to celebrate at least one day. Ho fully expected aerial retaliation, and he did not wish it to fall upon a nation at holiday.

Apparently no one in the South put any suspicious interpretation upon the shift. Other signals were similarly ignored or dismissed. The flow of Vietcong deserters had dried up, captured infiltrators spoke openly of "something big" impending, Northern newspapers freely predicted the approach of a "historic" campaign, while captured documents suggested that major onslaughts on the cities were close at hand. One of them actually contained the general instructions for the offensive. Printed as a press release by the U.S. mission, it was dismissed as a piece of enemy propaganda. Two days before the offensive was to begin, Vietcong agents arrested in Qui Nhon were found to possess a tape to be played over the captured Qui Nhon radio station exhorting the populace to rise in revolt. In Pleiku, the actual operation order for the assault there was also captured. Yet these warnings were discounted, probably because the Americans were deceived by the Khe Sanh feint and because they simply could not believe the battered enemy was capable of mounting such a grandiose offensive.

Fortunately for the Americans, Lieutenant General Fred Weyand, commander of the area around Saigon, became uneasy over reports of large movements of Vietcong forces, together with an unusual pattern of erratic behavior around the capital. He informed Westmoreland of his fears, and Westmoreland ordered 15 maneuver battalions to fall back on the area, giving Weyand a formidable force of 27 battalions.

Unfortunately, except for Weyand, the only signals the Americans heeded were the ones Giap prepared for them. A proposal for another Tet truce—to last from January 27 to February 3—was advanced by the Vietcong. Four days before D-Day, they appealed for a "scrupulous" observance of the cease-fire, hinting that it might be extended and perhaps, if the allied diplomats wished to read it that way, become a permanent armistice. They did; and to compound the atmosphere of wishful thinking and self-imposed euphoria, half of the men of the South Vietnamese Army were given holiday leave.

Neither Pearl Harbor nor Hitler's Ardennes Offensive of 1944 came as a bigger surprise than Vo Nguyen Giap's Tet Offensive of 1968.

Giap had planned full-scale ground assaults almost everywhere on the first day of Tet. Actually only six provinces were hit; the next night, seven more and Saigon; and then, the third day, eight additional provinces.

Giap's coordination had failed at the final moment. Counting so heavily on surprise, he had withheld vital information from his subordinates until the last minute; and although he did achieve surprise, he lost that condition of close coordination which is just as important for such a complicated operation.

Nevertheless the early assaults did not upset either the areas threatened or those still unharmed. Local commanders made routine dispositions calculated to contain the assaults, but no one attached any special importance to them. In Saigon on the second night, the celebrations continued with the streets thronged with revelers.

In Saigon also on that second night, in a garage close to the new American Embassy, about 20 soldiers from a Vietcong sapper battalion began loading a small truck and a dilapidated taxi with explosives and weapons. They moved quickly, quietly—tension etched on their faces, drawing their features taut. Their mission was to break into the U.S. Embassy, and as they entered the vehicles at 2:45 A.M. and drove slowly toward their objective, they knew that their chances of survival were slim.

At the embassy gate they opened fire on the U.S. military policemen on duty, missing them. The soldiers returned the fire, leaping inside the compound to swing the iron gates shut. At once, the sappers plastered a plastic charge against the embassy wall, blowing a hole in it three feet high. Inside, the two soldiers had radioed for help, turning to fire upon the sappers squirming through the hole before they were killed themselves. But they had killed several enemy soldiers, most importantly, the platoon leader. Now the sappers sprinted for the embassy building itself, just as the guards inside swung its teak doors shut. Frustrated, the leaderless sappers poured a useless fusillade of small arms and rockets into the empty lobby. They debated whether or not to detonate their way into the six-story structure, finally deciding against it. Eventually they were destroyed to a man, against five Americans killed and minor damage inflicted on the embassy.

Nevertheless, with that flair for the sensational no matter how inaccurate, the American media flashed the word to the U.S. that its embassy in the heart of Saigon had been captured. Eventually, of course, the report was corrected—too late. The psychological effect was enormous, and the truth attempting to overtake the falsehood was like the sound of an explosion trying to catch up with the flash. If the media had reported the total destruction of the U.S. Pacific Fleet at Pearl Harbor, or a successful breakthrough by the Germans in the Ardennes, the impact upon American morale could hardly have been greater.

Actually, the break-in at the compound was probably the smallest action in the general assault on Saigon. Larger attacks were launched on the Presidential Palace, the South Vietnamese joint General Staff headquarters, Tan Son Nhut Airfield and the giant airbase at Bien Hoa. All were repulsed in the first wave. South Vietnamese troops, fighting with Americans, showed that they could fight valiantly when their own homes were threatened.

They also fought well in all the other counterattacks which exploded across the land, and especially at Hue. Here in the ancient capital the Communists had captured the inner city or Citadel, the residence of Annamese emperors, and hung onto it doggedly in the face of counterstrokes by American Marines and South Vietnamese paratroopers and armored troops. On February 24 Hue was retaken— and by that time all the other cities held in whole or in part by the Vietcong had been torn from their possession.

Tet had failed. It was a crushing defeat, especially since the yearned-for general uprising of the people did not materialize. The vicious campaign of terrorism mounted by the Vietcong against the civil populations of the areas they held temporarily had had a reverse effect. General Giap's eleventh-hour disclosure of his plans had robbed his units of coordination, and in attacking everywhere—a violation of the cardinal precept of concentration which Giap knowingly committed—he did not have enough strength anywhere. He had also been wrong in believing that the South Vietnamese Army would fold and that the people would rise in revolt. Finally, General Westmoreland's decision to move battalions closer to the cities not only placed reserves within immediate call but also blocked enemy reinforcement routes.

By the end of March the Communists realized that they had suffered the most appalling defeat in the history of the war. Their losses were enormous: 60,000 dead and probably three or four times that number wounded. Perhaps worse, the agents of the infrastructure, and the members of the Front's shadow government who had eagerly surfaced to lead the anticipated popular revolt, had been destroyed. After Tet, it is safe to say, the Vietcong was hardly more than a name worn by a ragged band of demoralized, disillusioned soldiers.

The allies also suffered; chiefly from the terrorist war on civilians. Government figures placed civilian deaths at 7,721, with 18,516 wounded. Property losses were great. In Hue alone, barely 7,000 of 17,000 homes were left standing. A total of 75,000 homes and other buildings were destroyed, a major blow against the pacification program, creating an additional 670,000 refugees. Property losses were estimated at $173 million.

Military losses, however, were a small fraction of those suffered by the enemy: 2,600 killed and 12,727 wounded.

Tet, then, was for the Communists an unmitigated military disaster. By March, they were reeling—targets for the kill. A jubilant Westmoreland, backed by the Joint Chiefs, asked for 200,000 more troops to complete the job and break the enemy's back. President Johnson rejected the request, if only because news of the proposal had been leaked to the press, and by then, the American media and the antiwar dissenters—whether by accident or design or a mixture of both, only future historians can say—had turned the allies' most glorious victory in the field into a stunning, irretrievable psychological defeat.

Dissent in war is not, as some distraught Americans of 1965-75 appeared to believe, a departure from American tradition, but rather a return to it. Actually, the departures occurred during the two world wars, the "total" conflicts which shaped the concepts of war held by most Americans. True, Korea was a limited war, but most Americans had blocked Korea out of their mind. They remembered only World War I, when Wilson ruthlessly suppressed all dissent, or World War II, when dissent was made unpopular by the unifying burst of national outrage which succeeded Pearl Harbor. Most Americans either did not remember or did not know that all of America's other wars were limited, and that in them dissent was permitted. To protest against a war policy, therefore, was nothing new. Dissent was in the American tradition of free speech, and a dissenter might very well, in Emerson's phrase, be harking to "a different drum."

In 1965-75, however, the drumbeat of dissent was indeed different, so strident and vituperative that the "bloody graves" speech of Black Tom Corwin during the Mexican War seems by comparison the mildest bleat of disagreement. As in France during the war in Indo-China, the military was mocked and the widows of war heroes were subjected to obscene insults by anonymous telephone callers. Some college professors rooted openly for a Vietcong victory. Young men burned their draft cards and youth of both sexes burned American flags. Three Americans, perhaps influenced by the self-immolations of Buddhist protesters in Vietnam, burned themselves to death. Antiwar demonstrations were staged simultanteously in the nation's chief cities, and sometimes also in the chief cities of the world. Some leaders of the Civil Rights movement attempted to link the battle to secure equal rights for blacks with the fight to "end the war in Vietnam," and as numerous clergymen of all faiths joined in denouncing the war as "unjust and immoral," the floors of Congress resounded to debate between the so-called doves opposed to the war and the hawks who supported it.

Yet this was nothing new. Even the hatred and obscenity were only a matter of degree. What was entirely new in the Vietnam dissent was an impartial observer's difficulty in separating the sincere from the sham, the spontaneous from the manipulated, the informed from the ignorant, the patriotic from the personal and the naïve from the realistic. In truth, the Vietnam dissent was such a mixture of both that to separate the genuine from the counterfeit will probably not be possible for many years to come. Suffice it to say that in its effect on the nation's young men during the years 1965-67, the dissent was negligible. In 1966, only 353 of 1,100,000 draft-eligible men were convicted as draft-dodgers, in comparison to one-year totals of 8,422 in World War I, 4,609 in World War II and 432 in Korea. Similarly, the desertion rate for 1966 was 0.08 for every 1,000 draftees, against 3.7 in World War II and 0.89 in Korea. Its effect on President Johnson in those years 1965-67 may have been to compel him to consider public reaction to every decision to escalate the war, which, after all, is one of the purposes of free speech in a democracy. Its effect on his determination to prosecute the war, however, was negligible. In speech after speech he reiterated his determination to contain Asian Communism. " 'Hitherto shalt thou come, but no farther,' " he repeatedly declared, quoting from the Bible.

It was in its effect on the enemy that dissent was most deleterious to the American war effort. There seems to be little doubt that American dissent stiffened the enemy's resolve to fight on. Again and again, Hanoi spoke of "the mounting struggle of the people of the United States of America against Johnson's aggressive war in Vietnam." In truth, the bulk of the American people supported the war. In a nationwide poll taken in 1967, it was reported that 67 percent of the nation supported continued bombing of North Vietnam, 24 percent felt that it should be stopped and 9 percent had no opinion.

After the Tet Offensive, however, the uproar of protest and criticism that beat against the White House marked a turning point in the effectiveness of the antiwar dissent.

That single headline or bulletin flashed on TV screens—U.S. EMBASSY IN SAIGON CAPTURED!—was the spark that went flashing into the powder keg of protest. "What the hell's going on?" a famous commentator roared. "I thought we were winning this war!" His remark, reflecting the newsman's final delusion that he is making the news he is covering, as well as his ignorance of war and especially counterinsurgency, was typical of the ordinary American's reaction. General Westmoreland had only four days earlier submitted a summary of the fighting in 1967 which suggested that the enemy was on the ropes. In fact, he was; and by the time Tet was over, he was on his knees. Unhappily, Westmoreland's report created an atmosphere of euphoria; and now, here was the "beaten" enemy mounting another major campaign, killing and maiming more American boys. Subsequent reports putting the embassy action into its true perspective while making it clear that the Communists were failing simply could not restore that feeling of euphoria or of confidence. Even if the commentators or "anchormen" or correspondents had known or understood enough of warfare to point out that all desperation offensives succeed in the beginning, because of their very nature, or had possessed the sense of history to compare Tet to the Battle of the Bulge in which Hitler's opening success was even greater and his ultimate defeat more disastrous, it probably would have had little effect. World War II had been a popular war and there was no panic in the headlines. Vietnam was an immensely unpopular war— perhaps unpopular par excellence—and there were too many Americans who actually reveled and rejoiced in the initial bad news.

One of the chief sticks used to beat the war with was a photograph of General Nguyen Ngoc Loan shooting a man in the head in Saigon. The accompanying caption called the man a "Vietcong suspect," when he was actually a Vietcong colonel whom Loan knew personally, and who had been caught wearing civilian clothes while directing guerrilla warfare in the capital of Loan's country. By all the rules of warfare he could and should have been shot on the spot. What, say, would George Washington have done if he had found Benedict Arnold in civilian clothes directing a Tory uprising in New York?

Such questions, of course, were not asked by the infuriated dissenters and antiwar activists who made a *cause célèbre* of this single incident. The unsavory and ugly Loan was made to epitomize all that was foul and rotten in the South Vietnamese government. Denunciatory editorials and columns were written on this one photograph, sermons were pronounced on it—while little if any protest was raised against the enemy's deliberate murder of between 2,000 and 3,000 residents of Hue who were buried alive or clubbed to death for the crime of living peacefully under their own government.

It was after Tet that this double standard of thinking became more and more apparent among influential men and women of the nation's media. One after another, nationally famous commentators, anchormen and columnists turned against the war. None, of course, changed his colors. All still spoke or wrote under the banner of impartiality when, in fact, they had openly lent their names and influence to the antiwar movement. Members of the media, based as they were in South Vietnam, had few photographs or tapes of Communist cruelty to present their public. Instead, they concentrated on the shortcomings of America and her allies. Television shows were especially adept in serving up the nightly meal of misery. All that was heartrending and sickening in one day's filming in South Vietnam was cut and glued together in a single minute or so of film, which implied to its shocked and war-weary viewers that this was merely typical of what happened every day everywhere in the country. Battle after battle reported in the daily press spoke of the "mauling" of American and allied troops. Indeed, "maul" seemed to be many headline-writers' favorite word. "U.S. MARINES MAULED," the thick print would shout, until way down in perhaps the sixth or seventh paragraph of the story, it would almost invariably be discovered that the enemy got much worse than he gave. It was in such ways that a once-prized objectivity all but disappeared. Even *Newsweek* felt obliged to comment that for the first time in history the American press was more friendly to its country's enemies than to its country. What Ho Chi Minh said was believed; what Lyndon Johnson said was not.

Meanwhile the pitiless, relentless portrayal of the agony of Vietnam had a most demoralizing effect on the American public. Vietnam was actually the first conflict to be beamed into the living rooms of the world, and because of the selective nature of television coverage, the spectacle of so much suffering and destruction could hardly fail to produce anguish in the breast of the viewer. Moreover, after Tet the underlying purpose of all this death and destruction was seldom mentioned. Indeed, there was a tendency to belittle all administration explanations of "containment" or "the domino theory," the conviction that if South Vietnam were to fall, then the rest of Indo-China would fall "like dominoes"—as all but Thailand ultimately did. For its part, the government was inept at explaining these positions to the people. Probably they could not be explained, because the American people do not—perhaps even do not want to—understand that war is an instrument of policy. The idea of limited war, as Senator Taft perceptively observed during the Korean War, is abhorrent to them. Thus the distraught and agonized American public seemed to conclude that the war in Vietnam was being fought in a purposeless, mindless military morass. Oddly enough, they did not withdraw their approval of the war, as the polls continued to show; but Lyndon Johnson—the political animal famous for his pockets full of polls—was aware that they were withdrawing it from him.

On March 31, 1968, in a nationwide telecast, Lyndon Baines Johnson astonished the world by announcing that he would not run for re-election that year. He said the reason for his decision was to take the search for peace in Vietnam out of politics, disclosing that he had ordered a reduction in the bombing of North Vietnam and that preliminary peace negotiations were in progress.

Actually, Johnson did not choose to run because he knew that he faced almost certain defeat. A Louis Harris poll showed that public approval of his performance had dropped to 38 percent, a disheartening decline from his record-breaking victory in 1964 and the early days of his presidency, when his conduct merited as much as 70 percent approval. Moreover Senator Eugene McCarthy of Minnesota, an extreme liberal and outspoken opponent of the war, had openly challenged Johnson in the Wisconsin primary, where it appeared that he would defeat the President. So also had another prominent "dove," Senator Robert F. Kennedy, who actually went on to win primaries in California and South Dakota until, like his brother John before him, he was killed by an assassin's bullet in Los Angeles on June 5. Thus Johnson became, if not the first President to lose a war—a distinction which he dreaded—at least the first chief of state to be brought down by one.

He was undone by two factors: first, his determination to wage a

costly war while funding the expensive welfare programs of his
Great Society; second, the desertion of the antiwar liberals of his
own party. On the first count, a policy of "guns and butter," even
in a country as wealthy as America, is only possible for a short
while. Over the years it simply will not work. When it became apparent that money for "guns" was reducing the amount of "butter"
available for the Great Society, liberals such as the black leader
Martin Luther King—who was assassinated three days after Johnson
stepped down—openly associated his civil rights movement with the
antiwar forces. The influential Jewish community, almost always a
powerful factor in Democratic politics, was critical of the war because
it was considered a distraction from the Middle East, where Israel
in 1967 had been attacked by the Arabs once more and had again,
with incredible speed, been victorious. Meanwhile Democratic liberals
in both houses defected from Johnson's leadership. They had chanted
"All the way with LBJ" in 1964, but in 1968 it was apparent that they
were willing to go only one way: their own. While praising Johnson for
domestic programs such as Medicare, they denounced him for refusing
to withdraw from the war and leave South Vietnam to go it alone. Attacked from within his own party with a ferocity that must have been
at the least depressing, it is likely that if the dissent did not dissolve his
determination to continue the war, it certainly broke his heart. Day
after day the level of obscenity and vituperation among the antiwar
demonstrators chanting around the White House rose to a venomous
shrill pitch. "Hey, hey, LBJ—how many kids did you kill today?"[17]
Lyndon Baines Johnson knew that he could never be re-elected, still
less even gain his party's nomination. And when he made his announcement, he resuscitated the fallen political fortunes of Richard
Milhous Nixon.

After his narrow defeat by John F. Kennedy in 1960, Richard
Nixon returned to his native California. In 1962, he ran for governor—and was badly beaten. It seemed the end of the line, and
apparently Nixon felt that way, telling the press—which was, in
truth, openly hostile to him—"You won't have Dick Nixon to kick
around, anymore."[18] Retiring from politics, Nixon entered private
law practice, only appearing in public in 1964 and 1966 to campaign
for Republican candidates. Gradually, however, he began to mount
a presidential drive, and by 1968 he was at the head of a smooth,

efficient political machine which easily carried off the Republican nomination in a singularly dull convention held in Miami.

The Democratic Convention in Chicago was anything but boring. For months prior to the meeting, certain antiwar and "new leftist" groups had formed a coalition aimed at disrupting the convention and repudiating the Democratic leadership. "Parade marshals" were trained in the art of harassing police and penetrating security lines. They hoped to lead scores of thousands of dissenters—mostly students—in a violent confrontation with the police that would be televised nationally and further discredit the war. That it would also discredit their country all over the world seemed "acceptable" to them. To prevent the "takeover" of the convention and forestall a bloody riot, Chicago's 12,000-man police force was augmented by 13,000 Illinois National Guardsmen and Army regulars. Barbed wire was strung around the convention hall. It was a situation much to the liking of activists, who were careful to notify the media of where and when they would begin "harassing" the police. When they did, they came at the blue-shirted lines shouting obscenities and hurling rocks and bottles. Battles erupted repeatedly, the largest occurring on the night of August 28 when demonstrators chanting "The whole world's watching!" fought club-wielding police for 18 minutes in full view of television cameras. Some of the police, frustrated and enraged by the "harassment," seemed to enjoy beating the demonstrators, continuing to club them even after superior officers ordered them to desist. On the whole, however, the Chicago police force acted with restraint, and the bloodbath which radical demonstrators had sought did not occur. (It should also be added that the Chicago demonstrations were certainly not typical of the antiwar marches held before and after the Democratic Convention, most of which were peaceful and orderly.)

In this atmosphere of violence the Democrats nominated Vice President Hubert H. Humphrey of Minnesota. His selection enraged the antiwar people, who had backed Senator McCarthy. They believed that to nominate Humphrey, who had never publicly differed with his chief over the war, was tantamount to a vote of approval for Johnson's policies. Infuriated, they hung on Humphrey's campaign trail like a hairshirt, booing and heckling him wherever he appeared. For a full month, the Democratic candidate was literally drowned out by youths chanting: "Dump the Hump! Dump the Hump!" On one occasion, the antiwar hecklers would not permit the tearful Humphrey to finish his speech. Try as he might, Humphrey could not separate himself from Johnson, and although he picked up strength toward the end of the campaign, he went down to a narrow defeat.

Thus Richard Nixon became the first man since William Henry Harrison in 1840 to win the presidency after a previously unsuccessful attempt, as well as the 5th consecutive war veteran to occupy the White House and the 17th of 37 Presidents to have worn a uniform. An open supporter of Johnson's war policies, he had been the unintended beneficiary of that post-Tet dissent and antiwar activity which had demoralized the home front, brought down Johnson, driven Humphrey to distraction and defeat, and also, by the time Richard Milhous Nixon raised his right hand in January, 1969, helped to dissolve the discipline of American ground troops fighting in Vietnam.

Generally speaking, from 1968 onward, the American warrior was no longer the admirably trained and motivated fighting man that he had been in the preceding years. Bewildered by what seemed to many the "betrayal" of the home front, anguished at the spectacle of little brothers burning American flags during halftime at high-school football games, resentful of an unjust conscription system that had landed them in a detestable country among a people whom they despised, left in the dark by their government as to why they were there at all, it was perhaps inevitable that these young men should become chary of risking their flesh. And for what?, they sneered bitterly—a bunch of "gooks" and *Lyndon*? They were especially indignant over the widespread insinuation that the troops in Vietnam were mere cannon fodder, drawn from the "lower classes," and hardly the equal of those youths whose college deferments had gained them a minimum of four safe years in campus snuggeries. Nor could they swallow that other belittling implication, that the growing number of draft-dodgers and deserters were "the real heroes," or that, as the antiwar camp claimed, "The brave ones went to Canada." Thus, wherever esprit de corps, personal pride or native courage were inoperable, these young men simply did not want to fight. With such disgruntled troops, discipline, especially discipline in the face of danger, became most difficult to maintain. "Field refusal," that is, a soldier's refusal to advance against the enemy or, say, to enter a helicopter bound for the combat zone, was not uncommon. Nor was the punishment anything but mild: five years at hard labor for a conviction that heretofore was at least life imprisonment and sometimes death. Frequently junior officers would not give an order unless they were armed. Company and even battalion commanders often had no other way to halt their stampeding commands except to shoot the first to flee in the legs.

Inevitably, the men came to hate their officers with an unrivaled intensity. They boasted openly of holding "frag parties," that is, throwing fragmentation grenades into tents occupied by officers. Surely for soldiers to dislike their officers is not unusual, and reports of men in combat shooting their leaders in the back are also not rare. Normally, however, men in danger do not decimate themselves, and stories to the contrary are usually spurious. In Vietnam, however, the very coining of the phrase "frag party" seems to give credence to the claim that the practice existed. Two other problems which faced the military authorities in Vietnam were the widespread use of drugs— probably to be expected in Indo-China, where drug-taking is as normal as drinking in the West—and venereal disease. Much as the Americans might try to cleanse South Vietnam's army of prostitutes, they always found themselves shoveling sand against the tide. Drugs and VD complicated the task of motivating soldiers already demoralized by dissent, the unjust draft and antiwar activity at home. Finally, they had no desire to sacrifice themselves for the South Vietnamese, if only because they hated them at least as much as they hated the enemy.

In Vietnam, American ground troops fought what can only be described as surrealist war. Except for the rare conventional pitched battle, patrolling—searching for the enemy—was the war's chief tactical characteristic. Each day, soldiers and Marines crept with tense and fearful stealth through dripping jungles raucous with the shrill cries of tropical birds, or sloshed through swamps alive with squirming life—searching, searching, searching for an invisible enemy. They passed by tiny villages standing like Japanese gardens behind their bamboo hedges, silent little settlements eloquent of a strange exotic society that the Americans could not understand: a world of dainty miniatures inhabited by dainty miniature people with smooth golden skin and deceptively docile ways. Yet from these same villages came the sniper fire and mortar shells that killed and maimed, and the trails between the villages were sown with land mines and sharpened stakes planted by these same simple villagers. Gradually the American ground troops came to distrust and then to detest these people whom, according to the American government, they had come to save. Whether or not the villagers served the Vietcong willingly or under coercion was not a point to be mooted: either way they were a source of danger.

Whenever an American unit received fire from a village, its commander could choose between flattening the village with artillery fire or aerial bombing, or attacking it. If he chose the first, he might find among the bamboo ruins the bodies of only a few snipers, together with perhaps as many as 300 innocent villagers—men, women and children. If, however, he attacked, he might be leading his men into a trap. Not surprisingly, the officer frequently chose the first alternative—and he did frequently find many dead and wounded civilians in the rubble.

It did no good to denounce the Vietcong for their cruel cunning in compelling the Americans to make decisions which sometimes resulted in their killing and maiming their own allies, thus provoking South Vietnamese hatred of American troops. No, the Americans were on the horns of a bloody and unbearable dilemma. Too often it was either "them" or "us," and "they" were too often "us." Although appalled at first, the Americans gradually became inured to these horrible "mistakes." Naturally enough, they also sought to shift the blame. Cursing their own government for having put them in such predicaments was insufficient. The only sure way of assuaging guilt feelings was to hate the South Vietnamese as fiercely and as openly as they hated the Communists. Moreover there was to be no distinction between them. They were all "a bunch of gooks." They were "animals," and to kill one of them was not to destroy a human being.

All that was detestable about the South Vietnamese—their sloth, the filthy shantytowns they lived in, their incredible slowness and lethargy, the disorder and dirt of the refugee camps, their corruption —all this was seized upon, both to justify the American soldiers' hatred and to fuel it. The fact that American bombings were responsible for the shantytowns and the refugee camps; that the percentage of pilferage in South Vietnam was no greater and perhaps less than the rate of theft on the docks of the United States; that the corruption sprang in large part from the huge cornucopia of commodities that the United States had emptied over the country; or that the slowness and lethargy were a colonial people's surest ways of expressing their resentment of their new masters—all these were ignored or scarely considered by an embittered and enraged soldiery bent upon taking out their frustrations upon someone else.

To say that the foregoing was true of all ground troops who served in Vietnam is not accurate. Many American servicemen made great sacrifices and spent many hours working to help the people. Some returned to continue their works of charity after they had been rotated home and discharged. On their own and at their own expense, American servicemen organized welfare programs to feed and clothe the uprooted and homeless in their area. Medicines were dispensed out of unit stocks and doctors gave free medical care. Mills and schools were built out of funds contributed by American servicemen. Nevertheless, there is much evidence to support the antiwar groups' charges that American troops were frequently guilty of murder and maiming of South Vietnamese.

The supreme piece of evidence was unveiled in the fall of 1969, when the Pentagon disclosed that a year and a half earlier, in the wake of the Tet Offensive, American soldiers on a "clearing" operation had entered the village of My Lai and massacred many of its 300 inhabitants, mostly women and children. Eventually the unit leader, First Lieutenant William Calley, was court-martialled and convicted of the murder of 22 civilians. He was sentenced to life imprisonment, which was later reduced to ten years, and he was finally paroled. My Lai, of course, became a *cause célèbre* in America. Played up in all its repulsive gruesomeness in the media, investigated in Congress, My Lai became a kind of oriflamme for the antiwar movement. It shook a nation convinced of its own humanity. To realize that their own soldiers were no better than the Communists in their treatment of their allies was so wounding to American self-esteem that most of the people refused to believe it or else turned away from the war in disgust.

Almost as disturbing as the My Lai massacre itself was the attitude of those responsible for it. Although a congressional subcommittee investigating the incident concluded that the perpetrators could not have been sane, a team of psychiatrists who had examined the accused men insisted that Calley and his soldiers were eminently sane.

"It was no big deal," Calley declared repeatedly, suggesting thereby that it was "nothing new." After his trial he sought to attempt to justify what he had done by saying: "When my troops were getting massacred and mauled by an enemy I couldn't see, I couldn't feel and I couldn't touch—that nobody in the military system ever described them as anything other than Communism. They didn't give it a race, they didn't give it a sex, they didn't give it an age. They never let me believe it was just a philosophy in a man's mind. That was my enemy out there."[19] Obviously the incoherence of this statement suggests that if Calley was not insane, he was at least confused, and that My Lai, an unprovoked incident in which the commander was not hung on the horns of the bloody dilemma described earlier, may well have been born of panic. Still, it was wrong, terribly wrong, and the infuriating fact that the truth about the massacre had been suppressed by the Pentagon for 18 months hung like a millstone around the neck of Richard Nixon as he became the fourth American President to pursue the policy of "containment" in Vietnam.

9

☆

Richard Nixon also did not want to be the first American President to lose a war, and when he took office in January of 1969, his first priority in foreign affairs was to pursue the search for negotiated peace in Vietnam and to "wind down the war."

Lyndon Johnson had already set a tentative foot on the road to peace when, announcing his decision to retire from politics, he also revealed that he had ordered a halt to the bombing and naval bombardment of North Vietnam, except in areas where enemy build-ups threatened allied troops. A few days later Hanoi declared its "readiness" to discuss peace.

Preliminary peace talks were held in Paris in May of 1968. However, months of negotiation brought no progress, and on October 31 Johnson announced that all bombardment of North Vietnam would end the following day. He said that, in exchange for the bombing halt,

North Vietnam had agreed to permit South Vietnam to take part in the Paris talks, while the United States in turn had agreed to allow the National Liberation Front (NLF) to be present. At first President Thieu balked at seating the NLF, finally relenting and sending a delegation headed by Vice President Ky to the negotiations. A dispute over seating arrangements and the shape of the table stalled the talks into 1969, when Henry Cabot Lodge replaced W. Averell Harriman as chief of the U.S. delegation.

To break the deadlock, Nixon in May announced an eight-point peace plan based upon a mutual withdrawal of all foreign troops from Vietnam, together with internationally supervised elections. The Communists remained intransigent, the NLF insisting that the "puppet regime in Saigon" be removed before any productive talks could begin. Nixon thereupon wrote a conciliatory letter to Ho Chi Minh, meanwhile appealing to the Soviet Union to bring pressure to bear upon her balky ally. He also, at a June meeting with President Thieu on Midway Island, announced the first American troop withdrawal from Vietnam: 25,000 men, to be followed by 35,000 more in September and 50,000 in December. Gradually the war would be "Vietnamized," that is, Thieu's Army would be trained, equipped and motivated to assume responsibility for operations until, with the departure of the last American, it would be fighting on its own. It was Nixon's hope that evidence of his desire to "wind down the war," together with the continuing bombing halt, might break the peace-talk deadlock. However, Ho Chi Minh's reply to the President's letter was a flat rejection, demanding that Nixon end "the war of aggression of the United States against our people."[20] Ho's message was one of the last written by the aging revolutionary, for he died in September, to be succeeded by Premier Pham Van Dong.

In Paris, the wrangling and haranguing reminiscent of Panmunjom in Korea continued, until, on August 7, Lodge arose from his chair and told the Communist delegates: "We have done all that we can do by ourselves to bring a negotiated peace in Vietnam. Now, it is time for you to respond."[21] No response was forthcoming, however; nor was there any appreciable rise in battlefield activity, probably because of Nixon's earlier decision to bomb North Vietnamese troop sanctuaries in Cambodia.

Back in February, the Communists had launched a small but savage offensive against about 100 cities of South Vietnam, striking them with artillery and rockets. Obviously it was an attempt to test the new

American administration—and Nixon's reply was to order the secret bombing of some 40,000 North Vietnamese regulars massed in an area 10 to 15 miles wide just inside the Cambodian border. From there, they made their sallies into South Vietnam. The bombing was to be unannounced because Cambodia was supposedly "neutral." However, it was known that Prince Sihanouk resented the North Vietnamese presence on his country's soil. If the bombing of his country were secret, the White House reasoned, he would not protest. Nor would the North Vietnamese protest, inasmuch as they had repeatedly denied having troops in Cambodia. So the order was given, and waves of B-52s struck at the Communist sanctuary. Immediately afterward, Communist battlefield activity declined. Both Sihanouk and Ho Chi Minh, meanwhile, remained silent. Secret aerial attacks on North Vietnamese in Cambodia were launched again in April, after the Communist North Koreans shot down an American reconnaissance plane over the Sea of Japan. The strike was intended to warn both Communist countries that the new administration could not be intimidated. Once again, neither Sihanouk nor the North Vietnamese protested. But the American media did, after high administration officials in mid-May leaked details of the bombings to the *New York Times.* A storm of protest swept the country from editorial pages to the floor of both houses of Congress. Fortunately for the White House, the college students who had staged antiwar activity throughout early 1969 were busy with examinations and would soon be scattering for home.

In the fall, however, they were back on campus—ready to join the widely publicized Vietnam Moratorium scheduled for October 15 in Washington. On that date, with the public encouragement of Premier Pham Van Dong of North Vietnam, a quarter million protestors gathered for what were generally peaceful demonstrations. Across the country bells were tolled, the names of the war dead were read at religious services, wreaths were laid in parks and hortatory speeches delivered at seminars, teach-ins, vigils and folk-song concerts. Those who supported the war, meanwhile, displayed the American flag or drove with their automobile headlights on.

Although jubilant over what they considered a huge success, one which the Vietcong radio said had given "strong encouragement" to the Communists, the antiwar activists were dismayed when Nixon, obviously undeterred by the Moratorium, appealed to the nation for support of his war policies. In a nationally televised speech directed toward what he called "the great silent majority of my fellow Americans," Nixon declared: "the more divided we are at home the less likely the enemy is to negotiate at Paris. Let us be united for peace. Let us also be united against defeat. Because let us understand: North Vietnam cannot defeat or humiliate the United States. Only Americans can do that."[22]

To Nixon's delighted surprise, his appeal produced the greatest response ever accorded a presidential plea, almost all of it favorable. Even a majority in Congress approved, and a Gallup Poll showed 68 percent of the nation behind the President. Nixon was so gratified that he appeared personally before both houses of Congress to thank them for their support.

The antiwar dissidents, however, were enraged. It had been assumed that the Moratorium had so frightened the President that he was preparing to withdraw from Vietnam. To discover his opposite reaction infuriated them and drove some of them into the hands of the more radical dissenters, who openly advocated violence. A second Moratorium held on November 15, called the "New Mobe," was less orderly than its forerunner. In San Francisco, a black militant told a crowd of 125,000 persons shouting "Peace! Peace!" "We will kill Richard Nixon. We will kill anyone that stands in the way of our freedom."[23] In Washington, a few of the quarter million protestors who thronged the capital stormed the Justice Department building, screaming: "Smash the state!" They tore down the American flag, burned it and hoisted the Vietnam flag in its place. Such incidents brought surprisingly little condemnation from either Congress or the media. Indeed, the Washington *Post* said of the New Mobe: "To dig beneath the rhetoric is to discover something extraordinary, and quite beautiful. Those who were here . . . are here in support of what is best about this country."[24]

Most of the demonstrators undoubtedly believed that they were. But "what was best about the country" also included militant groups such as the Black Panthers, with their record of violence and murder, and the more palatable Yippies (Youth International Party), as well as youths fired by an intense hatred of "the establishment," who carried their grievances back from Washington and the other cities onto their college campuses.

Throughout the winter and spring of 1969 there had been antiwar demonstrations at the colleges and universities, where the student protestors against the "complicity" of the academic "establishment" in the war effort usually forced the authorities to submit to their demands. A typical reaction was the University of Pennsylvania's decision to put all its American flags in storage in order to avoid a confrontation. A few, such as Dr. S. I. Hayakawa of San Francisco State and Reverend Theodore Hesburgh of Notre Dame, would not, in Hesburgh's phrase, bow to those who substituted "force for persuasion."

In 1970, however, with the radicals in charge goaded by the shock of the news of My Lai, campus unrest was characterized by rioting, destruction and death. April perhaps was the most violent month. Rioting students at the University of California at Santa Barbara burned a bank to the ground, for the second time; at Ohio State, students demanding the abolition of the ROTC fought police for six hours; and at the University of Kansas students burned down a building valued at $2 million. Books also were burned, as libraries and cultural centers went up in flames. Throughout the academic year 1969-70 there were 1,800 demonstrations resulting in 7,500 arrests, 462 injuries—two-thirds of them to police—and 8 deaths. Property destruction was never calculated or estimated, but it must have been immense, to say nothing of the loss of irreplaceable books or research collections. Inevitably, the level of violence rose to a higher and higher pitch, driven there in great part by Nixon's description of some of the student protestors as "bums who burn books," and his decision to invade the Communist sanctuaries in Cambodia.

On March 18, while Prince Sihanouk was visiting Moscow, an anti-Communist Cambodian general named Lon Nol seized power in the capital of Phnom Penh. Although delighted, Washington did not immediately come to his support, fearing that Russia, China and North Vietnam would accuse the United States of having organized and financed the coup. In fact, not even the CIA had known it was impending. Washington also feared that Lon Nol did not have enough strength to hold off the Cambodian Communists, known as the Khmer Rouge. To support a government likely to be soon overthrown would not be wise. However, Lon Nol's forces at first fought surprisingly well against the Khmer Rouge, and the new chief of state also closed the port of Sihanoukville, thereby denying both the Cambodian and North Vietnamese Communists much of their supplies. However, the coup made rebels of supporters of Sihanouk eventually, who in Peking, became their titular leader. Thus strengthened, the Khmer Rouge continued to advance on Phnom Penh, and when it became clear that they had brought one-quarter of Cambodia under their control, President Nixon moved to send aid to Lon Nol.

Nixon feared that if Lon Nol were to fall and Cambodia go Communist, then South Vietnam would be open to attack from the west as well as the north. He also decided that the time had now come to launch ground attacks on the North Vietnamese massed in safety on that same vulnerable western border.

They were in two sanctuaries known, respectively, as the Parrot's Beak, the small area close to Saigon which would be invaded by South Vietnamese, and the larger Fishhook, to be entered by both Americans and South Vietnamese. In this narrow curving slice of land slashing into the heart of the south lay the nerve center or command post for both sanctuaries. Here also were most of the supplies, troops and fortifications. Nixon was convinced that as long as the Communists remained untouched in their Cambodian strongholds, they threatened the safety of American troops remaining in South Vietnam, while almost guaranteeing another invasion once the last American had gone home. Not all of Nixon's cabinet officers agreed, particularly Secretary of State William Rogers, who thought the strikes would be too costly with very little gain; and Secretary of Defense Melvin Laird, who did not like the way the operations were being organized. Laird thought General Creighton Abrams, who had relieved Westmoreland, would also oppose the operation. However, General Abrams told Nixon that an "attack on this area should have maximum unsettling effect on the enemy, who had considered until now his sanctuaries immune to ground attack."[25] On April 29 the invasion of the Parrot's Beak was announced, and that night President Nixon told the nation over television that U.S. and South Vietnamese forces would soon enter the Fishhook.

Although Nixon had explained that his purpose was to destroy enemy positions threatening the safety of allied troops, not to seize Cambodian ground or to expand the war into that unhappy country, in the storm of protest that succeeded the announcement he was accused of escalating the war and exposing Americans to heavier casualties. He was also charged with trying to end the war by military means rather than negotiation, while other critics called the Cambodian operations an admission of the failure of Vietnamization.

In fact, the Cambodian operation was militarily the most successful of the war. On June 30, two months after it began, the last allied soldier returned to South Vietnamese soil, leaving the sanctuaries utterly smashed. Enough weapons had been captured to equip 74 North Vietnamese battalions and enough food to feed all those Communist battalions then in South Vietnam for 4 months. More important, the Communists' capacity to launch the customary spring offensive into the South had been destroyed. American casualties, standing at 93 deaths a week before the attacks, dropped to 51 per week in the following 6 months, as the planned withdrawal of 150,000 men went forward on schedule, and the port of Sihanoukville remained closed. Such results, when properly understood, would seem to have been worthwhile. They were not, however, so understood by the antiwar faction in America, and thus the Cambodian operations, so beneficial militarily for the allies in Vietnam, produced, like many other similar successes, the exactly reverse psychological effect in the United States.

It was on the campus of Kent State University in Ohio that the perhaps inevitable tragedy overtook the outbreak of campus rioting. There, before cheering protestors, two young men threw lighted flares into the ROTC building and burned it down. Immediately Governor Rhodes sent in the National Guard, as he had done at Ohio State. The appearance of the armed Guardsmen angered the Kent State students. Some of them jeered at the troops, calling them obscene names. On May 4 a crowd of antiwar students began pelting the Guardsmen with rocks and chunks of concrete, driving them up onto a small hill. Some of the Guardsmen opened fire and four students—two bystanders and two protestors—were killed.

Now the student rioting spread from campus to campus. Hundreds of schools were thrown into turmoil. Within a week 448 colleges and universities had been closed down, and by the end of the month the National Guard had been called out 24 times in 16 states. Meanwhile a national day of protest was organized for May 9 in Washington. The night before, Nixon met the press in front of the television cameras. A reporter asked him if he understood why the students were converging on Washington. He replied: "They are trying to say that they want peace. They are trying to say that they want to stop the killing. They are trying to say that they want to end the draft. They are trying to say that we ought to get out of Vietnam. I agree with everything that they are trying to accomplish. I believe, however, that the decisions that I have made, and particularly this last terribly difficult decision of going into the Cambodian sanctuaries which were completely occupied by the enemy—I believe that that decision will serve that purpose, because you can be sure that everything that I stand for is what they want."[26]

In the dark of the following morning Nixon paid a personal visit to the Lincoln Memorial, where the protesting students had assembled. He spoke with about 30 of them until dawn, trying, as he said, "to relate to them," to explain to them what he had said at the press conference. But he failed. They were courteous but withdrawn. In this pathetic scene—the trim chief executive, dressed and groomed in such fashion as to suggest all that is "successful" in American life, appealing to grim-faced students, deliberately uncouth and "anti-establishment" in their faded blue jeans and long, unkempt hair, most of the boys bearded—may be seen the dreadful dilemma which had faced the White House since 1965. On the one hand, Nixon could escape the fate of his predecessor by listening to the protestors and unilaterally withdrawing from Vietnam; on the other, to do so would, he believed, cripple and perhaps destroy American credibility with her allies and make a travesty of her foreign policy. Standing in the dawning light beneath the heroic figure of Abraham Lincoln, Nixon might well have reflected on how the Great Emancipator, faced with the antiwar protests of the early days of the Civil War, had described the predicament: "Must a government, of necessity, be too strong for the liberties of its own people, or too weak to maintain its own existence?"

It was the immemorial dilemma of a democratic, free-speech society attempting to fight a limited war with a conscript army and a free press. It is perhaps possible against another open society similarly handicapped, but against a police state it cannot be done.

10

☆

In the summer of 1969, with the peace negotiations in Paris publicly and apparently hopelessly stalled, President Nixon opened a campaign of secret diplomacy.

He had already discovered in Jean Sainteny, a French business-man who had spent many years in Indo-China, an invaluable go-between and courier. Sainteny knew many influential Vietnamese in both the North and South, and was friendly with Ho Chi Minh. He had already acted as courier for the White House in delivering the Nixon letter which Ho had rejected.

On August 4, 1969, Henry Kissinger, Nixon's special diplomatic assistant and later his Secretary of State, met secretly with Xuan Thuy, chief of the North Vietnamese delegation to Paris, and his next in command, Mai Van Bo, in Sainteny's apartment on the fashionable Rue de Rivoli. Kissinger explained to both men that November 1 would be the first anniversary of the U.S. bombing halt. During that period, he observed, 25,000 American troops had been withdrawn and the United States had offered to accept free elections in South Vietnam. These measures had brought no response from Hanoi, so that now Washington was attempting to open another channel of negotiations. "I have been asked to tell you in all solemnity," Kissinger continued, "that if by November 1 no major progress has been made toward a solution, we will be compelled—with great reluctance—to take measures of the greatest consequences."[27]

Xuan Thuy's reply was a restrained reiteration of Hanoi's extreme position: complete withdrawal of all American troops and acceptance of the National Liberation Front's ten points; in effect, Communist control of South Vietnam. He also insisted that there were no North Vietnamese troops in the South and that President Thieu must be overthrown. It was not a very promising beginning, and the dismayed Kissinger suggested that both nations make an effort to find a solution before November 1. The three men then shook hands and departed one by one, so as to attract no attention. Throughout, the secret talks were conducted in this clandestine style: the participants arriving at airports on unannounced flights, driving to their destination in unmarked cars, assiduously eluding the press or inquisitive embassy officials.

Meanwhile Nixon used the intervening period between August 4 and November 1 to apply the pressure on Hanoi. His first move was to instruct Kissinger to inform Russian Ambassador Anatoly Dobrynin that the Soviet failure to help end the war had left both Moscow and Washington reduced to the barest basic diplomatic relations. Next, he cut off aid to Cyprus and Malta, two nations which had refused to halt shipping to North Vietnam, and then deliberately "planted" a story to the effect that he was considering blockading Haiphong and invading the North. As he expected, one of the nine Republican senators to whom he had spoken "leaked" the story to the press, thus attracting the attention of Hanoi.

Unfortunately for the President, his attempts to make Hanoi believe that he would carry out his ultimatum were undercut by the antiwar movement. Hanoi was not harking to the screams of the hawks but the cooing of the doves, and after the October Vietnam Moratorium Nixon realized with deep chagrin that his campaign had failed. Yet his counterstroke against the antiwar people—his November 3 speech to "the great, silent majority"—together with a Gallup Poll at the end of January 1970, showing that 65 percent of the American people approved of his conduct of the war, had the unexpected effect of bringing the Communists back to Sainteny's apartment.

When they met on February 21, Xuan Thuy was accompanied by Le Duc Tho, a ranking member of the Politburo. His presence suggested that Kissinger was now dealing with someone who could make decisions, and the American immediately alluded to the popularity of Nixon's position. Tho contradicted him, insisting that the Saigon government was opposed as much in America as in South Vietnam. Little more was said, and yet Kissinger reported to the President that the meeting was so far the most important and might lead to some thawing of the frozen negotiations.

Four weeks later, however, General Lon Nol seized power in Cambodia, and when the two sides met again in secret, the Communists bitterly reproached the United States for having arranged the coup. A five-hour wrangle led nowhere. When Kissinger proposed that a time limit be set for reaching some agreement in the secret talks, the Communists refused. Both sides again went their separate ways, agreed only that the channel between them could not be re-opened unless one party had something new to discuss.

It was not until after the operations against the Cambodian sanctuaries that another secret meeting took place. On September 7, an astonished Kissinger found the Communists friendly and affable. They said they were anxious to continue talking, dropping all reference to the NLF's ten points and promising to revise their proposals. They did, however, insist that Thieu be deposed.

They were especially intransigent on Thieu at the next meeting in September, making his deposition a *sine qua non* of any settlement. Because they also resumed their belligerent stance and could not agree on setting a date for another conference, Nixon decided to put pressure on them by publicly proposing a new peace plan. The American President had been encouraged by the success of the Cambodian operations and the progress of Vietnamization of the war, feeling that South Vietnam was now close to being able to defend itself. Accordingly, he went on television October 7 with a plan calling for a cease-fire in place throughout Indo-China, together with an all-Indo-China peace conference, to be followed by a negotiated timetable for the withdrawal of all U.S. troops. He also, four days later, announced that 40,000 more American servicemen would be withdrawn by Christmas. From Hanoi came no reply.

Although this negative position had the effect of producing an embarrassed silence among American antiwar forces, the Communists, during the ensuing year, played a cynical but highly skillful and successful propaganda game with the peace negotiations. Each time Kissinger made a major new proposal during the secret conferences, Le Duc Tho and his associates would reject it or haggle it to death. Then, in the public meetings, they would accuse the Americans of inflexibility, reiterating meanwhile their insistence that Thieu had to go.

They thus held up to the world a picture of a stubborn, unbudging Washington whose corrupt and supine puppet—President Thieu—was the only obstacle to peace. Such a portrayal was convincing to the antiwar movement, to the extent that one of its leaders—Senator George McGovern of South Dakota, already a major candidate for the Democratic nomination for President—was completely deceived. In September, 1971, McGovern flew to Paris to spend six hours conferring with Xuan Thuy. Afterward, he told reporters that he had secured from the North Vietnamese an assurance that they would return all American prisoners as soon as Washington set a date for U.S. withdrawal. McGovern, of course, was not aware that these were exactly the terms offered by Kissinger at a secret meeting May 31, rejected by the Communists four weeks later.

Yet, despite this duplicity, Washington proposed a new, more liberal peace plan, calling for withdrawal of all U.S. and allied forces within six months of an agreement, for a cease-fire throughout Indo-China, and an exchange of POWs on both sides. At the same time,

Thieu would accept an internationally supervised election throughout South Vietnam, even agreeing that he and Ky would resign one month before the election to give all candidates equal opportunities.

With this in hand, Kissinger suggested another secret meeting for November 1. The Communists declined, proposing November 20 instead. The United States accepted. On November 17, however, the conference was canceled with the excuse that Le Duc Tho—who frequently fainted at meetings in what Kissinger believed was an attempt to create sympathy for him—was too ill to attend. No further word was forthcoming from Hanoi, although there were by then ominous reports of a major Communist military build-up above the DMZ.

Nixon was alarmed. On the political side, he feared that the secret talks had been going on so long that reports of them would inevitably soon be "leaked" to the media, producing a political and diplomatic storm. On the military side, he was afraid that any new Communist attack would come at a time when Saigon was still unprepared to meet it, and also endanger the lives of the 69,000 American troops still in Vietnam. "Therefore," Nixon writes in his memoirs, "I decided to make a speech revealing publicly the peace plan that the North Vietnamese had not been interested in hearing from us privately, and, at the same time, to reveal the existence of the secret channel."[28] On January 25, 1972, Nixon appeared on television to disclose 30 months of secret negotiations, detailing each of his rejected peace proposals and accusing the enemy of publicly proclaiming what it had privately condemned in an effort to turn the American people against their government. He also warned the Communists that any escalation of the war on the battlefield would be met with force.

Again, there was no reply from Hanoi until, on March 30, 1972, the main force of the North Vietnamese Army—about 120,000 men employing armor and artillery—invaded South Vietnam across the DMZ.

Striking under cover of the monsoon rains, which grounded allied aircraft, a spearhead of 5 North Vietnamese divisions supported by 5 artillery, antiaircraft, missile, and tank regiments—about 54,000 men—swept through the northernmost provinces of South Vietnam in an attempt to establish control. Eventually, they were joined by 7 more divisions—12 of Hanoi's total strength of 15—together with more supporting troops. The purpose of the spring offensive, according to captured documents, was that "two-thirds of the countryside be liberated prior to the end of June, 1972."

In the beginning, the surprised and inexperienced Saigon forces below the DMZ fell back in the face of a three-pronged attack. Most of their forward bases were abandoned. President Thieu rushed his most battle-worthy troops—Marines, Rangers and airborne troops—north to the battle zone. "This is the final battle to decide the survival of the people,"[29] Thieu declared.

To the astonishment of the Communists, the Southerners fought with great spirit and bravery. They held firm in the face of enemy armor which had been very skillfully introduced in numbers for the first time in the war, and even though American airpower was chiefly responsible for the destruction of hundreds of enemy tanks, the South Vietnamese Army stood its ground with courage and tenacity. Quang Tri City was the only provincial capital to fall to the Reds, and this was eventually torn from their hands.

Meanwhile President Nixon, hoping to cut off Communist supplies while pinning down their army in the South, ordered a massive aerial and naval assault on North Vietnam. Once again, he sought to apply diplomatic pressure on the Soviet Union by publicly announcing that the North Vietnamese were attacking with Russian arms. Hanoi, however, buoyed by its early success, bluntly canceled the peace meeting scheduled for April 24. This was the conference which the Soviets had privately assured Kissinger would be the most decisive.

Nixon was dismayed. Once again he felt himself hooked on the horns—military and diplomatic—of a dilemma. A summit meeting with Soviet Premier Leonid Brezhnev aimed at strategic arms limitations and a general detente was approaching. So also was a historic trip to Red China and perhaps another detente. If he chose to soften his military response to the North Vietnamese invasion, he probably would be certain of both. If, however, he increased the pressure, he ran the risk of torpedoing both—especially the Soviet summit.

The decision was made for him by Hanoi when, at the peace meeting rescheduled for May 2, Kissinger found the Communists arrogant and insulting. Le Duc Tho was especially vituperative. Nixon thereupon decided that the enemy had launched his offensive to wring concessions out of the United States, and that the only way to bring him back to the peace table was to strike and strike hard.

Writing to Brezhnev to this effect—beseeching him not to allow the difficulty with Vietnam to keep their two great nations apart—Nixon ordered the blockading and mining of all North Vietnamese ports, maximum air and naval strikes against military targets, and the interdiction of enemy rail and communications.

The storm of protest arising from antiwar congressmen and most of the media came as Nixon anticipated, and did not deter him. He was, however, delighted with the mild Soviet reaction and the absence of an outpouring of rancorous criticism from Peking. In private, Ambassador Dobrynin assured Kissinger that the summit would go forward.

In Vietnam itself, the tide of battle was flowing against the Communists. American actions against North Vietnam's ports had vastly reduced the flow of supplies to the battlefront. Communist troops, stunned by the ferocity by which "the army that will not fight" had opposed them—particularly at An Loc near Saigon—gradually surrendered almost all of the territory they had seized.

After five months of fighting, another stalemate ensued. North Vietnam, with the Vietcong, controlled slightly larger portions of territory and had struck another savage blow against pacification, but had again suffered dreadfully. According to Saigon, enemy losses were 70,000 dead. The figure seems high, especially since, in a war in which the widespread use of automatic weapons increased the wounded to killed ratio from 3 to 1 to 4 or 5 to 1, this would suggest more casualties than the total number of soldiers used in the invasion. Nevertheless, Hanoi did suffer more severely than Saigon's announced losses of 14,000 dead, 5,000 missing and 50,000 wounded. More important, having failed once again to achieve on the battlefield what it could not obtain at the bargaining table, North Vietnam returned to Paris in October of 1972.

One of the reasons for the Communist spring offensive of 1972 was the belief that it might have a favorable effect upon the American presidential election in November. It might help defeat Richard Nixon. Early on, Hanoi was enthusiastic about the prospects of one of the front-runners, Senator George McGovern. McGovern's position was simply unilateral withdrawal, no matter what effect it might have on South Vietnam or American diplomatic credibility throughout the world; and on the question of the return of POWs, he said that he would "just ask" for their return. These, of course, were not the only planks in McGovern's platform. Activists who had made a turmoil of the Chicago convention succeeded in coalescing with feminists, blacks and youthful "anti-establishment" forces to seize control of the convention in Miami and nominate McGovern. Nevertheless an antiwar policy which, in its most basic stance, said simply, "We want out," did most to give McGovern the victory.

It also did much to guarantee the disaffection of many Democrats. McGovern's new alliance had shattered the fragile coalition forged by Franklin Roosevelt in 1932. Now, five decades later, this always uneasy amalgam of Southern Democrats, urban Jews, Irish and other Catholics, big-city bosses and their machines, as well as academic and aristocratic liberals and those Midwestern liberal descendants of the old Progressive Party and pacifist movement of the twenties, could not, with the exception of the latter, find much enthusiasm for a leader who, as they saw it, had joyfully nailed a white flag to his masthead. Veteran Democratic politicians, some of whom were compelled to stay home from the convention by delegate-selection reforms favoring McGovern's new people, regarded McGovern as "the Goldwater of the Left," an extremist whose candidacy would end in the kind of disaster that overtook the GOP in 1964.

Gradually the hardheaded, shrewd Politburo in Hanoi, always well informed by friends in America, came to realize that McGovern had no chance, and in August, 1972, still staggered by their defeat on the battlefield and the effect of the bombing and blockade on their supply line, probably believing that they could get better terms from Nixon before his re-election, signaled their willingness to resume secret talks. During sessions held on September 26 and 27, they presented their own ten-point program as a counter to Washington's earlier offers. Though unacceptable, it was no longer uncompromising, and the White House took hope.

At another meeting begun on October 8 and continuing four days, a major breakthrough was achieved. Le Duc Tho presented a new proposal meeting all of Nixon's major requirements: a cease-fire followed in 60 days by withdrawal of all American forces, and the exchange of POWs on both sides. Tho evaded the issue of the withdrawal of about 120,000 North Vietnamese troops still in South Vietnam by blandly insisting on the fiction that there were none there. However, he did drop his demand for a coalition government— in effect, eventually a Communist one—and accepted a National

Council of Reconciliation and Concord to be composed of the Saigon government, the Vietcong and neutrals. By requiring unanimity in all its votes, Thieu was protected against a coalition against him. Finally, they dropped their demand that Thieu resign—a major and astounding concession. Apart from minor differences, it appeared that the Communists had accepted all of Washington's proposals.

Now it remained to persuade Nyugen Van Thieu to accept the agreements. Understandably, Thieu was most disquieted at the prospect of allowing 120,000 enemy soldiers to remain in his country. Even though the agreement called for closing the Cambodian sanctuaries so that this force, denied supplies and replacements, would either have to return north or wither away, Thieu apparently remained adamant. Actually, he was noncommital, impressing Kissinger with his deep distrust of Communist cunning and his own lack of confidence at the prospect of American withdrawal. As President Nixon observed: ". . . . we were up against a paradoxical situation in which North Vietnam, which had in effect lost the war, was acting as if it had won; while South Vietnam, which had effectively won the war, was acting as if it had lost."[30]

In fairness to Thieu, he was in a difficult position. It would be up to him to explain to his people why he should accept an agreement which the Communist enemy, whom they knew and distrusted, might either dishonor or simply ignore. On one side he could be accused of selling out his country, on the other of dancing at the end of Washington's string. Nevertheless, by balking or at least dragging his feet, he was playing into Hanoi's hands. With clever calculation the Communists were compiling a perfect record of conciliation which, if made public, would embarrass Washington and leave the much-vilified Thieu as the villain who stood in the path of peace.

Thieu, however, did not budge, adhering to his announced policy of "the Four No's:" no abandonment of territory to the North, no coalition government, no policy of neutrality and no Communist participation in the political affairs of Vietnam. On October 22, meeting with Kissinger once more, he dismayed the American diplomat with the vehemence of his "insane demands." Nixon now wrote to Premier Pham Van Dong asking for more time in which to resolve "the difficulties" in Saigon, while reminding him that the United States had made it plain it could not make a unilateral agreement.

Like Harry Truman dealing in 1953 with a balkier and tougher

Syngman Rhee, Richard Nixon was exasperated. Once again an Asian ally, motivated by an implacable hatred of Communism born of a searing experience of it, was threatening to scuttle a hard-sought, hard-bought peace. True enough, Saigon, like Seoul, was much closer to the enemy than Washington; and yet, if loss of the peace would not actually result in loss of the war, it would certainly end in loss of the American public's will to continue it.

Of this the Communists were very much aware, and they began to strum a war of nerves intended to create friction between Washington and Saigon. Interviews were granted to the Western press to emphasize their "victory," or they changed the meaning of terms of the agreement when it was translated into Vietnamese. From their numerous agents who had infiltrated the Saigon government they had learned of the impasse between Thieu and Nixon, and they were aware that the American President was in desperate need of time in which to persuade the South Vietnamese President to accept the agreement. So they pressed for an early signing, even before the November 7 election. Then, as Nixon feared, on October 26 they turned the screws tighter by publicly broadcasting the terms of the agreement over Radio Hanoi, including the October 31 deadline for signing. The delay, Hanoi insisted, was nothing but a Washington cover-up for continuation of Saigon's "war of aggression."

When the appalled Henry Kissinger learned of this just before his own press conference that day, he attempted to torpedo the Reds' propaganda maneuver by announcing: "We believe that peace is at hand."[31] This unfortunate phrase caught the fancy and aroused the hopes of the American people. It also brought from the McGovern camp a charge of playing politics with the peace just before the election. Nixon, however, actually did not want a pre-election settlement; at least not one in which the United States would have to go it alone without Thieu. He desperately needed time in which to twist the arm of an ally who had already described the proposal as "an agreement to surrender."

Nixon also dared not deflate the rising spirit of optimism caused by Kissinger's "peace is at hand" statement. To do so might be the final disillusionment of a long-suffering American public. Therefore, he appealed to Hanoi for more time—for a November 1 meeting to precede a November 20 signing deadline—and wrote to Thieu telling him: "If the evident drift toward disagreement between the two of us continues . . . the essential base for U.S. support for you and your government will be destroyed."[32] Next, he made a televised campaign speech suggesting that the agreement was not quite right, but that it would be signed the day it became so. Finally, he withdrew restrictions on bombing the North begun October 13 as a concession to the Communists. Two days after, Hanoi agreed to another meeting on November 14—one week after the presidential vote.

That election was a Nixon landslide of enormous proportions: 47,169,841 votes to 29,172,767, or 60.7 percent to 37.5 percent. Nixon won everywhere but in Massachusetts and the District of Columbia, receiving the largest number of votes ever cast for a candidate and the second largest number of electoral votes. Only Lyndon Johnson, running in 1964 against arch-conservative Goldwater, received a higher percentage: 61.1. Although there were other issues, the votes showed overwhelming approval of Nixon's aim to achieve peace with honor and rejected McGovern's unilateral withdrawal without explicit provision for the return of American prisoners.

A jubilant Nixon immediately went to work putting more pressure on Thieu, sending General Alexander Haig, who was on friendly terms with the Southern chief, to Saigon to assure him of instantaneous American retaliation should Hanoi fail to abide by the terms of the settlement. Although Haig found Thieu still adamant, he reported his belief that he would eventually "come along." To bring him to that point, Nixon warned Thieu that if he did not join him in ending the war, then Congress would end it on its return in January by cutting off appropriations. At this juncture, it might well be asked: Why did Nixon continue to endure such a recalcitrant, uncooperative partner? The answer, it would seem, is that if the United States were to leave him on his own, he would go down immediately and Communism would conquer his country. In Thieu, for all his shortcomings, rested all the American hopes of building "a strong, free nation." It was he who had been elected and re-elected in national elections. Whatever he had done in suppressing almost all dissent and much of his political opposition, he had gotten where he was under American aegis. To leave him now, at the critical moment, would be to say that the sacrifice of nearly 50,000 American lives, of the bloody wounds of other hundreds of thousands, of a decade of suffering and self-torment and divisive internal discord unequaled since the Civil War—to say nothing of $165 billion—was all for naught. To leave

Thieu now would be to surrender all but the hope of gaining the return of American prisoners.

Probably for these reasons, Nixon continued to send his messages to Saigon, even after the new peace talks had opened in Paris. At the first meeting of November 20, Le Duc Tho read a lengthy speech accusing the United States of welshing on the October agreement. Kissinger replied by reminding Tho that he had always insisted that South Vietnam had to be consulted before any settlement could be signed. Kissinger next proposed changes in the agreement, almost all of them minor but, because there were 60 of them, thereby upsetting Tho. One change, however, embodied Thieu's insistence on the withdrawal of some of the North Vietnamese still in the South. He also proposed that the DMZ be respected by each side, meaning, of course, that the Northern troops would have to go home. Tho merely stated that he would take note of the proposed changes and that he would have some of his own to advance. Gradually however, throughout the November meetings, the Communist position hardened, even retreating to a stance held before the October 8 agreement. A subsequent threat by Nixon to repeat the aerial and naval assaults launched the previous May produced a momentarily softened attitude, but on December 4, Le Duc Tho rejected all of Kissinger's changes, even some agreed upon earlier, while introducing his own, unacceptable demands. Three days later, Tho was talking vaguely about "assessing regulations" for the movement across the DMZ, thereby questioning its validity. By December 10, it was clear that Hanoi was deliberately stalling, hoping to drive a deeper wedge between Nixon and Thieu. Their infiltrators in the Saigon government had probably informed the North Vietnamese of the American President's warning of a congressional funds cut-off in January, and they were trying to delay a settlement until Congress reconvened.

On December 13, it was obvious that no settlement would be reached. Le Duc Tho made it plain that he would agree to nothing, and the talks were recessed until sometime after Christmas. It was a frustrated, exasperated Henry Kissinger who reported to his chief in the White House that night, speaking in language which, it is hoped, may never become a language of diplomacy. "They're just a bunch of shits!" he exploded, gritting his teeth and clenching his fists. "Tawdry, filthy shits! They make the Russians look good, compared to the way the Russians make the Chinese look good when it comes to negotiating in a responsible and decent way!"[33]

Next day President Nixon put away the carrot and picked up the stick again. He ordered the re-mining of Haiphong Harbor and the resumption of bombing in the Hanoi-Haiphong complex. He did not announce this renewal of military pressure because he feared that to make public such an ultimatum would be to back North Vietnam into a corner where she could not but lose face before a watching world. He also notified Thieu that, if necessary, he would continue the negotiations alone. On December 22, he sent a message to Hanoi asking for a resumption of talks on January 3 which, if accepted, would lead him to halt the bombing by December 31.

In the United States, news of the renewed aerial attacks on the North provoked an outburst of vituperative protest. Nixon was called "a maddened tyrant" or "insane," the conductor of "senseless terror" or of "war by tantrum." It was as though the powerful or influential Americans who opposed the war did not comprehend the relationship between those contrary twins of foreign policy— the diplomat and the soldier, persuasion and force—or that in any conflict with Communists since the beginning of the Confrontation only force or the threat of force had brought them to the peace table. But in this instance, as in others before it, the naked fist had the desired effect: On December 26 the Communists asked to reopen the talks. On that afternoon, following 116 B-52 sorties against the North, Hanoi requested a meeting on January 8. Washington asked for technical talks to begin January 2, offering to stop the bombing once arrangements had been completed. North Vietnam agreed, and on December 29, the bombing came to a halt.

On January 8, 1973, Henry Kissinger and Le Duc Tho conferred for nearly five hours. The following day, Nixon's birthday, Kissinger reported that he had celebrated it by achieving a major breakthrough. Two days later the full text of the agreement was completed.

Meanwhile, Nixon continued to work on Thieu. On January 16, he warned him that if the United States were compelled to go it alone, he would have to explain publicly that Thieu was obstructing peace, a position that would inevitably result in a congressional cut-off of funds for South Vietnam. Thieu still would not budge. Not until it was jointly announced in Washington and Hanoi on January 18 that the Paris talks would resume January 23 for the purpose of completing the agreement did the embattled President of South Vietnam haul down his colors. "I have done my best," he told Haig. "I have done all that I can for my country."[34]

On January 23, the settlement ending the war was reached in Paris. It was, essentially, based on earlier American proposals, embodying all the terms of the October 8 agreement. North Vietnam's military force—now swelled to 145,000 men—would remain in place in the South, an ominous portent for the future, while responsibility for overseeing the cease-fire, which was to take place four days later, was given to an International Commission of Control and Supervision formed by Canada, Indonesia, Hungary and Poland.

For the first time in 12 years the United States was at peace. The longest war in American history was over. In point of casualties, it had been the fourth most costly: 46,572 battle deaths and roughly another 300,000 wounded (a figure usually broken in half between those requiring hospital care and those treated at the front). The wounds suffered within the body politic, the dreadful dissension that divided the nation, remain to be assessed.

Nevertheless, ending the war almost four years to a day after his inauguration—ending it as he saw it with honor, with the return of American prisoners and no loss of credibility among America's worldwide allies—was the triumph of Richard Nixon's political career.

Neither the Soviet summit nor the beginning of detente with Red China nor to have been President of the first nation to put a man on the moon compares to this achievement. And yet, by the time of the cease-fire, Richard Milhous Nixon was probably already afraid that the days of his second term were numbered. On December 29, the day that the news of the last bombing halt was flashed to the world, only slightly slimmer and shorter headlines proclaimed:

WATERGATE SPIES PLEAD GUILTY.

11

☆

On June 17, 1972, five men carrying electronic surveillance equipment were arrested inside the National Democratic Party's headquarters in the Watergate office-apartment-hotel complex in Washington, D.C.

At first, the public reaction was one of amused contempt for the "amateur burglars" who had bungled the break-in, or of mild disgust for what seemed to be typical "dirty politics." However, when it became known that the five burglars and two other accomplices had been financed with money from the Committee to Re-elect the President, Richard Nixon's 1972 campaign organization, the Watergate affair gradually escalated from "a prank," as Nixon called it, to a scandal unrivaled in American history.

After seven months during which the press charged the White House with trying to cover up a disgraceful record of political espionage, the so-called Watergate Seven had either pleaded guilty to or been convicted of felonies. With that, it seemed, the Democrats had been presented a not especially thick political stick with which to beat Nixon and the GOP—until, on March 23, 1973, the day set for sentencing, U.S. District Judge John J. Sirica read a letter from James W. McCord, Jr., one of the guilty men. McCord claimed that others were involved in the break-in, that perjury had been committed, and that pressure had been brought to bear on the defendants to persuade them to plead guilty.

McCord's letter gave the Watergate investigation the momentum it never lost. It caused formation of the Senate Select Committee to probe Watergate and to put Nixon on the defensive. From his earlier stance of silence and non-assistance, he immediately shifted to one of publicly proclaiming—but not actually giving—his full cooperation. On April 30 he appeared on television to say that he accepted full responsibility for any improper activities connected with his campaign. He also announced the resignation of four chief aides: H. R. Haldeman, White House chief of staff; John D. Ehrlichman, chief counsel for domestic affairs; John W. Dean, III, presidential counsel; and Attorney General Richard G. Kleindienst. There had been hints in the press that Ehrlichman and Dean had been the directors of the alleged cover-up. Kleindienst was to be replaced by Elliot L. Richardson, who was to take charge of the administration's Watergate investigation and to appoint a special prosecutor for it.

Meanwhile a seemingly unrelated case, the trial of Daniel Ellsberg and Anthony Russo in Los Angeles on charges of stealing the so-called Pentagon Papers, brought further opprobrium on Nixon's head. Ellsberg, a former State Department aide who had served in Vietnam, had provided the New York *Times* with a 7,000-page study of American involvement in Southeast Asia. All of this material was still classified as "Secret" or "Top Secret," although Defense Secretary Melvyn Laird later declared that 95 percent of it could have been declassified. The *Times,* of course, was not aware whether much or any of it was classified and made no effort to find out. After holding the document three months, the newspaper published it. Other newspapers subsequently obtained copies that they published. The study, called "The History of U.S. Decision-Making Process on Vietnam," soon came to be known by the more flamboyant name of "The Pentagon Papers." Nixon was outraged by what he considered to be a breach of national security. Even if as little as 5 percent of the material could still be regarded as classified, he argued, it could be of direct benefit to the enemy. Former Secretary of State Dean Rusk declared that it would be of help to the North Vietnamese and the Soviets, while the State Department said publication had exposed the Southeast Asia Treaty Organization's contingency war plans, the Central Intelligence Agency said that it would "blow the cover" off past and present informants and the National Security Council feared the documents contained code-breaking clues, while some of America's allies publicly protested exposure of their roles as go-betweens.

Nevertheless, publication was defended by the press on the ground that the Pentagon Papers proved that the Kennedy-Johnson administrations had deceptively involved the American nation in the war in Vietnam, and that Johnson, while publicly promising not to escalate the war, had privately agreed to raise the commitment from 17,000 to 185,000 men. Lyndon Johnson, himself outraged by the publications, bitterly denounced the authors of the study as having misconstrued his contingency plans for actual presidential decisions. As publication continued, Nixon called upon the Justice Department to seek an injunction against the *Times.* The U.S. Supreme Court, however, in a 6–3 decision, upheld the newspaper's right to publish—whereupon Nixon next moved against Ellsberg, securing his indictment by a Los Angeles grand jury.

During his trial, however, Judge William M. Byrne disclosed a Department of Justice memorandum revealing that two of the convicted Watergate Seven—G. Gordon Liddy and E. Howard Hunt, Jr.—had burglarized the safe of Ellsberg's former psychiatrist. Byrne later announced that he had met with Ehrlichman and been introduced to the President, after which Ehrlichman discussed with him the possibility of his being appointed director of the Federal Bureau of Investigation. Finally, the FBI made it known that Ehrlichman, on Nixon's orders, had begun a secret probe into the Pentagon Papers case which had ultimately led to the break-in at Ellsberg's psychiatrist's.

Such revelations gave Ellsberg's attorneys the opportunity to move that the charges of theft, conspiracy and espionage against their client and Russo be dismissed. Byrne agreed, ruling that "bizarre events have incurably infected the prosecution of this case."[35] The two men went free, never again to be questioned on the propriety of purloining the Pentagon Papers, while Ehrlichman, Liddy and Hunt were later convicted of burglary.

Related as the Pentagon Papers case was to Watergate, it helped to turn the Senate's Select Committee hearings in 1972 into a national and even international television show. James McCord, the convicted Watergater whose letter had broken the case open, testified that he had been offered executive clemency before his trial if he would remain silent. He was followed by John Dean, the former presidential counsel and key witness whose week-long testimony seemed to confirm McCord's charge, while accusing Nixon of having known of the cover-up.

Dean also implicated, among others, former Attorney General John Mitchell, who had resigned a few days after Watergate, and former Acting Director of the FBI L. Patrick Gray. These men and others were indicted by a federal grand jury almost a year later for conspiring to hinder the investigation. Mitchell, meanwhile, and some of the others, appeared before the Senate committee to deny Dean's charges.

So also did Ehrlichman and Haldeman. Ehrlichman admitted that he had approved a "covert operation" against Ellsberg but had not intended to authorize a break-in. He also insisted that both he and Nixon believed such a burglary to be "well within" the President's powers to protect national security. Here he was challenged by Senator Sam J. Ervin, Jr., the committee chairman, who retorted that no law empowered the President to commit an illegal act.

Haldeman's testimony was devoted chiefly to an attempt to refute Dean's charge that President Nixon had knowledge of the cover-up. He disputed Dean's contention that Nixon had told him, in Haldeman's presence, that it would not be difficult to raise $1 million to defend the Watergate Seven. Haldeman also created a sensation when he testified that he had listened at home to a tape recording of a conversation between Nixon, Dean and himself—thereby confirming earlier testimony that all of Nixon's conversations in the White House and the Executive Office Building had been taped since the spring of 1971. Thus, Nixon's talks with Dean were a matter of record and could prove or disprove Dean's charges of presidential knowledge of the cover-up.

Almost at once Archibald Cox, the special Watergate prosecutor appointed by Attorney General Richardson, the Senate Select Committee, and a federal grand jury conducting its own Watergate investigation, all demanded the tapes. The White House refused to surrender them. Both the Senate committee and Cox immediately issued subpoenas for the material, to which Nixon refused to respond under his insistent claim of "executive privilege." Judge Sirica thereupon directed Nixon to furnish him with the subpoenaed material for his private examination. Sirica said he could not judge the point of executive privilege without personally inspecting the tapes.

Nixon appealed Sirica's order in the U.S. Court of Appeals, where it was ruled that he must turn over the recordings to the U.S. District Court. "The Constitution mentions no executive privileges," the appeals court declared, "much less any absolute executive privileges."[36] Nixon next offered a "compromise" plan under which he would deliver a summary of the Watergate tapes to the District Court and the other Watergate investigators. Cox rejected the offer, whereupon Nixon directed Cox, an employee of the executive branch, to make no further efforts to obtain any material relating to presidential conversations. Cox refused, and Nixon immediately swung the executive ax in what came to be known as "the Saturday night massacre." With one sweep, the President fired Cox and Deputy Attorney General William D. Ruckelshaus while "accepting" the resignation of Attorney General Richardson. Rather than dismiss Cox, Richardson had resigned, and when Ruckelshaus refused to discharge the troublesome prosecutor, he too was ousted.

In the infuriated public protest that succeeded "the Saturday night massacre" were heard not only outraged expressions of the deepest disgust but the first angry demands for the impeachment of Richard Nixon. Three days later, the President announced compliance with Sirica's order. Not all the requested material, however, was there.

Noticeably missing was a vital conversation between Dean and Nixon during which, the White House explained, the recording machine had run out of tape. A record of another telephone talk between Nixon and Mitchell on the subject of Watergate was also not made, the White House said, because it was over a telephone not plugged into the taping machine. Moreover, an 18-minute portion of another Watergate tape was missing, and there were a number of silent spots in others.

Such disclosures aroused the suspicions of the American public. Various polls published shortly afterwards indicated that a great majority of the American people did not believe the President was telling the truth.

Meanwhile, reports of other suspicious situations involving the President helped further to erode his prestige and popularity. Questions were raised over Nixon's purchase of private homes at Key Biscayne, Florida, and San Clemente, California, with money furnished him by wealthy friends who, it would seem, might be expected to benefit from their generosity. Also suspect was Nixon's claim of a federal income tax deduction of $576,000 for pre-presidential papers turned over to the National Archives. Although such claims were not uncommon among other high-ranking officials—elected or otherwise—for Richard Nixon to have made one with such unfortunate timing was to draw down more contumely upon his head.

Perhaps the heaviest blow unrelated to Watergate was the resignation in disgrace of his outspoken Vice President, Spiro T. Agnew. Agnew, a constant critic of the media, admitted on August 6, 1973, that he was under investigation by the Attorney General's office for alleged kickbacks to him by contractors, architects and engineers when he was Baltimore County Executive from 1962 to 1967 and Governor of Maryland from 1967 to 1968. Eventually Agnew resigned and pleaded guilty to a single accusation of income tax evasion, in return for which all other charges were dropped. Because Nixon had often spoken openly of his admiration for his running mate in 1972, the scandalous end to Agnew's political career was another large chip knocked off the President's public image. Not even the selection of the popular and respected Representative Gerald R. Ford of Michigan as Agnew's successor did very much to restore it. Nor did it break the momentum of the Democrats' drive toward impeachment.

Nixon began 1974 by declaring in his State of the Union message:

"One year of Watergate is enough. As you know, I have provided to the special prosecutor voluntarily a great deal of material. I believe that I have provided all the material that he needs to conclude his investigations."[37]

Leon Jaworski, Cox's successor as special prosecutor, disagreed. Jaworski stated that Nixon had not turned over to him all the tapes and other documents he had requested. He also told the U.S. District Court that he had no evidence to suggest that Dean had lied in his testimony. To cap a bad beginning for 1974, the House on February 6 formally authorized its Judiciary Committee under Representative Peter Rodino, Jr., of New Jersey, to investigate the President's Watergate conduct to determine if any grounds existed for his impeachment.

Nixon was staggered again on April 3 by another blow unrelated to Watergate: an announcement by the Joint Committee on Internal Revenue Taxation to the effect that the President owed $476,431, including interest, in income tax for 1969-72. Although the White House quickly admitted the debt and said that Nixon would pay it, the fact that the man who held his nation's highest trust had not paid the taxes that are automatically withdrawn from the paycheck of every American wage-earner did not endear him to the ordinary citizen.

A few days later the President attempted to satisfy the Judiciary Committee's subpoena by furnishing it edited transcripts of 42 conversations. Widely published and even reprinted in book form, the vindictive and apparently profane (judging from the frequency of the phrase "expletive deleted") tone of the 1,308-page volume produced an immensely unfavorable impression in Congress and among the public. Moreover the Judiciary Committee, while accepting the edited transcripts, insisted on delivery of the tapes themselves.

Nixon was less conciliatory toward Special Prosecutor Jaworski, adamantly refusing to relinquish the 64 tapes demanded by him. To get them, Jaworski obtained a subpoena from Judge Sirica, and when Nixon refused to obey it, he asked the U.S. Supreme Court to hear the case.

The Supreme Court consented, hearing Nixon's lawyer, James St. Clair, argue that the President alone could determine the limits of executive privilege, while Jaworski contended that to allow any President to state that the Constitution means what he says it means would destroy constitutional government. The court agreed with Jaworski, and by an 8-0 decision ordered Nixon to turn over the tapes "forthwith."

On the same day—July 24, 1974—the Judiciary Committee began its nationally televised hearings, which quickly culminated in three articles of impeachment against the President: obstruction of justice in connection with Watergate, abuse of presidential powers and defiance of the committee in refusing to obey its subpoenas. Two other articles—one charging concealment from Congress of the secret bombing of Cambodia and the other income tax fraud and the unlawful use of government funds on his private homes— were rejected.

Still Nixon fought to hold his office, seeking a "strong political base" in Congress from which to continue the fight—until disclosure of a tape recording of a conversation between Haldeman and himself. When Haldeman informed the President that the FBI's probe of Watergate was leading to his 1972 campaign officials, Nixon told Haldeman to tell the FBI: "Don't go any further in this case, period."[38] Here was the end. Almost all support for Richard Milhous Nixon in Congress vanished clean away. Instead, his followers urged him to resign rather than risk certain impeachment and a scandalous trial before the Senate in full view of the nation. Nixon acquiesced. On August 8 he appeared on television to say that he no longer possessed the political base from which to sustain his struggle. "Therefore," he said somberly, his dry, sunken eyes staring straight into the camera, "I shall resign the presidency at noon tomorrow."[39] Shortly after noon on August 9, 1974, Gerald Ford, the first American appointed to succeed a Vice President resigning under fire, became the first Vice President to succeed a President resigning to escape impeachment.

The arrival of Gerald Ford in the White House was widely hailed in the United States as the advent of a decent, forthright new President who would be the "great healer" of the terrible wounds suffered by the body politic during Vietnam and Watergate. When Ford quickly announced a program of limited amnesty for Vietnam deserters and draft-dodgers, he was hailed by some in the antiwar movement as a man of vision and compassion. However, when he also promptly granted a "full and complete" presidential pardon to

Richard Nixon, he was immediately castigated by these same people and others as just another political hack who probably cooked up the pardon "deal" with Nixon before being appointed Vice President. Tragically, America was divided again.

On the one side were the haters of Nixon and the war in Vietnam and on the other the Nixon and Vietnam defenders minus many who, having supported both, were now disgusted and disillusioned. The antiwar people, together with the media, recovered quickly from their brief flirtation with Ford and now did their utmost to criticize his integrity and question hs judgment. Among the public there was an understandably bitter resentment of the injustice of sending 25 Watergaters—including Haldeman* and former Attorney General Mitchell —to prison, while the leader of the operation went free.

Not many fair-minded Americans, moreover, doubted the possibility of a deal between Ford and Nixon—and with good reason. Among power-hungry men, for such all politicians are, it is certainly not too much to suggest that the prize of the vice presidency offered Ford under the peculiarly attractive conditions then obtaining—the fact that Nixon was himself in danger of losing his own incredibly powerful office, which would then also succeed to Ford—could have been anything less than irresistible; and that no future favor requested in exchange for the appointment could possibly have seemed too great. For all these reasons, then, President Ford's public standing subsequent to the pardon was never very strong.

Nixon's defenders, meanwhile, bitterly charged that their former chief had been the victim of a conspiracy among those opponents of the war who were chagrined by his successful conclusion of it and angered by his refusal to submit to their demands for unilateral withdrawal. In this there is more than a little truth, if only because throughout the war in Vietnam and during the Watergate investigation these same Americans—liberal media, liberal academia, antiwar activists and liberal congressmen—were always comfortable bedfellows. However, there seems to be no truth in the other charges that Nixon was brought down by a "witch hunt" conducted by media that hated and despised him, or that he had been "railroaded" by a House

---

* It was Haldeman who, in a book written and published while he was in prison, claimed that the Watergate break-in was ordered by Nixon in an attempt to "get something" on Democratic National Chairman Lawrence O'Brien in his relationship with the late financier and industrialist Howard Hughes.

Judiciary Committee composed chiefly of vindictive Democrats eager not only for the scalp of their arch enemy but also for a Republican disgrace of such unprecedented proportions that it would all but guarantee a Democratic victory in 1976.

It is true enough that Nixon was never a popular President in the physically appealing sense of an Eisenhower or a Franklin Delano Roosevelt. It is also true that his historic landslide of 1972 was as much a rejection of McGovern as a mandate for Nixon. Finally, the liberal media did truly and openly abhor Richard Nixon, having consistently loathed him since 1948 when, as a freshman representative, he became a decisive factor in the conviction of the suspected Communist spy Alger Hiss on two counts of perjury; and when, two years later, using campaign tactics that earned him the sobriquet of "tricky Dicky," he defeated the liberal favorite of the press, Helen Gahagan Douglas, for the Senate. Nevertheless, however gleefully the members of the media might have pursued Nixon in their criticism and exposure of the Watergate crimes and cover-ups, they were actually fulfilling in the highest degree the role reserved for a free press in a free society, which is nothing less than criticism and exposure.

Nor was the Judiciary Committee a kind of kangaroo court, as charged. It is again true that even before the committee began its hearings, Chairman Rodino announced that all 21 Democrats on the 38-member board were going to vote for impeachment. Rodino later denied saying this, but the so-called anti-Nixon media confirmed that he had. Nevertheless, desite the obvious anti-Nixon, antiwar animus of a trio of extreme liberals, occasionally joined by two others, the conduct of the hearings was a model of sober decorum. If, indeed, Rodino had put in the "fix" before the hearings started, the comportment of his committee was again a very model of stagecraft. Actually, when compared to the only other congressional proceeding against a President in American history—the impeachment and trial of Andrew Johnson in 1867-68—the Nixon affair must receive high grades for fairness.

In Andrew Johnson's time, the Republicans controlled a "veto-proof" Congress, with 74 percent of the House and 78 percent of the Senate, in comparison to Democratic margins of 57 and 58 percent in 1974. Prejudice against Johnson was so widespread—especially among the radical Republicans—and so rancorous that it probably saved the Tennessee Democrat from conviction. Many moderate Republicans were sickened by the vindictive vituperation poured upon Johnson's head, and in the end one of them, Senator Edmund Ross of Kansas, cast a vote that acquitted him. Such conduct, again, cannot be charged to the Rodino committee.

Finally, the difference between the charges against the two Presidents was not one of degree but of kind. Andrew Johnson, with his so obvious sympathy for Southern politicians who had only recently been Rebels, together with his distaste for black enfranchisement, was accused of having ignored or countermanded the law. Richard Nixon, on the contrary, was accused of breaking it; not overtly flouting it, like Johnson, but secretly violating it and then using his presidential powers to try to cover his tracks.

And so it must be said that justice had been done through a provision of the U.S. Constitution so long in disuse that it had come to be regarded as a historical curiosity. "Let justice be done though the Heavens fall," runs the ancient Latin proverb, and yet how often in the affairs of mankind has the triumph of abstract justice produced just such cataclysmic results. Military history abounds with examples of the disastrous "law of the double effect"—the intended and the unintended—two of which may be cited here, if only to justify what may seem to have been an overlong and perhaps even irrevelant examination of Watergate.

The first was the famous Dreyfus Case in France at the end of the last century and prior to World War I. Captain Alfred Dreyfus, a Jew, had been convicted of betraying French Army secrets on evidence trumped up by the largely anti-Semitic officer corps. Although condemned in two subsequent retrials, Dreyfus was finally exonerated in 1906. Justice had finally been done, as the ardent defenders of Dreyfus had intended. What was not intended was that French Army Intelligence should have been so discredited that it was placed in civilian hands, with the result that when Germany attacked in August, 1914, the French Army not only "knew not the day nor the hour" but actually reacted exactly as the Schlieffen Plan envisioned.

The second example? As intended, Richard Milhous Nixon was brought to justice. What was not intended was that in the fall of 1974, when the Communists of North Vietnam began to lay their plans and commence their build-up for their "final" invasion of the South, they knew that the man whom they feared most and who might attempt to stop them was powerless and in disgrace.

12

☆

The "cease-fire" which ensued in South Vietnam after the Paris Agreement made a mockery of "peace with honor." There was no peace and the firing never ceased. Within nine months of the signing, the Saigon government charged the Vietcong with 26,000 breaches of the cease-fire while the Communists accused Saigon of 240,000 violations. An estimated 180 to 200 Vietnamese—civilians as well as soldiers—lost their lives daily in combat which the cease-fire was supposed to have stopped.

The International Commission of Control and Supervision was powerless to halt the fighting. Able to act only unanimously, usually hamstrung by the blatant bias of its Communist members, Poland and Hungary, with no power to enforce any decision if one could be made, the Commission quickly degenerated into an impotent debating society, from which Canada promptly resigned to be replaced by Iran.

Meanwhile the fighting continued, each side emphasizing the "defensive" nature of operations which were actually nothing less than attempts to expand or fortify territory already held. In fact, the only provision of the Paris Agreement faithfully observed was the withdrawal of all American and other allied forces. This was completed on March 29, 1973, when the last U.S. servicemen left Tan Son Nhut Airport. Their departure was hailed as a historic day by the North Vietnamese, the first time in 100 years that there were no foreign troops on the soil of Vietnam. There were, however, to be more North Vietnamese troops on the soil of the South: 70,000, armed with 400 tanks and artillery pieces, who quickly joined 145,000 fellow countrymen still in place menacing Saigon.

Politically, the "peace" for which both Le Duc Tho and Henry Kissinger received Nobel Peace Prizes was equally unpromising. Negotiations in Paris were suspended indefinitely after 28 sessions, with the Vietcong accusing Saigon of "continuous and flagrant violation" of the agreement and South Vietnam charging the Communists with "a discourteous and insolent attitude."

The National Council of National Reconciliation and Concord provided by the Paris Agreement was never formed, chiefly because the Communists regarded themselves as a second government parallel to Saigon while Thieu considered his government as the sole legal ruler. Neither could agree on who or what would form the "neutralist" third party. Thieu, meanwhile, strengthened his position not only *vis-à-vis* the Vietcong, but also at the expense of non-Communist opposition parties. Eventually Thieu came to dominate not only the executive but also the legislature; both the opposition and the Communists boycotting national elections held in August with the result that Thieu supporters were elected unopposed.

Economically, South Vietnam was in a state perhaps worse than the military and political situations. Withdrawal of the American troops had left 400,000 Vietnamese unemployed, and the $400 million poured each year into the country's economy by American servicemen was sorely missed. True, American spending had once been a cause of inflation, but in 1973 inflation was galloping at a rate of 60 percent annually, while exports were roughly 6 percent of imports, compared to 26 percent under Diem.

Self-sufficiency was simply impossible, and particularly so because more than half of the nation's annual budget was spent on defense, with the result that basic imports such as fertilizer, machinery and foodstuffs had to be reduced in favor of war material. Thieu maintained a huge army of 1 million men, including regulars, militia and national police. However, American aid had declined in two years from $2.1 billion in 1971 to $700 million in 1973, and the U.S. Congress was preparing further cuts for 1974, a well-known fact which led the jubilant Communists in Hanoi to remark that Thieu would soon be forced "to fight a poor man's war."

Hanoi suffered no such restrictions. It had, of course, lost much of its military aid from both the Soviet Union and Red China in 1972, when the Washington-Moscow detente reduced supplies from Russia (as American material was also withheld from Saigon), while Peking for some unknown reason also confined its assistance merely to small arms and mortars. North Vietnam had become in fact so destitute of arms that when the United States halted the late 1972 bombings which in effect ended the allied phase of the war, Hanoi had only one day's supply of surface-to-air missiles left. However, Communist Cuba came to its aid. Apparently unknown either to Moscow or to Peking, Cuba began shipping much of its own Soviet-supplied munitions to Hanoi, a ruse which enabled North Vietnam to become independent of both detente and whatever might ensue from the Sino-Soviet split. When the Soviet Union did discover the Moscow-to-Havana-to-Hanoi hook-up, it made no effort to interfere.

Indeed, by October of 1974, when the Politburo in Hanoi began to debate the proposal to invade the South once more, the USSR was no longer inclined to restrain its impetuous junior partner. This was because the Soviets believed that the United States was double-crossing them on an implied promise from Henry Kissinger that they would receive most-favored nation trade status in return for their help in promoting the peace. This was in 1972, when Kissinger and Soviet representatives negotiated what they considered a landmark trade bill.

Afterward, however, the United States began to express concern over mistreatment of Soviet Jews, and Congress began to talk of punishing Russia for it. Senator Henry Jackson of Washington, a consistent presidential hopeful whose campaigns for the Democratic nomination were based financially on his friendship with the American Jewish community, was the leader in the movement to compel Moscow to remove its restrictions on the emigration of Russian Jews. As the Politburo convened, Jackson and his followers offered an amendment to Kissinger's bill making its benefits to Moscow dependent on Russia easing her rules against Jewish emigration. The Soviets protested bitterly, and Kissinger warned Congress that the amendment would be construed as interference in the internal affairs of the USSR, with possible dire consequences. Nevertheless, it was passed and signed into law by President Ford on January 3, 1975.

By then, the "dire consequences" were a fact. Moscow had already sent General Viktor Kulikov, chief of the Soviet Armed Forces, to Hanoi with instructions to give North Vietnam all possible co-operation. The moment the amended trade bill became law, a thoroughly aroused Soviet Union publicly warned the United States of "retaliation," called home its ambassador for consultations, and gave the war hawks of North Vietnam its vigorous support for the invasion while promising unlimited supplies.

Such support from their chief and most powerful ally helped to give the Politburo hard-liners the victory over the moderates, who had been arguing against the invasion in favor of reconstruction of their war-torn country. It was not the only reason, of course. There were other considerations, such as the basic rot of the Saigon government and the declining morale of its people and its army—in which desertions had now reached the rate of 20,000 monthly. But the chief impetus came from an embittered Soviet Union which, so far from continuing to support the peace, was now actively encouraging Hanoi to strike. The American Congress, which had again trimmed its aid to Saigon that summer, was now unlikely to grant additional assistance, even in the face of an invasion, the Soviets counseled their junior partners. Diplomatic considerations? The sanctity of the Paris Agreement? To Communists bred to consider a treaty as a tactic rather than a commitment, these meant nothing. The agreement had served its tactical purpose in removing the Americans from Vietnam and now, it was clear, was the time to strike.

Militarily, South Vietnam's 44 provinces were divided into four Military Regions. Military Region (MR) 1 lay in the narrow northern quarter of the country, five rugged and uninviting provinces, except along the coastal lowlands where most of the area's 3 million inhabitants lived in and around the major cities of Hue and Danang. Military Region 2, 13 provinces occupying roughly 40 percent of the country, was a kaleidoscope of varying climate and terrain, in which the Central Highlands provinces of Kontum and Pleiku were of great strategic importance and the province of Ban Me Thuot further south absolutely vital. Military Region 3 was the zone surrounding Saigon, obviously the chief objective of the North's invasion; while in Military Region 4 lay the Mekong Delta, the richest and most populous area of the country, home of more than a third of South Vietnam's 19 million people and producer of 80 percent of its rice. Although the Delta had always been considered the prize of the war, little but guerrilla action was fought there because of its watery terrain.

In Hanoi once again, MR 2 had been chosen for the main blows in order to make the customary attempt to cut South Vietnam in two on a line running east from Cambodia through Kontum City south to Pleiku City then east to the ramshackle coastal city of Qui Nhon. Before these assaults were to be launched, however, the Communists decided to make three tests.

The first was of the efficacy of a new battle tactic of piecemeal attacks backed up by heavy artillery; the second was of the fighting prowess of Thieu's army; and the third, the paramount question, of possible American intervention or retaliation. Elated as the Politburo had been at the fall of its arch enemy Richard Nixon, confident as its members were of congressional opposition to a return to Vietnam, they still could not be sure of President Ford's reaction. So they chose the province of Phuoc Long, northernmost of those in Military Region 3, as the testing ground.

On December 6, 1974, the so-called mini-offensive was launched in Phuoc Long. North Vietnamese regulars cut the province into little pieces, overwhelming them one by one. First, they severed the roads to the target area, after which they overwhelmed South Vietnam artillery support with massed ground attacks. Next, they put the objective under siege with remarkably accurate heavy artillery, 130-millimeter guns made in the Soviet Union, and finally overran it with troops brought to battle in trucks and on tanks.

With no regular troops to defend the province—only a few thousand so-called Border Rangers—district after district fell to the Communists, and soon the provincial capital of Phuoc Binh came under siege.

Thieu, meanwhile, did nothing—until it was too late. On January 3, 1975, with both province and capital hopelessly lost, he ordered the 300-man 82nd Special Forces Airborne Battalion to Phuoc Binh with orders to hold the city "at any cost." This favorite phrase of the South Vietnamese leader reflected the utter fatuity of his conduct: first, to do nothing until too late; and second, to order a mere three companies of soldiers, no matter how elite or courageous, to turn the tide of battle against two full divisions, 20,000 men. The result was a tragic fiasco. Only one of the 82nd's companies took off by helicopter, to be driven away from the battle zone by enemy antiaircraft fire and dropped 5 miles outside the city with instructions to do its best on its own. Inevitably the unit fell apart, while Phuoc Long went to the North, the first time in the war that an entire province had been captured.

Militarily, Phuoc Long did not mean much. Morally, however, it was a staggering blow to be reckoned only less than Tet in its ultimate effects. Not only had the people and the troops of the province been the victim of Thieu's indecisiveness but a company of the most famous unit in the South Vietnamese Army had been casually and cruelly sacrificed for no end. Henceforth, no soldier of Saigon could be sure of support if he came under attack. In his mind, now, his only loyalty was to himself.

Phuoc Long had given the answers: the new tactic worked, Thieu's army was rotten and the U.S. government had announced that under no circumstances would Americans re-enter the war—on the ground, at sea or in the air.

Hanoi was jubilant. It was clear that the major offensive aimed at "liberating" the South in two years could go forward. Moreover, the Communists knew exactly where to strike, thanks to an amazing top-secret report furnished them by a still-unknown spy in Thieu's inner circle. From this they learned that although Thieu and his military chiefs expected the Communists to fight harder in 1975 than they had in 1974, they did not expect them to deploy nearly the numbers they had fielded in the Tet Offensive. (In fact, North Vietnam was to deploy 20 of its 23 divisions, a force, with supporting troops, of well over 200,000 men.) Thieu also did not believe the Communists capable of taking and holding major cities and therefore expected the main thrust in MR 3 in the westernmost province of Tay Ninh, where they would fight hard until the dry season ended in June. Because of this estimate, Thieu had decided not to reinforce the Central Highlands of MR 2 and was holding most of his reserves in the south.

Because of this information, Hanoi had already chosen Phuoc Long, rather than Tay Ninh where Thieu expected them, as the area in which the Communists could demonstrate their ability to capture and hold cities. Also because of it, the main thrust—called the Ho Chi Minh Offensive—was to fall in MR 2, which Thieu had not reinforced. Moreover, the enemy was to be duped into believing that the main blows would be delivered in the provinces of Kontum and Pleiku. A sham command post was to be established in western Pleiku from which radio signals would be beamed, indicating that strong Communist forces were still in the area. Large bodies of noncombat troops were to be drawn from the Cambodian border to mass openly for the benefit of Southern reconnaisance aircraft, while Communist agents who had penetrated the South Vietnamese Army were to prepare reports and maps all indicating that the enemy was concentrated in Kontum and Pleiku.

The true main body of combat veterans—3 divisions, or 25,000 men—was to move stealthlily south from these two provinces into Ban Me Thuot, the province which the French had always called the key to the South. There they would be targeted west of the town of Ban Me Thuot. After feints were made to keep the South Vietnamese forces north of them in place, they would overwhelm the town, opening the way to Saigon and isolating the enemy in Kontum and Pleiku.

By mid-January of 1975, all was in readiness. It remained only to appoint the field commander for this "historic" offensive. Obviously, it could not be General Giap, the Minister of War, whose health had been ruined by Parkinson's Disease. Instead, the appointment went to his second in command and chief of staff, General Van Tien Dung.

Van Tien Dung was number 11 in the 11-man Politburo, and at 58, the youngest member. He was also its only true "worker," having risen from a peasant background to become foreman of a French textile factory in Hanoi. By then he had become a Communist, and in 1939 he was imprisoned by the French during an anti-Red crackdown. Four years later he escaped, joining the American-sponsored resistance to the Japanese in World War II, during which period he journeyed to the Soviet Union for instruction in revolutionary training camps. Upon formation of the Vietminh, he was made chief of the army's political department and responsible for the indoctrination of its soldiers.

Ho Chi Minh was fond of this gruff, square-faced man with the thick peasant features, probably because he too had come of humble origins. He also admired Dung's daring and dedication and his capacity for work, qualities which soon impressed General Giap. With such sponsors, Dung rose rapidly, eventually becoming chief of staff. He had much to do with the planning and logistical support for the great victory at Dienbienphu, and with later campaigns for which Giap received credit. Audacious, politically astute and trustworthy, it was probably inevitable that the Politburo should turn to Dung for its last great gamble of the war.

By the end of January, all was in readiness. Three divisions were in place in MR 1 above Hue and Danang. Other units were targeted in the Saigon area and against Tay Ninh Province, and finally, the buildup against Ban Me Thuot was proceeding on schedule and undetected.

On February 5, General Dung moved south, traveling secretly to the airport while his "ailing" secretary followed in an ambulance.

From Hanoi, Dung's party flew to Dong Hoi in the North Vietnamese panhandle. They drove by automobile down the Ho Chi Minh Trail, by then a two-lane highway running from the western DMZ to within 75 miles of Saigon. A fuel pipeline with pumping stations ran alongside it. Obviously, the North Vietnamese Army engineers had been quite busy since the "peace" agreement was signed.

In Hanoi, meanwhile, every effort was being made to deceive the enemy as to Dung's whereabouts. National-day greetings to various countries signed by him before his departure were proclaimed as though he were still at his desk. Dung's double was driven back and forth from his office each day, and the soldiers who gathered in Dung's courtyard each afternoon to play volleyball were still to be seen leaping and running and striking the ball with a burly officer who could have been their general. The deception was successful. Not until it was far too late did either the South Vietnamese or their American friends realize that Hanoi had so valued the Ban Me Thuot operation that it had sent its chief of staff south to command it.

Dung's journey to his headquarters west of the target town had been immensely enjoyable. Wherever he could, he had stopped to talk to the combat troops. Expert indoctrinator that he was, he reminded them of the sacredness of the "Struggle" and called upon them to liberate their miserable Southern brethren who had been literally starving under the "American aggressors." He told them that they were the "musicians" in the great orchestration of battle that was soon to begin. When he lifted his hand in imitation of a conductor's baton, they would roar back at him in parrot-like unison: "We can do it! We can do it! Determined to win! Determined to win!"[40]

With such troops, and his own careful preparation, General Van Tien Dung told his aides just before the battle for Ban Me Thuot began on March 10, 1975, that it might be possible to liberate the South in less than the Politburo's estimate of two years.

The agony of war had not touched Ban Me Thuot for seven years. During the interval this sleepy city of 150,000 had revived its almost idyllic calm, returning to the untroubled rhythm of the prewar days. The plantations surrounding it were again peaceful with their symmetrical rows of coffee trees. The planters—Vietnamese, Chinese, French and Italian—having made their accommodations with the local Communists, were once again pursuing "the good life" on friendly terms with one another. Even the jungle had recovered the lush green cover once stripped from it by the American B-52 bombers, and the wildlife was again so abundant that a herd of wild elephants came close to ruining General Dung's carefully laid plans of conquest. Stampeding near his headquarters, they killed and maimed an unknown number of soldiers while ripping up or tearing down most of his communications wire. General Dung flew into a paroxysm of rage when he learned that he was out of contact with his divisions and Hanoi. A few days later, the incredibly quick and thorough restoration of the network of his Communications Corps earned from Dung a typically grudging grunt of approval. On March 8, he was enraged again to learn that one of his officer-couriers with full knowledge of the attack plans had been captured by the enemy. Dung knew that the Southerners, like his own interrogators, had irresistible ways of extracting information from their prisoners. Certain that the captured officer could not hold out for much more than a day or two, aware that Saigon troops were reconnoitering the area west of Ban Me Thuot, he immediately ordered the road north to Pleiku to be cut, thus isolating the South Vietnamese in Ban Me Thuot from their main body to the north.

General Pham Van Phu, commander of Military Region 2, had become convinced (or had convinced himself) that the main Communist threat would come against his forces in Pleiku and Kontum. Yet there had been reports that the enemy was slipping his forces south to Ban Me Thuot. A North Vietnamese defector had revealed the entire plan. If the prisoner was right, Phu reasoned, then it was imperative that he too displace his forces south, if only because he did not have enough men to defend both Kontum-Pleiku and Ban Me Thuot. But he was inclined to doubt the defector, believing him to be a plant, and to trust intercepted Communist radio signals indicating that the enemy was still in Kontum-Pleiku in force. Besides, General Phu was not an aggressive or daring commander and he preferred not to risk the dangers of massive displacement.

So he remained where he was until, aghast, he received the report that the enemy had cut Route 14 from Pleiku to Ban Me Thuot. Now he knew: the Communists had stolen south! At once he ordered another regiment to Ban Me Thuot, only to find that only one of his four giant CH-47 helicopters was flyable. In agony, he called upon Saigon for help—but none was forthcoming.

All that lay between the Communists and victory in the province of Ban Me Thuot were 2 battalions—about 1,200 men—in the city; another 2 just to the north of it, plus part of another regiment and a few formations of Rangers and militia: perhaps 4,000 scattered, uneasy and partially irregular troops against 25,000 concentrated, eager and superbly led Communist soldiers.

Shortly before dawn of March 10, the attack began.

Long-range artillery west and north of the city of Ban Me Thuot lighted the forests with their flashing and sent the echoes of their iron-tongued clanging reverberating around the highland hills. Almost at once, the lights of the city went out. At 7:30 A.M., the spearhead units of Dung's tanks clanked into its outskirts. A quarter of an hour later they were firing at South Vietnamese headquarters. Soon South Vietnamese aircraft struck at the invaders, only to prove as dangerous to friendly troops as to the enemy. Flying well above anti-aircraft range at 10,000 feet, they had hardly the slightest hope of achieving the accuracy required in such supporting strikes. After the South Vietnamese headquarters was bombed by mistake, the Saigon forces fell apart. By five o'clock that night, Dung's troops occupied the major part of the city. They had achieved most of their objectives, had knocked out the enemy's artillery, had seen the enemy's tactical air force neutralize itself, and had dug in for the expected counter-attack. When it came—and it came fiercely—it was repulsed. Next day they completed the conquest of the city, and although another week of battle remained to seize the smaller airstrip ouside of town and to scatter Saigon forces to the north of it, on that day Van Tien Dung could write jubilantly in his diary: "Basically, the battle is over."[41]

For days after the fighting began at Ban Me Thuot, President Thieu and his military chiefs lived in an agony of indecision. They could not decide whether the strike was a feint intended to draw off forces from Kontum-Pleiku or actually the main blow in MR 2. Reports from the front were spotty. Thieu did, however, send a reinforcing regiment to the area after it became clear that the Communists were actually after Ban Me Thuot.

By March 13, Thieu's eyes—those of a veteran professional soldier —were wide open. Obviously, the enemy was trying to strip Saigon of its defenses while luring him into overextending himself northward. On that day Thieu met with his Security Council to propose a radical change in strategy. He would withdraw all his strength in MR 2 and some of it from MR 1—the nonproductive and least populous part of the country—in order to protect the populous, productive lower half of the country by reinforcing the coast and counterattacking to regain Ban Me Thuot. He called this new concept: "Light at the top, heavy at the bottom."[42]

Thieu's advisers were stunned. But they did not object. They hardly ever objected. They merely sat silent and still while Thieu told them that the strategic withdrawal would begin in Kontum-Pleiku and that he was also pulling the Airborne Division out of the Hue-Danang area in MR 1.

Militarily, the concept of trading space for time, of gathering forces for a counterattack that might delay the enemy until the onset of the monsoon bogged him down, was completely sound. There even had been a plan for that purpose submitted to the President. Unfortunately he had allowed it to lie idle on his desk, neglecting to order the implementing staff work necessary for a retrograde movement of that magnitude. Still, his Security Council said nothing.

So the Airborne Division was ordered south and Thieu flew off to Cam Ranh Bay to confer with his MR 2 commander, Major General Phan Van Phu. Like the silent courtiers of the Security Council, Phu was not one to challenge his old friend, the commander-in-chief. His natural reticence, feeding on a morbid fear of being captured on the battlefield (he had been taken captive at Dienbienphu and imprisoned for years afterward), may have influenced his eagerness to carry out Thieu's orders. He asked only what route he should take on his withdrawal.

Thieu was for either of two major roads, one across the center of the region and the other directly south, until an aide pointed out that either could be interdicted by the enemy. Instead, he recommended Route 7B, an old logger's road running east to Phu Bon Province. Although it had not been used in years and was in disrepair, it had the virtue of being an unlikely selection. It was agreed that Phu would lead his forces down Route 7B—a fatal decision.

Route 7B was not only unserviceable; it was crisscrossed by streams, many of which were unbridged, and it was made for ambush. To choose it so casually was to compound the original error of calling for a strategic withdrawal without advance preparation and planning. In war, nothing is more difficult than a retreat: to disengage from the enemy and conduct an orderly retirement. To do so requires the most meticulous planning. The route must be carefully selected and reconnoitered. Stocks of supplies must be positioned along the way. Care must be taken to separate civilians from the soldiery. And when it commences, it is like a leapfrogging movement. The main body detaches and about-faces under cover of a rear guard occupying a blocking position. When the main body is sufficiently free, moving with flankers and a point out front to guard against ambush or attack from the side, preferably with air cover above it, then the rear guard begins to retire until it passes through another rear guard positioned below it and sets up another blocking position. The process is repeated throughout the retreat.

All of these precepts and tactics were violated in the withdrawal from the Central Highlands which came to be called "the Convoy of Tears." After General Phu flew from Pleiku City to Nha Trang on the coast to set up his headquarters there, his troops bulldozed the city while sound trucks went through the streets advising the residents to flee. They did, first setting fire to their homes, and they mingled with the retreating troops. Soon soldiers and civilians—women, children and old people—were inextricably mixed, on foot or aboard crowded vehicles, as the Convoy of Tears wound slowly south along Route 7B.

Within a few days all came under Communist fire. General Dung had learned of Phu's shift to Nha Trang and of an evacuation begun in the Central Highlands. At first he believed both moves portended a counterattack on Ban Me Thuot. But then, to his relief, a report from Hanoi stated that the Hungarians on the ICSS had flashed the word that the highlands were indeed being abandoned. Dung's relief quickly gave way to fury when he realized that his field commanders had allowed Phu's army to slip down 7B, a road which they had earlier described as impassable. He told General Kim Tuan, commander of the 320th Division, that if the enemy escaped, he would be held responsible. Mortified, Tuan quickly ordered two regiments north into Phu Bon Province to intercept the Convoy of Tears.

Perhaps 100,000 people were in the convoy. Because there were so many vehicles jam-packed together, they moved at a speed of about 3 miles an hour. There was not enough water or food for everyone, and almost all of it was held by the soldiers. By the second day many of the civilian marchers had begun to die. Thirsty and hungry, they collapsed beside the road, there to perish. The civilians pleaded with the soldiers for water, but got none. Those who attempted to take it were shot and killed.

On that day, the Vietcong began harassing the column from the rear. Shells crashed among the vehicles and machine-gun bullets cut down the refugees stumbling along on foot. Blood began to flow in a thick stream down the road. Moans and screams and the shrill shrieking of children counterpointed the chattering of the small arms and the roaring flash-and-crash of the artillery.

These were the people whom the North Vietnamese had come south to "liberate," and yet the slaughter of them continued. Revolutionaries do not really care about people. It is the "movement" that counts, the new order that is to be built. It was unfortunate that they had gotten in the way, but that was no reason to spare them. So the shooting and the shelling went on and the streams of blood on Route 7B grew thicker and wider.

Next day General Tuan's troops caught up with the column near a town named Cheo Reo and began attacking a unit of Rangers, the only organized formation in the convoy. The Rangers called for aerial support. When it arrived, the bombs fell on friendly units, destroying a full Ranger battalion. After that the North Vietnamese advanced and captured Cheo Reo. Phu's army was now severed, one part cut off and the other ready for destruction.

The withdrawal from the Central Highlands was ending in complete disaster. There would be no troops to reinforce the lower coast and any counterattack on Ban Me Thuot was out of the question. As General Dung was to write in his diary, Thieu had made a "fatal mistake."

On the very day that the Convoy of Tears began its journey into agony, General Giap in Hanoi eagerly expanded the offensive. The successes of the first five days had convinced him that the South Vietnamese Army was crumbling, and he called for two more drives: one directly south into Quang Tri, the northernmost province of South Vietnam, and the second eastward from Ban Me Thuot. In the first thrust Giap, seconded by Dung, hoped to test and perhaps even unmask the defenses of Hue farther south. Hue, they believed, would be a tough nut to crack, guarded as it was by the South Vietnamese Marine Division, considered Saigon's best. The Marines, however, had not seen action for some time and might have lost their fighting edge. Moreover, to defeat them and to seize Hue, the ancient capital which even modern Vietnamese of both nations still revered as the soul of the state, would be to strike two severe psychological blows. On March 19, the assault on Quang Tri began.

Ranks of tanks massed like platoons of men rolled through the Marine Division and sent its units backpedaling in terror upon Hue. Elated, the Communists now called the most momentous meeting of the war. It was held in a hall at Ba Dinh, the major square in Hanoi, and attended by both the political and military elite of North Vietnam. However, Le Duan, who had become the first among equals in the Politburo, dominated the gathering. In the typically long, windy, stilted speech that is the mark of the Communist bureaucrat world-wide, he argued that the time had come to strike for complete and total victory before the advent of the rainy season in early May. Le Duan's proposal was received and approved wih tumultuous joy, and the orders for the destruction of the enemy in Military Regions 1 and 2 were immediately transmitted south to General Dung.

On the morning of March 24, the North Vietnamese cut Highway 1 south of Hue, thus severing the escape route to Danang, after which they attacked the city. As the fighting spread, thousands upon thousands of refugees panicked and began streaming eastward toward the tiny port of Tan My. This had been the South Vietnamese commander's alternate escape route, but now it was clogged and blocked with terrified civilians. Ships brought to Tan My to evacuate troops began taking on civilians willing to hand over their life savings for a berth on a vessel bound for safety. Within the city, drivers of taxis and buses were charging the frantic refugees fees amounting to one or two years' salary. Soon rioting broke out in the central market. Civilians who could not forget the Communist massacres of the Tet Offensive grappled with soldiers for places on departing vehicles. Frequently, the soldiers shot them dead. By mid-afternoon, the Saigon forces defending Hue had disintegrated. Only a single Marine battalion remained in place north of the city, and because the commander did not wish to sacrifice what he considered his finest unit, he ordered it to withdraw. With this decision, he broke the spirit of the battalion's men—and Hue soon lay open to capture.

On March 25, it fell. And on the same day the Communists, with 21 of their 24 divisions now committed to combat, began the assault

on Danang. Soviet-made 122-mm rockets opened the attack, swoosh-
ing in and exploding upon the throngs of miserable refugees who had
flooded into the city from Hue and other northern points. Perhaps
500,000 military stragglers and refugees had entered Danang in the
past few days. The beaten, leaderless soldiers from the North were
of no use to Danang's defenders, actually demoralizing the troops
in place there, while the hungry civilians drained off supplies and
clogged the roads. Very quickly the dissolution of discipline and
rioting that had been Hue's undoing was repeated in Danang. Once
again, the race was on for transportation to the airfields or the sea.
Again and again, thousands of terrified Vietnamese broke through
airport guards to overwhelm arriving evacuation airplanes. Women
and children were trampled to death in the rush, and sometimes terrified pilots roared aloft, their craft only half loaded, with scores of
Vietnamese clinging to half-opened hatches or the wheel wells from
which they eventually fell to their deaths. The horrors on the waterfront were perhaps even worse, for there masses of deserting soldiers
had taken possession of some of the evacuation ships. An American
CIA official has described what he saw when he swung over the
railing of the *Pioneering Contender*:

Over 1,500 South Vietnamese troops were sprawled, lounging, fighting
among themselves on the main decks and the bridges, *practicing their aim*
at the hapless Vietnamese civilians in their midst. Less than thirty yards
away a [South Vietnamese] trooper was in the process of raping a Vietnamese woman while another soldier held her male companion at gunpoint.
The thirty-five or more American evacuees already on board were cringing
by the gangplank.[43]

Fortunately for the civilians on board, a band of U.S. Marines charged
the soldiers holding the bridge, disarmed them and freed the ship's
captain, whom the soldiers had captured and threatened to kill unless
he took them to the Philippines. Such were the agonizing death throes
of Danang, and on the 30th day of March the second largest city
in South Vietnam also fell.

Cambodia was falling, too. The Khmer Rouge's New Year's
Offensive was gaining momentum. By early February, it had cut the
Mekong River route to the sea. By mid-March, student riots in the
key town of Battambang, together with protest against corruption in

the capital of Phnom Penh, had unmasked the essential weakness of the Lon Nol regime. Although U.S. Ambassador John Gunther Dean pleaded for more aid for Lon Nol, in order to reach a "controlled solution"—i.e., a new leadership able to negotiate with the Communists—the Khmer Rouge had already made it plain that it would not deal. Its forces drove closer to the capital. On April 1, Lon Nol fled to Bali and thence to Honolulu, taking his family and close associates with him. Behind him, he left a governmental vacuum that was never filled, and on April 17 Phnom Penh surrendered.

At once the new masters ordered a seven-day celebration coinciding with the Cambodian New Year. Peace and forgiveness were proclaimed as the new watchword; until, with the emergence of Pol Pot as the Communist leader, there began a hideous bloodbath perhaps without parallel even in modern history. That the Communists should put to death the officials and servants of the fallen regime was not exactly unexpected, but that millions of Pol Pot's countrymen should be wantonly and cruelly murdered for no greater crime than to have lived in the cities, or gone to school or owned property, was an act of extermination so wanton as to rank with Hitler's destruction of 6 million Jews or Stalin's deliberate starvation of unknown millions of kulaks, or wealthy peasants, who resisted collectivization of farms.

Pol Pot's purpose was just as brutally simple: the building of a new social order. Human beings who did not fit the new design, or could be expected to oppose it, must be swept away. Cambodians not of either peasant or working-class stock, even peasants or workers with the slightest connection with the non-Communist past, were to be "eliminated." Whole families were exterminated because the Communists believed the children would resent the murder of their parents.

Cities, the special object of Pol Pot's hatred, became ghost towns after the mass deportations of their populations to heavily guarded resettlement camps in the wilderness. Even villages were cleaned out. Those chosen for slaughter were herded to mass graves, where, blindfolded, they were led to the ditch and beaten to death with axe handles or heavy garden hoes. Those granted life were rounded up and marched for days at bayonet point, under a scorching sun without food or water, medicine or shelter, to the resettlement camps. There, according to the Communists' prescription for the new order, husbands and wives were separated and set to work at hard labor while their children were placed in government youth camps.

The lowest estimate of those slaughtered over the next four years, until Pol Pot was ousted by rebel Cambodian Communists backed by Vietnamese troops, is 1 million, although most informed estimates place the number as high as 2.5 million, or, taking into account the civil war still in progress, perhaps 3 million. This out of a nation of 7.8 million! Such a calamity occurring in the United States would mean the destruction of 83 million of 220 million Americans.

It was on this horrid mound of bloody humanity that the Cambodian Communists began to build their new order.

In South Vietnam, meanwhile, General Dung had gradually brought all of Military Regions 1 and 2—more than half of South Vietnam— under his control. Patiently gathering his forces, he prepared for his next strike against Xuan Loc, the capital of Long Khanh Province only 38 miles northeast of Saigon. A city of 38,000 souls, Xuan Loc's importance was that it was a crossroads town, sitting astride vital Highway 1 running straight to Saigon. On the morning of April 9, a full division of North Vietnamese soldiers backed by heavy artillery struck at Xuan Loc. At first its defenders fell back, but then, to the enemy's surprise, they regrouped and counterattacked to force the Northerners back. General Dung was also startled, and a little dismayed. The division holding Xuan Loc—the 18th—was supposed to be the worst in Saigon's army; but here it was, fighting much more valiantly than its more famous brothers. Eventually the stiff fight put up by the 18th Division at Xuan Loc compelled Dung to bypass the town in order to move more quickly on Saigon.

As Dung knew, the capital city was in a turmoil. Everywhere everyone was crying for the head of Nguyen Van Thieu. All of them—even the Americans—had called upon Thieu to step down. But he had clung to power, even after the fall of Hue had brought about the resignation of his cabinet. Typically he went into isolation until, on April 20, amid reports that Xuan Loc was falling, one of his generals found Thieu sitting in his bomb shelter under Independence Palace and reported to him that not only was everything lost, but Thieu's own soldiers had bulldozed and desecrated his family's graveyard at Ninh Chu. Thieu was stunned, but he said nothing and the general left.

Early next morning, pale and nervous (he had not eaten for days), Thieu emerged from his bomb shelter and went to his office to prepare a speech to his commanders, which would then be shown on television.

During 90 minutes of wild, ranting, fist-pounding, rambling oratory—a rare performance for the normally dry and precise Thieu—he accused the Americans of having forsaken him and his country and at last announced that he was resigning in favor of the aging, if not senile, Vice President Tran Van Huong. "You Americans have not given us the aid you promised us," he sobbed. "Given that aid, I would not be afraid of the Communists."[44] Then, after turning to kiss Huong, he left the room. Five days later he was aboard an American airplane flying him into exile on Taiwan, taking with him four suitcases packed with the palace contingency fund of about $100,000. Earlier, his wife had provided for the exportation by ship to France of 16 tons of gold from the Bank of Vietnam, along with her priceless collections of jewels and antiques.

Behind them the Thieus left a political vacuum. The aged Tran Van Huong was simply unable to govern, even though U.S. Ambassador Graham Martin, a stickler for constitutional government, supported him tenaciously. It did not occur to Martin that it is regular that at times things should be irregular. Apparently he would have backed a cretin as president if he had gotten there by strict constitutional means. Martin, together with French Ambassador Jean-Marie Merillon and the pro-Thieu parties of the National Assembly, believed that the "Nationalists" now could sue for a peace based on their own interpretation of the Paris Agreement. Anti-Thieu legislators led by General Duong Van ("Big") Minh, whose political fortunes had risen with Thieu's fall, supported by left- and right-wing extremists, maintained that Thieu's resignation solved nothing, if only because the remaining rulers had been hand-picked by Thieu. The Communists agreed with Minh and his strange bedfellows. "This is a Thieu administration without Thieu,"[45] Radio Hanoi insisted.

Hanoi also began to mark time militarily. All forces were ordered to stand in place. They were not to surrender a foot of captured soil, but they were also not to attack unless it appeared that the Saigon Army was preparing for counterstrokes. Although victory in 1975 still seemed possible, the Politburo reasoned, Saigon might nevertheless be able to offer resistance which could delay the Ho Chi Minh Offensive until the monsoon arrived in a few weeks. Better to gain the victory through political than military means. Better to let the wolves in Saigon devour one another.

Nevertheless, troops still poured south toward the capital. An iron ring was being drawn around it. Artillery, fuel, trucks, tanks and bridging material were brought up. Inside Saigon, Ambassador Martin and those South Vietnamese politicians who either had not yet fled or were not busy arranging for their departure strove frantically to find a leader who would be able to negotiate with the Communists. In spite of Hanoi's blunt and unyielding refusal to negotiate with any Thieu men, Martin and others still hoped to preserve the constitutional forms by having Huong step aside for Senate President Tran Van Lam, with Big Minh entering the government as prime minister. Although Lam, who had always aspired to the presidency, still sought it even under such appalling circumstances, Big Minh would have none of the proposal. Eventually the National Assembly by a vote of 127 to 0 authorized Huong to resign in favor of Big Minh.

It was already too late. On Sunday, April 27, the day before Big Minh was to take office, the Communists attacked Saigon. A quartet of rockets—the first enemy missiles to strike the capital in three and a half years—swooshed into the city before dawn. Fighting erupted around the iron ring. To the east, a fierce Northern tank attack overran the Southern tank base. Saigon's defenses were crumbling fast. Too fast for Big Minh, who met with Martin that day and ordered all American military out of the country by Tuesday, the 29th.

It was again too late. Minh's move to cleanse himself of the American taint and make himself acceptable to the Communists did not deflect a single bullet. Hanoi was winning more easily and dramatically than either Dung or Giap or Le Duan could possibly have envisioned a week before, and there was now no need to negotiate with anyone ever.

Next day, Ambassador Martin ordered a final American evacuation, leaving the embassy himself by helicopter shortly after midnight; and on the following day, April 30, 1975, after the last U.S. Marine guards had gone whirling away to safety from the embassy roof, Big Minh surrendered his country and the Communists of North Vietnam made a fighting, triumphal entry into the fallen city of Saigon.

Almost 30 years of war were at an end.

13

☆

What happened in Vietnam?

Is it true that the United States—the most powerful nation in the world—was "beaten" in Vietnam by a small, semibackward Asian nation of 22 million people, albeit one supplied and technically trained by its mighty ally Soviet Russia, with lesser assistance from great China?

It is not true. At no time during the American military involvement in Vietnam was the United States incapable of destroying North Vietnam. Yet to have done so, of course, would have been to create a desert and call it peace, while earning world-wide opprobrium. Such a "victory," though possible, was unthinkable.

As in all wars of counterinsurgency, the objective was not victory but to deny the enemy victory. This was done, even under the hamstringing restrictions and limitations imposed by Lyndon Johnson, who now must enter history as the worst of American commanders-in-chief. But on the other side of the coin, the political side, the nation-building side, the attempt to forge a strong, free nation in South Vietnam, the United States was indeed defeated; and it was this failure which eventually resulted in the triumph of Communist arms.

Why, then, were five Presidents unable to contain Communism in Indo-China? Probably because of their naïve but mistaken belief that democracy can flourish in any soil. In truth, democracy—free-speech society with truly representative government—is a rare bloom, which has seldom blossomed outside Europe or the English-speaking countries of the world. To have attempted to graft it onto South Vietnam's population of peasants, ignoring their psychology, their traditions, their rigidly structured society, their indifference to the Western gods of Ballot Box and Freedom and their attachment to a charismatic leader, be he emperor, king or commissar, was the original and major mistake of the war.

Is it possible, then, that the line of containment could have been drawn in Indo-China if the Americans, practical and patient, had set up an intermediate, limited democracy, backing a leader who could match Ho Chi Minh's cohesive magnetism, a man in the mold of Syngman Rhee, a national hero strong and purposeful whose methods might sometimes be somewhat other than democratic? Perhaps, if one could have been found. But there were no such demigods in the South: only Ngo Dinh Diem, a pale, pudgy mandarin whose chief claim on patriotic loyalty was that he had broken with the French and refused to serve the Japanese. But Ho Chi Minh, a man of the people, had *fought* the Japanese and then the French. Uncle Ho was a true national hero who understood his people; so transparent, perhaps, to a Westerner, who would sneer at the photographs of Ho passing out oranges to laughing children or dabbing at dry eyes with a big red bandana; and yet, so effective among Vietnamese accustomed to the Confucian tradition of "doing the right thing." Ho and his colleagues on the Politburo skillfully inculcated in their people the spirit of crusade, the belief that they were engaged in a civil war and the liberation of their brethren in the South. To the Vietcong, the war was a battle for their homeland.

No such attitude existed in the South, especially not after the assassination of Diem. For Diem, for all his shortcomings, was at least an experienced civilian who knew something about government. After he was killed, all was chaos, and the familiar rhythm of coup and countercoup ensued, ending with Nguyen Van Thieu in power surrounded by a military junta of mostly corrupt generals. To remain in power, Thieu and his generals depended upon the American presence. Thieu may have been one of the five best politicians in the world, as Richard Nixon has insisted, but his political acumen served himself more than his country. He was no statesman, and no sense of dedication similar to the crusading zeal of Hanoi's soldiery existed under his regime. Still less in his army. From a captured North Vietnamese major comes this insight into the fighting spirit of the South Vietnamese soldiery. "I could command a division in North Vietnam," he boasted. "I have the ability to do that. But a platoon here, even a squad, I could not do that. What can you do? They have no purpose."[46] And from those hourly indoctrinated troops who greeted General Dung on his journey south to Ban Me Thuot comes that parrot-like roar that explains much of the difference between the South and the North:

"We can do it! We can do it! Determined to win! Determined to win!"

If the failure at nation-building was the ultimate undoing of the American effort to save South Vietnam, the fact still remains—and must not be forgotten—that on the military side North Vietnam was denied victory and was even, at the end of 1972, brought to its knees.

As early as 1965, when Westmoreland defeated Giap in the Battle of the Ia Drang Valley, Hanoi realized that it could never hope to beat the Americans in conventional, stand-up warfare. And as late as December, 1972, when President Nixon dropped the carrot of persuasion and swung the stick of coercion to force the Communists to accept his peace plan, the North was literally knocked out of the war. By 11 days of ruthless B-52 bombing, coupled with the blockading and mining of the chief port of Haiphong, the United States had rendered the entire nation defenseless against further attack. Supply by sea from the Soviet Union was cut off. All but three of Hanoi's SAMs were gone, and only a few more would be forthcoming overland from China. For the first time in the war the North Vietnamese rear base had been struck with all the American might, and it was now at the mercy of its enemy. Without a rear base, a nation cannot fight—and it was this realization and this alone that brought Hanoi back to Paris to sign the peace agreement.

At that point, should President Nixon have maintained the military pressure to knock North Vietnam out of the war? In no way could he have continued to strike at an enemy openly proclaiming his desire for peace. If he had attempted to, even the uproar that succeeded his announcement of the bombing would have seemed a gentle murmur in comparison to the volcano of protest that would have then erupted. Nixon would never have survived it. Furthermore, all that he had wanted was the agreement—which he got.

Unfortunately, the melancholy truth is that the decision to strike the enemy rear as hard as possible should have been made seven years earlier by Lyndon Johnson. Guided by his almost paranoid fear of Red China, persuaded by Secretary McNamara to ignore the advice of his military chiefs, Johnson opted for the disastrous policy of "gradualism." He did not attack the mouth of the funnel of supply and reinforcement but the bottom of it. Thus the North Vietnamese were granted time to prepare for the gradual escalation of aerial assault, resulting in much higher losses for the Americans. Instead of being targets, the areas around Hanoi and Haiphong became sanctuaries, and the enemy was permitted to organize his other havens along the South Vietnamese border. By not striking hard and at once, Johnson granted the Communists time to disperse their materials and manufactures and to train their nation for aerial defense. Gradualism also exactly suited the Soviet Union's design of involving the United States in a protracted, unpopular war which would alienate it from its allies and turn world opinion against it. Finally, it left the enemy's all-important rear relatively free from attack.

Not all the mistakes in Vietnam can be laid on the White House steps. The military also erred: chiefly by ignoring the French experience to the extent that, instead of preparing for guerrilla warfare, they trained both American and South Vietnamese and other allied troops for conventional warfare; and also by stifling its commands with an incredible flood of intelligence data; by permitting development of the "firebase psychosis"; by devising a system of rotation which, limiting a man's service in Vietnam to a year, had the unfortunate effect of encouraging the ordinary soldier to be cautious while restricting a company commander's time with his troops; and by building up an enormous body of service and supply troops so that the ratio of noncombat to combat soldiers was a lopsided 4 or 5 to 1. But these are minor in comparison to Johnson's refusal to allow his forces to isolate North Vietnam from the battlefield. A second mistake of almost equal magnitude—one for which the military bears equal responsibility with Johnson—was to underestimate the staying power of North Vietnam.

Until Nixon began to wind down the war, it was firmly believed that Hanoi could not stand the war of attrition which the policy of gradualism dictated. Yet in the end it was not the failure of North Vietnamese endurance that was decisive, but rather the collapse of the American will to wage the war.

War itself may be defined as socially approved armed conflict between hostile groups. Without social approval, war simply cannot be waged. Even absolute rulers—kings, khans and Caesars—depended upon the support of their nobles which, if withdrawn, made it impossible to continue the struggle. Thus, in the Revolutionary

War, the American victory at Yorktown made it clear to Lord North and King George III that Parliament would no longer condone the war. More recently, the Communist Revolution of 1917 took Russia out of World War I. Social approval had been withdrawn.

In Vietnam up until the Tet Offensive of 1968, the American people supported the war, not as freely or enthusiastically as in World War II, but supported it nevertheless. After Tet, when the media turned a great allied battlefield victory into a disastrous psychological defeat, social approval began to decline. The people were confused. Westmoreland had just reported great progress and they had been confidently expecting success. Instead, the "beaten" enemy proved capable of the Tet Offensive. And when the true figures on Tet were published, it was too late. Actually, the people had been confused throughout the war. The government never "sold" it to them, never clearly explained what its objectives were. Perhaps it feared that the people would never sanction a war being fought 10,000 miles away merely to serve a foreign policy of containment. To have described, say, the military value of the Strait of Malacca—the world's most vital narrow waters lying just below Indo-China, linking the Pacific with the Indian Ocean—would not have impressed the ordinary Americn who thinks of wars in terms of crusades. "Credibility with our allies all over the world" was also not a very persuasive point to make to a young man with only one life to lose. "Most men will die upon a dogma," wrote Cardinal Newman, "but few will be martyr to a conclusion."

Nor did the antiwar people make the reasons for their opposition any clearer. Father Hesburgh of Notre Dame has written that he came to "hate the whole involvement with a passion";[47] however, except to criticize the evils and injustices of the draft, he does not say why. When President Nixon talked to protesting students at the Lincoln Memorial, one of them said to him: "I hope you realize that we are willing to die for what we believe in."[48] But he never explained what that was. Protestors attacked the war as "wrong"; or, on the part of doctrinal pacifists, "immoral"; or said merely, "We have no right to be there." Some, echoing the Communist line, charged that the United States was interfering in a civil war; or shouted, "Stop the killing!"; or accused mighty America of wantonly destroying a tiny, defenseless Asian nation; or, with rare rationality, deplored the war's dreadful divisiveness; or called for an end to the

"Pentagon Plot" so that the money used to finance it might be diverted to cleaning America's polluted atmosphere. Most pitiful and poignant of all were the anguished outcries of those parents whose sons had been killed in what seemed to them a useless sacrifice. To many, many millions of other Americans the war did seem to be a hideous, senseless agony. Yet nowhere above the storm of debate and vituperation was a calm and influential voice raised to explain why the war was or was not in the best interests of the American nation.

Instead, the nation was torn apart by that divisive dichotomy of "hawk" and "dove." Sad to say, there were not many owls.* Small wonder that the American people were confused. After Tet and the disclosure of the My Lai Massacre, they did not know whom to believe. Unless they wanted to hear what either side was saying, their faith in their informants declined sharply. Misrepresentation was common on both sides. From the government and the military half-truths, exaggerations, or omissions could only be expected; but from the media, supposedly dedicated to speaking and writing the truth, nothing less than the truth can be acceptable. Yet members of the media also misrepresented facts. Instances abound, but perhaps the most incredible occurred when the writer Mary McCarthy, returning from her first trip to Vietnam, appeared on British television to declare that there was not a single documented case of the Vietcong deliberately killing a South Vietnamese woman or child. This in the face of the Vietcong's deliberate policy of terrorism and literal tons of documentation. Thus it is safe to say that during the Vietnam War, influential members of the American media lost that objectivity which is after all the soul of reportorial integrity; and some have yet to recover it. Perhaps worse is their conviction that they still have it, for there is no one more prejudiced than the biased man who insists that he is impartial.

It was in this way that social approval of the war was eroded, not in North Vietnam but in the United States of America. Richard Nixon was aware of this when he took office in 1969, and this consideration probably had much to do with his decision to begin "Vietnamization" of the war while withdrawing American troops;

---

* During the war when this writer appeared on a television program, he was asked by a famous commentator if he were a hawk or a dove. "I'd rather be known as an owl," he replied, and the commentator exclaimed: "But you can't *say* that!"

and also, in 1972, to dismantle the pernicious draft, almost as much an object of hatred as the war itself.

This, then, was what happened in Vietnam. Of the many mistakes of head and heart here catalogued, probably the greatest was to believe that democracy could be planted and spring forth full-blown—like Athena from the brain of Zeus—from the alien soil of an agricultural Asian country. Next was Lyndon Johnson's policy of gradualism, and the absence of any real strategy for achieving the grand strategy of denying the enemy military victory with one hand while building a strong, free nation able to defend itself with the other. Not actually a mistake but a major contributing factor was the escalating antiwar dissent and criticism of the war effort, both of which were inevitably helpful to Hanoi and harmful to American solidarity. And yet there was a perhaps deeper but unconscious error: the attempt of a free-speech society to fight a limited war with a free press and a democratic army.

If limited wars do arise in the future, they must be fought with professional armies paid well enough to compensate for the hazards of war, not with youths drafted against their will and permitted to exercise the civilian's rights of free speech. "War does not permit free speech," said Julius Caesar; and it is difficult not to agree with him, if only because free speech is not always free of falsehood, ulterior motive or harmful idealism, however sincere. Unfortunately, there is abroad in America the notion that everyone has the right to know everything, which is palpable nonsense. After Pearl Harbor, Franklin Roosevelt wisely suppressed the details of that disaster rather than risk a panic, only publishing them after the American counterattack had begun at Guadalcanal. In World War I, Wilson ruthlessly suppressed dissent while Pershing clamped an iron censorship over the front with no protest from the press. In both of these popular wars, the media understood that unrestricted reporting could be harmful to the Allies. So too in World War I the mutiny of the French Army was kept secret; in World War II, the death of thousands of French civilians killed in the saturation bombings of Normandy was not revealed. In that conflict an incident similar to My Lai would have brought the quiet court-martial of those responsible and perhaps even their secret execution, in the way that the now-famous execution of Private Slovik was not made public until after the war. The destruction of friendly troops by artillery or from the air—a tragic commonplace of modern war—was also not disclosed for fear of how it might agonize the home front, as repeated revelations of such events certainly did in Vietnam.

To fight these total wars, the United States had to become totalitarian itself, at least in the area of free speech. But the truth is that you must become what you fight, and nowhere more than in limited conflict with a police state, the power of which to wage protracted war simply cannot be overestimated.

All this should not be construed as a subtle attempt to undermine the First Amendment or to stifle honest criticism. The greatest mistake of World War II was Hitler's decision to turn away from an undefeated Britain, at a time when the United States was manifestly preparing to come to her aid, and to attack Russia. Errors of such magnitude are not possible in societies which permit criticism. Hitler heard none because he allowed none. Nevertheless it is paradoxically true that in wartime the First Amendment which makes us what we are must be limited lest it be useful to the enemy, and that if we do not limit it we may lose it.

This is the lesson to be learned from Vietnam. In a war of dilemmas, this was the dilemma par excellence: a free-speech society seeking to defend or extend the areas of free speech must limit free speech to do it.

PART ☆ XI

1981–1991:
America Recoiling,
Resurgent

EAST EUROPEAN REVOLT, TERRORISM,
LIBYA, GRENADA, PANAMA,
THE PERSIAN GULF
AND THE COLLAPSE OF THE U.S.S.R.

1

☆

It is now more than 16 years since that melancholy midnight when the last helicopter whirled aloft from the roof of the United States Embassy in Saigon carrying the last Americans out of the morass that had been the utter failure of America's attempt to reaffirm in Vietnam the policy of containing Communism that had succeeded in Korea and West Berlin.

During the decade between the end in Vietnam in 1975 and the appearance of Mikhail Gorbachev as leader of the Soviet Union, it did seem that Ho Chi Minh had opted wisely when he said: "I chose Marxism." Nikita Khrushchev appeared to be a true prophet when he told a group of Western diplomats in 1957: "Whether you . . . like it or not, history is on our side. We will bury you." His successor, Leonid Brezhnev, could hardly be challenged when he proclaimed the doctrine of Eternal Communism: the theory that once a nation chose socialism it would remain so forever. Everywhere inside the Soviet imperialist hegemony—that congeries of bullied and repressed nations and races of the Caucasus and Central Asia and the former democracies of Eastern Europe, that Ronald Reagan accurately described as "an evil empire"—any attempt to reverse that dogma was brutally suppressed. Before Vietnam the uprisings in Poland, East Germany, Hungary and Czechoslovakia had been crushed, and when the independent labor union Solidarity appeared in Poland in September, 1980, as a renewed challenge to the authority of the Kremlin, it was outlawed and martial law imposed on the country.

In Asia the Communist tide appeared to continue at the flood. Vietnam had been unified as a socialist state, Hanoi having found the National Liberation Front no longer a useful myth, and Saigon was renamed Ho Chi Minh City. But in Asia the tendency of neighboring socialist states to attack one another suggested that Communism—like the Western world in its two great civil wars—might divide and devour itself; for ideology, like civilization itself, is only a veneer. Scratch it, and you will uncover ancient hatreds and immemorial conceits: in a word, religion, race and nation. Rulers may change their ideologies, but people seldom shed their enmities. Thus Communist Vietnam, with the help of Cambodian socialist troops rebelling against Pol Pot, invaded Communist Cambodia on Christmas Day, 1978, and put Pol Pot to flight. But Vietnam, along with Thailand, has *always* scourged Cambodia and Laos, whether under a king or a commissar. Communist China on February 17, 1979, launched a seventeen-day invasion of Communist Vietnam, ostensibly to chastise Hanoi for its adventure in Chinese-supported Cambodia and its treatment of ethnic Chinese within its borders; actually because Vietnam had entered the Soviet orbit and was now an enemy of Beijing. But China has *always* been the tormentor of Vietnam whether under an emperor or a party chairman. And Russia and China? They, too, have quarreled since first they came into physical contact, and the so-called reconciliation of the late eighties seems to be more cosmetic than real. Thus ideologies change, enemies do not. Neighbors quarrel, but strangers—particularly those separated by great distances—do not.

During the post-Vietnam era the Soviet Union actually increased the tempo of its drive for world dominion, employing its customary tactics of interference and intimidation. Together with Communist Cuba, which supplied the troops, the Soviets were particularly active in Africa, seeking to influence or dominate the governments of emergent Third World societies such as Ethiopia. The U.S.S.R. also sought to sabotage the Israeli-Egyptian peace while cultivating client states among the Arabs, trying to capitalize on the fall of the Shah of Iran and thus move a step closer to the oil riches of the Persian Gulf. But the friendly outstretched paw of the Soviet bear could not dissuade the fanatical Ayatollah Khomeini from distrusting atheistic socialism. During this period the Soviet Union also built an impressive navy, using the modern seaports and airfields built by the Americans in South Vietnam to make her aerial and naval presence felt in Asian waters. Only Malaysia stood between these outposts and the Strait of Malacca, the world's most strategic narrow waters. In the

Mediterranean, the Soviet Navy became the dominant power. The Soviet bear's claws were again sheathed when it sought to extend its influence into South America, cultivating Catholic thinkers—most of them priests—when they evolved the theory of "liberation theology," as an alternative to the "sterile" theoretical thought of the Old World that is actually based on a Marxist analysis of society. It also preaches socialist capitalism, probably as another alternative, this time to the democratic capitalism of the Colossus of the North—the United States of America—hated for its prosperity, feared for its power. Even Catholic bishops became converted to the subtle socialism of liberation theology, provoking from the Vatican a sharp warning of its errors and a rebuke to its most outspoken propagandists.

Soviet influence also was extended into Central America, where a Marxist government came into power in Nicaragua and Communist rebels sought to seize El Salvador. Yet official Washington seemed more impressed by the Kremlin's friendly face rather than its greedy grasp. Détente was very much in fashion, and no one who was anybody seemed to remember Rudyard Kipling's description of the true Soviet bear:

> When he stands up like a tired man, tottering near and near;
> When he stands up as pleading, in wavering, man-brute guise;
> When he veils the hate and cunning of his little, swinish eyes;
> When he shows as seeking quarter, with paws like hands in prayer;
> *That* is the time of peril—the time of the Truce of the Bear!

Kipling's language describing America's former ally might in the immensely friendlier climate of the early nineties be regarded as intemperate. Nevertheless, it does suggest that a wide-eyed approach to the supplicating Soviet might not be exactly in America's best interests, especially if it is remembered that in 1979 Foreign Minister Huang Hua of China warned the United Nations that the Soviet Union still had designs on Western Europe and planned to fight the United States there with conventional weapons. This, of course, occurred during the "stagnant era" of Soviet Communism, under the aegis of Leonid Brezhnev, the hardest-liner to occupy the Kremlin since Josef Stalin.

The question then was: would the United States fight? It might not have, granted the lingering Vietnam psychosis and the vacillating leadership of the cautious Jimmy Carter. If it had, it would probably have been without the enthusiastic support of a unified people. It would have taken a shock of the magnitude of Pearl Harbor to make America fighting mad again, to overcome the influence of the paroxysm of pacifism and anti-militarism that seized the nation during the Vietnam War. It had so dissolved the American will that even when the struggle was in progress—in 1972—the U.S. did not possess the apparatus to mobilize if attacked. In that year Congress eliminated the truly despicable and divisive draft. It had been dodged by the sons of the rich and middle class, either by fatuous pretenses of disability, such as "thick toenails," by consulting draft-evasion experts or studying to become draft-deferred schoolteachers or else—among many of the young black males in the inner cities—simply by refusing to register for it. It had been so nonproductive of the necessary manpower that McNamara, with his delicate dross touch and myopic insight into human nature, sought to solve this shortage by creating a new class of draftees known as "Category IVs." A hundred thousand of these unfortunates were drafted, proving unreliable and almost impossible to train. Of them General Westmoreland said: "That's what brought the drugs and other unacceptable practices over there to the battlefield. These were men drafted from the ghetto, some of them had jail sentences . . . that lowest mental category used to bring about 85 per cent of the disciplinary cases."

But Congress also emptied out the baby with the bath water by failing to replace the draft with some workable system of calling up troops in America. Under Carter, legislation for a so-called "draft registration" was passed, but even this came under attack from the same coalition that discredited the military during Vietnam. "Hell, no! We won't go!" was their rallying cry, an echo of the Ludlow Amendment of 1938 and the shameful bleat of "Better Red than dead" that was popular in the fifties. Hitler and Mussolini to their regret attached much importance to the Ludlow Amendment and the Joad Resolution at Oxford, and the Soviets during their thrust for world domination could not have failed to be jubilant over the obvious decline of American military strength. Why else would the Soviet Union have so brazenly invaded Afghanistan in December of 1979?

Nor did the death of Brezhnev in 1982 suggest any slackening in the Stalinist thirst for still more satellites, especially not after Yuri

Andropov replaced him as General Secretary in November of that year. The son of a railway worker probably of Armenian origin, Andropov as a youth and young man was an ardent joiner of Communist organizations. Khrushchev sent him to Hungary as Ambassador in 1954, where he was instrumental in suppressing the national revolt, as well as the capture and hanging of the Hungarian patriot Imre Nagy. His next step up was as chief of the State Security Committee (KGB), where his zeal in carrying out his duties might have impressed Khrushchev, who often complained that his own chief did not torture or kill "with enthusiasm." With such a man leading the Soviet Union, the pathetically naïve faith in detente died a quick death. Fortunately for the world, so did Yuri Andropov. Although his brief tenure of only fifteen months might have suggested a mysterious end, he actually died of a combination of illnesses. His successor was Mikhail Gorbachev, whose appearance three years after Ronald Reagan's landslide election victory over Jimmy Carter in 1980 combined with that revolutionary event to bring a dismal end to Russia's 74-year-old experiment in dialectical materialism.

Mikhail Sergeyevich Gorbachev was born on March 2, 1931, in the territory of Stavropol, the son of peasant parents. Bright, self-possessed and ambitious, at the age of fifteen he followed the only reliable route to power in the Soviet Union by joining the Young Communist League. For four years he worked on a state farm as a combine harvester driver, until his native intelligence so impressed his superiors that he was sent to Moscow University, from which he was graduated in law. His rise was rapid, as much owing to his own abilities as the necessity of finding a powerful patron, and in this he chose unerringly in befriending the party ideologue Mikhail Suslov and his own predecessor, Yuri Andropov. Under the wing of these two powerful men Gorbachev's rise was so rapid that by the time he was 39 he was a full member of the Politburo. After Andropov succeeded Brezhnev, he assigned his protégé to the mission of reforming Soviet agriculture, an impossible task given the nature of a command society, and his inevitable failure did nothing to limit his growing popularity. Thus, on the death of his benefactor, in 1985 he became his successor.

In 1985 the citizens of the U.S.S.R. were on the edge of despair. To

them the prestige of living in a superpower was no consolation whatsoever for dwelling in a backward economy. Tiny, overcrowded and
dingy apartments or decrepit little houses with rudimentary furniture
and fixtures were the portion of everyone but the 19 million anointed
members of the Party, who, in varying degrees, could indulge themselves in spacious, comfortable quarters or elegant dachas with access
to the special well-stocked stores maintained just for them. They
knew nothing of the daily despair of shopping among empty shelves
or the frustration of shortages in every necessity. Restrictions were
everywhere: in travel or free speech by the government, in its system
of interior passports compelling almost all but Party members to
spend their lives in the areas of their birth. Even the size of a family
was limited by the size of an apartment or of a government-fixed
salary. To move from the country to a big city such as Moscow or
Leningrad required the proper permission, while to own property was
illegal.

Soviet products were so inferior that a foreigner might sometimes
be astonished to find stores seemingly stuffed with goods and appliances, unaware that Soviet shoppers rarely bought anything that was
not produced in the first third of the month. That was because in the
second third the workers were "storming" to meet their production
quotas and turned out shabby goods; while in the last third they were
so exhausted they refreshed themselves either with vodka or absen-
teeism—with the same results. When the first third rolled around
again, their hangovers gone or their bodies rested, they resumed a
normal tempo and improved their products. An American correspondent in Moscow watched as a construction battalion finished erecting
a concrete building to be followed next day by workers who painted
it. When he asked the foreman why they painted it so soon knowing
that without waiting three months for the concrete to cure the paint
would immediately begin to peel, the foreman replied: "Nobody owns
it so nobody cares." There in six words was the explanation of the
inevitable failure of the Soviet planned economy. Realism, the harsh
competition of the marketplace, simply did not exist. Thus a thimble
that cost five cents to make might be priced at a dollar and a toaster
costing three dollars to produce be sold at two.

For seventy-four years under eight leaders who were insatiable
gluttons for power and prestige—led by Josef Stalin, the immemorial
monster of all history—Soviet citizens endured every misery and

privation, including torture, murder and exile to concentration camps. Except for Lenin—a pathetic theorist who believed his own myth of the Russian proletariat and sought to regulate the revolution he had wrought by issuing daily ukases from his study—all of these leaders were obsessed by a passion for making the U.S.S.R. more and more powerful and the Communist creed more and more influential in the world. To do this they ignored their people, preferring to create and continue a monolithic state by suppressing dissent, sending refuseniks to Siberia, promoting either war or turmoil in the Third World, invading their neighbors and supporting any dictator who would at least give lip service to Marxist doctrine. Put simply: the Soviet people had no ally. Would they ever?

The answer came in 1985 and it was an emphatic "Yes!" given by Mikhail Gorbachev, affectionately known as "Gorby" in the West, which he frequently visited and could so easily charm. He was young—only fifty-four—vigorous, full of verve and vision and possessing a view of the empire unshared by any of his predecessors. He talked of *perestroika,* or the restructuring of Soviet society; of *glasnost,* or openness, meaning an end to official falsehood and a trial at least and at last for free speech. A thrill of hope seized the ordinary citizens, that vast suffering multitude unaffiliated with the Party, and the cold hand of fear clutched at the heart of those who were. Hardliners eager to perpetuate their privilege and power closed ranks around the Army and the KGB—the two most favored forces in Soviet life—in opposition to Gorbachev. But he was undeterred. Because of his youth and undeceived intelligence he believed in none of the shibboleths of the Old Guard: the fear of foreigners, the stultifying worship of Marx and Lenin, in which a text from either was supposed to solve any impasse; acceptance of terror as a tactic of government; the tendency to meet any crisis by squeezing the people harder.

When the hard-liners reminded him that *perestroika* had failed to stock the empty shelves and that *glasnost* had brought only popular complaint, he counterattacked by sending the people to the polls. In a nationwide election for the new 2,250-member Congress of People's Deputies fully a third of Communism's regional deputies failed to gain seats. Mikhail Gorbachev, however, was not out to destroy Marxism. He was still a dedicated Communist. What he sought at first was not democracy and a free market but "the revolutionary renovation of socialism, of our entire society." For he had learned from his mentor Andropov that the Soviet economy was in desperate straits—in fact, was a basket case—and that reform was desperately needed if Soviet society as it had been structured for seven decades was to endure.

He also knew that far too much money had been wasted on security—on the armed forces and KGB—and far too many of the brighter minds in the U.S.S.R. had been hogged by this duo. Much of these human resources must be reclaimed for the civilian sector. Gorbachev, perhaps alone, but possibly along with his astute Foreign Minister Eduard Shevardnadze, realized that the Cold War had been lost. The Soviet Union could no longer compete with the United States in the world arena, simply because it could not afford to. Since 1951 America alone had spent $4.3 trillion ($9.3 trillion when adjusted for inflation) in this unequal battle. Ronald Reagan's $2 trillion defense buildup during the eighties alone had made the pressure simply unbearable. But it cannot be maintained that these were the only factors that ended the Cold War. They contributed to it, of course, but the true cause of the Communist collapse was that the system was inhuman. The seeds of its own decay were inherent in its neglect of the human factor.

Because it discouraged competition it stifled innovation; because it was centrally controlled it rewarded conformism; because it was dogmatic it punished originality; because it was mystic it sanctified the foulest tactics in the belief that the end justifies the means; because it was doctrinaire it was incapable of change, renewal or reform; and, most corrupting of all its sins, because it was materialistic it ignored the human spirit. Marx made this plain when he said: "Religion is the opiate of the people." Opiates, he seemed to believe, are intrinsically evil. Food, drink and drugs may be considered opiates, and there is nothing evil in them per se, only in their addictive abuse. In the sense of its calming influence when it comforts and consoles, religion might indeed be considered an opiate: but a good one. Marxist materialists, however, regarded religion as the enemy simply because they could not understand Christ's meaning when he said, "Man does not live by bread alone."

It is possible that Mikhail Gorbachev, who was baptized in the Russian Orthodox faith, may have suspected this, although there is nothing in what he has said to suggest it. But he did open that little window of freedom, and to his everlasting credit did nothing to close it when there blew through it from Eastern Europe a howling hurricane of the human spirit that blasted the empire apart.

It was in long-suffering Poland that the first manifestations of discontent erupted in 1956, 1968, 1970 and 1976. All were either brutally suppressed or ended by some form of coercion. But in 1980 Polish opposition to Communist rule came under the leadership of Lech Walesa, a short, chubby, unemployed Gdansk shipyard electrician with a round, lively face and a magnificent mustache. Walesa had witnessed the 1970 demonstration, in which twenty Poles were slain, and had vowed to lead his country out of Kremlin domination. In this he had been supported by Cardinal Stefan Wyszyński, primate of overwhelmingly Catholic Poland. On August 14, 1980, Walesa led 17,000 Lenin Shipyard workers in a strike that shocked the Kremlin and spread rapidly throughout Poland like a forest fire. With only rudimentary education, this amazingly charismatic man—"I am a Christian. . . . Without [God] I am a nobody"—showed astonishing negotiating skill in obtaining from Polish authorities an agreement providing for "free trade unions, independent from political parties and employers." It was known as Solidarity. Ominously the Kremlin warned that it would not tolerate such an anomaly in the Soviet system. But nothing was done until after General Wojciech Jaruzelski became the new Polish Premier and Cardinal Wyszyński died, to be replaced as primate by Archbishop Jozef Glemp.

Although the Jesuit-trained Jaruzelski was a true Communist, he did understand that in Poland the Kremlin had allowed two anomalies to flourish: a system of private agriculture and the Catholic Church. He realized also that this third anomaly—Solidarity—would not be permitted to live, and that the hard-liners in Moscow were already preparing to drown it in the customary bloodbath. To preclude this, on the night of December 12–13, 1981, with the approval of General Viktor Kulikov, chief of the Warsaw Pact armies, who had been invited to Warsaw, Jaruzelski began his own crackdown.

It was, to Jaruzelski's credit, a bloodless suppression. Solidarity was outlawed, about 5,000 dissidents—among them Walesa—were "interned" and martial law was imposed, with Poland cut off from the outside world. Both Walesa and Glemp refused to cooperate with the Communists or to broadcast to the nation. Passive resistance continued and Solidarity went underground. Under duress, Polish workers refused to mine coal or make products, and farmers would not deliver their cattle to market. For seven years the Polish economy sank deeper and deeper into an economic morass burdened by debt, inflation, work stoppages, shortages and a near-worthless currency. At last Jaruzelski realized that the Party needed the union's help and Solidarity, under Walesa's calm and unvindictive leadership, agreed that this was true. For renewed recognition of the union, an amended constitution and truly free elections, he would trade an end to strikes. It was done, and in June of 1989 Solidarity, now a political party, won all but one of 100 seats contested in the Senate and 161 in the lower chamber. In August Tadeusz Mazowiecki, a dissident newspaper editor who had been jailed, was elected as the first non-Communist premier of Poland since Josef Stalin planted that foul weed forty years earlier. Eventually, the practical Walesa would supplant the theorist Mazowiecki as Poland's leader—and the first signs of rust had begun to appear on the Iron Curtain.

Fittingly, the revolt continued in Hungary, where, as in Poland in 1956, Hungarian freedom fighters were crushed in blood and steel. Perhaps shaken by the worldwide reaction of horror and outrage, the Kremlin decided to trade a little latitude in economic innovation in exchange for acceptance of Marxist orthodoxy. Nicknamed "goulash communism," this novelty for a time produced prosperity, but then, just as within the U.S.S.R. itself, the economic spiral sank steadily downward, until 1988 when the quisling János Kádár, who had replaced the executed Nagy, was compelled to resign. A moderate reformer named Károly Grósz took his place, but in January, 1989, a parliament no longer fearing the Kremlin—and emboldened by the absence of threats from Gorbachev—passed legislation permitting opposition parties and truly free elections in which Communism breathed its last.

On March 17 Hungary signed the United Nations Convention Relating to the Status of Refugees, promising not to compel fugitives to Hungary to return to their own countries. It also began taking down the barbed wire along its borders with Austria, thus making the first move to open the Iron Curtain.

East German malcontents were the first beneficiaries of this new route to freedom. By the literal thousands they streamed through Hungary into West Germany, where they received automatic citizenship. Enraged, the government in East Berlin demanded that Budapest honor a bilateral agreement and return the refugees. Hungary not only refused but deliberately allowed 15,000 fugitives to pass through its territory in three days. Other East Germans closer to Czechoslovakia poured into Prague to take refuge in the West German Embassy there. Premier Erich Honecker was infuriated. His country was losing its best and brightest citizens, skilled workers, trained scientists and engineers, people upon whom its future depended. When freedom marches began in Leipzig he ordered the police to use "all available force" to scatter them. But Egon Krenz, in charge of security, wisely persuaded the 77-year-old Party chief to rescind the order. Honecker knew that he was through when Gorbachev came to East Berlin on October 7 to mark the 40th anniversary of the Communist state and told him that if he planned to crush the revolt he could not depend on the Soviet Union for support. So the size of the Leipzig demonstrations grew: to 200,000 on October 23, then to 480,000 on November 6. On November 7 and 8 the demoralized Prime Minister with his entire cabinet and most of the Politburo resigned. Two days later ecstatic Germans on both sides of the Berlin Wall attacked that detested symbol of Kremlin oppression with hammers and chisels, pickaxes and sledgehammers and all other available tools, not only to chip away souvenirs but to begin the inevitable destruction of the structure that had divided them since 1961.

At the end of 1990 there were no longer East and West Germany, there was only one Germany, with neither West nor East Berlin but Berlin as its eventual capital.

Prague Spring returned to Czechoslovakia when the revered Alexander Dubček, the author of that aborted attempt to restore freedom to his countrymen, came back to the capital and was elected President of Parliament on December 28, 1989. Even greater adulation was bestowed on playwright Vaclav Havel, the oft-imprisoned leader of dissent, who hailed "the power of the powerless" as the one nemesis world Communism could not comprehend or crush. Havel eventually won a landslide presidential-election victory.

Most surprising of all was the defection of Bulgaria, the Communist state often regarded as the Kremlin's errand boy, and still suspected of having attempted to execute Brezhnev's order to assassinate Pope John Paul II. Demonstrations there began in September, snowballing until Todor Zhivkov, dictator for thirty-five years, was compelled to resign to be replaced on November 10, 1990, by Peter Mladenov.

Romania just across the border from the southern U.S.S.R. was also considered a "safe" Communist state. It had been ruled for twenty years by the blood-and-iron dictator Nicolae Ceauşescu. Like Tito in Yugoslavia, Ceauşescu operated independently of the Kremlin, although he was a thorough Communist. He thought so little of his despairing people that he and his wife called them "worms" and treated them as such. On December 22, however, the worms turned as a roaring crowd defiantly burned his picture in front of the incredibly ornate palace in which he lived. Ceauşescu fled, but was captured, tried in secret and executed—along with his wife.

Thus the collapse of the Balkan buffer which the xenophobic Josef Stalin deliberately created to protect his western flank.

2

☆

Before the death of Yuri Andropov and the rise to power of Mikhail Gorbachev, the Soviet Union had begun to eye possible expansion in the Caribbean and Central America. Castro's Cuba had already given Communism a firm base in the former and Daniel Ortega's Nicaragua had done almost the same in the latter. President Reagan made the U.S.S.R.'s purpose clear on March 10, 1983, in an address to the National Association of Manufacturers, declaring: "Soviet military theorists want to destroy our capacity to resupply Western Europe in case of an emergency. They want to tie down our forces on our own southern border and so limit our capacity to act in more distant places such as Europe, the Persian Gulf, the Indian Ocean, the Sea of Japan."

Seven months later—on October 23—Reagan received a message from the Organization of Eastern Caribbean States, a congeries of small island nations, requesting him to restore law and order to Grenada, where Prime Minister Maurice Bishop had been ousted the previous week by the hard-line Marxists of his ruling New Jewel Movement.

Bishop had studied law in London and after receiving his degree had become associated with the black civil-rights movement. Through his association with Black Power militants, though a Catholic, he had become a Marxist. Upon his return to Grenada in 1970 he joined the New Jewel (an acronym for Joint Endeavor for Welfare, Education and Liberation). He became bitterly opposed to the repressive government of Sir Eric Gairy. In 1973 Gairy's "Mongoose Gang" beat Bishop so badly that he had to seek medical treatment in Barbados, and in the following year his father, Rupert Bishop, was murdered—probably by the same thugs. That was also the year in which Grenada became independent from Britain. Determined to oust Gairy, Bishop became a champion of the poor, and in 1976 was elected to Parliament. In 1979 while Gairy was out of the country, he seized the radio station and proclaimed a revolutionary government.

Though popular, his refusal to lead Grenada into the Soviet camp enraged his deputy prime minister, Bernard Coard, who brought about his downfall. With this, General Hudson Austin of the Army quickly took control. His soldiers later murdered Bishop along with his cabinet. With a shipment of Soviet arms in Grenada warehouses and about 600 Cuban construction workers—actually combat engineers—at work on an airport, it seemed to Reagan that the Soviet expansion movement was at hand. So he decided to invade Grenada, on the grounds of the OECS appeal, and the fact that the safety of 1,100 Americans—half of them medical students—was at risk.

On October 25, 1983, a force of 1,200 Marines and 900 Army Rangers invaded Grenada. About 600 helicopter-borne Marines whirled aloft from the carrier *Independence* to land at Pearls Airport on the east coast, while a Rangers spearhead flew by Air Force jet transports to Point Salines airport in the southwest. The Rangers secured the perimeter and prepared the runway for the arrival of their comrades. Units of the 82nd Airborne Division joined the attack next day.

Although General Austin's militia and the Cubans put up a surprisingly strong resistance, they were eventually overcome, and on November 2 the United States announced that hostilities on Grenada had ceased and American troops were already being returned to their ships and bases. Except for a small peacekeeping force of about 300, all had left the island by mid-December. By then also the 600 captured Cubans—of whom about 40 were wounded—had been returned to their own island, and Governor General Paul Scoon—who had been under house arrest with 100 other political prisoners but was rescued on October 25—was in process of forming a provisional government and providing for new elections. American casualties were 18 dead and 39 wounded. Cuban casualties were 18 dead and 40 wounded, while 18 Grenadian civilians also lost their lives. On the whole, American casualties were much too severe for such a minor operation, and were probably the result of a hasty, patchwork venture thrown together in two days and following the fatuous guidelines that all services must be represented. The inevitable result was indistinct command lines and coordination so poor that the Navy and Marines could not cooperate with the Army and the Air Force because their radios were incompatible. Some units were even operating on different time zones. Finally, the shower of medals that fell on the participants was a travesty of military glory, especially when it is realized that these highly trained American combat troops were up against a ragtag force of noncombatant Cubans and a militia about as ferocious as the Keystone Cops. This is in no way intended to belittle the courage of the Marines and Rangers who secured the island, but rather to make mock of the officers' game of mutual medals: If I put you in for the DSC, how's about you putting me in for the Navy Cross?

Worldwide reaction was generally negative, even among NATO allies such as France, Germany and Britain, where Reagan's staunch supporter Prime Minister Margaret Thatcher said she had "considerable doubts" about the wisdom of the invasion and had advised against it. The Soviets called it "undisguised banditry and international terrorism." In Congress angry Democrats raised a storm of criticism of "Cowboy Reagan's" unilateral decision to invade, while Republicans rejoiced that for the first time in 20 years the Monroe Doctrine had had its teeth sharpened. Reagan defended his decision, claiming that it was necessary to protect Americans on the island and restore law and order after "a group of leftist thugs violently seized power." Two of these—General Austin and Deputy Prime Minister Coard—were arrested and charged with Bishop's murder.

Undeterred by the reaction, and winning another landslide presidential victory in 1984, Cowboy Reagan in 1986 was again riding herd on international terrorism.

Coincident with the outbreak and escalation of the war in Vietnam, there had also appeared a rise in terrorism. During that period this most hideous technique of unconventional warfare was used by a growing number of factions and minorities that were either too weak to mount a major insurrection or had tried and failed. Terrorism has been aptly described as "the weapon of the weak pretending to be strong."

It may begin with threats against life and property in order to compel a government or community to submit to the terrorists' demands; and, failing that, the use of bombs, firearms, arson, kidnapping and hijacking of not only airplanes but passenger ships as well. Such weapons of intimidation are aimed at publicizing a group's objectives or to create a climate of fear and hatred that will facilitate their attainment. Thus, if Great Britain were to reply to the murders and bombings of the Provisional Irish Republican Army in Northern Ireland by mounting a massacre of its own, such a bloodbath would be used to justify the IRA's own immoral tactics and to provoke in the world community a reaction of horror and outrage.

All terrorists seek to create in the minds of their targets a psychology of fear. They must strike without warning because a victim alerted in advance can take steps to protect himself. Thus if a bomb explodes on a crowded street or submachine guns are fired in a railroad station, innocent human beings are at risk of death or wounds, and in fact literal thousands of them have been killed or maimed during the last two decades. Although terrorists may speak of "warning time" or "selected victims," neither of these actually exist. Among poorly trained armed civilians there is also a high probability of error: i.e., the wrong person can be murdered.

Unpredictability and indiscriminate attacks are the *sine qua non* of terrorism. Without them the climate of fear that terrorism seeks to create would not be possible. Some nihilistic terrorist groups actually revel in mass atrocities, in which great numbers of civilians are wantonly killed. It gives them the publicity they crave. When the nihilistic Japanese Red Army committed the Lod Airport massacre in Israel in 1972, they were actually following the tactic of "mass slaughter in public places" advocated a century earlier by the anarchist Johannes Most. It would seem that such bloodbaths of innocent civilians—women and children, the elderly and infirm, even foreign nationals with no possible connection with the terrorists' enemies— are indeed hideous and need to be condemned by peaceful governments worldwide. But because the objectives of some states are often consonant with those of the terrorists, this does not always happen.

There is also a policy in some Western nations that condones the use of terrorism under certain conditions, providing, of course, it happens in some other, not exactly friendly country. It is excused in the holy name of "national liberation" or "revolutionary struggle."

Terrorism has many supposedly justifying arguments. First and foremost—and most illogical—is the theory that terrorism "transcends" all other means, such as peaceful and legitimate moves for change or liberation, because its ends are so imperative and overriding. Another is that because it has "worked" in the past it can be used. Here are two variations of the end justifying the means. Then there is the Old Testament law of "an eye for an eye, a tooth for a tooth": naked revenge. Or else terrorism is justified as the lesser evil: if it is not employed the immoral government or tyrant to be attacked will become even more unbearable. But Saint Augustine in his treatise on the just war specifies that if the evil that will ensue through a call to arms is greater than the one to be destroyed such a war is immoral and should not be waged. Of course, there are proterrorists such as the French philosopher Jean-Paul Sartre, who gloried in violence for its own "cathartic" sake, or the American poet e.e. cummings with his "necessary murder"; but these two, after all, are only Sartre and cummings enjoying themselves. Nevertheless such arguments also contribute to the reluctance of the international community to adopt a united antiterrorist policy. Sir Geoffrey Jackson, British Ambassador to Uruguay, who was himself the victim of terrorist kidnapping, has deplored this attitude with the remark: ". . . no injustice, however great, can justify an even greater injustice."

Finally, terrorism is no longer a tactic embraced just by minorities and factions, but in the Middle East has become official policy of legitimate governments. Among them are Syria, Iraq, Iran and Libya, all Moslem countries that have targeted Americans and the United States, the powerful ally of their arch-enemy Israel, as their chief victims. That is why in April, 1986, following the death of an American serviceman in the bombing of a Berlin discothèque believed to have been the work of Libyan terrorists, President Reagan decided to punish the virtual dictator of the small African country: Colonel Muammar al-Gaddafi.

Born in a Bedouin tent in the desert south of Tripoli, in September, 1942, Gaddafi was almost unknown until 1969, when he led a coup that deposed King Idris. Thereafter he became chairman of the Revolutionary Command Council—the true source of his power—commander-in-chief of Libya's armed forces, prime minister and defense minister. Although he later assigned the premiership to an aide, he remained in unchecked and unchallenged power.

Gaddafi—in J.F.C. Fuller's graphic phrase—could well be described as the Spanish fly of the Arab world, for his revolutionary objectives brought him into conflict with every Arab state except Algeria. He was particularly bitter against President Anwar el-Sadat of Egypt after he was kept out of the planning of the 1973 Arab-Israeli War. He and Sadat traded charges and countercharges until in July, 1977, open warfare between them erupted. After Sadat's peace initiative toward Israel, Gaddafi denounced him as a "traitor and apostate."

The Libyan dictator also moved closer to the Soviet Union, on which he depended for military supplies, and was the only Arab leader who sided with Marxist Ethiopia against Moslem insurgents from Somali and Eritrea. Why he became so virulent in his hostility toward Israel and the United States—except to out-Arab all other Arabs—is not especially clear, but his decision to export terrorism against Americans abroad very quickly brought vengeance upon his head.

On April 14, 1986, U.S. Air Force and Navy airplanes rising from land bases in Britain and the carrier decks of the 6th Fleet in the Mediterranean Sea launched surprise bombing attacks on Tripoli and Benghazi and their environs. It is not known exactly how many planes participated in the raids, but it could not have been many, for only one aircraft was lost and Libyan casualties both military and civilian totaled only 150. But the dictator in his patchwork tent pitched in the compound of his Tripoli residence remained unharmed. He certainly did not distinguish himself as the Libyan war chief, for his antiaircraft batteries did not open up until an hour after the last American jet dwindled into a speck in the sky above the Gulf of Sidra.

World reaction to the raids ranged from the support of a minority of countries—mostly Western nations anxious to eradicate terrorism—to denunciation from a large majority, most of them from the Third World. Momentarily, "the World Leader," as Libyan television called Gaddafi, became the hero of these poorer nations, even though he virtually vanished during the two months succeeding the attacks. In the conservative Arab World the only regret was that Gaddafi survived. At home Reagan was subjected to a barrage of criticism from liberals, but most of his countrymen were pleased that Gaddafi had been humbled and silenced, even though the spectacle of the world's most powerful nation pouncing on a tiny fourth-rater was somewhat akin to watching a lion chasing a chipmunk. Collapsing oil prices, cutting Libyan export revenues in half, multiplied Gaddafi's woes, along with growing evidence of bombings and assassinations carried out by his terrorist agents in Europe. British and American intelligence, however, eventually traced the Berlin bombing to Syria, suggesting that the master terrorist Abu Nidal was taking his orders from Damascus.

Meanwhile the Soviet Union backed away from a treaty of friendship with Libya, demanding immediate payment of an armaments bill totaling more than $5 billion, and other Libyan creditors did likewise. Once a nation of fairly comfortable citizens, Libyans found themselves so short of everything that one popular supermarket in Tripoli could offer nothing more than two brands of powdered milk, razor blades, shaving cream and tea. When the World Leader returned to public purview he was the same old obnoxious gadfly, flying around the Arab World like a witch on a broom, berating his peers for forsaking him, picking quarrels with President Hosni Mubarak of Egypt and King Hassan II of Morocco, whom he called a traitor for deigning to meet Prime Minister Yitzhak Shamir of Israel and for canceling the proposed union of Morocco and Libya.

But no one paid much attention to him anymore, especially the United States, which, having silenced one loud-mouthed dictator, was becoming increasingly distracted with another one almost on its front doorstep: Manuel Noriega of Panama.

3

☆

Manuel Antonio Noriega was born to a poor Panamanian family on February 11, 1938, in Panama City. He won a scholarship to study at a military academy in Peru, where, in the manner of Josef Stalin, he ingratiated himself with his instructors and picked up pocket money by spying on his classmates. Returning to Panama after being graduated he joined the National Guard, which he would eventually rename the Panama Defense Force (PDF), as a first lieutenant. In 1970 Noriega helped crush an attempted coup against the popular Omar Torrijos Herrera, for which the grateful general made him his intelligence chief. To Noriega this meant a license to blackmail his mentor's political rivals and to improve his spying techniques. It also made him the new commander of the national defense forces in 1982, after Torrijos died in an airplane crash many Panamanians believe was arranged by Noriega.

Flamboyant, derided as "Pineapple Face" for his plump, pock-marked features, Noriega sometimes attended formal events wearing a purple safari suit. Although a nominal Catholic, he was also suspected of dabbling in voodoo and black magic. By 1987 the self-promoted general as commander of the PDF was the real force behind the tiny nation's civilian government. But he was almost universally detested by the people, as well as by prominent Panamanians, all of whom accused him of election rigging, drug trafficking, drug-money laundering, the murder of a political dissident and passing of U.S. secrets and advanced technology to the Soviet Union and Cuba.

Noriega's connection with American intelligence agencies dated to the mid-fifties, when he was selling information about his fellow students at the Peruvian military academy. Later he went on the payroll of the Central Intelligence Agency at a reputed salary of

$200,000 a year. Noriega can be fairly described as a double-agent, if he was not also a "triple" or a "quadruple." His specialty seems to have been the double-cross, and among his victims were George Bush, when he was director of the CIA; Fidel Castro; the huge Medellín drug cartel in Colombia; and a procession of U.S. presidents stretching back to Richard Nixon. It has been said that Bush and the other chief executives did not listen too closely when informed of Noriega's drug-running activities for fear of losing a valuable intelligence agent. He had also been a cooperative host for the Southern Command, American military headquarters for Latin America.

His countrymen had no such reservations, especially after so many prominent Panamanians became convinced that it was Noriega who brought about the death of Torrijos. To disarm them, Pineapple Face in 1987 suspended all civil and political rights, after which the enraged National Civic Crusade, a group composed of civic, business and student groups, staged a two-day work stoppage that shut down 90 percent of Panama's commercial activity. This show of strength was not quite as disturbing to Noriega as the news that the U.S. was quietly collecting evidence of his drug-related ventures and seemed intent on prosecuting him. There had been inquiries among banks in France, Britain, Luxembourg and Switzerland about his accounts there, said to be more than $10 million. His other assets included a $600,000 mansion in Panama City in which at least 50 valuable paintings were on display, a châlet in Rio Hato and a 60-acre retreat in Chiriqui province, luxury apartments in Paris and the Dominican Republic, a Boeing 727, three Learjets and a trio of yachts named *Macho I, Macho II* and *Macho III.*

Inexplicably, aware that he was the object of investigation, Noriega turned bellicose when he should have adopted a low profile and a policy of wait-and-see. Widespread harassment of American servicemen assigned to the Canal Zone began. Panamanian troops at roadblocks outside Panama City detained and questioned American troops. There were hundreds of incidents, not all one-sided: a U.S. officer not supposed to be carrying a gun shot and wounded a Panamanian. In May of 1990 free elections were held and Noriega's candidates were badly beaten. So Pineapple Face calmly annuled the results. Also in that spring the Pentagon formulated a contingency plan for the invasion of Panama, with the capture of Noriega as one of its chief objectives. It was among the first things shown to General Colin

Powell when he became the first black to be appointed Chairman of the Joint Chiefs of Staff. Then in October Noriega crushed an attempted coup and ordered the execution of its leaders. Derisive criticism of Bush for having failed to intervene on the side of the rebels made Bush more than eager to send in American troops when the opportunity arose.

Pineapple Face obligingly gave him chapter and verse. He had his rubber-stamp People's Assembly designate him "Maximum Leader" and declare that "a state of war" existed between Panama and the U.S. Coincidentally Robert Paz, a U.S. Marine, was shot and killed at a roadblock. An American naval officer and his wife who witnessed the murder were pulled from their car and taken into custody, where they were rudely interrogated, the officer beaten and his wife threatened with gang rape.

Upon being informed of these incidents, an angry Bush declared: "Enough is enough! This guy is not going to lay off. It will only get worse." And so it was decided to invade Panama on Christmas Eve with a force of about 24,000 troops, many of whom had already been flown to U.S. bases in the Canal Zone. The operation was to be known as Just Cause.

General Noriega could not have failed to expect an invasion. Throughout the hours leading up to H-hour huge American military transports were landing at ten-minute intervals at Howard Air Force Base to disgorge troops. But Pineapple Face, like Gaddafi during the Libyan raids, was both unseen and unheard. To be sure he would not flee the country, just before midnight of December 24, Navy Seals (an acronym for sea, air and land capability) captured the private Paitilla Airport, where Noriega kept a getaway Learjet. They overwhelmed the guards, destroyed the airplane and secured the landing strip. But four Seals were killed, probably the first casualties of Just Cause. Others died while disabling that trio of *Macho* yachts. Whatever Noriega might do, he could now not leave Panama.

Next at 12:15 A.M. while American tanks rumbled through the streets of Panama City, U.S. gunships and other choppers attacked the Comandancia, Noriega's sprawling PDF headquarters. Their shells also struck the ancient, rickety wooden houses surrounding the Comandancia, setting them ablaze. Sleeping or reveling Panamanian civilians poured out of their flaming homes in terror, finding the streets jammed with roaring gringo tanks. An unknown number died in their homes, and many more were wounded. Before the invasion was over, as many as 600 civilians—and possibly more—lost their lives. In the meantime, at Fort Amador, a facility shared by both American and Panamanian troops, U.S. infantry turned their guns on adjacent enemy barracks, and a full-scale battle began. Before it was over, nearly 9,500 American troops joined the 12,500 already in Panama by parachuting out of the night skies or scrambling from those giant transports still arriving at Howard. With remarkable precision, they formed five task forces moving toward their objectives with equally amazing speed.

Probably the most critical assignment went to Task Force Atlantic, composed of paratroopers from the 82nd Airborne Division and troops of the Seventh Infantry Regiment, moving swiftly to secure vital facilities at the Panama Canal's Caribbean end at Colón. They seized Madden Dam, which stores water to raise and lower ships in the canal's locks, and captured the electrical distribution center at Cerro Tigre. Atlantic's soldiers also overcame stiff resistance from a naval infantry unit on the north coast and liberated 48 prisoners held in the failed October rising.

Vital Howard Air Force Base was secured against the PDF when Task Force Semper Fidelis, made up of Marine riflemen and light-armored troops, occupied the Bridge of the Americas, which crosses the canal and opens onto the road to the air base. Task Force Red, comprised of Army Rangers, hit both sides of the capital in a thrilling dual operation that went off precisely on schedule. Rangers in the west, led by Pathfinder aircraft dropping flares to illuminate the drop area, parachuted from heights as low as 500 feet to assault the Río Hato barracks of the 6th and 7th PDF companies, overpowering them and taking 250 prisoners. To the east other parachuting Rangers seized Torrijos International Airport. Next 82nd paratroopers in Task Force Pacific joined Rangers and Special Forces blocking the Pecora River bridge to prevent Noriega's best troops—Battalion 2000—from reaching Panama City. There Task Force Bayonet—an Army mechanized battalion and light armor—struck the Comandancia, igniting an enormous fire that gutted the building. In a room-by-room search, however, no trace of the Maximum Leader was found. Nor was he found in "the Witch House," another residence of his on the Pacific coast, where American soldiers found still-warm cigarettes in ashtrays, suggesting that someone at least had only just departed.

Noriega's whereabouts were still unknown when, at eight o'clock in the morning of December 26, 1990, a jubilant Colin Powell announced that "for the most part, organized resistance has ended." By fleeing, Pineapple Face actually did the gringos a favor: once his men realized that the Maximum Leader was on the run, they surrendered wholesale, turning in their weapons for a handsome bounty of $150 American. By then, Panama's new democratic government had been sworn in at Fort Clayton. Guillermo Endara, the rotund politician whose election victory in May had been annulled by Noriega, was the new President, with Ricardo Arias Calderón and Guillermo Ford his Vice Presidents. Meanwhile, as the search for Noriega continued—from an elegant hideout in the Hotel Marriott to a bug-ridden bed in a decrepit barrio shack—widespread looting erupted in Panama City, where ecstatic Panamanians waving pineapple-tipped poles danced in the streets, hugging and kissing their gringo liberators, whom they had been taught by Noriega to hate.

On Christmas night the telephone rang in the office of Monsignor José Sebastian Laboa, the Papal Nuncio to Panama. Manuel Antonio Noriega was on the other end requesting sanctuary. Laboa was of a mind to refuse, until the wily Maximum Leader reminded him that it was Christmas and in Rome Pope John Paul II would be repeating the ancient story of how Joseph and Mary in Bethlehem had been told "there is no room in the inn" and Mary had to give birth to Jesus in a cattle manger. Was there, then, no room in the inn at the papal nunciature? Laboa consented, had to consent, for as a trained diplomat of the Catholic Church he knew that a request for sanctuary is always granted: "Even if it were from Lucifer." Thus, accompanied by four aides, General Manuel Antonio Noriega knocked on the door of the nunciature and was met by the frail, dignified Spanish-born Nuncio.

At once Monsignor Laboa noticed that Noriega's aides carried a supply of weapons and injectable fluids, and he demanded that they be surrendered. They were, although a submachine gun was later found under the bed of the tiny bare room to which Noriega was assigned. It was a 10-by-6-foot cubicle with an opaque window and decorated only with a crucifix, and with only a Bible for diversion. Though accustomed to opulence, sex, drink and drugs, the Maximum Leader said nothing. In Rome a diplomat assigned to the Vatican pitied him, saying: "Poor Noriega! No drugs, no booze, no sex—and eating Vatican food."

Sometimes Laboa and Noriega talked. Laboa recalled: "He talked very little, nodded a lot. He is impenetrable." Meanwhile, a polite but intense tug-of-war ensued between the White House and the Vatican. Secretary of State Baker maintained that Noriega was not a political fugitive but a common criminal fleeing prosecution. There was no answer. Apparently the Vatican was depending on Laboa to solve the impasse. The Nuncio told Noriega that no country but Cuba would accept him, and Washington had vetoed that possibility. He told him that he had only two choices: to give himself up to the Americans or to have Laboa arrange for his surrender to Panamanian authorities. "You know, General," Laboa said softly, "what a Panama jail is like. In the U.S., the jails have air-conditioning and television." This was not exactly the clincher, but it conditioned Noriega for the clincher when it came: a U.S.-arranged visit from Vicky Amador, his 35-year-old mistress, who urged him to give himself up to the Americans. He would at least get a fair trial from them, and, who knows, might be acquitted. After she left, Noriega told Laboa he would surrender to the U.S. authorities. He put on a new tan general's uniform that Vicky had brought him, gave his aides a farewell salute, and then, clutching the Bible as a souvenir of his stay, went outside in the dark to surrender.

When his plane left Panama en route to Miami and a jail cell where he would await his trial on eight specific drug-connected charges, the Central American strongman, the dreaded Maximum Leader, began to sob.

At this writing—mid-September 1991—his trial has begun, his notoriety severely diminished by the appearance on the world scene of an even more baleful dictator: the self-styled "Father-Leader" Saddam Hussein of Iraq.

4

☆

Saddam Hussein was born in 1937, the son of peasant parents in the fiercely anti-Western town of Tikrit about one hundred miles north of Baghdad. Orphaned at only nine months, he was raised by his uncle, an Army officer named Khairallah Talfah. From him Saddam (he preferred to be called by his first name because there were so many Husseins in the Arab world) learned to revere his Mesopotamian homeland as the birthplace of civilization, and to honor the memory of its ancient and fierce kings, who ruled that world with an iron and bloody fist. His hero was Nebuchadnezzar, the somewhat mad Babylonian king who conquered Israel, destroying Jerusalem and carrying the Jews into captivity in 587 B.C. Tales of the bloodbaths of other Mesopotamian rulers, such as the Tiglath-Pilesers of Assyria, excited him. But not even the glory of Muhammad, the founder of Islam in the early seventh century—"There is no God but Allah, and Muhammad is his prophet!"—could eclipse Saddam's admiration for Hammurabi, the first and greatest of the Arabic lawgivers, who ruled in Babylon two millennia before Christ. To this inordinate racial and religious pride and a bloodthirstiness not exactly admirable in an unlettered child was joined a foaming hatred of the West for its humiliation of the Arab World, especially Britain with its policies of ruling the followers of Muhammad through puppet kings.

None of this distorted "education" came to Saddam in schools or through professional teachers, but rather at the knee and through the mouth of Uncle Talfah, a terrorist who was captured in an abortive anti-British coup in 1941 and imprisoned. Formal education for Saddam did not begin until the age of nine, and his wretched classroom performance thereafter disqualified him for admission to the elite Baghdad Military Academy. Like Adolf Hitler in 1907 when his crude drawings were rejected by the Vienna Academy of Fine Arts, Saddam Hussein was crushed. Oddly, this shattering of his dream of following in the footsteps of Uncle Talfah did not embitter Saddam, or turn him against the Army. Rather, it created in him a single-minded awe of the military mind fed upon imperatives and total reliance on armed might. After his rise to power he became fond of being photographed in a replica of Nebuchadnezzar's war chariot, as well as designing his own uniforms or firing a pistol into the air during public appearances.

But Saddam Hussein was never a soldier, not even a private let alone a general. The closest he came to combat was when, as a youthful member of the Baath Party, an anti-Western, pan-Arab socialist movement, he was placed on a hit squad assigned to murder Iraq's military ruler, Abdul Karim Kassem. In the way of all part-time soldiers, however, Saddam and his comrades, though armed with machine guns, were quite unable to hit Kassem as his station wagon sped through downtown Baghdad. But the dictator's body-guards, being somewhat more familiar with firearms, managed to kill two of these slipshod assassins while putting a bullet into Saddam's left leg. Here the aspiring successor to the great Saladin showed his true but unsuspected talent for fiction by concocting a lurid tale of how he carved the bullet from his flesh with a razor dipped in iodine (presumably standard equipment for socialist assassins), and then, disguised as a Bedouin tribesman, swam the Tigris River, stole a donkey and clip-clopped into Syria, expecting to be hailed as a hero. Instead, he was clapped into an unfriendly jail until President Gamal Abdel Nasser of Egypt—the Arab world's latest savior—was able to obtain his release and bring him to Cairo as another of these divinely anointed heroes of Islam.

Saddam, then twenty-five, decided to study law. His professors and classmates could not have been less than horrified by his unfailing solution to fine points of criminal justice: "Why argue about it?" he would shout. "Why don't you just take out a gun and shoot him?"

This was the credo that guided him when, in 1963, he returned to Baghdad to organize a militia for the Baath Party, which rose to absolute power five years later. Its nominal leader was General Ahmed Hassan al-Bakr, but everyone who understood Iraqi power politics knew that the real ruler was his relative and right-hand man: Saddam Hussein. Keeping things in the family was a typical tactic of low-born Moslems as well as noble, so that Saddam promptly married another relative, Sajida Talfah, the daughter of the uncle who had raised him. Sajida and Saddam are now supposed to be estranged. She lives in Geneva with her children in purloined opulence—Saddam is suspected of having squirreled away $10 billion of Iraq's oil revenues—while he consorts with a procession of mistresses in Baghdad.

In 1979 General al-Bakr retired, leaving Saddam completely in charge. He celebrated his ascent to power and gave his shocked countrymen a glimpse of its new gunsmoke-government by ordering the execution of twenty-one cabinet officers, among them his supposedly closest comrade. "He who is closest to me," Saddam warned, "is farthest from me when he does wrong." When such slaughter did not intimidate other "wrongdoers"—that is, dissenters from the dictates of Saddam—he led a collection of cabinet members and other officials to Baghdad's central prison to serve as the firing squad for a group of political prisoners. "It was to ensure loyalty through common guilt," a British official explained. It also could suggest that today's executioner might be tomorrow's victim. Hundreds of human beings are executed annually in Iraq, often on Saddam's slightest displeasure. Torture and secret police, the twin terrors of a police state, are his controlling tactics. Just to possess a typewriter without a license from the police is a crime akin to treason. So is failure to hang his picture in the living room. To speak against "the Father-Leader" is punishable by death, and Saddam himself was indignant— like Napoleon when he heard that Okinawans made neither weapons nor war—when he learned that in the United States there is no punishment for criticizing the President.

No one is safe who blocks or even just appears to block Saddam Hussein's demonic drive to dominate the Middle East just as his hero Nebuchadnezzar did 2,500 years ago. And yet he is neither paranoid nor megalomaniac. Says a senior British diplomat who has dealt with him: "He is an extremely shrewd, cold-blooded, clever thug. Human life means nothing to him." Neither does religion or patriotism. Nominally, he is a Sunni Moslem, that is, a follower of the main-stream of Islamic belief that Muhammad's successors were the four caliphs who came after him, as opposed by the Shiites, who regard Ali, the son-in-law of Muhammad, as his legitimate successor. Shiites form about 60 percent of Iraq's 17 million Moslems, but power is held by the minority Sunni. Patriotism to Saddam consists only in loyalty to him. "He does what he thinks is expedient," says another British diplomat. "He is not driven by ideology or whim. He coldly calculates every move. He is simply a brutal and very clever pragmatist." Newsmen who have met him speak of his "snake eyes. The eyes of a killer." The murderous John Brown, whose execution did so much to provoke the American Civil War, has been similarly described.

No European absolute monarch during the departed age of the despots ever thought so little of the lives or welfare of his people as Saddam, when, in 1980, he declared war on neighboring Iran, a nation twice as large and populous as his own. Forever two-faced, he had once given sanctuary to the Iranian Shiite leader, the Ayatollah Khomeini, but under pressure from the Shah of Iran next expelled him. When Khomeini ousted the Shah and began to curse Saddam's "blasphemous" regime, the now righteously religious Iraqi leader invaded his neighbor. The moment was propitious, for the politically and militarily naïve Khomeini was then also cursing the United States as "the world-devouring Great Satan" and had thus lost his own chief supplier of arms. When he also approved of the seizure of American Embassy personnel as hostages, he guaranteed an arms famine for Iran.

So Saddam, with an army trained by the Soviets as well as supplied by them and France, was confident that he would overwhelm Iran in a matter of weeks, thus emerging as the Middle East's irresistible messiah. But the ayatollah's ragtag Revolutionary Guards, inflamed by Khomeini's call to arms in a jihad or holy war, rushed into battle in search of a martyr's crown. Many of them found it, but they stopped Iraq's superior Army, not so much by their zeal—for spiritual power can never overcome firepower—but because Saddam's amateurish and inept conduct of the war effectively crippled his soldiers. After eight years of combat in one of the most futile and bloody wars in military history, these exhausted opponents finally agreed to a shaky cease-fire, which has never been converted into a peace. Saddam had lost an estimated 75,000 to 125,000 men. Destitute and desperate, saddled with a foreign debt of $80 billion almost evenly divided between loans from the West and the Arab world, Saddam Hussein's killer eyes turned covetously toward his puny Persian Gulf neighbor to the south: the emirate of Kuwait.

* * *

For thirty years Iraq and Kuwait had been engaged in a game of cat-and-mouse. Whenever the Iraqi cat bared its teeth and unsheathed its claws, the Kuwaiti mouse cowered and bought it off. But now Iraq meant business. Saddam Hussein had become exasperated by the quota cheating of both Kuwait and the United Arab Emirates farther down the Gulf. The Organization of Petroleum Exporting Countries (OPEC) had limited Kuwaiti production to 1.5 million 42-gallon barrels of crude oil per day and the UAE to 1.1 million barrels. But Kuwait was pumping an extra 200,000 barrels daily and the UAE from ½ to 1 million additional barrels, thus driving the price of crude down from $20.50 a barrel in January, 1990, to $13.60 in June.

In 1986 Saudi Arabia, the Gulf's chief producer, had sought to chastise the cheaters by unleashing a surplus of oil to bring the price down to a level unacceptable to them. But this had little effect on Kuwait and the UAE because both tended to favor low prices as a tactic discouraging Western customers from seeking alternative sources of energy.

At that time Saddam was still engaged in the eight-year war with Iran and the problem of quota-cheating did not concern him because his own wells were shut down and the price of crude was irrelevant to him. He even in a sense shared in the cheaters' profits through the $20 billion he received in loans from Kuwait and the UAE. But in 1990, struggling to rebuild his wrecked economy, it was not only relevant but vital. Every drop of $1 a barrel meant the loss of $1 billion a year to him. He simply could not accept such attrition. Even though experts estimated that his huge oil reserves would enable him to tap as many as 5 million barrels a day, thereby exceeding his own quota of 3.14 barrels and approaching the Saudi output of 5.42 million, the facts were that his own equipment was too antiquated to do so and he hadn't the money to modernize it. But tiny little Kuwait directly to the south of him had hundreds of wells, serviced by the most modern pumps and exportable through the excellent port of Kuwait City. Its immense oil reserves had enriched nearly all its minuscule population of 1.9 million Kuwaitis, making them the detestation of the poorer Arab nations such as Jordan or Iraq with its 17.5 million. With only 18 miles of coastline itself, Iraq would add about 120 through annexation of the tiny emirate, and remove forever the barricade of Bubiyan and Warba islands blocking his access to the Gulf.

If Iraq absorbed Kuwait and by intimidation forced the OPEC price up to $30 a barrel, his combined income would soar to $60 billion a year, enabling him to double his development budget and pay off his debts in four years. It was a tempting prospect and Middle Eastern experts now believe that Saddam resolved to devour Kuwait as long as a year before he actually moved.

In the meantime he embarked upon a campaign to unsettle Arab leaders and a war of nerves against Kuwait, both designed to disguise his true intentions. President Hosni Mubarak of Egypt thought his friend Saddam had lost his mind when he privately suggested a military coalition of Iraq, Egypt, Syria and Jordan to carve up both Kuwait and Saudi Arabia, with which Iraq had a nonaggression pact. Egypt's share of the loot would be $25 billion, but Mubarak declined with thanks. Then Saddam secretly offered Yemen two of Saudi Arabia's southern provinces and then promised impoverished Jordan's King Hussein that he could have the western half of the Saudi Peninsula. Next he shocked the Saudis' King Fahd by saying that the smaller countries of the Gulf "didn't make sense," declaring that he was going to seize Kuwait, adding, "You take Qatar." No one took him seriously then, and some Arab leaders actually thought that he was crazy.

He seemed even crazier when he began bullying Kuwait, complaining that while Iraq was busy fighting Iran the emirate stole $2.4 billion of his oil by slanting its own wells down into his side of the Rumaila Oilfield straddling their border. For this and Kuwait's alleged quota cheating he demanded $13 to $15 billion in reparations. He also accused Kuwait of moving its border 45 miles north while he was preoccupied with the war. He wanted the return of that pilfered territory, Kuwait's withdrawal from the Rumaila, a long lease on Bubiyan and Warba islands and forgiveness of his $10 billion war debt. No wonder the Kuwaitis also thought that he was dwelling in cloud-cuckoo-land, and this time they did not make the customary cringing capitulation to the menacing demands of the Iraqi cat. Angered by his ingratitude for their support during the war, believing that he was too weak to fight another one, even though their puny army of about 20,000 men could be easily brushed aside by his of a million troops and 5,000 tanks, they stubbornly stood their ground.

In Washington it was firmly believed that here was another Arab dispute that could be settled by concessions on both sides. Saddam had been America's friend, or at least the enemy of their sworn enemy Iran during the late war. He was not unreasonable. In spite of his rule by torture and terror, his chemical warfare against the Kurds, his ambition to possess nuclear weapons, his missile attack on the U.S.S. *Stark* that killed 37 American sailors, the American policy was to cultivate his friendship. "It is better talking to this man than isolating him," said April Glaspie, the newly appointed Ambassador to Baghdad. When Saddam called her to his palace on July 25 for their first meeting, he burst into an angry diatribe: America was conspiring with Kuwait to keep oil prices low, the CIA and the State Department were waging economic war against him. If America treated him as an enemy he would respond with terrorism.

Glaspie did not protest. Rather, she obeyed direct State Department instructions not to anger Saddam when she said: "We don't have much to say about Arab-Arab differences, like your border difference with Kuwait." Here was a blunder duplicating Secretary of State Dean Acheson's statement in January, 1950, that South Korea was outside the American defense triangle in the Pacific, thus inducing Stalin to order his North Korean puppet to invade the South. To Saddam, this also may have seemed a green light; but when Glaspie next conveyed President Bush's concern about his military buildup opposite Kuwait, Saddam replied that he would do nothing without consulting his Arab friends, actually picking up the telephone to give the same assurance to Egypt's Mubarak. Reassured, Glaspie told Saddam that she would now go ahead with a planned vacation.

Two days later at a meeting in Geneva both Kuwait and the UAE tamely accepted OPEC's decision to raise the price of crude from $18 a barrel to $21—and it seemed that Saddam's bluster had brought him a not insignificant bribe of $3 billion. At least everyone concerned hoped so, especially President Bush, distracted by the huge federal deficit, the savings-and-loan scandal, the end of the Cold War, with the concomitant collapse of East European Communism, and his earnest desire to help his friend Mikhail Gorbachev resist the growing insistence of the Kremlin hard-liners upon "saving" the turbulent Soviet Union by a return to a Stalinist command society.

During the six days following the OPEC meeting, Saddam Hussein alternated between threats and reassurances. While 3,000 Iraqi military vehicles carrying 30,000 soldiers wearing the red-and-black beret of Saddam's elite Republican Guard rumbled south to the Kuwaiti border, the Father-Leader declared: "Iraqis will not forget the saying that cutting necks is better than cutting means of living. O God Almighty, be witness that we have warned them." Evidently the $3 billion bonus was not enough. But Saddam still assured King Hussein and Mubarak that he had no intentions to invade. In Washington, photographs by a KH-II spy satellite showed 100,000 Iraqi troops on the Kuwaiti border. Saddam had tripled his forces. Other photographs portrayed a massive logistics train giving him all that he needed to strike. Still the CIA, the Defense Intelligence Agency and the State Department Bureau of Intelligence and Research agreed that there was little danger of war.

Intelligence estimates sent to Bush included predictions that (1) Saddam was bluffing; (2) he might seize Kuwait's portion of the Rumaila Oilfield, as well as Bubiyan and Warba islands, and would then withdraw to Iraq after these objectives were secured. "The line we kept hearing around here," said one senior Pentagon officer, "was that he's just massed there along the Kuwait border to drive the price of oil up. If people were saying he's for real and he's going to invade, it wasn't briefed to us as definite."

At the last minute Kuwait realized that the Father-Leader was indeed for real, and offered him a sizable buy-off for peace. But Saddam wanted Kuwait itself, and at 2 on the morning of August 2 the vanguard of about 100,000 Iraqi soldiers began rolling down the splendid 80-mile superhighway Kuwait had built—as a token of friendship—between the two countries. It took only four hours for the spearheads to come clanking into the sleeping capital at Kuwait City. Three hundred tanks—most of them the latest Soviet-built T-72 monsters—prowled the city, bringing it swiftly to its knees. Fifty more surrounded the Dasman Palace of Emir Jaber al-Ahmed al-Sabah, but the sheik and his family had fled to Saudi Arabia by helicopter.

Artillery shells shrieked and exploded in orange and yellow bursts, machine guns chattered, Iraqi jets and helicopter-gunships strafed and bombed at will. Throughout the darkened city, apartment and hotel lights flashed on, then quickly off again, as the terrified Kuwaitis realized that they had awakened in hell. Those who tried to flee were either shot at the wheels of their expensive autos, or else torn from them while their car phones—most of them could afford such luxuries—were ripped out to prevent communication with Kuwaiti troops. Meanwhile, the roaring tanks were roving everywhere. A squadron surrounded the central bank, where most of the emirate's cash and gold bullion was stored and seized it without opposition. The Ministry of Information housing Kuwait's radio and television facilities was taken just as easily, although a voice believed to be the Crown Prince's continued to broadcast from an unknown transmitter: "Oh, Arabs, Kuwait's blood and honor are being violated. Rush to its rescue! The children, the women, the old men of Kuwait are calling on you." Then the transmitter went dead.

But there was no rescue, although Kuwait's little Army, outnumbered five to one and facing even higher odds in guns and tanks, put up small but isolated pockets of resistance. One group at the palace, the heart of the emirate, fought gallantly, holding out during a two-hour artillery barrage. Here the Emir's younger brother Fahd was killed. But the palace also fell, along with the oil rigs offshore, where embattled Kuwaiti soldiers and missile-firing boats were able to sink an unknown number of enemy landing craft and escort ships. By early afternoon the assault had ended in complete success, and Kuwait for all intents and purposes had been conquered. Some 200 Kuwaiti soldiers had been killed and an unknown number—usually estimated at three times the death rate—wounded. Iraq issued no casualty figures.

Iraq immediately announced that it had entered the country at the invitation of the "Free Interim Government," a group of "young revolutionaries" who supposedly had seized power. But no one had ever heard of the movement—before or since—or seen a "young revolutionary." If it had ever existed—which it had not—it would be the first time in history that a coup d'état had been staged after an invasion.

At eight o'clock that night, 7,000 miles and 8 time zones away, the telephone rang in the family quarters of the White House. It was George Bush's security adviser Brent Scowcroft telling his chief that the crisis for which he had spent a lifetime preparing had finally come.

A silver-spooner with a pedigree as long as he was tall, George Herbert Walker Bush had been born into one of the wealthiest and most distinguished families of Connecticut. His father had been a U.S. Senator and his uncle a prominent Wall Street investment broker, who would one day raise the cash enabling young George to stake a claim in the rough-and-tumble oil fields of his adopted state of Texas. Although he had many advantages, he was constantly reminded of the responsibilities that came with them. The West Point motto—"Duty, Honor, Country"—might have been George Bush's own. At the age of eighteen, upon his graduation from Phillips Academy, Andover, Mass., he deferred his birthright of a Yale education to serve his country, joining the Navy to become that service's youngest torpedo-bomber pilot. Shot down over the Pacific on his forty-second mission, he was rescued and came home a war hero, marrying Barbara Pierce, herself a member of a wealthy and distinguished family. There followed a career eminently calculated to produce a unique candidate for President. A success in the oil business, George Bush earned a reputation for thoroughness, caution and calm confidence wherever else he went: whether to the U.S. House of Representatives, to China and the United Nations as an ambassador, to the CIA as chief or to the vice presidency for two terms under Ronald Reagan. Ten years ago during his unsuccessful challenge to Reagan for the Republican nomination, Bush gave the press a remarkable insight into his assessment of this most powerful office that he sought so earnestly.

"You work your behind off, get credit for stuff you're barely involved in and none at all for things you've put together behind the scenes. Domestic problems drag you down and nag you all the time. You're up in the polls and down and then up again. But sooner or later something happens, something abroad that only we [the U.S.] can do something about. Then you show if you can cut it. If you can't, everything else can be going beautifully and you're probably out of there next time. If you pull it off, a lot else can go wrong and you'll be all right. Because when people hit the [voting] booth, well, then they think: 'Hey, when the chips are down, this guy can defend us and what we stand for,' and that's what it's all about." To this Bush added, "I really would be a President we don't have to train," and then, later: "Maybe I'll turn out to be a Teddy Roosevelt."

Perhaps, for his training had indeed been quite similar to TR's; but at the outset of that momentous crisis for which he had spent that varied lifetime preparing, he did not exactly appear to be a Rough Rider.

* * *

In his telephone call, Scowcroft had made it clear that this was an outright invasion with intent to annex Kuwait, not the temporary incursion and withdrawal predicted by the intelligence agencies. Bush immediately summoned his top political and military advisers to an early-morning conference, and then tried to get a little sleep. At five o'clock the following morning, Scowcroft was knocking on his bedroom door with two executive orders freezing all Iraqi and Kuwaiti assets in the United States. Bush signed them. A half hour later he met Scowcroft in the Oval Office. Both men were quick to perceive the immediate problems: how to persuade allies everywhere to expand the freeze on assets into a worldwide economic boycott, how to keep Israel out of the confrontation so as not to discourage Arab states from joining an anti-Iraqi coalition, how to gain the all-important support of the Soviet Union. They also saw that Saddam's gamble was a daring challenge to American leadership of the emerging post–Cold War world.

"This cannot stand," George Bush said repeatedly. "This cannot stand." But how could it be repulsed? George Bush seemed not to know. Before he conferred with his advisers he twice told reporters that he had no plans to use American troops in the Persian Gulf. But then, after conferring with Secretary of Defense Richard Cheney, Chairman of the Joint Chiefs of Staff Colin Powell, White House chief-of-staff John Sununu and Scowcroft, he asked the penetrating question:

"What if we do nothing?"

To a man Bush's advisers warned their chief that if Saddam were to succeed all the good news of the past year and a half that had sent the stock of George Bush soaring higher, ever higher, on the popularity polls—the collapse of East European Communism; the fall of the Berlin Wall, that detested symbol of Communist oppression; happenings suggestive of a new and happier world order—would be engulfed in an earthquake of revulsion at home and a tidal wave of despair everywhere else. Hope would be drowned worldwide, and the United States, the last superpower, would be so distrusted that it would have to share world leadership with Germany and Japan, two nations now economic giants that had once sought a world order not exactly consonant with the American ideals of freedom and justice. Not all these warnings were so precisely detailed at this momentous meeting of the National Security Council, but though they came in a jumbled rush, they were clear enough to make Bush reply quietly:

"This must be reversed."

And yet, moments after the conference adjourned, the President told a few close aides that he wasn't sure how he was going to reverse it; and in his first public appearance since the invasion of Kuwait he appeared hesitant and vague. It was not until he took a trip on August 2 to Aspen, Colorado, and met Prime Minister Margaret Thatcher of Britain, there by chance on a visit, that Bush's resolve stiffened. He spent two hours talking to Thatcher, who knew and understood Saddam. "He must be stopped," she said. "This is no time to wobble, George." Bush, of course, was not wobbly, just unsure of how much support he could organize worldwide in a confrontation with Saddam. History and experience had taught him that military coalitions are at best uneasy alliances, difficult to form and easily unraveled by the first suggestion of defeat or disagreement. But Thatcher's insistence that the only way to stop Saddam was to send troops to the Persian Gulf immediately, and her instant offer of support, were the basis of George Bush's reconversion to the calm, confident commander-in-chief that his aides had come to know and respect.

He also knew that in such times of crisis the carrot of diplomacy must precede the stick of force, and so, even though now determined to use troops if necessary, he played his key diplomatic card: the newfound detente with the Soviet Union. With Mikhail Gorbachev his friend and Moscow now eager to show the world a more friendly face, especially the United States, from which it hopefully expected financial aid to stave off impending economic ruin, the President knew that he could forge a joint U.S.-Soviet condemnation of Iraq— and he was right. Even though Saddam had been a Soviet client, Gorbachev gave his solid support to Bush.

Secretary of State James A. Baker III had been headed for a hunting vacation in Mongolia when the invasion came. Reversing course, he quickly persuaded the Soviets to condemn the invasion and cut off all further supplies to Saddam. With this accord other nations could now join the growing alliance without fear of reprisal from a former superpower. Here Bush's assiduous courting of foreign leaders proved to be fruitful. As one of his aides recalled: "Call Fahd [King of Saudi Arabia], call Ozal [President of Turkey], say this to this guy, that to another. No memos were required. It was all in his head. . . . He knew that to be effective the lineup against Saddam had to be perceived as more than just the rich West against a poor Arab." Within days the United Nations Security Council had passed resolutions demanding Iraq's immediate and unconditional withdrawal from Kuwait while calling for worldwide economic sanctions against Saddam together with an economic boycott of Iraqi-Kuwaiti oil. Even Japan, which imported 12 percent of its oil from Iraq and Kuwait, joined the oil boycott after Bush made a persuasive telephone call to Premier Toshiki Kaifu—a move that was certainly not in Japan's best interest. But Arab nations were not so easily induced to join the anti-Iraq coalition, especially if force were to be employed. Prince Bandar bin Sultan, Saudi Arabia's Ambassador to the United States, told Cheney and Powell that King Fahd doubted that America sincerely intended to strike Saddam hard. It might tire of its mission and pull out. He reminded them of how the timid Jimmy Carter during an earlier Mideast crisis had sent only a dozen unarmed F-15 fighters to help defend the kingdom. Only an idiot would accept such a token force now. Was the U.S. really determined this time?

In response Cheney and Powell showed the prince a Pentagon contingency plan to defend Saudi Arabia against Iraq with two and one-third divisions, an air wing and a carrier task force. Though not exactly enough to stop Saddam, it was much more than Carter's empty gesture. More important, when Bush waived the controversial restriction on the sale of American jets to the Saudis engineered in the Senate by Howard Metzenbaum, the Ohio liberal who is Israel's unfailing friend, Prince Bandar told the American war chiefs that this would have a favorable influence on the King's decision. If the Americans could convince Fahd that they were sincerely determined to stop Saddam he would welcome American troops.

This was good news to Bush, but he still busied himself nailing down the diplomatic and economic isolation of Iraq. After the UN Security Council followed its condemnation of Iraq with economic sanctions against Saddam and U.S. naval surveillance of the Gulf to make them work, Bush turned to organizing the military coalition that would be needed should these measures fail.

By August 3 George Bush had already upon his return from Colorado convened the National Security Council with the question: "What are our interests?" His advisers replied: the threat to the vital

Persian Gulf oil, Saddam's persistent pursuit of nuclear weapons, the security of Israel and the challenge to America's credibility as the world's post–Cold War leader. It was in response to this summation that Cheney and Powell had met with Prince Bandar, and the Saudi Ambassador's reassurance had impelled Bush to reconvene the NSC that evening. Bush immediately asked CIA Director William Webster what he thought of Saddam's massing of troops on the Kuwaiti-Saudi border. Having been wrong on his prediction of what Saddam would do in Kuwait, Webster now did not hesitate to predict a second invasion, of eastern Saudi Arabia. Bush agreed, even though a few of his advisers were unconvinced. To him the threat to the immense Saudi oil reserves was unmistakable. For Saddam to control the combined wells of Iraq, Kuwait and Saudi Arabia would in effect make him commander of the Middle East and comptroller of the world economy. It would fulfill all the dangers to American interests reviewed in the earlier meeting.

Next General Colin Powell gave the advice Bush may have been seeking: he should "draw a line in the sand." He did not have to send many troops immediately, only enough for Saddam "to know that if he attacks Saudi Arabia, he attacks the United States." Asking the Joint Chiefs to meet with him next morning at the presidential retreat of Camp David in Maryland's Catoctin Mountains, he adjourned the meeting with the remark: "I believe we go."

At that council of war General H. Norman Schwarzkopf, the Army commander responsible for the Middle East, outlined for Bush the possibilities: what troops were available and how quickly they could get to the Gulf. A student of military history, Schwarzkopf was well aware of how the American virtue of striving for minimal casualties could become the vice of meeting a military crisis with air and naval power alone, and thus avoiding the bloodbaths that occur on the ground. He warned his chief that he would have to deploy ground forces as well. Bush asked: what about Egyptian troops? They were Moslems and Mubarak was anxious to help. No one agreed, except to say that Saddam would not be impressed. Just then a message was received from the head of a friendly state saying that the Saudis did not want American troops.

Bush immediately left the room and put in a call to King Fahd. Without mentioning the tip that he had just received, he told the King that he was absolutely committed to defending his kingdom, that he didn't want permanent bases and would withdraw his Americans as soon as was practicable. Then, in a clever stroke, he turned Prince Bandar's arguments to Cheney and Powell around and told Fahd that if all he wanted was a token force don't bother to ask. It was not an immediate clincher, but it stiffened Fahd's wavering spine. Bush returned to the meeting convinced that the Saudis would not reject American troops.

Now the question was: how many? Bush's military chiefs warned him that it would take months to deploy the forces needed to repel an invasion of Saudi Arabia. To attempt to do so with inadequate air, armor and infantry might end in an American bloodbath and a disastrous battlefield defeat. "This is the Super Bowl," General Powell said. "Don't count on the easy ways." Colin Powell had served two tours of duty in Vietnam, where he was wounded, winning a Bronze Star and the Soldier's Medal. With other officers he had sweated, squirmed and cursed inside the straitjacket of limitations and restrictions in which the jittery Lyndon Johnson had immobilized his forces. Now he told his chief: if you are going to use force, use all that you can muster. Bush readily agreed, for he too could remember the unclenched fist of "Nam."

Bush also did not flinch from the prospect of having to fight a war to dislodge the Iraqi dictator. But he still hoped to do so with diplomacy and the economic sanctions. So he was thinking defensively when he ordered a mere 2,300 men of the 82nd Airborne Division's lightly armed "ready brigade" to be flown to Saudi under the protection of Navy carrier aircraft and Air Force F-15 fighters. A Marine amphibious division of 16,500 men with heavy tanks was already aboard ship and would arrive next, followed by 19,000 soldiers of the 101st Air Mobile Division and 12,000 more of the 24th Mechanized Infantry Division, armed with 216 huge tanks and trained in desert warfare. It should have been more than enough to make Saddam Hussein rethink his low opinion of American resolve, but it didn't. Perhaps he was counting on Fahd's eventual refusal to allow infidel soldiers to desecrate the sands of the Holy Land of Islam.

The Saudi royal family could not make up its collective mind and the divided princes were still trying to persuade King Fahd to see it their way. Those who were terrified—and they were in the majority—feared to anger Saddam; those who were less timorous and understood American military force much more clearly argued that the disturber of Arab peace must be stopped. His Majesty was still undecided when Bush called again to suggest that he accept a visit from Secretary of War Cheney. King Fahd demurred: it would look too decisive and might provoke Saddam. A less prominent emissary would be much more acceptable. This was waffling, but there was nothing Bush could do about it—until Saddam himself angered Fahd by reneging on his promise to withdraw from Kuwait once he had installed his own government. Instead, the Father-Leader was doing everything possible to destroy Kuwait as a nation and a people. Kuwaitis were being tortured and murdered on a scale reminiscent of Hitler's Death's Head regiments that entered Poland in the wake of the Wehrmacht. Rape and robbery were even more widespread. Whatever an Iraqi soldier coveted or lusted for, he took. Kuwait's currency was worthless and its laws ignored. All of this intimidation, of course, was intended to cow the Kuwaitis into accepting the new status quo: they were Iraqis, the people of Saddam Hussein. Saddam was bent on nothing less than turning 1.9 million Kuwaitis into as many Iraqis occupying the 19th province of Iraq.

This angered the Arab world, especially King Fahd, who had also seen the American satellite photographs showing the ominous buildup of Saddam's forces on his border with Kuwait. He now invited Cheney to come to Riyadh. Cheney and Fahd spent two hours talking together in the presence of members of the royal family, such as Crown Prince Abdullah. CIA agents used maps and satellite photographs to show even more conclusively how Saddam had lied about his buildups in southern Kuwait. Not only troops but Air Force units had been moved forward, and the logistics train that had helped subdue Kuwait was now rumbling south. Abdullah, however, still opposed allowing infidels on sacred Saudi soil. The Saudi military could cope with Iraq, and as long as Kuwait existed as a country, there could be an Arab solution to the crisis. To this Fahd made the wry reply: "Kuwait is a country whose only territory is in hotel rooms in Saudi Arabia." Still Abdullah argued against accepting American troops. He was aghast when Cheney conveyed Bush's request to cut off the Iraqi pipeline across Saudi Arabia. This was nothing less than an act of war! It would provoke Saddam into an invasion! It is not known what King Fahd was thinking at that moment. Yet he was an intelligent man and it is possible that he saw the contradiction in Abdullah's feigned confidence in the Saudi military and his very real terror of enraging Saddam. But Fahd did say that if a war ensued he wanted to be sure that Saddam would "not get up again." After Cheney, scenting victory, repeated Bush's earlier assurances, the King looked into the eyes of the American secretary and said:

"We accept."

No single event—not even the American-Soviet detente or the UN's resolutions—was more important than this decision. With this, and Saddam's vicious indictment of his Arab "brothers" as traitors to Islam for accepting military aid from unclean unbelievers who were Zionist lackeys as well, many Moslem states, including Syria, the avowed enemy of the United States, pledged support of the economic sanctions and oil boycott and promised to send troops against Saddam. Saudi Arabia agreed to cut Iraq's oil pipeline and Turkey did the same, persuaded by an American promise to compensate it for lost revenue.

Within a week Bush and Baker had brought off a diplomatic tour de force. No fewer than 29 nations had rallied to American leadership to form what would be known as the Allied Coalition Against Iraq. They included Argentina, Australia, Bahrain, Bangladesh, Belgium, Britain, Canada, Czechoslovakia, Denmark, Egypt, France, Germany, Greece, Italy, Kuwait, Morocco, Netherlands, New Zealand, Niger, Norway, Oman, Pakistan, Poland, Qatar, Saudi Arabia, Senegal, Spain, Syria and the United Arab Emirates. Another eighteen others contributed economic, humanitarian or other assistance. These were Afghanistan, Austria, Bulgaria, Finland, Honduras, Hungary, Iceland, Japan, Luxembourg, Malaysia, Philippines, Portugal, Sierra Leone, South Korea, Sweden, Taiwan, Turkey and the U.S.S.R. Bush also persuaded some of these allies to pledge financial assistance to the coalition so that the U.S. would not be compelled to bear all the burden of the war's cost. With a projected bill of $36.4 billion for the war, Washington received a total pledge of $43.8 billion from Germany, Japan, Korea, Kuwait, Saudi Arabia and the United Arab Emirates, producing a surplus of $7.4 billion. Whether or not Washington plans to return the surplus is not known, but this second diplomatic coup was as pleasing to the President's conservative critics as it was annoying to Germany and Japan, both of whom used a constitutional ban on sending troops overseas as an excuse for with-holding military assistance. Of these final nails in Saddam's coffin, one of Bush's top-level aides remarked:

"In terms of directional clarity, this has all been an easy call. Even a dolt understands the principle. We need the oil. It's nice to talk about standing up for freedom, but Kuwait and Saudi Arabia are not exactly democracies, and if their principal export were oranges, a mid-level State Department official would have issued a statement and we would have closed down for August. There is nothing to waver about here." Quite true, but another White House aide observed that it was not all O-I-L—as some of Bush's liberal critics in Congress and elsewhere were maintaining—but a situation in which the obtuse Saddam in his messianic zeal to become another Nebuchadnezzar had offered Bush "a case where he knows what's right, he knows what the American people think, he knows what he should do. Most important, he knows these are all one and the same thing."

In a word, George Bush had been masterful and unwavering, and Saddam Hussein had been a stupid victim of his own wishful thinking. Perhaps more accurately he had been misinformed. He had believed what he had been told—not by his clique of sycophantic officers, who, like Hitler's toadies, told him only what he wanted to hear—but by the American media and academia. Writing and lecturing with endless glee about the American "defeat" in Vietnam, they had convinced this posturing pretender to the leadership of Islam that America did not have the will to fight. In this he joined the company of George III in the Revolutionary War, George IV during 1812, Santa Anna in Mexico, sundry Indian chiefs from King Philip to Tecumseh, President Jefferson Davis of the Confederacy, Aguinaldo in the Philippines, Kaiser Wilhelm in World War One, Hitler-Mussolini-Tojo in World War Two, Kim Il Sung and Chu Teh in Korea, Ho Chi Minh in Vietnam, Gaddafi in Libya and Noriega in Panama. All thought the same and all thought that the distinctly American privilege of dissent and criticism—even in wartime—was a sign of weakness and that the true voice of America came from those who disapproved of or opposed whatever war was current. So the dissident articles and lectures proclaiming "battlefield defeat" in Vietnam at a time when there were no American combat troops in Indo-China were swallowed whole by Saddam Hussein. He never read nor heard the true reasons for the failure of American foreign policy there; and if he had, it is doubtful that he would have believed them. There is no need to repeat them here because they have already been discussed.

In Ambassador Glaspie's report on her interview with Saddam she dwelt at length on his amazed delight that a Third World people could "defeat" the world's mightiest military power. That is why he made his sneering remark: "Yours is a society that cannot accept 10,000 dead in one battle." True enough, for to do all possible to keep casualties at a minimum is another American virtue often misunderstood. Saddam himself would in time learn its true meaning. Thus, in his ballooning self-esteem he misconstrued Bush's cautious policy in the Gulf and the restraint of Nixon and Johnson in Vietnam as indications of a flabby American will. "He thought he knew more about us than we knew about ourselves," said a senior State Department official, "and that was ultimately his most severe miscalculation."

5

☆

President George Bush made no such miscalculation of what Saddam could do. In that early August of 1990 the Father-Leader held the hammer, and time was his greatest ally. If he moved quickly against Saudi Arabia he would overrun that lightly defended kingdom almost as rapidly as he had conquered Kuwait. Eventually he would have 250,000 troops in Kuwait, but in the few days following the invasion he had only about half that many, still enough with his superiority in aircraft and tanks to overwhelm the Saudi Army of 45,000 men. If Saudi Arabia fell, the task of liberating that country and Kuwait too would be magnified many times. It would require counter-attack either by aerial or amphibious invasion: the two most difficult military operations. The prospect of the Allies having to attack an entrenched enemy either by air or sea or even air-sea might seem far too daunting to the nations pledging military support.

In many ways the situation in August was even more dangerous than the similar predicament in June, 1950, when the North Koreans were rolling relentlessly south and the collapsing South Korean Army appeared powerless to stop them. If the Reds had captured the southernmost port of Pusan they would have unified the peninsula as a communist state and all of President Truman's frantic efforts to weld the sixteen-nation United Nations coalition that eventually saved South Korea would have been fruitless. And for the same reason: for both diplomatic and military considerations, to strike an enemy from friendly territory is far easier than to attack him from the sea or the sky, with forces depending upon supply and support from far-off bases. Nations are usually far more reluctant to try to reverse an accomplished fact than to prevent it from happening. Thus George Bush and his top advisers were terrified that Saddam would act quickly. They knew that the spearhead of American paratroops winging toward Saudi Arabia might encounter Iraqi aircraft rising from captured Saudi airfields to attack and destroy them.

When Bush informed America by television that he had ordered American troops to the Gulf, declaring, "The mission is wholly defensive," he had this tableau of possible disaster at the back of his brain. But he also had the recollection of Jimmy Carter acting like a prisoner in the White House during the Iranian hostage crisis, and he had no desire to give his countrymen a similar image of a frightened, indecisive President. Indeed, his hostage situation was far worse: there were 3,000 Americans together with 1.5 million other foreign nationals trapped in Kuwait and Iraq, and there would eventually be media reports that if attacked Saddam planned to use them as human shields. Thus, to adopt a calm, business-as-usual stance intended to reassure his countrymen and deceive Saddam, he left Washington for the customary three-week vacation at his summer home in Kennebunkport, Maine.

There he staged what was almost a caricature of his passion for physical exercise and relaxing sports: marathon jogs, hard-nose tennis, golf and horseshoes and trolling for bluefish aboard his speedboat *Fidelity*. During those three weeks his top advisers knew how close Saddam Hussein was to seizing suzerainty of the Arab World. He could move in any direction: into Saudi Arabia, through Jordan into Israel, down the Gulf toward the lightly defended emirates of the Arabian Sea, although this last without any navy to speak of was highly unlikely. That was why Bush's decision to use the U.S. Navy to blockade Iraq in compliance with UN resolutions turned anxiety into dread, and the first time an American ship fired a shot across the bow of an Iraqi tanker many frantic officers and aides feared that a war was about to erupt.

But Saddam Hussein did not move, contenting himself with a fusillade of bloody threats so comical that it was a shame that there was no Charlie Chaplin around to do for the Father-Leader what he had done for *Der Fuehrer.* "We will tear your arms out of your shoulders." "We will drown you in your own blood."

At this writing there is no explanation of why Saddam granted this vital interval of twenty-one days to the American giant, known and feared for its masterful technology and organizing skill, able as no other nation to move men and arms rapidly over vast distances. Was he, beneath all this bluster, really a funker, something like the Union general Joe Hooker, who played a perfect game of poker up until the biggest pot and the last raise and final bluff, and then would go into a funk and fold his hand? Perhaps the delay can be explained by Hooker's own explanation of why he retreated from almost certain victory over Lee at Chancellorsville: "I just lost confidence in Joe Hooker."

So Saddam, like the biblical sun, stood still; much to the growing confidence and diminishing anxiety of the American chiefs. At Kennebunkport George Bush found that a fishing trip aboard *Fidelity* was the perfect place to make his plans: alone on the ocean with Scowcroft, within hail of boated Secret Service agents, but still alone. One day they talked for four hours. Sanctions: Would they work? What about Israel? Saddam would be sure to try to unravel the coalition by provoking the Israelis to attack him so that the Arab nations opposing him would withdraw in horror from an alliance with Jews. Could Israel be held on a leash? Would world leaders like Gorbachev stay aboard? He was Mr. Tilted-Both-Ways, pulled by Boris Yeltsin and the reformers on one side and the hard-liners and military on the other. What to do about the hostages? Bush had to be hard-headed about them. Both Jimmy Carter and Ronald Reagan had allowed emotion to draw them into bad decisions on hostages. And the American people most of all: their support had been marvelous, incredible, an outpouring of patriotism that had never been seen before in American history. But could it last? Americans had a fondness for the home run or the long bomb. They are not a stoical people. There were so many "ifs" to consider, and just one miscalculation might send an aroused Saddam plunging over the border. And there was as yet nothing there to stop him. Worse, as Bush and Scowcroft well knew, Saddam really didn't have to seize and hold the Saudi oilfields. For his immediate purposes all he had to do was blow them up.

George Bush was indeed frightened of the effect such a disaster would have on the world economy. But George Bush had not lost confidence in George Bush. The Kennebunkport Dance of the Nonchalant President would continue, for George Bush well knew, as he steered *Fidelity* back to shore, that while Saddam hesitated his own war chiefs were reacting with lightning speed.

Two days after the invasion General Colin Powell flew back to the Pentagon from Camp David to brief his admirals and generals on the decision to confront Saddam with American troops. On the same day he issued orders that sent fifty U.S. Navy warships steaming toward the Gulf, among them the aircraft carriers U.S.S. *Independence* and U.S.S. *Eisenhower*. Lieutenant General Hansford T. Johnson was told to begin mounting the biggest, farthest and fastest military deployment in the history of warfare. Next a top-secret order was flashed to Schwarzkopf at his headquarters in Tampa, Florida, directing him to prepare detailed plans for deploying forces Gulfward. But then, when Powell called for a general plan for that purpose, he found one that was to his dismay about as current as a propeller-driven fighter plane. It posited America and the Soviet Union engaged in a two-front war in Europe and Southwest Asia. The Gulf War was to be just a sideshow. This was actually the plan that Cheney and Powell had shown Prince Bandar, and it called for thirty days' notice from the Pentagon to get it started. Saddam, of course, had given not a moment's warning. But then to his joy Powell discovered that the aggressive and able Schwarzkopf had in 1989 updated and revised that plan in an elaborate war game or command-post operation—"CPX" in Army jargon—positing Iraq as the adversary. It convinced Powell that he could hold off Saddam with four and a third divisions, and this was the basis of Bush's decision to send 125,000 American troops to Saudi Arabia.

The deployment seemed so swift and sure that it revived a long-dead rumor that at the time of the oil crunch of 1974 the United States had offered to protect the Saudi oil wells, but was rejected. Nevertheless, so the rumor went, an elaborate contingency plan had been developed aimed at preventing a coup in Saudi Arabia led by fundamentalist Moslems similar to those who put the Ayatollah Khomeini in power in Iran. This, some media commentators were saying, explained the incredible celerity of the U.S.-led Allied buildup. In fact, it was not really so fast and so large; for the Pentagon had cleverly begun to issue a series of announcements of the arrival in the desert of various famous units, particularly the 82nd Airborne, the 24th Mechanized Infantry with their 216 mammoth M-1A1 tanks, the 1st and 2nd Marine divisions, the 1st Mechanized Infantry Division and so on—when in fact only spearheads or advance detachments of these formations were in place in the Saudi sands. It is highly possible that Saddam's hesitation could be attributed in great part to this deception. He had neither satellites nor spy planes to survey the Allied buildup. For intelligence he relied on the broadcasts of the Cable News Network, eventually the only American TV network that continued to broadcast without interruption from Baghdad. Because CNN had no more reason than anyone else in the American media to doubt the Pentagon's bulletins—and because handsome anchor men are usually neither perceptive nor skeptical nor expert in all the activities of mankind that they presume to expound upon—it is likely that Saddam swallowed the Pentagon's misinformation. Aware of this, the wily Schwarzkopf welcomed TV crews to the mushrooming Allied base at Dhahran to film the arrival every five minutes of giant C-5 Galaxy transports.

During this first critical month Norman Schwarzkopf proved himself as flamboyant a bluffer as his commander-in-chief. He knew that he was vulnerable, and would remain so for some time; and yet, student of military history that he was, he also realized that at the outset of an unexpected war—especially one in which the enemy scores spectacular early success, as in World Wars One and Two and here in the Persian Gulf—the reeling nation through its media and so-called expert analysts tends to exaggerate enemy strength. Thus the CIA and the DIA—the intelligence-gathering agencies that had been so completely wrong in their estimates of what Saddam could do—were now telling Schwarzkopf that he faced a million-man army of veterans of the eight-year war with Iran and that Saddam possessed 1,000 more Soviet-built tanks, 2,000 more armored personnel carriers and 250 first-line aircraft than had been estimated previously.

But Schwarzkopf did not panic. He knew better than to believe inflated media accounts of his rival's strength. If the Iraqi Army was so good how was it that, supplied by France and the Soviet Union and trained by the Soviets, it could not in eight years put away the Iranian Army, untrained and undersupplied after it alienated and lost its chief military ally in the United States? Were these Iraqi soldiers, dragooned into Saddam's Army, some of them still wearing the street shoes they had on when they were impressed, actually superior to the new American GI, the proud, intelligent and highly-trained and motivated warriors of the new All-Volunteer Armed Forces? Could Saddam's Soviet weaponry actually match the incredible array of "high-tech" arms in the American arsenal? To all of these questions General Schwarzkopf could certainly have replied with a quick and confident negative. And yet, during those tense early weeks of August, 1991, the physical giant that his men affectionately called "Stormin' Norman" was indeed scared to death.

For all his superb weaponry and soldiery he just didn't have enough of either if Saddam Hussein decided on an all-or-nothing gamble and sent his forces in Kuwait—then mistakenly believed to be close to half a million men, but actually only half that—plunging into Saudi Arabia. Even with the Saudi Army of 45,000 men Schwarzkopf did not possess 100,000, and the Saudi soldiers could never be considered the equal of the Americans. What Norman Schwarzkopf needed in those tense days was more of everything: more divisions, airplanes, ships and especially more of those fabulous weapons such as the A-10 attack plane known affectionately as "the Warthog" by the men who flew that slow-moving, ugly tank killer; fighter-bombers like the Harrier and F-16 Falcon; fighters such as the Tomcat and the Hornet; technological marvels such as the deadly F-111 fighter-bomber and above all the F-117A Stealth fighter-bomber, able to move to its targets undetected by enemy radar; and the Apache helicopters with their Hellfire missiles. Above all Schwarzkopf called for missiles like the Patriot and the Hawk to protect his troops and bases against Saddam's Air Force and Soviet Scud missiles. And he got them, all of them.

Even though the Navy was crippled by a shortage of American merchant ships, it was able to cut the delivery time for the arming of Desert Shield from 120 days to 95. Faced with a logistics problem much more daunting than the cross-Channel invasion of Normandy in World War II, and even greater than the biggest of all—the Tenth Army's amphibious assault on Okinawa in April, 1945—the armed forces, moving greater distances and with less time to deliver, managed by the end of August to arm Norman Schwarzkopf with an array of trained troops and marvelous weapons so astonishing that it dazzled the world. By the end of August cargo aircraft flying as many as 300 missions a day had shuttled 72,000 passengers and 100,000 tons of supplies to the Persian Gulf. When the 24th Mechanized Infantry Division arrived in the Gulf in early September with 216 of those monster M1A1 Abrams tanks—easily a match for Saddam's Soviet T-72s—General Schwarzkopf relaxed. He was in no strength yet to take the offensive, should that be ordered, but with what he possessed in mid-September he knew he could hold off Saddam.

President George Bush still hoped to avoid war with Iraq. With Baker and Scowcroft he hoped that the UN-authorized sanctions would compel Saddam to withdraw from Kuwait. By September, supported by a U.S. naval blockade, the sanctions had already cut off 90 percent of Iraq's exports and imports. Rationing of food and gasoline had begun in Baghdad and other cities. But eight years of war with Iran had accustomed Iraqis to shortages and misery. As was his wont, Saddam would solve the sanctions by squeezing his people a little tighter. By the end of September the CIA had notified the White House that "in the short or medium term" sanctions would not drive the dictator from Kuwait. The long term was not mentioned; and in fact no one wanted to mention it, if only because Bush and his advisers knew that coalitions and the American public had no stomach for marathon confrontations.

Cheney and Powell, never believers in the sanctions, now saw the opportunity to argue forcefully for shifting to the offensive. This would mean deployment of two more heavy divisions, probably a total of another 100,000 men. The plan was for the Marines and other Allied troops to pin down Saddam on the Kuwaiti border while Schwarzkopf sent his XVIII Corps on a long sweep to the west around Saddam's right flank. But then two months after his invasion of Kuwait the dictator began to redeploy his forces. He stripped the

Iranian border of troops and sent reinforcements into Kuwait, raising his strength there to the aforementioned 250,000. They dug protective earth berms for their tanks, built roads, planted minefields and erected formidable antiaircraft defenses—all measures aimed at a defense-in-depth. They also gave bite to their boast of blowing up Kuwait's oilfields if attacked by rigging the wells and refineries with plastic explosives.

Saddam also moved his elite Republican Guards—elite because they were politically trustworthy, receiving better pay, food and clothing in reward for their loyalty to the Father-Leader—from Kuwait into southern Iraq, reinforcing them with 150,000 of his ordinary or common denominator of cannon fodder. At the border were even more contemptible bodies, eminently expendable; but behind them were tougher, mechanized troops and formations of executioners trained to shoot fugitives from combat. Above both was the Republican Guard. Here was a carefully layered defense designed to cow the untrustworthy and crush any rebellion against the dictator; but, more important, also calculated to exact a fearful price in American lives should the enemy go over to the attack. Saddam, of course, like Nikita Khrushchev, still believed that "America was too liberal to fight." Every time an American was killed or maimed, a family would mourn. Kill enough of them, and President Bush would lose the social sanction necessary to sustain his war. Aware that those redoubtable 16,500 U.S. Marines were still boated and somewhere in the Persian Gulf, he feared an amphibious assault and thus moved heavy armored divisions and light infantry formations to the Kuwaiti coast, while shifting heavy armor into the neutral zone between Iraq and Saudi Arabia.

All these moves had the unintended effect of pulling the rug out from beneath the Pentagon's cherished plan for a long "end run" around Saddam's right that would envelop and destroy his best troops: the Republican Guard. But they were now too far north to be turned and trapped. In effect, they were a powerful reserve that could counterattack and punish the Allies entering Kuwait and also abort any uprising. In response to these unexpected moves, Schwarzkopf would need a new plan.

Instead, because of his fondness for daring and decisive strokes—like MacArthur's deep envelopment at Inchon that destroyed the North Korean Army—he proposed a variation on the old one: the end run had to be longer and deeper, long enough to outflank Saddam secretly, far enough north to surround the Republican Guard. For this he would need the powerful VII Corps stationed in Germany: two and a third armored divisions and an armored cavalry regiment, plus the First Mechanized Infantry Division from Fort Riley, Kansas—"the Big Red One."

Schwarzkopf sent an outline of his proposal to Powell, who was impressed enough to fly to Riyadh on October 21 to confer with his Middle Eastern chief. Here was probably the most crucial conference of the Gulf War. With his customary command of language, Schwarzkopf argued that the situation called for an imaginative and daring stroke. Nothing like Secretary of War Robert McNamara's idiotic "orchestration," i.e., gradual commitment of forces in Vietnam. It had to be massive and all at once. Powell flew home full of enthusiasm and convinced Cheney that what he called "the enhanced option" would bring the quick and decisive victory that the White House sought. Just to be sure, Cheney and Powell delighted Schwarzkopf by adding three aircraft-carrier battle groups and a battleship, plus the Second Marine Expeditionary Force and Fifth Marine Expeditionary Brigade to the Gulf commander's original request. They also alerted three National Guard brigades.

This meant doubling the Desert Shield commitment to 200,000 Americans, although it would take until January 15, 1991, to complete the buildup. Nevertheless, Bush approved "the enhanced option," believing that it was essential to confront Saddam with "a credible military threat." Although this was a definite shift from defense to offense, Bush still did not think it would automatically lead to war. Instead, he was confident a redoubled show of strength would make Saddam back down. Meanwhile, the time being late October and the November elections only a few days away, it was decided not to tell the country or even the Senate Armed Services Committee about the escalation until after the elections.

In the interval, the United States would try to persuade the UN Security Council to approve the use of force against Iraq if Saddam did not comply with the demand that he withdraw from Kuwait unconditionally. If this happened, Baker shrewdly observed, then it would be hard for Congress to refuse to grant its own war-powers resolution. It was also up to Baker to inform the Allies of this change in strategy, especially the Soviet Union. To this end the Secretary flew first to Saudi Arabia and then to Moscow. Baker was confident that Foreign Minister Eduard Shevardnadze would not balk at the use of force but was not so sure Gorbachev would approve. The Soviet leader had twice sent the Arabist Yevgeny Primakov to Baghdad. Primakov did not want the Soviet Union to abandon its longtime client in Iraq. If he, rather than Shevardnadze, had the last word with Gorbachev, the coalition might begin to unravel then and there. Although Gorbachev made no commitments, he did hold up two fingers together and say: "We have to stay like this." Baker was reassured, especially after Shevardnadze told him that certain situations might justify the use of force.

Two days after the election—which left the Democrats in control of Congress—Bush announced the redoubled troop commitment, only to be shocked by the storm of protest that erupted—not only in the Democratic Congress but in the country as well. "The public thought it meant that war was inevitable," a White House aide explained. "We saw it as part of the Big Bluff."

Senator Sam Nunn of Georgia, chairman of the powerful Senate Armed Services Committee, saw nothing but red. At a briefing in August Powell had assured Nunn's committee that the Pentagon's plan was to use mostly air power and a limited number of ground troops. He had said nothing about large numbers of foot soldiers. Enraged, Nunn scheduled a number of public hearings at which a selection of former chairmen of the Joint Chiefs or secretaries of defense testified that sanctions should be given time to work. This was exactly what House Speaker Thomas Foley and Senate Majority Leader George Mitchell wanted to hear. Sanctions not shooting became a Democratic rallying cry, and a great national debate of the kind peculiar to American public life ensued.

But it was not strong enough or antagonistic enough to dissuade George Bush from his chosen path. Accompanied by his wife, Barbara, he spent Thanksgiving among GIs in the desert, and both were deeply moved by the loyalty and determination of their young countrymen. They were also disturbed by the realization that if war came many of them might die, and Bush returned to Washington somewhat subdued. Reading Amnesty International's report on Iraqi atrocities in Kuwait, however, convinced him that Saddam was so evil that opposing him was of the essence of morality. When the Right Reverend Edmond Browning, presiding bishop of the Episcopal

Church, came to the White House to urge him to give sanctions more time, Bush the Episcopalian burst out: "You should read the Amnesty International report. *Then* you tell me what I should do." In other words: must I stand still while an entire people is being systematically raped and robbed, tortured and murdered?

Meanwhile, Baker was moving the Security Council steadily toward the resolution authorizing force. The only obstacle was a deadline. Baker wanted none, but when Gorbachev insisted, he suggested January 1. Moscow countered with January 15—and Baker accepted. Why not, when that was the date set for completion of the enhanced option? On November 30 the Security Council passed the force resolution.

Although jubilant, President Bush was disturbed by another outburst of war nerves afflicting the American public. To calm them, he invited Iraqi Foreign Minister Tariq Aziz to Washington and offered to send Baker to Baghdad. Saddam accepted the invitation for Aziz, and then resorted to one-upmanship on Bush by freeing all hostages. Sensing in this that Saddam might be softening his attitude, the administration adopted a wait-and-see attitude. Bush had been hinting to Saddam for months that *after* he withdrew from Kuwait the U.S. might be willing to call for a Middle East peace conference addressing such demands of Saddam as the plight of the Palestinians and new border accommodations with Kuwait. But the Father-Leader was still intransigent, which he made plain when he refused to receive Baker until the very eve of the UN deadline. In other words, he was stalling, not talking.

It is likely that this latest rebuff made up George Bush's mind. On the day after New Year's he met with his closest advisers in the White House and told them: "For me it boils down to a very moral case of good versus evil, black versus white. If I have to go, it's not going to matter to me if there isn't one congressman who supports this, or what happens to public opinion. If it's right, it's got to be done." Even so, he made one last proposal to Saddam: he would send Baker to meet with Aziz in Geneva, a gesture meant as much to influence a Congress about to debate its own war-powers resolution as to placate the dictator. But because Bush distrusted Aziz as just one more Saddam toady who would never violate the Iraqi eleventh commandment—"Bring no bad news to the Father-Leader"—he wrote Saddam a letter warning him to get out of Kuwait by January 15, six days thence, or face expulsion by the Allies. Baker gave the letter to Aziz for delivery. He also received a photocopy of it. Fluent in English, he read it. "I am sorry," he said, lowering his thick black-framed glasses. "I cannot receive this letter. The language in this letter is not compatible with language between heads of state."

Saddam not only did not see Bush's ultimatum, but also received the customary good news. His half-brother Barzan Tikriti sat next to Aziz through the six-and-a-half-hour talks, closely scrutinizing the Americans. Afterward he telephoned his brother to tell him not to worry. The Americans don't want to fight. They just want to talk. They are weak.

So Saddam Hussein failed to get the message, failed to believe Colin Powell when he said, "If we go in, we go in to win, not to fool around."

And that is what they did on January 16, 1991.

6

☆

In the dark of that night the art of rending entered its latest and most precise phase: push-button war. Operation Desert Storm—what Saddam Hussein was to call "the Mother of Battles"— began with the push of a button aboard a blacked-out U.S. battleship 200 miles from Baghdad. With a monster roar and a cloud of choking black smoke a Tomahawk cruise missile burst the seal of its launching tube—hanging momentarily in the air until its engine ignited—after which it vanished.

At the same time—just past midnight in Saudi Arabia—a vast armada of Allied aircraft, although mostly American, circled over the Desert Kingdom in silence broken only by orders from airborne command posts known as AWACS. They had been flying alerts for weeks to unnerve the enemy and on the last few nights had sent bogus messages to deceive him. He would not know when the war would erupt until he was hit.

First across the border were the latest technological marvels, the Stealth fighter-bombers. They were bound for communications centers in and around Baghdad. Called Stealth because with their radical batwing design they were invisible to radar, they could zero in on enemy targets without fear of antiaircraft fire. Because of this, they alone attacked Baghdad throughout the war.

After them came 15-C Eagles, matchless fighters intended to clear the skies of enemy interceptors, followed by more fighter-bombers: F-16s, F-15E Strike Eagles and F-11s, Navy A-6s and British Tornadoes. Leading them were jets loaded with radio equipment to detect, mislead and neutralize Iraq's air-defense radars. Though unarmed, they were as vital as any aircraft aloft on that momentous night; no fewer than eight of them assigned to guard a single strike force of twice that many F-16s. Each of these EF-111 electronic countermeasure planes carries ten powerful transmitters capable of jamming as many enemy radar stations from 100 miles away. Designed to disarm the Warsaw Pact's radar air defenses, five of them could immobilize the Communists from the Baltic to the Adriatic. No fewer than 100 of them joined the first night of battle in Operation Desert Storm.

Now there were other Tomahawk cruise missiles aloft, homing in on their targets at speeds of 550 miles an hour, headed for a landfall at the confluence of the Tigris and Euphrates rivers near Iraq's brief coastline. Twenty feet long and flying as low as 100 feet above ground, they are virtually impossible to defend against. Overland they are guided by comparing a radar image of the terrain below to maps pre-programmed into their computer memories. This means that in flight over the flat Arabian desert they cannot take the most direct route but must depend upon topographical features such as riverbanks or mountains. Reaching their targets, the Tomahawks flash brilliant strobe lights ahead in which to make final course adjustments for the buildings they are assigned to strike.

But the first hit came from a Stealth above Baghdad. While radar screens all over Kuwait and Iraq were going blank under the onslaught of hundreds of airborne jammers, a Stealth thousands of feet above Baghdad's main telephone building unleashed a 2,000-pound laser-guided bomb. It sped invisibly through the moonless night illuminated by tracers flashing skyward fired by panicking Iraqi AA men too terrified to turn on their radar screens yet pressing wildly on their firing keys. Below the Stealth stood the telephone building. One moment it was there, square and imposing; the next, there was a brilliant flash on its roof; the building swayed, and black smoke erupted from all four sides while all the telephones in Baghdad went dead. That was the image, replayed for days on videotape telecasts, that ushered in the new warfare.

Meanwhile, the vast and various Allied air armada roared through the night sky above Iraqi roads jammed with automobiles fleeing the cities for the safer countryside, their headlight beams piercing the darkness and looking like light pencils to the Allied airmen above them. It was excellent weather for a night attack: clear, moonless and chilly, perfect conditions for infrared imaging. The first wave's targets were communications centers, air-defense installations, military headquarters and bases, along with launchers for Iraq's Soviet-built Scud missiles—the brains rather than the body of Saddam's army—and in this Mother of Beatings the success of the strikes was an astonishing 80 percent; almost demonstrating, as the long-ago discredited "Bomber Barons" of World War II were fond of predicting, that strategic bombing can win a war. It still can't, because only men not machines can possess the enemy's territory, but on this fabulous January 16, 1991, the new technology of the new warfare showed that *guided* bombs and missiles, rather than those merely dropped or fired, are an improvement so enormous that it is almost a difference in kind rather than degree.

Saddam's airmen seemed to agree with that estimate. Only a handful roared aloft, and most of these became airborne to flee to safer bases in the north. Not then nor at any time during the war did they shoot down an Allied plane, and before they stopped flying altogether—or at least only to seek sanctuary in neighboring Iran—they lost 42 planes in aerial combat. One of these, if the lives of human beings had not been at risk, could be regarded as the most ludicrous freak in the history of aerial combat. Air Force Captain James Denton was flying an unarmed EF-11A Raven over a western Iraqi airfield when an enemy Mirage F-1 came up on his tail, launching an air-to-air missile from a mile away. Denton quickly released chaff and flares to confuse the missile's heat-seeking guidance and dived to within a few hundred feet of the ground, throwing his plane into a sharp right turn. The missile flew by him and struck the Mirage pilot trying to get into position for another shot. It was the first kill ever for an unarmed plane, and a Soviet news agency reported that Saddam was so incensed by such incompetence that he executed two of his top Air Force commanders. His AA defenses were hardly better. Though noisy and spectacular, they succeeded in downing only 8 Allied aircraft, flying 3,100 combat sorties in the first 48 hours alone. The reason: the Iraqi gunners quickly learned that as soon as they turned on their radar they became a target for American radar-seeking HARM missiles. Saddam might boast that when "the vultures were coming like rain . . . [the Iraqi gunners] never relinquished their guns. They never left their places." Nor did they switch on their radar.

The day after the first raid, Baghdad, except for those specifically targeted buildings that were destroyed or damaged, in no way resembled a German or Japanese city laid waste by the thousand-bomber British and American saturation raids of World War II. Although the streets were mostly deserted, Iraqi televisions showed a smiling Saddam strolling the sidewalks, shaking hands with civilians. The Father-Leader in a TV speech promised to make King Fahd "rot in hell" and to destroy "the poisonous whole nest in Tel Aviv." He did try to make good on the latter threat, anxious as he was to provoke Israel into attacking him and thus detach the Arab states from the Allied coalition—especially Saudi Arabia, host to the U.S.-led alliance. Saddam was believed to possess about fifty Soviet-made Scud missiles, obsolete weapons feared only because they were also thought to be armed with chemical warheads. Gas attacks by Scuds or conventional artillery were so dreaded by the Allies that not only were their soldiers provided with gas masks but civilians in Israel and Saudi Arabia as well. Actually the Scud was vastly overrated. It was a ballistic missile propelled from a launcher. Fired aloft by its rocket engines, it was carried to its targets by momentum, unlike the jet-powered Tomahawk guiding itself toward its prey. Grossly inaccurate, it was a ballistic blunderbuss that could hit a city, but nothing smaller. Eventually, it was realized that the Scud's warhead was conventional explosive and not poison gas.

Out of his inexhaustible reservoir of venomous hatred Saddam Hussein chose Saudi Arabia and Israel as Scud targets: the Saudi Kingdom for having welcomed infidel soldiers to the holy soil of Islam, Israel to unravel the Allied coalition. The Saudis were more fortunate because they were defended against the Scud by the American surface-to-air Patriot missile, a weapon about as martial looking as a garbage truck. It was a van filled with electronic equipment and a battery of tubes from which the Patriots were launched. Overall it looked like a nosed-over dumpster. But it picked off the first Scud fired at Dhahran. Air Force First Lieutenant Steven Kirik witnessed the event from his F-15: "I'm sitting in my jet, getting ready to go. I looked over at my port engine and there it was. It was like a big brilliant flare. It jumped off the ground, snaked back and forth a couple of times and then—boom! It was pretty spectacular." For the first time in military history an enemy missile was destroyed in flight, and it was done by a missile that was a by-product of the much-derided Star Wars program.

The Israelis had no such defenses, even though they had been working for years to develop their own anti-missile system. They could have had the Patriot, but refused two batteries shipped to them just before the Gulf War erupted. Defense Minister Moshe Arens rejected their American crews because, as he told Cheney, they had been defending themselves for forty years and weren't going to rely on anyone else's soldiers now. Nothing bothered George Bush more than this attitude. If Israel struck at Iraq in retaliation for a Scud attack, the guns of their American-made F-16s might very well chastise Saddam Hussein, but they would also chew the anti-Iraq alliance to shreds. And Hussein did fire Scuds at Tel Aviv: three of them in the first three days of the war. They hit a few cars and houses, but inflicted only minor casualties.

Nevertheless, news of the first strike shocked Cheney. He immediately called Arens on a direct satellite link and found to his dismay that a dozen Israeli F-16s were already airborne and prepared to attack Iraq. They were awaiting receipt of the pass codes that would identify them as friendly craft and not be shot down by Allied air or AA. Arens demanded that the codes either be supplied or the Allies suspend air operations for four hours to clear the way for his planes. Going further, he promised that if the Scud attacks continued he would send airborne troops into western Iraq to destroy launch sites. He even asked that Cheney secure permission for the Israeli squadron to cross Saudi or Jordanian airspace.

Stunned by this string of impossible and imperious demands, Cheney said that he could grant nothing on his own but would discuss the matter with the President. Within an hour Bush placed a personal call to Prime Minister Yitzhak Shamir. After expressing his condolences for the attacks, he again offered to ship Patriot batteries to Israel, and this time the offer was accepted. Bush also promised a widespread aerial hunt for Scud mobile launchers. He was able to make good on the destruction of most of Saddam's fixed-site launchers, but the mobile ones, hiding by day and firing only at night, were so difficult to find that in the first few weeks of the war as much as 15 percent of American air strength in Saudi Arabia was employed searching for them. So the Scud attacks—a total of 81 in all—continued until almost the end of the war. Several Israelis died in the raids, apparently of heart attacks rather than mortal wounds—victims nonetheless. To Israel's great credit, no more was said about retaliation.

Daniel Ellsberg was happy on the night of January 15, 1991. He was back in jail—arrested in Washington for an antiwar demonstration outside the White House. It was his 54th arrest, and the prince of professional war protesters thought it might be the most productive, even more salutary than the Vietnam War incarcerations. But Daniel Ellsberg was wrong.

The Persian Gulf War was not only the new kind of push-button war—at least on the victorious side; it was also a new American home front. The coalition of protest was between the old professionals such as Ellsberg, who hadn't found an incarnate evil to denounce since the Exxon Valdez oil spill, and the lunatic fringes of left and right: the customary pacifist groups screaming, "Support peace or I'll kill you"; Jewish-conspiracy theorists insisting that the whole, disgusting Middle Eastern mess was another Israeli plot—all of them vague and at a loss to explain how the Gulf War imperiled their causes, but none of them reluctant to wave a banner or shake a placard for the benefit of the TV cameras. There was also the American Civil Liberties Union, quite indifferent to the fact that the civil liberties of the soldiery that they were defending had already been severely limited the moment these so-called victims chose to put on a uniform.

There were some—but not many—wives of soldiers shipped out to the desert who protested; and an occasional soldier going into court in a vain effort to prevent his being made to do what he was paid to do; and there were families of servicemen claiming that their sons and daughters were being asked to risk their flesh for policies in which they had no voice. Some also simply maintained that no government had the right to ask its soldiers to fight, an argument so naïve, with anarchy as its obvious corollary, that it is not hard to doubt its sincerity, especially when applied to all-volunteer armed forces.

There was, however, a faint plausibility in the claim that the services had deliberately lured impressionable teenagers into their ranks with promises of high pay and quick promotion, as well as training that would one day qualify them for lucrative civilian jobs, while saying nothing of the possibility of having to go to war. But this again is naïve and self-serving: what else is the chief purpose of the armed forces that they joined? It was also an argument made chiefly on behalf of black servicemen, who constituted 29 percent of the military, nearly twice as much as their percentage of the overall population.

Judging from what service men and women said to inquiring reporters, they didn't see the war quite that way. They regarded combat as an unsought, unpleasant but necessary part of their calling, and a reasonable risk to take for the benefits that made them lift their right hands.

One of the most delightful surprises of these new armed forces was the character of the servicemen. Because they were issued high-tech weapons they had to be and were intelligent. They were patriotic, competent, disciplined, diligent and above all realistic—so different from most of the unfortunate and in the main reluctantly drafted armed forces of the Vietnam War: drug ridden and riven by class and racial hatreds. But the new armed forces, dealing only with volunteers, had the power to decree an end to racism, and the instrument of military discipline to enforce it. Black youths were probably the chief beneficiaries of this new policy, and those who were in Saudi Arabia were almost unanimous in their belief that they had a better chance of success in the military than in civilian life. Colin Powell was their role model, and they firmly believed that it was no accident that a black man could become chairman of the Joint Chiefs of Staff before there was a black chairman of a large American corporation. This is not to suggest that there was no racism in the American military. Bigots exist and always will exist everywhere. But there was no such policy. Off-duty whites went with whites and blacks with blacks, but on-duty they worked together with a minimum of racial incidents; and orders were obeyed without reference to the color of the skin of the person who gave them.

In its beginning, the antiwar movement was impressive indeed. The first big peace march drew 25,000 people to Washington on January 19, three days after the Allied aerial onslaught began. A week later six times that number gathered on the Mall. Even by Vietnam standards this was a most respectable throng. Unlike Vietnam, it was also commendably orderly, although a smaller crowd in San Francisco on the same day got unruly enough to cause nearly 1,000 arrests. But the anguish in the faces of many of these sincere people was indeed genuine—especially that of one elderly and stocky lady holding up a placard that said: "There *has* to be another way." But there isn't. Illegal and immoral force must in the end be countered by legal and moral force, else the criminal will triumph and look around for other victims. Anyone who has lived in this century need not be reminded of the tactics of Kaiser Bill, Hitler-Mussolini-Tojo and Stalin: and now Saddam Hussein. A policy of nonviolence is to invite an occupation and exploitation, if not actual destruction or enslavement. A citizen or a subject is not sovereign, able to pick and choose what taxes he will pay or what wars he will support. In his masterly discussion of the just war, Saint Augustine in maintaining that a war is just only if the evil that it seeks to erase is greater than the cost of eliminating it also observed that unless a citizen or subject is in possession of enough facts to demonstrate that the conflict in which he refuses to serve is indeed immoral, he must trust his government and bear arms.

Gradually, however, as the media began reporting interviews with the men and women in the desert, enthusiasm for the antiwar movement plummeted, reaching its nadir on a sunny February afternoon in New York City when a crowd of demonstrators opposite St. Patrick's Cathedral attracted a crowd of exactly eight: two four-person TV crews. One reason for this drastic decline in popularity was that it was hard to talk of "peace" when the Iraqi soldiery in Kuwait were torturing and killing, raping and robbing, as well as committing other atrocities—although the report that Kuwaiti infants had been yanked from hospital incubators was indeed apocryphal. Another sobering fact was that all the forecasts of an American bloodbath were similarly false. *Time* Magazine carried off the palm by predicting a ten-day war in which 200 American aircraft and as many tanks would be destroyed along with 3,000 Americans killed and 13,000 wounded. In actuality during four weeks of aerial war only 14 Americans died and 12 were wounded, with eight planes lost. In all of Desert Storm Americans killed in action did not exceed 150, and of these about a dozen were victims of friendly fire and 28 others lost their lives when a Scud broke up in flight over Saudi Arabia and fell on an American barracks. Rumors of planeloads of corpses and a Defense Department order for 60,000 body bags in Philadelphia were at best an exaggeration and at worst a lie.

One explanation of the phenomenal popularity of the antiwar movement during its inception is that most Americans still suffered from what President Bush called "the Vietnam syndrome." They feared to expose their pride to another pummeling, and those pig-sticking excursions in Grenada and Panama had not assuaged their badly bruised ego. There were also doubts about America's military prowess as manifested in the unfair and persistent attacks on General William Westmoreland's conduct of the war in Vietnam, when the actual culprits were Lyndon Johnson and his incredibly obtuse Secretary of War, Robert S. McNamara.

Then there was all that money—billions and billions, even trillions—spent on exotic military hardware: elaborate planes, ships and guns stuffed with electronic guidance that might never be used in combat. Such funds could better have gone toward alleviating poverty or cleaning up the environment, it was argued, while the Pentagon was denounced for its selfish infatuation with smart bombs, airborne computer surveillance and mammoth tanks that could go 40 miles an hour. It was even insinuated that the generals and admirals were hand in glove with munitions makers with their astronomical overruns of hundreds of millions of dollars in developing the prototypes of these new weapons. Even if they work, it was maintained, they were so expensive that the armed forces never could afford enough of them to win a major war.

But after two days of Desert Storm it was clear that they *did* work and *would* win the Gulf War. It is true that the Pentagon released only films of smart bombs darting inside bunker embrasures and blowing them up, no pictures of stupid bombs hitting only earth, or failing to explode. But why should they? One might as well expect Babe Ruth to include in his scrapbook all those pictures of him striking out. Much was also made of the fact that the incredibly expensive B-1 bomber would not appear in the Gulf because the entire fleet had been grounded a few months earlier because of engine trouble. Military analysts and commentators, ever eager to improve their reputations at the expense of the armed forces, found in the fact that all of this revolutionary technology had been in the American arsenal for years somehow embarrassing to the Pentagon. Having trumpeted the failure of the Stealth fighter-bomber and Tomahawk missiles during their early innovative years, they failed to report that in the interval the bugs had been ironed out of them. In Iraq there was no saturation bombing à la World War II when a thousand four-engine bombers might flatten an entire city district in its intent to destroy a concentration of factories. Instead, a single well-directed explosive could now do the job, leaving the neighborhood intact. And Americans did believe their government had been humane in its attempt to reduce enemy civilian casualties, so that there was no thunder of denunciation—not even from the antiwar people—when a Baghdad air-raid shelter mistakenly believed to be an enemy command post was bombed with great carnage. Even so, those two direct hits left the surrounding area undamaged.

That was why after two days of war the antiwar movement fizzled. American distrust of the military had vanished. The same Americans who in 1981 had been evenly divided in their trust or mistrust of the armed forces ten years later gave them a whopping confidence vote of 88 percent. The next closest was the churches at 58 percent, and TV and Congress, in a tribute to popular judgment, were last and next to last respectively with 30 and 33 percent.

In just a couple of days, then, Operation Desert Storm had restored to the American people their faith in their fighting men and women and their pride in their country.

7

☆

Bad weather that cut Allied air sorties proved a boon to Saddam's troops in another, unexpected way: it granted them a respite in which to dig themselves deeper into the sands. When clearing weather brought the Allied pilots swarming aloft again, they found that the enemy tankers had buried themselves up to their turrets and were very much more difficult to root out. Also the search for mobile Scud launchers diverted much Allied air from its primary purpose of destroying both the enemy army's brains and body: communications, command posts, armor and troops. The Iraqis made the hunt even more frustrating by parking decoy launchers out in the desert. General Schwarzkopf was not the least annoyed by this distraction, finding the Scud as a military threat beneath contempt. "I'd frankly be more afraid of standing out in a lightning storm in southern Georgia than I would be in the streets of Riyadh when the Scuds came down," he declared in a remark that he came to regret. Even worse, the Iraqi AA gunners were beginning to score hits. They still shrank from using their radar and thus drawing Allied radar-seeking missiles, but by firing blindly and continuously like the Mongolian archers of Genghis Khan, filling the air with volleys of arrows, they were nearly as effective—especially against the British Tornadoes flying some of the most dangerous missions of the war. They struck at targets so low that one British pilot returned to base saying that he knew now that some camels were more than ten feet tall because he looked up at one.

Saddam Hussein sought to make propaganda capital out of the persons of those American pilots who were shot down and captured. Warrant Officer Guy Hunter of the Marines and Lieutenant (S.G.) Jeff Zaun of the Navy flying off *Saratoga* were paraded before television cameras while denouncing the war in stilted monotones as though reading from a script. Hunter said: "I think this war is crazy and should never have happened. I condemn this aggression against peaceful Iraq." Zaun, his face bruised and swollen, declared that "our leaders and our people have wrongly attacked the peaceful people of Iraq." When free after the war, both fliers said their scripted remarks were so absurd they were certain that no one would believe they were voluntary, while Zaun said his bruises were not from being beaten but self-inflicted, intended to embarrass the Iraqis so that they would not put him on television a second time—and they didn't. Even so, Allied pilots thereafter gave only their first names or initials when interviewed after returning from successful missions, and the flamboyant practice of painting "kills" on the fuselage of their planes was abandoned: no one wanted to be captured and exposed to Saddam's hospitality.

Saddam meanwhile had become desperate. His water-bug fleet was useless, his Air Force another cipher because his pilots, like the New Zealand kiwi, could not fly, while his Army was dug in and on the defensive. Within a week it was clear to everyone—but perhaps not to him—that his dream of picking off Saudi Arabia could not be realized. Thus, either from spite or plain stupidity, he began to fight back with bizarre tactics based on oil. He had already filled his line of anti-tank ditches facing the Allies with oil and kerosene intended to be set ablaze when the enemy offensive began. Now he deliberately befouled the Persian Gulf by opening the taps on Kuwait's Sea Island Terminal, a supertanker loading dock designed to pump 100,000 gallons a day. He also emptied the holds of five tankers berthed nearby into the Gulf's waters. What he expected to achieve by this outlandish move still baffles his opponents. Obviously even Saddam had nothing against thousands of neutral birds. To fill the Gulf with oil might inconvenience but never prevent an Allied amphibious operation, and the threat to Saudi Arabia's desalination complex 200 miles downcoast never arose. The damage to the Gulf's ecosystem, of course, cannot be measured and may never be known; but "the oil weapon," just like his Scuds, fizzled when Allied planes stanched the flow of oil by bombing the terminal's pipe manifolds. At first, reconnaissance photographs seemed to disclose far and away the greatest oil slick ever: some 11 million barrels, compared to which the Exxon Valdez spill of 260,000 barrels off the Alaskan coast was a mere black spot upon the sea. But then it was realized that the photo readers had mistaken plankton fields and seagrass beds for floating oil, and that the actual discharge was only 1.5 million barrels, still the greatest ever. About 20 or 30 percent of this came from Allied raids on Iraqi coastal targets.

Saddam's next move was equally puzzling: in the last week of January his pilots took to the skies—but to fly to Iran, where they were interned and their aircraft impounded. Eventually a total of 137 planes of all descriptions—the heart of his Air Force, including treasured long-range bombers and MiG-29 fighters—were in the hands of his erstwhile enemy. Why? Were the pilots deserting? Probably not, because transports and support planes had joined the exodus, suggesting that Saddam had made some sort of deal with Iran to give them sanctuary until he needed them. During his war with Khomeini he had done something similar: fearing a counterattack by the Ayatollah's Revolutionary Guards, he had hidden several hundred planes in other Arab countries, among them his then allies Saudi Arabia and Kuwait. But the counter-stroke never came. Although Teheran promised to return the Iraqi planes after the war, the West interpreted this to mean: "Believe that, and I'll tell you another."

Without air power, Saddam Hussein was powerless to defend either his troops or his civilians. Allied pilots now could be restrained only by bad weather or to a much lesser degree by the blind blunderbussing of Iraqi AA gunners. Saddam's troops and his civilians were now utterly at the mercy of Allied air, although the populace was almost always made to feel the effects of bombing rather than attacked as targets. Smart bombs made selected targets possible, and ended forever Giulio Douhet's nonsensical "strategic bombing" theories of winning a war by terrorist bombing of enemy populations. Laser-directed bombs were so incredibly accurate that they actually could *hit* anything *seen* from the air. Videotapes of them smashing into enemy buildings and bunkers did not entirely describe their horrible efficiency. Private screenings of tapes too shocking to appear on living-room TV sets showed a terrified Iraqi pilot in his cockpit while his crew chief frantically tried to get him airborne before a smart bomb blew them both away. Another such missile actually chased and obliterated an Iraqi crewman sprinting for safety.

Unopposed aloft, the Allied airmen now began concentrating on tactical targets such as armor—tanks, trucks and personnel or ammunition carriers—and artillery. The Kuwaiti Theater was organized into "killing boxes"—a repugnant phrase reminiscent of the Boer War. These were areas of about 400 square miles into which aircraft were sent with orders to destroy anything that moved. F-16s carrying phosphorus rockets would mark targets for other heavily-armed F-16s called "killer bees" to attack. With typical Yankee ingenuity American pilots quickly discovered how to find camouflaged or dug-in enemy tanks. Aware that the tank's steel plates soaked up sun during the day, they went scanning just after dark with infrared detectors, and the hidden monsters sprang into sight as though framed in magic lanterns. By mid-February Schwarzkopf's headquarters was reporting kills of a hundred enemy tanks a day. Soon many enemy crews were living inside their tanks like moles, so deep in the sands they could never have been freed in time for battle.

Others were believed to have perished in tanks dug so deep that they were suffocated by sandstorms.

In the last week of January the Iraqis, without ears or eyes to keep them informed, began four probing movements in battalion strength. Actually, they were groping—and three of these were repulsed in brief but bloody clashes. One unit, however, found nothing to its front and continued for six miles into Saudi Arabia until it reached and captured the town of Khafji on the Gulf. This was the first seizure of enemy territory since the start of Desert Storm, and the Iraqi press made much of this Mother of Battles. In reality, said Schwarzkopf, it was "about as significant as a mosquito on an elephant." Khafji's population of 45,000 had long since been evacuated and the town was undefended except for a dozen Marine forward artillery observers. Holed up for 36 hours in a deserted apartment building, they mined the stairs and prepared to fight it out. They also called in artillery on passing armor.

But because Khafji was Saudi soil and the Iraqi media was hailing it as the most stunning Arab victory since the great Saladin drove the Crusaders from the Kingdom of Jerusalem eight centuries ago, this little-brother of battles had to be reversed quickly—and by Arabs. It was. After an occupation of less than two days, Saudi and other Moslem troops supported by American artillery drove the Iraqis back into Kuwait, leaving behind them 30 dead and more than 500 prisoners. Allied casualties were about 50.

The commander most impressed by Khafji was Stormin' Norman Schwarzkopf, for reports of the battle indicated that the Iraqis were poor or indifferent fighters, and he said later: "The Khafji attack was probably the time when . . . I really began to think: we are going to kick this guy's tail. The artillery couldn't put it together worth a darn . . . this was a lousy outfit."

But Saddam's soldiers continued to mass and maneuver on their side of the border, suggesting to some analysts that Khafji might have been a feint for a larger operation that never came off. Iraqi armor also appeared in strength, much to the delight of American fighter pilots tired of the hunt for mobile Scud launchers and dug-in Soviet T-72s. One column of 100 tanks was found rumbling like a herd of elephants down a Kuwaiti highway, only to be slaughtered in what one pilot called "a feeding frenzy." A-10s struck the first and last tank to trap the others and systematically destroy them. The Warthogs, firing up to seventy rounds a second of 30-millimeter shells about the size of an ordinary flashlight and made of depleted uranium denser than lead and able to pierce the thickest armor with ease, killed them all.

A single February week of tank- and artillery-busting from the skies had made it clear that Desert Storm was approaching the desired goal of 50 percent destruction of Saddam's armor and artillery that would signal that the ground phase of Desert Storm could begin.

The time and place of that great surge forward would be chosen by Stormin' Norman Schwarzkopf.

8

☆

Herbert Norman Schwarzkopf was born in Trenton, New Jersey, in 1935, the son of a West Point graduate and army officer of the same name and already famous as the Colonel Schwarzkopf who in 1934 as the first superintendent of the New Jersey State police conducted the investigation of the notorious Lindbergh baby kidnapping. From him, Stormin' Norman was to say, he learned "selfless service."

When he was twelve Norman joined his father in Teheran, where the U.S. Army had sent him as a brigadier general to train that nation's police. Seven years later General Schwarzkopf helped plan the coup that restored Shah Mohammed Riza Pahlevi to power. Ironically, the Shah's secular reforms so angered the Shiite conservatives led by the Ayatollah Khomeini that the Shah was driven from his kingdom, allowing Iraq, eventually led by Saddam Hussein, to emerge as a counter power to Iran. There thus began the younger Schwarzkopf's fascination with the Arab World. His father's globe-trotting career put an early polish on his son, who lived not only in Iran but in Switzerland, Germany and Italy, acquiring a fluency in both French and German.

When Norman could not accompany his father, he was placed in Bordentown Military Academy near Trenton, so that, as his sister

Sally said, he "wouldn't have to be home with three females." General Schwarzkopf's fears that too much feminine company might make his burly son effeminate were hardly justified, for he later starred as a big and bruising tackle at Valley Forge Military Academy near Philadelphia. At maturity Schwarzkopf stood six feet three and weighed 220 pounds, but as he grew older and developed a fondness for mint-chocolate-chip ice cream he reached 240. Although he would always be athletic, he did not play football at West Point, but rather showed more interest in military history and music, conducting the academy choir in his senior year. Apparently an affinity for music was a family trait, for a distant relative became an Austrian opera star. Schwarzkopf never lost his love of the opera.

But his first love was military history, in which he became profoundly learned. He also yearned for a combat command, and because he was only six when the United States entered World War II and fifteen when the Korean War erupted, he began to despair of becoming one of those "in-between" officers born at just the right time to miss all the big shoots. But then the Vietnam War erupted and he served two tours there, in 1964–65 and 1969–70, earning a reputation as an extremely brave and able officer, with a perceptive and original mind and a deep compassion for his troops that wisely stopped short of fraternizing or "leveling." "As a commander," he said, "you have to walk that difficult balance between accomplishing your mission and taking care of the men and women whose lives have been entrusted to you." During his second tour as commander of the Sixth Infantry Brigade this giant of a man showed the depth of his caring by crawling through a deadly minefield to rescue a wounded soldier. He was also deeply grieved by the number of American soldiers who fell victim to bombs and shells of their own aircraft and artillery. From this concern there came the book *Friendly Fire* by his friend C. D. B. Bryan.

Between his Vietnam tours Schwarzkopf met Brenda Holsinger, a 26-year-old TWA stewardess, at a football game—and they were married in 1967. They have three children: Cynthia, now 20; Jessica, 18; and Christian, 13. The general is a devoted family man, who believes that being a father gives a man moral strength. In times of stress, "you turn to the good Lord, and to your family, and more than anything else you call on that same inner strength that kept you going in a lot of other adverse times."

Like many another American officer, Norman Schwarzkopf was

shocked by the hostility of many civilians toward returning veterans of Vietnam, many of them wounded and decorated soldiers. He was stunned to find himself being called a "baby killer," and so outraged when his own sister Sally berated him in the typically abusive language of pacifism that he ordered her to leave his home. "I *hate* what Vietnam has done to our country!" he told the author Bryan. "I *hate* what Vietnam has done to our Army." Gradually Schwarzkopf began to doubt the morality of his own calling. "I was tempted to just bail out and go build myself a cabin in the wilderness," he told Bryan. But that, he knew, would have been a rabbity retreat, a victory for the pacifists and anti-militarists who took such gleeful comfort in contributing to their country's distress in Vietnam. Instead, he was one of those who fought for the all-volunteer armed forces, and there was no happier officer in the United States Army than Norman Schwarzkopf on the day when that revolutionary objective was obtained. An all-volunteer army is an army of professionals, well trained and well paid, proud of their calling and able to wage lightning war with clear objectives and massive concentration—the sort of war that Schwarzkopf hoped to wage in the Gulf.

General Schwarzkopf showed the world a commander of complex character not seen since the Union's William Tecumseh Sherman in the Civil War. As brave and brainy as Douglas MacArthur, he had none of that most illustrious American captain's hauteur, nor did he carry himself as the God of Battles like Robert E. Lee. Rather he was as warm, earthy and outgoing as Dwight Eisenhower. Like him, he had a quick, explosive temper that could instantly change, like the sun breaking through scowling storm clouds, into a reassuring grin. Sometimes called "the Bear" by his troops because of his size and massive head, he was actually "half-teddy, half-grizzly": as apt at consoling a frightened soldier as in chewing out a bungling subordinate. When in combat, he followed a spartan regimen—like Grant and Lee—sleeping in a bare bedroom devoid of furnishing except for a table on which rested a Bible covered in camouflage cloth, an exercise machine and a loaded shotgun. But of all his characteristics, his most outstanding quality was his deep compassion for his troops, a concern at least the equal of George Washington's. As he said: "Every waking and sleeping moment my nightmare is the fact that I will give an order that will cause countless human beings to lose their lives." But like Lee and Grant and John J. Pershing, once he was convinced that the order he was to give was the right one, his iron will would not allow him to alter it.

That was why during the Gulf buildup and the early stages of the fighting, which he had entrusted to Air Force Lieutenant General Charles Horner, he sat every morning in his Riyadh headquarters staring half-fearfully, half-eagerly at a wall map of Kuwait. Saddam, he knew, was thickening his fortifications, having given up all hope of conquering Saudi Arabia and preparing to keep Kuwait in a defensive battle. Directly across from the Allies in eastern Saudi Arabia he had created a vast network of minefields, oil-filled ditches, steep sand berms and deep trenches, all intended to channel the attacking enemy into killing lanes, fields of fire on which field artillery and tank guns were registered. This was the tactic that had worked against Khomeini's emotional Revolutionary Guards, fighting a 21st-century war with the religious fervor and arms of Saladin's twelfth-century suiciders. Norman Schwarzkopf had no desire to command an army of martyrs. He did not wish to gain victory by ardor alone rather than skilled bravery, to see his troops shredded by machine-gun crossfire or gasping in hideous death among clouds of poison gas, his tanks blundering into minefields and blown to bits. But how to avoid this and still get at Saddam?

It has been said that Schwarzkopf found the answer to this morose question when he remembered one morning how Bernard Montgomery had won the Second Battle of El Alamein in 1942 by a wide turning movement against the master tactician of World War II: Field Marshal Erwin Rommel. But this, granted Schwarzkopf's knowledge of military history, can hardly be true. The truth is that Rommel was then (late October) lying sick in a German hospital and that the little-known General Georg Stumme had replaced him, that Montgomery possessed an overwhelming superiority in men and arms of about six to one and that his forte was never maneuver but rather the set-piece battle, in a word, frontal assault—which is exactly what he ordered and very nearly lost. Rather what the American general probably realized as he studied his wall map of Kuwait was that this was desert warfare, on terrain made for maneuver because—like the sea—it has few or no physical features with which to shield an army or anchor a flank. This might have come from his reading of *The Seven Pillars of Wisdom* by the British Arabist T. E. Lawrence, in which he describes General Allenby's Arab campaigns in World War I. Whatever the reason, it is true that Schwarzkopf realized that on the desert you can, as in the jargon of baseball, "hit 'em where they ain't." And that was why he made a secretive trip to Hafar-al-Batin in far western Saudi Arabia to test the compactness of the sand there and discover that not only tanks but wheeled vehicles as well could pass over it.

Here was the critical decision of the Persian Gulf War, and it was reached in the light of Schwarzkopf's knowledge that Saddam had begun to concentrate his troops in eastern Kuwait in anticipation of an amphibious assault by U.S. Marines. This had left his right or western flank wide open. Here indeed was the opportunity for a wide and deep turning movement comparable to MacArthur's great stroke at Inchon in Korea in 1950. It could be made without detection because the destruction of Saddam's air power had left him without aerial reconnaissance, operable communications or spy satellites to track enemy troop movements: in a phrase, deaf, dumb and blind.

Thus, ten days before the ground offensive began, Stormin' Norman sent the U.S. XVIII Corps and VII Armored Corps, together with the British First Armored Division and the smaller French 6th Armored—a total of 200,000 men—on a silent, secret sweep into Saddam's empty western flank. Their mission: when the ground fighting erupted, they were to penetrate southwestern Iraq in the first hours of combat, moving north until opposite the Republican Guard, and then wheel to the east or right to trap and destroy Saddam's elite formations. Because of Schwarzkopf's devotion to lightning war, he had the parallel obsession with the importance of supply. Thus his trip to the desert to test the sand had been to make sure that his huge fleets of trucks carrying mountains of supplies—beans, bullets and black oil—would be able to establish forward supply bases. This was Schwarzkopf's *coup de main*—his decisive "left hook"—while with his right he would attack north through Saddam's barrier system, either penetrating it or so distracting it that it could not detach units to help the embattled Guard. Offshore were 17,000 U.S. Marines poised to assault the Kuwaiti coast. But they would never get their feet wet, for Schwarzkopf had wisely and humanely decided that they had already by their mere presence compelled Saddam to concentrate in the east and empty his western flank. Why, then, suffer unneeded casualties for an objective already obtained? Headquarters Marine Corps did not like this tame assignment at all, but Schwarzkopf remained firm, thereby earning the undying gratitude of thousands of young Leathernecks not quite so thirsty for glory as the armchair generals in the Naval Annex, and actually pleased at the prospect of sailing home in troop holds rather than inside body bags.

Thus, by February 21, 1991, with H-hour set for 8 P.M. Washington time, or between 4 and 6 A.M. in the desert, the ground assault that was to crush Saddam and drive the Iraqis out of Kuwait was to commence.

But on that same day Mikhail Gorbachev, still trying to save the face of his former client in Baghdad, seemed to have pulled the rug out from beneath the feet of his friend George Bush by proposing an eight-point "peace plan."

The Soviets on February 15 had already cooperated with Iraq in a peace initiative. On that day Baghdad Radio broadcast a proposal that some members of the Allied coalition at first believed to suggest the possibility of a peaceful solution. Actually, it was hardly more than another attempt to link the Palestinian question with any possible withdrawal from Kuwait, although it did for the first time use the word "withdrawal" and omitted the customary reference to the emirate as the "19th province of Iraq." It also made a vague reference "to deal" with the first of the UN's 12 anti-Iraqi resolutions ordering Saddam out of Kuwait. But it also described the Allied coalition as "an imperialist Zionist colonialist" conspiracy and repeated the demand that Israel withdraw from occupied Arab territory. In the end, President Bush, eager to move against Saddam now that Schwarzkopf had his offensive in place, refused to budge and described the "offer" as "a cruel hoax."

But Bush could not be so arbitrary with Gorbachev, whose cooperation had been and remained vital. So he adopted a conciliatory stance, never for a moment wavering in his inner determination to strike unless all 12 UN resolutions were accepted by Saddam. Unfortunately, Gorbachev's proposal of a "full and unconditional withdrawal" from Kuwait over three weeks and immediate release of prisoners of war fell on some accommodating ears among the Allied powers. They seemed willing to negotiate. In Washington one ranking State Department official cursed aloud and lamented: ". . . he [Gorbachev] has finally done it. He's split the coalition." Ever careful not to offend those super-sensitive Soviets, Bush pretended to consider the proposal. While supposedly "studying" the plan overnight, he and his aides spent hours on the telephone persuading their allies to reject it. But then Saddam Hussein, the high priest of blunder and bashaw of botch, came to Bush's assistance by setting the Kuwaiti oil wells on fire.

The Iraqis had already torched about 50 wells in what Allied intelligence misinterpreted as a minor nuisance intended to confuse American pilots by creating infrared hot spots and hiding targets. But on February 21 the systematic destruction of as much as three-quarters of the emirate's oil industry was begun. Well heads were packed with explosives to destroy valves and other controls, after which they were ignited, sending flames shooting fifty feet into the air and creating such a cover of greasy black smoke over Kuwait that actually created a darkness at noon. Pipelines, storage tanks and refineries were also wrecked. Saddam, it was clear, was now intent upon destroying Kuwait's single source of revenue. But he also gave the Americans the ineluctable argument that here was proof that he was an untrustworthy neurotic, and the Soviets said nothing when Bush flatly rejected their proposal.

The war would go on, and the ground offensive was scheduled to commence at noon Washington time, February 23—actually eight hours before Schwarzkopf's forces did go into action. All that the Soviets had done was to grant the Allied commander the two extra days of preparation time he had earlier sought and been denied.

9

☆

By General Schwarzkopf's calculations his Allied army possessed a slight numerical superiority: 500,000 Americans and 200,000 other troops facing about 540,000 Iraqis. Actually, postwar reckoning placed Saddam's strength in Kuwait at about half that number. Even so, traditional battle doctrine holds that an army in assault must possess a 3 to 1 advantage, and even 5 to 1 if the enemy is as well fortified as the Iraqis were supposed to be. However, Saddam's first-line troops were his worst—draftees eagerly awaiting the opportunity to surrender—while his best in the eight divisions of the Republican Guard were far to the north in reserve. Here was another of the amateur Saddam's numerous mistakes. He just could not help getting things backward.

Most of these troops were hunkered down along the Kuwaiti-Saudi border behind the layered barrier of minefields, sand berms, barbed wire and oil-filled trenches—all backed by tanks and heavy artillery. This was where Saddam expected the main thrust, just as he anticipated the amphibious assault from the 31-ship armada cruising opposite Kuwait City. Once again, by fighting according to Saddam the enemy was to be as obliging as Iran had been. But Schwarzkopf's battle plan was nothing like what the Father-Leader expected. That 200,000-man left hook was already in place 300 miles from the Gulf, across the border from the mostly empty desert of southern Iraq. The battle plan also provided for narrowly focused penetrations through the main Iraqi fortifications. Even if they did not succeed, they would serve the purpose of holding the enemy in place while that roundhouse left got into the Iraqi rear. There is nothing in battle quite as demoralizing as the cry, "The enemy is behind us!"

Out of Schwarzkopf's fear that his troops might be met by a full-scale poison-gas attack from heavy artillery firing chemical shells, the Allied chief had a week before ordered General Horner to concentrate his bombing attacks on Iraq's big guns. This was done, and with such spectacular effect that Saddam's artillery was neither as crushing nor as accurate as had been feared. Meanwhile, special-forces troops were already deep inside Iraqi territory. Landing by helicopter, they reconnoitered the terrain, fixing enemy tank, troop and artillery positions so that they could call air strikes upon them as well as guide advancing troops. As the deadline approached, tanks equipped with bulldozer blades began cutting lanes through the border berms so that Allied troops and tanks might pass through during the night in probing attacks. Also in darkness the giant B-52 bombers struck at Iraqi positions while helicopter gunships swarmed over Saddam's defense system, machine-gunning enemy troops in their trenches and firing rockets at tanks and field artillery. Allied howitzers and multiple-launch rocket systems also began to bay and swoosh, scouring Iraqi trenches with thousands of shrapnel-like bomblets. Between 4 and 6 on that momentous morning of February 24, 1991, in the last few hours of darkness so as to profit by their superior night-vision equipment, the Allied attack began.

All along the 300-mile front Allied troops moved out in their camouflage suits and coal-scuttle helmets, lashed by a heavy and pelting rain that turned the sands into a doughy goo. It sucked at their boots and sometimes pulled them off, but they still stumbled forward. Soldiers in these penetrations at selected points were hampered even more by their bulky chemical-warfare gear. But the clouds of poison gas that terrified Allied planners and haunted the dreams of Norman Schwarzkopf never appeared. On the right flank, the U.S. 1st and 2nd Marine divisions were hitting the critical junction known as "the elbow," where the border of Kuwait with Saudi Arabia turns north, and then "the armpit" where it abruptly sweeps west again. They were like the pipe fittings that a plumber would cut with his welding torch to destroy a system. Here the Leathernecks were led in person by Lieutenant General Walter Boomer, the top Marine in the Gulf, who was widely admired for his audacity, although not by those planners who got the chills when his final battle plan arrived in the Pentagon. But it was approved, and now his troops and all others hammering away at the border fortifications were discomfiting the enemy with ingenious tactics and devices that made the Saddam Line about as tough to crack as a custard pie. For weeks Allied troops had been building berms and replicas of other enemy installations, practicing assaults on them, like a football team rehearsing a play, until they could literally go through the proper motions in the dark. Pilotless drone planes or remote-controlled vehicles guided troops to the weak points in the enemy barriers. Minefields were safely passed by the use of "line charges," hundred-yard strings of tubing stuffed with explosives that blasted paths through them for tanks and armored carriers. They drove through them slowly and in absolute radio silence, the drivers communicating by hand signals. But they provided perfect penetration—even in the dark—by the use of night-vision glasses.

The fear of encountering trenches filled with burning oil was as baseless as the dread of poison gas. In the Marines' sector, American aircraft set the oil afire prematurely by bombing it with napalm. When the Saudis were confronted by trenches full of blazing petro-

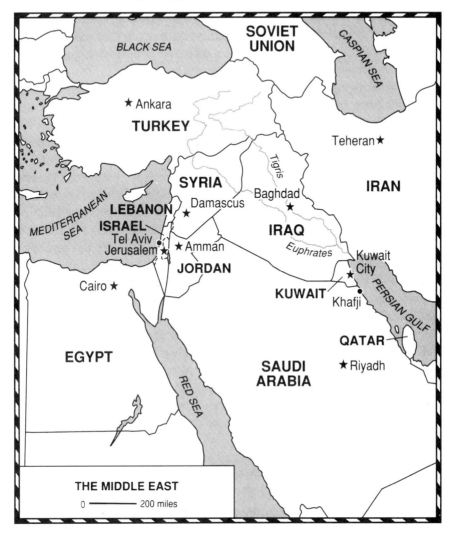

THE MIDDLE EAST

0 ——————— 200 miles

leum or sometimes just water, they passed them by the simple expedient of having tanks and bulldozers fill them with dirt. It was thus, in complete silence except for the rumble and rattle of the tanks and other combat vehicles, that the Saddam Line was penetrated: not in bloodbaths that were to endure for weeks or months as Saddam had predicted with gloating glee, but actually in near-bloodless hours. Total Allied casualties for the first day of combat were 4 killed and 21 wounded—including the fighting on the western front—and once the Allies burst through the supposedly impregnable enemy defenses they began a war of speed and lightning maneuver that left no doubt as to the outcome of Schwarzkopf's offensive, but only a question of how many days it would take to complete it.

Again and again the Allies bypassed heavy concentrations of enemy troops and armor, calling in punishing air strikes or tank and artillery fire whenever they encountered opposition. Except when the Iraqis began to surrender, it was seldom indeed that the troops of both sides ever saw each other face to face, let alone fought hand to hand. American technocracy, the new American volunteer troops, were simply too professional, too well tested in laboratories or proving grounds, too well trained on deserts or in helicopters or landing boats, to fight a war at anything but arm's length. As General Schwarzkopf was to say after the war ended, "Let me tell you why we succeeded: superb equipment." The enemy generals simply could not believe that anyone would attempt a flanking movement over the barren desert covering 200 miles in a period of two days. "Hey," Schwarzkopf continued, "nobody could drive over all that desert that far without their tanks breaking down and their equipment gone to hell." But they did, especially those much-maligned Abrams tanks, which, according to the Cassandra analysts, were prone to break down once a mile but never did. Even more astonished were Saddam's Republican Guards when those bellowing mammoths came bursting out of the west at speeds of forty miles an hour.

On the far left the first troops over the border were those of the French 6th Light Armored Division, who jumped off before dawn with the U.S. 82nd Airborne Division. Their objective was the fort and air base at As-Salman 105 miles inside Iraq. En route French Gazelle helicopter gunships firing HOT missiles and American artillery encountered and conquered an Iraqi force of armor and infantry, many of whom surrendered.

To their right the U.S. 101st Airborne Division launched a deep helicopter penetration of southeastern Iraq. Chinook choppers skimming low over the sands, some of them with Humvees—the newest version of the Jeep—slung under their fuselages, carried 4,000 men and their equipment deep into the desert, where they established a huge forward supply depot. Next they drove farther north toward the Euphrates, to cut or seize key highways and block any Iraqi retreat from Kuwait. Throughout that morning and the afternoon various other Allied formations swarmed into western Kuwait: seven U.S. Army divisions, the British 1st Armored and various Saudi, Syrian and Egyptian units. All moved with breathtaking speed, reaching their farthest objectives in a single day. Typical of this rapid movement was the 1st Marine Division's drive to al-Jaber Airport, half the 40-mile distance from the Saudi border to Kuwait City.

Speed was again the watchword the following day—Monday, the 25th—when all units measured their progress in miles. On the far left the French, having taken As-Salman in 36 hours, were ordered by Schwarzkopf to wheel and face west to guard against an Iraqi sally from that sector; on their right the 101st Airborne sped higher north toward the Euphrates; and as American, British, Syrian, Egyptian and Saudi forces drove deeper into Kuwait, on the far right the U.S. Marines clanked closer to Kuwait City. It was then that the phenomenon of mass enemy surrender witnessed during the first hours of combat actually exploded into a frenzy of capitulation. "They just keep dropping their gear and raising their hands," said one bored veteran of the Big Red One. "I've seen hundreds of them."

Waving white flags, handkerchiefs, scarves, opened copies of the Koran—anything white—as well as surrender leaflets the Allies had air-dropped by the millions, they greeted the Americans more as liberators than as captors. Many of them seemed to be well fed, but those tank crewmen who had been living like moles in their subterranean steel warrens were weak and emaciated. "When we fought Iran," said one of them, "we had breakfast, lunch and dinner, but here we had little to eat and almost no water." Another moaned: "Bombs! . . . Bombs . . . bombs . . . bombs . . ." Emerging from their bunkers by the hundreds, they began lining up in the desert until there were thousands of them, guarded by a few yawning military police, all awaiting transportation to the prison camps already constructed for them in anticipation of just such an event. To them imprisonment was sanctuary, not only from those ubiquitous American bombs and bullets but most of all from the detestable dictator who was the author of their misery.

Many of these disillusioned but now overjoyed Iraqi soldiers did not hesitate to embrace and kiss their captors. Sergeant Gary Mills of the Army engineers told reporters that when his bulldozer became stalled in the desert he saw a party of Iraqi soldiers approaching him and reached for his rifle. At once they threw down their own weapons and came rushing toward him smiling and crowding around him until his rifle muzzle was sunk in one man's stomach. "Get going!" Mills growled menacingly, but the Iraqi merely grinned and kissed him on both cheeks. In other ludicrous incidents, about forty of Saddam's soldiers tried to surrender to a pilotless drone plane circling overhead, while another motorized group, finding an American Humvee stuck in the mud, pulled it free and then made themselves the driver's prisoners. In two days no fewer than 30,000 Iraqi soldiers surrendered, and by the war's end an estimated 60,000 to 100,000 were behind barbed wire. Although it was indeed pleasurable to be kissed rather than shot by these reluctant soldiers, American battalion and regimental commanders were driven to distraction providing for them, and thus they had the effect of slowing the Allied advance: a novel tactic for which the discomfited Saddam Hussein made no haste to claim credit.

Schwarzkopf with becoming gallantry was quick to observe that these mass surrenders did not necessarily mean that the Iraqi soldiers were cowards. Most of them, he observed, were in uniform against their will and in Kuwait only because they had been ordered there. Often without food or water, many of them were sick and probably made sicker by a system of medical care that was either primitive or non-existent. Many had been terrorized by their own commanders, who had threatened to kill them if they tried to desert, employing roving execution squads to shoot anyone found in a rear area without satisfactory explanation.

On Monday also Baghdad radio broadcast an inexplicable order to withdraw from Kuwait, and although this was later repudiated, many of Saddam's soldiers obeyed with alacrity. Citizens in Kuwait City awoke with the joyous sound of tank and truck motors being revved up; but the noise did not signal the arrival of their Allied liberators, but rather the roaring engines of Iraqi soldiers heading north. Those who stayed behind to fight were mercilessly exterminated by the Allies. That afternoon when the 1st Marine Division's spearheads entered the Burgan Oilfield near Kuwait International Airport they met stiff resistance. At once the enemy was located and the order given to destroy them with a "time on target" (TOT) artillery bombardment. This is the opposite of a rolling barrage, in which the guns "walk" their salvos into and through the target, at intervals of about fifty yards. Thus during TOT all batteries fire at the same time on the same limited target until the enemy is either destroyed or flushed into the open. At Burgan they were routed from the oilfield by a combined blast of artillery, small arms and fire from Cobra helicopters and tanks. Some 50 to 60 Iraqi tanks and an unknown number of troops were lost in this brief but bloody engagement. There were no Marine casualties.

At almost the same time, however, one of the American tragedies of the war occurred. A Scud missile aiming for Riyadh broke up in flight, thus making it impossible for Patriot missile equipment to track it. The warhead fell on an American barracks near the great base at Dhahran, killing 28 soldiers and wounding 90 more.

When dawn broke over Kuwait City on Tuesday the 26th—the third day of battle—the sound of motors coughing into life was indeed that most desirable signal for which the Kuwaitis had yearned for seven long months: the unspeakable, detestable Iraqis were pulling out. Why they left is still not exactly clear, but their departure did spare the city the agony of the kind of street fighting that turned Stalingrad into a dreadful rubble of blood, flesh and fragmented concrete during World War II. By mid-afternoon Kuwaiti resistance fighters were in control of the city, gradually eliminating enemy snipers one by one. Above the town roads leading north to Basra, military headquarters for the Kuwait Theater, were so jammed with bumper-to-bumper vehicles that one pilot from the carrier U.S.S. *Ranger* compared the monster gridlocks to "the road to Daytona Beach during spring break."

Allied bombing of the bridges and roads was extensive. The few routes north that had been left undamaged drew traffic like magnets, producing bottlenecks that in turn created enormous traffic jams stretching for miles in either direction. The main road from Kuwait City to Basra attracted so many Allied planes that alarmed combat air controllers, fearing collisions aloft, redirected many of them to secondary roads.

Pilot after pilot described attacks on tank columns in which crews abandoned their steel colossi the moment the first Iraqi tank was hit, electing to trudge homeward on foot—a tiny, insignificant target not worthy of the smart missiles reserved for those enemy LSTs, "large stationary targets,"—the Soviet Tiger tanks. There were so many abandoned vehicles visible and *Ranger* pilots were so eager to refuel and return to the attack that they had their planes loaded with whatever bomb or missile was available on the flight deck, rather than wait for the correct projectile coming up on agonizingly slow ordnance elevators. Eventually a full mile along the Basra road was an enormous and hideous junk yard and choked from end to end with twisted, smoking, blasted, burning tanks, trucks and other vehicles, some of them torn open by smart bombs like can openers, many of them still crammed with pathetic loot: TV sets, toys, clothing, silverware, jewelry, radios, furniture, carpets and bottles of that perfume so cherished by Arabian males and females alike, its rare, subtle scent mingling with the pervasive sticky-sweet smell of decaying human flesh. Those Iraqi soldiers who did reach the Euphrates sought to replace its fallen bridges with pontoon spans, but these too were shattered by Allied air so that the more daring of these fugitives crossed the ancient river of civilization by walking tightrope over narrow earthen dams. Some Allied units had reached the Euphrates by Monday, and by Wednesday they were there in enough strength to prevent any further crossings. In the east British units cut the Basra road on the same day, after American Marines severed it farther south on Tuesday. The gate had been slammed shut on Saddam's army in Kuwait. It had no escape routes and was completely surrounded.

It was on Wednesday—the fourth and last big day of battle—that the two major tank engagements of the war were fought. At Kuwait International Airport the Marines, moving without aerial support under skies so dark with smoke from burning oil wells that Major General Michael Myatt had to read his map by flashlight, ran into a large force of Iraqi armor. Even without closeup air they attacked, destroying all 100 tanks that opposed them, with extremely light losses of their own.

Wednesday also saw the liberation of Kuwait City completed. Quite properly Arab troops—Saudis and Kuwaitis—entered the emirate's capital first, followed by the main body of U.S. Marines. A joyous, riotous celebration erupted, rivaling the arrival in Paris in 1918 of the U.S. 1st Infantry Division or the proclamation of V-E Day in New York City in 1945. Kuwaitis danced in the streets or indulged themselves in the Arab custom of firing automatic weapons into the sky. Many proper Moslems were shocked at the spectacle of pretty Kuwaiti girls kissing American Marines in the streets, but when a

Kuwaiti male knelt to kiss the feet of a Yank Leatherneck one of them cried aloud in anguish. "NO! No! No! Not even for Muhammad this! Such adulation is for Allah only." But the rejoicing continued far into the night, although it was somewhat tempered by reports that the departing Iraqis had dragged off some 40,000 Kuwaiti males as hostages, and that before they left had given rein to an orgy of sadism and sexuality, torturing and murdering men—poleaxing them in the forehead like so many cattle—and raping women. Such "horrible goings on" said General Khalid bin Sultan, the Saudi commander, would be punished, although he was unable to explain how the guilty would be located and identified.

On that same climactic day Stormin' Norman's decisive left hook surprised and finished Saddam's vaunted Republican Guard. These eight divisions were what the American commander had described as Iraq's "center of gravity." One of his staff officers explained: "The whole campaign was designed on one theme: to destroy the Republican Guard."

That destruction was begun as early as Monday night, when the British armored division struck some Guard units and destroyed a third of their tanks by concentrated artillery and tank fire. Fighting between Guard formations and the two American corps—XVIII and VII—also erupted Monday. An entire Guard division was knocked out of action. On Wednesday came the payoff as American and Iraqi armor exchanged body blows. Almost at once the Abrams tanks mastered the much-feared Soviet Tigers. In a one-on-one meeting an Abrams backed away to put itself out of range so that the Iraqi's first shot fell short. The American reply with its longer-range gun destroyed the Tiger, whereupon the Abrams swiveled around to seek other victims. In all, the so-called "elite" Guard was no more effective than Saddam's drafted cannon fodder. Some American officers insisted that they fought as well as could be expected without air and minimal, if any, communications, while under merciless aerial bombardment. But another Yank claimed that "basically we are chasing them across the plains, shooting as we go." Said Captain Kelvin Davis of a Marine armored battalion: "I hate to say it, but once we got rolling it was like a training exercise with live people running around. Our training exercises are a lot harder." A surer suggestion of the Guard's fighting prowess came when the men of one of its units actually took a cigarette break while the battle was raging around them. Unwarned by comrades fleeing for their own lives that onrushing American forces would soon engulf them, they were surprised and crushed. As Norman Schwarzkopf had said: "This was a lousy outfit."

By Wednesday, in a masterly briefing that was to make his name an American household word, General Schwarzkopf reported that 3,000 of the 4,700 tanks Saddam had in Kuwait had been destroyed, and added: "As a matter of fact you can add 700 to that as a result of the battle that's going on right now with the Republican Guard." What was left of Saddam's "formidable" army was a ragtag infantry force of reluctant soldiers, without armor, artillery or air power and certainly no navy. It was no longer capable of fighting modern warfare and therefore no longer a menace to its neighbors. Thus fulfilling the first objective of the war: to destroy Saddam's military power. The other, to evict Iraq from Kuwait, was actually in sight by the voluntary surrender and flight of his soldiers.

Thus on Wednesday, February 27, 1991, at 9 P.M. (5 A.M. in Kuwait), President George Bush went on the air to announce that he had decided to suspend ground operations. He had already been informed that in the 150 miles between the U.S. 24th Mechanized Infantry Division and the Iraqi capital at Baghdad there was nothing but empty desert. Said Colin Powell: ". . . there won't really be an enemy there."

"Kuwait is liberated," Bush reported. "Iraq's Army is defeated. Our military objectives are met."

The Persian Gulf War had been beyond question the most stunning feat of arms in modern military history, if not of all time. It had been won at an incredibly low price in human lives and suffering: at the latest count 148 dead and 513 wounded against probably 100,000 Iraqi casualties as well as those 60,000 to 100,000 who surrendered. No major war had ever been won with such speed: exactly 100 hours to deliver the knockout blows on the ground and about six weeks of aerial and naval bombardment, and thus shatter Saddam Hussein's dream of seizing Middle Eastern suzerainty.

There is, however, a melancholy postscript to this marvelous tale of minimal American casualties, and that is that 25 percent of them— 35 killed and 72 wounded—were due to "friendly fire." The dead numbered 21 soldiers and 14 Marines. No sailors or airmen were killed thus. There is nothing in any previous war to compare to this aston-

ishing percentage. In World War II there were 173 friendly-fire incidents and 90 in Vietnam, although the exact number of casualties is
not known. Here was grief indeed for the families of the bereaved, to
be informed that such an unsuspected wartime risk could exact such
a toll, and that their beloved sons, brothers or husbands were the
victims of their comrades' guns. And yet no other war was so swift-
moving and fought with such deadly weapons on such a broad front
in all kinds of weather and even at night, conditions almost guaranteeing fatal mistakes. Communications and identification simply cannot remain abreast of lightning warfare. An Apache helicopter pilot
armed with Hellfire missiles might be already aloft and homing on
his assigned target and never know that the men and vehicles below
him were not the foe but in fact friendly American troops who had
overrun their objective so rapidly that there had not been time to
inform him of who was actually beneath him. Casualties by friendly
fire are nothing new in warfare, not even in battles fought with spears
and bows-and-arrows, missiles that could also be misdirected. Probably the most notorious incident of deadly friendly fire occurred at
Chancellorsville during the Civil War, when Stonewall Jackson's own
men fatally wounded him. Nevertheless, this is scant comfort for the
relatives of the victims, and will do little to assuage their unspeakable,
uncomprehending grief.

As Sherman told the sorrowing people of Atlanta: "War is cruelty
and you cannot refine it."

10

☆

Winning the war had been incredibly easy, but winning
the peace was going to be difficult indeed. Moreover the question of
what to do about Saddam Hussein still remained unanswered. He had
been beaten and humiliated but at this writing (mid-November, 1991)
he was still in power. Still in power and still murdering and torturing.
Once the Shiites of the South and the Kurds of the north rose in

rebellion against the Father-Leader it became clear why he had so quickly accepted Bush's demands that he immediately release all prisoners-of-war, third-country nationals and Kuwait detainees; inform all authorities in Kuwait of the location of all land and sea mines planted there and comply with all UN resolutions, including the renunciation of all claims to Kuwait and reparation for all damage inflicted there. The reason: he needed what was left of his routed army—45 percent of his original 5,500 tanks, 39 percent of 3,500 artillery pieces and 51 percent of 500 aircraft—to suppress the Kurds and Shiites. This was done with the customary cruelty, so that the Allies, again led by America, had to intervene to prevent a war of extermination against the Kurds, hundreds of thousands of whom had fled from their homes to take sanctuary in the mountains of their homeland and in neighboring Turkey. Eventually, a protective cordon and construction of refugee camps lured them down from the hills. But in a country of 19 million people divided among the oppressed Shiites (55 percent) and Kurds (25 percent) and the oppressive Sunni (20 percent) chances of a peaceful reconciliation were very dim indeed, especially in a nation that has experienced five coups since 1958.

For the Middle East itself—that cockpit of ancient and abiding hatreds: between races and religions, haves and have-nots—the chances for peace or a stabilizing regional conference were hardly better. True, the good news is still that a dictator has been disarmed and that any potential strongman aspiring to that dangerous eminence will now have to exercise extreme caution. But this can change, once the special interests of all the nations occupying that mercurial region begin to collide again. When it becomes clear just how badly Iraq has been mauled—destruction of its roads and bridges, its power stations and telephone system, its desert sowed with unmapped mines and shells, its economy wrecked, and so many, many Iraqis dead and maimed or homeless, Shiites as well as Kurds—Arab rage among the shocked and grieving friends of Saddam, may erupt in a volcano of resentment that the present calm would have little chance to survive.

At present everyone in the coalition favors some sort of regional security apparatus made up of mainly Arab troops. Because the Western Allies made good so rapidly on their promise to withdraw their armies—a move that will reduce pressure on their partners from Moslem citizens still angry that the former colonizers and infidels had been called upon to suppress an Arab brother—there is also a feeling of gratitude. No one is now objecting to a continued U.S. presence in the region; heavy equipment left behind, joint military exercises, continued and increased American naval presence in the Gulf.

Even regional security is a local problem, and those oil-rich, sparsely populated Gulf states that would have been Saddam's chief victims are determined, in King Fahd's graphic phrase, that he or anyone like him "will never get up again." To prevent it they will provide their own security, and there has already been a meeting in Damascus between Egypt and Syria—the new powers in the Middle East—and the six Gulf states to plan just such a regional force. How Iran reacts to the discomfiture of Iraq is likely also to be a source of much secret speculation.

One problem that is probably insoluble is the region's enormous superabundance of arms. Israel, remembering the Scud attacks, has demanded that Iraq be stripped of all missiles and high-technology weapons, although Tel Aviv, along with Riyadh, obtained such arms during the war. But as much as President Bush and Prime Minister Major of Britain may press for a Middle Eastern arms-control agreement, there doesn't seem any likelihood that either the Arabs or Israel will agree to limit their arms.

This, of course—the Arab-Israeli conflict—is at the heart of all Middle Eastern turmoil. Although Bush and Baker hailed the great Gulf victory as the harbinger of "a new world order" and the chance to heal that enduring rift, these hopes have not been exactly realized.

At the beginning of the peace conference campaign launched by Secretary Baker it appeared that Prime Minister Yitzhak Shamir of Israel was unwilling to sit down with Arab nations if it meant trading captured land for peace or stopping Jewish emigrants from the Soviet Union settling those former Arab territories. These areas were the West Bank of the Jordan and the Gaza Strip seized by Israel from Jordon and Egypt, respectively, during the 1967 war, as well as the Golan Heights taken from Syria. He also insisted that he would sit down only with representatives from Arab states of his own choosing and would closely scrutinize any delegation from Palestine, where 1.7 million Palestinians remain in rebellion against Israel. Thus the Middle East peace conference sought so ardently by Bush and Gorbachev seemed to have been sunk, or was at least sinking.

But then came an unexpected lifeline from Lebanon. On August

8, 1991, the hard-line Arab allies of Iran freed the first of six hostages—three Britons and three Americans—eventually released by November 18. Even more dramatic, on September 11, Israel, in exchange for assurance that one of its missing servicemen was in fact dead, released 51 Lebanese prisoners and produced the remains of nine slain guerrillas, thus raising the possibility of a broad swap of prisoners, detainees and hostages. At this writing, that has not yet happened.

In the meantime Shamir made it quite clear that he does intend to people the occupied lands with Soviet Jewish immigrants. He had already requested that the U.S. guarantee $10 billion in American bank loans for Israel so that the money could be borrowed at reduced rates. Bush had agreed, providing that Israel promised the money would not be used to settle these areas. Shamir then made a calculated gamble on the ability of some 1,200 Jewish officials in forty states to persuade their numerous friends in Congress to enact legislation providing those guarantees with no strings attached, and also to continue to receive $5.6 billion in annual U.S. aid (the figure is often given as $3 billion, but it is actually much more) without seriously damaging the already strained Israeli-American alliance. This bombshell—for such it was—may have been motivated by Shamir's belief that time was of the essence in the settlement dispute, that to make the settlement of Soviet Jews an accomplished fact would win half the struggle before it could begin, and that time would assuage American displeasure. The speed with which these lobbyists in Washington did deploy suggests that this gambit had been well-planned and organized in advance.

Bush's response to it was immediate and decisive: he asked Congress to delay debate on the loan guarantees for 120 days, lest the fragile peace conference be shattered before the October conference could convene in Madrid. If it did not, and the law was passed, he would veto it. With American public opinion so solidly behind Bush, Congress turned a deaf ear to Shamir's appeal and the Madrid conference was indeed convened.

For the first time ever these ancient and bitter enemies—Arabs and Jews—did sit down at a peace table together. There was some acrimony, especially when the Syrian foreign minister, vowing nothing could be done *before* the Golan Heights were returned, also shook a "bloody shirt" before the assembly: a poster of Shamir as a youthful terrorist wanted for the murder of the Swiss diplomat Count Folke Bernadotte. But no one walked out and the Palestinian delegation did confer one-on-one with the Israelis, and it was agreed that another meeting among Israel, Syria, Lebanon and the Palestinian-Jordanian delegation would be held some time in the near future. At this writing the Arabs and Israelis are bitterly quarreling again over where the conference should be held, with the Arabs finally agreeing to Washington as a site, and the Israelis demanding Tel Aviv—thereby obtaining de facto recognition—or a venue somewhere in the Middle East. So the conference in Madrid did not accomplish much, but at least it was something; and it is better for old men to make war with words rather than for young men to kill and maim each other with bombs and bullets.

The hopes of Bush and Baker that the victory might create a political climate in which the first green shoots of democracy could sprout also seem to have been a bit too sanguine. Sheik al-Sabah of Kuwait still talks vaguely about "restoration" of popular elections, but none have so far been scheduled, even though the last of the hundreds of oil wells set afire on Saddam's orders have been capped and the tiny kingdom again basks in sight of the sun and hears the humming sound of oil pumps.

Nothing but lip service and very little of that has issued from the other kingdoms and emirates, while Kuwait, the special recipient of the Allied liberating triumph, has in its court-martial of "collaborators" with Iraq shown the world the same old cruel dynastic face. Twenty-nine of these pitiful people—stateless Arabs, Jordanians and Palestinians—were sentenced to death for the "crime" of doing for the Iraqi conquerors the same sort of menial labor that they had done for their Kuwaiti masters. Fortunately, worldwide horror at such absolute punishment for such minor crimes—if most of them were even that—and criticism by human-rights organizations changed the mind of Crown Prince Saad Abdullah al-Sabah, who commuted their sentences to life imprisonment shortly before the martial law of which he was governor expired at midnight June 27. This showed that Kuwait is at least responsive to outside outcry, although even life imprisonment seems to be rather harsh justice for mostly poor people who took petty jobs from the only available employers—the Iraqis—to keep soul and body together.

Only Iran among the Arab states seems to have been changed by the Gulf War. When President Hashemi Rafsanjani offered Saddam sanctuary for his airplanes, he placated his conservative critics who were pro-Iraq; by his failure so far to return them, he made friends with the Allies and also may have secured partial reparation for Iran's losses suffered in its own war with Iraq. Also Iran's neutral stance produced gratitude in the West, especially in Washington, and the weakening of Iraq made for a stronger Iran.

But by far the greatest change occasioned by the Persian Gulf War occurred in the United States of America.

When George Bush announced suspension of ground hostilities, he cried in exultation: "By God, we've kicked the Vietnam syndrome for once and for all!" He was right, and what he meant was simply that Americans had recovered their pride and sense of high moral purpose. Not since that melancholy midnight of April 29, 1975, when that last helicopter went whirling away from the roof of the U.S. Embassy in Saigon, had Americans as a people experienced anything but shame and dismay: shame that the Vietnam venture should be the one war their country did not win (although it also certainly did not lose); dismay at a succession of fiascos and failures ranging from seizure of the U.S. Embassy in Teheran together with its ambassador and staff of Americans in November, 1979, to the cowardly murder of 241 sleeping U.S. Marines in Beirut, Lebanon, in 1983, to a rise of terrorism in which Americans abroad seemed to be the chief targets, to the succession of space disasters in 1986, capped by the loss of the shuttle *Challenger* with all aboard, and, finally, to the growing embarrassment of the trade deficit, America's transformation from world creditor to world's chief debtor and what seemed to be its economic eclipse by the growing wealth of Germany and Japan. To these there may be added the government's obvious inability to win the so-called "war on drugs"—a policy as disastrously misguided as the attempt to enforce Prohibition—and thus restore law and order to the nation's streets. In truth, there seemed nothing to cheer about, and when Saddam Hussein swept into Kuwait on August 2, 1991, and George Bush spoke of sending American troops to the Persian Gulf, most Americans exchanged glances of apprehension and wondered aloud if here was not another Vietnam.

But it wasn't, chiefly because of the diplomatic skill of George Bush and James Baker, of the President's wise decision to allow the generals and admirals to fight the war, of the amazing American military technology, once so severely criticized if not gleefully derided, and the revolutionary shift from drafted to all-volunteer armed forces. Emergence of a commander of the caliber of H. Norman Schwarzkopf was also a great contributing factor toward the extraordinary unity and determination that characterized the American people during the Persian Gulf War.

Actually, it was incredible. Never before—NEVER—had Americans given such unreserved support to a war, not even to both world wars, probably the really only popular conflicts until the Gulf. All over America, in towns and villages, in cities and states, in schools and reception rooms, in stores and taverns, on rural front porches and from skyscraper windows, Old Glory was on display along with garlands of yellow ribbon or signs and banners proclaiming: "WE SUPPORT OUR TROOPS!" Enough yellow ribbon must have been manufactured to pave a four-lane highway from Maine to California and back again. And here was a puzzling facet of the Gulf War: this choice of color to salute brave men and women. Traditionally red has been the color of courage; as it is in the American flag or in the title of Stephen Crane's immortal novel: *The Red Badge of Courage.* Yellow has always been the color of cowardice. If a man is faint-hearted he usually is called "a yellow bastard," a phrase used by George Patton when he slapped that soldier in an Army hospital in France. But now yellow is also supposed to be the color of hope, and the custom of tying it around trees was begun by Penne Laingen, wife of L. Bruce Laingen, the senior diplomat in the U.S. Embassy in Teheran, who was among the 52 Americans seized there by Moslem revolutionaries. Mrs. Laingen made a huge yellow bow out of twelve feet of vinyl upholstery material and tied it around an oak tree in the front yard of her home in Bethesda, Maryland. She said her inspiration came from the hit song of the early 1970s, "Tie a Yellow Ribbon Round the Ole Oak Tree," which was based on a folk tale about a prisoner's homecoming. In January, 1991, Mrs. Laingen made another yellow bow for her two sons, Charles and James, who were naval pilots in the Gulf. After their safe return she donated the original bow to the Library of Congress.

Meanwhile, with astonishing speed all but about 28,000 of the 540,000 American troops assembled on the sands of the Saudi desert or the waters of the Gulf were brought home, and what a reception they received! Everywhere across America parades, brass bands, tearful embraces, joyous fathers hugging children born during their absence and festivals. It seemed that every tiny town and whistle stop had a hero to lionize, no matter whether he was a front-line tanker or rifleman or a rear-echelon specialist trained to interpret aerial photography. But the mothers of all parades were the one in Washington attended by a beaming George Bush and on June 10 in New York City, where about 25,000 marchers—including 12,000 troops from Desert Storm—strode up Broadway through the twenty-block Canyon of Heroes in a knee-deep blizzard of confetti. Reviewing them were the three grand marshals—Cheney, Powell and Schwarzkopf—and supposedly 4.7 million spectators, an estimate given by a New York police captain whose enthusiasm matched the crowd's. "U.S.A.!" they thundered. "U.S.A.!" Or else they chanted: "I love you! I love you!" They were saying what Ralph Waldo Emerson said in Boston at the outbreak of the American Civil War:

"We have a country again! Sometimes gunpowder smells good."

11

☆

On the last day of July 1991 thoughtful men and women throughout the world rejoiced to hear that in Moscow on that date President George Bush of the United States and President Mikhail Gorbachev of the Soviet Union had signed the historic Strategic Arms Reduction Treaty providing for the reduction by each power of 30 percent of its long-range nuclear weapons. Perhaps only slightly less important was the decision of Bush and Gorbachev to seize upon the rising impetus toward world peace by announcing that they would jointly convene a conference between Israel and the Arab states in October. Earlier, in another sign that cooperation might be replacing confrontation throughout a once bitterly bifurcated world, the Group of Seven—the globe's richest industrial democracies: Britain, France, Germany, Italy, Japan, Canada and the United States—

decided in London to provide technical assistance if not actual cash, to the U.S.S.R. to help steer it toward a market economy. It was expected that a later meeting might be held to discuss ways to provide humanitarian assistance—food, medicine, clothing, etc.—to the Soviet Union to help withstand its impending and inevitably brutal winter. No one was happier with these events than Mikhail Sergeyevich Gorbachev. It seemed to him that "the new world order," of which George Bush had spoken so enthusiastically after the Gulf War, was indeed at hand—and he could now turn from foreign policy, confident that his friendship with Bush was even firmer, to the domestic turmoil among the U.S.S.R.'s fifteen republics that threatened to tear the Soviet Union apart.

It had begun with the declaration of independence by the three Baltic republics of Estonia, Latvia and Lithuania, all forcibly annexed in 1940 by Stalin under the terms of a secret pact with Hitler. Gorbachev had told them that they could not secede except by "constitutional" means, meaning over a period of five years with his own foot on the brake and hand on the throttle. Nevertheless his failure to deny that the Baltics were inside the U.S.S.R. illegally, and his willingness to abide by their "constitutional" departure angered the hard-liners in his cabinet—all of them his cronies or appointees—just as they had been incensed by his cheerful farewell to the democracies of Eastern Europe. They did not realize that Mikhail Sergeyevich did not share their fear of foreign encirclement and believed that the Balkan buffer contrived by Stalin was too costly to maintain.

There were eight of these arch-conservatives, including Interior Minister Boris Pugo. A Latvian himself who had headed the KGB branch in the capital of Riga, Pugo conferred frequently with Gorbachev on the problem of the Baltic republics. He avoided discussing the legality of their presence in the Soviet Union, rather stressing the necessity of maintaining law and order lest the other twelve republics become infected by the secessionist fever. He also played to his chief's Russian sympathies by feigning concern for the many ethnic Russians planted in the Baltics by Stalin in accordance with his policy of diluting the racial consciousness of all but the peoples of the great Russian republic. Thus, when Pugo asked for permission to take "the necessary measures to assure that constitutional norms are upheld and the rights of minorities respected," it was granted.

In mid-January in the Lithuanian capital of Vilnius something called "the National Salvation Committee of Lithuania" made its appearance. It was supported by troops of the Soviet Interior Ministry: the dreaded "black berets." Early Sunday morning on January 13 formations of them attacked the television tower, defended by unarmed Lithuanian citizens, leaving fifteen dead and hundreds wounded. Appearing on television, Pugo said the National Salvation Committee had appealed to him for help and that the Lithuanian civilians had started the fight by "flashing bayonets" at his troops. Very few Soviets believed him, nor did they when the same sort of massacre occurred in Riga leaving five civilians dead.

Neither did Mikhail Gorbachev, who was furious with Pugo for organizing massacres aimed at him personally, which Gorbachev called "an attempt by reactionary forces to derail the process of reform." He denied responsibility for the bloodshed and ordered the military never again to attack civilians. But he did not move against the Old Guard, who, quailing at his show of infuriated authority, had retreated into the shadows.

Why not? The answer comes from one of Gorbachev's English-speaking aides with a fondness for the earthy idioms of the late Lyndon Baines Johnson: "Mikhail Sergeyevich felt it was better to have the camels inside the tent pissing out than outside the tent pissing in. He wanted to keep them where he could see them and where they would have to take orders."

History will show whether or not this had been the truth. More likely, the storm of discontent among the other republics following the Baltic massacres may have induced Gorbachev to move away from the reformers toward the hard-liners in order to preserve his own authority and reknit the unraveling fabric of the Soviet Union. History must also answer the question of whether or not Mikhail Sergeyevich actually understood that a new breed of Soviet citizens had emerged: better educated than their parents, less inclined to passive acceptance of the repressive decrees emanating from the Kremlin or to the dreadful regimentation of their lives, and also—most important—joyfully cherishing the free speech and freedom from fear granted them since 1985 by President Gorbachev himself. Nor is it yet exactly known how much of Gorbachev's toleration for his true enemies in the Old Guard was influenced by the steady encroachment upon his own power by his former protégé and present rival Boris Yeltsin, president of the huge Russian Federation.

* * *

Boris Nicoleyevich Yeltsin was born in 1931 in Sverdlovsk province of the Ural Mountains, growing up in a family so poor that all six members and their goat slept on the floor of a one-room apartment. His childhood, said Yeltsin, was "a fairly joyless time." As Yeltsin grew older he became what Americans would call "a wild kid." At age eleven he lost the thumb and forefinger of his left hand after he and his "hooligan" comrades stole two hand grenades from a military warehouse, unwisely fooling with them until one of them exploded. Something of a free spirit in grade school, he was expelled for denouncing a teacher as a sadist. Irrepressible and dogged, he pursued his tormentor relentlessly until the teacher was discharged.

At maturity Boris Yeltsin was a Russian of the Russians: tall, burly, with a thick shock of dark hair that would turn prematurely to silver, sunken bright blue eyes and a round, ruddy, cheerful Slavic face. In college his combative, often harsh personality and persistent questions annoyed his instructors, although he was eventually graduated with a degree in engineering. Thinking only of his profession, he did not join the Party until he was thirty. But his rise to become first secretary of the Sverdlovsk central committee was meteoric and he soon established a Party-wide reputation as a hard-hitting reformer and implacable enemy of sloth and corruption. When Mikhail Gorbachev became General Secretary in 1985 he quickly brought Yeltsin to Moscow as first secretary there and a member of the Politburo.

Yeltsin lost no time launching a scorching attack on the Politburo's moribund Old Guard. Scorning their love of luxury he rode on the subway or on packed, smelly, grimy workers' buses, scolding store managers because they had neither meat nor shoes to sell, trimming the dead wood from the city's payroll and arresting hundreds of dishonest officials. Eventually, Yeltsin's endless attacks on the waste and corruption of the Communist command society irritated his mentor Gorbachev, and in 1987 he forced him out of the Politburo—much to the dismay of the ordinary workers of Moscow. Given an unimportant sinecure as a sop and in the hope that it would silence his criticism, Yeltsin spent his fifteen months of banishment quietly building a political machine comprised of devoted followers who had been radical reformers during the bad days when indiscreet criticism brought exile or disgrace. They instructed him in the evils of the Stalinist past, including the rape of the Baltics, and how only a return to private property and conversion to a market economy could save an exhausted superpower that might possess 27,000 nuclear warheads and put cosmonauts in space but was powerless to feed its people.

In 1989 when Gorbachev went to the people in his campaign for reform, Yeltsin was ready. So were the people of Moscow. In the elections for a new Congress of Peoples Deputies—the first multicandidate nationwide election in the U.S.S.R. since 1918—the usually apathetic Muscovites gave Yeltsin, running as a delegate-at-large, a whopping 89 percent of the vote. Later standing for President of the Russian Federation, he crushed his Old Guard opponents with a landslide victory.

The disenchanted plotters of the Politburo Old Guard—who would one day be known as "the Gang of Eight"—now had to deal with Boris Yeltsin as well as Mikhail Gorbachev.

In the aftermath of the Baltic bloodletting, Mikhail Gorbachev was subjected to a storm of criticism from democrats and nationalists at home and democratic governments abroad. He found himself the man in the middle. On the right were Pugo and the other conservatives whose resort to violence had brought all this condemnation upon his head, and who were now further alienated by his refusal to allow them to complete the murderous suppression begun on Bloody Sunday, and on the left were Boris Yeltsin and his reformers steadily eroding his power. When Yeltsin exacerbated the Baltic crisis by flying to Estonia to sign "a mutual support pact" with all three breakaway governments, Gorbachev flew into an impotent fury, openly cursing Yeltsin as "that son of a bitch!" Yeltsin had already, with his frequently unsound judgment, called publicly for Gorbachev's resignation. Now it appeared a confrontation between the two presidents was inevitable.

But then came the crisis in the Persian Gulf, and Gorbachev's decision to side with the U.S. and most of the rest of the world against Saddam Hussein apparently placated Yeltsin and the left while further enraging the Gang of Eight. They did not see Saddam Hussein as Yeltsin's Foreign Minister Andrei Kozyrev portrayed him: "the child of our totalitarianism, who was nurtured under the care of our ideology and with the help of huge arms shipments." Rather the Father-Leader of Iraq was to them the victim of American imperialism and Soviet betrayal. The U.S.S.R. votes in favor of the UN resolutions were a sign of Moscow's toadying to Washington. In that frame of mind, when Shevardnadze resigned in December 1990, declaring that he feared a dictator was waiting in the wings, the hard-liners pressured Gorbachev to name their hand-picked candidate, Alexander Besmertnykh as his successor. To the democrats and nationalists, the president of the Soviet Union seemed to have taken another step away from them and closer to the Central Committee conservatives.

Outbreak of the air war upon Iraq had the hard-liners close to apoplexy. Most of Iraq's AA batteries were made in the U.S.S.R. and their gunners trained by Soviet officers. When the Allied air armada—mostly American—achieved complete surprise against these defenses and proceeded to scourge Saddam's armed forces at will, there were no cheerful faces among the generals and admirals assembled for the Defense Ministry's daily briefing and horror tapes on TV. The ground war was even more humiliating. Their client state's vaunted million-man army trained and armed by the Soviets collapsed in just 100 hours and with a casualty rate suggesting the most abject defeat in military history. Thus, in the late winter of 1991 the Soviet military leaders were extremely receptive to the appeals of the plotters.

And who were they?

Vice President Gennadi Yanayev was held in hilarious contempt by most perceptive Soviets as the faceless *apparatchik* and yes-man par excellence. His mediocrity was so obvious that the Congress of People's Deputies twice rejected his nomination to the country's number two office and approved it only after Gorbachev's unabashed arm-twisting campaign. Yanayev mechanically seconded all of his chief's reformist policies, but with no apparent enthusiasm.

Probably the most feared man in the Soviet Union was Interior Minister Boris Pugo. He was detested and reviled in his native Latvia as a traitor who killed and tortured with enthusiasm while he was the KGB chief in Riga. The son of a prominent Latvian Communist, his feigned devotion to the Soviet Union convinced Gorbachev that here was the ideal Soviet citizen, as it was intended to do, and the General Secretary made him the nation's top cop in response to hard-liners' complaints that the present one was too liberal.

Prime Minister Valentin Pavlov was an economist whose open

criticism of *perestroika* led his co-conspirators to select him for a verbal campaign intended to discredit Gorbachev. Among the people he was derided as "Porky the Hedgehog," a disparaging Russian nickname of unknown meaning, but probably expressive of Boris Yeltsin's hatred of him as a power-pig with seventy ministries under his control. During the attempted coup he would distinguish himself as a first-class coward and fence-straddler.

Gorbachev reappointed Defense Minister Dmitri Yazov in 1989 over the objections of the Supreme Soviet. Gorbachev was drawn to his levelheadedness and solid devotion to strict military professionalism. But this World War II veteran whose seamed and stony face seemed to suggest the heart of a hangman, while backing *perestroika,* attacked *glasnost* for allowing civilians to criticize the armed forces.

Oleg Baklanov was a Ukrainian and a weapons expert,. an important member of the Soviet Union's industrial-military complex who feared it would be emasculated by *perestroika.* He also sat on the shadowy but powerful Soviet Defense Council. Some Soviet experts believe that he was the Gang's mastermind.

Two other members of the Gang of Eight were Vasili Starodubtsev, a staunch advocate of collective farming who simply by protective reflex action opposed *perestroika,* and Alexander Tizyakov, a relatively unknown *apparatchik* in the mold of Yanayev.

Unsuspected as a conspirator at the time of the coup, Anatoli Lukyanov is now considered a leading conspirator if not the actual mastermind rather than Baklanov. He was a law school classmate of Gorbachev's who became one of his closest friends, rising to be Chairman of the Supreme Soviet, where he subtly used most of his power to subvert his benefactor's liberal legislation. Like Gorbachev himself, he would not hesitate to turn off the microphones of deputies who opposed him. He is believed to have set the conspirators in motion by assuring them that Gorbachev approved of their takeover. During the attempt, however, he remained offstage.

Valeri Boldin was another plotter not at first identified as a member of the Gang of Eight. Of him Gorbachev would one day say, with Julius Caesar, "*Et tu,* Boldin? You, too, Boldin?" He had been one of Mikhail Sergeyevich's closest aides since 1981, and had been elevated to the highly confidential and sensitive post of chief of staff in charge of the general secretary's agenda and appointments.

Of all of these men Gorbachev was to say ruefully: "These are people I have trusted. They have turned out to be not only participants against the President [but also] against the Constitution, against the people, against democracy. It was my mistake."

By mid-spring the conspirators felt strong enough to criticize Gorbachev publicly for continuing to tread the path to reform. Hoping to torpedo the growing rapprochement between the Soviet Union and the United States, Kryuchkov of the KGB repeatedly made the public charge that the CIA was secretly trying to sabotage Soviet society. Here was a subtle suggestion that advocates of reform were either dupes of America or its agents. He also insisted that throughout the world there were still "fundamentally conflicting interests" between the two superpowers. Some of Gorbachev's loyal aides began to have second thoughts. The tide seemed to have turned against their chief.

On March 17 a national referendum was held. It was sponsored by the Kremlin, and although it was typically vaguely worded, a negative vote would be considered support for Yeltsin. A positive vote would be a mandate for Gorbachev to reshape the relationship between the Kremlin and the republics as he saw fit. Although the referendum was close to a draw, the result was taken to be favorable to Yeltsin.

In joyful reaction to this moral victory Yeltsin and his followers announced that they would hold a rally in central Moscow to celebrate. Now the plotters acted. A meeting was held in Gorbachev's office at which Pugo warned that they faced the threat of "neo-Bolsheviks storming the Kremlin." He told Gorbachev that the rally was a direct challenge to his authority. In a fatal step, the president agreed to ban all rallies and to bring troops and tanks into the capital.

Alexander Yakovlev, the ideologue who was one of Gorbachev's most loyal and devoted aides, tried repeatedly to dissuade his chief from following such a dangerous course. A showdown with Yeltsin would only confirm suspicions that he had joined the reactionaries. It could backfire and strengthen Yeltsin. Gorbachev saw his peril and decided to take personal command of the forces marching into Red Square. He would order them to hold their fire. He did keep the troops in check, and the huge, orderly pro-Yeltsin demonstration was conducted without serious harm. Nevertheless, as Yakovlev concluded, it could never rectify the first serious mistake of attempting to intimidate Yeltsin and his people. It was probably this blunder that led Yakovlev eventually to join forces with Yeltsin. It also shook Gorbachev in his very soul. Although on reflection he had averted a disaster, for the second time he had unwisely listened to Pugo, Kryuchkov and the other hard-liners—and had again found that they were out for blood. Said one of his aides:

"March 28 was not just a turning point—it was *the* turning point for Mikhail Sergeyevich. He went to the abyss, looked over the edge, and was horrified by what he saw, and backed away."

Thereafter Gorbachev was ready to make common cause with Yeltsin and the other nine republics, which had had second thoughts about secession. His incisive legal mind immediately began to compose a new treaty between them and the Kremlin. It would transfer to them many powers, among them taxes, natural resources, and even state security apparatus. A new national cabinet would be named by representatives of the republics, meaning that such powerful ministers as Vladimir Kryuchkov of the KGB, Interior Minister Pugo and Defense Minister Dmitri Yazov would lose their jobs. Gorbachev set August 20 as the date for the treaty to be signed by the Russian and Kazakh republics, with the others to sign later. In the meantime, with his wife Raisa and his daughter and her husband, he retired to his vacation dacha at Foros in the Crimea. There he would relax and work on the speech he would deliver on signing day: August 20, 1991.

But two days earlier, the Gang of Eight, aghast at the prospective loss of their ministries and their power, as well as the democratization of the Soviet Union in what they considered to be the final humiliation of their Cold War defeat, decided that it was now or never.

As early as February 1991, according to British Intelligence, Soviet Army and KGB units were rehearsing a coup attempt not very well disguised as a counter-coup. In June Prime Minister Pavlov launched what might be called a probing operation by demanding that the Supreme Soviet authorize him to issue decrees without the consent or knowledge of Gorbachev. Rebuffed there, the Gang of Eight could see that the time to strike was not yet ripe. Here indeed was activity fairly shouting at Gorbachev to take heed, but he ignored it, perhaps because the plotters had been crying wolf so frequently that he could no longer listen. When Alexander Yakovlev warned him and actually gave him the true names of some of the plotters, he jeered at them as men who "lack the courage to stage a coup."

Ten minutes before 5 P.M. on Sunday, August 18, the telephone rang in Gorbachev's study at Foros. It was the head of the president's security guard reporting that "a group of people" were insisting on seeing him. Immediately wary, Gorbachev demanded to know who they were and how they got into the house. The guard replied that all he knew was that Yuri Plekhanov, chief of the security guards and his boss, had ordered him to allow them to enter. Now thoroughly alarmed, Gorbachev seized a telephone to call Moscow. "It didn't work. I lifted the second, the third, the fourth, the fifth. Nothing." His communications had been cut off. At once he hurried to warn his family that his unwanted visitors might "attempt to arrest me or take me away somewhere."

Hurrying back to his study he found Plekhanov with four others already there. The color drained from his face when he saw a somewhat sheepish Valeri Boldin among them. His own chief of staff, his most trusted aide—now his Judas! The other three were Oleg Baklanov; General Valentin Varennikov; and a party hack named Oleg Shenin. They identified themselves as members of the newly formed State Committee for the State of Emergency and demanded that Gorbachev sign a decree declaring an emergency and relinquish all his powers to Vice President Yanayev.

"You will never live so long," said Gorbachev.

Outside KGB troops had already surrounded the dacha and others drove tractors across the nearby airport runway to block the presidential jet from taking off. Mikhail Gorbachev and his family were trapped.

It was about twelve hours before the outside world knew that anything had happened to the Soviet president. But at 6 A.M. Monday, August 19 the Soviet news agency Tass reported that Gorbachev was ill and had temporarily delegated his powers to Yanayev. Later it announced formation of the Emergency Committee and the names of its members, half of whom were unknown to Soviet citizens. Yanayev was seen at once to be a puppet with the strings in the hands of Baklanov, Yazov, Kryuchkov and Pugo. Next the committee announced that it would rule for six months, promptly banning all protest demonstrations, ordering all but nine "loyal" newspapers to stop publishing while suspending all political parties.

Muscovites going to work that morning saw tanks and troops

moving through the streets to surround or seize key installations and strategic areas and realized with sinking hearts that a junta had seized power and that the gray old days of fear and fawning were coming back. There would be no more free speech except inside their own kitchens among trusted friends with the radio blaring and the shades drawn. And yet, eventually many of them sensed that there was nothing particularly ferocious or efficient about these conspirators.

In a coup it is imperative to move at once against all centers of power and all popular persons who might resist. But this clique of would-be revolutionaries was a half-hearted junta. They would speak admiringly of Gorbachev and hold out the prospect of working with him again. They seemed embarrassed by their illegitimacy and tried to cover themselves in a mantle of constitutionality, when they should have immediately killed Gorbachev and Yeltsin and scattered their followers, while letting the world know that they had seized the "black box" containing the Soviet Union's top-secret release codes for its 27,000 nuclear warheads. Ruthlessness and terror are the tactics of revolution, and these men showed when they appeared on television at 5 P.M. Monday, August 19 that, if they were not a pack of nervous clowns, they were still not to be taken seriously. Shaking and apologetic, they explained without conviction that because Gorbachev was so tired his authority had devolved constitutionally on Yanayev, a preposterous claim which, without Gorbachev present to support it or at least a letter from him, was also farcical. With starry eyes they professed a devotion to reform and would continue it. But their twitching eyes and trembling hands belied every word they said. "They said I was sick," Gorbachev observed later, "but they were the ones whose hands were shaking."

Gorbachev himself, though still a prisoner supposedly denied any communication with the outside world, had at least contrived to hear from it. His intensely loyal guards had found some discarded old radio receivers and rigged an antenna so that they could monitor worldwide coverage of the coup. Thus Gorbachev learned that the plotters had impressed no one, that Yeltsin was still defiant in his barricaded Russian Parliamentary building, and that his friend George Bush, though at first hesitant to condemn the coup as unconstitutional, had come out that very Monday in unstinting support of Yeltsin and against the takeover. From all this he took heart, and turned to composing his own condemnation of the coup. Fearing that he might be executed, he used his gadgeteer son-in-law's camera and recording equipment to make four tapes of himself to prove that he was far from "ill" or "tired." His final word on the tape was to the plotters: "Go to hell!" These he distributed among his family and guards to make sure that, if he were killed, one of them at least would reach the outside world.

From that outside world, Gorbachev heard the most joyful news. The Western powers had unanimously, though separately, denounced the coup and sworn to forgo any relations with the Soviet Union until the legitimate authority of Gorbachev was restored. They had cut off most of the economic assistance so direly needed by the U.S.S.R.

At noon Tuesday, August 20 an estimated 150,000 Muscovites, thrilled by the news of how Yeltsin on Monday had climbed on top of a tank turret to bellow his defiance of the clique and call for a general strike, assembled outside his headquarters known as "the White House" because of its marble facade. "We will win!" they roared. "We will win!" A thunderous ovation greeted the silver-haired Boris Yeltsin as he appeared on the balcony to shout: "We will hold out as long as we have to, to remove this junta from power!" That afternoon it became clear that the Emergency Committee was wobbling. Tass began broadcasting reports of the fierce spirit of resistance sweeping the U.S.S.R.: Patriarch Aleksei II of the Russian Orthodox Church had come out firmly against the coup, coal miners in Siberia had left their pits and resolutions condemning the coup were spreading like wildfire through the five time zones of the vast Soviet Union.

Nevertheless by Tuesday night Yeltsin and his followers realized that the showdown was at hand. Condemned throughout the world and vilified at home, the Gang of Eight had no choice but to back down or resort to force. As a Russian, Yeltsin expected the mailed fist. Throughout the night loudspeakers at the White House crackled with warnings that Kremlin troops and tanks were on their way . . . sixty huge aerial transports had begun taking paratroopers aboard. . . . Far from cowed, Muscovites began feverishly building barricades while human chains of unarmed protesters were formed to repel the expected onslaught with their bodies. An Orthodox priest in full vestments wielding a gold aspergillium sprinkled holy water and bestowed a blessing upon the throng, leading them in intoning the Lord's Prayer. Military reinforcements appeared in the tanks and troops of Major General Alexander Lebel's Tula Division. Lebel ordered his tankers to turn their turrets away from the White House. Although he issued them no ammunition, they became part of the barricade. About midnight shots and screams were heard nearby. Yeltsin's ragtag army braced for the assault. But no one came. There had been a scuffle between protestors and tanks around a trolley-bus barricade in which three civilians had died, the only casualties in the Muscovite Revolution.

By the morning of Wednesday the 21st hope lifted the hearts of the indomitable throng guarding Yeltsin's headquarters. The failure to storm the White House the preceding night was to them the signal of the junta's inevitable downfall. What they did not know was that a crack KGB unit ordered to storm the building had remembered Pugo's bloodbaths in the Baltics and refused to obey. Thus the despicable and detested interior minister had unwittingly been the instrument of the coup's failure. To atone for it, Pugo killed himself, after shooting and seriously wounding his wife. His comrades meanwhile were scurrying for safety. In mid-afternoon Yeltsin announced in the Russian Parliament that some members of the Gang of Eight were hastening to Vnukovo Airport to get out of town. A posse was quickly organized and eventually of the ten men actually involved, three were arrested and another four, flying to Foros to beg clemency from Gorbachev, were also taken into custody. The ninth—Lukyanov—was picked up later while protesting his innocence with starry-eyed dissimulation, and Pavlov was found cowering in a hospital which he had entered pleading a nervous breakdown. All nine—Pugo of course, was dead—were charged with high treason, a crime punishable by death. It is hoped that their trial will be an open one, for a closed one would lend credence to the absurd but still widely believed theory that Mikhail Sergeyevich arranged the entire affair himself.

Thus seventy-four years after Lenin's forces stormed the Winter Palace in St. Petersburg to launch the Russian Revolution that spawned the Communist Party and created the Soviet Union, a tumultuous, unarmed angry multitude of civilians led by Boris Yeltsin successfully defied the Kremlin and wrought the Muscovite Revolution that destroyed both the dreadful Utopian doctrine that tried to press them into a Procrustean bed and the evil empire that enchained them.

* * *

When Mikhail Sergeyevich Gorbachev returned to Moscow, jubilant but weary, making immediately for the White House to thank Boris Yeltsin for his decisive stand against the Gang of Eight, perceptive Soviets feared that the two men so disparate in method and personality—Gorbachev sophisticated and supple; Yeltsin blunt and triumphalist—could never work together. Their fears seemed justified by the flood of decrees issuing from Yeltsin's office, like the ukases of Lenin, some concerning sectors such as banking in which he had no competence, or his threat to "review" Russia's borders with the other republics. During Gorbachev's appearance with Yeltsin before the Russian Parliament his former protégé did not hesitate to bully him. Fortunately, most of Yeltsin's irritating declarations were withdrawn or modified, and after two weeks of heady, edifying glory he seems to have stepped back from center stage and left the role of arbiter to the president of the vanished Soviet Union. Probably Yeltsin is content to be president of the mammoth Russian Federation with more than 50 percent of the population and 74 percent of the land, and realizes that his enormous responsibilities there preclude him from attempting to run whatever new nation arises from the ashes of the U.S.S.R.

Though Gorbachev was probably completely—and pleasantly—surprised at this deferral, he did not hesitate to offer an olive branch himself. On Friday, August 23 the two men obviously in lockstep conducted a merciless purge of the central government, removing all top officials such as Foreign Minister Besmertnykh and others like him who didn't immediately denounce the coup and replacing them with trusted reformers. Next Gorbachev resigned as general secretary of the Communist Party, unreservedly condemning its record of oppression and repudiating it as a force in Soviet life. Together with Yeltsin he appeared on a television program beamed at America, and the very verb to beam adequately describes their performance.

"I think that the experiment conducted on our soil was a tragedy for our people," said Yeltsin.

Nodding, Gorbachev replied: "That model has failed. I believe that this is a lesson not only for our people, but for all people."

When the two men appeared together before the Congress of People's Deputies, Gorbachev remarked: "In any case, we are all one, side by side, and we shouldn't spit on each other." Yeltsin responded: "I personally believe in Gorbachev." And he reassured those deputies nervous about Russian power: "The Russian state, which has chosen democracy and freedom, will never be an empire, neither an older nor an elder brother. It will be an equal among equals."

After this exchange Gorbachev, who only a few days before was still an ardent Socialist, demonstrated that he was a living exponent of Nathan Bedford Forrest's famous dictum: "If'n you cain't lick 'em, jine 'em." He began by warning the deputies: "Let me tell you, The West is watching. If we are able to coordinate, unite within new forms, find new structures, the West will support us." Then to impress the West he put on probably the most masterful Parliamentary performance of his career, cajoling willing radicals and bullying unwilling hard-liners into entombing the stricken carcass of Soviet Communism and proposing in its place a new, free central government.

It would be composed of a State Council consisting of Gorbachev and the leaders of the ten participating republics charged with the conduct of foreign and military affairs, law enforcement and national security. A revamped Supreme Soviet would have a two-chamber parliament: the Council of the Republic to which each republic would send twenty to fifty-two deputies but each possess only one vote; and the lower Council of the Union with the size of each republic's delegation to be determined by population. An Inter-Republican Economic Committee would supervise the daily operation of a market economy and spearhead economic reform.

The proposal was approved 1,682 to 43, and the first act of the State Council was to recognize the independence of Lithuania, Latvia, and Estonia. On September 17 the trio of Baltic states was admitted to the United Nations, along with Micronesia, the Marshall Islands, and South and North Korea, the latter admissions suggesting that the great Communist watchword—"Nyet"—may also be dying in Asia. There was also later an indication that the new government would return to Japan the southern half of Sakhalin Island seized as loot by Stalin after about forty-eight hours of bloodless combat in the Pacific War. Next President Gorbachev gratified the United States and enraged an embittered Fidel Castro by promising to withdraw all 11,000 Soviet troops from Cuba and end all subsidies to that Communist island bastion ninety miles south of the American mainland.

To ram this not universally popular proposal through the Congress, Gorbachev used every wile and trick at a parliamentarian's command. First, to emphasize the importance of the republics, the plan was submitted by Nursultan Nazarbayev, the outspoken and immensely popular president of Kazakhstan. Thereafter Gorbachev actually cowed the deputies into submission, shutting off microphones to silence opposition, ignoring rules of order and scolding the deputies like so many naughty children. "If we can't agree on this," he told the deputies, "the Congress ceases to work." Finally, in a tour de force of persuasion, he induced the deputies to vote themselves out of existence, for which each received "perks" including apartments and automobiles and $175 monthly salary until 1994. Ironically, those who complained most bitterly about Gorbachev's "unconstitutional" conduct were the hard-liners who had supported—vocally or in silence—the aborted coup.

For the first time the concept of freedom and a market economy was embraced by the new government succeeding the Russian nation that came into being ten centuries ago, and by those sometimes backward buffer states that also never knew it. How long it will live cannot be stated with any certainty. There will have to be much improvisation and experimentation until the member republics and the central government come to agree on a viable confederation. Because of the welter of different races, languages and religions it can never emerge as a homogeneous federal entity such as the United States of America, where the melting pot forged together an amalgam of mostly Western races and the freed African slaves, all of them speaking English and professing the Judeo-Christian religious traditions, together with today's alloy of Asians eagerly learning to speak the language of the land with some of them erecting mosques and temples. But it will be at least contiguous, not as loosely bound as the so-called British Commonwealth, its members possessing no central government and separated by oceans and continents as well as languages, races, customs and faiths.

There are so many other questions: Who will wield the greater influence in the State Council, Gorbachev or someone like him or the republic presidents? Is a confederative president really needed? Will the political concepts of the writers of the new constitution be consonant or divided? If movements toward complete independence grow in the republics can the center hold the republics together? Finally, there is the possibility that the hardships and disagreements that necessarily must be endured to achieve real and voluntary cohesion may be found to be insurmountable by a people who never knew the Renaissance or the Industrial Revolution, most of them accustomed to a dependence on the state and given to envy anyone among them with a higher standard of living. If competition is rejected by them, a market economy will die, along with political freedom. To obtain and maintain freedom they will have to give up the dole.

Although the breakaway fever that spread from the Baltics to other republics such as the Ukraine, Moldavia and Georgia seems to have cooled, nationalism is still running strong. Actually, racism is a more suitable word—but the positive, not the negative kind. Ukrainians and Russians living in Moldavia are opposed to that republic's intention to become reunited with Romania. Oil-rich Chechen-Ingush in the Northern Caucasus, one of sixteen autonomous republics in the Russian Federation, declared its independence and its newly elected president General Dzhokar Dudayev has successfully defied Boris Yeltsin's attempt to force the republic back into his federation. Chechen-Ingush is also seeking to form an all-Moslem confederation of six mainly Islamic areas stretching about 310 miles from the Caspian to the Black Sea. That area's population would total 5.3 million people. Thus the nationalist divisions succeeding the demise of Communism are followed by subdivision, and the obvious question is: Where will it end? Like the name of the Unknown Soldier, the answer is known but to God.

Meanwhile, Boris Yeltsin has been steadily arrogating to Russia much of the Kremlin's power and authority. Although he relented on a cut off date of December 1, 1991, for funding of about 80 of the Kremlin's ministries and agencies, this is merely a postponement of the inevitable. Coal, gold and diamond exports will soon come under Russian control, and the printing of Soviet currency is also in Yeltsin's hands. Russia accounts for 90 percent of petroleum production in the U.S.S.R., which is the world's largest oil producer.

But a far greater threat to the existence of the Soviet Union occurred on December 1 when the Ukraine voted nine to one for independence and elected former Communist Leonid Kravchuk as president. "The Soviet Union has disintegrated," Kravchuck cried joyfully. "An independent Ukraine is born." He promised that the Ukraine, with Russia, Byelorussia and Kazakhstan—the other republics in which nuclear warheads are based—would establish collective control of these weapons.

No more devastating blow to Mikhail Gorbachev's attempt to forge a New Union could have been delivered, for Yeltsin had already declared: "As long as the Ukraine doesn't sign the Union Treaty, Russia won't put its signature on it either." Without these two industrial, mineral and agricultural giants, survival of the U.S.S.R. as a controlling center is simply not possible. With Russia gone, the U.S.S.R. becomes bereft of more than half its population and 74 percent of its land, plus the oil and other resources already described; and with the Ukraine absent it loses its second largest population of 52 million people, 56 percent of its corn, 25 percent of its wheat, 47 percent of its iron and 23 percent of its coal.

Only a starry-eyed lunatic could believe that the Soviet Union could continue to exist so emasculated, and even the ever-hopeful Gorbachev has already conceded that departure of the Ukraine was "unthinkable." Without the Ukraine and Russia, and possibly minus Kazakhstan and Byelorussia as well, a verdict of "stillborn" must be pronounced on the proposed New Union.

Its replacement—if there is one—will probably take years to evolve; although a strong possibility of economic cohesion remains. The twelve republics have been bound together commercially too long—as interdependent as the warp and woof of fabric—for them to split suddenly in a dozen different directions. To paraphrase Benjamin Franklin: if they do not hang together economically, they might then hang separately.

Nevertheless the immediate recognition of a free Ukraine by Poland and Canada, together with the American pledge of soon following suit, suggests that these emerging concepts of freedom and a market economy will continue to be welcomed with great enthusiasm in the West and especially in Washington, although President Bush has yet to move from simple humanitarian aid for the emerging federation to outright financial assistance, as Secretary of State Baker has been urging him to do. "Nationalism can turn to Fascism," Baker warned Bush and the Cabinet. "If they move to Fascism, or slip back to Communism, we will get the blame." Former Foreign Minister Shevardnadze seems to feel the same way, remarking: "The struggle between the democrats and the reactionaries is not over."

Among the myriad unanswered questions is what will happen to the new nation's four million-man armed forces and its 27,000 nuclear weapons. The Soviet armed forces were always controlled by the

Communist Party, which in turn was generous because it depended on force for its existence. But now it is likely that because of the Party's demise and General Yazov's treachery there will be a civilian defense minister and probably an army composed of volunteers and greatly reduced in size. If the Persian Gulf War proved anything it was that volunteers are much better soldiers than conscripts, most of whom hate the uniform they wear, and cheaper because far fewer of them are needed. The republics, of course, will probably want their own territorial forces, much like the American national guards, for use in emergencies or natural disasters and controlled from Moscow.

Only the national army would possess weapons of mass destruction. Probably the most frightening prospect in the failed coup was the fact that the conspirators in fact did possess Gorbachev's "black box." Because the other official in the Soviet Union's two-person release authority was Defense Minister Dmitri Yazov, who was in on the plot, the Gang of Eight did have in its hands the power to launch a nuclear attack. But strategic weapons are of little use in putting down internal resistance if only because the missiles are aimed at foreign targets and there would not be time to reprogram them. Battlefield nukes might have been used, of course, but the order to fire them probably would have met the same refusal made by the KGB formation ordered to storm the White House. Moreover, to incinerate 150,000 countrymen would have been too horrible to contemplate, even for the Gang of Eight. Thus with the black box back in Gorbachev's safekeeping and a civilian defense minister likely to be chosen there is no longer need for apprehension.

Even more reassuring the terribly costly and frightening arms race between the superpowers has also apparently been turned into a "*dis*armament race." In early October President Bush surprised and delighted the world by announcing that he would eliminate all its ground-launched nuclear weapons; withdraw all tactical nuclear arms from U.S. ships; take strategic bombers off 24-hour alert; and cancel the development of the mobile MX missile. Bush called upon the Soviets to take similar steps and to enter into negotiations to eliminate intercontinental ballistic missiles with multiple warheads.

On October 5 in what appeared to be a game of friendly one-upmanship, Gorbachev replied with a disarmament plan that surpassed Bush's: liquidate all nuclear artillery shells; remove nuclear warheads from surface-to-air missiles among battle-ready forces to central bases while destroying "some of them"; remove all tactical warheads from ships and multipurpose submarines, as well as from land-based navy planes, and store them at warehouses where "some will be liquidated"; take all heavy bombers similar to the U.S. B-52s and B-1s off battle alert and place their nuclear weapons in storage; freeze the number of railroad-based intercontinental warheads, place them at fixed locations and cease to improve them; and remove from service three nuclear missile submarines with 48 launchers aboard. Between the two chief executives they removed all nuclear weapons threatening Europe and brought the forty-five-year-old nuclear arms race to an end.

And so, almost like the end of a fairy tale, the long struggle is over. In all the wars of America there was no conflict as long and as important worldwide as the Cold War begun in 1946 between a fixed, monolithic command society on one side and a fluid, free, democratic competitive one on the other. Fortunately for America and the rest of mankind, it was won by the Free World led by the United States.

Epilogue

☆

It is now 382 years—almost four centuries—since Samuel Champlain began the wars of America with those fatal shots at the Iroquois on the shores of the lake that bears his name: and now, at this writing in mid-November of 1991, America is but nine months removed from its latest war.

It was by arms that the American colonials helped the British to subdue the French menace in Canada. By war the Americans learned to organize and rule themselves. In the crucible of combat they won their independence, failed to expand at the expense of Canada, did expand at the expense of Mexico and the American Indian, abolished chattel slavery and preserved the Union. They became imperialist to the discomfort of Spain, entered the international arena to thwart Imperial Germany, returned to it to do the same to Nazi Germany, and finally assumed Free World leadership in the confrontation with Communism known as the Cold War. In this, America was at first successful, preventing the North Korean Communists and later the Red Chinese from unifying Korea under the Red Flag and by the Berlin Airlift thwarting Stalin's attempt to drive the Allies from West Berlin; but next failing to foil the more determined North Vietnamese in turning all Vietnam into a socialist state; after which, though chastened, it still held firm against terrorism, deposed dictators and in the Persian Gulf War led a unique coalition of Western and Arab nations in an unprecedented war to restore Kuwait to its rightful rulers.

It has been by war more than by peace that our institutions have been proclaimed and defended, our industries developed, our culture enriched, our history made national, our arts and sciences improved and advanced—and our hearts broken. And yet, although there is much agonizing truth in that last phrase, it is also a fact that the chance of heartbreak—nay, of the destruction of the race—is now much less likely than it was in 1981 when those words were written. No longer need this author repeat his 1981 lament: "By the force of arms we are now the mightiest power on earth. But at what price! We stand surrounded by threats and hatred. Our European Allies falter and fall back. Our new Allies in Asia do not love us but only seek the shield of our military might against the Communist aggressor. At home we are divided and seem to be hating one another with an ideological fanaticism. And in a world gone mad with militarism—in which the leader who does not wear or has not worn a uniform is rare indeed—we are the foremost military power. . . . All this has transformed and agonized a nation which honestly loves peace. To no other country on earth has it been given to cry with such anguish: 'Peace! Peace! When there is no peace.'[1] No other people yearns so hungrily to let down this burden taken up so reluctantly."

But now—a decade later—the time has come, not to lay down the burden, but to rejoice that we no longer carry it alone. Because of the collapse of Communism everywhere but Cuba, China and Vietnam and the success of collective security in evicting Iraq from Kuwait, a truly new world order may be emerging through the growth of regional security organizations and a growing disposition to challenge the heretofore sacrosanct doctrine of the inviolable sovereign state. The problem in international relations has always been: how do you punish a sovereign state? No independent nation will accept interference in its internal affairs, and if it is embarked upon a policy of aggression and annexation as Nazi Germany was, it will change its policy only under the compulsion of arms. To resort to war to keep the peace is not, however, a very peaceful policy—as the eviction of Iraq from Kuwait demonstrates.

Iraq is also a prime example of the difficulty of encroaching upon national sovereignty. Although it agreed to accept the United Nations resolutions demanding destruction of its nuclear, biological and chemical weapons, it has not done so, and has admitted to only about a quarter of its real potential to make them. UN inspection teams have also discovered that Iraq, supposedly ten years away from building a nuclear device, was actually only a year or two short of that objective. Iraq has been so recalcitrant that as recently as September 19–20, 1991, President Bush has had to warn Saddam that if he did not stop harassing UN inspectors as they move by helicopter in search of hidden weapons he would order U.S. warplanes to protect them. Bush said that he was "plenty fed up" with Saddam, but was not looking for a new war—"a son of Desert Storm." Under the UN resolutions the U.S. has the authority to use force in such an impasse. Thus in Iraq at least collective security has been no more successful than it was in Korea.

True, Saddam has been evicted from Kuwait, just as the North Korean Communists were driven back above the 38th Parallel; but, like them, he remains in power and defiant. In fact, the 16-nation UN coalition that liberated South Korea dissolved so quickly afterward that Red China supplanted Nationalist China on the Security Council. It is possible that the U.S.-led alliance of 38 nations may follow a similar course.

Nevertheless this is not to suggest that the concept of collective security has died of inanition or a lack of enthusiasm for punishing what could be a sister state. It is rather to maintain that because of events in Yugoslavia, and among the Kurds of Iraq, *regional* collective security organizations may be a great step toward keeping peace in the world.

Moreover, Yugoslavia would hardly seem the place for this new concept to succeed. Its six republics were once provinces of the defunct Austro-Hungarian empire: "a melting pot on a cold fire." Jerry-built into a democratic nation by those inept political carpenters at Versailles, most of its people—with the notable exception of Croatia—bravely resisted Hitler, only to be undone by Marshal Tito, their wartime leader who compressed them into a Communist monolith, even though he remained independent of the Kremlin. Came the revolt of Eastern Europe and freedom seemed to blossom there also. But is was actually a horrid growth: a coalition of equal republics rotating a federal presidency among them.

Predictably in June, 1991, two of the republics—Slovenia and Croatia—proclaimed their independence from the Serbian-dominated federal center in Belgrade. Yugoslavia's answer was force, and the first clashes of an outright civil war ensued. Into this threat to the peace of Europe stepped the European Community. Although Yugoslavia was not a member of this body, EC delegates from the Netherlands, Portugal and Luxembourg invited—not to say summoned—the leaders of Yugoslavia to the Italian island of Brioni and there obtained from them an agreement to halt the fighting and resume negotiations on the proposed secession of Slovenia and Croatia. What was remarkable about this meeting was that the EC delegates did not suggest solutions but actually dictated the terms of the agreement, threatening economic sanctions and an end to financial aid if they were rejected. But they were accepted and the fighting ceased, only to break out again between Serbia and Croatia. Slovenia, meanwhile, had gone free and remains so.

Serbia wished to annex the portions of Croatia populated by ethnic Serbians, who were complaining of their treatment there, just as Hitler acted in the Sudetenland upon the complaints of ethnic Germans there and later did the same in Czechoslovakia. For the EC to accept this would be to repudiate the policy upon which it was founded: intolerance of military aggrandizement. And it did not accept it. Nor did the Euro-American alliance in Iraq permit Saddam to continue to persecute his disaffected Kurds. A security zone was established to protect them, and eventually those hundreds of thousands of Kurds who had fled for sanctuary into their own hills and those of neighboring Turkey returned to their old homeland.

Here, in both these cases, was nothing less than intervention by collective security in the internal affairs of another nation. Here was the challenge to the old theory of national sovereignty, which, it may be said, was first made by President Reagan in Nicaragua and again by President Bush in Panama, both in defiance of the International Court of Justice. Here was proof that military expansion may be prevented through collective security.

Unfortunately, no less than a dozen truces negotiated by the EC between Croatia and Serbia have been broken, some of them only moments after they had been signed. How could it have been otherwise, granting the deep disparities dividing this nation of 24 million sundered by three major religions, four languages and two alphabets, and five races and dozens of minor sects and ethnic groups. The deepest hatreds, some of them centuries old, dwell in the hearts of these people. Of the most recent hatreds, Serbia, which resisted the Nazis in World War II, can never forget how Croatia in the service of Hitler massacred its citizens.

Thus on September 18 the Serbian-dominated Federal Army launched a full-scale attack on Croatia in an apparent attempt to seize and annex a third of its neighbor's land, even though the 600,000 ethnic Serbs living there represented only about an eighth of Croatia's population of about 4.75 million people. So far the offensive has been eminently successful, although more than 2,000 people have been killed and Croatian towns and cities devastated, especially Dubrovnik, an Adriatic port city considered to be a medieval jewel and possessing no strategic value.

One ray of hope appeared on November 15 when Croatia and a Federal Army general signed the thirteenth truce, expressing unusually optimistic hopes that it would hold. The next day two United Nations diplomats—former U.S. Secretary of State Cyrus Vance and UN Undersecretary-General Marrack Goulding—flew to Yugoslavia in an attempt to seize this fragile opportunity to negotiate a permanent cease-fire. If they fail and this thirteenth truce is shattered, it is possible that a general civil war—"a combination of Northern Ireland, Cyprus and Lebanon," according to one gloomy Balkan scholar—might engulf all six republics. Although oil supplies and the world economy are certainly not at stake here as in Iraq, the peace of Europe is; and that may be just as important to the UN, the U.S. and the EC.

More important, the doctrine of national sovereignty will have been challenged as essentially selfish and immoral. Everywhere during this horrible century of neo-barbarism, of calculated and massive assaults upon human life and dignity, national sovereignty has been advanced as the excuse for non-intervention. But now, with the end of the Cold War and the triumph of democratic values, humanitarian intervention and the peacekeeping of collective security organizations—especially if they are regional with members who understand the area's problems—may be morally mandated. At the least the concept of national sovereignty must be reconsidered and rethought.

Having suggested the emergence of a new world order based upon a nascent international morality, it would be a pleasure to end this second updating and revision of this study by proposing the imminent end of the institution of war. But this work cannot be so ended, if only because it cannot be stated that war can be eliminated. War is endemic to society. Society is the root cause of war. War, as has been suggested, is socially approved armed conflict between hostile groups. If hostility is the condition of war, groups are its cause. What a man may gain from the structure and order of a group—a society—he loses in frustration and conflict. Man is not only up against himself but society as well. Hermits do not have wars, nor do they commit individual murder. Yet, if one hermit discovers a path to another's hut, they may socialize; and when they do, they will encounter disagreements over which they may have quarrels, which may end in violence and murder. That is because they will have become social men. Once men come together, their individual interests are in conflict. When this occurs and diplomatic efforts to resolve the conflict fail, what we call war ensues. Society itself, then, seems to be the root cause of war, and as long as great societies—sovereign nation-states—continue to possess great and unchecked power, war will remain inevitable.

Even if nations, like individual men before them, were to surrender all power to coerce to a higher, international body, to do so would not eliminate war because then the world authority would certainly depend on force to keep the peace or to restrain any government or group that unjustly disturbed it. What, actually, could be substituted for the traditional appeal to arms, the last resort of the downtrodden? It would seem nothing.

Thus, in this last decade of the twentieth century, the future of mankind still seems uncertain, but to a much lesser degree than in 1981, when the threat of nuclear war between the superpowers was a chilling reality. But there remains the fear of nuclear proliferation, especially among malevolent military adventurers such as Saddam Hussein, who came so close to achieving this objective in 1991. Arms control, of course, is a distinct possibility and is in the forefront of the minds of most of the world's responsible leaders. But it is fatuous to believe that even such incredible weapons as those contained in the American arsenal during the Persian Gulf War will not continue to be manufactured and even improved upon. Development of some revolutionary new defensive device such as the one envisioned in the Star Wars program may only provoke research into an offensive weapon even more horrible than those already possessed by the nuclear powers. Even worse than the dread of their using them is the possibility that some unbalanced leader craving either world or regional dominion may come into possession of ultimate weapons. So the hideous genie is out of the bottle and loose among us, and there is no way we can put it back in.

The solution to the problem of war, of course, is to develop the good society. But as Thomas More wrote nearly five centuries ago at the conclusion of his *Utopia,* society will be good only when men are good—and that, he thought, would not be for some time.

Until then, the wars of America will continue.

Notes

☆

PART I: THE COLONIAL WARS

1. Francis Parkman, *The Pioneers of France in the New World* (Boston: Little, Brown, 1888), p. 350.
2. Francis Parkman, *The Jesuits in North America* (Boston: Little, Brown, 1888), p. 247.
3. *Ibid.*, p. 248.
4. Michael Kraus, *The United States to 1865*, "The University of Michigan History of the Modern World" (Ann Arbor: University of Michigan Press, 1959), p. 91.
5. Alvin M. Josephy, *The Patriot Chiefs: A Chronicle of American Indian Leadership* (New York: Viking, 1961), p. 58.
6. *Ibid.*, p. 59.
7. Francis Parkman, *Count Frontenac and New France under Louis XIV* (Boston: Little, Brown, 1888), p. 15.
8. *Ibid.*, p. 214.
9. *Ibid.*, p. 233.
10. *Ibid.*, p. 268.
11. *Ibid.*, p. 270.
12. Francis Parkman, *A Half-Century of Conflict* (Boston: Little, Brown, 1892), Vol. I, p. 135.
13. *Ibid.*, p. 171.
14. *Ibid.*, p. 174.
15. *Ibid.*, p. 177.
16. Alfred Thayer Mahan, *The Influence of Sea Power upon History 1660–1783* (New York: Hill & Wang, 1957), p. 200.
17. *A Half-Century of Conflict*, Vol. II, p. 70.
18. *Ibid.*, p. 102.
19. *Ibid.*, p. 124.
20. *Ibid.*, p. 132.
21. *Ibid.*, p. 133.

22. Douglas Southall Freeman, *George Washington* (New York: Scribner, 1948), Vol. I, p. 310.
23. *Ibid.*, p. 318.
24. *Ibid.*
25. Francis Parkman, *Montcalm and Wolfe* (Boston: Little, Brown, 1888), Vol. I, p. 218.
26. *Ibid.*, p. 225.
27. *Ibid.*
28. *Ibid.*, p. 308.
29. *Ibid.*, p. 309.
30. *Ibid.*, p. 506.
31. *Ibid.*, p. 510.
32. *Montcalm and Wolfe*, Vol. II, p. 46.
33. *Ibid.*, p. 97.
34. Christopher Hibbert, *Wolfe at Quebec* (New York: World, 1959), p. 1.
35. *Ibid.*, p. 34.
36. *Ibid.*, p. 37.
37. *Ibid.*, p. 25.
38. *Montcalm and Wolfe*, Vol. II, p. 205.
39. *Ibid.*
40. *Ibid.*, p. 206.
41. Hibbert, p. 76.
42. *Ibid.*, p. 100.
43. *Ibid.*, p. 113.
44. C. P. Stacey, *Quebec, 1759* (Toronto: Macmillan, 1959), p. 179.
45. *Ibid.*, p. 35.
46. *Ibid.*, p. 276.
47. *Ibid.*, pp. 285–86. Some historians have challenged this incident, but none with proof that it did not occur. It does not seem likely that the scrupulous Parkman would have been taken in by a fable.
48. Hibbert, p. 135.
49. *Ibid.*
50. *Ibid.*, p. 136.
51. *Montcalm and Wolfe*, Vol. II, p. 291.
52. *Hibbert*, p. 149.
53. *Montcalm and Wolfe*, pp. 296–97.
54. *Ibid.*, p. 297.
55. *Ibid.*, p. 308.
56. Major General J. F. C. Fuller, *A Military History of the Western World* (New York: Funk & Wagnalls, 1955), Vol. II, p. 270n. (Hereinafter referred to as Fuller, MH.)

PART II: THE WAR OF THE REVOLUTION

1. Christopher Ward, *The War of the Revolution* (New York: Macmillan, 1953), Vol. I, p. 7.
2. Bruce Lancaster, *From Lexington to Liberty*, "Mainstream of America Series" (New York: Doubleday, 1955), p. 17.
3. Lawrence Henry Gipson, *The Coming of the Revolution*, "New American Nation Series" (New York: Harper & Row, 1954), p. 67.
4. *Ibid.*, p. 68.
5. *Ibid.*, p. 219.
6. Ward., Vol. I, p. 13.
7. *Ibid.*, p. 16.
8. Lancaster, p. 67.
9. *Ibid.*, p. 68.
10. Gipson, p. 227.
11. Henry Steele Commager and Richard B. Morris, eds., *The Spirit of 'Seventy-Six: The Story of the American Revolution as Told by Participants* (Indianapolis, New York: Bobbs-Merrill, 1958; new edition, Harper & Row, 1967), Vol. I, p. 65. (Hereinafter referred to as Commager.)
12. *Ibid.*, pp. 108–09.
13. Ward, Vol. I, p. 22.
14. Commager, Vol. I, p. 67.
15. Ward, Vol. I, p. 35.
16. Commager, Vol. I, p. 69.
17. Ward, Vol. I, p. 37.
18. *Ibid.*
19. *Ibid.*
20. Lancaster, p. 99.
21. Ward, Vol. I, p. 43.
22. *Ibid.*
23. *Ibid.*
24. *Ibid.*
25. Lancaster, p. 110.
26. John C. Miller, *Triumph of Freedom: 1775–1783* (Boston: Little, Brown, 1948), p. 42.
27. Commager, Vol. I, p. 103.
28. Ward, Vol. I, p. 68.
29. *Ibid.*
30. Freeman, Vol. III, p. 427.
31. Willard M. Wallace, *Appeal to Arms: A Military History of the Revolution* (Chicago: Quadrangle Books, 1964), p. 32.

32. Miller, p. 8.
33. Ward, Vol. I, p. 56.
34. Lancaster, p. 129.
35. *Ibid.*
36. *Ibid.*, p. 130.
37. Ward, Vol. I, p. 74.
38. *Ibid.*, p. 86.
39. Thomas J. Fleming, "Battle at Bunker Hill," *Reader's Digest,* July, 1960, p. 259.
40. Ward, Vol. I, p. 88.
41. Fleming, p. 263.
42. *Ibid.*
43. Commager, Vol. I, p. 133.
44. *Ibid.*, p. 137.
45. *Ibid.*, p. 130.
46. Fleming, p. 271.
47. *Ibid.*
48. Ward, Vol. I, p. 103.
49. Freeman, Vol. III, p. 520.
50. Ward, Vol. I, p. 195.
51. *Ibid.*, p. 194.
52. Miller, p. 82.
53. *Ibid.*, p. 58.
54. *Ibid.*
55. Commager, Vol. II, p. 1071.
56. Commager, Vol. I, pp. 313–14.
57. Burton Stevenson, *Home Book of Quotations* (New York: Dodd, Mead, 1958), p. 62.
58. Russel Blaine Nye, *The Cultural Life of the New Nation,* "New American Nation Series" (New York: Harper & Row, 1960), p. 198.
59. Ward, Vol. I, p. 205.
60. Wallace, p. 113.
61. Lancaster, p. 215.
62. Miller, p. 132.
63. Ward, Vol. I, p. 232.
64. Wallace, p. 122.
65. *Ibid.*, p. 123.
66. Commager, Vol. I, p. 500.
67. *Ibid.*, p. 503.
68. *Ibid.*, p. 504.
69. Freeman, Vol. IV, p. 309.
70. Ward, Vol. I, p. 298.

71. Lancaster, p. 245.
72. Freeman, Vol. IV, p. 321.
73. Ward, Vol. I, p. 305.
74. Lancaster, p. 249.
75. Commager, Vol. I, p. 520.
76. Wallace, p. 133.
77. Ward, Vol. I, p. 317.
78. Commager, Vol. I, p. 517.
79. Miller, p. 166.
80. *Ibid.*
81. *Ibid.*, pp. 165–66.
82. Ward, Vol. I, p. 347.
83. *Ibid.*
84. *Ibid.*, p. 351.
85. *Ibid.*, p. 354.
86. Commager, Vol. I, pp. 625–26.
87. *Ibid.*
88. *Ibid.*
89. Miller, p. 206.
90. Lancaster, p. 238.
91. Ward, Vol. I, p. 351.
92. *Ibid.*, p. 423.
93. Stevenson, p. 66.
94. Lancaster, p. 279.
95. Wallace, p. 164.
96. Lancaster, p. 238.
97. Wallace, p. 170.
98. Lancaster, p. 335.
99. Wallace, p. 140.
100. *Ibid.*, p. 181.
101. Lancaster, p. 354.
102. Ward, Vol. II, p. 584.
103. Freeman, Vol. V, p. 59.
104. Ward, Vol. II, p. 681.
105. Miller, p. 405.
106. Dudley Knox, *A History of the United States Navy* (New York: Putnam, 1948), p. 35.
107. Miller, p. 481; Lancaster, pp. 380–81.
108. Miller, p. 483.
109. Commager, Vol. II, p. 804.
110. John Richard Alden, *The American Revolution*, "New American Nation Series" (New York: Harper & Row, 1954), p. 220.
111. *Ibid.*, p. 221.

112. Miller, p. 518.
113. Ward, Vol. II, p. 724.
114. Miller, p. 524–25.
115. Lancaster, p. 369.
116. Miller, p. 527.
117. *Ibid.*, p. 528.
118. Ward, Vol. II, p. 741.
119. *Ibid.*, p. 742.
120. *Ibid.*
121. *Ibid.*
122. *Ibid.*, p. 760.
123. *Ibid.*, p. 761.
124. *Ibid.*
125. Bruce Lancaster, *The American Heritage Book of the Revolution* (New York: Simon & Schuster, 1958), p. 321.
126. Commager, Vol. II, p. 1217.
127. *Ibid.*, p. 1218.
128. Ward, Vol. II, p. 890.
129. Commager, Vol. II, p. 1233.

PART III: THE WAR OF 1812

1. Commager, Vol. II, pp. 1243–44.
2. Wallace, p. 266.
3. *Ibid.*
4. Samuel Eliot Morison, *The Oxford History of the American People* (New York: Oxford, 1965), p. 270. (Hereinafter referred to as Morison, O.)
5. William Addleman Ganoe, *The History of the United States Army* (New York: Appleton, 1928), p. 101.
6. Glenn Tucker, *Dawn Like Thunder: The Barbary Wars and the Birth of the U.S. Navy* (Indianapolis, New York: Bobbs-Merrill, 1963), p. 26.
7. *Ibid.*, p. 115.
8. Glenn Tucker, *Poltroons and Patriots: A Popular Account of the War of 1812* (Indianapolis, New York: Bobbs-Merrill, 1954), Vol. I, p. 224. (Hereinafter referred to as Tucker, PP.)
9. Henry Adams, *The War of 1812*, ed. by Major H. A. De Weerd (Washington: Infantry Journal Press, 1944), p. 1.
10. Harry L. Coles, *The War of 1812*, "The Chicago History of American Civilization" (Chicago: University of Chicago Press, 1965), p. 45.

11. Adams, p. 24.
12. *Ibid.*, p. 34.
13. Coles, p. 80.
14. Tucker, PP, Vol. I, pp. 174–75.
15. *Ibid.*
16. Adams, p. 43.
17. Tucker, PP, Vol. I, pp. 174–75.
18. Coles, p. 84.
19. Tucker, PP, Vol. I, p. 230.
20. *Ibid.*, p. 231.
21. Adams, p. 57.
22. Tucker, PP, Vol. I, p. 299.
23. *Ibid.*, p. 267.
24. Coles, p. 121.
25. Tucker, PP, Vol. I, p. 315.
26. Josephy, p. 168.
27. Coles, p. 120.
28. Tucker, PP, Vol. I, p. 327.
29. *Ibid.*, p. 331.
30. *Ibid.*, p. 337.
31. Josephy, pp. 169–70.
32. Tucker, PP, Vol. I, pp. 338–39.
33. Josephy, p. 170.
34. *Ibid.*, p. 171.
35. Ganoe, p. 132.
36. Adams, p. 91.
37. *Ibid.*
38. *Ibid.*, p. 92.
39. *Ibid.*, p. 93.
40. *Ibid.*, p. 102.
41. Tucker, PP, Vol. II, p. 427.
42. Marquis James, *The Life of Andrew Jackson* (Indianapolis, New York: Bobbs-Merrill, 1938), p. 130.
43. Tucker, PP, Vol. II, p. 439.
44. James, p. 153.
45. *Ibid.*, p. 154.
46. Tucker, PP, Vol. II, p. 442.
47. James, p. 154.
48. Coles, p. 197.
49. James, p. 165.
50. *Ibid.*, p. 166.
51. *Ibid.*, p. 178.

52. *Ibid.*
53. Coles, p. 163.
54. *Ibid.,* p. 248.
55. *Ibid.,* p. 249.
56. Alfred Thayer Mahan, *Sea Power in Its Relation to the War of 1812* (Boston: Little, Brown), p. 332. (Hereinafter referred to as Mahan, 1812.)
57. Adams, p. 218.
58. *Ibid.*
59. *Ibid.,* p. 215.
60. *Ibid.,* p. 225.
61. George Robert Glieg, *The Campaigns of the British Army at Washington and New Orleans* (London: 1821), p. 132.
62. Tucker, PP, Vol. II, p. 483.
63. Adams, p. 227.
64. *Ibid.,* p. 332.
65. *Ibid.,* p. 334.
66. *Ibid.,* p. 335.
67. Mahan, 1812, p. 364.
68. *Ibid.*
69. Adams, pp. 201–02.
70. Mahan, 1812, p. 364.
71. Tucker, Vol. II, p. 635.
72. *Ibid.,* p. 590.
73. *Ibid.,* p. 591.
74. *Ibid.,* p. 589.
75. Neil H. Swanson, *The Perilous Fight* (Toronto, New York: Farrar & Rinehart, 1945), p. 504.
76. Adams, p. 338.
77. *Ibid.,* p. 340.
78. *Ibid.,* p. 341.
79. Coles, pp. 206–07.
80. James, p. 201.
81. *Ibid.*
82. *Ibid.,* p. 217.
83. *Ibid.*
84. *Ibid.*
85. *Ibid.,* p. 225.
86. *Ibid.*
87. *Ibid.,* p. 228.
88. *Ibid.*
89. *Ibid.,* p. 236.

90. Adams, p. 313.
91. James, p. 239.
92. *Ibid.*, p. 240.
93. *Ibid.*, pp. 241–42.
94. *Ibid.*, p. 244.
95. *Ibid.*
96. *Ibid.*, p. 245.
97. *Ibid.*, p. 247.
98. *Ibid.*, p. 249.

PART IV: THE WAR WITH MEXICO

1. Fuller, M. H., Vol. II, p. 541.
2. George Dangerfield, *The Awakening of American Nationalism, 1815–1828,* "New American Nation Series" (New York: Harper & Row, 1964), p. 4.
3. Morison, O, p. 405.
4. *Ibid.*
5. Kraus, p. 424.
6. *Ibid.*, p. 421.
7. Ray Allen Billington, *The Far Western Frontier: 1830–1860,* "New American Nation Series" (New York: Harper & Row, 1956), p. 149.
8. *Ibid.*
9. *Ibid.*, p. 148.
10. Morison, O, p. 561.
11. *Ibid.*
12. Justin H. Smith, *The War with Mexico* (Gloucester: Peter Smith, 1963), Vol. I, p. 159.
13. Edward J. Nichols, *Zach Taylor's Little Army* (New York: Doubleday, 1963), p. 35.
14. Lloyd Lewis, *Captain Sam Grant* (Boston: Little, Brown, 1950), p. 137.
15. Robert Selph Henry, *The Story of the Mexican War* (New York: Ungar, 1961), p. 41.
16. *Ibid.*, p. 45.
17. Lewis, p. 142.
18. Henry, p. 47.
19. Lewis, p. 143.
20. *Ibid.*, p. 147.
21. Henry, p. 62.
22. *Ibid.*

23. *Ibid.*
24. *Ibid.*, p. 63.
25. Smith, Vol. I, p. 194.
26. Lewis, p. 160.
27. Samuel E. Chamberlain, *My Confession* (New York: Harper & Row, 1956), p. 31.
28. Glyndon G. Van Deusen, *The Jacksonian Era: 1828–1848*, "New American Nation Series" (New York: Harper & Row, 1959), p. 210.
29. Henry, p. 103.
30. *Ibid.*
31. Lewis, pp. 161, 168.
32. *Ibid.*, p. 161.
33. *Ibid.*, p. 162.
34. Lt. Gen. Winfield Scott, *Memoirs* (New York: 1864), Vol. II, p. 383.
35. Lewis, p. 175.
36. *Ibid.*, p. 176.
37. Smith, Vol. I, p. 260.
38. Henry, pp. 68–9.
39. *Ibid.*, p. 69.
40. *Ibid.*, p. 70.
41. Scott, Vol. II, p. 401.
42. *Ibid.*
43. Van Deusen, p. 240.
44. Morison, O, p. 562.
45. Lewis, p. 200.
46. Henry, p. 174–75.
47. *Ibid.*, p. 175.
48. Smith, Vol. I, p. 376.
49. *Ibid.*, p. 374.
50. Chamberlain, p. 116.
51. *Ibid.*
52. Lewis, p. 193.
53. *Ibid.*
54. *Ibid.*, p. 196.
55. Smith, Vol. II, p. 10.
56. Lewis, p. 199.
57. Scott, p. 423.
58. Lewis, p. 199.
59. Lewis, p. 201.

60. *Ibid.*
61. Scott, p. 425.
62. Henry, p. 287.
63. *Ibid.*, p. 296.
64. *Ibid.*
65. *Ibid.*, p. 305.
66. Scott, p. 460.
67. *Ibid.*, p. 466.
68. Smith, Vol. II, pp. 84–5.
69. Lewis, p. 234.
70. *Ibid.*
71. *Ibid.*, pp. 241–42.
72. *Ibid.*, p. 244.
73. *Ibid.*, p. 245.
74. Henry, p. 381.

PART V: THE CIVIL WAR

1. Kraus, pp. 445–46.
2. Morison, O, p. 571.
3. Kraus, p. 438.
4. *Ibid.*
5. Morison, O, p. 573.
6. Edmund Wilson, *Patriotic Gore: Studies in the Literature of the American Civil War* (New York: Oxford, 1962), p. 3.
7. Kraus, p. 451.
8. Bruce Catton, *This Hallowed Ground: The Story of the Union Side of the Civil War,* "Mainstream of America Series" (New York: Doubleday, 1956), p. 8. (Hereinafter referred to as Catton, HG.)
9. Kraus, p. 469.
10. *Ibid.*, p. 472.
11. *Ibid.*, p. 473.
12. *Ibid.*
13. *Ibid.*
14. Catton, HG, p. 8.
15. Morison, O, p. 602.
16. Clement Eaton, *A History of the Southern Confederacy* (New York: Macmillan, 1962), p. 17.
17. Carl Sandburg, *Storm Over the Land: A Profile of the Civil War* (New York: Harcourt, Brace & World, 1942), pp. 5–6.
18. *Ibid.*, p. 8.

19. Morison, O, p. 610.
20. Stephen Vincent Benét, *John Brown's Body* (New York: Holt, Rinehart & Winston, 1962), p. 141.
21. Douglas Southall Freeman, *Lee's Lieutenants* (New York: Scribner, 1942), Vol. I, p. 20. (Hereinafter referred to as Freeman, LL.)
22. Fuller, MH, Vol. III, p. 12.
23. Sandburg, p. 54.
24. Freeman, LL, Vol. I, p. 61.
25. Clifford Dowdey, *The Land They Fought For: The Story of the South As the Confederacy, 1832–1865,* "Mainstream of America Series" (New York: Doubleday, 1955), p. 121.
26. Freeman, LL, Vol. I, p. 72.
27. Lt. Col. Matthew Forney Steele, *Campaigns of America* (Washington: Combat Forces Press, 1951), Vol. I, p. 72.
28. Bruce Catton, *Mr. Lincoln's Army* (New York: Doubleday, 1962), p. 53. (Hereinafter referred to as Catton, MLA.)
29. Bruce Catton, *The American Heritage Picture History of the Civil War* (New York: American Heritage, 1960), Vol. I, p. 111. (Hereinafter referred to as Catton, AH.)
30. Morison, O, p. 636.
31. *Ibid.*
32. *Ibid.,* p. 616.
33. Maj. Gen. J. F. C. Fuller, *Grant and Lee* (Bloomington: Indiana University Press, 1957), p. 59. (Hereinafter referred to as Fuller, G–L.)
34. *Ibid.*
35. Ulysses S. Grant, *Memoirs of U. S. Grant* (New York: Webster, 1894), p. 149.
36. Catton, HG, p. 94.
37. Grant, p. 173.
38. Fuller, G–L, p. 72.
39. Grant, p. 181.
40. Catton, HG, p. 97.
41. *Ibid.,* p. 98.
42. Grant, pp. 183–84.
43. Fuller, G–L, p. 140.
44. Catton, HG, p. 103.
45. *Ibid.,* p. 104.
46. *Ibid.,* p. 111.
47. Col. Vincent J. Esposito, ed., *The West Point Atlas of American Wars* (New York: Praeger, 1959), Vol. I, 1689–1900, Map 33.
48. Catton, HG, p. 114.

49. Grant, p. 201.
50. *Ibid.*, p. 206.
51. Fuller, G–L, p. 75.
52. *Ibid.*, p. 148–49.
53. Sandburg, p. 112.
54. *Ibid.*, p. 119.
55. *Ibid.*
56. *Ibid.*, p. 149.
57. Catton, AH, Vol. I, p. 142.
58. *Ibid.*
59. Irving Werstein, *Kearny the Magnificent* (New York: John Day, 1962), p. 202.
60. *Ibid.*
61. Henry Steele Commager, ed., *The Blue and the Gray* (Indianapolis: Bobbs-Merrill, 1950), p. 337. (Hereinafter referred to as Commager, B–G.)
62. Catton, AH, Vol. I, p. 141.
63. Lewis, p. 266.
64. Fuller, G–L, p. 129.
65. *Ibid.*
66. Benét, p. 165.
67. Fuller, G–L, p. 107.
68. *Ibid.*, p. 102.
69. *Ibid.*, p. 101.
70. *Ibid.*, p. 100.
71. Werstein, pp. 224–25.
72. Fuller, G–L, p. 129.
73. Richard Harwell, *Lee: An Abridgment of the Four-Volume R. E. Lee by Douglas Southall Freeman* (New York: Scribner, 1961), p. 215. (Hereinafter referred to as Harwell-Freeman.)
74. Catton, AH, Vol. I, p. 165.
75. *Ibid.*
76. *Ibid.*
77. Fuller, G–L, p. 250.
78. Werstein, p. 231.
79. Kenneth P. Williams, *Lincoln Finds a General* (New York: Macmillan, 1964), Vol. I, p. 252.
80. Werstein, 235–36.
81. Sandburg, p. 144.
82. Catton, MLA, p. 50.
83. Catton, HG, p. 161.
84. Catton, MLA, p. 217.

85. *Ibid.*, p. 318.
86. Harwell-Freeman, p. 261.
87. Fuller, G–L, p. 169.
88. Morison, O, p. 653.
89. *Ibid.*
90. Commager, B–G, p. 200.
91. Sandburg, p. 158.
92. Esposito, Vol. I, Map 71.
93. Freeman, LL, Vol. II, p. 346.
94. Dowdey, p. 234.
95. *Ibid.*
96. *Ibid.*
97. Kraus, p. 500.
98. Harwell-Freeman, p. 278.
99. Morison, O, p. 656.
100. Catton, AH, Vol. I, p. 281.
101. Catton, HG, p. 191.
102. Williams, Vol. II, p. 555.
103. Sandburg, p. 181.
104. Esposito, Vol. I, Map 102.
105. Fuller, G–L, p. 180.
106. Richard S. West, Jr., *Mr. Lincoln's Navy* (New York: Longmans, 1957), p. 221.
107. Grant, p. 284.
108. Fuller, G–L, p. 183.
109. Commager, B–G, p. 663.
110. *Ibid.*, p. 677.
111. Bruce Catton, *Glory Road* (New York: Doubleday, 1952), p. 140. (Hereinafter referred to as Catton, GR.)
112. Commager, B–G, pp. 250–51.
113. Catton, GR, p. 165.
114. *Ibid.*, p. 141.
115. *Ibid.*, p. 169.
116. *Ibid.*, p. 177.
117. Harwell-Freeman, pp. 301–02.
118. Freeman, LL, Vol. II, p. 681.
119. *Ibid.*, p. 682.
120. Fuller, G–L, p. 128.
121. Freeman, LL, Vol. III, p. 46.
122. Harwell-Freeman, p. 321.
123. *Ibid.*, p. 322.
124. Catton, GR, p. 270.

125. *Ibid.*
126. Harwell-Freeman, p. 323.
127. *Ibid.*, p. 325.
128. *Ibid.*
129. *Ibid.*, p. 326.
130. *Ibid.*, p. 329.
131. *Ibid.*, p. 336.
132. *Ibid.*
133. *Ibid.*, p. 337.
134. *Ibid.*
135. Commager, B–G, p. 627.
136. *Ibid.*
137. *Ibid.*, pp. 627–28.
138. Harwell-Freeman, p. 338.
139. *Ibid.*, p. 340.
140. *Ibid.*
141. *Ibid.*
142. Commager, B–G, p. 1074.
143. Williams, Vol. II, p. 730.
144. Commager, B–G, p. 677.
145. Sandburg, p. 206.
146. *Ibid.*, p. 207.
147. Eaton, p. 271.
148. *Ibid.*
149. Catton, GR, p. 228.
150. *Ibid.*, p. 231.
151. Morison, O, p. 659.
152. Catton, GR, p. 233.
153. Bruce Catton, *A Stillness at Appomattox* (New York: Doubleday, 1953), p. 24. (Hereinafter referred to as Catton, S.)
154. Catton, HG, p. 273.
155. Commager, B–G, p. 887.
156. Catton, HG, p. 285.
157. *Ibid.*
158. Commager, B–G, p. 907.
159. *Ibid.*
160. *Ibid.*
161. *Ibid.*
162. Catton, HG, p. 300.
163. Harwell-Freeman, p. 376.
164. Fuller, G–L, p. 216.
165. Catton, S, p. 100.

166. Esposito, Vol. I, Map 126.
167. Sandburg, p. 252.
168. Catton, S, p. 116.
169. Commager, B–G, p. 998.
170. *Ibid.*, pp. 998–99.
171. Harwell-Freeman, p. 388.
172. *Ibid.*
173. Sandburg, p. 252.
174. Harwell-Freeman, p. 408.
175. Catton, S, p. 169.
176. Grant, p. 503.
177. Catton, S, p. 191.
178. *Ibid.*
179. Harwell-Freeman, p. 411.
180. Catton, S, p. 289.
181. *Ibid.*
182. Sandburg, p. 306.
183. West, p. 267.
184. Grant, p. 388.
185. Catton, HG, p. 352.
186. *Ibid.*, p. 348.
187. Catton, S, p. 275.
188. Grant, p. 417.
189. Catton, S, p. 285.
190. Commager, B–G, p. 1055.
191. Thomas Buchanan Read, "Sheridan's Ride," quoted in Stevenson, p. 2118.
192. Catton, S, p. 312.
193. *Ibid.*, p. 315.
194. Sandburg, p. 315.
195. *Ibid.*, p. 316.
196. Fuller, G–L, p. 50.
197. Commager, B–G, p. 925.
198. William Tecumseh Sherman, *Memoirs* (Bloomington: Indiana University Press, 1957), Vol. II, p. 152.
199. *Ibid.*, p. 126.
200. Sandburg, p. 331.
201. Harwell-Freeman, p. 447.
202. Sandburg, p. 384.
203. Catton, S, p. 355.
204. *Ibid.*
205. *Ibid.*
206. *Ibid.*, p. 357.

207. Sandburg, p. 390.
208. *Ibid.*
209. Harwell-Freeman, p. 466.
210. *Ibid.*, p. 475.
211. *Ibid.*, p. 479.
212. *Ibid.*, p. 483.
213. *Ibid.*
214. Catton, S, p. 378.
215. Fuller, G–L, p. 61.
216. Harwell-Freeman, p. 489.
217. *Ibid.*
218. *Ibid.*, p. 490.
219. *Ibid.*, p. 492.
220. *Ibid.*

PART VI: INDIAN WARS, THE SPANISH-AMERICAN WAR
AND THE PHILIPPINE INSURRECTION

1. Morison, O, p. 702.
2. *Ibid.*, p. 704.
3. Hodding Carter, *The Angry Scar*, "Mainstream of America Series" (New York: Doubleday, 1959), p. 31.
4. *Ibid.*, p. 25.
5. *Ibid.*
6. *Ibid.*
7. Foster Rhea Dulles, *The United States Since 1865*, "The University of Michigan History of the Modern World" (Ann Arbor: University of Michigan Press, 1959), p. 13. (Hereinafter referred to as Dulles, US.)
8. *Ibid.*, p. 14.
9. Grant, p. 641.
10. Carter, p. 94.
11. Dulles, US, p. 15.
12. *Ibid.*
13. *Ibid.*, p. 14.
14. *Ibid.*, p. 18.
15. *Ibid.*, p. 14.
16. *Ibid.*, p. 41.
17. Josephy, p. 340.
18. Foster Rhea Dulles, *America's Rise to World Power*, "New American Nation Series" (New York: Harper & Row, 1955), p. 19. (Hereinafter referred to as Dulles, WP.)
19. Dulles, US, p. 55.

20. *Ibid.*, p. 126.
21. Dulles, WP, p. 20.
22. Dulles, US, p. 159.
23. Harold U. Faulkner, *Politics, Reform and Expansion*, "New American Nation Series" (New York: Harper & Row, 1959), p. 217.
24. *Ibid.*
25. Dulles, WP, p. 27.
26. *Ibid.*
27. *Ibid.*
28. Faulkner, p. 225.
29. W. A. Swanberg, *Citizen Hearst* (New York: Bantam Books, 1963), p. 127.
30. Dulles, US, p. 165.
31. Faulkner, p. 227.
32. *Ibid.*, p. 229.
33. Swanberg, p. 162.
34. Faulkner, p. 230.
35. Frank Freidel, *The Splendid Little War* (New York: Bramhall House, 1959), p. 14.
36. Freidel, p. 22.
37. Knox, p. 338.
38. Freidel, p. 33.
39. Faulkner, p. 235.
40. Freidel, p. 59.
41. Wolff, Leon, *Little Brown Brother* (London: Longmans, 1961), p. 277.
42. Freidel, pp. 94–95.
43. *Ibid.*, p. 153.
44. *Ibid.*, p. 163.
45. *Ibid.*, p. 194.
46. *Ibid.*, p. 224.
47. *Ibid.*, p. 231.
48. *Ibid.*
49. Knox, p. 361.
50. Dulles, WP, p. 43.
51. *Ibid.*, p. 44.
52. *Ibid.*, p. 46.
53. *Ibid.*, p. 51.
54. Faulkner, p. 248.
55. Dulles, WP, p. 55.
56. Faulkner, p. 248.
57. Wolff, p. 252.
58. *Ibid.*, p. 253.

59. *Ibid.*
60. *Ibid.*, p. 279.
61. *Ibid.*, p. 271.
62. *Ibid.*, p. 276.
63. *Ibid.*, p. 274.
64. *Ibid.*, p. 344.
65. Morison, O, p. 810.

PART VII: WORLD WAR I

1. Fuller, MH, Vol. III, p. 95.
2. *Ibid.*, p. 133.
3. Dulles, WP, pp. 69–70.
4. *Ibid.*, p. 73.
5. *Ibid.*, p. 78.
6. *Ibid.*, p. 62.
7. Walter Millis, *Arms and Men: A Study of American Military History* (New York: Putnam, 1956), p. 175.
8. *Ibid.*, p. 200.
9. *Ibid.*, p. 163.
10. Fuller, MH, Vol. III, p. 171.
11. *Ibid.*
12. Karl Marx and Friedrich Engels, *The Communist Manifesto,* "Great Books of the Western World" (Chicago: University of Chicago Press, 1952), Vol. 50, p. 434.
13. Dulles, US, p. 223.
14. *Ibid.*, p. 210.
15. *Ibid.*, p. 248.
16. Fuller, MH, Vol. III, p. 179.
17. S. L. A. Marshall, *The American Heritage History of World War I* (New York: American Heritage, 1964), p. 8.
18. *Ibid.*, p. 19.
19. *Ibid.*, p. 27.
20. *Ibid.*
21. *Ibid.*
22. Fuller, MH, Vol. III, p. 181.
23. General Richard Thoumin, *The First World War* (New York: Putnam, 1964), p. 29.
24. Marshall, p. 39.
25. Morison, O, p. 848.
26. *Ibid.*, p. 849.
27. Barbara Tuchman, *The Guns of August* (New York: Macmillan, 1962), p. 119.

28. Richard M. Watt, *Dare Call It Treason* (New York: Simon & Schuster, 1963), p. 59.
29. Hanson W. Baldwin, *World War I* (New York: Harper & Row, 1962), p. 19.
30. Watt, p. 61.
31. Marshall, p. 52.
32. Tuchman, p. 412.
33. *Ibid.*, p. 400.
34. Marshall, p. 53.
35. Tuchman, p. 418.
36. Marshall, p. 57.
37. Watt, p. 91.
38. Marshall, p. 106.
39. Arthur S. Link, *Woodrow Wilson and the Progressive Era: 1910–1917*, "New American Nation Series" (New York: Harper & Row, 1953), p. 165.
40. Marshall, p. 106.
41. Morison, O, 852.
42. *Ibid.*
43. John Dos Passos, *Mr. Wilson's War*, "Mainstream of America Series" (New York: Doubleday, 1961), p. 138.
44. John Terraine, *The Great War: 1914–1918* (New York: Macmillan, 1965), p. 212.
45. Baldwin, p. 89.
46. Link, p. 218.
47. Millis, p. 232.
48. Link, p. 182.
49. *Ibid.*, p. 196.
50. *Ibid.*, p. 265.
51. Marshall, p. 203.
52. *Ibid.*, p. 204.
53. *Ibid.*
54. Fuller, MH, Vol. III, p. 270.
55. Morison, O, pp. 859–60.
56. Fuller, MH, Vol. III, p. 269.
57. Marshall, p. 222.
58. *Ibid.*, p., 223.
59. *Ibid.*, p. 224.
60. *Ibid.*
61. Dos Passos, pp. 232–33.
62. Baldwin, p. 114.

63. General John J. Pershing, *My Experiences in the World War* (New York: Stokes, 1931), Vol. I, p. 30.
64. *Ibid.*, p. 92.
65. Laurence Stallings, *The Doughboys: The Story of the AEF, 1917–1918* (New York: Harper & Row, 1963), p. 15.
66. Pershing, pp. 95, 101.
67. Stallings, p. 21.
68. Marshall, p. 216.
69. Watt, p. 283.
70. Fuller, MH, Vol. III, p. 329–30.
71. Marshall, p. 228.
72. Watt, p. 296.
73. Marshall, p. 270.
74. *Ibid.*, p. 274.
75. *Ibid.*, p. 281.
76. *Ibid.*, p. 280.
77. Robert B. Asprey, *At Belleau Wood* (New York: Putnam, 1965), pp. 127–28. This remark generally has been attributed to Colonel Frederic Wise, but Asprey seems to prove that it was made by Williams.
78. *Ibid.*, p. 174.
79. Stallings, p. 113.
80. Marshall, p. 284.
81. *Ibid.*, p. 287.
82. Fuller, MH, Vol. III, p. 295.
83. Marshall, p. 296.
84. Morison, O, p. 866.
85. Pershing, Vol. II, p. 273.
86. Douglas MacArthur, *My Reminiscences* (New York: McGraw-Hill, 1964), p. 63.
87. Cyril Falls, *The Great War* (New York: Putnam, 1959), p. 351.
88. Marshall, p. 330.
89. *Ibid.*, p. 291.
90. Fuller, MH, Vol. III, p. 296.
91. Marshall, p. 337.
92. *Ibid.*, p. 342.

PART VIII: WORLD WAR II

1. Dulles, US, p. 267.
2. Dulles, WP, p. 109.

3. Louis L. Snyder, *The War: 1939–1945* (New York: Messner, 1962), p. 15.
4. Dulles, US, p. 269.
5. Maj. Gen. J. F. C. Fuller, *The Second World War* (New York: Duell, Sloan & Pearce, 1962), p. 20. (Hereinafter referred to as Fuller, SWW.)
6. *Ibid.*
7. Marshall, p. 368.
8. Fuller, SWW, p. 20.
9. Dulles, US, p. 270.
10. *Ibid.*, p. 271.
11. *Ibid.*
12. Dos Passos, p. 486.
13. Morison, O, p. 882.
14. *Ibid.*, p. 883.
15. Dulles, WP, p. 127.
16. Fuller, MH, Vol. III, p. 324.
17. *Encyclopaedia Britannica* (Chicago: Benton, 1958), Vol. IX, p. 102.
18. Fuller, MH, Vol. III, p. 365.
19. Winston S. Churchill, *Memoirs of the Second World War* (Boston: Houghton Mifflin, 1959), p. 7.
20. Fuller, MH, Vol. III, p. 367.
21. Dulles, US, p. 277.
22. John D. Hicks, *Republican Ascendancy, 1921–1933*, "New American Nation Series" (New York: Harper & Row, 1960), p. 24.
23. *Ibid.*, p. 74.
24. *Ibid.*, p. 81.
25. *Ibid.*
26. William E. Leuchtenburg, *Franklin D. Roosevelt and the New Deal: 1932–1940*, "New American Nation Series" (New York: Harper & Row, 1963), p. 41.
27. Morison, O, p. 992.
28. Snyder, p. 57.
29. Churchill, p. 150.
30. *Ibid.*, p. 43.
31. *The Ciano Diaries*, ed. by Hugh Gibson (Garden City: Doubleday, 1947), p. 10.
32. Snyder, p. 50.
33. Fuller, SWW, p. 40.
34. *Ibid.*, p. 41.
35. William L. Shirer, *The Rise and Fall of Adolf Hitler* (New York: Random House, 1961), pp. 101–2.

36. Fuller, SWW, p. 37.
37. Shirer, p. 117.
38. Snyder, p. 89.
39. Fuller, WW, p. 67.
40. *Ibid.*, p. 69.
41. Robert Leckie, *The Story of World War Two* (New York: Random House, 1964), p. 42.
42. Churchill, p. 250.
43. *Ibid.*, p. 251.
44. *Ibid.*, p. 253.
45. *Ibid.*
46. *Ibid.*, p. 283.
47. *Ibid.*, pp. 284–85.
48. Desmond Flower and James Reeves, eds., *The Taste of Courage: The War, 1939–1945* (New York: Harper, 1959), p. 65.
49. *Ibid.*, p. 64.
50. A. Russell Buchanan, *The United States and World War II*, "New American Nation Series" (New York: Harper & Row, 1964), Vol. I, p. 13.
51. Ciano, p. 239.
52. Churchill, p. 290.
53. *Ibid.*
54. Snyder, p. 103.
55. *Ibid.*, p. 104.
56. Dulles, US, p. 422.
57. *Ibid.*, p. 423.
58. Robert Sherwood, *Roosevelt and Hopkins* (New York: Grosset & Dunlap, 1950), p. 123.
59. Buchanan, p. 14.
60. Leuchtenburg, pp. 320–21.
61. Dulles, US, p. 429.
62. Churchill, p. 350.
63. Snyder, p. 110.
64. *Ibid.*, p. 112.
65. Churchill, p. 366.
66. *Ibid.*, p. 410.
67. *Ibid.*, p. 381.
68. Kenneth S. Davis, *Experience of War: The United States in World War II*, "Mainstream of America Series" (New York: Doubleday, 1965), p. 47.
69. *Ibid.*, pp. 48–9.
70. Churchill, p. 385.

71. Ciano, p. 300.
72. Chester Wilmot, *The Struggle for Europe* (New York: Harper, 1952), p. 64.
73. *Ibid.*, p. 72.
74. *Ibid.*, p. 78.
75. *Ibid.*, p. 80.
76. *Ibid.*, p. 79.
77. Buchanan, Vol. I, p. 36.
78. *Ibid.*, p. 46.
79. Masuo Kato, *The Lost War* (New York: Knopf, 1946), p. 89.
80. Buchanan, Vol. I, p. 51.
81. *Ibid.*
82. *Ibid.*, p. 53.
83. *Ibid.*, p. 55.
84. Cordell Hull, *Memoirs of Cordell Hull* (New York: Macmillan, 1948), Vol. II, p. 1095.
85. *Ibid.*, p. 1096.
86. Samuel Eliot Morison, *History of U.S. Naval Operations in World War II*, Vol. III, *The Rising Sun in the Pacific* (Boston: Little, Brown, 1948), p. 132.
87. Louis Morton, "Japan's Decision for War," in *Command Decisions*, ed. by Kent Roberts Greenfield (Washington: Office of the Chief of Military History, Department of the Army, 1960), p. 87.
88. Fuller, SWW, p. 175.
89. Hanson W. Baldwin, *Great Mistakes of the War* (New York: Harper, 1950), p. 68.
90. Buchanan, p. 100.
91. Maj. Gen. Courtney Whitney, *MacArthur: His Rendezvous with History* (New York: Knopf, 1956), p. 53.
92. Louis Morton, *The Fall of the Philippines*, "The U.S. Army in World War II" (Washington: Office of the Chief of Military History, Department of the Army, 1953), p. 456.
93. *Ibid.*, p. 561.
94. Samuel Eliot Morison, *History of United States Naval Operations in World War II*, Vol. IV, *Coral Sea, Midway and Submarine Actions* (Boston: Little, Brown, 1960), p. 41.
95. Field-Marshal Bernard L. Montgomery, *Memoirs* (Cleveland, New York: World, 1958), p. 92.
96. Snyder, p. 280.
97. Dwight D. Eisenhower, *Crusade in Europe* (New York: Doubleday, 1948), p. 100.
98. Sherwood, p. 696.
99. *Ibid.*, p. 903.

100. Samuel Eliot Morison, *The Two-Ocean War* (Boston: Little, Brown, 1963), p. 238. (Hereinafter referred to as Morison, TO.)
101. *Ibid.*, p. 563.
102. Eisenhower, p. 165.
103. General George S. Patton, Jr., *War As I Knew It* (Boston: Houghton Mifflin, 1947), p. 61.
104. Snyder, p. 334.
105. Churchill, p. 709.
106. *Ibid.*, p. 710.
107. *Ibid.*, pp. 711–12.
108. Flowers, p. 754.
109. Luke, 11:26
110. Gen. Mark W. Clark, *Calculated Risk* (New York: Harper, 1950), p. 188.
111. *Ibid.*, p. 204.
112. Eisenhower, p. 203.
113. Robert Leckie, *Strong Men Armed: The United States Marines Against Japan* (New York: Random House, 1962), p. 189.
114. Snyder, p. 325.
115. Buchanan, Vol. II, p. 314–15.
116. Col. Conrad A. Lanza, ed., *Napoleon and Modern War: His Military Maxims* (Harrisburg: Military Service Publishing Co., 1954), p. 78.
117. Martin Blumenson, *Anzio: The Gamble That Failed*, "Great Battles of History Series" (Philadelphia: Lippincott, 1963), p. 58.
118. *Ibid.*, p. 61.
119. *Ibid.*, p. 62.
120. *Ibid.*, p. 65.
121. Fuller, SWW, p. 224.
122. *United States Strategic Bombing Survey* (European War) (Washington: Government Printing Office, 1945), p. 190.
123. Snyder, p. 363.
124. Cornelius Ryan, *The Longest Day* (New York: Simon & Schuster, 1959), p. 27.
125. Snyder, p. 336.
126. *Ibid.*
127. Gen. Omar Bradley, *A Soldier's Story* (New York: Holt, 1951), p. 272.
128. Snyder, p. 363.
129. Eisenhower, p. 279.
130. Fuller, SWW, p. 331.
131. Fleet Admiral William F. Halsey and J. Bryan III, *Admiral Halsey's Story* (New York: McGraw-Hill, 1951), pp. 207–08.
132. MacArthur, pp. 216–17.

133. Morison, TO, p. 447.
134. *Ibid.*, p. 461.
135. Whitney, p. 181.
136. Snyder, p. 464.
137. Hull, p. 1606.
138. Wilmot, p. 549.
139. Snyder, 427.
140. *Ibid.*, 429.
141. *Ibid.*, p. 430.
142. *Ibid.*
143. *Ibid.*, p. 437.
144. *Ibid.*
145. Fleet Admiral Chester W. Nimitz and E. B. Potter, *The Great Sea War* (Englewood Cliffs: Prentice-Hall, 1960), p. 447.
146. 1st Lt. Robert A. Arthur and 1st Lt. Kenneth Cohlmia, *The Third Marine Division* (Washington: Infantry Journal Press, 1948), p. 252.
147. Leckie, SMA, p. 472.
148. *Ibid.*, p. 481.
149. Buchanan, Vol. II, p. 593.
150. Kado, *The Lost War* (New York, Knopf, 1946), p. 26.

PART IX: THE KOREAN WAR

1. "The Summary Report on the Pacific War," Strategic Bombing Survey (Washington: Government Printing Office, 1946), p. 26.
2. Morison, TO, p. 1046.
3. *Ibid.*
4. Luke, 11:21.
5. Dulles, WP, p. 231.
6. *Ibid.*, p. 234.
7. *Ibid.*, p. 235.
8. Dulles, US, p. 493.
9. James Forrestal, *The Forrestal Diaries* (New York: Viking, 1951), p. 373.
10. Capt. Walter Karig, Cmdr. Malcolm W. Cagle and Lt. Cmdr. Frank A. Manson, *Battle Report*, Vol. VI, *The War in Korea* (New York: Rinehart, 1952), p. 5.
11. Robert Leckie, *Conflict: The History of the Korean War* (New York: Putnam, 1962), p. 37. (Hereinafter cited as Leckie, C.)
12. *Ibid.*
13. U.S. Department of State, *Guide to the UN in Korea* (Washington: Government Printing Office, 1951).

14. Roy E. Appleman, *South to the Naktong, North to the Yalu (June–November, 1950),* "U.S. Army in the Korean War" (Washington: Office of the Chief of Military History, 1960), p. 37.

15. Harry S. Truman, *Memoirs* (New York: Doubleday, 1956), Vol. II, p. 337.

16. MacArthur, p. 334.

17. Appleman, p. 60.

18. *Ibid.,* p. 76.

19. *Ibid.,* p. 119.

20. *Ibid.*

21. Leckie, C, p. 75.

22. Maj. Gen. William F. Dean, *General Dean's Story* (New York: Viking, 1954), p. 29.

23. Philip Deane, *I Was a Captive in Korea* (New York: Norton, 1953), p. 18.

24. Appleman, p. 180.

25. *Ibid.,* p. 208.

26. Malcolm W. Cagle and Frank A. Manson, *The Sea War in Korea* (Annapolis: United States Naval Institute, 1957), p. 65.

27. Appleman, pp. 347–48.

28. Leckie, C, p. 114.

29. *Ibid.*

30. Cagle, p. 81.

31. Karig, p. 167.

32. MacArthur, p. 349.

33. *Ibid.*

34. *Ibid.,* p. 350.

35. *Ibid.,* p. 353.

36. Whitney, p. 364.

37. *Ibid.,* p. 365.

38. *Ibid.*

39. Karig, p. 280.

40. *Ibid.,* p. 297.

41. Appleman, p. 759.

42. Trumbull Higgins, *Korea and the Fall of MacArthur* (New York: Oxford, 1960), p. 58; Truman, Vol. II, p. 365–67.

43. Allen S. Whiting, *China Crosses the Yalu: The Decision to Enter the Korean War* (New York: Macmillan, 1960), p. 92.

44. *Ibid.,* p. 96.

45. *Ibid.*

46. *Ibid.*

47. *Ibid.,* p. 99.

48. Appleman, p. 761.
49. MacArthur, p. 368.
50. Whiting, p. 138.
51. Whitney, p. 407; MacArthur, p. 369.
52. MacArthur, p. 370.
53. Robert Leckie, *The March to Glory* (New York and Cleveland: World, 1959), p. 169.
54. Leckie, C, p. 227.
55. *Ibid.*
56. Matthew B. Ridgway, *Soldier* (New York: Harper, 1956), p. 216.
57. Leckie, C, p. 102.
58. Truman, Vol. II, p. 358.
59. *Ibid.*
60. MacArthur, p. 379.
61. Truman, Vol. II, p. 442.
62. *Ibid.*, pp. 445–46.
63. *Ibid.*, p. 447.
64. MacArthur, p. 404.
65. Leckie, C, p. 282.
66. Robert F. Futrell, *The United States Air Force in Korea, 1950–1953* (New York: Duell, Sloan & Pearce, 1961), p. 266.
67. *Ibid.*, p. 284.
68. *Ibid.*
69. Leckie, C, title page.
70. *Ibid.*, p. 287.
71. John M. Miller, Jr., Major Owen J. Caroll and Margaret E. Tackley, *Korea: 1951–53* (Washington: Office of the Chief of Military History, 1956), p. 106.
72 Truman, Vol. II, p. 458.
73. Admiral C. Turner Joy, *How Communists Negotiate* (New York: Macmillan, 1955), p. 92.
74. Truman, Vol. II, p. 461.
75. Edward Hymoff, "The Day the Reds Humiliated Uncle Sam" (*True* Magazine, October, 1961), pp. 111–12.
76. Joy, p. 92.
77. General Mark Clark, *From the Danube to the Yalu* (New York: Harper, 1954), p. 111.
78. Rutherford M. Poats, *Decision in Korea* (New York: McBride, 1954), p. 295.
79. Dwight D. Eisenhower, *Mandate for Change* (New York: Doubleday, 1963), p. 179.

PART X: WORLD-WIDE UPHEAVAL AND THE WAR IN VIETNAM

1. Lt. Col. Erskine B. Crew, *"La Guerre d'Indochine"* (*Marine Corps Gazette,* April, 1966), p. 38.
2. Robert Shaplen, *The Lost Revolution* (New York: Harper & Row, 1965), p. 170.
3. "Lin Piao's Manifesto" (*Army Magazine,* December, 1965), p. 48.
4. Shaplen, p. 348.
5. "Lin Piao's Manifesto," p. 48.
6. Shaplen, p. 48.
7. *Ibid.,* p. 31.
8. Brig. Gen. Samuel B. Griffith, trans., *Mao Tse-tung on Guerilla Warfare* (New York: Praeger, 1961), p. 46.
9. Douglas Pike, *Viet Cong* (Cambridge: M.I.T. Press, 1966), p. 85.
10. *Ibid.,* p. 131.
11. Theodore Sorensen, *Kennedy* (New York: Harper & Row, 1965), p. 732.
12. *Ibid.,* p. 247.
13. Dave Richard Palmer, *Summons of the Trumpet* (San Rafael, Ca.: Presidio Press, 1978), p. 129.
14. Frances Fitzgerald, *Fire in the Lake* (Boston: Atlantic-Little, Brown, 1972), p. 306.
15. Newark (N.J.) *Star-Ledger,* April 12, 1978.
16. Fitzgerald, p. 352.
17. Richard Nixon, *Memoirs* (New York: Grosset & Dunlap, 1978), p. 755.
18. *Ibid.,* p. 245.
19. *New York Times,* March 31, 1971.
20. Nixon, p. 397.
21. *Ibid.,* p. 397.
22. *Ibid.,* p. 409.
23. *Ibid.,* p. 412.
24. Washington *Post,* November 15, 1969.
25. Nixon, p. 450.
26. *Ibid.,* p. 459.
27. *Ibid.,* p. 396.
28. *Ibid.,* p. 585.
29. *Book of the Year* (Chicago: *Encyclopaedia Britannica,* 1973), p. 724.
30. Nixon, p. 30.

31. *New York Times*, October 27, 1972.
32. Nixon, p. 706.
33. *Ibid.,* p. 733.
34. *Ibid.*, p. 751.
35. *Book of the Year* (Chicago: *Encyclopedia Britannica,* 1974), p. 710.
36. *Ibid.*, p. 712.
37. *Ibid.*
38. *Book of the Year* (Chicago: *Encyclopedia Britannica,* 1975), p. 714.
39. Nixon, p. 1083.
40. Alan Dawson, *55 Days: The Fall of South Vietnam* (Englewood Cliffs: Prentice-Hall, 1977), p. 30.
41. Frank Snepp, *Decent Interval* (New York: Random House, 1977), p. 182.
42. *Ibid.*, p. 185.
43. *Ibid.*, p. 248.
44. Dawson, p. 289.
45. *Ibid.*, p. 297.
46. Fitzgerald, p. 308.
47. Lawrence M. Baskir and William A. Strauss, *Chance and Circumstance: the Draft, the War and Vietnam* (New York: Knop, 1978), Foreword, p. xii.
48. Nixon, p. 464.

PART XI: 1981–1991: AMERICA RECOILING, RESURGENT

Because all of these events are so recent that there is as yet no general literature on them—memoirs, histories, operational details, interviews, etc.—this part of the narrative has depended mainly upon such periodicals as the *New York Times,* the Charleston (S.C.) *News and Observer* and *Post-Courier,* the Newark (N.J.) *Star-Ledger* and the weekly issues during the years of 1981–91 of *Time* magazine and *Newsweek,* as well as the Britannica *Book of the Year* volumes from 1978 through 1991.

EPILOGUE

I. Jeremiah, 6:14.

Recommended Reading

☆

THE COLONIAL WARS

Freeman, Douglas S., *George Washington*, New York: Scribner, 1948. Although inflated, Freeman's seven-volume biography remains the definitive work on Washington. Vols. I and II relate to the Colonial Wars.

Josephy, Alvin M., Jr., *The Patriotic Chiefs*, New York: Viking, 1961. A colorful chronicle of American Indian leadership beginning with King Philip in the Colonial Wars and ending with Chief Joseph in 1877.

Mahan, Alfred Thayer, *The Influence of Seapower upon History, 1660–1783*, New York: Hill and Wang, 1957. The chief book of the "bible" of seapower also gives a demonstration of its decisive role in the Colonial and Revolutionary Wars.

Morison, Samuel Eliot, ed., *The Parkman Reader*, Boston: Little, Brown, 1955. An excellent short trot with Parkman for those without the time to take the entire trip.

Parkman, Francis, *France and England in North America*, Boston: Little, Brown, 10 vols. 1887–88, 2 vols. 1892.* Parkman's work remains the classic on the Colonial period. Of the 12 volumes cited here, those dealing directly with the Colonial Wars are:

The Pioneers of France in the New World.
Count Frontenac and New France under Louis XIV.
A Half-Century of Conflict, 2 vols.
Montcalm and Wolfe, 2 vols.
The Conspiracy of Pontiac, 2 vols.

Stacey, C. P., *Quebec, 1759*, Toronto: Macmillan, 1959. A clear style and the most up-to-date research combine to present the best single account of the climactic battle of the Colonial Wars.

* All the editions cited here are those used by the author.

THE WAR OF THE REVOLUTION

Commager, Henry Steele, and Richard B. Morris, eds., *The Spirit of 'Seventy-Six*, 2 vols., Indianapolis: Bobbs-Merrill, 1958. A mine of documents, diaries, letters and eyewitness accounts of events of the Revolution.
Freeman, *op. cit.*, Vols. III, IV and V.
Lancaster, Bruce, *The American Heritage Book of the Revolution*, New York: Simon & Schuster, 1958. Text and lavish illustrations join to make an absorbing popular account of the Revolution.*
————, *From Lexington to Liberty*, New York: Doubleday, 1955. Although Lancaster's narrative here is neither so disciplined nor so lucid, the book is still crammed with entertaining incident and anecdote.
Miller, John C., *Triumph of Freedom, 1775–1783*, Boston: Little, Brown, 1948. The most complete single-volume work on the Revolution, and especially recommended for the balance struck between battle front and home front.
Wallace, Willard M., *Appeal to Arms*, New York: Harper, 1951. The finest short history of the Revolution, a brilliant small gem of military writing.
Ward, Christopher, *The War of the Revolution*, 2 vols., New York: Macmillan, 1953. This is a complete and masterful narrative, perhaps the best on the subject.

THE WAR OF 1812

Adams, Henry, *The War of 1812*, Washington: Infantry Journal Press, 1944. This excerpt from Adams's nine-volume history of the United States remains the most complete account of 1812.
Coles, Harry L., *The War of 1812*, Chicago: University of Chicago Press, 1965. A clear and concise narrative which should be attractive to modern readers.
James, Marquis, *The Life of Andrew Jackson*, Indianapolis: Bobbs-Merrill, 1938. One of the best biographies in American letters, and invaluable for its portraits of Jackson in the Creek Wars and at New Orleans.
Tucker, Glenn, *Dawn Like Thunder*, Indianapolis: Bobbs-Merrill, 1963. A stirring account of the Barbary Wars and the birth of the U.S. Navy.
————, *Poltroons and Patriots*, 2 vols., Indianapolis: Bobbs-Merrill, 1954. A highly readable popular history of the war.

* Again because of space limitations, the author is compelled to cite only American authors.

THE WAR WITH MEXICO

Henry, Robert Selph, *The Story of the Mexican War*, New York: Ungar, 1961. An affectionate and accurate narrative, with much emphasis on the character of the individual American soldiers.

Lewis, Lloyd, *Captain Sam Grant*, Boston: Little, Brown, 1950. A fascinating study not only of the young U. S. Grant but also of his comrades-in-arms who were to be the generals of the Civil War.

Nichols, Edward J., *Zach Taylor's Little Army*, New York: Doubleday, 1963. A short colorful account of the fighting in northern Mexico.

Smith, Justin H., *The War with Mexico*, 2 vols., Gloucester, Mass.: Peter Smith, 1963. Although flawed by a prejudice against things Latin, this remains the most complete work on the subject.

THE CIVIL WAR

Catton, Bruce, *The American Heritage Picture History of the Civil War*, 2 vols., New York: American Heritage, 1960. This is Catton's finest work, a lucid narrative that covers all the ground and is superbly served by marvelous maps and photographs.

Eaton, Clement, *A History of the Southern Confederacy*, New York: Macmillan, 1962. A short history notable for its accuracy and impartiality.

Foote, Shelby, *The Civil War*, 3 vols, New York: Random House, 1958, 1963. An exhaustive study of the war from a Southern viewpoint. The third volume has not yet been published.

Freeman, Douglas S., *Lee's Lieutenants*, New York: Scribner, 1942–43–44. A detailed account of the war waged in the East by the Confederate Army.

Fuller, Major General J. F. C., *Grant and Lee*, Bloomington: Indiana University Press, 1957. One of the most perceptive military writers of the century makes a fascinating study of generalship which challenges many of the conventional judgments on the war's two great protagonists.

Harwell, Richard, *Lee*, New York: Scribner, 1961. This is an excellent and readable abridgment of Freeman's four-volume study of the great Virginian.

Sandburg, Carl, *Storm Over the Land*, New York: Harcourt, Brace, 1942. Taken from Sandburg's four-volume *Abraham Lincoln: The War Years*, this profile of the Civil War is a colorful account of Lincoln's conduct of the war.

Williams, Kenneth P., *Lincoln Finds a General*, 5 vols., New York: Macmillan, 1956–64. A factual and sometimes controversial work, which, when read in conjunction with Freeman's volumes, presents a detailed and balanced account.

INDIAN WARS, THE SPANISH-AMERICAN WAR AND THE PHILIPPINE INSURRECTION

Crook, General George, *His Autobiography*, edited by Martin F. Schmitt, Norman: University of Oklahoma Press, 1960. All the flavor of the frontier is present in this remarkable personal narrative by "the greatest Indian fighter of them all."

Downey, Fairfax, *Indian Wars of the U.S. Army, 1776–1865*, New York: Doubleday, 1963. A stirring account of the Indian Wars of the "middle period."

———, *Indian-Fighting Army*, New York: Scribner, 1941. The same author carries the narrative to the end of the nineteenth century and also presents a picture of the regular army which later fought the Spanish-American War. Read with Parkman and Josephy, these two books complete the story of Indian warfare.

Freidel, Frank, *The Splendid Little War*, Boston: Little, Brown, 1958. This popular account of the Spanish-American War is also available with pictures in a book of the same title published by Bramhall House, New York, 1958.

Schott, Joseph L., *The Ordeal of Samar*, Indianapolis: Bobbs-Merrill, 1964. A chilling story of the vicious guerrilla fighting characteristic of the Philippine Insurrection.

Wolff, Leon, *Little Brown Brother*, London: Longmans, 1961. A skillful presentation of both sides of the unpleasant coin of American imperialism.

WORLD WAR I

Baldwin, Hanson W., *World War I*, New York: Harper & Row, 1962. A short, concise history which nevertheless covers all the ground while presenting the conflict's leading men and issues.

Falls, Cyril, *The Great War 1914–1918*, New York: Putnam, 1959. Among the best histories of the war. Though written with a slight British bias, it is nonetheless a compelling book which profits much from the author's own experience and literary style.

Marshall, Brig. Gen. S. L. A., *The American Heritage History of World War I*, New York: American Heritage, 1964. This straightforward, well-balanced narrative is General Marshall's most masterly work. The maps and photographs are equally good.

Stallings, Laurence, *The Doughboys,* New York: Harper & Row, 1963. An intimate and affectionate account of the men of the American Expeditionary Force.

Watt, Richard M., *Dare Call It Treason,* New York: Simon & Schuster, 1963. This book cannot be recommended too highly. It describes the political corruption and military blindness which brought the French Army to mutiny in 1917, and in doing so it becomes the best short account in America of the French effort in World War I.

WORLD WAR II

Baldwin, Hanson W., *Great Mistakes of the War,* New York: Harper, 1950. A hard-hitting little book indicting those grand errors of Anglo-American strategy which led to the fall of the Iron Curtain across Central Europe and prepared the drop of the Bamboo Curtain in Asia.

————, *Battles Lost and Won,* New York: Harper & Row, 1966. With customary clarity and thoroughness, the author describes 11 major campaigns in history's greatest war and analyzes their results and their effect upon warfare in general.

Buchanan, A. Russell, *The United States and World War II,* 2 vols., New York: Harper & Row, 1964. For its portrayal of every aspect of the American war effort—from the political through the social, technical, financial and scientific problems to the logistical and purely military—this masterly work is unsurpassed.

Churchill, Winston S., *Memoirs of the Second World War,* Boston: Houghton Mifflin, 1959. This is an abridgment of the British Prime Minister's six-volume history, and as such it is an excellent condensation of the scope and sweep of that monumental work.

Flower, Desmond, and James Reeves, eds., *The Taste of Courage,* New York: Harper, 1959. A book for browsing, an exhaustive compilation of eyewitness accounts of ordeal from the combatants of all countries as well as the correspondents who accompanied them.

Fuller, Major General J. F. C., *The Second World War,* New York: Duell, Sloan & Pearce, 1962. A terse and highly critical account which considers only the strategy and tactics of the war while eschewing the so-called "romance." It is pure Fuller, both irritating and inspiring.

Jacobsen, H. A., and J. Rohwer, *Decisive Battles of World War II: The German View,* New York: Putnam, 1965. German generals and historians analyze ten major campaigns in this authoritative account of the war as seen through German eyes.

Leckie, Robert, *Strong Men Armed,* New York: Random House, 1962. A popular narrative of the U.S. Marine Corps's campaigns against Japan, which, being related to the exploits of the Army, Navy and Army Air Force, also presents a picture of the Pacific War.

Morison, Samuel Eliot, *The Two-Ocean War,* Boston: Little, Brown, 1963. This thorough short history of the U.S. Navy in World War II is recommended to those without the time to read Admiral Morison's exhaustive 15-volume work on the subject.

Wilmot, Chester, *The Struggle for Europe,* New York: Harper, 1952. Far and away the most authoritative and sweeping account of the European war as it was conducted and fought by the leaders and armies of both sides.

THE KOREAN WAR

Cagle, Malcolm W., and Frank A. Manson, *The Sea War in Korea,* Annapolis: United States Naval Institute, 1957. Naval operations portrayed in detail describe the decisiveness of sea power in Korea as well as its importance in limited warfare.

Futrell, Robert F., *The United States Air Force in Korea 1950–1953,* New York: Duell, Sloan & Pearce, 1961. This is a clear, unvarnished account of what air power could and could not do in Korea. It also provides insights into the problems of war in the nuclear age.

Higgins, Trumbull, *Korea and the Fall of MacArthur,* New York: Oxford, 1960. The author styles his book, "A précis in limited war," which it is. It is also valuable for its impartial treatment of the MacArthur-Truman controversy.

Joy, Admiral C. Turner, *How Communists Negotiate,* New York: Macmillan, 1955. A primer in Communist intransigence at the truce table, as well as insights into Red propaganda techniques.

Leckie, Robert, *Conflict: The History of the Korean War,* New York: Putnam, 1962. As yet the only complete account of the conflict in all its complexities of command, politics, diplomacy, battle and international relations.

Whiting, Allen S., *China Crosses the Yalu,* New York: Macmillan, 1960. How and why Red China decided to enter the Korean War, as well as a detailed indictment of the failure of communications between Peking and Washington.

WORLD-WIDE UPHEAVAL AND THE WAR IN VIETNAM

There is not, as yet, a general history of the war in Vietnam, although there is a veritable flood of books on the various aspects of the conflict. Unfortunately, so much of this is polemical that it is difficult to make recommendations. For operations, the various studies of the late Brig. Gen. S. L. A. Marshall provide insights into the character of the war. Also, the following:

Pike, Douglas, *Viet Cong,* Cambridge: M.I.T. Press, 1966. A detailed and detached description of the National Liberation Front.

Shaplen, Robert, *The Lost Revolution,* New York: Harper & Row, 1965. Apart from a tendency to drive home the title's thesis, this is an excellent unraveling of the entire tangle from the years 1946 to 1965.

Baskir, Lawrence M., and Strauss, William A., *Chance and Circumstance,* New York: Knopf, 1978. A candid discussion of the draft, how it was evaded and dodged, which also details the institution's injustices and inequities.

Dawson, Alan, *55 Days: The Fall of South Vietnam,* Englewood Cliffs: Prentice-Hall, 1977. Except for a shaky and unclear start, this is a good account—from both sides—of Saigon's last days.

Thompson, W. Scott, and Frizzell, Donaldson D., *The Lessons of Vietnam,* New York: Crane, Russak, 1977. Transcripts of discussions at a colloquium on the war attended by top participants and analysts, such as General Westmoreland and Sir Robert Thompson.

Nixon, Richard, *The Memoirs of Richard Nixon,* New York: Grosset & Dunlap, 1978. Valuable for the fallen President's own account of the labyrinthine way he and Henry Kissinger had to follow to bring Hanoi to the peace table.

AMERICAN HISTORY

Morison, Samuel Eliot, *The Oxford History of the American People,* New York: Oxford, 1965. Although Professor Morison has a tendency to disdain all that was not born in New England, or at least educated there, this big and bursting book is still the most complete and current of all single-volume histories extant.

Commager, Henry Steele, and Richard B. Morris, eds., *The New American Nation Series,* 20 vols., New York: Harper & Row, 1954——.

Boorstin, Daniel J., ed., *The Chicago History of American Civilization,* Chicago: University of Chicago, 1953——, 23 vols.

Gannett, Lewis, ed., *Mainstream of America Series,* New York: Doubleday, 1953–66, 18 vols.

These three series complement and balance one another. The Harper volumes are valuable for their political and diplomatic history, the Chicago works for their emphasis on the topical and sociological and the Doubleday books for their treatment of the men and the movements which shaped the nation.

FOREIGN HISTORY

Nevins, Allan, and Howard M. Ehrmann, *The University of Michigan History of the Modern World*, Ann Arbor: University of Michigan Press, 1958–65, 15 vols. The purpose of this excellent popular series is to acquaint Americans with the history of all those peoples with whom their destiny is now irrevocably joined. It also includes a fine two-volume history of the United States.

Index

☆